The Soviet Union
and the Challenge
of the Future

The Soviet Union and the Challenge of the Future

Volume 3: Ideology, Culture, and Nationality

Edited by Alexander Shtromas and
Morton A. Kaplan

A PWPA Book

PARAGON HOUSE

New York

First edition, 1989

Published in the United States by

Paragon House

90 Fifth Avenue
New York, New York 10011

Copyright © 1989 by Paragon House

A Professors World Peace Academy Book

Library of Congress Cataloging-in-Publication Data
The Soviet Union and the challenge of the future.
"A PWPA book."
Includes bibliographies and indexes.
Contents: v. 1. Stasis and change—   —v. 3.
Ideology, culture, and nationality.
1. Soviet Union—Social conditions—1945-   —Con-
gresses. 2. Soviet Union—Politics and government—
1945-   —Congresses. 3. Soviet Union—Ethnic
relations—Congresses. I. Shtromas, Alexander,
1931-   II. Kaplan, Morton A.
HN523.5.S69   1988   306'.0947   87-6904
ISBN 0-943852-35-8 (v. 3)

The paper used in this publication meets the minimum require-
ments of American National Standard for Information Sciences—
Permanence of Paper for Printed Library Materials,
ANSI Z39.48-1984.

Contents

Introduction

The ideological and cultural crisis in the Soviet regime—the subject of Vol. III—is, perhaps, the most fundamental and fateful crisis in the Soviet Union. It may undermine the legitimacy of communist rule and call into question the political system that assures the Communist party absolute and undivided power over the state and society.

The economic, social, international crises treated in Volumes I, II, and IV do not challenge the regime's survival directly. As long as society, at least to some extent, identifies itself with the regime ideologically and culturally, it will support the regime's efforts to overcome the other crises. But if the ideological perceptions and the basic values and goals of the society clash with those of the regime, each crisis will be perceived and used as a valid reason for changing the regime.

Volume III consists of two main parts: the first is devoted to Russia proper; and the second, to the non-Russian nations of the USSR and the Soviet Bloc.

I

The authors of Part I attempt to disentangle the Russian and Soviet identities of the ethnic Russians and to discover underneath the Soviet facade the true orientation and authentic values and aspirations of the Russian people. They also evaluate the significance of Russian nationalism as a factor in the stability of the Soviet system.

The fifteen authors of Part I come to broadly similar conclusions. They more or less share the view that the Soviet regime's determined attempts to make Russia authentically communist and Soviet have failed. Mutilated by the relentless mass terror of the first decades of Soviet rule, demoralized by induced fear, benumbed by monotonous indoctrination, and corrupted by continuous alienation from the officially endorsed values and goals, the Russian nation, to a large degree, degenerated into a mass of cynical and ruthless individuals united only by their traditional national identity. This identity is coming to the fore with increasing intensity and the Russians, in self-defense, are asserting with increasing emphasis the ideals of their pre-revolutionary past.

The conflict between official Soviet values, goals and ideals and the contrasting true orientation of the Russian people is the fundamental Soviet crisis. It logically follows from this that *perestroika* will not be able to succeed, unless the regime in time renounces or redefines its communist identity; abolishes the restraints imposed by Marxist-Leninist ideology on social, economic and political change; and allows the Russian people, in concordance with their genuinely held values and beliefs, freely to engage in political, social, economic and cultural activities.

Part I opens with Andrzej Walicki's profound study of the intellectual tradition of pre-revolutionary Russia that lays the historical foundation for understanding the present conflict between Soviet and Russian identities. This theme is further developed by the English author Peter Kelly who in his subsequent chapter connects the traditions of Russia's past with the prospects for her future. In chapter 3, Alexander Shtromas investigates the nature and extent of Marxism's influence on the Russian intelligentsia before and after 1917. He explores the character and tragic fate of the Russian "true believers in Marxism" (now an "extinct species") and substantiates the thesis of Yury Kublanovsky, the young Russian poet, that at the present time in the USSR "Marx is of no interest to anyone, and only a few individuals still continue to hate him." "True Marxism," according to Shtromas, is dead in the USSR even as an ideology of opposition. "In the Soviet Union," he says, "there is simply no room any more for utopian ideologies and movements of whatever kind," and this means that the political transition that Russia is about to undergo, may, at last, naturally and painlessly bring her into a state of civilized pluralistic (though perhaps not immediately democratic) normalcy.

In Chapter 4, W. Bruce Lincoln analyzes *glasnost'* in Russia in historical perspective and attributes the first ("prototypical," as he calls it) *glasnost'* campaign to Catherine II (in the second part of the 18th century). *Glasnost'* under both Catherine II and, about a century later, under Alexander II, brought into the open the hitherto hidden Russian radicalism and precipitated political crises that ended in the ruthless suppression by the regime of the forces and ideas of the political opposition. Such suppression, however, only stimulated the growth of the Russian revolutionary movement which in 1917 finally brought down the oppressive Tsarist Regime. The discrepancy, indeed conflict, between the official ideology of the state and public opinion, now is incomparably greater than it has ever been in the past. In Lincoln's opinion, this does not bode well for the present *glasnost'* campaign launched by Gorbachev. Looking at present Soviet developments in the context of Russia's historical experience, Lincoln believes that the failure of Gorbachev's *glasnost'* will most certainly also bring about a revolutionary movement that, given the new circumstances, should be more massive and viable than that which in 1917 brought down Russia's *ancien regime*.

In chapter 5 the Yugoslav dissident and historian of ideas, Mihajlo Mihajlov, considers the problem of Russian and Soviet identities from the position of the spiritual substance of man, his inescapable commitment to transcendental religion. Mihajlov intrinsically links religion, fundamental beliefs and faith, to the problem of human rights. People in Russia, the rest of the Soviet Union and Eastern Europe, he believes, use "the invisible reality of human rights" to release themselves from "their physical bondage to the external idols of state, empire, nation, or any other political and social reality."

Mihajlov specifically stresses, and devotes much time to proving, that there is no fundamental difference in this respect between Russia and the so-called "kidnapped West," the term usually applied to Eastern Europe. In his view it was not Russia that kidnapped Eastern Europe, but totalitarian communism which since 1917 equally kidnapped Russia.

Mihajlov argues that the "pervasive existential *dualism* between the materially real social-political world and individual consciousness based on an invisible spiritual reality" makes collectivistic totalitarianism in Russia and the rest of the communist world unviable. This dualism, according to him, requires the introduction of individual freedom, pluralism, and, also democracy. The latest developments in Russia, China and Yugoslavia appear to vindicate Mihajlov's perspective.

The following three chapters: by respectively Nikolai Poltoratzky, Mikhail Agursky, and Darrell P. Hammer consider Russian nationalism as an ideological alternative to Soviet Marxism-Leninism. They explore Russian nationalist ideas and movements in the USSR in an effort to establish the content and extent of the challenge to which the so-called "Russorhile ideology" exposes the Soviet regime.

Agursky's argument is complex. He shows that radical Russian nationalism was, to a large extent, the inspirational force behind Bolshevik Marxism and that the Bolshevik ideology was thus a peculiar amalgam of Marxism and the radical program of changing Russia into a stronger and more viable entity which ultimately could become a globally dominant force. He then demonstrates how throughout its history the Soviet Communist Party-state tried to coopt "pure" (non-Marxist) Russian nationalism. Agursky maintains that the Bolsheviks were partly successful in this endeavor. They indeed managed to coopt the crudest imperially minded nationalists (the so-called *derzhavniki*, the statists, or, in Agursky's broader terminology, the radical nationalists). They also managed during World War II to coopt the main conservative stream of Russian nationalism. This alliance, however, did not survive the war. The reassertion of the Soviet state's communist identity after the war drove conservative Russian nationalists back into inner opposition to the Soviet regime. Agursky believes that in the ongoing confrontation between conservative Russian nationalism and Sovietism, the former will emerge as the victor. He also thinks that the West should welcome the victory of conservative Russian nationalism, as this victory will, in his view, eliminate the Soviet global threat and make Russia a peaceful neighbor of the Western world. Agursky concludes his chapter by stating that "conservative Russian nationalism . . . is by no means a threat. It is hope."

Hammer's argument is much simpler than Agursky's. From the outset he divides all Russian nationalists into two groups, the "National Bolsheviks" and the "Russophiles," and deals only with the latter group. Having analyzed their concerns and views (especially through the writings of Father Dimitrii Dudko), he comes to the conclusion that the "Russophile" trend represents a real challenge (and thus also a real and radical alternative) to Sovietism. For Hammer, as for Agursky, the "Russophiles" are a benign force able to incorporate a future Russia into the world community of nations as an organic and cooperative member. "Russophilism," as every other nationalism, is to Hammer a defensive orientation, a reaction to a threat to the nation's culture and identity. "Russophilism," Hammer argues, "begins with this perception of a threat to Russian culture and Russia's national identity. Out of the basic instinct for survival has developed a deep concern for the future of the village, a rejection of the cult of technology, and a quiet hostility to the Soviet system—hostility to the Marxist-Leninist philosophy and hostility to the ruling bureaucracy."

The editors share Agursky's and Hammer's views on Russian nationalism. They also see in it a positive opposition and a viable and welcome alternative to the Soviet communist political status quo. The editors, however, are not so sanguine about the inclusion into the Russian nationalist spectrum of the so-called National Bolsheviks (or, in Argursky's terms, radical nationalists).

The term National Bolshevism was coined in the 1920s and was applied to people (like General Aleksey Brusilov, Nikolai Ustryalov, et al.) who, although they were avowed Russian nationalists (or rather statists) and thus non-Marxists (or even anti-Marxists), accepted the Soviet party-state as the legitimate heir of the pre-revolutionary Russian Empire. Out of their commitment to Russia, they were ready faithfully to serve the Soviet regime without ever joining the Party or otherwise identifying themselves with the regime's communist ideals and goals. The term National Bolshevism made good sense at the time of the Soviet state's formation. However, under Stalin's levelling rule this term lost its meaning by the mid-1930s. At that time the toleration of any wavering about, or of conditions attached to, the approval of the communist substance of the Soviet state had stopped, and the people identified with such attitudes were resolutely repressed. Under Stalin, people had either fully to accept, and identify themselves with, the Stalinist variety of the Bolshevik political myth or, alternatively, face, if not immediate execution, then at least imprisonment in "labor-extermination" camps. For whatever inner-reason people under Stalin joined the Party or otherwise submitted themselves to the service of the regime—skin-saving, careerist, statist-nationalistic or even Marxist ideal-istic—they had unquestionably to assume the uniform Stalinist-Bolshevik identity and thoroughly hide any other identity that they may have had. Because of that their inner motives for serving the Soviet party-state were practically irrelevant. The outwardly adopted and practiced Stalinist-Bolshevik identity was the only relevant one.

Lenin used to complain that many Russian communists in essence were merely Russian chauvinists. Referring to the old proverb, "scratch a Russian and reveal a Tatar," he used to say: "Scratch a Russian communist and reveal a great Russian chauvinist." Lenin accused even Stalin (together with Dzerzhinsky and Ordzhonikidze) of great Russian chauvinism after the conquest of Georgia. The Trotskyite oppositionists were the first to call Stalin himself a National Bolshevik. However, this was no longer National Bolshevism proper. During Stalin's ascendancy Stalinism became Bolshevism incarnated and any nationalist or other deviation from the Stalinist Bolshevik orthodoxy (e.g. the original National Bolshevism of the Brusilov-Ustryalov type) was mercilessly suppressed and crushed. After World War II, scores of the Russian SFSR's leading Party workers were accused by Stalin of Russian nationalist deviation, arrested and, in most cases, executed (the so-called "Leningrad case").

The Stalin (and thus Bolshevik) loyalists may have presented (even to themselves) their unswerving loyalty to the Soviet party-state as loyalty to the Russian nation but this did not make them into nationalists of any kind, Bolshevik or not. Most of them were mere self-seekers. The *appar-*

atchiks who did well under Stalin and their party descendent believed that any change of the Stalinist system would put them in a losing situation. It is natural for such people to dress up their vested interests as concern about the fate of the nation and its state. It makes them feel more comfortable, however cynical they may be, for no human being likes to see himself as a total cynic.

Some of the Stalinist Bolshevik loyalists are what one could call "natural conservatives." Such "natural conservatives" having once, mainly out of conformity, accepted (and adjusted to) the political myth proclaimed and forcefully implemented by the powers that be, regard every challenge to, and revision of, that political myth as an attempt to disrupt the established and, for better or worse, routinized way of life to which they see no alternative but anarchy. The notorious letter of the Leningrad chemistry teacher Nina Andreeva, published in *Sovetskaya Rossiya*[1] with, one may reliably assume, the sponsorship of Politburo members Ligachev and Chebrikov, is a typical expression of such a naturally conservative orientation. (On the part of Nina Andreeva but certainly not on the part of Ligachev and Chebrikov who used her genuine conservatism for the advancement of their vested power-interests.) To call such a conservative orientation nationalist in any sense would be, in the editors' view, inappropriate.

Finally, there are Stalinist loyalists—whether of the self-seeking, conservative or any other variety—who, knowing well that Marxist-Leninist arguments will cut no ground with anyone anymore, opportunistically try to use nationalist arguments in order to oppose the "chaos of *perestroika* and *glasnost'* " and to restore "strict and clear order" along Stalinist lines. The writer Yury Bondarev is perhaps the most outspoken representative of such pseudo-nationalism; close to him are the editors of the literary journals *Moskva* (Moscow) and *Molodaya Gvardiya* (Young Guard), Mikhail Alekseev and Anatoly Ivanov, with groups of their respective collaborators. Although clearly nostalgic about the "good old days of Stalin," the *Moskva* and *Molodaya Gvardiya* literary groups try to acquire credibility by joining some authentic nationalist ventures such as the series of mass meetings calling for the preservation of Russia's cultural and religious heritage held in 1989 under the auspices of the Orthodox Church, the Russian Cultural Fund and similar bodies. At one such meeting in January 1989, the Deputy Editor of *Molodaya Gvardiya* Vyacheslav Gorbachev (no relation to General Secretary, Mikhail Gorbachev), tried to rouse the crowd by denouncing the oppressed and exploited situation of the Russian nation in the contemporary USSR and by reciting as evidence of that situation statistical data about the numbers of Jews in higher education, the Academy of Sciences, the Writers Union, etc. The hint here was quite clear: under Stalin the Jews were suppressed and stopped from dominating the Russians; now, however, after the Stalinist grip had been relaxed, the Jews were starting to dominate the Russians again. And, typically, in response to V. Gorbachev's speech, some specially prepared members of the audience put up a placard denouncing "rootless cosmopolitism," the code-phrase Stalin used in his anti-Semitic campaign of the late 1940s.

It is true, however, that at the time when the Soviet state seemed strong and invincible (especially during and in the aftermath of World War II), there were among Stalinist Bolshevik loyalists some people who genuinely believed that by serving Stalin and the Bolsheviks they indeed served the state and the national/imperial interests of Russia, and who for that reason alone decided fully to identify themselves with the Stalinist Bolshevik system of rule in Russia. One could call these people crypto-National Bolsheviks but there is no evidence of their continuing presence in the ranks of the Stalinist regime's loyalists today. For it is by now crystal clear that the Stalinist system has undermined the economic strength of Russia and the morale of the Russian people to such an extent that only a speedy replacement of that system could effectively preserve Russia's social, political and imperial integrity.

The ideological demise of National Bolshevism, its reduction to mere demagogy or to a device for justifying one's conformity with, or even adherence to, the Stalinist Soviet system, is perhaps best exemplified by the emergency in May, 1987, of the association *Pamyat'* (Memory) which now calls itself the National Patriotic Front (NPF) *Pamyat'*. The natural heir to National Bolshevism, *Pamyat'* is, however, by no means Bolshevik, even in pretense. The ideology of this relatively new "informal association" is based on the belief that Bolshevism was no more than the tool used by Zionist-Masonic plotters to undermine Russia and destroy her national identity and culture. In the words of Dimitrii Vasil'ev, until 1989 the leader of *Pamyat'*, it all began with the murder of the Tsar Nicholas II and his family in 1918, then developed "into the crucifixion of the people itself, of the whole country, of the entire fatherland," and continues unabated at present.[2] The Zionist-Masonic plot, according to Vasil'ev, is aimed at subjugating the whole world to the rule of those few who consider themselves to be "God's chosen" people. However, "Holy Russia" had to be destroyed first if this plot were to succeed on a global sale.

Pamyat' identifies as the champions of this plot in Russia today leading Politburo members Aleksandr Yakovlev and Lev Zaikov, the current editor of the magazine *Ogonyok* (The Little Spark) Vitaly Korotich and some other figures none of whom (in contrast to the main culprits of the past: Trotsky, Sverdlov, Kaganovich, et al.) are actually Jewish; (this, apparently, makes it necessary to add the Masons to the Zionists when identifying the source of the threat to Russia's survival).

Pamyat' is not directly imperialistic. It is even sympathetic, at least verbally, to the authentic hopes and aspirations of all Soviet dominated peoples to be truly sovereign and free; but it believes that all these peoples should nevertheless stick with Russia and each other in order to be able effectively to fend off together the subjugating attempts of their single and common enemy, the Masonic-Zionist plotters. Although the *Pamyat'* leaders do not say so directly, the implication here is that the separation of non-Russians from Russia is against the authentic interests of the non-Russian nations of the USSR and Eastern Europe themselves, for their natural and otherwise commendable inclination to independence, is in fact, according to *Pamyat'*, cleverly manipulated by, and used to the advantage of, the Masonic-Zionist plotters and thus to the equal detriment of all the nations involved. This newly found "internationalism" ("nationalist internationalism," as one could say) is what has effectively replaced today whatever had remained of National Bolshevism in Russia. Those who continue to stick to Soviet communism are by no means National Bolsheviks but sheer opportunists, either self seekers or mere conformists, who would be the champions of any stable order or any monocratic regime, Soviet or not, provided that order or regime assured their unperturbed existence.

Both Soviet and Western media have blown out of all proportion the significance of *Pamyat'* in Russia's social and political life. They usually present *Pamyat'* as if it were either the sole and single authentic voice of contemporary Russian nationalism or, at least, the most powerful and representative force in the extant Russian nationalist spectrum. This "image-making" serves the purpose of frightening the public, both in the USSR and worldwide, of a Russian nationalist alternative to the Soviet communist status quo. It, thus, serves the purpose of effectively mobilizing public support for the preservation of the present Soviet regime as the lesser evil. In fact, however, *Pamyat'* is a very marginal and extremely fragmented force which by no means could, on its own, provide an alternative to Soviet communism.

The most revered spokesmen for the Russian national revival in the country, such as Academician Dimitrii Likhachev, have publicly denounced *Pamyat'* and its xenophobia on many occasions. The mainstream Russian nationalist forces working within the official framework (e.g., most importantly, the influential "village prose" writers and other literary figures who write for the literary magazine *Nash Sovremennik* [Our Contemporary], such as Valentin Rasputin, Viktor Astaf'ev, Vladimir Soloukhin, Vadim Kozhinov, et al.) do not associate themselves with *Pamyat'* either. The same goes for the unofficial Christian Patriotic Union, led by a prominent national dissident and a long time political prisoner, Vladimir Osipov, and the people collaborating with his samizdat journal *Zemlya* (Soil) (e.g., another prominent Russian nationalist dissident writer and long time political prisoner, Leonid Borodin). Although the messages of the *Moskva* and *Molodaya Gvardiya* groups are heavily borrowed from the ideological arsenal of *Pamyat'*, these primarily regime-loyalist groups categorically refuse to have anything in common with *Pamyat'*, since *Pamyat'* is so strongly disapproved of by the Soviet officialdom.

The marginality of *Pamyat'* was irrefutably proved by the March-May, 1989, elections to the USSR's Congress of People's Deputies. In all cases *Pamyat'*'s support for a candidate proved to be counter-productive, as it diminished that candidate's chances to be elected. Indeed, among the elected deputies of the Congress there is *no one* who was directly associated with *Pamyat'*. One of the most notable examples of *Pamyat'*'s inability to get its way with the electorate was the failure of the *Pamyat'*-supported prominent writer Yury Bondarev (mentioned above as one of the Stalinist loyalists who is now posing as a Russian nationalist) to get elected to the Congress. The Russian electorate was sophisticated enough to discern under Bondarev's (and *Pamyat'*'s) nationalist rumblings the true Stalinist pro-establishment orientation of this otherwise well-known and quite popular figure, and voted overwhelmingly against him.

Pamyat' mounted an especially vigorous and noisy campaign in Moscow's Oktyabr'sky electoral district trying to prevent the election of a Jewish dissident Il'ya Zaslavsky, who was standing for a seat in the Congress against four ethnic Russians. Despite *Pamyat'*'s use of all its available resources for the "anti-Zaslavsky campaign," and the fact that the constituency in which Zaslavsky stood is predominantly a working class one, Zaslavsky, a typical young Jewish intellectual, was elected in the first round with a comfortable majority. Zaslavsky's election, despite *Pamyat'*'s virulent anti-Semitic campaign against him, does not mean of course that anti-Semitic arguments do not have an impact upon a Russian constituency or that those who voted for Zaslavsky were totally unprejudiced with regard to Jews. What the election has proved was the fact that Zaslavsky's dissident and impeccably anti-establishment credentials powerfully tilted the balance in Zaslavsky's favor, in spite of his being Jewish, which means that the primary concern of the Russian electorate in this election was not ethnic but socio-political. People were so eager to elect anti-establishment figures, whom they could trust to defend their rights, they did not care whether these figures were Jewish or Gentile.

Pamyat' also failed to attract to its ranks any prominent intellectuals. In contrast with most other "informal associations" now active in the USSR, *Pamyat'* is even unable to put out a periodical. During the two years of its existence *Pamyat'* published in *Samizdat* only a few separate documents, among which two acquired some currency—its Program which contains a lot of emotional rumbling but no comprehensible and consistent message, and the Declaration On the Leader that somewhat ineptly tries to reproduce in Russian Hitler's infamous *Fuhrerprinzip*. The only well known intellectual who in the beginning collaborated with *Pamyat'* was the popular painter Il'ya Glazunov; but after several months (by the beginning of 1988) he fell out with *Pamyat''s* Council's Chairman, Dimitrii Vasil'ev and left the movement.

Soon afterwards the movement split into the Christian and Pagan wings, the former led by Vasil'ev himself and the latter by the notorious author of anti-Semitic pamphlets, V.N. Emelyanov, the former Party official who was expelled from all his posts and who served time in prison for killing his wife. Nothing much has been heard since about the activities of the Emelyanov (Pagan) wing of *Pamyat'*, although in the spring of 1989 another anti-Semitic pamphlet by him, *One-Sided Internationalism or Stalinism— the Asiatic Mode of Production* (accusing the Zionists of forcefully imposing this mode of production upon Russia), started to circulate in *Samizdat*. Later in 1988, the Christian wing of *Pamyat'* underwent a further split. A group of *Pamyat'* members in Moscow, led by an artist Igor Sychev, formed a separate *Pamyat'* movement (as opposed to the Association and, later, the NPF *Pamyat'*, led by Vasil'ev). They called Vasil'ev's xenophobia a provocation that undermined not only the *Pamyat'* cause but its very existence. On the other hand, the most aggressive wings of *Pamyat'*, operating in Leningrad and the Ural-Siberian regions, split away from the Moscow leadership and accused it (both Vasil'ev and Sychov) of "flabbiness and compromises with the enemy." In 1989, in a coup-like event, Vasil'ev himself was removed from the Chairmanship of the NPF *Pamyat'* Council. The controversy about, and the ultimate failure of, the "anti-Zaslavsky campaign" was apparently the cause for this change of guard. It remains to be seen how Vasil'ev will respond to this move. Whatever his response is going to be, the "*Pamyat'* Association", as Roy Medvedev, the dissident historian, noted in an interview with a provincial newspaper, "is no longer monolithic. It disintegrated into "*Pamyat'-1*," "*Pamyat'-2*," and "*Pamyat'-3*." (He probably meant the *Pamyat'* groups, led, respectively, by Vasil'ev, Emelyanov, and Sychov.)[3]

In contrast with the fictitious National Bolsheviks, *Pamyat'* (or all the *Pamyat's*) is, indeed, a legitimate part of the Russian nationalist spectrum. It represents its extremist, one could even say, its proto-fascist sector.

On the more moderate side of this extremist sector there also exists the newly formed (in 1989) Russian Popular Front, practically led by an old hand in extremist nationalist politics, Valery Skurlatov. This new organization is, however, handicapped by the fact of its close association with the Institute of Press at the CPSU's Central Committee and is therefore likely to attract even less support than *Pamyat'*.

Mainstream Russian nationalist thinking has no identifiable organizational core, although Osipov's KhPS (or CPU, Christian Patriotic Union), mentioned above, is clearly representative of that mainstream. However, the major intellectual forces of that mainstream, such as Academician D.S. Likhachev, Corresponding Member of the Academy of Sciences Sergei Averintsev (both elected to the Congress of People's Deputies), the numerous supporters of Solzhenitsyn, "the village prose" writers and other intellectuals of the *Nash Sovermennik* group, have not associated themselves with it.

Ideologically this mainstream is quite diverse. People like Likhachev and Averintsev are Christian liberal democrats who are fully committed to the principles of human rights and individual freedom, while some others, e.g. the "Solzhenitsynites," are more committed to collectivistic religious and national spiritual values within the strict framework of which, they believe, the exercise of individual rights should take place. What, however, unites all shades of Russian mainstream nationalist opinion is their rejection, indeed aversion, to "rootless modernity" or what Tomas Venclova, in his recent study of nationality issues in contemporary Soviet literature, aptly called "presentophobia."[4] This "presentophobia" is first of all directed against contemporary Soviet society with its continuous destruction of Russia's spiritual substance and natural environment, but it is also directed against the overall *embourgeoisement*, associated with the impact on the Russian mentality of Western civilization which, in its narrowly rationalistic pragmatism, spiritless cult of money and science, and demoralizing absence of religious spirit, most of the mainstream Russian nationalists tend to reject.

Mainstream Russian nationalism is not anti-Semitic on the whole. Likhachev, Averintsev, and those who identify with them, sincerely and even passionately denounce anti-Semitism. They see in it not simply a shameful trait that undermines the decency of their nation, but also a dangerous seed from which a new tyranny may evolve. These Russian nationalists are the clear successors of the philo-Semitic traditions of the pre-revolutionary Russian intelligentsia which considered anti-Semitism the greatest sin of the Russians and did not tolerate anti-Semites within their ranks. However, some of the "Solzhenitsynites" are suspicious of Jews as the most likely carriers of decadent Western influence on Russia. They see them as people who would put individualism above the collectivistic spiritual (that is basically Christian) values of the Russian nation.

The *Nash Sovremennik* group of writers is ambiguous in its attitude toward Jews, too. This became clear in the confrontational correspondence between one of the leading Russian nationalist writers in this group, Viktor Astaf'ev, and the prominent historian Natan Eidel'man, which was made public by *Samizdat* and then reprinted in Russian emigre press.[5] In this correspondence, Eidel'man accused Astaf'ev of xenophobia generally and anti-Semitism in particular. Astaf'ev replied in kind, accusing the likes of Eidel'man of the murder of the last Tsar and his family, defilement of Russia's purity and integrity, and continuous destruction of Russia's nature and spiritual substance.

Eidel'man's letter was provoked by Astaf'ev's short story, "Lovlya peskarei v Gruzii" (Fishing for Carp in Georgia),[6] in which the modern Georgians were depicted with a hateful contempt that reached truly racist proportions. But, as Tomas Venclova showed in his analysis of this short story, Astaf'ev is not a Georgiophobe at all. On the contrary, Astaf'ev extols in the story the virtues of the traditional Georgian village, highly praises the 19th century Georgian romantic poet Nikoloz Baratashvili, and even associates the hero of Shota Rustaveli's celebrated medieval epic poem "The Knight in the Tiger's Skin" with Christ's driving the traders out of the temple. Astaf'ev's scathing remarks are indeed directed not against the Georgians as a race, but only at those contemporary Georgians who, because of Soviet influence, have lost their traditional identity as brave, decent and God loving people. Furthermore, as Venclova also shows, it is easy to find in Astaf'ev's other stories analogous invectives directed against degenerate contemporary Soviet Russians, his own compatriots. In fact, Venclova concludes, Astaf'ev's xenophobia (be it Georgiophobia, Mongolophobia or Judeophobia) "turns into an aversion to the *present of all peoples* including his own" (Venoclova's emphasis).[7] This conclusion could be equally applied to most members of the *Nash Sovremennik* group, among whom there are several Jews, including the deputy chief editor of the journal Anatoly Salutsky.

Anti-Semitism is thus a characteristic not of the whole Russian nationalist spectrum but only of some of its rather marginal sections. Although *Pamyat'* stresses that it is not anti-Semitic but only anti-Zionist, there is no doubt that anti-Semitism is an essential part and perhaps even the main pivot of its ideology. There are also prominent anti-Semitic overtones (again, vehemently denied by the group's leadership) in Skurlatov's Popular Russian Front. Certain elements in the mainstream Russian nationalism are to a greater or lesser degree doubtful about the ability of Jews as an ethnic-religious group to become an organic part of the Russian national community; some of these elements also believe that certain Jewish intellectual circles exercise a pernicious influence on the communal values and the "organic way of life" of the Russian nation; but very few members of the Russian nationalist mainstream could be identified as straightforward anti-Semites.

There is yet another steadily growing fringe of Russian nationalism that identifies Russian national interests with the nation's adoption and assimilation of Western liberal democratic principles and institutions. The National-Democratic Party created in the beginning of 1989 in Leningrad is the first identifiable organized body which, on the basis of a Russian nationalist orientation, fully approves of Western-type liberal democratic principles as the ones which are best suited for shaping Russia's new political system. This is the first organized political group in Russia which combines a nationlistic perspective with a liberal-democratic orientation and which considers the Jews an organic part of Russian national society.

As Hammer rightly stressed in his chapter, "nationalism is an idea, and not an ideology," that is why Russian nationalism is inherently pluralistic. No such body as the "Russian Party" exists or is likely to come into existence in the future. The phrase "Russian Party" could therefore be used only as a figurative expression, designating a broad and loose Russian nationally minded opposition—an opposition that is yet more moral and intellectual than political—to the communist status quo.

This inherently pluralistic structure of the "Russian Party" is the special topic of Poltoratzky in chapter 6. Poltoratzky, as well as Agursky and Hammer, would view the victory of the "Russian Party" as tantamount to the end of Soviet monocracy and to the institution in Russia of political pluralism. Poltoratzky effectively refutes the widespread belief, according to which Russian nationalism, if it replaced Soviet communism, may radically change the ideological content but not the ideologically monistic and thus fundamentally totalitarian (or authoritarian) nature of the Russian state. As a loose amalgam of various ideological groups with very different perspectives on what is best for Russian national interests, he says, the so-called "Russian Party" is organically pluralistic, and thus incompatible with any kind of ideological and/or political monism.

Poltoratzky vividly depicts the main organizations and ideas of Russian nationalist opposition to the Bolsheviks and the Soviet regime throughout the 70 years of Russia's post-revolutionary history. In the course of his thorough review of the Russian nationalist opposition, Poltoratzky marshals some new, and some less new but not easily available, evidence on the ideologies and activities of the Russian Whites and their organizations abroad; he also interestingly analyzes the Russian nationality ideas and organizations that evolved both in Russia and abroad in more recent times.

Although Poltoratzky convincingly argues that the victory of the "Russian Party" would irreversibly destroy the monocratic political structure of the USSR and resolutely open up the road for Russia's transformation into a modern liberal democracy, he is frankly partisan in his adherence to the view of certain sections of the older (post-1917) generation of Russian political emigres, according to which the fate of the USSR should be determined only after the common struggle of all Soviet ruled nations against communist oppression is victoriously concluded. That is to say that at present no Soviet ruled nation should be recognized as having an *a priori* right to separate itself from the USSR and establish its own sovereign statehood.

This view stems from the concept of "one and indivisible Russia." On the basis of this concept, he advocates "non-predetermination" (*nepredreshenie*), a position that is very seldom heard in the Western Sovietological literature. Although the editors firmly believe in the *a priori* right of all nations to self-determination and sovereignty, Poltoratzky's position is worthy of attention.

The editors, however, do not think that Poltoratzky presented his position on "non-predetermination" in a sufficiently coherent and convincing manner. Criticizing US Public Law 86-90, he concentrates on that Law's reference to the restoration of independence of "Idel-Ural" and "Cossackia," that is, of nation-states which, as he rightly notes, are unknown in history. But the Law's point is surely not about such incidental oddities as "Idel-Ural" and "Cossackia"; it is first and foremost about much better established and historically well known nation-states, such as, the Ukraine, Georgia, Lithuania and scores of others. Poltoratzky, however, remains silent on how these nation-states should be treated in regard to their right of separation from Russia. He says only, that "one cannot put on the same level nation-states which have had long independent existence, or at least internationally recognized status, and 'nations' which were created, and immediately disappeared, in the turmoil of the civil war. Or independent nations which were always outside the borders of Russia and nationalities which have long been a more or less organic part of Russia."

One can only guess what the adequate and proper treatment of one or another Soviet-ruled nation should be on the basis of that generalization. Does, for example, Poltoratzky's formula mean that the fifty million strong Ukraine should be treated as a 'nation' which was created, and immediately disappeared, in the turmoil of civil war, and Georgia and Lithuania as nations which had long independent existence? It is even less clear what kind of distinction Poltoratzky is trying to make between nations that were always outside the borders of Russia and those that have long been a more or less organic part of Russia. Does he want to say that the fate of Czechoslovakia or Bulgaria that have never been part of Russia should be decided differently from the fate of Poland (or even Finland) that before 1917 were "more or less organic parts of Russia"? And, if so, what should this difference consist of? These paradoxical questions, and one could think of many more similar questions, show only too well how unhelpful, and indeed confusing, Poltoratzky's arguments against US Law 86-90 (The Captive Nations law) are.

Three main propositions seem reasonable to the editors:

(1) Nations of the Soviet realm of rule that are formally independent, such, as Czechoslovakia and Poland, have to be granted full and real independence, regardless of their historical relationship with Russia;
(2) Nations which were independent before World War II and which had enjoyed international recognition, but which were annexed during the war by the USSR (such as Lithuania, Latvia and Estonia) have to be recognized as having an *a priori* right to full and real independence and should be unconditionally restored to full sovereign status;
(3) All other nations of the USSR should be allowed freely to decide their future status within or outside of Russia by a referendum or by other democratic means.

Poltoratzky's review of the "Russian Party" is not fully comprehensive. He did not mention some of the more unpleasant manifestations of Russian nationalism, such as, for example, the chauvinist manifesto *Slovo natsii* (The Nation Speaks) or the works of Gennady Shimanov. (At the time Poltoratzky wrote his chapter *Pamyat'* and other groups mentioned above were not yet in existence). Although he did discuss a number of other Russian nationalistic groups, he ignored their attitudes toward the non-Russian nations' future association with Russia. If Poltoratzky were to pay proper attention to the treatment of this problem by contemporary indigenous Russian nationalists, he would have discovered that none of them stick to the concept of a "one and indivisible Russia" or talk about "non-predetermination," a term that makes sense only as an ambiguous and uneasy compromise between the concept of a one and indivisible Russia and the right of nations to self-determination.

As is shown in A. Shtromas's chapter in Part II (on Soviet multinationalism) of this Volume, most indigenous Russian nationalists are first and foremost eager to create a culturally and religiously homogeneous state and therefore insist upon Russia's separation from the non-Slavic and non-Orthodox Christian nations of the USSR. Even those who, like Igor Shafarevich, want to preserve the unity of the Soviet state, speak not of one and indivisible Russia but of a confederation of free and equal nations united by their common and unique historical experience and fate. It follows from the above that Poltoratzky's open Russian nationalist partisanship may reflect the attitudes of some sections of the pre-World War II Russian political emigration but that it is out of tune with the current thinking on these problems in Russian nationalist circles within the USSR.

The subsequent seven chapters of Part I (chapters 9–15) are devoted to the exploration of specific aspects of Russian national consciousness and its relationship to Soviet official values, ideals and goals. William Fletcher looks at the crucial role religion is playing in the process of Russia's self assertion and evaluates the significance of the religious revival in determining Russia's path to a post-Soviet future. Michael Kreps, Maurice Friedberg, Nicholas Hayes, Alexander Gershkovich and Vladimir Frumkin base their analyses of the subjects under their scrutiny, and the conclusions they reach, mainly on the examination and interpretation of works of contemporary Soviet Russian art and literature.

Christie Davies concludes Part I of Volume III by examining political jokes, which are an important part of popular culture in all communist ruled nations, and perhaps the best indicator of authentic public opinion in these nations about the political circumstances under which they live. The fact that Davies includes jokes not only from Soviet but also from East European sources is here only of technical significance. Jokes travel from country to country rather quickly and, as many analysts have shown, all communist ruled nations are in fact in possession of a common bank of political jokes. This is to say that if Davies has heard a joke from a Bulgarian source it does not mean that the joke is necessarily Bulgarian— it may be Russian or Polish; and vice-versa, a joke heard from a Russian or Polish source may be originally a Bulgarian or Hungarian joke. According to most analysts, Russia (along with Poland) is the country where most of the political jokes circulating in all communist countries originate, and therefore Davies's analysis of the socio-political implications of all these jokes fully applies to Russia and indicates the contradictory nature of the relationship between the Russian and Soviet identities of the Russian people.

The Marxist-Leninist ideology and the Soviet communist regime which is based on that ideology, as Part I makes clear, have at present no surviving foundation in Russia. Whatever hold on Russia—through devices like National Bolshevism or missionary zeal (sometimes undistinguishable from imperialist endeavors) to introduce a new and better world order— Marxism-Leninism and Sovietism ever had, it has by now become obsolete. The only force that keeps the communist ideology and regime in Russia going today is the force of sheer inerita. Inertia can continue to keep the Soviet system in Russia operative for only a relatively short period of time. Thus, according to the collective verdict expressed in Part I of this Volume, the collapse of the Communist Soviet system in Russia is unavoidable. And with its crumbling in Russia, Communism will inevitably lose ground and go under also in the rest of the world.

II

Part II examines the ideological, cultural and political attitudes of the non-Russian nations of the USSR and the Soviet bloc. The authors evaluate the stability of the Soviet-type communist regimes governing these nations and the potential impact that political destabilization in the outskirts of the Soviet empire could have on political stability in the Soviet-Russian metropolis itself, and vice-versa.

Subpart "A," deals with nations within the USSR proper. The first two chapters are devoted to a general review and assessment of Soviet multi-nationalism, while the remaining chapters examine particular nations or groups of nations of the USSR.

All Soviet nations of union-republican status are surveyed, and the editors included a chapter dealing with Soviet Finno-Ugrians, a relatively large group of nations and nationalities of sub-union-republican status which usually do not receive enough attention in the specialist, let alone general, literature. Thanks to the inclusion of this especially extended chapter on the Finno-Ugrians, this Volume provides a unique insight on the Karelians, Izhors, Mordvins, Maris, Komis, Udmurts, Khantys, Mansis and other Finno-Ugrian peoples of the USSR.

Of the many non-territorial national minorities living in the USSR, only the Jews received special treatment in this Volume.

Although the editors tried to make Part II of the Volume as comprehensive as possible, they, understandably, could by no means include into it studies on all the 200 or so ethnic groups that inhabit the USSR. Despite the best efforts of the editors, the Muslim nations of the USSR received less attention in the Volume than they obviously deserve. The Tatars (both the Volga and the Crimean ones), the Bashkirs, the peoples of Dagestan and other sub-union republican Muslim nations of the USSR were not dealt with here, and there is even no substantial chapter in the Volume that discusses on an adequately detailed level the major Muslim nations of Soviet Central Asia. Chapter 7 by the late Alexandre Bennigsen, "Soviet Muslims and Self Determination," gives only a scant overview of these nations' problems and discerns those general trends of their development under Soviet rule that may determine the prospects for the Soviet Muslims' future. Robert L. Nichols's Chapter 6, which deals with Transcaucasia, gives a much more prominent place to the Transcaucasian Christian nations of Georgia and Armenia than to the Shiite Moslem nation of Azerbaijan.

The insufficient attention paid to Soviet Muslims is, no doubt, a serious defect of the Volume. The editors' only consolation rests on the fact that the specialist literature on Soviet Muslims is relatively ample and that most of this literature is of excellent quality. On the other hand, the specialist literature on Byelorussia, Moldavia and the Finno-Ugrians—nationalities that have been quite thoroughly scrutinized in this Volume—is relatively scarce.

In Part II's opening chapter, Sergei Maksudov gives an idiosyncratic and to say the least, an extremely controversial interpretation to the development of the USSR's nationalities, a view that is in stark contrast to all the other contributions to Part II. According to Maksudov, the process of assimilation and Russification of the non-Russian nations and nationalities of the USSR is by now well advanced and should come to completion before too long. The editors strongly disagree with this view. The statistical data used by Maksudov for substantiating his thesis on the "organic success of the Soviet policy of Russification" are of some independent interest, although the editors believe that they could be used to oppose Maksudov's thesis.

During 1987–1989, life itself convincingly refuted Maksudov's stance on the problems of Soviet multinationalism. Unleashed by *glasnost'*, the authentic attitudes and aspirations of the various Soviet nations and nationalities were powerfully and unequivocally expressed in the public domain. The Balts and the Transcaucasians have suddenly come out into the open with very radical demands. Although theirs are the most vocal and visible demands, the Ukrainians and Byelorussians, who had to overcome in this process the determined attempts of their republics' authorities to quell every sign and expression of national protest or unrest, also entered the fray. The real attitudes and aspirations of Soviet Central Asians were clearly demonstrated by the end-1986 riots in Kazakhstan's capital Alma-Ata and in Spring-Summer 1989 nationalist unrest in some other major cities of Kazakhstan, Uzbekistan, and Kirghizstan.

Even the minor ethnic groups of Russia's North and Siberia began to use *glasnost'* powerfully to reassert themselves. The Khantys, Mansis, Nentses, Khakasians, Yakuts, and scores of other formerly nomadic peoples of these areas started energetic campaigns for the preservation of their languages, cultures, and traditional ways of life generally. They demanded substantial revisions in Soviet industrialization and urbanization policies, policies that hitherto worked strongly against the vital interests of these ethnic groups. The indigenous writers Yury Rytkheu and Yuvan Shestalov took upon themselves the championship of the causes of these ethnic groups. Although himself a Mansi, Shestalov has come out in defense also of the Nentses, Khantys, and some other ethnic groups whose situation is similar to that of the Mansis; and Rytkheu, a Chukcha, spoke on behalf not only of the Chukchas but of some of their neighbors, too.

It is now apparent that, contrary to what Maksudov tried to prove in his chapter, these small and scattered peoples, although exposed not just to mere assimilation and Russification but to a slow process of virtual cultural elimination, have nevertheless managed to remain full-fledged ethnic entities, conscious of their tragedy and eager to assert and defend their specific identity and traditional way of life. Maksudov thus clearly mistook the terrible deterioration of ethnic integrity of the Soviet non-Russians, which the Soviet regime doubtlessly brought about, for their terminal demise. What he failed to notice were the remaining cores of all these ethnic groups that underneath the deteriorated surface carefully and inconspicuously kept their traditional identities alive.

The Buryats, a nation that Maksudov regarded as one that has been almost totally acculturated and uprooted, in fact preserved their national identity and cultural heritage with remarkable success. Under *glasnost'* and the toleration of the Buryat religion (lamaism) that it has provided, it became clear that the centuries' old and extremely rich literature in the Buryat language, which was for many decades forbidden and taken out of circulation by the Soviet authorities, has been in fact carefully preserved by the Buryats and circulated among them through unofficial channels. There were in Buryatia also some functioning underground schools where children were taught the Buryat language, religion and literature. The Buryat intelligentsia, led by the leaders of the Buryat Writers' Union, N. Damdinov, D. Dorzhgutabai, and some others, are engaged in a struggle to legalize these schools and to publish textbooks in the Buryat language. They are also campaigning for official republication of the classical (e.g., religious and philosophical) texts of the Buryat literature.

It is, no doubt, a fact that the Soviet nationalities' policy, especially from the late 1930s, was aimed at the cultural annihilation of all these "lesser nations and nationalities." Maksudov has accurately described the terrible damage that this policy of the Soviet regime inflicted upon all the nations under its control. But Maksudov is wrong when he credits this policy with almost full success and prematurely deplores the annihilation of these groups as ethnic entities as an inevitable result. For contrary to Maksudov's assertion, the most recent Soviet history, has proved that a territorially compact ethnic group, however oppressed and exposed to assimiliationist pressures, however minoritarian in its own territory it may be, is able as a rule, successfully to preserve its ethnic identity. Only physical extermination or mass deportations could eliminate such a territorially compact ethnic group as a socially cohesive and nationally self-aware entity. And these are not the policies that Soviet authorities are likely to adopt.

According to Shtromas's second chapter, no satisfactory solution of the nationalities problem is possible within the confines of the Soviet political system which deprives the nations and nationalities living under it of their basic liberties and free self-expression. Therefore, "the persistent and sharpening multinationalism within the USSR is the time-bomb ticking under the surface of the illusory Soviet monolith." Shtromas does not think, however, that the non-Russian nations of the USSR and the Soviet bloc could liberate themselves from Soviet oppression on their own. The prerequisite for the liberation of the non-Russians is the collapse of the Soviet system in Moscow, although such a collapse might be precipitated by a sufficiently strong nationalities crisis.

One of the most interesting features of the revival of non-Russian nationalist movements in the USSR in 1987–1989 was the reaction of Russian public opinion to these movements. The Russian public engaged in various manifestations of support for the Armenian claim to Nagorno Karabakh. Mass demonstrations and meetings in Moscow and several other Russian cities condemned the murderous suppression by the Soviet military in April 1989 of the Georgians who had peacefully petitioned for the restoration of their nation's independence. The Russian central press carried numerous articles that responded sympathetically to the plight of ethnic groups in North Russia and Siberia and backed their demands for unhindered national development. Substantial support was also given by Russians, living in Russia, to the Baltic nations' pleas for sovereignty and to demands of the Ukrainians and Byelorussians to enhance the status and usage of the national languages in their respective republics. These "pro-ethnic" manifestations on the part of the Russians corroborate the thesis of Shtromas's chapter that a substantial part of authentic Russian public opinion favors the cause of freedom and independence for non-Russians and sides with them in the common endeavor to get rid of the levelling communist Soviet yoke.

In chapter 3, Victor Swoboda disputes Shtromas's thesis about the willingness of the Russians to let Soviet non-Russians separate themselves from Russia's core and to form independent nation states. In the context of his own subject, Eastern Slavs, the Ukrainians and Byelorussians, Swoboda is, on the whole, right. Some Russian nationalist authors (Solzhenitsyn among them) talk vaguely about the natural union between all Eastern Slavs; some remain entirely silent on this issue; and some (such as Shimanov and Vagin) argue that the unity of the Slavic Orthodox Christians should be preserved under all circumstances. In effect, they would not mind the separation from Russia's core of the Western parts of the Ukraine and Byelorussia, where most of the inhabitants are Catholics and Uniates, but would oppose the independence of the mainlands of the Ukraine and Byelorussia which are overwhelmingly Orthodox.

Splitting the Ukraine and Byelorussia on religious grounds would be totally unacceptable to either the Ukrainians or Byelorussians, since for both the Catholic Uniate and the Orthodox the preservation of national unity takes clear precedence over their religious differences. Both nations are also equally and firmly united in their unswerving ultimate desire to become independent nation-states—a desire that they clearly demonstrated in 1917-1919, when for a short period of time they managed to establish, and successfully to run, their own sovereign polities. Swoboda's meticulous analysis convincingly proves that during the seventy years of Soviet rule the ideology of the Ukrainians and Byelorussians has remained basically unchanged; that today, as in 1918, their main goal is to establish sovereign and liberal-democratic nation-states.

Very few specialists doubt that Swoboda's thesis is true of the Ukrainians. But many accept Maksudov's thesis but the Byelorussians have lost their separate national identity and have become practically indistinguishable from the Russians. The events of the last two years, however, strongly support Swoboda's thesis and undermine Maksudov's. Scores of "informal organizations" devoted to the protection of Byelorussia's cultural and historical monuments, to the preservation and promotion of Byelorussian language and literature, and to other nationally relevant causes, have sprung up in Byelorussia under *glasnost'* literally overnight and were, somehow unexpectedly, joined by very large numbers of people. One of these informal organizations, *Tuteishyya* (the Locals), is a society of young authors who write in Byelorussian. It has launched bold and quite imaginative initiatives that are aimed at bolstering the Byelorussian national identity and traditions, an effort that has become quite popular.

On October 19, 1988, representatives of these "informal groups" gathered in Byelorussia's capital, Minsk, to form a United Byelorussian Historical-Educational Society, "Martyrolog," and also to elect a Working Commission for the Organization of the Popular Front for the Support of *Perestroika* that is modelled on analogous Popular Fronts formed previously in the three Baltic republics.

The Byelorussian Soviet authorities who were alarmed by such spontaneous developments decided to suppress them. On October 30, a mass meeting called by *Tuteishyya* with the support of the official Minsk Cultural Fund to commemorate deceased ancestors (*Dzyady*), was brutally dispersed. Water cannon and tear gas were used, many hundreds of people were beaten up, and even more were arrested and sentenced for hooliganism, some only for having dressed up in clothes containing white and red colors—the national colors of Byelorussia—which always have been treated by the Soviet regime as subversive.

The Byelorussian Soviet authorities also severely curtailed all other activities of the "informal organizations." The Byelorussian Popular Front was publicly denounced by the Party and Byelorussian official press as bourgeois nationalistic, and its "self styled activities" were suppressed by the authorities. The Byelorussian "informals" however have found a way to avoid the total suppression of their activities. They started holding their meetings and protest actions in neighboring Lithuania, where the national movement *Sajudis* generously provided them with accommodations and other facilities, while the Lithuanian Party authorities do not interfere. Lately, the Moscow press[8] has strongly intervened in defense of the Byelorussian "informals" and condemned the behavior of the Byelorussian authorities as inconsistent with the basic principles of *perestroika* and *glasnost'*. But this intervention did not change the basically confrontational relationship between the government and the active indigenous population of Byelorussia. All the main Soviet Byelorussian officials who initiated the intransigently intolerant policies towards the "informals" are still in office and continue to stick to their suppressive attitudes to any grassroot initiatives.

The recent events in the Ukraine and especially in Byelorussia, provide strong support for Swoboda's arguments. Similar evidence supports the chapters by V. Stanley Vardys on the Baltic States, Dennis Deletant on the Moldavians, and Robert L. Nichols on Transcaucasia.

In Chapter 4, Vardys has meticulously proved—(in a polemic against some claims in Helene Carrere d'Encosse's famous book *The Decline of an Empire*)—the coherence and high self-awareness of the three Baltic nations which, according to him, successfully adjusted to Soviet rule, but never accepted it as legitimate or stopped aspiring for the restoration of their authentic independence and freedom. In 1988–89 the Balts proved much more about their true national and political attitudes and goals than Vardys even tried to claim for them.

Among the Balts, the Estonians were in the most desperate demographic and ecological situation. That situation was so intolerable that the Estonian Soviet government itself had to initiate in 1987 some moves aimed at curbing the damage the Moscow central planners were thoughtlessly inflicting upon Estonia. The Estonian authorities vigorously opposed—in fact vetoed—Moscow's decision on full scale phosphate mining which would have terminally poisoned Estonia's fresh water resources; they also introduced a 16,000 rubles tax on each worker that Estonian enterprises hired from outside Estonia. Meanwhile, Estonian scholars elaborated plans for Estonia's economic autonomy (the so-called regional economic self-accounting) which the Estonian government approved and officially submitted to Moscow for adoption. The Estonian people enthusiastically responded to these moves and spontaneously began forming grassroot organizations for the support of *perestroika* as well as for generating new demands that advanced the progress of Estonia's freedom. This is how the Estonian Popular Front came into existence in the spring of 1988.

The Latvians and Lithuanians, who saw that the Estonians had succeeded in their unprecedented moves, decided to follow suit and formed their own popular fronts (called the Movement or Sajudis in Lithuania). In their cases it was not the governments but the public, led by the creative intelligentsia, that took the initiative. By 1989, the Lithuanians, who had previously followed Estonian initiatives, replaced the Estonians as the champions and leaders of the Baltic popular movement for freedom and democracy and, ultimately, for full self-determination and sovereignty. The Lithuanian equivalent of the Popular Front, *Sajudis*, is now practically in charge of the Republic.

These developments drastically changed the mentality of almost all the Lithuanians, and they started to behave as if they were already living in a free country that was independent of Moscow. In March 1989, Lithuanian institutions of higher education, without asking anybody's permission, abolished all the obligatory courses on Marxism-Leninism, Dialectical and Historical Materialism and similar disciplines and replaced them by instruction in Western style social sciences. State-run publishing houses printed uncensored works, and a whole range of independent newspapers and magazines were started. The youth organizations that functioned in independent Lithuania—the Scouts, *Ateitininkai* (a Catholic youth organization), the Neo-Lithuanians (a nationalist youth organization that in pre-war Lithuania was allied with the ruling Nationalist Party), et al.—were reestablished and quickly acquired mass membership in no time. The women's Catholic organization, *Caritas*, has been restored, too, and it held an inaugural meeting that was attended by more than 15,000 delegates in April 1989. The Christian Democratic Party was also restored with the official blessing of the Lithuanian Catholic Church and its Primate, Vincentas Cardinal Sladkevicius. The Lithuanian Democrats, a new political party formed ad hoc, joined the Sajudis movement which accepted the new party within its ranks as a part of the movement. The restoration of the Lithuanian Social-Democratic Party is now in the offing, too.

Lithuania's Communist Party and government, after some hesitation and change of leadership, decided to cooperate with these popular movements to avoid loss of control and to exercise a moderating influence. The traditional, pre-Soviet Lithuanian symbols (e.g. the three color yellow-green-red flag, the Vytis [Pursuit] coat of arms, and the old national anthem) were restored to official status; the "bourgeois" independence day (February 16) was officially celebrated and declared a national holiday in 1989 (its spontaneous celebration had been brutally suppressed in 1988); the Secret Protocols to the three Nazi-Soviet (1939–1941) pacts were tacitly acknowledged and their publication was permitted. In May 1989, the Lithuanian Supreme Soviet introduced unprecedentedly drastic changes in the Republic's Constitution. The Republic, not the Union, was proclaimed the owner of state property on Lithuanian territory; Union laws were declared subject to explicit approval by the Lithuanian Legislature; Lithuanian citizenship would no longer be granted automatically to every Soviet citizen residing in Lithuania, etc. These changes have far exceeded in their radicalism the changes in the Estonian Constitution that were introduced by the Estonian Supreme Soviet in November 1988 and that the Lithuanian Supreme Soviet at that time had refused to emulate in an effort to avoid confrontation with Moscow, which had declared the Estonian constitutional amendments null and void. At the same May 1989 session the Lithuanian Supreme Soviet also issued a formal declaration of Lithuania's sovereignty, a step that no other Soviet republic has yet emulated.

One can predict with some assurance that Latvia and Estonia will soon catch up with Lithuania. For the moment Moscow has left the Balts alone in apparent reliance on the local parties' and governments' ability to keep the overall situation from getting out of hand.

In chapter 5, Denis Deletant deals with the Moldavians from an historical perspective. Deletant's historical analysis shows the Rumanian identity of the Moldavians and somewhat dispassionately presents the unpalatably true facts about the forceful incorporation into the USSR in 1940 of the Moldavian part of Rumania. In doing so, Deletant explodes one by one the Soviet myths connected with Moldavia's annexation and its acquisition of union-republican status within the Soviet Union. The rich information in this chapter is generally unavailable elsewhere. Deletant's chapter does not, however, contain any specific information on Moldavia's present national attitudes and their aspirations for the future. At the time his chapter was written there was not much samizdat coming out of Moldavia and very little evidence of popular unrest. Artfully using available Soviet sources, however, Deletant came to the definitive conclusion that the so-called Moldavians continued to retain their Rumanian national identity and to withstand the vigorous attempts of Soviet authorities to "Moldavise" and "Russify" them. At the end of his chapter, Deletant states that "the strong sense of national identity that continues to be felt by the Rumanians in the Moldavian SSR, despite Soviet efforts to dilute it, suggests that their exercise of self-determination would produce the same results as in 1918, the last occasion on which they were able to do so," that is that they would choose to rejoin their Rumanian homeland. However, Deletant also admits that, given the circumstances of Ceausescu's rule in Rumania, the Moldavians would hardly rush to join Rumania now. They would, he thinks, rather prefer to remain, at least for the time being, within the USSR and do their utmost to get the Soviets to recognize their proper Rumanian, not Moldavian identity.

That these are the true preferences of the Moldavians was proved by the events that have transpired in the Moldavian republic since February 1987, when the long standing chairman of the Moldavian Writers' Union, Pavel Bocu, committed suicide and the writers decided to use this occasion to reshuffle the leadership of their Union. The new leadership of the Writers' Union began demanding the reintroduction of the Latin alphabet, which the Soviets, in order to justify their claim that Moldavia and Rumania were separate nations, had replaced with the Cyrillic. Following the Baltic example, the Moldavians, in June 1988, also formed their Popular Front which they called the Democratic Movement for the Support of *Perestroika*. This Movement started by demanding the elevation of the Rumanian language to the status of state language of the Moldavian SSR and the acceptance of Rumanian national symbols as official symbols of the Moldavian republic. Later, the issues of economic autonomy and separate citizenship were added to the Movement's agenda. The Movement also strongly challenged the policy of Russification and Soviet falsifications of Moldavian history.

Unlike the case in the Baltic states, the Moldavian Movement was immediately and strongly attacked by the Moldavian Party and government, which used the official press to accuse it of blatant "bourgeois nationalism" and of seeking to restore the kulaks in the countryside. According to the account of the official newspaper of the government of the Soviet Union, *Izvestiya*[9], the Moldavian authorities, led by the Party's First Secretary Semyon Grossu, initially refused to meet any of the Writers' Union's or the Movement's demands. In response to such high handed treatment, Moldavia's capital city Kishinev has become a scene of unending mass demonstrations and meetings in support of the Movement and its demands. Confronted with such a vigorous mass opposition, the Moldavian Soviet authorities started gradually and grudgingly to make concessions to these demands. But as soon as the issues of language and alphabet were thus more or less resolved, a new flair-up of popular unrest took place in Moldavia, this time in relation to the March 1989 election campaign to the USSR's Congress of People's Deputies. This time people protested against the Moldavian Soviet authorities' attempts to manipulate the lists of candidates for the election by eliminating from these lists those popular figures who enjoyed the support of the Movement. (One was a former Party worker, Anatoly Plugaru, to whose "electoral case" the *Izvestiya* article, noted above, was mainly devoted). The confrontation between the Moldavian Soviet authorities and the people, represented by the Movement and some other "informal groups," seems to continue unabated and it is rather significant that *Izvestiya* took a strong stand against the authorities.

Robert L. Nichols' chapter on Transcaucasia provides excellent background for proper understanding of the current Nagorno-Karabakh crisis between Armenia and Azerbaijan, as well as of the Georgian separatist unrest. This chapter also predicted the present turn of events in Transcaucasia and correctly identified separation from Russia as the ultimate aspiration of the Armenian, Georgian and Azerbaijani peoples.

It is interesting to trace how the evolution of the Armenian irredentist claim, concerning Nagorno-Karabakh, which the Armenians thought should be of no particular significance to Moscow, triggered a full-fledged national movement for Armenian independence. The blunt refusal by Gorbachev even to contemplate the possibility of changing Nagorno-Karabakh's present status as a province of Azerbaijan, the introduction of martial law in Armenia and of unconstitutional direct rule from Moscow in Nagorno-Karabakh itself, the scandal of the trial of the Azeri participants in pogroms against Armenians in Sumgait, the sly arrest and deportation for imprisonment in Moscow, in the aftermath of the tragic Leninakan earthquake, of the whole Karabakh Committee that had become at the time the recognized and popular leader of the Armenian nation—all these and scores of other instances of high handed treatment by Moscow convinced the Armenians, who traditionally had relied heavily for their national survival on Russia and who thus had been the most faithful allies of Russia in that area, that their continued membership in the USSR is incompatible with Armenia's national interests and its national dignity. It would be very difficult for Moscow now to appease the Armenians even with substantial concessions, and it is most likely that, once started, the movement for Armenia's national independence will not recede or change emphasis and goals.

The rough treatment of the Armenians and the decision to keep Nagorno-Karabakh Azerbaijani did not however endear the Gorbachev leadership to the Azeris either. On the contrary, they suspected that the whole issue of Nagorno-Karabakh was raised by the Armenians in cahoots with Moscow and that it represented only the first step in the process of separating Nagorno-Karabakh from Azerbaijan. The anti-Armenian mood of the Azeris has thus been extended to an equally anti-Russian mood. As a result, the Azeris started staging mass protest rallies in the central square of their capital city Baku, demanding the deportation from their territory, not only of all Armenians and Russians, but also of the whole "treacherous"

Central Committee of Azerbaijan's Communist Party with the First Secretary Vezirov at its helm. Green Islamic flags and portraits of the Ayatollah Khomeini gradually started to dominate these rallies and Azerbaijan's separation from the USSR became their main theme. There was however some disagreement among the Azeri protestors on what should be done with their country after its separation from the USSR, with some groups favoring Azerbaijan's integration into Iran (where about half of the Azeri population already lives) and most others advocating incorporation into Turkey with which, although the Turks are Sunis and the Azeris Shiites, the Azeris identify themselves ethnically and linguistically. Interestingly, the pro-Turkish groups used as an argument in favor of their view Turkey's membership in NATO, saying that, because of this membership, Turkey would be much better equipped than Iran to counter Soviet claims for regaining Azerbaijan.

How can one explain the fact that the leadership of each union republic deals with its own nationalist movements in the ways which it finds most suited? In the Ukraine for example, the authorities effectively prevented the formation of a nationwide Popular Front. They half-heartedly tolerated the existence of such locally based fronts in the cities of Kiev and Odessa, but when the representatives of a number of "informal groups," mainly from the Western Ukraine, had met in L'viv to form an All-Ukrainian Democratic Front for the Support of *Perestroika* in July, 1988, the Ukrainian authorities took drastic action to thwart this endeavor. The main activists of this would-be Democratic Front (e.g. Ivan Makar and Father Mikhailo Havryliv) were arrested and imprisoned. Together with the members of the Armenian Karabakh Committee and some leading members of Georgian separatist groups, they constitute the so far still small core of political prisoners of the Gorbachev era.

No official criticism was voiced in Moscow of these actions by the Ukrainian authorities, still led by the Brezhnevite old-timer Volodimir Shcherbitsky. On the other hand the Byelorussian authorities were severely criticized in *Literaturnaya Gazeta* and *Ogonyok* for taking analogous repressive action against Byelorussian "informal groups." Perhaps the explanation is that the Byelorussian authorities publicly suppressed a mass meeting whereas the Ukrainian ones let the mass meetings and demonstrations take place in L'viv in July 1988 without much interference and then took drastic action against the newly formed Democratic Front later in August when the crushing blow delivered by the authorities took everyone by surprise. One should note however that in the public criticism of the Byelorussian and Moldavian leaderships (the latter, as mentioned above, was voiced in *Izvestiya*), the main point was the unwillingness of these leaderships to listen to *legitimate* popular demands and the provocation by these leaderships of *unnecessary* confrontations between the authorities and the people. There was no such criticism aimed at the Ukrainian leadership although its attitudes and actions were almost identical with the ones undertaken by the Byelorussian and Moldavian leaderships.

It should also be noted that the Kremlin categorically denied any responsibility for the brutal suppression by troops, using sharpened shovels and poisonous gas, of the peaceful demonstration by Georgians demanding their nation's independence, which took place in Tbilisi in April 1989, and blamed that suppression on the local Georgian leadership.

The only place where there is very little confrontation between the republican authorities and the powerful grassroot supported popular fronts is the Baltic. But this present consensus had not been achieved there easily either. Although it was the Estonian government which first confronted Moscow by launching independent initiatives, the reaction of the same government to the "excessive demands" of "informal organizations" was initially very negative. The then First Secretary of the Estonian Communist Party's Central Committee, Karl Vaino, took a very confrontational stance towards the Estonian Popular Front, but, as a result, was removed from office by an extraordinary Plenum of the ECP's Central Committee and replaced by Vaino Valjas, a man who sympathized with the Popular Front and its goals. The same pattern was later repeated in Lithuania, where the confrontationally minded First Secretary, Rimgaudas Songaila, was replaced by a Sajudis sympathizer, Algirdas Brazauskas. No such changes of leadership have yet taken place either in the Ukraine or Byelorussia or Moldavia.

The very structure of authority in the USSR and Soviet political traditions suggest that, before taking a definite stance on any issue or engaging in any political action, the republican leadership would seek approval and direction from Moscow. It may be true that Gorbachev learned about the suppression of the Georgian rally, as Politburo member Edward Shevardnadze has stated, only several hours after the event, but some important official in Moscow had to sanction the use of troops. The Commander of the Transcaucasian Military District General Igor Rodionov, who issued orders to move the troops against the demonstrators, is subordinated not to local party and government authorities in Tbilisi but directly to Moscow. Only orders issued by the Minister of Defense or his deputy, or by the All-Union Central Committee of the Party, in the guise of a decision of the USSR's Defense Council, would cause him to act as he did. This fact shows that both the Georgian authorities and the military forces stationed in Georgia could have acted as they did only upon being instructed to do so by "someone" in the Kremlin, though both Gorbachev and Shevardnadze may have been totally unaware of it.

It is also apparent that both the Estonian Vaino and the Lithuanian Songaila took a confrontational stance towards their respective popular fronts with the explicit approval of, or even on direct orders by, *someone* in the Kremlin, whereas their successors in office, who were from the outset sympathetic to the popular fronts, could neither have entertained such an attitude with impunity nor won their first secretaryships without the encouragement and powerful support of *someone else* in the Kremlin. Again, the sharp criticisms of the First Secretary of the Moldavian Party and of the whole Byelorussian leadership could not have appeared in the official central press unless *someone* in the Kremlin had sanctioned their publication, while the fact that these publicly criticized leaders still remain in office shows that *someone else* in the Kremlin strongly supports them and effectively blocks the efforts of the other(s) to remove them from office.

In chapter 2, Shtromas suggested that "the Gorbachev administration has not yet worked out its nationalities policy and still keeps that policy under debate in the framework of the *glasnost'* policy." The above facts suggest, however, that the problem is not so much in the Kremlin's ability to work out a coherent nationalities policy as in its ability to agree upon one or another version of such a policy. For it is more or less obvious from the prior accounts that there are at least two groups in the Kremlin: one that is accommodating to popular demands, and another that prefers the Stalinist-Brezhnevite suppression of any ideas or demands that come from below or through any other officially unendorsed channel. These two groups in the Kremlin have their clients and cronies in the local Party and government organizations who do the respective biddings of their patrons in Moscow. Hence, the discrepancies and inconsistencies in the present Soviet nationalities policy.

In 1988 a movement gradually began to form among the sub-union-republican-Soviet nations and nationalities (which are, with the exception of Estonians, all Soviet Finno-Ugrians, that advocates the abolition of the hierarchical structure of the national-territorial units of the USSR and the equalization of the rights of all these units on the level of the union republics. This Movement was initiated by the Volga Tatars and is starting to gain momentum elsewhere.[10] This is yet another sign of the strength of national consciousness of the smaller and weaker peoples of the USSR, of their determination to acquire the necessary means for restoring their full-fledged ethnic selves and for assuring themselves a secure future.

In chapter 9, Mikhail Agursky gives an historical overview and an original and imaginative analysis of the role of Jews in Russia and of Russo-Jewish relations. Agursky does not see any future for Jews in Russia but he also does not believe that Russia can have a great future without her Jews. His concluding imaginary parallel between the decline of Spain after the expulsion of Jews and what could happen to a "Jew-less" future Russia, is significant.

The first two chapters in Subpart "B," 10 (by Radoslav Selucky) and 11 (by Aurel Braun), consider respectively the impact of changes in the USSR on the communist states and societies of Eastern Europe and, vice-versa, the impact of developments in Eastern Europe on the political stability of the USSR. Chapter 12 by Zdzislaw Rurarz examines the political and socio-economic alternatives that Eastern European countries could, and would, adopt, if and when the opportunity arose for them to do so freely. This chapter is complemented by chapter 13 in which Tadeusz Musiol expresses some ideas, related to the potential impact of the Eastern European political institutions in exile on choosing and shaping the socio-political alternatives for Eastern Europe.

While these four chapters of Subpart "B" discuss the problems of the inter-relationship between the USSR and the Soviet Bloc in a comprehensive manner, the next two chapters, 14 and 15, are devoted to Poland only. Christopher G.A. Bryant analyzes the problems of legitimacy in Poland, whereas Stanislaw Andreski looks at Poland in the hypothetical situation of cessation of Soviet control.

Finally, in chapter 16, Anthony Arnold examines the situation in Afghanistan in an effort to explore the extent to which the Soviet military and political engagement in that country has affected the moral-psychological situation in, and, consequently, the political stability of, the USSR.

Volume III could be used as a textbook for at least two different courses—on the ideological and cultural aspects of the Soviet society and polity (Part I); and on the Soviet Empire, its structure and problems (Part II). A course in Soviet nationalities could also usefully employ this Volume as a fully adequate textbook. Volume III is also an invaluable sourcebook on Soviet nations and nationalities, starting with the Russians themselves and including not only the major nations of the USSR but also some minor ethnic groups that are usually ignored by most books on the subject.

Another important aspect of Volume III is the fact that all of its contributors dealt with their specific topics from the perspective of assessing the long-term viability of the Soviet polity and of possible alternatives to that polity. The fact that the contributions to this Volume have remained consistent with the rapid and radical changes that the USSR and the whole Soviet Bloc are currently undergoing has, in the editors' opinion, validated such an approach.

A. Shtromas and M.A. Kaplan

Notes

1. *Sovetskaya Rossiya*, March 13, 1988, 3.
2. See "From the Conversations of V. Fefelov (Frankfurt-on-Main) with the Chairman of the Council of the National Patriotic Front *Pamyat'* " D. Vasil'ev (Moscow), June–August, 1988," in *Veche* (Munich), No. 31, 1988; 227–235; quote on 228.
3. See *Komsomolets Uzbekistana* March 22, 1989.
4. See Tomas Venclova, "Ethnic Identity and Nationality Issue in Contemporary Soviet Literature", in *Studies in Comparative Communism*, Vol. 21, Nos. 3/4, Fall/Winter 1988, 319–329; for the quoted expression see 324.
5. See N. Eidel'man and V.T. Astaf'ev, "Perepiska iz dvukh uglov", in *Sintaksis* (Paris), No. 17, 1987, 80–87.
6. *Nash Sovremennik*, No. 5, 1986.
7. T. Venclova, *op. cit.* 324.
8. See *Literaturnaya Gazeta* of December 28, 1988; and *Ogonyok*, Nos. 47 and 51, December 1988.
9. See V. Vyzhutovich and E. Kondratov, "Postskriptum: ob iskussvve sozdavat' sebe opponentov". (Postscript: On the Art of Creating Opponents), April 20, 1989, 3.
10. For arguments in favor of making all the fifty-eight national-territorial entities of the USSR equal in status, see the article by the Volga Tatar writer Dias Valeev, "Prioritet ravnopraviya" (The Priority of Equal Rights), published in *Literaturnaya Gazeta*, November 23, 1988, 3.

PART

I

Ideology and Culture: The Relationship Between Russian and Soviet Identities

1

The Intellectual Tradition of Pre-Revolutionary Russia: A Re-examination

ANDRZEJ WALICKI

We are witnessing today a quite remarkable revival of interest in the Russian tradition. In the years of the Cold War such interest was alive mainly among Westerners. Today Western intellectuals have become somewhat less interested in Russia *as a problem* and, often, too easily satisfied with the existing level of understanding about it; among Russians, however, both in the Soviet Union and in the Russian diaspora, the Russian past has once more become a frame of reference for the controversy over Russia's future. We now have the new Slavophiles and the new Westernizers among the Russians. The first follow Alexander Solzhenitsyn in stressing the need to return to "native roots," in trying to prove that all evils have come to Russia from without, and in hoping for a renaissance of truly Russian values, interpreted, as a rule, in national-religious terms, with the emphasis either on national uniqueness, and the need to isolate Russia from the West, or on the universal-Christian significance of the Russian heritage, and the need for a spiritual crusade. The second group is inclined to follow those Western historians, like Tibor Szamuely or Richard Pipes, who see the Russian past as paving the way for Soviet totalitarianism and proclaims the need for gradual Westernization, insisting, as a rule, that all attempts to revive the national heritage or pre-revolutionary Russia can only result in such evils as an awakening of the worst forms of Russian nationalism and their fusion with official "Sovietism."[1]

This is, of course, a very simplified picture, one which deliberately ignores some intermediate positions and some complicating factors. Nevertheless, one can safely say that the controversy over Russia's future has once more become inseparable from the controversy over Russia's past. The only major exception to this rule is the work of Alexander Zinoviev, who has revealed the phenomenon of *homo sovieticus*, explaining it in terms of a quasi-universal theory of society—as a product of pure collectivism, very different from Western man but yet having no traits of a specifically Russian national identity. It is obvious, however, that Zinoviev's views are significantly, although negatively, related to the contemporary debate on Russia's past and future: on the one hand, they try to destroy the distinction between the terms Russian and Soviet, presenting Soviet man as a perfectly normal phenomenon and thereby ruling out any hope of a Russian spiritual and cultural revival; on the other hand, they are even more effective in killing hopes for a gradual Westernization of Soviet Russia.

This chapter is not an attempt to deal with the problem of the contemporary significance of Russia's spiritual and cultural heritage in its entire scope and complexity. I propose to consider only part of this vast problem: the post-Enlightenment intellectual history of Russia or, to put it differently, the intellectual tradition of the pre-revolutionary Russian intelligentsia. But even this important restriction does not enable me to do justice to all the complexities of my subject. What I want to say must be summary and, therefore, subject to many possible misinterpretations. To avoid such misinterpretations, or, at least, to reduce their number, I have decided to introduce my argument with some personal declarations and a methodological distinction.

First, I should like to testify personally to the role of pre-revolutionary Russian thought in the early years of my mature life, a testimony which seems appropriate here since my work on Russian thought, at least in the beginning, could hardly be separated from my own intellectual biography. Elsewhere I have described this role as follows:

> For me Russian thought was *an antidote* to Stalinism in all its forms—against [the temptation of] the Stalinist "New Faith" and against its inseparable counterpart in the constant pressure of aggressive lies. I saw the threat in sovietization, not russification. The authentic Russian culture did not seem to me a stupefying and enslaving force; on the contrary, it was a liberating force, sharpening my criticism of official lies, shaping my self-awareness and strengthening my moral identity.[2]

This personal experience explains my positive attitude to the idea of a Russian spiritual revival—a revival of Russian *national* values. Such a national revival should not be seen as an alternative to Westernization; on the contrary, it should be treated as a necessary step toward a *genuine* Westernization. Russians must learn to understand and assimilate the contemporary culture of the West but their own heritage is too great, their own historical experience too terrible to be ignored, or forgotten. It is arguable that in order to develop they must first heal their wounds, and this cannot be done without returning to their own roots, rediscovering their traditions, defalsifying and rethinking their tragic history.

Second, I must concede that in later years, after the Polish thaw of 1954–56 which greatly diminished the danger of sovietization and the pressure of official ideology, the results of my studies in Russian intellectual history considerably weakened my first enthusiastic response to the Russian tradition. I was sometimes overwhelmed by evidence of an affinity between certain trends in Russian intellectual history and the totalitarian frame of mind. Willy-nilly I had to agree with the authors of *Landmarks*[3] that the mainstream tradition of the Russian intelligentsia contained many dangerous elements, explaining some aspects of the tragic fate of Russia. I defended myself against pessimism, trying to keep alive my conviction that a Russian spiritual and cultural revival was desirable and possible. This conviction, however, was increasingly based upon irrational feeling rather than rational analysis.

The rational element in it was closely bound up with a value judgment and political choice. This choice consisted in rejecting the view that Russia, whether because of her past or for any other reason, was doomed, as it were, to remain totalitarian, and that "sovietism," although repulsive to us, harmonized perfectly with the genuine Russian tradition. Historical diagnoses are not innocent since they can influence historical reality. Too much stress on the native roots of the Soviet regime could only help to give this regime a national justification and, at the same time, discourage all attempts to influence it. If Russian communism is indeed the logical outcome of Russian history, including Russian intellectual history, the rational attitude toward it must be either to leave it to its own fate (isolationist option), or to strive for its total destruction (Hot-War option). Both these options are in my eyes morally and politically unacceptable. Historians of Russia, I feel, must pay due attention to the Russian roots of Sovietism but should not be tempted to see Russia's fate as preordained, let alone deserved and morally tolerable.

At this point I should like to involve the methodological distinction between the so-called "objective interpretation of tradition," in which the heritage of the past is seen as something objectively given, and the selective approach to tradition, concentrating on those elements of a nation's heritage which can provide a historical basis for *changing* historical reality in a desired direction. This selective approach is sometimes called "subjective interpretation" which is rather misleading, as it exaggerates the element of subjective arbitrariness instead of stressing that selectivity is simply part of a critical and evaluative attitude.[4] Nevertheless, the intention of this distinction is clear enough. Let me try to apply it to my subject.

Historians are naturally inclined to explain the present by reference to the past and I would be the last to deny that study of the intellectual tradition (in an objective sense) of a given country can bring about a better understanding of its present state. Hence, if we study the intellectual heritage of pre-revolutionary Russia we should not omit to ask ourselves whether knowledge of it reveals the existence of certain links between the Russian intellectual traditions and the victory and relative stabilization of Soviet totalitarianism. Unfortunately, it is difficult to deny the existence of such links. I can agree with Solzhenitsyn that there is no "*indissoluble link*" between "the universal disease of communism" and "the country where it first seized control,"[5] but I cannot endorse his tendency to present pre-revolutionary Russia as a country almost completely free from the germs of totalitarianism, not differing in this respect from the West. It is possible, however, to ask another question—a question about the possibility of finding some elements in the Russian intellectual heritage which *cannot* be seen as paving the way for totalitarianism, elements which are inherently incompatible with spiritual sovietization and, therefore, can be subjectively accepted by those who do not want to abandon hope of Russia's political and cultural regeneration. To *such* a question I am ready to give a positive answer. Indeed, the intellectual heritage of pre-revolutionary Russia contains many elements which can be taken over by the different opponents of the various sorts of totalitarianism and used to create their respective "historical genealogies" or "subjective traditions."

Having given these explanations I can outline the subject of this paper. I shall concentrate on two questions: first, which traits of the pre-revolutionary Russian intellectual tradition seem to pave the way for the emergence of an "ideocratic" totalitarian state, i.e., a state committed to a single, positively formulated substantive goal, universalizing this goal and trying to achieve it by imposing on its citizens an all-embracing *Weltanschauung*, i.e., by controlling not only their external behavior but also their minds, their feelings, their consciences.[6] Second, which elements of Russia's intellectual heritage were especially valuable in resisting totalitarian temptations; which of them, if any, could be invoked today by those people who want Russia to have both political freedom and a national revival. In answering the first of these questions we shall try to come a little closer to an understanding of the *causes* of the Russian tragedy. In answering the second we shall adopt a different perspective and deal with Russia's past in relation to the question of Russia's future.

Let us turn now to the first of these questions. The literature on the subject is vast and the main contributions come from Russians, notably the prophetic analyses of the authors of *Landmarks* and Berdyaev's book on the origins of Russian communism.[7] I agree to a certain extent with some of the existing interpretations and, therefore, what I am going to say is, perhaps, not very original. But I am not deliberately striving for originality; my only aim in this attempt at clarifying my views on the subject is to achieve a closer approximation to the truth.

It has become commonplace to point out that the mainstream ideologies of the Russian intelligentsia, including Marxism, could be classified as quasi-religions, striving for terrestrial, collective salvation.[8] If so, they may justifiably be classified as variants of secularized millenarianism—sometimes intense, sometimes somewhat diluted, but always containing a strong element of terrestrial/collective salvationism. Even the militantly antireligious Russian scientism of the 1860s in fact differed widely from the usual positivist scientism of the epoch; it was rather an ardent quasi-religious *belief* in science as the means of a universal and final redemption. On the other hand, it should be remembered that mainstream religious thought in Russia was also permeated by eschatological utopianism and millenarian aspirations.[9] This tendency was strongly rooted in the tradition of the Orthodox church, with its emphasis on the Holy Ghost, the divinization of the world and eschatological fulfillment, a tradition deeply inimical to the rationalism and individualism of the West in its rejection of the scholastic (i.e., rationalist) approach to theology and its absorbtion of the mystical heritage of Christian neoplatonism, especially "certain elements of Christian gnosis."[10]

Eric Voegelin has described the revival of gnosticism as "the nature of modernity," defining it as the "fallacious immanentization of the Christian eschaton,"[11] produced by "the desire for a redivinization of society."[12] It is obvious that gnosticism conceived in this way is closely related to millenarianism: the latter is, in fact, a form of the gnostic desire to impart meaning to historical events and to cooperate in directing history toward its eschatological fulfillment. From this perspective both modern gnosticism and millenarianism can be defined as a reaction against Augustinian Christianity, which had radically separated redemptive events from profane happenings, *Heilsgeschehen* from *Weltgeschichte*.[13] "The Christian doctrine from Augustine to Thomas," wrote Karl Löwith, "had mastered history theologically by excluding the relevance of the last things. This exclusion was achieved by the transposition of the original expectations into a realm beyond historical existence." In spite of this, however, the temptation to see eschatology in a terrestrial form proved ineradicable and found expression in modern gnostic/millenarian ideas and movements.[14] All such ideas could perform, often simultaneously, two different functions: (1) promoting the terrestrial, this-worldly orientation, thus trying to reconcile the hope of salvation with the process of secularization, and (2) restoring the divine meaning to terrestrial history, thus bringing about its redivinization. The intellectual history of the radical Russian intelligentsia provides many excellent examples of the first category while Russian religious thought abounds with good illustrations of the second. Young Chernyshevsky linked his socialism to the concept of a "new Messiah, a new religion, and a new world,"[15] Vladimir Soloviev expressed his millennial dreams in the vision of a "free theocracy," but both were equally imbued with the hope of a terrestrial salvation.

Among the critics of the immanentization or terrestrialization of the Absolute was the Russian legal philosopher, Pavel Novgorodtsev. We find in his works the view later developed by such thinkers as Voegelin or Löwith: that any attempt to place the Absolute not *above* but *within* history creates false Absolutes and encourages the mortal sin of idolatry.[16] Typical forms of such idolatry are, on the one hand, the idolatry of progress combined with secular (or quasi-secular) utopianism and, on the other, various combinations of religious belief with millenarian hopes of a heavenly city on earth. All possible variants of such tendencies are to be found in pre-revolutionary Russian thought but undoubtedly the most widespread and dangerous was the idolatry of secular, or quasi-secular progress—especially when combined with a belief in possession of a "truly scientific" knowledge of the necessary laws and preordained end of history.

The authors of *Landmarks*, especially Sergei Bulgakov and Semyon Frank, described the radical Russian intelligentsia as militant monks of the religion of earthly salvation. How penetrating this observation was can be seen by comparing the characteristics of the Russian radicals with the results of contemporary analyses of the typical features of millenarian ideologies and movements. True, the revolutionary millenarianism of the Russian radicals was more or less deeply secularized, consciously avoiding religious terminology and therefore very different, outwardly at least, from narrowly defined *religious* millenarianism. Nevertheless, it shared almost all features of classical religious millenarianism, such as:[17] the belief that history has its predetermined, underlying plan and that earthly salvation will be achieved by an elite of the elect (a revolutionary vanguard, or a revolutionary class); a dualistic, Manichaean vision of the world dividing people into the elect and the condemned, saints and satans, followers and opponents ("progressives" and "reactionaries"), forces of light and forces of darkness; a readiness to accept evil as the price of the victory of Good, whether by accepting the sufferings of the present generation for the sake of future happiness, or by justifying blood and violence as a means of achieving an earthly paradise; finally, the gnostic belief in initiation into "true knowledge," providing ready-made answers to all questions and elevating its possessors above the uninitiated, ignorant masses. The presence of all these features, combined with intense commitment to "the cause," makes it clear that pre-revolutionary Russian radicalism, including a significant part of its non-revolutionary wing, should be described as a secularized, or quasi-secularized, millenarian movement. This movement undoubtedly expressed a search for absolute certainty, for an all-embracing ideology providing clear solutions to all problems, both intellectual and moral, and produced a powerful tendency to subordinate everything to the collective goal, and to absolutize this goal, i.e., to see it as the final fulfillment of human destiny, worthy of realization at whatever cost and demanding total commitment. In this sense it can hardly be denied that the intellectual and moral tradition of this movement had its share in paving the way for the victory of communist totalitarianism.

The famous nineteenth-century controversy over the role of objective and subjective factors in historical progress may be interpreted in this light as a dispute between the gnostic and the activist-voluntarist variety of secularized millenarianism. Belinsky's intellectual struggle with the dialectics of historical necessity—his "reconciliation with reality" as the embodiment of a dialectical phase in the unfolding of Historical Reason, followed by his rejection of existing reality in the name of the dialectical laws of progress—provides an excellent example of gnostic initiation.[18] A similar experience of initiation into deeper knowledge of the *objective* underlying plan of history is to be found in the intellectual biography of Plekhanov, "the Father of Russian Marxism," who was well aware of the structural similarity between his Marxism and Belinsky's Hegelianism.[19] In contrast to this, the populist "subjectivists," Petr Lavrov and Nikolai Mikhailovsky, emphasized subjective moral choice, rejecting the idea of objective necessity governing historical processes. However, despite appearances, this difference was not as great as it was thought to be. The "subjectivists" did not reject the idea of initiation; indeed their notorious attempts to define the "criterion of progress" expressed an ardent search for salvation through conversion to "true knowledge." Their emphasis on the existential aspect of truth, i.e., on "living in truth" and not merely knowing what is true, brought them even closer to religious millenarianism, while their fight against historical determinism did not, as a rule, involve a rejection of the notion of the inner meaning of history. Like the objectivists they recognized this idea in the movement towards socialism, which they saw as restoring, on a higher level, the communal values of the archaic past. This enabled them to treat Russia, because of its peasant communes, as the chosen nation of socialism. At the same time, of course, it reproduced the classical trinitarian scheme of the original paradise, then lost and to be regained. This scheme, in which socialism took the place of the millennial Third Realm and the Russians were endowed with a unique universal-historical mission, strongly appealed to the Russian radicals, both objectivist and subjectivist. Even Herzen, in spite of his ardent, though inconsistent, revolt against all attempts to find meaning in history (as expressed in his splendid book *From the Other Shore*), could not resist its fascination.

Lenin's version of Marxism represented an organic fusion of "objectivism" and "subjectivism." He took from Plekhanov the idea of an objective, teleological development of history while also stressing the importance—often *decisiveness*—of the "subjective factor." In this way he combined the dogmatic certainty deriving from gnostic initiation into the "higher knowledge" with a militant activism stemming from the firm conviction that ultimate fulfilment would not come by itself, that the pace (if not the general outcome) of historical events depended on human will, consciousness and organization. It is easy to see that this emphasis on will throws some light on the phenomenon of the so-called voluntarism, characteristic of all "real socialist" societies. But the most sinister, most totalitarian feature of Leninism is its emphasis on consciousness, a kind of consciousness, moreover, which supposedly reflects the inner logic of history but cannot be generated spontaneously and, therefore, must be brought into the movement from without, by the initiated elite. This view highlighted the need to raise people to the level of "correct consciousness" by means of organized mass indoctrination; in other words, it justified spiritual tyranny, the worst feature of a totalitarian "ideocracy."

To be sure, millenarian and messianic motifs were not monopolized by Russian radicals; they were conspicuously present in some currents of conservative nationalist ideology—Dostoevsky's case is typical and the best known in this respect and also in religious thought, irrespective of its political orientation (cf., Chaadaev, the Slavophiles, Vladimir Soloviev). Other common features of both radical and non-radical, antireligious and religious trends in Russian thought were also to be found. In the present context I shall restrict myself to a brief discussion of two: *Gemeinschaft*-type collectivism and the censure of law.

It is easy to see that these two features were interconnected: the censure of law was closely bound up with a commitment to collectivism of the *Gemeinschaft* type and with fear of the cold, impersonal, legalistic *Gesellschaft*. Both right-wing and left-wing Russian thinkers—the Slavophiles and Dostoevsky on the one hand, the Populists and Anarchists (from

Bakunin to Tolstoy), on the other—were strongly inclined to see the peasantry of earlier times as embodying the spirit of an authentic brotherly community which could dispense with written law and prevent the development of egoistic individualism. Both groups too easily condemned civil rights and political liberties as mere masks for capitalist exploitation. Both perceived capitalist development, and the formalization in legal terms of social bonds which it involved, as something peculiar to the West, coming to Russia from without and not worthy of acceptance. Law and legal rights were condemned in Russia for various reasons and by different groups: in the name of autocracy or in the name of freedom, in the name of Christ or in the name of Marx, for the sake of higher spiritual values or for the sake of material justice.[20] In this manner left-wing and right-wing Russian intellectuals supported one another in a suspicion of the law and in hostility to liberal values. Bogdan Kistiakovsky, one of the authors of *Landmarks*, wrote of it in his famous essay *In Defense of Law*—the only contribution to *Landmarks* which criticized not only the Russian radical intelligentsia but the Russian intellectual tradition as a whole. He also pointed out that ordinary members of the Russian intelligentsia could easily combine such a contempt for law with a tendency toward the detailed formal regulation of all social relations—a tendency characteristic of the police state, as opposed to the rule-of-law state. Reading his essay (written in 1909) creates an impression that the final outcome of the Russian revolutionary movement was unavoidable and that Russian intellectuals of almost all political and philosophical persuasions had their share in paving the way for it.

At this juncture it is proper to stress that collectivism combined with disrespect for law was equally characteristic of Russian democratic radicals and of the supporters of autocracy. In Russia democracy was opposed to aristocracy rather than to autocracy; this particular feature of Russia's political culture[21] affected even in the Russian language in which it is perfectly possible to talk of a "democratic autocracy" while a "noble democracy" (as in Poland) sounds like a contradiction in terms. The Russian democratic tradition was not liberal-democratic but populist, and populism is known to be perfectly compatible with a strong paternalistic authority. Russian monarchism, on the other hand, was often ostentatiously anti-aristocratic, stressing its popular roots and presenting itself as curbing the strong in the interests of the weak. In both cases the individual was seen as weak, dependent, incapable of self-reliance, needing support from a tutelary state, whether autocratic or socialist. Even Russian anarchism was strongly collectivist, explicitly condemning individualist values. Bakunin and Kropotkin saw the *political* and *juridical* organization of society as their chief enemy, while at the same time, in sharp contrast to the anarchism of Thoreau (not to mention Max Stirner), fully accepting man's dependence on the "natural," unwritten laws of society, as manifested in the bonds of tradition and custom. They wanted maximum disalienation through participatory democracy but did not care about the "negative" freedom of the individual. On the contrary, they agreed with the Slavophiles that freedom individualistically conceived, freedom *from* the pressures of community, could lead only to maximum alienation and a dangerous disintegration of both personality and society.

Thus, I must admit that certain features of the intellectual heritage of the pre-revolutionary Russian intelligentsia and of Russian political culture in general might legitimately be seen as explaining the relatively easy victory of totalitarian dictatorship in Russia. It is necessary to stress, however, that all these features of this intellectual tradition explain only some weaknesses of the non-totalitarian forces and their insufficient resolution in resisting totalitarian temptations, but not the actual emergence of a militant totalitarian ideology. The example of Nazi Germany has shown that totalitarianism can win even in a country well known for its respect for law. The millenarian patterns underlying so many currents of both Western and Russian thought cannot be treated as by themselves producing totalitarian consequences; neither Norman Cohn nor Jacob Talmon has demonstrated a *direct* and *necessary* relation between millennial dreams and the emergence of modern totalitarianism.[22] Even more doubtful is the claim, made by F. A. Hayek among others, for an inner connection between totalitarian socialism and traditional communalism,[23] i.e., the type of collectivism which was so idealized by the various Russian admirers of the peasant commune. The fundamental difference between these two types of collectivism was aptly shown by Georg Simmel: "Modern socialism has one main feature which is totally antipathetic to the earlier collectivism of landed property and quite alien to the farmer's impulses in life, namely the complete control of production by reason, the will and the organizing calculations of man."[24]

At this point we can at last, grasp the crucial element in the structure of totalitarian thought: the idea of seizing total control over social forces, of subjecting them to reason and becoming thereby masters of our own collective fate; in other words, the idea of subjecting history to man's conscious will and rational planning. While millenarian tendencies, a penchant for collectivism and a failure to properly understand the value of law can be seen as native to Russia (although not *distinctively* Russian), the idea of man's rational control over his collective life was certainly something peculiarly Western, reflecting the Promethean ethos of the process of rationalization which characterized modern Western history. It is arguable that this idea was not bound to generate totalitarianism, that it could produce a non-totalitarian socialism, and that such was the intention of its greatest representative, Karl Marx. Possibly, although the historical function of a given ideology and its inherent logic are, obviously, two different things. It seems fair to say that Marxism, an organic product of the West, contained in itself, though not in a fully developed form, the best ideological justification of Communist totalitarianism,[25] while Russia, because of some features of her national heritage, was especially exposed to the danger of becoming its first victim. In Russia Marxism was bound, as it were, to give a new quality to the native collectivism and a new dimension to the old "teleocracy,"[26] which then provided ideological justification for subordinating everybody to total control in the name of the collective goal—a goal, supposedly, predetermined by history and freely chosen at the same time. In this way Communist totalitarianism was born. Its first representative in Russia was Petr Tkachev, but he was too obsessed with equality and too little concerned with the task of rational modernization. A full-fledged, modern form of Communist totalitarianism is to be found only in Leninism.

Thus, in spite of all qualifications, the answer to my first question, whether the Russian intellectual tradition did contain traits which could be seen as facilitating the victory of totalitarianism, must be in the affirmative. Yes, there were such traits. At the same time, I want to insist that although the origin of some of these traits can be linked with certain features of Eastern Christianity their function in nineteenth-century ideologies is to be explained by the historical conditions in which Russia as a country and the Russian intelligentsia as its intellectual elite had to develop, and not by centuries-old peculiarities of "Russianness."

The millenarian tendencies among the Russian intelligentsia are easily explained by such normal causes of millenarianism as deprivation, frustration, and isolation.[27] If we agree with Yonina Talmon that millenarianism is typical of people who are alienated, cut off from their traditional order and unable to satisfy their wants, confused and disoriented by the incongruity between indigenous and external influences, permeated by an increased feeling of self-importance combined with a feeling of isolation and political helplessness, depressed and frustrated by multiple deprivations and, at the same time, imbued with enormously inflated expectations, then we are forced to conclude that for historical reasons the Russian intelligentsia provided a milieu particularly responsive to millennial dreams. We should add to this that the phenomenon of the intelligentsia, i.e., of an intellectual elite alienated from the existing social system and painfully aware of its inalienable responsibility for the freedom and progress of "the people," is typical of backward agrarian countries facing the tasks of modernization. The more intense the feeling of social duty among such people, the more they are inclined to see themselves as a collective Messiah and to attribute messianic characteristics to their nation, or to the oppressed class with which they identify themselves. Finally, we must realize that the very nature of such an intelligentsia makes it prone to believe in the salvationist function of initiation to "true knowledge"—even without any direct influence from Christian gnosticism.

Other features of Russian thought with which I dealt above—a strong penchant for idealizing traditional agrarian collectivism and a notorious disrespect for classical liberal values, both equally characteristic of the Russian Left and the Russian Right, are also explicable without assuming any predetermined qualities of Russian national character. A clinging to communal traditions and a suspicious attitude to bourgeois freedom safeguarded by rational law is typical of all underdeveloped countries experiencing modernization as Westernization, i.e., as something alien to their native heritage, posing a threat not only to the values of the past but also to their national identity. As a rule, the uneven development of the world creates conditions which strengthen such tendencies through the ideological influence of the more advanced countries, when criticizing their own achievements as deeply disappointing, or merely "formal." George Lukács has shown how the Western critique of democracy—a critique stemming from "a certain disappointment with democracy on the part of the masses and their ideological spokesmen"—helped to engender the militant ideologies of the German radical Right.[28] In a similar way the retarded development of Russia created conditions in which the powerful influence of the Western criticism of capitalism, its "formal freedom" and its "juridical world-view," merged with certain elements in the native heritage and called into being an intellectual tradition deeply suspicious of law and hostile to liberal values. It is worth while to remind ourselves in this context that the influence of Marx's ideas in Russia was not restricted to those Russians who defined themselves as Marxists: as I have tried to show elsewhere,[29] Marx's critique of capitalism, liberalism and "bourgeois democracy" was instrumental in crystallizing the ideas of Russian populism and became an integral part of all currents of Russian populist (as well as anarchist) thought.

Let us turn now to my second question: what elements, or currents in Russian thought can be regarded as especially valuable for resisting totalitarianism on an intellectual level?

The first of these is the heritage of nineteenth-century Russian Westernism whose main contribution to Russian thought was the elaboration of the idea of a free, autonomous personality. Although the classical Westernism of the 1840s was not long-lived, its ideology influenced not only those thinkers who continued to believe that Russia should follow the general pattern of European progress. Its main heritage, the idea of personality, survived disillusionment with the bourgeois West and, thanks to Herzen and Lavrov, became an important part of the mainstream tradition of Russian populism. Although often combined with different forms of disrespect for law, it was invaluable as an antidote to collectivism, whether as exclusive concern with the happiness of the popular masses or as treating the individual as merely a means to future collective salvation. As a rule, the left-wing Russian thinkers were deeply critical of Western "bourgeois individualism" but, at the same time, they shared Belinsky's commitment to the "idea of personality" and tried to reconcile it with communal values. For this reason the mainstream tradition of the pre-revolutionary Russian intelligentsia was never *dominated* by pre-totalitarian currents of thought, although the presence of and relative strength of these attitudes and tendencies was undeniable. It is arguable, moreover, that the last two decades of Imperial Russia saw a conspicuous increase in awareness of the positive sides of individualism. Ivanov-Razumnik's *History of Russian Social Thought* (1908)—a book extolling the populist tradition but, at the same time, giving "individualism" a strongly positive connotation and presenting it as the main virtue of the radical intelligentsia—was very typical in this respect.

Secondly, I should mention the well-known tradition of Russian antirationalism, which included many currents and stages, from the backward-looking romanticism of the Slavophiles, through different variants of post-Slavophile conservative thought, to the forward-looking messianism of Vladimir Soloviev, politically allied to liberalism, and to the various thinkers of the so-called Russian religio-philosophic renaissance of the first decades of our century. True, there were also some dangerous tendencies within this tradition; its extreme right wing revived the old idea of Moscow as the Third Rome while its extreme left wing tended toward a chiliastically tinged mystical revolutionism. But the mainstream tradition of antirationalist religious philosophy in Russia deserves to be seen as a deeply anti-totalitarian spiritual force.

Let me try to be more specific. Antirationalist thought in Russia produced some of the best examples of the critical approach to that Promethean rationalism from which communist totalitarianism sprang. By this I mean the idea of man's conscious rational control over his own social forces; in other words, the project of subjecting human history—and thereby the whole of human life, both individual and social—to rational (or quasi-rational) collective planning. The Slavophiles, who saw this idea as peculiar to the West, treated such strivings as inherent in rationalist thinking and as leading inevitably to what they called "unity without freedom"—an artificial unity superimposed upon a deeply atomized society, destroying both genuine social bonds and the inner unity, "integrality" (*tselnost'*) of the human individual. Apollon Grigoriev, the ideologist of the "return to the soil" movement, added to this a profound criticism of the idolatry of progress and of the "goal-oriented" model of society, arguing that life was directed by divine creativity, and not by man's purposive reason; that man should listen to the irrational pulse of life instead of trying to control it. In Dostoevsky's novels these ideas were presented as the struggle between the religion of Man (Mangodhood) and the religion of God (Godman-hood), and it is widely recognized that his image of the Grand Inquisitor, seen as the logical result of replacing the first with the second was a prophetic anticipation and a powerful critique of the totalitarian ideal (in its most benevolent form, be it added).[30] From Dostoevsky a straight line runs to Soloviev's critique of "false theocracy" and to Berdyaev's warnings against the totalitarian dangers inherent in socialism as a religion[31] and in other forms of the terrestrialization of soteriology.

I fully realize that this is a somewhat over-idealized view, that Russian antirationalism—like its German counterpart to which it owed much—also contained many dangerous ideas. Nevertheless, it may justifiably be claimed that on the whole it offered deep insights into the nature of totalitarian temptations and was at the same time, well equipped to struggle against them. One of the reasons for this was its Christian character, markedly distinguishing it from certain currents in German antirationalism (Cf., the *Lebensphilosophie* of Nietzsche, or of Klages). It is arguable that the more Christian Russian thinkers were (Christian in substance, not necessarily in form), the more immune they were to the temptation of absolutizing any forms of earthly existence. Dmitry Merezhkovsky, who proclaimed a "new revelation" which was to rehabilitate the flesh and accord divine quality to matter by establishing a messianic Kingdom of God on earth, was, in spite of his transient popularity, less representative of the Russian religio-philosophic renaissance than those thinkers who, like Berdyaev, wanted to reconcile the Neoplatonic striving for godliness with the Orthodox-Christian view of the suprahistorical, transcendent nature of the Absolute. Because of this, Russian religio-philosophical thought culminated in the development of a Christian personalism, consciously and consistently opposed to all forms of material and spiritual enslavement.[32]

Another tradition of Russian thought which is worth mentioning in this context is much less known and was rather marginal in its effective influence on the pre-revolutionary Russian intelligentsia. It is not marginal, however, to a consideration of Russian thought from the point of view of its *potentialities*, i.e., if we look in it for traditions which were developing and consolidating themselves in the last decades of Imperial Russia and which might have become much more influential if the Bolshevik Revolution had not broken the continuity of Russian history. Moreover—from the point of view of the "subjective" approach to tradition, as explained above, this development should, I think, be singled out as especially attractive, deserving thoughtful study and practical continuation.

The tradition I mean is that of Russian liberal legal thought from Boris Chicherin to the legal theorists of the Kadet party.[33] It may sound odd, since Russia is rarely associated with liberalism or with law, and justly so. But precisely because of this it is important to realize that the liberal intellectual tradition in pre-revolutionary Russia was, in fact, much stronger than is usually believed, that the main concern of Russia's liberal thinkers was the rule-of-law state (*pravovoe gosudarstvo*), and that the most precious legacy of Russian liberalism was its contribution to the philosophy of law, as well as to what might be called the controversy about law, the debate in which the value of law as such was seen as a controversial issue.

The Russian liberal thinkers whom I have in mind were organically rooted in Russian intellectual history because they were deeply committed to the struggle against the prevailing negative attitudes toward law. Their legal philosophies were very different but these differences may be seen as links in a remarkably continuous process: that of transforming classical liberalism, as represented by Chicherin, first into a "new liberalism" (as represented, in its different variants, by Vladimir Soloviev, Pavel Novgorodtsev and Leon Petrażycki) and then, with Bogdan Kistiakovsky, into a "rule-of-law socialism." The differences in their strictly philosophical views and in their attitudes towards religion were often very sharp but all of them wanted to save the idea of law and to clarify it by clearly distinguishing between law as general rules of justice and law as administrative or governmental commands, by putting law above the state, and refusing to reduce it to the role of an instrument of political power. In other words they were united in opposing all forms of legal positivism, especially the command theory of law and Ihering's "jurisprudence of interests." They accused legal positivism of putting political authority, "the sovereign" (whether individual of collective), above law and thus paving the way for tyranny. They disagreed with the legal positivist view that law, as Kelsen put it, "can have any content whatsoever," and that jurisprudence should be concerned only with positive law, *ius qua iussum*, dismissing the problem of just law, *ius qua iustum*; they argued forcefully, however, that legal justice (i.e., justice enforced by law) should not be confused with morality because such a confusion brings about results equally disastrous for both morality and law. They all tried to develop a theoretical justification for the subjective rights of man, which would limit the scope of political power, including the power of a democratic majority. All placed law within the context of a general, often metaphysical, philosophy of man and a philosophy of values, trying to avoid the cynical relativism inherent, as they saw it, in positivism, and to find an independent criterion by which the value of existing positive laws could be judged and which could serve as a guide for future legislation.

Another common feature was their emphasis on the autonomy of law from politics, on the logical and axiological priority of the rule of law over political freedom. All the thinkers to whom I here refer were concerned with developing legal culture and to defend it against excessive politicization. They were quite clear that the rule of law was conceivable without full political freedom, but not the reverse; they opted for a rule-connected society (as opposed to an end-connected one), a society, in which political decisions could not be arbitrarily made, in which law would set the rules for politics, and not *vice versa*. Their increasing support for the tenets of the new, social liberalism, proclaiming the need to use the power of the state to secure to everybody his "right to·a dignified existence," was bound up with an effort to preserve classical liberal values in a changing world by creating an alternative to increasing government regulation and control. This alternative—*legal* regulation and *legal* control—was to bring about a partial socialization of economic relations without abandoning the classical-liberal principle of limited government. This applied also to the conception of rule-of-law socialism, as elaborated by Kistiakovsky and, later, Sergius Hessen.[34] The originality of this conception consists in seeing liberal socialism not simply as an extension of the democratic principle of popular sovereignty (through its application to the economic sphere), but rather as a higher stage in the development of the rule of law, i.e., as a further extension of the scope of human rights. Thus it was not a concession to populist democracy but a fusion of socialist and classical-liberal principles, emphasizing subjective rights and safeguarding them not only against all forms of arbitrary political power but also against the mechanisms of social conformity or the moral pressures of the community. The idea of law was seen as inseparable from the central idea of nineteenth-century Russian Westernism—the idea of personality. Law was to protect human personality against external compulsion exercised by the state; legal consciousness (as distinct from moral conscience) was to help individuals in defending their intellectual and moral autonomy against collective pressure.

It is obvious that such an intellectual tradition is impenetrable to totalitarian temptations. The existence of this tradition in Russia cannot change the overall view of Russian thought as permeated by deeply rooted anti-legal prejudices and containing many elements from which a totalitarian cult of the absolute ideocratic state could be built. On the other hand, however, the emergence of this tradition, its growing strength, and the high intellectual quality of its representatives provide arguments against the concept of Russian "exceptionalism" as, allegedly, an inherent enmity between the Russian nature and the spirit of law and an inherent affinity between the Russian mind and totalitarian strivings. It is important to add that this liberal tradition was not incompatible with the mainstream tradition of Russian religious thought: Vladimir Soloviev belonged to both and his influence on some liberal philosophers in Russia, including Novgorodtsev and Hessen, should not be neglected.[35]

To sum up: the intellectual tradition of pre-revolutionary Russia contains many currents, some explaining the relative ease of the victory of totalitarian communism in Russia, others throwing light on its national features, still others providing intellectual tools and spiritual resources for combatting it. The very fact of the richness, complexity and pluralism of this heritage makes it a powerful support for all those, Russians and non-Russians, who are battling against totalitarian tyranny. True, it also contains some pitfalls, especially dangerous for those Russians who have lost their faith in communism and are now looking for a new religion and a new collective purpose; in view of the increasing de-ideologization of the Soviet system, or, rather, the crisis of its ideological legitimacy, this danger should not be underestimated. But the best way of avoiding danger is knowledge—in this case a thorough, deep and critical knowledge of Russian intellectual history. Only such knowledge can provide us with both understanding and criticism, and only critical understanding enables us to select those ideas in the Russian heritage which are worthy of continuation and, on the other hand, to point out where the pitfalls lie and how to avoid them. For Russian patriots the knowledge of the intellectual tradition of their country should be not only a means of returning to their native roots but also a means for the attainment of critical self-awareness. The long-awaited spiritual and cultural revival of the true Russia, about which they dream, must be accompanied by a raising of the Russian national consciousness to a higher level and this is clearly impossible without a thoroughly critical attitude toward the Russian past.

Notes

1. A. Yanov, *The Russian New Right, Right-Wing Ideologies in the Contemporary USSR*, Institute of International Studies U. Cal., Berkley Press, (Berkeley, CA., 1978)
2. A. Walicki, *Spotkania Miloszem* [Encounters with Milosz], (London, 1985,)
3. See the contributions of Berdyaev, Bulgakov, Gershenzon, Izgoev, Kistiakovsky, Struve, Frank, to *Landmarks: A Collection of Essays on the Russian Intelligentsia, 1909.* (Boris Shragin and Albert Todd, New York, 1977.)
4. See J. Szacki, *Tradycja. Przeglad problematyki* (Tradition: A Survey of Prob-

lems), (Warsaw, 1971): 147–54. Cf., Max Radin, "Tradition." In *Encyclo-paedia of Social Sciences*, Vol. XV (New York, 1949): 62–67.

Szacki distinguishes between the three concepts of tradition which occur together in scholarly literature: The first might be termed *functional*, since attention is focused on the function of transmitting, in a given community, certain elements of culture from generation to generation. . . . The second has been termed *objective*, since the researcher's attention shifts from the transmission of elements to the elements themselves. The third might be termed *subjective*, since it is neither the operation of transmission, nor the object transmitted, that comes to the fore, but the attitude of a given generation toward the past, its acceptance of the heritage or its protest against it. (Tradycja 280–81, Summary in English).

5. A. Solzhenitsyn. "Misconceptions About Russia Are a Threat to America," *Foreign Affairs*, 58, No. 4, Spring 1980: 797.

6. For a definition of totalitarianism stressing "commitment to a single, positively formulated substantive goal" see Herbert J. Spiro, "Totalitarianism," in *International Encyclopedia of the Social Sciences*, Ed. by David L. Sills, Vol. 16, (1968): 106–13. Spiro, however, clearly underestimates the "ideocratic" character of communist totalitarianism, i.e., the aspect of it which is felt by Russian dissidents as the most hateful and the most oppressive.

7. See N. Berdyaev, *The Origin of Russian Communism*, (London, 1948), idem, *The Russian Idea*, (London, 1947)

8. A very good summary of the vast literature on millenarianism is to be found in Yonina Talmon, "Millenarian Movements," in *Archives Européennes de Sociologie*," Vol. 7, No. 2: (1966) 159–200. A shortened version of this study was published under the title "Millenarianism" in the *International Encyclopedia of the Social Sciences*, Vol. 10, (1968): 349–61.

9. Cf., V. Lossky, *The Mystical Theology of the Eastern Church*, (London, 1957): 112.

10. *Mystical Theology*, 104.

11. E. Voegelin, *The New Science of Politics: An Introduction*. (Chicago, 1952): 121.

12. *The New Science*, 110. For an interpretation of pre-revolutionary Russian ideologies as a kind of politicized gnosticism see Alain Besançon, *The Intellectual Origins of Leninism*. Trans. by S. Matthews. (Oxford, 1981.)

13. Cf., K. Löwith, *Meaning in History: The Theological Implications of the Philosophy of History*, (Chicago, 1949): 203.

14. *Meaning in History*, 114, 159, 202–3.

15. Chernyshevsky's diary, entry of 10 December 1848.

16. P. Novgorodtsev, *Ob obshchestvennom ideale*. 3rd ed. Berlin, 1921.

17. "Millenarian Movements."

18. Cf., My *History of Russian Thought From the Enlightenment to Marxixm* (Stanford, 1979 and Oxford, 1980): 121–27.

19. For an analysis of the relationship between Plekhanov's and Belinsky's views see A. Walicki, *The Controversy Over Capitalism: Studies in the Social Philosophy of the Russian Populists*, (Oxford, 1969): 153–65.

20. For a detailed analysis of these negative attitudes toward law see Chap. I of my forthcoming book *The Legal Philosophies of Russian Liberalism* (to be published by the Clarendon Press).

21. For the concept of "political culture" and its application to Russia see Archie Brown, ed. *Political Culture and Communist Studies*, (Macmillan Press, 1984)

22. N. Cohn, *The Pursuit of the Millennium*, (London, 1957) and Y. L. Talmon, *Political Messianism: The Romantic Phase*, (London, 1960). Cf. also Y. L. Talmon, *The Origins of Totalitarian Democracy*, (London, 1952).

23. See F. A. Hayek, *The Road to Serfdom*, (London, 1946) I should add that I agree with Hayek's argument that "our present moral views undoubtedly still contain layers or strata deriving from earlier phases of the evolution of human societies." (F. A. Hayek, *Law, Legislation and Liberty*, (London, 1982) Vol. II, 42). What I am critical of is only his assertion that there is a necessary connection between atavistic views on social justice and totalitarianism.

24. G. Simmel, *The Philosophy of Money*. (Boston, 1982) 352.

25. See my article on Marx in *Concepts of Liberty*. Cf., also A. Walicki, "Marx and Freedom," *New York Review of Books*, XXX, No. 18, (24 November 1983): 50–55.

26. For the distinction between "teleocracy" and "nomocracy" see Hayek, *Law, Legislation and Liberty*, Vol. II, 15, 38–42.

27. "Millenarian Movements," 181–91.

28. G. Lukács, *The Destruction of Reason*, London, 1980: p. 68.

29. See my *Controversy Over Capitalism*, 60–63, 132–53.

30. For a detailed study of the Slavophile and post-Slavophile critique of rationalism in nineteenth-century Russian thought (including Grigoriev, Dostoevsky and Soloviev) see my book *The Slavophile Controversy: History of a Conservative Utopia in Nineteenth-Century Russian Thought*, (Oxford, 1975.)

31. See N. Berdyaev, "Sotsyalizm kak religiya," in *Voprosy filosofii i psikhologii*, 17, No. 85, (1906):508–45.

32. See V. V. Zenkovsky, *A History of Russian Philosophy*. (London, 1953) 2; N. P. Poltoratzky, ed., *Russkaya religiozno-filosofskaya mysl' xx veka*, (Pittsburgh, 1975), S. A. Levitsky, *Ocherki po istorii russkoi filosofskoi i obshchestvennoi mysli*, 2, (Frankfurt/Main, 1981)

33. For a detailed presentation of this current of Russian thought see my *Legal Philosophies of Russian Liberalism*.

34. See S. Gessen (Hessen), "Problema pravovogo sotsyalizma," *Sovremennye Zapiski*, Paris, 1924–7, 22–30. For Kistiakovsky's views on rule-of-law socialism see his "Gosudarstvo pravovoe i sotsyalisticheskoe" in *Voprosy filosofii i psikhologii*, No. 85, 1906 and "Gosudarstvo i lichnost" (in B. Kistiakovsky, *Sotsyalnye nauki i pravo*, Moscow, 1916).

35. See A. Walicki, "Vladimir Solov'ev and the Legal Philosophies of Russian Liberalism," in *Russian Thought and Society 1800–1917. Essays in Honour of Eugene Lampert*. Ed. by R. Bartlett. Keele, 1984, 153–80. See also chapters on Soloviev, Novgorodtsev and Hessen in my *Legal Philosophies of Russian Liberalism*.

2

The Other Russia—Past and Future

PETER KELLY

Russia, according to the Great Soviet Encyclopedia, is now the RSFSR;[1] and the RSFSR, still according to Soviet thinking, is one component of a new advanced form of society called the Soviet Union, which has already achieved socialism and will go on to achieve communism. The Soviet patriotism which animates Soviet society has, allegedly, subsumed within itself previous narrower forms of national consciousness; and, while national characteristics, whether Russian or other, continue to exist, they are of secondary importance in the new society. For instance, local cultures provide the language in which the regional party newspaper can most conveniently be printed without, of course, any difference arising between the substance contained in the paper and that contained in *Pravda*; alternatively, local "folklore" can find innocuous expression in an evening of national dances.

If the assertions about the phasing out of Russia were as correct as they are familiar, this book would have no purpose; and the "Other Russia," which I have been asked to consider in this chapter, would be a topic for historical research, or an account of some quaint customs surviving among the older generation.

In considering whether some other Russia, "other" that is than the subsumed Russia of Soviet propaganda, continues to exist and what part it might yet play, it will be convenient to look first at the New Man, the Homo Sovieticus who, in theory, has replaced or soon will replace, the various nationalities of the Soviet Union. I have attempted to define his characteristics.

1. The first and most obvious characteristic of Homo Sovieticus is his certainty. The philosophical and moral doubts which have troubled humanity from its beginnings are over. Homo Sovieticus *knows*.
2. The general basis of Soviet Man's knowledge is atheism and historical determinism. But, more specifically and immediately, it derives from the interpretations by Marx and Lenin of the interplay of economic forces.
3. Notwithstanding the seeming narrowness of this philosophy Homo Sovieticus claims to derive from it a Gospel of comprehensive scope and universal application; and, when the Gospel is fully realized, under communism, mankind will no longer be afflicted by such evils as poverty, crime, and social strife.
4. In the meantime Homo Sovieticus is, above all else, a social animal concerned constantly to bring about the millenium. In his work (and he is always working) he is self-sacrificing; towards his fellow men (if they are right thinking) he is endlessly cooperative; toward the foes of communism, whether external (such as those plotting to attack the Soviet Union) or internal (such as religion), he is a merciless (*bezposhchadny*) foe.
5. To judge by countless statues and medallions, and a hundred turgid novels (and, after all, what other evidence have we got?) Soviet man personally is a somewhat stiff and humorless fellow. With his resolute gaze, his firmly set jaw, his military stride and, like as not, his banner triumphantly upheld, he seems somewhat remote from us ordinary mortals. One has difficulty imagining him playing with his children or cracking a joke. And you would hardly want to ask him to a party.

Can Russians really have been cast already into the new mold of Soviet Man? Prima facie, there are obvious reasons for doubting it. After all, Russian culture is so rich, so old and so deep-rooted that it would not be easy to transmute it into some minor variation of the new Soviet culture. If some of the characters of Chaucer's *Canterbury Tales*, written five hundred years ago, are recognizably English, and if some of the characters of the Old Testament are recognizably Jewish, why should a mere 67 years suffice to wash away the nature of Russia?

To take another obvious consideration: repeated assertions in *Pravda* constitute in themselves a reason for doubting the correctness of what is asserted. *Pravda* does not tell us that the sun rises in the East or that the Volga is a large river, not because it is afraid of boring us (this is the last consideration which would deter a Soviet editor), but because these facts are self-evident, and nobody is in any doubt as to their correctness. What is drummed into our heads day after day, not only by *Pravda* but by every

organ of propaganda, is that the Soviet Union is the Soviet Union and
nothing else, and that a new Soviet patriotism has taken over. If these
claims are true, why is it necessary to state them? But if *Pravda* after all
goes on making the claims, one is perforce reminded of the treacherous
queen in *Hamlet*—"The lady doth protest too much, methinks."

If, then, we think that Russia is not, after all, just some subunit of Soviet
culture, and if we doubt that the Russians have yet become Soviet Men,
what has now become of "Russianness"? In an attempt to describe, if not
define, so undefinable a concept, I have identified five aspects of Russian
life which seem to me particularly important, and shall suggest how they
relate to the "Party-line" put forward by Soviet propaganda. Inevitably,
the aspects I have selected are based on subjective choice; and my assessment of their continued significance must be judgemental rather than mathematical. This is regrettable but unavoidable. If, in treating this theme, I
were to assign quantitative values to the factors considered and to claim
that a unique mathematical conclusion was derivable from them, then I
should myself be more suitably employed in writing for *Pravda*.

Looking then at "Russianness," the first characteristic I identify is a
certain "dukhovnost," a certain otherworldliness; a certain lack of satisfaction with the everyday material world, even perhaps a certain lack of
interest in it; a straining after God, or some substitute for God; a readiness
to live for ideas.

We need look no further than the theory of Soviet communism for one
illustration of Russian *"dukhovnost"* (spirituality). Its underlying doctrine,
namely atheism, is as much a faith as belief in God is a faith. What communism is all about is the perfectability of Man, and the realization of
Utopia. The followers of the true faith must be ready to accept all sacrifices
in order to bring about Utopia; and they have a missionary role—all humanity must be freed from its enthrallment to outmoded doctrines and
their attendant miseries. These heady concepts are, in fact, the stuff of
idealism and religion. They are very far indeed either from pure materialism
or from the sort of political programs which might be proposed to people
in Western Europe. For instance, you could certainly sit through a congress
of the British Conservative party without any speaker either denying or
affirming the existence of God. Such an issue, in such a context, would be
considered irrelevant, even in bad taste, and anyone who suggested that
Utopia was around the corner would be likely to provoke ribald laughter.
The program eventually adopted by our British Conservatives would consist
of whatever positions could be agreed on in relation to the short-term
problems of the day. It would be an unpretentious, pedestrian, not to say
materialistic, affair, by comparison with the Communist crusade to liberate
humanity.

Of course, whatever Soviet propaganda calls for, one may doubt whether the present Politburo, in fact, consists of selfless idealists. The point is, however, that the Communist program as it has evolved, and as it is presented in Russia, is an idealistic one. Nor do I at least doubt that, especially in the early days of the Revolution, very many Russians made great sacrifices, including their lives, for the sake of the Communist dream. In our time growing disillusion with Soviet propaganda has not yet led in the Soviet Union to the development of more simple and pragmatic political programs but rather to the spread of an all-embracing cynicism such as is reflected, for example, in the books of Aleksandr Zinoviev.[2]

A different manifestation of Russian *dukhovnost* can be found in the continued survival, and perhaps latterly, revival of Christianity in the Soviet Union, whether as Orthodoxy or in less traditional forms. Despite decades of persecution, particularly under Stalin and Khrushchev, despite the massive closure of churches, and despite the manipulation and penetration of religious movements by the Council for Religious Affairs and the KGB, religion still lives on, as attested, for instance, on the one hand by the crowded churches of Russia or the religious Samizdat; and, on the other, by the attacks on religious practice which constantly recur in the Soviet press. It is often said by Christians that the early Church drew its strength from the blood of the martyrs shed in ancient Rome. In our time Russia must have provided more religious martyrs than ancient Rome, and, so far as statistics in such an area can be meaningful, modern Russia's witness to religion is at least on a par with that of the early Christians.[3]

A third, and again quite different, illustration of Russian "*dukhovnost*" can be found in the National Labor Union or NTS, the main political movement among the Russian émigrés. The cards are heavily stacked against the NTS. To start with, Russians, whether at home or abroad, are somewhat apathetic politically; and, once they become emigrants, they tend to be both widely scattered from one another, and primarily concerned with making their way in the alien world of the West. Thus, while the NTS keeps secret the number of its members, it is certainly not a mass movement. It does not have great material resources; it does not enjoy official recognition by any Western government; and it is, of course, subject to the unremitting and hostile attentions of the KGB which among other things has sought (sometimes successfully) to kill or kidnap NTS leaders.[4] Notwithstanding all these difficulties, the NTS not only survives but continues to attract recruits from the younger emigration. NTS activists are prepared today to risk their lives on such ventures as the distribution of anti-Soviet material in Russia, or the stimulation, again in Russia, of independent trade unions.

The conclusion that can be drawn from these diverse examples is that today, as in the past, ideas of an other-worldly, nonmaterialist nature continue to exercise a powerful fascination on the Russian mind. Official Soviet ideology is an arid Marxism/Leninism which everyone pretends to believe, but which appears in practice moribund; but Russian "*dukhovnost*" lives on.

As a second aspect of "Russianness" I have selected patriotism or national consciousness—that inner feeling that makes a man think of himself and speak of himself, as a Russian rather than, say, a Georgian, an Uzbek or a Soviet citizen.

Let us start with something basic. If a Russian says to you "*Ya—grazhdanin Sovetskovo Soyuza*" (I am a citizen of the Soviet Union) or "*My Sovietskiye Lyudi*" (We Soviet people), do such formulations sound to you natural and spontaneous? To my ear they do not. The first reminds me straight away of Mayakovski's poem on the Soviet passport,[5] from which it is, in fact, quoted. The second formulation reminds me of Boris Polevoi, who gave this title to a book of war stories.[6] My subjective impression is that Russians, whether inside or outside the Soviet Union, tend to call themselves first and foremost Russians. Put another way: you can give Homo Sovieticus a philosophical Latin name, and speculate as to his characteristics; but you cannot meet him.

Before the Revolution the existence of Russian natural consciousness was not, of course, in doubt. Russia, under the name of Russia, was one of the greatest empires the world has known. There was a Russian czar at the head of it; in a symbiotic relationship with the czardom there was the Russian Orthodox church, to which, formally, most Russians belonged; the Russian language and Russian civilization dominated the old empire: the greatness of Russian culture was acknowledged worldwide.

And now? In some ways Russian nationalism, even Russian chauvinism, is recognized and encouraged in the Soviet Union. Thus it was "the great Russian people" which brought about the Revolution and played a main part in the "Great Patriotic War." The Russian language continues to predominate. The overwhelming majority of Politburo members and senior army officers are ethnic Russians. Achievements such as the expansion of Moscow's empire, the humiliation of Germany, the surpassing of the West in some aspects of space research, and the realization of an allegedly advanced form of society are presented in such forms as cannot but be flattering to the ego of the Russians, so long used to slavery, so long looked on as semi-barbarians by many in the West, so often told, by Russian writers above all, that Russia is a backward country.

But, along with this long-desired boosting of the Russian ego, there are other factors at work which tend rather to put its existence at risk. Thus, notwithstanding flattering references to the Great Russian People, it remains basic Soviet doctrine that Russian and other nationalities have been or will be subsumed. Of the main binding forces of Old Russia, one, czarism, has been killed, and the other, Orthodoxy, is subject to persecution or subversion. Then the proportion of Russians in the Soviet population is tending to decrease. At the moment it amounts to just over half, but can be expected to decrease much further, given the low birthrate in the industrial cities of the North, and the much higher birthrate of the Muslim peoples of Central Asia.[7] Russian writers and artists have been silenced, or have been driven abroad; historical buildings have been allowed to fall into decay; the countryside has been damaged by industrialization and pollution, and even wider damage is threatened if the course of rivers in the North is changed;[8] the traditional lifestyle of the Russian village has been destroyed.

In the face of the pressures enumerated, Russian national consciousness feels itself under siege, and this is what has led, for example, to the appearance of the *"Derevenshchiki"* (Countrymen) school of writers,[9] who praise the beauty of the Russian countryside and lament the vanishing life of the Russian village.

Another example of contemporary Russian nationalism is to be seen in Solzhenitsyn, with his longing for a traditional Orthodox Russia, at once freed from the accretions of empire, and set apart from the ungodly materialism of the West.

On purely general grounds, it seems reasonable to surmise that in Russia, as in other European countries, there has been a resurgence of national feeling, a desire to assert one's individual ethnic character in the face of the homogeneous industrial culture which threatens to overwhelm us all. Certainly, if we look at the emigration, we find that national feeling is far from dead. It is first and foremost along national lines that Soviet émigrés, including Russians, divide up. The NTS, mentioned above, is perceived by other emigrant groups as a Russian national body which seeks to perpetuate Russian ascendancy.

National feeling, then, is still there, and it still finds expression as something more than an aspect of party-line Soviet patriotism. But it is something different from the Russian nationalism of pre-revolutionary days. Formerly, one could say *"Rossiya—et mir"* meaning that Russia was a whole world of its own.[10] One would say one was Russian rather as St. Paul said he was a Roman citizen, though he was far from being of Latin descent; or rather as, fifty years ago, Nigerians, Malays, Australians, and many others might have described themselves as British. With the British Empire gone, the nationalism that you find in England nowadays is more narrow, more strident, more chip-on-the-shoulder, more anxious to assert that, despite all, "British is best," a truth once regarded (at least by the

British) as self-evident and not needing to be said. Something similar is happening to Russian nationalism, now that the Russian Empire, in its old form, has passed into history. It has become more inward-looking, more sensitive, more xenophobic and more resentful than in the past. As Russian nationalism feels itself more and more under threat, it seems likely to become yet more intractable and hostile, and this could give rise to difficulties both within the Soviet Union and internationally.

As the third characteristic of Russianism I have selected the intelligentsia. This peculiarly Russian class, sandwiched between the autocracy on top and the great amorphous "*narod*," the untutored masses, below, represents the narrow stratum which, over the past two hundred years has produced some of the greatest of world literature; which has made immense contributions to art and science; which has been the conscience of Russia; and which brought about the Revolution.

What now of the intelligentsia? Has it been reduced to a class of hacks who regurgitate, in their different spheres, the well-worn platitudes of Sovietism? Certainly not. For instance, some of Russia's best poetry has been written in the Soviet Union by Blok, Esenin, Akhmatova, Tsvetaeva and Mandelshtam, even if, in different ways, all of them were eventually silenced. A pleiad of prose writers (for instance Bunin, Pasternak, Solzhenitsyn) have produced works in the Soviet Union or in the emigration, which are comparable with the classics of the nineteenth century. In other fields of art (e.g., ballet, music, films) there is ample evidence of continued Russian creativity. In Soviet books and newspapers lively minds continue to discuss quite fundamental questions, though they have to do it in an oblique manner so that, for instance, a discussion about an art exhibition, or the *Derevenshchiki* school of writers, may really be a discussion of Soviet political trends (Soviet readers, used to reading between the lines, understand this very well). Poets, like Andrei Vosnesenski or Okudzhava, have been particularly successful in conveying through allusions and symbols reflections of Soviet life diverging very far from the party line.[11]

The intelligentsia maintains its concern for social justice, as shown, for instance, in Solzhenitsyn's monumental indictment of the *Gulag*, and by the *samizdat*. The mere existence of *samizdat* is in itself evidence that people continue to think independently in the Soviet Union, and are willing to take considerable risks to spread their ideas. Perhaps not all the *samizdat* can claim the forcefulness and articulateness with which Herzen denounced the Russian government of his day. On the other hand the circulation of "*Kolokol*" was less hazardous than the furtive writing and copying of nonofficial literature in which thousands of people now engage in the Soviet Union.

In some respects the position of the Russian intelligentsia has weakened.

Before, in the nineteenth century, the intelligentsia could, and largely did, exist outside of government. Now, willy-nilly, everyone in Russia belongs to the state, and must perform some function which the state thinks useful. Again, although far more Russians receive higher education today than in czarist times, such learning is often specialized, and designed to equip the recipients for particular roles in industry or defense. On the other side, however, the increasing technical sophistication of our world, and the complexity of the Soviet Union's economic and military problems, put the intelligentsia in a stronger position than before. The case of A. D. Sakharov serves to illustrate the point. He rendered great service to the Soviet regime and was highly rewarded for so doing, when, in the early 1950s, he helped to solve the then unsolved and, as some thought, insoluble problem of bringing about a high-yield nuclear explosion. Sakharov, in fact, was a clever man who was allowed to think; and he thought to such effect that he arrived at a new scientific idea. The trouble is, however, that if you allow people of Sakharov's calibre to think, their thoughts may carry them in directions very far from the party line, as indeed happened with Sakharov. This presents the Soviet regime with a dilemma. They need intellectual advances in many fields, not just in the making of hydrogen bombs, if they are to overcome the backwardness of Soviet industry and agriculture; but, if they allow intellectuals to ponder freely, especially on economic problems, who is to say that they will not get more Sakharovs and more Novosibirsk economists of the kind who, in 1983, attacked the whole concept of centralized planning?[12] In my view the logic of events and the severity of their economic problems must in the end drive the Soviet leadership to seek new solutions, and if this is right the position of the intelligentsia will be strengthened.

In any event, it seems that ultimately Soviet rule of the present style and the Russian intelligentsia are irreconcilable. The one represents, in an intensified form, the same regimentation of minds which a line of czars (Nicholas I, for example) endeavored vainly to impose; the other, at its best, embodies the same longing for truth, freedom, and justice which was unconquered in the nineteenth century and remains so today.

The fourth aspect of "Russianism" which I have selected is the political tradition of Russia. Looking back over the past five hundred years, to the times of the Great Dukes of Muscovy, this is fairly easily characterized: there has been almost unbroken autocracy. One must make some qualifications, but they are comparatively unimportant. There was the disorderly period between the death of Boris Godunov and the coming of the Romanov's; Alexander II established a measure of local government, though his son and successor blocked further constitutional advance; and there were the four successive Dumas which attempted to function between 1905 and 1917, but were never given a proper chance to develop, largely through the folly of Nicholas II and, perhaps still more, the czaritsa. Subject to these qualifications Russia has been more influenced by its individual rulers than other European countries, and, indeed whole epochs of Russian history have been characterized by the personality of particular rulers.

The almost untramelled autocratic tradition of the czars has been continued into Soviet times; and many of the negative features of czarist rule have been taken over and, alas, greatly developed by the Soviet "czars." One could instance: censorship; political policing; internal passports; deportation or execution of dissidents; arbitrary interpretation of laws; manipulation of the Russian Orthodox church.

A particularly important carryover from czarist rule to Soviet rule has been the continuation of the Caesaro-papist tradition deriving ultimately from Byzantium. The czars were thought of as inseparable from Orthodoxy, the official religion of the state. Through the intertwining of czarism and the Orthodox Church, the czars, as it was supposed, were not ordinary terrestrial rulers but the "Anointed of God" who would uphold and be upheld by the True Faith. (As a converse of the belief that there could be no czars as such without Orthodoxy, it must have seemed to many, including the early Bolsheviks, that there could be no Orthodoxy without czarism; but the later development of Orthodoxy has shown this to be untrue.[13]) Taking over the tradition, the Soviet leaders have assumed responsibility not only for civil rule but also for the determination of true doctrine (i.e., the correct interpretation of Marxism-Leninism) and for the upholding of this doctrine through the suppression not merely of non-Marxist creeds, but also of "deviations" from orthodox Marxist-Leninism (as from time to time determined). The disadvantage of Caesaro-papism for the Soviet rulers is that, as communism becomes less and less plausible,[14] they will need to find some new justification for exercising power.

Thus both autocratic rule and its claim to be linked to orthodox doctrine are in the Russian tradition, and, subject to occasional disorderly explosions of popular sentiment, they have been accepted by the people as a whole. One cannot find in Russia a tradition of pluralism, or the mechanisms for making government accountable, or the will among the people to be sovereign, factors which have grown up over centuries in certain Western countries, and which have made it possible for the frail flower of democracy to take roots and, though with difficulty, to survive. Certainly, it is to be hoped that Russia will turn to Western-type democracy in our lifetime; but it is not to be expected.

Going further, it would be correct, following Berdyayev and Dan,[15] to recognize that the communism to be found in the Soviet Union has acquired a specifically Russian character. In the beginning Marxism could have been regarded as alien to Russia insofar as it was developed outside Russia by a non-Russian; in that its theories related to national economies were very different from that of nineteenth century Russia; and in that Marx himself took little account of the possibility of a Russian revolution. But native thinkers (e.g., Plekhanov, Lenin, Bukharin) contributed to the creation of a specifically Russian Marxism. The radical revolutionary tradition of Russia, deriving from the *narodniki* (the common people) and others, helped to transform the Bloomsbury-type dreams of economic theorists into a program of action; and the unrestrained Russian character helped to make of bolshevism not merely a promotion of alternative policies but an elemental explosion of pent-up fury, a wholesale ruthless rejection of the past, on a scale rarely, if ever, seen in history.

But, if Soviet rule is to a large extent in the Russian tradition and of Russian making, there are nevertheless differences, some bad, some good, which set it apart from anything that went before.

The first and obvious difference lies in the completeness of the state control practiced in the Soviet Union. Monopoly of information, the most powerful single weapon in the hands of the Soviet regime, is exercised with a comprehensiveness and efficiency which make Nicholas I look like a bumbling amateur. Along with the monopoly of information goes another weapon, a system of political policing exercised by the KGB. The experience, the technical resources, and the quality of its staff make the KGB an effective organization by comparison with which the *Oprichina* looks simply primitive. These twin instruments—information control and skilled political policing—help to distinguish the Soviet Union from czarist or other autocracies of the past and turn it into a sophisticated totalitarian state such as became possible only in our own century.

Another less immediately obvious and less academically classifiable peculiarity is the sheer burdensomeness of Soviet life. The vast distances that one needs to travel in Soviet cities; the crowded trolleybuses; the deep escalators of the Metro;[16] the lines in the shops; the recurring shortages, even of paper; the bureaucracy; the documentation; the unending meetings—all this on top of one's daily work, combines to make of the Soviet citizen, and especially of the Soviet woman, a person who is continually harried. If a Soviet citizen wishes not merely to survive but in some way to expand his life, say, by having a family, or finding somewhere to think and write on his own, or (getting progressively more difficult) to travel abroad, or even to emigrate, the sheer cumbersomeness of the procedures confronting him are a deterrent. If a Soviet citizen should wish to step yet further out of line by, say, starting some new religious community, or initiating some movement for social or political reform, the mere logistic and bureaucratic obstacles are sufficient to overwhelm all but the most committed. When you further take into account the repressive activities of the KGB, the result is such a conformism, not to say stagnation, of society that it is difficult to conceive of any movement at all, unless it be brought about from above.

There are other respects, however, in which the Soviet regime at least offers the potential for development. One lies in the formal adoption of democratic practices. Elections do take place, both to the Party congresses and to the Supreme Soviet, and both bodies now meet regularly. Government policy is presented and justified to the Supreme Soviet, and the budget is submitted for approval. Of course, it can be objected that the elections are stage-managed, and that much of what the government is really doing is kept secret. Maybe so. Nevertheless, it is thought necessary to represent Soviet rule as a democracy, and to observe punctiliously all kinds of democratic forms, which is more than happened under the czars. If you go on drilling soldiers long enough on the parade ground, they eventually acquire the habit of obedience. Rather similarly, if you go on exercising the Soviet population long enough in the forms of democracy, they may eventually acquire something of the substance, even though that may not be your intention.

Another hopeful development can be found in some signs (admittedly slight) that public opinion is taken into account. It has long been known (e.g., from the "Smolensk Archives")[17] that the Soviet rulers go to great lengths to inform themselves in detail about what people think. Nowadays, just occasionally, newspapers and television programs canvas public opinion openly, if only on points of little political importance. Another change for the better is that contemporary Soviet leaders have felt a need to cultivate goodwill by public appearances and frequent speeches in a way that Stalin would have found superfluous, not to say incongruous. (In Western countries television has put new pressures on political leaders who now need not merely to win support for their policies in parliaments, but to appeal directly to the people in their living rooms; and it may be that Soviet leaders, too, will have to learn to "sell" themselves in this way.)

Another strength of the Soviet system is that its leaders come to be leaders neither through birth nor alleged divine right but by merit (supposing that you include in "merit" the ability to manipulate the Party apparatus). Indeed, as far as class-feeling of a social type is concerned (meaning the belief of certain groups that they are superior to their fellow men by reason of birth, education, accent or the like) the Soviet Union is a comparatively classless and "democratic" society, more so, certainly, than the United Kingdom.

A further hopeful point of the system is its comparative flexibility. Historically, the rule by Lenin and his associates was very different from the dictatorship of Stalin, and that dictatorship in turn differs from the rule of *apparatchiki*, which is what we appear to have now. Geographically, too, there are differences. At present, life in the Estonian Republic is better organized than in most other parts of the Soviet Union; and the atmosphere in the Georgian Republic appears lighter than that of Moscow. Outside the boundaries of the USSR, Hungary and (for the time being) Poland demonstrate the surprising variations of life-style which can be accommodated within communism.

Thus, potentially evolutionary aspects of Soviet rule are: the observance of democratic forms; an incipient regard for public opinion; an opportunity for the lowest born (if they are ruthless enough) to advance; and flexibility.

Taken all in all, if we consider the Soviet regime purely politically, I cannot myself find that it is either non-Russian, or wholly out of line with what Russians at present want. Certainly, you will find plenty of cynicism in the Soviet Union; you will meet a frustrated intelligentsia; you will hear widespread complaints about shortages of goods, especially outside the big cities; and you will be told more anecdotes than you can possibly remember. What you will not find, at least in my judgment, is any kind of revolutionary mood, or a readiness to contemplate overthrowing the Soviet system. Indeed, my guess would be that if Gorbachev were to hold genuinely free elections in the Soviet Union, his candidates would win them, at least for the next few years. Partly because of the absence of any organized opposition;[18] partly because Russia is at present little disposed to accept pluralism and would regard an opposition with suspicion; partly because the Soviet regime, with all its faults seems to offer Russia what it wants above all else, namely stability and peace. Better take a chance on Gorbachev than risk a new revolution; better the KGB and the half-empty shops than the new war which, as the Soviet population is constantly told (and partly believes), is being prepared by external aggressors.

Unfortunately—or should it be fortunately?—there is no chance of genuinely free elections putting matters to the test. The theory, and still more the practice, of Soviet rule, is that the supposedly enlightened minority at the top decides what is good for the country, and the rest of the population is constrained to carry it out.

As the fifth and last aspect of "Russianism," some comments are offered on the contrast between the characteristics of Homo Sovieticus as above described and the characteristics of the living Russians one actually meets. It would, in fact, be difficult to imagine a greater contrast. To start with, in place of Soviet Man's certainty, modern Soviet Russians display rather a rueful disillusion, of a kind that finds reflection in the anecdotes; and they hold a variety of views. In place of Communist faith you find in some a turning to religion; among the youth there is a leaning toward Western pop-culture; in the liberal intelligentsia, a longing for Western democracy; among the traditionalists a hankering back to the old pre-revolutionary Russia. Some Soviet citizens, disoriented by recent changes, even long for the certainties of the Stalinist era. And among the Russian emigration you will find more or less any views you like.

As for the moral regeneration of man, the Soviet press alone gives you cause for doubt with its constant references to corrupt practices and to alcoholism; in Solzhenitsyn, among other authors, you can read about the criminal elements who shared the camps with the political prisoners—murderers and thieves, with their own ruthless code of behavior; Bukovsky and others have described the psychiatric "hospitals" where people, who must themselves be psychopathic criminals, are prepared to inflict the most refined cruelty on their fellow men. All but the tiniest handful of these criminals, drunkards, and perverts were born and educated in the Soviet Union. One must reluctantly, but without surprise, conclude that human nature, whether Russian or non-Russian, is not so easily transformed.[19]

The enthusiasm of the Soviet Man for work is a particular travesty of the truth. At the best of times, the Russians work in sudden fits, when the short summer, or their mood, stirs them to outbursts of frenzied effort. Not for them the steady meticulous labor of the Germans. Nowadays, in the Soviet Union, the sheer futility of many jobs (e.g., the endless checking of *propusks* (passes), the compiling and verification of meaningless statistics, the waiting hour after hour at the wheel of a car until the boss leaves the meeting) combined with poor material reward, has led to a "could-not-care-less" attitude to work, and probably to the lowest overall productivity of any industrialized country. The supposed land of the work-zealot is in fact the land of the *"perekur"* (break for a smoke).[20]

As for the upheld banner, this, for the real Russian, is just a chore which he has to carry out with his workmates on May Day (having first made sure that the right words are written on the banner[21]). But, in private life, he is no flag-waver. When talking to foreigners, certainly, the Soviet Russian is somewhat on the defensive about the Soviet regime, though he prefers (like Lenin) to make his case by attacking the opposition and assailing the real or imagined evils of the West. Toward the regime, his inner attitude might be guessed as resigned acceptance. He is not, however, cowed, and is more watchful than in the past. Gorbachev is on trial in a way that his predecessors were not.

If in the above significant features of "Russianness" have been selected, and if they have been rightly assessed, two conclusions can be drawn. First, that Soviet Man is a myth; and second, that the real, non-Soviet Russia lives on. It does not, however, live on just in some corner of the emigration, or even in the emigration as a whole. The other Russia is there today, before our eyes, in the Soviet Union; and what we see, as Soviet history develops, is the interaction of two opposed forces. The political power, with almost all the material weapons in its hands, is trying to cast the Russian people into an artificial mould, in the name of a moribund doctrine;[22] but the spiritual, intellectual, and human qualities of the Russian people live on and make themselves felt.

In the long run it is not to be doubted that Russia will win, and that some new, more Russian, phase of Russian history will evolve from the present phase. But the qualification "in the long run" is important. I should not wish to associate myself with the dramatic predictions of an imminent "system breakdown" in the Soviet Union, meaning, apparently, a collapse of Soviet power. I do not doubt that there are serious economic and other difficulties in the Soviet Union; but there have been difficulties before, including the huge devastation caused by the war. Russia, however, is a rich country; the main wish of Russians, at this stage, is for a quiet life; and the present Soviet rulers are at least as capable as some of their predecessors. Changes will certainly come, and they will be big; but big changes will not, in my view, come quickly.

Postscript

Alexander Shtromas's contribution to volume I of this series, "How the End of the Soviet System May Come About," was made available to me after I had already written this chapter. Since it bears in part on themes treated in my paper, I should like to add here a few comments on it. Shtromas represents the fruit of first-hand experience and prolonged research in a number of key areas, for instance the background of Gorbachev or the attitude of the Soviet army. It helps us to understand that the Soviet ice age is approaching its end. It will, I hope, stimulate Western readers to take a more lively and constructive interest in Russia, instead of "writing it off" as many people, alas, now do in the West.

I hope nobody will be put off from reading it by the argument at the beginning that revolutions take place according to a definable pattern, or by the repeated references to first and second "pivots." I doubt that Man will ever comprehend the workings of history. It seems to me *prima facie* implausible that Marx, basing himself on some hundreds of years of economic history in a small corner of our planet, should thereby come to understand the destiny of the human race which has now continued for two million years. By the same token, it is unlikely that Shtromas, and the *samizdat* writer to whom he refers, have identified a formula governing the change of political regimes.

Of more substance, I think that Shtromas exaggerates the wish and capacity of technocrats to play a political role. On the whole, industrial managers are one thing, and politicians are another. Looking around the world today you can find leaders who seem to embody the social aspirations of their countries; leaders who are eloquent; leaders who are demagogic; and leaders who know how to run a political police force. But few political leaders have gotten to where they are because they are good technocrats; and the technocrats I know do not aspire to exercise political power.

In any case, as far as Russia is concerned, the ultimate issue is not about gross domestic product but about God. Soviet communism believes it can do away with God, and that humanity can be perfected, materially and spiritually, provided it believes whatever Agitprop says. In my view, the Russians no longer believe, if they ever did, that Soviet communism really embodies all the answers. Major changes in Russia are bound to come, and will come because, as Agitprop becomes less and less credible, more traditional and less synthetic Russian values, including religious values, will increasingly reassert themselves.

Notes

1. "Russia is now usually called the RSFSR," Big Soviet Encyclopedia, 22, 1975.
2. One could instance *Ziyayushchiye vysoty* (The Yawning Heights), (Lausanne: L'Age d'Homme, 1976), or *V predverii raya*, (In Heaven's Antechamber), (Lausanne: L'Age d'Homme, 1979). Just as Joseph Heller in *Catch 22* satirized war as a nonsense, so Zinoviev seeks to show the Soviet Union as an absurdity, where nothing makes sense any more and nobody believes anything. Zinoviev will never achieve the wide readership of Heller because (as often with Russians!) his books are formless and far too long. However, while Heller wrote pure fantasy, Zinoviev's books have the ring of truth. Both the books mentioned were allegedly written in the Soviet Union; and the bitter understated conversations they contain sound like genuine exchanges between Soviet intellectuals.
3. Exact statistics in this area are unobtainable, but a broad comparison is possible. In ancient Rome (population up to one million) there was general tolerance for all religions; but the Christian minority, who refused to acknowledge the emperor as a God, were the exception, and from the time of Nero (A.D. 54–68) up to the coming of Constantine (A.D. 324) they were subject to intermittent campaigns of persecution. However, when Saints Peter and Paul were put to death under Nero (around A.D. 67), the number of their converts can hardly have been more than a few hundreds, perhaps thousands. At the time of the severe persecutions of A.D. 257–58, the total number of

Christians might have been around 50,000, of whom not all, of course, were killed. So, overall, we seem to be dealing with some thousands, or perhaps tens of thousands, of martyrs (see, for example, the *Dictionnaire de Théologie Catholique*, Paris, 1928). In the Soviet Union (population over 264 million) all religions were, from the beginning, subject to ruthless repression. Taking the Russian Orthodox church alone: it could count some tens of millions of adherents before the Revolution; and there were some 50,000 parish churches and other places of worship. A. Kojevnikov of Keston College, England (which specializes in the study of religion in the USSR) has estimated that some hundreds of thousands of Orthodox priests and laymen were killed or imprisoned in the subsequent wholesale persecutions. To these must be added large numbers of Uniates, Baptists, and other religious believers. These figures are based on a paper A. Kojevnikov gave at a conference on "Church-State Relations in the Soviet Union and Eastern Europe" at Baylor University in April 1985 (proceedings in the course of publication).

4. N. Khokhlov, then a captain in the MGB, was sent to kill the NTS leader Okolovich. Now a member of the NTS, Khokhlov has told his story in *Pravo na sovest'*, (The Right to Conscience), (Frankfurt a.M.: Possev, 1957).

5. V. Mayakovsky, "*Stikhi o sovetskom pasporte.*" (A Poem on the Soviet Passport).

6. Boris Polevoi, *My sovetskiye lyudi*, (We Are Soviet People), (Moscow: Sovetskii Pisatel', 1948). The book claims to be based on real incidents of which Polevoi learned while a war correspondent for *Pravda*. The melodramatic tales recounted are full of heroic Russians and wicked Germans; but, notwithstanding the book's title, the specifically Soviet inspiration of the heroes is little explained. *Mutatis mutandis*, the stories could have been told about France under German occupation.

7. *Narodnoe Khozyaistvo SSSR*, (The Economy of the USSR), published periodically by the Central Statistical Directorate of the USSR, among other Soviet publications provides basic data on the question. The present population of the Soviet Union is 270 million (rounded) of which half are Russians. The average birthrate of the Soviet Union (1982) was 18.9 per thousand, with wide variations between the different republics. The RSFSR (lowest) had a birthrate of 16.6 per thousand; the Tadzhik SSR (highest) had a birthrate of 30.2 per thousand.

8. The concept of diverting certain northern rivers in order to irrigate the Central Asian desert and raise the level of the Caspian Sea has been approved for study at the last two Party Congresses. The possibly calamitous consequences, and the threat to the survival of certain ancient towns and historical sites (e.g., the Solovetski Monastery), have given rise to widespread concern in the Soviet Union. The "*derevenshchik*" writer V. Belov expressed his disquiet in the *samizdat* (see: *Russkaya mysl'*, Paris, July 15, 1982). Subsequently, *Grani* (133/1984) published papers which were submitted to the Soviet government by a number of academicians, writers and others, and which express deep misgivings about the project. Finally, at the 27th Congress of the CPSU,

in March 1986, it was proclaimed that this project is not going to be implemented.

9. One might class in this school, among others, V. Belov, V. Soloukhin, V. Rasputin. Their writings at best are distinguished by a lack of propaganda, and by realistic descriptions of the Russian countryside, in which love for its beauty does not exclude frank references to the hardships of life on the collective farms, to the lack of roads, and to the damage done by industrial pollution. A number of the *"derevenshchik"* writers have been published in the RSFSR literary journal *Nash sovremennik*, (Our Contemporary), and they are sometimes associated with the concept of a "Russian Party." It is probably premature to think that there is as of now any organized nationalist opposition in the Soviet Union. On the other hand, the *"derevenshchiki"* could not have existed and flourished unless there had been at the least some tolerance for their ideas in the higher reaches of the Soviet government.

10. Dostoevsky in *"Dva lagerya teoretikov,"* (Two Camps of Theoreticians) "Narrow nationalism is not in the Russian spirit"; or S. M. Soloviev in *History of Russia*, 8: "Russians are not given to unpleasant boasting about their nationality."

11. Poets have long occupied a high place in Russian literature, and have attracted a wider readership than in many countries—a further example of Russian *dukhovnost'* (spirituality). Nowadays they are the more attractive because they can convey ideas which, if in prose, would be unprintable.

12. See, for instance, *Posev*, No. 9, September 1983. The Novosibirsk branch of the Academy of Sciences prepared the paper for a closed economic conference. Whether by accident or (more likely) by design a copy fell into the hands of Western journalists.

13. Despite the difficulties that beset it at home and the divisions that beset it abroad, the position of the Russian Orthodox church has in some ways strengthened. Faced as they were with the challenge of Western Christianity, a line of thinkers (Bulgakov, Florensky and others) enriched Orthodoxy with an intellectual base. In a number of Western countries Orthodoxy now attracts converts on a greater scale than heretofore.

14. Khrushchev, one of the last believing Communists among the Soviet rulers, himself struck a grave blow to the credibility of the doctrine when he forecast that communism would be achieved in twenty years (i.e., by 1982). This embarrassing prediction (like Khrushchev himself) is passed over in silence by today's Soviet propaganda; and discussion of when communism will come and what it will look like in detail appears to be discouraged.

15. N. Berdyaev in a number of books, e.g., *Istoki Russkogo Kommunizma*, (The Sources of Russian Communism), (Paris: YMCA Press, 1955). T. Dan, *Proiskhozdenie Bolshevizma*, (The Origins of Bolshevism), (New York: Chekhov Publishing House, 1946).

16. The underground railway systems of Soviet cities are distinguished by their extensiveness, their depth, and the vast size of the stations. If only the convenient transportation of the public were in question, Soviet Metros, which

often follow the main axial roads, could have been built like the Paris Metro, just below the surface. In fact, however, Soviet Metros are likely to be built first and foremost as bomb shelters, and they constitute a more serious preparation for nuclear defense than can be found in Western countries. Soviet Metro passengers contribute towards the cost of this preparation as they spend hundreds of thousands of hours on the escalators each week.

17. See: *Smolensk Under Soviet Rule* by Merle Fainsod, (London: Macmillan, 1959). Fainsod collates and presents detailed documentation showing how the Soviet Party and government apparatus actually functioned at ground level. The Smolensk papers fell into German hands during the war.

18. How could it be other than absent? After decades of brainwashing, Soviet citizens do not dispose of the information on which to base alternative policies; and while, as individuals, they often doubt what they are told, the conditions of Soviet life do not allow them to establish even discussion groups unless the government approves.

19. In 1976 Brezhnev told the 25th Congress of the CPSU that the creation of Soviet Man was the main achievement of the preceding sixty years. But five years later none other than M. Suslov, the Party ideologist, admitted to a conference of social scientists that much still remained to be done (*Pravda*, October 15, 1981).

20. The writer recalls with amusement a discussion with a Los Angeles taxi driver who had, until shortly before, been a Soviet citizen, and was none too pleased with the transition. In tones of mingled amazement and indignation he complained: "*A zdes' rabotat' nuzhno!*"—"You actually have to *work* here!"

21. There is a story of the late 1930s according to which some hapless woman called out, during a May Day procession: "Long live our glorious Soviet leaders!"—and was promptly arrested for anti-Soviet agitation (on the ground that she had not specified *which* leaders). Perhaps it is apocryphal, but to minimize the chances of any such incident, *Pravda* prints approved slogans for banners in advance of each main procession.

22. Once again, Marx got it wrong. He foresaw that his doctrine would triumph when communism was realized, and the state would wither away. But for most people in the Soviet Union today, Marxism is no more than a doctrine one formally pretends to accept, whereas the state shows no signs of withering away, and still less any inclination to do so.

3

Marxism-Leninism in Contemporary USSR

ALEXANDER SHTROMAS

Marxism-Leninism and Soviet Society
in the Context of History

When, after having seized power in Russia in November 1917, the Bolsheviks imposed upon that country the Leninist variety of Marxism as the sole foundation of Russia's new political myth, the great majority of that country's established and traditionally minded population had inevitably become politically alienated. This is not to say that Marxism was entirely alien to Russia. Indeed, from the beginning of the twentieth century Marxism had a significant influence on Russia's intellectual and political life but this influence was minor in the sense that it had never acquired a larger appeal among the masses, and only a certain part, by no means a predominant one, of the intellectual elite was affected by it. The Bolsheviks tried very hard to build upon that existing influence of Marxism in order to make it universal but their success in this respect was rather limited.

The new Marxist-Leninist political myth was internalized and fully accepted only by a certain, not large, proportion of idealistically minded young people from all sections of Russian society, as well as by some assimilatory minded representatives of national minorities (the assimilationist Jews figured prominently among them) and some declassed people who in Russia were rather more numerous than in any other European country. All this amounted to a very strong zealot-type support for the revolutionary Bolshevik regime from a relatively small minority of committed people. Such support was enough for effectively ruling the country by dictatorial-terroristic means, but in no way was it sufficient for establishing rule by consensus.[1]

Under the circumstances, the majority of Russians had little choice but to adjust to the Marxist-Leninist political myth without ever having internalized or otherwise accepted it. People simply tried to survive in adverse conditions by pretending that they were converted to the regime's ideology and, then, to improve the conditions of their existence by positively responding to a variety of incentives which the Bolsheviks offered to "working people" in exchange for their outward loyalty to the regime and the values of Marxism-Leninism on which it was allegedly based. These opportunists, total strangers to the Marxist-Leninist ideology, were actually destined to form in time the largest bulk of good Soviet citizenry and even of the membership of the Soviet Communist party.

The opportunistic intake into the new Soviet elite became especially prominent in the late 1920s with the demise of the NEP. It had quickly overtaken the small regular idealistic intake and had reduced it, together with the politically committed Bolshevik Old Guard, to a small minority.[2] This minority was, however, to remain for some time in the top echelon of the Party's hierarchy. Stalin was not yet powerful enough to replace it with his own promotees and devotees. Moreover, he still needed its commitment to the Bolshevik cause for the successful accomplishment of drastic revolutionary changes, such as the collectivization of agriculture, aimed at the "socialist transformation of Russia."

The situation changed drastically when this "socialist transformation" was accomplished and the country, in the 1930s, entered into the period of "socialist stability." Under these circumstances, Stalin needed only obedient and unscrupulous executioners of his will; the idealists became to him not only superfluous but, as potential challengers of his decisions, extremely dangerous too. Hence, they had to go and to be replaced by the opportunists in all significant offices of the country. By the mid–1930s Stalin had already enough power to realize such a replacement, but he was well aware that, if simply removed from office and left at large, the members of the Bolshevik Old Guard could be even more of a challenge than when in office where the inevitable bounds of collective discipline would have a restricting influence on their challenging activities.

The Bolshevik Old Guard were political figures with established names and reputations, large clienteles, and constituencies of support. But, most importantly, they had a lot of experience in revolutionary political and organizational work which, when left outside the disciplining framework of the office, they could easily and devastatingly turn against Stalin and his cronies in the newly staffed power hierarchy. Hence the only way for

Stalin to get rid of them safely was to dispatch them directly from their offices to the gallows and the *Gulag*. This is what Stalin chose to do by skillfully using Kirov's assassination on December 1, 1934, for launching the Great Purge that was successfully accomplished by 1939.

Marxism-Leninism and the Soviet Officialdom

The Great Purge signified the triumph of the opportunists and the almost total annihilation of the idealists.[3] The Party's intellectuals, people like Nikolai Bukharin, David Ryazanov, Aleksandr Slepkov, Nikolai Krylenko, Evgeniy Pashukanis, and many thousands of their likes, were eliminated practically to a man by Stalin. Those left, mainly former Mensheviks and other professional "left-overs" of the old regime, being by then concerned much more about saving their skins than about ideals (people like Andrei Vyshinski and David Zaslavsky), were ready to follow every whim of Stalin's with extreme zeal.

Most of the few nonintellectual genuine believers in communism perished in the Great Purge, too, being thoroughly beaten in the ferocious struggle for survival by the cynical schemers swelling the Party hierarchy in ever-increasing numbers. By the rules of natural selection, evolved during the Great Purge, the genuine believers were the "unfittest species," destined to be mercilessly swallowed by the Stalinist terror machine in the first place. Most of them were actually entirely devoted to Stalin, identifying communism exclusively with his leadership, but this did not help them. Under Stalin, for a functionary to be fit to survive, it was even not enough to renounce all personal convictions, all moral principles, replacing them with one single belief in Stalin's infallibility—as Mikhail Isakovsky declared in his poem on Stalin: "We so trusted you, Comrade Stalin,/ As, may be, we did not trust even ourselves"—it was necessary, in addition, to develop special intuitive skills and pliancy allowing one rightly to foretell, and to be in step with, Stalin's next move at the right time.

A few genuine believers in communism and even some true Marxist-Leninists did, however, survive Stalin's purges. Indeed, neither Stalin's nor any other rule by terror known to history has ever been able to annihilate totally all those against whom the terror was directed. Although the Party and government machinery was perhaps the place most thoroughly cleansed from the presence of true believers, a few of them managed to remain in place even there. Among them was Nikita S. Khrushchev, Stalin's ultimate successor.

Khrushchev was of course a great survivor. He earned his right to stay alive by ably playing the role of the fool at Stalin's court and by ruthlessly executing Stalin's will in both Moscow and the Ukraine where, intermittently, he used to be placed as Stalin's all-powerful proconsul. Being semi-literate (he learned to read and write only at the age of 23), Khrushchev was of course unable to grasp the intricacies of Marxist-Leninist theory, but in his own peasant way he religiously believed in the communist ideal and, when in power, seriously tried practically to implement it, assuming that the Soviet system over which he now presided was, for this purpose, the only suitable vehicle. As an avowed populist and experienced political practitioner, he no doubt knew only too well that the Soviet system in its rigid Stalinist shape did not work, but, as a believer, he was convinced that, if properly reorganized, that system could start working well enough to produce in the USSR an abundant communist society in a not-too-distant future—actually the Party's program, reflecting Khrushchev's personal beliefs and officially endorsed by the 22nd Congress of the CPSU in 1961, scheduled the dawning of communism in the USSR for 1980.

With the view of finding the right formula under which the Soviet system would at last become functional with regard to this purpose, Khrushchev kept the country's apparatus of power and management in a state of constant reorganization as none of the newly introduced configurations and shapes of that apparatus made it work to his satisfaction. He acted like the monkey in Krylov's fable, who, being unable to play a musical quartet with three other animals, believed that the fault lay not with the musical skills of the players, but with their wrong sitting order, and constantly made them change their seats. This reorganizational urge only further paralyzed the system, endangering its overall operational capacity, and ultimately threatened its very survival.

Communist convictions practically turned the deeply frustrated and increasingly impatient Khrushchev into a *de facto* enemy of the Soviet system without him ever being able to realize that this was the case. His off-the-cuff speeches often matched, and sometimes even surpassed, the most radical dissident standards for the criticism of the system. Khrushchev's reorganizational drive had, by 1962, reached the critical point of undermining the basic foundation of the system—the monocentric domination of the Party apparatus over all other power apparatuses and all walks of Soviet life—as exemplified by his abolition during 1962–63 of most of the rural *raykoms* (Party district committees) and, even more importantly, by his 1962 division of the provincial and territorial Party committees (*obkoms* and *kraykoms*) into two such committees, one for industry and one for agriculture. (That latter, major blow to the "Party's leading role" had been preceded by the replacement in 1957 of the central industrial ministries by the local councils for national economy, the *sovnarkhozy*, which substantially undermined not only the power of the central authority but to some extent also that of the provincial and territorial Party committees, as the territorial areas of the *sovnarkhozy* did not always coincide with the boundaries of the established administrative-territorial units over which these committees exercise their rule.) Khrushchev's 1962–63 moves went much too far to be tolerated by his purely system-preservation-*oriented*, cynically pragmatic colleagues. On October 14, 1964, they staged a palace coup against Khrushchev, trying to save the system by removing him from office.

Khrushchev was indeed the sole member of the Soviet leadership that he himself had handpicked, and certainly the last Soviet leader, who was a believer in communism. His case demonstrates best the Soviet system's inability to accommodate and tolerate within the ranks of its functionaries the true believers who, trying to behave in accordance with their convictions, invariably break the rules of conformity with the system, thus endangering its continuous existence. Those who, instead of unquestioningly serving the system's needs, try to make the system serve their own Communist or any other ideals can either break the system or, if the system survives their tinkering, will inevitably be rejected by it and, consequently, thrown out into the wilderness of "extra-structural" existence to which in the USSR all identified dissidents are automatically relegated. Only those who could convincingly pledge themselves once and for all to fully submit their entire personalities to obediently serving the system, may be allowed back into its fold. This is how Boris Yeltsin, after having undergone the humiliating ritual of public repentance, was readmitted into the ranks of the ruling elite, although on a much lower scale in the hierarchy than before, one that explicitly excluded personal decision making. (He was appointed *Deputy* Chairman of the State Committee for Construction.) Yeltsin is indeed a curiosity among the post-Khrushchev Soviet leaders whose only concern always was and is the preservation, whatever the costs, of the system that comfortably keeps them in power but that, as they are fully aware, is totally unfit for achieving Communist affluence or any other ideal goals. Their policies may change but not the preservationist substance of these policies. They realize that the defensive immobility practiced by Brezhnev and Chernenko had served its course and become counterproductive. They branded it as stagnant and as "fostering" "brake-putting mechanisms" (*mekhanizmy tormozheniya*). They revert under Gorbachev to *perestroika* and *glasnost'*, but they practice these policies, however, only insofar as they sustain the system as it stands, without interfering with its basic structure.

Whatever policies the post-Khrushchev Soviet leaders opportunistically applied, they always claimed them to be based on Marxist-Leninist ideology and aimed at the construction of a Communist society. Like the notorious medical orderlies in Chekhov's famous short story who, though convinced that no such thing as a pulse exists, have to keep themselves in business by pretending to measure it, the Soviet leaders, in order to defend their rule, have to uphold their Marxist-Leninist identity and enhance the official status of Communist ideology, without believing in the values, ideals and goals enunciated by that ideology. Indeed, Marxism-Leninism and the Communist ideal are their sole claims to, and legitimation of, power. Moreover, only as the "high priesthood" of this supposedly ultimate scientific creed, are they invested with a primordial and inalienable right to rule without being responsible in exercising it to anyone but themselves and the future. Without believing in communism, the Soviet leaders are thus bound to stick to their Communist credentials and, in order to warrant these credentials, have to set themselves Communist political goals both nationally and globally. To renounce Communist ideology, or even substantially to sidestep from Communist politics, would be for them tantamount to relinquishing power, and to some of them such abdication may mean not merely the loss of status and position but also liability for crimes they committed on their way up the social ladder. The Soviet leaders are indeed trapped by their ideology and have no way of escaping from that ideological trap. And so they have to soldier on along the route laid down by that ideology as no alternative route is available to them.

This is, however, only one part of the story. The other part of it is that Marxism-Leninism provides an ideal instrument for an unrepresentative political clique to exercise absolute and unlimited power in an unchallengeable way. The idea of socialism, translated into the Party-state's ownership and direct management of all the means of production and also into what is known as the concept of the leading role of the Party, entitling the Party-state to be in direct charge of all socially-relevant activities of the people, reduces every member of society into a mere servant of the ruling clique which alone is entitled to set him or her tasks and to assess his or her performance in fulfilling these tasks either by reward or punishment. Any decentralization which would entail true autonomy for economic units and public bodies (and thus responsibility of people running these units and bodies not to the Party-state's officialdom but to themselves and their workers and customers) would immediately alter that relationship between the rulers and the ruled. Not only would such autonomous social units stop being servants of the ruling political clique, but that ruling clique itself would either have to start providing these units with qualified political services or quit and give way to a government which the autonomous actors on the social stage could trust and consider qualified to render them such services. As the present ruling clique has no qualifications or experience in rendering political services, and as it knows no other way of ruling than through complete mastership over the totality of people's activities, for it to allow such decentralization would be equal to committing political suicide. (If the top leadership even were to try, in a volte-face, to transform itself into a normal, political-service-rendering government of the country, that would amount to nothing less than a revolution from above, deviously perpetrated by the top leadership against the Soviet system and the rest of the ruling clique which it is supposed to represent and lead. The checks and balances characteristic of the present Soviet oligarchic system would hardly allow the top part of the oligarchy successfully to perpetrate such an about-face. For a revolution from above to become possible, an autocratic regime must replace the oligarchic system first, and this the oligarchs, who learned the lessons of Stalin's purges very well indeed, will resist it as much as a revolution against the system itself.)

Marxism-Leninism, by declaring the natural and ever-growing social demands for authentic decentralization anti-socialist and rejecting them outright on ideological grounds, effectively performs today the most important pragmatic task of sustaining the present Soviet ruling clique in power. Furthermore, Marxism-Leninism provides that ruling clique with a most powerful device for thoroughly controlling the political behavior of each individual. All Soviet people, including school children and pensioners, are on a daily basis requested to manifest in one form or another their adherence to the Marxist-Leninist ideology and the Soviet system of rule based on this ideology. Attending celebratory demonstrations, speaking or at least clapping at self-congratulatory meetings, voting several times a year for Party-selected candidates to various positions, attending political-education classes, performing various "voluntary social duties" (e.g., the propagandistic ones), observing regular ideological rites and participating in all sorts of public performances, is the usual routine of every Soviet citizen's daily life. Roman Redlikh, when trying to distinguish totalitarian systems from all other systems of dictatorial rule, referred to these practices as to a regime of "active unfreedom." According to him, the regime of "active unfreedom," forcing people constantly to show their enthusiastic approval of, and admiration for, their oppressors, is a distinguishing trait of a totalitarian dictatorship. The non-totalitarian dictatorships are satisfied with establishing a regime of "passive unfreedom" which demands of their subjects only to refrain from actively opposing or criticizing the established dictatorial rule.[4]

Any attempt of a Soviet citizen to escape from the duties the regime of "active unfreedom" imposes upon him or her is noticed and recorded by the authorities who, when such attempts reach beyond the level of "pardonable laziness," single out the "guilty person" for punishment. In the beginning that punishment is relatively mild: exclusion from the regular line for promotions or, in a graver case, demotion; prohibition to travel abroad or official ignorance of legitimate pleas for improvement of housing conditions. In most cases such relatively mild pressures, amplified by an increasingly tense atmosphere of official suspicion and disapproval, are sufficient to change the person's ways and bring him back to the conformist fold. If that does not work, heavier measures of punishment are applied. People are thus forced into either active participation in the official lie or dissent.

It was the late Leonard Schapiro who said that the Soviet official ideology and the lie come "to the same thing, since in view of the fact that the ideology does not correspond to the reality which people see around them, its dogmas have to be reiterated with increasing persistence in spite, or because of, their falsity. . . ."[5] It was also Schapiro who observed that this ideology, or the lie, "acts as a binding force on those who might be ready to reject the Party and the system which it represents."[6] Indeed, in the USSR a person's continuous, though purely formal, public acknowledgement of adherence to the official ideology has become the standard way of proving that person's political loyalty to the Soviet Party-state. A person's readiness publicly to repeat the official lie is accepted by the Party-state as this person's solemn pledge to seek the advancement of his or her personal interests and goals exclusively within the extant socio-political framework and be totally bound by its constraints. Only those people who are prepared to lie in order to avoid trouble and live as obedient members of the Soviet Party-state, satisfied with the rewards that thus may come their way, are treated by that state as its good and reliable subjects. All others are rejected and suppressed. Ideology in the Soviet Union has thus lost its traditional meaning of a set of people's genuine values, ideas and goals. Instead of being "internalized," the Communist ideology in the Soviet Union has thus been entirely "externalized" and transformed into a mere instrument of political rule and control. As Milovan Djilas succinctly summed it up: "Ideology in the Soviet Union is both *dead*—and very much *alive*! Dead at the level of faith, alive as an indispensable (tool and) rationale of policy."[7]

The Marxist-Leninists Who Survived Stalin

Among the few Marxist-Leninists who survived Stalin and his purges, many were Stalin's victims themselves. Having been rehabilitated by Khrushchev, they returned to their places of residence and gradually got reintegrated into the current pattern of Soviet life. There were also some believers among the members of the younger generation, those who in Stalin's time were mainly at school and who, because of young age, largely escaped the axe of Stalin's terror. Almost all of these younger people lost to Stalin's terror some members of their families and friends but this sometimes only hardened their resolve to be good Marxists and Communists. These surviving Marxist-Leninist idealists were typically either students or people in the beginning of their careers; and some were already reaching the end of their active life as were most of the rehabilitated returnees from the Gulag. Almost none of them were established members of the current political or managerial elite.

The "idealistic communist remnants" in Soviet society divided into two broad categories based on their different attitudes toward Stalin:

First were the "idealistic left-overs" of Stalin's purges and other people affected by them in one or another way, who came to the conclusion that Stalin was a traitor to the lofty Marxist-Leninist cause and that his grip on power was the main obstacle on the way to the triumph of that cause. These people nurtured a dream about such a time when Stalin would be finally removed from the USSR's political stage and the country would become able to revert to its genuine Marxist-Leninist and socialist origins, a process in which they aspired to participate actively and enthusiastically.

Second were those, mainly younger people, who accepted the official version of the purges and who continued to identify totally and unequivocally their belief in Marxism-Leninism with the personality of Stalin, seeing in his leadership the ultimate (and, perhaps, the sole remaining) guarantee of the country's, and the world's at large, following the right course toward the victory of communism.

It is important to note at this stage that these people, i.e., the remaining genuine Marxist-Leninists, were the ones who originated Soviet dissent as we know it today.

Many of the remaining Marxist-Leninist idealists of the first "anti-Stalinist" category were people who either have themselves been victims of Stalin's purges (for example, among the well-known later-day dissidents, the Medvedev brothers, Pyotr Yakir, Elena Bonner, Raisa Lert, et al.) or who were old enough consciously to witness the purges and develop grave doubts about Stalin's consistency with genuine Leninism (among the well-known later-day dissidents, for example, Naum Korzhavin and Alexander Solzhenitsyn, who were themselves imprisoned for expressing such doubts; Alexander Zinoviev, et al.). They were the enthusiasts of the de-Stalinization process initiated by the Party under Nikita Khrushchev after Stalin's death and entertained high hopes for the country and for themselves in relation with it. Many of them who at the time of Stalin's death were not in the Party joined its ranks during this period—the most notable example is that of Elena Bonner, the present wife of Academician Andrei Sakharov; the best explained one (in a most penetrative autobiography) is Dora Shturman[8]—and those who already were members but had kept a distinctively low profile became publicly visible, boldly outspoken and even "pushy." These people very soon discovered, however, that their hopes about the Party's intentions were misplaced and that, like in Stalin's days, the Party was not prepared to tolerate any independent initiatives or views, let alone attempts at pushing it into doing anything it did not itself plan to do beforehand. The rebuke by the Party of these enthusiasts of de-Stalinization was swift, clear-cut and strong. However, not all the rebuked complied with the Party and some intransigently continued to stick to their critical points in spite of severe repercussions. (Among the many victims of this rebuke were the chess grandmaster Mikhail Botvinnik who complied and Professor Yuriy Orlov who did not and who became later one of the leading Soviet dissenters.) That is how, in 1956, dissent for the first time appeared on the visible surface of Soviet politics. It has continued unabated ever since, mainly along the same lines of defending the principles of Soviet legality, of enlarging the extent of human rights (individual and collective), as well as of some other issues related to the liberalization and democratization of the Soviet society.

One should stress once more that up to this point all these newly emerged dissenters were firm believers in Marxism-Leninism and in the very principle of the Soviet system of rule which, in their view, needed only to rid itself radically of Stalinist perversions and deviations in order to become perfect again. Soviet dissenters of the early and mid–1950s were typical products of the minority participatory political culture and therefore dared to challenge the powers that be on the consistency of their actual performance with the principles of Marxism-Leninism which the frightened conformist majority would never have dreamed of doing.

The Marxist-Leninist idealists of the second category ("the believers in Stalin"), in the aftermath of Stalin's death, underwent a much more drastic change of mind. Some of them realized that Stalin was, to a large extent, personally responsible for the evils of the Soviet system on April 4, 1953, when the "killer-doctors" were rehabilitated and it became clear that Stalin personally was responsible for their false accusation. For some, however, that realization came about only in 1956, after the 20th Congress of the CPSU, where Khrushchev officially revealed the horrible crimes of Stalin. These revelations meant the collapse of their whole belief in the Soviet system of rule as such; but one should stress—not in the ideals of Marxism-Leninism which remained for the time being their unshaken symbol of creed.

To these people who saw the ills of the Soviet regime only too well, Stalin had represented the last hope for the system's progressive improvement and for its staying on the right course to communism. The shocking discovery that Stalin himself was an initiator of the system's gross violations of justice and of its virtual degeneration into a fascist-type dictatorship convinced them that the system was totally irredeemable. Accordingly, these people started to develop their own radical Marxist-Leninist programs for the revolutionary change of the existing "fascist-type" Soviet system into a genuinely socialist one. They counted on massive support from the working class and the honest Marxist-Leninists in the Party itself. In other words, they were advocating a new socialist revolution and were prepared to take a lead in it.

No wonder that these people preferred to remain anonymous and to conduct their activities clandestinely. The first such dissenters who became publicly known were the members of the Krasnopevtsev-Rendel group at the History Faculty of the University of Moscow. Their activities were disclosed by the KGB and in 1956 (in the very aftermath of the 20th Congress of the Party) they were sentenced to long terms of imprisonment. This was actually the first recorded political trial that took place in the USSR after the 20th Party Congress.[9]

Perhaps the most outspoken summary of the views of this category of Marxist-Leninist idealists was given by a person who wrote in Soviet *samizdats* under the pseudonym of F. Znakov and whose identity has remained undisclosed.[10] In Znakov's view, in the USSR, under the name of socialism, super-monopolistic capitalism was, in fact, coercively and voluntarily established. As the result of Stalin's "great leap forward," by the mid–1930s the ownership of all the means of production in the USSR was concentrated in the hands of one supermonopolistic body (organized as the self-coopting and self-perpetuating leadership of the Party) which combined its total economic domination with direct and unlimited exercise of political power. A fascist-type totalitarian dictatorship is the natural superstructure over the basis of super-monopolistic capitalism and this is into what the USSR's political system had in fact developed. F. Znakov claimed that from the Marxist-Leninist point of view the USSR had thus reached (though by coercive and artificial means) the last and the most reactionary stage of capitalist development—the one which Karl Kautsky used to call ultra-imperialism—and was therefore fully ripe for a genuinely socialist change. In other words, according to him, the general Marxist rule about the inevitability of a socialist revolution in a capitalist society had acquired in the present-day Soviet Union (and, as yet, nowhere else) its really concrete and practical expression. The author, by addressing his 1956 work to the Italian Communist leader, Palmiro Togliatti, wanted to enlist the understanding and support of the international Communist movement for that "imminent, and this time real, leap from the realm of necessity into the realm of freedom." In his second essay, written ten years later, F. Znakov gives essentially the same analysis of the Soviet system and predicts its imminent collapse. This time, however, he does not make any references to either Marxism-Leninism or socialism and, instead of addressing himself to foreign Communists, appeals for understanding and support to the public opinion at large, both at home and abroad.

It follows from the above that Soviet dissent which has emerged during the mid–1950s-early 1960s was in all its varieties entirely Marxist-Leninist. It is perhaps natural that in a Soviet-type system people with a participatory political culture are the first to react to indications of change from above by entering the dissident arena, whereas the real dissidents, those who remained alien to official Marxism throughout all the years of Soviet rule, were skeptical about any changes within the same Marxist-Leninist framework and continued to live their lives in the way that was shaped in the preceding Stalinist period, that is, mainly as conformists—people keeping their genuine oppositionist views and values to themselves or expressing them publicly in an inoffensive manner such as, for example, participation in religious life.

Marxist-Leninist Convictions Fade Away

With the passage of time the Marxist-Leninist ideological framework within which the early Soviet dissenters used to express their views has gradually faded away. Those belonging to the first category of the Marxist-Leninist idealists (i.e., the "anti-Stalinists"), after having realized that the Soviet system is neither willing nor able to change in accordance with their views and values (it took them quite some time to realize this fact; the turning point here being the Soviet invasion of Czechoslovakia in August 1968), were forced by the sheer logic of life to reexamine their Marxist-Leninist convictions. The process of such reexamination was prompted also by their concentration on the issues of legality and human rights. Slowly but irreversibly they came to the conclusion that these are best catered to in conditions of a pluralist Western-type liberal democracy which, as they knew only too well, were incompatible with the very idea of the socialist state as conceived by Marxism-Leninism. In the end these people had to make their choice between the two and most of them made this choice by rejecting their original Marxism-Leninism and wholeheartedly embracing the Western-type liberal-democratic views. (The personal stories of Andrei Sakharov and especially of his wife, Elena Bonner, are here the most typical and eloquent cases in point.)

Today the only people in this category who still claim to be Marxists are the twin brothers Roy and Zhores Medvedev. Their Marxist convictions,

however, are highly questionable since their assessment of the Soviet society is not based on either class analysis or on the analysis of the relationship between that society's economic base and its superstructure.
Neither do the Medvedev brothers reason about the USSR from the clear-
cut standpoint of the interests of the working class. They talk rather about
the abstract rights and freedoms of the people in the typical bourgeois-
democratic way. In fact, therefore, their self-proclaimed allegiance to
Marxism seems to be nothing else but a politically motivated explicit declaration of total loyalty to the Soviet system, loyalty not only to its political
formula but also to its entire political myth. Proclaiming this loyalty under
the "code-name" of their adherence to Marxism-Leninism, the Medvedev
brothers believe that they are the only dissidents realistically contributing
to the liberal-democratic change of the Soviet system. For they are convinced that such a change could be introduced only from above, i.e., by
the Soviet leadership itself. It therefore seems to them that the most important task of the dissidents consists not in confronting and opposing the
Soviet leaders (an activity which will only provide the "reactionaries"
within the leadership with arguments against liberalization), but in persuading those of them who are in the "progressive camp" (of course, in
their own Marxist-Leninist language) to opt for such a change and in
assisting them in introducing changes. But the only way in which any Soviet
leaders could be thus persuaded is, according to the Medvedev brothers,
the way of convincingly showing them that the proposed liberal changes
are entirely compatible with the Soviet political myth, do not entail any
dangers for the system's continuity, and should even increase the system's
stability and strength.[11]

It should be clear from the above that the controversy between the
Medvedev brothers and the rest of the Soviet liberal-democratic dissidents
is not so much about ideas as about political tactics. Marxism as a philosophy or ideology has nothing to do with it.

The most drastic change of mind took place among those people in both
categories of the surviving Marxist-Leninist idealists who were unable to
reconcile themselves with the ideological vacuum which was left by their
disillusionment with and/or their rejection of Marxism-Leninism. The urge
to fill this vacuum with a different creed turned some of them to older
traditional ideologies, such as religion and/or nationalism. The ideological
biographies of such people as Alexander Solzhenitsyn, Igor Shafarevich,
Vladimir Maksimov, Vladimir Osipov, to name but a few, are here the
relevant cases in point. So is also the revival of Zionism among the formerly
Marxist-Leninist-oriented Soviet Jews.

F. Znakov tells us that by 1963 he "overgrew" his Marxism, too, and
in philosophical terms became a "self-conscious eclectic." A few years

before this happened, he, a professional scholar, was constantly mocked by his numerous academic friends and colleagues as "the last Marxist of the Soviet Union."[12] These friends and colleagues of Znakov's apparently became "Marxist agnostics," and many of them "militant Marxist atheists," much earlier than Znakov himself. The autobiography of the former Soviet general, Petro Grigorenko,[13] confirms that this process of "evaporation" of Marxist beliefs, however firmly they were held in the past, is not limited to the Soviet scholarly community but is rather typical for former "Marxist believers" in all sections of Soviet society. As N. Korzhavin, himself formerly an ardent Marxist-Leninist, pointed out, in the Soviet Union today only the unashamed cynics are still pretending to be Marxists; in fact, they are not; even the present Soviet rulers abandoned Marxism a long time ago, and for good, but they have to continue to use its phraseology for entirely pragmatic reasons.[14]

It follows from the above that Marxism, which was in the beginning the sole ideology of Soviet dissent, had by the mid–1960s almost entirely disappeared from the dissident ideological spectrum. Instead, Soviet dissent gradually developed a variety of ideologies most of which were based on a modern reinterpretation of the pre-Soviet non-Marxist ideological creeds, such as democratic liberalism, religious idealism, different shades of nationalism and combinations of all these.[15]

In personal terms the former Marxist-Leninists, as people with a participatory political culture, still dominated the dissident stage but now their views were in most cases virulently anti-Marxist. This provided the possibility for the "silent majority" of the traditional non- and anti-Marxists to abandon their long-standing position of silent and inconspicuous loners and to join the ranks of Soviet dissent. Some of them eventually did so. In the first place the Soviet dissidents were joined by the members of such national and religious minorities who had their special acute grievances. Their presence in the all-Union dissident movement became especially apparent after the "rights-defending" wing of Soviet dissent, in particular Andrei Sakharov himself, had actively involved themselves in the protection of their specific rights. (The Crimean Tatars, Pentecostalists, Adventists, Evangelical Baptists, Zionists, and many other similar minorities provide the illustration of this point.) But not only such specific minorities represented the traditionalist intake into the originally Marxist Soviet dissent. A number of mainstream religious individuals (such as Anatoly Krasnov-Levitin, Gleb Yakunin, et al.) as well as nationalists, none with any Marxist background in their past, both the Russian and the non-Russian ones, started to make their presence in its ranks felt too.

It would, however, be untrue to say that Marxism as an ideology of Soviet dissent is already entirely dead. In his *samizdat* works the late historian Alexandr Zimin continued to discuss the acute problems of Soviet society in purely Marxist terms.[16] Marxist methodology was manifestly present in the proposals for an integral reform of the Soviet system on which the scholars Len Karpinsky and Otto Latsis were working in the early 1970s and which were seized by the KGB in 1975.[17] A group of young scholars (mainly from the Institute of World Economics and International Affairs of the Academy of Sciences of the USSR) who were trying to revise Soviet communism from a Euro-Communist perspective and whose activities were disclosed by the KGB in 1982 is in this context of special significance because it shows that there are signs of a Marxist revival among the younger, yet very little known, generation of Soviet dissidents. This fact is partly substantiated by the arrest in October 1984 of four young members of Moscow's Engineering-Physical Institute who, as the *samizdat* report indicated, were trying to "reassess Soviet reality from a Marxist position."[18]

In spite of the above, Marxism as a dissident ideology is of marginal importance today in the USSR. During the 1960s and most of the 1970s Marxism, although already rejected by the mainstream of Soviet dissent, still played an important role at least as an ideology the dissidents had to overcome and to combat. As Marxism before, anti-Marxism during this period of time was increasingly becoming the common ideological denominator for the dissidents who by now already greatly varied in their respective values and views.

This is no longer the case. For the dissidents of the 1980s Marxism becomes increasingly irrelevant, a subject not even worth discussing seriously. As the young Russian poet Yuriy Kublanovskiy pointed out, Russians of his generation (he is in his late twenties) are completely indifferent to Marx although they have to study him in schools and colleges; "Marx now," he continued, "is in the USSR of no interest to anyone and only a few individuals still continue to hate him."[19]

Is There a Common Denominator for People's Authentic Sociopolitical Orientation in the USSR?

It is in my view significant that Soviet dissent has not developed or acquired a radical political ideology calling for a revolutionary destruction of the Soviet system of rule and the establishment of another utopia, whatever its name. As was pointed out above, such an ideology was, in fact, offered by some Soviet dissidents in the mid–1950s-early 1960s in the form of a Marxist reinterpretation of the nature of the Soviet society and state (by F. Znakov, et al.), but it did not attract any significant following and was soon almost completely forgotten. It seems that the Soviet experience of an ideologically based revolution and its repercussions made both the intelligentsia and the people immune, indeed idiosyncratic, to any repetition of such an experience.[20]

The Soviet dissident movement as a whole, a few marginal exceptions, such as VSKhSON,[21] notwithstanding, is based on political moderation. It totally rejects political violence, unequivocally condemns terrorism wherever it takes place and by whomever, and for whatever purpose, it is exercised, vehemently opposes the very idea of having any definitive blueprints for an alternative organization of society, and does not even believe in political struggle or any kind of activities that have to be conducted by conspiratorial or insurrectionist means. It considers patience to be the greatest and most important political value, is unequivocally committed to the rule of law and, accordingly, relies on making a feasible impact on the ongoing processes of social and political development which should by themselves, in a natural and spontaneous way, decide the fate of the Soviet system of rule.

This is why the Soviet dissidents, many of whom were released by the Gorbachev administration from prison camps and places of exile during 1986–1987, on the whole support that administration's policies of *perestroika* and *glasnost'*, constructively criticizing the inconsistencies, limitations and contradictions that mark the practical implementation of these policies. These dissidents participate in the activities of scores of newly formed informal pressure groups (the so-called *neformaly*), openly (though without explicit official approval) publish new periodicals, such as *The Express Chronicle* that operatively reports the developments in the country's human rights situation, *Glasnost'* in which a wide range of issues related to the present situation in the country are freely discussed, and scores of others. They are also ready to cooperate fully with the official media and do so whenever this is possible. The qualified support that Sakharov, without conceding any of his principles or views, lends to Gorbachev's policies is a classical illustration of the dissidents' constructive attitudes to Soviet political reality. The dissidents fully recognize the tremendous positive potential that *glasnost'*—the demand for which marked the beginning of the dissident movement in the USSR in the late 1950s— if it is to develop and acquire an unstoppable momentum, may have for the USSR's transformation into a truly pluralistic and tolerant society, and do whatever they can to enhance its chances to take proper root in Soviet social life, e.g., by using as much as possible the opportunities opened by it, to express publicly their views.

There is in the Soviet Union simply no room any more for utopian ideologies and movements of whatever kind. In this respect, one could say that the politically backward Russia pioneers a new sociopolitical mentality which, if mankind is to survive, has to conquer the world.

Notes

1. For a more detailed substantiation of this thesis see Alexander Shtromas, *Political Change and Social Development: The Case of the Soviet Union*, (Frankfurt a.M. & Bern: Verlag Peter Lang, 1981): esp. 23–66.
2. This started with the so-called "Lenin levy" of 1924 when 200,000, mainly young career-minded workers were recruited to join the Party "to compensate for the Party's loss of Lenin"; this one year's intake comprised about a third of the then total membership of the Party of 472,000 (see Thomas H. Rigby, *Communist Party Membership in the USSR, 1917–1968*, (Princeton: Princeton University Press, 1968). By 1928 the total membership of the Party was already 1,304,471 (see *Bol'shaya Sovetskaya Entsiklopediya*, /The Large Soviet Encyclopedia/, 1st edition, 11, XI, 533, which means that in three years after the "Lenin levy" had been completed, the membership of the Party had almost doubled, making the career-minded opportunistic element in the Party's ranks overwhelmingly dominant.
3. According to Robert Conquest's carefully analyzed data, among the 6 to 8 million people repressed during the Great Purge at least 1.5 million were members of the Party. Of them only 50,000 were released alive from the *Gulag* by Khrushchev; the rest had perished. *The Great Terror*, 2nd edition, (London: Macmillan, 1970; Appendix A.) This shows that the number of eliminated party members greatly exceeded the total membership of the Party as it stood in 1928 (see previous note), which means that, along with the idealists, many "unfortunate" opportunistic recruits to the Party also fell victims to the Great Purge.
4. See Roman Redlikh, *Stalinshchina kak dukhovnyi fenomen*, (Stalinism as a Spiritual Phenomenon), 2nd edition, (Frankfurt a.M.: Possev, 1971).
5. Leonard Schapiro, "Epilogue: Some Reflections on Lenin, Stalin and Russia," in George Urban, ed., *Stalinism: Its Impact on Russia and the World*, (Aldershot: Wildwood House, 1985): 416.
6. Schapiro in Urban, *Stalinism*, 424.
7. Milovan Djilas, "Christ and the Commissar", in Urban, *Stalinism*, 197.
8. See Dora Shturman, "Tetrad' na stole," in *Vremya i my* (Time and We), 53, 1981; 152–181. This is the most relevant part of a bigger *memoir* serialized in that magazine.
9. For a more detailed account on the Krasnopevtsev-Rendel case see, Cornelia Gerstenmaier, *The Voice of the Silent*, (New York: Hert, 1972.)
10. There were two documents signed by F. Znakov which circulated in Moscow's *samizdat* at the time: *Otkrytoe pis'mo Pal'miro Tolyatti* (Open Letter to Pal-

miro Togliatti), dated 1956, was one, and *Pamyatnaya zapiska*, dated 1966, was the other. Only the latter has reached the West and is available in its original Russian version, in Radio Liberty, *Arkhiv samizdata*, 374, 1966: 1–31. For a rather detailed summary of F. Znakov's views in English, see Shtromas, *Political Change*. There were more similar critical-programmatic documents circulating in Moscow's *samizdat* at the same time; one of the most prominent among them was the so-called "Testament" of Academician Evgeniy Varga (for its English translation see *New Left Review*, 62, 1966: 134–53).

11. The political views of the Medvedev brothers are elaborately presented in Roy Medvedev, *On Socialist Democracy*, (New York: A. Knopf, 1975). For their polemics with fellow dissidents see Roy Medvedev, "The Problem of Democratization and the Problem of Détente," in Radio Liberty's *Special Report*, 359, 1973; Roy A. Medvedev, *Political Essays*, (Nottingham: Spokesman Books, 1976); and Roy Medvedev, *On Soviet Dissent: Interviews with Piero Ostellino*, (New York: Columbia University Press, 1980). In the latter work Medvedev already concedes that he is a socialist rather than a Marxist. For a very well substantiated scholarly account on the progression of Soviet dissenters from Marxism-Leninism to Western-type liberal democracy see Ferdinand J.M. Feldbrugge, *Samizdat and Political Dissent in the Soviet Union*, (Leiden: Sijthof, 1975).

12. See Znakov, *Pamyatnaya . . .* ; 28–30.

13. See Petro Grigorenko, *V podpol'e mozhno vstretit' tol'ko krys*, (One Can Meet Only Rats in the Underground), (New York: Detinec, 1981). An abridged English version is *Memoirs* published in New York in 1982.

14. Naum Korzhavin, "Psikhologiya sovremennogo entuziazma," (The Psychology of Contemporary Enthusiasm), in *Kontinent*, 9, 1976; 123–33. It seems that by now the fact that Marxism-Leninism is in the Soviet Union in terms of faith a dead ideology has ceased to be a subject for controversy and is admitted by everyone who touches upon this subject. All the authors of Urban's *Stalinism* agree on it and so do all Soviet dissidents from Solzhenitsyn to Sakharov. See Alexander Solzhenitsyn, *Letter to Soviet Leaders*, (London: Fontana, 1974): 28, 46–49; Andrei Sakharov, "On Aleksandr Solzhenitsyn's *Letter to Soviet Leaders*," in Michael Meerson-Aksenov and Boris Shragin eds., *The Political, Social and Religious Thought of Russian Samizdat—An Anthology*, (Belmont, Mass.: Nordland, 1977): 291–301.

15. There were also a few manifestations of outright fascist ideology. One of the most outspoken examples of it is an anonymous document *Slovo Natsii* that widely circulated in Soviet *samizdat*. (For its English text, see "The Nation Speaks", in *Survey*, 17, No. 3, 1971.) For interesting attempts at classifying the ideologies existing in the USSR, see Andrei Amal'rik, "Ideologies in Soviet Society," in *Survey*, 21, No. 2, 1976; and Carl A. Linden, *The Soviet Party State: The Politics of Ideocratic Despotism*, (New York: Praeger, 1983), chap. 4. See also Vladislav Krasnov's contribution to Vol. I of the present series. A short survey of fascist ideological tendencies is given in Mikhail

Agursky, "The Intensification of Neo-Nazi Danger in the Soviet Union," in Meerson-Aksenov and Shragin (eds.); 414ff.

16. Aleksandr Zimin, *Sotsializm i neostalinizm*, (Socialism and Neo-Stalinism), (New York: Chalidze Publications, 1981).

17. The original text of Karpinsky and Latsis is not available. Its content is known only from brief summaries in *samizdat* reports concerning the event.

18. Published in *Russkaya Mysl'*, (Russian Thought), 3568, (1984); 2.

19. Yuriy Kublanovsky, "Marks i SSSR" (Marx and the USSR), in *Russkaya Mysl'*, 3456, (1983); 5.

20. F. Znakov in *Pamyatnaya zapiska* (1966) himself recognized that facts have not borne out his predictions made in 1956. He complains that all sections of Soviet society, including the working class and the Party's rank and file, instead of developing a revolutionary socialist orientation, are getting increasingly permeated by bourgeois consumerism and, gradually, also by the spirit of capitalist entrepreneurship which manifests itself in the rapid growth of the "second economy," and wonders whether socialism is not merely the longest way for transition from feudalism to capitalism.

21. For a detailed account of VSKhSON, see John B. Dunlop, *The New Russian Revolutionaries*, (Belmont, Mass.: Nordland, 1976).

4

Glasnost' and Russia's History

W. BRUCE LINCOLN

Ever since Peter the Great launched Russia's first crash program of modernization some three centuries ago, the Russians have borrowed science, technology, and practical know-how from the West and have used Western yardsticks to measure their achievements. Yet, Russia's rulers have attempted to match the technological and economic progress of the West by imposing modernization from above in an effort to produce more quickly the achievements that the West came to enjoy only after undergoing a series of long and complex revolutionary experiences. While Western peoples combined the political consequences of the French Revolution of 1789 with the economic achievements of the Industrial Revolution to destroy despotism and foster free enterprise, the Russians have relied upon their heritage of absolute authority, all-powerful bureaucracy, and closely guarded secrecy to weaken individualism, strengthen the government's ability to impose change from above, and minimize the political and social threats posed by the Western experience.

Few phenomena have posed this conflict in Russia's national heritage more starkly than *glasnost'*, the policy of "openness" currently associated with the leadership style of the Soviet Union's Mikhail Gorbachev. Gorbachev's *glasnost'* contrasts sharply with the rigid, closed regimes of his predecessors in that much that used to be hidden behind a wall of official silence now is held up to public scrutiny. The Soviet press continues to publish reports about Chernobyl and other catastrophes, to criticize corruption at high levels in the Party and government, to point to the failings of the stumbling Soviet economy, and to lament such social ills as alcoholism and drug abuse. Gorbachev's *glasnost'*, hopeful Westerners believe, may herald the Soviet Union's coming of age and mark the opening of a new era in which its leaders will confront reality rather than sweep it behind a wall of propaganda that for so long proclaimed that reality was not what it seemed to be.

Yet, *glasnost'* is not an invention of the 1980s, and Gorbachev is not its creator. The Russians have trod this path before on those infrequent occasions when their rulers and statesmen have moderated their usual curbs upon the expression of public opinion. But, if they have permitted public criticism of national policy in rare instances, Russia's leaders have never relinquished their authority to make decisions and impose them from above. Historically, *glasnost'* has been, at best, an attempt by Russian rulers to respond to extreme economic and political crises by bringing an awareness of public opinion into their government's decision-making processes while providing a very limited outlet for political discontent. The limited criticism of government policies that *glasnost'* has allowed has seemed unprecedented at the time, but it has never obliged Russia's policy-makers to act upon that criticism, nor has it ever taken decision making outside closed government circles. *Glasnost'* in Russia has never been synonymous with its Western equivalent of public and open policy-making. In years past, this has bestowed meanings very different from those used in the West upon such terms as "democracy," "constitution," and "publicity."

Primarily a product of the West's political experience, the public nature of *glasnost'* has always threatened the absolute authority, rigid bureaucracy, and jealously guarded secrecy upon which Russia's long-standing competition with the West has been based. On the rare occasions when they have turned to *glasnost'*, Russian rulers and policymakers therefore have attempted to subject it to those same influences with which they have moderated other borrowings from the West. This has meant that *glasnost'* has had limits, and these have to be understood as more than crude attempts by an absolute government to prevent public criticism from going beyond prescribed boundaries. Russia's rulers have limited *glasnost'* in a far more subtle fashion by insisting that those who would comment critically upon the shortcomings of state policy must share political, social, economic, and cultural values in common with their government. Before the twentieth century, these accepted values were the precepts of Orthodoxy, Autocracy, and Nationality upon which the Romanovs based their defense of Imperial Russia's government. Now, they encompass the precepts of Marxism-Leninism, uniquely reshaped by the Soviet political experience under Stalin, Khrushchev, Brezhnev, Andropov and, now, Gorbachev.

Glasnost' first appeared in Russia in a prototypical form during the last third of the eighteenth century when Empress Catherine II encouraged educated men and women to debate the failings of their nation's recently Europeanized aristocracy. Why, Catherine asked, had so many Russian nobles acquired the trappings of Western culture without learning about the ideas that underlay them and without developing that strong sense of civic duty and social responsibility that formed such a central part of the lives of their counterparts in the West? What was needed to develop that sense of civic responsibility which would lead Russia's nobles to serve their government loyally and willingly?

However well-intentioned she may have been, Catherine quickly found that the public debate she had encouraged could not be confined within the limits she thought proper or useful because some of her subjects hurried to challenge the very principles and institutions that she thought most vital to her people's well-being. None did so more persistently than Nikolai Novikov, publisher of four short-lived satirical journals between 1769 and 1774, and the first writer of consequence to question Russia's eighteenth-century social and economic order. Not content to embroider upon Catherine's criticisms of the personal foibles of Russia's semi-Europeanized nobility, Novikov turned his pen against the venality of his country's judges, the manner in which provincial lords abused their serfs, and the corruption of some of Russia's leading statesmen. Clearly, Catherine found Novikov's criticisms disturbing, all the more so because Russia's government did not have at hand the instruments to control the new and awesome force of a private press that her brief flirtation with *glasnost'* had unleashed. Although the evidence to support historians' claims that she forced Novikov to close his journals remains inconclusive, it was hardly coincidence that Catherine established the first institutions of press censorship in Russia soon afterward.

Novikov's broad criticisms of autocratic politics and Russian society was a direct consequence of Catherine's experiment with *glasnost'*. From it sprang the first radical challenges to her autocracy and her government. These found their most dramatic statement in *Journey from St. Petersburg to Moscow*, a fictional travel account cast in the style of Laurence Sterne's *Sentimental Journey*, that Aleksandr Radishchev published in 1790. Designed to comment upon the indignities of serfdom, the corruption of the bureaucracy, the immorality of the clergy, and the failings of Russia's ruler, Radishchev's book (which was published because of a censor's arrogant carelessness) forced Catherine to choose between continuing her effort to foster enlightenment or defending the autocratic government which she considered essential for protecting Russia against the ideas of the French

Revolution. Unhesitatingly, the aging empress chose the latter course, condemned Radishchev to death (although she commuted his sentence to exile in Siberia), and, two years later, sent Novikov to prison.

Catherine's experiment with a prototypical form of *glasnost'* thus gave birth to political radicalism in Russia. Although this played a part in the easily suppressed Decembrist Revolt against Nicholas I on December 14, 1825, it posed no serious political threat to Russia's stability until after the middle of the nineteenth century. While European monarchs nervously faced waves of revolutionary violence in 1820, 1830, and 1848, Russia's rulers and their counselors therefore drew a false sense of confidence from their nation's apparent political tranquillity. Yet there was greater danger than they knew, for the unmodernized, servile Russia that defenders of autocratic government cheered during the middle of the nineteenth century suffered serious ills that could not be left untreated much longer. For too long her rulers and statesmen had made policy in secret and had endowed state officials with the absolute authority to enforce it. Russia's laws served not as sensitive instruments for bringing justice to all, but as rigid regulations destined to be applied by men who never dared to interpret them as special circumstances might require. Men bearing the emperor's commission thus had wielded power that mirrored his own. The result was a society that continued to suffer from a chronic lack of civic responsibility that had only worsened during the three-quarters of a century after Empress Catherine had first sought remedies for that defect in the 1760s and 1770s.

With a limited sense of duty to the government they served, and with no understanding that, as citizens, they bore a responsibility to the society in which they lived, many Russian state officials therefore served themselves before they served others. It was no accident that their army was the worst fed of any in Europe, or that its officers on occasion issued their men musket balls made of clay and paper cartridges filled with millet because they had sold their rations, gunpowder, and lead for profit. Nor was it mere chance that many judges in Russia's courts, and officials at all levels of her government, sold their influence as a matter of course. Russia in 1850, a contemporary observer remembered, "resembled a lake, in the depths of which great fish devoured the smaller ones, while near the surface everything was calm and glistened smoothly, like a mirror."

In Russia, arbitrarily bestowed privilege and the government's stubborn refusal to draw upon the talents of private citizens produced a chasm between governors and governed that continued to deny rulers those native wellsprings of new ideas that had enabled Europe's rapidly industrializing nations to flourish. Without public debate about national policy, and with no public discussion of the failings of their government and society, Russia's rulers found it impossible to defend themselves and their government against abuse by their servants. Emperors and senior statesmen therefore relied upon undercover surveillance by secret agents to expose the misbehavior that an independent press in an open society would have reported all too readily. The very fact that surveillance functioned in secret and derived its authority to seek out corruption in government from the emperor's unlimited personal power only made the absence of civic responsibility more acute. Most of the men who abused the people they governed escaped punishment because so few in Russia had any sense that such crimes transgressed against the body politic of their nation.

At the same time, the Industrial Revolution that transformed Europe so dramatically during the first half of the nineteenth century remained a mere shadow upon Russia's horizon. While the populations of England, France, Belgium, and Germany began to move from farms to factories in order to lay the base for those modern, industrialized societies that were to enjoy the unheard-of standards of living that came to Europe during the second half of the nineteenth century, Russia remained overwhelmingly rural and without the technological fruits of Europe's Industrial Revolution. The rapidly industrializing nations of the West therefore posed a far more serious threat to Russia's well-being at the middle of the nineteenth century than any of her rulers or statesmen imagined. Perhaps most important, the growing might of European nations threatened Russia's jealously guarded military superiority, the single claim to Great Power status that she had enjoyed ever since the armies of Peter the Great had defeated the Swedish forces of Charles XII at Poltava in 1709. Since then, Russia had reminded Europe's Great Powers of her claim at regular intervals. Cossack cavalry had ridden into the outskirts of Berlin in 1761 to threaten Frederick the Great with defeat in the Seven Years War and, in 1814, a triumphant Alexander had led a victorious Allied parade down the Champs-Elysées after his armies had driven Napoleon back from Moscow in defeat. A mere forty years later, Russia's claim to Great Power status crumbled as the armies of France and England defeated her forces in the Crimea.

Russia's defeat in the Crimean War threatened her membership in Europe's community of Great Powers and confronted her with an urgent choice. If she wished to compete with Western nations on a more equal footing, she had to follow the path taken by the nations of Europe during the first half of the nineteenth century and modernize rapidly. Yet, the reason Russia's rulers had not chosen that course earlier was because serfdom, and the society that had been built around it, had barred the way to economic progress. Now thoughtful Russians had to question the very social and economic order that had won them a place among the Europeans in the first place. How must Russia modernize? What social and economic changes were needed? What institutional renovations must be undertaken? Never had modern Russia faced such a crisis. To find the answers upon which their nation's survival as a Great Power depended, Russia's young Emperor Alexander II and some of his more progressive advisers looked to *glasnost'*, the policy of "openness" which, they hoped, might give them access to Russian public opinion without depriving them of their decision-making authority.

For a few years after the Crimean War, it seemed that Russia's new policy of "openness" might succeed. Most Russians shared a common outlook shaped by their belief in the principles of "Orthodoxy, Autocracy, and Nationality," and, on that basis, the emperor and his advisers hoped that a p7blic debate about state policy could help them decide what course to follow without obliging them to allow public opinion to have a voice in defining that course. At the same time, *glasnost'* seemed to many progressive-minded Russians to offer a way for the voices of responsible citizens to be heard within a government that had closed its ears to public opinion for so long. It would be more than enough, one of Russia's leading liberals wrote early in 1855, "if only the voice of public opinion, bit by bit, will reach [the new czar]."

Called by some "the best physician for the ulcers of the state," *glasnost'* seemed about to bring public opinion and government together in a new and fruitful union that would set Russia and the Russians upon an evolutionary path to modernization and progress. "By permitting all civic interest groups to express themselves openly," one enthusiastic Russian wrote, it would become possible to "supply the government with information about the needs and requirements of Russia" at a time when most government officials had "no more acquaintance with the internal life of Russia than with that on the Isle of Ceylon." Such men hoped that *glasnost'* could become the mortar that would at last cement czar, public opinion (including radical opinion), and the inarticulate masses into a force that could overwhelm all self-interested opposition to reform and modernization in Russia.

As the Russians embarked upon this new era of "openness" between the spring of 1856 and the spring of 1862, most of the so-called "cursed questions" that had concerned thoughtful men and women came into the public forum for discussion, beginning with serfdom, perhaps the problem that troubled the Russians the most. Less than two weeks after the Crimean War had ended, Alexander II himself told the assembled nobility of Moscow that it was "better to begin to abolish serfdom from above than to await that time when it will begin to abolish itself from below" and asked them to "think seriously about how to bring all this about." Just how clearly Alexander understood what *glasnost'* meant when he issued that invitation, and just how far he intended to extend it, are matters open to some question for he never spoke the fateful word "emancipation" himself. Nevertheless, by 1858, Russians had begun to debate the question of emancipation in their nation's press. That, in itself, had seemed beyond the wildest imaginings of progressive men and women less than three years before when the liberal publicist and jurist Konstantin Kavelin had expressed the timid belief that it would be enough for Russia's czar just to listen to "the voice of public opinion" for "ten or even fifteen years" before the nation embarked upon "any further reforms or transformations."

A sense of liberation filled the air in the late 1850s and early 1860s as Russians spoke of freeing their serfs, electing their local governments, reforming education and the penal code, bringing justice into their nation's courts, and liberating women from the tight patriarchal constraints that had bound them to hearth and home for centuries. Wearied of having the emperor's gendarmes and censors pose as the moral and political guardians of Russia, public opinion also began to seek emancipation from that loathsome combination of government tutelage and government control which had allowed censors to choke the life from Russian arts and letters during the so-called "era of censorship terror" that had spanned the difficult years between Europe's revolutions of 1848 and the end of the Crimean War.

Now, Russians hurried to reverse that process as *glasnost'* began to lift the weight of government repression. In elegant parlors and in humble rented rooms, men and women conversed publicly about ideas that would have caused their arrest just a few years before. No less a figure than Alexander II's aunt, the Grand Duchess Elena Pavlovna, became the hostess of one of St. Petersburg's most daring salons, in which even publications that still could not survive the censor's scrutiny were read aloud and discussed. Rarely had attitudes changed so quickly in Russia. In 1849, the authorities had condemned a group of young men, including Dostoevsky, to forced labor in Siberia for discussing the writings of a number of French utopian socialists in the privacy of their own lodgings. Now, just more than a decade later, a censor passed *What Is To Be Done?*, a novel in which the radical publicist Nikolai Chernyshevskii set forth a plan for liberating women by means of a considerably more concrete form of socialism. A diplomat who had been away from Russia for some time viewed these dramatic changes with optimistic amazement. "Arriving in Russia now, one runs the risk of not recognizing her," he wrote when he returned home to St. Petersburg in 1858. "One feels that a new era is beginning."

As it had in Catherine's time, the very openness of *glasnost'* quickly raised unexpected and difficult problems. Once the authorities loosened the restraints that had kept public opinion in check, Russians' expectations rose much faster than the government's willingness—or ability—to meet them. Between 1861 and 1864, the Great Reforms emancipated Russia's serfs, created institutions of local self-government, opened the universities to more lower class students, and transformed the nation's court system. In village assemblies, former serfs cast ballots to determine what direction their lives would take and elected deputies to represent them in district councils charged with improving public education, health, and welfare. Aided by attorneys (there had been none in Russia before 1864), men and women defended themselves in public trials presided over by judges who had been trained in the law, while juries of their peers judged their guilt or innocence. Yet, these reforms, which went further than men and women had even dared to dream less than a decade before, now met with sharp criticism for being less than they ought to have been. Spurred by their brief taste of *glasnost'*, Russians called for broader reforms than any autocratic government could grant without relinquishing its power to direct the nation's course. Perhaps most striking of all, a number of sober and sensible Russians with close ties to the "establishment" called for a national assembly in which *glasnost'* would have the potential for producing legislative action independent of the czar's initiative and, even, against his wishes.

Of course, there were good reasons for such daring proposals and stern criticism. Most important, *glasnost'* itself very quickly had eroded that common body of aspirations and values based upon "Orthodoxy, Autocracy, and Nationality" that had ruled Russians' lives between the 1830s and 1850s. Depending upon their vision of their nation's future, Russians' views and values now ranged across as wide a political spectrum as any in Europe. Some men still stood to the right of the government, but others now stood at the other extreme as well. When Russia's emperor and government failed to satisfy their newly—and rapidly—inflated expectations, prominent publicists and thinkers moved sharply leftward. The very same Aleksandr Herzen, who had thought that *glasnost'* could bind czar and people together in 1858, hurried in 1861 to condemn the emancipation statutes as "an act of Judas" and warned that "the peasant community, the will of the people, and the rights of man [will be raised] against the Czar and the great lords in revenge for their betrayal."

Alexander II and his advisers thus faced the same dilemma that had confronted Empress Catherine about how to control public discussions of state policy once it had begun. As Catherine had done nearly a hundred years before, they looked to censorship to prevent public opinion from stepping beyond the bounds they thought permissible. Indeed, censorship and *glasnost'* could readily coexist, Alexander once explained, because the "judicious vigilance" of Russia's censors need not "inhibit thinking" so long as the Russians and their government shared a common set of values and aspirations. That such shared values no longer existed meant that the sources of conflict between the government and the governed could only grow more bitter. The only *glasnost'* possible under "judicious censorship" that did not "inhibit thinking" was that which clarified and elaborated the views that the government itself set forth. At best, such *glasnost'* could criticize the improper or ineffective application of policy, not the content of policy itself.

Nowhere was the government's view of *glasnost'* set forth more energetically in the 1860s than by Oskar Przhetslavskii, one of the leading members of Russia's Central Censorship Office. The fault of *glasnost'* as it had developed in Russia since the Crimean War, Przhetslavskii insisted, was that it had failed to conform "to our civic order, the peculiarities of our national character, the level of our present development, or our future requirements." For *glasnost'* to have any "real value in stimulating discussions about serious issues within a framework permissible to the government," he argued, it "must always have an indissoluble link with, and conform to, the bases and forms of the state and civic structure." To accomplish that end, Przhetslavskii defined public opinion as openly stated public support for the government's policies. Only if it were made to conform to Russia's national character and national institutions, he concluded, could *glasnost'* cease to stand "in opposition to the spirit and bases of state institutions and to Russia's system of administration and legislation."

The efforts of such senior officials as Przhetslavskii to balance those dichotomies of *glasnost'* that had been expressed by Alexander II's belief that judicious vigilance need not stand in the way of independent thinking quickly curtailed public debate about Russia's renovation and modernization well before the Great Reform era reached its end. Embittered because the expectations raised by *glasnost'* had not been met, Russia's radicals turned violently against their czar. Catherine's far more modest experiment with *glasnost'* in the 1770s had produced the beginnings of Russian radicalism in the 1780s; now, the failure of Alexander II's much broader effort brought Russia's first revolutionary movement into being. No longer did concerned young Russians believe that the czar might be convinced to redirect their nation's path as they had during the stern regime of Alexander's father, Nicholas I. Now certain that the only way to better their nation's future was to substitute a different social and political order for that defended by autocracy, Russia's newborn revolutionaries declared war against their emperor and his government. They first spoke of assassination in 1862. Four years later, they made their first serious attempt to assassinate Alexander II as he walked in St. Petersburg's Summer Gardens and, in 1881, the czar who had liberated his nation's serfs, became their victim. Clearly, Russia's experiment with *glasnost'* in the 1860s had encouraged far greater expectations among educated and thoughtful Russians than any autocratic government dared satisfy if it intended to preserve its authority.

The bitterness that such unfulfilled hopes produced among Russia's intelligentsia spawned a revolutionary movement at just the moment when Russia's effort to renew her economic and political competition with the West after the Crimean War brought her firmly into the embrace of Europe's revolutionary experience. Russia had been spared the revolutionary upheavals of 1830 and 1848, but she would not go unscathed much longer. The Russian anarchists Bakunin and Kropotkin, and, later, the Marxists Plekhanov and Lenin, all figured prominently in European revolutionary circles between 1860 and 1900 as they struggled to fit the precepts of Marx, Engels, and a score of others into the framework of their homeland's historical experience. Yet Europe's revolutionary heritage could not become Russia's because the specific historical experience of Russia inevitably transformed Western revolutionary doctrines into unique Russian forms. Bolshevism proved to be the most notable result of that process. In competition with a host of more "Western" and less "Russian" revolutionary alternatives in 1917, bolshevism made Marxism all the more effective in Russia, for it preserved those traditional elements of secrecy and arbitrary authority imposed from above that had been a vital part of Russian politics for centuries. At the same time, the Bolsheviks remained unencumbered by those Western trappings of constitutionalism and lawfulness that so effectively crippled their rivals when they tried to transplant Western ideologies and political programs across Europe's eastern frontier.

In 1917, such Western systems as constitutional monarchy, liberal parliamentarianism, and trade-union socialism all failed to take root in Russia's revolutionary turmoil and the Bolsheviks launched their nation upon an experiment with an authoritarian form of Marxism designed to prevail in a backward country unready to embark on such a radical revolutionary path. As a result the Bolsheviks have created in Russia a Marxist-socialist state which had to draw its strength from Russia's autocratic tradition. Given this already seventy-years-long experience with bolshevism, does *glasnost'* now offer more promise for success in Gorbachev's widely acclaimed new version than it did in the 1770s or the 1860s? For *glasnost'* to succeed, both society and government must respect the law and observe it—yet neither lawfulness nor openness can coexist with the absolute power, censorship, and bureaucratic tyranny that remain a part of the Russian experience today even more than in the late eighteenth or mid-nineteenth century. Nor can *glasnost'* and lawfulness function amidst the corruption that has become second nature to so many Russians. This problem cannot be dealt with merely by punishing Party officials who take bribes and abuse their authority; it can be resolved only when Russians are not obliged to buy Western clothing on the black market, pilfer computer and auto parts from their workplaces because they cannot buy them through legitimate channels, and bribe officials in order to have a private telephone installed in less than six months or a year.

If the aspirations of present-day Soviet society exceed the government's ability to meet them on such modest material levels as fashionable, well-made clothing, decent housing, and (by Western standards) a reasonable demand for consumer goods and spare parts, the gap between the two can only grow much larger if *glasnost'* follows its natural course and leads Russians to expect easier access to Western culture and more meaningful involvement in their own national political processes. The chance for any sort of peaceful transformation along Western lines therefore may very well be less in Russia now than was the case in the 1860s, while the consequences of failure remain far more ominous from the government's point of view.

The revolutionary movement that grew out of Russians' disillusionment with *glasnost'* a century ago involved a mere handful of people, had the support of only a small segment of Russian society, and functioned in a world in which the limits of time and space had barely begun the explosive expansion they would undergo in the twentieth century. Communication between revolutionary groups spread across a sixth of the globe's surface in those days posed logistical problems that nineteenth-century Russian revolutionaries found all but insurmountable. Compelled to work in a society that still suffered from widespread illiteracy, and without any form of modern telecommunications, Russia's nineteenth-century revolutionaries therefore found it a painfully slow process to increase their numbers and organize new converts effectively. This meant that, as a few thousand standing against tens of millions, they always faced overwhelming odds. For, right down to the beginning of 1917, Russia's lonesome revolutionaries could not count upon the support of their nation's masses.

The Soviet establishment faces a very different situation. Although the power of their government is even greater now than it was during the last third of the nineteenth century, so are the pressures that Russians can exert upon their leaders should *glasnost'* again raise their expectations as it did during the Great Reform era in the 1860s. Russians now have a sense of national community that was foreign to their nineteenth-century predecessors, and unofficial networks that have spread from one end of their country to the other make it possible for Russians to communicate with an ease and certainty that was impossible a century ago.

Now assured of at least minimal shelter and sufficient food, large numbers of Russians can dare to be much more daring in demanding that the limits of *glasnost'* be broadened more than they were in the last third of the nineteenth century, when the struggle for food and shelter kept their proletarian ancestors perpetually off balance and uncertain of their fate from one day to the next. If embittered by the failure of *glasnost'* to fulfill their expectations, such men and women now have the potential to exert mass pressures against the Soviet authorities that their predecessors could not hope to bring to bear against the government in czarist times. To Western observers, whose views remain conditioned by the Soviet experience under Stalin, massive antigovernment demonstrations in the Soviet Union may seem impossible, even in the late 1980s. But, in the context of Russia's historical experience, they appear much more likely now than the development of a viable revolutionary movement seemed even on the eve of the 1905 Revolution, that is, about a decade before the victorious Revolution of 1917.

A quarter-century ago, an early post-Stalinist dissident posed the question: "Will the Soviet Union Survive to 1984?" It has done that to be sure. But, whether Gorbachev can succeed with *glasnost'* where his eighteenth and nineteenth century predecessors failed is much less certain. Soviet authorities must struggle to make good on decades of broken promises that have to be met before they can raise the national standard of living substantially above the subsistence level. Likewise, broadened contacts with the West can only emphasize the widening gap in living standards and remind Russians how modest their demands for increased material comforts are when compared to those enjoyed by their counterparts elsewhere. Both factors place the Russians, who must suffer the consequences of a minimal living standard, in a much more antagonistic relationship with their government than was the case in the late 1850s when the mystique of czar and Orthodoxy bound rulers and masses together.

What makes this situation all the more volatile now is that, as in the late 1850s, the Soviet government appears to have no clear sense of direction to guide its search for new paths toward desperately needed renovation and reform. Such ideological baggage as collectivized agriculture and centralized industrial planning was discredited decades ago, yet it continues to burden Soviet policymakers and cloud their vision of the course to be followed. Such rigidity in the Soviet establishment can only raise further antagonisms should it confront the aspirations that any new experiment with *glasnost'* must inevitably raise among the Russians. Gorbachev therefore can no more expect to use *glasnost'* to clarify his government's uncertain views about the reform and renovation of its ponderous system than could Alexander II, and there is no indication that the Russians will be any more charitable now than they were then in forgiving their leaders' failure to satisfy the legitimate aspirations to openness, lawfulness, and economic progress that *glasnost'* is bound to raise. *Glasnost'* therefore poses dangers to the stability of the Soviet Union that remain every bit as acute as they were more than a century ago. And the outcome of such an experiment is no less uncertain now than it was then.

5

The Spiritual Roots of Political Confrontation Between Totalitarianism and Democracy

MIHAJLO MIHAJLOV

In October 1985, at the Conference of European Bishops, Pope John Paul II argued for a United Europe and recalled the Millenniums of Christianity in Poland in 1966, in Hungary in 1972, and in the Ukraine and Russia in 1988. He underlined that the development of Christian roots in the East and West experienced different evolutions that were nonetheless "not opposed but complementary and mutually enriching instead."[1] Analyzing present-day Europe, he noted that the lack of unity, the fracture that separates the peoples of the East and the West, is a result of historical, political, and ideological vicissitudes that should be overcome. The pope even stated that East-West unity is the wish of Jesus.

Speaking at the 1985 Cultural Forum in Budapest, the German writer Günther Grass stated that instead of the concept of East Europe or West Europe the forum should take up the dream of one Europe, which was so crudely divided by Yalta and Potsdam.[2] The argument about the world being artificially divided into East and West and the necessity of achieving at least the world's spiritual unity dominated also the 1986 Cultural Conference in Venice, the 1985 European Conference in Madrid, and has always been in the background of every major political, cultural or scientific international forum.

Dissidents from Eastern Europe and the Soviet Union took part in these discussions, too. The issue of East-West divide even became one of the most important points of ideological division inside the Russian dissidents' movement. This East-West controversy turned out to be especially important for intellectuals from central European countries—countries that belonged to the Western cultural circle until 1945, and now are part of Eastern Europe. Probably the most provocative and interesting essay was written by the Czechoslovak dissident, Milan Kundera, who lives in Paris. Among the most important essays by Western participants in the discussions were those published in 1985 by the late Hugh Seton-Watson, an English historian, and Peter L. Berger, an American scholar.

In the now so greatly revived old controversy about the "East" and the "West" nobody uses these terms any more in their geographical sense. For Hugh Seton-Watson "Europe is more than a geographical expression,"[3] and for Milan Kundera "Europe is a spiritual and not a geographical conception."[4] Solzhenitsyn in his Harvard speech named Japan the "Far West." On the other hand, almost all authors debating this issue use the terms "Western" and "European" as interchangeable and some even as identical. Europe is thus considered as the symbol of the Western world, and the line dividing NATO from the Warsaw Pact is seen as its boundary. Some of the authors include American civilization within the European one, some of them do so only partly.

There is nothing new about attempts at defining the boundaries of Europe or the West in a spiritual rather than geographical sense. At the end of the eighteenth and the beginning of the nineteenth century, the Germans regarded France, and to some extent Britain, as being the West. German romanticism was a reaction to "Western rationalism." Later, after the Napoleonic Wars, a similar situation was repeated in Russia; for the Russians, Germany, together with France and Britain, was the West, and the Slavophile movement was the Russian reaction to it. In the second half of the nineteenth century and the first decade of the twentieth century, the Asiatic nations already considered Russia as the "West." The Islamic fundamentalist movement in Iran and elsewhere is an Asiatic anti-Western reaction *par excellence*, and even in Japan there are many signs of such anti-Western reactions, as the public hara-kiri committed by the famous Japanese writer Mishima, exemplified several years ago.

Sometimes the contradiction between East and West in the cultural sphere reminds of the contradiction between rural and urban civilizations. In fact, the contradiction is much deeper and it rests at the bottom of human existence—in the sphere of the ontological and metaphysical structure of every human being. Contemporary divisions between the Communist and the democratic worlds also raise the question of the origins of totalitarianism and the influence of old historical traditions on today's events.

The Kidnapped West

An essay by Milan Kundera, "Kidnapped West or the Tragedy of Central Europe,"[5] expressed very strongly the political and existential situation of the peoples of Soviet-dominated Eastern Europe. Kundera tries to prove that, in the aftermath of World War II, East European countries did not only lose their political freedom but also their entire culture and national personality. Kundera believes that Russia has a civilization different from the European one and that "Russian communism rejuvenated the old Russian anti-Western obsessions and sharply cut Russia from Western history"; Russia, in other words, is "anti-West." According to Kundera, central Europe is, in fact, the essence of Western civilization, "the maximum of diversity on the minimum of territory," whereas Russia is "the minimum of diversity on a maximum of territory." To him, central Europe (in fact, the present Eastern Europe)—the area situated between Germany and Russia and populated by a variety of small nations—from the nineteenth century onward became the very center of European culture, which gave it Sigmund Freud and Franz Kafka, Antonin Dvořák and Gustav Mahler, Hermann Broch and Robert Musil, Barocco and structuralism. The fate of the whole of Europe is therefore bound to be determined by the destiny of its central part and in this sense the latter's political catastrophe in 1945 represents a lethal threat to the entire Western civilization.

All anti-Communist revolts in Eastern Europe after World War II were linked with the cultural sphere. For Kundera the most tragic fact is what he sees as Western Europe's loss of its sense of a common European culture. Poetry, music, architecture, philosophy, in present times do not unite Europe as they did in previous centuries. In Kundera's view this should be regarded as having the same importance as the decolonization of Africa. During the Renaissance, religion was replaced by culture and the Czech dissident writer is facing the big question: What is going to replace European culture now? As he wrote: "Culture already left. In Prague we felt its disappearance as a catastrophe, as a shock, as a tragedy, and in Paris this is considered something banal and insignificant, a non-event." According to him, "Central Europe does not exist any more." And this, in his view, has happened not only because the civilization of Russian totalitarianism, which has submerged central Europe, "is a radical negation of that West which . . . is based on the thinking and doubting 'Ego' and distinguished by cultural creativity expressing the unique and irreplaceable 'I'." It has happened also because at present "the feeling of its cultural identity is being lost . . . in Western Europe itself . . . where Europe is not conceived anymore as a value." Kundera concludes that central Europe, if it is to be resurrected, "has to countervail not only the destructive power of its giant neighbor but also the immaterial tread of time that leaves behind the epoch of culture."

In a recent article published in the United States, he wrote a paragraph which can be used as a summary for all of his philosophy: "Faced with the eternity of the Russian night, I had experienced in Prague the violent end of Western culture such as it was conceived at the dawn of the modern age, based on the individual and his reason, on pluralism of thought and on tolerance. In a small Western country I experienced the end of the West. That was the grand farewell."[6] In the same article he expresses his animosity even toward Dostoevsky's novels because he considers them to be a part of the entire anti-Western civilization.

Similar attitudes have been expressed by a few other East European intellectuals. The Hungarian author, Mihaly Vajda, is arguing that . . . "in Eastern Europe proper the social relations and the political structure are more or less in harmony, whereas in central Eastern Europe the state and society are in fundamental conflict . . ." In these countries "the ruling elite has to strive to annihilate most European values . . . , namely the social and individual autonomies." According to Vajda, "Moscow tolerates Romania's extravagant foreign policy because all manifestations of Europeanism are systematically quashed there."[7] There are also many similar statements written by Polish dissidents and it is obvious that a significant section of the intellectuals of East European countries (i.e., central European states) identify the Russian civilization and even the Russian culture with Soviet communism. Sometimes however, Kundera himself—being conscious that Communist totalitarianism is, in fact, a new historical phenomenon—tries to differentiate between those two. Thus, he stated that Russia was the first victim of communism, and that at the end of the nineteenth century she almost belonged to Western civilization, so that the German poet, Rilke, could consider Russia as his spiritual homeland.

Kundera clearly sees that Russian communism, inside of Russia, is the negation of Russian traditional, cultural, historical roots; but, at the same time, outside of Russia, it remains for him an incarnation of traditional Russian imperial ambitions.

Kidnapped Russia

Such a strong statement about different types of civilization—Russian and Western—provoked an answer by a Russian dissident poet, Joseph Brodsky. Brodsky reminded Kundera that Marxism was imported to Russia from Western Europe, that in 1939 the totalitarian invasion of Czechoslovakia came from the West and not the East, and that the establishing of totalitarianism in Kundera's country did not meet as many obstacles—long civil war, dozens of bloody revolts, etc.—as was the case in Russia.[8]

Brodsky's statement made an important point. Fascist and Nazi movements were really born within Western cultural circles. One of the French "new philosophers," Henri Glucksman, developed a theory that Russian communism is a direct product of Western rationalism.

Dostoevsky is, indeed, an inseparable part of European culture and if it is possible to understand Kundera's animosity toward Dostoevsky at the time when Warsaw Pact armies occupied Czechoslovakia in 1968—it is very difficult to make a link between the great Russian novelist and the Communists. It is true that in his political articles Dostoevsky often proclaimed Russian imperial goals, and in this sense he can in a way be considered as an ideological supporter of the Soviet Empire. For example, only under Stalin did Dostoevsky's dream that all Slavic nations should be united under Moscow's rule become, in fact, reality. Curiously enough, it was Dostoevsky who first expressed the idea that the Crimean Tatars should be expelled from the Crimea. And in 1944 Stalin realized this idea. But in his novels Dostoevsky used his genius not for the advocacy of Russian imperialism, but rather for asserting the autonomy of every man against Marxist socialism, nationalism and what was later called "Nietzscheanism"; as well as against social and religious institutions, against everything that attempts to enslave the individual human soul. Just because of this, Dostoevsky became an important pillar of West European culture of the twentieth century, when, as never before in history, individual autonomy was threatened by all types of collectivist ideologies and movements.

There is no division or serious dispute regarding the East-West problem within East European dissident circles. The entire East European dissident movement is pro-Western. The situation is different with the Russian or Soviet dissidents. If for East European dissidents, the question about the relation of pre-Communist Russian culture and the Soviet Union is merely theoretical, for Russian dissidents the explanation of the origins of totalitarianism is the most important philosophical, historical and even practical political problem. Indeed, this problem divides the Russian dissident movement into two parts, both in the Soviet Union and in exile. The division depends on the answer to the question: Who is more responsible for the

Communist totalitarianism—the Marxist ideology, imported from Western Europe (that means, Western influence) or the tradition of many centuries of historical Russian autocracy, linked with the Orthodox church. The most important representatives of the first view are well-known dissident authors such as Aleksandr Solzhenitsyn, Igor Shafarevich, Viktor Trostnikov and dozens of others. (Trostnikov and Shafarevich are still living in Moscow.) Sometimes this wing of the dissident movement is described as "new Slavophiles" and they insist that the real Russia was kidnapped by the totalitarian movement based on the Marxist ideology which originated in, and was conceived by, the West.

The second part of the divided Russian dissident movement is also represented by some very important writers and thinkers such as Academician Andrei Sakharov, Andrei Sinyavsky, Lev Kopelev, and many others. Recent developments in the Soviet Union hold signs that the official line, step by step, is coming ever closer to the ideas of the anti-Western wing of the dissident movement. As was written, not long ago, by an analyst of Soviet events: "Today, Soviet patriotic propaganda, with its Russian nationalist overtones, is used to counter external (i.e., Western) influences, not to destroy internal enemies. The notion of Russian cultural and historical superiority over the West is being used to prove the superiority of the Soviet way of life. Soviet propagandists, faced with the growing enthusiasm of the Soviet youth for everything Western, have countered by affirming the superiority of spiritual—that is, Russian-Soviet—values over materialistic—that is, Western—values."[9]

So, the link between the current situation and previous historical traditions has become a real and important political question: Did the Communist movement kidnap the West, or the East (Russia), or—both.

The Western Thesis

In general, Western authors stress that there is a strong link between Western (i.e., European) culture and Christianity. In fact, there is virtually a unanimous agreement among them that Western culture is based on the concept of the autonomous individual which, historically, has been derived from Christianity. Christianity was born fighting the nationally collectivist religion of Judaism, and this is how the fundamental force in Christian religion became the individual human soul. This is the reason why Hegel stated that before Jesus Christ only nations existed, and after him, individuals. Berger, in his recent article, "Western Individuality: Liberation and Loneliness,"[10] writes: "The very fact that we can intelligently speak of 'Western civilization' implies that this particular aggregation of human acts and meanings differs in significant ways from other aggregations, such as, say, those of southern and eastern Asia. In this 'Western aggregate,' we would contend that there is a strategically central item—the autonomous individual, both as an idea and as a reality of human experience. . . . It is also quite clear, we would contend, that the working out process began in earnest when the Hellenic and Israelite traditions met in Christianity. It was the Christian synthesis that gave birth to Western civilization, and it was the Christian version of individual autonomy that is with us today, albeit very frequently in a secularized form. . . . Both the Hellenic and the Israelite elements of the Christian synthesis reemerged with particular power in the Renaissance and Reformation. It is these two revolutions that gave birth to the modern world. . . . The modern philosophical and legal tradition of human rights derives from Europe. Through an accident of history the Universal Declaration of Human Rights promulgated by the United Nations, which today is given lip service by virtually all states, is couched in the concepts and terminology of this Western tradition."

Berger understands that the idea of individual freedom is linked with the idea of individual responsibility for the individual's entire life and for society.

This American scholar considers Marxism—an ideology which by adopting the radical, "scientific" materialism, denies individual freedom and, consequently, individual responsibility—to be a European self-criticism. Actually, Berger believes that there "can be no liberation without the cost of alienation." Milovan Djilas, the first East European dissident, shares the same view on liberation and alienation, which he has expressed in his writings on the Marxist theory of alienation.[11] They both, contrary to Marxism, agree that "alienation" is similar to "liberation." The majority of Western scholars and philosophers make a link between genuine Christianity and the European Renaissance. Several Russian anti-Marxist philosophers, like Nikolai Berdyaev, for example, share the same point of view. On the other hand, Solzhenitsyn, Trostnikov and many other representatives of the anti-Western wing of the dissident movement, consider the European Renaissance as a tragic, anti-Christian breakdown, and Communist totalitarianism only as the final logical result of the Renaissance and especially of the Enlightenment.

Berger is fully aware of the vulnerability of individual freedom even in the Western civilization: "Looking at the world today, it is certainly not fanciful to fear that freedom might 'pass like a shadow and a dream.' Western individuality and its drama of liberation may well turn out to have been *an episode* in human history, to be recorded (if at all) as a strange aberration. The 'common human pattern' in its collectivism, may reassert itself once and for all, and the institutional structures that allowed individual autonomy may be demolished ('disaggregated'), never to reappear. . . ." What is even more important, the American scholar has a clear notion that it is possible to destroy the ideas of freedom by means of pure violence: "One of the silliest contemporary notions is that 'you cannot fight ideas with weapons.' Of course, you can—and, over and over again in history, not only ideas but entire worlds of human experience linked to these ideas were quashed by brute violence."

In his posthumously published article, "What is Europe, Where is Europe," Seton-Watson agrees with Kundera's thesis that Christianity was replaced by the European idea (European culture—as Kundera said), but, contrary to the Czech dissident, he believes that the idea of Europe as former Christendom is still very much alive. Seton-Watson in his essay came to the point of distinguishing two types of civilization within Europe in spite of the fact that both were Christian. This is, according to him, the reason why nowhere else in the world is the belief in the European cultural community as strong as it is in contemporary Eastern Europe. He even sees a similarity between the present East-West political division and the situation in previous centuries. Thus, he points out the similarities of the Carolingian Empire with the European Common Market. Most important, however, is Seton-Watson's drawing of a parallel between the Russian mentality of the sixteenth and the twentieth centuries. Muscovy in the sixteenth century, under Ivan the Terrible, was considered to be the only land with a Christian ruler: "Muscovy was Christendom. It faced a hostile world, on the one hand schismatic Romano-German Europe, on the other hand the infidels. Today the Soviet Union is the land of socialism. Socialism *is* the Soviet system. . . . The outside world is hostile. On the one hand are the infidel exponents of unregenerate capitalism. On the other hand is the realm of the renegades to socialism, the Chinese Maoists. The main difference between the situation of the Soviet Union today and of Muscovy then is that then the schismatics were in the West and the infidels in the East, and today the positions are reversed."[12]

As we can see, the dispute on East-West division is far from being limited only to political contradictions between the open and closed societies, between the one-party and pluralistic states. Several old and new philosophical questions arose in 1985 East-West disputes. Is genuine Christianity really the basis for political pluralism and democracy or can it also be the basis for an anti-Western autocracy linked with the Orthodox church? Was the European Renaissance based on Christianity, or was it anti-Christian? Is Marxism a legitimate product of Western civilization, or just a negation of Western culture, in the same way as national-socialism? Is there really such an immense difference between the two wings of Christianity—Catholicism and Orthodoxy—that in contrast to the Catholic church the Orthodox church has prepared the human being for the collectivist ideology of modern totalitarianism? Where are the roots of totalitarianism: in the weak and permissive democracy, or in the long-standing authoritarian tradition? The answers to these questions has, in our time, important political implications. Discussions among Westerners and dissident authors prove this.

Lux ex Oriente

A few years after World War II, an English historian, Arnold Toynbee, had an argument with the Russian émigré author, Vladimir Weidle. The cause for this was Weidle's criticism of Toynbee's theory. Arnold Toynbee, following the nineteenth-century Russian historian Danilevsky and the German historian and philosopher of the twentieth century, Oswald Spengler, in his books describes Russia—in fact, Orthodox Christianity—as a separate civilization similar to the Western, Islamic, Hindu and Far Eastern civilizations. Weidle criticized this thesis and tried to prove that the two types of Christianity, two Europes in fact, do not exist: "the Hellenic world a little bit romanticized on the one hand, and the Hellenic world in Roman incarnation on the other hand." Arnold Toynbee answered: "The Western world did not appear one thousand years before Christ, when ancient Greeks settled at the coast of Asia Minor and the Aegean Sea. The Western world was born when Christian dualism was married with Roman Law. In Russia this never happened, perhaps of our fault—in the nineteenth century, Russia strongly inclined towards the West. . . . Our civilization, our Western world was born when the division between 'God's and Caesar's' was included in the classical conception of the law."[13]

Here is the main point—the division between spiritual and political, between "God's and Caesar's." The implicitness of this division belongs to genuine Christianity, but only in the context of the historical-political reality of Western Europe, the successor to the Roman Empire, had it created the divided social institutions which provided the basis for pluralism, individual autonomy and human rights. The Orthodox Christianity of the eastern part of the Roman Empire fell under the absolute control of the state. The Byzantine emperor, as well as in later centuries the Russian emperor, was both the head of the state and of the church at the same time. This political—spiritual *monism* was called "symphony." This was the main reason why, in the Orthodox Christian part of Europe, divided social institutions were created so late, if ever at all.

On the other hand, the Catholic church in Western Europe tried for centuries to create a similar type of "symphony" but of an opposite kind, whereby the church would have held the state under its control. The entire West European history of the last millennium is the story of the struggle between the two powers—the Roman Catholic Church and the state. The history of the Reformation and the Counter-Reformation may also be included in this story. The result was the final *dualism* between the spiritual and state powers which subsequently led to the division of the sociopolitical powers, thus establishing pluralism and democracy. Modern ideologies of collectivism—such as Marxism, fascism, National Socialism—being fully *monistic*, are fighting dualism in the West solely on the ideological level; on the political level it is a confrontation between one-party and the pluralistic society. This explains why Communist totalitarianism up to now has always been successful in establishing itself in nations with a long authoritarian tradition, that is, in those nations which have not developed divided sociopolitical institutions.

Hence, paradoxically, Christianity, which in Roman times was considered as an import from the East—*lux ex oriente*—became the seed from which the Western civilization has grown. But even in Western Europe, when the Catholic Church succeeded in putting society under its full monistic control, as it was the case in Spain during the period of the Inquisition, the result was not much different from the situation in any totalitarian state today. To assure the rebirth of Christian dualism it was necessary for the Renaissance to overcome the Church's ideological monism of the Middle Ages first.

Political Implications

The importance of the question of human rights has been steadily growing during the 40–odd years since World War II and is becoming increasingly central in the ongoing confrontation between democracy and totalitarianism.

During his trip to Paris in October 1985, Mikhail Gorbachev, the general secretary of the Soviet Communist party, fielded reporters' questions on the issue of human rights, saying at one point, "Questions on human rights present no difficulty for us. We are ready to discuss the problem in any place. . . . We have much to say."[14]

He was, in fact, correct in a way. The Soviet media indeed had much to say about human rights, especially about human rights in the West. Although this Soviet media campaign appears to reflect new tactics for dealing with this important issue developed since the onset of the "Gorbachev era," there is nothing much new in its contents.

From the acceptance of the Universal Declaration of Human Rights in

1948 to the signing of the Helsinki Accords in 1975, and especially after President Carter's campaign for human rights, Soviet ideologists have developed standard arguments in defense of their internal policy on this matter. Soviet mass media and diplomats have argued that *basic* human rights exist in socialist countries but not in the Western world and that without these basic rights all other individual human rights are senseless. According to the Soviets, these "basic" human rights are:

1. The right to work. There is no unemployment in socialist states.
2. The right to education. Education at all levels is free.
3. The right to health protection. The entire population is entitled to free health services.
4. The right to housing. The lease of housing is a social service not a commercial enterprise.
5. The right to social insurance. All types of social insurance—old age and disability pensions, temporary disability allowances, etc.—are paid out of the state budget.
6. The right to rest and leisure. All working people are entitled to a holiday every year.[15]

Added recently to this list of basic human rights is the "most fundamental human right," the right to live, now alleged to be threatened by the use of nuclear weapons in future world conflicts. Individual human rights—such as the freedom of expression, freedom of traveling, freedom of the press, freedom of assembly, freedom of information, and the dissemination of ideas, are considered secondary in socialist states. Western concern about these individual human rights has usually been described as a "propaganda maneuver that hopes the abstract babble about human rights will silence the gun shots . . . (of the American aggressors. M.M.)."[16]

The Soviet basic human rights are "collectivistic" (economic and social) rights, and individual rights belong to a qualitatively different category, namely to the civil and political rights. Moreover, the right to work in the Soviet Union and its satellites is, in fact, an obligation to work.[17] Individuals who are not employed by state enterprises (other enterprises do not exist) and who are without "socially useful work" for three months in the Soviet Union (four in Bulgaria) are violating the law and are tried and punished according to a specific article on parasitism in the Penal Code. The recent development connected with the proposal to introduce in the USSR a three months' unemployment benefit may radically change the situation and probably explains certain changes of Soviet tactics in the human rights issue.

The "right to live," apparently understood as the protection of human physical existence, appears to conflict with the fact that capital punishment in the Soviet Union and other Eastern European countries is used on an extremely wide scale unknown in any other legal system. Hence, the slogan is used only in "anti-war" propaganda.

The Soviet press has recognized only one real "right" in the Western world: "The right to hate us—this is in fact the only right that capitalism definitely guarantees their citizens. This right is very expensive. This right requests 'star wars,' not the bread that hungry people desperately need. This right means killer satellites and not housing for the homeless."[18]

AIDS was also used as an example of the perverted conception of human rights in the USA. "The AIDS virus is a kind of boomerang result of the highly praised bourgeois freedoms. In the USA, for example, all types of prostitution are legal. Bourgeois morality recognizes it as compatible with human nature, and thus permissible, what is not even peculiar to the majority of animals. This is how they understand human rights."[19]

The new tactical element in this human-rights-related propaganda battle that was developed after Mikhail Gorbachev came to power and bloomed on the eve of the Geneva summit is the broad orchestration of accusations of violations of *individual* human rights in the West. In fact, these tactics were used in previous decades from time to time, and from one specific case to another, but never before on such a large scale and as an orchestrated campaign. Hundreds of articles were published in the USSR about the trial of Angela Davis; for many years the Soviet press was full of indignation because of "McCarthyism" in the USA: Soviet newspapers, especially *Literaturnaya Gazeta*, "supported" the case of the "Wilmington ten," the "three from Charlotte," and some others; even psychiatric abuses were attributed to the USA (allegedly there exists in New York one secret psychiatric clinic for political dissenters, wrote *Izvestiia* in 1984), etc. etc. Of course, the execution of Sacco and Vanzetti remains a never-ending story. The CIA was also accused of attempting to assassinate Pope John Paul II after the "Bulgarian connection" came to light.

In Gorbachev's time all these sporadically used accusations have been collected, developed and elevated to the highest level of propaganda priorities. They were supported by the Supreme Soviet, the Union of Soviet Writers, the Synod of the Russian Orthodox church, and dozens of other organizations.

The Soviet mass media in a distorted reflection methodically now accuses the West of every violation of human rights that the USSR has been rightly accused of in *samizdat* publications or the Western media. Harassment of dissidents, anti-Semitism, repression of religious believers and churches, abuses of psychiatry, prohibition of travel abroad, tapped telephones, censorship of mail, repression of trade unions, the persecution of members of pacifist movements, banning of books and disinformation in the press, abominable prison conditions and hunger strikes of protest—all this is ascribed to the United States. Even the existence of hundreds of thousands of political prisoners and concentration camps for dissidents—all these evils are allegedly present in America. A few Western journalists have noted this new Soviet tactic with justified amazement.[20]

This is the list of the most important Soviet accusations directed at Western violations of human rights:

1. For years the Western world, its statesmen and its public opinion have tried to come to the aid of the renowned Academician Andrei Sakharov, who was sent into internal exile without a trial. In a tit-for-tat action, the Soviet media launched a campaign in support of Leonard Peltier, an imprisoned American Indian convicted of killing two FBI agents. (His case was already used by the Soviet media in 1984, i.e., in the pre-Gorbachev era, when Sakharov began his first hunger strike.) Millions of members of Soviet Communist youth organizations are now writing letters to the Soviet press and American authorities in support of Peltier. The Soviet media has described the horrible prison conditions in which Peltier is held and his hunger strikes.[21] Similar treatment is given in the Soviet media to a certain John Harris whom the Soviets call a prominent American civil-rights activist sentenced to life imprisonment in 1970 on a fake theft charge. "That courageous black American worker has been languishing behind prison bars for fifteen years only for daring to come out in defense of the rights of the working people and of national minorities," wrote *Tass* correspondent Maxim Knyaz'kov.[22]

2. For two years, the Western world attempted to sway the Soviet government to permit Elena Bonner, the wife of Andrei Sakharov, to travel abroad for urgently needed eye surgery. In response, the Soviet mass media launched a campaign in support of a certain Ruben Carter, a former boxer and released prisoner. According to Soviet sources, Carter was tortured in prison and one of his eyes was injured. He is allegedly not allowed to travel to Canada for eye surgery.[23]

3. The plight of the Crimean Tatars, who were expelled from their homeland in 1944 and who are seeking the right to return, has been discussed in the Western press for years. As a counterpoint to this, the Soviet mass media and Soviet authorities have raised the question of the status of the American Indians in the USA. "The status is intolerable from the human point of view and from the position of international law."[24] Fourteen members of the Supreme Soviet sent a petition to the United

States Senate in which they stated: "How can America call itself a free, democratic nation and assert that it sets an example for other nations as regards democracy, if the policy of genocide against American Indians is carried on in the United States? This is what our electors say at the meetings with us, and we can only support their views."[25]

4. Anti-Semitism in the Soviet Union and the problem of Jewish emigration has always been of concern to the Western press. In response a persistent campaign against anti-Semitism in the USA was launched in the Soviet media last year. The Soviet press protested against the "social discrimination of the Jews in the USA." "At the nineteenth national convention of the Communist Party of the USA, it was stated that Jews are discriminated against at work, when renting apartments, in education. The Jewish population is one of the main targets of a dirty racist propaganda."[26] Ten members of the Supreme Soviet, all of them of Jewish origin, once again sent a letter to the United States Congress protesting against anti-Semitism in the USA.[27]

5. The Western world has protested against Soviet repression of religious believers and clergymen for decades. In 1985, the Soviet mass media started a systematic campaign against the trial of twelve clergymen in Arizona, who were accused of supporting illegal immigration from Central America. *Izvestiia* published an article on the front page containing the following statement: "The Reagan administration is preparing a political massacre of American religious figures who oppose the administration's criminal course in Central America."[28]

The Synod of the Russian Orthodox church has sent President Reagan a protest "on behalf of the clergy and the believers." "We, the members of the Holy Synod of the Russian Orthodox Church, are deeply worried by the events in the United States of America where yet another trial of U.S. pastors, members of the Church movement 'Shelter,' was started in the city of Tucson (Arizona) with the secret backing of the country's present administration."[29]

6. Soviet psychiatric abuse is an old story in the Western press. The Soviet media has now accused the United States of abusing psychiatry for political purposes. This accusation was prompted by the case of the KGB defector, Vitaly Yurchenko, who, after having returned to the USSR, stated that he was constantly drugged by the CIA. According to Soviet press agencies, the CIA is intensely experimenting with drugs and electric shocks in an effort to find a way to destroy the human personality and enslave the human mind.[30]

7. It is commonly known how difficult it is for Soviet citizens to get a passport for traveling abroad. Soviet mass media has stridently accused

the United States of depriving their citizens, usually members of the Communist party, of traveling abroad. Of course, the black singer Paul Robeson is always mentioned in this context.[31]

8. It is a common Western assumption that Soviet telephones are tapped and that the mail is censored. The Soviet media now state that this is also the case in the United States. According to Radio Moscow, the "citizens of the United States corresponding with foreign governments without official permission will be punished—up to five thousand dollars and up to three years imprisonment."[32]

9. Everyone knows of the plight of the members of the unofficial antiwar movement in the USSR. We now read in the Soviet press about a similar situation occurring in the United States and Western Europe with the pacifists.[33]

10. In the Soviet Union and in Eastern Europe, the widespread banning of literature has resulted in a second "grassroots" culture—"*samizdat.*" The Soviet media points to a similar situation in the United States. It claims that books by Mark Twain, Ernest Hemingway and Kurt Vonnegut are prohibited in school libraries.[34] The Western press, according to Soviet sources, in order to provide "an ideological cover for militaristic foreign policy,"[35] constantly indulges in various kinds of deliberate disinformation of the public.

11. Members of the first two independent Soviet trade unions are still in prison or in psychiatric wards. Any attempt to strike is considered a dangerous criminal act by Soviet authorities. Now the Soviet press and the official Soviet trade unions have expressed deep concern about the violation of the rights of American trade unions.[36] The Soviet press also argues that the absence of strikes in the Soviet Union does not mean that the rights of workers are violated: after all, the Soviet trade unions are able to solve any labor conflict arising within the framework provided by Soviet law.[37]

12. The Western world has read with great horror about Soviet concentration camps in books written by former Soviet prisoners. One of these books, Solzhenitsyn's *Gulag Archipelago*, became a symbol of modern totalitarian enslavement. These days we can learn from the Soviet mass media that the number of political prisoners in the USA is about 250,000. "Imagine almost a quarter of a million Americans sentenced, many of them to life imprisonment, only because they do not agree with the ruling system."[38] The Soviet newspaper *Pravda* further informs us that "the U.S. is living through a period of a kind of prison boom. . . . Camps for dissidents are hastily being built there."[39]

13. In his recent interview for the Soviet press, President Reagan men-

tioned that "one of the weapons being used by the Soviets against the people of Afghanistan consists of toys—dolls, little toy trucks, things that are appealing to children."[40] The Soviet press immediately reacted with the same accusation. Of course, toy weapons are used against Afghan people by the anti-Soviet rebels, who are supported by America.[41] The same goes for the accusation about supporting international terrorism.

It is highly doubtful that these new tactics will be in any way successful. The accusations are often contradictory. So, for example, the Jews, "Zionists," are usually described by the Soviets as an omnipotent minority in the U.S. which controls the American mass media. One can also learn from the Soviet press that Peltier is allowed to use the telephone to speak to people outside his prison, that he freely and without limitations corresponds with Soviet people and gives interviews to Soviet correspondents. Prison conditions such as these seem unbelievable to the Soviet people when compared to the conditions existing in the Soviet Union. When describing the repressions against labor organizations, the Soviet press quoted the president of the AFL-CIO—Lane Kirkland—who had protested against the administration's policy toward the trade unions. The Soviet press reports that the persecuted writer Kurt Vonnegut is free to travel, publish his books and give interviews in which he accuses the American society of injustice and lack of rights. At the same time, Soviet readers discover that Vonnegut was a member of the American delegation at the Budapest Cultural Forum. They can also discover in the Soviet press that the twelve clergymen really violated immigration laws. Soviet mass media also frequently states that religious "obscurants" are an extremely powerful force in America and Western Europe. The Soviet press carries many articles with quotations from public statements—opposing the present American administration—made by dozens of American scientists, authors, politicians and ordinary citizens. Even the information about the number of prisoners and the establishment of concentration camps are quoted from Communist magazines that thus appear to be freely published and distributed in the U.S. Taking all this into account, it would indeed be very difficult for anyone to believe in the existence of a quarter of a million political prisoners and in concentration camps for dissidents in the USA.

Whatever the Soviet propaganda efforts, the basic underlying Soviet argument on human rights remains unchanged. In all official publications and international negotiations related to the issue of human rights, the Soviet Union and its allies continue to argue that these rights are meaningless as long as the risk of an atomic conflagration exists, that the prime

and most important right is the "right to live," that the right to development, medical treatment, economic welfare, and employment, are the only
truly meaningful basic human rights. It is here that we are faced with the
authentic Soviet attitude that reflects a typical collectivistic and monistic
ideology of the nation or the state, a certain class or the "entire society"
(in the latest, 1977, Soviet Constitution, the formula of the dictatorship of
the workers' class was replaced by that of the power of the entire Soviet
people). It is also fully logical that the Soviet Union and all other East
European states consider human-rights problems as an interference in the
affairs of a sovereign state.

On the other hand, when representatives of democratic countries consider human rights as the individual rights of free expression, free flow of
ideas, freedom of travel, assembly, etc.—this is precisely linked with the
dualistic concept of humanity. The spiritual essence of each individual is
considered here to be an independent sphere that cannot be put under the
control of either the state or the nation, or class or party. The most important contradiction between totalitarian and pluralistic societies, and
between East and West, is the ideological concept of the foundation of
human existence. Is this foundation the individual with an actually or only
potentially free spirit, or is it the omnipotent historical forces of the nation,
class, race or state? This is the basic question of our times from which
everything else derives.

It is worth noting that the majority of these "collectivistic human rights"
(the right to live, to be fed, to have medical treatment, full employment,
etc.), in fact, already exist in any West European and American prison.

Conclusion

At present, individual human rights have become one of the most important
topics of international confrontation, an issue dominating the global scene.
In fact, today only the global scene is the one that really exists, for modern
communications' technology has made our globe a very small and interdependent place. At the same time, the problem of individual human rights
is linked with the ontological and metaphysical spheres—with the fundamental beliefs and faith—with religion. The historical development which
began several centuries ago—when modern science and rationalism were
born—has made a full circle arriving back at its starting point. Once again
the problem of atheism and religious belief has become a major problem,
but in a different sense from that which was expected by the Marxists.
Once again, in totalitarian societies Christianity is being reborn, repeating
the experience of the first century's Christians. In the Roman Empire the

believers in the *Deus Absconditus*—the Hidden God—used to release individual human minds in a spiritual sense from their physical bondage to the external idols of state, empire, nation, or any other political and social reality. People in the Soviet Union and Eastern Europe, actively fighting for human rights, consciously or unconsciously, are doing precisely the same. They are following the spiritual, invisible reality of human rights. Freedom and pluralism depend on the persistence of this existential *dualism* between the materially real sociopolitical world and individual consciousness, based on an invisible spiritual reality. Any collectivistic ideology, no matter whether it is the ideology of the nation, race or class, is a deadly enemy of the autonomous individual, and thus the enemy of human rights.

Berger concludes his brilliant essay with the following words: "History is not an inexorable process, but the sum of human actions. Individual autonomy did not appear in history of necessity; conversely, it will not necessarily disappear. For those who believe in its worth, therefore, the enterprise of understanding the phenomenon leads to a political agenda."[42]

He also writes: "Freedom, as a quality attributable to men in one place, must be attributable to all men in all places, at least potentially, if the attribution is made as a statement about human nature."

The fact that in all totalitarian countries dissident movements have appeared show that freedom is indeed an inherent part of human nature. Even in China, several years ago, dissidents demanded classical "Western-type human rights," in spite of decades of Communist totalitarianism and total lack of historically established democratic tradition. We can thus conclude that the notion of the West, of the Western civilization, is not confined to Western Europe and its various civilized offsprings. It is a truly universal phenomenon synonymous with an autonomous individual and his natural craving for freedom everywhere in the world. Consciously or unconsciously, this craving for freedom is inextricably linked with man's true religion, with his believing in the higher spiritual sphere, which is his own and which demands ideological dualism. If this demand for ideological dualism in the sociopolitical realm were based not on the universal human nature but represented a mere product of a particular European historical development, democracy would then really "pass like a shadow and a dream" (words of Don Quixote before his death). Fortunately, all the existing evidence overwhelmingly points to the fact that freedom is part of human nature and a prerequisite for any historical development (even toward totalitarianism).

This, in my view, is the main factor which will decide who will win the present global battle between totalitarianism and democracy or, which is one and the same thing, the East and West.

Notes

1. DPA, October 13, 1985, Vatikanstadt.
2. RFE Correspondent's Report (Budapest), 4 November 1985.
3. Hugh Seton-Watson, "What is Europe, Where is Europe," in *Encounter*, Vol. LXV, No. 2, July–August 1985.
4. Milan Kundera, "*Pokhishchenyi zapad ili tragedija central'noi Evropy*," (The Kidnapped West or the Tragedy of Central Europe), *22*, 42, (1985).
5. Kundera, *Pokhishchenyi*.
6. Milan Kundera, "An Introduction to a Variation," in *The New York Times Book Review*, 6 January 1985.
7. Mihály Vajda, "Central Eastern European Perspectives," in *East European Reporter*, (Spring 1985).
8. Joseph Brodsky, "Why Milan Kundera is Wrong About Dostoevsky", in *The New York Times Book Review*, 17 February 1985.
9. *Russian Nationalism in the 1980s: Echoes of Stalinist Policy*, RL Report, 7 November 1985.
10. In *Partisan Review*, 52, 4, (1985).
11. See, for example, his article in *Encounter*, 39, 5, (May 1971).
12. Seton-Watson, *What is Europe*.
13. Quoted from G. Agar (ed.), *Vo chto verit zapad*, (In What the West Believes), (New York: Chekhov Publishing House, 1955), 123, 132–133.
14. "Kremlin Stays Tough on Human Rights Ahead of Summit," *Reuters*, (Moscow), 14 November 1985.
15. Gennady Pisarevsky, "Socialism and Human Rights," *Novosti Press Agency*, (Moscow), 16 September 1985.
16. Hanzadyan, "Tol'ko sotsialism obespechivaet vse prava cheloveka," (Only Socialism Guarantees All Human Rights), in *Literaturnaya Gazeta*, 18 September 1985.
17. *Unemployment in the Soviet Union*, RL Research, 10 December 1985; *Yet Another Bulgarian Campaign on the Employment of Idle Youth*, *RAD RFE*, 4 October 1985.
18. Vitaly Korotich, "O podlinnoy demokratii i pravakh cheloveka," (On True Democracy and Human Rights), in *Pravda*, 15 September 1985.
19. S. Lyapich, "SPID," (AIDS), in *Sovetskaya Belorussiya*, 24 November 1985.
20. Celestine Bohlen, "Soviets Attack US Record on Human Rights", in *Washington Post*, 17 September 1985; "Soviet Press Steps Up Charges Against US in Advance of Summit", *AP*, (Moscow), 25 October 1985.
21. Many articles and letters in *Komsomol'skaya Pravda*, 5 November 1985 and 12 November 1985; *TASS* Report, (New York), 8 November 1985; *TASS* Report, (Washington), 29 November 1985; *Radio Moskva*, 8 November 1985.
22. "Soviet Press Steps Up Charges Against US in Advance of Summit", *AP*, (Moscow), 25 October 1985.
23. *Radio Moskva* I and II, 15 November 1985.
24. *TASS* Report, (Moscow), 15 November 1985. P. Khyaz'kov, "Na ringe s

rasizmom," (In the Ring with Racism), in *Sovietskaya Rossiya*, 18 December 1985.

25. Ibid.

26. Yu. Dzhufarov, "Sionizm protiv SSSR," (Zionism Against the USSR), in *Pravda Vostoka*, 19 September 1985; *Radio Moskva* I, 24 November 1985.

27. "Otkrytoe pis'mo sovetskikh parlamentariev kongressmenam SShA," *APN*, (An Open Letter of Soviet Parliamentarians to the USA Congressmen), 15 November 1985.

28. "Gotoviatsya raspravy," (Reprisals in Preparation), *Izvestiia*, 12 October 1985.

29. "Pozornoe sudilishche," (Shameful Trial), in *Izvestiia*, 17 November 1985; *TASS* Report, (Moscow), 5 November 1985; "Russkaya Tserkov' protestuet," (The Russian Church Protests), *APN*, (Moscow), 13 November 1985; *TASS* Report, (Washington), 11 October 1985.

30. Vladimir Kirilov, "Voyna CRU za kontrol' nad soznaniem cheloveka," (CIA's War for Control Over Man's Consciousness), *APN*, 26 November 1985; "CRU ispol'zuet metody natsistskih vrachei," (CIA Uses the Methods of Nazi Physicians), *APN* Report on an Interview with a Prominent Soviet Psychiatrist, Professor Nikolay Zharikov, *APN*, 18 November 1985; A. Palladin, "Ya tshchetno vzyval k ikh sovesti," *Izvestiia*, 6 November 1985.

31. *Radio Moskva* I, 15 November 1985.

32. *Radio Moskva* I, 25 October 1985; *AP* Report, (Moscow), 25 October 1985.

33. "Politicheskie repressii i podavlenie grazhdanskikh svobod v SShA i drugikh kapstranakh," *TASS*, 5 December 1985; *Radio Moskva* I, 21 October 1985; "Human Rights in the U.S.", *TASS*, (Washington), 25 December 1985.

34. Martin Walker, "Soviets Accuse BBC and VOA", *The Guardian*, 14 November 1985; G. Gerasimovich, "Neopkhodimyi dialog," *Sovetskaya kul'tura*, 16 November 1985; *Radio Moskva II*, 30 November 1985.

35. "Two Approaches to Information Policy," *TASS*, (Moscow), 28 November 1985.

36. "VTsPS. Otkrytoe pis'mo prezidentu SShA g-nu Ronal'du Reiganu," *APN*, 18 November 1985.

37. Gleb Spiridonov, "Prava cheloveka: SSSR–SShA," *APN*, 6 November 1985.

38. *Radio Moskva* I, 17 September 1985.

39. Vitaly Korionov, "Demokratiya po amerikanski," in *Pravda*, 6 October 1985.

40. Text of the Reagan interview with Soviet media, Washington, 4 November (Special Report).

41. "Chemu uchat v Sovetskom Sojuze afganskikh detey?" *Moskovskie novosti*, 24 November 1985.

42. Berger, *Partisan Review*, 52, 4, (1985).

6

Would the Victory of the "Russian Party" Preserve Political and Ideological Monism?

(Politico-ideological Platforms of the 'Russian Party')

NIKOLAI P. POLTORATZKY

First of all, some terminological and methodological remarks.

I believe most would agree that political monism means one-party dictatorship, and ideological monism means imposition of a single ideology, exclusive of all others. At least that is the way these terms will be used in this chapter.

As for the "Russian Party," there would be, probably, much less unanimity. What is the proper definition of this term? Who belongs to the "Russian Party," i.e., who is to be included and who excluded? In my opinion, almost any person (or organization), independently of ethnic origin, who is striving for the very existence, liberation, and renascence, of Russia and the Russian people, and who sincerely perceives himself as belonging to the "Russian Party," does, indeed, belong to it. And this means a very large spectrum of individuals and groups do belong to it. However, in this chapter I will have to leave out a number of such persons and organizations, especially those on the fringes, both right and left, and shall instead concentrate on what, in my perception, could be considered to be the mainstream of the "Russian Party."

Besides "extremism," an additional, though secondary, consideration for my choices would be the fact that certain Western powers, at one time or other and in some form or other, have also recognized a given person, group or movement as representative of the "Russian Party."

Another important terminological problem is connected with the very word "Russian." The Russian language knows not one but two terms, having related yet different contents: *russkii* and *rossiiskii*. *Russkii* (both an adjective and a noun) has usually an ethnic connotation and may refer to either Great Russian or, jointly, Great Russian, Small Russian or Ukrainian, and White Russian or Belorussian (*velikorusskii, malorossiiskii, belorusskii*). Moreover, departing from narrowly ethnic content, the term may refer also to any person, irrespective of national origin, who can be in some way or other related to the former Russian Empire. The term *rossiiskii* (from *Rossiia, Rossiiskaia Imperiia*) has a more political, state, all-national character, implying the multitudinous ethnic base, but concentrating on the "superstructure," i.e., the principles that unite all those disparate elements. The post-1917 Soviet policies, with their emphasis on ethnic origin, their reduction of "Russia" to the territory of only one of the 15 national republics of the USSR, and their introduction of the term *sovetskii* (Soviet), representing a poor substitute for the former *rossiiskii*, only further complicate the problem of the proper terminological usage. In any case, since there is just one term in English, standing for both *russkii* and *rossiiskii*, it is important to note from the very beginning that in this chapter "Russian" may, depending upon the context, refer to either *russkii* or *rossiiskii*, though, normally, it stands for *rossiiskii*.

One more preliminary remark, this time methodological. Since I was asked to deal mainly with the future, one may expect me to proceed entirely from the present situation. I shall deal briefly with the present too, but only as the last stage in a process. And this for two main reasons. Firstly, the past may be actually much more revealing than the present, which is still in flux; and secondly, the present is sufficiently familiar and has been already subjected to many descriptions, analyses, revelations, and public debates by persons more immediately immersed in the current scene than I am.[1]

To end this introductory part, the purpose of this chapter is to present a condensed picture of the political and ideological positions taken by the mainstream of the "Russian Party" since the victory of the Bolsheviks in Russia and up to the present. This is not a history of the Russian anti-Bolshevik and anti-Communist movement (though, in part, it unavoidably is). My task is more limited: I am concentrating my attention on the mainstream and the highlights in a retrospective chronological approach that would help to answer such questions as: What have been the aims and goals and aspirations of the "Russian Party" during the nearly seventy years of Communist rule in Russia? What are the lessons that could be drawn from such an historical survey? And, of course: Would the eventual victory of the "Russian Party" preserve political and ideological monism in Russia?

The White Movement

The Bolshevik overthrow of the Provisional Government almost at once threw Russia into a Civil War, which in Europe lasted until the end of 1920, and in Asia until 1922. The first and, till the end of this phase of anti-Bolshevik struggle, the most important expression of Russian opposition was the so-called White movement. It was started immediately after the Bolshevik seizure of power, on 15 November 1917, in Rostov and Novocherkassk on Don, where the former Chief of staff and later supreme commander of the Russian army, General Mikhail Vasil'evich Alekseev, raising the flag of struggle for the honor and freedom of Russia, formed the so-called Alekseev organization. He was joined soon by Generals Kornilov, Denikin, Markov, Romanovskii, and by a few hundred other officers, soldiers, Cossacks, and students from military and public schools and universities. Generals Alekseev, Kornilov (another former chief of staff and the supreme commander of the Russian army), and Kaledin (the first elected *Ataman* of the Don Cossacks), formed the first White government.

This southern front against the Bolsheviks, who managed to establish themselves in the center of the country, lasted three years. Half a year after the formation of Alekseev's organization, the Czechoslovaks started their uprising in the East, leading, as a result of Admiral Kolchak's coup, to the creation, in November of 1918, of the eastern front of the White movement, which lasted one year and three months (until 7 February 1920). Nine months after the Bolsheviks seized power, the British disembarked in Arkhangel'sk; this resulted in the formation of the White's northern front under General Miller, which remained active for almost a year and a half (August 1918–February 1920). After eleven months of Bolshevik rule, the Germans finally allowed the recruitment of Russian volunteers in Pskov, and the newly created White western front under General Iudenich functioned for over a year (October 1918–December 1919).[2]

Thus, of the four fronts of the White movement, the southern front lasted the longest. It was also the most important in every other respect. (True, for a while it seemed that the entire resistance movement would be headed by Admiral Kolchak, who was proclaimed supreme ruler—and was recognized as such also by the leadership of the southern and north-western

White fronts. However, Kolchak was later betrayed by his Czechoslovak and Western allies and executed by the Bolsheviks.)

The situation of the southern White front was tragic, too—and was perceived as such by its initiator from its very inception. But he and his associates equally clearly perceived the moral and national necessity for the creation of this movement. Leaving the Don region for the inhospitable Southern steppes (the famous first "Icy" campaign) General Alekseev said: "We leave for the steppes. We may return, if God is merciful. But we must light the light, so that there will be at least one light point in the midst of the darkness which has enveloped Russia."[3]

Thus, the White movement was a reaction to the national, political, and cultural degeneration which followed the Revolution of 1917, and to the seizure of power by Lenin's Bolsheviks. The political and ideological preferences and ideas of the White movement's leaders and its rank-and-file participants were as variegated as their social origins.[4] To represent it, as do its detractors, as a reactionary movement bent on the restoration of monarchy and the old regime, in general, is to represent part for the whole. Such a view is counterbalanced, moreover, by the accusations coming from the Russian political right which always maintained (and still maintains) that the founder of the movement, General Alekseev, was a republican and that the main cause of the final defeat of that movement lay in the refusal of its leaders to put forth monarchic slogans and raise the banner of monarchy.

The general mood which sustained the Whites was well expressed in the famous song of the Kornilov units: "For Russia and Freedom, /If called into battle, /The Kornilovites into water /And fire will go"; "We do not long for the past, /The Tsar is not an idol for us,/We cherish only one dream: /To bring Russia peace."

This was, then, the psychological and ideological platform of the early White movement: Russia, its honor, freedom, integrity, and peace.

Fate was, however, unmerciful to both the ranks and the leadership of the movement. Soon after its beginning, General Kaledin, crushed by the growing political confusion and anarchy among his beloved Don Cossacks, committed suicide; General Alekseev died from old age and exhaustion; Generals Kornilov and Markov fell on the battle field; General Drozdovskii died from wounds received in battle.

During most of its existence, from October 1918 to April 1920, the White movement in southern Russia was headed by one of its early organizers and commanders, General Anton Ivanovich Denikin (1872–1947), who, in political and administrative matters, was assisted by *Osoboe Soveshchanie*, a special deliberative body representing various political tendencies and headed by General A. Dragomirov.

In 1918 and at the beginning of 1919, Denikin's government consistently abstained from declaring its political program. However, the general political and ideological position of the White movement was expressed by General Denikin on several occasions. He himself singled out two of his public speeches, in Stavropol and at the opening of the Kuban Extraordinary Assembly. They served as the basis for official propaganda, political discussions, and formal representations in foreign countries.

The speech at the Kuban Assembly of 1 November 1918, had the character of a political declaration. In it General Denikin pointed out that from the very beginning of the White movement "a sole sacred thought, a sole bright hope, a sole desire inspired all—to save Russia." Calling for unity of forces in the struggle against the Bolsheviks, he emphasized that in order to succeed in this struggle, it was necessary to have a unified provisional authority, responsible only to the Russian people as represented by a future supreme authority, and a unified military force, on which the provisional authority could lean.

He continued: "Such unity of all national formations and of all nationally thinking Russian people is all the more possible, as the Volunteer Army, conducting a struggle for the very existence of Russia, does not pursue any reactionary goals and does not predetermine either the form of the future mode of government, or even the methods, by which the Russian people shall express its will. Some demand that we hoist a party flag. But isn't the tricolored banner of Great Russia higher than all party flags? Don't you see how the valiant warriors of the Volunteer Army, in bloody battles, day after day, under this banner selflessly fight 'for holy Russia,' die and prevail? Unity is possible also because the Volunteer Army recognizes the necessity, both now and in the future, of the widest autonomy of the component parts of the Russian state and of an extremely considerate attitude toward the age-old Cossack tenor of life."[5]

In addition to the importance of the principle of unity of forces and authority, General Denikin emphasized also the principle of faithfulness to agreements and treaties with Western Allies, which the Volunteer Army has always maintained, in spite of all external and internal pressures.

In a telegram to S. Sazonov of 2 January 1919, which was intended for Western Allies, General Denikin briefly and clearly formulated his political platform:

"We fight for the very existence of Russia, do not pursue any reactionary goals, do not support the interests of any single political party, and do not patronize any single class. We do not predetermine either the future state structure, or the paths and methods, through which the Russian people shall declare its will."[6]

In his later study of this period, Denikin explained that this political platform of non-predetermination (*nepredreshenie*) was the result of both his personal conviction and objective necessity. With the exception of Separatists and Federalists, the participants in the struggle against the Bolsheviks could have kept in common ranks only by proceeding from a few general propositions: "Struggle to the end against Bolshevism," "Great, United, and Indivisible" Russia, "autonomy and self-government," and "political freedoms." To go further than that would have meant to reawaken some of the discordances among the participants and, consequently, to lead to the disintegration of the achieved unity. Even among the representatives of the politicized intelligentsia there was no conformity of ideas concerning such an important question as, for instance, the acceptability of a Constituent Assembly. As for the fighters at the front, some were just shedding their blood without sophistry, others declared categorically that they wouldn't fight for any *uchredilka*, as the Constituent Assembly was derogatorily called. "That is why," explained Denikin, "I called the Army to fight simply *for Russia*."[7]

However, the pressure on Denikin to publish a political declaration of the government of south Russia, addressed to all, continued from Russian and foreign, especially British, circles. Finally, on 10 April 1919, a declarative note, signed by General Denikin and all members of the Special Council including its chairman, Dragomirov, was sent to the British, French, and American representatives. The goals of the government were expressed in seven points:

1. Liquidation of Bolshevik anarchy and introduction of legal order in the country.
2. Restoration of a strong unified, indivisible Russia.
3. Convocation of a People's Assembly on the basis of universal suffrage.
4. Carrying out of decentralization of authority through establishment of regional autonomy and broad local self-government.
5. Guarantee of full civic liberty and freedom of religion.
6. Immediate beginning of agrarian reform for the elimination of the agrarian need of the toiling population.
7. Immediate introduction of labor laws, guaranteeing the working classes from their exploitation by the state and capital.[8]

After the initial great successes of Denikin's offensive in the direction of Moscow, there came a great retreat at the front and a collapse of the rear. Following numerous political consultations, Denikin decided that the circumstances required introduction of a military dictatorship. On 14 December 1919, he presented the Special Council (*Osoboe Soveshchanie*)

with a new platform containing 11 points,[9] the most important of which
were the first four:

1. Unified, Great, Indivisible Russia. Protection of Religion. Introduc-
    tion of order. Restoration of the productive powers of the country
    and of the national economy. Increase in the productivity of labor.
2. Struggle against Bolshevism to the end.
3. Military dictatorship. All pressure from political parties should be
    cast aside, all resistance to the authorities, be it from right or left,
    should be punished. The question of the form of government is busi-
    ness for the future. The Russian people will create the supreme au-
    thority without pressure and without imposition. Unity with the
    people. A speedy union with Cossacks through the creation of South-
    ern Russian authority, without, however, detriment at the same time
    to the rights of an all-national authority.   Attraction to the Russian
    statehood of Transcaucasia.
4. Foreign policy, only national Russian.
    In spite of the occasional oscillations of the Allies with regard to the
    Russian question, to continue to move with them. Because another
    combination is morally censurable and impossible to realize. Slavic
    solidarity. For the help, not an inch of Russian land.[10]

A. I. Denikin was a famous and experienced general, a patriot, and a
man of great personal integrity and sense of duty. He was, nonetheless,
lacking the political and diplomatic qualities necessary for the leadership
of an all-national military, political, and ideological movement in the conditions of Revolution and Civil War.

It was only with the advent of General Baron Petr Nikolaevich Wrangel
(1878–1928) that the White movement acquired at its head, in early April
1920, a person with all the qualities of military and political leadership
suited to the unusual and exacting circumstances. He transformed the by
then demoralized army into a fighting force, installed a civil administration
on the territory under his authority, carried out a most important land
reform, introduced the *zemstvo* and implemented a number of other
significant reforms.

Wrangel expressed his political and ideological principles on several
occasions. His most concise statement was a formal "Appeal" (*Vozzvanie*)
to the population, dated 20 May 1920:

Hear, Russian people, what we are fighting for:
For the desecrated faith and its abused holy things.
For the liberation of the Russian people from the yoke of Communists,

tramps and convicts, who have brought Holy Russia to total ruin.
For the cessation of the internecine war.
For giving a chance to the peasant, acquiring full ownership of the land
   he tills, to devote himself to peaceful labor.
For the reign of genuine liberty and law in Russia.
For the opportunity for the Russian people to independently choose
   their own Master.
Help me, Russian people, to save our Motherland.[11]

Simultaneously with this "Appeal," Wrangel, in his capacity as ruler
and supreme commander of the Armed Forces of Southern Russia, signed
an order in which, declaring that his army was advancing to free Russia
from the "Red scum," he stated that a decree on the introduction of self-
government in rural districts had been signed and *zemstvo* institutions were
being created on liberated territories and that land, both public and private,
would be distributed by district *zemstvos* to those who were toiling on it.
He called for the defense of the Motherland and peaceful work and promised forgiveness to all the misguided who would join him. Asking for God's
blessing, he proclaimed:

Land and liberty in the organization of the State (system)—to the people.
   A Master, installed by the will of the people—to the land."[12]

This new direction in the domestic policies of the Whites' government
was supported by corresponding foreign policy initiatives and representations. Thus, P. B. Struve, who was in charge of the Office of Foreign
Relations, addressed to the chairman of the Council of Ministers of France,
A. Mitterand, a letter, in which he expressed the three basic principles of
domestic and foreign policies of the Wrangel government: 1) legalization
of the agrarian revolution, including the seizure by peasants of the landed
gentry's estates, and consolidation of the peasant's right to full ownership
of the land on which he toils; 2) building future Russia in the form of a
broad federation, based on a contractual relationship and proceeding from
common interests and needs, between actually existing new political formations; 3) "Whatever the relations of various parts of Russia, at the
present time divided, will be in the future, the political organization of
their territories and the construction of their federal union must be based
on a free expression of the will of the population, through representative
assemblies elected on democratic principles." In the conclusion of his letter
Struve stated that Wrangel realized that the peasant majority of the Russian population was opposed to both the restoration of the old order and
the installation of a Communist tyranny; Wrangel's main goals were:

"To satisfy the needs of the peasant population, to sanitate the moral life of the country, to restore economic life, to unite all elements of order. . . ."[13]

A month later, in an order dated 26 June 1920, Wrangel indicated that governmental institutions are required "to introduce legality, to safeguard freedom and security of peaceful citizens, and to give agrarian order and self-government to the population."[14]

Believing that the authorities should be judged not simply by their public pronouncements but by their actions and that governmental policies based on new principles do not need to be accompanied by artificial measures of influencing public opinion, General Wrangel ordered the shutting down of all special military and civil organizations of political propaganda and information, first of all the discredited *Osvag* (*Osvedomitel'noe agentstvo*, Information Agency). All affairs of the press were transferred to the jurisdiction of the head of the civil administration. A number of other measures pursuing the same general goal of liberty and order based on law were introduced in a very short time.

But time was running out on the Whites. The successes of the Bolsheviks in their war against Poland further convinced Lloyd George and his associates that they should strive for a rapprochement with Lenin. The British pressured Poland to conclude peace with the Bolsheviks, and with Wrangel—to cease military actions. Italians were also inclined to compromise with Lenin. Only France, which supported Poland and recognized de facto Wrangel's government, and the United States still remained faithful to their former policy of support to the White movement.

In early September 1920, Rear Admiral N.A. MacCully, who was a special agent of the U.S. State Department for Russia, on the orders of his government, wrote eight questions to the Wrangel government in order to clarify the general policies of the Whites.[15] He received an immediate answer:[16]

1. General Wrangel confirms what he has stated on many occasions before: that his goal is to give the Russian people the opportunity to freely express its will concerning the future form of government in Russia. Conditions will be created for the convocation of a National Assembly, elected by universal suffrage, and this Assembly will decide the form of government in Russia.

2. General Wrangel has no intention at all to impose on Russia a form of government functioning without people's representation and lacking public support.

3. General Wrangel does not believe that law and liberty can be restored in Russia by military means alone and this has been proven by the

whole set of reforms already implemented by the government. Restoration of the State and satisfaction of the needs of the peasant majority of the Russian population is of utmost importance. The immediate goal is to strengthen the political and economic center created on the territory held by the Russian Army and the Cossacks, so that this healthy center can serve as a point of attraction, around which could begin the national renascence of the Russian people.

4. The government of General Wrangel is indeed bent on important reforms. The purpose of the reform connected with the introduction of small district (*volost'*) *zemstvos* is to transfer to the people local authority and the care for local economic needs—through freely elected representatives of the population. The law on district *zemstvos* is to be followed by a law on larger district (*uezd*) *zemstvos*, and the two of them would serve as the basis for still larger elective institutions. The purpose of the agrarian reform is to radically solve the entire agrarian problem by eventually creating a new strong class of small farmers, owning and tilling their own land.

5. The number of refugees from Bolshevism, seeking the protection of General Wrangel's government in Crimea is over 500,000. A similar number of people, representing all social classes and professions, have fled to the Middle East, Egypt, and Europe. The government feels responsible for all of them.

6. General Wrangel believes that his government is the only custodian of the idea of national renascence and restoration of the integrity of Russia. At the same time, he acknowledges that only a government, installed after a National Assembly decides the problem of the future form of government, will be in a position to conclude treaties bearing on the sovereign rights of the Russian people and to dispose of the national patrimony.

7. The political program of General Wrangel with regard both to the unity of Russia and to the fate of Poland fully coincides with the recent political declaration of the U.S. government.

8. General Wrangel believes that his deeds even more than any oral statements will prove that there is no danger at all of his regime degenerating into either a military adventure or political reaction. He is ready to cease all fighting as soon as there will be real guarantees of inviolability of his and Cossack's territories and as soon as the Russian people, languishing under the Bolshevik yoke, receives a chance to freely express its will. The same freedom of expression will be given, of course, to the population under his jurisdiction. As for himself, General Wrangel will without any hesitation obey the sovereign decision of the Russian people.

Thus ends the programmatic answer of General Wrangel's government to the U.S. governmental inquiry.

Unfortunately for Russia—and for the rest of the world—the events overtook Wrangel and his actual and potential allies. Poland and the newly created Baltic republics having ceased armed struggle against the Bolsheviks, the latter concentrated their forces on the southern front and forced Wrangel to evacuate his troops and a great number of refugees to Turkey in November 1920.

Independently of the actual outcome of the first, and till now, main phase of the anti-Bolshevik struggle, there is no question concerning the genuine aspirations, aims, and deeds of the White movement, especially in its initial and its final stages. With all its mistakes and transgressions, it was, in essence, an idealistic and heroic movement fighting for Russia, its existence, honor, and renascence and for the victory of liberty, law, and sovereignty of the Russian people. The mainstream of that movement never presented any danger of introducing in Russia political and ideological monism. On the contrary, it actively fought for the elimination of the political and ideological monism already established by Lenin's Bolsheviks in the center of the country and bent on spreading its power to the rest of the country and the entire world.

Between Two World Wars

The Russian Army and ROVS

After the evacuation of Crimea and while the resettlement of the evacuees in various European countries was progressing, an acute struggle for Wrangel's cadres began, both from the Left and from the Right. The Left strived for the complete political and organizational liquidation of the Russian army as such, and hoped to lure into resurrected Party factions at least some of the military personnel. The Right, which, on the contrary, desired to preserve the army, wanted, however, the army to raise the banner of monarchy, considering this banner to be a national one, and not a party one.

General Wrangel, who had great difficulty in dealing with his foreign allies, especially with the French, had to face also the double onset coming from the Russian Left and Right. Withstanding the pressure from the Right proved to be even more difficult than from the Left. In spite of such pressures, Wrangel remained faithful to his earlier principle of non-predetermination of the form of the future government of Russia. Thus, in a letter to General P. N. Krasnov, dated 16 January 1922, Wrangel wrote:

> I paid the greatest attention to that part of your letter, where you wrote that, in your opinion, the time has come to raise the standard "For Faith, Tsar, and Fatherland" with complete frankness. You cannot doubt that by my convictions I am a Monarchist and that equally monarchic is also the majority of the Russian Army. However, in Imperial Russia the concept of "Monarchism" was identical with the concept of "Motherland." The revolution tore asunder these two historically indissoluble concepts, and at the present time the concept of "Monarchism" is connected not with the concept of "Motherland," but with belonging to a specific political party. Prolonged work is required for the two concepts to be again blended together in the people's consciousness. As long as this unavoidable process is not accomplished, and at that without any forcible influence from the outside, as long as these two concepts do not become again homogeneous, as long as the concept of "Monarchism" does not transcend the narrow frames of a political party, the Army will live only with the idea of "Motherland," considering that its restoration is the real primary task.[17]

Answering another direct appeal to raise the standard of monarchy during his visit to the Russian community in Turski Begei on 21 August 1922, General Wrangel again affirmed that, irrespective of political views of individual members of the Armed Forces, the army as a whole, being the last remaining nucleus of national Russia, should not become a tool of a singular political party; it should stay out of party politics. "The standard that passed to me from the hands of Generals Alekseev, Kornilov, and Denikin, I," said General Wrangel, "will preserve in exile. I would rather burn that standard than betray the sacred word 'Fatherland' that is inscribed on it."[18]

The growing political activization of the Monarchists culminated in the Manifesto of 31 August 1924, proclaiming the ascendance to the Russian throne of the "Emperor Kirill Vladimirovich." The manifesto aroused a negative reaction even among members of the Imperial family. The dowager Empress Mariya Fedorovna wrote that such a manifesto was premature, and expressed her belief that, with God's will, the future emperor would be designated according to the Constitution, in union with the Orthodox church, and conjointly with the Russian people. The eldest of the Romanovs, Grand Duke Nikolay Nikolaevich, in making public this letter of Mariya Fedorovna to him, added: "I have on several occasions expressed my constant conviction that the future organization of the Russian State can be decided only on Russian soil, in accordance with the expectations of the Russian people."[19]

On his part, General Wrangel, desiring to preserve the cadres of the Russian army as an autonomous nucleus of national Russia, by order No. 35 of 1 September 1924, created *Russkii Obshche-Voinskii Soiuz* (*ROVS*)—Russian All-Military Union, whose membership included persons representing the units of the former Armed Forces of Southern Russia, the Russian army in the Crimea, and volunteer armies of other White fronts (Siberia, North, Baltic, and Poland), as well as the old Russian Imperial army.

Politically, *ROVS* was functioning in accordance with still an earlier order,[20] by which General Wrangel established the organizational and ideological independence of the army from party politics of both the Right and the Left, thus confirming the principle of nonpredetermination of the form of government and state system of future Russia. This, in turn, protected the right of each member of *ROVS* to hold his own political and ideological views, as long as they did not contradict the common ideal of a sovereign, free, and renascent Russia.

Vozrozhdenie (Renascence)

By the middle of the 1920s the political differentiation of the Russian emigration became rather complex. The Right (Legitimists, the Supreme Monarchical Council, etc.), though quite active, was lacking the financial means and foreign support enjoyed by the Russian émigré Left: those former Left Kadets who renounced the tenets of Constitutional Monarchy and proclaimed themselves Republicans under the leadership of P. N. Miliukov, the moderate socialists headed by A. F. Kerenskii, and the more radical socialists—the Social-Democrats Mensheviks of Martov and Abramovich and the Socialist-Revolutionaries of Victor Chernov.

The various political groupings had their own newspapers and journals. The main mass of the Russian emigration wishing to pursue the struggle against bolshevism, represented mostly by the "Army in civil dress" led by General Wrangel, also had its own publications. However, none of its newspapers could compete in scope and authority with Miliukov's Paris newspaper *Poslednie Novosti* (Latest News). This situation was changed only on 3 June 1925, when, due to the material help of the wealthy financier and public figure A. O. Gukasov, the first issue of a new daily, *Vozrozhdenie* (Renaissance, Renascence), appeared in Paris.

The title and the subtitle (*Nezavisimyi organ natsional'noi mysli*, An independent organ of national thought) were in themselves quite indicative of the political and ideological direction of the new organ of the press. Another indication was the name of its editor in chief, the prominent publicist, editor of many earlier publications, public figure, and Member of the Russian Academy of Sciences, Petr Berngardovich Struve. Though two years later Struve was actually pushed out of the newspaper, the general political and ideological platform of the newspaper which he formulated from the beginning, remained basically the same under the next editor, another former Kadet (Constitutional Democrat), Iu.F. Semenov. Besides Struve, a most important political and ideological pillar of the newspaper was I. A. Il'in.

In 1955, on the thirtieth anniversary of *Vozrozhdenie*, Georgii Meier (who was then editor of the review *Vozrozhdenie*, a postwar offspring of the newspaper), wrote that soon after the newspaper's birth its main collaborators (*Vozrozhdentsy*) split into two groups. One group, headed by Struve, Iu.F. Semenov, A. A. Saltykov, S. S. Ol'denburg, N. N. Chebyshev, and later G. A. Meier himself, became grounded in the state, imperial, religious *Fatherlandish* (*Otechestvennye*) ideas of Konstantin Leont'ev. The other group, led by D. S. Merezhkovskii and I. A. Il'in, and supported emotionally by B. K. Zaitsev, I. S. Shmelev, I. S. Lukash, I. D. Surguchev, K. A. Korovin, A. M. Rennikov, V. I. Gorianskii, and many others, was nourished by *Motherlandish* sources, and thus, in one way or another, was following Dostoyevsky's legacy.[21]

This attempt to classify the main authors of *Vozrozhdenie* into two ideological categories, though interesting in itself, is, however, very questionable, both in its fundamental opposition of *Otechestvo/Rodina* (Fatherland/Motherland), and in the specific allocation of names to one or the other category. Even the author himself wrote that these were "two apparently unavoidable for Russian life categories which essentially only complemented each other and always required their synthetical blending."[22] And, indeed, that is how it actually was in this instance, at least with the two ideological leaders, P. B. Struve in the first category, and I. A. Il'in in the second. It would be wrong to oppose these two names and to connect Struve with the concept of Fatherland and Il'in with that of Motherland. In reality, for each of them, Struve and Il'in, these two concepts were inseparable and obligatory, and depending upon the context, either one of them would occupy either the forefront or the background.

It would be equally misleading to present Struve's ideological genealogy as proceeding from K. Leont'ev and Il'in's from Dostoyevsky. Il'in valued Dostoyevsky with significant reservations, while Struve "discovered" (actually, reevaluated) K. Leont'ev at a very late stage in his life, when Struve's final political *Weltanschauung* had been already formed. B. Chicherin, for instance, had for Struve a much greater importance than K. Leont'ev, among whose ideas Struve cherished basically only two: his perception of Christianity as a teaching of individual salvation and his analysis of state as a phenomenon having religious-mystical roots.[23] On the whole, however,

Meier presents Struve's and *Vozrozhdenie*'s political and ideological principles convincingly and extensively.

After everything that Russia experienced in the two revolutions of 1917, the short republican period of the Provisional Government, the Civil War, and the new Soviet Republic under Lenin's dictatorship, *Vozrozhdenie* had no taste at all for creating a republican Russia in the future. On the other hand, it was opposed also to the restoration of monarchy along any party lines. It took the same position of nonpredetermination with regard to a future governmental system in Russia, as did the White movement under Alekseev, Kornilov, Denikin, and Wrangel, both in Russia and in exile. As long as the former supreme commander of the Imperial army and senior representative of the Romanov dynasty, Grand Duke Nikolay Nikolaevich, was still alive, the newspaper tried to unite national public opinion around his personal authority, considered as an authority of service (*sluzhenie*) and not of dominance (*gospodstvo*). Viewing the Russian army as the force which had been defending the very existence and honor of Russia from the onslaught of destructive antinational sedition, the newspaper was fully supportive of the Russian army and of the White movement.

Though published in emigration and for the Russian emigration, *Vozrozhdenie* under the pen of its editor in chief called its readers to turn away from settling small émigré scores and disputes and to devote their attention to the mainland, to internal Russia.

Rejecting the Revolution as a national, political, and cultural catastrophe, Struve and his *Vozrozhdenie* considered it necessary to take into account the great displacements and significant changes which took place in the people's life because of and since the Revolution. What Russia needs, Struve wrote, is renascence, and not restoration, a universal renascence based on the ideas of nation and Fatherland, liberty and private property, yet free from the evil spirits of self-interest and vengeance. History teaches us that spiritual strength and freedom of the individual, as well as the power and greatness of a nation or a state, are directly dependent on their religious principles and sources. Once separated from these sources, both individual and nation droop and grow shallow spiritually.

Having deep roots in Russian culture and nationhood, perceived as inseparable from their historical-spiritual-religious soil, *Vozrozhdenie* unavoidably found itself in conflict with the political views and general a-religious or anti-religious *Weltanschauung* of the leading contributors of Miliukov's *Poslednie Novosti*, and, to a lesser extent, Kerenskii's *Dni* (Days).

A still greater gulf separated *Vozrozhdenie* from *Poslednie Novosti* with regard to their attitudes toward Soviet authorities and the Communist regime. In this respect, a new delineation of political positions arose that removed some old barriers between the Right and the Left and created some new ones. Being unconditional revolutionists (or counter-revolutionists) with regard to bolshevism-communism, Struve and his colleagues found themselves in total opposition to Miliukov and Kuskova, with whom certain of them were in the past political allies (before the Revolution, Struve and Miliukov were both prominent Kadets)—and found much in common with Melgunov, many of whose past and present political and historical views were still alien to *Vozrozhdentsy*.

For Miliukov and his *Poslednie Novosti*, the evolution of bolshevism was unavoidable, which signified that at the end of this process bolshevism would self-destruct. For Struve, it was always clear that politically and economically Bolsheviks can only zigzag, but not evolve.

"Of course," wrote Struve, "Bolsheviks, the Soviet authorities evolve, i.e., the situation or milieu which surrounds the Bolsheviks, the Soviet authorities are evolving, but the Bolsheviks, as a political force, cannot evolve. This can be formulated still differently: *the political evolution of Soviet authorities is impossible police-wise (politseiski)*. The meaning of the events developing in Russia consists exactly in that the Communist party ruling over Russia, *remaining as it is by nature*, sometimes permits concessions, in order at this price to preserve itself intact at the head of Russia."[24]

The general political *Weltanschauung* reflected in the writings of Struve and his collaborators in *Vozrozhdenie* was defined by Struve as *Liberal Conservatism*. This unorthodox combination of terms meant an equal love for the elements and ideas of liberty and authority, freedom and order, reform and tradition, culture and state. Struve singled out eight major names as bearers of such a *Weltanschauung* in the Russian past. Chronologically, they were: Catherine the Great, Admiral N. S. Mordvinov, N. M. Karamzin, Prince P. A. Viazemskii, A. S. Pushkin, N. I. Pirogov, B. N. Chicherin, and A. D. Gradovskii. The combination of liberalism with conservatism required that, depending on historical circumstances, either the elements of liberalism or of conservatism would come to the fore in one's pronouncements and actions. Thus in pre-revolutionary Russia, Struve was essentially a conservative liberal; after the Revolution of 1917, a liberal conservative.

Vozrozhdenie remained fundamentally faithful to Struve's general platform of liberal conservatism throughout its long existence.

As this condensed exposition of the basic principles by which the mainstream *ROVS* and *Vozhrozhdenie* lived indicates, there was never any danger of political or ideological monism coming from these two quarters of the "Russian Party." On the contrary, both *ROVS* and *Vozrozhdenie* most definitely adhered to the principles of political and ideological pluralism.

The Russian Liberation Movement

During the late 1920s and in the 1930s the mainstream of the nationally active part of the Russian emigration suffered severe losses. The demise of the Grand Duke Nikolay Nikolaevich and the death—as many believed, poisoning by the Bolsheviks—of General Wrangel was followed by the Bolshevik kidnapping—and presumed murder—of General A. P. Kutepov, who succeeded General Wrangel as the head of *ROVS*, and then by the kidnapping and presumed murder of Kutepov's successor, General E. K. Miller.

The formerly quite unified White movement, organized in exile into *ROVS*, did become—contrary to the intentions of *ROVS*' founder—politicized to a certain extent, with such politicized elements breaking away and either joining existing political parties and groups or forming new ones. Thus broke away the more extreme Monarchist elements, mostly *Legitimists*. The representatives of the younger generation formed—first inside or by the side of *ROVS*, and later outside and, to a great extent, against the *ROVS*—a new political organization, which in the 1930s was called *Natsional'no-Trudovoi Soiuz Novogo Pokoleniia* (*NTSNP*, The National-Labor Union of the New Generation) and is currently called *Narodno-Trudovoi Soiuz* (*NTS*), Russian Solidarists. The left flank was occupied by still another new organization, under the name of *Mladorossy* (Young Russians), who—replacing the earlier political groups of National-Bolsheviks, *Smenovekhovtsy* (Change of Landmarks movement), and *Evraziitsy* (Eurasians), all of them compromised by their association, in one way or another, with bolshevism—tried to combine in their political platform monarchism with sovietism (they became famous for their slogan "Czar and Soviets!"). Later on, a new military-political organization of veterans was formed under the leadership of a prominent White general, A. V. Turkul. But the bulk of the military emigration and of their children remained on the general political and ideological positions of the White movement and Wrangel's and Kutepov's *ROVS*.

The beginning of World War II and, especially, the starting of the German-Soviet War on 22 June 1941, created a completely new situation and presented new opportunities and dangers. In various parts of Europe, particularly in the Balkans, those Russian anti-Communists, for whom the Bolsheviks always were and remained the foremost national enemy, used every possibility for organized and individual action. Organizationally, the most significant effort was the creation in Yugoslavia of the so-called Russian Corps on the Balkans. Its participants believed that the corps would be sent to Russia, to continue the military and political struggle against bolshevism begun a quarter of a century earlier. But Nazi Germany had its own political and strategic plans, and the corps remained in Yugoslavia, fighting mostly Communist partisans, till the end of the War.

A somewhat different situation was evolving on the German eastern front in Russia itself. The hatred for Stalin and communism was such, that millions of Red Army soldiers gave themselves up in the first months of the war and among the tens of millions of the civil population the advancing German army was usually received as liberators. The most active anti-Communist elements among the prisoners of war and the civil population, believing at first that the Germans came, indeed, as liberators, cooperated with them in one form or another, joining even German units in very great numbers as so-called *Hiwis* (*Hilfswillige*, Volunteer Helpers) or fighting the pro-Soviet partisans. Thus, when, a year later, the Soviet military hero, General Andrei Andreevich Vlasov, became a German prisoner of war and decided to join the anti-Stalinist side, there was already in existence a mass movement. This movement, however, lacked a recognized leader. Vlasov became such a leader, and he and his name gradually became the rallying point for all active anti-Stalinist and anti-Communist elements. As a result, the so-called Vlasov movement grew into a most important political phenomenon of the German-Soviet War of 1941–1945. Its main significance was that, after the White movement, it became the second (and, till now, last) mass anti-Communist movement, in whose ranks representatives of the many peoples of Russia were able to join forces, of all possible social and professional groups and ranks, and of various political and ideological persuasions. This was, indeed, a large national coalition of forces fighting for the liberation of Russia and its peoples.

The first documents connected with Vlasov's name, including a leaflet (without Vlasov's signature) dated September 1942 and containing thirteen specific political recommendations, bear the marks of direct German intervention.[25]

In Berlin, at the end of 1942, a new "Open Letter" and a "Smolensk Declaration" concerning the creation of a Russian Committee were prepared, with Generals Vlasov and V. F. Malyshkin, and M. A. Zykov contributing. Though the committee itself was a fiction, a German propaganda act for the eastern front, the new "13 points of the Russian Committee," edited by M. A. Zykov, represented a clear political program. They were:

1) Abolition of forced labor and guarantee of genuine right to work, creating the worker's material well-being.
2) Abolition of kolkhozes and a planned transfer of land to peasants into private ownership.
3) Restoration of commerce, trade, and handicraft, and an opportunity

for private initiative to participate in the economic life of the country.

4) Giving the intelligentsia the opportunity to freely create for the welfare of its people.

5) Guarantee of social justice and defense of toilers from any exploitation.

6) Introduction for toilers of real rights to education, rest, and secure old age.

7) Liquidation of the regime of terror and coercion, introduction of real freedom of religion, conscience, speech, assembly, and press. Guarantee of inviolability of person and home.

8) Guarantee of freedom for nationalities.

9) Liberation of political prisoners of Bolshevism and return to the homeland from prisons and labor camps of all, who were repressed for struggling against Bolshevism.

10) Restoration, at the State's expense, of cities and villages destroyed during the war.

11) Restoration of factories and plants belonging to the State which were destroyed during the war.

12) Renunciation of slave treaties, concluded by Stalin with Anglo-American Capitalists.

13) Guarantee of an existence minimum for invalids of war and their families.[26]

For its authors, this social and political program, produced in conditions of extreme difficulty, was only a first step. However, for Hitler and his associates, who were enemies not simply of Stalin and bolshevism, but of Russia and the Russian people, whom they considered to be *Untermenschen* (Subhumans), this was already an enormous concession. Departing somewhat from his initial maximalist position, Hitler agreed that Vlasov could be used for propaganda purposes on the front, but he was dead set against the creation of an, albeit allied but autonomous, Russian army and Russian government.

After the 20 July 1944 abortive military plot against Hitler, Himmler, who previously stood on the same racist anti-Slav and anti-Russian positions as Hitler, saw that there was no other hope for the salvation of Germany and the regime, and agreed to the formation of something like a Russian government in exile. A Committee for the Liberation of the Peoples of Russia (*Komitet Osvobozhdeniia Narodov Rossii, KONR*), with General Vlasov at its head, was created and a *KONR* Manifesto was made public at a solemn ceremony in Prague on 14 November 1944. A lengthy preamble was followed by a statement of goals and principles of *KONR*. The three main aims were formulated as:

a Overthrow of the Stalinist tyranny, liberation of the peoples of Russia
  from the Bolshevist system and return to the peoples of Russia of
  the rights, which they conquered in the people's revolution of 1917;
b Termination of the war and conclusion of an honorable peace with
  Germany;
c Creation of a new free people's state system without Bolsheviks and
  exploiters.[27]

This statement of *KONR*'s aims was supplemented by a list of fourteen
main principles and measures on which the new system was to be based.
They included the thirteen points of the Smolensk declaration but contained also a number of important new elements. Here is the entire text:

1) Equality of all peoples of Russia and a real right for them to national
   development, self-determination and state independence.
2) Establishment of a national-toiler's state system, under which all
   interests of the State are subordinated to the goals of improving the
   well-being and development of the nation.
3) Preservation of peace and establishment of friendly relations with
   all countries and development of international cooperation of every
   kind.
4) Extensive state measures for the strengthening of family and marriage. Real equality for women.
5) Abolition of forced labor and guarantee to all toilers of a real right
   to free labor, creating their material well-being; establishment for
   all kinds of work of such wages that would ensure a cultured standard
   of living.
6) Liquidation of kolkhozes, transfer of land to the peasants into private ownership without compensation. Freedom of forms of toiling
   usage of the land. Free disposal of products of one's labor, abolition
   of forced deliveries and annulment of debts to the Soviet authorities.
7) Introduction of inviolability of private ownership resulting from
   work. Reestablishment of commerce, trade, handicraft, and allocation to private initiative of the right and opportunity to participate
   in the economic life of the country.
8) Giving the intelligentsia the opportunity for free creative work for
   the good of its people.
9) Guarantees of social justice and defense of toilers from any exploitation, independently of their origin and past activity.
10) Introduction for all without exception of a real right to free edu-
    cation, medical care, rest, and secure old age.
11) Liquidation of the regime of terror and coercion. Abolition of forced

resettlements and mass deportations. Introduction of real freedom of religion, conscience, speech, assembly, press. Guarantee of inviolability of person, property, home. Equality of all before the law, independence and open proceedings in the courts.

12) Release of political prisoners of Bolshevism and return home from prisons and camps of all who were repressed because of their struggle against Bolshevism. No revenge and persecution of those, who cease the struggle for Stalin and Bolshevism, independently of whether one fought out of conviction or was forced to fight.

13) Restoration, at the expense of the State, of people's property— cities, villages, factories, and plants, destroyed during the war.

14) State care for war-disabled persons and their families.[28]

The *KONR* Manifesto expressed, further, the belief that "The annihilation of Bolshevism is an urgent task of all progressive forces" and that "the united efforts of the peoples of Russia will find the support of all freedom loving peoples of the world." It was pointed out also that the present liberation movement headed by *KONR* has behind it a definite tradition: it is "a continuation of the perennial struggle against Bolshevism, for liberty, peace, and justice." Emphasizing the diverse yet unifying character of the entire movement and its striving to defend the national dignity and independence of Russia, the manifesto continued:

"The Committee for the Liberation of the Peoples of Russia sees the main condition for the victory over Bolshevism in the consolidation of all national forces and their subordination to the common task of overthrowing the authority of the Bolsheviks. For this reason the Committee for the Liberation of the Peoples of Russia supports all revolutionary and oppositional to Stalin and Bolshevism forces, decidedly rejecting at the same time all reactionary projects, connected with an infringement of the rights of the people.

The Committee for the Liberation of the Peoples of Russia welcomes the help of Germany on conditions which do not infringe upon the honor and the independence of our Motherland. At the present time, this help represents the only real opportunity to organize the armed struggle against the Stalinist clique."[29]

The manifesto, especially in its preamble, contained some elements which reflected the abnormal conditions under which it was formulated and promulgated. What is surprising, however, is not that there were such elements, but that there were so few of them—despite the enormous pressure exercised on Vlasov and his associates by the entire Nazi machine. One should recall that in the fall of 1944 Germany was still a powerful country which, the successful Allied landings in Normandy in June notwithstanding, was now preparing for the impressive December offensive in the Ardennes. Moreover, after the 20 July attempt on Hitler's life, Himmler's and his sinister institutions' authority was increased even further. Dealing with them required strong conviction and great courage.

According to Iu. Pis'mennyi, a former member of the presidium of *KONR*, who relied on the testimony of some close associates of Vlasov, the German side demanded initially the inclusion in the manifesto of two cardinal negative points, one against the "World Jewry," the other against the "Anglo-American Plutocrats." Vlasov categorically refused. After much discussion, the Germans offered, as a last concession on their part, a compromise: to leave at least one of these two points, otherwise the impending deal would be off. Not wishing to give up the whole manifesto and the entire liberation movement, Vlasov preferred to eliminate from the manifesto any anti-Semitic references, and keep the anti-Plutocratic ones, and, at that, only in the introductory part of the manifesto, but not in its basic fourteen points.[30] In the conditions of November 1944 that was an incredible achievement.

No matter how one regards the Vlasov movement, in the final analysis one must acknowledge that in its aspirations, aims, and even in heavily censored official statements, it was antithetical not only to Stalin and bolshevism, but also to the foundations on which the Nazi regime was built. This was clearly understood by the Nazis themselves, as evident, for instance, in a secret Nazi document, a survey of the work of Dr. Taubert's department in Goebbels' Reich Ministry of Propaganda. Dr. Taubert's department, "Antibolschewismus," was in charge of anti-Bolshevik and anti-Soviet activities. The document, covering the period up to 31 December 1944, was, apparently, prepared in 1945. In its final section, "Perspectives," the document concludes that: "2) The Vlasov movement does not feel itself bound with Germany to such an extent as to go with her 'neck or nothing.' It has strong Anglophile sympathies and plays with the idea of a possible change of course [i.e., an alliance with Western democracies. -N.P.]; and 3) The Vlasov movement is not National-Socialist. . . . the Vlasov movement is a watery infusion of liberal and Bolshevist ideologies. It is important also that it does not fight the Jewry and generally does not recognize the Jewish problem. The Vlasov movement ridicules the national-socialist Weltanschauung."[31]

With all its defects, the Vlasov liberation movement was an essentially pluralistic movement.

After World War II

The victory of the Allies over Nazi Germany resulted in the occupation of eastern and part of central Europe by the Red (by then Soviet) Army and in the gradual establishment in the occupied countries of a Stalinist Communist regime. This dealt a severe blow to the cadres and organizational structures of the Russian anti-Communist emigration. Very many were forcibly repatriated to the Soviet Union or otherwise delivered into unmerciful Soviet hands. Despite these adverse conditions, the political and cultural life of the emigration resumed, even while the forced repatriation and all types of repressive screenings were going on—not only in the decimated Germany and Austria, but also in France.

At the beginning, *NTS* was the main political force among Russian émigrés in West Germany. Gradually, other groups were revived or created anew. Thus, the surviving Vlasovites became active again. However, instead of uniting, they broke into several organizations, each one of them pretending to be the true heir to the Vlasov movement. Eventually, the most important among them turned out to be *SBONR* (*Soiuz Bor'by za Osvobozhdenie Narodov Rossii*, Union of Struggle for the Liberation of the Peoples of Russia). The rightist organizations, among them the Supreme Monarchical Council, were also reactivated. Such elements representing the prewar mainstream "Russian Party" as *ROVS* were revived too. And a new political trend, connected mostly with the name of S. P. Mel'gunov, came to the fore.

Nashi Zadachi and Vozrozhdenie

After the Bolsheviks kidnapped (and, presumably, murdered) Generals Kutepov and Miller, *ROVS* was headed by General Arkhangel'skii. The former representative of General Wrangel in Berlin and head of *ROVS* in Germany, General A. A. von Lampe, moved to Paris after the war and became General Arkhangel'skii's main assistant (and later successor). In 1948 he became the editor of a new *ROVS* publication, *Nashi Zadachi* (Our Tasks), which continued through 1954. Mimeographed, called "leaflets," and distributed initially "only for like-minded persons" (i.e., members of *ROVS*), it dealt with a multitude of political, ideological, and cultural problems. The first issue, bearing the very characteristic title "*Odin v pole i tot voin*" (Even alone in the field, one is still a warrior), emphasized that the banners are not folded and the struggle against communism and for Russia continues. It gave, in an extremely brief and clear form, a definition of the political and ideological platform of both the author of *Nashi Zadachi*, and of *ROVS* in general:

All our fundamental ideas turned out to be justified; they are true and unshakable, we have nothing to change. Service to Russia, and not to parties (even then, when someone has become a member of a party). Struggle for the liberation of our people from the anti-national tyranny, terror, and infamy. Unity and indivisibility of Russia. Safeguarding of a free Orthodox Church and national culture. Rejection of all kinds of Totalitarianism, Socialism and Communism. Faithfulness to conscience and to honor till very death.

It is difficult to suppose that someone among us would believe in the possibility of the existence of Russia in a Republican form. But a sincere and convinced Monarchist can not avoid to understand that a Tsar must be deserved, that a place must be prepared for him in the *hearts* and *on the throne*. A Sovereign should not be again abandonned to isolation, treason, and profanation. Loyalty demands of us political tact, self-education, a selection of men of honor and experience.

All other problems of a political program are open to discussion.[31]

They were, indeed, open to discussion—in the next more than 200 issues of *Nashi Zadachi*. Later it became known that the sole author of *Nashi Zadachi* was Ivan Aleksandrovich Il'in (1883–1954). A former professor of Moscow University, a religious philosopher, philosopher of law, political philosopher, and publicist, Il'in left behind him a printed legacy of some thirty books and booklets and several hundred articles. After his death, all existing issues of *Nashi Zadachi*, with some important supplementary materials, were published as two large volumes under the same title, in standard typographical form. They represent the most elaborate treatment of the elements comprising the political and cultural ideology of the White movement component of the "Russian Party."[32]

Another important source for the understanding of the world outlook of the "Russian Party" was the review *Vozrozhdenie* (Renascence).

The Paris newspaper *Vozrozhdenie*, which started to appear as a daily in 1925, was later transformed into a weekly. Its last issue came off the press on 7 June 1940, on the eve of the *Wehrmacht*'s entrance into Paris. From January 1949, *Vozrozhdenie* resumed publication as a review (formally, *tetradi* or *cahiers*, note-books), appearing first 6 times a year, and from January 1955 till its expiration in 1973, as a monthly. During most of those years it was published by A. O. Gukasov (who died in 1969). Editors changed quite frequently. First the review was edited by S. S. Tkhorzhevskii, then by S. P. Mel'gunov, afterward by a number of other people, including the previously mentioned G. A. Meier; at the end the main role belonged to Prince S. S. Obolenskii.

Though the editors changed, the general political, ideological, and cultural-philosophical platform of the review remained more or less constant, with some secondary fluctuations to the right or to the left (under S. P.

Mel'gunov, somewhat to the left, under Prince S. S. Obolenskii, more—and in the last few issues visibly more—to the right). On the whole, however, the centrist "Russian Party" course set for the newspaper *Vozrozhdenie* by its first editor P. B. Struve, remained the same. The general political philosophy expressed by Struve in his formula of *liberal conservatism*, was further concretized in three brief formulas: "Greatness and freedom of Russia. Dignity and rights of man. Continuity and growth of culture." This motto, printed at the head of the first issue of the review *Vozrozhdenie* (under S. S. Tkhorzhevskii), was then repeated, as a kind of political, civic, and cultural credo of the review, in every subsequent issue, as long as the review continued to appear.

SBSR

S. P. Mel'gunov's postwar contribution to the activities of the "Russian Party" was by no means limited to his editorship of the review *Vozrozhdenie*. Born in 1879, he was well known already in prerevolutionary Russia as a liberal publicist, Russian historian, and political figure, belonging to the Populist Socialist organization. An enemy of bolshevism, he continued his editorial and political activities in the emigration, in France. Gradually, however, he devoted himself to an extensive study of the Russian Revolution and Civil War, which resulted in several important books.

Mel'gunov's political reactivation took place in the immediate postwar period, when persecution of enemies of bolshevism and former Soviet citizens not wishing to return to the Soviet Union became especially acute. At that time French Communists were still part of the government and the Soviet embassy in Paris with its Beria detachments had almost a free rein. Mel'gunov bravely stood up to these persecutors and began the publication of an anti-Communist review, which, because of Soviet pressure on French authorities, had to change titles several times before becoming finally *Rossiiskii Demokrat* (Russian Democrat). When things became more normal and contact with émigrés in other countries was reestablished, Mel'gunov organized a political association, *Soiuz Bor'by za Svobodu Rossii* (*SBSR*, Union of Struggle for the Freedom of Russia). The purpose was to form a national-democratic kernel around which a politically active center could be created that would direct the struggle for the liberation of Russia from bolshevism. From the very beginning, this was conceived to be a tactical and not an ideological organization. The membership consisted of those who accepted a political "Platform," consisting of six sections:

I. The purpose of the Union is liberation of Russia from Soviet authority, unshackling of the spiritual and material forces of the peoples of Russia, enslaved by Communism, and establishment in it of a democratic regime, founded on social justice in the rights of man and citizen.

II. The Union is an association of active opponents of Bolshevism from all peoples of Russia and includes in its ranks individuals and representatives of various political currents based on personal criteria, and not as delegates and representatives of parties. Members of the Union are those, who join the platform, drawn up by the Union.

III. After the overthrow of the existing totalitarian-Communist regime, during the transitional period the following measures should be implemented:

1) restoration of the inviolability of person and home, freedom of conscience, speech, assembly, unions, freedom of press, and independence of court system;

2) abolition of terror, concentration camps, liberation of all political prisoners;

3) abolition of all kinds of coercive labor. Restoration of freedom of choice of professions and place of work, as well as of the independence of professional associations. Establishment of real labor protection;

4) organization of State help for the return to their native places, if they so wish, of those groups of the population and of peoples who were forcibly deported by the Soviet authorities;

5) liquidation of kolkhozes and transfer of the land to the population on the principles of free peasant landownership;

6) a decisive course toward a) abolition of the Soviet military-economic policy and organization of the national economy in the interests of large masses of the people; b) rebirth of private and cooperative initiative in industry and commerce (domestic and foreign) along with safeguarding of state property and control in enterprises of a national importance; c) inviolability of private property recognized by law;

7) abolition of the aggressive imperialistic foreign policy of the Bolsheviks.

IV. At the earliest possible date an all-Russian Constituent People's Assembly must be convoked on the basis of universal suffrage, secret ballot, and with complete freedom of political agitation.

V. The internal structure of the reborn Russian State must grow, in the view of the Union, out of a free expression of the people's will and in all its stages to lean on broad democratic self-government. In order to achieve this aim:

1) in Russia a federation on the principles of equality of all peoples inhabiting it is established;
2) its territory is divided into large regions (lands-states) based on a national, geographic, economic, and cultural-historical principle. Each region has a local parliament, ensuring its legislative, administrative, and way-of-life independence;
3) to all nationalities inhabiting Russia, independently of territory, is guaranteed freedom of language, teaching, and cultural autonomy;

> *Note*: Taking into account that the solution of the problem of federation belongs to the Constituent People's Assembly, the Union accepts into its ranks also persons, who recognize other forms of federation of the state, on the condition that the principle of the unity of historical Russia is preserved as inviolable.

4) the Supreme authority is conceived as consisting of a Head of State, elected according to a Constitution established by the People's Assembly, of a responsible central government, and of legislative chambers—all-Russian People's *Duma* from the entire population and an all-Russian People's Council of representatives of regions-lands;
5) the foreign policy, command and guidance of the armed forces, monetary affairs and other state functions of all-Russian importance are in the hands of the central authority.

VI. A detailed elaboration and establishment of political, economic, and social structure of Russia, as well as an exact delimitation of competence between the federal and the regional legislation and organs of administration belongs to the future Constituent People's Assembly."[33]

This political platform of the Union of Struggle for the Freedom of Russia, important in itself, was significant also in that it allowed to bring together, in one common political effort, such ideologically divergent personalities, as, on the one side, the prominent Populist Socialist I. M. Khezaskov and, on the opposite, the former right Constitutional Democrat (Kadet) and later tactical ideologist of the White emigration and *ROVS*, N. A. Tsurikov. Their ideological confrontation on the pages of *Vozrozhdenie*, then edited by S. P. Mel'gunov, was in itself a good illustration of the pluralistic character of Mel'gunov's *SBSR*. Under the general heading "Sovereign People and Free Man," Mel'gunov published N. Tsurikov's brief but challenging "Democracy or Freedom?" and Iv. Kheraskov's longer and affirmative "Democracy—Freedom." Kheraskov ended his response by stating that what separates him from Tsurikov is much less important than what unites them. The real task facing Russian democracy now is the struggle against the Communist evil that is destroying Russia. There ought to be an amalgamation of all democratic forces into a single union. "One of the nuclei of such a union," concluded Kheraskov, "is the 'Union of Struggle for the Freedom of Russia,' of which we both, with N. A. Tsurikov, are members with a completely equal right, in spite of all our party divergences."[34]

Besides a common enemy, a most important factor in keeping together such disparate ideological elements under one roof was also the personal authority of the leader of the union, S. P. Mel'gunov. It was this personal authority of Mel'gunov and the centrist, essentially non-deterministic nature of his union and its political platform that played such an important role also in the creation of a new émigré political center.

KTsAB and KTsONR

After the Soviet Berlin blockade and American airlift bridge to Berlin in 1948–49 and the North Korean invasion of South Korea in 1950, the American response to Communist aggression became more active. Greater attention was given to the internal forces of resistance in the Soviet Union and to the political emigration. Through a newly formed American Committee for Liberation from Bolshevism financial and technical means were provided for three major initiatives: 1) creation in Munich of a radio station "Liberation" (currently, "Liberty"), broadcasting to the Soviet Union in Russian and a number of other languages of the peoples of that country; 2) strengthening of the Munich based research Institute for the Study of the History and Culture of the U.S.S.R.; and 3) unification of various émigré political groups under the umbrella of a center.

Radio "Liberation" began broadcasting on 1 March 1953, i.e., on the eve of Stalin's death. The institute significantly expanded and deepened its activities. But the unification of anti-Communist forces met with serious problems.

After several meetings and lengthy and passionate negotiations a new unifying organ, *Koordinatsionnyi Tsentr Antibol'shevistskoi Bor'by* (*KTsAB*, Coordinating Center for Anti-Bolshevik Struggle), was finally formed in October 1952. Headed by S. P. Mel'gunov, it consisted initially of his *SBSR* (Union of Struggle for the Freedom of Russia), the Vlasovite *SBONR* (Union of Struggle for the Liberation of the Peoples of Russia), the League of Struggle for People's Freedom, the membership of which consisted mainly of Russian Social Democrats-Mensheviks and Socialist Revolutionaries living in the U.S.A., and *RND* (Russian Populist Movement), headed by A. F. Kerenskii. These four Russian organizations were joined by five political organizations representing the non-Russian peoples of the Soviet Union, who were ready to cooperate with Russians proceeding from the *KTsAB*'s platform of non-predetermination.[35]

However, the American Committee, supported by the essentially Socialist League of Struggle for People's Freedom represented mainly by the Menshevik B. I. Nikolaevskii, wanted to unite *KTsAB* with the so-called Paris Block of separatist anti-Russian organizations. Since these organizations rejected the only possible ground for a common action during the period of struggle for the overthrow of bolshevism, the principle of non-predetermination of the future state system of Russia, further unifying efforts by the American Committee led to nowhere and the committee discontinued all financial support of *KTsAB*.

A conference of organizations remaining faithful to the initial platform of *KTsAB*, in Munich on 30 August 1953, ended with the adoption of a special "Appeal"[36] to the emigration, signed by fifteen Russian and non-Russian groups. On the Russian side, besides the initial *SBSR, SBONR* and *RND*, they were: *NTS* (National-Labor Union), *TSOPE* (The Central Association of Postwar Emigrés), and two Vlasovite organizations, *KOV* (Committee of United Vlasovites) and *SVOD* (The Union of Warriors of the Liberation Movement). In addition to the seven Russian organizations, there were eight non-Russian.[37]

In the "Appeal," it was stated that this enlarged *KTsAB* continues to proceed from the two basic principles, around which the statutes of *KTsAB* were formulated, the principle of non-predetermination and the principle of equality of all currents of democratic thought inside each of the national (non-Russian) emigrations representing the peoples of the Soviet Union. This, in contrast to the American Committee of Liberation from Bolshevism, which initially adhered to the same two principles, but later practically abandoned them and insistently tried to introduce into *KTsAB* avowed predeterminist-separatists as the only genuine spokesmen for their nationalities.

Later, by a resolution dated 29 September 1954, the name of *KTsAB* was changed to that of *KTsONR* (*Koordinatsionnyi Tsentr Osvobozhdeniia Narodov Rossii*, Coordinating Center of Liberation of the Peoples of Russia). The resolution said in part:

"Recognizing, as always, the unconditional right of every people to self-determination and non-predetermining the people's will after the victory of the people-liberating revolution of the entire territory of the contemporary Soviet Union, the Coordinating Center struggles for the liberation of *the united family of the peoples of Russia* from Communist rule, decidedly rejecting attempts to substitute for this struggle a struggle of non-Russian peoples against the Russian or among themselves, as a conception rotten at its root and actually working in favor of Communism."[38]

This concept of the "unity of the family of the peoples of Russia," i.e., the unity of historical Russia as a single political organism, was put forth at the very beginning of the discussions about the creation of a center in Stuttgart, in August 1951,[39] but later, in the search for a working compromise between non-predeterminists and determinist-separatists, became moot. Now that the split with separatists became final, this principle was ressurected—and accepted by sixteen Russian and non-Russian political organizations.[40]

The creation of *KTsONR* was a significant political achievement, but it turned out to be short-lived. Lack of financial support and diminishing political prospects on the international scene resulting from the advent of Khrushchev and the famous *détente*, as well as the grave illness and ensuing death of the leader of the united front, S. P. Mel'gunov, led to the eventual demise of the new center.

NTS

With *NTS* (*Narodno-Trudovoi Soiuz Rossiiskikh Solidaristov*, People's Labor Union of Russian Solidarists) we find ourselves on a rather familiar current scene.

NTS, which under various names has been in existence since 1930, had a complex, and sometimes painful, history. With the years, not only its name, but also its policies and political platform (and program) changed.

For the last several years *NTS*'s main organ, *Posev*, has been publishing the text of a political platform which is openly pluralistic. Since not everyone reads *Posev*—and for the sake of completeness of the present record—here is that platform:

> The basic idea of the *NTS*, reflected in the name of the organization, is the building of a free Russian (*Rossiiskii*) state founded not on coercion and class struggle, but on the elicitation of the people's will, free labor of citizens, and solidarity of all strata of the society in service to the common good. *NTS* is struggling for the elimination of the existing regime. At the present *NTS* considers necessary the carrying out in our country the following changes:
>
> —renunciation of the planting in the entire world of 'brotherly' regimes and of help to them; normalization of relations with the West; return of all our troops from foreign countries; preservation of the fighting capacity of the Army on a level sufficient for the repulsion of foreign intervention in our affairs;

—use of all means and efforts for the solution of the internal, deepening crisis in all spheres of life;

—elevation of the standard of living, for which it is necessary: to free the enormous means, spent on ideologically determined aims, for which our people have no need; to renounce the system of total planning; to introduce into the economy the principles of free market, to encourage private initiative, peoples' interest in the results of their labor;

—restoration of truth about the past of Russia; elimination of obstacles for the development of national cultures of all peoples of our country; ensuring the freedom of religion;

—creation of an open society and of conditions for political pluralism; introduction of legal norms of regulation of public life; liberation of political prisoners; enlisting of the entire population in the discussion of further measures for the normalization of life in the country; preparation and conduct of elections for organs of administration on all levels.[41]

As is known, *NTS* was able to establish direct contacts with Soviet citizens, and has been the object of regular attacks by the Soviet propaganda and secret services.

This brings me to manifestations of the Russian liberation movement inside the country in the post-Stalinist period. With regard to the "Russian Party," besides the advent of Solzhenitsyn, the most significant was, as many would agree, the emergence of *VSKhSON* and, still later, of a current that has been directly designated as "the Russian Party."

A. I. Solzhenitsyn

Though this chapter deals, essentially, with organized efforts, it would be unthinkable to speak about the "Russian Party" without at least a reference to A. I. Solzhenitsyn. He heads no formal movement or organ of the press, and he insists that he is first of all and foremost a writer, not a political figure. However, no matter what his innermost preferences, he did become a publicist and a public figure—of such a stature that, speaking of him, one cannot fail but think of the famous story about Stalin and the pope. Solzhenitsyn, too, has no tank divisions (a political organization or his own newspaper, radio or TV network) but his actual and potential political influence is enormous. Some would even claim that he is now the "Russian Party."

I can not discuss here Solzhenitsyn's political, historical, philosophical, and cultural ideas. They are sufficiently well known. But, bearing in mind the main theme of this chapter, I must at least mention that, in my opinion, Solzhenitsyn himself has convincingly repudiated the accusations of "monism," directed against him by the so-called "pluralists."[40] And he was right in saying that he is not a critic of the West, but a critic of the West's weakness.

VSKhSON

Vserossiiskii Sotsial-Khristianskii Soiuz Osvobozhdeniia Naroda (*VSKhSON*, the All-Russian Social-Christian Union for the Liberation of the People) was formed by Igor' Viacheslavovich Ogurtsov in Leningrad in early 1964 (the program was adopted on 2 February 1964). Three years later, the organization was crushed: some 60 people were arrested or detained in Leningrad, Tomsk, Irkutsk, Petrozavodsk, and other cities. The penalties were very severe: the main leaders received from eight to fifteen years.

VSKhSON's "Program" is a bulky detailed document consisting of an introduction and two parts divided into fifteen sections. The titles of the five sections forming the first part give a good idea of its contents: "Marxism-Leninism—the totalitarian ideology of the Communist bureaucracy," "The tasks of the Russian revolutionary movement of the 20th Century and the general line of the Communist oligarchy," "The Communist System," "The predestinated doom of Communism," "The bankruptcy of Marxist-Leninist teachings in the face of history. The international anti-Communist liberation movement."

While the first part of the "Program" represents primarily a critical analysis of Marxism-Leninism-communism and the Soviet system, the second part formulates the positive program of *VSKhSON*. After a section devoted to "The basic principles of Social-Christianity," come nine sections, dealing each with one or another aspect of the future social, economic, political, and cultural system: "On ownership," "Land relations," "Industry and services," "Credit; Banking; Commerce," "Culture; Science; Education; Public Health," "Religion and Church," "Justice," "State," and "Rights of man and citizen."[41]

In the *Chronicle of Current Events, VSKhSON*'s "Program" was briefly summarized in the following way:

"Establishment of a democratic regime. The head of the State is elected by the entire population, is subordinated to the parliament. The controlling organ is *Sobor* (representatives of the clergy), has the right of 'veto' with regard to the head of state and the parliament. Land is the property of the State, is alloted to private persons or collectives (exploitation is forbidden), hired labor is allowed only on an equal footing. Most enterprises are property of collectives of workers, the main branches—transportation, electronics, etc.—are state owned. The basic principle of the economy is Personalism."[42]

As the term alone, Personalism, indicates, the fundamental ideas of *VSKhSON* were greatly influenced by N. A. Berdiaev, in particular his *Novoe Srednevekov'e* (New Middle Ages) and his later writings on Personalism.[43] Generally speaking, Berdiaev's influence was such that another important representative of the "Russian Party," Vladimir Nikolaevich Osipov, who until his arrest in 1974[44] had been publishing the *samizdat* review *Veche* and, while still imprisoned, met some of the imprisoned members of *VSKhSON*, directly characterized that organization as *Berdiaevskii kruzhok* (Berdiaev circle).[45]

In spite of the very definite and detailed nature of views and ideas of *VSKhSON*'s "Program," one must point out that they did not, even for their authors, represent something final and exclusive. This is clearly stated in the "Program" itself:

"Advancing a Social-Christian program as a basis for a future structure of social relations in the country the Union of Liberation of the People is not inimical to programs close in spirit, but having their own peculiarities, considering that the final selection must take place after the overthrow of the Communist dictatorship . . ."[46]

Thus *VSKhSON*'s program, though definitely Social-Christian and personalist, was, in principle, a nondeterministic program—and not only with regard to the future form of government in Russia.

"The Russian Party" of the 70s and 80s

As for the current situation in the Soviet Union, the writer G. N. Vladimov who emigrated from the Soviet Union on 26 May 1983, characterizes the general platform, cadres, fate, and importance of what is actually called there "the Russian Party," in the following way.

The main goal of "the Russian Party" is the renascence of Russian national consciousness and culture. Those who belong to this "Party," "wanted to awake the memory of Russia, to return it to its history, they fought for the restoration of spiritual values, in many ways contributed to the awakening of religious consciousness." In Vladimov's opinion, the contemporary Russian idea, positively received in many hearts, is, basically, an isolationist idea ("Leave alone Cuba, leave alone China, enough of feeding others. Let us live within our own state").

This "Russian Party" is most strikingly represented by writers, especially writers-*derevenshchiki* and *pochvenniki*, but people of other professions, and not just of the humanities, belong to it too. Besides writers and publicists, one finds here also artists, technical intelligentsia, and military personnel (usually, in higher ranks: majors, lieutenant-colonels, colonels).

The "Party" is by no means an organized political movement. Generally speaking, in the Soviet Union "everything is so scattered that often people not only professing but expressing the very same ideas may not meet one another—as have never met Vladimir Soloukhin and Vasilii Belov with Vladimir Osipov, with Leonid Borodin. Their thoughts are similar, but situation, is different."[47] "The Russian Party" is the more broader as it includes, besides people who do not protest when others directly connect them with this "Party," also people who, without belonging to it and without sharing all its ideas, at the same time are very sympathetic to it. According to Vladimov, even in the machinery of the Central Committee of the CPSU and in the Council of Ministers of the USSR there are patrons and sympathizers of those who frankly speak for "the Russian Party."[48]

The "Party" faces, however, a double danger: from its own extremists and, especially, from the Communist regime. Thus, under Andropov it was exactly in "the Russian Party" that the authorities saw the main menace to the regime. "People tell that Fedorchuk, having been for a brief while chief of the KGB, had enough time to give instructions: 'The main thing is Russian nationalism; dissidents come after, we will catch them in a single night.' "[49]

In Vladimov's opinion Andropov was right: "the Russian idea is, indeed, the main danger (to the Communist regime), and not without reflection: you see, this is in essence a second positive program, which is both newer and more attractive than the Marxist-Leninist, and, well, this is, moreover, good literature: Vasilii Belov, Boris Mozhaev, Vladimir Soloukhin, the recently deceased Fedor Abramov . . ."

But no matter how hard the Communist authorities persecute "the Russian Party," "national movements are not just the inevitability of our century, but they have much better chances to stand against the furiously aggressive 'proletarian internationalism,' than those not always capable of defending democracy. . . . As any idea, opposing the official rotten ideology, the Russian national idea is both inevitable and (life)saving."[50]

This brings to an end my brief historical survey of the highlights of the various manifestations of the mainstream of the so-called "Russian Party," as it expressed itself in two mass movements, several organizations and currents and their organs of the press and their political programs and platforms.

All of these political and ideological platforms had to deal, in one way or another, with the problem of Russia and the West. But a no less important problem has always been the reverse relationship. It requires at least a brief treatment here.

The West and the "Russian Party"

Looking back at the long history of Russian opposition to bolshevism-communism, one is left with a very sad impression: it is not the "Russian Party" that did not seek and accept the alliance of the West, but the West that did not truly understand and unselfishly support the "Russian Party."

The help to the White movement was slow in coming, uncoordinated, and insufficient. The allies of Russia acted in a selfish and quite often near-sighted way (culminating in Lloyd George's conclusion, that one can trade with cannibals too, for which purpose the British government stopped supporting the Whites and sought reconciliation with Lenin's Reds).

There was no support for the "Russian Party" by any major Western power between the two world wars. When Germany attacked the Soviet Union in 1941, the West became allied with Stalin, and since Hitler was betting on the dismemberment of Russia and the enslavement of the Slavic peoples, the "Russian Party" found itself between hammer and anvil. After the war, the West handed over to Stalin—for immediate or slow death—thousands of the most active anti-Communist elements of the "Russian Party," as well as hundreds of thousands of less active opponents of the regime.[51]

When America finally began a search for the "Russian Party" as an ally in the struggle for the containment of communism in the early 1950s, and a political center coordinating the activities of various organizations representing the peoples of Russia was created, the whole undertaking was immediately stifled by the American Committee for Liberation from Bolshevism. Though formally neutral, the committee actually sought to impose on the "Russian Party" a union with the anti-Russian groups, which the "Russian Party" could not accept without both sides espousing the principle of non-predetermination for at least the duration of the common struggle against bolshevism.[52] Nowadays there is still very little understanding of, and visible support for, the "Russian Party."

Also, apparently, there is no sufficient understanding of the fact that we are dealing not with one, but with two essentially disparate forces: communism, and Russia, the Russian people. These two forces can, and sometimes do, unite or even amalgamate, as in the case of the so-called Soviet patriotism. It was primarily this amalgamation that led to the eventual destruction of Nazi Germany. America and the free world in general cannot allow themselves to repeat these self-destructive German policies with regard to Russia. Every effort should be made to separate Russia from communism and to direct the force of Russian patriotism against the force of communism.

It seems that many people in authority in the U.S.A. and throughout the world continue to underestimate the danger of communism. Yet the doctrine of Marxism-Leninism and organized communism are a force much more dangerous, and certainly no less cruel, than National-Socialism and Hitlerism. The latter, because of racial and national exclusivity, had an incomparably more narrow appeal. Communism is appealing to all races, to all peoples, to all declassed elements, and its specter is moving now around not just Europe, as the authors of the *Communist Manifesto* had proclaimed in their time, but on all continents, throughout the entire world.

If the force of communism is not separated from the force of Russian (or Soviet) patriotism, and if they become, on the contrary, united and amalgamated, as a result of wrong Western policies, the struggle will be long, cruel, and costly, and its outcome dubious. Even if, in the end, the anti-Russian coalition turns out to be victorious, it may be a Pyrric victory. For it is impossible entirely to defeat, conquer, and rule by means of occupation a country as great and as vast as Russia. Only a victory over communism, and not over Russia and the Russian people, can lead to the establishment of freedom, law, order, and a genuine and lasting peace.

Is not the relationship of the Western allies to Nazi Germany and Imperial Japan teaching us something in this respect? Whether or not one agrees that the Allies' World War II policy of unconditional surrender addressed to an entire nation and not just to its temporary rulers was a reasonable one, one cannot deny that it was absolutely necessary to gain later the support of the German people and of the Japanese people in the free world's struggle against Soviet imperialism and aggression. Even the totalitarian Communist China has been courted as part of this global strategy.

Who can guarantee that in the future there will not emerge some new center of aggression and that America and Western Europe will not have to face a new danger requiring their alliance with Russia? And what if the Russian people, repeatedly betrayed by the West in its best hopes and aspirations will find itself allied with the enemies of the West? Is it not better to start now cultivating in the Russian people a friend, and not an enemy?

Summary and Recommendations

In the introduction I expressed my hope that this chapter would supply material for answers to three basic questions:

—What have been the aims, goals, and aspirations of the "Russian Party" during the nearly seventy years of Communist rule in Russia?

—What are the lessons that could be drawn from a historical survey of the various manifestations of the "Russian Party" during this period of time?

—Would the eventual victory of the "Russian Party" preserve political and ideological monism in Russia?

Reiterating some of the points made and adding a few new ones, I should like to say the following. With regard to the aspirations, aims, and *goals* of the mainstream "Russian Party," the essence of the numerous political programs and ideological platforms of that "Party" could be presented, tentatively, in the following condensed way:

1) Liberation of Russia and of the peoples of Russia from the yoke of Marxism-Leninism, bolshevism-communism, and the Soviet totalitarian regime.
2) Establishment of a free Russia, regenerated spiritually, nationally, politically, economically, and culturally.
3) Non-predetermination of the form of the future government and the composition of the future state. Whether this future Russia will be a monarchy or a republic and whether it will be structured as a single state, a federation, or some new kind of a commonwealth, and within what borders, should be determined in accordance with the freely expressed will of its peoples.
4) Independently of the form and structure of the government and the state, future political and cultural life in Russia should be motivated by an adherence to the principles of human and civil rights, including freedom of conscience and worship, cultural expression, speech, assembly, and press.
5) The new economic order should be based on the principles of private ownership and social justice.

Such a minimal political program as this one could, probably, serve also as a platform for any future coalition of forces struggling against communism, for a free Russia.

With regard to *lessons*, there are, essentially, three:

1) From the very beginning of the Bolshevik seizure of power and the establishment of a Communist regime in Russia, there has always been an active "Russian Party" opposing the usurpers and oppressors. This opposition resulted in two mass movements and a great number of organizations, organized initiatives, and trends, of which only some of the most important could have been mentioned here.

2) The "Russian Party" has never been a monolithic block. It always had its left, right, and center. This chapter concentrated on what could be considered the center, the mainstream. As the various political platforms of the "Russian Party" presented here demonstrate, even within that mainstream there has always been, alongside a common core program, a plurality of positions on a number of important questions—and no danger of political or ideological monism.

3) Russia was the first victim and the "Russian Party" the first, and permanent, deadly opponent of bolshevism-communism. However, the "Russian Party" has never received, neither then nor later, adequate outside support in its struggle against bolshevism-communism, which, from the very beginning, was, after all, intent on subjugating not just Russia but eventually the entire globe.

While there is every reason to reject the extreme left manifestations of the "Russian Party" (which could be labelled, collectively, national-bolshevism or national communism), as well as its extreme right manifestations (to which the term *Chernosotenstvo*—Black Hundred—could be applied), the center and center-left and center-right deserve the favorable attention and full support of the United States and the free world in general.

The ways in which this support can manifest itself are numerous and may vary in accordance with changing international and Soviet domestic circumstances. Recently, a valuable attempt to present a list of practical policy recommendations has been made by Professor John B. Dunlop. They are:

1) Western governments, diplomats, and media representatives should cease using interchangeably the words "Russia" and "Soviet Union" or "USSR", "Russians" and "Soviets."

2) In Public Law 86–90, adopted by the U.S. Congress on 17 July 1959, with the purpose of commemorating the "captive nations" each year in the third week of July, Russia should be added to the list of captive nations.

3) The West should begin to properly understand and deal with the so-called "Slavophile" and conservative currents in Russia's past and present, which would include also a proper knowledge and understanding of Russian Orthodoxy.

4) Western scholarship should cease to consider contemporary Russian nationalism as monolithic and as anti-Semitic and should be able to disentangle the various strands of that nationalism, paying particular attention to moderate Russian nationalists.

5) Foreign radio broadcasting—in the case of the United States, the Voice of America and Radio Liberty—should lend more support to

moderate elements in the Russian national movement and to Christian elements among its listeners.

6) Similar efforts should be made also in the area of cultural exchanges. Thus, leaders of the Soviet Society for the Preservation of Historical and Cultural Monuments or the so-called *derevenshchiki*-writers could be invited to visit the West; while Western ecological groups could send their members to the Soviet Union, where exhibitions on the work of Western cultural figures popular among Russian nationalists (such as the novelist William Faulkner) could be held.

7) Western books and monographs on Russian nationalist currents and Russian history, on monarchism, fascism, democracy, and law should be regularly translated into Russian and published, and thus made available for circulation in the Soviet Union.[53]

I must add that I fully agree with all of Professor Dunlop's practical recommendations except one, recommendation number two: Public Law 86–90 dealing with the so-called "captive nations" was promoted by anti-Russian separatists living in America, and is based on such historical and political misinformation and errors that it is, in my opinion, beyond redemption. In American terminology, we are dealing with nation-states.[54] History knows of no such nation-states as "Idel-Ural" or "Cossackia." One can not put on the same level nation-states which had had long independent existences, or at least internationally recognized status, and "nations" which were created, and immediately disappeared, in the turmoil of a civil war. Or independent nations which were always outside the borders of Russia—and nationalities which have long been a more or less organic part of Russia. Adding the name of Russia to the list of such "captive nations" would simply perpetuate the historical and political errors of Public Law 86–90, including the greatest political error: an implied call for the dismemberment not only of the coercive Soviet-Communist empire created by Stalin, but also for the dismemberment of Russia itself.[55] It is possible that, taking into account American domestic electoral conditions, Professor Dunlop sees no other practical remedy, except adding to the list the name of Russia. Contrary to his and, incidentally, that of many Russian Americans' opinion, I believe that, the abrogation of the law being impossible, the only remaining solution is to let the law fade away. If this is impossible too, let the law stand as one more example of historical ignorance and political myopia.

And now the final question: Would the victory of the "Russian Party" preserve political and ideological monism? The short answer is clearly: *No, it would not.*

Of course, in human affairs there are no absolute guarantees. With the experience of the twentieth century almost behind us we can affirm: In history everything is possible. But there are, nevertheless, some very strong grounds to maintain that the victory of the mainstream "Russian Party" will result in the advent of a pluralistic society and state.

First of all, as has been demonstrated, the historical survey of movements, organizations, initiatives, and political programs of the "Russian Party" contains a very strong and consistent promise of a pluralistic future. Secondly, the mainstream "Russian Party" is characterized by or is related to certain phenomena, which in themselves are pluralistic. Thirdly, the "Russian Party" is in itself a plurality of different, and sometimes conflicting, views and opinions and thus a pluralistic phenomenon in its own right. It has as its core a special brand of centrist conservatism, either national-ethical-religious (as in the case of A. I. Solzhenitsyn and like-minded people), or avowedly liberal and pluralistic (as in the case of P. B. Struve and his followers), but always recognizing the rights of others.

However, for all those contributing factors to be fully effective, and, first of all, in order for the mainstream "Russian Party" to eventually prevail over Soviet communism and totalitarianism, the U.S.A. and the free world in general should clearly recognize that the true enemy is, indeed, communism—and unequivocally throw their support not behind forces inimical to Russia and the Russian people, but behind the mainstream "Russian Party" itself.

Notes

I should like to acknowledge my indebtedness to the Illinois Summer Research Laboratory on Russia and Eastern Europe, University of Illinois' Russian and East European Center at Urbana-Champaign, where I was an Associate in 1984 and 1985 and where many of the documentary and background materials necessary for the preparation of this chapter have been collected.

1. For a clear and comprehensive picture of the current situation, see the following works by John B. Dunlop: *The Faces of Contemporary Russian Nationalism* (Princeton, N.J.: Princeton University Press, 1983); *The New Russian Nationalism*, in the Washington Papers/116 (New York: Praeger, 1985).
2. See General A. A. von Lampe, *Puti Vernykh: Sbornik Statey*, (The Paths of the Faithful. A Collection of Articles) (Paris, 1960), 17–19, 28, and 72.
3. von Lampe, *Puti:*, 19.
4. Nowadays, the "pluralist" political composition of the White movement is recognized sometimes even by Soviet scholars. Thus, the recently published Soviet Encyclopedia of the Civil War mentions that the first White government

in Novocherkask (*Donskoy Grazhdanskyi Sovet*) included, on its left flank, representatives of Constitutional Democrats (Kadets), Socialists, and Socialist-Revolutionaries. [See: *Grazhdanskaya Voina i Voennaya Interventsiya v SSSR, Entsiklopediya*, The Civil War and the Military Intervention in the USSR, An Encyclopedia, Ed.-in-chief S.S. Khromov, (Moscow: Sovetskaya Entsiklopediya, 1983), 200.]

5. The text of this speech is printed in General A. I. Denikin, *Ocherki Russkoy Smuty*, (Essays on Russia's Discord), vol. IV: *Vooruzhennye Sily Yuga Rossii* (The Armed Forces of the South of Russia) (Berlin: Knigoizdatel'stvo "Slovo", 1925): 45–48.

6. The text of this telegram is printed in Denikan, *Ocherki*, 210.

7. ———, 211; author's emphasis.

8. ———, 215, footnote 2.

9. The full text of this document is reprinted in the fifth volume of Denikin's *Ocherki*, 280–81.

10. ———, 280. The first four points are to be found, in a somewhat different English rendition, also in General Baron Peter N. Wrangel, *Always with Honor*, with a Foreword by Herbert Hoover (New York: Robert Speller & Sons, 1957), 120.

11. *Vospominaniya Generala Barona P. N. Vrangelya, kn. V i VI Belogo Dela: Letopis' Beloy Bor'by; Materialy, sobrannye i razrabotannye Baronom P. N. Vrangelem, Gertsogom G. N. Leikhtenbergskim i Svetleyshym Knyazem A. P. Livenom* (Memoirs of General Baron P. N. Wrangel, Vols. V & VI of the White Cause: The Chronicle of the White Struggle; Materials collected and elaborated by Baron P. N. Wrangel, Duke G. N. Leikhtenberg and the Lightest Prince A. P. Liven) (Berlin, 1928); 2nd ed. in one volume (Frankfurt/ Main: Posev, 1969), 76. The word "Master" (*Khozyain*) in the "Appeal" was spaced out. This enabled the Left to accuse Wrangel that by that word he meant a czar, and the Right—that he meant himself, as a supreme ruler. Both interpretations were wrong: as it is clear from the text of the "Appeal" and of the accompanying order, Wrangel spoke of the master that the Russian people will elect and inaugurate—as a result of a free expression of the people's will. Thus, the Russian people itself was considered to be the master of its own destiny. Later, Wrangel returned to this problem in an important interview, having the character of a political declaration. The interview was given to N. N. Chebyshev, representing the newspaper *Velikaya Rossiia* (Great Russia), on July 5 (unless both dates are indicated, in his memoirs, Wrangel uses the old style, which was in existence in southern Russia during the Civil War). Wrangel explained: " 'The Master' is the Russian people itself. As it desires, so also the country must be organized. If it wants to have a Monarch, Russia will be a Monarchy. If it recognizes as useful for itself a Republic, there will be a Republic. (. . .) My personal tastes have no importance at all. From the moment I accepted authority, I gave up, in my official activities, my personal inclinations to the one or the other regime. I unquestioningly submit to the voice of the Russian land" (Wrangel *Vospom-*

inaniya, 123). In addition to the question of monarchy and republic, Wrangel dealt in this interview with three other important questions: his general purpose, the Jewish question, and Russia and Europe. He defined his purpose as struggle for freedom, against Bolshevik despotism, reaction, and enslavement. Recognizing a growth of anti-Jewish feelings among the masses, Wrangel declared: "Any pogrom-movement, any agitation in this direction I consider a State calamity and will fight it with all the means at my disposal," (Wrangel, *Vosposmaniya*, 124; as Wrangel mentioned earlier, on p. 122, when the monarchist newspaper, *Russkaya Pravda*, /Russian Truth/, published in Sevastopol, printed a number of articles having a pogromist character, he reprimanded the censor and closed down the newspaper). With regard to Russia and Europe, Wrangel said that his greatest desire was to end the Civil War in Russia, but until a regime based on law, guarantees of personal and economic rights, and respect for international agreements is established in Russia, Europe will never know real peace and normal economic and international relations. It is here that the importance of the White movement lies: "The cause of the Russian Army in Crimea is a great liberation movement. It is a sacred war for freedom and law." (Wrangel, *Vospominaniya*, 124).

12. ———, 92. This order (No. 3226), signed in Sevastopol on 20 May 1920, was published on the 25th, because of delays in the printing of the land-reform order.

13. ———, 108,109; the Russian text of Struve's letter, dated 7 (20) June 1920, is reprinted in its entirety on pp. 107–9.

14. ———, 118; order No. 3372.

15. The English text of Admiral McCully's letter is reproduced in General Wrangel's *Vospominaniya* on pp. 165–66, followed by a Russian translation, pp. 166–67. (In both editions of Wrangel's memoirs, the Russian and the English, i.e., *Vospominaniya* and *Always with Honor*, N. A. McCully's last name is spelled as MacCully; in the Russian text it is also hyphenated: Mac-Cully.)

16. ———, 168–69; the answer, dated 24 August (6 September) 1920, is given in Russian.

17. Quoted in V. Davatts, *Gody: Ocherki pyatiletney bor'by*, (The Years: Essays on the Five-Year Struggle) (Belgrade: *Russkaya Tipografiya*, 1926), 61. While writing his book Davatts had Wrangel's permission to use the general's archives and thus had access to materials both generally available and confidential.

18. ———, 62.

19. ———, 101. Nikolay Nikolaevich's letter is dated 7 (20) October 1924; Mariya Fedorovna's to him, 21 September (4 October), 1924.

20. Order No. 82, signed by Wrangel on 8 September 1923.

21. Georgy Meier, "*Vozrozhdenie* i Belaya ideya, (K tridsatiletiyu so dnya osnovaniya *Vozrozhdeniya*)" (*Vozrozhdenie* and the White Idea /To the thirteenth anniversary from the day of *Vozrozhdeniya*'s foundation/), *Vozrozhdenie*, No. 42 (Paris, June 1955), 7. Meier's study, published first in three consecutive issues of the review in 1955 (No. 42, 5–41; No. 43, 61–86;

No. 44, 79–107), was later included in his book *U istokov revolyutsii*, (At the Sources of the Revolution), (Frankfurt/Main: Posev, 1971), 121–242.

22. *Vozrozhdenie*, No. 42, 7.

23. See, among others, N. Poltoratzky, *P. B. Struve kak politicheskyi myslitel'*, (London, Canada: Zarya, 1981), (P. B. Struve as Political Thinker), especially Section IV, "Leont'evets ili chicherinets?" (Leontevite or Chicherinite?"). 33–40, G. Meier's statement that, while in emigration, a "meeting-blending" of Struve's and Leont'ev's views took place (Denikin, Ocherki, 10: "Ideynaya vstrecha-sliyanie Struve s Leont'evym . . ." /The meeting of ideas—the merger of Struve with Leont'ev/), is, in this form, untenable.

24. Quoted from Meier, *Vozrozhdenie*, 27.

25. See Polkovnik V. V. Pozdniakov, *Andrei Andreevich Vlasov* (Syracuse, N.Y., 1973), cf., 50. Colonel Pozdniakov was General Vlasov's operative adjutant.

26. The Russian text used here is the one to be found in Pozdniakov; Vlasov, 52–53. Pozdniakov, in his turn, used as his source M. Pershin's book *Pravda o bol'shevizme*, (The Truth About Bolshevism), published by the Courses for Propagandists of *ROA* (Vlasov's *Russkaya Osvoboditel'naya Armiya*, Russian Liberation Army), in Dabendorf near Berlin, in 1943.

27. The Russian text of the manifesto used here is from Pozdniakov, Vlasov, 125–33. The quotation is from p. 129. (Pozdniakov's original source was *KONR*'s newspaper *Volya Naroda*, (The Will of the People), No. 1, 15 November 1944, 1.)

28. ———, 129–130.

29. ———, 130, 131.

30. See Yu. Pis'mennyi, "Ob odnom voprose, svyazannom s manifestom," (On One Question Related to the Manifesto), in M. V. Shatov, *Materialy i dokumenty osvoboditel'nogo dvizheniya narodov Rossii v gody Vtoroy mirovoy voyny (1941–1945), Trudy Arkhiva ROA v N'iu-Yorke, Tom Vtoroy, 2* (New York: Vseslavianskoe Izdatel'stvo, 1966), 151–54. (Original source: *Vlasovets*, No. 3, 1950)

31. The quotations here are from B. Dvinov, *Vlasovskoe dvizhenie v svete dokumentov (S prilozheniem sekretnykh dokumentov)*, (The Vlasovite Movement in the Light of Documents /with the Addition of Secret Documents/) (New York, 1950), 121. Dvinov, an enemy of the Vlasov movement, translated the German text into Russian. Although the text here is a retranslation on my part, the ideas expressed in the secret German document are so unmistakably definite, that distortion due to translation and retranslation is hardly possible.

32. Professor I. A. Il'in, *Nashi Zadachi: Stat'i 1948–1954 gg.* (Our Tasks: Articles 1948–1954), in two vols. (Paris: Izdanie Russkogo Obshche-Voinskogo Soyuza, 1956). The quotation above is from I, 13. Not being able to go into greater detail for lack of space here, I am referring interested readers to three of my own studies of Il'in: *I. A. Il'in i polemika vokrug ego idei o soprotivlenii zlu siloy*, (I. A. Il'in and the Polemics Around His Idea on Resisting Evil by Force), (London, Canada: Izdatel'stvo "Zaria", 1975); *Monarkhiya i respublika v vospriyatii I. A. Il'ina*, (Monarchy and Republic in Il'in's Perception)

(New York: Sodruzhestvo, 1979); and "Ivan Aleksandrovich Il'in: K Stoletiyu so dnya rozhdeniya, 1883–1983," (Ivan Aleksandrovich Il'in: To the Hundredth Anniversary of His Birth, 1883–1983), *Russkoe Vozrozhdenie*, 6, No. 24 (New York, 1983), 38–109.

33. I am using here the Russian text of the "Platform" as reprinted in *Rossiyskiy demokrat*, (The Russian Democrat) No. 2 (27) (New York, 1957): 62–64. The "Platform" was published initially in *Rossiyskiy demokrat*, No. 2 (18) (Paris, 1949).

34. N. Tsurikov, "Narodopravstvo ili svoboda?" (Rule of the People or Freedom?), *Vozrozhdenie*, No. 5 (September–October 1949), 123–27; Iv. Kheraskov, "Demokratiya—svoboda" (Democracy—Freedom), Vozrozhdenie, 127–34. Kheraskov's words are from p. 134.

35. The five non-Russian political organizations were: The Georgian National Council, The Committee of the Azerbaijan National Association, The Association of Armenian Fighters for Freedom, The North-Caucasian National Association, and The Turkmenistan National-Liberation Committee TYuRKELI.

36. The "Appeal" ("Obrashchenie k zarubezhnoy obshchestvennosti") was published in, among others, *Rossiyskiy demokrat*, No. 3 (24) (1953), 3–5.

37. The eight non-Russian political organizations were: The Belorussian Democratic Association, The Georgian Democratic Union, The Kalmyk Committee for Struggle against Bolshevism, The Crimean-Tatar Anti-Bolshevik Association, The Association of Armenian Fighters for Freedom, The Association of Ukrainian Federalists-Democrats, The Ukrainian Liberation Movement, and the Tatar-Bashkir Committee.

38. *Rossiyskiy demokrat*, No. 2 (26) (1954), 3. In the text the words "the united family of the peoples of Russia" were printed in boldface and spaced out.

39. Earlier, at the August plenary session of the revitalized KTsAB, the North-Caucasian National Association (SKANO) was admitted conditionally. Like SKANO, two other organizations, the Turkmenistan National-Liberation Committee TYuRKELI and the Azerbaijan National Association, were also in a state of turmoil as a result of their leaders finding themselves apparently outvoted by the membership, which favored the Mel'gunov political line.

40. *Posev*, No. 11 (1318) (November 1983), 63; No. 11 (1330) (November 1984), 52; No. 5 (1386) (May 1985), 90, etc..

41. See A. Solzhenitsyn, "Nashi plyuralisty," (Our Pluralists), *Vestnik RKhD*, (The RKhD Messenger), No. 139 (Paris, II-1983), 133–60.

In addition to his unique artistic and publicistic contribution, Solzhenitsyn's achievements include: 1) the foundation of the All-Russian Library of Memoirs; 2) Research Studies on Recent Russian History under his editorship; and 3) *From Under the Rubble*, a collection of essays by Alexander Solzhenitsyn, Mikhail Agursky, A. B., Evgeny Barabanov, Vadim Borisov, F. Korsakov, and Igor Shafarevich; translated into English by A. M. Brock, Milada Haigh, Marita Sapiets, Hilary Sternberg, and Harry Willetts under the direction of Michael Scammell, with an introduction by Max Hayward (Boston-

Toronto: Little, Brown and Company, 1975; the original Russian edition was published by YMCA-Press in Paris, in 1974). Both the title and the contents of this collection of essays connect it with two previous very important Russian collections of essays, *Vekhi*, (Landmarks, 1909) and *Iz Glubiny* (De Profundis, 1918). On these collections, see, among others, two of my articles: "The 'Vekhi' Dispute and the Significance of 'Vekhi,' " *Canadian Slavonic Papers*, 9, No. 1 (Spring 1967), 86–106, and "Sbornik 'Iz Glubiny' i ego znachenie," (Collection *De Profundis* and Its Significance), *Iz Glubiny: Sbornik statei o russkoy revoliutsii*, (*De Profundis*: A Collection of Articles on the Russian Revolution), 2nd ed., with introductory articles by N. Poltoratzky and N. Struve (Paris: YMCA Press, 1967), ix–xxii.

42. In my discussion of *VSKhSON*, I am using the Russian texts from John B. Dunlop, ed.: *Vserossiyskiy Sotsial-Khristianskiy Soyuz Osvobozhdeniya Naroda, VSKhSON: Programma, Sud, V tiur' makh i lageryakh*, (Paris: YMCA Press, 1975). There is also an English edition: John B. Dunlop, *The New Russian Revolutionaries* (Belmont, Mass.: Nordland Publishing Co., 1976). In the Russian edition, *VSKhSON*, the text of the "Program" is on pp. 31–79, i.e., it consists of almost 50 pages.

43. *Khronika tekushchikh sobytiy*, (The Chronicle of Current Events), No. 1 (April 30, 1968), and *Posev*, Special Edition No. 1 (1969), quoted in Dunlop's *VSKhSON* on p. 85.

44. On Berdiaev and the problems connected with his ideas, see, among others, my book, *Berdyaev i Rossiya (Filosofiya istorii Rossii u N. A. Berdyaeva)*, (Berdyaev and Russia/The Philosophy of the Russian History in Berdyeav's Works/) (New York: Obshchestvo Druzey Russkoy Kul'tury, 1967), and my article "The Russian Idea of Berdiaev", *The Russian Review*, 21, No. 2 (April 1962), 121–36.

45. This was Osipov's second arrest; for his earlier *samizdat* activities, he was imprisoned first from 1961 to 1968.

46. VI. Osipov's research on VSKhSON resulted in a study which contained this very definition: "Berdyaevskiy kruzhok v Leningrade," (The Berdyaev Circle in Leningrad) (January, 1972). The text was later included in his book *Tri otnosheniya k rodine*, (Three Attitudes to the Motherland) (Frankfurt/Main: Posev, 1978).

47. J. B. Dunlop, *VSKhSON*, 61.

48. See "Chto proiskhodit v strane. Rasskazyvaet Georgy Vladimov," (What is Going on in the Country. The Talk by Georgy Vladimov), *Posev*, No. 7 (1314), (July 1983), 22–29. The second part of the interview was published under a somewhat different title: "KGB protiv literatury. Rasskazyvaet Georgii Vladimov," (The KGB Against Literature. The Talk by Georgy Vladimov), *Posev*, No. 8 (1315), (August 1983), 37–43. The interview was conducted on 19–20, July 1983. In the same month another interview was published in the Paris-based *Russkaya Mysl'*, (Russian Thought), " 'Ot yunosheskoy obidy, cherez period illyuziy, k novomu ponimaniyu, chto my zhivem v strane nesvobody . . .' Interv'iu s Georgiem Vladimovym vedet

Vladimir Rybakov" (From a Youthful Offense, Through a Period of Illusions, to the New Understanding that We Live in a Country of Unfreedom. An Interview with Georgy Vladimov conducted by Vladimir Rybakov), *Russkaya mysl'*, No. 3472, (7 July 1983), 13. The quotations are from *Posev*, No. 7, 27, 28.

49. ———, 27. In his interview to *Russkaya mysl'* Vladimov said that Fedorchuk, unquestionably, was repeating the words of his boss Andropov. As a result of this new policy, some representatives of "the Russian party" were pinned to the ground. Vladimov interprets the severe sentence given to the writer Leonid Borodin as a warning to others: "a mortally ill man, who would hardly last there three years, was given ten years of special regime. They (the Communist authorities) needed to thunderstrike all, to frighten all"; and Borodin was so severely punished "not so much because of religion, as for the Russian idea."

50. *Posev*, No. 7, 27.

51. The subject of forced repatriation has been dealt with in many articles and books. Among the latter the following should be singled out: B. M. Kuznetsov, *V ugodu Stalinu, Gody 1945–1946*, (Pleasing Stalin. The Years 1945–1946), 3 vols. (New York: "Voennyi Vestnik"; a condensed one-volume edition was published later by Izdatel'stvo SBONR, Canada, 1968); General V. G. Naumenko, *Velikoe predatel'stvo: Vydacha kazakov v Lintse i drugikh mestakh (1945–1947)*, (The Great Betrayal: The Delivery of the Cossacks in Linz and Other Places /1945–1947/), 2 vols. (New York: Vseslavyanskoe Izdatel'stvo; I, 1962; II, 1970); Julius Epstein, *Operation Keelhaul: The Story of Forced Repatriation from 1944 to the Present*, Introduction by Bertram D. Wolfe (Old Greenwich, Connecticut: The Devin-Adair Co., 1973); Nicholas Bethell, *The Last Secret: The Delivery to Stalin of Over Two Million Russians by Britain and the United States*, Introduction by Hugh Trevor-Roper (New York: Basic Books, 1974); Nikolai Tolstoy, *The Secret Betrayal* (New York: Charles Scribner's Sons, 1977; the British ed. was published, under the title *Victims of Yalta*, by (Hodder and Stoughton, London-Sydney-Aukland-Toronto, 1977).

52. To be sure, representatives of the American Committee denied that this has been, indeed, their policy. As one of its members wrote at the time, "The Committee has taken its stand on the middle ground of two principles: self-determination for all peoples in the Soviet Union and no 'predetermination' of their political status or frontiers." (William Henry Chamberlin, "Emigré Anti-Soviet Enterprises and Splits," *The Russian Review*, 13, No. 2, (April 1954): 96). But the results speak for themselves. There is no political center coordinating the anti-Communist activities with any respectable Russian participation—because of what was interpreted as pro-separatist American actions. Neither are the two other initiatives of the American Committee (now defunct) in any commendable state. The Research Institute has been closed down altogether, and Radio Liberty, which, since its inception, has been facing one crisis after another, is in continuously poor political health.

53. J. B. Dunlop, *The Faces of Contemporary Russian Nationalism*, 276–90. The numbering of the recommendations is mine, not the author's.

54. The law lists the following nations: "Poland, Hungary, Lithuania, Ukraine, Czechoslovakia, Latvia, Estonia, White Ruthenia, Rumania, East Germany, Bulgaria, mainland China, Armenia, Azerbaijan, Georgia, North Korea, Albania, Idel-Ural, Tibet, Cossackia, Turkestan, North Vietnam, and others" (*United States Statutes at Large*, Containing the Laws and Concurrent Resolutions Enacted During the First Session of the Eighty-Sixth Congress of the United States of America, 1959, and Proclamations, vol. 73, in one part (Washington: GPO, 1960): 212.

55. The adoption of the law did not remain without objection. Thus, "A Statement on U.S. Public Law 86–90", dated 17 November 1960, and signed by 16 American scholars, was published in several organs of the press (I am using here the text of the "Statement" as it appeared in *The Russian Review*, 20, No. 1 (January, 1961), 97–98). The "Statement" pointed out that "The Public Law 86–90 calls in effect for the complete dismemberment of Russian territories according to an overall geographical pattern which closely resembles the one advanced in the past by Pan-German and Nazi invaders of Russia and of the Soviet Union for the aggressive purpose of their political subjugation and economic control." The "Statement" ended with a call "for an official review by the U.S. Congress of the erroneous premises of P. L. 86–90, and for its repeal." The "Statement" was signed by the following American scholars: Arthur E. Adams, Oswald P. Backus, III, Robert P. Browder, Robert F. Byrnes, Harold H. Fisher, Andrew Lossky, Fred Warner Neal, Nikolai P. Poltoratzky, Nicholas V. Riasanovsky, Gleb Struve, Edward C. Thaden, N. S. Timasheff, S. P. Timoshenko, D.W. Treadgold, Gregory P. Tschebotarioff, and Serge A. Zenkovsky. The "Statement" was published a quarter of a century ago. The "Law" is still in effect.

7

Soviet Communism and Russian Nationalism: Amalgamation or Conflict?

MIKHAIL AGURSKY

Any reasonable observer might admit pessimistically that the actual character of international relations is determined not by the real nature and intentions of states, and often even not by their real power, but by their images, which may differ considerably from reality. A country *"an sich"* may be completely opaque both as a result of misunderstanding and of deliberate misinformation on its part. Pragmatic, reasonable, and even benign states are often viewed as exploiters and aggressors, while genuine aggressors are often regarded as peace-loving altruists.

Unfortunately, such is the nature of things, and we must honestly own to the limits of our knowledge, those limits which have long been stressed by neo-Kantian critics of historical knowledge.[1]

Essentially, wrong perceptions of international affairs and of their actors, do not differ greatly from wrong perceptions of behavior on the personal level. It goes without saying that a personality can produce completely different impressions on various people, and there may be no consensus among close acquaintances concerning both the actual behavior and the motivation of almost any personality in their circle. Almost any person may inspire genuine attraction and violent hatred among his acquaintances;

nations and states as collective entities enjoy the same dubious privilege. They are always controversial.

There is no doubt that the Soviet Union is in this respect the most enigmatic country in the world, and Winston Churchill's remark to this effect is still applicable. This quality of the Soviet Union is due both to the natural limits of our knowledge and also to her active policy of disinformation in which huge resources are invested.

One of the most obscure problems, which evokes heated debate, is whether Soviet domestic and international behavior is motivated and regulated by the official, self-declared Communist ideology, or whether it is largely nonideological, statist, and nationalist? This problem is difficult not only for foreign observers, but probably also for Soviet statesmen themselves, due to the lack of a clear identity, and also very often due to their own self-deception.

The very fact that a man or a state declares himself or itself as a standard-bearer of some kind is not at all decisive—for example, the claim of Byzantium or of the Hapsburg monarchy to embody the former Roman Empire, or the claim of American Blacks in the Israeli town of Dimona, who came to this place from Chicago, to be the only authentic sons of Abraham.

It is quite understandable that the majority of foreign observers, academics and politicians, would like to grasp first and foremost the background of Soviet foreign policy, because of the enormous destructive impact exercised by the Soviet Union on international affairs. For a long time this country, which has become a real global power, has been provoking permanent international tensions, escalating the arms race, kindling local wars, instigating international terrorism, causing devastation of world natural resources by criminal mismanagement in all countries which fell under the Soviet sphere of influence, including the USSR itself.

A former American ambassador to Moscow, Foy Kohler, remarked in 1974 that "the Kremlin probably stands in the world as guilty of criminal negligence for the inefficiency of its agriculture in a world of mounting population and mounting hunger."[2] The violation of ecology by the USSR has also become a real international danger.[3]

Morton Schwartz asks the crucial question: "Of the numerous uncertainties surrounding the foreign policy of the USSR, few have caused greater confusion than the relationship of ideology to foreign policy. If we take them at their own word, we must begin by believing that the Soviet leaders are Marxist-Leninist. Does this really matter? Does official doctrine actually shape Soviet policy, or is it mere scholastic ideology whose only real function is to provide the slogans which decorate public buildings and party posters?"[4]

Indeed, the relationship between Communist ideology and Russian nationalism (as the alternative legitimacy of the Soviet system) is an old issue of concern to Western observers. It is evidently not a purely academic problem, since it has extremely important political implications in the Western decision-making political process.

Is Soviet aggressive imperialism conditioned by Communist ideology (as too many people believe) or is it conditioned by the internal dynamics of the giant Russian superstate simply inherited by its Communist successor?

Here we must have recourse to some samples of the variety of opinions on this subject in the West, not in order to use *ad hominem* arguments relying on most eloquent opinions, but in order to provide a fresh view of the real scope of the controversy which makes the Western decision-making process so difficult.

* * *

The ideological background of the Soviet system has been stressed by many Western scholars and politicians, and I would like to refer first of all to such authorities as Gustav Wetter,[5] Alain Besançon,[6] Luciano Pellicani,[7] Annie Kriegel.[8]* Alexander Nekritch and Michel Heller call the Soviet system "Utopia in power,"[9] which is equal to the comprehensive ideological qualification of the Soviet system.

A leading American diplomat and former ambassador to Moscow, Charles Bohlen, discussing de Gaulle's policy toward the Soviet Union, noticed that de Gaulle "realized that Soviet Russia was inherently a malignant power, but since he did not worry about the threat of Communist ideology he did not see the degree of danger that we did. He was mistaken. Fifty years from now he might be right. By then, I doubt if there will be any remnants of the Bolshevik theory left as guides to an active political belief. But now the ideology plays its part. . . . Once adopted, the Soviet ideology imposes obligations and leads to consequences that would not otherwise be present. De Gaulle never saw these truths."[10]

Those who believed in the ideological interpretation of the Soviet system dismissed the relevance of Russian nationalism for the Soviet Union, as did, for example, the German historian Georg von Rauch. According to him, "Stalinist patriotism is a multinational collective patriotism of a group of nations brought together through the strong universalist feeling of space and a common political ideology."[11] The so-called Soviet patriotism was for von Rauch "one of deliberate, pre-planned usage and manipulation of existing historical and popular-psychological premises, and is a further development of Marxism through adoption of additional elements."[12]

Since official Soviet self-identification is that of Marxism-Leninism, ide-

---

*I shall not mention various intellectuals and writers, such as Alexander Solzhenitsyn, who regard the Soviet system as ideological *par excellence*.

ological interpretations of the Soviet system look more or less self-inviting, regardless of how the Soviet system is estimated: positively or negatively.

* * *

However, not only Charles de Gaulle, but many observers, academics and politicians alike, try to interpret the Soviet system as non-ideological, with Marxism as only a cover, while the real driving force of the Soviet society is Russian nationalism.

Such an interpretation had already been explicitly suggested just after 1917 by many Russian intellectuals: pro- and anti-Bolshevik; as well as by many Western politicians. They all claimed that Communist ideology should not deceive anyone, that it was a new historical mask of that same Russian state, which was only taking advantage of an internationalist ideology as a successful instrument of the assertive Russian foreign policy, and also for internal cohesion.

The early historical development of this interpretation has been dealt with elsewhere by the present author,[13] and we shall quote here only a few later outstanding interpretations of the Soviet system seen as full-fledged Russian nationalism.

José Ortega-y-Gasset wrote in 1930: "In every instance of historical camouflage we have two realities superimposed: one genuine and substantial, underneath; the other apparent and accidental, on the surface. So, in Moscow, there is a screen of European ideas—Marxism—thought out in Europe in view of European realities and problems. . . . That Marxism should triumph in Russia, where there is no industry, would be the greatest contradiction that Marxism could undergo. But there is no such contradiction, for there is no such triumph. Russia is Marxist more or less as the Germans of the Holy Empire were Romans. . . . I am waiting for the book in which Stalin's Marxism will appear translated into Russian history. For it is this which is Russia's strength, what it has of Russian, not what it has of Communist."[14]

In 1931 Carlton Hayes treated the Soviet system as demonstrating what he called the "integral nationalism of Russian Bolsheviks." He wrote: "One may also note the development of the Bolshevists in Russia who, beginning as economic and social reformers, with loud protestations against militarism, imperialism and nationalism, soon discovered . . . that the world is not equally prepared for their messianic altruism, and have ended by exalting a peculiarly integral nationalism in the USSR—living to themselves alone, serving their own interests, brandishing a sword, destroying democracy and liberty, and worshipping at the shrines of their dictators that are now their national heroes. . . . The extreme nationalism of the Russian Bolshevists is likely to be remembered when the details of their economic experiments shall have been forgotten."[15]

The German historian Walther Biehahn, challenging the official Nazi ideological interpretation of Soviet society, claimed in 1934: "It is not the Marxist form that determines Bolshevik policy, but the Russian content."[16] The British Royal Institute of International Affairs, in 1939, noted the rise of Russian nationalism in the USSR, and the war against Nazi Germany brought new fuel for this interpretation, which survived World War II.[17]

Maurice Hindus, an American journalist who lived in the USSR for a long time and who moved from a stance of uncritical sympathy with the USSR to that of violent criticism of the USSR, wrote just after Stalin's death: "I can conceive of no more hopeless task than to interpret the Bolshevik revolution, especially since Stalin's rise to power, as either Marxist or international. . . . Though Lenin was a Marxist, Marxism did not make the Bolshevik revolution. . . . Whatever the ideological seeds Stalin shook out of his Marxism, they fell on Russian soil and were nurtured by a Russian climate . . ."[18]

Zbigniew Brzezinski, a leading American expert in Soviet studies and President Carter's national security adviser, wrote: "Stalin consummated the marriage of Marxism-Leninism and Soviet (particularly Russian) nationalism. The increasing stress on Great Russia's state traditions, on frontiers, on national aspirations, and on a civilizing mission vis-à-vis the non-Russian Soviet nations, went hand in hand with the physical transformation of the CPSU from one dominated by a rather mixed lot of cosmopolitan and internationally oriented intellectuals of Russian, Jewish, Polish, Baltic or Caucasian origins, into a party dominated primarily by Russian (and, to some extent, Ukrainian) peasants turned into party apparatchiks . . ."[19]

A leading American historian, Robert Tucker, who served in the American embassy in Moscow, claimed that "Communism as a culture underwent a definite Russification from an early time,"[20] and he treated it as a Russian national communism. This was repeated by the British Soviet expert, Vladimir Kusin, who said: "That Soviet Communism is National Communism there can be no doubt. . . . Communism, having found the internationalism of its doctrine impractible, lifted Russia onto the pedestal of supreme nationalism."[21]

In 1974, a group of American former diplomats and journalists who had spent some time in the USSR, participated in a roundtable discussion of the Soviet system, which took place in Miami. The highlights suggested to the roundtable clearly stress the inherent Russian nationalism of the Soviet system: "Expansionism appears inherent in the Soviet system, as well as one of the strongest heritages from the Russian past. . . . A given action may be part of the world revolutionary movement or an expression of the nationalist ambition of the Russian state, very often a combination of both."[22]

Scholar-diplomat and American ambassador to Moscow in 1952, George Kennan, whose influence on American Soviet studies should not be underestimated, said during this roundtable discussion that "if there is any enthusiasm for the regime in its undertakings vis-à-vis the outside world . . . such enthusiasm today is much more of an old-fashioned, patriotic nationalist nature than it is of an ideological nature."[23]

Many discussions emerged around the well-known ambivalent slogan, Soviet patriotism, introduced officially in 1934. Many observers treated it as a symbolic expression of assertive Russian nationalism. For example, the German historian, Günter Stökl, said in 1960 that "fundamentally Soviet Patriotism is nothing other than an expression of the relationship of a politically conscious nation to its national state. The Soviet nation means first and foremost the Russian nation, although at the moment the latter is neither the only Soviet nation nor even the homogeneous Soviet nation."[24]

The lack of clarity concerning the relationship between Communist ideology and Russian nationalism can be seen in too many cases, but one particular case is especially obvious: the case of the Russian emigrant scholar, Nikolai Timasheff, who hesitated between one extreme and another. In 1946 he solemnly declared that there was a "great retreat" of the Soviet system from Communist ideology to peaceful Russian nationalism. "After 1928," he said, "the internationalism of Russian Communists was no longer as it had been; perhaps it could be termed ambivalent."[25] He continued: "It was only natural that the change in the international policy of the Soviets and the reversal of the trend, from internationalism to nationalism within the Soviet Union was accompanied by a significant reversal of the trend in the interethnic policy . . ."[26] He said, too, that "in turning nationalist once more, Russia proved that in the very depths of her national soul she had never abandoned her historical way, which on the surface seemed lost in 1917."[27]

However, within a few years Timasheff had to reconsider his previous views, and accordingly, in 1953, he claimed that Soviet aggressive behavior was motivated by Communist ideology, not by Russian "imperialism." He attacked "the men in the Kremlin as the legitimate successors of those who in 1917 achieved power over Russia in the name of Communism." Unable to ignore nationalist propaganda in the Soviet media, Timasheff explained it away by saying that "the ultra-nationalism of the present day is much more a governmental affair than a current in public opinion."[28] As late as 1962 Timasheff spoke of the Soviet Union as an "ideocracy."[29]

Taking up views probably already in existence, Morton Schwartz, quoted previously, claimed in his excellent (but not faultless) exposition of the domestic factors in Soviet foreign policy, that Communist ideology played no significant role in Soviet foreign policy, and was used mostly for internal cohesion. "Cynical manipulations of doctrine," Schwartz said, "leads inevitably to the conclusion that Marxism-Leninism does not determine Soviet politics but functions merely to rationalize decisions made by the Soviet government on other grounds. . . . Ideology is less a fountainhead of policy than a system of propaganda. . . . Although still wedded to a revolutionary doctrine, the Soviet authorities see their international responsibilities in largely traditional terms. . . . The focus today is on national interest, traditionally conceived; on power, security and prestige."[30]

* * *

We can now see that both points of view are defended with vigor, sophistication and confidence, which may tend to discomfit the innocent bystander. Let us now attempt to make our analysis, keeping in mind the foregoing, mostly for the purpose of orientation. And to start, we should ask first of all: What is Communist ideology and what is Russian nationalism? and: Which parts of Communist ideology and which aspects of Russian nationalism are indeed relevant to Soviet reality?

There is no doubt that at least some parts of Communist ideology play an enormous role in not only the USSR, but also in any country which declares itself Communist; and this is not only a matter of self-identification.

The comparative approach to various Communist societies demonstrates clearly that "a communist world does exist . . . as a set of reference groups, a source of moral and intellectual support for authority, and a source of economic and technological support—and increasingly as a group whose members compete among themselves and may even fight each other in the name of truth versus heresy."[31] Robert Tucker also commented that "Communism . . . is not inherently a local phenomenon but a form of society or civilization than can spread and take root in virtually every part of the globe where circumstances are propitious."[32]

Indeed, the existence of such virtually independent countries as Albania, Yugoslavia, China, Vietnam, or strong Communist parties in the Western world, indicates that there is something that can safely be called communism. But it would be a grave mistake to regard communism only as a set of philosophical or social ideas which are pursued for their own sake. There is no doubt that communism as a pure ideological phenomenon did exist in the USSR in its early period; and it still exists today, mostly among Communist intellectuals in the non-Communist world. However, as a distinct phenomenon, communism has long since become transformed into a political philosophy which teaches first of all how, by using or even by provoking a crisis and capitalizing on the ensuing widespread popular frustration, a political minority (even a minute political group) can achieve and maintain absolute power against the will of the whole nation. According to that philosophy this is done not simply by the means of blunt, outdated military dictatorship and terror, but chiefly by imposing on the nation such social changes that make almost any resistance against the new system impractical, and thus ensure the system's impregnability. Hence, the social changes pursued by the Communists are not an end in themselves, but primarily a prerequisite for assuring power to the above-mentioned political minority. The original Communist ideology, as a system of personal beliefs, therefore becomes increasingly irrelevant, and Communist slogans calling for "social justice," "humanism" and "internationalism" form a purely "declaratory ideology" necessary to disguise the true goals of power-seeking personalities and groups.

Yet, as a normative set, providing a quasi-religious system of beliefs, Communist ideology plays an extremely important role in the mobilization of support for Communist rule during the period of Communist seizure of power and in the early stages of consolidation of that power. In that sense, communism is a genuine "preparatory-for-transition" ideology which later can be also successfully used as the source of legitimation of an established and routinely entrenched Communist system. The so-called "Utopia" therefore is serving only as a transient ideological appeal which as such will be abandoned after the power of the new Communist system has been properly consolidated.

However, even in the initial stage this appeal is insufficient to attract substantial popular support for Communist rule. Therefore even the most idealistically minded Communists, in order to seize and entrench themselves in power, have to use ruthless repression amounting to wholesale terror. In that sense, as Alexander Shtromas has remarked, the Soviet state from its outset was "bound to be a clique state—a state whose only purpose is to enhance and promote at all costs the interests and goals of the small, ideologically zealous ruling clique against those of the people at large. In this respect it is of secondary importance whether, as in the beginning, this ruling clique consists of idealistic believers in a higher and better order of things, which they are determined to bring about against all odds by a revolutionary (e.g., terrorist) action, or of cynical opportunists who do not believe in any ideals at all but who, in order to survive, do everything they can to perpetuate the single ideology and teleology of the power they have inherited. The clique nature of this state remains exactly the same at all times and so remain also its basic policies and activities."[33]

In essence, communism has become a very attractive and efficient philosophy of power, the philosophy of a power-oriented and power-centered group *par excellence.*

It goes without saying that this philosophy has integrated some major elements of Marxist dogma, which obscure the frontiers between the pure philosophy of power and authentic Marxism. Moreover, the very fact that Russian Bolsheviks came to power in 1917 under Marxist slogans, made these slogans extremely attractive for authoritarian personalities who seek to achieve political power by violently destroying the existing political system.

There are several basic elements of Communist ideology which were introduced by Russian bolshevism and accepted by other Communist systems, and these are not necessarily Marxist:

1. The strict centralization of the economy which renders all opposition to the new system utterly helpless, and even hopeless, due to lack of resources. Therefore, any potential Communist ruler will perform such a centralization not in order to bring about "utopian" social changes but to deprive the opposition of any resources.
2. The strict suppression of all political freedom and of the free press under the pretext that the harsh reality of class struggle makes it necessary; the first victims of such suppression usually are anti-Communist socialists (in Russia these were the Mensheviks, Social Revolutionaries and Anarchists) and Communist dissidents themselves (e.g., the Trotskyists in Spain).
3. The creation of the one-party system which, in fact, is soon replaced by one-person rule or by the rule of a small clique, while the party is reduced merely to an administrative body in the service of that leader or that clique.
4. The centralization of the economy does not mean that a planned economy has been established, but rather that the national economy has been transformed into a system of military mobilization of a society which, having been deprived of the possibility of a normal economic life, has had to concentrate its resources for the achievement of certain military and strategic goals (and not all of them simultaneously). Such an "economy of mobilization" that Soviet Russia introduced at the time of the Civil War by simply aping the organization of the German military economy during World War I, has nothing to do with a normal, "harmonious" economic system. The first to notice this was Karl Kautsky, who at the end of the 1920s completely dismissed all the ambitious claims about the Soviet society having established a planned economy.[34] By the way, even in the sphere of mobilization of the economy, the

Soviet system has demonstrated its inferiority. The "capitalist" American war economy was incomparably more efficient, supplying as it did military equipment, strategic resources, and food to the entire anti-Nazi world. The Soviet economy survived the war due only to enormous American supplies. Amitai Etzioni later introduced the concept of "mobilization society" and in our opinion, this is the best definition of the Communist economy.[35]

5. Political manipulation of arts and literature in order to consolidate the political power of the ruling clique.
6. Active rejection of any philosophy or religion which may challenge Communist rule, this notwithstanding the fact that religion could sometimes be used in its more passive form as an auxiliary to the political legitimacy of the ruling class.

Hence, however spiritually irrelevant it may be, the fundamentally "declaratory ideology" is politically extremely useful for any Communist régime since:

1. It is a highly respectable legitimization of the new oppressive rule.
2. It aids in the cohesion of multi-national or multi-ethnic Communist societies (the USSR, Yugoslavia, Albania, etc.)
3. It is a respectable legitimization of Soviet expansion.
4. It is a source of mobilization of support for achieving and consolidating power.

It is clear, therefore, that the declaratory internationalist and social-justice oriented Communist ideology is in full contradiction with the actual philosophy of power which dominates the Soviet political mind; every Communist society has, however, adapted to this contradiction. Any power-thirsty dictator is now aware that his rule will be much more stable, and even unchallenged if he declares himself a Marxist, nationalizes the economy, introduces one-party rule, and takes shelter under the Soviet political umbrella. The first such dictator to "convert" to communism on these premises was Fidel Castro, and his example has proved very attractive.

Such dictators introduce social changes not because of ideological commitments but as efficient means of power politics securing their tyrannical rule. It is well known that the international network which organizes pro-Soviet upheavals, never fully relies on committed Communists, seeing them as dangerous fanatics and troublemakers, and prefers to deal with power-seeking groups. Soviet defectors, such as Alexander Kaznacheev in Burma,[36] Vladimir Sakharov in Yemen and Egypt,[37] among others, have testified to this effect. This has also been the case in Ethiopia, Nicaragua, Mozambique, et al.

Some Western left-wing intellectuals believe that the Communist system in the USSR and in other Communist countries was the only feasible way to modernize and industrialize these nations.[38] It is harmful, wishful thinking; one can easily argue that the Soviet pattern of economy only disseminates backwardness and inefficiency. Potential dictators who are desirous of using the Communist model for their countries may well be aware of this, but they are less likely to care about it since their overriding consideration is the stability of their political power, not the economic progress in their countries.

One of the reasons for the relative stability of the Soviet political system is that since the Revolution, Bolshevik leaders, who as a tiny minority had to expand their very narrow base of power, were forced to appeal to the national sentiments of the dominant nationality, the Russians, representing themselves as the only authentic Russian national force struggling against sinister foreign intervention whose goal is to strip Russia of her national independence and enslave the Russian people. This was publicly declared by Lenin himself already in November 1918[39] and the idea was given free rein during the Russian-Polish war.[40] The Bolsheviks cynically played their national card by appealing to Russian nationalism for whom the only meaningful value was Russian state power. The Bolsheviks, with their universalist ambitions, could not make this appeal a part of official ideology but after consistent efforts their theoreticians succeeded in elaborating highly important political concepts which tied official internationalism to national appeals such as "Socialism in one country," "Soviet patriotism," and so on. These controversial concepts, which might be called "National Bolshevism," while ostensibly internationalist, had a second meaning directed only at Russians.

Edmund Demaitre noticed that, "The contradiction between the terms 'national' and 'communist' is of more than semantic significance, since it was the conflict between the universalistic international content of Communism and the specificity of the conditions in which it was implemented that determined the transfiguration of the Soviet Communist system into a political and ideological model that was to inspire all successive national-communist trends."[41] Soviet Russian nationalism has been very succinctly explained by the American diplomat and scholar, Frederick Barghoorn, who came to the conclusion that it was used in the USSR only because the regime was forced to do so in its search for a broader base of support.[42] "The Russian supremacy," he noted, "is used to support Kremlin policies which do not necessarily have the enthusiastic support of the Great Russian element within the Soviet Union. It is important to make this point strongly because it might be easy to conclude from some of the evidence examined here that Soviet Russification is a mere confirmation of pre-revolutionary Tsarist policy, or at least that it is a Russian nationalist policy. There is of course an element of continuity with the Tsarist régime, and there is also at least some reflection of Russian popular sentiment in the policy of the régime. The Soviet régime utilizes traditional and other elements of national culture if it is forced by circumstances, or if it is advantageous for it to cloak its policies in traditional or national guise."

We have seen that one must have a finely tuned approach to what is called Communist ideology. But the same approach must be used in relation to Russian nationalism in order to avoid misunderstandings. Russian nationalism is too broad an abstraction. In fact, it covers a variety of nationalisms: liberal and oppressive, racist and cultural, radical and conservative. These variations of nationalisms can be totally and mortally hostile to each other and their nominal common denominator (nationalism) cannot prevent that.

Eugene Kamenka made a very important contribution to the study of nationalism when he commented on a very important point: "Nationalism can be, and has been, democratic or authoritarian, forward-looking or backward-looking, socialist or reactionary. . . . Definitions, if they are useful at all, come at the end of an inquiry and not at the beginning."[43]

For example, John Plamenatz distinguished between "Western" and "Eastern" nationalism: "We have also the nationalism of peoples recently drawn into civilization, hitherto alien to them and whose ancestral cultures are not adapted to success and excellence by those cosmopolitan and increasingly dominant standards. This is the nationalism of peoples who feel the need to transform themselves, and in so doing to raise themselves . . . It is both imitative and hostile to the models it imitates, and is apt to be illiberal. . . . It has involved, in fact, two rejections, both of them ambivalent: rejection of the alien intruder and dominator who is nevertheless to be imitated and surpassed by his own standards, and rejection of ancestral ways which are seen as obstacles to progress and yet also cherished as marks of identity."[44]

Indeed, already before the Revolution, bolshevism had become a type of such an Eastern nationalism, and in this specific case might safely be called a continuation of the Radical Russian nationalism which had originated with Herzen and Bakunin. Herzen, for example, preached the conquest of the rotten West by young and barbaric Slavic hordes as a progressive revolutionary act which would bring about a new civilization. Bakunin appealed to the socialist and anarchic revolution essentially as to a Slavic national liberation movement. According to Bakunin only a socialist revolution would save Slavs from German colonization since the socialist world would be stateless and therefore the Germans would lose their deadly state power directed against the Slavs.[45]

Radical Russian nationalists hated the actual Russian nation as it was, seeing it as degraded and backward, and at the same time they were dreaming of making those degraded Russians not only equal to leading Western nations, but even surpassing them. With its strong antitraditional and anti-personalist background, this nationalism could even conceive of a physical extermination of those Russians who turned out to be unfit for the dreamed-of transfiguration and therefore represented only harmful ballast.

A tremendous boost for such a philosophy of human engineering was the amalgamation of Nietzscheanism and Marxism which infected many Russian left-wing radicals at the end of the nineteenth century and the beginning of the twentieth century. Though many of them personally opposed Lenin, for example in the framework of the group "*Vpered*" (Forward), they exercised an enormous impact on Soviet politics, ideology and culture after the revolution. Maxim Gorky, Alexander Bogdanov, Anatoly Lunacharsky, Mikhail Pokrovsky, Via Cheslav Menzhinsky, Dimitry Manuilsky, belonged to this group, whose so-called philosophy of collectivism was in fact the manifestation of Russian radical totalitarian nationalism.[46]

Though Lenin violently criticized this group for its empiriomonism,[47] a philosophical conception which was not the most important part of its general outlook, he largely shared other views of this group, and in 1915 himself claimed that there was no contradiction between the critical attitude to the actual state of one's nation and the ardent wish to reeducate it.[48]

If one can legitimately contest the extent of social "utopianism" in Bolshevism and regard it merely as a philosophy of power, one must nevertheless admit that the genuine Bolshevik wish to change the nature of the Russian people was definitely a utopian concept which cost the Russians so dearly.

It is interesting to note that such patterns of thought are not unknown in human history. There was the Divine "example" of the Flood, which exterminated the whole sinful body of humanity as unfit, except for Noah and his family. Biblical Jewish nationalism implied all kinds of mass reeducation—for example, that which was practised by Moses on his own people, the former slaves, whom he did not see as worthy of the Promised Land. The Hebrew prophets were always eloquent in their radical criticism of their own people, although they always dreamed of improving them. Ancient Jewish nationalism was never narcissistic.

Zionism, which emerged almost simultaneously with bolshevism, acted on the same premises, leveling devastating criticism at the Jewish people and trying to destroy their corrupted, traditional ways of life by building the "Alt-Neu" utopian land with entirely new and perfect people. However, the Zionist leaders never resorted to the physical extermination of their own people as the Bolsheviks did.

The most frightening example of Bolshevik genocidal practice was collectivization, which deliberately sacrificed many millions of Russian peasants—the harmful human ballast that was not fit for the radiant kingdom of the Third Rome. Scholars who studied Soviet collectivization ignored the extremely significant fact that the political philosophy of Russian peasant genocide was publicly suggested by Gorky in 1922 and was implemented six years later by Stalin, just after Gorky's triumphant return to Russia from self-imposed exile, to become one of Stalin's closest advisers for several years.

Gorky suggested, already before the Revolution, that there are two souls in the Russian people. One soul is Slavic, i.e., European, active, creative, dynamic. The second is Mongol, i.e., Oriental, passive, conservative, destructive. The Mongol soul is a genetic heritage of the Tatar-Mongol invasion, a harmful impact of Asia on Russia.

The Russian peasant was in his view a manifestation of this dreadful Oriental infection which could be cured only by a surgical operation and more precisely by amputation.[49]

The influence of Gorky on the Soviet system and ideology has never been fully understood and rightly evaluated but it was, in fact, he who was one of the founding fathers of the Soviet system, and his impact on that system might be ranked just after that of Lenin and Stalin. Gorky was also the most important Russian radical nationalist, and he became the main bridge linking pre-revolutionary radical Russia with the Bolshevik system. One of the central ideas of this radical nationalism was its pride in Bolshevik Russia so vividly expressed in the ambitious wish of making it into a new world center. Everything could be sacrificed to this national goal: traditional values, countless human lives. Radical Russian nationalism pointed at Peter the Great as the first Russian Bolshevik.[50]

As a result, a very dangerous amalgamation of Communist ideology and radical Russian nationalism emerged, where Communist ideology was regarded as a very valuable political philosophy which served first and foremost Russian national interests as they, the Bolsheviks, understood them. One can thus extend what was said by Barghoorn, about the Bolshevik leaders having to resort to Russian nationalism in order to extend their narrow popular support.

This triumph of Russian radical nationalism was, however, only a time bomb which undermined the very national existence of the Russians. The Russian people did not rise as a new phoenix from under the rubble of the old Russia, but on the contrary, they suffered a terrible, and probably irreversible, blow.

The Bolshevik leaders treated the Russian people itself as a natural resource which could always be replenished by simple reproduction.

Wars provoked by the new system, emigration of much of the population, genocide of peasants, political terror, starvation, extermination of millions of prisoners of war, and much more, undermined the demographic strength of the Russian population. Instead of the new utopian nation which impressed Gorky so much after 1928, the Russians suffered a terrible demographic blow, both quantitative and qualitative, which was clearly manifested only at the end of the 1960s.[51] The first reaction of the Soviet leadership to this new demographic situation was to forge, as quickly as possible, a new Soviet nation into which non-Russian Soviet nations equipped with the Russian language as *lingua franca* would also be included. They hoped that intensive intermarriage between Russians and non-Russians would ease the process of the formation of that new nation. Essentially, they would have liked to do what was anticipated by Georg von Rauch, as previously noted.

The Soviet leaders did not care for the Russian people as a value *per se*. They needed the Russians only as a matrix for that new national entity. It can easily be seen that as a minority, the Russians would not achieve Russification of other Soviet nations, but their denationalization, which, for local nationalists opposing Russification by all means in their power, would be probably even a more distasteful and unacceptable policy than that of Russification.

But this was exactly the point that created controversy among Soviet leaders. Some Soviet leaders could legitimately cast doubt on the political wisdom of pursuing such a policy of national integration.[52] They could argue that this policy was extremely dangerous for Soviet political stability, since what was ostensibly called national integration, in which they did not believe anyway, could only escalate the demands for real political influence on the part of other Soviet nations, allow the penetration of their representatives into the heart of the Soviet political system, which has been dominated by ethnic Russians at least since 1938. In this case the inherent Soviet factional political struggle could easily acquire a national dimension. Some Soviet leaders did not believe that multinational Soviet leadership could be stable. Nobody believes in the reliability and commitment of "Soviet minorities" to the Soviet system. At any rate, it was evident that the Russians as a distinct national group were seriously endangered, with no clear prospects for revival.

If a part of the Soviet leadership was merely concerned about its power within the new system, real national concern was expressed by Russian intellectuals and writers as from the end of the 1960s. This concern was duly covered by many observers, all of whom agreed that without serious top-rank political support, its open expression would not have been tolerated. Indeed, this was one of the points mentioned in the roundtable of former American diplomats referred to above: it was said that "Another type of opposition was also stressed, a very strong Great Russian nationalist opposition which works within the party."[53] Participants in the discussion, such as George Kennan and Henry Shapiro, tried to interpret this Russian nationalism as internationally more dangerous than the familiar and, on the whole better, acceptable "Internationalism" and "Integrationism."

Shapiro, for example, said: ". . . Wouldn't it be more correct to call it (i.e., nationalist opposition, M.A.) an internationalist opposition in the sense that most of the members of the Politburo, most of the rulers of the Soviet Union, are the Russian nationalists, Great Russian nationalists, rather than internationalists."[54] On the other hand, George Kennan claimed: ". . . there is a center of sharp discontent within the Party that is headed by strong Russian nationalists, ones who would really like a war with China, ones who are strong Russian as opposed to Soviet nationalists."[55]

In fact, Kennan and Shapiro were unable to distinguish between two forms of Russian nationalism—radical and conservative—which are totally hostile toward one another. Opposition Russian nationalism is conservative, but not in the sense that it is eager to restore the traditional Russian society. It also embraces the basic features of the original Communist ideology. It has no intention of giving up its political power. It is strongly statist but includes some traditional Russian values, also even some ambivalence toward the Orthodox church.

The Soviet system has already discarded many parts of the original Communist ideology. The problem is now whether it would be able to get rid of its universalist ambitions and the policy of national integration.

One could even imagine such a version of assertive Russian conservative nationalism that would refuse to reject communism and try simply to accommodate it to itself, as was the case during World War II when Soviet propaganda stopped stressing the ideological background of Soviet society and explained the Bolshevik ascent to power as a Revolution of national liberation. For example, the main Soviet ideologist of that period, Alexander Shcherbakov, was keen to stress in his official speeches that the Bolshevik Revolution saved Russia from foreign colonization.[56] By the way, Lenin himself also resorted to such an explanation immediately after the 1918 November Revolution in Germany, when he said that through the October Revolution and the Brest-Litovsk Treaty in 1918, the Bolsheviks had saved Russia's independence.[57] A more recent example of

Russian conservative nationalism retaining the national power-oriented elements of the Soviet system and thus amounting to what one could call National-Bolshevism, are the books of a popular Soviet novelist, Petr Proskurin in which the Party is portrayed as a system of national administration.[58]

Anyway, there is already now an acute political crisis in the USSR, while the conservatives challenge the radicals for their support of suicidal trends expressed in further expansion, the arms race and the unconstrained Soviet national integration. A very interesting sign of this is the heated debate among establishment Russian nationalists as to what is Russia, the West or the East.[59] Such Russian nationalist ideologists as Vadim Kozhinov or Lev Gumilev regard Russia as an organic part of the East which is irreconcilably opposed to the West. Meanwhile, their opponents, for example Apollon Kuzmin, the late Vladimir Chivilikhin, Vasily Lebedev, and Vladimir Shubkin claim that Russia is an organic part of the West and that Asia is her mortal enemy. An evident implication of this claim is the criticism of Soviet policy in the Third World, for its support of radical movements and an appeal for Russian isolationism. Such dissenting views obviously cannot be publicly expressed in the USSR without strong top-rank political support.

However, it would be wrong simply to assess those who see in Russia a part of the East as an aggressive faction while treating those who place Russia into a Western context as a peaceful one. For some the identification with the West may mean the wish to dominate it while the identification with the East may simultaneously mean isolationism. Here is another trap resulting from over-simplification or over-generalization of the issues to do with nationalism, which can lead to various tragic misconceptions.

Even Conservative Russian nationalism is heterogeneous. It, too, might be a battlefield between different trends such as xenophobia and tolerance.

However, in spite of its controversial character, conservative Russian nationalism is to be welcomed, for under its aegis there will be no more danger to international stability and peace. This nationalism, though committed to keep Russia as strong as it is, and maybe even stronger, is by its nature nonexpansionist—it looks for security of the status quo rather than to aggrandizement. Essentially, what we are witnessing now is an awesome historical drama, the drama of the disintegration of the largest world empire which, for many decades, has been destabilizing the life of the rest of the world, provoking great and local wars, the arms race, violence, terror, and causing a terrible waste of natural resources.[60] And the Russian conservative nationalists are trying to do their utmost to stop this process even if in its course they will have to lose some of Russia's present possessions.

* * *

One can now be tempted to make a paradoxical statement: the dichotomy of ideology and nationalism in Soviet domestic and foreign policy is probably untenable. In fact, the Soviet system is a power-oriented society which may use different appeals, ideological or nationalist, in order to survive.

The term "power-oriented" may need some clarification. It would perhaps be sufficient to say that this term implies power to be the highest value, regardless of how that power has been achieved and maintained. Ideology is so highly placed in the USSR only because it helps to consolidate political power. If ideology would seem detrimental, as it was during World War II, its impact would be minimized accordingly, too. The Soviet rulers will use every appeal, ideological or nationalist, in order to consolidate their position. The trend toward unlimited expansion is not so much motivated by ideology as by power politics. It is a manifestation of the Soviet internal weakness. To quote Alexander Shtromas, "There is probably even more real substance in the Soviet rulership's commitment to communist world domination at present than there was at any other time. For now it is not any more only abstract ideals but the plain survival of a ruthless and cynical power clique which is at stake, depending on the success or failure of communism worldwide. In order to keep its people in submission, the Soviet state has to impress them constantly and convincingly with its irresistible might. Expansion serves this purpose best. It shows the peoples ruled by the Soviets that resistance is pointless. Indeed, how could their resistance stand any chance of success if even the most powerful countries of the world can do nothing about stopping Soviet expansion and choose to comply with Soviet constant infringements upon their best interests? This attitude could, however, drastically change if the Soviet expansion failed to succeed and proceed. Such a failure would convey to the people the message that Soviet power is becoming weaker and that, after all, resistance to Soviet rule may be meaningful. That, in itself, could have fateful repercussions for the survival of the unpopular Soviet regime. Hence, without successfully expanding to the outside world, the Soviet rulers would by now hardly be able to sustain themselves firmly enough in power at home. No other credibility is left to them except that of their unfailing ability to exercise repressive power effectively, and this very last credibility the Soviets cannot afford to lose."[61]

The Soviet system from the very beginning has been politically and economically unstable and has always tried to survive by expanding and relentlessly undermining its external enemies. In spite of the fact that Soviet official ideology is very fluid, Soviet leaders violently resist any challenge to its current form, not because of their ideological fanaticism, but because they know full well that any challenge to the current version of their ideology is first of all a challenge to their power. The so-called ideological disputes between Russia and China, Russia and Yugoslavia, and so on, conceal interstate conflicts exactly in the same way as minor dogmatic differences between various Christian rulers in the past essentially concealed their struggle for power, with each party in the dispute trying to accord to itself, by ideological means, a more respectable position in that struggle.

The same is true for nationalism. Nationalism, as well as ideology, is used by Soviet leaders as a way to secure popular support. It was not Russian radical nationalism which conditioned Soviet expansionism. On the contrary, Soviet leaders resorted to a Russian nationalist appeal in order to secure popular support for their policy of expansionism. There is no doubt that in a situation of heavy crisis, Soviet leaders would not hesitate to resort to a conservative and isolationist national appeal, exactly as Stalin did in World War II.

All this should clearly demonstrate that both ideology and nationalism are vitally important as they provide rulers with sufficiently reliable means to secure their grip on power over their people. Exactly because of this it is also vitally important to encourage isolationist forms of Russian nationalism for the sake of international peace and security. Already in 1956 Frederick Barghoorn understood this need when he said: "There is an intriguing element of paradox in the relationship between militarism and nationalism in Soviet Russia. War contributed to the development of totalitarianism by stimulating centralism, chauvinism and anti-foreignism. But at the same time the revival of Great Russian nationalism in the Soviet Union must to a certain extent at least be regarded as an anti-totalitarian development. We should not, of course, exaggerate the contradiction between these two elements in Soviet ideology. The Kremlin has, to a considerable degree, succeeded in synthesizing them. And yet it is not impossible that the concessions made by the Kremlin to Great Russian nationalism may have introduced modifications in Soviet ideology which contain a promise of easier Soviet-Western relations in the long-term future."[62] It would be a grave mistake to anticipate an ideal solution to the grave problems that are tormenting the Soviet Union today. Nobody must nurture an eschatological vision of a new free beautiful model country emerging in place of a former monster. But this should not perturb the international community too much. What the international community needs most is a peaceful neighbor, a neighbor that would not interfere in the life of other countries, trying to impose on them its own way of life.

Even if the triumphant conservative Russian nationalism were to try to integrate the experience of Soviet history into the new Russian national myth, that should not worry other nations either. After all, history knows many examples of such integration which proved to be, in terms of international politics, absolutely innocuous. Conservative Russian nationalism, whatever form it takes, is by no means a threat. It is hope.

Notes

1. Cf., R. Aron, *Introduction à la philosophie de l'histoire*, (Paris: Gallimard, 1938).
2. F. Kohler, et al., *The Soviet Union: Yesterday, Today, Tomorrow. A Colloquy of American Long Timers in Moscow*, (Coral Gables, Fla. Center for Advanced International Studies, University of Miami, 1975), 148.
3. Cf., B. Komarov, *The Destruction of Nature in the Soviet Union*, (White Plains, N.Y.: M.E. Sharpe, 1980).
4. M. Schwartz, *The Foreign Policy of the USSR. Domestic Factors*, (Encino, Ca.: Dickenson Publishing Co., 1975), p. 97
5. G. Wetter, *Dialectical Materialism*, (New York: F. Praeger, 1958).
6. A. Besançon, *Court traité de soviétologie á p'usage des autorités civiles, militaires et religieuses*, (Paris: Hachette, 1976).
7. L. Pellicani, *I rivoluzionari di professione*, (Firenze: Wallechi, 1975).
8. Cf., A. Kriegel, *Israel est-il coupable?*, (Paris: R. Laffont, 1982).
9. M. Heller, A. Nekrich, *L'utopie au pouvoir*, (Paris: Callman-Lévy, 1982).
10. C. Bohlen, *Witness to History*, (New York: W.W. Norton, 1973), p. 513.
11. Cf. his *Letter to the Soviet Leaders*, (London: Fontana, 1974).
12. G. von Rauch, "Sowjet Patriotismus?," in *Zeitschrift für Geopolitik*, Bd. 22, 1951, p. 104.
13. M. Agursky, *The Ideology of National Bolshevism*, (Boulder, Col.: Westview Press, 1986) (forthcoming)
14. J. Ortega-y-Gasset, *The Revolt of the Masses*, (London: G. Allen & Unwin, 1972), 105.
15. C.J.H. Hayes, *The Historical Evolution of Modern Nationalism*, (New York: Russel and Russel, 1931), 166–67.
16. W. Biehahn, "Marxismus and Russentum im Bolschewismus", in *Osteuropa*, Bd. 10, 1934–35, 506.
17. "The Rise of Russian Nationalism," in *Nationalism*. Report by a Study Group of the Royal Institute of International Affairs, (London: Oxford University Press, 1939), 57–80.
18. M. Hindus, *Crisis in the Kremlin*, (New York: Doubleday, 1953), 32–34.
19. Z. Brzezinski, "The Soviet Past and Future," in *Encounter*, 34, No. 3, (March 1970), 7.
20. R.C. Tucker, "Communist Revolutions, National Cultures, and Divided Nations," in *Studies in Comparative Communism*, 7, No. 3, (Autumn 1974), 242.
21. V. Kusin, "Socialism and Nationalism," in L. Kolakowski, S. Hampshire eds., *The Socialist Idea*, (London: Weidenfeld & Nicolson, 1974), 148.

22. Kohler et al., *The Soviet Union*, 4–5.
23. ⸻, p. 31.
24. G. Stökl, "Creation of a Homogeneous Soviet Nation," in *Problems of Soviet Internal Policy*. Proceedings of the Conference, (Munich: Institut zur Erforschung der UdSSR, 1960), 110.
25. N. Timasheff, *The Great Retreat. The Growth and Decline of Communism in Russia*, (New York: E.P. Dutton, 1946), 156.
26. ⸻, p. 187.
27. ⸻, p. 191.
28. N. Timasheff, "Russian Imperialism or Communist Aggression?" in W. Gurian ed., *Soviet Imperialism*, (Notre Dame, Indiana: University of Notre Dame Press, 1953), 35, 41.
29. N. Timasheff, "Soviet Ideology for the 1960s," in *Current History*, 43, No. 254, (October 1962), 224.
30. Schwartz, *The Foreign Policy*, 123.
31. Ch. Johnson, ed., *Comparing Communist Nations*, Ch. Johnson, "Change in Communist Systems," (Stanford, Ca.: Stanford University Press, 1970), p. 4.
32. Quoted from Johnson, 5.
33. A. Shtromas, "To Fight Communism: Why and How?," in *International Journal on World Peace*, I, No. 1, (Autumn 1984), 37.
34. Cf., M. Salvadori, *K. Kautsky and the Socialist Revolution*, (London: NLB, 1979).
35. A. Etzioni, *The Active Society*, (London: Collier-Macmillan, 1968).
36. A. Kaznacheev, *Inside a Soviet Embassy*, (Philadelphia: Lippincot, 1962), 207.
37. V. Sakharov, U. Tossi, *High Treason*, (New York: Ballantine, 1981).
38. Cf., T. von Laue, *Why Lenin? Why Stalin?* (Philadelphia: Lippincot, 1964).
39. V. Lenin, "The Valuable Admission of P. Sorokin," in *Collected Works*, 28, (Moscow: Progress Publishers, 1965), 187–88.
40. Cf., K. Radek, "O kharaktere voiny s Pol'shei," (On the Character of War Against Poland) in *Pravda*, 11–12 May, 1920.
41. E. Demaitre, "The Origins of National Communism," in *Studies in Comparative Communism*, II, No. 1, (January 1969), 1.
42. F. Barghoorn, *Soviet Russian Nationalism*, (London: Oxford University Press, 1956), 60.
43. E. Kamenka, "Political Nationalism," E. Kamenka ed., *Nationalism*, (Canberra: Australian National University, 1976), 3.
44. J. Plamenatz, "Two Types of Nationalism," in E. Kamenka ed. *Political Nationalism* 34.
45. Cf., M. Bakunin, "Gosudarstvennost' i anarkhiya," (Statehood and Anarchy) in *Izbrannye sochinenia*, I, (Peterburg-Moscow: "Golos truda," 1922).
46. Cf., *Ocherki filosofii kollektivizma* (Outlines of Collective Philosophy), St. Petersburg: "Znanie," 1909.
47. V. Lenin, "Materialism and Empirocriticism," in *Collected Works*, 14, (Moscow: Progress Publishers, 1962).

48. ———, 21, 103–5.
49. M. Gorky, "On the Russian Peasantry," in *The Journal of Peasant Studies*, 4, No. 1, (October 1976).
50. Cf., A.N. Tolstoi's book on Peter the Great.
51. Cf., M. Agursky, *Sovietskiy Golem*, (The Soviet Golem) (London: Overseas Publications Interchange, 1983), 47–55.
52. For more details, see Ibid., pp. 36–39.
53. F. Kohler, et al., *The Soviet Union*, p. 12.
54. ———, 62.
55. ———, 62–63.
56. See, for example, *Pravda*, 22 January 1944.
57. V. Lenin, "The Valuable Admission of P. Sorokin," *op. cit.*, pp. 187–88.
58. M. Agursky, "The New Russian Literature," Research paper No. 40, The Soviet and East European Research Center, The Hebrew University of Jerusalem, 1980.
59. Cf., M. Agursky, "Les idéologues du PCUS dans le débat," in *La documentation française, Série URSS*, No. 467, 1983.
60. Cf., M. Agursky, "Can Soviet Russia Remain a Superpower?," in N. Oren, ed., *When Patterns Change: Turning Points in International Relations*, (New York: St. Martin's Press, 1984).
61. A. Shtromas, To Fight Communism, 23–24.
62. Barghoorn, *Soviet*, 264.

8

The Challenge of the Russophile Ideology[1]

DARRELL P. HAMMER

Chekhov's tale of "The Lady with the Dog" illustrates an important point about Russian ethnic identity, which is relevant to contemporary Russian nationalism. It is the story of a worldly man from Moscow, Gurov, who is on vacation in Yalta, and there meets a young woman whom he knows, at first, only as "Anna Sergeevna." Gurov inquires at her hotel, and finds that her last name is von Diederitz. At their next meeting he asks her the obvious question: "Is your husband German?" And she replies:

"No, his grandfather, I believe, was German, but he himself is Orthodox."[2] Not *German*, but *Orthodox*. As if baptism carried with it a new ethnic identity. This close identity between Russian nationality and the Orthodox faith will help us to distinguish between various trends of thought which have appeared in recent years, which are generally (and mistakenly) grouped under the rubric "Russian nationalism."

In 1970 a *samizdat* writer who signed himself "Vol'ny" wrote about the relationship between Orthodoxy, nationalism, and political dissent:

The new generation is not very intellectual and makes its religious choice on the basis of moral intuition. It is not a matter of conflict between reason and faith, but between two faiths. Frequently an attraction to the persecuted, martyred church will draw pure hearts away from the power of a false Communist propaganda. An Eastern, socialist Russia—heavy-laden, crude, grasping for bread yet proud of its power—a Russia of tractors and missiles cannot be a country of great culture. And it cannot be a country of great morality, because the great enemies of mankind, class hatred and national hatred, cannot be overcome in the conditions of Communist totalitarianism . . .

Some call for a free society, others for the morality of Christian ethics. This is why we see the masses leaving the church at the same time that we see a significant part of the intelligentsia returning to her fold. Christianity once again, as in the days of the early church, is becoming a religion of a spiritual aristocracy.[3]

We find here three terms that are common in the discussion of Russian nationalism: power, culture, and morality.

One of the disputed questions of contemporary Russian life is the "renaissance" of religion, and specifically of Orthodoxy, in the USSR. Some knowledgeable émigrés, such as Chalidze, insist that there is no such renaissance.[4] Chalidze acknowledges the phenomena discussed in this chapter—the conversion of some intellectuals to the traditional church, and the organization of unofficial groups such as the Christian seminar. But he denies that there is a "renaissance"—or if there is, that it brings any prospect for change in the system. He argues, first of all, that there has been no mass return to the church, and second, that of all the major religious faiths, Orthodoxy is the one most likely to adapt to the existing political structure, and therefore the least likely to inspire political change.[5]

Vol'ny, just as clearly, believes that there is a renaissance of sorts, and its ultimate consequences are unpredictable. We find a similar view in another *samizdat* author, writing under the name "Zelinskii."[6] They would agree with the major Orthodox dissenters, Dudko and Iakunin, on the prospects for a religious rebirth.

In this chapter I propose to discuss the ideas of the intellectuals who belong to the group described by "Vol'ny." They represent the philosophy that I shall call, following Osipov's suggestion, the Russophile idea. I shall concentrate on the political writings of the dissident Orthodox priest, Dimitrii Dudko. Dudko is not the most original or the most important of the Russophile writers. I have chosen to look at him, however, because after Aleksandr Solzhenitsyn, he was the most visible living symbol of the Russophile idea, and because his writings sum up so well the basic Russophile beliefs. My emphasis will be on political ideas. At the end of the chapter, however, I want to discuss some of the ramifications of the Russophile ideas for some current issues of public policy in the USSR.

I must begin, however, by making a distinction between the Russophile idea and other contemporary currents which are loosely labeled "Russian nationalism." Nationalism is an idea, and not an ideology. I would agree with Plamenatz, that it can best be understood as an effort to preserve or protect the cultural identity of a people when that identity is under threat.[7]

Nationalism thus is, first of all, a reaction to a threat. Russophilism begins with this perception of a threat to Russian culture and Russia's national identity. Out of the basic instinct for survival has developed a deep concern for the future of the village, a rejection of the cult of technology, and a quiet hostility to the Soviet system—hostility to the Marxist-Leninist philosophy and hostility to the ruling bureaucracy.

Most of the Russophile writers are dissidents. Their writings can be found in *samizdat*; the writers themselves can be found in the camps, or in exile. But we can also find the influence the Russophile idea in legally published writing. The obvious example is the "village writers," who have many Russophile themes. For example Rasputin, in his tale *Money for Maria* (perhaps his most openly political statement), relates the story of an uneducated peasant woman who takes charge of a village store. No sooner has she assumed her responsibilities, than a government inspector appears to conduct an inventory. He discovers a shortage of 1,000 rubles, and she must make it good. Here is the expected description of village life, and the contrast between the city and the village. But the villain in the story, it seems to me, is the bureaucracy—a mindless institution which oppresses ordinary people and threatens to destroy Russian life.

The Russophiles must be distinguished from another ideology that I shall call (following Solzhenitsyn's suggestion) "National Bolshevism." The National Bolsheviks owe their loyalty to the state and not to the nation; they do not fear power, and they look on the Soviet state as the legitimate successor to the Russian Empire. Their "nationalism" (if that is the correct term) is very different from that of the Russophiles.

Dimitrii Dudko

In his writings and in his sermons, Dimitrii Dudko expresses all the basic themes of the Russophile idea. He is concerned with the breakdown of traditional values, the problems associated with urban and industrialized societies and, in particular, the disintegration of family life. On these points he has a familiar message—familiar, at least, to those who have read the works of Osipov and *Veche*, or Aleksandr Solzhenitsyn.[8] Like Solzhenitsyn, Dudko believes that much of the "progress" made since the Revolution has been a "mad rush into a blind alley." Like other Russophile nationalists, Dudko calls for a period of moral regeneration, and for a rebirth of Russian national culture. But Dudko has another message as well. For those who would listen, he was calling for a return to Russian religious philosophy and, in particular, for a rediscovery of the ideas of the Slavophiles, Solov'ev, and Berdiaev.

Dimitrii Sergeevich Dudko was born in 1922 in a peasant village near Briansk.[9] In later life he would recall a difficult childhood, the catastrophe of collectivization when food was literally confiscated from their house, and the time when his father was arrested. His town was occupied by the Germans at the beginning of the war but was liberated in 1943, and Dudko was called into the Red Army. Later, when Dudko had become a well-known dissident, there were vague charges that he had collaborated with the occupation.[10] No formal charge was ever brought against him, and these accusations can probably be dismissed as propaganda. After leaving the army in 1945, he went to Moscow to enter the new theological seminary. It was here that he first met Anatolii Levitin.

In 1948, while still a student, Dudko was arrested and charged under article 58–10 of the criminal code. The basis for the charge was apparently poetry of a religious content, and for this crime Dudko received a seven-year sentence. He completed this term in the labor camps. In the post-Stalin "thaw" of 1956 he was rehabilitated, returned to Moscow, and resumed his theological education. In 1958, at the age of 36, he completed the course of the Moscow Theological Academy, and after some delay he was ordained to the priesthood by Bishop (later Patriarch) Pimen. In 1963 he was assigned to St. Nicholas Church in the Preobrazhenskii cemetery, where he served for eleven years, until the scandal that first brought him to public attention.

During this period Dudko lived the obscure life of a parish priest. But he seems to have been a closet dissident, and a reader of *samizdat*, although he took no part in public dissident activities. He maintained a close friendship with Levitin, the leading Orthodox *samizdat* writer, and it was Levitin who introduced him to Vladimir Osipov.[11] Dudko also continued to write, although what he wrote was not circulated even in the closed world of *samizdat* literature, and it did not reach the West until Dudko had emerged into the open world of public dissent. He kept a notebook called "Diary of a Priest," parts of which have been published in the West.[12] Of somewhat greater interest is a series of dialogues under the name "The Two-way Current," apparently written between 1970 and 1972.[13]

In these early sketches we encounter a remarkable cross section of the Russian population: the sick and dying, whom the priest visits, peasants who have come to the city because their village churches are closed, children brought to the church who are bewildered by what they find, and intellectuals whose spiritual wanderings have brought them, finally, to the Orthodox faith. These sketches are a mixture of fact and fiction, but they bear witness to Dudko's deep faith that Russia was experiencing a religious rebirth. At one point he describes an encounter with a woman professor who, in turn, relates the story of a student who had been a witness to the murder of Nicholas II and his family. The young man is tormented by this recollection, and it frequently comes back to him in his dreams. He finds some solace in the company of the professor, because she is a religious believer.[14] This image of the murdered czar is to reappear in Dudko's other writings.

In these early writings, his concern is for the oppressed and the sick in spirit, but it is also for the Church, which has been insulted and injured as an institution. He writes, of the Church, that it is "the only power in Russia," and eventually "she will prevail."[15] He also writes of frequent encounters with former political prisoners who had found Russia, and found religion, in the camps (possibly a reference to Osipov). He writes of hearing confession from Party members, and the first sin they confess is that they belong to the Party. And he describes some of the adults, many of them intellectuals, whom he has converted:

> Recently I baptized an artist, who had been born in an atheistic family.
>
> In the thirties he had begun to think about religious questions. He went from one extreme to the other: Buddhism, Islam, even Judaism, but finally came to realize that a Russian can only be Orthodox.[16]

Cautious as he was, Dudko still came to the attention of the political police. In July 1972 he was summoned to the procuracy and some of his books and papers (including the Sakharov memorandum) were confiscated.[17] In October of that same year, he delivered a short sermon in which he asked for his parishioners' support.[18] A few days after this provocative sermon, Dudko was summoned to the Moscow representative of the Council for Religious Affairs. Here he was warned that he was under investigation because of his "anti-social activity" and because the books that had been seized from his apartment were "slanderous."[19] These were potentially serious charges, because the possession of books which "slander" the Soviet system is a criminal offence.

The October sermon marked the beginning of his public activity. He became bolder, and at the end of 1973 his sermons in St. Nicholas' Church took on a different character. They became an open forum in which the priest responded to questions from his listeners. Word of these "discussions" (*besedy*) spread through the city, and large crowds began to gather at the Saturday night services where he spoke. The discussions were taken down and circulated in *samizdat*, and eventually published in the West.[20] By May 1974, the sermons had become an embarrassment to the Patriarchate, and Dudko was ordered to break them off. Then there began one of the petition campaigns so characteristic of the early 1970s and a number of such petitions, defending the priest, began to appear in *samizdat*.[21]

The Patriarchate tried to solve the problem by transferring Dudko to the jurisdiction of the metropolitan of Krutitsa and Kolomna, i.e., to Moscow region. This made it possible to reassign him to a parish outside the city, in an area closed to foreigners. Dudko at first announced that he would retire, but then he accepted a transfer to the church in the village of Kabanovo, about 50 miles from Moscow. He also discontinued his "discussions," and returned to the more traditional form of sermon. At the end of 1975 he left this church because he was dismissed by the parish council, although the dismissal apparently came as the result of external pressure. A few months later he found employment in another village church, in Grebnevo, somewhat closer to the city. He now resumed his "discussions," and in 1978 he began to publish a *samizdat* newspaper, in the form of a weekly parish bulletin.[22]

He remained a parish priest in Grebnevo until his arrest in January 1980, which occurred just a week after the forced exile of Sakharov. During his service in Grebnevo, Dudko continued to live in Moscow, where he took an increasingly active part in the public dissident movement. His arrest was part of a general sweep of dissidents. After six months' incarceration in a KGB jail, Dudko recanted. He made a remarkable appearance on Moscow television in which he repudiated his writings and admitted that his dissident activity had a criminal character. After this tragic event he was released. Since then he has not been completely silent. He circulated a detailed explanation of his television statement, and in November 1980, his *samizdat* newspaper appeared once again.[23]

Dudko must be approached as a priest and a teacher. He is an important figure in contemporary Russia not because of the originality of his ideas, but because of his courage and his influence. Dunlop has written that during the height of his fame, Dudko was virtually a "shadow patriarch."[24]

This description may be a slight exaggeration, but it is true that Dudko acquired enormous influence among certain Moscow intellectuals, and especially among youth. We know that Dudko became religious mentor to Osipov, after Osipov was released from his first term of imprisonment.

I would say of Dudko what Berdiaev said of Dostoevsky: He is profoundly Russian, and it is hard to imagine a Father Dimitrii Dudko outside of Russia. In part this is true because Dudko was deeply influenced by Dostoyevsky, as well as by Berdiaev. Dudko does not quite make Russia equal to God. But running through all his writings is the symbolism of Russia on the cross, of Russia crucified. And at one point Dudko reminds his reader of the words of the Roman centurion: "Truly this man was the Son of God."[25]

Dudko's long essay, "Overcoming Temptation," is the most systematic statement of his political philosophy. The essay was written between 1972 and 1974, and circulated widely in *samizdat*.[26] But I use "systematic" in a relative sense. Like Dudko's other *samizdat* writings, "Overcoming Temptation" is rambling and discursive. It reads more like occasional notes than a logical statement of a philosophy. Indeed, Dudko himself tells us that he is not trying to write a treatise but to give expression to his ideas. The truth, he insists, is not always found through logic but may be discovered through feeling or intuition.[27] Nonetheless a careful reading of this essay reveals not only Dudko's worldview, but a consistent argument about Russia and her place in the world.

Dudko is an unembarrassed Russian nationalist. But he also admits that nationalism is one of the "temptations" that men must overcome. Nationalism is a "healthy human instinct" but cosmopolitanism, on the other hand, is cold and soulless.[28] However, Dudko's Russophile philosophy carries no hatred or even antipathy for other nationalities. On this point Dudko is close to Vladimir Solov'ev. Solov'ev had argued that no man can exist apart from his nationality (*narodnost'*): what we would today call "national character" is an essential part of the human personality. Patriotism thus is a natural instinct, and no one should be ashamed of it. But patriotism should not be allowed to degenerate into "national egotism," and love for one's own national culture should not become hatred toward others. Finally Solov'ev concludes that if we are to love one another as we love ourselves, then we must love other nations as we love our own.[29]

Dudko clearly accepts this argument and furthermore, like Solov'ev, he goes on to apply the argument to the Jews. The Jews have the same right as all other men to cling to their own national culture. Zionism (by which Dudko simply means Jewish nationalism) thus, is a phenomenon to be welcomed. Indeed he insists that the Russians and the Jews have much in common. Both are nations that have lost their homeland, and both are the object of senseless hatred. Dudko's nationalism thus is a pluralist nationalism, in which all nationalities deserve respect and love.

For Dudko there are two Russias: the Russia of the Orthodox tradition and the Russia of the imperial tradition. He recognizes that much of the criticism of the Russophile idea comes from a failure to make this basic distinction, which is so clear in his own mind. His faith and his hope are fastened on "Holy Russia" (*sviataia Rus'*). The critics confuse loyalty to Holy Russia with crude chauvinism, and Dudko's own idea of Russia's mission with the myth of the Third Rome—a myth which Dudko rejects.

I know that even now, after all that we Russians have experienced and all that we have lost, there are men who cannot stand to hear about Russia. They immediately think of the Third Rome, of Russian national chauvinism, and more recently, of national Bolshevism. They become terrified, as if Russia had subjugated them and they have fallen under her despotic rule. True, there is some basis for this. But the basis for it comes from misunderstanding or from blindness, from confusing Russia with the USSR.

Dudko's message is that Russia herself was the first victim of this terror and despotism. This is what gives Russia the right to speak out and perhaps to teach the rest of the world.[30] But if, indeed, Russia has such a mission to the world, that fact does not make Russia a superior nation. "We Russians are not better than others. We are worse than others. It is for this reason that we hunger after repentance.[31]

Russia, for me, is not merely a state, not just the land in which I was born. Russia is the most sacred thing in my soul. Here is the sacred thing [*sviatinia*] and the culture which I love. Holy Rus' is her true name. Anyone can love Holy Rus', and not just those of Russian nationality. The other Russia has the same faults [*poroki*] as other countries, and perhaps more. Only a believing Christian, one who is Orthodox, can love Holy Rus'. An atheist can love the state and the land. But for an atheist, Russia could someday come to the end of its existence. For a believer, when all else comes to its end, Holy Rus' passes into the next world.[32]

It is what Russia has suffered that makes her the "messenger of God." This, at least, is my interpretation of a phrase that appears frequently in Dudko's writing: "*bogonosnaia strana*" (literally, "God-bearing country"). "Truth," he wrote about 1968, "is to be found not in logic but in suffering." Russia herself is not "logical" and seems inferior in education and culture to the West. But through her suffering, Russia will come to find the truth.[33] Russia's mission is to carry this Truth to the rest of the world.

Russia will be reborn, and from Russia a light will spread to the entire world. What began in the West, and thence spread to Russia, will finally perish in Russia. After the Russian tragedy never again will we dare to call evil "good."[34]

"What began in the West" was, of course, the Revolution. But in the hands of the Russians, the revolutionary idea itself was transformed. The Revolution in the West was a struggle for social justice; more specifically it had been a struggle to improve the material conditions of the oppressed. In Russia the Revolution was transformed, from a struggle for material betterment into a struggle for Eternal Truth.[35] In the name of Eternal Truth the country was destroyed and then rebuilt [*peredelyvanie vsekh i vsia*]. Sixty years later Dudko surveyed the wreckage, and found that nothing positive had been achieved. "Now the time has arrived when we can judge what the reconstruction of society has accomplished, and we can see that the evil has not diminished but has become worse."[36]

Dudko's analysis of the Revolution and its "mystique" is not entirely new. His thinking is derived in part from a reading of *Vekhi* and in particular from Berdiaev.[37] What is new in Dudko is his gentle suggestion that the Christians could have done it better, without the shedding of blood, and without encroaching on individual freedom. The Marxists have charged that the Christians cannot contribute to the rebuilding of society, because they place all their hope in God. Dudko sardonically quotes from the Soviet Constitution—"Who does not work, neither shall he eat"—and reminds his readers that this supposedly "socialist" principle had been taken from the Scriptures.[38] Dudko suggests that the Christian would be a good worker, and an honest worker, because he not only perceives a "Higher Control," but he knows that this control cannot be deceived.[39]

Dudko's career as a political dissident was a short one, from 1974 until the end of 1979. During this period he lived not only under surveillance, but under constant fear of arrest. But his influence was considerable, even if it is hard to measure. Not only did he influence Osipov, but the religious and philosophical seminar of the later 1970s was organized by Dudko's disciple, Aleksandr Ogorodnikov. Despite this short career, Dudko is a significant figure because he succeeded in articulating a philosophical point of view that remains the basis of the "Russophile" idea. It is a highly eclectic philosophy, which (as we have already noted) borrows heavily from Dostoyevsky, Vladimir Solov'ev, and Berdiaev. It is clear that one of the reasons that this philosophy appealed to many of Dudko's disciples was its sharp contrast with the official ideology of Marxism-Leninism. But a more important reason is that Dudko and his ideas seemed so fundamentally Russian. His writings express the total Russian experience, for Dudko is a victim of collectivization, a veteran of the war, and a veteran of the labor camps.

The Alcohol Epidemic

In the programmatic statement of *Veche* (1971), Osipov referred to the "epidemic of alcoholism." In calling for protecting national culture, Osipov was crying out for a return to traditional values and, in particular, for a solution to the problem of drunkenness. The second issue of *Veche* contains an appeal from an anonymous priest who has the same concern. He called for a return to the church: "Give us ten years and we shall not recognize ourselves."[40] Dudko too, in his writings, frequently refers to the problem of drunkenness.

There can be no doubt that alcohol abuse is a major problem. Drinking on the job is one of the causes of the country's low labor productivity. Treml has published some statistics which show the magnitude of the problem. Per capita consumption of alcohol has risen sharply in the last quarter century. What is of interest to our theme is that there are significant regional differences, with consumption highest in the Russian republic and lowest in the traditionally Islamic regions.[41]

Treml's findings are confirmed by a *samizdat* document written in 1983. The document seems to be a summary of a report by the Academy of Sciences. According to this document, the major cause of the country's health problems is alcoholism, and it also blames the sharp increase in the birth of retarded children on alcohol. It shows a deep concern about the effect of alcoholism on the Russian nationality, which is faced with a "progressive degeneration." "To encounter a sober male in a village in the evening, is about as common as encountering a Martian." On the other hand: "In the Central Asian villages, where there is almost no drinking, there are well-kept houses, autos, motorcycles. This makes it even more heart-rending to look at the dying Russian village." The report adds, finally, that most violent crimes can be attributed to alcohol abuse.[42]

In May 1985 the government announced tough new measures to cure this social problem.[43] There seems to be serious doubt that the anti-drinking policy will work. There is also considerable skepticism about whether the government wants it to work. According to popular myth, the government makes more than 1,000 percent profit on every bottle of vodka sold. To cut down on vodka sales would cut into the government's income. The *samizdat* document just quoted takes the same view. It quotes *Mein Kampf* to the effect that all the Slavs need is liquor and tobacco—and accuses the government of following Hitler's policy toward the Russian people.

The "Demographic" Problem

One of the first Russians to take up the "demographic" problem was a Russophile writer who contributed a thoughtful analysis to Osipov's *Veche*.[44] The "demographic problem" is a code word for what some Western writers call the "Islamic threat": the high birth rate among the traditionally Islamic nationalities which threatens to make the Russians a minority in the USSR. Western analysts have invariably attributed the

Comparative Figures for Population Growth

	Death Rate	Birth-Rate	Crude Rate of Natural Increase
Tadzhik SSR	6.0	36.0	30.0
Turkmen SSR	7.0	37.2	30.2
Pskov oblast	11.3	11.9	0.6
Kalinin oblast	10.4	11.8	1.4

SOURCE: Voronov, "Demograficheskie problemy Rossii," 256–57.

"demographic problem" to cultural differences. Inevitably the predominantly rural Islamic culture, with its cult of the family, will produce more children than the more advanced and urbanized Russians. If this analysis is correct, then we could expect that as the Islamic areas become more industrialized and urbanized, their birthrate will level off.

What is interesting about Voronov's argument is that he rejects this view entirely, insisting that the decline in the Russian birthrate is not the result of economic growth, and social change. He notes that a low birthrate is also observed among the Russian peasants, the more "backward" part of the population. What is happening to the nation as a whole is also happening in the village: "The nation shares the fate of the peasantry"; the nation is dying because the village is dying.[45] Behind it all: lack of concern, on the part of the regime, for the future of the Russian nation. If the usual analysis were correct, then Pskov, one of the economically backward, rural areas of the Russian republic, should have a high birthrate. Voronov calculated the natural population growth (difference between death rate and birthrate) for certain oblasts of the Russian republic, and compared them with two Islamic republics. The results are shown in the accompanying table. Voronov proposed several measures: payments should be made to support a family with two or three children and there should be an improvement in living conditions for young families. More specifically, the Russophiles and some of their supporters argued for a differentiated population policy, making an effort to stimulate the birthrate in the Russian regions. It is possible to find, in published Soviet sources, a position very close to the Russophile argument of Voronov: (1) the Soviet budget favors the minority nationalities, so that the smaller republics receive a larger share of the resources of the country, at the expense of the Russian republic (RSFSR); (2) the agricultural regions of Central Asia are better provided for than those of the RSFSR; (3) family policy should aim at achieving a uniform birthrate throughout the USSR, and change a situation where the Central Asian population is growing much faster than the Russian population.[46]

The government appears to have settled on a compromise policy, meeting partially the Russophile demands for a differentiated policy. The new policy, beginning in 1981, was to give more generous grants for child support and maternity leave. The policy was to begin at once in some areas of the Russian republic, and gradually be extended to the rest of the USSR. Curiously enough Pskov oblast, from which Voronov took his example, was one of the regions where the new policy went into effect right away.[47]

Conclusion

My title refers to the "challenge" of the Russophile idea. Is there, in fact, a challenge from a group of misguided youths and religious fanatics? I believe that there is a challenge, and it can be considered at two levels. First is the level of public policy. I have discussed only two issues on which the Russophiles have spoken out. But there is a larger range of issues on which a clear Russophile program is emerging—on matters of urban policy, religious policy, and caring for the environment, to mention only a few points. In this sense the Russophiles can be said to comprise a "party": they have a point of view but they are not pressing a single issue.

The other level concerns that most sacred event, the October Revolution. At his trial Vladimir Poresh, the Leningrad leader of the Christian Seminar, gave his opinion of the Revolution: "It was a great tragedy."[48] Dudko would say that it was worse than a tragedy; it was a failure.

Notes

1. For a more detailed discussion of this topic see the careful study by John B. Dunlop, *The Faces of Contemporary Russian Nationalism* (Princeton: Princeton University Press, 1983), and two recent articles: Dimitry Pospielovsky, "The Neo-Slavophile Trend and Its Relation to the Contemporary Religious Revival in the USSR," *Religion and Nationalism in Soviet and East European Politics*, ed. Pedro Ramet (Durham, N.C.: Duke University Press, 1984), 41–58; Darrell P. Hammer, "Russian Nationalism and Soviet Politics," *Soviet Politics: Russia after Brezhnev*, ed. Joseph L. Nogee (New York: Praeger,

1985), 122–49, 41–58; see also Darrell P. Hammer, "Vladimir Osipov and the *Veche* Group 1971–1974," *Russian Review* (forthcoming, 44, no. 4).

2. A.P. Chekhov, "Dama s sobachkoi," *Sobranie sochinenii*, (Moscow: "Khudozhestvennaia literatura," 1956) 8, 394–410. Ronald Hingley's translation misses this nuance: "No, his grandfather was, I think, but he's Russian." *The Oxford Chekhov* (Oxford: Oxford University Press, 1975), 9, 139.

3. K. Vol'ny, "Intelligentsiia i demokraticheskoe dvizhenie," AS No. 607.

4. V. Chalidze, "O nekotorykh tendentsiiakh v emigrantskoi publitsistike," *Kontinent*, 23 (1980): 151–75.

5. ———, 168–69.

6. Vladimir Zelinskii, "Prikhozhdenie v Tserkov' " (1980), AS No. 4706.

7. Eugene Kamenka, ed., *Nationalism: The Nature and Evolution of an Idea*, John Plamenatz, "Two Types of Nationalism," (Canberra: Australian National University Press, 1973), 22–36.

8. See V. Osipov, "Na Veche!" in *Tri otnosheniia k rodine* (Frankfurt: Posev, 1978), 7–8.

9. A.E. Levitin-Krasnov is the author of two short biographical articles with the same title: "Otets Dimitrii Dudko," AS No. 1975 (May 1974), which appeared in the *samizdat* journal *Zemlia* No. 1, and "Otets Dimitrii Dudko," *Posev*, 1 (1975): 26–36. The first article was written in the USSR, while the second was written after the author had emigrated. An abbreviated version of the *Posev* article appears as an appendix to *Vovremia i ne vovremia* (Brussels: Zhizn' c Bogom, 1978). Dudko also figures in Levitin's memoirs: *Vospominaniia, 2, "Ruk tvoikh zhar" (1941–1956)* (Tel-Aviv: Krug, 1979), and in later volumes.

10. A. Belov and A. Shilkin, *Diversiia bez dinamita* (Moscow: Politicheskaia literatura, 1976), 100.

11. Levitin-Krasnov, *Vospominaniia, 4, Rodnoi prostor: demokraticheskoe dvizhenie* (Frankfurt: Posev, 1981), 236–37.

12. "Kreshschenie na Rusi (iz dnevnika sviashchennika)," *Vestnik RKhD*, 117 (1976): 188–208; "Pokaianie na Rusi (iz dnevnika sviashchennika)," *Vestnik RKhD*, 119 (1976): 254–80.

13. Dm. Drozdov (pseud.), "Dvoinoe techenie," (Part 1) *Russkoe vozrozhednie*, 6 (1976): 15–49; (Part 2) 7–8 (1979): 235–50; (Part 3) 10 (1980): 106–26.

14. ———, (Part 1), 22.

15. ———, 30.

16. ———, 46–47.

17. AS No. 1691.

18. *Vestnik RKhD*, 106 (1972): 340; English translation of this sermon, *Religion in Communist Lands*, 4–5 (1973): 54–55.

19. AS No. 1692.

20. D. Dudko, *O nashem upovanii* (Paris: YMCA Press, 1975); Dmitrii Dudko, *Our Hope*, (Crestwood, N.Y.: St. Vladimir's Seminary Press, 1977). *Our Hope* also contains Dudko's recollections about his interview in the procuracy, and his meeting with the representative of the Council for Religious Affairs.

21. *Vestnik RKhD*, 112–13 (1974): 269; *Russkaia mysl'*, 30 May 1974; AS No. 1794, 1795.
22. *V svete preobrazheniia: ezhenedel'naia pravoslavnaia gazeta*. The first issue was dated 3 September 1978; *Vol'noe slovo*, 33 (1979): 52–119. Material from this *samizdat* newspaper was also published in *Pravoslavnaia Rus'*, and in other Western periodicals.
23. *Khozhdenie po krugam* . . . (unpublished *samizdat* document, dated 31 July 1980); *V svete preobrazheniia* 1980–1981 (unpublished samizdat document). The second document contains eight additional numbers of the newspaper, and other material written after his recantation.
24. Dunlop, *Contemporary Russian Nationalism*, 190.
25. Mark 15: 39. Dudko, "Chto znachit mif o Rossii," *Russkoe vozrozhdenie*, 10 (1980): 59.
26. "Preodolenie soblaznov," in Dimitrii Dudko, *Premudrostiiu vonmem* (New York: "Free Word," 1980), 7–133. Portions of this work had appeared earlier in *Posev*, 4 (1980): 2–3, and *Russkoe vozrozhdenie*, 1 (1978): 71–102. We have confirmation from a Soviet source that the essay was circulated in *samizdat*. According to *Diversiia bez dinamita* (p. 100): "Dudko learned nothing from life (read: the labor camp). While finishing the seminary and starting his service in the church, he did not change his views. In his sermons and writings he continued to speak out from his earlier position, as an enemy of the Soviet system, fighting for a restoration of the monarchy. These positions are expressed quite clearly in his typescript opus 'Overcoming Temptation.' "
27. Dudko, *Premudrostiiu vonmem*, 15–16.
28. ———, 29.
29. Vladimir Solov'ev, *Opravdanie dobra* (St. Petersburg, 1897), 387–89.
30. Dudko, "S russkoi golgofy /dlia razmyshleniia/," *Vrag vnutri*, in *Vol'noe slovo*, 33 (1979): 44–45.27. *Premudrostiiu vonmen*, 15–16.
31. Dudko, "O chem propovedovat'," *Vol'noye slovo* p. 19.28., p. 29.
32. Dudko, *Premudrostiiu vonmem*, p. 58.
33. Dudko, *Veriu gospodi!*, pp. 243–44.
34. Dudko, "Chto znachit mif o Rossii," p. 60.
35. ———, p. 64, and *Premudrostiiu vonmem*, p. 66.
36. Dudko, *Veriu, gospodi!*, p. 237.
37. Leonard Schapiro has pointed out that the basic criticism in *Vekhi* was that the revolutionary idea had been transformed into a "sacred dogma." "The *Vekhi* Group and the Mystique of Revolution," *Slavonic and East European Review*, 34 (1955): 56–76.
38. This phrase (2 Thes. 3: 10) was written into the Soviet Constitution of 1936, article 12. It was omitted from the Constitution of 1977. Lenin, in *State and Revolution*, refers to this rule as one of the basic principles of socialism. Vladimir Soloukhin, who has recently been criticized for his "religious" views, has reminded us that the contemporary language contains many aphorisms from the Bible, although average Russian is usually unaware of the source. *Kameshki na ladoni* (Moscow: "Sovetskaia Rossiia," 1977), 55–56.

39. Dudko, *Veriu gospodi!*, p. 55.
40. *Veche* 2: 103–4.
41. V.G. Treml, *Alcohol in the USSR: A Statistical Study* (Durham, N.C.: Duke University Press, 1982).
42. "Pravda ob alkogolizme v SSSR," *Russkaia mysl'*, 7 February, 1985.
43. *Izvestiia*, 17 May 1985.
44. K. Voronov [pseud.], "Demograficheskie problemy Rossii," *Grani*, 98 (1975): 255–76. This is a slightly shortened version of the article from *Veche*.
45. ———, 266.
46. See G.I. Litvinova and B.Ts. Urlanis, "Demograficheskaia politika Sovetskogo Soiuza," *Sovetskoe gosudarstvo i pravo*, 3 (1982): 38–46.
47. *Sobranie postanovlenii pravitel'stva SSSR*, 24 (1981), item 141.
48. AS No. 4022.

Religion and the Soviet Future

WILLIAM C. FLETCHER

One of the most intractable dilemmas facing the Gorbachev leadership is the problem of religion.

Religion showed absolutely that it could survive the most unrestrained use of force in the arrests, imprisonments and executions under the pre-war Stalin and the Khrushchev administrations. When leniency was the norm (as during the NEP and, perhaps, since 1975) or even neglect (as during and immediately after World War II, during the middle fifties and, again, since 1975) religion not only failed to wither away: it grew, sometimes at a fearsome rate.

The result is that the Gorbachev leadership remains confronted with a problem for which the Soviet government has not yet found a solution. Not only is religion alive and well in Soviet society, but it is handily surviving, and at times flourishing under, the best efforts of the state to suppress or even contain it. Far worse from the point of view of the present government is the very real possibility that religion is currently experiencing a surge of growth, perhaps massive growth.

The Intelligentsia

There is an abundant accumulation of evidence concerning a resurgence of religion among the Soviet intelligentsia, especially in Moscow and Leningrad. This tiny, but immensely influential, sector of the population which is university educated traditionally has served as the vanguard of intellec-

176

tual and social development in Russia. And here religion's growth and spread are thoroughly documented.

The beginnings of this return to religion on the part of the secular intelligentsia can be traced to the earliest days of the Soviet experiment.[1] A certain portion of Marxism's thinking adherents seem to find that over the course of time, the doctrine's grandiose claims to intellectual, ethical and social integrity do not stand up well. Certainly by the end of Stalin's reign the brutalities and horrors could scarcely be ignored, and Nikita Khrushchev's "Secret Speech" of 1956 forever terminated the myth that paradise and justice must inevitably result from obedience to the leader of the Communist party.

This revelation of a dark reality contradicting the bright promise was an overwhelming trauma for some parts of the intelligentsia, particularly among the youth.[2] A part of the intelligentsia, particularly the literary intelligentsia, almost immediately upon the death of Stalin began to search elsewhere. Non-conformist literary experimentation began as a trickle and quickly swelled into a flood in what came to be known "the Thaw" of the middle fifties. The Khrushchev regime was unable to stem the tide and by the next decade literature dissenting from the old ways, the Stalin ways, proliferated. Some of this new direction was in the published literature (as, for example, Solzhenitsyn's *One Day in the Life of Ivan Denisovich*); more of it was in *samizdat*.

The dissenting movements were symptomatic of a deeper unrest within the intelligentsia. There was a wholesale, virtually universal abandonment of Marxism-Leninism as a philosophy of life. By the middle sixties it began to be evident, and by the seventies it was obvious, that nobody among the younger generation—and very few from the older generations—believed in Marxism.

The intelligentsia had lost its secular faith; but it had not yet embraced religion. There were straws in the wind, however. The received dogma that only the illiterate can be religious began to give way, as here and there religious believers were discovered who had completed the higher levels of Soviet education. Initially surveys of religion and atheism among university students found a comfortable level of only a few percent who were not convinced atheists, and believers numbered far fewer than one percent of the sample. Even findings of 1 or 2 percent might be tolerable. But inconsistencies began to appear and the complacency of the atheist establishment began to erode.[3] (In one survey, for example, the researchers first classified the university students into categories according to religious belief. Then they administered a questionnaire, one of whose questions was, "Do you believe in God?" The researchers discovered that 91 percent of the atheists and 88 percent of the non-believers did not believe in God.[4])

And more and more evidence began to accumulate showing that religion was, in fact, becoming a significant factor in this elite population group. The situation finally became so clear that even the most hostile propagandists could not credibly claim that fewer than 10 percent of the population of advanced students were believers in the supernatural.[5]

But it was only in the middle sixties that a direct link between the intelligentsia and traditional religion began to appear. Late in December of 1965, two Moscow priests, Nikolai Eshliman and Gleb Yakunin, together wrote open letters protesting the state's treatment of the Orthodox church.[6] These letters (which may have been modeled on an earlier protest movement among the Russian Baptists) quickly elicited an echo throughout the Russian Orthodox church, and the Church intelligentsia almost immediately joined in.

This development within the Church had the potential to bridge the gap between the secular intelligentsia and organized religion. It was some years, however, before it became apparent that people were indeed crossing over from the intelligentsia into the Orthodox church.

Not that there has ever been a complete separation between the intelligentsia and the Church. Some of the poetry of Boris Pasternak, for example, was deeply religious and carried many overtones of Orthodoxy. When the poetess Anna Akhmatova died she had requested, and she received, an Orthodox funeral, which a great many of the intellectual elite attended, openly demonstrating their allegiance to or, at least, respect for Orthodox Christianity. But, by and large, the secular intelligentsia during the sixties and on into the seventies conducted their search for religious values outside the official Russian Orthodox church, considering that the Moscow Patriarchate was thoroughly tainted by collaboration with the regime and that its churches were intellectually stultified, fit only for elderly illiterates.

It was Alexander Solzhenitsyn who made the first public, dramatic return to the church. His "Prayer" confirmed his deep religiosity; his "Lenten Letter" of 1972 established him as a firm and loyal son of the Russian Orthodox church.[7]

Nor was he alone, for the evidence soon began to proliferate that an army of intellectuals was moving rapidly back to Orthodoxy.[8] In 1974, continuing seminars were formed in Leningrad and Moscow for discussion of religious and philosophical issues. These groups began to issue regular *samizdat* journals, and their influence grew apace. Despite the concerted efforts of the secret police to harrass and disrupt it, the Leningrad seminar continued its regular meetings into the 1980's. The Moscow seminar was finally broken up by the arrest and imprisonment of its members, but not before it had begun to attract members from other cities of the USSR.

Subsequent evidence demonstrated that during these years other, less well-known seminars for religious instruction and discussion began to spring up among the Moscow and Leningrad intelligentsia.

Late in 1976 an even more vigorous endeavor was undertaken by the Orthodox intelligentsia. A "Christian Committee for the Defense of Believers' Rights in the USSR" was formed and began actively to publicize cases in which believers, not only of the Orthodox church but of all faiths, were denied their legal rights because of their faith. In 1979, Gleb Yakunin and the other founding members were imprisoned, but this did nothing to inhibit the committee's work. To the contrary, it was galvanized with a flood of applications for membership and its work continued even more vigorously.

Obviously, there was great religious ferment in the intelligentsia. Perhaps our most complete picture of this ferment is to be found in the *samizdat* documentation concerning the Moscow priest, *Dimitry* Dudko.[9] Especially vivid evidence can be found in the Dudko materials which have reached the West, particularly in notes from his journals, concerning a growing influx in the late seventies of highly qualified scientists and intellectuals into full membership in the Orthodox church. By the end of the seventies hundreds of such intellectuals were presenting themselves to him for baptism into the Church each year. This confirms the mountain of other reports of a widespread return to Orthodoxy among the intelligentsia.

The Churches

This phenomenon is very much evident in the institutional church, although here the data are much less abundant. Nevertheless, the outlines of a picture are beginning to emerge. Of particular importance is the rejuvenation of the episcopate in the Russian Orthodox church.[10] A new generation of younger, more dynamic bishops is beginning to make its way in the hierarchy. Much less compliant than their predecessors, these new church leaders are succeeding in revitalizing church life even over the opposition of state authorities.

One of their most effective endeavors is to increase the numbers and the quality of the priesthood. Large numbers of new priests have been ordained by some of these more aggressive bishops, and many of them have a much better theological preparation than had been the norm. In part, this is due to a more dynamic system of informal training of candidates for the priesthood in the parishes. It is also due, however, to the effectiveness of the theological school system.

Even though the theological schools were severely truncated during the

Khrushchev anti-religious campaign of the sixties, during the past few years the three remaining seminaries and the two theological academies have managed to break out of their former confines. The student body has more than doubled in the last ten years, and the stream of new graduates is beginning to make itself felt throughout the Orthodox church.[11]

This new confidence on the part of religious leaders is by no means confined to any one denomination: instead, it seems to be operating across the board. In the western Ukraine, for example, Uniates (Catholics of Byzantine Rite) and other denominations have been especially vigorous since early 1984.[12] No longer cowed, clergy are beginning to confront their adversaries directly. Indeed, it is one of the scandals of contemporary atheism that some people, at least, were first introduced to anti-religious materials at the home of their priest, who subscribes to the materials in order to refute them.[13] And the believers themselves are reflecting this new attitude:

> Here is a typical example. In one of the district centers of our region a young man broke with religion. . . . The district newspaper publicized the testimony of this man, and an article about him appeared in the regional paper. For a time he was popular, he gave speeches on the story of his life. And then they forgot him. But the believers sent him letters, they visited him. No, they did not abuse the "apostate from religion," but they expressed sorrow about his decision, they invited him to think it over, they debated with him, they persuaded him.[14]

Given these new, dynamic winds blowing in the churches, one would expect growth (or, at least, pressures for growth) in the number of functioning churches in the USSR. Unfortunately, this is one of the most difficult subjects to assess, for in no other area are the authorities, secular and (as a consequence) ecclesiastical, so reticent. Reliable data occur most rarely, and often many years late.[15] There are scattered data from the sixties about new churches which had been built here and there; and Soviet spokesmen occasionally give estimates for the number of churches functioning in 1960 which are somewhat higher than estimates for the latter forties. But no firm data are available.[16]

We have rather better data for the attrition suffered by the churches during the campaign of the sixties, for authoritative figures during the next ten years indicated that half or more of the churches had been closed during the campaign.[17] Thus the number of functioning churches by the middle sixties was approximately 7,500 for the Orthodox and 3,200 for the Baptists; similar (or greater) losses were recorded for other denominations.

Apparently these figures remained fairly stable for a decade. In 1975, however, the situation began to change, and since then there has been some evidence of churches expanding their facilities to double or treble their capacity, some few new churches being built, and some old churches being renovated and restored to use. A Catholic parish in Belorussia had more than tripled its size by 1975 and, presumably, has continued to grow.[18] Although the numbers of Baptist churches have been suspiciously stable, an additional two thousand churches, with perhaps one hundred thousand members, are estimated to be functioning in the unregistered Baptist movement.[19] There is some evidence that donations to mosques have increased and mosques are being restored or built in Soviet Central Asia.[20]

There are curious indications that a considerable number of Catholic churches have been closed in the western Ukraine, Trans-Carpathia and elsewhere.[21] However, during the forties the Uniate Catholic church was eradicated entirely and thereafter could maintain its existence only deep in the underground in furtive, illegal movements. Since such churches are recently reported closed, this necessarily implies that some of the suppressed Catholic congregations have been allowed to function openly as churches during the past ten years.

One possible explanation of this anomaly is a change in state policy which took place in the middle seventies. Whereas previously the Soviet regime had been adamantly opposed to registering new churches, the policy was reversed in the seventies and the authorities began to encourage illegal congregations to register as legally functioning churches. This certainly was the case among the Uniates in the Ukraine, for example.[22] The protest movement among the Baptists, which has functioned illegally (but often quite openly) since the early sixties, was now allowed and even encouraged to register as legally permitted, fully functioning churches even though they refused to join the legalized Baptist denomination.[23] Other formerly illegal movements also were embraced by the new policy. The Pentecostals, for example, fairly rapidly acquired 230 legal Pentecostal churches and 320 joint Pentecostal and Baptist churches.[24]

Thus there is some scattered evidence that the number of churches in the USSR may be increasing. It should be reemphasized, however, that the data are much too sparse to support any confident assertions concerning increasing numbers of churches to any widespread (or indeed, even necessarily significant) degree—hard, reliable knowledge on this subject must await the accumulation of more data.

There are similar indications that church attendance has increased, perhaps dramatically. The observance of religious rites, once thought to be moribund, is apparently very widespread at present. "Why, even today," wonders one atheist, "is this religious rite [baptism] widespread, even more than the others, and many parents, even though they do not believe in god,* baptize their children?"[25] The main anti-religious journal, commenting on letters it receives, echoes this dismay:

> Often in these sad letters such a note as this sounds forth: Contemporary families are unstable because the spouses do not believe in god and the wedding is not sanctified by the church. As a rule this is the opinion of people of elderly age, the uncles and the grandmothers; however, a fairly similar point of view is expressed by young people also, who view the distant past in a rosy light.[26]

There are many reports that the churches are crowded, and the influence of organized religion seems to be widespread regardless of denomination.[27]

> Young people waste their best years in "comprehending god," and then they want but are unable to make up for lost time, I know such cases. How can one help them escape this? Young people easily give in to the influence of religion, they are not fixed in their views.[28]

With unconscious irony, one Soviet observer admits going to the cathedral sometimes "to hear the music of the choir" and while there he wonders what attracts all the young people.[29]

A large number of examples of widespread church attendance can be cited, but given the vast size of the country, and the number of discrete denominations and faiths which permeate the society, the evidence is far from adequate to draw sweeping conclusions. It indicates fairly persuasively that there is an increase in the interest in religion; the size and significance of this increase remains to be determined.

Religiousness

The resurgence of religion is by no means confined to organized religion, however. More and more it is becoming apparent that a strong stream of religious attitudes pervades the society and indeed may be increasing.

In the sixties and the early seventies the anti-religious establishment of the USSR apparently discovered sociological surveys.[30] A growing number of surveys were conducted, some of them very large indeed, to attempt to isolate precisely what portion of the population was still religious. At the start of this effort, it was confidently asserted that only small remnants of the past remained religious, certainly no more than 10 percent of the

---

*Soviet anti-religious propaganda insists on "orthographic atheism," whereby references to the divinity are denied the dignity of capitalization.

population. Indeed, some of the early studies purported to demonstrate this.

However, as the studies became more sophisticated and as the sociological researchers became more proficient in their craft, this earlier confidence began to erode. Regardless of how desperately the data were manipulated (e.g., counting only "convinced believers" in the religious sector of the population and consigning "wavering believers" to the other categories) even in selected populations it was becoming impossible to maintain the earlier confidence. By the early seventies these sociological surveys were uncovering an incidence of religiousness in the population which indicated that as a minimum, some 45 percent of the population were believers. After this had become increasingly apparent, for some reason such research was all but abandoned, and subsequent sociological data became exceedingly rare.[31]

One of the great reasons for this unexpectedly high incidence of religiousness was the rise of nationalism, which has become increasingly important in the USSR. In one area, for example:

> The materials of the research showed that a great part of those questioned do not distinguish between confessional and national adherence, equating the understanding of "Tadzhik" and "Moslem," that religious holidays and rites contribute to national [observances] and refraining from them leads to renunciation of one's national independence.[32]

More and more, religion began to accompany nationalism; whatever other functions it may have performed, religion served as one more means of demonstrating loyalty to one's own nation, rather than to the USSR as a whole.

Nor were the Russians themselves free of the similar phenomenon. In the search for their own roots, many Russians discovered how closely religion was intertwined with their own history. "An educated man must know all this," responded one Russian to explain his interest in religion.[33] Even in the Russian areas it became increasingly difficult for the state to quarantine pride in Russian history from a similar fascination with religion.

Among the general population, more and more indications are cropping up that materialism has not taken hold and at least in oblique ways the population retains its accustomed fascination with the supernatural. Atheist spokesmen are much disturbed, for example, at the persistence of pectoral crosses in the population. "Even men and women who are already grown up are beginning to wear a cross around their necks as though they were baptized—it is not only the youth who are rushing to follow a fad."[34] Even though some anti-religious commentators may try to trivialize the practice—one noted that one girl, when she grew tired of the neck cross, had it made into a gold crown for a tooth[35]—the problem is not disappearing. Other atheist observers go to great lengths to find rationalizations from popular psychology to explain away the pervasiveness of neck crosses and icons, but in fact they are unable to make any suggestions other than calling for more of the same anti-religious propaganda which has failed to eradicate this phenomenon even after a half century of trying.[36]

Just as worrisome is the persistence of religious practices even when the atheist observers find no residuum whatsoever of a real faith in the people themselves.

> Delirium, nothing more, in our times!" her daughter writes to us. "I know that Mama needs to go to the psychiatrist, but there is no possibility at all of convincing her of this. I cannot say that Mama is a believer—she does not pray, does not attend church, does not know the prayers, although she writes them down on slips of paper and carries them with her, saying they help her.[37]

The main antireligious journal was much annoyed when in a work of its fiction a reader noticed an incantation to the devil for healing and asked the magazine for the full text so that she could use it; she called it a "prayer."[38] "Many people, especially the elderly, refuse Soviet medicine, and instead go to the grannys or uncles for potions."[39] (While the atheist propagandist rightly views this as a failure of the materialist worldview among such people, it may also imply something about the quality of Soviet medicine in the countryside.)

Along with religion, outright superstition seems to be on the rise among the Soviet people. The atheist establishment, of course, considers religion as just another form of superstition and deplores the number of works of contemporary fiction which promote superstition.[40] Belief in house spirits is widespread, and explaining that the noises are due to a building's architectural resonances really does not seem to help much.[41] In what must surely be desperation, one propagandist attributed "the rise and strengthening of mystical prejudices" to two highly improbable factors: "First, the targeted export of mysticism from abroad, specifically the attempt of imperialist circles to use it together with religion as one of the arms of ideological diversion directed against the USSR, and second, the revival of propaganda activities of partisans of mysticism in our country."[42] With regard to occupation, the greater the danger the more likely it is that superstition will be present.

> To a great degree [it] appears in professions connected with risk (among flyers, sailors, chauffeurs, hunters, fishers), among athletes and participating youth.

When a person is unsure of the final result of his efforts, whether they will turn out beneficial to him, there is soil for mysticism. This is the source among some of belief in fate, luck, chance, signs and similar superstitions; among others it elicits hidden currents of the psyche, bringing out "reserve possibilities of the human organism," which often leads to reinforcement of mysticism.[43]

The picture that is emerging among the general population is an increasing ferment, a growing search for answers that transcend the drab, disappointing world of the official ideology.

So there are churches, so there are old men and women, abandoned by the children, their grief flows, and I ask you, dear editor, write something about god for them, let them think that god does not desert them if people have deserted them,"—this was the sad letter sent by a woman from the Ukraine, naive in its request to an atheist journal, but demonstrating one of the reasons why people turn to god: because they hope with the help of religion to fill a lack which they have in their lives.[44]

The converse of this widespread interest in the supernatural is the virtual collapse of atheism. Very much a growth industry in the fifties and sixties, anti-religious propaganda began to stagnate in the seventies, and during the eighties it has become entirely moribund.

The presses continue to produce the propaganda, but in nothing like the volume of years gone by.

The All-Union "Knowledge" society conducts not only oral but also printed propaganda of political and scientific knowledge. For the five years [1976–81] it published more than 15,000 books, pamphlets, journals, scientific-methodological aids and other publications with a general press run of around 700 million copies. Among them were the mass journals, "Science and Life," "Science and Religion," "Knowledge—Power," "International Life," "The Word of the Lecturer," the international annuals "Science and Humanity," "The Future of Science," 34 signed series of pamphlets in the cycle "What is New in Life, Science and Technology," and others.[45]

Impressive though it might seem, this list is radically truncated when compared to the heyday of a decade earlier. And the decline accelerated. *Problems of Scientific Atheism*, the crowning achievement of the scholarship of atheism, was published semi-annually from its inception in 1966. Thus it remained through volumes 29 and 30 in 1982; volume 31 appeared in 1983 and volume 32 only in 1985. In all of 1985, only seven articles on religion or atheism appeared in the national journals (excluding articles in the specialized periodicals).[46] *Science and Religion*, the flagship of anti-religious propaganda, continues to appear each month. But it has aged. The format has been unchanged for 20 years, the contents of each issue repeat with numbing monotony the handful of tired themes which are the entire brief of the Old Guard of atheism. Each issue contains articles on elderly heroes reminiscing about the glory days of their atheistic youth, and these sad elegies characterize the entire journal.

"Research has shown that the level of religiousness nevertheless remains high, and atheist work requires further perfecting."[47] The problem, however, is that the atheist establishment does not seem to have the capacity to accomplish this.

> One of the important problems is highly qualified cadres. It is no secret that some of the scholars who defend Doctoral and Candidate dissertations on scientific atheism then, because of various circumstances, leave this field.[48]

In what may have been an act of desperation, *Science and Religion* announced a nationwide contest to uncover new authors of anti-religious propaganda. First prize was 300 rubles, there were two second prizes of 200 rubles and three third prizes with no monetary reward. The winners would be recommended to a publishing house for consideration of a mass edition of their work.[49]

The anti-religious establishment continues to compile impressive statistics concerning the number of lectures delivered (with rather less data about how many people actually attend these tedious non-events) and how many courses on atheist themes are given each year.[50] Television programs are prepared,[51] and the cinema continues to be pressed into the service of atheism.[52] But there is a real question of how effective these efforts are. Reporting on letters received from readers, the editor of the leading atheist journal asks, "And another question: in fact do they make few atheist movies, or do they exist but are poorly publicized?"[53]

The quality of the anti-religious propaganda is appallingly low. "Unfortunately, in a number of published works the contents have no new ideas, there is no useful information, no deeply worked through guidelines for atheist education or recommendations which have useful actual data."[54]

> Some of our propagandists "usually prefer to prove the proven instead of thinking about new phenomena of life." Now and then lectures lack concreteness and conviction. Their themes, as has already been stated, do not reflect the full scope of the new achievements of the theory and practice of scientific atheism nor, similarly, the process of the modernization of religion. The nationality of the population of one region or another, the character of

the religiousness and the degree of atheist conviction of the people are not always taken into account.[55]

For all their concern, the professionals of atheism have not yet been able to find any real answer to these problems. Usually they have to fall back to the time-honored but totally ineffective pleas for greater efforts to indoctrinate the people with rationalist education, when it is becoming increasingly obvious that at its core it is not a problem of rationalism at all.[56] "Unfortunately, atheist literature addressed to the young reader is often excessively rationalistic, it does not have the emotional content which is able to grip the youth, to make them think about serious worldview and moral questions."[57]

Indeed, in many respects the teeth of the propaganda have been drawn; it has become almost domesticated. In place of the former militance and aggressiveness, today's anti-religious propaganda has taken on a more tentative, almost apologetic note. Referring to letters from readers, *Science and Religion* editors commented:

> With some (a very few) it was not possible to agree, insofar as they took a position foreign to ours. Thus, one cannot accept the advice "not to stand on ceremony with believers," "to quit debating with them and fight them actively." Even though it renounces religious ideology, our society does not come out against the believer. And we, naturally, will never take up arms against a believing person, "to fight them."[58]

In place of the earlier clarion calls to militance, now the propaganda almost begs its practitioners to be nice. "It is especially necessary to explain that atheists do not allow themselves to turn to sincere believing young people with words of condemnation."[59] The earlier doctrinal commitment that religion must be eradicated as a horrible evil which is totally incompatible with the new socialist society has been replaced by the mildest of all opinions that in socialism society will realize its socialist goals more quickly if fewer people are religious.[60]

So far has this transformation gone that at times the anti-religious propaganda has been turned completely around and now performs functions that used to be in the domain of religious propaganda in the Soviet Union. Thus, one atheist article cautioned its readers that a church wedding does not necessarily guarantee domestic tranquility.[61] An article in *Science and Religion* went to great lengths bragging about Patriarch Pimen's peace conference in May 1982, taking special pride in the statements of the Rev. Billy Graham confirming that there is religious liberty in the USSR.[62] And in 1985 *Problems of Scientific Atheism* contained a very strange article listing in great detail and praising all the recent activities of the Moscow Patriarchate, and Patriarch Pimen, on the peace front.[63] Such an article in earlier times would have graced the pages of the *Journal of the Moscow Patriarchate* over the by-line of a bishop, but would never, never have appeared in the anti-religious propaganda.

State Policy

Aside from the actions taken by believing citizens themselves, the key determinant of the status of religion remains what it has always been in the USSR: state policy. Whether religion flourishes or braces itself for attack is determined almost exclusively by the state, for when the policy is harsh and relies on force, religious believers have less room for action than when policies are lenient. And during the past ten years state policy toward religion has undergone major changes.

The first ten years of the Brezhnev period were far from promising for religious believers. While Khrushchev's anti-religious campaign leveled off, in all but the most brutish respects, the state's policy toward religion remained harsh. It was only in the middle seventies that this situation began to change.

At first it seemed that it would be a change for the worse. In 1975, amendments to the 1929 laws on religion were enacted which radically centralized the control over churches and religious believers. Nearly all the important decisions were taken away from local and regional bodies and were given to the central government's Council for Religious Affairs.[64] It was widely feared that this would be a bitter blow to the churches, greatly increasing their difficulties.[65]

Even more ominous were the changes in the 1977 Constitution. Of particular importance was the Constitution's specification of the citizen's duties in the civic education of his children. One of the most severe sanctions introduced during Khrushchev's anti-religious campaign and continued since then had been the denial of parental rights: parents guilty of teaching religion to their children were stripped of parental rights, and their children were forcibly removed to atheistic state boarding schools. The strictures concerning civic education in the new Constitution seemed to threaten a wholesale application of this measure:

> The rights of parents are intimately connected with their obligations and responsibilities to their children for education. The Constitution of the USSR and the legislation on the family and marriage require of each citizen of the USSR, whether believer or unbeliever, the education in children of feelings

of social duty, civil obligations, patriotism, readiness to defend the motherland and participation in socially useful labor.[66]

Events were to prove, however, that the 1975 amendments and the 1977 Constitution were the last hurrah for advocates of a harsh state policy against religion across the board. In fact, the Constitution remained a dead letter insofar as denial of parental rights was concerned, for no cases of this penalty based on the Constitution have come to light since then. The 1975 amendments which centralized policy decisions in the Council for Religious Affairs had the opposite effect of what was feared. In practice, the Council for Religious Affairs has acted in many cases to restrain anti-religious excesses on the part of local administrators, and with regard to registering churches these amendments have had exactly the opposite effect to what was feared.

Beginning in the middle seventies, the state introduced the most radical change in its policy toward local churches in a half century. The policy had been almost without exception to deny any requests by local believers to register as a legally functioning church. The state went to great lengths to keep the number of such permitted churches as low as possible. Suddenly, in the middle seventies this policy was reversed. Now the state itself began urging groups of believers who had been meeting illegally to accept registration as a legally functioning church.

A great many such groups took advantage of this unexpected windfall. Many others, however, did not, for they rightly perceived that the reasons for the state's change of policy were, first, a tacit admission that it could not prevent believers from worshiping together illegally and, second, that once they accepted legal registration they would gradually come under controls which could not be applied when they met in clandestine circumstances. "There is great significance in activity directed toward the liquidation of the extremist, primarily sectarian, underground by the registration . . . of religious congregations which accept the legislation on religious cults."[67] But regardless of the state's motivations, this *volte-face* whereby the state became the agent, rather than the enemy, of the creation of new, legally functioning churches, was unprecedented.

The next surprise in the state's policy came in 1981. The state decreed that as of 1 January 1981, the category of taxation for clergy and all other church employees would be revised downward one bracket, from a tax rate ceiling of 81 percent to 69 percent. In effect, this removed the special stigma attached to clergy by the state and placed them in the same category as any other privately employed professionals.[68]

As these new policy directives were applied in practice, state officials sometimes became defenders of the rights of believers rather than, as had been the case almost without exception, their enemy. The central anti-religious journal, for example, began to denounce job discrimination against religious employees.[69] In one case a trio of thieves specialized in burglarizing churches, on the theory that the authorities would be less likely to protect such property. Two of them received four year sentences and the other got two years.[70]

But there was another side to the coin. These indications of an unprecedented leniency in state religious policy were accompanied by a vigorous, indeed brutal, use of force against selected targets. Key religious leaders, especially those who attracted a large following, were arrested, and it soon became apparent that while the rank and file might enjoy unprecedented freedoms, the most vigorous of their leaders would come under furious attack. For example, between 1979 and 1984 the number of Baptists known to be in prison increased from 35 to nearly 200,[71] and in the spring of 1985 there was another considerable crackdown on selected activists of the unregistered Baptists.[72]

What had happened was a full scale, more consistent application of the Andropov approach to social controls. After the fall of Khrushchev, Brezhnev's new head of the KGB, Yurii Andropov, established a carefully calibrated policy to contain and eradicate the secular dissent. Significant concessions to the rank and file were coupled with extreme measures against the leading dissidents, including imprisonment, confinement in psychiatric hospitals, exile to remote locations within the USSR, and expulsion from the country. Obviously, the approach was to offer concessions sufficient to draw off the main body of followers while simultaneously decapitating the dissent by removing its leadership. Consistently applied, this approach worked wonders in the secular dissent, and by the end of the seventies such dissenting movements were virtually a thing of the past.

The same approach was applied in the religious sector. Wherever there was dissent—whether in Orthodoxy following the Eshliman-Yakunin letters, among the dissenting Baptists, or among the illegal groups such as Pentecostals, Mennonites, underground Orthodox, Uniates, Lithuanian Catholics and a host of others—concessions were made to meet the needs of the rank and file while the leaders were abruptly removed through arrest, imprisonment, and other uses of force. By the middle seventies this policy was becoming plainly evident; during Andropov's brief reign following the death of Brezhnev and for several years thereafter the policy was implemented most vigorously, with a great many individual leaders arrested and unprecedented leniency shown toward the churches at large.

But it did not work. Among the secular dissent, where the concern ranged from parochial matters of artistic license to more amorphous questions of human rights, the Andropov approach was eminently successful: once minor concessions were made and the leadership was removed, the movements collapsed. Not so in the churches. Yielding to the believers resulted only in demands for further concessions, for even the most lenient policies of the state stopped well short of any real religious freedom. And no sooner would leaders be incarcerated than new leaders, equally brave, equally talented, and equally committed, would arise to take their place. What had worked beautifully in the secular intelligentsia, completely disrupting the dissenting movements, had the opposite effect in the churches. This two-pronged approach, by giving the believers much greater room in which to operate and by creating local martyrs among their leaders, resulted only in an explosive growth of religious sentiment.

While the policies of the KGB were fairly clear and applied with some consistency, there was great and increasing disarray in the central leadership with regard to religion. In his last years in power, Brezhnev sowed no end of confusion in religious policy just as he did in other realms. At the 26th Congress of the Communist Party of the Soviet Union in 1981, he announced:

In certain countries of the East in recent times Islamic slogans are being actively promoted. We Communists respect the religious convictions of people who profess Islam, as also other religions. The important thing is what goals are pursued by forces proclaiming one slogan or another. Under the banner of Islam a liberation struggle may be unfolded. The experience of history, including the most recent history, testifies to this but it also says that reaction also operates with Islamic slogans, supporting counter-revolutionary insurgencies. Consequently, the whole matter is what is the real composition of one movement or another.[73]

While such ambivalence may be understandable in a nation whose foreign policy must simultaneously face the Ayatollah Khomeini and Afghanistan, this statement certainly provided small guidance for policymakers concerned with Islam—or any other religion—domestically in the Soviet Union.

Two years later, Konstantin Chernenko, who had succeeded Andropov, provided leadership which was no less muddled. At the June plenum of the Central Committee he turned his attention briefly to religion:

Communists are consistent atheists," he said, "but they do not force their world view on anyone. Our method is enlightenment, conviction, propaganda, but when we come across facts of transgressing socialist laws or subversive political activity, which is only disguised by religion, then we act as our Constitution requires.[74]

The plenum which occurred in December of the same year tried in vain to clarify this perplexing approach by noting that "the strengthening of socialist consciousness comes through the struggle against recidivist idealist psychology, against the intrigues of bourgeois propaganda, which often comes forth in religious 'garments.' "[75]

> The first task of this work," said A. S. Onishchenko, "is to unmask ideological diversions in religious form, to show the true nature of the political, moral, philosophical and theological doctrines of contemporary clericalism. An important place in the counter-propaganda should be occupied by unmasking clerical speculation on the nationality question.[76]

The Present Situation

Even if the central leadership had been able to devise more coherent statements of policy, it is highly doubtful that the situation could have been reversed throughout the vast country. During the later Brezhnev years inefficiency and corruption had proliferated in all areas of Soviet public life, but Brezhnev and his aging lieutenants remained inactive; Andropov's fulminations were fruitless; Chernenko's torpid reign was irrelevant; and it remains to be seen whether the best efforts of the Gorbachev leadership can stem the tide. The nation was gripped in a rising tide of incompetence.

The ethical and moral decline of contemporary Soviet society has escalated the problem of religion. What was formerly a backwater of Soviet policy, of interest and concern only to third-rate bureaucrats and (according to them) pensioners and crones, suddenly has begun to appear at the highest levels among the educated elite.

What triggered this development was *glasnost'*, or "openness," proclaimed by Gorbachev as a fundamental policy. The literary intelligentsia seized upon this as an opportunity, and the deep ethical and moral problems of society began to surface in print.[77] Newspapers began to publish letters from their readers equating social problems such as alcoholism with the decline (or suppression) of religion.[78] Nor were such opinions confined to the rank and file. Three of the nation's leading writers, Chingiz Aitmatov, Vasyl' Bykov and Viktor Astaf'ev, added their weight to the discussion.[79] They were of towering reputation—two were winners of the Lenin Prize and one of the State Prize, respectively, and for them to equate society's moral decline with religion lent great authority to the opinion.

The state was quick to counterattack. Ivan Kryvelev, an old warhorse of the antireligious campaigns, denounced their views, reasserting the dogmatic attachment to atheism which has been the official position for seventy years.[80] Kryvelev, in turn, was attacked for being out of step with the present by another philosopher;[81] and he, consequently, was threatened with expulsion from the cadre of state-sanctioned lecturers on atheism.[82] The affair had become such a *cause célèbre* that Yegor Ligachev, then the Party's chief ideologist, apparently felt constrained to turn to the subject in a ringing attempt to buttress the state's fading commitment to atheism.[83]

But the incompetence in the government and throughout the leadership structures had paralyzed religious policy. With the best will in the world, there is a real question whether any consistent policy, harsh or lenient, could successfully be initiated by the central government and have any chance at all of effective application in the countryside. Venality was rampant, and local administrators either did not pay attention to instructions from the center or carried out the instructions so haphazardly as to achieve nothing but chaos locally. At all levels bribes became the expected norm in any church leader's relations with the local government representatives.[84]

This situation leaves the religious believers with vast new areas in which to operate. The various indications summarized above are admittedly episodic and far from complete. No confident assertions concerning the extent and significance of the current religious resurgence in the USSR can be made on the basis of this sparse evidence. However, in the situation which currently prevails in the USSR, certain key areas of silence in themselves raise questions concerning what may be happening.

For example, although the flow of religious *samizdat* has by no means diminished, the current materials seem to be curiously lacking in some of the traditional complaints of earlier years. Protests against widespread closings of churches have disappeared entirely. Nor are there the accustomed number of reports of the militia or the KGB disrupting illegal services. Fewer and fewer atrocities are reported at shrines and places of pilgrimage. Perhaps most significantly, the earlier demands for the freedom to give religious education to children have all but disappeared.

On these issues, and on many others, current *samizdat* is virtually silent. The public press, too, is devoid of some of its earlier staples, particularly newspaper reports and articles on large-scale arrests or exposures obviously designed to intimidate believers. Where the earlier anti-religious efforts, which did enjoy some success in suppressing or perhaps even reducing religion in the society, had been accompanied by vast press campaigns bearing all sorts of veiled and open threats, today's anti-religious propaganda, what there is of it, is anemic, insipid, often apologetic, and non-threatening.

Prospects for the future

Given such a situation, the demoralization of the anti-religious forces is understandable, and perhaps the current, contradictory policies combining sporadic severity with unprecedented lenience are the most that can realistically be accomplished by the government. No truly attractive alternatives have yet appeared: while recent policies have been ineffective, none of the other approaches which have been tried in the past seems any less so. With a rapidly deteriorating situation (from point of view of the ideology) in the religious sector the Gorbachev government can choose only between two distasteful alternatives.

First, it might contemplate complete abandonment of the policies of severity which have failed utterly to eradicate religion; the remaining remnants of this approach are only complicating a hopeless situation. But then the predictable result would be a massive, perhaps explosive growth of religion. And sooner or later (perhaps a great deal sooner) this religious floodtide might break out from the reservoirs of the purely religious, where its effects are mostly trivial from the Party's point of view, into regions of real danger to the government.

Alternatively, Gorbachev might seek to reverse the deteriorating situation by a return to force. This never worked well in the past, but at least it served temporarily to contain the problem of religion within manageable limits. There is real question, however, whether he could find the cadres needed to implement such a reversion to force and discipline.

Religion is not like other problems faced by the government. The much heralded anti-corruption campaign, for example, has a problem which is similar (*quis custodiet ipsos custodies?*) but it can add two assets to the purely ideological appeal. The first is an appeal to self-interest on the part of the anti-corruption cadres, for denunciation of corruption can promote one's advancement (by getting rid of superiors) and reinforce one's position (by removing unreliable inferiors). Second, it can appeal to basic morality, the almost instinctive aversion to bribery and swindling which seems to infuse all civilized societies.

But an anti-religious campaign lacks these supra-ideological advantages. Religion has never been a career track of promise in the USSR, and to engineer the removal of corrupt or lenient officials would only confirm one in an intrinsically undesirable career. Nor is the appeal to morality at all effective: excepting only the small band of zealots of atheism, morality and religion are all but synonymous in the minds of most people.

What is left is only the ideological appeal, that religion is bad because Marxism-Leninism says it is bad. And it is one of the Party's greatest disappointments that the ideology has proven woefully ineffective in inspiring most of the population, and it must be buttressed by some less-noble sentiment—patriotism, nationalism, economic self-interest, privilege or even outright careerism—if it is to mobilize any large-scale cadres. Certainly in the field of atheism the impassioned appeals to the ideology have fallen on the deaf ears of four generations of Soviet citizens.

With nothing better in sight, then, the Gorbachev government most probably will decide to live with the present situation, leaving its religious policies, and the current conditions, largely unchanged. But there are huge risks in such a *laissez-faire* approach. Religion may be building up so much momentum, there may be so much suppressed demand, that a massive breakout may be imminent.

The areas of silence, the sectors where no data are forthcoming, do not in themselves necessarily indicate that any sort of religious revival is beginning. However, history provides precedents which must disturb the anti-religious establishment. Every time similar silences have occurred in the past—during the fifties, during and immediately after World War II, during the middle thirties, and during the twenties—subsequent evidence has demonstrated that religion enjoyed a revival in the country. Sometimes it was slight, as during the brief thaw of the thirties; but sometimes, as during the fifties, it was massive. Today's large areas of silence, coupled with the increasing fund of positive evidence which has been outlined above, may combine to suggest that the USSR now may be on the verge of a religious revival of historic proportions.

And such a revival, when it takes hold, must have huge effects on the destiny of the USSR.

There is no way to foresee precisely what the effects of such a resurgence of religion will be. The nation is too vast, its resources, both natural and of the mind, are too great, its nationalities are too diverse, and its religions are too variegated to permit any confident assertions about the future. Three recent analogies, however, may be of some interest.

After the Poznan riots in 1956, the Polish regime virtually ignored religion (except for occasional *pro forma* contacts and statements by the highest representatives of church and state). Two decades later 96 percent of the Polish population were members of the Roman Catholic church, 70 percent were in church on a given Sunday, and Solidarity rose up to shake the very foundations of the state. The Church was not involved in Solidarity's formation, not directly; but the growth of religiousness, of which church membership was an index, was definitely one of the driving forces of the deep commitment to human rights which was intrinsic to the movement.

If this kind of history should repeat itself in the USSR, the results might be profound. Like it or not, the state might be tempted to enforce the martial discipline, and, failing that, the regime, or its successor, might have to accept a return to the local control ("the czar is far away") enshrined in the nostalgia for the village democracy of the *veche* (old Russia's people's assembly).

Events in the United States may also give evidence of the power of religion to influence a modern nation. For a generation it was assumed that religion was fading out of the secularized society which was emerging in America, with the mainline denominations collapsing and the more enthusiastic forms of Protestantism already dead. Suddenly in the latter seventies the evangelicals exploded into the national attention, with their churches growing at an unprecedented rate. Immediately thereafter the political life of the nation was transformed with a resurgence of conservatism, and society itself began to edge away from its earlier easy acceptance of promiscuity, abortion, drugs, and an array of other practices with which the newly awakened evangelical sensitivity was not comfortable. To say that the religious revival was responsible for these political and social changes would be to go far, far beyond the currently available evidence; but it would be parlous to divorce the evangelical movement from these changes entirely.

Whether the effects of a religious revival in the USSR would be similar is, of course, highly problematical. However, the current resurgence is taking place against a backdrop of profound concern with the erosion of public morality, and many of the dimensions of the return to religion are couched in the terms of recapturing the moral purity of an earlier era. Pietism has always held a huge fascination for the Russian people, and, excepting only the aristocracy, the society has been saturated with puritanical attitudes. Should the growth of religion effect a marriage between the prudishness of the political leadership and the deeply conservative morality of Russia's past, then the effects on the society would be incalculable.

Finally, and ominously, the example of Iran presents itself. After a generation and more of heroic efforts on the part of the state to leave the religious past behind and enter into the twentieth century, traditional Islam returned to Iran with a vengeance. Under the Ayatollah Khomeini, Islamic fundamentalism has triumphed absolutely. Practices which the modern mind had thought safely relegated to the nightmares of medieval fanaticism now are normative throughout the society, and the nation is being goaded on a forced march back to religious purity.

Should a similar return to the past occur in the USSR, an awesome possibility arises. The remotest chance, the merest premonition that Russian messianism might enter an unholy alliance with the dark places of the country's religious history—such a dire prospect must give one pause.

One thing is certain. If there is a religious revival under way in the USSR, and the evidence is increasingly persuasive that there is, then the nation and the society are on the brink of profound changes. And on a shrinking, interconnected globe, these changes must have great importance for the world's future.

Notes

1. Indeed, some of the leading Orthodox theologians of the twentieth century, Nikolai Berdyaev among them, were themselves Marxists before their conversion to Orthodoxy. See Nikolai Zernov, *The Russian Religious Renaissance of the Twentieth Century* (New York: Harper and Row, 1963).

2. Dimitry Pospielovsky has written eloquently on this intellectual trauma, presenting it as perhaps the chief cause of the growth of the Church and the renewal of anti-religious severity in the latter fifties. *The Russian Church under the Soviet Regime 1917–1982* (New York: St. Vladimir's Seminary Press, 1984), 2: 350–52.

3. Such data are surveyed in some detail in William C. Fletcher, *Soviet Believers: The Religious Sector of the Population* (Lawrence, KS: The Regents' Press of Kansas, 1981), 91–99.

4. A. A. Lebedev, "Studencheskaya molodezh' i ateizm," in Academy of Sciences of the USSR (hereafter AN SSSR), *Voprosy nauchnogo ateizma* (Problems of Scientific Atheism—(hereafter *VNA*) (Moscow: AN SSSR, semiannually) 15 (1973): 202.

5. V. F. Milovidov, "Kritika sovremennoy mistiki," [A critique of contemporary mysticism], in AN SSSR, *VNA* 32 (1985): 131.

6. The most extensive, and best, treatment of the Eshliman-Yakunin affair is Michael A. Bourdeaux, *Patriarch and Prophets* (London: Macmillan, 1969).

7. See *Vestnik Russkogo Studencheskogo Khristianskogo Dvizheniya*, (The Messenger of the Russian Students' Christian Movement) 103 (1972): 145–9.

8. The materials on the Christian seminars are nicely summarized by Pospielovsky, *Russian Church*, 2: 433ff.

9. The Dudko affair is summarized in some detail in Dimitry Pospielovsky, "Intelligentsia and Religion: Aspects of Religious Revival in the Contemporary Soviet Union: The Orthodox Church," in Dennis Dunn, ed., *Religion and Communist Society*, (Berkeley, CA: Berkeley Slavic Specialties, 1983), 20–30. In this volume it is dealt with at greater length in Darrell Hammer's contribution.

10. See Pospielovsky, *Russian Church*, 2: 400–22 *et passim*.

11. ———, 403.

12. Andrew Sorokowski, "The Chronicle of the Catholic Church in Ukraine," *Religion in Communist Lands* 13, 3 (Winter 1985): 292–97.

13. "Iz 'Ankety-83,' " *Nauka i religiya*, 2 (1984): 33; "Chitatel' i zhurnal," *Nauka i religiya* 9 (1984): 2.
14. E. Takello, "Byt' posledovatel'nym," *Nauka i religiya* 1 (1982): 22.
15. William C. Fletcher, "USSR," in Hans (J. J.) mol ed., *Western Religion: A Country by Country Sociological Inquiry*, (The Hague: Mouton, 1972), 565–86.
16. The data are surveyed in Pospielovsky, *Russian Church*, 2: 327, 403–7.
17. See, e.g., Donald A. Lowrie and William C. Fletcher, "Khrushchev's Religious Policy, 1959–1964," in Richard H. Marshall, Jr. ed., *Aspects of Religion in the Soviet Union, 1917–1967* (Chicago: University of Chicago Press, 1971), 131–55.
18. Tadeusz Poleski (pseud.), "Pastoral Work by the Catholic Church in Belorussia (1927–1984)," *Religion in Communist Lands* 13, 3 (Winter 1985): 309–10.
19. Lawrence Klippenstein, "An Unforgotten Past: Recent Writings by Soviet Emigré Baptists in West Germany," *Religion in Communist Lands* 14, 1 (Spring 1986): 29.
20. "Sources," *Religion in Communist Lands* 131, 3 (Winter 1985): 317, summarizing *Pravda vostoka* (Truth of the Orient), 17 February, 24 March, 1985 and *Turkmenskaya iskra* (Turkmenian Spark), 7 April 1985.
21. Sorokowski, "Chronicle," 293, 295.
22. ———, 295.
23. A. V. Belov, *Sekty, sektantstvo, sektanty* [Sects, sectarianism, sectarians] (Moscow: "Nauka," 1978), 53.
24. ———, 22.
25. V. Shevelev, "Uverennost' v zavtrashnem dne," [Confidence in the coming day], *Nauka i religiya* 1 (1984): 7.
26. Editorial commentary introducing Inga Ballod, "Dvoe v odnom dome," [A couple in one house], *Nauka i religiya* 6 (1984): 18.
27. Cf., "Iz 'Ankety-83,' " [From "Questionnaire 83"], *Nauka i religiya* 5 (1984): 43.
28. "Chitatel' i zhurnal," 3.
29. "Iz 'Ankety-83,' " [From "Questionnaire 83"], *Nauka i religiya* 5 (1984): 43.
30. See Fletcher, *Soviet Believers, passim*.
31. E.g., S. Iu. Dadabaeva, "Konkretno-sotsiologicheskie issledovaniya v praktike ateisticheskoy raboty," [Concrete sociological research in the practice of atheist work]. *VNA* 31 (1983): 257.
32. ———, 258.
33. "Iz 'Ankety-83,' " [From "Questionnaire 83"], *Nauka i religiya* 1 (1984): 14.
34. ———, 2 (1984): 33.
35. E. Sergienko, "Chto stalo s krestikom," [What became of a cross], *Nauka i religiya* 2 (1981): 32.
36. V. Ostrozhinskii, "Printsipy i moda," [Principles and fashion], *Nauka i religiya* 4 (1982): 23–24.
37. E. Sergienko, "O 'tserkovnom' uteshenii, domovom i noevom kovchege,"

(On "church" consolation, a house spirit and Noah's Ark), *Nauka i religiya* 12 (1984): 19.

38. ———, 19.
39. ———, 19.
40. Milovidov, "Kritika," 138.
41. V. Simbirtsev, "Otkuda berutsya sueveriya" (Where Do Superstitions Come From), *Nauka i religiya* 2 (1981): 30.
42. Milovidov, "Kritika," 138.
43. ———, 137.
44. "Chitatel' i zhurnal," 4.
45. *Nauka i religiya* 6 (1981): 3.
46. According to the *Letopis' zhurnal'nykh statey* for 1985 there was one article on religion each in *Druzhba narodov* (Friendship of Peoples), *Voprosy filosofii* (Problems of Philosophy), *Novoe vremya* (New Times), *Partiinaya zhizn'* (Party Life), *Politicheskoe samoobrazovanie* (Political Self-Education), *Priroda* (Nature) and *Sovety narodnykh deputatov* (Soviets of People's Deputies). There were also eleven articles in journals dealing with foreign countries (*Aziya i Afrika segodnya* [Asia and Africa Today] (8), *Inostrannaya literatura* [Foreign Literatures], *Latinskaya Amerika* [Latin America], and *SShA* [USA]. The complete absence of religion from authoritative journals such as *Kommunist* is striking.
47. Dadabaeva, "Konkretno-sotsiologicheskie issledovaniya," 253.
48. "Aktual'nye voprosy ateisticheskogo vospitaniya v svete resheniy iyun'skogo (1983 g.) Plenuma TsK KPSS," (Essential Problems of Atheist Education in the Light of the Decisions of the June (1983) Plenum of the CC CPSU), in AN SSSR, *VNA* 32 (1985): 13.
49. *Nauka i religiya* 4 (1982): 39.
50. ———, 6 (1982): 3.
51. ———, 7 (1982): 8.
52. V. Zots, "Poedinok s temnotoy i lozh'yu," (A Duel With Darkness and Falsehood), *Nauka i religiya* 4 (1982): 49.
53. "Iz 'Ankety-83,' " (From "Questionnaire 83"), *Nauka i religiya* 2 (1984): 39.
54. "Aktual'nye voprosy," 14.
55. *Nauka i religiya* 7 (1982): 8.
56. Ostrozhinskii, "Printsipy i moda," 23.
57. "Aktual'nye voprosy," p. 8.
58. "Chitatel' i zhurnal," 4.
59. *Nauka i religiya* 10 (1984): 29.
60. D. Ugrinovich, "Religiya kak sotsial'noe yavlenie," [Religion as a social phenomenon], *Nauka i religiya* 10 (1982): 18.
61. Ballod, "Dvoe v odnom dome," 18.
62. V. Makhin, "Ostrye problemy na 'Kruglom Stole,' " [Critical problems at the "Round Table"], *Nauka i religiya* 10 (1982): 39.
63. V. V. Yashin, " 'Russkaya pravoslavnaya tserkov' i antivoennoe dvizhenie,"

[The Russian Orthodox Church and the anti-war movement], in AN SSSR, *VNA* 32 (1985): 251–66.

64. The translated text of these amendments is in Pospielovsky, *Russian Church*, 2: 493–500.

65. ——, 397–99.

66. "Novye tendentsii v ideologii i deyatel'nosti khristianskikh sekt i voprosy ateisticheskogo vospitaniya," [New tendencies in the ideology and activity of Christian sects and problems of atheist education], in AN SSSR, *VNA* 24 (1979): 216.

67. E. Filimonov, "Religioznyi ekstremizm: ideologicheskaya i sotsial'naya sushchnost'," [Religious extremism: ideological and social essence], *Nauka i religiya* 8 (1984): 22.

68. Pospielovsky, *Russian Church*, 2: 431.

69. A. Maslova, "Gumanisticheskaya sushchnost' Marksistskogo ateizma," [The humanistic essence of Marxist atheism], *Nauka i religiya* 12 (1982): 30.

70. Ya. Shestopal, "Ikony v stogu," [Icons in a stack], *Nauka i religiya* 2 (1982): 34.

71. *Religion in Communist Lands* 13, 1 (Spring 1985): 64.

72. John Anderson, "Renewed Harassment of Council of Baptist Prisoners' Relatives," *Religion in Communist Lands* 14, 1 (Spring 1986): 100.

73. Ugrinovich, "Religiya," 17–18, quoting from *Materialy XXVI s"ezda KPSS*,[Materials of the 26th Congress of the CPSU] (Moscow, 1981), 13.

74. "Aktual'nye voprosy," 4.

75. I. Malakhova, "Na uroven' aktual'nykh zadach," [At the level of contemporary tasks], *Nauka i religiya* 6 (1984): 4.

76. ——, 5.

77. For a convenient summary, see Vera Tolz, "Soviet Writers Criticized for Christian Leanings," *Radio Liberty Research*, RL 418/86 (5 November, 1986), p. 1–5.

78. *Sovetskaya Belorussiya*, 28 June 1986.

79. See note 77, Tolz, p. 2.

80. *Komsomol'skaya pravda*, 30 July 1986.

81. *Literatura i iskusstvo*, 5 September 1986.

82. *Komsomol'skaya pravda*, 3 October 1986.

83. *Pravda*, 28 September 1980.

84. Pospielovsky, *Russian Church*, 2: 401.

10

Religious Values in Contemporary Soviet Fiction and the Level of Official Tolerance

MICHAEL B. KREPS

This chapter aims at examining a phenomenon new in kind for Soviet literature—appearance in the official Soviet press of works which treat contemporary life, as well as events of the recent past, from the standpoint of the religious ethic. While briefly discussing such writings I will also analyse the reaction to this phenomenon on the part of the Soviet authorities responsible for ideological control in the field of literature. In stricter terms, I try to define the general pattern of the interaction between literature and censorship today, from which can be derived an abstract but important concept, which I call the level of official tolerance.

This level is an imaginary boundary that separates the realm of the permitted from the sphere of the uncontrolled or forbidden. The writer crosses this boundary at his own risk, since the very act, whether involuntary or purposeful, may be defined by censorship as a transgression which provokes automatic retaliatory reaction.

The level of official tolerance is a variable quantity—it depends on the state of affairs at any given period of time, and is susceptible to fluctuations. It is never discussed in the official press or defined by law, though the involved parties know about it only too well. It is also a composite structure consisting of a number of smaller units, each of which pertains to its own sphere of cultural and political reference. Thus, it should not be imagined as a flat plane, but rather as a curved one, since the level of official tolerance for one sphere of activity may be higher than for another. I mainly deal with one of its constituents concerning the topic of the religious in literary works.

The presence of religious allusions, characters and themes in contemporary Soviet fiction is not a feature inherited by it from its previous Stalinist period. The orientation of Soviet writers toward religious values— a cultural movement, originating in the late fifties, and still going on—is an unexpected phenomenon, which could hardly have been predicted in the early fifties. After Stalin's death one could have made a number of prognoses on the possible development of Soviet literature in the following decades. In fact, such prognoses were made predicting the proliferation of such genres and topics as war, industrial and teenage novels, psychological, urban, science-fiction, and even detective and modernistic stories. The most daring analyst could have even foretold the emergence of writings on the hardships endured by the Soviet people during the time of the personality cult, in the vein of *Gulag* and village themes, though in reality they hit Soviet readers as a bolt from the blue. But to predict the appearance of literary works involving religious topics in the country of militant atheism, would have been utterly unimaginable.

But the unimaginable happened, and now we have a number of stories and poems where these topics are given prominence. These works are, however, far different from the conventional, superficial antireligious pieces of earlier times. Quite the reverse—in these recent works religious problems are treated seriously and with a large measure of compassion by the author, even if he himself tries to avoid expressing his own clear-cut attitude toward these themes, as is the case in the long stories of Vladimir Tendryakov's "Apostolic Trip" ("Apostol'skaia komandirovka"), and "The Eclipse" ("Zatmenie"). It is noteworthy also that this interest in religious values has been displayed by the most talented of the contemporary Soviet writers: Solzhenitsyn[1], Trifonov, Rasputin, Aitmatov, Shukshin, Bykov, and others. The religious ethic in their works, whether open, concealed, or veiled, is the main, and sometimes, the only moral yardstick by which men and their actions are measured.

As distinct from Soviet published literature, the sympathies of *samizdat* and *tamizdat* writers toward religious values are expressed more candidly, as in the later works of Alexander Solzhenitsyn, in Vladimir Maximov's "The Seven Days of Creation" ("Sem' dnei tvoreniia"), in Felix Svetov's "Open the Doors unto Me" ("Otverzi mi dveri"), in Leonid Borodin's "The Third Truth" ("Tret'ia pravda"), and "The Parting" ("Rassta-vanie"), and in the poems of Joseph Brodsky, Inna Lisnyanskaya, and others. Probably the first work in the post-Stalin era dealing with religious themes in prose and poetry was Boris Pasternak's *Doctor Zhivago* which, though published outside its borders, became widely known in the Soviet Union among intellectuals. Since Soviet official literature, as well as *samizdat* and *tamizdat* are, in fact, parts of the same cultural process, not only may we speak about their common features, but also about a definite influence of the so called "second" uncensored literature on the "first" official one. It is a universally known fact that uncensored literature is obtainable without much difficulty in the circles of the intellectual elite, and it is difficult to imagine a talented official writer who is completely unacquainted with it. However, since this chapter analyzes the interaction of official writers with Party censorship, the works of "the second literature" fall out of its scope.

There are definite difficulties in assessing the religious sympathies of contemporary Soviet authors since they are not displayed in pure form, but linked with other themes and sometimes even dissolved in them. In the writings of Russian authors, for example, among such themes are: pride in Russian national character, in Russian art and architecture, interest in Russia's historic past, national customs and traditions, awareness of the peculiarities of the Russian soul, appreciation of patriarchal village life as the epitome of Christian morality, etc. A keen interest in patriarchal, religious and national forms of life is very characteristic of non-Russian Soviet writers also.[2] It goes without saying that the involvement of all these themes in the artistic texture of the writing and peculiarity of their combinations vary from author to author.

The sometimes purposeful, sometimes unconscious non-separation of the religious and the humanitarian spheres in a number of Soviet writings represents another difficulty, which may render vulnerable a scholar's conclusions regarding a given writer's orientation toward religious values. However, this second difficulty does not arise from the writer's whim, but has understandable reasons in the very essence of official Soviet literature, whose fundamental principle—*partijnost'* (adherence to the Party goals and ideology)—has always been the yardstick applied to a work of art by the censors and official critics.[3]

As it has always been, since 1917 to the present, religious philosophy is understood to be in opposition to Marxist philosophy, incompatible with and inimical to it. Scientific atheism is promulgated by the government by all available means, and is fully used in the struggle against the religious worldview.[4] This is why the existence in the open in the Soviet Union of the religious writer, philosopher, scientist, artist or poet is out of the question. However a clandestine, concealed, or camouflaged existence is in theory possible. The same applies even to the mere orientation of a writer toward religious values—which also must not be declared openly. A writer, unlike other cultural agents, has at his disposal a powerful tool which permits him to say what he wants, and remain for a time unpunished—the artistic talent which enables him to express what is inadvisable to say. It is not only religious morality which is refracted artistically in whimsical form in a story, but at times the idea of the existence of God as, for example, in Valentin Rasputin's "Farewell to Matyora" ("Proshchanie s Materoi"), through the image of the invisible and unknown Landlord of the Island, or Mother-Doe in Chingiz Aitmatov's "The White Steamship" ("Belyi parokhod"), or Woman-Fish in his "Dappled Dog, Running at the Edge of the Sea" ("Pegii pes, begushchii kraem moria").

The inclination to the religious ethic and religious themes varies from work to work and appears in each writer in a different way. We can trace four basic modes of reference to the religious in contemporary Soviet fiction.

In the first of these modes the religious ethic may appear as backlighting, illuminating the events of the narrative, serve as a touchstone for the character's behavior, or become apparent through his feelings, desires, and thoughts. This is the most widespread manifestation of the religious in literature, and is highly characteristic of the so-called "ruralists." The old woman, Darya, in Rasputin's "Farewell to Matyora," as the bearer of patriarchal religious values, exemplifies this mode. She does not discuss religion directly, but the reader gathers her ethical attitude from her thoughts and views on various subjects. It is as if Rasputin offers the reader, that is, the Soviet reader, brought up on the atheistic Marxist ethic, the opportunity to reexamine his relationship to the world and the people, to penetrate to the essence of Darya's moral stance. In her moral position we find reservations about the omnipotence of human reason, doubt that man is the ruler over nature with the right to change it at will, faith in the uninterrupted spiritual link between generations, belief that the eternal concept of good and evil does not depend on the expediency of the moment, confidence that man is created for the fulfilment of defined tasks, that his life is full of meaning, and that every man's first responsibility is to his ancestors and descendants, not to the state, political system or party. The difference between the Marxist and patriarchal perspectives defines a divergence in the attitude of the old and new generations to the same actions and events; for Darya the destruction of the cemetery is a desecration of the memory of her ancestors and an act of blasphemy, while for the clean-up brigade, who intend to burn the wooden gravemarkers and crosses, this is an ordinary act of sanitation, for which they bear no moral responsibility: they do as they are ordered. The same difference in perception and evaluation of reality exists between Darya and her grandson, Andrey, in their relationship to the island-village, Matyora. For Darya it is the homestead, the earth of her ancestors, the motherland; for her grandson it is only a worn-out island, standing in the way of the great transformation of nature, a place with which he feels no spiritual kinship.

The whole story is permeated with the religious ethic, though expressed indirectly; it characterizes the entire mode of Darya's thought and feeling, with which the author sympathizes, and which in the final analysis emerges as morally and spiritually superior. While an example of permeation with religious values was taken from Rasputin, others could, with equal effect, have been taken from Vasilii Belov, Victor Astafyev or Vasilii Shukshin. This form of expression is characteristic, however, not only of the "ruralists," but of writers on urban themes as well (such as Jurii Trifonov), and writers on war themes (such as Vasil' Bykov).

Perhaps the best of the early examples of the unobtrusive religio-moral position of an author, expressed not as a declaration, but through the character of the protagonist, and through the entire artistic structure of the story, is Solzhenitsyn's "Matryona's Household" ("Matrenin dvor"). Matryona who has lived a life unremarked and unnoticed by others, achieving nothing and accumulating nothing, but who has always responded compassionately and helped others without recompense, emerges, in the author's evaluation, as the sole righteous person without whom not a single village would stand.

Concluding the discussion of this type of religious expression, it is necessary to note that a general examination of recent Soviet prose makes us aware of the appearance of a new positive hero. If previously he was a chairman of the kolkhoz farm, exemplary worker, scientist-inventor, young creative intellectual, etc., now the positive hero is represented very often by an old man or woman—the bearer of patriarchal morality. Similar to them are simple older people of the village, such as Ivan Afrikanovich in Vasilii Belov's "Everyday Business" ("Privychnoe delo"), and Fedor Abramov's Pelageya, the title-character in the story of the same name.

The second mode in which a writer's attraction to religious values is expressed is the representation of certain characters, often secondary ones, as spontaneous carriers of those values. Their views may be criticized by more sophisticated and up-to-date protagonists, but they are treated by the author with unmistakable warmth and sympathy. Sometimes such characters carry on detailed, serious conversations with others regarding God and morality. Although these questions are, more often than not, peripheral to the theme and to the ideological content of the story, the author's serious attitude toward them as the very possibility of including such material in a literary work testifies, on the one hand, to a new orientation of authors to the religious ethic, and leads, on the other hand, to the idea of a certain "permissiveness" on the part of the official censorship. The allusions to the religious of this type can be found today even in writers who, until recently, were indifferent to religious themes. Even Evtushenko's characters in his last novel *Berry Places* ("Iagodnye mesta") speak about God, the meaning of life, and man's purpose on earth. Overall, the general trend of Soviet prose of the last two decades may be defined as moral-philosophical, which fundamentally distinguishes it from the previous politico-demagogical period. It also becomes apparent that talented Soviet writers no longer pay attention to the demands of socialist realism, to the principle of the Party-Line, or to the recipes and recommendations of the official Party critics. Today it is evident as never before that literature exists in its own right, and criticism in its own, and that the two seem to intersect only in some special cases. An amusing and at the same time characteristic example is the activity of Chingiz Aitmatov as a writer, on the one hand, and polemicist, on the other. In the pages of *Novyi Mir* and *Literaturnaya Gazeta* he often appears with pronouncements on the fruitfulness of socialist realism, on the new Soviet positive hero, even on the party line, while there is not the slightest reflection of any of these in his writings which often even reject them. This gives rise to the impression that Soviet writers continue to lead double lives, although now they try not to lie in literature. However, two-facedness still continues to characterize such authors as Fedor Abramov, Iurii Bondarev, and Sergei Zalygin, to say nothing of writers of lesser caliber.

The third widespread mode of reference in Soviet literature to the realm of the religious is a flirtation with it. This condition can be explained, on the one hand, by the emergence among the literary-artistic elite of a special interest in all things religious, almost a fashion, and, on the other, by their sincere desire to understand the sources of such an interest. In prose this orientation goes hand in hand with heightened attention to everything national and patriarchal; in poetry with a return to eternal, universally human, timeless themes.

However, to analyze poetry with respect to its religious orientation is much more difficult, since it never broke with it—religious motifs have represented one of the most stable conventions of the system of poetic expression and were rarely seriously criticized, except, of course, where they appeared distinctly and consistently, as in the Christian poems of *Doctor Zhivago*. The latitude to use religious metaphors at present is indirectly attested to by the fact that they are employed by those poets who previously had been very indifferent to such a mode of expression. One would hardly imagine that the following verses of Andrey Voznesensky from his collection "The Master of Stained-Glass" ("Vitrazhnykh del master") (1976) could have been written by the Voznesensky of "The Triangular Pear" ("Treugol'naia grusha"):[5]

In the garden washing my car
I will go to the curb
And wash the feet of the aspen
As the sinful woman did Christ's feet.

And the downpour, which fell afar,
Will return to the rye and the oats.
And the light will wash my soul,
As Christ washed the sinner's feet.

Finally, the fourth mode of reference to the religious ethic in contemporary Soviet literature is the direct discussion of questions of faith, the direct exemplification of the complex paths man takes to religion, of the conflict between believers and the atheistic milieu, of contemplations on God, on the meaning of life, and religious precepts; that is, exactly the instance in which religion itself is the theme of the work. We find these themes in their most distinct manifestations in the previously mentioned stories of Vladimir Tendryakov: "The Apostolic Trip" and "The Eclipse." Since such writings are very rare in Soviet literature, and since there could have been no question of publishing them just twenty years ago, it is worth dwelling on them here in little more detail.

The protagonist of "The Apostolic Trip" is a Moscow journalist in his thirties, well-established and externally well-off. He has a solid family, challenging work, and a comfortable private apartment. But for some time he has not been able to find himself emotionally. He has come to believe in God, and now can not live as he did before hiding his views from his colleagues or his wife, and he wants to speak openly of his religious concerns. In search of more hospitable surroundings and the chance to meet like-minded people, he quits his job, secretly leaves his family, and settles in a small village near Moscow. There he works as a laborer, meets several ordinary Christians, and tries to understand them. As a result, he reaches the conclusion that he is very alien to these people, and they to him, that the elite philosophical Christianity to which he is attracted has little in common with their dogmatic Christianity. After living several weeks in the village, he becomes disillusioned with these people, doubts the correctness of his decision, and finally thinks of returning to his wife and daughter in Moscow. Thus ends his short-lived "apostolic trip." Regardless of the main idea of the incompatibility of popular and elite Christianity, the image of the main hero, his thinking about God and his religious quest are shown with a great deal of seriousness, sympathy, and occasionally even concealed authorial approval.

In "The Eclipse" the romantic love of two young people, Pavel and

Maya, is described. One day Maya meets Gosha, a former acquaintance of Pavel, who is a philosophizing proponent of homespun Christianity. Unlike the talented and positive Pavel, Gosha is externally plain, physically weak, unkempt, and shabby. He leads a disorganized life, does not work, lives on air, but he is able to attract people with his discourses on God, love, and kindness. The story ends with Maya breaking up with Pavel and going off with Gosha to bring love and spiritual aid to the suffering and deprived of the world.

Having now completed the overview of the four modes of reference to the religious in contemporary Soviet literature, I must note that an analysis of concrete writings with the aim of defining the degrees of their religious orientation falls outside the scope of this chapter—this would take an entire book. Taking the religious orientation as a fully established fact, I will attempt to analyze briefly its appearance, its sources, the reasons for its emergence, its social and cultural significance, its viability and the possible trends in its future development. For this purpose, let us make a brief excursion into history.

Russian classical literature undoubtedly was built upon and permeated with the Christian religious ethic; Tolstoy and Dostoyevsky were actually its ardent propagandists in literary form. Russian classical writers could debate or reject this or that form of Christian orthodoxy, but would never challenge the very essence of the religious ethic; in other words, while they might subject some of its premises to criticism, they would never transgress its boundaries, never oppose to it anything new in principle. The same kind of religious orientation was also highly characteristic of pre-revolutionary non-Russian literatures.

The literature of the Soviet period, in this sense, taken as a whole, is torn by two opposite tendencies: on the one hand, by traditional pursuit of the old religious values, and, on the other, by a sharp rejection of them. It is proper to call "Soviet" those works which propagate the new ethical values of the period, not those which simply belong to it chronologically. In contradistinction to religious values, these new ethical standards can be defined as Communist class values. The literature of the Soviet period may be viewed as a reflection of the struggle between the Communist ethic and the religious ethic. If we detach ourselves from the concrete subject matter of writings, we will discover that the collision of these two ethics and their mutual irreconcilability have even become a new theme in Soviet literature. However, a defeat of religious morality in many works was dictated not so much by the ongoing realities of Soviet life, as by the calculations of writers under the dictates of a regime which handed them their social orders.

The Communist ethic[6] differs mainly from the religious ethic in its disregard for the problem of personal guilt and personal responsibility for one's own fate, the fate of one's children and the fate of the whole society. According to the Communist ethic, the morality of acts depends on the practical results they lead to. The state authority removes the feeling of moral responsibility from an individual, provided he acts in accordance with its orders which are declared to be leading toward a common good. The individual conscience of each person, from this point of view, should ideally be a mirror image of the collective conscience—that is, to be in no kind of contradiction with it. This collective conscience, however, is not a quality inherent to the masses, but a modified artificial "class consciousness" imposed from above as a result of continuous and coercive brainwashing. The thesis of the first years of the Soviet regime that all acts resulting in consolidation of the proletarian dictatorship were moral, was not canceled by subsequent leaders. Sixty years later Leonid Brezhnev expressed the same idea in the following aphoristic form: "In our society everything is moral that serves the interests of communism."[7]

In theory the Communist ethic, or "class consciousness" which incorporated it, can be assimilated by any person independent of his class or social origin; thus many Communist leaders of Lenin's time were neither workers nor peasants, though they claimed to be bearers of working class consciousness. In practice, however, representatives of other classes were often considered by Party ideologists alien to Communist principles and goals. In many cases the very belonging of a person to a non-proletarian class relegated him to the status of potential enemy, and no personal strategy could save him from suspicion of disloyalty. In Soviet fiction this oversimplified understanding of class values resulted in even more simplified and primitive portrayals of people and events. All members of the "wrong classes," regardless of their spiritual and intellectual gifts were depicted as "bad guys," while the representatives of the dictatorship turned out to be positive heroes.

Only in a small number of writings were "bad guys" given a chance to be led to the true path in the process of Communist "reforging" and in this way to join the good company. The Communist ideology with its components of class struggle, militant atheism and proletarian internationalism was most instrumental in ruining two main constituents of the traditional religious mentality: the national identity and the families loyalty. In Soviet fiction these processes were reflected in stereotypical plots of families split when one member served with the Whites and the other with the Reds.

To summarize, not human but class traits defined the face of the hero in Soviet literature, so that the reader knew in advance that aristocrats, noblemen, White Guards, priests, believers, kulaks, Nepmen, émigrés, and in later literature, defectors, displaced persons, criminals, speculators, and so on, could be nothing but negative characters. Into the description of their complicated psychologies (to say nothing of showing sympathy and empathy) writers never ventured; and even where there might have been such attempts, these personalities were presented in a lopsided and tendentious way. When authors did create works in which such characters were treated sympathetically, these works would not pass censorship, and remained unknown to the Soviet populace.

In the past two decades, a new attitude to the traditionally negative characters has appeared—they are explored not only from the class or ideological, but from the human point of view; writers present a deep analysis of their inner worlds, giving elaborate, well-delineated logical and psychological bases to their actions. Consider, for example, the character of a traitor, Rybak, in Vasil' Bykov's "Sotnikov," a deserter, Gus'kov, in Rasputin's "Live and Remember" ("Zhivi i pomni"), a defector, Ramzin, in Yury Bondarev's "The Choice" ("Vybor"), the images of kulaks in Petr Proskurin's novels. The traditional evildoers obtained their right to express their views, became full-blooded, "round" characters. Religious people in fiction underwent an even more surprising metamorphosis. Previously humiliated and ridiculed, now they not only began to be depicted as sympathetic and attractive, but sometimes were shown to be on a higher moral level than their atheistic milieu; the earliest example of this being the Baptist Alyosha, in Solzhenitsyn's "One Day in the Life of Ivan Denisovich" ("Odin den' Ivana Denisovicha").

It should be noted, however, that in the majority of recent Soviet writings the religious ethic is not openly or straightforwardly declared, but is smuggled in obliquely. A slow, inexorable reevaluation from the standpoint of religious moral criteria, of almost all the historic events of the Soviet period is going on (thoroughly and skillfully camouflaged), along with a simultaneous covert denunciation of the Communist ethic and its cruel adherents.

Every artistic work published in the Soviet period with the approval of the censor, must be viewed as the outcome of a struggle between what the writer, in quest of truth, wanted to say, and what he was allowed to say by the Party censorship. (Here we are, of course, not referring to the writers who are indifferent to the truth, or who distort it in order to please the authorities.) In the vast majority of cases the writer himself knows what the censor may allow to pass, whether out of ignorance or as a result of the author's refinement in the art of camouflage; thus the author is himself his first and chief censor. Self-censorship is an important theme almost untouched by literary criticism, though it is a very prominent feature of the current Soviet life. What the author may or must not say (we speak here only of those cases where the author's aim is publication in official Soviet print) depends entirely on the transient social and political situation. In stricter terms, the degree of artistic freedom at any given moment is defined by the level of official tolerance which, however, is not unchanging, but vertically mobile, fluctuating, rising or falling.

However, the main law of artistic creativity—freedom of creative expression—enters into an irreconcilable contradiction with the level of official tolerance. That is why true talent always tries to exceed this level, to circumvent or ignore it. Sometimes this happens even despite the intentions of the author, as though involuntarily, according to the law of the dominance of the artist over the man. In other words, art is always struggling with the level of official tolerance, and always in the long run wins out over it by elevating it. But if art always wins, the same can not be said about the artist himself—the writer who has exceeded the level of official tolerance is, in the best of cases, subjected to criticism and attacks, and in the worst of cases, is deprived of professional benefits, forbidden to publish, expelled from the Union of Writers, incarcerated, exiled from the country, or annihilated, depending on the severity of the current regime.

If we examine Soviet literature with respect to this criterion, we can conclude that there has been a marked rising of the level of official tolerance, beginning with the Khrushchev era, and continuing to the present. Otherwise stated, what can be published today with official sanction, could never have been printed in the days of Stalin's rule.

Such easing of official tolerance by no means always results through pressure from below. Sometimes it can also take place with the sanction of the leadership, according to its notion of what is useful under present economic, political and cultural conditions. Almost always such a concession from above is not freely chosen—it may be a preventive measure against a possible proliferation of dissent, dictated by the fear that some intellectual movement may get out of Party control.

It is necessary to note that in the Soviet Union the level of official tolerance was always much lower (and to this effect strictly controlled by the government) than any level of artistic freedom which could conceivably represent a danger to Communist ideology. We can safely assert that the majority of rejected works by Soviet writers offered for official publication (that is, already self-censored works), could have been published without any apparent negative consequences for the regime.

Some rank-and-file Soviet writers in their fear of transgressing it, write significantly below the level of official tolerance, some unintentionally reach it, others play with it, and still others consciously try to exceed it, recognizing its basic property—its tendency to fluctuate, at times unexpectedly and unpredictably. Each refusal by the censorship to approve a book for publication defines for its writer, and for all others, the current level of official tolerance. Direct disregard of it by the writer, manifested by the appearance of his book in *tamizdat*, always has the actual effect of raising the level of official tolerance at home, and thus is regarded by the Party ideologists as an extremely undesirable and subversive act. And the appearance of a work in *samizdat* is treated in the same way, though this phenomenon, as an internal matter, is easier to combat, since it is not attended by reverberations in world public opinion, or by external pressure.

An examination of a series of the best writings of the last twenty years makes the fact of the discrediting of the Communist ethic in Soviet literature abundantly clear. But if Communist values have given way to others, then these other values undoubtably have a religious character, or in any event a religious origin, since we cannot speak of any third ethic at the present time. In contemporary Soviet fiction there is a gradual reevaluation of the events of the Soviet period from the perspective of the old, patriarchal religious values. The reader perceives the de-kulakization according to Sergei Zalygin, the Second World War according to Vasil' Bykov, labor camps through the eyes of Solzhenitsyn and Shalamov, the life of the Soviet countryside through Vasilii Belov, Fedor Abramov, Vasilii Shukshin, Valentin Rasputin, and other "ruralists."

This process of return to the old ethic began, however, not under the influence of literature, but as part of a wider Russian national and religious revival, which started in the late fifties and early sixties, and which constituted to an overall disillusionment with Communist rule among all strata of the Soviet population, and a universal disbelief in the construction of communism in the USSR. The religious and patriarchal elements were inseparable from the national elements of Russian tradition. The regime overlooked the strong religious stream which flowed in the center of the national revival; when it took notice it was already too late to gain effective control over it.

We should take account of several peculiar forms of religious-national interdependence characteristic of the Soviet period.

Although on paper an unremitting struggle was to be waged against nationalism as a bourgeois tendency (even if it was sometimes used by the regime for its own ends), it always had its own level of official tolerance. In particular, in Stalin's time, nationalism was promoted, but cloaked in the dress of national pride, which embraced not only the idea of pride in culture, literature, art, and outstanding technical achievements, but also pride in Soviet patriotism and the Russian national character. In fact, since the Stalin period this component of nationalism was never suppressed, but, to the contrary, was used to distract the people from economic and political difficulties. Of course, nationalistic movements that aimed at overthrowing the Communist regime have always been brutally suppressed.

The reciprocal relationship between Church and state was more complex. On paper, religion was actually the only form of legal and organized nonconformity. In reality, religious activity was systematically persecuted, and the fierce antireligious propaganda sanctioned and supported throughout all periods of the Soviet rule, aimed at putting an end to it. From the late fifties on, despite individual persecutions and show trials, despite strict governmental control of the church,[8] the level of official tolerance of religious activity rose constantly. This provided a pretext for some observers to speak about a religious revival in the Soviet Union.[9]

It would be more correct, however, to speak of a religious-national revival. Nationalism and religion in Russia have always been tightly intertwined. Because of this cultural phenomenon, the national and religious movements which began in the late fifties proceeded in lockstep with one another.

The originality of today's religious-national revival is in its elite character. It did not arise as a movement of the masses, but of the cultural elite in search of national and spiritual roots. This intellectual elite included also some members of the Party elite—that is, the movement did not begin as an ideological, but as a cultural phenomenon. The movement promoted the restoration and preservation of the national culture; above all, the restoration of architectural treasures, and of old masterpieces of painting, sculpture, and literature. Though this movement was characteristic of all the national cultures of the Soviet Union, the more pronounced and apparent it became for Russian culture. Since Russian ancient and folk art was basically religious, the restoration of churches, the discovery and cataloging of icons, and the publication of old Russian literary texts and related scholarly works, necessarily brought about not only a heightening of interest in religious art, but in the religious values which had nourished it as well. Many intellectuals went over from a conscious atheism to a spontaneous religious feeling; others became advocates of the rebirth of religious ethics; still others perceived the revival as a religious fashion—they wore crosses, collected icons, visited churches, chatted with clergy. This fashion became the property of mass culture, which simply is an indirect indication of the serious attitude of both masses and elite toward religion. Theoretically, to the achievement of the triumph in the Soviet Union of the religious ethic (that is, the total ousting of the Communist ethic), there remained but one step—for folk and elite religiosity to coalesce and to act in concert. At that point the Party realized that the level of official tolerance for religious matters had risen too far and a strict ideological control was needed.

Soviet literature of the last two decades has, in its best works, truthfully reflected this mass shift of Soviet society toward religious values. It has done so either by taking the religious ethic as the general moral background of the actions of characters, or, as in several instances—by choosing plot lines in which the protagonists turn out to be people who are religious, or sympathetic to religion, leaning toward it, or playing with it.

The religious national revival, as has been already stated, was not an organized, but a spontaneous movement. It had developed without any organizing and directing group, without supporting circles, definite plans for action, or worked-out ideological program. Not only from the point of view of the Soviet Constitution was there nothing prejudicial in this movement, but more often than not it proceeded under the banners of conventional Soviet patriotism. It was for this reason that the leadership realized too late the true nature of the movement, and decided to give the impression that it had never transgressed the legal framework, that it had even been sanctioned from above. From the way this happened, people might have been left thinking that the level of official tolerance had been raised by the regime without any pressure from below. But since this was not so, a special type of interaction of ethical movements and the regime was created, which was characterized by constant vertical fluctuation in the level of official tolerance, ending inevitably in a progressive heightening of that level. The dynamic of this process seems likely to go on as long as Soviet society develops under peaceful conditions. This dynamic is expressed through the repetitive working of the mechanism of the interdependent relationship between the regime and the literary world—the regime attempts to restrain the rising level of official tolerance at the lowest possible point, in response to which literary works are channeled into *samizdat* or the émigré press. To avoid this in the future the regime again raises the level of official tolerance at home, adjusting it a bit higher. This process is slow and evolutionary, but results in an ever-increasing ousting of the Communist values by religious values. The mass and spontaneous character of this movement, along with the constitutional legality (at least on paper) of religious non-conformity, makes it much less conspicuous and vulnerable, than any other types of ideological dissent. On the other hand, if the regime is to contend with this movement, it will have to search out more refined, complicated and illicit means to do so, which will greatly increase for it the difficulty of this struggle. Such an entanglement of the regime in this mechanism of inexorable elevation of the level of official tolerance must be acknowledged as a potential crisis within the system.

The marked shift in Soviet fiction toward religious values (together with a keen interest in patriarchal and national forms and norms of life) seems to be only one facet of a strong undercurrent cultural movement directed against the Communist outlook. Nowadays, more than ever before, it becomes apparent that neither the Soviet people nor the Party elite believe in building a Communist society in the USSR. Thus, the survival of the regime depends entirely on strict ideological control and coercion. Under such conditions religion may turn out to be the only more or less "safe" outlet for the Soviet people to express their opposition toward official Communist dogma. The return of the Party to the old methods of ideological control at present may be fraught with difficulties. The entanglement of the regime in unsolvable confrontation with religious dissent appears to be the counterpart of a much broader and more dangerous entanglement in the fight with a spontaneously rising mass cultural opposition in the country, which may lead the regime to a greater and more comprehensive crisis.

Notes

1. Solzhenitsyn is named here "Soviet" in relation to his pre-émigré period and in accordance with the working definition of a "Soviet writer" in this chapter— a native of the country who was officially published in the Soviet press.
2. See George Luckj, ed., *Discordant Voices: The Non-Russian Soviet Literatures*, (Ontario, 1975.)
3. For a detailed discussion of the principles of *ideinost', klassovost', narodnost',* and *partiinost'* see N.N. Shneidman, "The Russian Classical Literary Heritage and the Basic Concepts of Soviet Literary Education," *Slavic Review* 31 (1972), 626–38.
4. A comprehensive study of the question in its historical perspective can be found in David E. Powell, *Antireligious Propaganda in the Soviet Union: A Study of Mass Persuasion*, (Cambridge: MIT Press, 1975).
5. Not to mention his poem "Longjumeau" (1963), where not Christ, but Lenin appears to be the final judge of people's acts:

> One day, having become mature,
>   out of everyday haste
> we enter the Mausoleum,
>   like we enter an x-ray room,
> stripped of gossip and legends,
>   without hats and embellishments,
> and Lenin, like an x-ray machine,
>   examines us.

6. The principles of the Communist ethic as seen by Communists are discussed in the following works: V.I. Lenin, *O kommunisticheskoi nravstvennosti*, third

edition, (Moscow, 1969); E.G. Fedorenko, *Osnovy marksistsko-leninskoi ètiki*, (Kiev, 1972); A.I. Titarenko, *Marksistskaia ètika*, (Moscow, 1976).

7. "Doklad tovarishcha L.I. Brezhneva na 25 s'ezde KPSS," *Pravda*, 25 February 1976.

8. In order to combat the rising religious consciousness a new popular antireligious magazine *Science and Religion* ("Nauka i religiia") was established in 1959 and a new compulsory course "Fundamentals of Scientific Communism" was introduced by 1962 to all institute and university curricula in all the republics of the USSR.

9. Robert C. Tucker, "Religious Revival in Russia" in A. Inkeles and K. Geiger eds., *Soviet Society: A Book of Readings*, Boston, 1961, 424–28; Dennis J. Dunn, "Religious Renaissance in the Soviet Union," *Journal of Church and State*, (Winter 1977), 21–36.

11

Authentic Russian Values and Aspirations:

The Literary Evidence

MAURICE FRIEDBERG

When first asked to produce an article on the subject of *authentic* Russian values and aspirations (as distinct from those fostered by the Communist regime), and how these are reflected in *Soviet* Russian literature, my misgivings were probably much the same as those of many readers of this chapter's title. How can this information be gleaned from a doubly censored body of writing, I wondered—censored not only by the Soviet editors and censors, but, more importantly, preemptively censored by the Soviet authors themselves? After all, nearly all of these men and women have no experience in writing for non-censored journals and publishing houses. On a subconscious level, such authors, one may legitimately assume, censor themselves as routinely as they proofread their manuscripts for typographical errors.

As I delved into the subject, some of my doubts began to dissipate, and gradually I arrived at the following conclusions. *Certain* completely authentic Russian values and aspirations—say, a yearning for political freedoms or a striving for a truly religious perception of the human condition—simply cannot be overtly articulated in Soviet literature. (On the other hand, excessive camouflage may render the message "hermeneutic" to the point of incomprehensibility to all but a chosen few.) Such goals are, politically, glaringly incompatible with the Soviet ethos. Hence, the non-articulation of such principles in Soviet writing does not necessarily preclude their existence, or even their popularity. At the other end of the ideological spectrum are the values and hopes advanced and promoted in a significant body of Soviet literary evidence with the apparent encouragement of the authorities. Such transparently tendentious motifs, however, may be identified readily enough. In contrast to "authentic" values, they are also, as a rule, ostentatiously advertized and systematically disseminated by the Soviet mass media and the Soviet social sciences. Indeed, on occasion these state-endorsed values (as distinct from those merely tolerated) may even be traced to public pronouncements of Soviet leaders and solemn resolutions of the Communist party's Central Committee. Such officially inspired goals and principles must, of necessity, gently overcome, by persuasion and not by command, the reader's resistance or at least indifference to them. In my view, it was the failure to recognize this last consideration, rather than mere artistic ineptitude, that accounted for much of the public hostility toward the emotionally unacceptable Socialist Realist potboilers of the Stalin era. Similarly, the artificiality and meretriciously shrill optimism of Soviet novels, plays, and verse of the Stalin period were caused, in large degree, by an insistence that the merely *desired* beliefs and purposes fostered by the Soviet authorities be presented *as already universally held, as long accepted by the population*. It was the latter features of Soviet writing of the late 1940s and early 1950s that imparted such transparently false, unbelievable quality to the psychology of its protagonists. All too often, they appeared driven only by concern for the welfare of the Party and the government, and not their personal needs and aspirations.

It is my contention that Soviet writing of the post-Stalin age differs from that which preceded it in that side by side with values fostered on demand from above, it also reflects many genuinely held beliefs and desires of its readers. Indeed, this particular concession may now be the last remaining gain of the great expectations engendered by the literary-political "thaws" of 1956 and 1962 that had, otherwise, ended in a defeat of the liberal forces. This concession accounts for the sharp contrast between the writing of the Stalin era and the post-Stalin literary output, including that of the late 1950s, the 1960s, the 1970s, and the early 1980s. However uneven its literary merit, post-Stalin Soviet literature is definitely found appealing enough by large segments of the reading public, a fact corroborated by statistics gleaned from the libraries and the book trade, and in the case of poetry and songs for the stage (e.g., the late Vladimir Vysotsky's or young Yevgeni Yevtushenko's) quite literally by the public acclaim. This point is worth emphasizing because during the Stalin era concern for ideological crusading was so great, that no significant concessions were made to the readers' predilections—even if readers retaliated with the deadliest weapon at their disposal, namely with downright refusal to read books they found repugnant.

For purposes of this chapter, then, we define as "authentic" those values and aspirations that recur again and again in a very large and representative sample of recent Soviet Russian literary production, and which *do not coincide* with values and aspirations fostered in official Soviet sources. From time to time we shall expand the definition of Soviet Russian literature to include also writing that was, technically speaking, *printed* abroad. Such instances, not very numerous, will be limited to books that were, to all appearances, written in the expectation that they might be published in the USSR. It may come as some surprise that émigré and Soviet writing is not all *that* different. My own observations are corroborated by a leading Western student of the subject. Deming Brown writes:

> In it [literature published in the USSR] one often finds the same concerns and themes as in literature that has to be published abroad although, as a rule, these domestic publications cannot be as candid and comprehensive in their exploration of social, moral, and ideological problems. But, regardless of whether works are published inside or outside the USSR, all of them have emerged from the same society. The kinship among them is so close that, for purposes of the present book, the term Soviet literature will be applied to all of them.[1]

Indeed, a large part of the body of writing now synonymous with the concept of emigration was originally created in the USSR and with the Soviet reader in mind. In many instances, such books had actually been submitted to Soviet literary journals and publishing houses, and were printed abroad only when their authors had become convinced that there is no longer any hope of their appearance at home. The list of such books is impressive. It includes Boris Pasternak's *Doctor Zhivago* and Georgi Vladimov's *Faithful Ruslan*; Vladimir Voinovich's *Private Chonkin* and Alexander Solzhenitsyn's *The First Circle*, as well as the same author's *Cancer Ward*. In fact, a strong argument can be made for the proposition that it is precisely works such as these that reflect most faithfully certain truly popular Soviet values and aspirations. Their non-publication in the USSR may well be due to the fact that these were ultimately found incompatible with those promulgated by the Soviet establishment. Values espoused in such literary texts do not, as a rule, clash head-on with those officially promoted by the Soviet authorities, and that is hardly surprising in Soviet conditions. (More unexpectedly, much the same is true of the bulk of recent émigré fiction, even though the latter often raises such taboo subjects as political persecution or anti-Semitism—or sex.) As a rule, these cautious expressions of, to use a Tolstoyan formula, "What men live by," emphasize their "unofficial and private nature." This point is stressed by means of such stratagems as their articulation by individual fictional personages, and certainly without any hint of authorial endorsement. Moreover, the Soviet author's ideological alibi is supported by protestations that mere reportage of such phenomena does not in the least aspire to the status of generalizations, *obobshcheniia*. Outwardly, to be sure, no claims are made that such "unofficial" beliefs are widely held. Surprisingly, perhaps, such often transparently insincere claims are on occasion tacitly accepted by Soviet editors and censors who pretend not to see the sham. We submit that these scattered pronouncements of Russian literary protagonists of the three post-Stalin decades do contain a number of identifiable themes. When multiplied by scores and hundreds of instances in novels, plays, and verse written by hundreds of Soviet authors ranging from sophisticated artists to purveyors of very unsubtle potboilers (the kind the Germans call *Kitsch* and the Russians *nizkoprobnoe chtivo*) they offer us a reasonable approximation of many popularly held values and beliefs. The entire body of post-Stalin writing is considered here, with particular emphasis on the most recent. In particular, we base our findings on the contents of ten-year runs (from 1975 to 1984) and four literary journals—*Novy mir, Moskva, Nash sovremennik*, and *Druzhba narodov*—and five-year runs of *Molodaya qvardia, Znamya, Zvezda*, and *Roman gazeta* (from 1975 to 1980), and of *Neva, Prostor, Sibirskie ogni*, and *Literaturnaya Armenia*, for 1980 to 1984. It is our contention that this very sizeable and representative sample reflects traits that are characteristic of Soviet writing as a whole.

* * *

The elementary human longing for freedom from fear could not, for obvious reasons, be as much as hinted at during the decades of Stalinist terror when fear was a foremost tool for the implementation of government policies. Quite understandably, this subterranean longing began to be articulated, if ever so timidly, almost immediately after the tyrant's death in March of 1953. The caution, as subsequent experience confirmed, was well advised. The authorities, even at the height of Khrushchev's liberal "thaws"—that of 1956 and the other of 1962—were willing to tolerate only understated literary portrayals of Stalinist terror and expressions of hope that it may never be repeated. Moreover, the terror (Marxist theory of history notwithstanding) was to be ascribed to one man's, Stalin's, caprice euphemistically designated as "cult of personality" rather than to "objective" political, social, and economic realities. Its victims, however unbelievable psychologically, were to be shown unshaken in their belief in the justice of the Soviet cause. Last, but not least, no specific Soviet institutions as a whole—not even the secret police—and almost no specific individuals were to be indicted as culprits, and for obvious reasons. Stalin's successors, including those who, like Khrushchev, were to denounce the dead dictator's crimes, were themselves Stalin's lieutenants and accomplices in his crimes, and none of Stalin's mechanisms of terror, were wholly dismantled. Post-Stalin Russia was what post-Hitler Germany would have been had Hitler's immediate entourage succeeded him, with only minor shakeups in the Gestapo, the SS and the Nazi party, and without any trials of war criminals.

In recent years there has been a disquieting proliferation of militaristic Soviet novels, with Yulian Semyonov's spy thrillers and Alexander Prokhanov's colonialist opus *A Tree Grows in the Center of Kabul* among the most notorious. This has tended to obscure to a degree a far more pervasive theme, that of *hatred of war*, which is the undercurrent of a vast volume of recent Soviet fiction with World War II settings. While outwardly describing hatred of Hitler and the Nazis, these books promote in reality *hatred of war as such*. One finds it in Vasyl Bykov and in Georgi Baklanov, as well as in scores of lesser authors. Indiscriminate pacifism in literature has never been tolerated in the USSR, and, to be sure, an antimilitaristic novel of the power of Vladimir Voinovich's brilliant satire *Private Ivan Chonkin* could not appear there.[2] It is, therefore, not entirely surprising that Mr. Voinovich now lives in Western Europe. (It should be noted, incidentally, that *Chonkin's* crime is compounded by the fact that it mocks the army not only in peacetime—which would be bad enough—but also during the war. In battle, regular Soviet military is portrayed in it as confused, stupid and often ridiculous. As for the uniformed secret police, they are cowards as well.) Still, the principle of *hatred of war*—quite different from the disquieting glorification of war that may be found in much of officially inspired patriotic fiction—is enunciated frequently enough to be viewed as an *authentic Russian* value of our time. Traumatic episodes from World War II, particularly defeats with enormous casualties have repeatedly been portrayed in recent Soviet fiction with occasional overtones of outright pacifism. This contrasted sharply with the emphasis on glory, heroism, and patriotic fervor in Soviet writing of the Stalin era. Thus, there was Konstantin Simonov's *The Living and the Dead* that was published in 1959 amid much controversy and there were others, too. Still the tragic and unglamorous view of the war is linked, above all, to the name of Vasyl Bykov, a Belorussian novelist who also writes in Russian. Bykov's *The Dead Feel No Pain* (1966) showed how some officers' careers were made of the blood, sweat and tears of ordinary soldiers—a subversive enough observation, but one that was overshadowed by *Sotnikov*, a novel published four years later. In it, Bykov portrayed the metamorphosis of some staunch Communists into Nazi collaborators and revealed also that a number of ostensible collaborators were actually trying to ease the lot of their countrymen. Bykov's novels and others like them created a view of the war that was more shaded and complex. Readers could now obtain accounts of the war that were intellectually, emotionally, and artistically more satisfying than the black-and-white two-dimensional literary posters of the Stalin era—and with more subtle implications for the present as well. The new books, to paraphrase Yevgeni Yevtushenko, still proclaimed—no, the *Russians* want no war—but as for their government, that was, of course, quite another matter and the answer was more equivocal here. Curiously, as memories of the war fade from collective consciousness—only the middle-aged now retain any personal recollections of it—interest in Soviet writing and films dealing with the subject of World War II is gradually declining. Some interesting statistics are cited in Ellen Mickiewicz's excellent book on Soviet communications.[3] Thus, the Soviet authorities' effort to promote literary works that extol military valor and which call for vigilance and preparedness, now meet with increasing apathy. And so will, paradoxically, the older generation of Russians' attempts to convey to the young the message that war is hateful.

Significantly, hatred of war (including even "just" wars, those of which the USSR approves) is occasionally extended even to revolutions, including even—sacrilegeously—of that which begot the Soviet regime. Intimations of such disapproval of violent upheavals that begin with an explosion and proceed to disrupt private lives and the social fabric (however imperfect the society) are first encountered in Pasternak's *Doctor Zhivago* in the late 1950s, but they recur two decades later in Yuri Trifonov's *The Old Man* and Valentin Katayev's *Werther Has Already Been Written*. Trifonov's book is significant because it suggests that among the casualties of the Communist Revolution of 1917 and of the Civil War that ensued were such precious human attributes as loyalty, friendship, and justice. As for Valentin Katayev, a Soviet writer now nearing the age of ninety (and of the counted few to have published before World War I!), his wistful evocations of the past, including the labor pains of the Soviet state, occasionally sound an ambivalent note about the social and moral costs these entailed.

Russian nationalism, often with religious overtones, is another authentic and, by all accounts, popular value reflected by recent Soviet writing. Agrarian, anti-industrial, and with a Luddite flavoring, it has been often articulated by authors identified with the so-called "village school" of Russian literature. Because some of this Russian nationalism is overly gentle, too historically oriented, excessively religious, and unappreciative, it seems, of the twin virtues of electrification and the Soviet regime—as was Valentin Rasputin's *Farewell to Matyora*—it has been at times subjected to criticism. Neither were the authorities altogether happy with Victor

Astafyev's *Kingfish* with its strong environmentalist concerns, or with Vasili Belov's idealized portrayals of Russian peasants only superficially affected by Soviet modernity. The Soviet establishment, of course, prefers the strongly anti-Western Russian nationalism of a Vladimir Soloukhin (even if his championship of the traditional Russian costume may be viewed as going a bit far), because it clearly and unambiguously identifies the Western enemy. (Indeed, as Deming Brown rightly notes, Soloukhin's distrust of the West extends even to the relatively innocuous realm of cultural contacts: "Soloukhin is strongly opposed to the notion of an international culture. He feels, in fact, that the chief danger threatening contemporary Russian art is denationalization."[4] Presumably, it also favors Konstantin Skvortsov's *We Don't Forsake Our Fatherland*, a novel that glorifies Nicholas I, a staunchly reactionary nineteenth century monarch, for his refusal to admire the West. There are reasons to believe that it also finds Valentin Pikul congenial, who went so far as to attempt the rehabilitation of Grigori Rasputin, one of the most odious figures in Russian history, by demonstrating that the poor monk had been manipulated by Jewish capitalists. Pikul and Skvortsov, and, to a degree, Soloukhin, are all, one suspects, at least partly officially inspired. By contrast, there are good grounds to assume that *moderate* Russian nationalism, nationalism tinged with nostalgia after an agrarian and vaguely religious past, is, indeed, an *authentic* and widely held sentiment which modern Russian literature merely reflects.

What was ultimately to blossom forth into a major tendency in modern Russian writing, that of the *derevenshchiki*, the "village school" or, more precisely, "agrarians," began modestly enough during the first post-Stalin thaw of 1956 as cautious revival of literary interest in the Russian countryside. For all the ludicrously idyllic novels and films about life on the collective farms (as Khrushchev was to report after the dictator's death, these pastorales of abundance and contentment actually made Stalin believe that all was well with the peasantry), Soviet culture as a whole has traditionally been city-oriented, a reflection in part, no doubt, of Marxism's contempt for the "idiocy of village life." Hence, Valentin Ovechkin's and Efim Dorosh's reportages (*ocherki*) from the Russian provinces were as remarkable for the candor with which they described the poverty and squalor of the countryside (suggesting, in fact, that the collectivized peasants retain some nostalgia not only for religion—which would be bad enough—but for private property as well), as for the fact that these were portrayed as a serious social problem with implications for the entire nation. The factual findings of Ovechkin and Dorosh were then corroborated by an impressive array of novels and short stories which suggested, in effect, that the pre-Soviet pattern of exploitation of peasants by absentee landlords from the big city, a major concern of Russian literary classics, continues to this day. Fyodor Abramov's *Around and About* (1963) suggested that both the Soviet landlord and the destitute peasants would stand to gain if some private initiative and private property were to be reintroduced—an idea smacking of ideological heresy. A disciplined Communist, the late Fyodor Abramov eschewed such concrete proposals in his later works, but not his profound disquiet—indeed, alarm—at the extreme poverty of the peasant and also the privations and ultimately even moral degradation this destitution engenders. In "Pelageya" (1969), the heroine agrees to go to bed with the manager of a bakery because it is the only way to get a job that would provide bread for her and for her daughter. A similar incident is described in *Two Winters and Three Summers*, a novel from *The Pryaslins* cycle (1975). In it a teenage farm girl is pressured into a loveless marriage that will bring a calf into a family struggling to stay alive in a village ravished by war. Examples can be multiplied. In Boris Mozhayev's *From the Life of Ivan Kuzkin*, the central protagonist, a war invalid, tried to make ends meet by tending a private garden plot, for which "crime" he is hounded by the Soviet authorities. (To think that Voltaire's Candide believed such activity would meet with approval in royalist France!) The peasants in Vasili Belov's *The Usual Thing* and *Carpenter Stories* are plagued by poverty, alcoholism and ill health, they are undisciplined and downtrodden. And yet, Belov and the other "agrarians" emphasize, it is they who are the real Russians on whom the nation can depend in an hour of need. That this idealization of the peasant extends also to non-Russian is demonstrated by Chingiz Aitmatov's major novel *One Day Lasts Longer than a Century* which is set in the steppes of Central Asia. Ultimately, such novels pose a crucial question—what price industrial progress? The dilemma, real enough elsewhere, is particularly painful to face in Soviet conditions. What is at stake in Rasputin's *Farewell to Matyora* is not only a choice between economic advancement and—to use an anti-industrial American locution from the 1960s—"the greening of Russia." Industrial progress, we should recall, is a central article of the Soviet faith.

Because of its emphasis on active and socially useful protagonists, conventional Soviet writing favors male characters over female, young over old, healthy over ailing, and prefers for its settings public over private life, factories and laboratories and collective farms over bedrooms and nurseries. And that is, in a way, inevitable. Hospital patients, retirees, and even full-time mothers and housewives are poor material for Socialist Realism's Positive Heroes, those repositories of official virtues that Soviet readers are expected to emulate. All the more interesting because of that are the departures from these norms that began to appear in post-Stalin Soviet writing. There is Yuri Trifonov's contemplative octogenarian in *The*

Old Man; there is the harassed young mother trying against all odds to reconcile the demands of her job and family in Natalya Baranskaya's *A Week Like Any Other Week*; there are the lonely and infirm old ladies in I. Grekova's *A Ship of Widows* and the professionally still active middle-aged unmarried mothers in the same author's *Ladies' Hairdresser* and *The Hotel Manager*. Exceptional popularity of these otherwise different books in the USSR since their publication attests to public approval of the legitimacy of concerns for the infirm, for the working mother, and the senior citizen—concerns rarely raised earlier by establishmentarian Soviet fiction.

The most elementary of human aspirations, freedom from fear for the safety of one's person, an aspiration understandably rarely even hinted at during Stalin's reign of terror, began to surface soon after the dictator's death, albeit always guardedly, camouflaged with euphemisms, understatements, hints and protestations of loyalty to the regime that had engendered the plague. These qualities pervade nearly all officially sanctioned writing on the subject, from Daniil Granin's *One's Own Opinion* in 1956 to the most recent important work tackling that theme, to Trifonov's 1976 *House on the Embankment*. Not even Solzhenitsyn's *One Day in the Life of Ivan Denisovich* is entirely exempt from it. It is important to remember that following its publication in 1962—we have it, as Grigorii Svirsky has shown, on the authority of Khrushchev himself—Soviet journals received some *ten thousand* manuscripts describing the horrors of Soviet concentration camps.[5] Khrushchev's admission demonstrates that *samizdat* camp literature that subsequently began to circulate and in particular those works that were ultimately to be published abroad—from Evgeniia Ginzburg's *Journey Into the Whirlwind* and Varlam Shalamov's *Kolyma Tales* to Georgi Vladimov's *Faithful Ruslan* and Solzhenitsyn's own *Gulag Archipelago*—were a natural expression of a widely held emotional need. A vast nation's collective soul, as it were, had to be purged of the pain and horror of decades of mass arrests, deportations and death before any confidence could be instilled that the nightmare would not return.

The moderately repressive administrations that followed Khrushchev's relatively liberal regime, those of Brezhnev, Andropov, Chernenko, and the early Gorbachev period did not encourage further exploration of the subject. But then, in all fairness, even at their harshest, none of them came close to duplicating the agony of Stalin's police state, and memories of Stalinism itself gradually began to fade. Concerns are now much more modest, and they are voiced in guarded tones. Thus, Yuri Nagibin, a well known author of moderate views, appeals for a recognition of a citizen's *right to a degree of privacy*, to an area of activities and beliefs with which the state would not even attempt to interfere. Two recent works of Nagibin's come to mind, *The Forest of Berenday* and *The Strange Woman*, as well as *The Fortieth Day* by Vladimir Krupin, a less established author. Similar concerns are expressed in other works.

As so many other facets of human existence, the problem of privacy, of man's inner, intimate life—concepts seemingly so impervious to politics—have long been the subject of political controversy in the USSR. Suffice it to recall that in the Soviet scheme of things the collective is officially viewed as a repository of virtue, while individualism is, ultimately "morbid." (It was, accordingly, quite fitting that, as already mentioned, in 1956 Khrushchev was to blame the horrors of the Stalin era on the "personality cult" of one particular individual, while conveniently exempting the Party as a collective body of any guilt, even if only as an accomplice.) Monarchs of yore, the Russian included, would have, as suggested, been more than content to see their subjects forsake all interest in public concerns for private ones. Not so those professing Marxist esthetics. Writing on the eve of World War I, Georgi Plekhanov suggested in *Art and Society* that avoidance of social issues is an artist's way of venting his hostility to values of his society. It was these considerations, we submit, that underlay the public excommunication in 1946 of the humorist Mikhail Zoshchenko and the lyric poet Anna Akhmatova. They also help explain the failure to publish in the USSR, a quarter of a century after its author's death, Boris Pasternak's *Doctor Zhivago*, a resolutely apolitical novel, except in the sense that its hero chooses to remain in his private world with the woman he loves, oblivious to the Civil War raging around them.

Understandably, the right to privacy in one's emotional life ranked high among the concerns of nonconformist writing of the late 1950s. It was the subject of Nikolai Pogodin's play *Petrarch's Sonnet* which described the love relationship of a middle-aged married man and a much younger woman; not only was there gossip and hatred, but both lives were destroyed, his by expulsion from the Party, hers from the Young Communist League. (That the battle for this cause is far from won, is attested by such later works as I. Grekova's *The Hotel Manager*.)

Before long, however, the range of issues was broadened and made more controversial. Alexander Yashin's story "The Levers" suggested that sensitive and intelligent *individuals* turn into levers, automatons when acting as a *collective*, while the two most celebrated novels of the mid–1950s, Ilya Ehrenburg's *The Thaw* (which bestowed the name on the period) and Vladimir Dudintsev's *Not By Bread Alone*, advanced the thesis that mindless conformism of the *collective* threatens to stifle the creative *individual*. Indeed, literary works began with increasing frequency (the late Yuri Kazakov's short stories are a good example) to depict solitary protagonists—or romantic couples—against the background of nature, and not, as was customary, of a factory, farm, school, or a military collective. Cheerfully upbeat protagonists of conventional Soviet fiction, now frequently competed for the reader's attention with literary characters, such as Viktor Konetsky's, whom an American scholar describes as "brooders, burdened with grief, disappointments, or feelings of guilt. They are responsible, mature men of proven courage, but they are also alienated, lonely and troubled."[6] Vladimir Lugovskoi, a leading poet of the older generation wrote:

> Tell me, how will it end, the eternal quarrel
>   Between the individual, unique in the world,
> And the state.
>   Between personal happiness
> And the state.
>   Between personal freedom
> And the state.
>   Between personal truth
> And the state?[7]

Not unexpectedly, the poet offers no answer. And not only because no definitive response is possible, but also because the query is pregnant with weighty ideological implications. When all is said and done, it argues, in effect, that men and women not only have the right to moral autonomy, but also an obligation to make their own ethical choices. Acting merely in accordance with orders received from above does not absolve us of moral responsibility for our acts. It would be unfair to expect a Soviet poet writing in a book published in the USSR to dot the i's and cross the t's on an idea ultimately so subversive of Soviet values. We should marvel, instead, at the degree of human courage that posing this question certainly required.

Reference has been made earlier to official Soviet writing's preference—vigorous and youngish protagonists. Another, and unexpected, parallel comes to mind when one examines its portrayal of personages of different age groups. As if continuing the tradition of Byzantine icons in which infants and children are portrayed as merely small adults, establishmentarian Soviet literature stubbornly refuses to recognize the legitimacy of aspirations peculiar to the young, and is quite adamant in its denial of the very existence in the USSR of a conflict of generations. This conflict, however, does exist, much as it did over a century ago when Ivan Turgenev wrote *Fathers and Sons*, and this fact is often reflected in less conventional Soviet writing of the post-Stalin era. Clashes of conflicting values and attitudes of the young and the middle-aged were shown in Daniil Granin's *I Walk Into the Storm* and the late Vera Panova's *How Are Things, Fellow?* On the stage, theatergoers could observe it in Victor Rozov's *Unequal*

Struggle, A,B,C,D,E and, most recently, in *The Nest of the Woodgrouse*.
In ostentatious defiance of traditional Soviet policy of closed borders (as
a result of which only a miniscule number of older Soviet citizens have
ever been to the West), Yevgeni Yevtushenko proclaimed the young generation's desire to see the world:

> I don't like frontiers.
> It's embarrassing
>   not to know Buenos Aires and New York
> I want to wander
> To my heart's content
> Around London
> And to talk to everybody (so what if in broken English)
> And to ride around Paris in the morning
> Hanging, like a little boy, on the back of a bus.[8]

Yet it was Vassily Aksyonov who surely was the foremost literary spokesman of the aspirations of the Soviet young. The son of a long-time inmate
of Soviet concentration camps (the author Evgeniia Ginzburg, referred to
earlier), Aksyonov portrayed a gallery of rebellious Soviet youths, somewhat cynical and suspicious of adult authority. His *Ticket to the Stars*,
Colleagues and *Halfway to the Moon* bore a degree of resemblance to the
writings of J. D. Salinger and were as popular with Soviet young as *Catcher
in the Rye* was with their counterparts in the United States. Perhaps there
is some symbolism in the fact that Aksyonov was later stripped of Soviet
citizenship and now lives in America.

Glaring social inequality in the ostensibly egalitarian Socialist state was
among the first shams to be exposed in literature in the flush of enthusiasm
in the wake of Stalin's death. In Vladimir Tendriakov's "Potholes" a bureaucrat refuses the use of a tractor to save a man's life: rules and regulations, after all, are more important than the life of an ordinary citizen.
Similarly, in Yuri Nagibin's "A Light in the Window" a chambermaid, in
an act of rebellion, allows children to watch television in a hotel room
always kept vacant should the Boss ever deign to visit the town. And in
Nikolai Zhdanov's "A Visit Home" a Communist party functionary arrives
in a village after his mother's death only to discover that he has nothing
in common with his erstwhile neighbors and relatives. They view him as
a powerful and privileged stranger, not very different from the aristocratic
landowners in the countryside of Imperial Russia. That conditions of social
inequality which breed privilege side by side with deprivation have not
changed much in the post-Stalin quarter of a century is shown by some

striking similarities between Leonid Zorin's 1954 play *The Guests* and the late Yuri Trifonov's 1978 novella *The Old Man*.

Various shortages continue to plague Soviet citizens even now, four decades after the war. Lack of adequate housing and consumer goods are depicted as debilitating, while humiliation at being denied goods and services that are available to the elite—including decent medical care—is unmistakably felt in scores of literary works. For all their muted tone, pronouncements of fictional protagonists dealing with the subjects of shortages, inequality, and privilege are often, in effect, not merely *pleas for fairness but outright, if muted, demands for justice*. In order to diffuse the politically subversive overtones of such motifs, recent Soviet prose and drama (social issues are, for obvious reasons of limitations of the genre, rarely dealt with in poetry)—in marked contrast to writing of the Stalin era—do not, as a rule, openly, identify privilege with the Soviet *political* establishment. The rich and the influential are no longer Communist party secretaries or even factory directors as they were in Stalin's days.[9] Instead, they are ostensibly members of the scientific jet set and the artistic intelligentsia, much safer targets of social resentment—although, one suspects, the ruse is much too obvious to deceive the majority of seasoned readers. The *nomenklatura*-level secret police chief in Yuri Trifonov's *House on the Embankment* lived during the Stalin era, but many readers probably suspect that his successors are no less adept at using their positions to bully and blackmail those around them. Be that as it may, anger and envy of privilege, cast differentiation and unequal distribution of creature comforts in Vladimir Kommissarov's *Old Debts* is shown against the setting of a research institute, but surely a similar reaction might be expected in a different milieu as well. In Gennadi Nikolaev's *The Apartment*, a homeless young married couple obtains housing only when one of them submits to sexual demands of an influential older citizen (the "modernity" of the story is attested by the fact that traditional sex roles in fiction are reversed here: it is a young *man* who must yield to a rich older woman!). Important people in Yulii Krelin's *What Are You Complaining of, Doctor?* obtain medical services unavailable to ordinary mortals and so forth. The common denominator of these works, and of scores like them, is, to use the Orwellian formula, that while all Soviet citizens are equal, some are clearly far more equal than others. And the angry grumbling of those "others" is quite audible even in recently published "official" Soviet writings that tackle the old questions of Nikolai Nekrasov's poem—*komu na Rusi zhit' khorosho*, (who lives well in Mother Russia?) That the resentment of privilege and status is widespread is attested also by the thunderous applause that greeted Yevgeni Yevtushenko's denunciation of such evils at the congress of Soviet writers in December of 1985.

Finally, there is the quest for a code of ethics. A central preoccupation of much of Soviet Russian literature, this theme attests to the refusal of a significant number of authors—and also of readers—to wholeheartedly accept the implications of official Soviet pronouncements on the subject that, in effect, bestow the state's blessings on whatever may benefit the state, oblivious of the moral vacuum this inevitably engenders. Vladimir Lugovskoi's eloquence may not have been matched by others, but he was not the only Soviet author to discern the problem. If a search for a Russian ethnic identity—and perhaps also a religious one as well—is to be found most often among the "agrarians," the quest for ethical and moral codes is particularly pronounced in works of authors identified with urban settings and youthful protagonists. Attempts to formulate a set of ethical principles, of standards of honesty and integrity that are not politicized by familiar Soviet cant, can be traced back to Semyon Kirsanov's 1956 poem "Seven Days of the Week" with its message that the crowning achievement of Creation, Man with a capital "m," is yet to come. A very similar title, *Seven Days of Creation* was chosen by Vladimir Maksimov for one of his novels in 1973. Together with Yevgeni Ternovsky's *The Strange City*, (1977), the novels are among the few in modern Russian writing to reflect a religious *Weltanschauung*. Both were published abroad.

The most important modern Russian author inspired by a religious vision of life is, of course, Alexander Solzhenitsyn. His writings posit a multitude of religious and quasi-religious questions and even those published in the USSR, such as "Matryona's Hut," occasionally portray traditionally religious "righteous" human beings, *pravedniki*, reminiscent of Nikolai Leskov's or Turgenev's *Living Relics*. Moral categories are elucidated in *Cancer Ward*, and the lack of a minimum of human decency results in a denial to a Soviet bureaucrat, Rusanov, of that instant of *prosvetlenie*—a glimpse of redemption, as it were—that was granted a century earlier a more attractive Russian bureaucrat dying of cancer, Tolstoy's Ivan Ilyich. Solzhenitsyn, now an émigré, is a devout Russian Orthodox Christian. Yet quasi-religious quests and religious imagery are also characteristic of some of Soviet Russia's officially atheist authors, such as the late Yuri Trifonov. The anti-hero of his 1976 novel *House on the Embankment* is evil because, like Judas Iscariot, he betrayed his Teacher; the central character of *The Old Man*, published two years later, is haunted by memories of a crime to which he may have been an unwitting accessory, the murder of a wartime comrade half a century earlier. Significantly, perhaps, moral searchings were particularly characteristic of the writings—prior to their departure from the USSR—of such authors as Victor Nekrasov, Anatolii Gladilin, Georgii Vladimov and Vasilii Aksyonov. Perhaps there is a connection between these writers' emigration and the moral and ethical concerns of their books. Among living novelists still in the USSR one should single out Yuri Bondarev, a well known writer, and Yuri Galkin, a lesser author of prose. Preoccupation with so-called "accursed questions"—*prokliatye voprosy*—is one of the hallmarks of prerevolutionary Russian writing. It is, indeed, the fearless probing of man's relationship to God, to his neighbor, and to his conscience, that imparts the quality of high seriousness to the great Russian novels of the nineteenth century. If anything, in the absence of widely accepted religious or secular ethical values (official rhetoric notwithstanding, the Soviet idea today survives more as a set of rituals than as a dynamic creed) there may well be an even greater thirst for such discussion today. The Soviet authorities appear to encourage the creation of a literature that would pervert such quest for their own ends. Thus, for instance, concern with honesty was used meretriciously in Alexander Gel'-man's film *The Prize*, in which "honest" workers refuse a monetary award they do not deserve. An analogous situation was portrayed in Vadim Koz-hevnikov's staunchly Stalinist novel *The Field of Life*, in which a much decorated Soviet worker is tormented by pangs of conscience—is he *still* worthy of these medals?

Next to the quest for moral and ethical norms and for a reconciliation of reason with faith in God, compassion for the underdog was the foremost concern of prerevolutionary Russian writing. This "philanthropic" tradition is not entirely extinct today even though it, too, is alien to the Soviet ethos and the "official" writing inspired by it. Orthodox Soviet prose emphasizes intolerance of weakness; at the very least it celebrates *victory* over weakness. Suffice it to read such stalwart Communist novels of recent years as Boris Polevoi's *Anyuta*, Semyon Babayevsky's *The Cossack Village*, Anatoli Ananyev's *The Years When There Was No War*, Mikhail Koles-nikov's *Altunin Makes Up His Mind*, or Vil' Lipatov's *Igor Savvovich*.

By contrast, the idea of *compassion and forgiveness*, (though, to be sure, in its less objectionable secular form), is very prominent in some of the most popular works of recent Soviet fiction. It is the scaffolding on which I. Grekova's *A Ship of Widows* and *Hotel Manager*, already referred to, rest. It serves as the underpinning of Pavel Nilin's *Married for the First Time* and Yuri Skop's *Industrial Safety*, both of them chronicles of travails of single motherhood. It permeates Vladimir Tendriakov's *The Reckoning*, Valeri Prokhvatilov's *The Hour of Rest*, Boris Shustov's *An Arctic Tale*, and scores of other works that describe the ravages of alcoholism. It is felt in two otherwise quite different novels, Nilin's *Cruelty* (English title *Comrade Venka*) and the late Vasili Shukshin's *Snowball Berry Red*, the latter a Dostoyevskian story about a young man's thwarted desire to forsake crime and embark on a new and godly life on a farm.

The unofficial Russian *Weltanschauung* that emerges is thus a combination of painful memories, social norms, political attitudes and moral searchings. There is the feeling of revulsion toward wars—*all* wars, the "good" included, and perhaps also the revolutions as well. The Stalinist past is remembered with horror and pity, and also with hope that it will never return. There is a sense of moderate Russian nationalism with vaguely religious overtones. Social injustice and inequality is resented. Admiration for industrial progress is no longer blind. It is often accompanied with concern for its destructive impact on the ethnic, historical, and environmental landscape. An individual's right to a degree of privacy in their personal life is recognized, and of individual responsibility for moral choices, as well as the need to grant the young a degree of autonomy, and that the collective is not *always* right: sometimes, it may be the loner and eccentric. Compassion is shown for the less fortunate, the peasants, working mothers (particularly, if unmarried), the aged and the infirm. Finally, there is a continuing search for a code of personal ethics, as distinct from the quasi-official values of what may be termed polite Soviet society. In the final analysis, these unofficial hopes and beliefs bespeak a society far more decent, tolerant, and humane than official Soviet slogans may lead an observer to believe.

Notes

1. D. Brown, *Soviet Russian Literature Since Stalin*, (London, New York, and Melbourne: Cambridge University Press, 1978), 1–2.
2. Thus, in a letter to Maxim Gorky on 17 January 1930, Joseph Stalin warned against excessive enthusiasm for pacifist writing inspired by revulsion of World War I: "The book market is filled with a mass of literary tales inculcating a revulsion against *all* war (not only *imperialist* but *every other kind* of war). These are bourgeois-pacifist stories, and not of much value. . . . Besides, we are not against *all* wars. We are against imperialist wars, as being counter-revolutionary wars. But we are *for* liberating, anti-imperialist, revolutionary wars, despite the fact that such wars, as we know, are not only not exempt from the 'horrors of bloodshed,' but even abound in them." J.V. Stalin, *Works*, (Moscow: Foreign Language Publishing House, 1955), vol. 12, p. 182. Italics in the original.
3. E. Mickiewicz, *Media and the Russian Public*, (New York: Praeger, 1981).
4. D. Brown, *Soviet Russian Literature*, 241.
5. G. Svirsky, *Na lobnom meste*, (London: Overseas Publication Interchange, 1979), 253.
6. D. Brown, *Soviet Russian Literature* 209.

7. V. Lugovskoi, *Seredina veka*, (Moscow: Sovetskii pisatel', 1958), 238–39. Deming Brown trans.

8. For a very concise description of "public" Soviet poets of the 1960s, of whom Yevtushenko is one, see Edward J. Brown, *Russian Literature Since the Revolution*, (revised and enlarged edition, Cambridge, (Mass.) and London: Harvard University Press, 1982), 336–41.

9. The subject of mores and values of the Soviet bourgeoisie of that age, and its reflection in Soviet literature, is perceptively analyzed in Vera Dunham's *In Stalin's Time*, (London, New York, and Melbourne: Cambridge University Press, 1976).

12

A Crisis of Belief:

Reflections on Soviet Youth Culture

NICHOLAS HAYES

I've revalued
I undervalued
   that seething Sanhedrin beneath an
      azure dome and tall white pillars
   cold not red sequoias
   you made appeal to the sequoia
   in Lenin's likeness
   try appealing to the sharks
   with sharklike mouths and chins receding
   the shocked dismay of all your friends
   when faced with this menagerie
   the roar of this menagerie
   Tallyho, tallyho, chase them abroad
   into asylums into the grave
   but for us the caviar
   delicious meats and fats and juices
   if need be through our nostrils
      through our ears
   or through our pores
   so long as it keeps flowing

From Vasily Aksyonov, *The Burn*
(1969–1975)

For it is an open secret that there has
occurred among the young a certain
reappraisal of our convictions and our
values; the soul and consciousness of
our youth have been seriously undermined.

> E.A. Shevardnadze, then (1976)
> First Secretary of the Central
> Committee of the CP of Georgia
> now full member of the Politburo
> and Minister of Foreign Affairs
> of the USSR.

In its broadest terms the description of differences between the generation that came of age in the Stalinist 1930s and 1940s and the post-Stalin generations invariably includes emphases on: an upbringing not under the shock waves of "building socialism" but under the measured confidence in the material progress of the Khrushchev and Brezhnev eras; education not in the hastily improvised Party institutes and vocational schools of the 1920s but in the baccalaureate and graduate programs of a stabilized system of Soviet higher education; a perspective on international affairs shaped less by the national struggle for survival in the "great patriotic war" than by the "positive correlation of forces"; consumer expectations that take for granted the provision of basic subsistence but expect the quality and diversity of an advanced industrial society. What is more, there has been sufficient evidence of youthful protest in the Soviet Union in the 1960s to the 1980s along the lines of the youth countercultures in the West, and also of "grumbletonian" complaints from the Bolshevik Old Guard, to draw the conclusion that a "conflict of generations" was generic to the post-industrial world and embraced the socialist East as well as the capitalist West.[1]

Soviet analyses of the younger generation may admit to problems of communication between the young and the old but they persistently deny the existence of a "conflict of generations" in Soviet society. A "conflict of generations" in the Soviet view results from class struggle in the capitalist nations and has specific causes today in the problems of youth unemployment and their sense of the impending doom of the capitalist system. Any affinities between Soviet youth and their Western peers stem mainly from their shared antipathy toward capitalism. The Soviet view admits, however, that Soviet youth are unfortunately the prime targets of the psychological warfare waged by imperialism against the USSR. Aided and abetted by the Voice of America and the BBC, some Soviet youth are seduced by nihilism, faddishness, and vulgarity of youthful fashions in the West—which is, in actuality, the swan song of the decadent stage of capitalism—and confuse what is trendy under capitalism for what should be the contemporary mentality and life-style for youth generally.[2]

The term youth culture, as used in this essay, means a certain style, value judgments, and aesthetic tastes by which the Soviet young generation consciously separates itself from the older generation raised in Stalin's time. In part, a description of the Soviet youth culture is to be found in the history of the generation that came of age in the 1960s. The youth culture is not simply a demographic phenomenon, however. The aging of that particular generation did not bring about the end of the Soviet youth culture. What is significant about the youth culture is that it continues to develop in a non-conducive Soviet environment and breeds a "youthful foreign tribe" out of place in Soviet official culture.[3]

To trace the themes of the youth culture, we turn to its sources. Its manifestations are most obvious in the life-style of the so-called *stilyagy* (translated loosely as "beatniks" or "the hip"), who were thus identified by Soviet media in the latter 1950s and who, through their fetishising Western pop culture and sprouting native Soviet rock culture, continued into the 1970s and 1980s. This development represented a spontaneous expansion of the new space opened up for artistic expression since the mid-1950s. Innovative modern currents started then to permeate and transform Soviet poetry, prose, and visual arts. In poetry, it was the "magnificent pentad"—Evtushenko, Voznesensky, Rozhdestvensky, Akhmadullina and Odkudzhava[4]—and their public poetry readings in the late 1950s and early 1960s which became the public rites of the young. It was, however, in prose, and specifically the so-called "young prose" of the early 1960s, that the most important public debate of the 1960s on the problems of the youth culture surfaced. The central publication of the "young prose" was the literary magazine *Yunost* (Youth) under the editorship from 1955 to 1962 of Valentin Kataev and later, even if through benign neglect, under Boris Polevoy. The most persistent, and to the eyes of the older generation the most impertinent, themes of "young prose" were found in the short stories and novels of Anatoly Gladilin, Vladimir Voinovich, Andrei Bitov, Viktor Konetsky, Vladimir Maksimov and especially Vasily Aksyonov.[5] While the controversies over "young prose" ebbed in the late 1960s, the "new wave" of Soviet paintings and films of the 1970s and 1980s took on the themes raised in these controversies with renewed vigor, developing them in concordance with the changing experience of the young generation.

The connection between the new writing and the political critique of Stalinism had been stressed repeatedly. The young writers' public success had an obvious coincidence with Khrushchev's politics of de-Stalinization, first in the "thaw" of 1954–1956 and, again, in the second spring, or more accurately phrased, the false spring of 1962. The young writers were direct in the critique of their parents' ties to the crimes of the "cult of personality," and to discuss their writings without reference to that issue is not unlike discussing American student radicalism in the 1960s and omit reference to the radicals' opposition to the Vietnam War.

However, the distinction of the young culture was not its antipathy to the more notorious crimes of the "cult." The *stilyagy* disdained not simply what fell under the reproach of "our dear Nikita Sergeevich" but, more importantly, what remained beyond reproach in a society still contently married to the *kitsch* that graced High Stalinism. The young culture loathed not so much the excesses but the norms of the new respectability of their parents' world. When Anatoly Gladilin's hero in "First Day of the New Year" confronts his father with the following words:

> You don't repair the consequences of the cult of personality by limiting your-self to the removal of portraits and the renaming of cities. The cult of per-sonality is sluggishness of thought, it is the fear to think for oneself, it is the dream of tranquility and hatred for the new.[6]

He suggests that a compromise with Stalinist social conservatism, without the terror, will not placate the defiance of the young of the early 1960s or preempt the return of that defiance in an amplified form later.

Much of the polemics about the "youth culture" focused on whatever is flippant, impertinent, wilfully deviant and indiscreet in the literature and life-style of the defiant youngsters. The "youth culture" was accused of encouraging juvenile delinquency, social deviance, and unhealthy habits among the young. What was at issue, however, were of course not so much the causes of delinquency as the promotion of social impertinence and of Western styles among the young people. Aksyonov's *Oranges From Mo-rocco* (1962) was controversial for its lack of discretion in divulging the problem of shortages. The novel, however, was more socially invidious for its depiction of the easiness with which "normal" Soviet society, when confronted with non-conformist behaviour, can be transformed into a brawling and raucous mob. Much later, in *The Burn*, Aksyonov revels in the carnival side of Soviet life. His Russia is not the discreet order of the new Soviet bourgeoisie but the "decor of our native pigsty with its per-manent sense of being just about to erupt into a noisy brawl."[7]

While much of the conservative criticism of youth's impertinence could have been found in Western conservatives' responses to its own young, the Soviet youth culture always faced the peculiar charge of the beatnik ways and jazz and rock 'n' roll serving imperialism. Jazz and rock, with their expression of spontaneity, inextricable association with Western culture, and performances verging on anarchic rites of individual passage, proved, however, to be so attractive to the young that no amount of political accusations could stop their acute interest in, and association with, these forms of music. Thus, the Soviet officialdom had to tone down its criticism and, though reluctantly and in limited ways, admit jazz and rock into the category of legitimate forms of the USSR's "socialist culture." Although jazz and rock are, in principle, not amenable to co-optation within the establishment, one can imagine a neo-Stalinist solution to the problem through the creation of state institutions for the study and promotion of jazz and rock compositions and for the management of their performance in the Komsomol clubs across the Soviet Union. This solution would, however, hardly work to the satisfaction of the guardians of ideological purity.

Rock in the 1970s seemed to have replaced jazz as the focus of musical controversy in Soviet cultural life. The decade witnessed a proliferation of Soviet rock bands and fans. New groups sprung up right under the noses of the cultural authorities. As if by spontaneous generation, properly authorized folk ensembles or variety theatre troupes reportedly turned up overnight and most frequently on the concert tours into rock bands with names like *Karnaval* (Carnival), *Kruiz* (Cruise), *Zemlyane* (Earthmen), *Akvarium* (Aquarium), *Korobeiniki* (the Peddlers), and the most publicized *Mashyna vremeni* (Time Machine). The rock concert circuit expanded from Moscow and Leningrad to include festivals in Tbilisi and Erevan as well as performances throughout the whole of the Soviet Union. Rock, and especially rock concerts, are rites of primal festivity that in the Soviet Union, as in the West, take on the character of a spontaneous and elemental carnival of youth culture. In the Soviet case, moreover, as a reviewer of the Soviet rock opera *Orpheus and Eurydice* (1975) noted, rock

> . . . reflects young people's strong attraction to the carnivalization of life itself and a challenge to the dreary grayness of standardization that one sometimes encounters in life.[8]

Not surprisingly, the response of the cultural establishment took aim at the lack of inhibition in the emerging rock culture. During the summer of 1984, *Sovetskaya kul'tura* (Soviet culture) featured a series of exceptionally perturbed commentaries on rock groups that made a mockery of traditional Russian folk melodies and generally indulged themselves in "violations . . . of the ethical norms of behavior on stage." The Ministry of Culture of the Russian Soviet Federated Socialist Republic responded with a model solution for the problems of "vocal and instrumental groups" or "collectives" (the official euphemism for rock groups) in the 1980s. Stricter supervision and controls were to be placed on concert tour associations and the Composers' Union in the Russian Republic. Several groups were banned from performing, several were placed on probation, and others given the opportunity of a "rehearsal period for the purpose of improving their program." What is more, the ensembles were restricted to presenting in their performances no more than 20 percent from works composed by an artist who was not a member of the Composers' Union. These regulations received a strong endorsement from the Ministry of Culture of the USSR which promised to extend the efforts undertaken in the RSFSR to an All-Union-wide campaign.[9] In sum, the response to the proliferation of Soviet rock culture in the 1970s was to envelop it in the 1980s within an admonishing and parental embrace knowing full well that the children will not be prompted to disturbing behavior by Komsomol songs even when set to the sound of heavy metal.

This reminds us that the arguments over *stilyagy* and beatnik ways in Khrushchev's times centered not so much on the substance of the new values but on whether there existed at all a youth culture distinct from the traditional one. The excitement generated over the publication in 1956 in *Yunost'* (Youth) of Anatoly Gladilin's *The Chronicle of the Times of Viktor Podgursky* stemmed primarily from the desire of the young to see a public confirmation of their own idiom and milieu. Gladilin's fiction disavowed any grand political re-orientation and promised only to

look at life as Viktor Podgursky saw it . . . no more grandiose task . . . (than) to show life as it was and characters (who) did not express themselves in fancy literary language, but spoke the living language of the street.

He found his constituency in

. . . high school and college students (who) read the story right during class, tore it out of each other's hands. . . .[10]

Gladilin was deliberate in the choice of his generation's street language; he was also politically indiscreet for having fomented a rush of youthful enthusiasm over the precious opportunity for a new generation to see itself in its own, not its parents', light.

In the early 1960s, the young prose chronicled the coming of age of this generation and how its members fulfilled their parents' high and predictable expectations. The source of conflict here was the young people's insistence on their right to doubt the values behind those expectations and to negotiate on their own terms their place in Soviet social reality. Aksyonov's first novels—*Kollegi* (Colleagues) (1960) and *Zvyozdny bilet* (A Ticket to the

Stars) (1961)—have the common theme of a generation's coming of age while mistrusting and malingering the demands of the Soviet professional work ethics and the conformism of their parents toward those ethics. In *Colleagues* Aksyonov questions the clichés that surround the mystique of the socially useful and personally fulfilling career of a Soviet doctor. *A Ticket to the Stars* takes Aksyonov much further into the defiant psyche of youthful skepticism, relieved only by the urge to have fun. The novel's popularity owed to the early section depicting Aksyonov's young heroes as they most unconventionally jived, talked, and raucously celebrated their upcoming "Soviet manhood." More importantly, Aksyonov expressed a generation's insistence on questioning society's preconception of the lives for its young members. His hero rejects in his elder brother the paradigm for the hopes of the parents of the 1960s:

> Your life, Victor, was devised by Papa and Mama when you were still in the cradle. A star in school, a star in college, graduate student, junior scientific worker, M.S., senior scientific worker, Ph.D., Member of the Academy, and then . . . a dead man, respected by all. Never once in your life have you made a truly important decision, never once taken a risk. To hell with it. We are scarcely born when everything has already been thought out for us, our future already decided. Not on your life: It's better to be a tramp and fail than to be a boy all your life, carrying out the decisions of others.[11]

The young people of the 1960s were quite aware of the ties of this complaint to the Salinger generation. The young prose played on this association for ironic effect. For example, Vladimir Voinovich's story, *Dva tovarishcha* (Two Comrades) (1967), holds up Salinger's mirror to the face of the new generation as if to tease the suspicions of the older generation and the pretensions of the younger:

> "And what did you do yesterday?" asks Tolik.
> "Nothing. Layed down, read a book."
> "What kind of book?"
> "*The Catcher in the Rye.*"
> "About espionage?"
> "No, about life."[12]

The young people who, however, negotiated a compromise in the 1960s did not hold to it in the 1970s. Youth literature of the 1970s showed the rebellion in mid-career at compromises made in youth. To follow this theme we can turn to Soviet film where we find an aged Soviet Holden Caulfield at mid-life career and in rage with his own complacency and acceptance in respectable society. That rage at compromises made forms the underlying psychology of key characters in two of Nikita Mikhalkov's films—*An Unfinished Piece for Mechanical Piano* (1977) and *The Slave of Love* (1978). The first, an adaptation based on an eclectic selection of Chekhov's later short stories, centers on the character of Platonov (played by Aleksandr Kalugin). He brings the film to its conclusion with a raging monologue protesting against the last decade of his life, spent in social comfort and stupor, blaming himself not only for failing to answer the questions of his youth but for stopping asking these questions altogether. In *The Slave of Love*, a generation's disappointment with itself surfaces again in the character of a film director (again played by Aleksandr Kalugin). The setting is a small film troupe in the Crimea in about 1919 faced with the dilemma of either collapsing with the White army or following it abroad. This dilemma could be taken as an allegory for Russian artists' debates on the merits of emigration and of their reflections on the meaning of their careers. Re-assured that he is a success, that everyone loves him, and that he has no enemies, the director responds:

> Look at our films! Who needs them. They're stupid. . . . What? No enemies.
> . . . I have no enemies? Look at Chekhov. He had enemies.

Mikhalkov brings us back full circle to the questions of the young generation. They insisted on the right to doubt and to challenge; they refused to please but nevertheless some of them negotiated their compromise with Soviet social reality. Thus, in the 1970s the Soviet "youth culture" refuses to accept the complacency of aging and throws back at itself the questions it raised in its youth with regard to the older generation.

After a long banishment under the cultural prudery of Stalin's time, eros also returned into the writings and artistic creations of the "youth culture." Like the life-style of the *stilyagy*, the youthful pursuit of the erotic had the sense of the illicit, the outlawed, and the scent of a love that in Evtushenko's phrase consisted "not of bought but of stolen apples."

The "youth culture" drew the metaphors and symbols for eroticism from traditions that, if one looked for Russian antecedents, belonged to the Silver Age and the 1920s. The young turned to an eros imaged in metaphors of vertigo that, like in Chagall's "Birthday," inspired dreamlike discreet symbols of light and floating freedom. Aksyonov's *Half-Way to the Moon* (1962) is best understood if read as a metaphor for such a vision of the erotic. The hero, Kirpichenko, spends a vacation flying back and forth on the Moscow-Khabarovsk flight in search of a flight attendant he had seen once on an earlier flight. But, once he encounters her—Tanya—at the Moscow airport, he shies away and prefers to have only her memory, not her company. Both conservatives and feminists may be justified in suggesting that Aksyonov's hero is a stunted male adolescent unable to have a mature relationship with a woman.[13] The force of the novel, however, lies in the metaphor for the ethereal dream of eros as ". . . a woman of the kind that doesn't really exist, the kind that's as far away from you as the moon".[14]

The new eroticism was nevertheless not a cult of celestial goddesses but a longing for love that is as heavy as our physical desire but, at the same time, as light as our dreams. Thus, the new eros took to images of floating as if in Malevich's fourth dimension or in Evtushenko's reminder to a lover ". . . we have to embrace so we won't fall down".[15]

The scene from Andrei Tarkovsky's autobiographical film, *The Mirror* (1981), where a child sees in a dream the sensual embrace of his parents floating on their bed in the cottage and beckoning toward him, is perhaps one of the most precise expressions of such a vision of eroticism. The eroticism of the Soviet "youth culture" is political only in the oblique. As Evtushenko says of Nefertiti: "when in reality, authority comes face to face with beauty, its value depreciates".[16]

Also, when Evtushenko in his autobiographical film *Kindergarten* (1984), takes up the story of his generation's childhood during the "Great Patriotic War," he deftly avoids making yet another epic on the older generation's favorite theme. He sets the primary inspiration for the child narrator not in the politically predictable sources but in the child's erotic visions of Lily. She is the beautiful, but fallen, woman who befriends and protects the child refugee in Siberia. In one scene, we see—through his eyes—Lily emerging from the bathhouse into the fresh Siberian snow. Shot in slow motion, the scene suspends our sense of narrative time and distorts the perspective of place as Lily bounds into the snow, rolls over again and again, laughs, and beckons to us with her hand. This is Evtushenko's metaphor for his generation's aspiration for the genuine beauty and spontaneity of the erotic. It is also, though indirectly, political. Evtushenko suggests an erotic inspiration that is powerful enough to distract a generation even from such emotionally tenacious political lessons as those of the war.

Since the 1950s there has been an increasing discrepancy between an officially sponsored constant proliferation of international youth congresses, days of solidarity with the struggles of the young in various Third World nations, the marking of UNESCO's international year of the child, and similar events, designed to cast the image of Soviet youth as a younger clone of the old in their struggles for the world's progress toward communism, and the Soviet youth's genuine interest in Western life-style, literature, and art. The real behavior of Soviet youth provides more than ample evidence that the USSR today is a net importer, not an exporter, of the cultural artifacts attracting the young. Soviet youth even renders the chewing of Juicy Fruit gum or wearing of Calvin Klein jeans into an act of protest against the square side of Soviet life from the admonishments by Komsomol *druzhiniki* (the vigilantes), who monitor their parties, to the baggy suits of the *nomenklatura*. A knowledge of the latest fads is complemented by the Soviet young people's more than respectable knowledge of contemporary Western authors with a special affection shown by them for such Americans as Hemingway, Fitzgerald, Salinger, Kerouac, Tennessee Williams, Updike, Arthur Miller, Kurt Vonnegut, and many more.

By eagerly following Western culture the Soviet youngsters do not so much identify with contemporary European and American youth politics as try to reassert for themselves the genuine cultural internationalism, the one with a pre-Stalinist face. This is, in the first place, the face of Mayakovsky with his conviction that the new Soviet generation represented whatever was genuinely modern in cultural life. From Mayakovsky's poetic of futurism to his relish in coining advertising jingles, there is a direct link to Aksyonov's experimental novels and the youth's black market in pirated cassette tapes. What is, however, markedly different in the neo-futurism of Soviet youth culture today from the futurism of Mayakovsky's generation, is the unshakable assumption that whatever is most advanced rises in the hip West, not in the square East.

There is also in Soviet youth a sense of the parochialism of the culture artificially fostered behind the Soviet frontiers and a genuine longing for a larger cultural world. The desire to again be an inseparable and organic part of Europe is very strong indeed among the Soviet young, as Aksyonov conveys in one of the narrative voices of *The Burn*:

> . . . I was not alone and could feel behind me the presence of mother Europe. She did not leave me, her flesh and blood; silent, great nocturnal, she was there. Where are you now?[17]

In its most naive and honest form, this longing admits to a youthful restlessness with frontiers and a certain embarrassment at the lack of exposure to the world out there. Evtushenko's poem "Frontiers" was controversial in the 1950s because it expressed a generation's desire to roam and travel freely:

> Frontiers are in my way;
>   It's awkward
> Not to know Buenos Aires

Or New York.
I want to knock around
As much as I need in London,
I want to talk to everyone
Even in pidgin,
I want to strap-hang like a kid
Through morning Paris.[18]

The Soviet "youth culture" had its own international dreams—not of marching in step with abstract history but of knocking around Europe and simply being, at least for a while, there, where the life of the young generation was being freely formed.

"The older generation grew up in fear," Viktor Konetsky once remarked to a French journalist, "but our generation—in hope and faith."[19] The new generation's was indeed a culture of hope which had bluntly rejected the old culture of optimism. Optimism marks time in progressive stages of history; it is objective and rational in viewing the present and the future. Hope is aesthetic, not scientific. It looks to the future with a melancholic and nostalgic sense of the past. Hope sees the future in dreams—as Evtushenko has noted, "My generation liked to dream"—while optimism plans agendas for the future. In its early stages, the mood of hope prevailed in young writing. Aksyonov's youthful heroes of *Colleagues* and *A Ticket to the Stars* pass through skepticism and doubt only to reaffirm a generation's faith in itself and society. Evtushenko's famous *A Precious Autobiography*, published in 1962, was a most forceful testament to his generation's determination to look critically at the "false" and "artificial" optimism around them and to prevail in hope for their future.

The face of youthful hope inevitably ages and changes over time and over disappointments. The image of hope in the 1960s gave way in the 1970s to an anxious brooding passing over to depression. The poet of the darker mood of his generation was the late Vladimir Vysotsky. The tone of his voice and guitar strokes so hard, angry, guttural and grating as if in singing his poems he can hardly contain the impulse to scream. It is also his images and idiom of gut physicality, street and convict language, hard drinking and uncourtly sex that conveys the generation's tragedy. Take a few lines from "The Red Haired Broad" for example:

What's with you, shaving your eyebrows, slut?
How come you've put on your blue beret, whore?
And where are you off to, bitch?

Beyond profanity, Vysotsky shares with the young art of the 1960s the mood of restlessness, of being caged in and wary of the aggressive designs of the world outside. It is most typically expressed in the metaphor of the wolf hunt seen with the eyes of the hunted wolf:

A wolf should not, cannot do otherwise . . .
So this is the end of my life:
The one I was destined for
Smiled and raised his gun . . .

or that of racing cars moving in Vysotsky's "The Horizon," compulsively and suicidally to crash the boundaries:

What if there's a boundary at the edge of the world?
And is it possible to push aside horizons?
I wind the miles onto the axle
I'll not let them shoot at my tires.
But the brakes refuse to work—coda!
And I cross the horizon at full tilt.

Vysotsky presumes the worst on the other side. He quite frankly, and unequivocally states:

Things aren't right,
They're not right, friends,

but his resolution lies in the freedom of despair, not of hope:

I've had it up to here, up to my gullet.
Ah! I'm fed up with singing and playing.
Oh, to go to the bottom like a submarine
So nobody can get a bearing on me.

Vysotsky's mass funeral in the summer of 1980 was the rite to the depression of his generation's mood in the 1980s, just as in the 1960s poetry readings had been rites of their youthful hopes.[20]

The portrait of this mood is found in the "figurative expressionist" paintings in mixed media of the Moscow artist Pyotr Belenok. His works combine photographic elements of human figures set against expressionist backgrounds of menacing brushes of grays, blacks, and whites. In one work, young men in a line appear to gyrate or perhaps to dance. Are they dancing, falling, or being pushed as the white landscape at their feet slips away and they are enveloped into a morbidly white background? Another work shows a young man poised and about to jump. Why? Is he being forced, is there no other alternative but to take the inevitable plunge or yield to the push from behind that was always there and fall into the angry vortex suggested in the swirling brushes of black? That metaphor of the young man on the edge of uncertainty, tempered only by distrust and a suspicion of the hostile, brings the "youth culture" of the 1970s back full circle to the opening images of the heroes in young prose of the early 1960s. The common ground remains here the will of youth determined to reject the falsity and complacency of their social environment and re-structure the socially customary expectations so that they could become their own. The difference consists, however, in the experience of having applied the skepticism addressed toward the official ideals of society to their own hopes and concluded from it that only doom lies on the other side. On the edge, young culture is poised in the 1980s not with another of Aksyonov's tickets to the stars but with the landing, like Vysotsky's submarine, "on the bottom."

Grumbling about the youth culture took on a more directly political tone in the mid–1980s. Andropov included some elements of Soviet youth in his published remarks about . . . "drifters, shirkers, loafers and botchers, who are essentially parasites living at the expense of the mass of the con-scientious workers."[21] In July 1984 the CPSU's Central Committee drafted a special resolution on the problem of youth. The resolution added little that was new to the discussion and, summarizing what the Party avowed to preempt, provided a convenient summary of the complaints that had been directed against the "youth culture" for over a decade.

It is important," the resolution stated, "that young men and women not indulge in shallow amusements in their free time and that all forms of leisure time activity facilitate their ideological enrichment and physical development, the formation of lofty cultural interests and aesthetic tastes, and an acquaint-ance with the best achievements of our country's and the world's culture. Political indifference, immorality, and the blind imitation of Western fashions must not be permitted to infiltrate the youth's environment . . .[22]

This resolution coincided with the drafting of the new political agenda for a changed Soviet leadership in 1985. The latter identified the youth problem as part of the malaise left over from the Brezhnev years and proclaimed itself determined to solve it in the nearest future. It is, however, doubtful that Gorbachev will succeed in fulfilling this commitment.

The youth culture persists because it is the congenital side effect of the basic compact of Stalinist and post-Stalinist society. The appearance of the youth culture in the 1950s was the unwanted offspring of what Vera Dunham calls the "Big Deal"—the compact of Stalinism and the new Soviet bourgeoisie.[23] This "Big Deal" forged the alliance between the Soviet leadership and the bourgeois appetites of a generation raised in the poverty, deprivations, and hardships of the 1930s and 1940s. What distinguishes the youth culture from the old and, for that matter, from other modes of cultural discontent in the contemporary Soviet Union was the revulsion of the young people at the embourgeoisement of Soviet society as well as at the temptation of their own embourgeoisement. The youth culture characteristically refuses to be pleased as stubbornly as it refuses to please. What renders the problem so invidious for the leadership arises from the fundamental paradox that the régime's success in expanding the consensus of bourgeois comfort is precisely the cause of its failure with the young.

The new Gorbachev look is the imaging of Soviet leadership as the top graduates of the Soviet Union's finest universities, true believers in Soviet patriotism and dedicated servants of the official society, competent professionals and slightly sentimental family people with spouses in the latest from European fashion—a model for Soviet everymen and women. This new look may play well to the Soviet bourgeoisie but it will only aggravate the youth culture's rejection of the official Soviet society with all its growing Philistine comeliness. Furthermore, because the new look diffuses but does not answer the key socio-political questions about the freedom of expression, plurality and free competition of views, tastes, and life-styles, it will fail to entice to accept Soviet society not only the young but also those of every generation who did not conform to its norms and standards before. Within the Soviet systemic framework nothing but uniformity may be proclaimed and tolerated, though now this uniformity may include some bourgeois values and ideals—and it is exactly this stifling uniformity against which the "youth culture" has been rebelling all the time and is most likely to continue to rebel in the future. Only time will tell how this continuing rebellion of the young people will affect the stability of the Soviet system and what part in the process of overcoming that system's narrow uniformity the youth culture will assume.

Notes

1. Stephen F. Cohen et al., eds., *The Soviet Union Since Stalin*, (Bloomington, Ind., Indiana University Press 1980), contains John Bushnell's, "The New Soviet Man Turns Pessimist," 179–199, which includes a summary of much of the more recent writings on Soviet youth and its attitudes. Walter D.

Connor, "Generations and Politics in the USSR," *Problems of Communism*, September–October 1975, 20–31, provides an interpretation of the broader issues represented by the changing generations in terms of their respective political cultures.

2. See, for example, G.T. Fedorov, *Molodezh'i sovremennaya ideologicheskaya bor'ba*, (Kiev, 1978; 21–22, 33–34, 68–86, 97).

3. The quotation is taken from Anatoly Gladilin, *The Making and Unmaking of a Soviet Writer* (Ann Arbor, Mich.: Ardis, 1979), 95.

4. ———, 81.

5. On the "young prose" movement, see Deming Brown, *Soviet Russian Literature Since Stalin* (New York: Cambridge University Press), 1977; 180–217; A. Makarov, "Cherez piat' let," *Znamya* (The Flag), No. 2, (February 1966), 207–225; No. 7, (July 1966), 201–19; No. 8, (August 1966), 217–27; and Priscilla Meyer, "Aksenov and Soviet Literature of the 1960s," *Russian Literature Triquarterly*, No. 6, 1973, 447–63.

6. Quoted in Brown, *Soviet Russian Literature*, 181.

7. Vasily Aksyonov, *The Burn*, trans. Michael Glenny (New York: Random House, 1984); 307.

8. M. Provorov in *Yunost*, No. 5, (May 1976), 108.

9. *Sovetskaya kul'tura*, 26 July 1984; 4.

10. Gladilin, *The Making*, 29, 30.

11. Quoted in Brown, *Soviet Russian Literature*, 180.

12. ———, 216.

13. Meyer, Aksenov, 450.

14. *Half-Way to the Moon*, Patricia Blake trans., (New York: 1965; 92.)

15. Evgeny Evtushenko, *Love Poems* (London: Victor Gollancz), 1977; 3.

16. From *The Poetry of Evgeny Evtushenko 1953–1965*, selected, edited and translated by George Reavy (New York: October House, Inc.), 1965; 191.

17. From *The Burn*, 21.

18. Quoted from Evgeny Evtushenko, *A Precious Autobiography*, Andrew R. MacAndrew trans., (New York: E.P. Dutton), 1963; 113–14.

19. Quoted in Gladilin, *The Making*, 19.

20. Quotations from Vysotsky are taken from translations by H. William Tjalsma in *Metropol: Literary Almanac*, V. Aksyonov et al., eds. (New York: W.W. Norton & Co., 1979); 4–5, 156, 170, 173.

21. *Kommunist*, No. 3, February 1983, 9–23.

22. *Pravda*, 7 July 1984.

23. Vera Dunham, *In Stalin's Time: Middle Class Values in Soviet Fiction* (New York: Cambridge University Press, 1976), 3–5.

13

The Alternative Messages in Recent Soviet Art and Literature

ALEXANDER GERSHKOVICH

1. Two Approaches

In the free world two views exist of Soviet literature and art. According to the first, pessimistic view, free creation in the USSR is altogether impossible; Great Russian culture has been completely crushed by totalitarian power and is incapable of spawning true artistic values. Even the best that appears, advocates of such an approach believe, is produced with the permission of the higher ups and the KGB. Art is used by the authorities to misguide public opinion within the country and especially abroad, for *appearance sake.* In particular, Alexander Zinoviev, in his satirical book, *The Yawning Heights,* espouses such a view, when speaking about one of the unique phenomena of artistic life of the post-Khrushchev era—the Taganka Theater.[1]

The second, so-called optimistic view is less politicized, and places special emphasis on the artistic aspects of a work. Its adherents believe that in culture as a whole, and in Soviet culture in particular, not one, but two arts exist—the real and the "pseudo." To be more exact: all that is genuinely Soviet is not art, while all real art is not Soviet and, in the final analysis, works against the regime. From this point of view, *And Quiet Flows the Don,* for example, or the symphonies of Shostakovich, the works of Eisenstein, Meyerhold, and, from among current authors, of Rasputin,

Akhmadulina, Trifonov, and Okudzhava, among others, belong under the second rubric, for no one is likely to deny that this is real art.

In my view, neither of these approaches can be regarded as totally satisfactory, as corresponding to the true state of affairs in contemporary Soviet art. While reflecting a part of the truth, both approaches have at least one common flaw. Namely, they underestimate the relative independence and irregularity of development of art in the life of any society and for this very reason make it directly dependent upon external conditions and circumstances. It goes without saying that art is not free from the surrounding environment. But, first of all, even this environment, like everything in nature, is not unchanging, and, secondly, art has its own immanent laws which require special, more subtle criteria.

In addition, an extreme categorical approach to the state of affairs in current Soviet art does not aid in understanding the true processes taking place. It serves only to confuse matters further and adds fuel to the Soviet ideological fire. It is well known that the leaders of the USSR attempt to create the impression among their people that *all* changes occurring in the country, including those in the spiritual sphere, are the result of their own conscious, carefully considered decisions and actions. The very notion that something can happen in the country without their knowledge and beyond their control enrages them, as in the case of the human rights movement and the dissidence of Sakharov. But at the same time the authorities understand that the hidden "doublethink" that today permeates Soviet society from top to bottom cannot be eradicated by either prisons or by obsolete slogans or by demagoguery.

The historian Richard Pipes, in his book, *Survival Is Not Enough*, writes about the problem Communist regimes of the post-Stalinist era have had to confront. It is, in essence, that:

A way has to be found of reconciling the interests of the state and its ruling elite with the creative energies of the people. This cannot be accomplished unless the elite is prepared to sacrifice some of its authority and bring society into partnership, if only of a limited kind.[2]

I would not venture to judge about other areas of national life, but in the artistic practice of Soviet society this postulate has already been corroborated to a substantial degree. Gradually, even if with caution, with concessions on both sides, the general climate in Soviet art is changing. The regime, of course, is still attempting to keep the most restless artists, who are violating the obsolete maxims of "socialist realism," within relatively safe limits. But when reading certain stories of Rasputin, Asatfiev, and Trifonov; when watching the latest films of Andrei Tarkovsky, Gleb

Panfilov, Nikita Mikhalkov, Larisa Shepitko, and Eldar Ryazanov; when attending performances at the Taganka Theater, not only under Liubimov, but also under Efros; when listening to the songs of Okudzhava and even of the apolitical Alla Pugacheva, one cannot help but be amazed. How are such "freedoms" possible, given the general ossification of the regime, how did they pass through the sieve of ideological censorship? An art which since the Stalinist period has been bred to be a lackey of the regime finds strength within itself to oppose lying, to express shifts in the psychology of society, to reexamine many moral and aesthetic standards, to awaken people's creative and critical faculties. While shaking the regime's ideological supports, art, as in the famous Russian fairy tale, is carrying on a debate about how it is better to live in this world: by Falsehood or by Truth?

The peculiar position of Soviet art today reflects the Communist party's vacillations in ideology and cultural politics. Having banished the principal rebels, involved in open protest, from the country—Solzhenitsyn, Voinovich, Aksyonov, Oskar Rabin, Neizvestny, and others, the regime is now attempting to win artists—practicing more covert protest—over to their side. It rewards them with medals, posthumously publishes the books of those it did not recognize and did not publish in their lifetime, sprucing them up in the general Soviet style. It elects them to the Supreme Soviet, appoints as heads of theaters directors who until then had been out of favor, sends them abroad, gives them prizes—if only to keep them within the bounds of loyalty.

On the other hand, however confused and complex today's relations between artists and the government might be, art, while changing masks, takes advantage of any opportunity, any indulgences on the part of the regime, to acquire ever-greater artistic freedom. Taking this away from art would not, of course, present any great difficulty, but what can the regime offer the people in its place? The forces working for changes in Soviet art are operating under conditions that are virtually insurmountable. Under these conditions an art is appearing and forming which, for lack of a better term, we arbitrarily call "alternative."

2. In Search of a Third Way: The Taganka

Alternative art is being created by those Soviet artists who are seeking a detour where the straight road to free creation is closed. By its very nature, alternative art is twofold, palliative. To a certain extent this is an art that does not speak out fully. Its goal is not to answer questions that have piled up, much less to resolve them. It formulates these questions only in a country where questions are not meant to be asked. It is perhaps precisely on the strength of its duality that it is so attractive to the masses, who are infected by "doublespeak," so comprehensible and near to them.

Alternative art, diverging from the official doctrine of "socialist realism" while not making up its mind to openly oppose it, does not try to persuade its reader, listener, or viewer of one thing or another. Perhaps it does not yet know clearly itself *what, how*, and *where to?* It only lets people think that all is not yet lost, that a choice is still possible in art and, therefore, in life as well. "Alt-art" shows the artist the possibility of finding his own path, even under conditions of non-freedom. For a society with a totalitarian frame of mind and ideology this in itself, let us agree, is already quite a lot.

Alternative art is bound to its own time. It blooms and thrives during agonizing and often prolonged periods in the life of society—in times of stagnation. Former idols and ideals have been overthrown, and new ones have not yet appeared. Everyone feels it is impossible to go on living in the same old way, but a new way is not yet known. It seems one can *already* say something, but one is not *yet* free to say it all fully. Under such conditions the famous Taganka Theater—the headquarters of alternative art in the USSR—was born.

The theater was formed in 1964, during the twilight of the Khrushchev era, an outgrowth of the studio of the Shchukin Theater School. Instead of naturalistic, experiential theater, it played at being a theater of the public square, full of spectacle and convention, clearly violating the rigid rules of normative socialist aesthetics, laughing at them. It should have been brought to a halt from the very beginning. But the acting company of the Taganka, with the support of the liberal intelligentsia, held out for twenty years, in constant battle with the bureaucrats of the Ministry of Culture.

Taganka, under the leadership of director Yuri Liubimov, did not only bring together young actors, but also famous writers, artists, and composers. Among its admirers and friends were eminent national figures—scientists (the academician P. Kapitsa, for example), cosmonauts (Yuri Gagarin, Titov), students, and, strange as it may seem, Party veterans who had passed through the Stalinist camps. (The latter were especially active, and wrote letters to the highest levels in defense of the theater when they wanted to close it.)

The Taganka, the half-forbidden, half-permitted fruit of an exhausted, docile, but still living, unbroken Russian theater, during the 1970's became a sort of banner for those who believed that art, like life, need not follow just one path prescribed from above, that various quests and solutions are possible. This principal idea of alternative art in the USSR liberated dor-

mant spiritual forces and creative energy from the power of socialist realism's dreary standardization. The theater's program was proclaimed
openly and loudly. From the very beginning, the Taganka demonstratively
hung two portraits at the entrance to the auditorium—those of Stanislavsky
and Meyerhold, whom Party ideologists had always set off against one
another as irreconcilable enemies. This aroused fierce attacks from orthodox critics (Abalkin, Zubkov). But most important, Taganka's productions
themselves, so different from those appearing on other stages throughout
the country, served as a ferment for a subdued art. The plays at the Taganka
were not only events for the theater, but for society as a whole: *Ten Days
that Shook the World*, after John Reed's book; Brecht's *Galileo*; *What Is
to Be Done?*, after Chernyshevsky's novel; *Mayakovsky, Mother*, after
Gor'ky; Esenin's *Pugachev*; Bulgakov's *Master and Margarita*; and Shakespeare's *Hamlet*. Every play brought with it a whole moral and aesthetic
program: "arise from despondency," "feel sufficient strength in yourself . . ."

Artistically Liubimov strove for a synthetic theater, in which the means
of stage expression is not limited to the word, but includes other arts—
music, mime, songs, and even film. A Taganka actor should know how to
do everything—move, sing, read poetry, play the guitar, work in mime,
and with shadow puppets. Taganka created a whole system of stage techniques that help convey the idea to the viewer, at times without words.
The curtain of light; Taganka's well-known, disturbing "blinking" light;
the living curtain in *Hamlet*, which moves with the hero, experiences everything with him; the nonperiod costumes, stressing the connection between
the modern world and past history. "Theater is not for the blind," Liubimov
said at the very beginning of his career, "it is not only an audible art, but
is also *visual*.[3]

The ideas this theater introduced forced the audience to shake off their
mental lethargy, to think, compare, sympathize, come to their own conclusions, participate in the theatrical action, forget that there is a wall
between the stage and the auditorium. For this reason, Liubimov often
began his plays in the lobby, or even on the street, forced the audience to
cross the stage or made the action unfold in the auditorium, continuing it
after the play had ended in the theater cloakroom.

The director had his actors play their attitude toward an image. In
Brecht's *The Good Person of Setzuan*, the actress Slavina played two
roles—the good Chinese woman, Shen Te, in love with a pilot who is only
after her money, and her evil brother, the "dog" Shui Ta, who talks to
the extortioner man to man, in the way he deserves. In her impulse toward
good, Slavina-Shen Te is fluttering, inspired, flowing. But when she sees
that goodness is weak, that in order to conquer one must become evil, she

assumes the image of the "dog" Shui Ta—her brother. A bowler, black glasses, pants, a cane—that is all she needs and she is transformed right before our eyes. Her voice now sounds cold and apathetic. Her movements are dry, abrupt, arrogant; the actress does not know compassion. Such are the two—incompatible, it would seem—halves of one soul.

And gradually, with the help of the theater, it occurs to the viewer that in Shen Te's world goodness is a danger and a weakness; goodness borders on destruction. To save itself, goodness must betray itself and become a force, sometimes even evil . . . perhaps the viewer also ponders that this is true not only there, where Shen Te lives.

Thus art imperceptibly becomes politics.

It is with envy that I quote the impeccably exact observation of the Soviet critic, V. Gaevskii, who describes the acting style of Slavina, perhaps the most brilliant actress in Liubimov's theater. He writes:

> Slavina acts in a way one is not supposed to act, not allowed to act. Those frenzied screams, that overwrought emotional quality, that merciless expend-iture of nervous energy. . . . Slavina's best moments are when she, tearing herself from the context of the role, from the interrelationships, from the presumed circumstances, hurls her ringing and sobbing phrases at the audi-ence. . . . Slavin's art intermingles two simple abilities, but ones not granted to everyone—to pity people who have come to grief and to defend her own rights, human and feminine.[4]

The second well-known production at Taganka, which for a long time defined the image of the theater, its aesthetics and civic ideas, was this time taken from our own, non-Chinese life. *Ten Days that Shook the World*, based on John Reed's book, is a colorful, vivid, noisy, poster-like *spectacle*, with music, mime, shadow puppets, and rifle shots. It already begins on the street, in front of the theater, where a song resounds from loudspeakers over all of Taganka Square, muffling the roar of automobiles:

> Our locomotive, fly forward,
> Our stop is at the commune . . .
>
> (Nash parovot, uperyod leti,
> v Kommune ostanovka . . .)

At the theater doors stand Red Army soldiers with rifles instead of the usual ticket collectors. As they let the crowd of viewers through, they thread the tickets on their bayonets, giving them instead red bows for their buttonholes. In the lobby, sailors play the accordion and sing ditties from the time of the Civil War in Russia:

To the sorrow of all the bourgeois, we
Will fan the world-wide fire . . .

(My na gore usem burzhuyam
Mirovoy pozhar razduem)

In 1918
There was a revolution.
From fright my sweetie
Gave birth to a piglet . . .

(V vosemnadtsatom godu
Revolyutsiya byla
Moya Milka s perepugu
Porosyonka rodila)

My sweetie-boy is a Menshevik
And I'm a Bolshevik.

(Moy Milyonok–Men'shevik
A ya bol'sherichka)

A most unusual spectacle unfolds on stage and in the auditorium, re-creating the atmosphere of the stormy, chaotic time that determined the fate of the peoples of Russia for long decades. Within the chaos and diversity of the spectacle one can make out something integrated, fateful, half-forgotten. The figures and situations, familiar since childhood, are not presented in a complex way; on the contrary, they are simple, poster-like, grotesque: the soldier with his rifle, the potbellied bourgeois, the Social Revolutionary with his little beard, the hysterical Kerensky, the little ladies from the "death battalions," cripples, peasant petitioners, a sailor-*bratishka*, the Russian plowman in a field . . .

Techniques from the realistic, psychological theater were not, of course, suitable for a production of this sort, and Liubimov, boldly violating the laws of socialist realism, turned to the discoveries of Vsevolod Meyerhold's conventional theater, condemned by the Party for "formalism." In contrast to the first Brecht production, where art was turned into politics, here, on the contrary, politics was transformed into art.

Ten Days . . . opened a cycle of plays at the Taganka that might be called a "reflection of Russian history as mirrored by the theater." And this was not only a reflection, but also a reinterpretation. This play was the first link in the chain of the people's historical memory: 1917. It was followed by *The Master and Margarita* (the 1920s) and *House on the Em-*

bankment (the 1930s and 1940s). When I asked Liubimov in 1980 whether or not he was doing this consciously, he answered in literally the following words:

> If you've noticed it already, then you have to go farther. The segment begins with *What Is to Be Done?*, then comes Gorky's *Mother*, and then the pro-ductions you named. These are the historical turning points in our society's life for the past hundred years. *And the Dawn Is Quiet Here?* Isn't that really a reflection in theatrical language of the war years? And *Wooden Horses?* What is it, if not the story of the fate of our countryside?

And the Dawn is Quiet Here, by B. Vasiliev (1971) is perhaps the most integrated, poetic, and harmonious of Liubimov's productions, in which he shows that his is not only a director's, but also an actors' theater, that psychological theater is not alien to the art of the Taganka. More than that: the further it develops, the more the theater includes the truth of subtle human experiences into its stage conventions. This play does not show the splendid facade of war; rather, it is seen from within, through its sacrifices and losses. The fine young women of Sergeant-Major Vaskov's anti-aircraft battery perish right before our eyes, one after another, during August of that difficult year, 1942. They do not utter lofty words and do not feel that they are heroes. They behave at the front just as one would expect girls of their age to behave: they joke, sing, remember, love or dream about love, squeal in the soldier's bathhouse, cry from fear in the dark forest, are terrified of death and, in essence, meet it fearlessly, because they do not yet know what death is, just as many of them have not yet known their first kiss. They perish without having tasted the joys of life, and therefore war seems especially monstrous. The war is not Great, as Soviet propagandists have tried to present it, but "simply war," a slaugh-terhouse, a bloody meat grinder, as Bulat Okudzhava later called it, in an interview for the Hungarian *Literary Gazette* in December 1983. He de-clared—and this appeared in black and white: "It was not a Great, but a Terrible War. A Disgusting War. It ravaged our souls, it made us cruel. We had to become adults before our time . . . —this is by no means the best thing that can happen to a person. It is not an object of pride, not a merit."[5]

We have discussed the activities of Liubimov's theater in such detail because in it were concentrated the main ideas of alternative art in the USSR of the 1970s and 1980s, ideas which are directly relevant to all forms of artistic creation, not only to the stage. In the area of form—liberation from the oppressive routine of socialist realism; in content—reinterpre-tation of key problems from Russian history, distorted by Soviet falsifiers;

in the realm of cultural politics—struggle with Party control of art, with the bureaucratic-administrative method of governing it. Liubimov's last production at the Taganka in December, 1982, Pushkin's *Boris Godunov*, was the culmination of this struggle.

Pushkin's tragedy had bad luck on the Russian stage. Both in Pushkin's time and afterward, on the imperial stage, in the Moscow Art Theater under the direction of Nemirovich-Danchenko, and in the 1937 production by the brilliant Meyerhold, when everything, it would seem, was ready, even the set design and the music, specially written by Sergei Prokofiev. Then they ran scared and closed the play right before the premiere; they were not so much afraid of Pushkin's text as of the directors' vision of the eternal Russian problem of "the people" and "state power."

In his production Liubimov embodied the idea of a national folk drama, an idea proposed by Pushkin himself and picked up, but not brought to fruition, by Meyerhold. This was a play without a central hero, the role of main character assigned to the people and performed by a chorus, which did not quit the stage from beginning to end. The chorus personified the people, who had lost hope in their rulers, who had been duped by them, and who only in songs could unburden their hearts. This chorus, dressed in costumes from various periods—from multicolored old Russian *sarafans* to contemporary jeans and leather jackets—lived an independent life on stage, which had only an indirect relation to the scenes about the czar. It served as a motley, folk background, against which the intrigues and struggle for power at the top took place. This mixed chorus, which consciously violated historical concreteness, created a colorful and dynamic idea of the simple Russian people, united by the folk songs they preserved through the ages. Their singing, free and mischievous, lyrical and plaintive, their round dances, laments, and wailing, carried the play as if on the waves of a folk sea, bringing coherence to the free arrangement of short and vivid scenes.

The main characters of the play were also dressed in "meaningful" costumes. Grishka Otrepiev (played by V. Zolotukhin) was dressed like a "sailor boy" of the Civil War period, Godunov (Gubenko) wore an Asiatic robe, while the main schemer, the courtier, Shuisky, was in a long leather coat. A leather coat may not say anything to a person from the West, but it means a great deal to a Soviet viewer. If, in addition, a goatee was glued on to the actor playing Shuisky and he strode headlong, making the flaps of his coat flutter, then one need not say another thing—the entire era of "Iron Felix" arose lifelike before one's eyes.

Liubimov also introduced another substantial innovation: he showed the people losing faith in their leaders. In the Taganka production Czar Boris grew virtually to the dimensions of a tragic figure—the ruler-favorite. Attempting during the Time of Troubles to establish order with a firm, punitive hand, Godunov himself fell victim to court intrigues in the Kremlin. And the people remained entirely uninvolved in his fate, both in his rise and his speedy death. This also suggested a number of topical allusions.

At the conclusion of the play the actor Nikolai Gubenko, who played Godunov, changed from his Tartar robe into contemporary street dress. He emerged from the auditorium, climbed onto the proscenium, and addressed the last words of the play to today's Muscovites: "Why are you silent?" The people in the auditorium "kept silent." Thus Liubimov, true to his aesthetics of involving the viewer, made him the main participant in the present-day production.

Need one add, after this description, that the fate of Taganka's production was a foregone conclusion, that the authorities prohibited its showing before the public? The news, however, that under Andropov it was forbidden to play Pushkin perhaps undermined the position of the authorities more than the production itself would have.

As often happens in such circumstances, aesthetic and political problems were intermingled, and resulted in an explosion. Liubimov, as a sign of protest against bureaucratic capriciousness, wrote a letter to the head of the state announcing that he would leave the theater if not allowed to put on *Godunov* and two other plays forbidden earlier. In this atmosphere of conflict, when the theater's fate was hanging by a thread, it was suddenly suggested to Liubimov that he go to London with his family to stage Dostoyevsky. Everyone is familiar with the consequences. This specious proposal allowed the authorities to get rid of Liubimov and his unruly theater. The director who was appointed in his place—Anatoly Efros, who himself had been out of favor once—should, according to the plans of those who had organized Liubimov's persecution, have turned the Taganka into yet one more of the ordinary, docile theaters of the country. However, last year the two new post-Liubimov productions at the Taganka—Gorky's *The Lower Depths* and *War Has an Unfeminine Face*—show that the actors' opposition to state administrative pressure and the search for new ways and means to practice alternative art have merely taken new, yet more refined forms.[6] Only the future will tell where they will lead.

A Longing for History: Okuszhava, Akhmadulina, et al.

Taganka's initiative in joining the present and the past, in freely surveying the remote and recent history of its homeland in order to understand and orient itself among the false values Soviet ideology imposed upon the people, was engendered by the spirit of the time. Artists representing various views and tendencies, and at times lacking an overt fighting spirit, followed in Taganka's footsteps.

Historical unconsciousness, imbibed with your political milk in kindergarten and school, where you were taught that the history of Russia begins with "grandpa Lenin," where at best the entire past exists for you as a prehistory of "Great October," this artificially inculcated gap in historical memory is gradually beginning to avenge itself. In society there is arising what sociologists call a "restoration consciousness." This appeared in England after the Industrial Revolution and in France during the Napoleonic era. Something similar can also be seen today in Soviet Russia. Bold voices are reaching us from there:

> We must understand, if we in Russia value historical existence, that the discovery of memory is now the equivalent for us of the discovery of the historical future. . . . Not one of the problems facing awakened Russian thought today can be solved, or even properly formulated, without taking historical experience into account.[7]

Now a second generation of Soviet people is already gradually aging under Soviet rule without having seen either living "Whites" or real "Reds" face to face, as they were during the Civil War years. Soviet historians have fabricated many legends about both sides. Two generations have been taught that the "Reds" are good and the "Whites" are always bad. But now a third generation has come of age, and at this point we observe something new and strange in the social consciousness. History's main characters have begun perceptibly to change places.

In my childhood all the kids, without exception, around Moscow worshipped Chapaev, and played "Reds" and "Whites" in the yard, with no one, of course, wanting to be the "Whites." Everyone wanted to be "Chapaevists," "Petkas," "the machine gunner Anka." The weakest and shakiest were forced into playing the White Guard "Kapelevists." After all, you had to have someone to fight with! The famous film by the Vasiliev brothers, *Chapaev* (1934), starring Boris Babochkin, was, of course, to blame for all of this.

In the 1960s, our children no longer played "Chapaev." Art, called upon to create official legends, set out in one way or another to destroy them. Numerous anecdotes about "Vasily Ivanovich" now arose, and no incantations by the Party could return Soviet art to the "Chapaev" days. The new KGB ideologist Aliev recently voiced an appeal at the plenum of the Cinematographers' Union to create films like *Chapaev,* but it is unlikely that anyone in the hall could restrain a smile at these words.

Even more noteworthy is the fact that, with the dethroning of "Chapaev" and other "Red heroes" in the mind of the masses, a reevaluation of the entire nature of the "White movement," of the image of the Russian officer class at its best, is occurring. Rather than the official stereotype of "Chapaev," Soviet young people today prefer the chivalric qualities of his former enemies. In the 1960s, millions of viewers enthusiastically watched the serialized television film, *Adjutant to His Excellency,* in which the actor Yuri Solomin brilliantly performed the title role. Solomin's hero—a military aristocrat with noble manners and motives—remained the idol of the young for a long time. Even his sympathy for the Bolsheviks, with which the scenario's authors endowed him in the pardonable desire to avoid ideological censorship, was not a hindrance.

Several years later, the success of *Adjutant* was built upon by the favorite of the public, Vladimir Vysotsky, who elevated the image of the White officer to the level of high poetry. His impetuous Lieutenant Brusentsov from the film *Two Comrades Served* was selflessly devoted to Russia and experienced the defeat of the volunteer army as a series of fatal failures. In Vysotsky's portrayal a genuine tragedy, with a barely perceptible touch of melodrama, took place during the hero's flight from Russia. Brusentsov-Vysotsky stood on the ship's deck, miserably bidding farewell with his eyes to his faithful horse, left on shore. The ship cast off and the horse, neighing, rushed after it along the shore and then threw itself into the open sea, swimming toward its master. The face of the lieutenant, who had confronted death in battle without a tremor, became contorted. With a desperate effort of will he pulled out his pistol and shot at the splendid white head of his friend, as if sensing his own imminent end as well. People cried uncontrollably in the movie theater. Lieutenant Brusentsov-Vysotsky took his place alongside the heroes of *The White Guard* by Mikhail Bulgakov, who had forced many of us to ponder upon the historical injustice that had taken place in Russia.

Following in the footsteps of the cinema, poetry also rehabilitated and sang of the old Russian officer. Bulat Okudzhava devoted songs to this theme which, thanks to the tape recording, became famous all over the country. In "Farewell, Cadets," he sang to the accompaniment of his guitar:

Our life isn't a game, it's time to get ready to go!
Our trim is raspberry, our horses are gray.
Gentlemen cadets, who were you yesterday?
Today you're all officers.[8]

(Nasha zhizn—ne igra sobirat'sia pora!
Kant malinov, i loshadi sery.

Gospoda yunkera, kem vy byli vchera?
A segodnya vy vse ofitsery.)

In another well-known song, "Battle Painting," Okudzhava presented the splendid image of the czarist army, wrapped in a romantic veil.[9]

A longing for and reevaluation of the past finds entirely unambiguous, almost overt and clear, expression in current Soviet literature and art. In Bella Akhmadulina's latest book of verse (1983), permeated from beginning to end with a tragic sense of living through a stagnant period, we find insistent appeals to return to the past, to "call to Pushkin" for help:

So let's start our game, dear friend,
Let's remain in a garden of the past century.[10]

(Nachnyomte zhe igru, lubeznyl drug, au!
Ostanemsya u sadu minuvshego steletya.)

The poetess says:

Let eternity breathe on my cheek tenderly-tenderly,
I find it so sweet to cling to her warmth.

(Pust' nezhno—nezhno dyshit vechnost' v shcheku,
Isladko mne k ego teplyni l'nut.)

In "A Comic Epistle to a Friend" (Bulat Okudzhava), Akhmadulina's voice burst through the self-control that is characteristic not only of her verse. She expresses the awakening historical consciousness of a duped people through confessional lines such as these:

Why does it have to be this way?
Why do we feel at home
With the beauty of alien lands, alien times?
Bulat, it's the same thing everywhere.

Bulat, get in! Coachman, drive on!
How the snow is flying! So much snow!
How much you are beloved by me, my brother!
What a long road it is from Petersburg to Leningrad.[11]

(Zachem dano? Zachem my vkhozhy
V Krasu chuzhbin, v chuzhye dni?
Bulat, vezde odno i to zhe.
Bulat, sadis'! Yamshchik goni!

Kak shey Petit! Kak shegu mnego!
Kak mnoyu ty lyubin moy brat!
Kakaya dal'nyaya doroga
Iz Peterburga v Leningrad.)

The last two lines involuntarily call forth another associative image in the reader's mind—that of the road from Leningrad to Petersburg: will it be just as long?

A turning to the past for a lesson to the present and future is perhaps the main theme in alternative art. It has an added advantage in allowing one to say, on the basis of historical material—not necessarily Russian, incidentally—what it is impossible to express when depicting the contemporary world. The poet N. Nekrasov, who, of course, knew a thing or two about such matters, already taught Russian literature how to avoid the censorship. He gave the following advice to his fellow writers:

The action is moved to Pisa
And a multi-volume novel is saved . . .

(Perenosita deystvie v Pizu
I spasyon mnogotomny: Roman.)

Times have changed, but the good advice continues to hold true. The poet Bulat Okudzhava recently wrote a song about "The Roman Empire":

The Roman Empire at the time of the decline
maintained the appearance of firm order.
The leader was in his place, with his comrades in arms at his side,
Life was wonderful, judging by reports.[12]

(Rimskaya imperiya vremeni upadka
sokhranika uidimost' tvfordogo poryadka
Glavnyi byl na meste, soratniki ryadom,
Zhizn' byla prekrasha, sudya po dokladam.)

The song's refrain is entirely ironic, even providing the slow-witted with the key to its meaning:

But the critics will say that the expression
"comrades in arms" is not a Roman detail,
that this mistake deprives the whole song of meaning.
Perhaps, perhaps, perhaps it isn't Roman, no pity,
this doesn't hinder me at all, and I, in fact, find it ennobling.

(A kritiki skazhut, chto sloro "soratniki"—ne rimskaya detal',
Chto eta oshibka vsyu pesenku smysla Pishaet.
Mozhet byt', mozhet byt', mozhet i ne Rimskaya, ne zhad'
Mne eto sovsem ne meshaet, i dazhe menya vozuysheet.)

Further on the song says that:

The men of the Empire at the time of the decline
ate any old thing, got disgustingly drunk.
Then the following morning had a powerful taste for pickle brine—
apparently they didn't know that they were in decline.

(Muzhiki imperii veremeni upadka
eli, chto pridyotsia, napivalis' gadko.
A s pokhmelya kazhdyi ma rassol byl padok—
Vidimo, ne znali, chto u nikh upadok.)

And once more:

But critics will say: pickle brine, oh come on:—is no Roman detail," etc.

(A knitiki skazhut, chto slovo rassol, mol, ne Rimskaya detal' . . .)

Another song with the same context, which received wide circulation in Soviet Russia in our day, tells of Anton Pavlovich Chekhov, who once noted that "a clever person likes to study, and a fool to teach." "When they get rid of all the fools," sang the poet:

an epoch will dawn,' which can be neither dreamed up nor described.
It's troublesome with the intelligent man, bad with the fool,
what is needed is something in between—but where can one find it?

(. . . nastanet epokha,
Kotoroy ne vydumet' ne opisat.
S umnyn Khlopotno, s durakom–plokho,
nuzhno chto–to srednee–a gde ego uzyat?)

The moral of this fable, according to Okudzhava, is:

To be a fool is profitable, but who wants to be one?
One wants to be intelligent, but that will end in a beating.
Nature has a shrewd prophecy on her lips . . .
Maybe someday we'll find something in between?

(Durakom byt vygodno, da ochen' ne Khochetsia–
Umnnym–ochen' Khochetsia, da Konchitsia lit'em.
U prirdy na ustach Kovarnye prorochestva . . .
A mozhet byt' Kogda–nibud' srednee naydyom?)

The spirit of social outrage, which at times adopted defiant, low, carnival-like forms, also took hold of large, important genres. In 1982, in the first issue of the journal, *Soviet Dramaturgy,* the Soviet playwright Edvard Radzinsky published a play with the strange title, *Theater in the Times of Nero and Seneca.* True, the editorial board covered itself by warning the reader that the play deals with "characters from a remote era" and that one should not look for any contemporary allusions in it. In the introduction to the play, Professor V. Tolstykh, doctor of philosophy, states explicitly:

> While not evoking in the reader's consciousness any direct parallels with any other historical figure, the play at the same time is an artistic denunciation of dictatorship, despotism, and tyranny as such. While historically concrete and fully recognizable, . . . Nero forces us to recollect all his future imitators, right down to Hitler, Somoza, and Pinochet. However, the essence of the play cannot simply be reduced to a denunciation of dictatorship. It is also about that which brings tyranny to life and nurtures it—about social and moral impassiveness, behind which toleration of evil always lurks.[13]

We are prepared, of course, to agree with the professor's interpretation if the rules of the game are such in present-day Soviet art. And so I propose to examine Edvard Radzinsky's play from this position, which everyone finds convenient.

Of course it is purely by chance that Radzinsky took a subject and documents from the period of the decline of the Roman Empire. He had no ulterior motive, since that is not fitting for a Soviet dramatist. And of course the author was interested exclusively in the character of Nero (57–68 B.C.) and not in the least in the universal model of the relations between Despot and the People, as it has appeared to some. (If I am mistaken, let my older colleagues correct me.) The exceptionally cruel Roman despot was thus able with impunity to instill fear and horror in his subjects and rule them, trampling upon their freedom and dignity, dragging all that was most holy through the mud. True, a few have asserted that even without Nero analogous situations have occasionally occurred in history, under Hitler, let's say, and, well, under Somoza, or, as a last resort, under Pinochet today. But of course this can have no relation to Soviet Russia. Neither a Despot of the Nero type nor the other hero of the play, the philosopher Seneca—a cowardly moralist, a spineless timeserver, and a shifty person who holds his tongue when he should speak out—could be born on Russian, not to mention Soviet soil. Seneca, through endless concessions, fear for his own hide, finally, through his silence, helps his pupil carry out abominable acts; and gets away with everything. Such a thing also can happen only in an exotic land, of course, one where grapes are cultivated, by no means in one where birches grow. This is entirely obvious to everyone and requires no special proofs.

Something else, by the way, that shows that all the Soviet dramatist's thoughts are directed toward the first century B.C. and, more concretely, toward Rome during the decline of the empire—and not, God forbid, toward the Soviet period—is the special language of the play, not comprehensible to all foreigners. At every step one encounters such strange expressions as, for example, *"byt' v kurse"* (be up on something), *"postanovili . . . schitat' "* (they have resolved . . . to consider), *"Genial'no!"* (Great!), *"Grandiozno!"* (Stupendous!), *"uchenie o edinstve protivopolozhnostei"* (doctrine of the unity of opposites), or even more racy: *"I vse dela!"* (That's it!) or—*"Vot i ves' razgovor"* (That's the whole story).

In the excellent English translation of the play by Alma Law—the well-known popularizer of Russian drama in the United States—these virtually untranslatable "Neroisms" have somewhat lost their brilliance.

What, in fact, is E. Radzinsky's play about? Its idea, expressed, it is true, in Aesopian language, but very transparently, is related to an old but very painful question in Russia, one which was already discussed among the Russian intelligentsia at the very beginning of this century: should one resist evil with force or must one practice non-resistance? In Radzinsky's play the answer is twofold: it all depends on your view of things. If you do not value your life—resist, but if you want to survive—put up with things, say yes, in the last resort—be silent, hide in Diogenes' barrel. However, as the dramatist shows us, This is no way out either—sooner or later you will be crucified.

Into the Depths of Man: Rasputin, Trifonov, etc.

For alternative artists—from Rasputin to Okudzhava—it is as though the artistic text has *changed its addressee*. They appear to be writing for themselves, abstracting themselves from external circumstances. When the director Tarkovsky, at a discussion of his film *The Mirror* at a workers' club, was asked for whom he made his films, he answered heatedly, "For myself and for my friends," thus arousing the indignation of the audience.

Having lost faith in utilitarian Party art, the artists avoid generalizations, seek self-expression in their work. New concepts have appeared in art: the authorial film, authorial directing, bards. It is hard to overestimate the

importance of this artistic turnabout in the aesthetics and poetics of so-
ciologized, Soviet art. It is consciously moving away from general social
questions, concentrating upon the depiction of the individual, exclusively
personal element in man, upon the individual fate, the victory of the spirit
over the transitory outer shell of existence.

The spiritual and national rebirth of Soviet people belonging to various
cultures is expressed today not only ritualistically, in the collecting of icons,
the wearing of crosses or stars of David, the baptizing of children, the
rebirth of Islam. The loss of faith in revolutionary ideals, in fictitious state
ideology, is being replaced by a search for eternal underpinnings, not
mirages. This general process provides excellent proof that "even a society
of non-believers cannot get by without faith." Art could not help but reflect
these changes in society's psychology.

In Valentin Rasputin—an extremely important Soviet prose writer—the
old woman Anna from his story "Borrowed Time" thinks while dying:

> Where would her life go? She would have liked to know why and for what
> purpose she had lived, trodden this earth in a fever of activity, carrying the
> heaviest of burdens on her back. Why? Only for her own sake, or for some
> other purpose as well? Who had needed her for anything serious, or for any
> amusement?[14]

It is not by chance that Anna's inner speech is transmitted not in her
own words, but obliquely, through the lips of the author himself, filtered
through his heart.

In the works of Viktor Astafiev—another major poet "of the soil," the
narration flows slowly, like a Siberian river, one knows not where and
why. The nature description is given as an end in itself, as poetic meditation.
Here is a berry shrub, which has caught on to a hummock of the mighty
Siberian *taiga,* disfigured by greedy humanity. Here is a duel between a
poacher and a fish. Here is a dog that a prisoner escort has shot down
because it recognized its arrested master. Social life is harsh; man is alone
and powerless on this earth and he himself gradually becomes a beast.
There is one way out—to recognize one's guilt before nature and oneself.

In analyzing the difference between Astafiev's story "King Fish" and
the ideologized Soviet novel *The Russian Forest* by L. Leonov, the Swiss
professor Georges Nivat, a shrewd interpreter of Russian literature, notes
correctly: "There are no dialectics of the social struggle, there is nothing
demiurgic, no hidden enemy. . . . People are not divided into activists and
hidden parasites. The main thing is moments of communion with something
higher."[15]

The urban writer Yuri Trifonov, through a thick layer of everyday detail, reveals the increasing shallowness of the Soviet people, their psychological insensitivity, their moral capitulation to the harsh pressures of the times. In his story, "The Exchange," the hero sets out for the funeral of his grandfather, a selfless old Bolshevik, but on the way he sees a line standing in a grocery story where they have put out cans of high quality sardines. He waits his turn on line, receives the cans, and hides them in his briefcase. "When he entered the premises of the crematorium from the courtyard," the author narrates, "Dmitriev quickly passed to the right and placed his briefcase on the floor in the corner, behind a column, so that no one would see it."[16] The author does not comment, but the reader understands that it is not his grandfather that Dmitriev is burying, but the morality, the ideals, that his grandfather, the selfless revolutionary, embodied.

Another hero, from the novel *The Old Man,* an old retired revolutionary, rethinks his life during a hot summer at a *dacha* outside Moscow. He is within the circle of his offspring, who are occupied with everyday concerns: "What is bad is that they don't want to think about anything, remember anything." The novel's two planes—the everyday and the historical—interweave, but they do not merge. Rather, they contradict one another, "like a double image on a broken television," the author remarks.

And the "old man" returns mentally to his revolutionary youth, when everything was simple and clear—isn't this indeed the cause of all the misfortune which has been revealed only now, at the end of the 1960s, when he is already too old and helpless to change anything? "Black and white," thinks the Old Man, "obscurantists and angels. And no one in between. Yet everyone is in between. There is something of the angel and something of the fallen angel in everyone,"[17] he sums up the lesson of his life. But it is too late, life has passed.

The solitary Professor Ganchuk from Trifonov's last story, "House on the Embankment," embodies the same theme of belated insight. While he goes to return empty bottles at the dairy, he repeats to himself that Aleksey Maksimych (i.e., Gorky) turned out to be wrong, while Fyodor Mikhailovich (i.e., Dostoyevsky), whom he had underestimated, was right, that "everything *is allowed* if nothing exists but a dark room with spiders."[18] The turn from Gorky to Dostoyevsky is occurring today along the entire front of Soviet art. There have even been attempts to read Gorky himself "according to Dostoyevsky," as, for example, in Efros's 1984 production of *The Lower Depths* at the Taganka has shown.

"The spiritual is essential to real creation," the film director Andrei Tarkovsky tersely formulated this growing requirement of Soviet official art, squeezed out and wrinkled like a lemon.[19] What is capable of resurrecting art is not the Party and class consciousness that the Central Committee demands of artists, but the spiritual.

His film, *Andrei Rublev,* banned for five years, shows ancient Rus laid waste by the Tartar invasion. The icon painter Rublev, the young bell maker, and the wandering minstrel whom the guards finish off by hitting his head against a tree with all their might, all embody a single image—of the artist as an eternal spiritual treasure of the people. In their souls the image of the Mother of God is one of temporal continuity, of the succession of generations of culture. For the young apprentice in the film, it would seem that the secret of casting a bell was hopelessly lost with the death of the Master, his father. But he finds within himself the strength and inspiration to discover this secret once again, and casts the miraculous bell.

This artistic metaphor is sharply projected upon the contemporary world. Is the secret of Russian culture lost today after seventy years of arbitrary Bolshevik rule? Where does this secret lie—in submission to, or, on the contrary, in surmounting the power of circumstances? Such writers as Yuri Bondarev, throughout his entire career and in all his works (see his latest novel, *The Game*), tends toward the former, asserting that "you can't swim against the tide." But artists such as Rasputin and Trifonov, having chosen another ethical position, prove through their writings and their behavior that one must resist the widespread delusion that art has only a utilitarian duty to the state and society. They insist that art has its own spiritual goals, standing higher than the "class struggle" and various forms of political speculation.

The debate on this question has been going on for a long time within Russian culture, beginning with Pushkin and Zhukovsky and continuing with Dostoyevsky and Chernyshevsky and followers of the latter's theory of "useful art." It is entirely logical that Russian literature has turned from the simplified illusions of Gorky to the aesthetic program of Dostoyevsky, who wrote in opposition to the utilitarians:

> The first business is not to constrain art with various goals, not to prescribe laws for it, not to confuse it, because even without that it has many stumbling blocks, many temptations and deviations inseparable from man's historical life. The more freely it will develop, the more normally it will unfold, the faster it will find its genuine useful path . . . the freer its development will be, the greater use it will bring to humanity.[20]

"In essence you despise poetry, the artist," says Dostoevsky to Dobroliubov and other revolutionary democrats with whose aesthetics Soviet ideology is armed, "first and foremost you need some business, you are business-like people. But the thing is," he emphasizes, "the artistic quality is the very best means, the most persuasive, the most indisputable, and the most comprehensible to the masses, of presenting in images that very same business for which you are pleading,"[21] you business-like people.

If one examines more closely the position of adherents of alternative art, one cannot help but see that they are resolving this old argument in favor of liberating creative forces from a servile psychology, from state pressure on the mind of the artist. They are shedding obedience and control, in various ways going from quiet rebellion to open protest, but the goal is the same—to defend the right of the artist (as of any person) to be his or her self. This urge is apparent, as we have attempted to show, in all forms of artistic practice in the Soviet Union—from the classic novel to a youthful genre born in our own time—tape-recorded guitar poetry.

"The Free Opinion of the Street": V. Vysotsky

Three singers—Okudzhava, Galich, and Vysotsky, are the products of a single period, and have themselves brought about a new period in Soviet art. Right before our eyes they have broken through the censorship, to the astonishment of many. They were united by the desire and the bravery to say about their time what official art does not say. With guitar and tape recorder, they moved against the mighty barrier of the state and broke through it. They have different voices, performance styles, repertoires, but a single goal—not to lie.

Vysotsky burst into Soviet art like an active volcano spewing its lava across the country. To Okudzhava's elegaic softness, to Galich's intellectual civic-mindedness, was added the coarse, vulgar, frenzied voice of the down-and-outs, singing of the world of communal apartments, of beer halls, bathhouses, of inhabitants of dormitories, trade schools, sailors' quarters, of barracks, construction battalions. The singer merged with them and expressed their lives with his strained, frenzied singing.

His semi-criminal performance style gained him the immediate love of the down-and-outs while at first arousing the indignation of the snobs, until they, too, grew used to it. At the same time it was precisely the criminal style and themes of his early songs that saved him from persecution by the authorities, who saw less danger in them than in the more refined "pieces" and hints of Galich and Okudzhava. The criminal jargon deluded them. Vysotsky seemed like "one of the guys." He sang of a crude, half-drunk, cruel world, of the crude ways of people warped by their dreary life and spewing out their bitterness it doesn't matter at what—whether at their wife at the television set, or at an elephant in the zoo, or at their neighbor who owns a Zhiguli car, or at an educated person earning more than a simple "working man" ("They're rolling in dough, and we don't have enough for vodka"), or at a geologist ("For that kind of money I would have found uranium in Moscow myself"), or at an instructor at a Party city committee, telling a Soviet tourist how to behave in "Bulgarian Budapest," or at Jews—Karl Marx and his neighbor Rabinovich, or at guys who wear glasses, or at policemen—it isn't important who. He sang as if from their point of view, not so much condemning as *pitying* people for their spitefulness, ignorance, stupidity.

And he also dreamed. Vysotsky has few lyrical songs. His dreams are those of a common soldier, someone who has led an ordinary life and labored a fair amount along the way. He dreamed of a "Neutral Zone," the way a soldier dreams while sitting in a trench and looking at the world from the bottom up, at a hostile world, divided into our side and theirs by a neutral zone. In this quiet, sunlit neutral zone he dreamed about, special flowers grew for Vysotsky, "flowers of unusual beauty": rare human qualities—friendship, loyalty, pride, truth.

Okudzhava preferred the elegy, sadness, while Galich made a more difficult choice, preferring overt civic spirit, political protest. Vysotsky chose another path or, rather, the path chose him. "Let life be the teacher," he sings in one of his songs. And life taught him to balance himself along a narrow path over an abyss. He, as it were, was called upon to legitimize a forbidden genre—the uncensored song—right in front of the leadership and of ideological censorship, to make truth in art an everyday phenomenon. His popularity was so great that he was permitted what no one else was permitted. He became a leading actor at the Taganka Theater, made films where he played Cheka agents, married a Frenchwoman of Russian descent, traveled abroad, performed not only in student and workers' auditoriums, but for the military, at the cosmonaut settlement, at the MGB club, for border guards, at government *dachas*, for the families of Central Committee members, and for workers at OVIR.

His life was a desperate balancing act, and every day it became more and more difficult. In his songs the image of a tightrope walker is supplanted by that of an exhausted beast, and here he is already, a wolf being tracked down in the hunt:

> The wolf hunt is on, the hunt is on!
> For gray prowlers, old ones, and cubs;
> The beaters shout, the dogs howl themselves sick
> There's blood on the snow and the red spots of flags.

> (Idyot okhota na volkov, idyot okhata!
> Na serykh khishchinikov, matyorykh i schenkov;

Krichat zagonshchiki i layut psy do rvoty,
Krov' na snegu i pyatna krasnye flazhkov.)

This desperate cry, this terrible image, sums up all of present day Russia, the Vysotsky era:

The wolf cannot violate traditions,
It seems in childhood we blind pups,
wolf cubs, sucked the she-wolf
And imbibed: "It is not allowed to go beyond the flags.

(Volk ne mozhet narushit' traditsiy,
Vidno, v detstue–slepye shchenki,
My, volchata, sosali volchitsu
I vsosali: "Nel' zya flazhki.")

And so that no doubt whatever would remain about the meaning of the song, Vysotsky reveals its intent fully, directing it at himself:

But I've transgressed my obedience and gone
Beyond the flags—the thirst for life was stronger!
And behind me I heard with joy
The amazed cries of the people.

I'm straining my utmost, every sinew,
But today's not the same as yesterday:
They've surrounded me,
But the hunters have been left empty-handed![22]

(Ya iz povinoveniya uyshel–
Za flazhki, zhazhda zhizni sil' ney.
Tol'ko szadi ya radostno slyshal
Udivlyonnye Kriki lyudei.

Rvus' iz sil i iz vsekh sukhozhiliy.
No segodnya ne tak, kak uchera.
oblozhili menya, oblozhili,–
No ostalis ni s chem ergerya.)

The people acknowledged Vysotsky's greatness on the day of his funeral, five years ago, when tens of thousands of people who had not been notified by anyone, who had not asked anyone's permission, gathered at Moscow's Taganka Square in an elemental, irrepressible crowd. They cut off traffic and, silently, wilfully, with their feet, voted for free Russian art as Vysotsky had seen it and created it—a poet without titles, without medals, without books, the first genuine people's artist of the Soviet Union, who in a difficult struggle had defended his right to create freely.

To paraphrase Vysotsky's words in his poem, "I Keep Vigil": "The authorities have declared war on me because I disturb the peace, but I will continue to write my songs and in them I will curse those who want to forbid my singing, and at the same time I will bow low to those people who write me not to surrender. Even if I perish I will not betray their hopes."[23]

The more time passes since Vysotsky died, the dearer he becomes to all Russians both in the Soviet Union and in emigration: and the more important his inimitable, precious contribution to the present and future of Russian culture is.

The Soviet authorities are attempting to belittle Vysotsky's significance, to compromise his art in the eyes of the people. Antagonistic fellow poets—Robert Rozhdestvensky, Stanislav Kunyaev, among others—are involved in this dishonorable affair. The Black Hundreds poet Kunyaev, recently decorated, attempted to prove that Vysotsky was also unfree and fell victim to his own popularity with the people. Kunyaev complains in the Soviet press that he received thousands of letters cursing him for daring to criticize Vysotsky. Here is what he writes—and this was published in a Soviet magazine in 1984:

> Nine out of ten cursed the author of the article with such ferocity that if words had material force he would have turned to ashes. Time and again the telephone would scream out at night: "You're still alive!" "Now, just you wait . . . ," "You're just envious! Your own verses are a failure. . . .

Kunyaev cites the opinions of Soviet people such as: "Maybe in a hundred years Vysotsky will stand alongside, maybe higher than Shakespeare and Pushkin. . . . You mustn't touch the people's favorites, our heroes, our idols" (Milena Milkovskaya, Stavropol). "You're no better than Salieri" (R. Orlova, Magadan). "And I don't believe a single contemporary poet except Vysotsky" (V. Maksimova, Aldan), etc., etc.

How can one explain this impassioned defense of Vysotsky by millions of Soviet people, who openly express their solidarity with him, with his songs, with his valor? "Student, worker, engineer," Kunyaev enumerates the social positions of those who wrote letters supporting Vysotsky (for which we thank him), "schoolboy, tradesman, Ph.D. There were more women than men . . ." "Millions of hands will push their way through to you and grope in the dark until they find you!" he quotes one unsigned letter. "Yes, this isn't a matter of taste, which you can't argue with," concludes the far from stupid Kunyaev, "but of something much more. As Lev Tolstoy said in his story, 'The Death of Ivan Ilich': 'It is not a matter of a kidney, but of life . . . and death.' "[24]

He turns out to be entirely correct, this decorated Soviet poet, attempting to prove that Vysotsky, by having become so extraordinarily popular with the people, is, according to the law of mutual bond with his audience, not free from the people in whom he has inculcated a grain of civic valor with his songs. The poet does not, indeed, wish to be free from them, he wants to remain true to his ideas, to be worthy of his songs, to the very end.

Vysotsky's songs continue to be heard from the windows of Soviet houses in the capital, in cities large and small, in villages and workers' settlements. The pilgrimage to his grave at Vagankovo Cemetery in Moscow continues.

Conclusion

As the dissident writer, Arkady Belinkov, wittily remarked, it is impossible to take a taste of Soviet power and spit it out if you do not like it. They took a taste in 1917 and, as you can see, we are pining away to this day, and the end is not in sight. But . . . the most dangerous thing is to lose heart. Times do change, all the same, and art is sensitive to that.

When people in the West today express skepticism about the possibility of nonconformist art existing under Soviet conditions, they usually judge according to Western standards. Nonconformism in Western and Eastern Europe, however, are not at all the same thing. In Russia it does not take the form of political opposition, but rather of moral and aesthetic resistance. And the forms are different: within the framework of Western democracy, art speaks openly, while in the harness of socialist democracy, it speaks in code, is understood only by those who also go around in harness.

Vassily Aksyonov is entirely correct, I believe, when he disagrees with those critics who, forgetting about the conditions under which Soviet artists are forced to live, reproach them for timidity, half-heartedness, for not speaking out fully.[25] Do we have the right to judge them for this? Can we apply the same standards when evaluating the creative work and behavior of artists working in freedom and those creating under the weight of totalitarianism?

An obvious example for me of this form of creativity is a case I myself witnessed at the avant-garde Taganka Theater, in 1980. They were rehearsing Trifonov's *House on the Embankment*—a tragic chronicle of Soviet life in the 1930s and 1940s. In one scene, evoking the atmosphere of 1937—the year of raging "Ezhovism," the director brought a Pioneer detachment on stage, which recited poems in honor of the Stalinist People's Commissar

Ezhov. The commission charged with approving the play objected to the mention of this name: "Why," they said, "stir up the past?" In order to save his production, the director removed the name, which rhymed with the preceding line. During the performance everything proceeded as at the rehearsal, but when the Pioneer rapturously read the verses and reached Ezhov's name, he paused for a second and another actor, looking mockingly at the audience, slapped his hand over his mouth. The effect was stunning, because of its unexpectedness and its twofold, hidden, psychological truth. What was not said had a more powerful effect than if the theater had said everything fully, having shown itself to be better than it was, in fact. In human terms, not saying everything brought art closer to the audience.

Soviet alternative art sometimes bears unexpected fruit as, for example, in Anatoly Efros's latest production in Liubimov's former theater. He did not show the tramps and murderers of Gorky's *The Lower Depths* in a basement, at the lowest rungs of the social ladder, as they were intended to be. Instead, they were unexpectedly elevated to the Pinnacle, to the height of power, to the upper stories of a red brick building erected on stage. Soviet criticism, including E. Surkov's article in *Pravda,* lavished praise on this production, which was extremely dubious from the point of view of orthodox ideology. After this should we reproach Efros, Eldar Ryazanov (director of the films *Garage* and *Railroad Station for Two*), Nikita Mikhalkov, and others, who create, well, let us say, semi-truthful films? Should we accuse them of being "cunning," "evasive," of not being overly squeamish about compromising with the leaders? At the plenum of the Cinematographers' Union in December, 1980, within a narrow professional circle, Eldar Ryazonov declared unambiguously:

> On my way here, I did not think about what to say but rather about what should not be said. We are all like icebergs—which, as you know, are nine-tenths under water. . . . In nineteenth-century Russia, democratic literature was always the conscience of the nation. When I think about this, I understand that we still are a long way from a conscience here. I would like to remind you that the people see all, know all, remember all . . . The deaths of Vladimir Vysotsky and Vasili Shukshin have shown very clearly who had power over men's mind in our country.[26]

Here you have a "timid," "compromising" artist under the conditions of Soviet democracy. The difference, incidentally, between Soviet and Western democracy, as someone has joked maliciously, is no less than that between an ordinary and electric chair!

In conclusion, the main idea of alternative art in the USSR is, in my view, the defense by any means, including palliatives, of creative freedom, the liberation of art from the burden of utilitarianism and political speculation. It seems to me that this idea can help Russian art to fulfill its main social mission—that of awakening people's spiritual strength, of helping them to take heart and make *their own* choice in life.

Not so long ago, the famous German dramatist Peter Weiss—the son of emigrants who had escaped from nazism—died in Stockholm. It was his idea that *gullible hope is just as dangerous as hopelessness.* In my view, the author wanted to stress by this that you should let yourself hope only once you have thoroughly analyzed events and interconnections. At the same time, even in the most hopeless times, you should search for the opportunity to hope for something.

Notes

1. Aleksandr Zinov'ev, *Ziiaiushchie vysoty* (Lausanne: L'Age d'Homme, 1976), 386–87.
2. Richard Pipes, *Survival Is Not Enough: Soviet Realities and America's Future* (New York: Simon & Schuster, 1984), 206.
3. Iurii Liubimov, "Iskusstvo govorit obrazami," *Teatr,* No. 4 (1965), 59. Repeated in the newspaper *Sovetskaia Estoniia,* 28 March 1975.
4. V. Gaevskii, "Slavina," *Teatr,* No. 2 (1967), 75.
5. Bulat Okudzsava, "Tul korán kellett felnönünk," *Elet és Irodalom* (Budapest), 9 December 1983. See also: Alexander Gershkovich, "Neobychnoe interv'in Bulata Okudzhavy," *Obozrenie,* No. 8 (1984), 23–25.
6. About Efros's production, see: Alexander Gershkovich, "Nazad k Gor'komu?" *Novoe Russkoe Slovo,* 24 February 1985, 5. See also E. Surkov, Spor o cheloveke," *Pravda,* 7 Feb., 1985, p. 3.
7. A. Veretennikov, *Arkhiv Samizdata,* 1973 g., quoted by Boris Shragin, "Toska po istorii," in *Samosoznanie* (New York: Khronika, 1976), 243–59.
8. Bulat Okudzhava, *65 Songs,* musical arrangement, selection, and editing by Vladimir Frumkin. English translation by Eve Shapiro. (Ann Arbor: Ardis, 1980).
9. Okudzhava, *65 Songs,* 140–41
10. Bella Akhmadulina, *Taina* (Moscow: Sovetskii pisatel', 1983), 9.
11. Akhmadulina, *Taina,* 117.
12. Here and below the Russian originals and English translations of Okudzhava are cited from texts given to the author by the collector and popularizer of Okudzhava's songs, Vladimir Frumkin (USA). For this we offer him our deep gratitude.
13. V. Tolstykh, "Personazhi dalekoi epokhi," *Sovremennaia dramaturgiia,* No. 1 (1982), 88–89.

14. Valentin Rasputin, *Money for Maria and Borrowed Time*, Kevin Windle and Margaret Wettlin trans. (Sidney: University of Queensland Press, 1981), 349.
15. Georges Nivat, "K voprosu o novom pochvennichestve . . . ," in *Odna ili dve russkikh literatury?* (Geneva: L'Age d'Homme, 1981), 140.
16. Iurii Trifonov, *Izbrannoe* (Minsk: Vishaishaya Shkola, 1983), p. 243.
17. Yury Trifonov, *The Old Man*, Jacqueline Edwards and Mitchell Schneider, trans. (New York: Simon & Schuster, 1984), 52.
18. Iurii Trifonov, *Dom na neberezhnoi* (Ann Arbor: Ardis, 1983), 90.
19. Andrei Tarkovskii, "Nastoiashchemu tvorchestvu nuzhna dukhovnost'," *Russkaia Mysl'*, 10 January 1985, 10. See also "Ispoved' Andreia Tarkovskogo," *Kontinent*, No 42 (1984), 385–406.
20. F.M. Dostoevsky, *Dnevnik pisatelia za 1873 god.* (Paris: YMCA Press, n.d.), 95–96
21. Dostoevsky, *Dnevik*, 83
22. Vladimir Vysotskii, *Pesni i stikhi* (New York: Literaturnoe Zarubezh'e, 1–2, 1981), 1, 138. English translation from Gerald Stanton Smith, *Songs to Seven Strings. Russian Guitar Poetry and Soviet "Mass Song"* (Bloomington: Indiana University Press, 1984), 160–61.
23. Vladimir Vysotskii, "Ia bodrstvuiu . . . ," *Pesni*, 2, 86.
24. Stanislav Kuniaev, "Chto tebe poiut," *Nash sovremennik*, No. 7 (1984), 179–80.
25. Vasilii Aksenov, "Progulka v *Kalashnii riad*," *Grani*, No. 148 (1984).
26. Eldar Riazanov, "Stenographic Report of Speech at the Plenary Session of the Film-Makers Union of the USSR, December 2, 1980," in *Motion Pictures in the USSR, 1972–1982* by Val S. Golovskoy, as told to John E. Rimberg, with the assistance of Steven P. Hill (Ann Arbor: Ardis, 1985), 251.

14

Liberating the Tone of Russian Speech:

Reflections on Soviet *Magnitizdat*

VLADIMIR FRUMKIN

One of the first things that struck me on my arrival to the West was the difference in tone of Soviet and Western oral communication. As a musician who barely knew English, I automatically focused my attention on the musical aspects of the language of mass media. The contrast between this new tone, and the tone to which I had grown accustomed in the USSR was overpowering. Here the voices of newscasters, political figures, actors, lecturers, and poets reciting their verse all sounded simpler, warmer, and less formal. I immediately felt at home in this world. These voices came not from ideological puppets spouting standard formulae such as *"Istoricheskie resheniia partiinogo s'ezda"* (The historic decisions of the Party Congress), *"Proiski mezhdunarodnogo sionizma"* (The machinations of international Zionism), and *"Obil'nyi urozhai zernovykh"* (The abundant grain harvest), but came rather from real people, for whom the process of speaking was simultaneously a process of thinking. Furthermore, they thought independently, and not in reaction to an external prompting. They stated their case, disagreed with one another, constructed their arguments, made jokes, and lost their temper. The melody of their speech seemed more like spontaneous improvisation, full of unexpected turns of expression and contrasts. It was then that it occurred to me that if societies are constructed differently, then they will inevitably sound different; that each society has its own tone, its own melodic style of communication. In dis-

Ideology and Culture

cussing the contribution of Soviet poet-singers to the "thaw" of the Russian language, I would like to emphasize precisely that what is usually ignored—the importance of their music. For the poetry we are dealing with is *sung,* and draws on current, popular musical idiom. This idiom in addition has much in common with the prevalent spoken style of the era, and interacts subtly with it. Together these constitute what might be called the sound of the times.

Given the constraints of a short chapter, I will concentrate on the works of two poets only—Bulat Okudzhava and Alexander Galich.

I

The new independent song, which appeared in post-Stalinist Russia, immediately and unambiguously distanced itself from the official state-controlled song. Bulat Okudzhava, the father of free "guitar poetry" once said to me that he wrote his first song (not counting "Burn, Fire, Burn" of 1946 which, in his own words, appeared purely by chance) to prove a point to a friend. The song, as a genre, remarked this friend, is doomed to be foolish, like all the songs in the endless flow of Soviet popular hits. Okudzhava disagreed and "thought up" (as he likes to put it) his own song. And thus it all began. In Moscow in 1956 the tradition of oral, pre-Gutenberg poetry was reborn—a medieval troubadour tradition of sung verse unprecedented in the history of modern Russian poetry.

But Okudzhava's first attempts in this genre distinguished themselves not only by the depth and seriousness of the words. The music, too, was new. The poet sang his poems in a restrained and subtly ironic manner which represented a glowing contrast with the stilted, insincere tone of the official song. We sensed and valued the originality of the music, it seems, even before we had time to listen carefully to, and ponder about the meaning of, the lyrics. This led us to recognize the monotony of the tonal atmosphere in which we had lived for years. Our cantatas and songs, the speeches of our orators and superiors, and the voices of our announcers and actors sounded both overdone and bombastic by comparison. It seems that in a thoroughly organized and ideologized society not only are economics, morals, politics, and art degraded, but also speech and song. People forget how to express themselves. Intonation loses its richness and spontaneity, and becomes mechanical and stiff. It is no longer nourished by living thoughts and emotions, and struggles to conceal their absence in an exaggerated pathos, or a saccharine imitation of intimacy.

But it had not always been that way. The Soviet regime had a different sound in its youth. The dissident Soviet philosopher, Grigory Pomerants, once expressed the hypothesis that the victory of the Red Army in the

Russian Civil War was due in part to the Bolsheviks' ability to compensate for a lack of *military* hardware with expertise in the field of *rhetorical* bombardment:

> One of my bunkmates, a soldier of 1920, used to tell me about the powerful impression made by the visit of orator One or Two (the names of these men today are odious). Their speech was equal in its power to the force of 500 artillery barrels aimed at a section of the enemy lines one kilometer in length. . . . In other words, the Reds owed their victory in part to their command of the art of eloquence. Later they tried hard to forget their dangerous art.[1]

The "reds" did not, of course, lose the art of persuasion but they did lose their capacity for this particular kind of eloquence which they had already developed prior to the Revolution and which gradually degenerated until it disappeared in the early thirties. This first stage may be described as the "revolutionary phase" of Soviet rhetoric. Words flowed in a raging torrent seething with indignation, rejection of the old world and the call to battle.

The following step in the history of Soviet rhetoric came after the consolidation of power was complete, approximately in the mid–1930s. The spirit of struggle and negation was then replaced by the spirit of affirmation. An aura of glory and festive joy prevailed. The flow of official speech began both to slow down and take on a new ponderance and self-assurance—regardless of the subject at hand. This change did not escape the attentive ear of Lydia Chukovskaya. In her novel *The Deserted House*, written in the late thirties, we read:

> On her days off Olga Petrovna switched on the radio first thing in the morning. She liked to hear the confident, important voice announcing that perfumery store No. 4 had received a large consignment of perfume and Eau de Cologne, or that a new operetta was to have its première in a few days.[2]

Soviet intonation found its most obvious and fullest expression, however, during the Stalinist terror, in the mass song. The air resounded with a new style of glorious and cheerful tunes. (As an aside I would like to note that a similar change in tone was taking place at just that time among German National-Socialists: soon after Hitler came to power the voice of ideology changed from dynamic and aggressive to festive and self-assured. In the words of the Nazi composer, Hans Bajer, "the songs of struggle were replaced by the songs of joy".[3] The songs were similar to their Soviet counterparts not only in style; they also shared a number of melodies. For instance, Lenin's favorite, "Be bold comrades, keep in step!" which was translated for German Communists, was sung by stormtroopers without a single change in lyrics! It probably would not be an exaggeration to say that Stalin's Russia, Hitler's Germany, and Mussolini's Italy perfected a tone of international totalitarianism.)

But let us return to our brief history of Soviet rhetoric. The Second World War led to a thawing of state rhetoric. This new tone was set by Stalin himself in his famous speech of 3 July 1941. "I turn to you, my friends, my Brothers and Sisters!" Not a single Soviet ruler had spoken to the Soviet people in this way. Similarly, the tone of music sounded more human and more straightforward during those years.

But after the war had ended, and the state had recovered from its panic, the orchestra of Soviet propaganda geared up again and began to drum out its peculiar tune, in time more pompous and grandiose than ever before.

II

Spring 1953. In the first days after Stalin's death there was a vague expectation of changes to come. The word "thaw" had yet to be pronounced, but the feeling, if not the word, filled the air. We first became aware of the change in atmosphere when we realized that the state had again altered its voice; it sounded less grand. I remember how drastically the musical menu changed; suddenly the main dish—songs about Stalin—disappeared. Portraits of the deceased leader still hung everywhere—busts, statues and monuments stood firm—but hymns dedicated to him vanished.

The enormous, flawlessly adjusted machinery of the song industry began to break down. The mass hymns did not bring forth the mass enthusiasm they once had sparked, and were heard more and more rarely, whether at official public events or at private gatherings. In fact, these songs were increasingly becoming the target of a flourishing underground humor. The familiar lines and catch-phrases which had comprised the "sung codex" of our morals and faith suddenly began to whirl in the throes of some devilish dance, to wink mockingly and to take on new, suggestive tones:

The entire world of oppression we shall destroy
To its foundations. But what for?
    (self-explanatory)
We were born to make Kafka into fact . . .
    (i.e., our goal is to turn into reality
    the frightening, absurd world of Franz
    Kafka's fiction)
No one sitting at our table is a Lifshits . . .

(a not-so-subtle hint at the Soviet
regime's anti-Semitism).[4]

By replacing only one or two words within the familiar phrases of an
official song, the entire meaning could be turned upside down—and many
a pompous line thus somersaulted and landed on its head.

For almost a quarter of a century the state song had, for all practical
purposes, known no competition within the country. There now appeared
rivals: at first there were songs from the camps and prisons, brought to
freedom by those political prisoners who had survived long enough to be
granted amnesty. These songs, often naive and clumsy from an artistic
viewpoint, but containing genuine emotions and a sense of real life, vitally
refreshed the "tonal climate" of Russia. Then there came the homespun
songs of students, travelers, mountaineers, geologists, and other spontaneous, close-knit groups. And finally, at the end of the fifties, *"magnitizdat"*
appeared—the uncensored "guitar poetry" of B. Okudzhava, A. Galich,
V. Vysotsky, N. Matveeva, Yu. Kim and dozens of amateur poet-singers
whose songs began to circulate throughout the country on hundreds of
thousands of reels of tape.

But the renewal of tone and feeling was not limited to these new simultaneous, yet unofficial manifestations. It also occurred in the theatre—
in the plays of Alexander Volodin: *The Little Factory Girl* and *Five Eve-
nings,* and in the productions of young theatrical groups like the "Sovremennik" or the "Taganka." And a new more natural style was beginning
to assert itself in film, in part as a result of the first professional contacts
with the Western film world. For example, while the Franco-Soviet film
Normandy-Niemen was being made, the French director of the film was
on the brink of despair at the irreconcilable approaches of French and
Soviet actors when saying their lines. The Soviet actors infused with profound significance even the most prosaic lines such as "Come on lads, let's
have a cup of tea," while their French counterparts on the contrary resolutely "demystified" everything, by adopting a colloquial and everyday
manner for whatever they happened to be saying. All the director could
do was to try to reeducate the Soviet actors to speak more like ordinary
human beings. Soviet actors are still, I am afraid, learning that lesson. A
quarter of a century has passed since then, and the Soviet cinema is still
not free of the vestiges of bombastic rhetoric and a stylized melodic line
of speech. This is particularly obvious to former Soviet citizens, who have
already adjusted to the spoken style of the West.

During the thaw of the Khrushchev era, poetry was indisputably in the
forefront of the struggle to emancipate spoken Russian. The authentically
emotional and even confessional tone of the new poetry immediately broke

through the encrusted indifference that had arisen from years of artificial "civic poetry." Hundreds and thousands of young people poured into cultural centers, institutes, concert halls, and even stadiums to hear poetry readings. Young poets were the ones in the limelight, those who had discovered in themselves a new talent for communicating with vast audiences, the talent of the orator, the actor, and the variety artist. There was a rebirth of the tradition of oratorical poetry of Mayakovsky and other poets of the twenties represented by such young poets as Ye. Yevtushenko, A. Voznesensky, R. Rozhdestvensky, who ushered this tradition in a new era. Initially the voices of these poets virtually drowned those of others with a simpler and more direct message. These were the voices of poets who also worked in close contact with the public, but in an atmosphere that was worlds away from concert halls and sports stadiums. They had no ticket office and no stage, microphones or amplifiers. These poets performed in private apartments for a handful of like-minded people and friends. This atmosphere of an intimate chamber performance was probably most responsible for the emergence of a new sort of relationship between the poet and his audience: poems were neither read nor recited, rather they were sung to the accompaniment of a guitar.

III

The Leningrad geophysicist, poet and "bard," A. Gorodnitsky, who now lives in Moscow, once told me that when he tried to read his first poems to friends on a field trip he found it impossible to rid himself of a feeling of embarrassment and artificiality, because reciting them in the atmosphere of an intimate circle of friends seemed false and out of place. He then tried singing them—and the awkwardness vanished.

This would seem something of a paradox at first. Singing is in principle an activity that is more artificial and subject to convention than reading; from this point of view reciting is more natural, (somehow closer to life and to ordinary forms of oral communication). At the same time, however, singing is more intimate than a poetry reading; it is less imposing because there are fewer demands on the attention of the public. Singing by its very nature makes use of an apparent (and sometimes genuine) indifference of the singer toward the audience. Indeed we sometimes just sing to ourselves when we are completely alone. While seeming to have no need of our attention, a singer succeeds in capturing it. Simple melodies in a folk style, the unpretentious and untrained voice of the poet, an unsophisticated guitar accompaniment—all of this creates an atmosphere of immediacy, intimacy, and sincerity.

Those poets who decided on singing as a "means of communication" with their audiences were bound to have a considerable influence on the evolution of speech in post-Stalinist Russia. At first glance their songs are often similar in content to the majority of the poems and songs permitted by the authorities, songs about war and peace, about love, women, Moscow, about their contemporaries; songs about these things, and yet suggestive of something much deeper, because the entire poetic and musical structure of their "sung verse" is strikingly different from the stereotype of Soviet mass culture.

Let us take, for example, the theme of war and peace. Those in the West, who are inclined to lend credence to Soviet pacifist propaganda, would do well to actually listen to a Soviet official anti-war song. How little they have in common with Western antiwar songs! To the Soviet ear these songs sound too "peaceful." A Soviet journalist in America, a correspondent for the newspaper *Pravda,* once wrote about a young American folk singer who sang an antiwar song in what the journalist considered to be a very surprising manner; he sang softly, lightly, almost cheerfully. The correspondent, accustomed to the heroic and aggressive tone of the Soviet so-called "songs of struggle for peace," was taken aback by the simple tone of the American singer. He had probably heard something along the lines of Bob Dylan's "Blowing in the Wind."

Soviet antiwar songs of the late forties and early fifties had a particularly militaristic sound. One joke popular in those years comes to mind: "What do you think, Rabinovich, is there going to be a war or not?" "Who needs a war, when such a fierce struggle for peace will easily do us in." Even the "musical envoys" of the later period of Soviet pacifism, with their milder tone, provided an easy target for anonymous wits. The following musical joke arose in the mid-sixties when Yevtushenko's "Do the Russians Want War?" resounded throughout the country. (Music by E. Kolmanovsky):

Why was the male quartet disbanded in Odessa?
For their arrangement of this popular song:
Soloist - Do the Russians Want War?
Chorus - Don't they though, don't they though!

This song certainly provided fertile soil for such a parody. It was not so much the text of the song, which continuously asserted that Russians are against war although they fight superbly ("Yes, we know how to fight a war"), as the ominous implications, hidden in the music of this slow, steady and stern song, which gave occasion for ridicule.

According to Novella Matveeva militarism is one of the characteristic aspects of Soviet musical culture as a whole. "Many of the songs are now

didactic to the point of being bizarre," she has said. "They are written in
a tone ranging from the dissatisfied to the threatening, as if they were
created specifically for the enemy and not for a peace-loving listener. As
a result even popular singers perform them with clenched fists and grim
faces. In such cases if one applauds at all, it is more out of fear than out
of admiration for their art."[5]

But it is doubtful that these jokes and parodies, ridiculing the "peaceful
offensive", would have occupied such an important position in Soviet underground humor if it had not been for songs of a somewhat different
nature which began to appear at the same time. These songs provided an
artistic and moral standard for the antiwar theme.

> Oh war, what have you done, you villain!
> Our courtyards have all grown silent.
> Our boys have raised their heads,
> They've become men too soon.
> They appeared in the doorway a moment
> and departed—soldier after soldier . . .
> Good-bye, boys—
> > Boys —
> Do your best to come back!

> Akh, voyna, chto zh ty sdelala, podlaya:
> stali tikhimi nashi dvory,
> nashi mal'chiki golovy podnyali—
> povzrosleli oni do pory.
> Na poroge edva pomayachili
> > i ushli
> za soldatom soldat . . .
> Do svidaniya, mal'chiki!
> > Mal'chiki,
> postaraytes' vernutsya nazad!

(1958)

Here, Bulat Okudzhava, in "Goodbye Boys," is not pressuring his listener, or exhorting any particular moral stance. Rather, in straightforward
terms, he suggests the hopelessness of war. Although he tells the boys "Do
your best to come back," he ironically implies the terrible unlikelihood
that they will. The narrator seems to be a contemporary of these boys who
by chance survived the hell of war, and who is now "attempting by means
of invocation to alter what has already occurred".[6]

And our footsteps falter
On the rickety stairs—there is no salvation . . .

(Ishagom nevernym
po Pestnichke shatkoy—spaseniya net . . .)

So speaks Okudzhava in another of his early songs (1961). He returned
to this tone of despair a few months ago in one of his most recent poems:

. . . Thursday the war began . . . and there's no salvation.

(Schetrerga voyna—i net spasen'ya

In the following excerpt from one of Okudzhava's early songs, as the
poet Naum Korzhavin notes, soldiers and women are robbed of their youth,
and relationships are laid bare with a frightening clarity, while underlying
this is both an acceptance of the unavoidable situation and an acute sense
that it is terribly wrong. " 'It could have been different' is never uttered,
but it is present throughout, and makes the events described both more
tragic, and more meaningful:"[7]

And where are our women, friend,
When we come through our doors?
They meet us and lead us in,
But our home reeks of deceit.

Yet we'll brush the past aside—it's all lies!

(A gde zhe nashi zhenshchiny, druzhok,
Kogda vstupaem my na svoy porog?
Oni vstrechayut nas i uvodyat v dom,
a v nashem dome pakhnet vorovstrom.

A my ru rukoy na proshloe—vran'ye!

I would like to add, however, that this unspoken "it could have been
different" is hinted at not only in the lyrics but also in the stern but heart-
rending melody of this gentle and quiet march. Finally, it is felt in the
subtle modulations of the poet's unique voice.

IV

The challenge that Okudzhava presented to the ethics and aesthetics of Soviet music was not entirely spontaneous. His own words attest to this fact:

> Before that the songs in vogue were official . . . cold, without a sense of human fate, permeated by a cheap cheerfulness (this was called optimism), by primitive, routine rhetorical thoughts about Moscow, about man, about the homeland. This was called patriotism. . . . I began singing about what was troubling me: about the fact that war is not a holiday and not a parade, but a terrible, absurd inevitability, that Moscow is amazing, melancholy and not always happy, and that for me, a Moscow ant, things don't always work out . . .[8]

But the poet never suspected that his invasion into the closed realm of Soviet song would cause such a brusque and decisive reaction:

> I started to sing my poems, not imagining what a scandal was to break out in a short time. . . . Guitarists accused me of lack of talent . . . composers of lack of professionalism . . . singers of having no voice at all, and all of them generally of impudence and banality. . . . The officials accused me of pessimism, antipatriotism, pacifism and the press backed them up.[9]

Although in the Soviet Union the lyrics to Okudzhava's songs from time to time managed to find their way into print the music long remained "non grata." Only in 1976, twenty years after he pioneered the genre, was an album of carefully selected songs released.

At one point in the late sixties the state publishing house for music works, "Muzyka," in Moscow, agreed, at my suggestion, to print a small collection of Okudzhava's songs *with music.* I selected twenty-five songs from the hundred or so composed by the poet up to that time. The manuscript safely passed editorial proofreading; on the first page was stamped the promising and long awaited "For Typesetting." But it ended up not on the printing press, but in the desk of K.A. Fortunatov, the director of the publishing house, where it remained for several years until I returned to pick it up upon my departure from the Soviet Union in 1974.

What actually prevented the publication of the book? After all, most of the lyrics in the collection had already appeared in print, so from an ideological standpoint "Muzyka" was safely insured from risk. Strange as it may seem, the book fell through not on account of the lyrics, but because of the music. Okudzhava's melodies were a source of doubt and anxiety to the administration of the publishing house. To publish Okudzhava's poems the way they were performed by the author—that is, in combination with his melodies and guitar accompaniment—would imply official recognition of a doubtful, unofficial genre which was not planned anywhere or approved by anyone, and which was outside any of the norms and rules by which songs are composed, selected and distributed in the Soviet Union.

But there was something else which alarmed the officials at the music publishing house and the Union of Soviet Composers: the very *nature* of Okudzhava's music, the way it actually sounded. What was frightening was its simplicity, unpretentiousness and sincerity. To the official Soviet ear it was like some unknown tongue, a strange and alien accent, although Okudzhava's songs are deeply rooted in Russian culture. The poet had found a new voice by turning to a forgotten (or half-forgotten) old one. His melodies revived the motifs of Russia's once popular waltzes and marches, student songs, love songs and Russian gypsy songs, street ditties, and the tunes of organ grinders—motifs far removed from the conventional sound of Soviet official songs.

Some of Okudzhava's melodies are close to the style of the French chanson (with which the poet became familiar in 1956, when the French singer Yves Montand toured the Soviet Union), and some to Soviet lyrical songs of the Second World War. All of these widely different styles were transformed to unity by the unique voice and manner of the poet.

It was precisely the individuality of Okudzhava's sounding which the Soviet musical establishment could not forgive him. The authorities were prepared to tolerate his words but not his manner of singing. Attempts were made to force Okudzhava's poems into the mold of the Soviet songwriting industry and leech them of their originality. One of the most striking attempts of this kind was the cycle of five songs put to music by Matvei Blanter.

It so happened that I learned from Blanter himself that he was planning to compose a song-cycle to words by Okudzhava. I got to know the author of the legendary "Katyusha" in August of 1965. We were then both members of the group of Soviet musicians sent to the Edinburgh Festival in Scotland. Knowing that I felt drawn to the art of our Soviet "minstrels" and "bards," Blanter told me in confidence that the popularity of these artists with young people was particularly instructive. What these "minstrels" and "bards" said was new, far better written and more interesting than the stock "text" of Soviet songs. But why did these poets sing and who allowed them to? They had not studied at the conservatory, they could not even read music! We should use their poetry to recapture the interest of young people and revive the Soviet song, which was suffering from mediocre themes and uninspiring lyrics. Their music, however, was primitive, vulgar and in the worst possible taste! "You know," he said, "when I realized this, I began to write my own music to Okudzhava's songs. I'd like to show him and all these 'bards' and 'minstrels' how to write music. These amateurs, without any professional training, are interfering in our business by writing songs!"

As soon as Blanter completed his project, his cycle was printed in the magazine *Muzykal'naya zhizn'* (Musical Life) and, subsequently, as a separate issue by the publishing house "Sovetskii Kompozitor." Soon after that a record of the songs came out, performed by the well-known singer Eduard Khil and the instrumental ensemble "Kamerton."

Blanter and Khil´'s efforts forced Okudzhava's poetry into a tonal environment entirely foreign to it. The poems sounded strained and flat. The underlying shades of meaning disappeared, Okudzhava's melancholic irony vanished along with his sense of moderation; the manner and character of the poems were deformed as if they had been forced to wear a mask.

This was, of course, only my personal view of Blanter's experiment, and I wondered what would be the reaction of the public. Blanter was addressing a young audience. To find out, I decided to carry out an experiment of my own. Blanter's cycle was performed and discussed on six separate occasions involving a total of about seven hundred people of between seventeen and thirty-five years of age. After each of Blanter's "arrangements" a recording of Okudzhava performing was played. The following reactions are taken from a transcript of one of the discussions (broadcast 5 March 1969 on Leningrad Television) and one of the surveys, which was carried out at the Union of Leningrad Composers on 11 March of the same year:

"Song of Moscow by Night" (or "The Little Orchestra of Hope"):

- Blanter's music doesn't reflect the worry and anxiety, it's much too lyrical. (Female student, twenty-one years old.)
- The tension and pointedness of Okudzhava's words have been completely lost. (Literature student at Leningrad University.)
- What is attractive about Okudzhava's poems is their quiet strength. Blanter's song lacks this quality. The lines sound clumsy and there seems to be heavy underlining under each one, as if to say "Look how important this is!" Of course, Okudzhava has fewer musical resources at his disposal than Blanter. But that is precisely what makes the quiet strength of his words so striking, that's why they are so attractive. (Physics student at Leningrad University.)
- Gets on my nerves. (Female student.)
- The philosophical meaning of the song has been completely blurred. It sounds more like *restoranny romans* (i.e., like romance intended for performance in restaurants). (Female student.)

- The poetry has been stripped of virtually everything it had. Its warmth and gentle irony have been replaced by soulless bombast. Khilź's performance is carefully controlled and the tune is not unpleasant, but the words have been made superfluous. (Male student, eighteen years old.)
- Blanter's accompaniment is more varied and enjoyable, but the rhythm of the verse has been lost, the song has lost its soul. (Male student, nineteen years old.)

"The Old Jacket":

- Too much show, inappropriately cheerful. (Technician, twenty-one years old.)
- No irony, and as a result the sense of the words is lost, they come across as empty. (Female student, twenty-one years old.)
- These are poetic reflections of a philosophic nature, and brass band treatment is out of place. (Female student, twenty-one years old.)
- Taken as such, Blanter's version is musically more intense. But the poet has something else to say and this is completely drowned out by the inane joviality of the composer's music. The song of the poet is far richer than that of the composer, which is one-dimensional and dull. (Conservatory graduate, twenty-five years old.)
- The poet's performance makes you think about the words, you realize that it's quite a serious song commenting on events and saying something about our lives. (Female student.)

"Song of the Open Door":

- A great tune, but the words don't fit. (Working girl, eighteen years old.)
- There's no relationship between the words and the music. It's much too bouncy. (Radio technician, twenty-five years old.)
- According to the words, this song is supposed to make each of us think about our relationship to society. When the poet himself sings, the incentive to do so is much greater and more powerful. (Female student, seventeen years.)

In every audience, without exception, the overwhelming majority preferred Okudzhava's version. Although some of those present did say that Blanter's music sounded more professional, richer, and more enjoyable, they were won over by Okudzhava's interpretation because of its inner strength, seriousness, and gentle irony. They felt that the poems sounded more profound when performed by the poet himself, as he managed to hint at the inner meaning, the real nature of the poetry, while Blanter's music never got beyond the surface. This confrontation between two completely different aesthetics—one official, the other unofficial—resulted in a resounding defeat for the official style.

V

Alexander Galich, who came to "guitar poetry" shortly after Okudzhava in the early sixties, brought with him a spoken manner which broke even more decisively with the legacy of the Stalinist years. In his songs is heard for the first time a style of speech which had been avoided by Soviet literature in general and by official songs and popular music in particular: the vital, at times crude, unstylized language of laborers and soldiers, inmates and prison guards, inspectors and Party bureaucrats, chauffeurs and their bosses. The rhythms and inflections of Galich's poetry were drawn largely from genres which had been banished from official life and disdained by official aesthetics. We find in his poetry the folklore of criminals, the "cruel romance," Russian gypsy dances, the village limerick and the street-talk of working-class neighborhoods.[10]

Before Galich, the state song and independent song existed on two separate, parallel planes, confronting each other only indirectly. Galich brough them into direct confrontation. Like a surgeon, he constantly excises lines, phrases, melodies from official songs, transplanting them into the body of his own poetry, where, by the virtue of being put into such an alien context, they are devastated by Galich's bitter and merciless irony. In his "Dance Song" he tells of Stalinist *"palachi"* (hangmen)—high ranking KGB members, who were forced to retire under Khrushchev, but continued to lead lives of luxury. So as not to see the bloody ghosts of their past at night, they have sumptuous dinner parties together. On their tables is a rich assortment of delicacies, all from special stores:

And the masters of torture sit
And sing softly, but with feeling
"About Stalin, the wise, the dear and beloved . . .

I sidiat zaplechnykh del mastera
I tikhon'ko, no dushevno poiut:
"O Staline mudrom, rodnom i liubimom . . .

The last line is a quote from the famous "Cantata about Stalin" of 1936 by A.V. Aleksandrov with lyrics by the amateur poet M. Iniushkin. In

Galich's song this last line appears in toto, with the original melody. The shift is unexpected and abrupt: a lively dance tune at a gathering of retired (temporarily?) KGB officers abruptly reverts to a majestic cantata, which, since times are bad, is sung "softly," but "with feeling."

Galich is unequaled in his ability to integrate into the simple form of the song cinematic and dramatic effects such as flashbacks and montage, sudden changes of rhythm, tempo, intonation, style and setting, creating colorful musical collages. Galich is particularly fond of using these effects in his satirical compositions:

> When the car has knocked me down
> The sergeant will write up a report
> And an imposing man
> Will place that report in a drawer.
>
> Another man of lower rank
> Will take this report from his boss,
> Will read it in decorous silence
> And will draw up the hole-puncher . . .
>
> And having punched holes along the edge,
> He'll say: "There's no good fortune in this world!
> The deceased was a singer, and I play an instrument—
> We could have formed a duet!

> Kogda sob'yot menya mashyna,
> Serzhant napishet protokol,
> I predstavitel'ny muzhchina
> Tot protokol polozhit v stol.
>
> Drugoy muzhchina–nizhe chinom,
> Vzyav u nachal'stva protokol,
> Prochtyot ego v molchan'i chinnom . . .
> I pododvinet dyrokol.
>
> I prodyryaviv list no krayu,
> On skazhet: "Schastya v mire net—
> Pokoynik pel, a ya igrayu . . .
> Mogli b sostavit' s nim duet!

Galich wrote this song in the early seventies when he suspected that the KGB was planning to eliminate him, probably by a staged hit-and-run accident. By writing "Happiness was so possible" the poet got rid of his fear. Originally Galich sang the song to a simple, mournful waltz. The bitingly grotesque lyrics are juxtaposed with music reminiscent of the pathetic songs of the war wounded on commuter trains, intensifying the irony present in the lyrics alone.

This kind of incongruity is sometimes carried even further, becoming the sole source of humor in a text. For example, there is nothing amusing about an Aeroflot advertisement, and even less humor in Chopin's funeral march, but it occurred to some anonymous comic genius to combine the two, using this most famous of funeral themes:

TU-104 is the best airplane!
TU-104 is the best airplane!
Economize your time!
Economize your time!
TU-104 is the best airplane!

TU-104 samy luchshy samolyot!
TU-104 samy luchshy samolyot!
Ekonom'te vremya!
Ekonom'te vremya!
TU-104 samy luchshy samolyot!

When Galich decided to rewrite the music to "Happiness was so possible", he proceeded in exactly the same way as the author of this macabre musical joke: the lyrics were set to the music of the Russian version of the Marseillaise. The resulting contrast is even more striking and meaningful than in the earlier waltz version: the irony of the event—secret police filing the death report of their own victim—is intensified by setting it to the tune of a heroic revolutionary march.

VI

Galich used to say: "In my songs I often play the part of an idiot" as a reminder that one must not confuse him with the narrator/hero in his songs. He knew perfectly well that his form of satire did not have a long tradition in Russian song, where theatrical character development has been rarely employed. Russian popular songs, in fact, are characterized by the use of monologue, where there is no distinction between the performer and the narrator/hero. It immediately follows, as the Soviet critic A. Sokhor points out, that "the hero of a song, that is, the character assumed by the popular performer, cannot be a negative one," and on those occasions when satire does play a role in folk songs "the narrator is inevitably the positive character who exposes and ridicules the negative character (whereas, for instance, the operatic aria can and often does convey the point of view of the villain)."[11]

The structure of Galich's satires has nothing in common with such a scheme in which the heroic protagonist reveals the true character of the antagonist. Although they are not quite the idiots that he makes them out to be, Galich's characters are brought to life through self-expression, and for the most part are not morally irreproachable. These satires bear a closer resemblance to the French chanson, from Béranger to Brassens, and to the songs of Brecht's "epic theater" than to the operatic aria in which the actor fully assumes the character of the hero. In other words, in these songs the performer does not lose himself in his hero, but rather remains slightly removed from him. He is able to conduct a subtly ironic, unspoken dialogue with the audience, while at the same time transforming himself into a given character. The lyrics stem simultaneously from two separate points of view: that of the hero, and that of the singer, who is appraising the hero, mocking him, and at times even ridiculing himself.

This intriguing polyphony of viewpoints could hardly be accomplished within the boundaries of the traditional strophic song. It demands more complex poetics and more flexible devices—compositional, verbal and tonal. Taking the traditional song as his starting point, Galich has substantially modified it, adding to it elements from other genres including the romance, the ballad, vaudeville, the musical, radio drama, and film scripts. The masterful use of the parody of traditional genres is yet another sign of the author's voice which breaks through the voice of the hero-narrator. Let us look at how Galich parodies at least one genre—the ballad.

The parody is immediately apparent in the title: "The Ballad of Conscientiousness" or "The Ballad of how N.A. Kopylov, the director of antiquarian shop No. 22, almost went mad, as told by the director himself to Doctor Yu.I. Belen'ky." Galich's choice of music for his farcical ballads is also mocking. For example, having announced the title "The Ballad of Surplus Value" with the epigraph "A specter is haunting Europe, the spectre of Communism," Galich begins to sing a melancholy salon waltz.

The melody of the waltz is at times languishing, at times unexpectedly passionate and even hilarious (due to the incongruities of text and music). This type of music, which is seemingly detached from the poetry but is, in fact, mocking it, is unthinkable for the real ballad, but it works superbly in the ballad-parody.

The "Ballad of Conscientiousness" is the only one of Galich's ballads which opens on a serious note, and it is also the only song in which the hero is not the narrator. Egor Maltsev is referred to in the third person by yet another character who shares Egor's language and uneducated background:

Hey, look here, listen, buddy.
We're startin' to get mad.
You make the press look shoddy
An' it makes us all look bad.

Poymi, chto s etim, koresh,
Nel'zya ozornichat',
Poymi, chto ty pozorish
Rodimuyu pechat'

But the author has not disappeared from the scene entirely; we can hear
his voice in the masterful use of parody. Although the "Ballad of Conscientiousness" starts off as an apparently serious march in a nervous minor
key, this gravity is immediately transformed into parody by the lyrics:[12]

Yegor Petrovich Maltsev*
Was ailing really bad,
Life going out of fingers
And going out of glands.

Out of his other members
His life was going as well.
It looked as if before long
There would be nothing left.

And then suddenly the mood takes an unexpected turn: in charges a
lighthearted and decidedly un-ballad-like street waltz:

When like a herd of cattle
His local in-laws come,
Of all that poor Yegor was,
What will be left for them?

This is the very same melody as Ckudzhava's "Song of the Old Organ-
Grinder." The similarity is not immediately obvious, since Okudzhava sings
the tune with gentle intellectual irony, while Galich's delivery is harsh and
grating. The waltz quatrain is immediately followed by the return of the
romantic march theme:

There'll just be one old raincoat,
A pillow for the bed,

* In view of a professional translation, the Russian text is not provided.

One book, one savings-bank book,
Worth just a couple of quid.

One bowl, one pair of saucepans,
One torn subscription form,
A used-up season ticket
For buses, trains and trams.

And then once again the lively waltz:

That's all, Yegor has left us,
A man's been here and gone!
And the obituary column
Will tell us of it soon.

And so it continues—the humorous verses are set to a frenetic march while the more somber moments lilt to the accompaniment of an irrepressibly joyful waltz, intensifying the absurdity and irony.

The polyphonic interference between music and text reaches its peak when the Red Army Chorus proclaims over Egor in his coffin:

One of our big newspapers
Has given the world the news
That in the Soviet Union
Diabetes has been cured!

The weighty official pronouncement, as one would expect by now, is set to the raucous strains of the waltz. How, after such a barrage of ingenious effects, can one help but sense the powerful presence of the author himself? And indeed, finally, at the very end of the ballad, the song stops short, the guitar falls silent, the stylized hero/narrator is abandoned, and Galich appears in person to pronounce in his own voice the following words:

It's only Soviet power
Can make things work like this!

VII

One day in March of 1968, I arrived at the Academgorodok House of Scientists outside Novosibirsk where I was supposed to say a few words about Galich to introduce him at his performance there. (It was at that concert [part of the 1968 Festival of Bards] that Galich's serious troubles began.) Backstage someone was playing Gershwin's "Rhapsody in Blue."

When I took a look I found it was Galich who was playing. I did not ask him whether he was playing by ear or whether he had learned the piece from sheet music, but later, one day in Moscow, Galich told me that although he did read music, he was reluctant to write down his own compositions. Instead he asked me to do it for him so that they could be published in the West.

It was only as I started transcribing Galich's music from tape recordings that I realized with what whimsy Galich wove his melodies. It was an awful job. At first I imagined I could simply set down the music for the first stanza and it would then fit the rest of the verses, too, as is usually the case with songs by Soviet composers such as Dunayevsky, Blanter or Pakhmutova. When the music did not quite fit each verse, I would use footnotes to indicate variations from the main theme, just as I did when transcribing Okudzhava. There turned out to be so many variations in the melody that footnotes were simply not enough, and as a result I had to write out almost every verse in full. The matter was further complicated by Galich's frequent use of montage-like shifts and alterations in his music and vocal delivery.

In addition to the above difficulties, pitch and rhythm in Galich's singing are often blurred to the point where his delivery at times seems to border either on recitation of poetry or on everyday speech. As a result, the melody often strays from established pitches, and cannot be adequately described with traditional musical notation. In attempting to convey on paper the various effects of rhythm, tempo, and pitch through notation borrowed from the field of ethnomusicology, I became aware of yet another facet of Galich's singing: his ability to create an entire spectrum of ideas and emotions with a single melodic phrase. His simple folk-like melodies are extremely sensitive to subtleties of plot, and like chameleons they take on different colors in response to the slightest nuances in the text.

Galich inherited from his predecessor Alexander Vertinsky this art of manipulating intonation and using it to create meaning through contrast between words and music. Vertinsky, the foremost Russian singer-poet-actor, "exploited the technique of a calculated and very powerful contrast between words and presentation. The everyday 'scène de moeurs' vig-nette—'On the chair the whiteness of your blouse . . .' was presented as a piece of great solemnity, significance and grandeur. He sang the words as a chorale. Such an unexpected juxtaposition of everyday situations and a lofty, high-flown style—or the reverse a capricious singing style and grandiloquent 'meaningful' words—is very characteristic of Vertinsky. Pathos is combined with real sadness, arrogance with genuine anguish, and false merriment with despair. The key to his art in these poignant and daring balancing acts is his virtuoso ability to manipulate changes of mood."[13] The difference, however, is that Vertinsky's technique of unexpected juxtaposition of words with music is used by Galich not for the refined manifestation of a mood, but to enrich his satiric range, play off points of view against each other and heighten the irony.

Bulat Okudzhava, Alexander Galich, Vladimir Vysotsky, Yuly Kim and hundreds of other less well known "bards" and "minstrels" in a very short period of time—literally in only a few years—have managed to bring about a revolution in the tone of speech in the Soviet Union. These "singing poets" have dealt a mortal blow to the glib and uninspired intonation of the official speech of the state media which for so long dominated communications in almost every sphere of Soviet life. Having thus revived the humanity and natural simplicity which had before always been the fundamental characteristic of Russian speech, song, and poetry, these "singing poets" have foiled yet another long-term attempt of the Soviet regime to achieve exclusive control over the souls and minds of the Russian people— the attempt at subjugating and manipulating their speech.

Notes

1. G. Pomerants, "Antikrasnorechie Dostoevskogo v istorikokul'turnoy perspektive", in *Rossiia/Russia* (Torino), No. 4 (1980), 154.
2. Lydia Chukovskaya, *The Deserted House*, Aline B. Werth, trans., (New York: Dutton, 1969), 31.
3. Hans Bajer, "Lieder machen Geschichte," in *Die Musik*, No. 9 (June 1939), 592.
4. The first example is a variation of the "Internationale," the original of which is:

> The entire world of oppression we shall destroy
> To its foundation, and then
> We'll build our new world . . .

> (Ves' mir nasil'ya my razrushim
> Do osnovan'ya. A zatem
> My nash, my novyi mir postroim . . .)

The twist in meaning is achieved almost effortlessly, by using the words "a zachem" (but what for) in place of similar sounding "a zatem" (and then).
The classic Soviet song "Aviamarsh", the official song of the airforce, begins with the captivating line:

> We were born to turn a fairy tale into fact . . .
> (My rozhdeny, chtob skazku sdelat' byl'iu . . .)

By replacing "skazka" (fairy tale) with the name "Kafka", again a totally different message is delivered.
Finally, in the extremely popular "Song of the Motherland" there is a line which goes:

> At our table, no one is unwanted . . .
> (Za stolom nikto u nas ne lishny . . .)

Here the single word "lishny" (unwanted) becomes the common Jewish surname "Lifshits," and a new effect is achieved.

5. From the unpublished article "What to Do With Songs" written by the poetess for *Poetry and Music: A Collection of Essays*, V. Frumkin, ed. and comp., (Moscow: Muzyka, 1973). The article was rejected. The same fate befell my article for that Collection, "The Poet-Singer," written in collaboration with K.V. Chistov, and dedicated to the creative genius of B. Okudzhava.

6. N. Korzhavin, "Poeziya Bulata Okudzhavy", in Bulat Okudzhava, *Proza i Poeziia*, (Frankfurt/Main: Posev, 1984), p. 333.

7. ————, 345.

8. V. Frumkin ed., *Bulat Okudzhava, 65 Songs*, (Ann Arbor: Ardis, 1980), 16.

9. Ibid.

10. In the Roundtable section of the Soviet weekly *Nedelya*, (1966, No. 1), Galich made the following remarks: "Not only the lyrics, but also the music of our songs serves a purpose. It is sensitive to the inflection of everyday speech which is heard in the streets, on subways, in buses. The intonations are conversational and familiar to every ear. It's as if you've heard it somewhere before, but you can't quite think where."

11. A. Sokhor *Russkaya Sovietskaya Pesnya* (Russian Soviet Song) (Leningrad: Sovetsky Kompozitor, 1959), 9.

12. Alexander Galich, *Songs and Poems*, Gerald Stanton Smith, trans., (Ann Arbor: Ardis, 1983), 62–64.

13. K. Rudnitsky, "Alexander Vertinsky" (Manuscript).

15

Humor for the Future and a Future for Humor

CHRISTIE DAVIES

It is often stated that jokes in an authoritarian society are one of the few avenues of political criticism open to people and that jokes are a way of expressing political resentments, grievances and grumbles.[1] At this point the argument often dissolves into a sterile wrangle as to whether political jokes are a means by which political dissent is kept alive and the morale of the dissenters maintained or a safety valve which protects authoritarian regimes by channeling political resentments into a harmless form. The purpose of this chapter is to try and get away from the pointless debates of functionalists and conflict theorists and to look at the actual content of the jokes as a form of *implicit* politics. The sociologists of religion have long ago extended their studies to embrace "implicit religion," the taken-for-granted values and metaphysics of the everyday world as well as conventional organized religion. Cynics may well feel that this is merely a way of fending off the demise of their art in an increasingly secular world where there is not enough organized religion to go around. This is an unfair half-truth for the decline of the organized religious bodies does not mean that people have ceased to hold views or to speculate about the moral and eschatological issues which lie at the core of religion. There is still an important human phenomenon here and one that should be studied.

Similarly even peoples who, from compulsion or choice, from frustration or apparent apathy take no active part in politics, have an internal map of the political world that impinges on them, its nature, its failings, and its prospects. Equally they have a notion of what that political world ought to be like, of the future they would like to see, even if it appears impossible right now. In a free society there are many ways of studying this *implicit* politics. It can be inferred from certain consistent patterns of behavior and comment (often in non-political contexts) that indicate their view of the nature of social and political organization, of power, of political morality. It is also possible simply to go and ask people either by the use of questionnaires whose answers can be coded and quantified or by in-depth interviews. Yet despite the plethora of data that is available, it is still possible to learn new and sometimes unexpected aspects of people's implicit politics through the study of their folklore in general and their jokes in particular. Alan Dundes's book *Life is Like a Chicken-Coop Ladder*,[2] for instance, is a study of German social and political life through folklore which provides insights into the "implicit politics" of the German people that it would have been difficult to obtain by other methods. Similarly the study of ethnic jokes and the stereotypes they employ can tell us a great deal not merely about the joke-teller's attitudes to the butts of the jokes but about the relationship between them and about the kind of negative qualities that the joke-teller's wish to "export." Thus while both the British and the Americans agree in telling jokes which pin "stupidity" on familiar ethnic groups living on the periphery of their society, the Americans alone also depict these groups as dirty. Why? It is not because they are dirty but rather because the American evaluation of hygiene and the American view of the nature of the boundaries of their society differ from those of the British. One of the trickiest of political questions that can be asked is, "Where are the boundaries of our people, of our land, of our nation?" Most citizens do not regularly grapple with such problems or even think about them very much except perhaps in a crisis but they frequently tell jokes that explore this very issue.

Similarly most people—quite rightly—do not bother their heads with, say, the labor theory of value which still survives despite being either false or circular depending on how it is formulated. They know it is daft, for everyday experience teaches people the meaning of scarcity, the value of land, location, rare talents, intangible services—and they demonstrate the fact by their willingness to pay for these things. Admittedly, there are a few implicit believers in the labor theory of value but they are soon put in their place—by jokes:

An old man came into town to have a tooth extracted by the dentist. Afterwards he asked how much it would cost and was told, five pounds. "Five pounds!" he exclaimed in astonishment, "Why it only took you a minute. The blacksmith in my village took a tooth out for me a year ago and it took him nearly two hours. He dragged me all round the room and lost his grip half a dozen times at least. I never saw such hard work, and after all that, he only charged me two pounds. And now you want five pounds for a mere minutes work!

An engineer was called in to repair a large piece of machinery in a factory. He examined it carefully and tapped it gently with his hammer until it sprung to life. Later he sent in the following bill:
For tapping machine £5
For knowing where to tap £50

If the study of jokes is a useful part of the analysis of the implicit politics of a free society, it is even more valuable in relation to the exploration of the implicit politics of authoritarian societies.

Here jokes are more important both because other forms of political expression are limited and because of the difficulties a researcher faces in exploring a people's implicit politics—for quite different reasons neither the regime nor the people would be willing to trust him or her. The regime would seek to prevent or at least to curtail such research lest the findings prove embarrassing while the people might well feel inhibited from expressing critical views that could lead to repercussions. These problems also face the collectors and interpreters of jokes but at least it is possible to assess those that are in common circulation in the Soviet Union and Eastern Europe and to compare them with the jokes told in freer societies. On this basis it is possible at least to say something about the joke-tellers implicit views of the present and hopes and expectations for the future.

One of the most striking features of East European jokes is the way in which politicians are depicted in these jokes as utterly stupid, not merely in their political role but in ordinary everyday life. Some of them no doubt are stupid but they are not all stupid and even the stupid ones are not that stupid. The jokes are not descriptions of individuals or even a class of individuals any more than, say, the similar ethnic jokes told in the West about the alleged stupidity of the witty Irish, the enterprising Belgians or the canny Calvinists of French-speaking Switzerland. They are rather a ritual statement about the legitimacy of a certain category of politicians. The range both of subjects and of targets in the jokes about stupidity from Eastern Europe and the Soviet Union is quite remarkable:

After the successful Apollo-Soyuz space flight Leonid Brezhnev called to congratulate the cosmonauts. However, he also reproached them with: "The Americans are winning the space race. We must accomplish something to outdo them. They've already landed on the moon so we in the Politburo have decided to send you for a landing on the sun."

The cosmonauts groaned: "But, Comrade Brezhnev, we'll be burned alive."

"What do you think," interrupted Brezhnev, "that we don't understand anything? Don't worry, we've already planned all the details. First of all you are going to complete the landing at night."[3]

(Russian)

Husak one day held a reception for Mrs. Gandhi and the staff of the Indian Embassy in Prague. He and his wife arranged a curry buffet and had all the Czechs dress up in Indian costumes. Half way through the reception, Husak's wife came over and said: "Gustav, we've not dressed right."

"What do you mean?" asked Husak.

"You've got to paint a red spot on your forehead like Mrs. Gandhi." said his wife.

"Why?" said Husak.

"Well," said his wife, "all the Indians are looking at you and tapping their foreheads with a finger.[4]

(Czech)

What is the average I.Q. of Poland?

Fifty Ochab.[5]

All Brezhnev's speeches at the Olympic games in Moscow carried as a heading the Olympic symbol. As a result Brezhnev began all his speeches with the phrase "Oh! Oh! Oh! Oh! Oh!,"[6]

(Russian)

Antonin Novotny (president of Czechoslovakia from 1957 to 1968) wanted to take his wife to the annual ball of the Academy of Sciences but his advisers tried to dissuade him. "They are a nasty lot. They will ignore you." The Novotnys went all the same.

The next day he bawled out his advisers: "Ignore us my foot! Nobody took the slightest notice of us!"

At the same ball Mrs. Novotny had noticed the beautiful complexion of some of the ladies. Novotny set his spies to work: "Find out how they do it."

They report back within a few minutes: "They use eau de toilette, Mr. President."

"Oh—d—what?"

"Toilet water, Mr. President."

When he comes home next evening his wife has a big bump on her head. "What happened to you?" he asks.

"I tried this thing with the toilet water," says the first lady "but the lid dropped on my head."[7]

(Czech)

When Gierek was secretary of the Polish Communist party, he was renowned for making long, dull and boring speeches. After one particularly tedious three-hour speech one of his colleagues hinted that a shorter speech might go down better with his audience. Gierek took the hint and told his secretary to limit his speeches to twenty minutes. At his next public appearance, however, he spoke for a full hour to the great irritation of his colleagues. The next day Gierek said angrily to his secretary: "I gave you definite instructions that my speech was under no circumstances to be longer than twenty minutes."

"But, Comrade Gierek," replied the secretary, "I wrote you a twenty minute speech just as you requested and as usual I gave you two carbon copies to go with it."[8]

(Polish)

The phone rang in the Kremlin one night. Brezhnev woke up, put on the light, put on his glasses, fumbled in his pajama pocket for the appropriate scrap of paper, picked up the phone and read out carefully: "Who is it?[9]

(Russian)

The uniform total stupidity assigned to the politicians is quite striking when compared with the jokes that have been told about politicians in the Free World which refer to particular traits of recognizable individuals—jokes about the deviousness of Lloyd George, the taciturn Calvin Coolidge, the bluntness of Harry Truman, the aloof pride of General de Gaulle, the self-effacing modesty of Clement Attlee, the toughness of Barry Goldwater, the wobbling vacillation of Jimmy Carter (How I went from peanut butter to jelly in four years), Richard Nixon's selling of a used car to Edward Kennedy, the logic of Enoch Powell, the monarchical style of President Kekkonen of Finland. Whether these jokes are true or fair is besides the point. What is crucial is that they represent a very varied pattern of mockery of the politicians. The only two politicians in the English-speaking world in recent years who have been the butt of East European type jokes about stupidity, were Gerald Ford and Sir Alec Douglas-Home, both of them able and by no means unpopular politicians.

Harold Wilson versus Sir Alec Douglas-Home—a case of smart alec versus dull Alec.[10]

R.A. Butler introducing Lord Home at a meeting: We are very lucky to have Sir Alec Douglas-Home here with us this evening. He will be talking about foreign policy, a subject he knows something about.[11]

The jokes about the alleged stupidity of Gerald Ford were even collected and published as "The Jerry Ford Joke-Book edited by Max Brodnick":[12]

Only last week Mr. Ford was riding a White House escalator when it broke down and he was stuck there for three hours.

Irked by Ronald Reagan's Hollywood sophistication, Mr. Ford has signed a contract to star in one film comedy. However, he isn't thrilled by the title— Mr. Clumsy goes to Hollywood.

Ford and Douglas-Home were intelligent respected politicians and it was perfectly possible for anyone to criticize them as part of the normal democratic political debate. The only thing these two men had in common with the despots of Eastern Europe is that they had not been elected to the office they held. Gerald Ford was the only American president never to have been elected as either president or vice-president. He was the accidental president who came to that position as a result of the unprecedented resignation of both President Nixon and Vice-President Agnew. When in office he had the kind of minor banana-skin physical accidents that happen to everyone and also made embarrassing verbal slips of a kind since repeated by Carter and Reagan. However, only in Ford's case were these seized upon and turned into jokes so that he became the president who "stumbled into office and has gone on stumbling ever since." Sir Alec Douglas-Home was Lord Home, a hereditary peer holding office in Harold Macmillan's government. It had long been felt in Britain that it would be undemocratic for a peer to be prime minister and indeed this was one of the factors that prevented Lord Curzon and Lord Halifax from attaining that office. Lord Home got around this convention by resigning his peerage and being elected to the House of Commons in a specially arranged by-election for a safe Conservative seat. He was then eligible to become prime minister.

The election of Sir Alec Douglas-Home to Parliament created a vacancy in the House of Lords—and another in the House of Commons.[13]

The penalty both men paid for their unorthodox routes to office that circumvented the usual process of democratic competition, was that they became the butts of jokes about stupidity. It is more difficult for people to make jokes about the stupidity of political leaders whom they have elected for, like Barrabas, they are the people's choice. After every election in a democratic country bumper stickers proclaim "Don't blame me, I voted X" (i.e., for the losers). It is this process of competition and choice that is the basis of political legitimacy in a democracy. Those who lack it are labeled "stupid" whether they are or not. If we extend this argument to Eastern Europe and the Soviet Union then it is clear that the entire political class is seen as illegitimate, because they have not been chosen, they have not won office in open competition and are thus a "stupid" group. By implication the joke-tellers share the concepts of democratic legitimacy applied in the West and not those of "democratic centralism."

At the Central Committee Plenum: After his unanimous election as General Secretary, Andropov announces: "When you have voted, you may lower your arms and come away from the wall."[14]

Only when Soviet and East European politicians are chosen in open competition and the people have the fundamental political right "to turn the rascals out" will jokes about stupid politicians wither away. The implicit political message of the jokes is that this is the future the joke-tellers want and mean to have.

The politicians are by no means the only group in Eastern Europe and the Soviet Union who are the butts of jokes about stupidity. Party hacks, official heroes, and especially militiamen are also ridiculed in this way.

The fearless hero of the Civil War, Vasiliy Ivanovitch Chapaev and his loyal orderly Pyetka were sky-diving.

"We're only 100 meters from the ground" said Pyetka, excitedly. "Its time to pull the ripcord, Vasiliy Ivanovitch!"

"Its still kind of early," Chapaev answered calmly.

"Its only fifty meters now," screamed Pyetka. "Pull the ring Vasiliy Ivanovitch!"

"Calm down, Pyetka," said Chapaev. "There's still time before we hit."

"Only three meters remaining!" cried Pyetka. "Pull!"

"Its not worth it," answered Chapaev. "From this height I can land without a parachute . . . ![15]

(Russian)

Why was Grechko made a Marshal of the Soviet Union?
Because he was too stupid to be a General.[16]

(Russian)

Two Czech militiamen were on duty in Wenceslas Square in Prague. A foreigner came up to them and asked them in German how to get to the main railway station but he received no reply. The militiamen simply shrugged their shoulders so he tried in English. Again no reply. In French—still nothing. In Russian—not even then. Finally the foreigner also shrugged his shoulders and went away.

"You know, I think it would be a good idea to learn a foreign language," said one of the militiamen.

"Whatever for?" asked the other. "Just look how many languages that chap spoke and it didn't help him one bit.[17]

(Czech)

A Czech militiaman with severe burns on both his ears went to see his doctor. "How did this happen?" asked the doctor.

"Well, someone telephoned while I was ironing," said the policeman.

"Yes, but how did you manage to burn both ears?" asked the doctor.

"Well then I had to call an ambulance," said the militiaman.[18]

(Czech)

Why do Czech militiamen go around in groups of three?

One can read, one can write and the other is keeping an eye on the two intellectuals.[19]

(Czech)

Why do Polish militiamen have a stripe around their elbows? So that they can remember where to bend their arms.[20]

(Polish)

A Polish militiaman took his car into the garage to have it serviced. "There's something wrong with the indicator lights," he told the mechanic.

The mechanic got into the car and turned them on. "How are they now?" he asked.

"They're working. They're not working. They're working. They're not working." . . . replied the militiamen.[21]

(Polish)

The jokes about stupid militiamen are not simply an expression of resentment at the behavior of the day-to-day enforcers of state power, for there are after all much more powerful and sinister agencies of state control in the East who are the subject of different kinds of jokes. The key to the jokes about stupid militiamen lies in their mode of recruitment. The role of policeman in Eastern Europe and the Soviet Union is not a respected one and those who are in a position to choose other careers do so. In consequence, the militia recruit unskilled rustics who lack a trade or an educational qualification and for whom joining the militia is their only means of obtaining a permit to live and work in a city.[22] Police officers of a similar breed in other countries such as Italy, South Africa; nineteenth-century American cities are or were the butts of similar jokes about carabinieri, van der Merwe and dumb Irish cops. The key element is the political appointment of the unskilled, uneducated, unsophisticated to positions of crude power. In Italy it is the clients of the entrenched politicians of the poor and backward South; in South Africa, Afrikaner Red-necks (as distinct from rooineks) who support the National Party (or did in the days before the H.N.P. and Treurnicht's Conservatives); in America it was the nominees of Tammany Hall who fill or filled the police force. Thus the unfortunate militiamen of the Soviet Union or Eastern Europe are doubly illegitimate, for not only are the rules he has to enforce often illegitimate, but so, in the eyes of the citizenry, is the mode of his appointment.[23]

Political appointees who have not had to compete in the marketplace, the examination hall or even through the ballot box are always likely to be regarded as stupid for in the eyes of the joke-tellers they lack merit. They are not professionals. This point has been neatly made by Fox Butterfield in his description of the Chinese telling political jokes:

These cadres are viewed by the more sophisticated natives of Peking and Shanghai as urban Americans would view hillbillies from Kentucky or Tennessee. Our friends the Wangs liked to tell jokes about the typical cadre.

"In a village the county authorities had announced they were going to form the militia and issue rifles," Li began one of his favorites stories. "It was a big event in a place where nothing ever happens and the peasants got very excited. But then days and weeks passed, and the county authorities were having trouble reaching a decision.

"Finally, after two years, a jeep came down to the village. An important-looking cadre got out and declared there would be a big meeting about forming the militia.

"At the meeting, he got up and began speaking slowly, 'I-am-the-county-Party-secretary,' and with those words the audience burst into thunderous applause. It was a great honor to be visited by such a high cadre.

"But then the speaker added, 'That is, I was sent by the county Party secretary.' " Li told the story employing the thick dialect of Hunan province, where Mao and many other cadres came from.

" 'We have decided, about the guns, that one gun for each person,' and again there was a chorus of applause, 'is absolutely impossible.

" 'We have reached the conclusion that one gun for every two people,' and there was still clapping, 'is not right.

" 'So I want to announce the final decision of the county Party committee is, one gun for every three people,' which set off more applause. 'But they are wooden guns,' the cadre concluded.[23]

The point of the jokes is not the mere snobbish rejection of crude peasant manners and speech though that in itself can be the basis of jokes but (a) the fact that the cadres/militiamen, etc. are stupid in the sense that they lack the skills and knowledge necessary for their job, (b) the fact that political rectitude is seen as a sufficient qualification for resolving technical issues and, (c) the inverse snobbery that sees proletarian or peasant ancestry as a qualification *in itself* in much the same way as an aristocratic lineage would have been in a traditional society. In open societies where tradition is still an important force both peasants and aristocrats are the butt of jokes about stupidity. The sons of peasants who come to town are derided as stupid rustics, ignorant bumpkins, dumb yokels, slow-witted hill-billies, hoosiers, red-necks because their traditional skills and attainments are not relevant to the changing and cosmopolitan city where they are seeking employment. Aristocrats are equally the butt of jokes about stupidity because their claim to status is not a meritocratic one, not one based on success through competition. Hence the English jokes about upperclass twits,[24] the American jokes about tongue-tied English aristocrats,[25] the Austrian and German jokes about Graf Bobby[26] and their Hungarian equivalents which still survive long after the demise of the Hapsburg social order. The aristocratic preoccupation with social origins rather than the abilities of the individual has its Communist counterpart and the fate of both is jokes about how stupid they are. The Russian official hero Chapaev who was lauded for his humble origins is the butt of jokes about stupidity for the same reason as aristocrats in other societies.

Why is an aristocrat like Euclid's definition of a point?
He has position but no parts and no magnitude.[27]

Why are the upper classes like turnips?
The best part of them lies under the ground.[28]

Why are the upper classes the cream of the country?
They are rich and thick.[29]

The implicit message of the jokes is a meritocratic one that stresses mobility through competition and legitimacy through skill, as against arbitrary sponsorship on irrelevant social or political grounds. There are also many jokes that spell out this message directly:

Two comrades met in the street. "Heavens, you've changed!" said one. "You've lost so much weight."
"Well you see I got married and my wife can't cook," replied the other.
"Why don't you send her on a state cookery course?" asked the former.
"That's exactly what I did just after we got married six months ago."

"Well?"
"The course has only just reached the revolution of 1905.[30]
(Russian)

It was finally decided to introduce striptease into the Soviet Union, and since this was thought to be an extremely avant-garde concept, it was decided only to employ women who had been members of the Party for at least 20 years. One day Brezhnev himself came along to watch the imported novelty. To ensure absolute ideological correctness, a girl who had been a Party member since 1917 was the main star. Brezhnev watched her act for a while and when with palsied hand, she removed the last veil he said in a bored voice: "I can't understand why those westerners are so enthusiastic about striptease."[31]
(Russian)

A (Czech) interview: "What was your father's occupation?"
"I don't rightly know. . . . He used to mingle with the crowds in marketplaces and at soccer games and come back in the morning loaded with money."
"In other words, a pickpocket. And your mother?"
"I don't rightly know. She used to leave at night and come back in the morning loaded with money."
"In other words, a prostitute. Anybody else in the family?"
"There was an uncle. He used to go from door to door selling combs and brushes."
"A petit bourgeois businessman! You fool, you could have been a first-class cadre but your uncle spoiled it all for you!"[32]

Politics is of necessity an irrational activity. It cannot be reduced to a technically rational system of administration.[33] There is no way of deciding that a person is qualified (or unqualified) to be a politician in the sense that a surgeon, a mathematician, an electrician, or a pilot has to be and they do not require the bits of paper demanded of the would-be bureaucrat. Politicians are experts in doing nothing in particular and they do it very well. They are the ultimate fixers and politics is the point at which the final arbitrary bargains of interests, values and resources must be struck. There are no right answers, only possible ones and the only qualification for being a politician is being a politician. The qualified, the specialist, the bureaucratic office-holder retires at an arbitrary fixed age beyond which they are quite unfairly held to be too old and incompetent through age, but the politician who has ultimate responsibility can go on to become the Grand Old Man or his rival "Der *Alte* Jude—dass ist der Mann."[34] Old politicians only die, they never fade away. Adenauer and Hindenburg, De Gaulle and de Gasperi, Kekkonen and Reagen, Tito and Franco, Mao and Meir, Clémenceau and Churchill, Khomeini and Morarji, Petain and Perone *Le roi est demi-mort. Vive le roi.* Very old politicians represent in their own persons the bargains of today and yesterday, survival, continuity, a link with safer or more successful times.[35] But before Gorbachev, there was no gerontocracy like Soviet gerontocracy—not respected as the G.O.M. or Der Alte but mocked as a dubious oligarchy of senile survivors:

What did Chernenko inherit from Brezhnev?
Senility.[36]

Why is it that Brezhnev travelled abroad but Andropov doesn't?
Brezhnev was supplied from a battery but Andropov is plugged into the mains.[37]

Political life is of necessity irrational and the legitimacy of politicians does not depend on any specialized expertise or knowledge. This is fair enough—but there is a corollary, viz., that politics should be limited in scope and the range of politicians' power restricted by constitution or convention. It is when the politicians step far outside their true sphere and try to settle technical, economic or social issues that require expertise or are best left to the forces of "spontaneous order" that they gain a reputation for stupidity like the apocryphal politicians of the Indiana State Legislature who came within two crucial votes of declaring that the value of the ratio of the circumference of a circle to its diameter was in the area of their jurisdiction to be 3.2 exactly.[38] Had they got to the point of trying to enforce such a law, the politicians would have been the irrational fraction of Indiana. The point is *not* that politicians are stupid or grossly fallible, for the world contains a multitude of scientists, businessmen, academics, plumbers who are one or the other or both. Politicians alone possess the final power to enforce their decisions and it is this combination of power without expertise that makes their stupidity more dangerous and more risible than that of other people. This is particularly the case in totalitarian societies where they have a monopoly of political power, where they may be filled with a sense of their own ideological righteousness and where there are no clear limits to what is political, so that they are able to extend the range of their arbitrary decisions into areas that need autonomy. Political attempts to *decree* the findings of pure science or the nature of mathematical relationships, to denounce bourgeois science, Jewish science, Machism or to proclaim the virtue of Black mathematics or proletarian physics really are stupid. The wisdom of scientists is fallible and provisional, but that is its virtue, and the worst thing one can say about influential scientists who try to use their position to enforce their views and to exclude dissent is that they are behaving like politicians. Scientific paradigms are not enforceable or even dogma. The jokes about the politicization of science in the Soviet Union and Eastern Europe have mainly related to the stupid impositions of an arbitrary ideological cage on scientific findings, though Polanyi noted on his various visits to scientific institutions in the USSR that attempts to plan the advance of science were themselves the subject of "contemptuous jokes."[39] The Lysenko affair[40] in particular gave rise to such jokes, the main butt of them being the unfortunate horticulturalist Michurin who allegedly had produced wonderful hybrid proletarian fruit that defied "bourgeois" Mendelian genetics.

> Do you know how Michurin died?
> He broke his neck when he fell off one of his strawberries.[41]

> Do you know how Michurin died?
> He crossed his legs and could no longer urinate.[42]

> Who invented barbed wire?
> Michurin. He crossed earthworms with hedgehogs.[43]

Professor Beckmann, a Czech electrical engineer who is a connoisseur of jokes about stupid politicized science, has also recorded a number of true incidents about the exercise of political power to supress rational criticism in the physical sciences:

> For example in Ostrava, an industrial town in East Moravia, a worker had proposed a machine that in essence was to throw rocks in the air and the rocks would then do work coming down. The chief engineer tried to explain the principle of the conservation of energy to him, but to no avail. The worker turned to the party, the engineer was fired and the proposal wandered all over the country, one expert handing it to another like a hot potato.[44]

The aspect of political control that impinges most directly on the common people in the Soviet Union and Eastern Europe is the supression of the marketplace, the lack of enough private ownership of the means of production, the attempt to replace the price mechanism by central planning. The results of this are lines and shortages, and a black market in Western goods and currency which are recognized as having value.[45] The black markets, moonlighting, speculation and even corruption are all attempts by individuals to create a spontaneous order in the face of the chaos left by planning.[46] The jokes about the state of economic life told in Eastern Europe and the Soviet Union also implicitly recognize the failure of socialist planning, and the necessity for a system of market prices and a meaningful currency. *Quid rides?* (Who laughs?)

A hundred people were standing on line for food in Warsaw when Jaruselski drove past in his car. He stopped. "What are people waiting for?" he asked. "We are waiting for meat. There is no meat." Jaruselski said: "It is dreadful that you should have to stand like this. I must do something about it." An hour later a truck drove up and unloaded a hundred chairs.[47]

A Soviet economist visited France and told the French economic Minister, "Your economy is in a terrible state. I have never seen such poverty." "What do you mean," replied the Frenchman. "The shops are full of all kinds of goods and produce." "But," replied the Russian "No one can afford to buy them. During the whole of my visit to France I haven't seen one single line."[48]

There are three classes in the classless society of Poland. Those who have dollars, those who have zloty, and those who have neither.[49]

What is the common factor between the Polish and the American economy? In neither country can you buy anything with zloties.[50]

The use of Marxist jargon and special pleading to excuse chronic economic failure is equally subject to ridicule in jokes:

Soviet economist: The reason why Canada and the United States supply the Soviet Union with so much grain is due to the catastrophic over-production of capitalism.[51]

Under capitalism you get rigid discipline in production and chaos in consumption. Under socialist economic planning you get rigid discipline in consumption and chaos in production.[52]

When will the Cubans know that they have achieved the same level of socialist development as the Soviet Union?
When they start importing sugar.[53]

The free market, science, and jokes are all forms of spontaneous order created by the autonomous actions of individuals and groups. In a competitive system prices and production depend on the hidden hand not the clenched fist. Discovery, invention, innovation cannot be predicted let alone planned with any accuracy except *in limited* areas over short periods of time. Jokes are not produced by ministries of humor and their invention and circulation are inevitably the result of millions of spontaneous individual initiatives. They are but the sum of people's uncoordinated humorous responses to widely shared predicaments. There is an order to the jokes told in a society albeit one that is often difficult to pin down but it is not an order designed by any one. There is no director of Radio

Armenia[54] but the broadcasts have a recognizable style; no transmitters but a common wavelength.

No complex industrial society is based only on spontaneous order. There always exists also a planned and corporate order, a state that is not going to wither away, a degree of necessary and beneficial central control and intervention, a role for politics. The fallacy on which Marxist states are based is the idea that the equally necessary forms of spontaneous social order which require the autonomy of individuals, groups, institutions can and should be made subordinate to political authority and directives. It is singularly appropriate that jokes should be one of the means by which people express their mockery of the manifest failures of such a system, a mockery which reveals popular insight into its central, tyrannical yet self-defeating, oppressive yet risible weakness, viz., the attempt to supress spontaneous order and to deny autonomy.

The absurd promise of Marxism is that it can enable man to determine his own future. An understanding of the forces of spontaneous order teaches us that long-term future patterns of demand, of scientific discovery, of technological innovation, of supplies of raw materials are unknown and unknowable and that political attempts to control that future are futile. At best we can simply try and avoid tomorrow's total disasters, but we don't even know which of these is most threatening or what new ones will arise. Joke-tellers are no better at telling the future than anyone else and there is no more *esoteric* wisdom to be found in jokes than in the dimensions of the pyramids. There is nonetheless an impressive implicit political common-sense in the jokes of the Soviet Union and Eastern Europe. They are the jokes of people who have seen the future and it doesn't work, who have recognized the stupidity of a politicized society, who have no illusions about either the realities of present-day socialism or its utopian promises for the future:

In twenty years," proclaimed the Soviet economist, "our socialist society will be so advanced that everyone will have their own private helicopter."

"But why would anyone need one?" asked a puzzled listener.

"Well," said the economist, "supposing you lived in Moscow and one day you heard that potatoes were available in Kiev—look how quickly you could get there.[55]

The three stages of socialism: Early socialism where goods are readily available and there are no ration cards.

Advanced socialism where there are few goods but plenty of ration cards with which to obtain them.

Full communism where there are neither ration cards nor any goods left in the shops.[56]

A Muscovite inherited millions of dollars from America. The government offered to do him any favor he wants in return for the money.

He asks to run the biggest food shop in Moscow for three days and to have all the supplies he needed. He then put up notices all over Moscow saying "all the food you want free."

There were huge crowds, total chaos, fifty shop assistants were killed, the buildings were demolished and all the food in Russia eaten up.

The members of the Politbureau asked him "Why did you do it?"

"I'm an old man. I'd have never lived to see what Communism will be like. But now I've seen it![57]

There is, however, a promise for the future implicit in the people's (not the People's) humor of the East. Their jokes display an insight into the failures of the social and political order that indicate a sophisticated implicit politics and a willingness to enter the uncertain worlds of spontaneous order. It is a humor *for* a future very different from their recent past. It is a humor of autonomy, based on limited but valued autonomy, and a wish for much greater autonomy. In the humor of present disillusionment, there is thus a hope for the future. Every joke is a tiny counterrevolution. Yet the dreams of the joke-tellers involve a withering away of their jokes. In a free society there is less work for humor to do and the future of humor is play—they have only their jokes to lose.

At the time of writing in the years immediately following 1984, it is clear that the subject peoples of the Soviet Empire often feel trapped in a long dark tunnel with no end, no light in sight.[58] Some indeed know only the intermediate stage between socialism and communism known as alcoholism. Cuban sucrose has become in turn bellicose, lachrymose and comatose. Yet many others see hope in the very deadliness indeed decadence of the system which is now displaying the symptoms of decay that their ancestors mocked in czarist Russia, in the Ottoman or Austro-Hungarian empires. New Gorbachev is but Old Procházka and this particular Johnny Walker[59] is growing weaker. In the outposts of empire there is still no freedom of speech but there is freedom of conversation and in bars,[60] cafés, private homes critical, hopeful jokes predict the end of Soviet socialism:

A citizen of Moscow went into a restaurant and ordered: "Borsht, veal cutlets, rhubarb pie, a cup of coffee. . . . oh and a copy of *Pravda* please."

"Certainly," said the waiter, "we have all that you have ordered but not *Pravda*. That newspaper ceased publication when the old Communist regime collapsed."

The waiter duly brought the borsht, the customer ate it with relish and said: "And now bring me the veal cutlets and don't forget my rhubarb pie, coffee and my copy of *Pravda*."

The waiter said patiently, "I'm sorry but I can't bring you a copy of *Pravda*. It doesn't exist any more. It died with the Communists."

The cutlets in turn were brought and eaten. "Now said the customer, please bring me my rhubarb pie and then my coffee and the copy of *Pravda*."

"The rhubarb pie is no problem," said the waiter, "and there's plenty of coffee but there is no longer any *Pravda*—like the old Communist government, it's finished, done away with, no more."

The customer consumed his pie and called the waiter over to his table. "That was excellent," he said, "and now I'm ready for my coffee and the copy of *Pravda*."

The waiter exploded: "How many times do I have to tell you, there is no *Pravda*. There is no Communist government. We've got rid of all that!"

"Yes, I know," said the customer, "I just wanted to hear you say it again.[61]

Notes

1. See Egon Larsen, *Wit as a Weapon*, (London: Muller, 1980.)
2. Alan Dundes, *Life Is Like a Chicken-coop Ladder*, (New York: Columbia University Press, 1984).
3. Emil Abramovitch Draitser, *Forbidden Laughter*, (Los Angeles: Almanac, 1978), 56.
4. Anonymous Czech source, 1981.
5. Folklore Archives, University of California, Berkeley, Polish source.
6. Told to the author by Emil Draitser (see note 3) in England in 1980.
7. Petr Beckmann, *Whispered Anecdotes*, (Boulder, Colorado: Golem, 1969), 94.
8. Anonymous Polish source 1981, see also John Kolasky, *Look Comrade the People are Laughing*, (Toronto: Peter Martins, 1972) 38–39 for a similar joke about Gomulka.
9. Anonymous Bulgarian source, 1982.
It may be objected that the stress I have placed on the jokes about the politicians being *stupid* is one-sided and that I have neglected jokes about their more evil and sinister qualities such as, say, the jokes about Stalin being a cruel tyrant. These jokes, however, tell us nothing new for they are literally true, they simply restate in comic form a ghastly historical fact known to us in great detail from other sources (e.g., see Robert Conquest, *The Great Terror*, [Harmondsworth: Penguin, 1971]) and even half-acknowledged by the Soviet elite. The jokes in a sense do not even exaggerate for no exaggeration is possible. Admittedly it is gratifying to see the "sacred" figure of Lenin revealed in his true viciousness and the nonsense of the cult of Lenin mocked as soundly as the worship of saint's relics were by Chaucer. Nonetheless, these jokes mean just what they say and are comparable to other jokes about individual politicians. The jokes about the *stupidity* of politicians,

however, are jokes about a *category* in the same sense as similar jokes about an ethnic group or a social class. The members of these social categories are not literally stupid individuals in the sense that Stalin really was a monster. The jokes about stupidity are an index of social position—in this case a statement about the monopoly of power and the absence of truly competitive achievement by the members of the category. This inference can *only* be made on the basis of a comparative analysis of these and similar jokes from other societies.

A similar point can be made about the militia jokes which are quite different from, say, the jokes about the brutality of the security police. The brutality is real; the stupidity may or may not be and is primarily a signal of their social origins and lack of legitimacy through merit.

10. British, 1964.
11. Told to author by a British student in early 1960s.
12. Max Brodnick, *The Jerry Ford Joke-Book*, New York, 1975
13. British, 1964.
14. Dora Sturman, "Six leaders in search of character," *Survey*, 28 (Autumn 1984), 28, 3:(122) 213.
15. Draitser, *Forbidden Laughter*, 50.
16. Kolasky, *Look Comrade*, 70.
17. Anonymous Czech source, 1981
18. Anonymous Czech source, 1981
19. Anonymous Czech source, 1981
20. Anonymous Polish source, 1981
21. Anonymous Polish source, 1981
22. The comments concerning the militia are based on discussions with East European criminologists. See also Robert Conquest, *The Soviet Police System*, (London: Bodley Head, 1968): 32–33, *and We and They*, (London: Temple Smith, 1980) 98.
23. Fox Butterfield, *China, Alive in the Bitter Sea*, (London: Hodder and Stoughton, 1982) pp. 289–90.
24. English jokes about this group need to be *told* as the identity of the "stupid" person is conveyed by their peculiar mode of speaking—what has been termed 'the old school tie in the mouth voice." See also W.S. Gilbert, *Iolanthe*, Act II.
25. American ethnic jokes about the English usually refer to this class. It is a good example of how one country's jokes about a class can become another's ethnic jokes.
26. These jokes were popular in the last years of the Austro-Hungarian monarchy but have recently had a revival. The traditional jokes depict a wise fool, the new jokes a complete fool.
27. British, 1960s.
28. British, 1960s.
29. British, 1960s.
30. Anonymous Russian source, 1981, See also Larsen *Wit* 95.

31. Anonymous Russian source, 1981.
32. Petr Beckmann, *Hammer and Tickle*, (Boulder, Colorado: Golem, 1980): 84.
33. See K.G. Robertson, *Public Secrets, a Study in the Development of Bureaucracy*, (London: Macmillan, 1982). Chapters 1, 2 and 10 for a discussion of the boundary between "politics" and "rationality."
34. The G.O.M. was Gladstone. "Der alte Jude" was Disraeli. The praise of Disraeli came from Bismarck.
35. See C. Davies, "Women as Rulers in Modern Times, a Study in Democratic Inheritance," *New Quest*, 35, (September-October 1982): 271–89.
36. Sturman, "Six Leaders" 215.
37. ——, 214.
38. John Grant *A Book of Numbers*, (Bath: Ashgrove, 1982), 34. See also C. Morgan and D. Langford *Facts and Fallacies*, 1981 and Stephen Pile *The Book of Heroic Failures*, 1979.
39. M. Polanyi, *The Contempt for Freedom, the Russian Experiment and After*. (London: Watts, 1940). It is a dialectical nightmare where Joseph K. merges with his antithesis. Under socialism thesis and antithesis leads to paralysis.
40. See John Langdon-Davies, *Russia Puts the Clock Back, a Study of Soviet Science and Some British Scientists*, (London: Gollancz, 1949). See also Beckmann (1969) p. 78 and Mark Popovsky, *Science in Chains*, (London: Collins and Harvill, 1980).
41. Beckmann, Hammer, 67 and Kolasky, *Look Comrade*, 110.
42. Beckmann, Hammer, 67.
43. Beckmann, Hammer, 67 and see also Kolasky, *Look Comrade*, 111.
44. Beckmann, Whispered, 123. For a contrast between Beckmann's account of a true incident with a British fantasy satire on bureaucracy see Evelyn Waugh, *Put Out More Flags*, (London: Chapman and Hall, 1942). Truth is stranger than fiction though not as funny.
45. Note the *skill* with which the citizens of socialism can create a market.
46. See M. Hirszowicz, *The Bureaucratic Leviathan, a Study in the Sociology of Communism*, (Oxford: Martin Robertson, 1980), 130–48 and C. Davies, "Corruption Versus Competition," *New Quest*, 12, (1978): 383–92 for a discussion of how these processes work.
47. Told by Russian émigré at International Conference on Humor, Washington, D.C., 1982.
48. Anonymous Russian source, 1981.
49. Polish taxi driver quoted in *Time*, September 1980.
50. Anonymous Polish source. See also Larsen, *Wit* 90.
51. Anonymous source.
52. Greg Benton and G. Loomes, *The Big Red Joke-Book*, (London: 1976), 98.
53. Kolasky, *Look Comrade*, 132.
54. Dr. A.M. Kirakosian was said in 1972 to be the director of Radio Erivan/Armenia broadcasting on 74, 26 m; 347, 6 m; 41,27 m; 248, 42 m; 1181, 1 m; 4,5 m; 4, 25 m. See Michael Schiff *Radio Eriwan antwortet* and Wolfgang W. Parth and Michael Schiff *Neues von Radio Eriwan* (Frankfurt: Fischer, 1972).

According to Emil Abramovitch Draitser formerly of *Krokodil*, meetings in Moscow at which a speaker from Radio Erivan/Armenia was announced, used to dissolve into laughter.

55. Anonymous Russian. See also Armand Isnard *"Raconte . . . Popov,"* (Paris: Mengès, 1977), 79.

56. Polish, 1980s.

57. Told by A. Shtromas, 1981. See also Lewis Carroll, *Sylvie and Bruno* in John Fisher, ed. *The Magic of Lewis Carroll*, (London: Nelson, 1973), 259.
The implication of these jokes for the future is to be seen in terms of what people know is both impossible and undesirable. The people know that the present socialist societies are doomed to economic, technological and social stagnation—they know they are trapped in stupidity and the official view of a rosy future following the "transition to communism" is a meaningless mirage. It is not possible to know much about the future in a positive sense but we can know what it will *not* be. We *can* know that communism in a complex industrial society is impossible in the same sense in which it is impossible for a cat to swim the Atlantic (Polanyi, 1940) and we *can* know that the tragedy of past socialism will not repeat itself as farce (if it did the audience would boo and walk out and the theatre would close down). The jokes indicate a profound disillusionment, a sense that the system has failed and is doomed, which is a humor for a future but an uncertain future. The inner contradictions of the system are much clearer to people than the likely direction of its evolution or even the possible alternatives available. There is a discussion of this point in Jaroslaw A. Piekalkiewicz, *Public Opinion Polling in Czechoslovakia 1968–69.* (New York: Praeger 1972). The surveys bring out the people's low opinion held of politicians (124–25) their lack of confidence in political organizations (133–34) their distrust of political monopoly (171–75) their knowledge that the economy had failed (274, 286–90). However, no clear popular view of the kind of radical change needed emerged. People knew what they wanted but not how to get there though a different set of questions might have produced different results.

58. It has often been pointed out that political jokes languished in Poland in the period when there was a directly political confrontation between Solidarity and the government. At this time there was open discussion of political issues and widespread hope of rapid political change. It would be false to say that jokes are a substitute for political activity but it is true that when opportunities for real opposition and resistance to socialist tyranny are lacking, people turn to jokes instead. Jokes are a mere barometer of political pressure.

59. In the last years of the crumbling Austro-Hungarian Empire, the Emperor Franz Josef II was known in the Czech lands as Old Procházka (see for instance Jaroslav Hašek, *The Good Soldier* [Harmondsworth: Švejk Penguin, 1974], 261.) A photograph of the Emperor appeared in a newspaper with the title "Procházka na moste,' 'A walk on the bridge." However, this phrase can also mean Mr. Procháska on the bridge, Prochaska being a common Czech name with the same pronunciation. The joke soon caught on and provided

the Czechs with an irreverent nickname for the emperor such that even advertisements for walking sticks or "sticks-for-the walk," i.e., "sticks to beat the Emperor with" could be seen as a subversive joke. Today the Czechs have recreated this tradition of seeing or planting subversion in everyday objects—ask a Czech to show you the subversive symbols concealed in the design of their paper currency.

60. The decor and atmosphere of many bars in Prague is such as to create a feeling of a Western oasis where one can forget or even mock socialism. Sexist naked ladies and racist gollywogs advertise American, British, Canadian, and German drinks, Western pop music is played, the customers wear shirts that feature the Stars and Stripes, the Union Jack or the Maple Leaf, and only the shortage of decent food reminds the customers that it is a socialist country.

61. Told to the author by Alexander Shtromas, 1985.

The Issues of Multinationalism and the Fate of the Soviet Empire

A

THE USSR

1

Prospects for the Development of the USSR's Nationalities

SERGEI MAKSUDOV

"As I understand Russian history," wrote D.I. Mendeleev at the beginning of this century, "the Russian nation has never been inclined towards conquests, and if it has fought and subdued more than a few peoples, it has done so solely from the force of circumstances. It was impossible not to fight the Cherkeses, Turkmens, Kirghizes, Khivins and other such peoples when they gave no peace to Russian lands and when they could not form state relationships in any way satisfactory for life as neighbors. Evolution of this sort has apparently come to an end in our historic times. We have more than enough to do where we have settled. We attempted, in a manner unsuited to us, to enrich ourselves at China's expense and learned a lesson which showed that it was not for us to grow to excess. A better approach, one which is rapidly becoming a necessity, is to busy ourselves with what has long been ours, to examine what we have here at home, for which without an external push there was never enough motivation, knowledge, or will."[1]

This advice was not given in vain and no small effort is being expended today on the development of the northeastern region of the country—a spacious, unspoiled dwelling, which has been saved by history as if solely for further development by the Russian state. "The CPSU's CC values highly the labor of BAM's builders, and expresses its firm confidence that they will labor selflessly in the future . . . and doing so, will hasten the development of the rich natural resources of Siberia and the Far East."[2]

The expanses of Russia are one-sixth of the world's land masses taken together. While all other grand empires fell apart, Russia's not only preserved itself, but successfully rounded off its borders and formed a covering detachment of vassal states around itself.

The vastness of Russia! How indeed endless and indistinct are its limits. "O Russian land, you are already here beyond the hill," exclaimed Prince Igor, nearing the border of Voronezh District. "And all of the tongues native to her shall mention me," proudly declared the poet, "and the Finn, and the still wild Tungus, and the friend of the steppe, the Kalmyk." But not included in his count were the Armenians, Uzbeks, and Koreans, then living beyond the state's boundaries.

"Vladivostok is a city of our own (*nashenskiy*)," cleverly noted Vladimir Ilich Lenin, but could he have suspected that the city of Koenigsberg would be "nashenskiy," too?

Immense are Russia's expanses. "From the cold Finnish cliff to the fiery Kolkhida" and back "from the southern mountains to the northern seas." Immense and untouchable.

And suddenly again, in the last quarter of the twentieth century, as at the turn of the century, anxious voices are heard telling of a threat hanging over the Russian people. It has, they say, crept up from within, coming from the rapid growth of the Moslem peoples, and threatening the dominant role of the Russians in the country.[3] Inasmuch as the main arguments of such kind are demographic in nature, let us examine the quantitative side of the question with a broad historical perspective.

Peter the Great, after having founded the empire, ordered a census of the population. According to the 1719 data there were approximately 7.8 million inhabitants in the country—among them not more than 5.9 million Russians.[4] At that time, the eastern giant seemed almost a dwarf. Neighboring countries were much more heavily populated. More than 12 million people lived in the Kingdom of Poland, mainly Eastern Slavs (forebears of the contemporary Ukrainians and Belorussians). Austria-Hungary's population was close to 17 million, also-to a large degree of Slavic origin; the population of the German principalities numbered 17 million, the French 20 million, the Italians, Spaniards, and English (including the Irish) 10 million each.[5] Russians were first neither among Europeans nor among Slavs.

The heirs of Peter managed to redress this situation, and toward the end of the nineteenth century Russia surpassed European states not only in the extent of its domain, but also in its population—it was 125 million according to the 1897 census, of which 55 million named Russian as their native language; among Europeans at this time only Germans were slightly more numerous. In eighty years (by 1979) there were 137.4 million Russians by nationality and a total of 153.5 million people were using Russian as their native language.[6] No European nation is equal today to the Russians. In the 260 years since the time of Peter, Russians have increased their population 26 times and were this tendency to continue for the same period, Russians would outnumber all other inhabitants of the world at present. And in another 500 years there would be approximately 20 Russians for each square meter of the earth's surface.

However, this fantastic perspective has no chance of becoming reality. As with the other peoples of Europe, Russians have curtailed their birthrate and their growth rate has slowed. At the same time, the southern Moslem regions of the USSR, which fell into the sphere of interests of the Russian state during the nineteenth century, are experiencing a demographic boom. This boom is leading to a reduction in the proportion of Russians among the general population of the country (Table 1-1). It is evident from the table that the absolute size of population growth of Russians and Moslem peoples of the south has equalized in the recent past. In the decade of 1970–79, both populations grew by approximately 8 million people, while other nationalities of the country grew by considerably smaller numbers.

This phenomenon is evidently not just a matter of high birthrates among some groups and low rates among others. A complicated process of inter-action between races, peoples, and languages is taking place, determined by both general historical tendencies and the state's policy. In order to picture the general prospects, these tendencies should be examined.

Some Are More Equal

The nationalities policy of autocracy was quite resolute and harsh. Not just a "prison of peoples," but a camp of forced reeducation and national annihilation was organized on the expanses of the empire. Russian ortho-doxy, which occupied a privileged position as the state religion, exerted strong religious pressure. Under more humanitarian emperors this pressure took the form of missionary activity and the curtailment of participation in the state's life of the so-called "*inorodtsy*" (aliens); under harsher em-perors this pressure expressed itself in pogroms and the burning of syn-agogues and mosques. As well as religion, the concept of Russian nationality included use of the Russian language. Instruction was conducted in Russian in all schools except primary and religious ones. In some schools the language of instruction was German. Printing of literary works in many

Table 1–1
Population of National Groups from Census (in thousands)*

	1897[1]	1926	1939[2]	1959	1970	1979
Russians	55,668	77,791	100,392	114,114	129,015	137,397
Ukrainians, Belorussians, Moldavians	29,388	36,213	45,946	47,380	52,503	54,778
Europeans[3]	15,240	5,197	8,240	6,325	6,298	6,104
Finnic group[4]	2,499	3,090	3,290	3,214	3,280	3,230
Peoples of Siberia[5]	636	716	714	734	902	986
Baltic peoples	4,099	347	4,805	4,715	5,102	5,310
Georgians, Armenians[6]	2,693	3,730	4,794	5,887	7,338	8,297
Turkic peoples of Volga region[7]	6,266	5,270	6,662	7,533	9,002	9,586
Azerbaydzhani and peoples of the Northern Caucasus[8]		3,204	4,185	5,020	7,283	8,958
Moslems of Central Asia[9]	10,946	10,755	11,198	13,295	20,055	26,470
Others[10]	205	325	374	610	972	969
TOTAL	127,640	146,638	190,600	208,827	241,720	262,085

*1897 by language, other years by nationality

NOTES:
1. Without Finland, Bukhara and Khiva (about 2 million Moslems lived in the latter two areas).
2. With territories annexed in 1939.
3. Germans, Poles, Jews, Greeks, Bulgarians, Rumanians, Gagauzes, Czechs, Slovaks, Western Europeans.
4. Finns, Karelians, Komis, Mordvins, Maris, Udmurts, Vesps, Izhors.
5. Altayans, Yakuts, Buryats, Khakases, Shorts, lesser peoples of the North.
6. Also Abkhazians, Adygeyans, Abazins, Kabardinians.
7. Tartars, Bashkirs, Chuvashes, and closely related peoples.
8. Mountain peoples of Dagestan and all others living in the northern Caucasus and Transcaucasia.
9. Kazakhs, Uzbeks, Tadzhiks, Kirghizes, Turkmens, Karakalpaks, Uygurs, and lesser Moslem groups of Central Asia.
10. Koreans, Chinese, Gypsies, Tuvins, and other small nationalities.

Table 1–1 (*continued*)
Percent of Population by Nationality from Census

	1897	1926	1939	1959	1970	1979
Russians	43.6	53.0	52.7	54.6	53.4	52.4
Ukranians, Belorussians	23.0	24.6	24.1	22.7	21.7	20.9
Europeans	11.9	3.6	4.3	3.0	2.6	2.4
Finnic group	2.0	2.1	1.7	1.5	1.4	1.2
Peoples of Siberia	0.5	0.5	0.4	0.4	0.4	0.4
Turkic peoples of Volga region	4.9	3.6	3.5	3.6	3.7	3.7
Lithuanians, Latvians, Estonians	3.2	0.2	2.5	2.3	2.1	2.0
Georgians, Armenians, Abkhaztsi, Adzhartsi	2.1	2.5	2.5	2.8	3.0	3.1
Azerbaydzhani and other peoples of the Caucasus		2.2	2.2	2.4	3.0	3.4
Moslems of Central Asia	8.6	7.3	5.9	6.4	8.3	10.1
Others	0.2	0.4	0.2	0.3	0.4	0.4
TOTAL	100	100	100	100	100	100

SOURCES:

1. *Vsesoyuznaya perepis' naseleniya 17 dekabrya 1926* (All-Union Census of 17 December 1926), Moscow-Leningrad: TsSU, 1929, Vol. 17; 26–33.
2. *Itogi Vsesoyuznoy perepisi naseleniya 1959* (The Results of the All-Union Census 1959), Moscow: TsSU. Gosstatizdat, 1962; 184–89.
3. *Itogi Vsesoyuznoy perepisi naseleniya 1970* (The Results of the All-Union Census 1970), Moscow: Statistika, 1972; 9–60.
4. *Chislennost' i sostav naseleniya SSSR. Po dannym Vsesoyuznoy perepisi naseleniya 1979* (The Quantity and Composition of the Population of the USSR. Based on the data of the All-Union Census of 1979), Moscow: Finansy i Statistika, 1984; 283–322.
5. Kozlov, V.I. *Natsional'nosti v SSSR* (The Nationalities of the USSR), Moscow: Statistika, 1975; 34–35.

languages, e.g., the Ukrainian language, was forbidden. Russian was the language of administration, of the army, press, and judicial system.

Even after the introduction of the so-called constitution, the state Duma in its 1907 resolution declared: "The aim of all education for the *inorodtsy* living within the borders of our Fatherland should be their Russification and merger with the Russian people."[7] Co-opting of the elite was one of the most important elements used by the authorities in their assimilationist policy. The Ukrainian, Polish, Tatar, and Georgian elites were co-opted by their incorporation into the Russian nobility, invitation to serve at the Imperial Court, granting of lands, and inclusion into the bureaucracy.

The national policy of the czarist government was, on the whole, successful. Russians, while comprising only 44 percent of the country's population, in practical terms, experienced no difficulties because of the country's multinational makeup. In the most serious incidents (the insurrections in Poland, riots in the Caucasus and Turkestan), the army quickly restored order.

A small crack was opened in the doors of the "prison of peoples" by the February Revolution, and demagogically thrown wide open by the October Revolution. The Bolsheviks were supporters of a single, centralized state. "We want a state as large and as closely-knit as possible, with the greatest number of nationalities living side by side with the Great Russians . . ." Lenin wrote.[8] However, wishing to hold on to power, the Bolsheviks took steps in the opposite direction. On 2 November (15), 1917, the Sovnarkom issued the "Declaration of the Rights of the Peoples of Russia" in which it was proclaimed that all peoples of Russia are equal and sovereign and that the right of free self-determination, inclusive of the right of secession and formation of an independent state, is accorded to them. By this declaration all national and national-religious privileges and restrictions were abolished, and the freedom for the development of national minorities and ethnic groups had been instituted.[9] Lenin at that time wrote that: "No matter how many independent republics there are, we won't be frightened by it. For us it's not important where a state boundary lies, but that the union of workers of all nations be preserved for the struggle against the bourgeoisie of whatever nation."[10] However, in practical terms, any attempt at separation was treated as a counter-revolutionary act and efforts were made to suppress such attempts by armed force. In the majority of cases this was successful. "After the October Revolution, only the bourgeoisie of Poland and Finland, the religious-feudal orders of Tuva, and, in 1919, the Baltic bourgeois republics managed to achieve secession," writes a contemporary Soviet historian.[11] The verb "managed" is especially expressive here, as it indicates that it was not so easy for the minority peoples of the country to translate their right to self-determination into reality.

Curious are the subsequent changes in the number of Soviet republics, that is, of peoples whose theoretical right to secession and to an independent existence was recognized. At the beginning of 1922 there were nine republics (RSFSR, Ukraine, Belorussia, Georgia, Azerbaijan, Bukhara, Khorezm, and the Far East Republic). Later in that same year there were only four. The Stalin Constitution of 1936 recognized the right to form Soviet republics and to secede from the Soviet Union for peoples numbering more than one million and living in a territory bordered on a foreign country. At the end of Stalin's life there were sixteen such republics. Today fifteen republics possess the right to become independent. The scores of remaining nationalities of the USSR are treated as second or third-rate and are not supposed to gain independence under any circumstances.

The problem of sovereignty, however, even on a purely theoretical level, is gradually losing its substance. Lenin considered the "communality of economic life"[12] to be the main trait of a nation. And this determining factor has lost its national character in the USSR. Economic life has become united there throughout the whole country, a fact which was affirmed by the Basic Law of the land which proclaims that: "The economy of the USSR is a *single* national-economic complex embracing all elements of social production, distribution and exchange on the country's territory"[13] (author's italics). But even in the first post-revolutionary years national independence was almost a complete fiction. Lenin then wrote that, "We should know and remember that the entire legal and actual constitution of the Soviet republic is built on the basis of the Party's correcting, determining and building everything according to a single principle. . . ."[14] In the Soviet press one can hear voices declaring that the Soviet Union has ceased to be a federal and has, in fact, become a unitary state, that the time has come therefore to abolish the right of union republics to secede from the Union, all the more so since the population makeup of many territories has become mixed and no longer corresponds to their original national character.[15] While it is considered premature to own up to these proposals, in practical terms they have long been realized and the question of bringing the substance in correspondence with a formal arrangement is put off only out of reluctance to lose still another attractive ornamentation.

Whereas independent statehood for non-Russian nationalities of the USSR was always only a subject for mere political speculations, the development of national cultures and languages was treated seriously until the mid-thirties. Each national group, occupying any kind of compact territory, was granted the right to use its national language in the courts, schools, and so forth. In addition to the large national territorial units (republics and provinces), there existed national districts and even national village Soviets. In 1930, in the Ukraine alone, there were 28 national districts and more than a thousand national village Soviets (German, Polish, Jewish, Bulgarian, Greek, and others). Instruction in schools was conducted in Ukrainian (18,905 schools), Russian (1,001), Polish (656), Yiddish (470), and in other languages (939).[16] Today students are taught only in Ukrainian and Russian and the data on these matters have disappeared from statistical reference books. Some sporadic and incomplete information is, however, occasionally published. It is known, for example, that during the 1967–68 academic year in the Ukraine, 2,512,000 pupils of the 5th to the 10th grades, or only 60 percent of the whole number of pupils in those grades received instruction in Ukrainian.[17] Even taking into account the growth of the Russian population in the republic, one cannot help but notice the sharp decline in the use of the Ukrainian language by the native population. The situation in the country as a whole is much worse. In 1975, in the entire country, there were 225,700 school teachers of the Russian language teaching in Russian language schools, while their number in non-Russian language schools was only 114,500.[18] Since Russian children make up approximately 40 percent of all schoolchildren, one can conclude that about half of non-Russian children do not study in their native language.

In the first years of Soviet power one of the most important ideas with regard to national and cultural policy was the creation of written languages for each national group. As a rule, the Latin alphabet was used as the basis, and about 50 nationalities gained the opportunity to read and write. The national languages were obligatory in the Party and government apparatuses of the republics. But it was much more difficult to carry out these good intentions since the bureaucratic ranks preferred the more familiar Russian. Here is an example of what took place in 1933 at the Ministry of Education in Kazakhstan: "Eighty-seven people worked there, among them sixty-one were Kazakhs, who essentially did not know their native language. They could not write in it, only in Russian, typed the text out, and then gave it to a translator for translation into Kazakh or even into Arabic.* The Arabic text was then given to a typist to type in Latin script."[19]

By the second half of the thirties, attempts to advance national cultures were set aside. The Cyrillic alphabet in its Russian form became the graphic basis of most written languages. As a graphic basis, Arabic disappeared

---

*Before the Revolution the graphic basis for Kazakh was Arabic, then the Latin alphabet was introduced and, finally, at the end of the 1930s, the Cyrillic alphabet.

completely; the Latin alphabet was preserved only in the Baltic countries, which were incorporated into the USSR in 1940, that is, after these reforms were introduced. Only the Georgians and Armenians managed to save their ancient writing systems. The number of nationalities deserving their own written languages decreased noticeably and equality of languages in administration came to an end. All nationalities of the country were locked into a strict framework of a homogeneous mass culture with common norms and values, with a single dominating ideology, with an ever more uniform way of life. The centrally determined content of mass media, the films, and plays shown around the whole country, the uniform curricular programs in schools, colleges, and universities, the universality of production processes, a centrally administered hierarchy of academic institutes with degrees and titles accorded centrally by the VAK (the All-Union Highest Attestation Commission), and many other features, have formed a high degree of communality among the country's inhabitants. In the USSR, this communality is viewed as the hallmark of what is referred to as a socialist nation. Soviet scholars argue whether such a nation also possesses ethnic features. Evidently, it does. The common economic system, the similarity of daily life, the uniform pressure on people exercised by the authorities, and the single source of information about the outside world permits the formation of a common national consciousness, identical psychological characteristics, a standard uniform reaction to the outside world. Former national traditions and customs are relegated to the realm of memories, increasingly acquiring the character of mere festive rituals. A single Soviet culture is thus being formed by the representatives of the most diverse peoples. More and more national authors such as the Belorussian Vasil Bykov, the Kirghiz Chinghiz Aitmatov, and the Abkhazian Fazil Iskander, are now being co-opted into Russian literature and are counted among the most brilliant Russian writers.

It would not be entirely correct to call the contemporary consumer of Soviet culture Russian, but at the same time it cannot be refuted that the Russian language serves as the common basis for this new Soviet culture. Language has become the universal means of uniting the country. The talk of the equality of languages, of their influence on one another, of their convergence, is all in the past. Russian has become central and obligatory; in many ways it is the only relevant language. Here is how today's Soviet scholars formulate the problem: "First of all, languages, unlike distinct cultures, cannot converge. . . . Secondly, languages, unlike cultures, cannot merge. Thirdly, the task of equalizing the level of the functional and inner-structural development of all languages of the peoples of the USSR cannot be posed because of objective, socially conditioned laws. . . . Except for Russian, there is no language which could reflect the entire contents of the encyclopedia and all branches of Soviet society's material and spiritual culture. Moreover, except for Russian, no other language of the USSR could be effectively used for communication between different peoples within the country. Among the languages of the USSR, Russian is the only one to possess the status of a world language. Furthermore, Russian is the only language adequate for the exchange of cultural heritage between different nations in the USSR.

"This can all be explained by the action of objective, socially conditioned laws: by the relatively small number of speakers of each language; by the limited size of the territory of their use; by the limited sphere of their usage and so forth."[20]

Everything here is stated quite specifically and frankly, but among the reasons the main one—the political resolve of the Soviet leadership—has not been mentioned. Taken fifty years ago, this political resolve was continuously reaffirmed in a series of decrees, the latest of which was enacted by the CPSU's Central Committee and the Council of Ministers of the USSR in May 1983—"On additional measures for improving the study of the Russian language in schools and other educational institutions of the union republics." This decree asserts that a fluent command of the Russian language has become under the conditions of developed socialism an objective necessity and a requirement.[21]

Many Soviet authors justify the advance of Russian to a primary position in relation to all other languages, not simply for the reasons of practical necessity, but by virtue of the exceptional historic qualities of the Russian people.

"The language of intranational intercourse in the USSR is not a foreign, artificially introduced language (as it is the case in some former colonies that recently gained independence). It is the language of the most numerous, most advanced people of the country. The sons and daughters of the Great Russian people, by virtue of their devotion to socialism, have earned the deep respect of all the peoples of the country, and are by right marching in the vanguard of the friendly family of nations of the USSR. For these nations the Russian language is as near and dear as their own native language."[22] The Uzbek poet, R. Farkhadi, shared with his readers even more remarkable thoughts: the Russian language is necessary "for life, for glory, for truth . . . in it the shining genius of the Hellenes and the exalted spirit of the Romans have not grown dim and died."[23] According to such logic, less remarkable languages, the ones which are so much more distant from Greek and Latin and whose speakers do not march in the vanguard, naturally stop being an objective need and necessity—they rapidly exit from the societal stage into the realm of the family, occupying within it a place somewhere between the national costume and an ethnic culinary delight.

The majority of lesser nationalities (Izhors, Vepses, Saamis, Itelmans, Udegeyans, Shorts, and many others) have already lost their recently acquired written languages.[24] The primers in the Mansi languages have become the exclusive property of libraries. The Gagauzes (a people living in Moldavia and numbering about 170,000), 90 percent of whom consider their native language to be the language of their nationality, recently turned to the government with a request to stop instruction in the schools in their native language. The parents prefer their children to speak, read, and write in the language of the more advanced and respected people that is indeed suited "for life and for glory."[25]

The Buryats are taking similar steps. A people with an ancient and distinct culture, famed for its rich epical folklore, they exceed several nations of Asia and Europe by the size of their total population (350,000 in 1979). There are more than one thousand schools, dozens of technical colleges and four institutes of higher education in their republic and regions. The Buryats could study in their native language, however, only until the sixth grade before 1973, and now only until the fifth. And yet the majority forego even this opportunity, "sending their children to schools where Russian is the language of instruction."[26] Similarly, the Chuvashes, a people numbering over two million and not yielding in size of population to such boisterous nations as Lybia or Nicaragua, study in their native language for only four years.[27] In Soviet scholarship this phenomenon is usually defined either as the replacement of the native language, or as the acquisition of a second native language or simply as second language. (Table 1–2)

Today, however, even a complete transition to the Russian language does not mean in formal terms the Russification of the persons concerned. The Soviet passport system is such that it fixes the nationality in an almost immutable way—it can be changed only in instances of mixed marriages, since the children born of such marriages are entitled to choose at the age of 16 the nationality of one of their parents. Such a race-based approach fictitiously preserves nationalities that have long since lost their ethnic identity except for the appropriate notations in the passports. In such a way the authorities of the USSR have achieved two mutually opposed results simultaneously—the practical assimilation with the Russians of many nationalities and the preservation of the appearance that all these nationalities continue to exist. Let us look at how this is happening.

Table 1–2
Percent of Given Nationality Who Named Russian as a
First or Second Language Based on Census Materials

			First Language				Second Language	
	1929	1959	1970	1979	1979[1]	1979[2]	1979[3]	1979
Ukrainian	12.6	12.2	14.3	17.1	26.0	11.0	56.0	49.8
Belorussian	27.6	15.3	19.0	25.4	40.5	16.3	63.0	57.0
Moldavian	3.2	3.6	4.2	6.0	18.5	13.0	25.5	47.4

1. Cities
2. Those living within republic's borders
3. Those living outside republic's borders

SOURCES:

     1. *Vsesoyuznaya perepis' naseleniya 17 dekabrya 1926*; 26–33.
     2. *Itogi Vsesoyuznoy perepisi naseleniya 1959*, 184.
     3. *Itogi Vsesoyuznoy perepisi naseleniya 1970*; Vol. IV, 9; Vol. VII; 272–303.
     4. *Chislennost' i sostav naseleniya SSSR. Po dannym Vsesoyuznoy perepisi nase-leniya 1979*; 71, 284–322.
     5. Kozlov, V.I., *Natsional'nosti v SSSR*, Moscow: Statistika, 1980; 240–41.

NOTE: The minor changes during the period 1926–1959 can be explained, first by the na-tionalities' policy of the late 1920s and early 1930s, emphasizing national cultures and languages, and secondly, by the annexation in 1939 of territories which included millions of Ukrainians, Belorussians and Moldavians who had not yet been subjected to the process of Russification.

"The old quarrel of the Slavs among themselves"

The "brotherly" Slavic peoples, the Ukrainians, Belorussians, and the Moldavians who are closely related to the Ukrainians, and, although not Slavs, will also be examined here—serve as the most significant sources for increasing, by means of assimilation, the Russian population of the country. While not yielding to the Russians in the natural rate of their populations' growth, these nations, nevertheless, grow more slowly than the ethnic Russian population itself (Table 1–1). The closeness of their languages, the long-standing colonizing efforts of the Russians, resulting in the absorption by Russians of the cultural elites of these peoples, the high percentage of Russians living among the urban population of these republics, lead to their rapid Russification. Emigration of the members of these nations beyond the borders of their republics plays here an especially important role. Ukrainians and Belorussians, living in another national environment—in Siberia, Kazakhstan, or the Caucasus—as aliens, easily begin to identify themselves with the more numerous and, in some ways, more privileged Russians. In the southern region of the Omsk District at the beginning of the century, Ukrainians formed a majority, but by 1979 they constituted only 5–10 percent of the population. Research conducted in 1973 showed that, in villages where formerly the Ukrainian population was predominant, it now numbers only a small proportion of the inhabitants, at times only a few individuals. Only 18 percent of the Ukrainians questioned during this survey were fluent in their national language. Not one of them read political or scientific-technical literature in the Ukrainian language; only 27 percent read Ukrainian newspapers and magazines and 2.5 percent Ukrainian literary works. Among young people (under the age of 25) this proportion was even smaller (7 percent read newspapers and magazines, 1 percent literary works). Only culinary memories appear to persist for quite some time: 48 percent of those questioned knew four or more national dishes. In 1973, 86.4 percent of all Ukrainian marriages were mixed.[28] A similar picture can be observed throughout the country. Only 15–20 percent of Ukrainians and Belorussians living outside their own republics belong to single-nationality families. (Table 1–3)

The situation in the republics themselves is somewhat different. In 1979, 3 percent of Moldavians, 10.9 per cent of Ukrainians, and 16.5 percent of Belorussians living in their own republics, named Russian as their native language.[29] It is true, however, that the numbers of members of these nationalities whose native language is Russian are rapidly growing. In 1970, the respective percentages were 2.0, 8.6 and 9.8.[30] The major factor contributing to the loss of the national language is mixed marriages, the share of which has noticeably grown in each of these republics. (Table 1–3) That the family plays a decisive role in determining the first language can be witnessed in the distribution of the loss of the national language throughout various age groups. According to the 1970 census, in the Ukraine 10.8 percent of Ukrainian children in the 0–10 age group, 10 percent of the 11–15 age group, 10.3 percent of the 16–19 age group, 10.1 percent of the 20–29 age group, 8.9 percent of the 30–39 age group, used Russian as their first language. That percentage gradually decreases in the following age groups.[31] These figures illustrate that schooling and occupational activity have little influence on the choice of a first language. The case is completely different for a second language. In the age group under 10 years, 7.9 percent; in the age group 11–15, 43 percent; in the age group 16–19, 67 percent; and in the age group 20–29, 63 percent named Russian as their second language.[32] A similar picture is observed in Belorussia.

In Moldavia the loss of the national language is much weaker; there are also fewer mixed marriages here. However, specialist investigations, conducted in the early 1970s, showed that the transition to Russian there, too,

Table 1–3
Population Living in Single Nationality Families
(in thousands)

| Nationality | Year | Within Territory of USSR | | Within Territory of Republic | | Percent Living in Single Nationality Families | | |
		Total	Single Nationality Families	Total	Single Nationality Families	in USSR	Within Republic	Outside Republic
Russians	1970	129,015	99,812	107,747	90,027	77.4	83.6	46.0
Russians	1979	137,397	105,343	113,521	91,508	76.7	80.6	57.9
Ukrainians	1970	40,753	29,157	35,284	27,392	71.5	77.6	32.3
Ukrainians	1979	42,347	28,902	36,489	27,844	68.3	76.3	18.1
Belorussians	1970	9,051	6,224	7,290	5,860	68.8	80.4	20.7
Belorussians	1979	9,463	6,055	7,568	5,778	64.0	76.3	14.6
Moldavians	1970	2,698	2,090	2,304	1,917	77.5	83.2	43.2
Moldavians	1979	2,968	2,194	2.526	1,992	73.9	78.9	49.8

SOURCES: See Table 1–2.

NOTE: The "Total" column includes family members living separately and single members. In 1970 they made up approximately 12.5 percent of the total population. In order to calculate the percentage of mixed marriages, it was necessary to take this figure into account.

is already quite widespread, especially in the cities. In the urban single-nationality families, for example, Moldavian women spoke both Russian and Moldavian at home in 30 percent of the cases, while at work Russian was used by 70 percent of them. For men, the transition to Russian takes place even more rapidly. Among the Moldavian village population, unskilled laborers use Russian least (9 percent); among supervisors and workers with middle to high qualifications, the use of Russian already amounts to 20–27 percent and among office workers, to 44 percent.[33]

It is important to note that the Russian population of these republics almost never turns to the use of the language of the indigenous population. In the Ukraine and in Belorussia, more than two-thirds of the Russian inhabitants named the national language neither as their first nor the second one. In Moldavia, between 1970 and 1979, the percentage of Russians who knew Moldavian declined from 13.9 to 11.2 percent.[34]

A rapid transition to the use of the Russian language by the indigenous population thus takes place in the Ukraine, Belorussia, and Moldavia. This transition embraces, in the first place, city dwellers, youth, persons engaged in skilled labour. National traditions are preserved comparatively firmly only in single-nationality families, especially in the countryside: approximately 15 million Ukrainians, 3 million Belorussians, and 1.5 million Moldavians still predominantly use their native languages. The remaining population groups, especially those living outside the national republics, quickly lose their language and with it their national-cultural identity.

Chud' Chanced, While Meri Measured

The Finnic peoples are undoubtedly the most ancient inhabitants of the northern parts of the country.* They have been neighbors of the Slavs for centuries, mingling with them, adopting their customs, life-style and faith. In the Volga region Orthodoxy and Islam fought stubbornly for the souls of the Mordvins and the Meris. Their struggle continued with variable success until the religious question under the Soviet regime lost its significance. In the short post-revolutionary period of the 1920s and 1930s, each Finnic people gained a written language, which in most cases was later put out of use. Even the written languages of the larger national groups (Erzyas, Mokshas, Komis, Karelians, Votyaks) are in a quite deplorable situation. Instruction in the general curriculum is not continued beyond the third grade in any of these languages, and the Udmurtian and Mordvinian languages are not present as special subjects in the last years of the secondary school programs.[35]

The centuries-old process of Russification of these peoples is rapidly gaining momentum. In 1926, only 3.9 percent of them named Russian as their native language; even among the Vepsians and Izhors only four thousand (8 percent) had made a transition to Russian. But by 1959, Russian had become the native language of 16 percent of the Finnic peoples, and by 1979 of 25 percent. According to the census of 1979, 11 percent of them did not know Russian and 19 percent did not know their national language at all. Ten years before, the corresponding figures were 17 and 13 percent.[36] It is evident that if the native languages were used as the factor determining ethnicity (as this is the case in other countries), the numbers of these peoples would be cut by one-fourth. They are, however, fictitiously maintained by the passport system which deprives individuals of the free manifestation of their national consciousness. Therefore, considering themselves Russians both by culture and language, the Komis and Maris have

---

*For a more detailed treatment of these peoples see V. Uibopuu's article in this volume.

no possibility of changing the formal description of their nationality except by means of mixed marriages. The frequency of such marriages is growing and the children born of them in a great majority of cases choose Russian nationality. In practical terms, already today 70–80 percent of all Finnic peoples are Russians by their language, culture, religion, and way of life.

The peoples of the Paleasiatic and Turkic languages groups, as well as the ancient inhabitants of Siberia and the Far East, find themselves in a similar position. In the course of the seventeenth to nineteenth centuries these peoples not only avoided assimilation, but, on the contrary, successfully assimilated the few Russian settlers. Here, for example, is how the matter stood in the Baikal region according to the testimony of eyewitnesses: "Few Buryats, however, can read, write or even speak Russian, perhaps because Russians in their neighbourhood, both young and old, all speak Buryat extremely well. . . . Native Russians, who live here, (Aginsk District—S.M.) never spoke Russian, only Buryat. This was before the revolution. . . . After the revolution people here began to speak Russian . . ."[37]

The mass colonization of the twentieth century changed the situation completely. Russians who arrived in the East during the Soviet period have not bothered to learn about what kinds of economic activity would suit the territories in question best. They came bringing with them their own plans for radical change and found the local traditions, as well as the native peoples themselves, cumbersome and therefore expendable. The apotheosis of such a resolute policy was the expulsion of great numbers of local inhabitants in the Far East (Koreans and Chinese) to Central Asia or abroad. When the forest is cut, the chips fly. In such a way, the native inhabitants of Sakhalin, the Ainis, found themselves beyond the country's borders. Many dozens of lesser peoples of the North were driven to the edge of extinction. Their material culture has been transferred to ethnographic museums, and specialists in Moscow and Leningrad know their national languages better than the Udegeyans or the Itelmans living in their homelands themselves. Their numbers are, however, preserved since the children of mixed marriages prefer to choose the nationality of the minority parent.[38] This they do because it provides them with certain material and social advantages: financial assistance, easier release from service in the army, preferential admission to institutes of higher education.

As Soviet researchers assert, Russian becomes a native language for these peoples simultaneously with their national languages. Yu. Rytkheu writes, for example, that, "Today a Chukcha child begins to speak in the family simultaneously in two languages. Russian for him is not even a second language but one that he learns on an equal footing with the Chukchan language."[39] The most numerous peoples of Siberia—the Buryats,

Yakuts, Altais—have not yet lost their national languages completely, but the process of their assimilation is accelerating. The intelligentsia, the urban population, the migrants to other regions and the members of the skilled labor force are gradually abandoning their national languages. Here is how Soviet scholars describe the function of the Buryat language before and after the Revolution. Before the Revolution Buryat was "the language of religious-Buddhist writings; of instruction in the monasteries; of translations and, also, of some original works on philosophy, logic, astronomy, medicine, poetry, geography, linguistics; of dictionaries (primarily in the nineteenth century); of epics, historic-literary monuments; of judicial documents; of communication within the family and with fellow villagers; of folklore, and of social-political communication in the village." Today Buryat is the language of "literature, translations of literary works from various languages; of periodicals; the language of instructional literature in schools until the fifth grade and of a special subject in higher grades; the language of the theater and the arts; of propaganda; of folklore and radio; of communication in the family and in a single-language environment; of personal correspondence."[40] One will note the absence of works about philosophy or astronomy (to say nothing of works on, and instruction in, Buddhist religion) in contemporary Buryat; one will not even come across textbooks on these subjects. It is natural that, under such conditions, Buryat and the other languages of the relatively lesser peoples of the USSR are destined to degradation.

A Loan's Well That's Paid Well

Western colonists and inhabitants of Europe who became Russia's subjects with the expansion of the country's borders to the West played an enormous role in the life of Russia. Germans and Poles set the tone for a long time in Russia's administrative system, in her sciences, arts, the army, and the whole socio-political and economic life. At the turn of the twentieth century Jews also began to take an active part in Russia's life, and their influence grew to tremendous proportions during the years of the Revolution and the first post-revolutionary decade. At present, however, the civilizing role of these peoples has come to an end. In practical terms, Germans have been completely removed from participation in cultural and political life, and since their resettlement in the East during the war, access to higher education for them has been made more difficult. Jews are being pushed aside in a similar fashion. Germans, Jews, Poles, and other European nationalities who do not possess their own national territorial units in the USSR rapidly lose their distinctiveness, e.g., the language, and ultimately

Table 1–4
Percent of Population Using Language of Their Nationality as Their Native Language

Nationality	1926		1959				1970				1979			
	T¹	C²	T	C	WR³	OR⁴	T	C	WR	OT	T	C	WR	OR
Russians	99.7	99.7	99.8	99.8	100	99.3	99.8	99.9	100	99.2	99.9	99.4	100	99.9
Ukrainians	87.1	64.9	87.7	77.2	93.5	51.2	85.7	75.9	91.4	48.4	82.8	73.7	89.1	43.8
Belorussians	71.8	37.5	84.2	63.5	93.2	41.9	80.6	63.4	90.1	40.9	74.2	59.1	83.5	36.8
Lithuanians	46.9	39.3	97.8	96.6	99.2	80.3	97.9	97.0	99.5	71.8	97.9	97.4	97.9	63.9
Latvians	78.3	66.1	95.1	93.1	98.4	53.2	95.2	93.2	98.1	51.1	95.0	93.3	97.8	55.3
Estonians	88.4	68.3	95.2	93.1	99.3	56.6	96.5	93.8	99.2	53.5	95.3	93.4	99.0	33.3
Moldavians	92.3	74.2	95.2	78.4	98.2	77.7	95.0	82.5	97.7	79.1	93.2	81.3	96.5	74.3
Georgians	96.5	97.2	98.6	96.8	99.5	73.4	98.4	97.1	99.4	71.5	98.3	96.9	99.4	67.3
Armenians	92.4	88.0	89.9	84.4	99.2	78.1	91.4	87.8	99.8	78.0	90.7	87.6	99.4	73.9
Azerbaydzhani	93.8	98.4	97.6	96.4	98.1	95.1	98.2	96.7	98.9	95.8	97.9	96.2	98.7	92.7
Kazakhs	99.6	98.4	98.4	96.7	99.2	95.6	98.0	95.8	98.9	95.0	97.5	97.1	98.6	92.8
Uzbeks	99.1	99.2	98.4	96.7	98.6	97.4	98.6	96.9	98.9	97.4	98.5	96.1	98.8	96.9
Turkmens	97.3	98.8	98.9	97.3	99.5	92.0	98.9	97.2	99.3	93.5	98.7	97.0	99.2	90.4
Tadzhiks	98.3	99.3	98.1	96.4	99.3	94.6	98.5	96.7	99.4	95.6	97.8	95.9	99.3	92.8
Kirghiz	99.0	96.1	98.7	97.4	99.7	92.3	98.8	97.6	99.7	91.6	97.9	97.3	99.6	84.8
Karakalpaks	87.5	99.3	95.0	96.8	99.1	56.4	96.6	97.6	99.5	62.2	95.9	97.3	98.7	59.1
Karels	95.5	70.3	71.3	51.7	80.9	61.3	63.0	50.4	71.7	51.0	55.6	43.4	61.7	46.9
Mordva	94.0	64.2	78.1	52.2	97.3	70.9	77.8	56.6	96.2	72.6	72.6	55.1	94.3	63.9
Mariitsi	99.3	87.4	95.1	75.8	97.8	91.6	91.2	73.2	95.8	86.5	86.7	72.3	83.7	79.9
Udmurts	98.9	85.6	89.1	69.7	93.2	75.9	82.6	64.3	87.7	71.4	76.5	60.6	82.3	64.4
Chuvash	98.7	82.2	90.8	71.2	97.5	83.2	86.9	68.0	94.5	79.1	81.7	64.7	89.8	73.4
Tartars	98.9	96.2	92.0	87.5	98.9	89.3	89.2	83.3	98.5	85.9	85.9	81.0	97.7	81.8
Bashkirs	53.8	72.8	61.9	73.3	57.6	75.1	66.2	73.2	63.2	73.8	67.0	72.8	64.4	72.6
Kalmyks	99.3	92.2	91.0	83.8	98.2	79.6	79.6	91.7	90.0	97.3	76.2	91.3	90.1	62.3
Peoples of Dagestan	99.3	97.0	96.2	90.3	98.6	87.9	96.5	91.6	98.7	88.9	95.9	—	98.6	86.8
Buryats	98.1	89.5	94.9	81.5	97.3	84.9	92.6	79.6	95.0	84.4	90.2	78.8	93.1	86.0
Yakuts	99.7	96.8	97.5	90.7	98.2	82.8	96.2	87.0	97.1	72.4	95.4	86.1	96.4	72.3
Jews	71.9	67.4	21.5	21.0	—	—	17.7	17.4	—	—	14.2	12.3	—	—
Germans	94.9	77.4	75.0	66.3	—	—	66.8	58.3	—	—	57.0	48.5	—	—
Poles	42.9	49.7	45.2	38.6	—	—	32.5	32.3	—	—	29.1	27.8	—	—

1. T – Total Population   2. C – City Population   3. WR – Within Republic
4.   OR – Outside Republic

SOURCE: Kozlov, V.I., *Natsional'nosti SSSR*, Moscow: Statistika, 1982; 240–41.

assimilate (Table 1–4). Only the passport system prevents these peoples from dissolving completely into the surrounding population. Practically all children from mixed marriages of these peoples abandon their respective national group, and the proportion of mixed marriages among them is very large.

The emigration of Jews and Germans has shown how far this process has gone; abroad, both preserve their Russian way of life, language, culture, and consciousness. While we have spoken about the rates of assimilation with regard to other national groups, in these cases we can confidently speak about the process of assimilation nearing completion.

Civilization's Rearguard Battles

Stating that a number of the oppressed peoples of the Russian Empire were more developed than the Great Russians, Lenin probably had in mind principally the nations of the Baltic and the Caucasus. In any case, in 1936 only the Georgians and Armenians (and later the Latvians, Lithuanians and Estonians) avoided conversion to the Russian Cyrillic alphabet. To the present day, these peoples, in their own territories, are successfully coping with the onslaught of Russian. Even among city dwellers, not less than 93–97 percent of the population preserve their national language.

Russians living in Armenia, Georgia, and Lithuania have appreciably bettered their knowledge of the local languages, listing them as their second, conversational languages in increasing numbers. The study of Russian as a second language by the local population is similarly expanding—more than half of Latvians and Lithuanians and 40 percent of Armenians know Russian (the latter figure, however, also is significantly inflated by inclusion into it of Armenians living outside their national republic). In Georgia and Estonia, 28 percent of the indigenous population named Russian as a first or second language. Between 1970 and 1979, however, the number of those who knew Russian increased in Georgia by 6 percent but decreased in Estonia by 5 percent. At the same time the number of Russians living in Estonia and knowing Estonian decreased from 14.1 percent to 12.9 percent. It appears that intranational communication in this republic is becoming increasingly more difficult. These figures indicate the strengthening in Estonia of national consciousness, which limits the encroachment of an outside language on the national culture. The situation in Estonia in this respect is especially favorable because of the influence of Finland, which is felt particularly strongly thanks to television broadcasts from Helsinki which can be received in Tallin.

Data concerning the knowledge of the Russian language by age groups in these republics shows that learning of Russian starts at school and expands and improves at the workplaces. In 1970, among the Georgians and Armenians in the 30–39 age group, 31 percent and 40 percent respectively knew Russian. The figures for Estonians, Lithuanians, and Latvians were 47 percent, 57 percent, and 69 percent respectively. These figures show that the working population of the above republics know Russian fairly well. However, among people in the older age brackets, and also children under 10, those who know only the national language prevail.[41]

National identity plays a large role in the choice of nationality by the children of mixed marriages. In the capitals of the Baltic republics between 1963 and 1968 children aged 16, from nationally mixed families, comprised 20 percent in Vilnius, 18 percent in Riga, and 11.3 percent in Tallin. More than half of these children, when receiving their passports, chose the nationalities of these republics. In the case of Estonia, 62 percent of young people became Estonians and only 38 percent Russians. These choices were not accidental as the children tended to choose the nationality of their fathers.[42] Hence, despite the growth of the Russian population and the high number of mixed marriages (35 percent in Latvia),[43] the process of assimilation in the Baltic republics is proceeding quite slowly.

"East is East and West is West"

The "Moslem threat," which, as previously noted, provokes the most heated debates, according to the students of this problem, consists in the rapid increase of the Turkic peoples of the USSR, in the devotion of these peoples to their national languages and religion, and in the high levels of their concentration in the southern regions of the country where the proportion of Russians is gradually declining.[44] (Tables 1–1 and 1–4). These factors deserve more detailed examination.

As a result of the general aging of the population and of other demographic processes, the growth rate of the Turkic-language nationalities is already in decline. The growth of these people will not cease but it will most likely continue to decrease. Toward the end of the century, the birthrate of the Uzbeks, the most populous people of Central Asia, will apparently be somewhat less than 30 per thousand, and as their mortality will reach 12 per thousand, their net increase should be around 18 per thousand. The number of Uzbeks at that time will thus be close to 20 million, while the three other major Turkic-speaking nations of Central Asia will number about 12 million. In the past decade the Kazakhs birthrate has been lowered to the extent that their population by the end of the century will not exceed 9 million people. The Turkic peoples of the Caucasus will reach approximately 12 million and those of the Volga region approximately 10 million. The general total, without considering assimilation, will thus be 60–65 million (20–22 per cent of the country's entire population). In one hundred years, the proportion of Turkic peoples in the country has nearly doubled (Table 1–1). However, if one discounts the seceded Poles, and takes into consideration the Bukhara and Khiva which were incorporated into the Russian Empire later, then it turns out that the proportion of Turkic peoples in pre-revolutionary Russia was about 18 percent of the population. And then they were settled much more compactly and their assimilation was appreciably less. The current colonization of the northern Caucasus, Kazakhstan and Kirghizia by Russian and Ukrainian settlers has advanced considerably. Before our eyes the assimilation of the Turkic population of the Volga region is coming to completion. Even at the turn of the century, the majority of peoples of this region were under strong Tartar influence. The Tartar language was used for intranational contacts, and Tartar merchants and mullahs successfully spread Islam. Now, the three main Turkic peoples of the Volga region—the Tartars, the Chuvashes and the Bashkirs—are being increasingly Russified. More than 15 percent of Tartars and Chuvashes consider Russian their native language, and two-thirds of Tartars, Bashkirs and Chuvashes use Russian as their second language.[45] The active groups of the population (working-age men, city dwellers, scientists and administrators) all know Russian and even make a complete transition to it; one-half of the Tartar population of Kazan speak Russian even in their homes.[46] In other parts of the country, Tartars and other peoples of the Volga region serve as bearers of Russian culture and of the Russian language. Mixed marriages are becoming more and more frequent, especially in the cities. In Kazan, for instance, 10–20 percent of all marriages in the 1960s were Russian-Tartar. Children born of marriages between Russians and Tartars, Bashkirs or Chuvashes choose, as a rule, the Russian nationality. In Cheboksary (Chuvashian ASSR), only 2.2 percent of young people born from Chuvash-Russian marriages consider themselves to be Chuvashes.[47]

The realm of usage of the national languages of the Turkic peoples of the Volga region is ever narrowing. As a rule, they are used only in rural areas, in the home, and only sometimes at the workplace. In the Tartar ASSR more than one-half of the rural intelligentsia speak Russian.[48] Rural Chuvashes, Tartars and even Bashkirs are overtaking rural Ukrainians and Belorussians in their knowledge of Russian (Table 1–4). The peoples of the northern Caucasus are in a similar situation—they are rapidly mastering the Russian language and absorbing Russian culture.[49]

The Kazakhs and Kirghizes are following in the footsteps of the peoples of the Volga region and northern Caucasus. They no longer constitute a majority in their respective national territories. The predominance of the Russian language is in those territories a fact of life, and many Central Asian Moslem people themselves prefer Russian to their national languages

(Table 1–5). Russians, Ukrainians and even Tartars living in these territories categorically refuse to use the local languages (only 1–1.5 percent know them), which testifies to their narrowing usage.

The situation in the territories of the other four Moslem union republics—Azerbaijan, Uzbekistan, Tadzhikistan and Turkmenistan—is, however, entirely different. Here the indigenous population consistently strengthens its predominant position, a process which is accompanied also by a wider spread of the national languages (Table 1–5). The proportion of Russians in the general population of these territories is rapidly decreasing, which points to demographic decolonization.[50] However, in reality, the situation is not that serious. Some curtailment of the size of the Russian population is more than compensated for by the wide distribution of the Russian language and contemporary culture. The uniform educational system imposed by the authorities; standard patterns of material and spiritual consumption; the system of administration; science; compulsory military service; and urbanization itself—push aside the traditional Moslem way of life, culture, and languages. Almost one half of the Uzbeks in the 20–24 age bracket preferred contemporary music to traditional. Eighty percent of the 60–year-old age group preferred the latter.[51] According to research conducted during 1971–1976, 42 percent of Uzbek city dwellers and 30 percent of Uzbek villagers learn Russian in school. A further 8–11 percent learn Russian in the army. Four percent of city dwellers learned Russian even at home, before school, and 7 percent in communication with friends.[52] Only slightly more than one-third of the Uzbek population speaks exclusively in their native language at the workplace.[53] Russians, Ukrainians, Germans, and Koreans living in Uzbekistan get by practically without any knowledge of the Uzbek language (Table 1–5). As a result, Russian offers serious competition to the national language. In 1979, 60 percent of Uzbekistan's population knew Russian and 72 percent knew Uzbek (Table 1–5). The number of those who know Russian is rapidly increasing. Investigations show that the national languages are successfully preserved only in the least-educated milieu, among collective farmers and other people engaged in unskilled manual labor. Schoolchildren, especially those enrolled in Russian language schools, begin to use Russian at work, in their social life and even at home. These children prefer Russian for reading and even more so for television and film viewing.[54]

The preservation of instruction in the national languages in schools, however, as well as the compactness of rural population, decrease the rate at which Russian is spreading. It is evident, on the other hand, that the process of transition to the Russian language will eventually outstrip the rate of the population's growth, and toward the end of the century,

Table 1-5
Population Size and Language Fluency from 1979 Census

	KAZAKHSTAN			UZBEKISTAN			KIRGHIZIA			TURKMENISTAN			TADZHIKISTAN			AZERBAYDZHAN		
		Language (%)			Language (%)			Language (%)			Language (%)			Language (%)			Language (%)	
	Pop.[1]	Russ.	Kaz.	Pop.	Russ.	Uzb.	Pop.	Russ.	Kirg.	Pop.	Russ.	Turk.	Pop.	Russ.	Tad.	Pop.	Russ.	Azer.
Total Population	14864	79.5	36.8	15389	60.1	71.7	3523	54.9	49.1	2765	38.5	70.6	3806	38.0	62.3	6026	38.5	81.1
Russians	5991	100	0.8	1666	100	5.9	912	100	1.1	349	100	1.0	395	100	2.7	475	100	9.2
Ukrainians, Belorussians, Germans, Jews, Tartars, Koreans, Armenians	2385	83.8	0.8	1026	89.5	5.6	282	90.4	1.4	104	89.4	3.1	169	91.2	5.3	568	53.2	8.3
Kazakhs	5289	52.0	98.6	620	49.8	9.4	27	70.4	18.5	80	31.2	16.2	—	—	—			
Uzbeks	263	42.6	4.3	10569	57.0	98.8	426	32.4	4.0	234	23.5	13.3	873	22.3	15.1			
Tadzhiks	—	—	—	595	35.7	33.8	23	23.8	4.3	—	—	—	2237	28.3	99.2	—	—	—
Kirghiz	—	—	—	142	37.3	40.8	1678	28.8	99.6	—	—	—	48	14.6	12.5	—	—	—
Turkmens	—	—	—	92	38.0	22.8	—	—	—	1892	24.9	99.2	14	30.7	2.0	—	—	—
Azerbaydzhani	73	68.5	6.9	60	56.7	26.7	—	—	—	24	85.1	4.5	—	—	—	4709	28.9	98.1
Karakalpaks, Dungans, Uigurs, peoples of Dagestan	170	54.1	10.1	298	45.3	4.4	57	63.2	5.2	30	34.5	34.3	—	—	—	220	28.6	56.2

1. (in thousands)

SOURCE: *Chislennost' i sostav naseleniya SSSR. Po dannym Vsesoyuznoy perepisi 1979 goda*, Moscow: Finansy i Statistika, 1984; 110–35.

60–70 percent of the indigenous population of the Moslem republics will know Russian.

Demographic Policy

What has been the demographic policy of the Soviet government during these years? In the postrevolutionary period it was quite radical—legalization of abortion and easing of divorce laws. Later abortions were prohibited and assistance to mothers with many children introduced. During the post-Stalin period, abortion was again legalized and at the same time some measures were undertaken to ease the conditions for mothers of newborn children. These included an increase in the length of pregnancy leave, widening of the system of women's health centers and nurseries, and the introduction of one-year maternity leaves, which have now been increased to one and a half years.

From time to time calls are heard from Soviet demographers for the execution of differential demographic policies in the European and Moslem regions of the country. For the time being, however, the government has not undertaken any such measures. The printing of wedding announcements in newspapers, which was recently permitted in Latvia, or similar moves, are in this respect of very little significance. Although the government exerts very little influence on changing the structure and distribution of the country's birthrate, the general tendency of social development toward stabilization of the birthrate is, in the government's eyes, a favorable phenomenon.

A more universal problem of social rather than demographic nature is being energetically addressed by the Soviet leadership. This problem concerns the formation of a unified Soviet nation that should be based not on common ethnographic roots, but on the communality of language, culture, way of life, and outlook. Numerous measures are undertaken on a massive scale to this end, and expenses are not being spared. One must acknowledge that these actions are producing an appreciable and accelerating effect. Russian has become the only language of intranational communication, the only language of science, administration, medicine, and many other spheres of life. The Russian language bears the fundamental weight of ideological propaganda, mass culture, and contemporary technology. The Soviet government will probably never succeed in completely eliminating the country's multinational character, but its efforts in this direction certainly contribute to the population's increasing homogeneity.

Conclusion

The ever-increasing Russianization of the USSR is an ongoing and inexorable process. Among the peoples of the USSR, the Russians are the only ones who are accorded the official label of a "great people" and who are treated as the "first among equals," and the "older brother." The Russians "are like the sun, the interaction with which is decisive for the movement of the Earth and for its entire fate, and yet for the sun that interaction has no such great meaning," wrote with true Eastern servility and obvious astronomic expertise, the famous Armenian astronomer, Academician Ambartsumian.[55]

Some of the lesser peoples will indeed soon exit from history's stage, having left their remaining representatives only with their ancient names and a few ethnographic and culinary artifacts. The national cultures of these peoples will retreat to the countryside, where for some time their languages will apparently be preserved. This is, most likely, to be the fate of the Ukrainians, Belorussians, Tartars, and other peoples of the Volga region.

The peoples of the Baltic and Caucasus will, however, survive, although they will pay no small price in captives by, and deserters to, the Russians. The inhabitants of Central Asia, who have come into the sphere of Russian mastery relatively recently and who possess enormous masses of conservative rural population, are nationally threatened least, although even they are making a transition to the Russian language.

Toward the end of the century the proportion of Russians by a passport count will be not less than one-half, but Russians by language will grow to about two-thirds of the population. The adherents of racial purity will, no doubt, justifiably note that from the viewpoint of blood, these Russian speakers will not be true Russians. Here, as the saying goes, there is nothing one can do. And in some sense, it is too late to do anything in this respect, anyway. The anthropological Russian type of today hardly exemplifies genetic purity. Studies have shown that Russians of the Volga region differ appreciably from Russians of Novgorod. Moreover, both the former and the latter, by most indicators, are more similar to their immediate Finnic and Turkic neighbors than they are to one another.[56] However, this does not prevent the natives of Gorki and Pskov, each speaking a distinctive dialect, from considering themselves equally Russian.

The process of Russification, which I have attempted to sketch, was described surprisingly accurately by Alexander Herzen:

Russia is rising around like water, surrounding tribes from all sides, covering them with the uniform ice of autocracy, and, underneath, turning Kalmyks into soldiers, worshippers of the Dalai Lama into defenders of Orthodoxy, and Germans into desperate Russian patriots.

Notes

1. D.I. Mendeleev, *K poznaniyu Rossii*, (To the Knowing of Russia) (Petersburg: A.S. Suvorin, 1906), 45.
2. L.I. Brezhnev, *Sochineniya*, (Moscow: Gospolitizdat, 1976), 5, 432.
3. A. Bennigsen, *Musul'mane v SSSR*, (Muslims in the USSR), (Paris: YMCA Press, 1983).
4. Ya. E. Volodarsky, *Naselenie Rossii v kontse XVII—nachale XVIII veka*, (The Population of Russia in the End of the XVIIth–Beginning of the XVIIIth Century), (Moscow: Nauka, 1977), 192–93.
5. J.S. Spengler & O.D. Duncan, eds., *Demographic Analysis*, (Glencoe, Ill.: The Free Press, 1956), 13–14; *Slownik Historii Polski*, (Dictionary of Polish History), (Warsaw, 1973), 618–21.
6. *Chislennost' i sostav naseleniya SSSR. Po dannym Vsesoyuznoy perepisi 1979 goda*, (The Quantity and Composition of the Population of the USSR. Based on the data of the All-Union Census of 1979), (Moscow: Finansy i Statistika, 1984), 7–10.
7. A.M. Lar'kov, *Natsii i natsional'nye otnosheniya razvitogo sotsialisticheskogo obshchestva*, (Nations and National Relations of a Developed Socialist Society), (Moscow: Moscow University Press, 1980), 113.
8. V.I. Lenin, *Polnoe sobranie sochineniy (PSS)*, (Collected Works) (Moscow: Gospolitizdat, 1962), 35, 11.
9. *Dekrety Sovetskoy vlasti*, (Decrees of the Soviet Government), 1, (Moscow, 1957), 40.
10. Lenin, *Polnoe*, 115.
11. M.I. Kulichenko, *Natsional'nye otnosheniya v SSSR i tendentsiya ikh razvitiya*, (National Relations in the USSR and the Tendencies of Their Development), (Moscow: Mysl', 1972), 172.
12. V.I. Lenin, *PSS*, 24 (1961), 148.
13. Art. 16 of the Constitution of the USSR (Quoted from Sharlet, R., *The New Soviet Constitution of 1977. Analysis and Text*, [Brunswick, Ohio: King's Court Communications, 1978], 82).
14. V.I. Lenin, *PSS*, 41 (1965), 403.
15. See, for example: Semyonov, P.G., "Programma KPSS o razvitii sovetskikh natsional'no-gosudarstvennykh otnosheniy," (The Program of the CPSU on the Development of Soviet National-State Relations), in *Sovetskoe gosudarstvo i pravo*, (Soviet State and Law), 1961, 12, 25. A number of other authors holding similar views are quoted in Kulichenko, *Natsional'nye*; 417–18.
16. Lar'kov, *Natsii*, 60; Kulichenko, *Natsional'nye*, 348.
17. Based on: *Mezhnatsional'nye svyazi i vzaimodeystvie kul'tur narodov SSSR*,

(Intranational Links and Mutual Influence of Cultures of the Peoples of the USSR), (Tallin: Eesti Raamat, 1978), 99; *Naselenie SSSR 1973*, (Population of the USSR 1973), (Moscow: Statistika, 1975), 71; *Narodnoe obrazovanie, nauka i kul'tura v SSSR*. *Statisticheski sbornik*, (People's Education, Science and Culture in the USSR. Statistical Data), (Moscow: Statistika, 1976), 35.

18. *Narodnoe obrazovanie, nauka i kul'tura v SSSR*, III.
19. S. Kenzhebaev, *Sovety v bor'be za postroenie sotsializma*, (The Soviets in the Struggle for the Construction of Socialism), (Alma-Ata: "Kazakhstan", 1969); 272–73.
20. *Mezhnatsional'nye svyazi i vzaimodeystvie kul'tur narodov SSSR*; 100–101.
21. Postanovlenie SNK i TsK VKP/b/ v marte 1938, "Ob obyazatel'no izuchenii russkogo yazyka v shkolakh natsional'nykh respublik i oblastey," was the first in this series of decrees. For the latest ("O dopolnitel'nykh merakh . . ."), (On Additional Measures . . .), see *Pravda*, 27 May 1983.
22. A.T. Baziev & M.I. Isaev, *Yazyk i natsiya*, (The Language and Nation), (Moscow: Nauka, 1963), 214.
23. Quoted from Kulichenko, *Natsional'nye*, 496.
24. See, Baziev & Isaev, *Yazyk*, 120–24.
25. See *Problemy mira i sotsializma*, (The Problems of Peace and Socialism), No. 8, (1972), 40.
26. *Razvitie natsional'no-russkogo dvuyazychiya*, (The Development of Russian-National Bilingualism), (Moscow: Nauka, 1976), 85–94.
27. Kulichenko, *Natsional'nye*, 494.
28. Kalashnikov, A.D., Pervykh, S.Yu., Provatorova, O.M., "Nekotorye napravleniya sovremennykh protsessov sredi ukraintsev yuga Zapadnoy Sibiri," (Some Directions of the Contemporary Processes Among the Ukrainians of the South of Western Siberia), in *Sovremennye etnicheskie protsessy u narodov Zapadnoy i Yuzhnoy Sibiri*, (Sbornik), (Contemporary Ethnic Processes Among the Peoples of Western and Southern Siberia/Collection/), (Tomsk: Tomsk University Press, 1981), 74–85.
29. *Chislennost' i sostav naseleniya SSSR*; 102–29.
30. *Itogi Vsesoyuznoy perepisi naseleniya 1970 goda*, (The Result of the All-Union Censue 1970), 4, (Moscow: Statistika, 1973), 152–310.
31. ———, 377.
32. Ibid.
33. See M.N. Guboglo, *Sovremennye etnoyazykovye protsessy v SSSR*, (Contemporary Ethno-Linguistic Processes in the USSR), (Moscow: Nauka, 1984), 193–206.
34. *Chislennost' i sostav naseleniya*; 102–109; *Itogi*; 152–310.
35. *Sovremennye etnicheskie protsessy v SSSR* (Contemporary Ethnic Processes in the USSR), Moscow: Nauka, 1977; 272–73.
36. See sources for Table 1–1.
37. Quoted in *Razvitie natsional'no-russkogo dvuyazychiya*; 85, 94.
38. *Mezhnatsional'nye svyazi i vzaimodeystvie kul'tur narodov SSSR*, 33.
39. Quoted in Guboglo, *Sovremennye*, 265.

40. *Razvitie natsional'no-russkogo dvuyazychiya*; 85–98.
41. For all the quoted figures see: *Chislennost' i sostav naseleniya*; 102–29; *Itogi*; 152–331.
42. L.N. Terent'eva, "Opredelenie natsional'noy prinadlezhnosti podrostkami v natsional'no-smeshannykh sem'yakh," (The Determination of National Identity by Adolescents in Nationally-Mixed Families), in *Sovetskaya etnografiya*, (Soviet Ethnography), No. 3, (1969), 20.
43. For more details, see: V.I. Kozlov, *Natsional'nosti v SSSR*, (The Nationalities of the USSR), (Moscow: Statistika, 1975), 237–239.
44. Bennigsen, *Musul'mane*, 6–9.
45. *Chislennost' i sostav naseleniya*, 71.
46. Guboglo, *Sovremennye*, 197.
47. *Sovremennye etnicheskie protsessy v SSSR*; 482, 471.
48. Guboglo, *Sovremennye*, 201.
49. For statistical data confirming this thesis, see: Guboglo, *Sovremennye*, 140, and *Sovremennye etnicheskie protsessy v SSSR*; 362, 528–29.
50. See Bennigsen, *Musul'mane*, 6–9.
51. See *Mezhnatsional'nye svyazi i vzaimodeystvie kul'tur narodov SSSR*; 92–93.
52. See Guboglo, *Sovremennye*, 78.
53. ———, 206.
54. *Razvitie natsional'no-russkogo dvuyazychiya*; 35–54.
55. V. Ambartsumian, "Naveki s Rossiey," (For Ever With Russia), in *Nauka i zhizn'*, (Science and Life), (1979), 1.
56. See the substantiation of this in *Proiskhozhdenie i etnicheskaya istoriya russkogo naroda*, (The Origins and Ethnic History of the Russian People), (Moscow: Nauka, 1965), *Etnicheskaya odontologiya SSSR*, (The Ethnical Odontology of the USSR), (Moscow: Nauka, 1979).

2

Multinationalism and the Soviet Future

ALEXANDER SHTROMAS

Soviet "Socialist Federalism" vs. the Imperial-Colonial Model of the Organization of a Multi-national State

The Soviet approach to multinationalism is based on the country's primary administrative-political division into national-territorial units which, if they border on a foreign country (by land or sea) and have a population of not less than one million, are formally accorded the equal status and rights of a union republic. The whole territory of the Soviet Union is thus divided into fifteen such "equal" union republics, each bearing the name of a different nation, the biggest of which is Russia with a territory of 17,100,000 square kilometers (76 percent of the whole territory of the USSR) and a population of 137,410,000 people (about 53 percent of the total population of the USSR), and the smallest—Estonia, with a territory of 45,100 square kilometers and a population of 1,464,000 people. Furthermore, within a few union republics that are themselves multinational, there exist—alongside with merely territorial administrative-political units, such as territory (*kray*), province (*oblast'*), city (*gorod*), and district (*rayon*)—also specific national-territorial units: the autonomous republic, autonomous province and autonomous region (*okrug*), within which nations and nationalities of a "sub-union-republican status" are accommodated. There are no precise criteria for according to the "sub-republican" national-territorial unit one of these statuses but usually the more numerous (over one million strong) nations (such as the multimillion Volga Tatars or Bashkirs) not bordering

353

on foreign countries or smaller nations bordering on foreign countries (such as the 166,000 strong Tuvans) are given the status of autonomous republics, whereas smaller "inner" nations get the status of autonomous provinces. The status of autonomous regions is reserved to the remnants of formerly nomadic tribal groups of Russia's north and Siberia. The autonomous republics and provinces are structured as separate administrative-political units directly subordinated to the union-republic's authority,[1] whereas the autonomous regions are created within a *kray* or *oblast'* and are directly subordinated to the local authority of that *kray* or *oblast'*.[2]

The arrangement under which nationally definable territorial areas are given first priority in devising the country's administrative-political structure forms the essence of Soviet "socialist federalism."[3]

The Russian republic, which is the more complex of all the republics, contains 16 autonomous republics, 5 autonomous provinces and all the 10 autonomous regions of the country. Because of this great variety of different nations and the extensive number (thirty-one) of territorial units accorded to them, Russia, within the socialist federal structure of the USSR, is defined as a "Federal Soviet Socialist Republic" in its own right.[4] However, certain other union-republics which have not been accorded such a special status contain a few separate national-territorial units, too. There are two autonomous republics and one autonomous province in the Georgian SSR, one autonomous republic and one autonomous province in the Azerbaijan SSR, one autonomous republic in the Uzbek SSR, and one autonomous province in the Tadzhik SSR province. Altogether, there are thirty-eight additional national-territorial units in the fifteen union republics that are also directly represented in the Soviet of Nationalities, one of the two "equal-rights" houses of the USSR's Supreme Soviet—the country's official Parliament.

Within each of the fifty-three (fifteen union republics, twenty autonomous republics, eight autonomous provinces and ten autonomous regions) national-territorial units of the USSR, some room is provided for the development and self-assertion of the ethnic entitites whose name (or names, in the cases of dual- and multinational entities) these units bear. Local national languages are in public usage there, along with Russian, which is effectively the official language of the Union as a whole, although such a status is not accorded to it legally.[5] In national schools, where Russian is the second language, certain elements of the national history and cultural tradition are taught, and there also are in each such unit officially functioning cultural institutions dealing with selected aspects of the national heritage. The media use national languages extensively and native literatures of the "socialist realism" variety are generously sponsored, sometimes even artificially, by the authorities.

The "socialist federalism," whose basic features are described above, was conceived by the founding fathers of the Soviet system as a political form which would be capable of definitively putting an end to the traditional imperial-colonial model of a multinational state which hitherto was, with very few exceptions (such as Switzerland), the only one history has known. It was considered to be entirely adequate also for the purpose of abolishing old-standing suspicions and antagonisms between nations and for drawing them all together ever more closely, until they gradually merged into one supranational Soviet socialist people, which eventually would embrace the whole of mankind. The experiment with Soviet "socialist federalism" is still continuing, but now, after 70 years of its practical functioning, one could definitely say that it has failed to live up to the expectations of its creators.

It would be futile to try to find the explanation for this failure by searching for certain inadequacies or shortcomings within the formal structure of Soviet "socialist federalism" itself. In fact, this structure, however imperfect and contradictory, was sufficiently imaginative and innovative to lend at least some hope for getting different nations satisfactorily accommodated within a single political unit and thus to provide a significant departure from the prevalent imperial-colonial tradition.

If this has not happened, if Soviet "socialist federalism" has proven to be incapable of overcoming even the worst traits of the imperial-colonial organization of a multinational state, to say nothing about the realization of its other much grander goals, it is not because of any inadequacies in its formal structure, but chiefly because of the purpose to which the ruling Bolsheviks have chosen to put it to use. The task they set themselves to was indeed enormous. What they wanted to achieve in the shortest possible time was no less than a complete transformation of the different traditional cultural-religious identities of the several scores of various nations under their rule into a single and uniform Marxist-Leninist identity for all of them. And they made sure that the allowances for the official usage of various national languages and other cultural forms provided by the constitutional arrangements of Soviet "socialist federalism" served this purpose solely and exclusively. Every deviation from it has been treated as hostile activity deserving unequivocal suppression.

Milan Kundera, the prominent Czech writer, succinctly defined the essence of Bolshevik rule as that of "organized forgetting."[6] In order to explain what he meant by so saying, Kundera quotes the following words of the Czech dissident historian Milan Hubl: "The first step in liquidating a people is to erase its memory. Destroy its books, its culture, its history. Then have somebody write new books, manufacture a new culture, invent a new history. Before long the nation will begin to forget what it is and what it was. The world around it will forget even faster."[7] The trouble, however, was that the by now "socialist nations" were not at all prepared to forget what they are and what they were. On the contrary, the harder they were pressed to succumb to the newly manufactured Marxist-Leninist culture, the more determined they became to stick to their traditional national identities.

In the beginning this determination manifested itself in various forms of active resistance to Bolshevik rule—such as the Civil War (in Russia during 1918–1920), the formation in 1917–1918 of independent non-Bolshevik states and their armed resistance to the Bolsheviks and the advancing troops of Russia's newly formed Red Army (successful in the cases of Finland, Estonia, Latvia, Lithuania, and Poland), national guerrilla warfare (in the whole of the Ukraine during 1918–1922, and in its later annexed western part during 1944–1952; in Central Asia during 1918–1933; in the Baltic states during 1944–1952, etc.), and different other rebellious outbursts throughout the years and in different national areas, which the Bolsheviks have managed to put down in a determined and merciless fashion. But this was far from being enough to have the Bolshevik grip on power properly consolidated and maintained. The Bolsheviks also had to make sure that people are prevented from ever relapsing into active resistance again, and the most direct way in which this could be done reliably was by terror which the Bolsheviks did not hesitate to introduce on a massive scale and maintained for the following decades as a constant and common practice of their rule.

Conducted in the name of the "proletarian class struggle," the Bolshevik terror was supposed to suppress the "exploiting minorities" on behalf of the "exploited majority." In practice, however, it turned out to be suppressing the great mass of both the "exploiting minorities" and the "exploited majority" of all Soviet nations on behalf of one particular, rather tiny, minority—that of the Bolsheviks and their political supporters. The "proletarian class struggle" has thus come to be fought by the Bolsheviks mainly against the proletarians themselves.

There was nothing in this situation that took the Bolsheviks by surprise or forced them to reconsider their position. They always knew only too well that the lower classes of society are, on the whole, much more dependent on the established national traditions and values than the better educated (and thus more cosmopolitan) middle and upper classes, and that therefore the majority of the "exploited majority" is not simply unlikely to lend its support to the Bolshevik "transformatory" plans but is going to resist their implementation as resolutely as possible. That is why the Bolsheviks, from the very moment of their accession to power, were ready to engage themselves in a confrontation with the masses of the "working people" and did so without the slightest hesitation or doubt.

Such a stance, superficially looked at, may appear to be cynical or at least inconsistent. But on the part of the Bolsheviks it was neither. According to the Marxist-Leninist theory of class struggle, in which they believed without reservations, the workers by themselves were *in principle* unable to develop an adequate class consciousness. This consciousness could only be instilled into them by their Bolshevik vanguard. Therefore, properly class conscious could be only those workers who already followed the Bolshevik Party as their undisputed leader, and such workers were by necessity still only a small minority of the working class. Those in the majority who had as yet failed to take the lead from the Bolsheviks were bound to be culturally and ideologically dominated by their exploiters, besieged by "bourgeois prejudices" such as nationalism and, thus, prone to become "bourgeois stooges" in all other respects. Acting as such, these workers—whether a minority or a majority—had to be treated as enemies of their own class and dealt with accordingly. This, in the Bolshevik view, was the harsh but inescapable logic of the class struggle.

The ultimate task of the Bolsheviks consisted, however, in the bringing of the workers to that side of the class struggle to which they should have naturally belonged in the first place. Everything had to serve this purpose, even the harshest repression. The workers had, at any cost, to be submitted to the leadership of the Bolshevik party and made to follow it unquestioningly, as a properly self-conscious working class indeed should. Hence, the Bolshevik-led "proletarian class struggle," which in form seemed to be directed against the proletarians, was, from the Bolshevik viewpoint, in substance, a fight for the proletariat—for the transformation of its "false bourgeois consciousness" into a "true proletarian self-consciousness," that is for the transition of the proletariat, using Karl Marx's expression, from a "class in itself" into a "class for itself" (*The Poverty of Philosophy*).

It was in this sense that the Bolsheviks claimed that the class struggle they were conducting was, in essence, nothing less than a *cultural revolution*. This was indeed a succinct term. On the one hand, it provided a justification for the necessity of conducting the class struggle on behalf of the majority against that majority itself, and, on the other hand, it gave a respectable code name to what in Kundera's much more realistic terms amounted to the rule of "organized forgetting," the inevitable resistance to which fueled the endless confrontation between the Bolshevik rulers and all the nations encompassed in the realm of their rule.

The cultural revolution was at the heart of everything the Bolsheviks were doing at all times, and since, in spite of all their efforts, they are today as far as ever removed from the accomplishment of their ultimate goal of replacing various national identities by a supranational ideological uniformity, the Bolshevik-conducted cultural revolution, though in somewhat milder forms, continues unabated and there is as yet no end to it in sight.

Under the circumstances of that ongoing cultural revolution, Soviet "socialist federalism" did not stand a chance of achieving (or even of starting to achieve) any of the goals for which it was originally conceived. These goals were simply incompatible with those of the cultural revolution and the latter took clear precedence over the former. It was also mainly because of the ongoing cultural revolution that Soviet "socialist federalism" was rendered incapable of transcending in any significant way the boundaries of the "imperial-colonial model" of the organization of a multinational state, although the pure form of "socialist federalism" contained some potential for accomplishing such a transcendence.

It is very hard for the non-Russians to recognize the universal oppressiveness of the Soviet state, its determination to deprive of their true national identities all nations equally, including the Russians themselves. To the great majority of the non-Russians the Soviet state remains indistinguishable from a Russian nation-state and its policies of cultural revolution from those of assimilatory Russification and direct national oppression of their respective nations by the Russians. Indeed, in spite of all the rather generous linguistic and cultural provisions allocated to the non-Russians under the arrangement of "socialist federalism," Russia remains a dominant nation in the country at large, as well as a decisive presence within every separate non-Russian nation of the USSR.

It is common knowledge that the Russians form a large proportion of the population in every non-Russian area of the USSR, especially in the bigger cities, where their presence is in many instances absolutely overwhelming.[8] In the governmental apparatus of the non-Russian areas the number of Russians is also disproportionately high and as representatives, and sometimes direct envoys, of the central authority, they are the most influential force in it.

But the forced coexistence of the relatively small non-Russian nations in a single-state union with such a giant as Russia has many other less visible but not less significant implications insofar as national self-preservation of the former is concerned. All non-Russians aspiring to higher stations in their lives must in this state become fluent in Russian, considered to be in the Soviet Union "the means of intranational communication," and thus acquire, in addition to, and very often at the expense of, their own national identity, also a Russian one. It is therefore very difficult for the non-Russians living in a predominantly Russian state to defend themselves against acculturation and, in the long run, assimilation with Russia, even if Russification were not a part of the state's official policies.

Furthermore, the central authority, which is in actual charge of every aspect of life in the country and which effectively controls every single national area, is in the view of an average non-Russian a purely Russian institution. It sits in Moscow, the center of Russia; it is composed almost entirely of ethnic Russians and thus appears to be willy-nilly bound to act for and in the exclusive interests of the Russians. However wrong it may be in essence, this view of the non-Russians of their situation within the USSR, as follows from the above facts, is not entirely unjustified.[9] One really cannot blame the average non-Russian, who is unfamiliar with the authentic Russian cultural tradition, for his thorough conviction that, in fact, he is an alien subject of the Russian Empire which for some obscure reasons postures itself as the a-national USSR.

To be sure, for the average non-Russian the USSR is not just a mere continuation of the pre–1917 Russian imperial state. It is much worse. The pre–October 1917 Russian state had never even contemplated affecting the traditional cultural-religious fabric and the way of life of the non-Russians to the extent to which the socialist Soviet state has done. Neither had it ever tried to change totally the customs, institutions and the whole identity of any of the nations it was politically and militarily controlling. The conclusion that the average non-Russian inevitably draws from this comparison is that the Soviet Union is nothing more than a disguised Russian imperial state which, thanks to the Revolution, has become unrestrained in practicing oppression of its non-Russian subjects. This is to say that for the average non-Russian the only real substance of the 1917 October Revolution consisted in the liberation of the "evil spirit of Russia" from attempts by the czars to tame it by imposing upon it some elements borrowed from the traditions of Western civilization. Thus, in his view, the more oppressive the Soviet state is, the more genuinely Russian is its substance. This is the main reason why Soviet "socialist federalism" has not only failed to overcome the basic pattern of the imperial-colonial model of the organization of a multinational state, but rendered the old strifes and rifts between nations fostered by imperial-colonial rule even more acute than they ever had been before.

It is true that the linguistic-cultural allowances the non-Russians enjoy under Soviet "socialist federalism" are incomparably greater than whatever was granted to them in this respect by the czars. But, on the other hand, under the czars, the absence of those allowances was to a large extent compensated for by a significantly lesser interference of the Russian state in the inner social fabrics of the different nations the czars ruled. As a matter of fact, in Soviet conditions of total state control over all walks of Soviet nations' lives, these allowances, instead of alleviating, made the situation of various non-Russian nations of the USSR, in some substantial respects, even more adverse. Totally subordinated to the centralized pursuit of the goals of the cultural revolution, these allowances were, in fact, turned into an additional source of mental coercion of the non-Russian nations by the "Russian" central authority. The combination of vigorous censorship with the promulgation into the native cultural frameworks of cheap and boring "Russian" propaganda material led to the bastardization of the respective national cultures which, in their officially accepted guise have become, to quote Stalin's motto, national only in form and socialist in content. This has created even more animosity and significantly increased the latent hostility of the non-Russian nations toward the Soviet ("Russian") "super-imperial state," indeed to the whole Soviet ("Russian") way of life, bringing the national situation in the country to a potentially explosive level.

But is the situation of the Russians within the USSR really significantly different from that of the non-Russians? Is it indeed so dominant and nationally satisfying as the average non-Russian would have it? Solzhenitsyn never tires of telling us that it is not; if anything, it is much worse than that of the non-Russians.[10] It is, of course, true that the Russians are much more sure than their smaller and weaker counterparts of their ability nationally to survive under the Bolshevik oppression. Because of their great numbers, and centrality for the state, they also enjoy some special privileges which no other Soviet nation does and which the non-Russians are so quick to point out. All this notwithstanding, the Russians have their own profound national grievances which leads them to consider their situation to be much worse than is the situation of the non-Russians. In this sense, Solzhenitsyn speaks for a great many Russians and his words should be taken with the utmost seriousness.

One should never forget that from the outset the Soviet rulers were extremely suspicious of anything truly Russian, treating it almost automatically as reactionary, if not directly anti-Soviet. Russia, as the former ruling imperial nation that during the Civil War resisted the Bolsheviks more staunchly and massively than perhaps any other nation did, always was for them a bogey of which they were extremely afraid and which they were trying to keep in fetters more vigorously than any other nation under their control. Indeed, originally the Bolsheviks had less trouble with the non-Russians than with the Russians. This was due to the fact that in the beginning they quite successfully claimed to have liberated the non-Russians from Russian oppression and got substantial support from them in fighting against their Russian enemies, all of whom were thought of by the non-Russians as carriers of Russia's imperial legacy. The Bolshevik terror of the 1920s and 1930s affected the Russians, in proportional terms, much more gravely than any other Soviet nation, perhaps with the exception of the Ukrainians. (The heavy population losses suffered by the Central Asian nations, especially the Kazakhs, were mainly the result of the protracted guerrilla warfare which, in Soviet Central Asia lasted until 1933, while in Russia and in the Soviet part of the Ukraine, armed struggle was practically over by 1922 and the huge loss of population that took place there between 1926 and 1939 could only be explained by the direct terror the state conducted against the civilian population.) At the same time, the Russian nation was the Soviet rulers' prime target for transformation into an uprooted body of a "model Soviet people" for all the other peoples to follow. Its traditional national-cultural identity was therefore exposed to the biggest threat of all, and continues to be so.

Furthermore, in comparison with every other Soviet nation, maybe with the exception of the Belorussians, the Russians have the poorest standard of living. This is no wonder since they are made to pay the price for keeping the Soviet Empire going and are compelled to reduce their own level of consumption so that that of the non-Russians can be artificially increased in order to keep them quieter. The Russians have also one of the lowest birthrates and one of the highest death rates in the whole of the USSR, and are about to become a minority in the land. This situation worries them a lot. They are feeling beleaguered, exploited, abused, and become increasingly hostile to the powers that be, whom they blame for their deplorable existence. Their frustration is eloquently demonstrated by the rapid increase in alcoholism which, even according to the official pronouncements made public on the eve of Gorbachev's introduction of his anti-drunkenness campaign, has in the last few years reached the proportions of a real plague of the nation.

Certain Russians, among them the prominent philosopher and writer Alexander Zinoviev, think that "every minority nation . . ." (of the USSR—A.S.) "has been enjoying a privileged position in comparison with the Russian people," that "for them Russia is a colony" and that "the colonization of Russia and the Russian nation" was "one of the most significant features of the October revolution."[11]

After having assessed Russia's, in his view abysmal, situation, Zinoviev stated: "As I want the Russian people to obtain independence as a sovereign state, I must logically hope for the destruction of the Soviet Empire."[12] No doubt, Zinoviev is a paradoxical thinker and could be accused of exaggeration, but what he said is only a sharpened reflection of a very widely held view. After all, Russian nationalist *samizdat* authors, such as Igor Shafarevich, Vladimir Osipov, Leonid Borodin, to say nothing about

Alexander Solzhenitsyn, are expressing basically the same opinion and do so in a most serious and non-exaggerated manner. And not only *samizdat* authors, but also those whose works are officially published in the Soviet Union, among them such prominent Russian authors as Valentin Rasputin, Viktor Astafiev, Boris Mozhaev, to name but a few.

All this shows clearly enough that the USSR is a very peculiar imperial state—an imperial state where all nations, including the dominant one itself, are oppressed by a clique of self-appointed rulers busy reshaping the living bodies of all the nations under their control in accordance with their pre-set image of what these nations should be like. Indeed, the Soviet Union is by no means a normal nation-state extended into a multinational empire. It is a typical example of a clique-state in charge of an empire where the real confrontation runs not so much between the ruling and ruled nations (although it often takes on such an appearance), but between all the nations forcefully incorporated into that empire and its fully self-centered, a-national and antinational, ruling clique.

In spite of all these traits which normally should spell weakness and instability, Soviet "socialist federalism" proved itself to be quite an effective political device for exercising firm control over a complex multinational environment. To be sure, no multinational state, organized along the lines of the "imperial-colonial model," can remain fully effective and stable in the long run. It has, in the end, either to overcome multinationalism or disintegrate. In the short run, however, it can sustain imperial rule either in a more or in a less stable and secure manner, and in this sense Soviet "socialist federalism" deserves a rather high mark. Within the framework of the "imperial-colonial model" of the organization of a multinational state one can perhaps even rate it as the optimally effective political form to have ever been evolved.

Why this is so and what the inherent advantages and disadvantages of Soviet "socialist federalism" are will be explored below in more detail. But in order to set the framework of discussion of these problems it is necessary to give first a brief review of the theoretical and historical foundations from which Soviet "socialist federalism" has emerged, and upon which it rests, as both an idea and political reality.

Marx and the National Question

In Marx's view the nationality problem was not of very great social significance. According to him, it was a problem totally subordinated to that of class in the way in which form is subordinated to essence. Moreover, for him the nation was the form of social entity specific only to the capitalist stage of social development. It did not exist before capitalism and will surely disappear with the developments conducive to a socialist revolution within capitalism itself; and under socialism it will finally be replaced by an entirely new social entity—that of mankind as a monolithic whole. Marx saw in the proletariat—the bearer of the socialist revolution and the ruling class after its triumph—the growing internationalist, indeed global, force and was absolutely convinced that with its accession to power the framework of a nationless global community would be automatically established. Hence, Marx's famous dicta: "The proletariat does not have a fatherland" and "proletarians of all countries unite"; hence, also, Marx's opposition to national separatist movements of less developed nations if they lived under the rule of the more developed ones, i.e., those who were *ipso facto* closer to the transition to socialism (as in the case of the Croatians and Czechs vis-à-vis the Austrians and Germans), and, on the other hand, his support for the more developed nations striving to rid themselves of the rule of the less developed ones, i.e., those who were *ipso facto* farther removed from socialist transformation (as in the case of Poles and Lithuanians vis-à-vis the Russians). For Marx a socialist nation-state, or even a multi-nation state, was a contradiction in terms; so also was a federal socialist state. The dictatorship of the proletariat, according to him, necessitated a strictly unitary state structure.

The Post-Marxian Revision of Marx's Views. The Pre-1917 Position of Lenin

The post-Marxian Marxists, especially the ones who acted in multinational environments, such as Austro-Hungary and Russia, were forced by the circumstances of their political activities to revise Marx quite radically on the national problem. In order to be able to strive for power and socialism in their multi-national countries, they had to accommodate somehow the still existing different nationalities of these countries within the framework of the socialist society they aspired to establish there. The Austrian socialists arrived for this purpose at the concept of national-cultural autonomy which was to be granted within the framework of the unitary, though multinational, socialist state equally to each of its nationalities, whether territorially compact or scattered in a territory predominantly inhabited by a different nation. According to the Austro-Marxist concept of national-cultural autonomy, every ethnic group should become a self-governing entity insofar as the organization and management of its schools, theatres, and other educational and cultural institutions and activities are concerned. The authority of the thus-conceived organs of national-cultural autonomy should extend to the whole territory of the multinational unitary state and cater to the interests of the ethnic groups in preserving and enhancing their respective identities not only in the territories compactly inhabited by these groups but wherever the members of such groups happen to live, and independently of their having an identifiable national territory at all.

The Russian Bolsheviks rejected the concept of national-cultural autonomy outright. They made a sharp distinction between nonterritorial national minorities scattered among territorial nations and these nations themselves. According to the Bolsheviks, the quicker the national minorities assimilate with the dominant territorial nation the better. To sustain their separate identities is a reactionary and class-divisive enterprise to which true socialists should not be a party.[13] (This was the reason for Lenin's protracted and relentless fight against the Bund, a Jewish socialist organization that had a separate status within the Russian Social Democratic party.) However, with regard to territorial nations, the Russian Bolsheviks were prepared to go even a longer way than the Austro-Marxists in the revision of Marx. They proclaimed themselves ready to grant to all territorial nations in the aftermath of the socialist Revolution the right of self-determination and, if they so wished, of secession from the original imperial state with the view of creating their own separate statehoods. This was, however, a rather tactical device which had very little to do with principles. Lenin, who was more serious about having a socialist Revolution here and now than the Austro-Marxists or his own native Mensheviks, was adamant to secure for this Revolution as much support as possible from all quarters of discontent, e.g., from the oppressed nations, too. He understood all too well that this would be impossible without promising the latter full self-determination. So he promised it. Lenin did not entertain at that time (I mean before the revolution, more precisely in 1912–1913, when he discussed these problems in his works criticizing Rosa Luxemburg's anti-self-determination stance) any ideas about creating a socialist federation of nations which to him, as to any other Marxist, was pure anathema.[14] After all, self-determination did by no means entail federalism; on the contrary, they were rather mutually exclusive concepts.

Lenin's concept of self-determination was double-bottomed in itself. As socialists, he said, we must stand for the unity of nations and thus against their using the right to self-determination in favor of secession; in other words, we must fight for every nation's joining of the multinational socialist unitary state. But as democrats, he continued, we must recognize the right of all the nations to free self-determination (in any direction) and respect it without being necessarily in agreement with the decision of the nations exercising this right. Practically, this meant for Lenin two things: first, that he would like to include into the newly created socialist state as many nations as he possibly could manage to incorporate into it; secondly, that he would not have in this state any nations which he, for one reason or other, would not be able to take over for socialism, preferring to leave such nations to their own devices (i.e., to independent existence) until such time when they would be ready to undergo a socialist transformation and, subsequently, to join the socialist state.

Lenin's subscription to the "bourgeois slogan" of self-determination of nations gave him significant tactical advantages; on the one hand, it attracted the nations striving for their independence from Russia to the support of the Bolsheviks in preference to other metropolitan Russian parties; and, on the other hand, by allowing to secede from Russia such parts of the former empire that, for one reason or other, could not be assimilated in its new socialist structure, it secured the monolithic unity of the prospective Bolshevik-led, Russian socialist state.

The Bolshevik Adoption of Federalism. Stage 1: The Creation of the RSFSR

The idea that federalism could be adopted as the form of organization of the multinational socialist state occured to Lenin only after the Bolsheviks had seized power in Russia. Although in the immediate aftermath of their seizure of power the Bolsheviks failed to get control over most of the nations living on the outskirts of the former Russian Empire, they still found themselves ruling many different territorial nations within Russia's inner borders—the Bashkirs, the Volga Tatars, the Chuvashes, the Mordvins, the Komis, the Maris, to name but a few—and had to decide how to deal with, and to treat, them. The solution of that problem came in the form of giving each of these nations what was called the national-territorial autonomy (this concept being consciously opposed to the Austro-Marxist one of non-territorial and thus non-political national-cultural autonomy). Because of the presence within Soviet Russia of such national autonomous territorial units and because, in accordance with Soviet Russia's Constitution of July 1918, these units were given special representation with veto powers within the All-Russian Congress of the Soviets and its Central Executive Committee,[15] it was decided to call the Bolshevik-led Russian state the Russian Soviet Federal Socialist Republic, or the RSFSR.

In fact, there was not much federalism in this so-called federal Russian Soviet republic at all. The powers of the Soviets of the autonomous national-territorial units were not (and were not supposed to be) different from the powers of all other local Soviets (except for the special representation these units got within the highest bodies of the state, as mentioned above). It was assumed that the Soviet system as such transfers power to the grassroots, i.e., to the workers and working peasants organized in the local Soviets (the latter, of course, working under the wise guidance and supervision of the Bolshevik party), and therefore the fact that territorial nations became now such separate administrative units with their own Soviets at the helm was supposed to mean that the political power had been transferred to them as to "worker-led" nations in the same way as it was transferred to working people in local areas everywhere else. One should note here that the first Soviet Constitutions (the above-mentioned RSFSR's of 1918 and the USSR's of 1924) disenfranchised all those who did not belong to the working classes and by using unequal representation also discriminated against the voting power of the working peasants (who in the non-Russian national areas represented the overwhelming majority of people and, in some cases, even their totality), but this is beside the point as the real power, the constitutional provisions notwithstanding, was in the hands of the Bolsheviks and, subsequently, within the national-territorial units, in the hands of the local Bolsheviks who, although totally subordinated to the center, locally were very much in command and had a lot of influence with the center. This latter fact is not to be dismissed in discussing the real extent of national autonomy in the early RSFSR, but it would be farfetched to use it to argue that Soviet federalism was genuine.

This is how the concept of Soviet "socialist federalism" was born and reached its first stage of practical application. As one can easily see, this first, Russian, model of Soviet "socialist federal" arrangement meant nothing more than the establishment of a unitary state within which territorial nationalities (i.e., nations) received the status of separate administrative political units headed, as in all other such units, by the local soviets but led, in fact, by the Party.

Soviet "Socialist Federalism" Matured.
Stage 2: The Creation of the USSR

With the end of the Civil War some non-Russian territories of the former Russian Empire, which in the meantime managed to establish themselves as independent "bourgeois" nation-states (such as the Ukraine, Belorussia, Azerbaijan, Armenia, Georgia), had fallen under Bolshevik control. They became now, as Russia was already, Soviet socialist republics, but their formal independent status remained unaffected by this fact. As states, these republics continued to exist independently of, and alongside with, Soviet Russia and each other although, in fact, they were all ruled by one and the same Bolshevik party which at all times remained even formally an integrated and highly centralized organization extending to all the territories formerly belonging to Russia, whether at any time independent of her or not, and firmly run from the center located in the capital of Russia.

By the end of 1921 the problem of how to bring into closer correspondence with one another the actual and formal patterns of rule over these legally separate Soviet socialist republics prominently figured on the agenda of the Bolshevik party. For the working out of the question of further mutual relations of the independent Soviet republics, the Politburo of the Central Committee, Russian Communist Party (Bolshevik) formed a commission of the representatives of the CC RCP(B) and of the Central Committees of the Communist Party (Bolshevik)s of Azerbaijan, Armenia, Bukhara, Belorussia, Georgia, the Far Eastern Republic, Ukraine and Khorezm. The first draft of the theses on unification was prepared by Stalin, the then RSFSR's Peoples Commissar for Nationalities, and presented by him to the commission under the title "Draft Resolution on Mutual Relations of the RSFSR with the Independent Republics." In it he expounded his "autonomization" idea, and proposed: "To recognize as expedient concluding a treaty between the Soviet Republics of Ukraine, Belorussia, Azerbaijan, Georgia, Armenia, and the RSFSR concerning the formal entry of these into the RSFSR" (as ASSRs, i.e., autonomous SSRs). The commission adopted the draft "without substantial changes" and circulated it to the CC CP(B)s of the republics. It soon transpired that the republican CC CP(B)s not only did not approve this draft but even launched a campaign against it. Thus, the Ukrainian CC opposed "autonomization" because "the centralized leadership of independent republics can be fully achieved through appropriate directives along Party channels." The CC CP(B) of Georgia also rejected Stalin's draft as "premature" and demanded "the preservation of all attributes of independence" for the republics. The CC CP(B) of Belorussia spoke in favor of the preservation of previous treaty-based relationships between the RSFSR and the other independent Soviet republics. Some Georgian, Bashkir, and Tatar functionaries suggested the liquidation of existing federal creations (such as Russian SFSR and Transcaucasian SFSR) and the formation of a union of republics in which all republics, including the autonomous ones, would be members as union republics. Suggestions were also made concerning the creation of a Union of Soviet Republics as a confederated state.[16]

In this controversy, Lenin strongly opposed Stalin's idea of "autonomization," too, for which stance he was quite viciously attacked by Stalin. The majority, however, followed Lenin and carried the decision which he had proposed. According to that decision, one had to establish an entirely new union state into which all the existing separate Soviet socialist states, including the RSFSR itself, would have to enter as equal members. A mutual treaty to this effect had to be concluded among the future members of the proposed union state, which had to remain open for other states later to join it. It was essential, in Lenin's view, that members of the newly formed union state retain the right to secede from it, if they so wished, since without such a right the very idea of the treaty of equals would become null and void. In fact, Lenin proposed to use as a model for "state integration of socialist nations" not the Russian but the Transcaucasian federal arrangement which had been set up in 1921 when the three independent Caucasian republics (Georgia, Armenia, and Azerbaijan), after having been conquered by the Bolsheviks (in fact, by the Russian Red Army), entered by such a treaty into the Transcaucasian Soviet Federal Socialist Republic (TSFSR). In the TSFSR all its three constituent members retained their separate and inviolable territorial integrity, the right to secede freely from the Union, and an equal status vis-à-vis each other and the Union itself.

From the two already available models of Soviet "socialist federalism"— the Russian and the Transcaucasian—Lenin chose the latter, first of all, for global reasons. At the 12th Congress of the RCP(B), a Ukrainian CP(B) delegate, Zatons'kyi, thus argued against the "Russian" federation and in favor of the "Soviet" one proposed by Lenin: "If, for instance, Romania is Soviet, if there is a Soviet Germany and another series of federations, will they also be called Russian? No. The fact that the federation is 'Russian' causes enormous confusion in the minds of Party comrades. This name should simply be removed, or only the name 'Soviet federation' should be preserved, or some other name should be invented."[17] Indeed, by choosing the Russian model one would have stressed the Russian national identity of the world's first socialist state thus showing only that under socialist conditions the once collapsed multinational integrity of the "original" state could be effectively restored and organically consolidated. No organizational framework for the future growth of the socialist community of nations by integration into it of new ones from outside of the realm of former Russia would be thus established, and Lenin was too ambitious a zealot of the world socialist revolution to forego such an opportunity. Indeed, he was not only prepared but keen to sacrifice the integrity of Russia for the sake of creating here and now, from the "material" provided exclusively by Russia, a nucleus of what should eventually develop into a world union of Soviet socialist republics. Such a union-state, even in its very name, was not to have any specific national overtones, these being given full expression only on the sub-union ("union-members") layer; it also had to be organized in such an open-ended fashion that each nation of the world could in its own time join it without feeling any loss of national identity and/or integrity. The Transcaucasian model was exactly the one which answered all these needs and thus was perfectly suitable for global adaptation. Along the lines of this particular model the new a-national state union of nations, the USSR,[18] was, in fact, created at the end of 1922 by Soviet Russia (RSFSR), the Ukraine (USSR), Belorussia (BSSR) and Transcaucasia (TSFSR) having concluded between themselves, as equal parties, the Treaty on the Formation of the USSR and entering this newly formed state as its first four equal founding members.

Founded on the same idea as the Transcaucasian Federation, the USSR was by no means its replica. The Transcaucasian Federation consisted of three member states of almost equal size and influence and, therefore, as a union-state, had no particular national overtones. This was not so in the USSR, which inevitably was dominated by Russia, and had a distinctly Russian character reminiscent of the former empire which it had now replaced. Lenin was, however, convinced that this "Russian bias" of the USSR would not last for too long. He believed that with the spread of the world revolution Germany, China and then other countries, too, would soon be brought into the USSR effacing its "annoying Russianness" and thus making it a truly internationalist socialist union-state with no more specific national overtones whatsoever.

How Federal is Soviet "Socialist Federalism"?

There was not much federalism in this newly created state of the USSR either. In comparison with the RSFSR, there was only one important difference—the USSR consisted wholly of nation-based administrative-territorial units, whereas in the RSFSR such units occupied only a certain part of that republic's territory.

The federal arrangements in the USSR were established in its first (1924) Constitution and did not undergo any fundamental changes in the subsequent constitutions of the USSR, the Stalin (1936) and the Brezhnev (1977) ones. True, in the constitutions previous to the Brezhnev one now in force, the rights of the Union were defined exhaustively; both these constitutions also clearly stated that the functions which were not explicitly named as all-Union ones belonged to the exclusive competence of the union republics. But what was the real realm of the so-called exclusive competence of the union republics? The republics never had the right to raise their own revenue and were always entirely dependent for all their finances, without exception, on the allocations in the all-Union budget which also defined all the main targets on which the money thus allocated should be spent. The whole structure of the USSR's budget was generally vertical, with each level of administrative-territorial authority getting all the finances for its own budget from the immediately higher level. The same principle applied also to the economic plan. And what independent functions could one fulfill without independent money and, moreover, without an independent economic plan which in a rigidly planned economy determines every small item on which money should be spent? The answer is straight and clear: none.

According to all Soviet constitutions the organization of the republican and local bodies of authority is an exclusive prerogative of the Union, too. Moreover, these bodies are supposed to act as direct agents of the central authority and, in fact, are nothing more than merely local extensions. This role of the republican and local bodies of Soviet authority is fully consistent with the principles of democratic centralism and the legal concept of double subordination according to which each level of authority below the union one is subordinated, on the one hand, to its immediate electors and, on the other hand, to its immediate superiors on the higher level of the administrative-territorial hierarchy. In fact, this means that the legal concept of double subordination, which is fundamental for all Soviet constitutions, puts the Union firmly in charge of exercising authority in the union republics and accords to the authorities of the latter a purely subsidiary role. In this respect Soviet reality is more or less adequately reflected in the Soviet constitutional law which, by the way not only in this instance, is much more often the case than one is usually ready to admit.

Finally, the legislative powers of the union republics have always been restricted to passing only such laws which do not contradict the laws of the Union. This restriction, in fact, means that the republics are entitled to legislate only for the sake of providing an adequate framework for the application of the all-Union laws to the particular conditions of the republics. It is worthwhile to note that in the case of any discrepancy between all-Union and republican legislation all the constitutions of the USSR make the all-Union law automatically valid and the republican one void. The Union's authority on authentic interpretation of any of the USSR's laws is (e.g., in the case of a clash with a republican law) made absolute and irrevocable by all constitutions of the USSR, too.

The latest (1977) Soviet Constitution abolished even that formal separation of powers between the Union and the republics which was present in all of its predecessors. Clause 12 of Article 73 of this Constitution states clearly and unequivocally that the Union has the right to deal with all matters without exception if it considers them to be of all-Union importance. A federation without any formal separation of power and competence between the Union and its member states, indeed with total concentration of all powers by the Union, this is what today the concept of Soviet "socialist federalism" is all about, not only in practice but also in constitutional theory itself.

The Real Meaning and the Advantages of Soviet "Socialist Federalism"

It follows from the above that even in constitutional and legal terms the USSR is a straightforward unitary state. Actually, the present Soviet Constitution directly proclaims the USSR to be a unitary state. According to the official translation of its Article 70, the USSR is an "integral, union and multi-national state" or, what is one and the same thing if one translates this text properly and in full: "a unitary, federal and multi-national state formed on the basis of the principle of socialist federalism and as a result of the free self-determination of nations and the voluntary union of equal Soviet Socialist Republics. The USSR embodies the state unity of the Soviet people and unites all nations and nationalities for the purpose of joint construction of communism."[19] The usage in one definition of the otherwise mutually exclusive terms, "unitary" and "federal," is, in fact, totally consistent with the concept of "socialist federalism" since this concept does not entail anything else but a unitary state of different nations qualifying for the union-republic's status which, as long as national differences persist, will be accorded a formally equal position of the basic administrative-territorial unit of this state. The generally known fact that the USSR is the most centralized country in the world, the most unitary of all the unitary states, is thus officially admitted and explained.

"Socialist federalism," far from hindering the central authority's exercise of absolute power, actually provides it with certain quite significant advantages which would be inconceivable in a full-fledged unitary state negligent of its multinational composition.

The *first* such advantage is related to international politics and propaganda. "Socialist federalism" makes more credible the Soviet official claim that the USSR is the practical embodiment of a harmonious socialist commonwealth of different nations in which, for the first time in human history, the otherwise insoluble national problem has been successfully solved. This, in turn, makes the Soviets better able to induce other states to associate themselves closely with the USSR and to choose the socialist road for their development. Moreover, "socialist federalism" provides the USSR with a succinct device of eventually swallowing into its own structure the states that made such a choice.

Indeed, all Soviet constitutions contain special regulations concerning the order in which other states can join the USSR. These regulations were used for the last time as long ago as 1944 when the Tuvan Peoples' Republic (Tanu-Tuva), before that an independent state of "socialist orientation" for almost a couple of decades, was incorporated into the USSR as an autonomous province, later transformed into an autonomous republic, of the RSFSR. Since then, the USSR has preferred to retain the formally sovereign status of the states newly "converted" with its help to socialism and always has stopped short of their official incorporation into the Soviet Union. However, this does not mean that the practice of incorporation has been abandoned by the USSR for good and will never be used again. It will all depend on the changing circumstances of international politics. The legal mechanism ensuring the possibility of incorporation of other nations into the USSR is being kept intact and ready to be used as soon as the Soviet leadership decides that it is appropriate again.[20]

The *second* advantage is related to domestic politics and administration. "Socialist federalism" is a unique arrangement which enables Soviet central authority to be in direct control of every particular nation as a whole. This not only makes centralized rule more adaptive to the specific circumstances of a certain national environment but, more importantly, allows the central authority to focus its undivided attention simultaneously to the whole spectrum of each nation's collective activities and movements, thus keeping them all in vigorous check and, at the same time, manipulating all of them so that they could be channeled into the direction desired by (or at least acceptable to) the central authority.

The *third* advantage is related to both domains mentioned above—international politics and propaganda, and domestic politics and administration. It consists in the central authority's "benign" tolerance (and, to a certain degree, even encouragement) of the use by the various nations under its control of their particular languages and other cultural forms not only in private but also in public life. This provides the central authority with another unique opportunity to translate its uniform policies and decisions more aptly into the different national environments over which it rules. The central authority thus becomes able to penetrate much more deeply and fully into each nation's inner life than would otherwise be possible. Moreover, the central authority, by using for its purposes the specific national-linguistic forms of each nation, becomes much more effective in enhancing cultural and ideological uniformity in all of them. (As mentioned above, the official definition of Soviet culture is national in form and socialist in content.) It thus tries to undermine from within the traditional spiritual foundations of all national cultures and to substitute for them Soviet-made surrogates. This is how the national cultures are bastardized and the policy of "all-round . . . drawing-together (*sblizhenie*) of all the USSR's nations and nationalities,"[21] pursued, according to the Soviet central authority's ideological and cultural whims. At the same time, the "generous" allowances for the various national-linguistic and cultural forms provide the Soviet central authority with the opportunity to boast nationally and internationally that it has discovered a unique way of combining the promotion of every nation's separate identity with the process of drawing all of them together into a new historical community of the Soviet people. This, no doubt, gives the USSR a not-at-all negligible propaganda advantage in its ideological struggle at home and abroad.

The *fourth* advantage consists in the central government's ability and willingness to use in its administration of nations the so-called national cadres, i.e., local nationals who form the partocratic elite of their respective republics and are in charge of exercising locally the authority of the central government. Being induced to such service by substantial social and economic privileges which go together with the job, the national cadres acquire a vested interest in the maintenance of the status quo and thus become in the hands of the central government an effectively manipulable tool. Of course, these cadres, although selected and approved by Moscow and constituting its own *nomenklatura*, are not totally trusted and each local "supreme" boss who, as a rule, is a member of the indigenous nation is being usually supervised on behalf of the center by an "alien" (but not in all cases necessarily Russian) deputy whose job is to make sure that his indigenous superior does not in his job overstep the center's directives. The two of them together perform the central government's tasks much better than each of them would have been able to perform separately. This is another clever device enabling centralized rule in national areas to be almost optimally effective.

The Disadvantages of Soviet "Socialist Federalism"

The subdivision of the USSR into national-territorial units, the union republics, contains, however, along with the above advantages, also a strong disruptive potential which, in the long run, could become an important factor contributing to the disintegration of the Soviet state. This disruptive potential could also be expressed in the form of four substantial disadvantages affecting the exercise by the Soviet authority of its centralized rule over the nations of the USSR.

The *first* disadvantage consists in the official endorsement of the separateness of each territorial nation and nationality of the USSR. In the form of its own administrative-territorial unit every such nation and nationality acquires a formidable battleground of its own for asserting and constantly enhancing its self-awareness and separate identity. This proved to be an effective counterforce to the "drawing-together (*sblizhenie*) of nations" policy of the Soviet central authority. Indeed, all available evidence points to the consistent growth of nationalism and of resistance to sovietization (especially if conducted by means of Russification) in *all* non-Russian areas of the USSR. Because of that, the official goal, of creating the new supranational entity of the Soviet people becomes practically ever more remote as time goes by. This was, in fact (though in a roundabout way), admitted by Brezhnev, when in the Report on the New Constitution of the USSR, submitted to the Supreme Soviet on 4 October 1977, he explained why the Constitutional Commission of which he was the chairman had to reject the proposals "to introduce into the Constitution the concept of one Soviet nation, to abolish the union and autonomous republics or (at least) to limit rather drastically the sovereignty of union republics."[22] According to Brezhnev, the rejection of these proposals was necessary because "we would be putting ourselves on a dangerous path if we started to speed up artificially this objective process of nations drawing together."[23]

Practically the same admission was repeated by Brezhnev's immediate successor, Yuriy Andropov in his Report of 21 December 1982 on the 60th anniversary of the USSR. He said that "success in solving the nationalities problem does not mean that all problems generated by the very fact that numerous nations and nationalities live and work within the framework of a union-state have been settled. This is hardly possible as long as nations and national distinctions exist. And they will survive for a long time, much longer than class distinctions will do." Moreover, Andropov had directly stated in this report that "occasionally in evidence" are such "negative phenomena" as "national arrogance and conceit" which "generate trends toward self-isolation, a disrespectful attitude to other nations and national minorities" and that these phenomena are not "survivals of the past alone" but "are nourished . . . by our own errors at work."[24]

Andropov's report, when properly analyzed, appears to be not at all a simple endorsement of Brezhnev's line. It endorses only Brezhnev's critical comments on the national situation in the USSR and then develops into nothing less than a severe attack on Brezhnev's nationalities policy which consisted in stressing the predominantly Russian identity of the Soviet state and in attempting to achieve the merger (*sliyanie*) of Soviet nations by means of their straightforward Russification. This policy, according to Andropov, was counterproductive and divided the Soviet nations more than it drew them together.

Andropov proposed a policy of promoting the "indigenous nationalities" and of their increased involvement in all-Union affairs. It is true that such a policy may have given to certain party-career-oriented sections within the "indigenous nationalities" some satisfaction and thus certain tensions in the official structure of Soviet intranational relationships could be temporarily reduced; but it is doubtful, to say the least, that it could have advanced any further the process of "drawing-together," let alone of "merging," the Soviet nations and nationalities into one entity. On the contrary, these nations and nationalities would have most probably taken every advantage offered to them by this policy to assert and enhance even further their separate identities and positions within the Soviet union-state. The Soviet nationality policy apparently has reached the stage where, in whatever direction one may try to shift it, the result will unavoidably be one and the same—the unabated growth of different nationalisms leading to a gradual disintegration from within of the Soviet multinational society and to its *de facto* demise into the existence of separate national units only superficially linked by whatever political bonds there are left (as is now the case in Yugoslavia which, in this respect, is much ahead of the USSR and leads the race). The Soviet Union increasingly becomes, if not yet an *"empire éclaté,"* as Hélène Carrère d'Encausse suggests, then surely an *"empire éclatant"* which, in favorable conditions of destabilization of power in the center, may indeed be suddenly transformed into an *"empire éclaté."*[25]

This probably explains why all attempts by Andropov to revise and change Soviet nationality policy were to no avail. His ferocious, all-around attack on Russian nationalism, dissident as well as official, which he launched as soon as he had replaced Suslov as secretary of the CPSU's Central Committee (CC) in May 1982 and further invigorated after succeeding Brezhnev in November 1982, had started to relent already by the end of March 1983, and after the "ideological" plenary session of the CPSU's CC in June 1983 fizzled out almost completely.[26] When Chernenko succeeded Andropov in February 1984 no visible trace of it was left, and in a few months the Party quietly restored officially endorsable Russian nationalism approximately into the same position which it occupied during the years of Brezhnev's ascendance. Apparently Chernenko's Politburo had decided to opt for the safety of well-tried policies and deemed all policy shifts to be more dangerous than their mere continuation, however ineffective or even counter-productive it may be in the long run.

Under Chernenko the veteran "within-system" champions of the "Russian idea" who under Andropov were either banned from further publishing of their works (such as V. Kozhinov and A. Lanshchikov) or strongly reprimanded for what they already had published (such as M. Lobanov) or even arrested (such as A. Semanov), were gradually returning to favor. In the summer of 1984 the newspaper *Sovetskaya Rossiya* (Soviet Russia) published a review article of several Western books on Russian history by

S. Tikhvinsky where the author vigorously defended the "excellent" historic record of imperial Russia against Western attacks. Tikhvinsky accused Western authors whose books he reviewed of blatant Russsophobia and, responding to them, highly praised Russia's czars and their generals as wise, strong, peaceful, and welfare-minded Russian national leaders. To his Russian readers he appealed "to be proud of their ancestors' glory" and concluded by saying that "Russophobia has become the main trend of recent anti-communism."[27]

The significance of this article is not so much in its content—articles extolling Russia's glorious past and achievements, the excellent "eternal" qualities of her people, etc., were proliferating in all Soviet media—as in the name of its author. For Tikhvinsky is neither a professional literary critic nor a writer with any record of commitment to the "Russian idea," but a high Soviet official in the Ministry of Foreign Affairs. As such he could not have written anything without being specifically commissioned to do so by the highest authority in the land. And this means that the stimulation of Russian nationalism had become, under Chernenko, official policy again. At the same time attacks on non-Russian nationalism came back into fashion as exemplified by the CPSU's CC summer 1984 decision in which Estonian Party organization was severely criticized for its deficiencies and errors in combating the threateningly growing Estonian nationalism; this decision called for its effective suppression by the Party in the shortest possible time.[28]

The Soviet nationalities policy in a relatively short time moved full circle. If Andropov, in contrast to Brezhnev, launched an offensive against the Russian nationalists and showed some unusual leniency to the non-Russian ones, Chernenko started to do just the opposite. Moreover, Chernenko's support for Russian nationalists exceeded even Brezhnev's.

So far, under Gorbachev, there have been no shifts in the Soviet leadership's nationalities policy. Being so critically outspoken on most of the other burning social and economic issues, Gorbachev, for a long time after having assumed the number 1 office in the land, remained conspicuously silent on the nationality question. On the other hand, however, problems related to nationalities policy became the subject of an increasingly prominent and unprecedently free discussion in the official media, mainly of the union republics. In the absence of new policy decisions or tone-setting articles in the central organs of the Party's press, one started to gain the impression that the problem of nationalities has been, at least for the time being, withdrawn by the leadership from the active policy-decision-making area and transferred into the realm of *glasnost'*, that is, into that of a relatively free discussion, which would allow the Party to take a sample of authentic public opinion before starting to make any policy adjustments or to issue authoritative pronouncements on how best to ensure and consolidate the overall cohesion of the multinational Soviet state.

In the Ukraine and Belorussia the writers and educationalists at their meetings and in the press in 1986 boldly started to raise the problems related to the demise of their national languages in schools, cultural life, and public affairs, offering drastic solutions with the view of restoring the prevalence and enhancing the status of the national languages in their respective republics. The intellectuals in other republics did not simply take up this theme but widened it substantially to include criticism of the deplorable state of cultural and historic monuments, neglect of specific national traditions, and even the official suppression of significant parts of historic and literary heritage. These latter themes were in turn echoed also in the Ukraine and Belorussia. All of them, together with the problem of the decline of the Ukrainian language, were eloquently raised by Ukrainian writers at the plenary session of the Steering Committee of the Ukrainian Union of Writers in June 1987, and surprisingly received a sympathetic review in Moscow's *Literaturnaya Gazeta* which published an unusually detailed report about the proceedings of the session.[29] At the same time, other articles, frequently appearing in the same magazines, strongly attacked the revival of local nationalisms and stressed the necessity of strengthening "internationalist education" and developing unity with "the great Russian people and other peoples of the USSR."

Without directly interfering or taking sides in these discussions, Gorbachev's administration has, however, in practice time and again demonstrated an amazing insensitivity to nationality problems. The replacement in December 1986 of the discredited Kazakh, Dinmukhamed Kunaev, at the helm of the Kazakhstan Party's Central Committee by an ethnic Russian, Gennadiy Kolbin, is only the most prominent among a number of examples of such an insensitivity, as it provoked violent nationalist riots in Kazakhstan's capital, Alma Ata.

Both the absence of innovation in the established (under Brezhnev and Chernenko) Soviet nationalities policy and Gorbachev's administration's insensitivity to the nationality problem have been, perhaps, best exemplified by the Soviet authorities' treatment of the Crimean Tatar problem in July 1987, when over 600 representatives of the Crimean Tatars descended on Moscow from the areas to which they had been exiled in 1944, publicly to demand full rehabilitation, the right to return to the Crimean homeland, and the restoration to that homeland of its Tatar autonomous status. Since this bold action of the representatives of the Crimean Tatar people made the headlines in the world press, the Soviet authorities could not remain silent and pretend that nothing of the kind had happened. On 23 July 1987, the official news agency TASS issued, on behalf of the Soviet government, a statement the gist of which consisted in the Soviet authorities' refusal to do anything about the Crimean Tatar problem there and then. In the statement, TASS announced the creation of a governmental commission, headed by President Gromyko, which would inquire into the problem, and declared that no decision on the Crimean Tatar situation would be taken until the commission had completed its work. By issuing such a statement Gorbachev's administration clearly admitted that it has no new policies to offer with regard to the nationalities, e.g., the Crimean Tatars, and that, even more importantly, as long as this is the case, it will stick to the old policy line which, in the particular case of the Crimean Tatars, means the continuation of their exile. Such an attitude demanded additional explanation and the statement gave it in quite impertinent terms. According to it, the accusations leveled by Stalin against the Crimean Tatars (collaboration with the Nazis, active participation in their atrocities, etc.) were on the whole correct but, since they were applicable only to "a part of the Tatar population," the deportation of "the whole people from its homeland was a mistake." Trying to justify the present administration's postponement of action with regard to correcting that "mistake," the statement consciously diminished its gravity and by referring to "the severe conditions of war," "the concrete situation in the Crimea" and "the mood of the time," made it look excusable. To add insult to injury, the TASS statement quite rudely condemned the public action the Crimean Tatars took for presenting their grievances to the government and grimly warned that any further attempt on their part thus to disrupt the normal process of the government's work would result only in the competent authorities' diminishing willingness to look at the Crimean Tatars' case favorably.[30]

Gorbachev's pronouncements on nationality issues during his visit to Latvia and Estonia in February 1987, provide another eloquent example of continuity in the Soviet conduct of the nationalities policy and the Gorbachev administration's amazing insensitivity to nationality issues. Addressing the *aktiv* in Estonia, Gorbachev simply contrasted the basic inability of the bourgeois order to solve the nationalities' problem with the "ideal solution" of that same problem in the USSR. For him, in other words, the nationalities problem in the USSR has been solved once and for all on entirely satisfactory grounds, and there was therefore no need to introduce changes in the "Leninist nationalities policy that the Communist Party was pursuing at all times during the last 70 years." "Of course," he added, "in the implementation of this great cause there were some slips and miscalculations (we also know this, do not hide, and remember it). And there were aggravations too. But all this does not change the main result of the Party's fruitful work in uniting nations and nationalities in the Soviet Union. This does not change the results of the great community of peoples that forms today the Soviet Union. Most important is the fact that we have created a powerful, multi-national, prospering state, where wide opportunities are secured for each people, for its social, cultural and national development under the conditions of a socialist order."[31] It was obvious from this speech that the summer 1984 CPSU's CC decision on the decisive suppression of nationalism in Estonia was excluded by Gorbachev from among the "slips, miscalculations and aggravations" and that it remains firmly and ominously in force, as do all other post-Stalin decisions and policies of the Party on the nationality problem.

In the Estonian speech quoted above, Gorbachev mentioned only in passing the "voluntariness" of the Baltic states' joining the Soviet Union. He devoted much more attention to that problem in his preceding speech to the Latvian *aktiv* in Riga and therefore did not need to repeat the same remarks in Tallinn. In his Latvian speech, Gorbachev, without any qualifications or doubts, repeated the old Stalinist legend according to which the establishment in 1940 of the Soviet regime in the Baltic states was the natural result of the relentless struggle of the Baltic peoples in the inter-war period "for social justice and national independence." According to him, "the whole heroic struggle for the establishment, restoration and consolidation of Soviet power in the Baltic bears witness to the fact that it is impossible to break the revolutionary resolve of peoples, that it is impossible to turn the movement back."[32] As if speaking in the name of the Balts, he said how much they enjoy the tremendous beneficial results of their decision voluntarily to join the Union of Soviet Socialist Republics and how determined they are never to turn back on this decision. This was a blunt warning to the Balts not to expect any changes of Soviet policy with regard to their fate. Gorbachev's message had an infuriating effect on many Balts and no doubt served as powerful incentive for their unusually numerous participation in the 1987 annual 14 June and 23 August protest demonstrations and meetings commemorating the victims of Stalin's first (1941) deportations and demanding the publication of the Secret Protocols amending the 23 August and 28 September 1939, Molotov-Ribbentrop Pacts, their abrogation and the restoration of the Baltic states' independence that was abolished in accordance with the Secret Protocols. In 1987 they also demanded the acknowledgement of the horrendous genocide-type crimes (mass deportations and executions) committed by the regime against the Baltic nations during the whole period of Stalin's rule. The regime responded to those demands with the usual self-righteous suppression.

On 18 November 1987, Latvian Independence Day, the regime took a number of strong preventive measures aimed at making impossible the planned popular demonstration commemorating this event in Riga, but, nevertheless, people—some groups over 5,000 strong—gathered in different parts of the city to join the demonstration. Under the circumstances—police and vigilante units patrolled the streets of the city in force—the demonstration did not stand a chance of properly forming and reaching, as planned, the sealed-off city center, where a meeting was to be held at the Liberty statue.

Official propaganda blamed all these demonstrations and other "nationalist outbursts" on foreign radio stations and "centers of anti-Soviet subversion operating in the USA and other Western countries." But the government inevitably also had to launch an attack against the "remnants of local nationalisms" that led some Balts, Kazakhs or Kirghizes to respond readily to these "foreign provocations."

Concurrently, the "Tikhvinsky line" has not only never been revoked but has been confirmed on many occasions in articles appearing mainly in the central and Russian republican press.[33] This imbalance in official propaganda output has helped to create among the non-Russians the impression that Gorbachev's administration continues to pursue the Brezhnev-Chernenko policy of stressing the prevailing Russian identity of the Soviet state and of imposing that identity over the identities of all the other nations and nationalities of the USSR although, in fact, Gorbachev's administration has not yet worked out its nationalities policy and still keeps that policy under debate in the framework of the *glasnost'* policy. It goes without saying that whatever adjustments to nationalities policy the Soviet authorities will see fit to make, these adjustments will be dictated by the necessity of strengthening the Soviet multinational state's cohesion. It is not excluded, however, that for the very sake of that cohesion some modest national demands could be accommodated by the regime. Be that as it may, the present position of the Soviet authorities on the nationality problems alienates even further the non-Russian nations from the Soviet state and enhances their determination to strive for secession and thus the breakdown of the Soviet Empire.

The *second* disadvantage expresses itself in the increasing difficulty with which the Soviet central authority manages to provide and secure the USSR's social and political integration. The deterioration of the USSR's integrative pattern is caused by national-territorial units insistently, and not unsuccessfully, trying to advance their self-interests in preference to all-Union interests. Outwardly totally submissive to the Union, the functionaries of these units are trying to get from it for their own republics as much as possible and at the same time to keep the maximum amount of their own resources to themselves. Localist or regionalist trends which are characteristic of all political systems without exception, acquire in the USSR a national (and thus a patriotic) dimension which is so much more difficult to curb. Indeed, in the USSR one strives for what could be called one's partial and basically selfish local goals with that self-righteous resoluteness, slyness, and strength which only the fulfillment of a patriotic duty to one's own nation can bring about and justify, and which can never be the same in political systems where patriotism is identified not with a particular region but with the nation-state itself.

Gorbachev's administration is trying to attack regionalism with all its resolution and strength. The effective recentralization of the Union, the elimination of "feudal laxity" that crept into the system under Brezhnev is one of the main tasks of Gorbachev's reforms program. Local Party and government officials are no doubt determined to defend their "feudal privileges" by all means in their power and, if necessary, defeat Gorbachev as they previously defeated Khrushchev who also tried to limit their power and privileges. In order to defeat the resistance to *perestroika* of the local *nomenklaturas* Gorbachev badly needs, as he always himself stresses, the unequivocal support for his policies of people from without the power apparatus—in the first place the intelligentsia and the industrial workers. While he still may receive some support from these sections of the population in the ethnically Russian areas, the intelligentsia and the population at large in the national republics are much more likely to side with their deviant, "republic-enhancing" local leaderships than with Gorbachev. This is to say that Gorbachev's drive for recentralization and reestablishment of an effective system of control from the center is unlikely to succeed easily. If, however, Gorbachev's administration were to insist on having its way and would consider applying against "national deviationists" stronger measures, e.g., by putting in charge of the republican Party and government apparatuses "new Kolbins," i.e., ethnically alien representatives of the center, the result may be massive national unrest threatening the overall stability of the regime. Hence, in this respect Gorbachev's administration seems to find itself in a rather deadlocked situation.

The same patriotic nationalism increasingly induces the nations and nationalities in the national-territorial areas to do their utmost to preserve their homelands by "keeping the Russians out," which in times of rapid industrial development and the massive migration of labor required by such development, is an extremely difficult task. The case of Kazakhstan under Kunaev's leadership provides a good example of how this is done. Kazakhstan is the only union republic where the indigenous nationality is in a minority. This minority status was for the first time confirmed by the 1939 census, according to which only 38.2 percent of the population living in Kazakhstan were Kazakhs (the previous census of 1926 gave the figure as 57.1 percent). The census of 1959 was, however, the last which showed the continuing decrease of the Kazakh proporition of the population in

Kazakhstan (30 percent). By 1970 the Kazakh proportion of the population rose to 32.6 percent and in 1979, to 36 percent.

The same development took place in Uzbekistan (the lowest proportion of indigenous population was registered there also in 1959 at 62.1 percent but in 1970 there were 65.5 percent and in 1979, 68.7 percent of Uzbeks living in Uzbekistan), Turkmenistan, Tadzhikistan, Kirghizstan, Azerbaijan, Armenia, Georgia, Bashkirian ASSR, Dagestan ASSR, Kabardino-Balkarian ASSR, Kalmukian ASSR, North Osetian ASSR, Tuvan ASSR, Checheno-Ingushian ASSR, and a number of autonomous provinces.[34] The political analysis of the dynamics of the demographic situation in all these national-territorial units shows that the indigenous Party and government leaders were in the first place quite successful in trying to promote as many of their landsmen as they could into responsible administrative positions and, after having thus reasserted their own fellow-nationals politically, gradually started to reassert them also territorially.[35]

In the republics where the proportion of local nationals continued to decrease the mechanism of national reassertion took a different turn. First of all, one should not readily attach dramatic implications to the relative decrease of the indigenous populations in these republics. The example of Kazakhstan cited above eloquently tells us why. Another example is presented by the Baltic republics. The Slavic newcomers in these three republics are mainly industrial workers, some sort of *Gastarbeiter*, who occupy the lowest social positions and have not too much impact on the life of the local nations. The second most significant part of the newcomers—the Party workers sent by Moscow to occupy certain administrative posts in the Baltic area—form a relatively small and exclusive group which, anyway, because of its status, does not easily mix with the main bulk of the local population. Even in the cities where the newcomers constitute the majority, they and the local national community exist as separate entities, almost like oil and water put into one vessel. Mixed marriages are extremely rare, so are friendships, and the language barrier keeps these two groups relatively isolated from each other on a rather permanent basis. Whatever mixed marriages there have been, in the overwhelming majority of cases, they have not led to Russification. Rather, on the contrary, it is the Russian element that has tended to be assimilated into the Baltic environment, which is best manifested by the fact that most of the children of those marriages have retained the local national identity and attend national schools with tuition in the local language. If one adds to this the facts that cultural life in all three republics is almost entirely dominated by the local nations, that tertiary education, with a few exceptions, is conducted in the local nation's language, and that local nationals have a clear priority in career promotions over the "non-assigned" new-comers, it is not surprising that the Russian settlers in the Baltic states tend to see themselves as an oppressed national minority.

It is interesting to note that the less numerous the local nation is, and the more beleaguered it feels, the more defensively it behaves and the more isolated from the ethnically alien environment it tends to become. For example, a large proportion of the Estonians, who comprise only 53.7 percent of Estonia's population, claim that they do not know Russian at all, whereas most of the Lithuanians, who form a compact 80 percent majority in their republic, list Russian as their second language without much apprehension. The result in both cases is, however, roughly the same—these nations, as well as the Latvians at 64.7 percent, remain equally coherent national and social entities, with a very high degree of national self-awareness unaffected by any numbers of foreign stock that live in their republics alongside them.

Could this situation be seen as a lasting one? I am sure it can. The experience of the last several decades has proven that the more pressurized by the Russians the Baltic nations have been, the more cohesive socially and self-aware nationally they have tended to become. The official policies of Russification exercised by making the Russian language, as the "means of intra-national communication," obligatory, or by imposing on the Balts a general Soviet identity above the Lithuanian, Latvian or Estonian one, have not simply failed—in fact, these policies have been counterproductive, for their only tangible result has been a tremendous increase in Baltic nationalism and strong proliferation of national dissent. Looking from a historical perspective, one may now rest assured that nothing short of outright genocide—mass deportations or extermination—could eliminate the Baltic nations as socially, perfectly cohesive and nationally, strongly self-aware entities. As long as the Balts remain in their lands, no number of foreign immigrants and no policy measures will be able to Sovietize them to the degree that Moscow would find satisfactory. But since it is most unlikely that the Kremlin may in the foreseeable future put the gen-ocide of the Balts on its agenda—on the contrary all the signs indicate that it is going to continue with the present policies of assimilation via accom-modation—the comfortable survival of the three Baltic nations in their original shapes is as good as guaranteed.

The same conclusion applies to all major nations and nationalities of the Soviet Union compactly inhabiting at least certain (e.g., rural) parts of their respective territorial units, and to those Soviet nationalities which were either coercively deprived of their territorial units by deportation and wish to return to their homelands (e.g., the Crimean Tatars) or identify themselves with nation states outside the USSR and wish to emigrate to them (e.g., some sections of the German, Jewish, and Polish populations of the USSR, and the Meschs wishing to go to Turkey).

The above conclusion clearly puts me at odds with Sergei Maksudov who, in the preceding chapter, has tried meticulously to substantiate the view that complete Russification is the final and inescapable destiny of the non-Russian peoples of the USSR, with only some of these peoples meeting this destiny sooner and some later. I believe that Maksudov is wrong and that what I regard to be his mistake is rooted in:

(a) his failure to distinguish between proper territorial nations and nationalities, forming self-sufficient communities at least on a village (or rather series of villages) scale, and national minorities interspersed with a dominant territorial nation and inevitably incorporated into the latter's communal life;

(b) his drawing of the conclusion concerning assimilation and acculturation of the non-Russians with Russia mainly from the data concerning the knowledge and usage of Russian by the non-Russians which, in my view, on their own, do not warrant such a conclusion.

Let us examine each root of Maksudov's mistaken conclusion separately:

(a) Historic experience shows that territorial (e.g., rural) nations are able to survive unassimilated through long centuries of foreign rule and eventually assert themselves as, to borrow Hegel's terminology, historical nations by creating their own nation-states, while national minorities, with a few rare exceptions (e.g., most notably the Jews), tend rather quickly to become assimilated and acculturated by the dominant nation.

Some of the minor Soviet nationalities, even if they possess an identifiable territory, have in the course of time practically become national minorities living among the dominant Russians. This applies in the first place to the Finno-Ugric Izhors and Vepses who are by now almost completely assimilated and have become indistinguishable from ethnic Russians. The Saamis, Itelmans, Udegeyans, Khakases, Shorts, Khantys, Mansis, and many other nationalities of predominantly Mongoloid racial origins, although they are today, in fact, also national minorities within Russia, mix with the Europeanoid Russians much less easily and willy-nilly retain their ethnic identity, despite of so many of them having lost their national languages and cultures. These nationals are in a peculiar "in-between" situation, neither *natsmeny* nor Russians, and only the future will tell in which direction they will tend to develop. (Outright refusal by the Russians to treat them as fellow-Russians may push them back to the rediscovery of their roots and full identification with them.)

Russia, along with the U.S.A., was always one of the most effective melting pots for foreign settlers. People of French, Scottish, German,

Dutch, Danish, Greek, and many other national origins who settled in imperial Russia usually already in the second generation turned out to be more Russian than the Russians themselves. The same was true of the members of the many nationalities incorporated into the Russian Empire who left their homelands and came to live in Russia proper. I was therefore rather surprised to learn from Maksudov's chapter that so many among the Ukrainians and Belorussians who were settled such a long time ago in Siberia, Kazakhstan and the Caucasus have to the present day retained their national languages and customs. However, one has to agree with Maksudov's general assessment of the national-cultural situation of these peoples as well as of the Soviet Jews, Germans, and even of the Koreans and the Chinese. Whatever of their specific national identities is left, or rather newly acquired, is basically the result of the discriminatory policies of the Soviet regime with regard to these national minorities. I believe that if these nationalities were not officially discriminated against and not reminded of their ethnic identity in such an insistent manner, the process of their acculturation and assimilation would be by now at a much more advanced stage.

(b) The fact that many non-Russian nationals speak Russian as their native, let alone second, language does not at all imply that they have lost or are about to lose their separate national and cultural identity. Russian is, after all, in the Soviet Union the "means of intra-national communication" and each educated person has to speak it as well as he or she can master it. One should also not forget that for Soviet Asians the mastery of Russian is the most natural means to getting themselves Westernized and becoming a party to global culture. Russian in the Soviet realm of rule performs a similar function to that which English performs today, and French performed before World War II, in the Western world, and therefore only the most backward, least culturally advanced sections of the non-Russian population of the USSR, the ones who could hardly play a significant role in the national-cultural revival, do not speak, write or read it. The strongest nationalist core in all the non-Russian nations of the USSR consists of speakers of perfect Russian which, bearing in mind what has been said above, is only natural, as the more educated and nationally aware the non-Russian national is the better he speaks, reads, and writes Russian.

In all national-liberation and anticolonial movements the leading and most active group always consisted of people who culturally and linguistically were almost undistinguishable from the nationals of the country of their nation's oppressor. English-educated Indians started the National Congress and led India to independence. Francophone Algerian, Moroccan, and Tunisian Arabs waged liberation wars against French rule. One of the finest writers in the Spanish language, Jose Rizal, became the Filippinos' leader in their uprising against Spain. And the Irish, having lost their native language almost entirely, have never stopped being Irish and fought for their independence from Great Britain throughout centuries crowning this fight in the aftermath of World War I with the creation of the Irish Free State.

Maksudov is right when he condemns the Soviet nationalities policy by the means of which the Soviet state is trying to deprive the non-Russian nations and nationalities of the USSR of their traditional identities and to impose upon them the uniform Soviet-made surrogate of Russian culture. This policy culturally impoverishes the affected nations and artificially stagnates their progress. The quotation from a Soviet source about the former and contemporary usages of the Buryat language which Maksudov cites in his article is the most apt illustration of this fact.

However, Maksudov is wrong in asserting that the Buryats, Chuvashes, Volga Tatars, and many other nations and nationalities of the USSR are destined soon to disappear from the world's ethnic map. His evidence does not warrant such conclusions. On the contrary, the evidence shows that, except for the national minorities, the nations and nationalities of the USSR are very much alive, self-aware and not at all ready to succumb to Soviet policies directed at their acculturation. As long as Soviet nationalities policy will be based on the principles of "socialist federalism" the various non-Russian nations and nationalities in the USSR will take full advantage of the opportunities it offers them for further consolidating themselves in all possible respects—demographically, linguistically, culturally, historically, environmentally, and spiritually.

All members of a national community, including the "national cadres" themselves, are to a greater or lesser degree involved in activities directed at using the given circumstances of Soviet "socialist federalism" for the preservation of their nation and, as far as this is possible, for the enhancement of its status and general improvement of its lot: the "national cadres" mostly for the sake of getting more autonomous powers to themselves but also in order to reconcile their national consciousness with their Moscow-serving political function. Hence, we observe in the USSR's national republics an extraordinary phenomenon of all-embracing national dissent which in this overall form could best be described as *national conservationism*. Within its wide spectrum we can then distinguish different degrees and forms, ranging from almost complete conformity to outright national resistance.

The *third* disadvantage consists in the officially definite boundaries of the territorial nations within the USSR which can be regarded as those of their potential sovereign states. There is very little doubt that the very existence of precise boundaries between the union republics is a factor that under the right conditions can facilitate secession and, ultimately, the break-up of the Union. By proclaiming (in Art. 72) that "each union republic retains the right freely to secede from the USSR," the Soviet Constitution even provides for such a break-up a legitimate foundation which, although in conditions of political stability, is of no practical significance, can in changed circumstances become an issue of the highest legal and political relevance.

Many of the Ukrainian, Baltic, Armenian, and Georgian national dissenters are already now using this legal-constitutional argument every time they raise the issue of national rights, e.g., the right of their nations to self-determination. By doing so, they try to stress the law-abiding nature of their separatist activities and, when indicted for such activities, gain a plausible legal position not only for defense but also for accusing the prosecuting authorities of gross violation of the country's Constitution and laws which they are supposed to enforce. Legal fictions, as a rule, have a powerful potential for being translated into political and, consequently, legal realities, and should never be dismissed as irrelevant.

The *fourth* disadvantage consists in the fact that the Soviet federal state structure has caused a radical change in the political self-awareness of the Russians who, because of it, have become fully conscious of their existence in a complex and, in most cases, hostile multinational environment and do not consider themselves any more the sole relevant nation of the state. In other words, the Russians took account of the fact that theirs is not the whole country but only its one part (though the overwhelmingly biggest one), out of fifteen such parts. This fact contains many significant political implications, all wholly inconsistent with the Soviet political status quo.

The reports of Brezhnev and Andropov quoted above clearly state that there are within the Soviet officialdom certain forces which have a dismissive attitude toward the non-Russian nations and which would like to abolish the multinational structure of the Soviet state altogether, thus practically restoring the Russian Empire in its original, fully unitary and Russian-chauvinist, shape. Expressing an attitude quite widely held among Russian and even some non-Russian *apparatchiks*, such views hardly represent, however, a significant segment of the authentic Russian public opinion, as they have never been aired in *samizdat* literature that provides the only reliable source from which one could get a realistic idea about what the authentic Russian public opinion may really be like.

It is well known that Russian liberal-democratic dissenters, people like Andrei Sakharov, and those associated with him in the Soviet human rights movement (e.g., Vladimir Bukovsky, the late Andrei Amalrik, Sergei Kovalyov, Andrei Tverdokhlebov, Yuriy Orlov, to name but a few), unequivocally adhere to the right of all Soviet nations to self-determination and on many occasions—by coming out in support of the demands of Ukrainian, Armenian, and Baltic dissenters for their countries' independence—have shown that they mean it. One may argue, however, that these people are a minuscule minority of maverick intellectuals who are not truly representative of the mainstream Russian public opinion and that it would make more sense to listen to what the avowed Russian nationalists have to say on that issue.

It may sound paradoxical, but it is nevertheless a fact that, as far as the non-Slavic nations of the USSR are concerned, the Russian nationalists are more firmly committed to letting them go their own way than even the Russian liberal-democrats. This is, for example, what Alexander Solzhenitsyn, the recognized spokesman for unofficial Russian nationalism, has to say on that issue: "There is one way out for us (and the sooner we take it the more effective it will be), namely, for the state to switch its attention away from distant continents—and even away from Europe and the south of our country—and make the North-East the center of (Russian) national activity and settlement and a focus for the aspirations of young people. Of course, a switch of this kind would oblige us sooner or later to withdraw our protective surveillance of Eastern Europe. *Nor can there be any question of any peripheral nation being kept within the bounds of our country*" (emphasis added).[36] Later Solzhenitsyn developed this thesis into an overall theory of repentance and self-limitation according to which, in order to be able to solve her manifold problems, Russia has to withdraw first from all foreign lands and then concentrate on healing her deep wounds inflicted during Bolshevik rule within strictly defined Russian ethnic boundaries.[37]

Solzhenitsyn could, however, be classified as someone whose position is one in-between of liberal-democratic and nationalistic orientation. This could not be said about Evgeniy Vagin, one of the founders and leaders of the underground Russian nationalist organization, *VSKhSON*, and himself an ardent monarchist. But even in his view, the Russian imperial idea should be limited only to the unity of Orthodox Christian nations.[38] Such is also the position of the most reactionary, one could say fascist-oriented, Russian nationalist authors of the notorious underground document *Slovo Natsii* (The Nation Speaks).[39]

I know only of one Russian nationalist[40] and of one Russian liberal democrat,[41] both of whom are equally in favor of keeping, after the breakdown of the Soviet regime, the present Soviet Union intact, because, in their view, in conditions of genuine national and individual freedom, a union-state of nations sharing the same historic experience will be to their mutual benefit as well as to the benefit of the rest of mankind. All the others are firmly against it. Therefore, one should fully agree with John Dunlop who, after having thoroughly analyzed various shades of Russian nationalist opinion, came to the following conclusion: "On the controversial question of Russia's future boundaries, it seems that the majority of Russian nationalists would tend to agree with the views of 'The Nation Speaks' and of Evgeniy Vagin, which would imply that at least Latvia, Estonia, Lithuania, the Western Ukraine, Armenia, Azerbaidzhan, Tadzhikistan, Turkmenia and Uzbekistan might be offered the choice of secession."[42] One has to add to this list Georgia which "The Nation Speaks" explicitly singles out for secession, albeit without Abkhazia whose people, the document states, actively expressed their will to be separated from Georgia and reunited with Russia.

The majority of Russian nationalists are not only in favor of granting the non-Slavic republics full independence (their attitude to the future association among Russia, the Ukraine, and Belorussia, except for their mainly Catholic or Uniate western parts, being yet very ambiguous) but sees it as mandatory from the point of view of Russia's own national self-interest. The reasons for drawing such a conclusion are manifold. Some of them were briefly explained in the introductory portion of this chapter. One should be reminded here of one of them—the Russians are getting increasingly worried about becoming a minority within the USSR.[43] This situation in particular fosters among them the same separatist and isolationist attitudes which are common to minoritarian nations within a multinational state. As follows from Russian nationalist dissident writings, the Russians start resenting their situation within the USSR so much that, if given a choice, they may prefer to dissociate themselves altogether from "all the aliens whom we have to feed," even if that would mean the loss of their imperial status and ambitions.

In recent years the pattern of migration within the USSR has changed dramatically; nowadays not only the Russians are populating the non-Russian areas but the non-Russians in increasing numbers inhabit the Russian mainland itself,[44] taking away a certain proportion of "good jobs" from the Russians. This is another powerful source of Russian resentment of the multinational environment in which under Soviet "socialist federalism" they have to live.

Finally, the Russians see themselves as the primary victims of the Soviet system and "hungry providers" of other Soviet nations' well-being. They, therefore, refuse to comprehend and accept the overwhelming anti-Russianism of the non-Russians. They assume that, as co-victims of the regime, the non-Russians should naturally and increasingly identify themselves with the Russians—"you are also victims and, by that, Russianized" (*"vy tozhe postradavshye, a, znachit, obrusevshye"*), typically cries out the Russian hero of Vladimir Vysotsky's song. They are literally baffled by the blunt and insistent refusal of the non-Russians to differentiate between

Russia proper and the USSR, between the Soviet policy of sovietization, adversely affecting all nations, and first and foremost the Russians themselves, and Russia's policy of Russification, benefiting the Russians and adversely affecting only the non-Russians.

This mutual incomprehension intensifies the animosity between the Russians and the non-Russians but it also increases their common desire to get separated from each other. The threat to the country's unity comes now, because of that, equally from both sides of the Russian-non-Russian tension. It is not by accident that some Russian nationalist dissenters are putting forward the idea that Russia should be the first union republic to use the right of secession from the USSR.[45] Ironic in form, this idea expresses in a nutshell what many Russians genuinely and strongly feel.

This may be seen as a remarkable achievement of the Soviet national policy aimed at "drawing-together" the Soviet nations. It seems that all the Soviet nations, the Russians and the non-Russians alike, in their common resentment and rejection of the Soviet multinational state, were drawn by this policy very closely together indeed. That this kind of drawing-together of Soviet nations is exactly the opposite of the one the Soviet authorities intended is a different matter altogether.

The deep animosity between the Russians and non-Russians notwithstanding, the growing awareness of the nationalist dissenters of whatever party of the fundamental unity of their "splintering" purpose has initiated in the USSR the process of gradual unification of the—by definition, particularistic—national dissenters into a single all-Union pattern. This is especially well demonstrated by the close cooperation between the Russian democratic and "law-defending" dissidents with almost every existing non-Russian nationalist and religious movement in the country. As an anonymous Soviet dissident has aptly put it in one of the *samizdat* documents: "The preposterous Marxist slogan 'proletarians of all countries, unite' was definitively and irreversibly replaced in the USSR by the only realistic and operational one: 'nationalists of all nations, unite.' "

Implications for the Future

The nationalist threat to the Soviet Union's integrity should not, however, be overestimated. Nationalist dissent, whatever its intensity and scope, will hardly be able to produce by itself the collapse of the Soviet system of rule; first, because of the inherently fragmented nature of different nationalisms which cannot be totally overcome by any unifying pattern; and, second, because of national issues being played out on the various margins of the Soviet state, which minimizes their possible impact on the effective exercise of power over the whole country by the center. For national issues to start playing a decisive role in the USSR's disintegration, the authority in the center of the Union must collapse first. Of course, national unrest, if sufficiently widespread and strong, could precipitate such a collapse provided the disruptive factors within the system of central authority itself were mature enough to burst out if thus incensed. Today the Polish and Afghan national movements are putting the system of authority in Moscow to such a test, but for the time being that system is quite successful in standing up to it. As long as this is so, there is hardly any real chance for either the Poles or the Afghans or, by the same token, for any other nation under Soviet control to change their present situation in any significant way. However, if the authority in Moscow collapses—and this could happen at any time, because of many different reasons and pressures most of which are quite remote from the purely national ones[46]—all the nations now under Soviet control, those within the USSR as much as the ones formally outside its "socialist federal" structure, will equally for the first time acquire a real chance to assert themselves as genuinely autonomous entities. It is most likely that under such circumstances all these nations would take up that chance vigorously enough to become able, by the means of each of them striving for their own freedom, to finalize together the process of the USSR's disintegration begun with the collapse of the central authority in Moscow. The era of Soviet "socialist federalism" could thus be brought to a close.

As Valeriya Novodvorskaya, a prominent dissident Russian poet, has succinctly put it in one of her poems:

What can one see there, in that remote blueness,
Behind the line of dawn?
Most probably Russia,
Certainly not the country of Soviets.

(Chto tam, v dalekoy sini,
Za kromkoyu rassveta?
Navernoe Rossiya,
A ne strana Sovetov.)

One should add that not only restored national Russia is to be seen there, "behind the line of dawn," but also Georgia, Uzbekistan, Lithuania, and many other genuine nation-states restored after so many years to their true selves.

Soviet nationalities policy, in general, and the peculiar federal arrangement of the Soviet state, in particular, have produced a very effective, maybe even an optimal, instrument of firm centralized rule over a multi-

national country. What they have failed totally to achieve is the rapprochement between the nations thus ruled which would lead to them gradually
withering away and organically merging into a new historical community
of the Soviet people. The experience of the Soviet state has shown that its
nationalities policy and structural arrangements for within-state accom-
modation of many different nations were in principle unable to achieve
such a goal; moreover, that they were totally counterproductive insofar as
its achievement was concerned.

The Soviet nations living under the conditions imposed upon them by
the Soviet regime have proved to be absolutely unemergeable (or, if using
a paraphrase of the Soviet official terminology, *"unsliyable"*) and, as things
in the USSR stand now, probably nothing short of genocide would be able
to deprive them of their firmly entrenched separate national identities. The
persistent and sharpening multinationalism of the USSR is the time bomb
ticking under the surface of the illusory Soviet monolith, and there is no
conceivable force in the whole world which would be powerful enough to
defuse it.

Notes

1. USSR's Constitution, Art. 85, in Robert Sharlet, *The New Soviet Constitution of 1977: Analysis and Text*, (Brunswick, Ohio: King's Court Communications, 1978) 101–102.
2. ———, USSR's Constitution, Art. 87, Sharlet, 102.
3. ———, This is how this arrangement is defined in Art. 70 of the USSR's Constitution, ibid.; 97.
4. ———, USSR's Constitution, Art. 71, ibid.; 97.
5. In the sub-union autonomous national units within the non-Russian union republics, these languages are used alongside with a third one, that of this particular union republic.
6. Milan Kundera, *The Book of Laughter and Forgetting*, (Harmondsworth, England: Penguin, 1983), 159.
7. ———.
8. The sole exception to this rule is the Armenian Republic where, according to the 1979 census, only 2.3% of the population are Russians. For the statistics on Russian presence in non-Russian areas of the USSR as established by the census of 1979, see the officially published Soviet study by V.I. Kozlov, *Natsional'nosti SSSR: Etnodemograficheskiy obzor*, (The Nations of the USSR: Ethnodemographic Review), 2nd ed., (Moscow: *Finansy i Statistika*, 1982), esp. 117ff.
9. Some nations of the autonomous national-territorial units existing outside the

Russian SFSR feel themselves oppressed in addition by their respective "union-republican nations." They consider themselves as suffering under a double national yoke which they would be keen to exchange for the single Russian one. Thus, the Abkhazians who suffer from Georgian oppression and want to get rid of it, mounted a vigorous campaign for the transfer of their autonomous republic from the Georgian SSR to the Russian SFSR. For facts on this Abkhazian protest movement, see well-documented reports in RFE-RL, *Materialy samizdata* (Samizdat Materials), esp. issues No. 20, 29 June 1984; and No. 24, 3 August 1984.

10. See, for example, Alexander Solzhenitsyn, *Letter to Soviet Leaders*, London: Fontana, 1974; 56ff. See also Alexander Solzhenitsyn (ed.), *From Under the Rubble*, (London: Collins and Harwill, 1975); *A. Solzhenitsyn Speaks to the West*, (London: Bodley Head, 1979); and a number of his other texts.

11. See Alexander Zinoviev's "Conversation with George Urban" in *Encounter*, 63, No. 4, (April 1984), 17.

12. ———, 23.

13. I would like to draw the reader's attention to Georg Brunner's excellent analysis of national discrimination of scattered national minorities in the USSR which stems from this theoretical attitude of the Bolsheviks and which is practiced in direct violation of Article 27 of the International Covenant on Civil and Political Rights to which the Soviet Union is a party (see G. Brunner's contribution to Vol. I of the present series).

14. One should remember that in *State and Revolution* written in the summer of 1917, i.e., on the eve of Bolshevik seizure of power, Lenin devoted a full chapter to the theoretical denunciation of federalist, i.e., to him anarchist, deviations in the ranks of the Marxist socialists. For the relevant references to Marx's, Engels's and Lenin's works on the national question see Walker Connor, *The National Question in Marxist-Leninist Theory and Strategy*, (Princeton: Princeton University Press, 1984), especially the notes to chapters 1–3.

15. According to that Constitution, they were supposed to be the highest organs of Soviet Russia's state power. For the full text of, and a detailed commentary on, the 1918 Constitution of the RSFSR, see A.L. Unger, *Constitutional Developments in the USSR: A Guide to the Soviet Constitutions*, (London: Methuen, 1981), 7–41.

16. See V.V. Pentkovskaya, "Rol' V.I. Lenina v obrazovanii SSSR," (The Role of V.I. Lenin in the Formation of the USSR), in *Voprosy istorii* (Problems of History), 3/1956; 16–18; and S.I. Yakubovskaya, "Rol' V.I. Lenina v sozdanii SSSR" (The Role of V.I. Lenin in the Creation of the USSR), in *Kommunist*, 10/1956; 36. These two sources, first presented to the English speaking readership by Richard Pipes (see his *The Formation of the Soviet Union: Communism and Nationalism, 1917–1925*, 2nd edition, (Cambridge: Harvard University Press, 1964), contain such a wealth of previously unavailable information that their study is indispensable for anyone seriously interested in the problem of the USSR's origins. I am greatly indebted to Dr.

Victor Soboda for pointing out this fact to me and for bringing to my attention some data of which I was hitherto unaware.

17. See *Dvenadtsatyi s'ezd RKP(b): 17–23 aprelya 1923g.* (The Twelfth Congress of the RCP(B): 17–23 April 1923), (Moscow: Partizdat, 1923); 209–10.

18. The name "USSR" was simultaneously proposed by the Ukrainian and the Transcaucasian Congresses of Soviets on 13 December 1922. See *Istoriya sovetskoy konstitutsii (v dokumentakh): 1917–1956*, (Moscow: Yurizdat, 1957), 383–88.

19. For the official Soviet translation of the 1977 USSR's Constitution into English, see *The Times*, London, 6 June 1977; the one quoted in full is R. Sharlet's (see R. Sharlet, *The New Soviet*; 96–97).

20. There are, by the way, no regulations at all concerning the order of the union-republics' secession from the USSR, although Art. 72 of the Constitution proclaims that to be the fundamental right of every such republic. It shows that the USSR's "practical mind" is fully concentrated on further expansion and excludes even the theoretical possibility of the Union's shrinking or even getting looser.

21. *The New Soviet*, USSR's Constitution, Art. 19; R. Sharlet, 83.

22. *Izvestiia*, 5 October 1977; 3.

23. ——.

24. *Pravda*, 22 December 1982; 2.

25. Hélène Carrère d'Encausse, *L'empire éclaté*, (Paris: Flammarion, 1978).

26. At that time Andropov was already gravely ill and Chernenko in full charge of the ideological policies of the Party.

27. For a detailed report of Tikhvinsky's article in English, see: Dusko Doder, "Soviet Blame Chilled Relations on Reagan-led Russophobia," in *Washington Post*, 27 July 1984; A25–A26.

28. *Pravda*, 1 August 1984; 1.

29. See "Plenum pravleniya SP Ukrainy: Obogashchat' dukhovnuyu zhizn' naroda," (The Plenary Session of the Steering Committee of the Ukrainian Union of Writers: To Enrich the Spiritual Life of the People), *Literaturnaya Gazeta*, 24 June 1987; 2.

30. See, "Zayavlenie TASS," (The TASS Statement), *Pravda*, 24 July 1987; 2.

31. *Pravda*, 22 February 1987; 1.

32. *Pravda*, 20 February 1987; 1.

33. For example, see O. Trubachev, *"Slavyane, Yazyk i istoriya"* (The Slavs, Language and History), in *Pravda*, 28 March 1987; 3, which not only typically exemplifies the continuity of the "Tikhvinsky line" but, in conditions of *glasnost'*, presents that line much more aggressively and with clear Russian-chauvinistic overtones.

34. The quoted figures are taken from V.I. Kozlov, *Natsional'nosti*; there one could also find the relevant figures for the republics that were listed in the text but the exact figures for which have been omitted.

35. Similar conclusions were drawn by Murray Feshbach in *The Soviet Union:*

Population Trends and Dilemmas, (Washington, D.C.: Population Reference Bureau, Inc., 1982).

36. A. Solzhenitsyn, *Letter to Soviet Leaders*; 31–32.
37. See Alexander Solzhenitsyn, "Repentance and Self-Limitation in the Life of Nations", in A. Solzhenitsyn ed., *From Under the Rubble*.
38. Vagin stated his willingness to grant independence to the non-Orthodox nations in a conversation with another dissident, Yuriy Händler, when both were serving their sentences in a Soviet prison camp. For details of this conversation, see: John B. Dunlop, *The Faces of Contemporary Russian Nationalism*, (Princeton, N.J.: Princeton University Press, 1983), 160.
39. For the English text of this document, see, "The Nation Speaks," in *Survey*, 17, No. 3, (1971); especially 196–97.
40. This is Igor' Shafarevich. For his views on the expediency of the present Soviet nations remaining in one state after liberation from Bolshevik oppression, see: "Separation or Reconciliation? The Nationalities Question in the USSR," in A. Solzhenitsyn ed., *From Under the Rubble*.
41. This is Roy Medvedev. His "internationalist" views on the subject are expressed in R. Medvedev, *On Socialist Democracy*, (London: Macmillan, 1975).
42. J.B. Dunlop, *The Faces of*; 164.
43. Growth rates of populations of various nations of the USSR are sharply different: the Muslim nations have the highest ones and the Russians one of the lowest. This is elaborated in more depth by Sergei Maksudov in the preceding chapter. See also Mikhail Bernstam's contribution to Volume II of the present series, and M. Feshbach, *The Soviet Union*.
44. For substantiation, see sources mentioned in the previous footnote.
45. Beside Zinoviev, quoted above (Zinoviev, *Conversation with*), most notably Vladimir Balakhonov, a Russian dissident at this time (November 1987) serving his 15th year in prison camps, who believes that the RSFSR's secession from the USSR is the only possible and the easiest way for Russia to save herself from "sinking into the sea of neighbors who hate her and thus turning not even so much into an Ulster as into a Lebanon". (Quoted from Sergei Grigoryants, *"Imperiya ili soyuz [Natsional'nye problemy v SSSR],"* /Empire or Union [Nationality Problems in the USSR]/, in *Russkaya Mysl'*, No. 3689, 4 September 1987; 5; originally published in Moscow's unofficial magazine, *Glasnost'*, of which Grigoryants is Chief Editor.)
46. For a detailed analysis of the possible causes of such a collapse of authority in Moscow and the forms in which this collapse may take place, see R.V. Burks's, F. J. M. Feldbrugge's and my own contributions to Volume I of the present series.

3

Prospects for Soviet Slavs in Conditions Favorable to the Establishment of National Freedom

VICTOR SWOBODA

The Decree about Peace was proclaimed by Lenin on 26 October 1917 (old style) at the Second All-Russian Congress of the Soviets and passed unanimously at 11 P.M., mere hours after the Revolution of 24–25 October. It is significant that Lenin's new Workers' and Peasants' Government defined "a just and democratic peace" as "an immediate peace without annexations (i.e., without the seizure of other [*chuzhikh*] lands, and without forcible joining of other peoples)." The concept of "annexation" was defined with specific reference to the democratic sense of justice:

> By annexation or seizure of other lands the Government understands, in accordance with the sense of justice of democracy in general and of the working classes in particular, every joining of a small or weak people to a large or powerful state without this people's agreement and wish precisely, clearly, and voluntarily expressed, irrespective of when this forcible joining was effected and also irrespective of how far developed or backward the nation is which is being forcibly joined or forcibly retained within the borders of the given state.

The concept of a nation's "wish" is interpreted widely: "irrespective of whether this wish is expressed in the press, in people's assemblies, in the decisions of parties, or in rebellions and uprisings against national oppression." A nation's wish thus expressed should be met by granting it "a right to decide by free vote, after the complete withdrawal of the armed forces of the annexing or generally more powerful nation and without the slightest coercion, the question of the forms of the state existence of that nation."[1]

"Annexations by Great Russians" are specifically mentioned in Lenin's decree,[2] thus obviously implying that the "non-Great-Russian" Slavs, Ukrainians, and Belorussians, are as much victims of annexations as all other of "Russia's borderlands."

The nearest approximation to the free vote requirement occurred in the elections to the short-lived Constituent Assembly in November 1917, when a two-to-one majority in the Ukraine voted for the Ukrainian socialist candidates as against socialists associated with Moscow, and Lenin himself, writing two years later, was still quite aware of this fact's importance.[3]

The intimate connection between peace and national freedom, so clear in Lenin's decree, was strikingly emphasized six decades later by the Ukrainian scholar Iurii Badz'o in his analysis of Soviet policy, in particular in the Ukraine, which is comparable to Ivan Dzyuba's famous 1965 critique of Russian and Soviet nationalities policy.[4] Badz'o knows that national freedom, just as human rights in general, are attainable only in a democratic society; and, in turn, "only the democratization of the Soviet Union, of Soviet socialism can . . . reduce ideological and the also political tensions between states with different social systems." He sees one possible way out of the Soviet blind alley in Eurocommunism:

> The future, and possibly even the immediate, political fate of Soviet society depends to the significant degree on the firmness and consistency of the Eurocommunists: whether democratic forces will prevail in the ranks of the party-state stratum, or whether the Stalinists will again gain the upper hand . . . increasing the threat to world peace. Yes, in today's world stuffed with nuclear explosives . . . the problem of the democratization of Soviet society is directly connected with the problem of war and peace. Every despotism and antidemocratism is a threat to peace. If the antidemocratic Stalinist forces triumph in Soviet society . . . the threat of a world war will increase. I urge you, those who stand at the helm of state power, not to treat lightly the fate of the peoples of the USSR and of the entire world, the fate of world peace![5]

Thus appealed Badz'o in April 1979 to the highest Party and Government agencies in Moscow whose great concern for world peace found its speedy and typical expression: on 23 April 1979, he was arrested and sentenced to seven years' in a concentration camp and five years of internal exile.

Nevertheless, the basic assumption being that history does not stand still, so that systemic political change is inevitable, and its probability is better than even within the next five years,[6] historical precedents may be used to generate possible scenarios of the way the end of the Soviet system may come about.[7]

I

What may be the likely nature of the "new Russian nation state" which is postulated by a number of writers? Dr. Shtromas's conjecture is that "Political change in the Soviet Union is less likely to involve the establishment of democratic rule than to establish a *rational* and nationally-minded government as opposed to the present *irrational*, single-ideology-based . . . regime . . ." While the new government "would have the full support of the technocrats, as well as of the overwhelming majority of people, it may also be authoritarian for a significant period of time." "There is little doubt that it will be technocratic in character and nationalistic in ideology."[8] Similarly, Liudmila Alekseeva observes that the adherents of the Russian national movement concentrate all their efforts, both in *samizdat* and in *tamizdat*, on criticizing the imperfections and defects of democracy, both American, all varieties of West European, and the short-lived (eight months in 1917) Russian one. All of this is declared by them to be unsuitable for the future new Russia. While some of the adherents of the Russian national movement lean toward monarchy as the traditional Russian mode of government, the majority accept the idea of "authoritarian rule" without clarifying what this idea entails. The determining role in the elaboration of the contemporary Russian Orthodox *Weltanschauung* belongs to Solzhenitsyn; in 1973–74, he asked in this connection rhetorically:

> So should we not perhaps acknowledge that for Russia this [democratic] path was either false or premature? That for the foreseeable future, perhaps, whether we like it or not, whether we intend it or not, Russia is nevertheless destined to have an authoritarian order? Perhaps this is all that she is ripe for today? . . .
>   Let it be an authoritarian order, but one founded not on an inexhaustible "class hatred" but on love of your fellow man . . .[9]

Petr Samorodnitskii puts it more bluntly, saying that nationally thinking Russians see the only alternative to communism in the old form of despotism traditional to Russia, while he himself believes that Russia can be reborn from communism only as a country of the Western type, as a democratic country.[10] A military dictatorship occurs in a number of scenarios. The *samizdat* author A. Kronidov fears that it may come in some fifteen years' time, and he is quite pessimistic as regards its effects, though he still has a residual belief in a "historical miracle."[11] Bukovsky is convinced that "any liberalization of the Soviet system will necessarily pass through a phase of absolute power for the military."[12] Pliushch is of the opinion that "the circumstances tend rather toward a military-technocratic coup (*Umsturz*)," and after a while the rulers will be faced by a dilemma: "either democratization or war."[13] Kronid Liubarsky fears a military coup, which will if anything result in a stronger version of the existing regime.[14] P. Abovin-Egides believes, like Samorodnitsky and in disagreement with opinions such as represented by Shtromas, Bukovsky, and Pliushch, that the way to democracy via autocracy is unrealistic.[15] The editors of the Moscow *samizdat* journal (*al'manakh*) *Varianty* (embracing social democratic, socialist and "Eurocommunist" opinion) surmised in October 1981 that "in a situation of acute crisis, the bloc in power will split, and one part of the bloc will collaborate with the opposition. For what concerns us, this is not of course a matter for the near future."[16]

Some scenarios stress the importance of the national factor; thus, Liubarsky warns that the popular idea of Russian-Orthodox authoritarianism will repel non-Russian national opinion; "it is the national opposition which now presents the chief danger to the regime"; thus to reject an alliance with that opposition would mean "unconsciously strengthening the regime."[17] Similarly Aleksandr Galich:

Soviet leadership sees in national liberation movements a powerful force. And it is afraid of this force, and perhaps it is afraid of it more than of anything else. Uprisings in national republics are unavoidable and irreversible, and it is they that may serve as the beginning of the end of the system.[18]

Bohdan Hawrylyshyn examines the feasibility of a peaceful evolution:

Some of the Russians in the power élite are likely to start having quiet doubts about the benefits of keeping their power monopoly over the other nationalities within the Soviet Union. The key benefit they derive is the "national ego massage." But the economic and political costs of such dominance are high.

They may realize that economic benefits may be derived from concentrating their energy on a smaller territory "if they would give up the burden of 'managing' the Soviet Union. They might become willing to share the power more equitably with other nationalities." But the probability for peaceful evolution is very low, and Hawrylyshyn proposes the following as the most likely scenario:

The probable consequences of the attempt to maintain the status quo would be more dissatisfaction, alienation, and dissidence; then, violent eruptions that would be amplified by some catalytic event, leading to the disintegration of the Soviet Union. As a result, most of the present constituent republics would become independent states. They would wish to maintain their independence for a number of decades. After tasting the joys and bitterness of such independence, they would likely voluntarily integrate into bigger entities, such as a United States of Europe or Central Asia, respectively, while maintaining their full cultural autonomy, as is the case in the present European Economic Community. A Russian republic would also find its place in some such supranational construction, the way West Germany did in the EEC—a strong partner, but just a partner.[19]

Let us now examine the various present-day Russian views of national freedom in general, and specifically as applied to the Soviet, or Eastern, Slavs. On the extreme right is Gennadii Shimanov's vision of "the Orthodoxization of the whole world and . . . a certain Russification of it"; for him, "the Soviet Union is not a mechanical conglomerate of disparate nations but a mystical organism . . . , a small mankind with the Russian people at its head"; and he reproaches Solzhenitsyn for his recognition of the border nations' right to secession.[20] But this form of National Bolshevism has no wide currency,[21] which cannot be said of the National Bolshevism of the Soviet establishment, which emphasizes not the Orthodoxy, as done by Shimanov, but the imperial, great-power idea. Within the country with regard to the non-Russian nations this turns into discrimination and Russification, and the subordination of economic and all other interests of individual nations to the interests of the whole, the USSR, where the Russian people is proclaimed, according to the official formula, *primus inter pares*. . . . Chauvinism is coupled with the conviction that democratic transformations in the USSR . . . would be fraught with the successes of separatist trends in the non-Russian Soviet republics and in the countries of Eastern Europe included in the Soviet block, and therefore such democratic transformations are to be resisted.[22] Similar is the chronologically earlier anonymous Slovo natsii which advocated the rebirth of "the great, one and indivisible Russia" and opposed any national freedom for non-Russians, among whom the Belorussian nation was said to be a fabrication, while the tiny Ukraine would not be able to stay independent for long because large parts of it, sufficiently Russified in the author's opinion, would stay with Russia in the first place, while the western Ukraine would be claimed by Poland; the small agricultural rump would soon, like the prodigal son, return to the forgiving Russian parents.[23] Vladimir Osipov's *samizdat* journal *Veche*, the focus of the Russian national trend in 1971–74,[24] welcomed the formation of the USSR, "the fraternal union of peoples having equal rights," though regretting Russification, and denied the existence of any oppression of nationalities in the pre-revolutionary Russian Empire; moreover, Osipov believes that Ukrainians and Belorussians are really Russians.[25] The All-Russian Social Christian Union for the Liberation of the People rejected the right of independence for the Ukraine, Belorussia, and the smaller nationalities of the USSR.[26]

Solzhenitsyn favors national freedom but hopes that it will result in voluntary unity. Thus, he asks in his *The Gulag Archipelago*:

> . . . why does their [Ukrainians'] desire to secede annoy us so much? . . . Like it or not, the time is at hand when we must pay out on all promissory notes guaranteeing self-determination and independence. . . . We must leave the decision to the Ukrainians themselves—let federalists and separatists try their persuasions. Not to give way would be foolhardy and cruel. And the gentler, the more tolerant, the more careful to explain we are now, the more hope there will be of restoring unity in the future.[27]

Also in his letter to the Toronto [McMaster University] Conference on Russian-Ukrainian Relations and to the Harvard Ukrainian Research Institute he maintained that "all questions (regarding 'separatism or federation' or otherwise) can really be solved only by the local population," but also insisted that "from the sufferings and national hurts of our peoples (all peoples of Eastern Europe) one should be able to extract not the experience of discord but the experience of unity."[28] But in his *Letter to Soviet Leaders* he seems to bracket Ukrainians with Russians ("It is the fate of the Russian and Ukrainian peoples that preoccupies me above all"), so that when he says, "Nor can there be any question of any peripheral nation (*okrainnye natsii*) being forcibly kept within the bounds of our country," he could hardly have thought of Ukrainians as "peripheral"; the same must apply *a fortiori* to Belorussians.[29] Again, in his article "Repentance and self-limitation" Solzhenitsyn declares that "with regard to all the peoples in and beyond our borders forcibly drawn into our orbit, we can fully purge our guilt by giving them genuine freedom to decide their future for themselves"; however, for him the Ukrainians and Belorussians are included in "us," not in "them": thus, when he talks about Poland in previous centuries "annexing our territory and oppressing us" he includes under the heading of "our territory," "Galician Ruthenia and Podolia; . . . Polesia, Volynia and the Ukraine"; "our own country," "our own people" are for him "Russians, Ukrainians and Belorussians."[30] All in all, Roy Medvedev seems to be right in his summing up that Solzhenitsyn would keep both the Ukraine and Belorussia.[31]

Solzhenitsyn's associate and a fellow-contributor to *From under the Rub-*

ble, Igor' Shafarevich in his article on the nationalities question has nothing specific to say about the Ukraine or Belorussia but he invokes "centuries-old alliances" against Estonian demands for independence (it must be admitted that it is rather a strained invocation; similar alliances could have been claimed for most other non-Russian nations with as much—or as little—justification) and asserts that "a common history has welded the nations of our land together," though admitting that "each people must of course consult its own conscience and decide whether to take . . . upon itself" "the historic mission of the peoples that inhabit what was once Russia and is now the Soviet Union," which he sees in their ability "to perceive and tell the world things that nobody else can tell . . . they can point the way out of the labyrinth in which mankind is now lost." Shafarevich admits Russian power-mania and imperialist proclivities as well as the Russians' inability to see other nations' right "to exist within their own national identity," and finds it "easy to understand how other peoples . . . are horrified and infuriated by the sight of the immense Russian tide advancing on them, ready to swallow them up without a trace." He hopes that his vision is a feasible one, "but to be honest I am not sure it will work out. There is too much deep-seated resentment and perhaps too little time left to neutralize it." He fears the specter of "national hatred," and concludes apocalyptically:

> And who can say which nations will survive yet another cataclysm, perhaps more terrible than any they have been obliged to endure so far? Herein lies the last reason for the extreme acuteness of the national question—it may well become a question of the continued existence of our peoples.[32]

Another contributor to the same volume, Vadim Borisov, in his article "Personality and national awareness" admits that

> Exacerbated national feeling among the various peoples of the Soviet Union is now a fact not to be concealed by braggart phrases about a "historic new community." In fact this community reveals itself as a none too solid ideological crust which can barely restrain the underground tremors of forcibly suppressed national energies.[33]

Academician Sakharov is of the opinion that the republics' constitutional right to secede should be guaranteed by law, though he believes that "the number of republics tending toward secession is, to all appearances, very small,[34] and those tendencies would doubtless become even weaker with time as a result of the future democratization of the USSR."[35]

"The Moscow Helsinki Group advocates unambiguously the strict observance of the equality of national rights and the right of all peoples to manage their own future".[36] The *samizdat* author V. Gorskii (pseudonym) wrote in 1969:

> The collapse of the Soviet empire will not be humiliating or unnatural for Russia. Deprived of her colonies Russia will not become economically impoverished. Likewise, it will not lose its political importance. Freed from the yearnings for occupation and coercion, it will confront its true problems: the building of a free democratic society, religious renaissance, and the creation of a national culture.[37]

The social democrat N. Arguni in his *samizdat* blueprint, "What is to be done after the fall of the totalitarian Communist dictatorship?" proposes under the rubric "National question":

> All Union Republics shall have the right to full separation—the right to secession from the USSR. The question about remaining within the USSR or about secession shall be solved by means of a general [*vsenarodnogo*] referendum. Citizens of all nationalities shall be equal before the law. Discrimination of citizens with respect to nationality shall be a crime punishable under criminal law.[38]

Writing in February 1984 in the *Chronical of Catholic Church in the Ukraine*, Iosyp Terelia sums up that "since the end of the 1970s, a certain part of Russian intelligentsia has begun to have a favorable attitude to our struggle for independence."[39]

A broadly similar spectrum of opinion can be found among recent Russian émigrés. Thus, A. Mikhailovskii writing in the Munich journal *Veche* operates with the concepts "the Russian Empire," "a multinational Russian nation" (*rossiiskaia* in both phrases) the core of which will remain the Russian (*russkaia*) nation, or more precisely "the Russian Orthodox nation" which includes "all branches" (presumably the Russian, Ukrainian, and Belorussian peoples) of "the Russian people-tribe and all so-called allophylians (*inorodtsy*) who have adopted Christianity."[40] Rather curious is Igor' Siniavin's view: He fears that, if the country were entrusted to the "Westernizers," such as Sakharov, they would allow it to disintegrate as it happened in February–October 1917 under Kerensky; in order to gather all the parts together again even tougher (*pokhleshche*) measures would be necessary than on the previous occasion. The aim of this would be "the pledge of freedom of all peoples comprising the historically established union of nations."[41] Boris Paramonov is another representative of the view that the retention of the Ukraine, the Baltic states, and all other republics is a foregone conclusion and not open to discussion.[42]

Against this, many émigrés centered around *Kontinent* expressed their anti-imperialism in a joint "Declaration on the Ukrainian question," signed by Amal'rik, Bukovskii, Galich, Natal'ia Gorbanevskaia, Maksimov, Nekrasov, as well as nine Poles, Czechs, and Hungarians:

> The Soviet Union today is the last colonial empire of the world, and sooner or later the universal tide of national liberation must hit also its anachronistic existence.
> There will be no really free Poles, Czechs or Hungarians without free Ukrainians, Belorussians or Lithuanians. And in the final reckoning—without free Russians. Without Russians freed from imperial strivings, developing their own national existence, respecting the right of other nations to self-determination.
> We strive, in any case, to achieve such a situation in which Ukrainians could freely say whether they wish to live in an independent state.
> We appeal to the Russian participants of the human rights movement in the USSR and to the Russian political emigration to strengthen and deepen cooperation with the fighters for the Ukraine's independence.[43]

Among the human rights activists, Kronid Liubarskii thus formulated mutual dependence between national freedom and democracy:

> There can be no democracy without a full realization of the rights of nations. . . . The USSR is an empire, [and] its democratization is impossible without its break-up. But the opposite is also true: without the democratization of the system, it is impossible to hope for the break-up of the imperial structure.[44]

Boris Vail', on the other hand, believes that "if the Soviet empire collapses it will apparently do so primarily as a result of national movements,"[45] while Samorodnitskii points out that the forcible retention of the Ukraine, Transcaucasia, the Baltic states etc. within the Russian state is disastrous and destructive for Russia herself for it demands of her great efforts and exhaustion of all her strength; for this very reason she has been, and still is, short of that strength needed for securing her own prosperity that could be created by her people's intelligence and work and her own natural resources.[46]

Finally, Aleksandr Zinoviev's views on the nationality question are remarkable for their Alice-in-the-looking-glass quality. He asserts

> . . . that every minority nation or nationality has been enjoying a privileged position in comparison with the Russian people—that they have regarded Russia as their colony,[47]

. . . the Russian people is the poorest and the most oppressed in the Soviet empire,[48]

. . . the great bulk of the citizens of various nationalities are interested in the preservation of the unity of the country,[49]

. . . the Russian people ought to struggle first of all for equality among other peoples and for independence from them,[50] [and] if the Soviet leadership does not radically change its policy with regard to the Russian people it has altogether a chance to suffer a grave defeat in the struggle with national mafias of all kinds and sizes.[51]

II

Before examining Ukrainian and Belorussian views of national freedom, a few basic remarks on the historical background of the Eastern Slavs may be in order. The three nations are rooted in tribal groupings which existed in the prehistoric period, before the formation of the state of Kievan Rus',[52] which was the creation of the Ukrainian (Ruthenian) people, and flourished in the tenth to twelfth centuries. The Galician and Volynian principalities of the thirteenth century continued Ukrainian statehood, and in the following century they were incorporated into Poland and Lithuania respectively. The history of Muscovite Russia begins in the thirteenth–fourteenth centuries with the rise of the Grand Duchy of Vladimir and the Principality of Moscow.[53] The early Belorussian Principality of Polotsk was within the Kievan state, and "the main content of the political history of the Polotsk Principality in the second half of the eleventh and the first half of the twelfth century was the struggle . . . for political separation"[54] (viz, from Kiev). During the thirteenth and fourteenth centuries all Belorussian lands were incorporated into the Grand Duchy of Lithuania, and in 1569 Lithuania entered into a federation with Poland, ceding the Ukrainian lands to her.[55] In the middle of the seventeenth century, the Ukrainian Cossacks' Hetman Bohdan Khmel'nyts'kyi broke away from Poland and sought allies—in his war against Poland—among the Ukraine's neighbors: Turkey, Muscovy, Wallachia, Transylvania, and Sweden, ultimately opting in 1654 for an alliance with Muscovy but continuing negotiations with Sweden and Transylvania. Meanwhile, Muscovy was not treating the relationship as an alliance but as a subjection, and was endeavoring to gradually make the Ukraine an integral part of Muscovy. Dissatisfied with this, Khmel'nyts'kyi was preparing a break with Moscow, but his death in 1657 foiled this. His successors renewed similar attempts, the most dramatic of which—Mazeppa's alliance with Charles XII of Sweden—ended in the Poltava defeat of 1709 which marked the beginning of the end of Ukrainian autonomy; its end came by the late eighteenth century.[56] It should be noted that the Ukraine had never been under Moscow until 1654, nor indeed had Belorussia until her annexation by Russia in the course of the three partitions of Poland in 1772, 1793, and 1795.

The highlight of the modern Ukrainian revival was the outstanding poetry of Taras Shevchenko (1814–61), the Ukraine's national poet; it carries ideas of national independence, human equality, and social justice. In particular, Shevchenko roundly condemned the 1654 alliance with Muscovy for its disastrous consequences for the Ukraine.[57] He was a member of the Brotherhood of Saints Cyril and Methodius (1845–47), the first political organization in the Ukrainian national movement with a definite program. This was embodied in *The Books of the Genesis of the Ukrainian People*, written by the prominent historian Mykola Kostomarov; its concluding lines are:

> 103 . . . And the Ukraine will rise from her grave . . . and Slavdom will rise, and there will be left no tsar or prince . . . or count . . . no lord, no boyar . . . no serf—not in Muscovy, in Poland, in the Ukraine, in Bohemia, in Croatia, in Serbia, not in Bulgaria.
>
> 104 . . . And the Ukraine will be an independent Common Wealth in the Slav Union . . .[58]

The last decade of the nineteenth century saw the appearance of a variety of Ukrainian political parties, and the Ukraine's independence within her ethnic boundaries was often among their aims. Thus, a member of the Ruthenian-Ukrainian Radical party (the western Ukraine, in Austria-Hungary) wrote in 1895 that the Ukraine must sooner or later become an independent state, and "Political independence of the Ukraine is the *conditio sine qua non* of her economic and cultural development, the condition, indeed, of the *possibility* of her existence."[59] Similar formulations appear in the program of the Ukrainian National Democratic party founded in L'viv in 1899 (Ivan Franko and Mykhailo Hrushevs'kyi were among its members), in a resolution of a meeting in L'viv of Ukrainian students from all Austrian establishments of higher learning in 1900, in the program of the Ukrainian Socialist party (in the Russian Ukraine) in 1900, and in the Program of the Action Committee of the Ukrainian Independent Union organized in the Ekaterinoslav *guberniia* in 1915.[60] The fatal 1654 alliance with Muscovy recurs in these contexts, such as in a pamphlet, *The Workers' Question in the Program of the Ukrainian People's Party* (Chernivtsi, 1902), where it is denounced as the beginning of "our nation's misfortune,:[61] or in a speech by M. Mikhnovs'kyi, a leader of the Revolutionary Ukrainian party (RUP) from Kharkov, who demanded adherence to the original 1654 treaty, with the corollary that "the one and indivisible Russia does not exist for us!"[62] This is echoed three quarters of a century later by Badz'o:

> The Ukrainians are a separate people, yet you talk of its "reunification" with the Russians. The Ukraine in the seventeenth century became part of the Russian state with the rights of an autonomous entity, yet now you talk of "the reunification" of the Ukraine with Russia in a single state![63]

Ivan Franko, the Ukraine's major writer and intellectual and political figure, distinguished between his contemporary reality, the longer-term freedom aim, and the distant future of international peace and cooperation:

> The ideal of national independence in every respect, cultural and political, lies for us for the time being . . . beyond the bounds of the possible. . . . But let us not forget that thousands of paths which lead us to its realization are here under our feet. . . . We must use all power and means in order to approach it.
>
> It may be that sometime there will come a time to consolidate some free international unions for achieving higher international aims. But this can happen only when all *national* struggles are fulfilled and when national injuries and subjugation depart into the sphere of historical memories.[64]

Sometimes there would be a change of emphasis between the long-term and short-term aims; thus, the Program of the Ukrainian Democratic party (UDP) (in the Russian Ukraine) of March 1905 included a demand for Ukrainian autonomy within a Russian state with a parliamentary system, while in the autumn of the same year a faction of the UDP formed the Ukrainian Radical party which added a long-term aim, a fully independent Ukraine; at the end of the year both parties united, forming the Ukrainian Democratic Radical party whose program did not include the long-term aim.[65] Similarly, the RUP (Kiev-based) 1903 draft program declared that the RUP

> puts as its most immediate task the complete destruction of Tsarism in alliance with revolutionary parties of all peoples of the Russian state; its replacement by a federative republic . . . with full autonomy of each region in internal affairs on the basis of a democratic constitution . . . and retaining the right of each constituent federative part to a complete state separation in accordance with the wish of the majority of its population expressed by vote.

A rider to the draft pointed out that autonomy was now more important for the Ukrainian proletariat than independence, though the former was undoubtedly a transitional point to the latter, which remained an avowed ideal though meaningless in the program-minimum. A subsequent draft adopted in 1905 demanded a Russian democratic republic and the Ukraine's autonomy. A faction of the RUP, the Ukrainian Social Democratic union (USDU), broke away in 1904 rejecting the independence aim and adopting the task of "introducing the Ukrainian proletariat into the proletarian family of the whole world so that the Ukrainian proletariat would contribute its share to the world-wide proletarian work of liberating the workers." It joined the RSDWP as a national organization, but soon lost its autonomy and became a regional RSDWP organization of Menshevik persuasion. Depleted by arrests, the USDU became defunct in 1912.[66] The Ukrainian faction of the Second State Duma, comprising 47 deputies, in 1907 formed a parliamentary club, the Ukrainian Labor Association; in its program it rejected the secession of non-Russian peoples as impossible and undesirable while advocating national and regional autonomy and self-government.[67]

The fall of czarism in the February 1917 Revolution tilted the balance in favor of autonomism-federalism; thus, though the proclamation of the Provisional Ukrainian Revolutionary Committee of Petrograd, within a week of the event, emphasized national state independence, the nearest practical task was proclaimed to be turning the Russian state, in cooperation with the democracy of other peoples of Russia, into a federative democratic republic with the widest national territorial autonomy of the Ukraine.[68] In March–April, the Society of Ukrainian Progressives, having changed its name to the Union of Ukrainian Autonomists-Federalists, called for the Ukraine's immediate autonomy within a free federative order in the Russian state; a similar declaration was issued by the constituent congress of the Ukrainian Party of Socialists-Revolutionaries.[69]

On 17 March (NS) the Ukrainian Central Rada[70] (UCR) was set up as an all-Ukrainian representative institution. In its first proclamation to the Ukrainian people it referred to "a harmonious family of free peoples" in a new Russia.[71] In March–April, the leader of the UCR, the eminent historian, Prof. Mykhailo Hrushevs'kyi, thus characterized the new political situation:

The demand of people's rule (*narodopravstvo*) and of an essentially democratic order in the Ukraine, in a separated . . . autonomous Ukraine, tied only by federative ties, be it to other Slav peoples, be it to other peoples and regions of the Russian state, is our old slogan. . . . Undoubtedly it will remain that middle political platform on which the uniting of the Ukraine's population will proceed without difference of strata or nationalities; the middle between the program of a simple cultural-national self-determination of nationalities and the demand of political independence.

A broad autonomy of the Ukraine with state rights for the Ukrainian people in federative ties is the program of the given moment from which there can be no retreat. Any obstacles, any hesitation in satisfying it on the part of the leaders of the Russian state or of the leading circles of Russian society can have only one result: that is, the shift to the centre of gravity to the side of Ukrainian independism.[72]

The UCR proclaimed repeatedly its adherence to the autonomy-in-federation principle and support for the Provisional Government (PG), and in May it sent a delegation which handed over a memorandum to the PG saying *inter alia*:

For people who are little acquainted with the history and character of the Ukrainian movement, the scale which it has shown since the very first days of the Revolution is completely unintelligible. That which was considered an affair of a small group of intelligentsia has suddenly acquired a mass character: national slogans and demands have become popular in the masses of the people.

Taking into account unanimous demands of the Ukraine's autonomy voiced by Ukrainian democracy we hope that the Provisional Government will express . . . in principle a favorable attitude to this slogan.[73]

The PG rejected the UCR's demands on the grounds that the decision must be left to the future Constituent Assembly. In June, the UCR declared:

Having rejected the Central Rada's demand, the Provisional Russian Government has consciously acted contrary to the interests of the working people in the Ukraine and contrary to the principle of the self-determination of peoples proclaimed by the Government itself.[74]

And then, in its First Universal, the UCR called for "organizing an autonomous Ukraine," and, in view of the PG's rejection, proclaimed: "From now on, we ourselves will create our life."[75] The UCR elected a government, called the General Secretariat, consisting of individual secretariats (ministries), among which the Secretariat for Inter-National Affairs

has as its aim to unite the work of all nationalities of Russia for struggle towards the autonomous federative order of the Russian Republic and for the Ukrainians' understanding with other nationalities on this basis. First and foremost there stands before the Secretariat for Inter-National Affairs the convoking of a congress of representatives of the peoples and regions of Russia and the preparation of materials for this congress. Next to it is the matter of the speediest understanding with the democracy of national minorities in the Ukraine.[76]

Such a Congress of the Peoples was indeed convoked in September, and Hrushevs'kyi addressing it extended the concept of federation, as a free union of fraternal peoples, from the new Russian Republic to Europe and the whole world, leading to the ideal of a universal free association and world peace. He asserted that

> for federalist Ukrainians, i.e., the dominant current in the Ukraine, . . . federalism is not a transitional stage to state independence. . . . We regard federation . . . as a road to the federation of Europe, and in future to the federation of the whole world. . . . To imperialism, wherever it may develop, outside Russia or within the limits of the federative Russian Republic, we shall oppose the idea of a free union of fraternal peoples. . . . In order to save herself from disaster (Russia) must without fail become federative.[77]

In the meantime, in mid-July, three PG representatives, including the then Prime Minister and Minister of War Alexander Kerensky, arrived in Kiev for negotiations; this resulted in the UCR issuing its Second Universal which declared that the PG recognized the right of the Ukrainian people to self-determination; but, as also in the First Universal, "opposition to the separation of the Ukraine from Russia" and support for "the unity of all of Russia's democratic forces" was expressed. Moreover, the universal provided for the inclusion in the UCR of representatives of the non-Ukrainian nationalities living in the Ukraine and thus made the UCR "the sole supreme organ of revolutionary democracy in the Ukraine." The General Secretariat, which was the Ukraine's government, was referred to as "operating in matters of state government as an organ of the PG." At the same time, the PG representatives issued a declaration according to which the PG recognized the General Secretariat as the supreme organ for the administration of territorial affairs but insisted that it (the PG) determine the composition of that body in consultation with the UCR. Essentially, this was a negation of sovereignty of the General Secretariat, and a month later this was spelled out in the PG's "Instruction to the General Secretariat," which, instead of recognizing the General Secretariat as the supreme organ of the UCR, defined it as "the supreme organ of the PG in the Ukraine." It also reduced the number of portfolios in the General Secretariat from fourteen to nine. The General Secretariat was to enact laws for the Ukraine but only with the approval of the PG. The latter was to treat with local officials only through the General Secretariat, but in the event of urgency retained the right to transmit orders directly to local authorities. In practice, however, the PG consistently used to send administrative directives directly to its own personnel in the Ukraine rather than through the UCR government.[78]

The record of relations between Petrograd and Kiev was rather uneven and it seems that the PG in its last days was considering prosecuting the members of the General Secretariat for their allegedly separatist stand. In fact, in October, on the eve of the Bolshevik seizure of power in Petrograd, the independence option begins to be mentioned again. V. Vynnychenko, while reaffirming the UCR's federative republican stand, added, "but no political form, even independence, must be renounced if it assists the aim of every socialist, that is, socialism."[79] The Ukrainian Social Democratic Workers party, which stood to the left of the UCR majority, also oriented itself on a European federation in the resolutions of its Fourth Congress:

> Close political and economic ties (of the Ukraine and Russia) can be preserved in appropriate political forms in the interest of the proletariat of both countries under condition if the centralistic and imperialistic strivings of Great Russian bourgeoisie are removed. . . . The formation of a political and economic connection between Russia and the Ukraine . . . corresponds to the trend of the political development of Europe which is proceeding to the transformation of Europe into an all-European federation on the basis of the self-determination of nations. . . . The Congress . . . finds it necessary to place on the agenda of Party activity the construction of a Ukrainian Democratic Republic which has to stand in federative relationship with the Russian Republic, and, if it were possible, also with other European republican states.
>
> The Congress regards that the All-Russian Constituent Assembly must in no way violate the right to full self-determination right up to secession of individual nations of Russia.[80]

The Ukrainian Democratic Farmers' party, on the other hand, proclaimed a struggle for the Ukraine's state sovereignty as the main point of its draft program, while the option of a federation was not entertained at all.[81]

A fortnight after the October Revolution, the UCR issued its Third Universal proclaiming "the Ukrainian People's Republic (UPR)," but still "without separating from the Russian Republic," which had to be helped to become "a federation of equal and free peoples";[82] at the same time, the support of the majority of the Ukraine's population for the UCR was demonstrated by the elections to the All-Russian Constituent Assembly held at last in late November 1917, where Ukrainian parties received almost two-thirds of the votes, while the Bolsheviks had only one-tenth. In mid-December, in order to take power, the Kiev Bolsheviks called the First All-Ukrainian Congress of Soviets; but instead of the hoped-for majority for themselves, there, too, there was an 89 percent support for the UCR. The Bolshevik delegates then walked out and left for Kharkov which had just been occupied by Soviet Russian forces. There they joined a local congress of Soviets which then on 24 December 1917 voted itself to be the "true" First All-Ukrainian Congress of Soviets. This "All-Ukrainian" Congress had, however, a very comfortable Russian majority: 76 percent Russian Bolsheviks and 21 percent Russian Socialist Revolutionaries. It proclaimed the UCR "deposed" and formed a Soviet government of the UPR which was installed, in the words of a Soviet historian, with the energetic participation of military units and detachments of Antonov which arrived from the north, chiefly from parts of the Petrograd and Moscow garrisons.[83]

Back in Kiev, a month later the UCR's Fourth Universal of 25 January 1918 proclaimed that "from now on, the Ukrainian People's Republic becomes an independent, subordinate to no one, free and sovereign State of the Ukrainian People," which fact was also embodied in the Constitution of the UPR adopted on 29 April 1918.[84] This was anticipated by the Ukrainian Party of Independist Socialists standing in its December 1917 program "on the basis of full independence of the UPR," which was confirmed in the resolutions of the Party's Central Committee of 1 January 1920.[85]

At the same time, on 19 October 1918 "on the Ukrainian Lands of the former Austro-Hungarian Monarchy there was created a Ukrainian State," named 'the West Ukrainian People's Republic' (WUPR) with its capital in L'viv, and on 3 January 1919 in Stanyslaviv (now Ivano-Frankivs'k) its Ukrainian National Rada proclaimed the merging of the WUPR with the UPR "into one, integral, and sovereign People's Republic," which was accepted and confirmed by the then Kiev Government of the UPR, the *Dyrektoriia*, on 22 January.[86]

Meanwhile, in July 1918 the First Congress of the Communist party (Bolsheviks) of the Ukraine (CP(B)U), held in Moscow, incorporated the CP(B)U into the Russian Communist party (Bolsheviks) and declared that the Party's task was "to struggle for a revolutionary uniting of the Ukraine with Russia on the principles of proletarian centralism within the boundaries of the Russian Soviet Socialist Republic, on the road to the creation of the world-wide proletarian commune."[87] But also "among the Bolsheviks there are advocates of complete independence for the Ukraine," as Lenin had to admit in November 1919;[88] in 1918–19 they tried to organize an independent national-territorial Ukrainian Communist party (Bolsheviks) (*sic*: not 'CP(B)U'); an independent Communist Ukraine, they thought, would be a more reliable ally of Soviet Russia than a Ukraine forcibly incorporated into the Russian state.[89]

There were also two non-Bolshevik Communist parties: the Ukrainian

Communist party (Borot'bists) which in August 1919 in its memorandum
to the Comintern advocated the Ukraine as "a separate Soviet Republic,
to be an independent member of the impending World Federation of Soviet
Republics"; and the Ukrainian Communist party *tout court*, which supported, in the program adopted by its First Constituent Congress in June
1920, "the independence of the economic and political order of the Ukrainian Socialist Soviet Republic" while advocating close alliance and cooperation with other Soviet republics in military and economic respects
"proceeding from the interests of communist construction of the whole of
humanity."[90]

By early in 1920, the Soviet Russian armies finally defeated the independent Ukrainian *Dyrektoriia*, occupied the Ukraine, and installed the
Moscow-sponsored Soviet Ukrainian government and the CP(B)U. It is
significant that, although several Soviet governments which controlled
smaller or greater portions of the Ukraine in the seesawing fashion were,
together with the CP(B)U, entirely dependent on Soviet Russian armies,
nevertheless the CP(B)U saw it politic to make the specific point in a May
1921 resolution that since 1918,

> there were periods of full independence of the Ukrainian SSR (the First
> Secretariat, the Soviet Government of the second period), periods of feder-
> ative ties (the Fourth All-Ukrainian Congress), and of political independence
> on the basis of military and economic union with the RSFSR (today's *status
> quo*).[91]

Nor can this be dismissed as being only lip-service: many Ukrainian
CP(B)U members, both old Bolsheviks and former members of the "other"
Communist parties (which had been forced into liquidation), were genuinely concerned about the independence of the Soviet Ukraine. Thus, the
old Bolshevik, Lenin's comrade-in-arms, Mykola Skrypnyk, said at the
Eleventh Congress of the RCP(B) in March 1922: ". . . A certain indicative
significance has for me Comrade Lenin's statement thrown in passing that
the Ukraine, by the way and fortunately, is an independent state." At the
same time, Skrypnyk had no illusions that *de facto* it was not so: ". . . in
practice the line of the Soviet *apparats* is quite different from that line
which is laid down by our Party."[92] By the end of that year, the hitherto
de jure "politically independent" Soviet republics formed the Union of
Soviet Socialist Republics (USSR). According to the Declaration on the
Formation of the USSR, adopted by the 1st Congress of the Soviets of the
USSR on 30 December 1922, "This Union is a voluntary association of
equal peoples. . . . Every republic is assured the right of free secession
from the Union."[93] This right has been enshrined in all subsequent con-

stitutions of the USSR and each union republic. It must be noted, however, that the RCP(B)'s original plan was, in fact, to incorporate all "independent" republics into the RSFSR, reducing them to the status of "autonomous" republics within the Russian Republic and thus fully depriving them of their newly won sovereignty; this plan was opposed chiefly by Ukrainian and Georgian Bolsheviks who ultimately achieved an equal status for all republics—the Russian SFSR, the Ukrainian SSR, the Belorussian SSR, and the Trans-Caucasian Federation, the removal of the word "Russian" from the name of the proposed state, and the preservation of the right to secede as a symbol of the individual republics' sovereignty.[94]

After several years of considerable national development in conditions of relative freedom (the NEP period), the end of the 1920s marked the beginning of an all-out onslaught on nationalities, notably in the Ukraine. In 1929–31, the OGPU (political police) arrested several thousand persons who were tried on the charges of belonging to the Union of Liberation of the Ukraine (ULU), the Union of Ukrainian Youth, an underground Ukrainian National Center, and several small underground organizations including the National Party of Liberation of the Ukraine in Vinnytsia; according to the charges, the first two organizations had branches in all the main cities of the Ukraine and were working toward an insurrection which would restore an independent Ukraine. The Ukrainian Autocephalous Orthodox church was also heavily implicated at the trial of the ULU, and it was annihilated subsequently by the OGPU.[95] This was the beginning of Stalin's genocide of the populations of the Ukrainian and Belorussian SSRs by means of total confiscation of grain and starving millions of peasants to death; mass deportations or executions of intelligentsia, and CP(B)U leaders and members; and allowing Hitler to occupy the two republics, exterminate most Jews, many prisoners of war, whole villages for aiding the partisans, former Soviet functionaries and Party members, and many militant nationalists, especially in the western regions. Total 1929–53 losses may have been of the order of 20 million people.

Guerrilla fighting on a considerable scale, with the Ukraine's independence as its aim, went on during 1943–53, chiefly in the western Ukraine which had escaped the prewar destruction. A leading member of the postwar Ukrainian underground, P. Poltava, wrote in 1947 about "the concept of an independent Ukrainian state created by the Ukrainian people in its ethnic lands" as deriving from its organic, natural desire to independent state life which has always been inherent in the Ukrainian people and manifested itself in the creation of the Kievan state of the tenth–eleventh centuries, of the Cossack Republic in 1648, and the UPR in 1918.[96] Osyp Diakiv-Hornovyi, another underground writer, asserted in 1949 that the reconstruction of the USSR into independent states is the most just and progressive solution of the nationalities question, for it cuts the root of Russian imperialism and creates possibilities for the all-sided development of each people. It leads . . . to the broadest cooperation and friendship among peoples, for it builds them on the principles of real independence, equality and voluntariness.[97]

After de-Stalinization, a number of groups arose in the Ukraine aiming at achieving her independence. Thus, in 1960 an attempt was made in L'viv to create a Ukrainian Workers' and Peasants' Union (UWPU) whose draft program stated:

We are struggling for an independent Ukraine such that, while providing to a high degree for the material and spiritual needs of her citizens on the basis of a socialized economy, she would develop towards communism, and secondly, a Ukraine in which all citizens would truly enjoy their political freedoms and determine the direction of the economic and political development of the Ukraine—such is the purpose of the ultimate struggle of our party.
. . . our specific ideal . . . is the independence of the Ukraine with a broadly developed socialist state system . . .
. . . the curtailment of the Ukraine's political and economic rights was pointed out, as were the facts that the Ukraine is deprived of sovereignty and of the right to enter into political and economic relations with the other states on our planet . . . it was concluded that, within the USSR, the Ukraine lacked the opportunity for normal political, economic and cultural development, that in certain respects her position was much worse now than it had been under the Tsarist regime, and that she was actually a colony of Moscow or, at best, had only cultural autonomy.[98]

Some time before 1959, a United Party for the Liberation of the Ukraine was formed whose goal was the creation of an independent Ukraine. About the same time or a few months later, a Ukrainian National Committee was formed "the aim of which was also to demand secession of the Ukrainian SSR from the USSR." According to the contemporary testimony of Ivan Kandyba who participated in the UWPU, "there are many similar, though smaller, group cases (apparently I.K. means groups having similar aims; the UWPU and the other two groups have seven, eight and twenty members respectively), while cases involving individuals from various regions of the Ukraine are numbered in hundreds."[99]

In December 1964, an "Action Committee" penned an appeal "to all communists of People's Democracies and capitalist countries and to leading organs of communist and workers' parties of the world," signed anonymously "Communists of the Ukraine," denying the truth of *Pravda*'s assertion that " 'separatist ideas' in the Ukraine are futile and artificial."[100] In April 1966, a Ukrainian National Front appealed "to the Ukrainian people":

> In the present era of great technological and social progress, when in the remotest corners of the globe the most backward peoples rend their colonial fetters and wake to an independent state life—the Ukrainian people cannot sleep any longer. It must start a struggle for its legitimate, sacred rights common to all humanity and for its freedom. . . . The struggle is carried on for a Ukrainian Independent State . . .[101]

The international dimension is stressed also in a letter from a Ukrainian political prisoner, H. Prykhod'ko, to the USSR Supreme Soviet of 17 November 1975: "To the outside world, the Soviet Union opposes colonialism and defends the right of nations to self-determination while inside the USSR it suppresses any moves of non-Russian nations to secession from Russia and creation of independent states."[102] The text of Vasyl' Ruban's manuscript written before September 1972 seems to be unknown in the West, but its title, *An Independent Communist Ukraine*, is explicit enough, and in November–December 1976 the Ukrainian Helsinki Group commented that "such way of thinking is typical of Ukrainian political prisoners."[103] Their stand is also elaborated by two prisoners, Oleksii Tykhyi, a member of the Helsinki Group, and Fr. Vasyl' Romaniuk, writing late in 1977 or in early 1978:

> We are democrats. Supreme principles of social and national life are for us the UN Universal Declaration of Human Rights, the UN covenants and documents about sovereignty and independence of nations and peoples. . . . We regard all forms of tyrannies, dictatorships, contempt of the rights of any nations and peoples and disregard for human rights as hateful and unacceptable. We regard the strivings of all peoples to independence, and help to such strivings from democratic countries and the UN as close to us and understandable.
>
> We are against: the support of struggle for independence which is achieved at the cost of millions of victims, fratricidal wars, millions of refugees, millions of political prisoners.[104]

Badz'o, writing in 1979, encompasses the questions of historical necessity, world peace and the USSR's democratization in his discussion of national freedom:

. . . the requirements of progress and of the natural development of history do not abandon us to chance, but guarantee support for our aspirations to national freedom as aspirations that are objectively progressive and such that are in the mainstream of the world's natural historical development. . . . Various forms of voluntary political union of socialist peoples based on equality could have become an important factor in preserving and strengthening world peace, a pattern for the future harmonious and dynamic coexistence of the world's peoples. Unfortunately, Russian great-power nationalism ruined things also here. The democratization of Soviet society is inconceivable without a cardinal reexamination of the interstate relations between the Soviet peoples. Many Ukrainians, myself included, consider that for the Ukrainian people a free, dignified life as a nation is impossible within the limits of political and state unity with Russia. The great-power traditions of viewing the Ukraine as Russia's legitimate "younger brother," that is, as her historical property, are too strong and persistent in Russia. There can be various views about the form of the state self-determination of the Ukraine, but there can be no compromise whatsoever on the point that the secession of the Ukraine from the federation of Soviet Republics is our constitutional and moral right, and the Ukrainian people alone is qualified to decide this question, in the conditions of democracy and free discussion of the problem.[105]

Among the most recent is Terelia's declaration in his July–August 1984 open letter "To the friends of the Ukraine in China" that "today the Ukrainian national movement under the leadership of the Ukrainian National Front[106] carries on its great work for the creation of an independent Ukrainian state; this is chiefly a movement from among the Catholics."[107]

Some writers try to look beyond the all too natural attitude that "if the Ukrainian SSR in reality becomes a sovereign republic, that is, we ourselves will solve our own problems without Moscow, then everything will fall into its own place," as Terelia said in a conversation with a secretary of the Presidium of the Ukrainian SSR Supreme Soviet and other Soviet officials in April 1984. Indeed, he went on to specify certain basic attributes of sovereignty:

But this will be possible only when customs barriers are established between Russia and the Ukraine, the Ukrainian SSR has its own currency, own army which will defend the nation's interests from Moscow's encroachments, and, what is most important, that the parliament of the Ukrainian SSR should not consist of Communists alone of which there are considerably fewer than Christians.[108]

Poltava envisages, writing in 1947, that the social order in the future Ukrainian state will be such that there will be no exploitation of man by man, with extensive nationalization and a cooperative ownership system, with nationalized land used either privately or collectively according to the wish of the population; return to capitalism is rejected as this would be regress.[109] In 1949, Diakiv-Hornovyi had this to say about relations with Russia:

> The separation of the Ukraine from Russia is not a hostile action against the Russian people. . . . (They) do not need the Ukraine. It is needed only by Russian imperialists. . . . The Russian lands are rich enough, and the Russian people are industrious enough, to provide well for themselves. . . . Moreover, if the Russian people need Ukrainian coal, iron, or grain they can get them by means of exchange with the Ukraine for economic goods of their land (for instance, timber or industrial goods) which are needed by the Ukraine. . . . We strive towards the closest collaboration in the political, economic and cultural spheres with the Russian people as well as with all other peoples. The Russian people are our immediate neighbor, we have many interests in common and our cooperation can develop very successfully if it is going to be built not on imperialist relations but on genuine friendship and equality. . . . We stand resolutely against ascribing "a leading role" and the duties of "the elder brother" to the Russian people. . . . They must realize that Russian imperialism has been the reason also for their grave situation during their entire history.[110]

A recent declaration by members of the Ukrainian Patriotic movement who describe themselves as "victims of political repressions in the Ukraine" thus states the principles of future relations with other nations:

> The Ukraine's freedom will enable both the Russian people and other peoples enslaved by the present regime to free themselves. A free Ukraine guarantees all rights to the peoples living in the Ukraine: the Russians and Poles, the Jews and Tatars, the Romanians and Hungarians. We have learnt too well what the enslaved colonial existence is, and therefore we declare that we will grant the broadest political, economic, and social rights to people living in our Motherland. All rights of national minorities and of various religious associations will be observed without reservations.[111]

The postwar examples of the advocacy of national independence reviewed above (and many more could be quoted) stem from unofficial "dissident" writings, and represent a virtual consensus in Ukrainian thought. On the official side, there have been no recent outspoken advocates of Ukrainian independence of the towering stature of a Skrypnyk, but the important case of Petro Shelest, the first secretary of the Central Committee (CC) of the Communist party of the Ukraine (CPU) between 1963–72, must be mentioned. He promoted the Ukrainian language and the study of Ukrainian history, in which he was attracted to the Cossack period of independence, and was after his ouster accused *inter alia* of advocating "economic autarkism" in his book,[112] i.e., economic self-sufficiency; and from this it is surely but one step to postulating the feasibility of independence. He is said to have been very popular in the Ukraine, and had numerous followers in the CPU at all levels;[113] they included Oles' Honchar, at that time the head of the Writers' Union of the Ukraine, and a member of the CC CPU and an alternate member of the CC CPSU, the author of the novel *The Cathedral* (1968) which was banned for, *inter alia*, stressing former Cossack freedom,[114] enabling the reader to draw implications for the present.

III

Belorussia's modern national revival begins with the 1863 uprising led by Kastus' Kalinoüski who advocated political autonomy of the ancient "Lithuanian Belorussian" lands,[115] and the activities of Belorussian populists in the 1870s–80s who "were among the first in Russia to define most fully the essential traits of nationhood and on the basis of these proved the existence of an independent Belorussian nation."[116] Among them, a "Social-Revolutionary Group of Belorussians" was organized in the early 1880s, and in 1884 it started an illegal newspaper, *Gomon*, in which autonomy for Belorussia within a federal republican Russia was advocated.[117] In 1902, Belorussian students in St. Petersburg founded the Belorussian Revolutionary Hramada (Association), in 1903 renamed Belorussian Socialist Hramada (BSH); its members' long-term aim was to establish a Belorussian national state.[118] In 1906 the first weekly, *Nasha dolia*, appeared, but was soon suppressed by Russian authorities for "revolutionary and separatist" tendencies. Its successor, *Nasha niva*, advocated national freedom for the peoples of Belorussia; it survived until 1915.[119] After 1905 the BSH played a leading role in national revival. In 1906, at its Second Congress, it worked out an ambitious program demanding for Belorussia not only "cultural autonomy," as it did three years earlier, but also "the federation of all free peoples within the empire."[120] It cooperated closely with the Ukrainian national movement.[121] Ianka Kupala, the Belorussian national poet, was even more radical in his national freedom demand than the BSH: *"Viarni nam Bats'kaüshchynu nashu, Bozha!*—'Return our Fatherland to us, O Lord!'"[122]

Soon after the February 1917 Revolution, on 25 March, the Belorussian National Congress, in which the BSH and other parties and organizations participated, elected a National Executive Committee composed of representatives of all ethnic groups and social classes, charging it with organizing the administration of Belorussia in agreement with the Provisional

Government.[123] The Second Congress of the Belorussian political parties held in July 1917 established a Belorussian Central Rada (BCR). At its first session on 5–6 August it was declared to be "the responsible and leading agency (*organ*) of the whole Belorussian national movement." It was composed of "deputies sent by all Belorussian organizations as well as districts, cities and small towns, refugee organizations and military units, if they recognize self-government, the native language and the development of national culture."[124]

After the October Revolution, in December 1917, the First All-Belorussian National Congress affirmed a republican mode of government in Belorussian lands. On 9 March 1918 the Executive Committee of the congress proclaimed the Belorussian People's Republic (BPR) "within the boundaries of the settlement and numerical majority of the Belorussian people." On 25 March 1918, the Rada of the BPR proclaimed the BPR "an independent and free state."[125]

After the Soviet Russian military reconquest of Belorussia, and having become aware of the strength of the Belorussian national movement, on 23 December 1918 the CC RCP(B) decided to create an independent Belorussian Soviet Socialist Republic (BSSR), and on 30 December the Northwestern Committee of the RCP(B) in Smolensk changed its name to the "Communist Party (Bolsheviks) of Belorussia." A group of Belorussian Communists tried to form a Belorussian Communist party but this was vetoed by Moscow.[126] The BSSR was proclaimed on 1 January 1919.[127] The First All-Belorussian Congress of Soviets, meeting on 1 February, legally established the independence of the BSSR and adopted its first Constitution.[128] On 30 December 1922, the BSSR joined the USSR with the other three Soviet republics.

The next few years saw the blossoming of Belorussian culture. But in June 1930 mass arrests were carried out, and the arrested were charged with belonging to an underground "Union of the Liberation of Belorussia."[129] In November 1930 more arrests of "conspirators" were carried out who were accused of having "striven to take Belorussia away from the path of Socialist reconstruction and to direct it to the path of restoration of capitalism." In summer 1933, the Party announced the discovery of a "Belorussian National Center," which was charged with seeking the establishment of an independent Belorussian Democratic Republic.[130] The 1933–34 purge carried off many thousands of victims, almost completely destroyed the Belorussian national and cultural leadership and, in fact, broke Belorussian national resistance,[131] and "not a single man who had labored for the establishment of the Belorussian Home under the Soviets in the 1920s was alive or free in 1939."[132]

It was only in the very last days of the German occupation in World

War II, on 27 June 1944, that a reconstituted BCR was able to call the Second All-Belorussian Congress in Minsk to reaffirm the principles of Belorussian independence and democracy.[133]

Little is known about the post-Stalin Belorussian national movement and demands for national freedom. This is to a considerable degree attributable to the fact that Belorussia is even more isolated from the outside world than the Ukraine, and this is aggravated by a large part of Belorussia's territory being a military zone. Thus, in the early 1970s a marvelous anonymous poem, *Skaz pra Lysuiu Haru*, written obviously by a member of the official Writers' Union of Belorussia and satirizing Belorussian establishment intellectuals for neglecting their native culture, began circulating among the reading public including high office holders in the Union;[134] and it was only in 1981 that it reached, and was published in, the West.[135] In 1963, a student of the Belorussian Polytechnical Institute, S. Khanzhankov, was arrested and sentenced to ten years for "an attempt to create an anti-Soviet organization"; this became known in the West only in 1971. In 1970, 2,000 students of the Belorussian State University signed a petition that teaching in that university should be conducted in Belorussian, and several hundred students were expelled for this; and it was only in 1979 that this became known in the West. Not much earlier was it learned here about an attempt, in 1974, of a group of Minsk secondary school pupils from upper forms together with a university student to create an independent youth organization; they pasted the rules of their organization on the walls of houses, the KGB intervened, they were expelled from school and their parents sacked from their jobs and expelled from the Party.[136] In 1972, it was learned that a *samizdat* periodical, *Listok*, appeared in Belorussia at irregular intervals,[137] and soon after a report arrived about a religious bulletin appearing in Belorussia,[138] but no parts of either periodical are so far known in the West. On the other hand, the important *Letter to a Russian Friend* was written in 1977 and reached the West in 1979. The anonymous Belorussian author writes his letter in answer to his friend's doubts about the viability of the Belorussian language. His friend is one of those "educated Russian minds" "who are nowadays anguishing over the rebirth of the Russian idea," and the author relies

on the understanding and support of my Russian friends for the current aims of Belorussians partly outlined in this letter. . . . Our complete support for the rebirth of the Russian national idea is also perfectly natural, because without the spiritual self-cleaning of the Russian people we cannot count on the success of our own Belorussian cause.

At the same time, he is distressed to note that

Among those visiting the BSSR a difference in outside observers' views on the present position of the Belorussian language can be observed between (on the one hand) Ukrainians, Poles, Czechs, Slovaks, and Bulgarians and (on the other hand) *Russians*. The former fail to understand the artificial obstacles placed on the development of the Belorussian language in Belorussia; the latter cannot grasp why the language is being "artificially inflicted" on the population.

And he is distressed that even those Russians like his addressee have a similar attitude. In a "historical digression" he traces Belorussian individuality to prehistoric times, and connects the nineteenth–twentieth century Belorussian renaissance with the rebirth of the language; but he is alarmed by the official disdain for Belorussian, and by the policy of the "merging" of nations, in fact, assimilation and Russification, in contrast to the official promotion of Belorussian in the second half of the 1920s (Belorussification). His view of national freedom is not explicitly expressed; on the one hand, he agrees with the idea of "Slav unity" as expressed by Vladimir Solov'ëv, that is, without compulsory Russification; on the other hand, he says:

> Providence has deigned to make Russia relinquish "her" borderlands (author obviously means Poland and Finland) as well as part of her statehood (i.e., through the *federal* structure of the USSR, as against the old *unitary* Russian Empire) in favor of related peoples. Neither the power nor the glory of the Russian people, nor the respect that Belorussians and Ukrainians (and Poles and Finns even more so) feel for them has suffered one iota.[139]

The unspoken, though clearly implied, conclusion is that Belorussians and Ukrainians would respect the Russian people even more (and this would surely be desirable)—as much as Poles and Finns do—if they were to have the status of Poland (as in 1977) or Finland, that is, national independence.

Another example of Belorussian *samizdat* to have reached the West recently is a pair of postcards, one inscribed "1000 years of Belorussia 980–1980" and the other, "Best wishes in the jubilee year! 980—Belorussia—1980" (cf., their reproductions, two-thirds of the original size; the background color of the second one is red in the original), the year 980 being the date of the first political conflict between Polotsk and Kiev.

A remarkable feature of Belorussian intellectual life is a considerable degree of divergence from the Party line, manifested in publications coming from official presses when concern is voiced about the threat of Russification, and thus ethnocide, hanging over the nation; this being opposed by national assertiveness, belief in the indestructability of the language and the nation's cultural individuality.[140] The most noteworthy example, belonging to the same period (1979–81), only partially fits this category: it is a 250–page book by Aleh Bembel', a 40-year-old historian of philosophy, *Our Native Language and Moral and Aesthetic Progress*, which *was* intended for official publication in the BSSR, but was not accepted, started circulating in typescript and was ultimately published in London late in 1985.[141] Its bulk, preceded by quotations from Belorussian writers and poets about their native language, comprises numerous interviews with intellectuals and older schoolchildren on their opinions about the Belorussian language, with answers ranging from hostile and disdainful through indifferent, or accepting its decline as inevitable, to voicing demands that "the leading Party (viz., the CPSU) and the Government itself of the BSSR must safeguard the creation of favorable conditions for the continuation of the as yet uncompleted process of the Belorussian Renascence and for the further development of the Belorussian language and culture."[142] Bembel' himself in a carefully documented essay persuasively argues the case against the merger of all nations and their languages in the postulated future worldwide Communist society,[143] and supports his argument *inter alia* by a like-minded quotation from a book, which *was* published, by a senior colleague of his, V. Konan, a Doctor of Philosophical Sciences and a highly placed member of the academic establishment, being as he now is head of the Sector of Aesthetics and Social Psychology of the Institute of Philosophy and Law of the BSSR.[144] Nor has Konan apparently been made to recant his views which he reinforced in a recent article. While pleading for the preservation of all facets of Belorussian culture he again asserts that "mankind . . . will always be a family of dissimilar and unique peoples," which is in flat contradiction to the official Soviet doctrine of the rapprochement and ultimate merger of nations and a challenge to the *de facto* official stifling of Belorussian culture and language.[145]

The best known Belorussian human rights activist, M. Kukabaka, a worker, is the author of several *samizdat* articles, among them "Protection of Human Rights and Détente Are Inseparable," and "The Stolen Fatherland."[146] This latter article, whose title sounds like an allusion to the Kupala line quoted above, is remarkable for its date, 25 March 1978, which happens to be exactly the sixtieth anniversary of the proclamation of the BPR "an independent and free state," and the title together with the date are an unmistakable demand for national freedom. This is emphasized by a paragraph about the old cathedral in his native city of Babruisk which was demolished to make way for a "Sports complex. Built in 1967 in honor of the Fiftieth Anniversary of the Great October Socialist Revolution," as the plaque informs. Kukabaka comments: "So this is how the local communist bosses marked the jubilee of the seizure of power! With similar barbarity as half a century before." Looking at a tank on a concrete pedestal—a memorial to some general who was apparently the first one to burst into Babruisk, then being liberated from the Germans, Kukabaka remembers:

> Similar generals in similar tanks were bursting into the Baltic states, into Bessarabia and into Poland. And already after the war they were crushing people in the streets of Budapest and Prague. But why Prague—what about their own Novocherkassk![147]

He praises Ukrainians for a more stubborn defense of their national individuality. "And they rarely have a good word for their 'foolish son'[148] Bohdan Khmel'nyts'kyi who over 300 years ago committed the fatal deed bordering on national treason"[149] *mutatis mutandis*, the conclusion is obvious: joining *Belorussia* to Russia was similarly fatal to *Belorussian* national freedom.

IV

It seems to transpire from the above that Russian opinion on the post-Soviet future is divided. The "Democrats" either regard the separation of non-Russian republics from Russia and the establishment of democracy in Russia as being two sides of the same coin, or consider that the constitutional right to free secession existing now only on paper should be made genuinely available. The "Nationalists," rejecting Communist atheism, tend to idealize the pre-Revolutionary favored status of Orthodox Christianity and hence "the historically formed community of peoples" of the Russian Empire—and, as it happens, of the Soviet Union. Some "Nationalists" do not see any centrifugal forces among the non-Russians, while others regard them as insignificant, or as such that can be overcome by persuasion or by the force of arms, while a few of them realize that the injuries inflicted upon the non-Russians may well make the breakup of the empire inevitable. In this context, a distinction often is made between the non-Slavs and the Slavs; while the departure of the former from the future new Russia is seen either as permissible or even desirable, the Ukrainians and Belorussians are expected to stay within that state. Reasons advanced for this distinction are ethnic (common origin), historical (common heritage of the medieval Kievan Realm as well as of the post-seventeenth-century Russian Empire and the USSR), and/or religious (common Orthodox Christianity). This latter principle sometimes leads to the conclusion (e.g., Solzhenitsyn, though not consistently) that central and eastern Ukrainians and eastern Belorussians must be retained while the Catholic western areas of these nations could, or should, be allowed to go, or even should be cut off.[150] It may be noted here that, although some precedents can be quoted in favor of dividing a nation according to religion, there also exist other precedents against this; in the case of the Ukraine, in modern times her unity has been axiomatic for Ukrainian political and social thinkers, and it found its expression in the 1919 short-lived merger of the WUPR with the UPR,[151] and now in nearly half a century of unity in the Ukrainian SSR. The principle of the Ukraine's unity is probably the only one that is shared by all Ukrainians entirely irrespective of their political views or religious beliefs. Similar considerations apply to the question of Belorussia's unity.

In contrast to the Russian opinion, Ukrainian and Belorussian opinion on the post-Soviet future is united. The "Nationalists," as well as the "Democrats" and the "Communists," have never idealized the pre-Revolutionary Russian Empire, do not consider themselves as a part of "a historic community" with the Russians as the senior partner (having, in fact, never been Moscow's subjects until the seventeenth–eighteenth centuries, thereafter being oppressed by, and struggling to free themselves from, Moscow/St. Petersburg/Moscow), and state independence is to them the only future that can be envisioned.

Some scenarios for the future new Russia have visualized "nationalistic," "authoritarian rule" supported by "the overwhelming majority of people." How will this support be demonstrated? The ballot box is an obvious tool; even Solzhenitsyn was wondering, "would it be still within the bounds of realism or a lapse into daydreams if we were to propose that at least some of the real power of the *soviets* be restored?"[152] Similar sentiments are expressed by many Ukrainians: the editors of the *Ukrainian Herald* of the early 1970s who obviously favored "democratically elected Soviets as a form of citizens" participation in governing the country,"[153] Anton Koval', "a voter," whose proposal was "to transform the Soviets into organs of real power,"[154] or Badz'o, who noted that "Stalinism was a true social counterrevolution that finally defeated the power of the Soviets."[155] It is significant that even in Communist Hungary, as from 1985 not less than two candidates must stand in elections for each one seat; in 1970, in the Trans-Carpathian Region of the Ukrainian SSR, just across the border from Hungary, four "unofficial" candidates were put up (unbeknown to them) in addition to the official ones in four electoral districts; of the four, Pavlo Kampov, a University lecturer and Party member, has been put away into the Gulag for the total of twenty–two years where he is held illegally—being an invalid—and subjected to inhuman treatment, while another, Ivan Chendei, a writer, got away lightly, being only excluded from print for four years.[156] There can be little doubt that a non-fraudulent poll with a genuine choice enabling people to register their support for one of the political options will be welcomed or demanded by the people from any "provisional government," which will purport to be less totalitarian than the present Politburo rule. But even if it is taken for granted that Russian "nationalistic" rule will be endorsed by a process of this kind in Russia, it is inconceivable that Russian "Nationalists" could possibly find support among Ukrainians or Belorussians. Therefore, the governments in the Ukraine and Belorussia will be politically different from the government of the former RSFSR (there being "independent" governments in the three republics today, any *less* totalitarian regime cannot arbitrarily merge them). Moreover, a new *Russian*, no longer Soviet, state will by definition repel the Ukraine and Belorussia; after all, even the Bolshevik-governed Ukrainian SSR and BSSR entered the Union only *after* the adjective "Russian" was dropped from its name.

The problem of secession as a constitutional right of a union republic is often regarded as fraught with unresolved difficulties.[157] On the one hand, they would seem to apply only to the USSR, the pre- and non-Soviet world offering enough precedents, including also of peaceful and orderly secession; on the other, the Union of SSR is a state structure with a specific character. Its purpose was to unite, without the loss of sovereignty, several republics, each of which had a ruling party which was a branch of the RCP(B), now CPSU. All the republics, including the RSFSR, were to have equal rights. But once the Union of SSR is succeeded by a new Russia it must *ipso facto* simultaneously be succeeded by a new Ukraine and a new Belorussia and the other republics since Russia can properly only be a successor to the RSFSR. When a Union ceases to exist its former members automatically revert to their original sovereign independence, nor will there be any longer a uniting force in the form of a common political party. On the international level, the Ukraine and Belorussia will continue to be members of the UN (unlike the other republics, which will have to apply for new membership).[158]

Hrushevs'kyi's uncannily perceptive essay in the "what if" futurology— "what if the Ukraine had managed to liberate herself in 1709," written nearly three quarters of a century ago, also gives much food for thought regarding the present and future relations of the three East Slav nations:

The Battle of Poltava was a critical moment: the victory of 27 June [1709] gave the Russian Realm not only a decisive predominance in Eastern Europe but also pushed it on the path of imperialism, policy of expansion and of ever more conquests and annexations for two whole centuries. This expansionist trend not only brought political death to a whole series of political organisms which could have lived even now but also very harmfully influenced the internal development of the Russian State itself and its state people, the Great Russians, having retracted all resources from the internal, societal and cultural progress and having applied them to the task of an external unremitting expansion. Without the Poltava victory all this could have gone along other paths. Poland would probably not have fallen. The Ukraine would have remained a separate organism, if not independent then discrete, even having ultimately entered the bounds of the Russian State. Instead of one centralized state burdened with endless "separatisms" and national problems, and with one-sidedly developed energy of imperialism which has in the end not only brought to a complete ruin its state people itself but also placed the state itself on the edge of an abyss—we would perhaps now have been the witnesses or the citizens of a better organized great East European federation, balanced and strong, which by the force of its inner characteristics could have attracted a whole series of lands which have forever remained outside the borders of the centralized Russia.

In particular, Ukrainian-Russian relations could have formed better. I do not doubt that, if the Ukraine had been freed from the coercive Muscovite centralism and leveling, in her (and similarly in Belorussia) there would have developed free attraction (gravitation) to the Great-Russian world as the nearest and closely connected by cultural community, historical tradition and Kiev's common heritage. If instead of the merciless annihilation and suppression of all political, social and cultural forms of Ukrainian life which began after the Poltava victory, instead of that devastation and terror which reigned after 1708–9 there had come at least several decades of a free development of the Hetman State, its national life would have been assured, and there would have been no place or temptation for all those Russifying measures—bans on the Ukrainian book, the Ukrainian language, the Ukrainian pronunciation and accent—which were undertaken beginning with the Petrine times (the 1720 Ukase) and in the course of all subsequent time. The 'Rus' peoples' would not have been experiencing such a grave internal struggle which now threatens to separate them forever, having extirpated by police persecution those internal, moral ties which used to connect them.

Also the inner evolution of Great-Russian life could have taken a different path if apart from the bureaucratic, centralist Muscovite order there had lived and developed next to it a free, elective and constitutional Ukrainian order. Perhaps not only Ukrainian but also Great-Russian popular masses would not have lived through those evils of serfdom which they had to live through in the century after the abolition of the remains of the Ukrainian order. And the grave heritage of Russian centralism and imperialism might have been spared us.

The Poltava victory was a triumph only of Russian imperialism, and not a triumph of Russian life, not a triumph of progress and culture even from the standpoint of state Great-Russian people, not to mention the standpoint of the whole East Slav, or still broader, the whole Slav world, its harmonious development and its free and common progress. Even from the Great-Russian standpoint, not only from the "Rus" standpoint in general, or the East Slavdom standpoint, perhaps it would have been better if the day of the 27th of June had not brought that memorable triumph. This explains the restrained attitude to it on the part of the true friends of progress and freedom.[159]

Such is Hrushevs'ky's wistfully optimistic scenario of how a different outcome of the Battle of Poltava might have saved Russia from embarking upon an expansionist imperialist path and might have resulted in an East European federation, a free community of a number of equal nations, including the three East Slav ones; at the same time, the Russian people itself would have gained a degree of freedom impossible under despotic imperialism. This view seems to be a corollary of the Marxian formulation—of which Hrushevs'ky could hardly have been aware—that "No nation can be free if it oppresses other nations,"[160] though it is possible to think of a number of twentieth-century examples where an ostensibly "free" nation manifestly "oppresses" others. Therefore, it does not necessarily follow that, if the Russians achieve their own "national freedom," similar freedom will *ipso facto* be enjoyed by the non-Russians, and the other two East Slav peoples among them. Thus, although the topic formulated in the title of this chapter may be taken as positing an "indivisible" national freedom, let us now consider some contrary scenario variations regarding the possible fulfilment of the Eastern Slavs' aspirations which have been elucidated in the preceding parts of this chapter.

The simplest scenario may be derived from the "Iron Law of International Relations":

That law, of which there are no exceptions throughout the course of human history, states simply that nations will seek to expand their influence into places and situations as far from their national borders as their power will allow.[161]

Therefore, if this law is to be accepted, no Russian, or any other, government can be expected to grant national freedom to a subject people, or to reduce the degree of that people's dependence, unless its power has waned. (The latter situation may be adduced as the cause of many instances of achieving independence in the course of this century.)

It may be objected that such policies are typical of totalitarianism rather than of authoritarianism which is posited in the present scenario for a New Russia; but it is precisely the policies of suppression by sheer military power which are typical of colonial rule, not only by authoritarian powers (e.g., Salazar's/Caetano's Portugal) but even quite impeccably democratic ones (e.g., the French government's bloody war against, Algerians before de

Gaulle's accession to power). The future Russian government is expected to be "nationally minded" and "have the full support . . . of the overwhelming majority of people,"[162] while the present Soviet government is generally believed to lack such support (*pace* Zinoviev); but this applies only to Soviet Russian domestic policies, while it is also generally agreed that Soviet policies toward the empire and the satellites are endorsed by the overwhelming majority of Russians (thus, the invasion of "ungrateful" Czechoslovakia was practically universally approved of, and likewise most Russians feel that non-Russians must always be made to show their undying gratitude to, and love for, the Russians for their constant selfless aid). Any retreat from the positions of strength in these areas while the power to maintain such positions exists (and there is no reason to suppose that it will cease to exist in the foreseeable future) will only contravene the "Iron Law."

It must be noted in this connection that the government of New Russia will have no legal right to grant or refuse sovereignty to any non-Russian nation now possessing a union republic's status since no such right is included in the current Constitution; instead, each such republic has, according to that Constitution, the right to *free* secession. Of course, everyone knows that this right is worth very much less than the paper it is printed on, but none the less this right has to be openly denied to the union republics *before* the central government could effectively arrogate to itself the new *discretionary* right to grant or refuse them sovereignty. But this may not be a simple matter: when, in 1978—the Party wanted to omit—from the new constitutions of the three Transcaucasian republics—an express designation of Georgian, Armenian and Azerbaijani as the respective republics' official (*gosudarstvennye*) languages (for they were indeed thus designated in these republics' previous constitutions of 1937) there was a large wave of protests, and the Party retreated on this point. Similar, or probably even much greater, protests may well be expected against any attempts to abolish the republics' right to free secession, which is surely an even more important issue than that of the official language, especially in the time of change when secession would start acquiring the shape of a realistic possibility. As far as the Ukraine and Belorussia are concerned, there is the additional complication of their full membership of the UN; again, although it is a universally known fact that this was due only to Stalin's desire to gain fifteen additional votes, none the less it has grown into an outward (albeit fictitious) symbol of these two countries' sovereignty, which it will be necessary to abolish in parallel with the abolition of the secession right, and this will doubtlessly cause similarly vigorous protests. The new Russian government will then be faced with a dilemma: to retreat, and to be confronted by a series of secessions, or to suppress by force non-Russian popular protest or to retreat in some areas and use suppression in others.

What the consequences of any of these policy choices might be only future can tell.

Notes

1. 'Dekret o mire' in *Dekrety Sovetskoi vlasti*, I (Moscow: Gospolitizdat, 1957), 12, 15.
2. ———, p. 15.
3. V.I. Lenin, *Collected Works*, 30, (Moscow, 1964), 270.
4. Ivan Dzyuba, *Internationalism or Russification?* (London: Weidenfeld, 1968 and 1970; New York: Monad Press, 1974; also in five other languages).
5. Iurii Badzo, "An Open Letter to the Presidium of the Supreme Soviet of the USSR and the Central Committee of the CPSU . . .," *Journal of Ukrainian Studies* 9, 1 (Summer 1984): 87–88. The original Ukrainian text: Iurii Badz'o, *Vidkrytyi lyst*. . . (New York: Zakordonne predstavnytstvo Ukrains'koi hromads'koi hrupy spryiannia vykonanniu Hel'sinks'kykh uhod, 1980), 64 pp.
6. R.V. Burks, "The coming crisis in the Soviet Union," in Vol. 1, present series, 115.
7. Alexander Shtromas, "How the end of the Soviet System May Come About: Historical Precedents and Possible Scenarios," in 1, present series.
8. Alexander Shtromas, *Political Change and Social Development: The Case of the Soviet Union* (Frankfurt am Main: Peter Lang, 1981), 131–32, 138.
9. Liudmila Alekseeva, *Istoria inakomysliia v SSSR: Noveishii period* (Benson, Vt: Khronika Press, 1984), 405–6, 411; Alexander Solzhenitsyn, *Letter to Soviet Leaders* (London: Index on Censorship/Fontana, 1974), 53, 55.
10. Petr Samorodnitskii, "Bran' za pravdu" *Forum* (Munich) 10 (1985), 161, 169.
11. A. Kronidov, "Skol'ko prosushchestvuiet Sovetskii Soiuz? (*Samizdat*)," *Forum* 3 (1983), 155–79.
12. Patrick Wajsman, "Peut-on reveiller le monde libre? Un entretien avec Vladimir Boukovsky," *Le Figaro*, 16 December 1983, 4.
13. Leonid Pljuschtsch, "Dissidente konnen positive Reformen anregen" [Interview], *Die Weltwoche* (Zurich), 22 March 1984, 7.
14. Kronid Liubarskii, "Zametki o nedalekom budushchem," *Forum* 6 (1984), 5.
15. P. Abovin-Egides, "Zlokliucheniia deval'virovannogo poniatiia," *Tribuna* (Fontenay-aux-Roses, France) 2 (April 1983), 8.
16. *L'Alternative* (Paris) No. 15 (March–April 1982), 7, 12.
17. Liubarskii, *Zametki*, 12–13.
18. "Konferentsiia o svobode slova," *Russkaia mysl'*, 29 May 1975, 5.
19. Bohdan Hawrylyshyn, *Road Maps to the Future* (Oxford: Pergamon, 1980), 43–44.

20. Alekseeva, *Istoriya*, 398; *A Chronicle of Current Events: Numbers 34, 35 & 36* (London: Amnesty International, 1978), p. 81.
21. Alekseeva, *Astoriya*, 399.
22. ——.
23. "Slovo natsii" in *Sobraniie dokumentov samizdata*, 8 (Munich: RFE-RL), AS No. 590, pp. 16–17; *A Chronicle of Current Events: Issue No. 17* (London: Amnesty, 1971), 93.
24. Alekseeva, *Istoriya*, p. 403.
25. "Veche, No. 6" *Arkhiv samizdata*, No. 1599, 7–8; *A Chronicle of Current Events: Issue No. 24* (London: Amnesty, 1972), 164; Vladimir Osipov, *Tri otnosheniia k rodine* (Frankfurt: 'Possev', 1978), 205.
26. John B. Dunlop, *The New Russian Revolutionaries* (Belmont, MA: Nordland, 1976), 195, 214–15, 292; Roman Szporluk, "History and Russian nationalism," Survey 24, 3 (108) (Summer 1979, 9–10; Alekseeva, *Istoriya*, 401–2.
27. Alexander Solzhenitsyn, *The Gulag Archipelago 1918–1956: An experiment in literary investigation*, 5–7 (London: Collins & Harvill Press, 1978), 45–46.
28. A. Solzhenitsyn, "Konferentsii po russko-ukrainskim otnosheniiam v Toronto Garvardskomu Ukrainskomu Issledovatel'skomu Institutu," *Russkaia mysl'*, 18 June 1981. Also in *Novoe russkoe slovo*, 21 June 1981.
29. Solzhenitsyn, *Letter* . . . (as Note 9 above), 7, 32.
30. Alexander Solzhenitsyn et al., *From under the Rubble* (London: Collins & Harvill, 1975), 117, 131, 135.
31. Michael Meerson-Aksenov and Boris Shragin eds., *The Political, Social and Religious Thought of Russian 'Samizdat': an Anthology* (Belmont, MA: Nordland, 1977), p. 77.
32. Solzhenitsyn, *Letter*, 99, 101–2, 104.
33. ——, 196.
34. This is an ambiguous phrase in the Russian original; it could equally well be translated, "Tendencies to the secession of any republic from the USSR do not have, to all appearances, a mass character . . ."
35. Andrei Sakharov, *Sakharov Speaks* (New York: Vintage, 1974), 149.
36. *Khel'sinkskoe dvizhenie* (New York: Chalidze Publications, 1982), 105.
37. Meerson-Aksenov and Shragin eds., *The Political*, 393.
38. N. Arguni, "Russkie sotsial-demokraty i budushchee Rossii (*Samizdat*)," Forum 4 (1983), 175.
39. *Materialy samizdata*, AS No. 5405, 16, 32. A recent emigre notes more specifically that "Russian human rights activists, as distinct from Russian nationalists, not only recognize the right of nations to self-determination but also actively support concrete demands of the oppositionists from the non-Russian republics," (V. Malinkovich, "O lozungakh i real'nosti," Forum 10 (1985), p. 18).
40. *Veche* 1 (1981), 141.
41. Igor' Siniavin's letters in Forum 9 (1984), 61, 63.
42. Boris Paramonov, 'Paradoksy i kompleksy A. Ianova', *Kontinent* 20 (1979), 231–74.

43. A. Amal'rik et al., 'Zaiavlenie po ukrainskomu voprosu', *Kontinent* 12 (1977), 210–11, and 14 (1977), 332. Cf., also an earlier editorial note on adhering to the principle of the right to self-determination: "Ot redaktsii," *Kontinent* 4 (1975), p. 339.

44. Kronid Liubarskii's answers to an editorial questionnaire, *Forum* 2 (1983), 11.

45. Boris Vail' (as note 44), Cf., also Boris Shragin's and Sergei Pirogov's answers to the same questionnaire, pp. 27, 42–43.

46. Samorodnitskii, Bran' Za Pravdu, 171.

47. George Urban, "Portrait of a Dissenter as a Soviet Man: A Conversation with Alexander Zinoviev," *Encounter*, 4 (April 1984), 17.

48. Aleksandr Zinov'ev, *Ni svobody, ni ravenstva, ni bratstva: Stat'i. . . 1980–81* (Geneva: L'Age d'Homme, 1983), 87.

49. ———, 90.

50. Aleksandr Zinov'ev, 'Stabil'no li sovetskoe obshchestvo?', *Kontinent* 37, 148.

51. Zinov'ev, *Ni svobody . . .*, 87.

52. Yury Serech, *Problems in the Formation of Belorussian* (Supplement to *Word*: Monograph No. 2) (New York: The Linguistic Circle of New York, 1953), 93.

53. Mykhailo Hrushevs'kyi, "Zvychaina skhema 'russkoi' istorii i sprava ratsional'noho ukladu istorii skhidn'oho slov'ianstva," in V.I. Lamanskii ed., *Stat'i po slavianovedeniiu*, Vol. I (St. Petersburg: Imperatorskaia Akademiia nauk, 1904), 298–304.

54. *Historyia Belaruskai SSR*, Vol. I (Minsk: Navuka i tekhnika, 1972), p. 110.

55. Hrushevs'kyi, Zvychaina 300–301.

56. Mykhailo Hrushevs'kyi, "250 lit," *Literaturno-naukovyi vistnyk* [*LNV* in the following], 1 (January 1904), 1–6, and Mykhailo Hrushevs'kyi,'Vyhovs'kyi i Mazepa', LNV, 6 (June 1909), 417–28.

57. Victor Swoboda, "Taras Shevchenko and the censors," *Scottish Slavonic Review* 2 (1983), 118 and 107–34 passim.

58. Georges Luciani, *Le Livre de la genese du peuple ukrainien* [the original text with a translation into French, introduction and notes] (Paris, 1956), 140–42.

59. Iulian Bachyns'kyi, *Ukraina irredenta (po povodu emigratsii): Suspil'no-politychnyi skits* (L'viv, 1895), 72, 131. In a footnote (72–73) Bachyns'kyi thus defines his term: "Here I use the term 'Ukraine' not so much in the national [viz., ethnic.—V.S.] meaning as rather to signify the south-western Russian territory which comprises: Volynia, Podolia, so-called "Little Russia" (the Kiev, Chernyhiv, Poltava and Kharkov provinces) and so-called "New Russia" (the territory up to the Black Sea). Struggle for the Ukraine's political independence likewise relates not exclusively merely to the Ukrainians as a nation but generally to *all* who live in the Ukraine irrespective of whether he is an autochthonous Ukrainian or a settler: a Great Russian, a Pole or a German. Their common interest will Ukrainize them and will make all of them become Ukrainian 'patriots'."

60. Taras Hunchak and Roman Sol'chanyk eds, *Ukrains'ka suspil'no-polytychna dumka v 20 stolitti: Dokumenty i materiialy* [*USPD* in the following], I (s.1.: Sucasnist, 1983), 57, 78, 89, 96, 228–29.
61. ———, p. 110.
62. ———, p. 65.
63. Badzo, *An Open Letter*, p. 88.
64. Ivan Franko, 'Poza mezhamy mozhlyvoho', *LNV*, 10 (October 1900), 8–9.
65. "Vid Ukrains'koi Demokratychnoi Partii," *LNV*, 6 (June 1905, 272–74, and "Prohrama ukrains'koi demokratychno-radykal'noi partii," *LNV*, 4 (April 1906), 194–9; *USPD*, I, 139–40, 142, 147–52.
66. ———, 116, 121, 129.
67. ———, 161.
68. ———, 257.
69. ———, 258–62, 264–66.
70. Ukrainian and Belorussian *rada* means 'council' (as also Russian *sovet*).
71. USPD, I, 259–60.
72. ———, 270–72.
73. ———, 263, 283–84, 286, 292, 308–10.
74. ———, 293.
75. ———, 297.
76. ———, 301–2.
77. ———, 328–30.
78. For more details see: John S. Reshetar, Jr., *The Ukrainian Revolution, 1917–1920*, (Princeton, N.J.: Princeton University Press, 1952) 65–80.
79. USPD, I, 323.
80. ———, 335–36.
81. ———, 305.
82. ———, 341, 343.
83. M. Popov, *Narys istorii Komunistychnoi Partii (bil'shovykiv) Ukrainy* (Kharkov, 1931) 134 ff.
84. *USPD*, 1. 372, 375.
85. ———, 347, 362. Among other political groupings, the Ukrainian National Union (a "United Front" against the monarchist Hetmanate) in August 1918 declared as its first aim "the creation of a strong independent Ukrainian state" (ibid, 400).
86. ———, 405–6, 422–23.
87. *Komunistychna partiia Ukrainy v rezoliutsiiakh i rishenniakh z"isdiv, konferentsii i plenumiv Tsk*, 1 (Kiev, 1976), 20, 23.
88. Lenin, *Collected Works*, (vol. 30, p. 295).
89. The most important document of the Ukrainian independist Bolshevik trend is Serhii Mazlakh and Vasyl' Shakhrai, *Do khvyli* (Saratov, 1919), translated with a useful introduction and notes as Serhii Mazlakh and Vasyl' Shakhrai, *On the Current Situation in the Ukraine* (Ann Arbor: University of Michigan, 1970). See also a review of the latter in *Soviet Studies* 23, 4 (April 1972), 659–62.

90. *USPD*, I, pp. 434, 438–39.
91. *Komunistychna . . .* (note 84), p. 149.
92. *Odinnadtsatyi s"ezd RKP(b)* (Moscow: Gospolitizdat, 1961), 73–74.
93. *Istoriya Sovetskoi Konstitutsii (v dokumentakh): 1917–1956* (Moscow: Gosiurizdat, 1957), 393.
94. Jurij Borys, *The Russian Communist Party and the Sovietization of Ukraine* (Stockholm: Norstedt, 1960), 297–323, 343–44.
95. *Ukraine: A Concise Encyclopaedia*, 1 (Toronto: University of Toronto Press, 1963), 818–19. It is uncertain whether discussions, in 1930, in Bukharin's opposition circle about the Ukraine's and Belorussia's national independence which he mentioned at his trial in 1938 (according to G.A. Tokaev, *Comrade X* (London: Harvill), 1956, 97) were in any way connected with those arrested at that time in the Ukraine. (The late Professor Leonard Schapiro expressed doubts to the present writer concerning the reliability of Tokaev's testimony.)
96. P. Poltava, *Zbirnyk pidpil'nykh pysan'* (Munich: Ukrains'kyi samostiinyk, 1959), 13.
97. *USPD*, 3, 148–49.
98. Michael Browne ed., *Ferment in the Ukraine* (London: Macmillan, 1971; Woodhaven, N.Y.: Crisis Press, 1973), 59–60.
99. ———, 69–70.
100. "Do vsikh komunisitiv narodno-demokratychnykh i kapitalistychnykh krain . . .," *Suchasnist'* 9, 12 (December 1969), p. 97.
101. "Na Zakhid prodistalosia odne chyslo 'Voli i Bat'kivshchyny' z 1966 roku," *Svoboda*, No. 148, 7 August 1982, 1, 3.
102. *USPD*, 3, p. 292.
103. ———, 302. Many more instances could be quoted. Thus, in 1976 Ukrainian nationalists imprisoned in Vladimir Prison declared the Ukraine's secession and state independence as their aim (280), and so did in 1979 eighteen political prisoners, "representatives of the Ukrainian National Liberation Movement" (374) and in 1980, the Ukrainian Patriotic Movement (on this, see p. 24 above). In 1979, Iurii Lytvyn of the Ukrainian Helsinki Group rated the question of national self-determination to be the most urgent problem for the Ukraine, ("Pravozakhysnyi rukh na Ukraini . . .," *Suchasnist'* 19, 10 (October 1979), 103).
104. Oleksa Tykhyi and Vasyl' Romaniuk, "Pozytsii ukrains'kykh politychnykh v'iazniv," *Suchasnist'* 18, 6 (June 1978), p. 76.
105. Badzo, An Open Letter, 81, 91–92.
106. Not identical with the homonymic organization active in the 1960s.
107. 'Khronika Katolyts'koi tserkvy na Ukrain: Ch. 8' *Visti z Rymu* 19, 12 (December 1984), 11.
108. *Materialy samizdata*, AS 5410, pp. 11, 47. In part similar demands were included in a "Common declaration of the Romanian Group of Renascence and the Ukrainian National Front" to the chairman of the USSR Supreme Soviet dated 27 January 1984 (*Visti z Rymu* AS 5372, 11, 12).
109. Poltava, Zbirnyk, 15–16.

110. *USPD*, 3, 149, 151–52, 157.
111. ———, 378.
112. P. Iu. Shelest, *Ukraino nasha Radians'ka* (Kiev: Politvydav Ukrainy, 1970).
113. Jaroslaw Pelenski, "Shelest and his period in Soviet Ukraine (1963–1972): A revival of controlled Ukrainian autonomism," in Peter J. Potichnyj (ed.), *Ukraine in the Seventies* (Oakville, Ont.: Mosaic Press, 1975), 283–305.
114. Victor Swoboda, "The Party guidance of a Soviet literature: The case of the Ukraine, 1968–1975" in Evelyn Bristol (ed.), *East European Literature* (Berkeley: Berkeley Slavic Specialties, 1982), pp. 87–89. On many other similar cases, including Shelest's, see pp. 85–106 passim.
115. N.P. Vakar, *Belorussia: The Making of a Nation* (Cambridge, Mass.: Harvard University Press, 1956), 72.
116. S.M. Sambuk, *Revoliutsionnye narodniki Belorussii* (Minsk: Nauka i tekhnika, 1972), 176.
117. *Istorya BSSR*, 1 (Minsk: Navuka i tekhnika, 1961), 397–98.
118. Aleksandr Charviakou, *Za Savetskuiu Belarus'* (Minsk, 1927), 25, as quoted by Ivan S. Lubachko, *Belorussia under Soviet Rule: 1917–1957* (Lexington: University Press of Kentucky, 1972), 6.
119. Lubachko, *Belorussia*, 9.
120. Vakar, *Belorussia*, 85–86.
121. Lubachko, *Belorussia*, 9.
122. From Kupala's poem, "Tsaru neba i ziamli" (written 1912; first published in 1920).
123. Mykhailo Hrushevs'kyi in *USPD*, 1, 274; *Revoliutsionnoe dvizhenie v Rossii posle sverzheniia samoderzhaviia: Dokumenty i materialy* (Moscow, 1957), 737, 739; Richard Pipes, *The Formation of the Soviet Union: Communism and Nationalism, 1917–1923* (Cambridge, Mass.: Harvard University Press, 1980), 73; Lubachko, *Belorussia*, 17.
124. *Revoliutsionnoe dvizhenie v Rossii v avguste 1917 g.: Razgrom kornilovskogo miatezha* (Moscow, 1959), 342, 626.
125. R. Astrouski ed., *Druhi Usebelaruski Kanhres: Matar''ialy sabranyia i apratsavanyia na padstave pratakol'nykh zapisau kamisiiai Belaruskai Tsentral'nai Rady . . .* (Munich: Belaruskaia Tsentral'naia Rada, 1954), 89–90.
126. S.P. Marhunski, *Sozdanie i uprochenie belorusskoi gosudarstvennosti: 1917–1922* (Minsk, 1958), 147–50; T. Gorbunov, 'Lenin i Stalin v bor'be za svobodu i nezavisimost' belorusskogo naroda,' *Istoricheskii zhurnal*, 2–3 (1944), pp. 15–16; *Istoriya BSSR* (note 114), Vol. II, p. 121; S. Ahurski ed., *Kastrychnik na Belarusi: Zbornik artykulau i dakumentau* (Minsk, 1927), 287, as quoted by Lubachko, *Belorussia*, 28.
127. Ahurski, *Kastrychnik*, 123, as quoted by Lubachko, *Belorussia*.
128. *S''ezdy Sovetov Soiuza SSR, Soiuznykh i Avtonomnykh Sovetskikh Sotsialisticheskikh Respublik: Sbornik dokumentov v trekh tomakh, 1917–1936 gg.* (Moscow, 1959–60), 2, 229.
129. Anthony Adamovich, *Opposition to Sovietization in Belorussian Literature (1917–1957)* (New York: Scarecrow Press, 1958), 160, 162–64.

130. Walter Kolarz, *Russia and Her Colonies* (New York, 1952), 155–56.
131. Lubachko, *Belorussia* 115–16.
132. Vakar, *Belorussia*, 150.
133. Astrouski ed., *Druhi*, 67, 79–80, and passim.
134. Ivan Shamiakin in his reminiscences of Mikhas' Lyn'kou, "Spakoinaia mudrasts', muzhny talent," *Polymia* (Minsk), 10 (October 1977), 216, called it "an anonymous masterpiece of a poem," while the anonymous author of *Letter to a Russian Friend: A 'Samizdat' Publication from Soviet Byelorussia* (London: Association of Byelorussians in Great Britain, 1979), 21, 48, 63 note 22, refers to it as "an example of Belorussian folk literature of the 1970s."
135. *Belarus* (Jamaica, N.Y.) 287–92 (March–September 1981).
136. Ianka Zaprudnik, "Inakodumstvo v Bilorusi," *Suchasnist'* 19, 7–8 (July–August 1979), 159–60.
137. *Homin Ukrainy* (Toronto), 21 October 1972.
138. Zaprudnik, Inakodumstvo, 162.
139. *Letter to a Russian Friend . . .* (note 134), pp. 6–13, 32, 33–40, 57–58.
140. Zaprudnik, Inakodumstvo, 163.
141. A. Bembel', *Rodnae slova i maral'na-estetychny prahres* (London: Association of Byelorussians in Great Britain, 1985).
142. ———, 204.
143. ———, 159–195.
144. V. M. Konon, *Esteticheskaia mysl' Sovetskoi Belorussii* (Minsk, 1978) 71, as quoted by Bembel', *Rodnae*, 163.
145. V. Konan, 'Vasilek na rodnai nive', *Chyrvonaia zmena*, 6 May 1984, 2; Ann Sheehy, "Belorussian scholar upholds importance of nationhood and national languages," *Radio Liberty Research* RL 204/84 (23 May 1984).
146. Mikhail Kukobaka, "Ukradennaia rodina," *Forum* 3(1983), 146–54. See also a recent article about him by Caroline Moorhead, "Mikhail Kukobaka," *The Times*, London, 4 March 1986, 9.
147. Kukobaka, Ukradennaia, 149, 151.
148. The phrase was used by Shevchenko (the Ukraine's "foolish son") in his poem "Rozryta mohyla" (The Plundered Grave) (1843). Significantly, the poem was found equally objectionable by the political police in 1847–1917, as well as in 1950–55 and 1976–80; see Swoboda, 'Taras Shevchenko . . .' 114–16, 128.
149. Kukobaka, Ukradennaia, 152.
150. See the sources in notes 20 to 32 above and, for a summary of Russian nationalist opinion on that matter, Alexander Shtromas, "Prospects for Restoring the Baltic States' Independence—A View on the Prerequisites and Possibilities of their Realization," in *Journal of Baltic Studies*, 17, No. 3 (Fall 1986), especially 274–276.
151. Documents collected in USPD, 1 (n. 60) and evidence presented in J. S. Reshetar, Jr., *The Ukranian Revolution*, clearly show that to be the case.
152. Solzhenitsyn, *Letter*, p. 54.

153. Victor Swoboda, "Cat and mouse in the Ukraine," *Index on Censorship* 2, 1 (Spring 1973), 89.
154. Anton Koval', 'Vidkrytyi lyst', *Suchasnist'* 9, 10 (October 1969), 99.
155. Badz'o, *An Open Letter*, 84.
156. On Kampov: Iakiv Suslens'kyi, "Vhamuitesia, neliudy! Koho karaiete . . ." *Suchasnist'* 22, 6 (June 1982), 118–27; Kampov's appeal to the UN, *Suchasnist'* 22, 4–5 (April–May 1982), 175–80; "Khronika Katolicheskoi tserkvi na Ukraine," Nos. 6, 7, *Materialy samizdata*, AS No. 5410, 4–5, 36–37, AS 5413, 5. On Chendei: Swoboda, *USPD* 3, 96, 98. The other two seem to have escaped punishment having made appropriate statements.
157. Cf., a detailed discussion by Valerii Chalidze, 'O prave natsii na samoopredelenie,' *SSSR: Vnutrennie protivorechiia* 1 (1980), 121–39.
158. As to a likely "post-independence" scenario, cf., Hawrylyshyn on page XX above.
159. Mykhailo Hrushevs'kyi, 'Vyhovs'kyi i Mazepa', *LNV*, 6 (June 1909), 192–95.
160. Karl Marx and Friedrich Engels, *Sochineniia*, 15, (Moscow, 1935) 223; originally published in *Der Volksstaat*, no. 45, 1875.
161. Thomas W. Robinson, "Soviet and Russian Interests in Asia Under Communist and Non-Communist Governments," in Vol. 4 of the present series.
162. A. Shtromas, *Political Change* (n. 8), pp. 131–32.

4

The Baltic States in the Soviet Union:

Their Present State and Prospects for the Future

V. STANLEY VARDYS

The Baltic nations are among the smallest compactly living national groups of union republic status in the Soviet Empire. Their republics cover less than one percent of the immense Soviet land mass.[1] Their combined population totals less than 3 percent of the Soviet total.[2] Sitting on the northern edge of the Central European flatland and open to the East while hemmed in by the Baltic sea to the West, since the early Middle Ages they served as a missionary and colonial outlet for West European crusaders.[3] In later time, they became the main battleground between the aggressively expanding Russian Slav and Teutonic German empires. Estonia and Latvia were occupied and colonized by a succession of conquerors, foremost among them the Germans, and then for two centuries (1710–1918) they were submerged as provinces of the czarist Russian Empire. Locally, however, they remained under the domination of the original Western colonists, the "Baltic barons." In the thirteenth century, Lithuanians rose as a nation and rode into Russian and Ukrainian flatlands to create an empire stretching out between the Baltic and Black seas. However, under the pressure of the Knights of the Cross who had taken over Prussia, they felt a need of strengthening themselves by a union with Poland into which they were almost absorbed as a nation; that is, until both Poland and Lithuania lost their statehood to Russia's Catherine II in 1795.

While all three nations were reborn for independent existence between the two world wars, 1918–1940, their identity in modern times has been frequently blurred. They were either unknown, or if discovered by Russian or by German scholars of the eighteenth–nineteenth century, considered dead or dying. They did not disappear, of course, but their occupation and annexation by the Soviet Union in 1940 gave new reasons to question not only the viability of their statehood but also the permanence of their individual national identity.

In a thought-provoking book entitled *L'Empire éclaté* (*Decline of an Empire*) (1978), Hélène Carrère d'Encausse distinguishes three groups of non-Russian nations in the Soviet Union. In her view, the first group is being assimilated or is "assimilable" by the Russians. The second group, consisting of nationalities with a high degree of national consciousness, by circumstance is condemned to weakness or even to physical extinction. The third group, "equally conscious of their national existence," is strong demographically and will survive and develop in the future. Belorussians as well as many smaller nationalities belong to the first group. Central Asians, Caucasians, and the Ukraine belong to the third. The Baltic nations, particularly the Estonians and Latvians, however, belong to the group destined to disappear. Professor Carrère d'Encausse explains:

> Despite the strength of their national feeling, despite of everything distinguishing them historically and culturally from the other peoples of the USSR, these nationalities are headed not toward assimilation, but toward physical extinction. The possible disappearance of nations endowed with such strong personalities is an historical tragedy of which every Balt is conscious, and yet no one seems able to prevent it. Faced with this fate, the Baltic nationalities seem not even able to react by forming a Baltic bloc. Each becomes weaker still by isolating itself in its particularism and the things which separate it historically from the other nations in the region. This isolation and withdrawal heighten the extreme vulnerability of this part of the USSR, which from every point of view is the most modern, the most impregnated with outside influences, the least Sovietized. Yet, apparently none of this can impede the Baltic people from advancing toward the annihilation of their nations.[4]

This is a judgment by a distinguished scholar of Soviet nationalities. It therefore must be taken seriously.

Is the existential condition of the Baltic peoples really so life-threatening that they have no future? Are they to be counted as players on the Soviet stage only in the short run but to be consigned to oblivion a generation or two later? Is their demographic decline—if it is a decline—fatal? Have the enormous political and economic changes produced correspondingly altered cultural and political attitudes, which endanger their cultural and political individuality? Should we assume, as a result, that in a possible though currently unlikely case of international political realignment or even domestic structural change in the Soviet Empire, the Baltic nations will be too exhausted and demoralized to play a part as they did in 1918–1920?

Answers to such questions need be sought, first, in an analysis of those radical changes that were forced on the Baltic societies by the Kremlin since their annexation and absorption in 1940; and, second, in an examination of their current political attitudes.

Economic and Social Revolution

Today's Baltic republics in many respects differ from the Baltic States of half a century ago, especially in economy, demography, and political leadership. The differences that have existed between the Baltic nations themselves due to peculiarities of their historical development have diminished but still exist between Estonia and Latvia on the one hand and Lithuania on the other. The most dramatic remaining difference between these two northern republics and Lithuania rests in their recent demographic development.

Students of Soviet nationality affairs are familiar with the story of Baltic economic, social, and political development under Soviet rule. Generally, this development may be characterized as modernization according to Moscow's Communist model.[5] Broadly understood, modernization can be defined as complex social change triggered by industrialization and largely determined by its effects. The Soviet model is distinguished from the modernization process in non-Communist systems by a number of important features, especially by central planning, guided management, collectivism, subordination to political and ideological goals, preoccupation with economic production figures, and insensitivity to the needs of non-Russian ethnic communities. In the Baltic countries, the process began under virtual military occupation. Since the passage of time forces new perspectives of consideration, a new look at the results of Soviet modernization is not only justified but also required, especially for the appraisal of Baltic strength as national communities.

The modernizing economic and social revolution the Kremlin brought to the Baltic States is rooted in industrialization. Started under Stalin, first in Latvia and Estonia which already possessed an industrial infrastructure of importance, industrialization transformed these agrarian peasant countries into urban agricultural-industrial societies. The traditional organic bond of the farmer to the land was cut.[6] Even in Lithuania over 55 percent of the gross social product now comes from industry.[7] Latvia receives 56 percent of its social product from industry[8] and Estonia 63 percent.[9] The pace of growth has also been very rapid, on the whole faster than the Soviet average. In 1981, Lithuania's industrial production was sixty times larger than in 1940, the last year of independence. Latvia's production increased forty-six times and that of Estonia fifty times.[10] In our context it is important to note that having somewhat slackened in the 1970s, the speed of industrial development doubled since 1980.[11]

To further demonstrate the industrial emphasis, it must be added that agricultural recovery and expansion have been relatively slow. True to the Stalinist model of development, initially agriculture was neglected. By 1965, Soviet statistics indicated only a 50 percent growth of agricultural production in the twenty-five years in Lithuania while in Estonia the growth was only 30 percent and in Latvia a mere 20 percent.[12] At the same time, the 1965 industrial growth percentages increased 1,800 percent for Lithuania, 1,700 percent for Latvia, and 1,800 percent for Estonia.[13] By 1981, Lithuania claimed to have doubled its agricultural production in comparison to 1940, while Estonia was reported to have it increased by 70 percent and Latvia by 50 percent.[14]

This type of growth had an enormous impact on the composition of social classes and on occupational distribution of population not to speak about a rapid and sustained rise of the cities. By 1980, of the total Estonian working force, 43.2 percent were employed in industry and only 13.5 percent in agriculture.[15] In Latvia, the percentages were 41 percent and 16 percent,[16] and in Lithuania 39.1 percent and 22.3 percent.[17] This again demonstrated a very radical social and occupational shift from the farm to the city and from agriculture to industry. For example, in comparison to prewar years, the Latvian percentage of industrial workers grew more than twice while that of agricultural workers declined more than four times.[18]

Since the Baltic countries have virtually no natural resources needed for smokestack industries, the Kremlin promoted labor-intensive industries requiring imported raw materials and more skilled labor than nations with a very low birthrate could provide. In Estonia and Latvia, as a result, labor shortages have existed for decades. The only currently exploited natural resource of consequence is the Estonian oil shale which makes the republic the largest shale oil producer in the Soviet Union. Lithuania has some oil. Additional deposits were recently found off shore in the Baltic Sea, but the amounts discovered were not considered sufficient for commercial exploitation.[19] For energy, in addition to oil shale, the Baltic countries use natural gas from the Ukraine, coal from European Russia, locally generated hydroelectric and nuclear electric power. Construction of the largest nuclear power plant in the Soviet Union is already partially completed in a beautiful lake region of Ignalina in eastern Lithuania.

With the exception of the food processing and fishing industries, most other materials for industrial production have to be imported from Russia or other Soviet republics. The three republics make most of their contribution in light machine building, communications, chemical, transportation and service, and textile industries. On per capita basis, Latvia ranks first in the Soviet Union as a maker of railroad and street cars, diesel generators, automatic telephone stations, telephone equipment, radio receivers, refrigeration equipment, washing machines, mopeds, woolen and linen textiles.[20] In the 1970s, Estonia accounted for 1.6 percent of Soviet electric energy production, 1.9 percent mineral fertilizers, 12.1 percent oil extracting equipment, 5 percent excavators, 2.5 percent cotton textiles, and 2.1 percent butter.[21] In 1981, Lithuania made 11.4 percent of Soviet metal cutting lathes, 5.4 percent of hosiery, 6 percent wide screen TV sets, 5 percent refrigerators, 4.3 percent meat, 2.7 percent furniture, 2.6 percent construction bricks, 2.3 percent mineral fertilizer, and 2 percent paper.[22] Baltic input into the Soviet economy is considerably larger than their population figures or richness in natural resources would suggest.

During the last forty years, Baltic industries not only grew in size and sophistication but also were fully integrated into the centrally planned Soviet industrial complex. Currently, for example, Estonia exports 50 percent of its production to Russia.[23] In 1977, again, 82 percent of all raw materials for the Latvian chemical industry were imported, while in the same year 75 percent of finished products were exported.[24] Professor Juris Dreifelds refers to such industrial development as contradicting "standard economic logic."[25] This may be the case. But the logic is not so much economic as political. It subordinates local developmental needs and social consequences of such expansion to the goals pursued solely by Moscow.

This represents a complete reversal and reorientation of economic policies of the independent Baltic States, 1918–1940. At that time, markets were in the West, primarily Germany and Great Britain. In case of a structural economic readjustment, as it was needed in independent Estonia and Latvia fifty years ago when they had to reorganize industries inherited from the czarist Empire, all three Baltic countries now would have much greater problems.

This rapid industrial development gave a strong boost to urbanization. By 1984, Estonian city dwellers constituted 71 percent of the republic's total population as compared to 34 percent in 1940. Latvian city population increased from 35 percent in 1940 to 70 percent in 1984. Lithuanian growth was even more impressive, from 23 percent to 65 percent.[26] With almost one full percentage of annual urban increase, the Baltic region belongs to one of the fastest growing urban areas in the world.

The Demographic Picture

Growth of the cities touches on a sore demographic problem which invites somber reflection by the Balts. The problem is associated with the Baltic ability to maintain proportional ethnic strength in their homelands allowing a continuous and vigorous functioning of national Baltic communities.

Under Soviet rule, the proportional ethnic strength of Estonians and Latvians in their republics has been severely impaired. The percentage of Estonians has dropped from 88.2 (92.4 percent in adjusted postwar boundaries) in 1934 to 64.7 in 1979.[27] The percentage of Latvians sank even more dramatically, from 75.5 (77.0 in adjusted postwar boundaries) in 1935 to 53.7 in 1979. Three basic reasons account for this threatening change: low birthrate, immigration from Russia, industrial development. Traditionally, the predominantly Protestant Estonians and Latvians married late and had small families. Their birthrate was the lowest in the Czarist Empire at the end of the nineteenth century.[28] It stayed the lowest in the Soviet Empire. At one point—the year of Soviet occupation, that is, 1940—Estonia even reached minus population growth.[29] The low Latvian growth rate of 3.6 in 1940 went down to 1.4 in 1981 but shot back to 3.4 in 1983.[30] After fluctuating during the Soviet period, the Estonian Republic's growth rate showed 4.0 in 1983.[31] It is, however, not clear whether this increase is due to native Estonian or immigrant Russian fertility or both. The average size of a family in Estonia is 3.6, that of a family in Latvia 3.7.[32]

These are the growth rates of survival only. They do not compensate for very serious ethnic population losses suffered at the hands of the Nazis during World War II and at the hands of the Communists in 1940–41 and again in 1944–53.[33] Neither do they provide an adequate population increase to maintain the Estonians in a relative position of strength in Estonia. In the last twenty years, 1959–79, for example, the ethnic Estonian population in the entire Soviet Union grew only by 31,000, from 989,000 to 1,020,000. The Latvians increased by 39,000, from 1,400,000 to 1,439,000.[34]

Such population increases in Estonia and Latvia have been insufficient to offset the growing Russian and other ethnically alien immigration. Since Moscow's economic plans paid little attention to the availability of local labor market, a sizable working force had to be imported. In the early postwar period, workers in Russia were recruited by government agencies for employment in the Baltic countries, primarily in Estonia and Latvia. In addition, a good number of Russians came as Party or government administrators. Finally, the higher standard of living and gentler physical as well as cultural climate attracted many others who sought positions in Estonian or Latvian enterprises or offices. Between 1951–1970, 51 percent of Latvia's population increase came from immigration. In the last years of the decade of the 1970s, this percentage grew to 64.[36] In Estonia, immigration accounted for 47–48 percent of the republic's population increase while between 1959–70 it was 61 percent.[37] The immigrants came mostly to larger cities making them multinational. Estonian and Latvian cities were rather multinational also in the Czarist Empire, but neither the Germans nor the Russians—the ruling groups in those times—posed a demographic danger to the ethnic influence of the autochtonous population. This is not the case now. By 1979, the percentage of the Russian population had grown to 27.9 in Estonia and 32.8 in Latvia and higher in their major cities.[38]

In the 1970s, there were fluctuations but emigration did not slow down. In 1979–84, it constituted 54 percent of the Estonian population increase and a whopping 62 percent of the population of Latvia.[39] Some observers expect that the modernization of industrial performance, now accentuated by Mikhail Gorbachev, may put brakes on further immigration.[40] This does not seem likely because industrialization rates in the Baltic region keep increasing instead of subsiding.

In predominantly Catholic Lithuania, the demographic problem is not yet serious. The percentage of Lithuanians in the republic has not declined while the percentage of Lithuanians in various Party and administration positions has been on the rise. Lithuania remains 80 percent Lithuanian and the percentage of Russians—while quadrupling in the last fifty years—is still below 10 percent (8.9 in 1979).[41] Enormously large population losses during World War II and afterward inflicted by the hands of both Hitler and Stalin, including the virtual destruction of Lithuanian Jewry, did not allow Lithuania to recover its 1940 population size until the early 1960s. However, the number of Lithuanians in the Soviet Union between 1959–79 increased by 18 percent, from 2,326,000 to 2,851,000.[42] This is a considerably lower increase than that of the Caucasian or Central Asian peoples but so far has been sufficient to insure the Lithuanian position in their republic.

However, the Lithuanian birthrate has been steadily declining and the family size now approaches that of the other two republics. In 1983, the population growth rate seemed to settle for 6 per thousand but is likely to go down again as it did earlier.[43] Average family size is 3.8, just slightly higher than that of Latvia.[44]

Immigration into Lithuania so far has been small; however, this is quickly and ominously changing. Between 1951–74, immigration provided only 12 percent of the population increase.[45] The republic, apparently, was not as attractive to the Russians as its northern neighbors. The eight-year-long partisan war, 1944–52, made life in the republic insecure. Industrialization really started only after Stalin's death. It is also possible that the policies of First Party Secretary Antanas Sniečkus (1903–1974) helped to steer emigration away from Lithuania.

However, all of this now has changed. Between 1979–83, already more than one-third of the population increase for those four years came from immigration.[46] It has been estimated further that less than 55 percent of this population growth came from autochtonous Lithuanians.[47] If the trend continues, Lithuanian demographic development trends will become similar to those of Latvia and Estonia though, of course, it will take a rather long time until the ethnic proportions of the population become as upset as they are in the sister republics.

The Ruling Elite

Similarly as the economic and demographic structure, so the changes in the ruling elite reinforce the view that the Baltic States have been not only sovietized but also considerably Russianized and fully integrated into the larger Soviet Russian system of power.

Communist parties in the Baltic States had been very small. In Estonia, the Communists attempted a coup d'etat in 1924, but failed. In 1940, the year the Kremlin claimed the Communists made a revolution and seized power, the total Estonian Party membership consisted of 133 people,[48] way too few for any radical action like a forcible seizure of government. The Latvian Communist party has glorious traditions. A split in Latvian Social Democracy in 1917–18 gave Lenin and the Bolsheviks the Latvian Communist party and the Latvian Rifleman who sustained the early revolutionary victories. A number of important leaders beginning with the Red Army chief Joachim Vacietis and the Commissar of Justice Peteris Stučka also came from the Latvian ranks. In 1917–18, the Bolsheviks almost won power in Latvia, in some provinces, through the ballot box. But by 1940, the underground Latvian Communist party could report a membership of only 967.[49] The roots of the Lithuanian Communist party are not as deep but at the end of the independence period it had a larger membership. Operating in the underground, in 1940 it had between 1,308–1,780 members,[50] though years later Communist historians claimed a membership of 2,200 for that time.[51] Even if one adds underground Komsomol members and supporters of MOPR, Communists were a conspicuous but not a large or significant force during the period of independence.

After the incorporation of the Baltic countries into the Soviet Union, Communist party membership began to increase steadily, but the growth in numbers was slow and continued so until the late fifties and early sixties. The basic reason for the slow membership growth at that time was the overwhelming hostility to the regime and doubts about its staying power. With the exception of scattered ideological converts, the majority of Balts considered the Party an instrument of a foreign power fit for joining only by local quislings. During the partisan war in Lithuania, 1944–52, and in many areas affected by partisan struggle in Estonia and Latvia, it was often personally unsafe to become a member of the Party. Attitudes gradually changed in the fifties, when armed struggle came to an end and people realized that the Soviet system was there to stay for a significant period of time. Socialization of the younger generation into the system had the effect of persuading larger numbers that acceptance of the system and participation in its ruling group might be absolutely necessary for reasons both of personal welfare and of national well-being. Post-Stalinist relations between the Soviet Union and the Western nations, furthermore, pointed to the permanence of the Soviet occupation. The watershed years seemed to be 1956 and 1962, the autumn of the Hungarian revolution and the fall of the Cuban crisis. Results of both dramatic confrontations were interpreted as Western acquiescence and acceptance of the *status quo* achieved by the Soviet Union after the war. The Cuban crisis was also seen as indicating a lack of resolve and unwillingness by the Western powers to push back Soviet influence even in regions which did not fall under Soviet domination as a result of World War II.

It is also important to stress that in the 1940s and 1950s a very large percentage of the Party membership was not native but immigrant, mostly Russian. With native Balts joining at a later time, the predominance of membership of Russian and other immigrant origins was somewhat reduced. In Estonia, in 1970, 52.3 percent of Party membership was already Estonian.[52] Ethnic composition of the Latvian Communist Party has never been revealed. Western estimates show that the percentage of Latvians in that organization is 43 percent at best.[53] Only the Lithuanian Party in which Lithuanian minorities, primarily the Jewish, had an disproportionately high percentage before the war, became more strongly ethnic Lithuanian, despite the quadrupling of Russian population. In 1970, 66.5 percent of the Party was Lithuanian,[54] though it slightly declined by 1980.[55] Generally, the percentage of native Balts in each Party was below their proportion in the total republic population. This is not the case in the Caucasus, a region where autochtonous populations show greater demographic strength and vitality.

This development indicates that on the one hand the Balts have become more integrated into the Soviet system and on the other that the main ruling group is unduly dominated by the Russians. This becomes even more true when the lists of ruling nomenclature are examined, primarily in Latvia and Estonia.

Impact on Perception of National Identity

It is now appropriate and important to inquire whether this dual process, that of more intense participation and integration into the Soviet system on the one hand and the concurrent weakening of the Baltic ethnic strength and decision-making power on the other, has affected Baltic national consciousness, identity, and political attitudes.

The postwar expansion of industry propelled a considerable growth of educational institutions and opportunities for learning various skills needed by the new or expanded branches of industry. Similarly, economic and political needs made it necessary for the regime to enlarge the network of communications, from newspapers to television. After the death of Stalin, the three nations experienced a resurgence of cultural initiatives, a revival of national traditions, a creativity—common to the Soviet Union at the time—which in the Baltic case was crowned by many achievements in which all the Balts, without regard of political persuasion, take great pride.

It should also be stressed that at first, most communications and activities were conducted in the native languages. But gradually the intensification and the broadening of the scope of interaction with Moscow, the rise of Russian immigration, the need for economic or other reasons to establish ties with non-Russian republics brought about an extensive use of the Russian language. It now dominates or is used on a par with native languages in economic enterprises as well as in government institutions and schools, including of course the meetings of republic Communist parties. Where before World War II, and virtually yet in 1940, only the native Baltic language was used in public affairs, at the workplace, or in general communications, now there are two. The prewar monopoly of the native tongue or its virtually total domination in 1940 has been effectively destroyed; to a large degree, even in Lithuania. In the wireless media, for example, time now is shared by two languages. Similarly, the educational system and many social activities are now linguistically divided between two communities, the Baltic and the Russian, on a presumably equal footing. While before the war or even shortly afterward, the Russians were a diaspora minority; today they live compactly in many Baltic districts. In effect, there now exist two societies in the Baltic republics: the native Baltic and the Russian.

Among the indices that may be used to measure how sovietization and Russianization has affected Baltic national consciousness and identity, the most practical are figures on the use of native language and the expression of national self-identification. Neither, of course, can claim precision because neither consciousness nor identity can be subjected to solely statistical evaluation. However, the availability of statistical data makes them the most practical technique to be used for our purpose.

Generally, Baltic data on the use of native language in publications reveals three seemingly contradictory though actually parallel trends. First, Baltic publication activity has grown vigorously both in quantity of titles and the size of circulation. Second, native language publications have lost a large portion of total republican publication percentage to a single minority language, the Russian. Third, the Russian language has steadily accumulated considerable gains in all printed media.

Soviet statistics on book, journal, and newspaper publication provide the needed evidence to demonstrate these trends.[56] Thus, the number of Estonian book and brochure titles jumped from 788 in 1950 to 1,380 in 1983. It is probably of significance that the real increase occurred before 1970. In the last decade, 1970–80, the number of Estonian book titles grew only by 39. In Latvia, the equivalent figures were 977 and 2,209. Lithuanians published 916 titles in 1950 and 2,439 in 1983. The Latvian and Lithuanian increases reveal a strong and rising growth curve. The number of published copies has increased in a similar fashion, in Estonia from 3,588,000 in 1950 to 12,800,000 in 1983, without the corresponding slackening, as in book titles, and in Latvia from 6,124,000 in 1950 to 12,200,000 in 1983. In Lithuania, it almost tripled, from 6,592,000 in 1950 to 17,500,000 in 1983.

During the same period of thirty-three years, the number of Estonian journals grew from 24 to 111. Their circulation, however, increased not five but ten times, from 1,981,000 to 20,900,000 copies. It also may be noted that the Estonian journal growth occurred before 1970, similarly to the case with books. In Latvia and Lithuania, journal circulation increase was not as dramatic as in Estonia, but nevertheless very large. The Lithuanian increase in journal titles was similar to the Estonian, from 17 to 85, or fivefold, while in Latvia the growth was threefold, from 27 to 86.

These data attest to an undiminished thirst for native language print and to an increased Baltic creativity in the field. The decline of local newspaper publishing activity is most likely due to technical reasons, such as improved transportation. The slackening of Estonian vigor in both book and periodical publication since 1970 is puzzling. Since cultural activities are controlled by the Party, the decline may simply reflect brakes the rulers put on Estonian initiatives.

It is clear, however, that under Soviet rule the energies of the Baltic nations have not been turned away from furthering cultural development in the native idiom. The hunger for native language publications is still sharp and even growing. It is a well-known fact, for example, that Baltic publishing houses can never publish sufficient number of copies of non-political book titles to satisfy the public. Russian publications, on the other hand, if and when used, are used in addition rather than instead of native language works.

Hand in hand with this growth of Baltic language publications there has occurred its relative decline in terms of total publication activity and a concommitant increase of Russian language print. The Baltic States always had numerous publications in other than Baltic languages. The qualitative difference between the prewar and the current situation is that at the present time actually all non-Baltic publications are Russian, the language of a single minority in the Baltics but also the language of the ruling group in the Soviet Union. Thus, the percentage of published Estonian book titles went down from 84 of the total book publication percentage in 1950 to 62 in 1983 and the number of Russian titles increased in a corresponding manner. The percentage of Latvian book titles decreased from 74 to 50 percent, Lithuanian books lost 10 percentage points, from 85 to 75. A very similar decline has been registered in Estonian, Latvian, and Lithuanian journal and newspaper publication.

A similar but, for the Baltic languages, less advantageous situation exists in the wireless media. Data on radio and television broadcasting are less available and more difficult to study. Published Estonian data suggest that Baltic radios broadcast overwhelmingly in native languages. In 1980, for example, the average daily total of 34 hours of radio transmission included 30 hours of the Estonian language and only 1.5 hours of Russian programming.[57] In television, however, the situation was decidedly unfavorable to the Estonian language. Of the daily average of 35.3 hours of telecasting, only 6 hours were in Estonian while over 80 percent, or 29.3 hours, were telecast in Russian.[58] Considering that television is the medium overwhelmingly preferred by the youth, its effect on the Estonian youth must be correspondingly great. If telecasting is attractive and persuasive, in time the effect may become devastating for the use of the Estonian language.

Finally, it is obvious that the Baltic languages now have to compete against the Russian in the printed and the wireless media. In television—the most important of these media—Baltic languages are put at enormous disadvantage. Since neither the scope or volume of publications nor the telecasting time is apportioned without Communist party approval, development trends in the Baltic communications industry must mean that Moscow has purposefully decided not only to promote but also to impose the use of Russian language on the autochtonous Baltic populations. The Balts have been put on the defensive, as under the czarist rule.

However, data on the use of native language obtained by Soviet census takers in 1959, 1970, and 1979 reinforce the conclusion warranted by the findings on the media, namely, that the Baltic national communities remain strong, competitive, and very self-conscious.

Since language is the main characteristic of a nationality, its use can be taken as a reliable index of national self-identification. Soviet figures show that within republic boundaries there virtually has been no decline in the use of their native language by the Balts. In 1959, 99.3 percent of Estonians regarded Estonian as their native language. In 1979, the percentage was 99.0. The Latvians and Lithuanians registered a decline, the Lithuanians from 99.5 to 97.9 percent, the Latvians from 98.1 to 97.8 percent. These two figures are puzzling and cannot be explained without further information. For the first time ever, they show a considerably large decline in the use of native language. In total terms, of course, such decline does not impair the strength of a nation. The Balts, however, rather easily lose their language and resistance to assimilation outside of republic boundaries. In 1959, 80.3 percent of Lithuanians, 53.2 percent of Latvians, and 56.6 percent of Estonians living in diasporas of the Soviet Union still considered their respective Baltic languages as native, but in 1979 the percentages were 63.9 percent, 55.3 percent, and 33.3 percent. The largest losses were registered by the Lithuanians and the Estonians.

Sources of Baltic Political Culture

Eastern and Western social theorists generally agree that modernization has an impact on political attitudes, especially on the feeling of nationalism. Marxists, especially Soviet theorists, have expected that modernization will reduce nationalist emotions and identities and even will further assimilation of nationalities. As we know, however, this did not happen in the Baltic States. Marx and Marxists have been proven off the mark. In 1982, no lesser an authority than Yury V. Andropov, the general secretary of the Soviet Communist party admitted that "economic and cultural progress of all nations, large and small, is inevitably accompanied by the growth of national self-awareness." In other words, modernization sharpens rather than dissipates national feelings. According to Andropov, "this is a legitimate, objective process."[59]

However, before discussing the Soviet impact on Baltic political and national consciousness, it is necessary to briefly identify and characterize the forces that have shaped Baltic political attitudes in the past, particularly their nationalism.

Despite the fact that the Baltic nations have been historical neighbors of Russia, the culture that had a prevailing influence on the historical development of the Baltic nations has not been Russian but West European. It is generally agreed that even today the Baltic nations are the most Western Soviet republics, both in heritage and in the style of life.

For the Russian people, as Vasily Aksionov has depicted it in his short novels *Zvezdnyi bilet* (The Star Ticket) (1961)[60] and *Pora, moy drug, pora* (It is Time, My Friend, High Time) (1964)[61], the Baltic region is a land of Western mystery and foreign adventure. The Russians regard the Baltic republics as *sovetskaya* or *russkaya zagranitsa* (Soviet or Russian foreign countries).[62] It is a surrogate for the West, a "halfway house,"[63] so recognized both by the Soviets and by Western observers. The Balts, too, consider themselves different from the Russians not only ethnically but also culturally. In their view, their work habits, style of life, cultural, and religious attitudes are much more Western than Russian and, as such, superior to Soviet civilization. One must agree with the recent Western observer that "the Baltic nations might be called Europe's guerrillas in the Soviet empire" because "so much of their life is still fed from old European roots that Russia never knew."[64] As such, the Baltic nations have exerted some cross-cultural influence on certain spheres of Soviet life.[65]

Western influence came to the Baltic region through two different routes, the Germanic and the Western Slavic. Estonia and Latvia were dominated by the Germans, Lithuania by the Poles. The Knights of the Sword conquered the Estonian and Latvian tribes in the twelfth century. Their successors controlled the area for almost seven hundred years, though for long periods of time under Swedish, Russian or even Polish-Lithuanian sovereignty. The new cities the conquerors built belonged to the Hanseatic trading system. The Germans brought Christianity, a version of late feudalism and their own ethical and political codes. Reformation, which escaped Russia, painlessly swept over the Baltic establishing the Estonian and Latvian provinces as strongholds of Lutheranism. Since the sixteenth century Lutheranism was very influential in molding the Estonian and Latvian outlook on life. As was the case in other Lutheran countries, Estonian and Latvian society eventually became considerably secularized. Lutheranism remained an influence but it played a more modest role in public affairs generally and in national affairs specifically, than Catholicism in Lithuania, especially in modern times. Russian Orthodoxy won some adherents but never penetrated deeply into Estonian or Latvian society. Catholicism preserved the loyalties of a portion of the Latvian population— about one-third in recent times—but its role in Latvia has been confined both regionally and in scope.

This development, of course, was completely different from Russia. Similarly different was the social and cultural evolution. Serfdom was abolished in Latvia and Estonia half a century earlier than in Russia, or even in Lithuania. An early introduction of native print and native schools, under

Lutheran influence, made the historical Baltic provinces the most literate in the Russian Empire.

In Lithuania, the historically dominant influences were Catholic and Polish. In distinction to the Estonians and Latvians, the Lithuanians can also claim a much longer historical tradition of statehood. An important power in thirteenth–fifteenth century Eastern Europe which stopped the expansionism of the Teutonic Knights of the Cross in East Prussia and contained Tartar advances to the West in central Russia, medieval Lithuania was pagan and at first attempted to balance between Catholicism that the German Knights were pressing on it and Russian Orthodoxy, which was the religion of its Russian subjects. To gain strength against the German Knights, by the end of the fourteenth century, it chose an alliance and political union with Poland. With this union came the Latin-rite Christianity from Rome but via Poland. These twin influences, Catholicism and Poland, have shaped the Lithuanian political and social tradition through the nineteenth century. At first aiding in the polonization of the ruling elites, in the nineteenth century Catholicism became a catalyst for the emergence of modern Lithuanian national consciousness and has strongly influenced Lithuanian political, cultural and national development. The Soviets suppressed the Church, but it remains unbowed, and still exercises a vigorous and vital influence. Lithuania, however, has now become secularized and the role of religion in societal behavior and the acceptance of Catholic moral code, especially in family relations, has substantially declined.

Since the end of the nineteenth century, Baltic political culture has been strongly affected by three other forces, namely, nationalism, democracy, and socialism.

The origins of Baltic nationalism are found in the nineteenth century movements of national awakening. These movements united the national intelligentsias and the peasantry into a force which eventually gained national independence. The establishment of statehood and the demonstration of viable existence as political communities and sovereign nations, inspired the Estonians, Latvians, and Lithuanians to spare no effort to regain independence when it was lost in 1940. The wars of independence of 1918–1920, the resistance movements against the Soviets in 1940–41, the insurrection against the Soviet rule on 23 June 1941, followed by a similar rebellion in Latvia, the subsequent resistance movements against the Nazis combined with determination to defend themselves against the returning Soviets, all were inspired by this nationalist self-confidence and commitment. Its culmination came in a bloody eight-year-long partisan war in Lithuania fought against the victorious Soviets, 1944–52, and a more modest but extensive guerrilla activity in Latvia and Estonia during the same period of time. Sacrifices and sufferings accepted and endured by the

Balts seeking independence from 1917–1918 were enormous, much higher than the price most Third World countries paid for their sovereignty after World War II. These sacrifices were possible because nationalism had deep popular roots. It was the overarching ideology which united all social classes and political movements except the Communists.

Nationalism, it must be added, normally has philosophical and social underpinnings. At the end of the nineteenth, and the beginning of the twentieth century, the growth of the national awakening movements overlapped with the time of political differentiation of Baltic societies. This gave Baltic nationalism an articulated democratic philosophy. Consequently, in 1918–1920, it did not enter into anyone's mind—except the supporters of Lenin—that the new Baltic countries should not be founded on democratic principles. As a matter of fact, all three, especially the Estonians, chose the path of radically defined democratic systems. However, ideological divisions, economic problems, and an uncompromising style of political exchange put burdens on the fledgling democratic institutions that they could not carry for long. Mechanisms needed for solutions were not built into the assembly-type systems. As a result, democracy was eclipsed early in Lithuania, 1926–30, and somewhat later in Estonia and Latvia (1934). But democratic thought had, in the meantime, penetrated too deeply into the national consciousness to allow its demise. By 1939, democracy was already returning to Estonia and Lithuania.

Fascism, identified with extremist nationalist factions, was never well organized, but pro-Fascist movements and tendencies existed in all three. All three countries had to deal with extremist nationalists and succeeded in containing their influence; the Baltic extreme Right did not enjoy much popular support. Political systems, established by Konstantin Päts in Estonia, Karlis Ulmanis in Latvia and Antanas Smetona in Lithuania had some pro-Fascist institutional features, primarily in Latvia, but only Soviet propagandists can label these moderate personal dictatorships as Fascist. In the 1960s and 1970s, Soviet Lithuanian scholars and intelligentsia began to look nostalgically toward Smetona's regime referring to it as democratic rather than Fascist. First Party Secretary Antanas Sniečkus sternly warned the students of this last decade of the period of independence against such interpretation. From the perspective of Soviet reality, apparently, Smetona's system looked rather free.[66]

Socialism, too, had an enduring impact on Baltic political culture. Its origins go back to the end of the nineteenth century. The socialist movement was the strongest in Latvia, the most industrialized province of the czarist empire which also had the largest working class. The Socialists, it must be said, had adherents also among the landless peasants. The intelligentsia of Estonia and Latvia, as indeed a large portion of Lithuania, also was politically leftist, some even revolutionary oriented. While on the surface Marxist, early Socialist movements, however, contained large portions of nascent Baltic nationalism. Directed against czarism on the national level, Baltic socialists in Latvia and Estonia were anti-German at home. The most severe Russian revolutionary outbreaks of 1905 took place in Latvia and were directed mainly against German estate owners. Early socialist attitudes toward the Russians exhibited by all three Baltic socialist movements were ambivalent.

As elsewhere, the Bolshevik coup d'etat of October 1917 in Russia split the Baltic Social Democratic parties into Democratic and Communist factions. Democratic Socialists actively supported national independence while the Communists opted for joining Lenin's Soviet Russia. In 1918–20, the Communists lost and were banished from public life. As explained earlier, however, they survived in the underground though never acquiring either sufficient political strength or popular following successfully to challenge the "bourgeois" governments. Domestic political influence of Social Democratic parties was greater in Estonia and Latvia than in Lithuania where not the Social but Christian Democracy was the much stronger force.

In 1940, however, Communist parties were catapulted to power by the Red Army. This victory guaranteed the Communist monopoly of both power and ideology over the rather differentiated public life of the Baltic nations. The price the politically weak Communist parties paid for this sudden victory was very high: they became tainted by collaborationism with a foreign power. This made their ambition of governing and reeducating the Balts extremely difficult, actually impossible, without the aid of foreign troops and secret police. Without even realizing it, Baltic Communists became puppets in the Kremlin's designs on the Baltic nations, that were not foreseen nor anticipated by the underground idealists.

Soviet Impact on Political Attitudes

It is not the purpose of this chapter to analyze the ways and means by which the Kremlin and the Baltic Communist parties now took advantage of their victory to remake the political philosophy and the national consciousness of the Balts. We are interested, however, in the achieved results.

After first rejecting Soviet rule and even militarily fighting the regime, most Balts were forced to change their attitude if they wanted to survive. Partisan war casualties, cruel deportations of hundreds of thousands, absolute control of access not only to careers but also to the daily breadbasket exhausted the population and induced most of it to bow to the disagreeable reality. In time, most people accepted Soviet power as a fact of public life though even today it remains deeply ingrained in the consciousness of all postwar generations that this power is illegitimate.

The Soviets spent an enormous effort to win acceptance by the population and to socialize the young generations. However, this effort has produced only limited results. Sovietization has remained very shallow. The Baltic peoples still resemble the radishes; they may have red skins, but they are white on the inside. According to the testimony of Alexander Shtromas who grew up in Lithuania and for twenty-five years observed political life, "by the first half of the 1950s there were no more indigenous Baltic people who continued to support the Soviet regime out of idealism or conviction. Nor did any of the indigenous Balts still believe in Communism as represented and implemented by this regime."[67] It has to be kept in mind that the number of such ideologically committed Balts was very small to begin with.

Nevertheless, Marxist-Leninist indoctrination and experience with the Soviet political code has left an imprint on Baltic philosophy of life. Two major effects may be noted: first, political conformism combined with escapism and resignation from politics; and, second, radical secularization of society and of individual consciousness.

The attitude toward politics has been insightfully characterized by Alexander Shtromas. He describes Lithuanian attitudes but other evidence suggests that on the whole the characterization is valid for all the Balts. According to Shtromas, the disenchantment with official ideology or its rejection, combined with the impossibility of questioning it or articulating alternate political views, has produced a feeling of political resignation. The population has been left either disillusioned with communism or without any political ideology, alienated and cynical, "instinctively seeking to withdraw from everything political."[68] People withdraw into small circles of family or friends; they seek solely private pleasures. They have become, one should add to Shtromas's observations, very selfish, interested only in personal gain. It is paradoxical that an ideology that preaches selflessness and idealism should reap the opposite in reality. To escape the void, the old, but especially the young, took to the bottle. Drinking became not just an occasion for weekend enjoyment but a way of life, a ritual that accompanies public and private interactions. The Lithuanians and Latvians drink somewhat less than the Russians, but the Estonians drink more. They hold the record in the Soviet Union, and the Soviet Union holds the world drinking record among major nations of the world.[69] Drinking is a national scourge that the Kremlin's leadership under Mikhail Gorbachev has found to be very dysfunctional to Soviet economic progress though Gorbachev's predecessors preferred to cater to Soviet drinking habits because drinking was useful to the regime, one suspects, as a political tranquilizer.

In addition to the high degree of a-politicization, Shtromas identifies two other consequences of political alienation, namely, what he calls the "numbing" and the "antagonizing" effects. The "numbing" refers to insensitivity to acquisition of information, which is made very difficult by Soviet censorship. Fed only propaganda or half-truths, average people become "misinformed and disoriented." The "antagonizing" effect refers to "indiscriminate feelings of revenge and hatred to everything alien, threatening or merely insufficiently understood," which is caused by hostility to the Communist system. This is Shtromas's explanation for the antagonism frequently displayed by the Balts toward the Russians.

The Baltic dislike for the Russians is indeed well known. It has been demonstrated in the shops of Tallinn where Vasily Aksionov's hero Valya in *Pora, moy drug, pora* has to speak English to buy liquor after hours, in the settlements of Riga where violent antipathy and "chauvinism" toward Russians has been observed by foreign correspondents, in the stormy demonstrations against the Russians by soccer fans in Vilnius during and after games Lithuanian teams play against those from the Russian republic.

The existing evidence on the Baltic republics, as recorded and perceived both by the insiders and in the West, shows that, generally, political conformism has become a necessity and has discouraged many to see in political activity an instrument, which can help to produce a national alternative to communism. Life has become politically antiseptic, a-politicized; it also has been compartmentalized, alienating people not only from politics but from each other as well.[70] However, there are so many exceptions in the Baltic republics to this prevailing attitude that the Balts cannot really be considered politically resigned, though this varies from republic to republic and from one social group to another. Widespread dissident activities, *samizdat* publications, numerous involvements in private circles from prayer meetings to political discussions, search for information and contacts from abroad, use of officially published literature for articulation of otherwise forbidden thoughts frequently break the a-political pattern of behavior and pierce the ideological void. Balts, similarly, remain better informed than citizens of most of the Soviet Union. Finally, their dislike, even hatred, of the Russians—though widespread and "instinctive," as Shtromas says—is tempered by a realization articulated in *samizdat* that there are "good" and "bad" Russians. For example, Estonian, Latvian, and Lithuanian dissidents have collaborated with Russians not only in Moscow but also locally. Sergei Soldatov has been a leader in the Estonian democratic underground. Estonians have collaborated with Russian naval officers who drafted an early political program for Russia, the Ukraine, and the Baltic States. Latvian Baptists, especially, have worked together with their Russian coreligionists. Lithuanian dissidents have showered praise on Academician Andrei Sakharov and other Russian luminaries, but especially on Russian scientist Sergei Kovalev who spent years in prison for collaboration with Lithuanian religious dissidents. While the Russians are disliked and even vilified by many, on the whole Baltic intelligentsias have not become xenophobic.[71]

The Soviets have further impacted Baltic attitudes by interferring with religious beliefs and practices. One of the objectives of Marxist-Leninist indoctrination has been "secularization and atheist indoctrination."[72] The Soviets have not only completely isolated the churches and the clergymen from public life but also made inroads into religious consciousness of the young generation.[73] The achievement has not been crowned with the production of militant or radical atheists—though this has been the objective—but has resulted in the separation of large segments of the youth from religious influences. This is especially important in Lithuania where Catholicism in times of great adversity has helped to articulate and defend Western values and national traditions. Even in Lithuania, however, there are now many young people who know nothing of their religious traditions. They do not, as a rule, become atheists, but agnostics,[74] for whom religion is an irrelevant social phenomenon and who are not obsessed, as Dostoyevsky was, with the problem of God's existence. They remain positively disposed toward religion, especially when they see it persecuted, but they are not believers themselves. It may be, of course, debated whether the loss of religious consciousness affects national self-awareness, but the elimination of religious differences, be they Catholic or Lutheran, make the Baltic youth more like the Russian, thus eliminating one important obstacle to sovietization as well as to Russification and assimilation. With the loss of religious traditions, furthermore, the young Balts also lose ties to many symbols and concepts of their West European heritage.

Nationalism in Baltic Consciousness

Baltic hostility to the Russians reflects the feelings of intense nationalism, the traditional enemy of the Kremlin in the Baltic States. The Kremlin's attitude toward domestic and world nationalism has been ambivalent. On the one hand, the power of nationalist feelings is respected as an important social force which is antagonistic to communism but which can be manipulated to advance the Kremlin's interests. On the other hand, domestic non-Russian nationalism is regarded as an enemy of the system which has to be destroyed or at least contained.

Since nationalism may have several meanings, it may be useful to better identify it. In our context, it connotes a conscious and instinctive defense and promotion of the interests of ethnic collectivity, the most visceral of which is the interest in self-preservation and the most lofty of which is the attainment of independent statehood. It also should be pointed out that as political ideology nationalism integrates two major elements, the goal of national sovereignty and a political philosophy associated with that view.

If the Soviets have impaired religious consciousness, particularly in the more deeply religious Catholic Lithuania, the same cannot be said about nationalism. As a military force, it was crushed by the destruction of the partisan movement in the late 1940s and early 1950s,[75] but as a political force it suffered only a setback. Nationalist feelings and nationalist dispositions of the Balts were not substantively affected. Soviet authorities claim that nationalism as ideology was destroyed by the abolition of the capitalist economic system and the social classes—the bourgeoisie and the independent farmers—which sustained it but this is a highly exaggerated claim they themselves do not believe, as demonstrated by Yury Andropov's remarks in 1982. Nationalist consciousness, it seems, has been least affected by the process of modernization and radical sovietization.

Copious data[76] recorded not only by Western scholars and journalists but also by the Soviets themselves, in addition to dissident sources, demonstrate rather pervasive nationalist feelings in public and private life, even among the ruling Communist bureaucracies.

In the early years of Soviet rule many native Communist or pro-Communist leaders misunderstood Moscow's policies toward their republics and paid the usual price for it; they were purged. Others, unable to reconcile their consciences with the Kremlin's demands, became alcoholics or committed suicide. One of them, in 1946, was the chairman of the Presidium of the Estonian Supreme Soviet Johannes Vares-Barbarus who reportedly killed himself because he felt that he had betrayed his nation. This probably reflected the feeling of other Estonian Communists. The Kremlin accused several Estonian leaders of nationalist leanings and, in 1949–51, a number were purged, chief among them First Party Secretary Nikolai Karotamm.[77] In 1959–62, even a larger number of Latvian Communists were removed in Latvia, again for various nationalist deviations. Eduards Berklavs, deputy chairman of the Council of Ministers, was considered to be the chief culprit.[78] Emboldened by Khrushchev's anti-Stalinism and upset by the skyrocketing Russian immigration into Latvia, these Latvian leaders demanded that Latvia be allowed to draft its own economic plan, that the Latvian market be supplied before various Latvian-made goods were exported to other republics, and that the immigrant cadres be required to learn the Latvian language.

Arvids Pelše, then second party secretary, helped Khrushchev who had come to Riga to investigate the situation. Pelše's collaboration in the purges was eventually rewarded with a seat on the Politbureau. It is not known that—as a member of this supreme Communist decision making body in Moscow—Pelše did anything to promote or protect Latvian national or cultural interests. After he took over as the first Latvian Party secretary from Janis Kalnberzinš, he suffocated the relaxed cultural atmosphere possible in the other Baltic republics in the 1960s and kept Latvia under a strong hand that reached to Riga all the way from Moscow. The purge of Berklavs and his colleagues and the reign by Pelše silenced the Latvian Party and intelligentsia for years to come.

In Lithuania, pro-nationalist behavior in the party and government apparatus was efficiently managed and controlled by First Party Secretary Antanas Sniečkus, a confidant and ally of the dogmatic ideologist Mikhail Suslov. A possibly disenchanted[79] but loyal and tough Communist, Sniečkus is nevertheless credited with surrepetitiously aiding traditionally Lithuanian cultural initiatives and managing economic development without excessive Russian immigration. Already in 1957–58, Sniečkus sent a discreet signal to Lithuanian intellectuals emboldened, as were the political leaders of Latvia, by the spirit of de-Stalinization. The signal was delivered by means of a trial labeled the "trial of eleven intellectuals," which led to the sentencing of the several accused for various allegedly nationalist activities.[80] The very sparse information about the trial indicates that the alleged crimes were more of the type of cultural deviation rather than political conspiracy. Among the sentenced was Viktoras Petkus who had just been released from the *Gulag* and who would, twenty years later, again play an important role as organizer of the stillborn National Baltic Committee and as a cofounder of the successful Lithuanian Helsinki Watch group.[81] In 1958–59, Sniečkus fired and expelled from the Party the president of Vilnius University and purged its Departments of Lithuanian Language and Literature.[82] The president of the university apparently had been laying off Russian personnel, whom the school had been compelled to hire when Stalin was in power. Department of Lithuanian Literature was becoming a hotbed of "bourgeois" nationalist views. Sniečkus's purge covered the Party's Central Committee as well; some members were identified as "bourgeois" nationalists. Differently from Estonia and Latvia, cultural figures degraded by Sniečkus were allowed in time to return rather quietly to their original research, publication, or other activities.

These purged Baltic Communists were not "national" Communists in the West European sense; that is, they were not Communists who challenged the necessity of membership in the multinational Soviet state for the achievement of a Communist society in their native lands. According to Ukrainian Party secretary and CPSU Politbureau member Vladimir Shcherbytsky who once acknowledged the existence of national communism in the Soviet Union, this idea is not workable either economically or politically. In Shcherbytsky's view, national communism is not feasible.[83] Shcherbytsky is correct in the sense that the Kremlin refuses to tolerate national Communists in the Soviet Union. Non-Russian Communist leaders are removed for considerably lesser deviations than "national" Communist transgressions as was the case with Shcherbytsky's predecessor Petr Shelest[84] and with the Baltic Party functionaries. These unfortunate rejects of the Kremlin may be labeled "autonomists", that is, Communists who expect Moscow to pursue the original, idealistic, "Leninist" nationality policy. But Moscow has made it clear that even autonomists are not acceptable. The plight of these Communist loyalists disillusioned with the Kremlin's behavior in the Baltic republics has been best articulated in the 1972 letter by seventeen Latvian Communists addressed to the Western European Communist leaders in which the authors sent a desperate S.O.S. to their ideological peers imploring them to help stop the drastic Russification of Latvian life.[85]

Currently we do not know of conspicuous nationalist behavior in the ruling bureaucracies of Estonia, Latvia, or Lithuania though serious problems with ideological work have been acknowledged in Estonia. On 14 August 1984, the Central Committee of the CPSU strongly criticized the Estonian Party's managing cadres for not participating in political-educational work.[86] The Estonian Party responded in its own Central Committee plenum of the same month.[87] Nationalist sins were not discovered but enormous disaffection from work the Party organizes to keep the ruling managers ideologically doctrinaire and *au courant*.

In the 1960s and 1970s, observers of the Baltic scene suspected the existence of national Communist groups in Estonia, but this has not been confirmed. In Lithuania, an important *samizdat* journal *Perspektyvos* published a discussion of the merits of "real" socialism and an appeal signed by the national Lithuanian Communist Association, but at the trial of the arrested editors of the journal it appeared that such a movement really did not exist.[88] Its manifesto was authored by Gintautas Iešmantas, a former Communist who quit the Party as well as his journalistic profession. He became a coeditor of this *samizdat* publication intending to discuss diverse ideological alternatives to Soviet communism.

While, on the whole, the ruling bureaucracies must be considered loyal and pliant, recent defections to the West of high officials from the Estonian ministries of culture and justice, of a KGB agent from Latvia, and other officials as well as scholars from Lithuania raise doubts about the reliability of such Baltic cadres. Similarly serious is the problem among Baltic intelligentsia which in recent years lost important personalities of its cultural and artistic life to the West.

Since survey research on such sensitive questions as nationalist attitudes is not possible in the Soviet Union, the scope and depth of nationalist sentiments have to be gauged in different ways. A reliable though imprecise measure can be obtained from examining participation in public events which involve masses of young, Soviet-educated Estonians, Latvians, or Lithuanians.

Similarly to Poland, Lithuania has periodically registered such upheavals. The first massive outbreak against the government was inspired by the Hungarian Revolution of 1956 and took place on All-Souls-All-Saints days in November in the city of Kaunas. The second, too, occurred in the same city in 1972.

In the early 1970s, the Lithuanian situation was comparable to a powder keg which needed only the lighting of a match to explode. The events in Czechoslovakia in 1968 but more likely the already swelling wave of dissent catalyzed by concentration on civil rights and religious issues, inspired a youth rebellion which eyewitnesses characterized as a real insurection. To attract President Nixon's attention to the plight of Lithuania—he was coming to Moscow to conclude the SALT I agreement and officially to launch the American Soviet détente—on 14 May, a graduating high school student Romas Kalanta poured gasoline on himself, lit a match, and burst into flames in the theatre square of Kaunas, the second largest city of the republic.[89] Kalanta was a member of the Komsomol and his father a Soviet war veteran—both had loyalist credentials—but the nineteen year old student immolated himself, as he declared, for the "freedom of Lithuania." The event was apparently planned by a group of youths. Estonian and Latvian students were reported as intending to sacrifice themselves together with Kalanta but were arrested on the train on their way to Kaunas.[90] However, the city, an educational as well as industrial center, was seething with young students and workers who wanted to honor Kalanta's sacrifice. They were not given a peaceful opportunity for such a purpose. After the city police deceived the representatives of Kalanta's numerous friends about the time and circumstances of Kalanta's funeral, on 18 May, thousands of angered youths spilled into the city, raised the old national flag, overturned police cars, marched on the city's main boulevard, and seemed to be bent on taking over the city. Placards they carried demanded freedom, some for Lithuania, others for the youth, still others for the Jews. A restless night followed. On the afternoon of 19 May, special troops arrived to quell the rebellion. Over five hundred were arrested. Two hundred were detained. Eight were selected for trial and eventually sentenced. The old Party secretary Sniečkus rushed to the city, admonishing factory and school audiences from which the rebels came that there existed a problem with the young workers and students which needed to be repaired. He blamed the upheaval on lax discipline and foreign influences.

The Kaunas events reverberated throughout the republic. Whether in concert with Kalanta or spontaneously, self-immolations occurred in at least half a dozen other localities, involving protestors of all age brackets.

A decade later, a similar upheaval took place in Estonia. The Estonian series of events seemed to have been inspired by the example of Poland's peaceful revolution of 1980. They, too, clearly demonstrated that the loyalties of young Estonians—who knew about independent Estonia mainly from their grandparents—were not with the regime but with the ideal of Estonian freedom. During 1–3 October 1980, over 2,000 (some report 5,000) high school students demonstrated in Tallinn, demanding not only improved school facilities but also "freedom for Estonia."[91] They waved old Estonian national flags and exhorted the Russians to "go home." Similar though smaller demonstrations took place in a number of other towns. Some hundreds of demonstrating youth were detained but only few arrested. This dramatic rejection of the Communist system brought Yury Andropov, still the chief of the KGB, to Estonia's capital. As in Lithuania, the local newspaper, radio, and TV were mobilized to quiet down the population. On 11 October, the minister of internal affairs made a TV appearance to warn against further disturbances. Unlike in Lithuania, parents were called to special meetings in which they were admonished to keep their children disciplined.

The Estonian upheaval brought forth an articulated protest and warning by some forty leading Estonian intellectuals and artists, several of them of Communist background.[92] The group signed a letter to *Rahva Hääl* and to *Pravda*, Communist party papers respectively in Tallinn and Moscow, in which they suggested that the demonstrations were the bitter fruit of the discriminatory nationality policies Moscow applied in Estonia. These policies, the letter claimed, divided Estonia's society into two hostile, Estonian and Russian, camps. The letter warned that if Estonians were not given clear-cut assurances that their national future in Estonia would be preserved and secured, the relations between the Russians and the Estonians would further deteriorate. A number of signers were interrogated by the authorities though none were detained for trial.

Student rebellion was not the only event that shook the republic during October of 1980 and later in 1981. In October, 1,000 workers struck in a machine tractor factory in Tartu, and, shortly before the imposition of martial law in Poland in December of 1981,[93] a group calling itself the Democratic Front of the Soviet Union called workers to participate in a quiet half hour strike to force changes in a number of Soviet policies in the Baltic republics. The appeal was not widely followed but the authorities became very agitated and incensed. Quick arrests followed and later Karl Vaino, first secretary of the Communist party of Estonia, publicly complained about the strike action, first in Moscow's *Kommunist* and later in the plenum meeting of the Estonian Communist party in June of 1983.[94]

These two events tell as much about the actual feelings of Estonian and Lithuanian populations as it is possible in the Soviet Union. Paradoxically, Estonia is a fiefdom of the KGB. After Yury Andropov, who usually was the Kremlin's main speaker at official Estonian celebrations, such speeches now are made by Viktor Chebrikov. For the KGB, Estonia most likely serves as an experimental station for the implementation of current policies of Russification. Estonian reactions to it are probably studied by appropriate agencies and conclusions drawn on tactics to be applied in this field.

The leadership's responses to manifestations of Baltic nationalism further confirm the resurgence of the very wide scope of nationalist feelings among the Balts. There is hardly a republic or national Party congress in Moscow at which Baltic Party chiefs would not complain about some nationalist deviations. Such behavior is now attributed to "imperialist," "diversionary" incitement allegedly sponsored by the United States government and the CIA but implemented by Baltic emigration diasporas abroad, especially in the United States and in Sweden.[95]

Recent Latvian Communist reactions show that while the Latvians have been less articulate after Khrushchev and Pelše purged the Latvian Party, their nationalist feelings run deep and they remain intensively anti-Communist and anti-Russian.[96] In 1981, the concern of Latvian authorities with nationalistic activities rose to hysterical heights, exemplified by a trial on 25 May–5 June of two Latvians, Juris Burmeisters and Dainis Lismanis, on charges of espionage.[97] Both defendants were sentenced to fifteen and ten year terms, respectively, in labor camps. Their main crime, however, appears to have been communication with the old Bolshevik antagonist, the Latvian Social Democratic party, whose core in exile has found refuge in Sweden under the leadership of Bruno Kalniņš. Both Sweden and the United States—and inevitably the CIA—were denounced as nests and instruments of diversion and espionage. In the past, other Latvians drew severe sentences for such attempts at communication but no trial was given as much publicity as this one, indicating the Kremlin's fear that such activities may be widespread and may enjoy too much popular support.

Lithuania provides an example of how the Party attempts not only to contain but also to manipulate nationalist feelings for Moscow's purposes. In 1985, Lithuanian First Party Secretary Petras Griškevičius made a blatently nationalistic appeal of support for Soviet foreign and nuclear policy. In the form of an interview, the appeal was first published in *Gimtasis*

Kraštas (*Native Country*), a weekly available at newsstands in Lithuania but aimed primarily at the Lithuanian emigration. That Griškevičius's thoughts were not solely directed at the Lithuanian diasporas abroad is clear from the fact that his entire interview was reprinted in the popular and influential periodical *Literatūra ir menas* (*Literature and Art*) read by Lithuania's artistic and professional intelligentsia.[98] In the interview, Griškevičius admonished the Lithuanians not to criticize the Yalta agreements of 1943. According to him, abrogation of these agreements between the war-time allies, as has been widely demanded in the United States, would mean for Lithuania the loss of the Vilnius and Klaipéda territories. Therefore, no patriotic, "good" Lithuanian would want to abrogate a treaty guaranteeing possession of these ancient Lithuanian territories even though, ironically, the Yalta treaty delivered the Lithuanians and other Balts permanently into Soviet hands. It is even more important, Griškevičius suggested, that all "good" Lithuanians support Soviet nuclear policy because nuclear war would mean the destruction of Lithuania itself. It therefore follows, he said, that every "clearly thinking" Lithuanian has to oppose the American armaments competition. Instead, he must support the Soviet policy of détente. Griškevičius, of course, failed to say that the Baltic countries have become nuclear targets not because of the American arms' competition but because they are now saturated with Soviet nuclear rockets inviting nuclear retaliation. The Soviets have installed in the region an estimated 174 land-based nuclear delivery systems, from the very short range Frog 7 type to SS5 which has a range of 4,100 kilometers.[99] In addition, Soviet naval facilities in Baltic harbors house about 140 submarine and naval delivery systems outfitted with conventional and nuclear warheads. Two nuclear-tipped SS20 missiles also have been stationed in Estonia in 1983.[100]

The appeal of Griškevičius may be hollow but it testifies to strongly nationalistic traditional Lithuanian feelings, which now the Kremlin's proconsul in Lithuania is attempting to mobilize for Soviet foreign policy purposes.

Baltic dissidents added still another dimension to the expression of nationalist feelings. They articulated what Baltic protest demonstrations have demanded in general terms, namely, the restoration of Baltic independence.

On 23 August 1979, the 40th anniversary of the Stalin-Hitler non-aggression pact, forty-five Baltic human rights activists—four Latvians, four Estonians, and thirty-five Lithuanians—signed an appeal addressed to the governments of the Soviet Union, West and East Germany, as well as to all the signatories of the Atlantic Charter, and, finally, to Kurt Waldheim, then secretary-general of the United Nations. In this appeal, the Balts explicitly rejected the legitimacy of Soviet rule declaring it to be imposed by force and demanding the reversal of the consequences of the Nazi-Soviet pact. After reviewing the dire consequences of the Nazi-Soviet alliance for the Baltic States, the signers declared that "the Molotov-Ribbentrop Pact was a conspiracy between the two greatest tyrants of history—Stalin and Hitler—against peace and humanity, and it inaugurated World War II. We consider the date of August 23 the day of shame."[101] Well argued, the document showed familiarity with the 1939 treaty provisions, which the Soviets have not yet published and the knowledge of international law documents which declare self-determination to be the right of nations. Curiously, however, the self-determination provision of the Helsinki agreement of 1975 was included only as an afterthought. This Baltic appeal was endorsed by Academician Andrei Sakharov and some of his dissident colleagues in Moscow. Needless to say, this letter created great difficulties to its sponsors. At least one half of the group were arrested and sent either to prison, to the *Gulag*, or to a psychiatric hospital. However, the appeal became widely known in the West as a courageous public expression of the views of the three silenced nations.

Another common Baltic document, in addition to protests against the Soviet invasion of Afghanistan and greetings to the Polish *Solidarność* with its leader Lech Wałęsa, has been the 1981 appeal for the inclusion of the three Baltic republics into the suggested nuclear free zone in northeastern Europe.[102] The signatories of this appeal were predominantly Estonians and Latvians. They opposed the stationing of nuclear weapons in the Baltic republics, a policy Soviet authorities found most annoying. The signers of this appeal suffered a similar fate as that of the signers of the earlier letter demanding the restoration of Baltic independence.

In view of this record of manifestations of nationalist feelings, one may be tempted to agree with Alexander Shtromas's conclusion that while pragmatic in daily political orientation, the Balts remain strongly committed to the idea of independence for the Baltic States. Shtromas also suggests that the Balts subscribe to a five-point vision of their political future which postulates: a) the reestablishment of the Baltic states' independence within ethnic boundaries; b) the creation of a political, economic, and social system which favors national interests and furthers individual initiative, especially in economic life; c) the establishment of close ties to the Western world; d) the restoration on the territory of each Baltic state of a "compact national society"; and e) the promotion of religious and cultural freedom.[103] This adds further credence to the opinions of numerous recent emigrants and defectors who maintain that the Balts remain committed to the ideal of independent statehood. It also amplifies the view of the Baltic dissent movement.

Dissent and Undercurrents of Democratic Thought

The Baltic dissent movement has been nationalistic but it also has given proof of the survival of currents of democratic thought among impressively diverse groups of Baltic intelligentsia and citizenry. One such representative of citizenry has been the Lithuanian sailor Simas Kudirka who jumped off a Soviet fishing boat at Martha's Vineyard in New England but was returned to the Soviets by the U.S. Coast Guard and had to stand trial on charges of attempted flight from the Soviet Union. Feeling that he had nothing more to lose, at his trial in Vilnius he lashed out at the Soviets, leaving us a remarkable political statement.[104] In it, Kudirka traced the forcible imposition of Soviet rule, rejected Soviet sovereignty over Lithuania, and demanded the establishment of a democratic system which he was too young to remember and about which he knew only from books, conversations, and foreign radio broadcasts.

A brief sketch of Baltic dissident movement may be helpful in appraising dissident influence on Baltic political attitudes.

The movement has a long history. An anti-Soviet, pro-nationalist underground thrived in the Baltic republics ever since their occupation by the Soviet Union, especially in Lithuania. According to the *Washington Post*'s Kevin Klose, Lithuania is the original home of Soviet *samizdat* as well.[105] Baltic dissent thus has its own independent local roots. In recent decades, however, it has been galvanized to articulate action not only by its own specific conditions but also by kindred dissident activity in Moscow, initiated by Academician Sakharov and the circle around the *Chronicle of Current Events*. The watershed year seems to have been 1968, the year of "Prague spring" which inspired hope in reform. The Estonians reacted very loudly when, around 1970, it became absolutely clear that Russian immigration threatened to inundate the native national community. Lithuanian émigrés were mobilized to a large degree as a reaction to drastically antireligious edicts which became public in the mid-1960s. This legislation had been kept secret and not fully implemented but now it became part of the criminal code and was enforced. These very stringent government policies led the more active Catholic clergy and laymen to conclude that the new limitations of religious activity, combined with criminal punishment, were meant not just to contain but also to strangle the Catholic church. The only way to defend the Church was by organizing domestic public opinion, confronting the regime in daily situations, and by crying out to the international world in hopes that world opinion will pressure the Soviets to alleviate the Church's situation. The same philosophy was adopted by the Estonian movement and by the Latvian groups, though their primary concerns were secular.

In Lithuania, thus, the dissent movement has a very strong religious Catholic component. Its main *samizdat* publication, *The Chronicle of the Catholic Church of Lithuania*—started in 1972 and still publishing—represents not only religious interests but also acts as the main spokesman for the entire movement of civil and national rights. Dissident activities are interlaced with religious concerns also in Latvia and in Estonia. In Latvia, the involvement, however, is not Catholic though Latvia now has a Catholic cardinal, the first in the Soviet Union, but mainly Baptist. Lutheran activism also shows signs of life in Latvia but more so in Estonia.

Baltic dissidents have been concerned with three basic issues: national rights, civil rights, and the rights of religion. These three issues easily overlap. Dissident groups differ from one another, therefore, not so much in the basic underlying philosophy as in the accents they place on concrete issues. It is clear from the written dissident documents and from their actions that their shared common beliefs are democratic. This fact is worthy of special attention for at least two reasons. It reconfirms again the superficiality of Marxist influence in Baltic political consciousness; and, second, it demonstrates that the pro-Fascist tendencies found among some Baltic circles during the period of independence left little lasting effect.

Concrete dissident activities are too numerous to be listed here. They include diverse efforts, all of them nonviolent, such as publication of periodicals, organization of groups for the preservation of historical heritage, gatherings for discussion of political or cultural issues, sponsorship of prayer meetings and religious pilgrimages (for example, to the Catholic shrines of Aglona in Latvia and Siluva in Lithuania), petition writing to the government in protest of official behavior or requesting remedial action.

In Lithuania, in 1976, also the Helsinki Watch group was established and worked energetically till the middle 1980s, when it was decimated by arrests, murder, natural death, or attrition caused by KGB pressures. After the election of Pope John Paul II, in 1978, a number of Catholic clergymen organized the Committee for the Defense of the Rights of Believers which, too, was immobilized after arrests and harrassment in 1983. These groups compiled copious data on Soviet violations of civil rights and published, as well as publicized abroad, a large number of documents defending the persecuted without regard to their religious or national background.

The scope of dissident activity as well as the basis of popular support seems to be largest in Lithuania. This is due to the fact that in Lithuania the struggle for national and civil rights is tightly interwoven with the Catholic church and with the defense of religious rights. This allows the movement to recruit massive support among committed Catholics. In the Lithuanian case, therefore, petitions sent to the government obtain tens of thousands of signatures, a rare and daring expression of dissatisfaction in the Soviet Union. Thus, the 1971 petition to Leonid Brezhnev sent through Kurt Waldheim demanding restoration of religious and civil rights was signed by 17,054 people. The petition asking Leonid Brezhnev to return to the Catholics their newly built church in the port city of Klaipèda—it was seized by the government and converted into a music hall—was signed by 148,149 people. Demands protesting the arrest of Rev. Alfonsas Svarinskas and Rev. Sigitas Tamkevičius, in 1983–84, were signed by some 50,000 Catholics.

Another characteristic, this one common to all three Baltic dissident movements, is the fact that its activists come not just from the intellectual circles as, with only a few exceptions, in Russia but from the lower middle-class intelligentsia, the professionals, the workers, and the collective farmers—in other words, from all walks of life. This really national in scope membership is a fruit of the rather harmonious development of social class relations in the independent Baltic States.

Dissident activities have demanded sacrifices. Scores of activists and participants have been sent to the Gulag from the three republics, among them professors, clergymen, engineers, workers, and nurses. The latest wave of persecution began in the fall of 1980, when the Soviets became seriously concerned with the perceived menace of the Solidarity movement in Poland. It was intensified under Andropov. In 1983, all three republics were carefully combed again. The numbers and the nature of arrests indicate not only a continued dissident activity in Estonia and Lithuania but also its resurgence in Latvia.

While on the surface overwhelmed by the official Soviet press and the bustle of official life, dissident publications and activities play a significant role in the development of Baltic political attitudes. All of the dissident endeavors are aimed at increasing peoples' awareness of their situation and at promoting participation in public affairs with the purpose of actively pressuring the government to extend protection to civil or national rights. As such, all of these activities have had a democratizing influence in the officially monolithic social and ideological Soviet system in the Baltic republics. They also have helped to transmit remnants of the democratic heritage to younger Baltic groups. Finally, they show that the currently articulated Baltic nationalism has democratic underpinnings.

The Balance Sheet

Are the Balts condemned to extinction, as Hélène Carrère d'Encausse suggests? Let us summarize our findings and propose some answers.

On the positive side, the evidence clearly shows that despite various depredations, the Estonian, Latvian, and Lithuanian communities have not only survived but also prospered culturally as well as economically. Institutions and activities necessary for the national growth, such as universities and publications, first established during the period of independence, have grown and expanded. There has been no loss of national identity, and while religious consciousness has suffered, national self-identification has not. Nationalism, though changed in many ways and its expression being frequently muted or frustrated, remains strong and indicates the unrelenting desire for independent statehood. The enormous economic and social changes thus have not destroyed Baltic national personalities or basically affected the respective national characters of the Balts.

Problems and uncertainties, however, remain. In the past, national identity was sustained and patriotism nurtured primarily in the Baltic villages. The social stratum that now has to play the role of carrier of traditional values is the city intelligentsia and the workers. It is not clear how this shift, produced by economic and social restructuring of societies, will affect future attitudes of the population on the preservation of national traditions and other values that make a nation viable and strong, such as language, culture, and commitment to the community's interests. Furthermore, how permanent will be the corrupting Marxist-Leninist influences on political attitudes and political consciousness? It is also not clear how long the Balts will be able to keep up their West European heritage. One of the institutions of this heritage, namely, religion, Catholic and Protestant, has been hurt. Eitan Finkelstein, a former member of the Lithuanian Helsinki Watch group, is of the opinion that the preservation of Western traditions in the Baltic region was benignly tolerated by Moscow as a show place for Europeans to demonstrate that communism is compatible with the Western outlook.[106]

Still another point is how long, especially the Estonians and the Latvians, will be able to maintain the élan needed for nationally oriented creativity in the rising sea of the Russian population. Will the loss of "critical mass" affect Estonian, Latvian, and eventually Lithuanian national consciousness to immobilize them as viable national communities? This is the most serious of problems related to demographic development discussed a few lines later in this chapter.

As of now, all of these raised points remain only question marks. There is, however, another side of the coin. As Alexander Dallin once wrote, the Baltic States fell victim to the Soviet Union not because of their own political sins.[107] Sandwiched in, as they were, between the Russians and the Germans, the "East" and the "West," the Balts could not find protection in geography. In modern times, their sovereignty depended on the relative relationship between the Russian and German empires. An alliance of these empires spelled the death of Baltic independence, as in 1939. The mutual weakness and conflict between these empires opened the doors to Baltic freedom, in 1917–20. In today's world, the German Empire has been replaced by the Atlantic alliance, but the geopolitical position which conditions political answers remains the same. The Baltic nations themselves cannot change this situation.

As a result of the 1939–45 shift in the relationship between the Soviet and Western powers, the Baltic nations were delivered into the present predicament which indeed has not only undermined their sovereignty but also created existential problems for them as national communities. They have been absorbed and integrated into the Russian living space militarily, economically, and demographically. The heavy military buildup necessitated by Moscow's strategic considerations targets the Baltic region as a war zone in case of an East-West conflict, thus not excluding a repetition of destruction wrought upon it during the two world wars. However, eventually military presence can be withdrawn, and if it is ever withdrawn by a Moscow leadership compelled to do so, the Baltic economic development in the last forty years have made the Baltic region rather dependent on the Russian resource and market base. The Baltic republics will likely remain tied down to Russia and the Ukraine economically for a very long time.

The greatest menace to Baltic existence is demographic. Frequently, it is assumed that this menace is caused by the declining fertility of the Baltic nations, in other words, by the Baltic refusal to reproduce themselves which would be tantamount to suicide. But this is not true. The Lithuanian population growth rate under the Soviets has declined but it is still above replacement levels. Latvian and Estonian birthrates have declined but their population growth is at least at replacement level, as it has been for almost a hundred years. It is not Estonian or Latvian unwillingness to extend the national life that causes the difficulty but an artificial population growth by immigration, fostered and furthered by Moscow's leadership. Full economic and political integration opened Baltic borders to immigration by the Slavs, basically, by the Russians. Immigration is not slowing down. It is already predicted that the next census will show the Latvians in minority in Latvia.[108] It is doubtful that economic reforms, if Mikhail Gorbachev is able to force them on his bureaucracies, will cause a slowdown of new arrivals seeking better conditions of life. Estonia and Latvia are immediately and directly menaced at the present time. Lithuania's turn will come as immigration has already enormously increased and is likely to continue at this rate. In the case of this republic, if Moscow ever decided to "return" to Lithuania its Prussian patrimony, that is, the present Kaliningrad region,

Lithuanians would suddenly find themselves in a situation not better but worse than the Estonians.

What the Balts need for a reversal of trends of economic dependency and demographic decline is full control of their economic development and territorial borders. In other words, they need sovereign independence, equivalent to the status of smaller Western European states in the Western European community of nations. Only such arrangement can secure the growth of their national communities while allowing the maintenance of regionally required—and already partially accomplished—degree of economic integration.

Is this possible in the foreseeable future? The answer depends on social and political change in the Soviet Union discussed in the four volumes of currently published studies. A policy of evolutionary adjustment of less efficient institutions that General Secretary Mikhail Gorbachev is now pursuing will not bring about the radical structural rearrangement required for the Baltic States. Together with other republics, especially with the Ukraine, the Baltic States, of course, have an impact on Soviet development, but as has been shown earlier,[109] this impact has been limited and largely confined to cultural and economic affairs. Baltic nations can be beneficiaries of only radical systemic and structural change in the Soviet Empire, analogous to those which took place in the Russian Empire in 1917. Current data, as reviewed and analyzed in this essay, show that there should be no doubt about the current Baltic national strength and determination to act on the Soviet stage for the restitution of the Baltic States' sovereignty in events similar to 1917–20.

Notes

1. The territory of Estonia covers 45,100 sq.km. (over 17,000 sq.mi.). Latvia is larger. Its territory covers 63,700 sq.km. (over 24,000 sq.mi.). Lithuania is the largest of the three. Its territory comprises 65,200 sq.km. (over 25,000 sq.mi.). In territory, only Armenia and Moldavia are smaller. Four European nation-states are smaller than either of the Baltic countries. They are Albania, Belgium, The Netherlands, and Switzerland. See: Tsentral'noe statisticheskoe upravlenie SSSR. *Narodnoe khozyaystvo SSSR v 1983 g* [The Central Statistical Directorate of the USSR. *The National Economy of the USSR in 1983*], (Moscow: Finansy i statistika, 1984), 12–17.
2. In 1984, Estonia had a population of 1,466,000; Latvia, 2,364,000; and Lithuania, 3,569,000. *Narodnoe*, 8.
3. For a brief history, see Georg von Rauch, *The Baltic States: The Years of Independence 1917–1940* (Berkeley: University of California Press, 1974).

4. Hélène Carrère d'Encausse, *Decline of an Empire* (New York: Newsweek Books, 1979), 267.
5. Cf., V. Stanley Vardys, "Modernization and Baltic Nationalism," *Problems of Communism*, 24, No. 5 (September–October 1975), 32–48.
6. See V. Vardys, "Sovietinio lietuvio paveikslas," (The Image of a Soviet Lithuanian), *Ateitis*, (The Future), No. 10 (1975) and No. 11 (1976), resp. 300–306; 15–18.
7. Tsentral'noe statisticheskoe upravlenie pri Sovete ministrov Litovskoy SSR. *Ekonomika i kul'tura Litovskoy SSSR v 1975 godu*, (The Lithuanian SSR's Council of Ministers' Central Statistical Directorate. *The Economy and Culture of the Lithuanian SSR in 1975*), (Vilnius: Mintis, 1976), 29.
8. Tsentral'noe statisticheskoe upravlenie Latviyskoy SSR. *Narodnoe khozyaystvo Latviyskoy SSSR v 1980 godu*, (The Central Statistical Directorate of the Latvian SSR. *The National Economy of the Latvian SSR in 1980*), (Riga: Avots, 1981), 39, 68.
9. Tsentral'noe statisticheskoe upravlenie Estonskoy SSSR. *Narodnoe khozyaystvo Estonskoy SSSR v 1980 godu*, (The Central Statistical Directorate of the Estonian SSR. *The National Economy of the Estonian SSR in 1980*), (Tallinn: Eesti Raamat, 1981), 50.
10. *Narodnoe khozyaystvo SSSR v 1983 godu*, 126.
11. ———.
12. Tsentral'noe statisticheskoe upravlenie SSSR. *Narodnoe khozyaystvo SSSR, 1922–1982*, (The Central Statistical Directorate of the USSR. *The National Economy of the USSR, 1922–1982*), (Moscow: Finansy i statistika, 1982), 74–75.
13. ———.
14. ———.
15. *Narodnoe khozyaystvo Estonskoy SSSR v 1980 godu*, 203.
16. *Narodnoe khozyaystvo Latviyskoy SSSR v 1980 godu*, 214.
17. Tsentral'noe statisticheskoe upravlenie Litovskoy SSR. *Narodnoe khozyaystvo Litovskoy SSR v 1980 godu* (The Central Statistical Directorate of the Lithuanian SSR, *The National Economy of the Lithuanian SSR in 1980*), (Vilnius: Mintis, 1981), p. 150.
18. *Narodnoe khozyaystvo Latviyskoy SSSR v 1980 godu*, 214.
19. On 7 December 1986, *The New York Times* reported that the Soviet government ordered "a halt in drilling for oil in the Baltic Sea off Lithuania after conservationist protests."
20. *Lietuviškoji Tarybinè Enciklopedija*, (The Lithuanian Soviet Encyclopedia), 6 (Vilnius: Mokslas, 1980), 374.
21. ———, 3, p. 388.
22. *Narodnoe khozyaystvo Litovskoy SSSR v 1980 godu*, 32.
23. *Lietuviškoji Tarybinè Enciklopedija*, 3, 388.
24. Juris Dreifelds, "Demographic Trends in Latvia," *Nationalities Papers*, 12, no. 1 (1984), 75.
25. ———.

26. *Narodnoe khozyaystvo SSSR v 1983 godu*, 17; V.I. Kozlov, *Natsional'nosti SSSR*, (The USSR's Nationalities), (Moscow: Finansy i Statistika, 1982), 80.
27. See Vardys, in *Problems of Communism*, 39; *Narodnoe khozyaystvo SSSR 1922–1982*, 36–37.
28. V.I. Kozlov, *Natsional'nosti SSSR* (Moscow: Statistika, 1975), 133.
29. *Narodnoe khozyaystvo SSSR 1922–1982*, 28. In 1940, Estonia had 16,100 births but 17,000 deaths.
30. ——.
31. ——.
32. *Vestnik statistiki*, no. 2 (1983), 69–80.
33. One estimate of such losses is found in Romuald J. Misiunas and Rein Taagepera, *The Baltic States: The Years of Dependence* (Berkeley: University of California Press, 1983), 276–79.
34. Kozlov, *Nats'onal'nosti*, 1982, 137.
35. P. Mežgailis and P. Zvidriņš, *Padomju Latvijas iedzīvotāji*, (Riga: Liesma, 1973), 86.
36. ——.
37. Tsentral'noe statisticheskoe upravlenie Estonskoy SSR. *Narodnoe khozyaystvo Estonskoy SSR v 1972 godu* (The Central Statistical Directorate of the Estonian SSR. *The National Economy of the Estonian SSR in 1972*), (Tallinn: Eesti Raamat, 1973), p. 20; also: *Vestnik statistiki*, No. 2 (1975), p. 83 and No. 9 (1975), p. 70.
38. *Narodnoe khozyaystvo SSSR 1922–1982*, 36–37.
39. Ann Sheehy, "Population Trends in the Union Republics, 1979–1984," Radio Liberty Research 166/85, p. 3.
40. Mark Frankland, "Ghosts Stalk Lost Baltic Republics," *The Observer*, 3 February 1985.
41. Tsentral'noe statisticheskoe upravlenie SSSR. *Naselenie SSSR* (The Central Statistical Directorate of the USSR. *The USSR's Population*), (Moscow: Izd. polit. lit., 1980), p. 29.
42. Kozlov, 1982, 136.
43. *Narodnoe khozyaystvo SSSR v 1983 godu*, 32–33.
44. *Vestnik statistiki*, no. 2 (1983), 69–80.
45. A. Stanaitis and P. Adlys, *Lietuvos TSR gyventojai*, (The Population of the Lithuanian SSR) (Vilnius: Mintis, 1973), 135.
46. Saulius Girnius, *Baltic Area Situation Report 3*, Radio Free Europe, 22 March 1985, 22.
47. ——.
48. A. Pankseev, et al., *Zhiznenaya sila leninskikh printsipov partiynogo stroitel'stva*, (The Vital Force of the Leninist Principles of Party Construction) (Tallinn: Eesti Raamat, 1975), 68.
49. Institut istorii Partii pri TskKp Latvii, *Kommunisticheskaya partiya Latvii v tsifrakh (1904–1971)*, (The Institute of the History of the Party at Latvia's CP CC). *The Communist Party of Latvia in Figures (1904–1971)*, (Riga: Liesma, 1972), 24–29.

50. Pankseev, et al., *Zhiznenaya*, 67.
51. Partijos istorijos institutas, *Lietuvos Komunistu Partija skaičiais, 1918–1975*, (The Institute of the History of the Party. *The Lithuanian Communist Party in Figures, 1918–1975*), (Vilnius: Mintis, 1976), 42.
52. See A. Pankseev in *Nekotorye voprosy organizatsionno-partiynoi raboty*, (Some Problems of the Organizational-Party Work), (Tallinn: Eesti Raamat, 1971), p. 74.
53. See estimate in Vardys, *Modernization*, 1975, 40.
54. *Mažoji Lietuviškoji Tarybinè Enciklopedija*, (The Short Lithuanian Soviet Encyclopedia) (Vilnius: Mintis, 1968), 2, 386.
55. *Lietuviškoji Tarybinè Enciklopedija* (Vilnius: Mokslas, 1980), 6, 545.
56. Data taken from Tsentral'noe statisticheskoe upravlenie SSSR. *Narodnoe khozyaystvo SSSR v 1970 godu*, (The Tsentzal Statistical Directorate of the USSR. *The National Economy of the USSR in 1972*), (Moscow: Statistika, 1971), 680–85; *Narodnoe khozyaystvo SSSR v 1983 godu*, 524–26. Soviet statistics put together books and pamphlets thus introducing an element of ambiguity in the data. However, this is all we have available.
57. *Narodnoe khozyaystvo Estonskoy SSR v 1980 godu*, 321.
58. ———.
59. Y. V. Andropov, "Report on the Occasion of the 60th Anniversary of the USSR in the Kremlin Palace of Congress, 21 December 1982," in Y. Andropov, *Speeches and Writings* (Oxford: Pergamon Press, 1983), 27.
60. *Yunost'*, no. 6 (1961), 3–34; no. 7 (1961), 33–66.
61. *Molodaya Gvardiya*, no. 4 (1964), 48–93; no. 5 (1964), 53–146.
62. *The Times* (London), 5 October 1964, 11; Madeleine and Marvin Kalb, "A Visit to Tallinn," *The Reporter*, 11 May 1961, 30 ff.
63. *Newsweek*, 29 August 1966, 32.
64. Mark Frankland, in *The Observer*, 3 February 1985.
65. V. Stanley Vardys, "The Role of the Baltic Republics in Soviet Society," in Roman Szporluk, ed., *The Influence of East Europe and the Soviet West on the USSR* (New York: Praeger Publishers, 1975), esp. pp. 159–66.
66. *Komunistas* (Vilnius), no. 9 (1976), 36.
67. Alexander Shtromas, "The Baltic States," in Robert Conquest, ed., *The Last Empire: Nationality and the Soviet Future* (Stanford: Hoover Institution Press, 1986), 201.
68. Alexander Shtromas, "The Soviet Ideology and the Lithuanians," *Russia*, no. 3 (1981), 26–29.
69. See Vladimir Treml, *Alcohol in the USSR: A Statistical Study* (Durham, N.C.: Duke University Press, 1982), 70–71.
70. V.S. Vardys, in *Ateitis*, No. 11 (1976), 18.
71. Cf., Lyudmila Alekseeva, *Istoriya inakomysliya v SSSR*, (The History of Dissent in the USSR), (Benson, Vt.: Khronika Press, 1984), 53–55.
72. J. Aničas and I. Mačiulis, *Katalikybés evoliucija socializmo salygomis*, (The Evolution of Catholicism Under Socialist Conditions) (Vilnius: Mintis, 1979), 230.

73. For more information, see V. Stanley Vardys, *The Catholic Church, Dissent and Nationality in Soviet Lithuania* (New York: Columbia University Press, 1978), 196–218; Vello Sallo, "The Struggle Between the State and the Churches," in Tönu Parming and Elmar Järvesoo (eds.), *A Case Study of a Soviet Republic: The Estonian SSR* (Boulder: Westview Press, 1978), 191–222.

74. Cf., V. Stanley Vardys, ed., *Lithuania Under the Soviets* (New York: F.A. Praeger, 1965), 248 ff.

75. A. Shtromas refers to the partisan war in Lithuania as "civil war." His contemporary witness Tomas Venclova disagrees. (See Aleksandras Štromas, *Politiné samoné Lietuvoje* [Political Consciousness in Lithuania] [London: Nida, 1980, p. 86.].) My own studies, based to a very large degree on Soviet sources, have led me to the conclusion that this was not a Civil War but a war of Lithuanians against the Soviet occupant. Lithuania at that time was already under Moscow's occupation. The local Communist regime was extremely fragile and could not keep itself going without Red Army troops. Lithuanian Communists were puppets. Neither in philosophy nor in numbers did they even represent a substantive minority. If Shtromas's label is used in analogy, the partisan war in Afghanistan is a "civil war." See my "The Partisan Movement in Postwar Lithuania," *Slavic Review* 22, (1963), 499–522.

76. See, for example, Alexander R. Alexiev, *Dissent and Nationalism in the Soviet Baltic* (Santa Monica: Rand, R-3061-AF, 1983); V. Stanley Vardys, *The Catholic Church, Dissent and Nationality in Soviet Lithuania*; Rein Taagepera, *Softening Without Liberalization in the Soviet Union: The Case of Juri Kukk* (Lanham: University Press of America, 1984); Thomas Remeikis, *Opposition to Soviet Rule in Lithuania, 1945–1980* (Chicago: Lithuanian Studies Institute, 1980); Tönu Parming and Elmar Järvesoo, eds., *A Case Study of a Soviet Republic: The Estonian SSR*; Romuald J. Misiunas and Rein Taagepera, *The Baltic States: The Years of Dependence* (Berkeley: University of California Press, 1983). My own articles, further cited in abbreviated form, include the following: "The Baltic Peoples," *Problems of Communism* 16, No. 5, (September–October, 1967), 55–67; "Recent Soviet Policy Toward Lithuanian Nationalism," *Journal of Central European Affairs*, 32, no. 3 (October, 1963), 313–32; "Human Rights Issues in Estonia, Latvia, and Lithuania," *Journal of Baltic Studies*, 2, no. 3 (Fall, 1981), 273–98; "Lithuania's Catholic Movement Reappraised," *Survey*, 25, no. 3 (112), (Summer, 1980), 49–73; "Polish Echoes in the Baltic," *Problems of Communism* 31, No. 4 (July–August, 1983), 21–35.

77. See Vardys, 1967, p. 62.

78. ———.

79. Cf. Shtromas, in *Russia*, no. 3 (1981), 27.

80. *Aušra* (Lithuanian *samizdat* magazine), no. 4, (October, 1976).

81. *Aušra*, no. 11 (51), (May 1978).

82. See Vardys, 1963, pp. 316–18.

83. *Kommunist* (Moscow), no. 17, (1974), 22.

84. Cf. Yaroslav Bilinsky, "Shcherbytskyi, Ukraine and Kremlin Politics," *Problems of Communism*, 32, no. 4 (July–August, 1983), 1–20.
85. For text, see George Saunders ed., *Samizdat: Voices of the Soviet Opposition* (New York: Monad Press, 1974), 427–40.
86. *Sovetskaya Estoniya*, 31 July 1984.
87. *Sovetskaya Estoniya*, 23 August 1984.
88. Cf., report on the court proceedings in *Perspektyvos* (*samizdat* magazine), no. 22. Iešmantas said at the trial that he supported Eurocommunist political philosophy. He did not deny authoring the program attributed to the Lithuanian Communist Association. Conclusion that this organization does not exist is based on the fact that the name has never reappeared in *samizdat*.
89. See Vardys, *The Catholic Church*, 1978, 173–78. André Martin and Peter Falke in *Christus stirbt in Litauen* (Aschaffenburg: Paul Pattloch, 1977), 19–26, gives a slightly different version of events stressing that Kalanta's sacrifice was an attempt by religious Lithuanian youth to attract the Vatican's attention to the plight of the Lithuanian church and to finally receive some response to the petition mailed to Kurt Waldheim of the U.N. charging serious Soviet discrimination against religion.
90. Testimony by Jonas Jurašas, former artistic director of the Kaunas drama theater. Text in *Violations of Human Rights in Soviet Occupied Lithuania: A Report for 1975* (Glenside: Lithuanian American Community, 1976), 10–24.
91. See Vardys, 1981, pp. 282 ff.
92. See text in Vardys, 1981, pp. 292–95.
93. *Le Monde*, 25 October 1980.
94. *Kommunist* (Moscow), no. 4 (March 1983), 52; also *Plenum Tsentral'nogo Komiteta KPSS, 14–15 iyunya 1983 goda: Stenografichesky otchet*, (The Plenary Session of the CPSU's Central Committee, 14–15 June 1983: Stenographic Report), (Moscow: Izd. pol. lit., 1983), 141.
95. For example, speeches by Estonian First Party Secretary K.G. Vaino and the Lithuanian First Party Secretary P. Griškevičius at the 26th CPSU Congress in 1981. *Izvestiya*, 26 and 27 February, 1981.
96. R.W. Apple, Jr., of *The New York Times*, discovered even "a racist overtone" in comments Riga's Latvians made about the Russians. See *The New York Times*, 10 December 1980.
97. Radio Riga, 14 June 1981, translated in FBIS-SOV, 17 July, 1981, pp. R/2-3; also Vardys, 1983, 29.
98. *Literatūra ir menas*, 12 January 1985, 2–3, 4.
99. Editorial, "Baltic Bondage," *The Wall Street Journal*, 14 June 1985; Arturs Sons, "Die Dokumentation über die sowjetische Aufrüstung im Militärbezirk Baltikum," *Acta Baltica*, 23, 1983 (Königstein im Taunus, 1984), 47–65.
100. Acta Baltica; *Christian Science Monitor*, 26 January, 1984.
101. Text in Vardys, 1981, 289–92.
102. *Christian Science Monitor*, 14 December 1983.
103. Shtromas, in Conquest's *The Last Empire*, 202.
104. Text in *The International Herald Tribune*, 7–8 August 1971, 7–8.

105. Kevin Klose, *Russia and the Russians: Inside the Closed Society* (New York: W. W. Norton and Company, 1984), 187.
106. Eitan Finkelstein, "Musical Chairs in the Kremlin and the Baltic Republics," *Baltic Forum*, 1, no. 1 (Fall, 1984), 62.
107. Alexander Dallin, "The Baltic States Between Nazi Germany and Soviet Russia," in V. Stanley Vardys and Romuald J. Misiunas, eds., *The Baltic States in Peace and War 1917–1945* (University Park: The Pennsylvania State University Press, 1978), p. 107.
108. Dreifelds, *Demographic Trends.*
109. See Vardys, *The Role of the Baltic Republics*, in R. Szporhik, ed. (1975).

5

What Would Self-Determination Mean for the Moldavians?

DENNIS DELETANT

I begin this chapter with a disclaimer. My use of the term "Moldavian" in the very question posed implies that I am party to the obfuscation perpetrated by the Soviet authorities of the ethnicity of the Romanians in the Moldavian Soviet Socialist Republic. For "Moldavian" one should read "Romanian in the Moldavian SSR"; I am obliged to use the former for reasons of clarity, but it should be clear from my historical presentation that the "Moldavians" share the origins and, for the most part, the history of the remainder of the Romanian people.

In attempting to answer the question this unique relationship of the Romanians in the Moldavian SSR with their mother country must be borne in mind. They represent in the Soviet Union the only minority of a fraternal socialist nation-state—the Socialist Republic of Romania. Romanian opposition to Soviet authority, both within and without the Moldavian SSR, is conditioned by this relationship. In the absence of any significant émigré community of Moldavians in the West, the only defender of Romanian interests in the Moldavian SSR is the regime in Bucharest.

I have already identified the "Moldavians" with the Romanians in the conviction that they are one and the same people. Yet this conviction, shared by all objective students of the history of the Romanians, is denied in official Soviet publications. Upon this denial is based the Soviet attempt to create an artificial nationality—"Moldavian"—to obscure the fact that

2.5 million Romanians live under Soviet rule in a territory that once formed part of the Romanian principality of Moldavia, and to justify the incorporation of the Moldavian SSR in the Soviet Union. The deliberate Soviet concealment of the Romanian ethnicity of the "Moldavians" is attested by the very use of the name "Moldavian" to denote the Romanian population and the Soviet republic which they inhabit.[1] Yet the artificiality of the "Moldavians" is recognized by the Soviet authorities themselves in their classification of nationalities based on the census of 17 January 1979. According to the results there were 2,968,224 "Moldavians" living in the USSR of whom 2,525,687 inhabited the Moldavian SSR and 293,576 the Ukrainian SSR.[2] Alongside the "Moldavians" in the USSR are to be found 128,792 persons classified as Romanians, of whom 121,795 inhabit the Ukrainian SSR and the remaining 6,997 are scattered throughout the other republics, with the exception of the Moldavian SSR where there is no category of Romanians.[3] That Romanian and "Moldavian" as linguistic and ethnic terms are synonymous is shown by the recognition of the Romanian nationality in the Ukraine and by the designation of the Romanians' language as "Moldavian" by the Moldavian Linguistic Atlas.[4] The difficulties faced by the census authorities in distinguishing between the existence of the Romanian and "Moldavian" languages were highlighted by the mother-tongue declarations of the Romanians in the Ukraine. Of the 121,795 Romanians, 49,910 declared that they spoke their own language, 12,532 that they spoke Ukrainian, 3,753 that they spoke Russian and 55,600 that they spoke "another language."[5] That almost half the Romanian population should declare that they spoke a language other than Romanian, Russian, or Ukrainian when the other major coinhabiting nationality in the Ukraine is "Moldavian," suggests either that the authorities did not wish to recognize that these Romanians thought of their language as "Moldavian" or that these Romanians were unable to distinguish between Romanian and "Moldavian" and gave an uncommitted answer.

Soviet efforts to give the area between the Dniester and Prut rivers a distinct identity can claim a precedent in the czarist choice of the name Bessarabia, given in 1812 to the roughly corresponding area of the Moldavian SSR. The partly synonymous names of Moldavia and Bessarabia have a historical pedigree which the Russian authorities have ably exploited and which therefore requires examination.

The origin of the name Bessarabia can be traced to the emergence of the Romanian Principalities. The first of these is considered to have been founded circa 1330 by the ruler Basarab I. It eventually included the territory that was later to be called Wallachia, as well as the southern part of the area between the Prut and the Dniester. The association of the name of the Wallachian dynasty of Basarab with the territory of the first principality was perpetuated in the use by medieval cartographers of the term Bessarabia. This term, however, was used very loosely, sometimes designating much of present-day Romania, or merely Wallachia or Moldavia. Later it was confined either to the land between the Prut, Dniester and the Black Sea, or to the southern part of this region—the Budjak. Moldavia was the name applied to the second principality of Romanians which was established circa 1350, its frontiers being the Dniester River in the east and the dominion of Basarab in the south. Moldavia extended its control over the latter area during the early fifteenth century. The Genoese port of Maurocastro (Akkerman) at the mouth of the Dniester was obliged to pay tribute to Alexander the Good of Moldavia (1400–32) and this same prince even secured the port of Chilia on the Danube for a brief period. Apart from the narrow strips of territory around Chilia and Akkerman which came under direct Ottoman rule following their capture in 1484, and to which the Turks sometimes referred as Bessarabia, Moldavia never formed an integral part of the Ottoman Empire although, like Wallachia, it was subject to Turkish suzerainty.

As a result of the Treaty of Bucharest of May 1812 which concluded the Russo-Turkish War, Moldavia was partitioned, the Porte ceding all the Moldavian territory between the Dniester and the Prut to Russia in return for the Russian evacuation of the rest of Moldavia and Wallachia. Alexander I incorporated this area into the rest of czarist Russia, but to distinguish it from the rest of Moldavia resurrected the name of Bessarabia. The Treaty of Paris of 1856 restored to Moldavia the south-western districts of Bessarabia bordering on the Danube—Cahul, Bolgrad and Ismail—for strategic rather than national reasons since Britain and France wished to deny Russia access to the Danube. When the union of Moldavia and Wallachia took place in 1859, these three districts automatically became part of the United Principality of Romania. In 1878 the Treaty of Berlin returned the three districts to Russia and they were incorporated with Russian Bessarabia.

The shuttlecock fate of Bessarabia, or, more accurately, eastern Moldavia throughout the nineteenth century may give the impression that the ethnic mix of its population cast doubt on Romanian claims to the province. Yet the Russian census of 1897 gave the Romanian element of the population as 47.6 per cent (as against Ukrainian 19.6, Russian 8.1, Jewish 11.8, Bulgarian 5.4 and German 3.1). The opportunity for the restoration of Bessarabia to the rest of the principality of Moldavia, now subsumed into the Kingdom of Romania, arose when the Bolshevik Revolution proclaimed the right of self-determination for all subject nationalities in the former czarist Empire. A national movement in Bessarabia rapidly crystallized in November 1917 in a National Council (*Sfatul Țării*) consisting of 138 delegates[6] from different bodies in the province, the bulk of them representing soldiers and peasants; Romanian soldiers of the former czarist army had forty-five representatives, and the provincial council of peasants twenty-eight. The remainder were representatives of local *zemstva* and national societies.[7] The Bolshevik authorities, principally Trotsky, dismissed the council as a bourgeois assembly which did not reflect the wishes of the peasant and proletarian classes, a charge emanating from the fact that the Social Democratic and Social Revolutionary parties were each represented by only one delegate. On 15 December[8] the council declared that it represented the "Moldavian Republic," reserving for itself the right to act as an independent provisional government until such time as the Russian Federal Republic was formed. The council arrogated to itself full powers in Bessarabia and declared the important questions confronting them to be the anarchic behavior of Bolshevik troops in the province, and the securing of supplies for the population. Since the council lacked the necessary forces to solve these problems, it invited the Romanian army to enter Bessarabia in January 1918 and several divisions occupied the principal towns.[9] Fear of dismemberment of the province at the hands of the Ukraine[10] and of the Bolshevik forces led the Romanian leaders in Bessarabia to work for union with Romania; the Russian and Ukrainian representatives on the council were more hesitant. Nevertheless, the Romanian majority ensured the passage of a resolution on 8 April 1918[11] proclaiming the union of Bessarabia with Romania.[12] On 3 March 1920 the Allied Powers represented on the Supreme Council of the Paris Peace Conference pronounced themselves "in favor of the reunion of Bessarabia with Rumania which has now been formally declared by the Bessarabian representatives",[13] and recognition of this declaration was given in the Treaty of Paris on 28 October of the same year. While the Bolshevik government refused from the outset to accept the union and bitterly protested when each of the Allied governments ratified the treaty,[14] it did display a more conciliatory attitude toward Romania over the Bessarabian issue at the time of the Allied declaration of March 1920. In an effort to reduce the young regime's international isolation and to forestall possible Romanian intervention in the Civil War in Russia, Chicherin, the Soviet commisar for foreign affairs, invited the Romanian government to open negotiations with a view to restoring diplomatic relations between the two countries and to settling their territorial differences. A combination of distrust of the Russians, abhorrence of bolshevism, and reluctance to fall out of step with French policy toward the Soviet government made the Romanians cautious of these approaches and, in retrospect, vulnerable to the charge that they did not take advantage of Soviet pliancy.[15] Once the Soviet regime had consolidated itself, it was no longer prepared to make concessions and reverted to its former hostile stance over Romanian rule in Bessarabia. Communist bands raided gendarme stations and villages in the province throughout 1923 and on 4 August 1924 a Romanian frontier post was attacked by a group of men in Russian uniforms. Soviet attempts at subversion culminated in the seizure of the town of Tatar Bunar on 15 September by a Communist group led by Andrei Kulshnikov, better known under his conspiratorial name of Nenin. After three gendarmes had been killed and the town's communications cut, Nenin proclaimed the establishment of the Moldavian Soviet Republic in Bessarabia and attempted to spread the revolt by sending a contingent of men to a neighboring town. Local German farmers intercepted the Communists and forced them to withdraw to Tatar Bunar, which was virtually besieged by Romanian troops on 17 September. Nenin gave the order to retreat from the town and most of his men were captured while trying to reach the Black Sea. He himself took to the marshes where he was shot and mortally wounded by a gendarme.

The Tatar Bunar "revolution," as it is described in Soviet Moldavian historiography, can be seen as an attempt to provide a nucleus for a Soviet Moldavian Republic, which Moscow had been intending to establish for some time.[16] Indeed, in April 1924 a Soviet propaganda journal *Plugarul rosu* (The Red Ploughman) was published in Romanian and a September issue printed a letter from a group of Bessarabian peasants who sought "permission" to form an autonomous republic.[17] On 12 October 1924 the Kharkov Council of the Commissioners of the People in the Ukrainian Soviet Socialist Republic announced the creation of the Autonomous Moldavian Soviet Socialist Republic in the southwest Ukraine on the left bank of the Dniester.[18] Of its half-million population, only about 30 per cent were Romanians, over two-thirds being Ukrainians. Thus a territory which had never before been called Moldavia, nor been part of the medieval principality of Moldavia, was created to give credibility to the Soviet government's claim to Bessarabia and to provide a magnet for the "reunification" of the Moldavians on the left bank of the Dniester (in the AMSSR) with those on the right bank (in Bessarabia).

In the new republic[19] teaching in schools was conducted, and newspapers published, in both Ukrainian and Romanian, the latter being heavily influenced by the former in both written and spoken forms. In official use Romanian was registered in the Cyrillic alphabet but with the waning of Soviet intransigence over Bessarabia at the end of the 1920s, the Latin alphabet was reinstated in 1932. Its use was short-lived, however, for the Stalinist purges of 1937 and 1938 involved the suppression of those Romanians in the republic who had sought to "Romanianize" their language by preferring words of Romanian to those of Ukrainian or Russian origin, and led to the reintroduction of the Cyrillic alphabet in 1938. The continued use of this alphabet in the enlarged Moldavian SSR of 1940 and post-1944 was, of course, one aspect of Stalin's policy to give the Romanians there a new "Moldavian" identity distinct from their Romanian brothers across the Prut River.

On the question of Bessarabia itself, the Soviet government did not maintain its obduracy for long since it was anxious to return to the international fold. The USSR's emergence from isolation was endorsed by her adherence to several agreements which, at the same time, strengthened Romania's title to Bessarabia. Between 1928 and 1934, as signatory to a series of conventions and pacts, among them the Kellogg-Briand Pact and the London Convention for the Definition of Aggression, the Soviet Union gave *de facto* recognition to Romania's possession of her entire state territory, including Bessarabia.[20] Further support to Romania's claim to Bessarabia had been given by the 1930 census figures which showed an absolute majority of Romanians in the province, with 56.2 per cent of the population, compared with 12.3 per cent for Ukrainians, 11 per cent for Russians, 7.2 per cent for Jews, and 5.7 per cent for Bulgarians.[21] The growing Soviet-Romanian rapprochement was confirmed by the resumption of diplomatic relations after an exchange of notes in June 1934 between Maxim Litvinov and his Romanian counterpart Nicolae Titulescu,[22] who had largely been responsible for steering Romanian foreign policy closer to the Soviet Union. Titulescu, on becoming foreign minister in October 1932, sought to consolidate the system of alliances between states that opposed revision of the peace treaties of 1919 and 1920. Realizing that Germany under Hitler posed a threat to the peace of Europe, Titulescu advocated the creation of a system of collective security based on France and the Soviet Union. It was he who played a significant role in bringing about the mutual assistance pact between Moscow and Paris in 1935. Titulescu hoped that this agreement would form the nucleus of a large coalition of anti-revisionist states, and to this end he took Romania down the road to alliance with the Soviet Union. Consequently, in September 1935 he began discussions with Litvinov over the conclusion of a Soviet-Romanian Treaty of Mutual Assistance. Unfortunately, the international situation and King Carol's personal dislike of his foreign minister conspired against him. Titulescu's condemnation of Italy's invasion of Abyssinia and of Germany's occupation of the Rhineland made him an enemy of both countries, and prompted Mussolini to call for his dismissal. Moreover, the Rhineland occupation exposed France's weakness and caused many Romanian politicians to question the wisdom of pursuing an alliance with the Soviet Union which, because of geographical considerations and the feebleness of France, might bring Romania into dependence on her eastern neighbor with fateful consequences not only for Bessarabia, but for the rest of the country itself. Titulescu was aware of this danger and therefore when he and Litvinov agreed, on 21 July 1936, upon the general principles of the Soviet-Romanian Treaty,[23] the question of its subordination to the Franco-Soviet alliance was the only article that divided the two foreign ministers.[24] Even though Litvinov gave *de facto* recognition to Romania's possession of Bessarabia in the draft treaty by stipulating that Soviet troops would withdraw to the east bank of the Dniester at the conclusion of hostilities,[25] there is no doubt that the specter of Soviet forces outstaying their welcome in a territory to which their government had never renounced its claim haunted King Carol and his ministers. Titulescu was playing with fire in the eyes of his colleagues whom he had never let into his confidence and who naturally regarded him as arrogant and cavalier. His progress with the Pact added the final chorus to calls from within and without the country for his dismissal, and Carol finally removed him in August 1936. After Titulescu's departure Soviet-Romanian relations began once again to cool, in spite of Litvinov's efforts to resurrect the Pact. The increasingly pro-German orientation of successive Romanian governments alarmed the Soviet government which was eventually stung into action when the pro-Fascist Goga government was appointed by Carol in December 1937. Soviet displeasure at this development was translated into a reminder that the Bessarabian question had still to be resolved. In its issue of 11 January 1938 *Le Journal de Moscou* warned that "the Soviet Union cannot be indifferent to events in a neighboring country. Moreover, Romania is the only neighboring state with which the Soviet Union has not regulated certain fundamental questions."[26] Soviet concern was emphasized by the withdrawal from Bucharest, on 4 February 1938, of Minister Ostrovsky, who was not replaced until July 1940, i.e., after the Soviet seizure of Bessarabia.[27]

The drift toward royal dictatorship, the signal of which was Carol's imposition of the minority Goga government, was completed when the king announced the suspension of the Romanian Constitution in February 1938. Although Carol had become master of the internal situation, he and his country fell victim to external forces to which Romania, with her geographical position, her multinational composition and her economic resources, was particularly vulnerable. Romania's territorial aggrandizement through the peace treaties of 1919 and 1920 at the expense of the USSR, Hungary, and Bulgaria, had made her a champion of collective security and a defender of the European status quo. Hitler's commitment to revise the Versailles agreements allowed both Romania and the Soviet Union to bury their differences over Bessarabia for almost a decade. This situation drastically changed in 1939, when Stalin decided to abandon the pursuit of a collective security arrangement with Britain and France and opted instead for an agreement with Hitler. On 23 August 1939 the Nazi-Soviet Non-Aggression Pact was signed. The Soviet interest in Bessarabia was explicitly recognized in the supplementary secret protocol to the treaty.[28] Hitler's magnanimity in conceding the Soviet interest in Bessarabia was founded on an optimistic assessment of German power and Soviet weakness in southeastern Europe, a view reflected in the prediction made by the German military attaché in Bucharest in December 1939 that "the Russians will not occupy Bessarabia as long as Germany is strong enough. However, should we suffer a serious setback, or have all our forces engaged, Russia might take advantage of a rare opportunity which may not occur for a long time."[29] The accuracy of the attaché's forecast was borne out by events. Shortly before midnight on 26 June 1940, when German forces were completing their victorious sweep through France, the People's Commissar for Foreign Affairs Molotov summoned the Romanian minister in Moscow, Davidescu, to the Kremlin and presented an ultimatum demanding that Romania should cede Bessarabia and Northern Bukovina to the Soviet Union. The Soviet note called for a reply from the Romanian government within 24 hours. According to an official communiqué issued in Moscow on 28 June, Molotov's "written representations" were made in the following terms:

In 1918 Romania took advantage of the military weakness of Russia and robbed the Soviet Union by force of a part of her territory, namely Bessarabia, and thus broke the century-old unity of Bessarabia (principally occupied by Ukrainians) and the Ukrainian Soviet Republic. The Soviet Union has never been reconciled to this enforced robbery of Bessarabia and has often and openly expressed its mind to the whole world.

At the present moment, when the military weakness of the Soviet Union belongs to the past, and the present international situation demands the most speedy solution of unsolved problems which exist as an inheritance from the past in order to lay the foundation of a permanent peace between states, the Soviet Union considers it necessary and timely, in the interests of reestablishing justice, to find mutually with Romania a solution of the question of the return of Bessarabia.

The Soviet government declare that the question of the return of Bessarabia is organically connected with the question of the return to the Soviet Union of that part of the Bukovina where the predominant majority of the population is connected with the Soviet Ukraine by common historical destinies, as well as through the similarities of their language and national composition. This act is even more just, as the handing over of Northern Bukovina to the Soviet Union may be regarded as a compensation, though only in a small degree,

for the tremendous loss which the Soviet Union and the population of Bessarabia have suffered through the 22 years of Romanian rule in Bessarabia. The Soviet government propose to the Royal government of Romania
1. the return of Bessarabia to the Soviet Union
2. the transference to the Soviet Union of the northern part of Bukovina, as shown in the attached map.
The Soviet government hope that the Romanian government will accept this demand, and thus permit the peaceful solution of the long-standing dispute between the Soviet government and Romania. The Soviet government expect the reply of the Romanian government in the course of 27 June.[30]

Davidescu vainly protested. He began to dictate the text of the ultimatum in code over the telephone to Bucharest but the connection was interrupted until 6 A.M. in the morning of the 27 June. The Romanian government was thus given eighteen hours to decide upon and convey its reply to Moscow. According to Davidescu, Molotov had made it clear to him that if an affirmative answer failed to arrive by the expiry of the ultimatum, the Soviet Union would invade both territories demanded.[31] King Carol summoned a meeting of the Crown Council at noon to discuss the Romanian response while Prime Minister Tătărescu sought the advice of the German and Italian governments. During the Crown Council's deliberations replies were received from both. Ribbentrop, the German foreign minister, strongly urged the Romanians to yield to the Soviet demands and his enjoinder was echoed by his Italian counterpart. The Romanians' sense of isolation was completed by the cautious and evasive replies from their Balkan allies, Turkey, Greece, and Yugoslavia. The decisive argument in the Crown Council against resistance to Soviet pressure was the probability of a simultaneous attack by Hungary and Bulgaria to regain Transylvania and the Dobrogea, respectively. The Romanian army could not fight on three fronts, France was defeated and the Nazi-Soviet Pact forbade Germany to supply arms to any country engaged in hostilities with the Soviet Union. The council authorized Foreign Minister Gigurtu to wire the following reply to Davidescu, which the latter handed to Molotov on the evening of 27 June:

Inspired by the same desire as the Soviet government to settle peacefully all questions which might disturb relations between the Soviet Union and Romania, the Romanian government declare that they are prepared to take all necessary steps in the widest sense to come to a friendly agreement on all proposals that have been made by the Soviet government. Accordingly, the Romanian government request the Soviet government to name the time and place for conversations.[32]

Molotov realized that the imprecision of the Romanian reply was an attempt to gain time but gathered from a conversation with Davidescu that the Romanians were prepared to meet the Soviet demands. He therefore handed the latter a further note which completely ignored the Romanian request for discussions and set out a timetable for the transfer of Bessarabia and Northern Bukovina to Soviet control:

1. The territories of Bessarabia and Northern Bukovina shall be evacuated by Romanian troops within four days, beginning at 2 P.M. on 28 June.
2. Soviet troops shall occupy Bessarabia and Northern Bukovina within the same period.
3. The towns of Czernowitz (Cernăuţi), Kishinev (Chişinău) and Akkerman (Cetatea Albă) shall be occupied by Soviet troops on 28 June.
4. The Romanian government shall be responsible for handing over in good condition all railways, rolling-stock, bridges, depôts, aerodromes, factories, power plants, and telegraph installations.
5. A commission consisting of two representatives of each government shall meet to discuss questions arising from the evacuation of the territories in question.[33]

Molotov reportedly told Davidescu that his colleagues, especially those in the armed forces, were dissatisfied with the Romanian government's reply, which did not seem to appreciate the situation on the frontier. He gave the Romanians till noon on 28 June to reply, after which time the Soviet Union would act.[34]

The Romanian cabinet, which had been reshuffled a few hours previously in the hope that it would be better able to meet the crisis, discussed Molotov's evacuation demands in the early hours of 28 June. The military chiefs stated that the evacuation could not possibly be carried out in four days for lack of transport, but as the decision to give in to Soviet pressure had been taken they had no alternative. The new foreign minister, Constantin Argetoianu, in his note of acceptance delivered to Molotov by Davidescu at 11 A.M. on 28 June, emphasized that Romania was yielding in order to avoid war in southeastern Europe:

The Romanian government, in order to avoid the grave consequences of a recourse to force, and the opening of hostilities in this part of Europe, is constrained to accept the evacuation conditions specified in the note of the Soviet government.[35]

Argetoianu requested that the four day period allowed for evacuation be extended and although the Soviet government was reported to have agreed to this,[36] Soviet aircraft and troops landed at Cernăuţi, Chişinău and Cetatea Albă on the evening of 28 June. On the same day motorized units of the Red Army crossed into Bessarabia and Northern Bukovina.[37]

The Soviet ultimatum of 26 June was an act of international plunder. While the USSR had a right to request negotiations with Romania for territorial revision in Bessarabia, the claim in the ultimatum that Bessarabia was principally peopled by Ukrainians was not supported even by the Russian census figures of 1897 for the province, which gave the Romanian element of the population as 47.6 percent (920,919), the Ukrainian 19.7 percent (382,169) and the Russian 8.05 percent (155,774).[38] By 1930 the population figures, according to the Romanian census, had risen to 2,864,402 of whom 1,610,752 (56.2 percent) were Romanians, 351,912 (12.3 percent) were Russians and 314,211 (11 percent) Ukrainians, 204,858 (7.2 percent) Jews and 163,726 (5.7 percent) Bulgarians. The Soviet claim to that part of the Bukovina "where the predominant majority of the population is connected with the Soviet Ukraine by common historical destinies" was less spurious despite the terminology of this phrase which left the Soviet authorities open to the charge of writing history backward. Bukovina was the name given by the Hapsburg crown to the northern part of the principality of Moldavia, annexed by Austria in 1775. Although it had never formed part of the Russian Empire, and its population, according to the 1930 Romanian census,[39] was 853,009 of whom 379,691 were Romanians (44.5 percent), 236,130 Ukrainians (27.6 percent), 92,492 Jews (10.8 percent), 75,533 Germans (8.8 percent) and 30,580 Poles (3.5 percent), in the northern part of the province demanded by the Soviet Union there was a Ukrainian majority of approximately 167,500 Ukrainians to 136,400 Romanians.

The rapacious attitude of the Soviet government was illustrated by the delineation of the new frontier on the map which Molotov handed to Davidescu as an annex to the ultimatum. Marked with a thick red pencil line on a small map on the scale of 1/1,800,000, the frontier represented a seven-mile band of territory throughout its course causing confusion over which localities fell on the Soviet side. Furthermore, the roughness of the pencil stroke cut across the northeastern corner of the truncated Moldavia which included the town of Herţa. Despite Romanian protests that this area was not mentioned in the ultimatum, the Soviet representatives on the joint Romanian-Soviet commission,[40] established in Odessa to supervise the application of the ultimatum terms, insisted that as the line passed through the area it must be included in the ceded territories.

In its issue of 29 June 1940, *Izvestiia* announced that "courageous units of the glorious Red Army have crossed the (Romanian) frontier . . . as a direct result of the Soviet Union's policy of peace." Soviet Moldavian historiography justifies the seizure of Bessarabia as a strategic necessity since the Soviet defensive buffer was thus extended. The Red Army was able to delay the German and Romanian advance into the USSR proper by resistance in Bessarabia.[41]

The total area annexed by the Soviet Union from Romania in June 1940 covered some 51,000 square kilometres (19,700 square miles) and contained a population of about 3.9 million. Northern Bukovina, an area of roughly 6,000 square kilometers and half a million inhabitants, together with the Herţa region, the northern Bessarabian district of Hotin and the southern Bessarabian districts of Cetatea Albă (renamed Belgorod Dnestrovskii) and Ismail, these covering about 15,000 square kilometers and supporting a population of one million, were incorporated into the Ukrainian Soviet Socialist Republic.[42]

On 2 August 1940, by a decision of the seventh session of the Supreme Soviet, the Moldavian Soviet Socialist Republic was created[43] from the union of the rest of Bessarabia with the western part (some 3,400 square kilometers) of the Autonomous Moldavian Soviet Socialist Republic (the areas around Tiraspol, Bubossary and Balta). The greater eastern part of the AMSSR (some 4,900 square kilometers) was returned to the Ukrainian SSR, thus revealing that its creation in 1924 was merely a political stratagem to give credibility to the Soviet claim to Bessarabia. By restoring most of the AMSSR's territory to the Ukrainian SSR the Soviet government recognized the fiction of "Moldavian" in the autonomous republic's official name. The new Moldavian Soviet Socialist Republic covered an area of 33,700 square kilometers with a population of some 2.4 millions.[44] Immediately after the annexation, or "liberation" according to Soviet literature,[45] of Bessarabia the Soviet authorities began to apply the practice of communism to the province. The land was nationalized by a decree of 28 June 1940 and, in October, 487 private enterprises were taken over by the state. The process of sovietization was facilitated by the transfer of 13,000 "specialists" from Russia, the Ukraine, and Belorussia.[46] While over 500 teachers from Russia and 380 from the Ukraine were introduced into schools in the republic, it is disingenuous to see in this solely an attempt at Russification of education, for provision for teaching in both Russian and Ukrainian had been neglected during the years of Romanian rule and the Soviet measures were partly designed to redress the anomaly. Certainly Russification was a concomitant of the reorganization of administration along the Soviet model, and if the election results of 12 January 1941 for the Supreme Soviet are to be believed, 99.5 percent of the population of the Moldavian SSR approved of these fundamental transformations by voting for Communist candidates! After such an expression of favor for the Soviet regime in Moldavia, it is hardly surprising that the authorities should start to deport the Moldavians of the republic to Central Asia in order to work in factories and collective farms as replacements for those drafted into the army. Estimates of the total number of Moldavians re-settled in this way are difficult to give but some idea of the scale of the operation can be gained from the testimony of a Romanian Jew from Beltsy who stated that between 14 June and 22 June 1941 almost half the town's population of 55,000 was deported to the interior.[47] The deportations were interrupted by the German attack of 22 June on the Soviet Union in which Romania, under General Antonescu, participated. In an order of the day Antonescu told his troops that the hour had arrived for the fight against the yoke of bolshevism, while his Vice-President Mihai Antonescu, in a broadcast on the same day, began with the words "Romanians, today our nation has begun a great holy war."[48] A crusade against communism was not, of course the principal motive for Romania's involvement in the attack, as King Michael acknowledged in a telegram to General Antonescu:

> At this moment when are troops are crossing the Prut and the forests of Bukovina to restore the sacred land of Moldavia of Stephen the Great, my thoughts go out to you, General Antonescu, and to our country's soldiers. I am grateful to you, General, that thanks solely to your work, steadfastness and efforts, the entire nation and myself are living the joyful days of ancestral glory.[49]

Antonescu, who promoted himself to marshal while commanding the combined Romanian-German armies in the campaigns in Northern Bu-kovina and Bessarabia, recovered these provinces, as defined by their boundaries prior to the Soviet seizure in June 1940, by 27 July 1941[50] at the cost of 10,486 Romanian dead. Most Romanian political leaders were content with the reconquest and advised Antonescu against crossing the Dniester into the Soviet Union proper. Iuliu Maniu and Constantin Bră-tianu, respective leaders of the National Peasant and National Liberal parties, urged the marshal to confine his help to the Germans for the rest of the war, to the use of Romania as a base. Antonescu did not heed this advice. The Romanian-German armies advanced across the Dniester and captured Odessa on 16 October.[51] Two days later a decree was passed proclaiming Odessa and an area beyond the Dniester to be Romanian and giving it the name of Transnistria. This part of the Ukraine contained only a small number of Romanian settlements and had never before been claimed by Romania. The proclamation by Antonescu of Romanian sov-ereignty over it was an act of provocation which, coupled with continued

Romanian aggression in the Soviet Union, prompted the British government to send an ultimatum on 28 November 1941 to the Romanian government warning it that unless it ceased military operations in the USSR within five days, the British government would have no option but to declare war. At this point it is pertinent to point out that the British government had not protested when Romanian forces crossed the Prut into Bessarabia and Northern Bukovina; its attitude hinged on the Dniester. Reconquest of Bessarabia and Northern Bukovina did not constitute aggression against the Soviet Union; crossing the Dniester did.

If deportation had been one of the sinister features of Soviet rule in Bessarabia, it was now the turn of the Romanian authorities to indulge in it. In the winter of 1941–42 there were massive deportations of Jews and Gypsies from Bukovina and Bessarabia to camps in Transnistria.[52] On 9 December 1941, General C.Z. Vasiliu, then inspector-general of gendarmes, reported to Marshal Antonescu that the evacuation of Jews from these two provinces had been completed and that 108,002 persons had been resettled in Transnistria. Many of the deportees were packed into goods wagons without sufficient food and arrived at their destination dead. An even more terrible experience awaited a large number of those that survived the journey. They were shot, burned or starved to death in the Transnistrian camps by German and Romanian units. A conservative estimate puts the number of Jews and Gypsies murdered in this way at 70,000[53] while another source claims that 217,757 persons were victims of the camps.[54] In March 1943, Antonescu gave the Central Jewish Office in Romania permission to repatriate all Jews transported to Transnistria, but this body managed to retrieve only 7,000 Jews from northern Moldavia, 2,000 orphans and several hundred deported from Bucharest for offenses under the compulsory labor scheme.

The tide of war turned against the German and Romanian forces in the USSR after the Battle of Stalingrad. The Red Army pushed the enemy westward and by 27 March 1944 had reached the Prut River. On 2 April Foreign Commissar Molotov made this statement to the press:

> After their victorious advance the troops of the Red Army have reached the river Prut, which constitutes the frontier between the Soviet Union and Romania. This is the first step towards the complete reestablishment of the Soviet frontier laid down in 1940 in the treaty between the Soviet Union and Romania, which the Romanian government, allied with Hitlerite Germany, subsequently perfidiously violated in 1941 . . . .[55]

By the early summer the Red Army had recaptured the entire area between the Dniester and the Prut. The Moldavian SSR was reconstituted in its August 1940 frontiers and the remaining areas annexed from Romania on 28 June 1940 were returned to the Soviet Union by the armistice convention signed in Moscow between Romania and the Allied Powers on 12 September 1944. The USSR's title to the territories—known formerly as Bessarabia, Northern Bukovina and Herţa—was confirmed by the peace Treaty with Romania signed in Paris on 10 February 1947.[56]

The Soviet reoccupation of Bessarabia in the spring of 1944 prompted a large exodus of Romanians to Romania proper. The appallingly high United States Army Air Force casualty figures resulting from the USAAF raid on Bucharest on 4 April 1944 were attributable to the fact that several trains packed with refugees from Bessarabia, Bukovina, and Moldavia were hit in the marshalingyards.[57] Under the armistice convention the Soviet Union demanded the repatriation of all inhabitants of Bessarabia and Northern Bukovina; as a result 18,456 persons were returned to the USSR.[58] Among these were probably some 7,000 citizens of Odessa who had withdrawn voluntarily with the retreating Romanians in the early spring of 1944. Soviet determination that former inhabitants of Bessarabia and Northern Bukovina should be repatriated is illustrated by a number of incidents in December 1944. A trainload of Romanian Jews bound for Palestine was stopped in Bulgaria to prevent those among them who came from the two provinces from leaving Soviet-controlled territory. One hundred Bessarabians jumped into the Danube near Turnu Severin from the ship taking them to the Moldavian SSR and only two were said to have survived the icy waters. By 1 January 1945, 22,856 "Soviet citizens" had been made to register for return to the Soviet Union in accordance with article 5 of the armistice.[59]

The fierce rearguard action fought by the German and Romanian armies in Bessarabia caused the virtual destruction of the province. Kishinev was reduced to ruins and the Soviet authorities were faced with considerable supply problems, which they were unable to resolve. The problems of the re-created Moldavian SSR, the economy of which was based almost entirely on agriculture, were exacerbated by the severe droughts of 1946 and 1947 which created famine across the border in Romania as well. Several thousand Party activists were brought from the Ukraine and Russia to supervise the establishment of the republic's organizational infrastructure while only those "Moldavians" of "healthy peasant origin" were permitted to occupy positions of bureaucratic responsibility. Most of the Romanian schools in the villages were given over to teaching in Russian for which teachers were imported from the other Soviet republics, and where the size of a village was deemed by the authorities to justify the continued existence of only one school, the language of instruction imposed was Russian, regardless of a Romanian majority in the village.

The ubiquity of Russian and Ukrainian activists in the republic's official apparatus provided an important practical argument in the Soviet authorities' justification for the priority given to the use of Russian in the affairs of the republic. At the same time the influx of Russians and Ukrainians diluted the Romanian proportion of the republic's population and acted as a check against potential nationalist agitation among the Romanians. The Soviet difficulty in winning over the latter to the Party is exemplified by the choice of first secretaries of the Moldavian Communist party, none of whom, it appears, were of Romanian origin. The best known is Leonid Brezhnev who held the position between 1950 and 1952.[60] Throughout the republic's postwar history the percentage of Soviet Romanians who have been members of the MCP (Moldavian Communist party) has been the lowest amongst any indigenous nationality in a Soviet republic. In 1963, for example, only 44 of the 159 members (27.6 percent) of the MCP's Central Committee were Romanian, the remainder being of Slavonic origin, even though the Romanians constituted 65.4 percent of the population and the Russians, Ukrainians, and Bulgarians 27.3 percent.[61]

A reduction in the Romanian proportion of the population of the Moldavian SSR could be achieved not only through immigration of Russians and Ukrainians, but also through emigration of Romanians. In March 1955 *Moldova Socialistă*, the organ of the Moldavian CP, carried an announcement from the Directorate for Emigration and Manpower of the Moldavian Council of Ministers that a program of migration from Moldavia to Kazakhstan and Astrakhan had been drawn up. Not surprisingly, the twenty-two districts[62] earmarked for participation in the program were mainly populated by Romanian peasants and from them some 40,000 people, according to Soviet sources, moved to Kazakhstan.[63] To what extent this movement of population was voluntary is difficult to assess but it certainly opened the way for further immigration from the Ukraine and Russia of non-Romanians.

As long as the Romanian Workers' party[64] on the west bank of the Prut remained completely subservient to Moscow, representations from Bucharest over the plight of the Romanians in the Moldavian SSR could not be expected. This relationship of servility changed in the early 1960s and brought in its train a carefully orchestrated campaign by the Romanian Party leadership to reassert its historic right to Bessarabia. It is to the RWP's rejection in February 1963 of Khrushchev's plans to give COMECON a supranational economic planning role that the beginnings of Romania's autonomous line in economic and foreign policy have been traced.[65] To legitimize this new course, which was formally proclaimed in a "statement" of the RWP on 23 April 1964,[66] the Central Committee of the Romanian Party authorized in October of the same year the publication of Karl Marx's *Notes on the Romanians*.[67] These notes had been discovered by a Polish historian, S. Schwann, in an archive in Amsterdam and included a contestation by Marx of Russia's annexation of Bessarabia under the treaty of 28 May 1812:

> The Porte renounced Bessarabia. Turkey could not give what did not belong to her because the Ottoman Porte never had sovereignty over the Romanian lands.[68]

That the profession of Communist ideology could be compatible with a challenge to the Soviet claim to Bessarabia was confirmed by the reprinting in a volume on the socialist press in Romania before 1900[69] of a letter written in 1888 by Friedrich Engels to a Romanian socialist journal. The pro-Romanian tone of the letter is evident from Engels's reference to the "twice-over snatching of Bessarabia" by Russia;[70] his sympathies were echoed in an article of his on the foreign policy of the czar which was republished in 1965 in the collected works of Marx and Engels:

> Finland is Finnish, Poland is Polish, Bessarabia is Romanian. There is no question of bringing together various populations dispersed and related who could be called Russian. This is a brutal and undisguised conquest of foreign territories, this is purely and simply theft.[71]

The Romanian Party's appeal to national sentiments and its defiance of the Soviet Union's supranational pretensions served to increase its popularity in Romania and marked a shift from reliance upon the Soviet Union to support from within the country itself for its authority. At the same time it offered a signal to the Romanians in the Moldavian SSR that Bessarabia was regarded by Bucharest as irredenta or unredeemed territory of the Romanian nation-state. The official sanction given to the publication of Marx's and Engels's views on Bessarabia was illustrated by the new Romanian Party leader's reference to the 1888 letter. In his report to the Party congress in July 1965 Nicolae Ceauşescu quoted Engels's praise of the Romanian socialists but refrained from going so far as to mention the condemnation of the Russian annexation of Bessarabia expressed in the same letter. Nevertheless, Ceauşescu's allusion was clear.

Soviet unease over this nascent Romanian irredentism increased when the chairman of the Chinese Communist party Mao Zedong, in an interview with Japanese socialists in 1964, denounced the Soviet Union's occupation of the Kurile Islands and Mongolia. Mao continued his remarks by commenting on Soviet actions in Eastern Europe:

[The Soviets] have appropriated part of Romania. Having detached part of East Germany, they drove the local inhabitants into the western part. Having detached part of Poland, they incorporated it into Russia, and as compensation gave Poland part of East Germany.[72]

While Mao may have used these examples to show that the Soviet Union had elsewhere annexed territories to which they had little historical right in an attempt to highlight the injustice of the Soviet acquisition of the Kuriles and Mongolia,[73] there is little doubt that his support of Romania's claim to Bessarabia encouraged the Romanian leadership to press home its propaganda advantage. The tameness of the Soviet response reflected the inherent weakness of its position over Bessarabia. Not only is the Moldavian SSR the only Soviet republic with a majority population of the same nationality as that of a nation-state outside the frontiers of the USSR, but the 2.5 million Romanians of the Moldavian SSR represent an unredeemed part of the 19 million strong Romanian nation in the Socialist Republic of Romania. Furthermore, since Romania is a fraternal socialist republic, the USSR could not justify its possession of Bessarabia on the ground that it was protecting the Romanian population there from "capitalist exploitation." Its response, therefore, was to emphasize the progressive and permanent nature of the Russian annexation:

> The annexation of Bessarabia to Russia had a progressive significance for the population of this region. It was an important turning point in the life of the Moldavian people, who as a result of this historic act forever linked their future with the fate of their friends, the Great Russian people.[74]

This progressive character of the Russian position was carried to an extreme in the first volume of the official history of the Moldavian SSR that appeared in 1965. The annexation of 1812 was justified because it joined:

> the people of Bessarabia with the all-Russian revolutionary movement led by the Marxist-Leninist party.[75]

A more authoritative defense was based by Soviet officials on the attitude of the Romanian Communist party toward Bessarabia during the interwar period. Ivan Bodiul, first secretary of the Moldavian CP, in a speech given in Kishinev on the fortieth anniversary of the founding of his Party, quoted a manifesto of the Romanian CP that was issued in 1940 on the "liberation" of Bessarabia:

Now, when the gigantic force of the socialist state has liberated Bessarabia and Northern Bukovina from the heavy yoke of Romanian imperialism, there is a real possibility for friendship between the Romanian people and the great socialist state.[76]

Repetition of similar Romanian Party statements during the 1930s supporting the return of Bessarabia to the Soviet Union[77] stung Ceauşescu into criticism not only of his Party's early policy of condoning the annexation of Romanian lands, but also of the Comintern's role in initiating such a policy. Without mentioning Bessarabia by name, Ceauşescu's speech of 7 May 1966 on the occasion of the forty-fifth anniversary of the foundation of the RCP (Romanian Communist party) constituted the strongest and most authoritative claim that Romania has made to Bessarabia. He criticized resolutions of the third, fourth, and fifth Romanian Party congresses, held in 1924, 1928, and 1932, in which "Romania was mistakenly called 'a typical multinational state' formed from 'the occupation of certain foreign territories.' " He added:

The indications given to the party to fight for the severance from Romania of some territories which were overwhelmingly inhabited by Romanians did not take into account the concrete conditions in Romania—a unitary state.[78]

Ceauşescu stated that the Romanian Party's mistaken stance over the territories acquired at the end of the First World War was a

consequence of the practices of the Comintern which laid down directives that ignored the concrete realities of our country, gave tactical orientations and indications which did not accord with the economic, sociopolitical and national conditions prevailing in Romania.[79]

The sudden and unexpected journey of Brezhnev to Bucharest only three days after Ceauşescu's speech may be an indication of how seriously the Soviet leader regarded the Romanian effrontery, although it may also have been prompted by the planned visit to Bucharest a week later of Zhou Enlai. While the Brezhnev-Ceauşescu talks may have taken the heat out of the exchanges on the Bessarabian issue, both sides reaffirmed their positions with Moscow by applying pressure on the Moldavian CP to counter Romania's arguments. Ivan Bodiul responded in February 1967 at a plenum meeting of the CC of the Moldavian CP by denouncing propaganda which prevented the "masses" from appreciating the justness of the Moldavian SSR's incorporation into the Soviet Union. Bodiul attacked

bourgeois falsifiers of history who attempted to deny the fact that Bessarabia
was amputated from the Soviet Union; attempts to prove that the region was
not occupied but united with the bourgeois-landlord Romania supposedly with
the people's consent.

He called upon scholars in the Moldavian SSR

to find ways to combat and unmask the foreign falsifiers who distort the truth
about Bessarabia and to defend actively the interests of the Moldavian people
and the unshakable friendship that has existed for centuries between our
people and the Soviet peoples.[80]

Bodiul's call was taken up by the Moldavian press and Party officials at
a number of public occasions. Specific Romanian publications and historians were singled out for criticism in a campaign that reflected increased
Soviet concern over nationalist feeling in the Moldavian SSR.[81] Expression
of such sentiments had been voiced during the late 1960s at concerts given
by artistic groups from Romania, the most notable being in 1970 at a
performance in Kishinev when the visiting dance troup was acclaimed with
shouts of "brothers."[82] It was also reported that in the autumn of the same
year the walls of the Ministry of the Interior and of the university in
Kishinev were daubed with slogans such as "Russians go home" and "Moldavia for the Moldavians."[83]

The low-point in Soviet-Romanian exchanges over Bessarabia was
reached with the publication in 1974 in Russian of a lengthy polemical
work entitled *Moldavian Soviet Statehood and the Bessarabian Question*
by A.M. Lazarev, the Russian president of the Supreme Soviet of the
Moldavian SSR.[84] Lazarev's book was a discredit to Soviet historiography;
while concentrating on the period from 1918 to the present it made a crude
attempt to turn the tables on the Romanian position by demonstrating that
because the "Moldavians" speak a language "independent" of Romanian
and have a historical tradition distinct from that of the Romanians of
Wallachia and Transylvania, they are not Romanians. The corollary to this
assertion, which is actually hinted at by Lazarev, is that the aspirations of
the "Moldavians" have only been partially fulfilled since it is only the
eastern half of the former principality, Bessarabia, that has been incorporated into the Soviet Union. In other words, Moldavia on the west bank
of the Prut River is considered by Lazarev as an irredenta of the Moldavian
SSR.

In arguing that the "Moldavians" were not Romanians Lazarev was
forced to rewrite the history of the Romanians by distorting their ethnic

origins. In considering the emergence of the principality of Moldavia in the middle of the fourteenth century Lazarev opines:

> In the middle of the 14th century the Moldavians, whom Romanian historians have tried post factum to present as the mythical "ancient Romanians," had formed their independent state, having had nothing in common with the imaginary, non-existent ancient unitary Romanian state.[85]

Lazarev's contention is that the Moldavian SSR can trace its legitimacy to the independent Moldavia of the 14th century whose inhabitants were ethnically different from the Romanians of Wallachia and Transylvania. He supports his argument with semantic sophistry by claiming that the name "Romania" and the concepts "Romanian people" and "Romanian language" have validity only after the union of Moldavia and Wallachia as the United Principalities. He conveniently overlooks the fact that the early Moldavian chroniclers recognized the ethnic relationship of the Romanians of Wallachia, Transylvania, and Moldavia whom they consider to be "one and the same people, Romanians."[86]

Not content with denying the Romanians in Moldavia part of their history, Lazarev then moves on to deny them their language by asserting that the language spoken by them is as distinct from Romanian as is Portuguese.[87] This language is termed "Moldavian" in Soviet sources but the absurdity of claiming that it is distinct from Romanian is borne out by publication in the Moldavian SSR of the poetry of such Romanian writers as Vasile Alecsandri and Mihail Eminescu in the original language, obfuscated only by the use of the Russian Cyrillic alphabet which, to the uninitiated, gives "Moldavian" a Slavonic veneer. Such defenders of the existence of an independent "Moldavian" language as Lazarev, who have, as yet, failed to concoct a Romanian-Moldavian dictionary, are even out of step with respected Soviet linguists such as L.I. Likht who, in a Soviet academy-sponsored study of the Romance languages, distinguished four dialects of the Romanian language: Daco-Romanian, Aromanian, Megleno-Romanian and Istro-Romanian. While the last three are found in various parts of the Balkan Peninsula and Adriatic coast, Daco-Romanian is spoken in "the contemporary Moldavian SSR and Romania."[88]

For Soviet-Romanian relations it was not the clumsy artificiality of Lazarev's contentions but the vehemence of his attack on pre-Communist Romania and on Romanian historiography, including that of the post–1965 period, that performed the greatest disservice. His claim to a monopoly of the truth is evident from the following:

Bessarabia's seizure by bourgeois boyar Romania in 1918 is an indisputable fact. This is the most shameful page in the history of royalist Romania. Any other evaluation of this anti-Soviet action is incompatible with the historical truth.[89].

Romanian historians are warned that

no matter for how many years they should assert that Moldavians are "Romanians," Moldavians will never and in no way become Romanians, while Soviet Moldavia will never become Romanian territory.[90]

Lazarev's position in presenting the history of Bessarabia since 1812 is summed up thus:

Romania as a state (together with its official name, which reflects its international legal status), appeared on the map of Europe long after Bessarabia became part of Russia. The attempt by Romanian bourgeois historians to give retrospectively a wider meaning to the terms "Romania" and the "Romanian people," and to use them to refer to foreign territories and foreign peoples, was not only a concrete example of historical falsification, but also the expression of the aggressive tendencies of the ruling classes in the Kingdom of Romania.[91]

Using this argument we are justified in pointing out that the USSR did not exist in 1812 to claim Bessarabia.

Curiously, Lazarev's book was not reviewed outside the Moldavian SSR in the major Soviet historical journals, perhaps because Soviet academics regarded it as an unscholarly diatribe unworthy of mention. In Soviet Moldavia itself reviewers gave an uncritical validation of Lazarev's views, one syncophant even hailing the book as "a major contribution to Soviet historiography."[92] Yet this unanimity in the republic was only apparent. A. Grecul's *Rastsvet Moldavskoi Sotsialisticheskoi Natsii* (The Blossoming of the Moldavian Socialist Nation),[93] published also in 1974, was much more sympathetic to the difficulties encountered in the Moldavian SSR in molding the Romanians in the image of "Soviet man." The author, whose name suggests a Romanian origin, recognized that after the creation of the AMSSR in 1924 "bourgeois nationalists" attacked the introduction of the Cyrillic alphabet for Romanian and eventually in 1932 these nationalists in the Moldavian Communist party secured the reintroduction of the Roman alphabet. Grecul observed that these Moldavian nationalists wished "to use only those cadres who have a command of the Moldavian language." Such selfishness among Moldavian "careerists" led them to forget that the representatives of the fraternal peoples, especially the Russians, have shared and continue to give a generous share of their deep knowledge and rich experience for the sake of Moldavian prosperity.[94]

The author intimates that nationalist tendencies are also to be found among the Russians:

The chauvinistic elements try to exaggerate the importance of a certain people in the development of the economy and culture of different republics and to minimize the importance of the contribution made by the local population.

In a clear allusion to the official policy of demoting the Romanian language in the Moldavian SSR, Grecul states:

Some peoples are inclined to believe that if a process exists whereby nations are gradually brought together, and if a new historical community of people— the Soviet people—was already being formed, then, it is claimed, the time has come to bridle the use of the national language.[95].

The different emphases given by Lazarev, a Russian, and Grecul, a "Moldavian" (i.e., Romanian) to the phases in the "Moldavians" transition from a bourgeois nation to a socialist one suggest the existence in official circles in the republic of divergencies over Soviet policy toward the Romanian nationality in the Moldavian SSR. Moldavian resistance to attempts to dilute their national identity was undoubtedly encouraged by the Romanian Communist party's stand over the issue. Far from deterring Bucharest, Lazarev's book had the opposite effect. In 1975 a new museum of national history opened with prominently displayed maps of Romania showing Bessarabia and Northern Bukovina as part of the national territory. In the following year two members of the Party's Institute of Historical Studies produced a work on Romanian politics between 1918 and 1921 in which they referred to Bessarabia as "this ancient Romanian territory."[96]

To give further illustrations of Soviet-Romanian sparring during the late 1970s is pointless; while it has diminished in intensity, the Romanian authorities still refuse to let the problem of Bessarabia fade into silence.[97] Of greater significance was the crisis which beset the Romanian economy during this period. The country's foreign debt rose rapidly to 13 billion dollars. Agriculture, largely neglected at the expense of industry in the three five-year plans of 1966–1980, was called upon to increase exports in order to pay off the debt, yet this policy exacerbated an already poor food supply situation. In 1982, rationing of bread, flour, sugar, and milk was introduced in some provincial towns, and in the autumn of that year drastic energy-saving measures were introduced nationwide which stipulated periods for provision of hot water and quotas of electricity and gas to be consumed in the home. Gasoline rationing was introduced in 1983.

Ceauşescu has turned to the Soviet Union to assist him with his economic difficulties and in 1984 concluded an agreement to purchase Soviet oil in exchange for Romanian produce. It is reasonable to expect that this rapprochement will lead to a softening of Bucharest's voice over the Romanians beyond the Prut River. However, a more important consequence of Romania's economic crisis is the dampening effect that it has had on nationalist sentiment in the Moldavian SSR. An answer to the question posed at the head of this paper is less easy to give in 1986 than it would have been a decade ago. Against the desire of the Romanians of the Moldavian SSR to live within a Romanian nation-state, albeit a socialist one, must be set their perception of economic well-being, and their assessment of how far that can be satisfied in present-day Romania. Nevertheless, the strong sense of national identity that continues to be felt by the Romanians in the Moldavian SSR, despite Soviet efforts to dilute it, suggests that their exercise of self-determination would produce the same result as in 1918, the last occasion on which they were able to do so.

Notes

1. In respect of the name of the republic the Soviet authorities can point to the fact that the Romanians of Bessarabia christened the autonomous republic proclaimed by them in December 1917 the "Moldavian Republic."
2. *Vestnik Statistiki*, 1980, 8, no. 7, 41–42; 11, 66. The remaining Moldavians were accounted for as follows: in RSFSR 102,137; Kazakhstan SSR 30,256; Uzbekistan SSR 3,152; Byelorussian SSR 2,923; Georgian SSR 2,329; Turkmenistan SSR 1,561; Azerbaijan SSR 1,397; Latvian SSR 1,392; Kirghizian SSR 1,375; Estonian SSR 738; Lithuanian SSR 724; Tadzhikistan SSR 580; Armenian SSR 334.
3. ———, 8, 64.
4. *Atlasul lingvistic moldovenesc*, (Moldavian linguistic atlas), (Chişinău: Cartea Moldovenească, 1964), 34–39. See also: N. Dima, *Bessarabia and Bukovina: The Soviet-Romanian Territorial Dispute*, (Boulder, Colorado: East European Monographs, 1982), 110.
5. *Vestnik Statistiki*, 8, p. 64.
6. R.W. Seton-Watson, *A History of the Roumanians*, (Cambridge: Cambridge University Press, 1934), 520. According to Seton-Watson, the delegates were divided ethnically as follows: 103 Romanian, 13 Ukrainian, 7 Russian, 6 Jewish, 5 Bulgarian, 2 German, 1 Pole, and 1 Armenian.

7. C.U. Clark, *Bessarabia*, (New York: Dodd, Mead & Co., 1927), 146–47, who gives the number of delegates as 135. This is probably a misprint for 138 since this is the total number listed on 151–57.

8. 2 December by the Old Style calendar.

9. Following the entry of Romanian troops the Soviet government broke off diplomatic relations with Romania on 26 January 1918. The Council of People's Commissars also resolved that the Romanian gold reserve, transferred to Moscow at the end of 1916 to protect it from the German advance, should not be touched "by the Romanian oligarchy" and should be held in keeping for the Romanian nation (*Soviet Documents on Foreign Policy*, selected and edited by J. Degras, 1, [London: Oxford University Press, 1951], 40).

10. The Ukrainian Rada (Governing Council) had declared Bessarabia to be part of the Ukraine in August 1917.

11. 27 March by the Old Style calendar.

12. There were 86 votes for, 3 against, and 36 abstentions, the latter from mainly Ukrainian, Jewish, Russian, and Bulgarian representatives. 13 delegates were absent.

13. H.F.A., "The Bessarabian Dispute", in *Foreign Affairs*, 2, no. 4 (June 1924), 666.

14. Britain did so on 1 January 1921, France on 11 March 1924, and Italy on 8 March 1927. As Philip E. Mosely points out, the treaty never came into effect technically because one of the signatories, Japan, never ratified it. However, the actions of Britain, France, and Italy provided moral support for Romania's possession of Bessarabia (P.E. Mosely, "Is Bessarabia Next?," in *Foreign Affairs*, 18, no. 3 [April 1940], 559).

15. Soviet-Romanian relations during this interval are chronicled by Dov B. Lungu, "Soviet-Romanian Relations and the Bessarabian Question in the Early 1920s," in *Southeastern Europe/Europe du Sud-Est*, 6, part 1 (1979), 29–45, which is partly based on archival material in Bucharest which is inaccessible to Western scholars.

16. In February 1924, secret information was received in Bucharest to this effect; see D. Lungu, *Soviet-Romanian Relations*, 43.

17. N. Dima, *Bessarabia*, 22.

18. Its total area was 8,300 square kilometers.

19. Soviet cultural policy toward the "left-bank" Moldavians before the creation of the AMSSR is expounded by Z.M. Ivanova, *Kul'turnoe stroitelstvo v levoberezhnoi Moldavii v pervye gody sovetskoi vlasti (konets 1917–oktyabr' 1924 g)*, (Cultural Construction in Left-Bank Moldavia in the First Years of Soviet Power [end of 1917 to October 1921]), (Kishinev: Shtintsa, 1984).

20. For details, see P.E. Mosely, *Foreign Affairs*, 560–61. Mosely states that by signing these agreements the Soviet Union gave *de jure* recognition to Romania's possession of Bessarabia. However, the USSR never renounced its claim to Bessarabia during the interwar period.

21. *Recensământul general al populaţiei României*, (General Census of the Population of Romania), (Bucharest: Editura Institutului de Statistică, 1938).

22. In his letter of 9 June Litvinov wrote: "The governments of our countries mutually guarantee each other the full respect of the sovereignty of each of our states and the abstention from any interference, direct or indirect, in the domestic affairs and developments of the other, and especially from any agitation, propaganda or any kind of intervention on behalf of or in support thereof . . ." (Mosely, *Foreign Affairs.*, 560).

23. Details in J. de Launay, *Titulescu et l'Europe*, (Strombeek-Bever: Editions Byblos, 1976), 157–58. A Soviet account of Titulescu's attempts to conclude an agreement with Litvinov is given in A. Shevyakov, *Sovetsko-rumynskie otnosheniya i problema evropeiskoi bezopasnosti 1932–1939*, (Soviet-Romanian Relations and Problems of European Security 1932–1939), (Moscow: Izdatelstvo Nauka, 1977), 197–200. A copy of the text of the pact was annexed by Titulescu to a memorandum on Romanian foreign policy that he sent to King Carol after his dismissal as foreign minister. The memorandum is held in the Arhiva Institutului de Ştiinţe Istorice şi Social-Politice de pe lîngă Comitetul Central al Partidului Comunist Român, Fondul XV, doc. 355 (information supplied by Romanian colleagues).

24. The Franco-Soviet pact was signed on 2 May 1936. It was followed by the conclusion of the Czechoslovak-Soviet pact on 16 May which was subordinated to the Franco-Soviet agreement in the sense that aid to Czechoslovakia or the Soviet Union by the other signatory would be conditional upon France taking action first. Titulescu wanted a similar condition to be part of the Soviet-Romanian pact. Litvinov was against this.

25. The original draft text of the pact read as follows:
    1. Assistance mutuelle dans le cadre de la SDN (League of Nations) (comme p. ex. celle du traité tchécoslovaque ou français) pas contre un pays spécialement visé mais générale contre tout agresseur européen.
    2. Entrée en action de chacun des deux pays seulement quand la France sera entrée en action.
    3. Le Gouvernement de l'URSS reconnaît qu'en vertu de ses différentes obligations d'assistance les troupes soviétiques ne pourront jamais franchir le Dniestre sans une demande formelle du Gouvernement Royal de Roumanie à cet effet, de même que le Gouvernement Royal de Roumanie reconnaît que les troupes roumaines ne pourront jamais franchir le Dniestre vers l'URRS sans une demande formelle du Gouvernement de l'URSS.
    4. A la demande du Gouvernement Royal de Roumanie les troupes soviétiques devront se retirer immédiatement du territoire roumain à l'est du Dniestre de même que à la demande du Gouvernement de l'URSS les troupes roumaines devront se retirer immédiatement du territoire de l'URSS à l'ouest du Dniestre.

    Against article 1 Titulescu and Litvinov had both signed: accepté. Against article 2 Litvinov: pas accepté; Titulescu: ne puis signer convention sans cette action. Against article 3 both had signed: accepté. Against article 4 both had signed: accepté. (J. de Launay, *Titulescu.*)

26. Quoted from J. Haslam, *The Soviet Union and the Struggle for Collective Security in Europe, 1933–1939*, (London: Macmillan, 1984), 164.
27. Ostrovsky's successor was Anatoli Lavrentiev who, after holding other positions in East European capitals between 1941 and 1952, was reappointed to Bucharest as ambassador in July 1952.
28. Article 3 of the protocol read: With regard to South-Eastern Europe, the Soviet side emphasizes its interest in Bessarabia. The German side declares complete political *désintéressement* in these territories (*Documents on German Foreign Policy 1918–1945*, Series D (1937–1945), 7, [London: HMSO, 1956]), doc. no. 229.
29. Quoted from M.G. Hitchens, *Germany, Russia and the Balkans. Prelude to the Nazi-Soviet Non-Aggression Pact*, (Boulder, Colorado: East European Monographs, 1983), 221.
30. *The Times*, London, 29 June 1940, 6.
31. A. Cretzianu, *The Lost Opportunity*, (London: Jonathan Cape, 1957), 47.
32. *The Times*, London, 29 June 1940, 6.
33. ———.
34. A. Cretzianu, *Lost Opportunity*, 54.
35. ———, p. 55.
36. See *The Times*, London, 29 June 1940, 6.
37. ———.
38. Bessarabskaia Gubernia, *Pervaya vseobshchaya perepis' naseleniya Rossiyskoy Imperii 1897*, (The First General Population Census of the Russian Empire 1897), St. Petersburg, 1905.
39. *Anuarul statistic al României 1939 şi 1940*, (Statistical Yearbook of Romania, 1939 and 1940), (Bucharest: Institutul central de statistică, 1940), 60–61.
40. Generals Koslov and Soldin.
41. S.K. Briaskin & M.K. Sitnik, *Triumful adevărului istoric* (The Triumph of Historical Truth), (Chişinău: Cartea Moldovenească, 1970), 154. (The artificiality of the imposition in the Moldavian SSR of the Russian Cyrillic script on the Romanian tongue is highlighted by the Western practice of transcribing Romanian names according to the rules of transcription from Russian; thus the publishing house in Chişinău emerges in transcription from Cyrillic as Kartya Moldovenyaske. The publishing house upon which the name is modeled is the Bucharest Cartea Românească.)
42. According to the 1930 Romanian census the population figures for the three Bessarabian districts were Hotin: 392,430 (163,267 Ukrainians; 137,348 Romanians; 53,453 Russians); Cetatea Albă: 341,176 (71,227 Bulgarians; 70,095 Ukrainians; 62,949 Romanians; 58,922 Russians; 55,598 Germans); Ismail: 225,509 (72,020 Romanians; 66,987 Russians; 43,375 Bulgarians; 10,655 Ukrainians).
43. *Bol'shaya Sovetskaya Entsiklopediya* (The Great Soviet Encyclopedia), (Moscow: Gosudarstvennoe Nauchnoe Izdatel'stvo 'Sovetskaya Entsiklopediya', 1954), 91.

44. The Bessarabian element of this was 28,800 square kilometers and 2.1 million inhabitants; see N. Dima, *Bessarabia*, 33.
45. e.g., *Bol'shaya*, 91.
46. A.A. Zavtur, *Formarea şi dezvoltarea structurii sociale socialiste în Moldova* (The Formation and Development of the Socialist Social Structure in Moldavia), (Chişinău: Cartea Moldovenească, 1972), 87, quoted from N. Dima, *Bessarabia*, 143.
47. ———, p. 45.
48. *Timpul*, 24 June 1941.
49. ———.
50. They were officially reunited with Romania on 3 September 1941.
51. Romanian casualties in the Russian campaign then stood at 131,317 (27,061 killed; 14,624 missing; 89,632 wounded).
52. Full details can be found in M. Carp, *Cartea neagră: suferinţele evreilor din România 1940–44* (The Black Book: The Sufferings of the Jews in Romania, 1940–44), 3. *Transnistria*, (Bucharest: Socec, 1947).
53. According to an unpublished manuscript of A. Gibson, correspondent of Kemsley Newspapers in Romania between 1944 and 1945.
54. J.S. Fisher, *Transnistria: The Forgotten Cemetery*, (London, New York: Thomas Yoseloff, 1969). Of this figure 87,757 were said to be Jews deported from Romania and 130,000 were Soviet Jews. Fisher overlooks the Gypsies.
55. *Foreign Relations of the United States, Diplomatic Papers 1944*, IV: *Europe, Rumania*, (Washington, D.C.: Department of State, 1966), 165–66.
56. *Treaties of Peace with Italy, Roumania, Bulgaria, Hungary and Finland*, (London: HMSO, 1947 [Command 7022]).
57. A. Gibson writes that 17,000 people were killed in the raid, 12,000 of them being refugees in these trains.
58. ———.
59. This provided that the Romanian government "hand over all Soviet and Allied prisoners of war in their hands, as well as interned citizens and citizens forcibly removed to Romania, to the Allied (Soviet) High Command for the return of these persons to their own country"; see *Roumania at the Peace Conference*, Paris, 1946, 116.
60. Subsequent first secretaries have been Z.T. Serdyuc (1954–61), a Ukrainian, and Ivan Ivanovich Bodiul (1961–80) and Semen Kuzmich Grossu. It is claimed that Bodiul, a native of the village of Alexandrovka which is now in the Nikolaev *oblast* in the Ukraine, never mastered Romanian despite living in the republic for over thirty years (see M. Bruchis, *Nations, Nationalities, People: A Study of the Nationalities Policy of the Communist Party in Soviet Moldavia*, [Boulder, Colorado: East European Monographs, 1984], 33). Of twelve members of the present Bureau of the Moldavian CC only two, Grossu and G.I. Yeremey, have names that could be called Romanian. The others are Y.P. Kalenik, I.P. Kalin, V.K. Kiktenko, N.V. Merenischev, P.P. Petrik, B.N. Savochko, V.I. Smirnov, G.A. Stepanov, I.G. Ustiyan and P.V. Vo-

ronin. Only twelve of the 125 full members of the CC have names that suggest a Romanian origin.

61. R.R. King, *Minorities Under Communism*, (Cambridge, Mass.: Harvard University Press, 1973), 229.
62. N. Dima, Bessarabia, 46, quoting *The Economist*, 23 July 1955, p. 322.
63. D.T. Ursul, *Înflorirea și apropierea națiilor sovetice* (The Flowering and Drawing Together of the Soviet Peoples), (Chișinău: Cartea Moldovenească, 1971), 115.
64. It changed its name to the Romanian Communist party in June 1965.
65. Had the RWP accepted the Soviet scheme, Romania would have been obliged to remain a supplier of raw materials to its industrialized partners, and to abandon its own plans for rapid and intensive industrialization.
66. In the Party newspaper *Scînteia*.
67. Bucharest: Editura Academiei Republicii Populare Romäne, 1964.
68. K. Marx, *Însemnări despre români*, (Notes on the Romanians), edited by O. Oțetea and S. Schwann (Bucharest: Editura Academiei Populare Romäne, 1964), 106.
69. *Presa muncitorească și socialistă din România* (The Workers' and Socialist Press in Romania), 1 (1865–1900), part 1 (1865–1889), (Bucharest: Editura Politică, 1964), 188.
70. R.R. King, *Minorities*, 226.
71. Marx-Engels, *Opere*, (Works), 22, (Bucharest: Editura Politică, 1965), 28–29.
72. R.R. King, *Minorities*, 228.
73. Chinese interest in the Soviet-Romanian dispute over Bessarabia is examined by Alexander Motyl, "The Problem of Bessarabia and Bukovyna: The Intersection of the Sino-Soviet and Soviet-Rumanian Disputes", in *Journal of Ukrainian Graduate Studies*, II, no. 1 (Spring 1977), 32–48.
74. R.R. King, *Minorities*, 229.
75. ———, 231.
76. ———, 230.
77. ———, 230.
78. ———, 233.
79. ———, 234.
80. S.K. Briaskin & M. Sitnik, *Triumful*, 4.
81. Details in R.R. King, *Minorities*, 239.
82. N. Dima, *Bessarabia*, 53.
83. *New York Times*, 6 November 1970, quoted from N. Dima, *Bessarabia*, 53.
84. *Moldavskaya Sovetskaya Gosudarstvenost' i Bessarabskiy Vopros* (Moldavian Soviet Statehood and the Bessarabian Question), (Kishinev: Izdatelstvo Kartya Moldovenyaske, 1974), 910. It was reviewed in detail by Jack Gold, "Bessarabia: The Thorny 'Non-Existent' Problem", in *East European Quarterly*, 13, no. 1 (Spring 1979), 47–74.
85. A.M. Lazarev, *Moldavskaya*, 529.
86. Miron Costin (1633–1691) writes in the preface to his chronicle *De neamul*

moldovenilor (Concerning the Moldavian People) that he had undertaken to show the origins of "the inhabitants of our land, Moldavia, and so too of those of Wallachia, as mentioned above, and of the Romanians of Transylvania, for they are all the same one people and settled in these lands at the same time." (M. Costin, *Opere alese*, L. Onu ed. [Bucharest: Editura ştiinţifică, 1967], 133.)

87. A.M. Lazarev, *Moldavskaya*, 739.
88. Akademiya Nauk SSR. Institut iazykoznaniya, *Romanskie iazyki* (The Romance Languages), (Moscow: Akademii Nauk SSSR, 1965), 130. Quoted from J. Gold, *Bessarabia*, 73.
89. A.M. Lazarev, *Moldavskaya*. There are echoes here of the language of a history of Northern Bukovina published in the Ukrainian SSR in 1969. The Romanian annexation of Northern Bukovina is qualified thus: "Having grabbed Bukovina, the Romanian occupiers instituted a savage régime of terror, economic and political oppression". (V. Kurylo, et. al., *Pivnichna Bukovyna, ii mynule i suchasne* (Early Bukovina: Its Past and Present), [Uzhorod: Karpaty, 1969]), 92, quoted from A. Motyl, *The Problem* of, p. 33.
90. A.M. Lazarev, *Moldavskaya*, p. 801.
91. ———, 531.
92. M. Sitnik, *Codri*, no. 12 (Dec. 1974), 137.
93. Kishinev: Kartya Moldovenyaske.
94. A. Grecul, *Rastsvet Moldavskoy*, 253; quoted from J. Gold, *Bessarabia*, 60.
95. ———, 256.
96. M. Muşat & I. Ardeleanu, *Viaţa politică in Romänia, 1918–1921* (Political Life in Romania, 1918–1921), (Bucharest: Editura Politică, 1976), p. 10, note 4.
97. *Atlas pentru istoria României* (Historical Atlas of Romania), (Bucharest: Editura didactică şi pedagogică, 1983), not only presents maps of Romania showing Bessarabia as part of the national territory between 1918 and 1940 (nos. 65–67), but also contains a map (no. 73) of Romania indicating the areas annexed by the USSR "in autumn 1940."

6

Transcaucasia and the Nationality Question

ROBERT L. NICHOLS

I

In its simplest, and perhaps most profound form, the "nationality question" in Transcaucasia asks how the people of the region live out their lives in relation to the inherited values of the historical past and in relation to the generally prevailing Soviet social, political, and cultural milieu. In answering this question scholarship treats it as an essentially political one, that is, as a question of power: who holds it and what are the purposes for which it is used; how lives are shaped and directed; how new political forces compel a redirection of old policy or even break it down, producing a crisis.

After studying current journalism and scholarship about the complex situation in the USSR in the 1980s, it is only too easy to write about the nationality question as a "problem," perhaps an insuperable one, a melancholy tale of "decline and fall" of the Soviet Empire, bringing in its wake a transition to "post-Soviet society."[1] An analogy is sometimes made with the "twilight" of Imperial Russia, when the czarist state succumbed to a new barbarian "dark age." As early as two decades ago, prophets such as Andrei Amal'rik predicted disaster (*Will the Soviet Union Survive Until 1984?*), and more recently Hélène Carrère d'Encausse has written a somewhat controversial book about the decline of the Soviet Empire.

Yet such sweeping conclusions may not be entirely warranted when one considers that in historical terms the whole Soviet period has been rather short and its relationship with the imperial Russian past can hardly be interpreted in terms of mere continuity. Of course, one can speak of certain obvious similarities between imperial and Soviet policies: the overriding importance of the state and its administration in managing, developing, and even settling non-Russian territories; the systematic and largely successful policy of co-opting local elites as colonial administrators. But by accentuating the "imperial failure," we obscure the fact that the dynamic social, economic, political, and cultural changes that came with the twentieth-century revolution in Russia have also meant astounding new beginnings. We study these beginnings to find out about the rise of all-embracing ideology, the experience of economic "modernization" in "backward countries," the desire for national expression and the limits put on it, the agonies of trying to preserve one's roots and get from them a sense of direction and purpose when adjusting in the period of drastic change to the newly arising circumstances.

Frequently, scholars and other Soviet watchers reduce the question of nationality in the USSR to a study of Soviet nationality policy, often analyzed and explained in terms of a "two-tiered" model of society that speaks of "elites" and "masses," the "enlightened" and the "backward," "exploiters" and "exploited."

Modernization theory is one variation of the two-tiered model: modern and traditional, with the former somehow ranking higher on the ladder of civilization's achievements. For one period of Soviet history the two-tiered model has been reduced to the simple formula: Stalin and a totally dependent society. In any case, in all such variants of the above model the primary relationship is one of power, of how the dominant elite uses it to effect its will over the rest. In this scheme, the masses merely respond to what is initiated from above.

The two-tiered approach is widely used also for understanding the nationality problem in Transcaucasia, especially when this problem is considered as being one of the center versus region, with centralization or totalitarian control providing the meaningful context in which genuine national expression takes the form of "protest" to distant alien rule. In a sketch of Armenia's modern history, Grigor Suny describes that Soviet republic in the 1930s and 1940s in such a manner:

By the outbreak of the Second World War, the essential features of Stalinism had been established. The Soviet Union had become a new kind of political and social order in which an all-powerful state had eliminated all centers of autonomy and resistance to its monopoly of power, in which civil society and economy had been swallowed up by the state. Political decision-making was tightly centralized in the hands of Stalin himself and his closest associates, Beria, Molotov, Malenkov, and Zhdanov. The remnants of the autonomous prerogatives of the national republics or local administrations had been entirely eliminated as the secret police rose to dominate all sections of the party itself. Terror was the instrument which guaranteed political conformity and passivity; the slightest deviations from the prescriptions of the central leadership were punished with imprisonment or death."[2]

In very similar language David Marshall Lang emphasizes the same pattern for Georgia and the USSR as a whole: "The Soviet formula for a federation of European and Asiatic peoples under the domination of Russian Communists is not a perfect one, especially as it takes absolutely no account of the personal preferences or political aspirations of each national group."[3] It seemingly follows that such preferences and aspirations, expressed as "dissent," are to be treated as a political problem at the center. Much obviously can be said for this view, and it is instructive that both in the USSR and in the West institutionalized research on the Soviet "nationality problem" dates from the late 1960s when public manifestations of national dissent substantially increased. In 1966 the Commission on Problems of Nationality Relations and in 1969 a Scientific Council on Nationality Problems were created at the Academy of Sciences of the USSR; in the West a Committee for the Study of Nationalities of the USSR and Eastern Europe was formed in 1970.

The two-tiered model is sometimes also employed to explain the Soviet "nationality problem" in terms of the wholly negative means Stalin devised to bind the national minorities to the center. It is no doubt true that by binding the various nationalities more closely the Soviet Union shared the broader experience of modern multinational states in most of which increased communication and contact between different civilizations fostered nationalism. Paradoxically, however, by actually bringing the minor nationalities into closer contact with the Russians and with each other—and thus by leveling the citizenship status of all of them—Soviet leaders actually stimulated the rise of increasingly self-assured ethnic elites.[4] Due to this fact the usual Soviet emphasis on a common "Soviet" loyalty, while still siphoning off potential national resistance into safer channels of personal self-seeking, does not in other respects work today as well as it used to do in the past. The general "modern" phenomenon of national awakening is further reinforced by demographic, linguistic, constitutional, and economic developments, as well as religious ones, creating "an explosive situation which in a number of occasions has already led to violent outbursts against the Russians. . . ."[5] The riots in Soviet Georgia in 1957 and the acts of self-immolation in Lithuania in 1972 are cited as examples. In this account the result seems to be a highly dangerous impasse: the Soviet Union is held together by forces containing the power of its destruction. ". . . If (the regime) ever began to decentralize it would be unable to control the process; in other words, . . . even moderate administrative concessions to the union and autonomous republics would inevitably lead to their demanding complete independence. . . . And so the Soviet government temporizes, fostering a vague ideal of ultimate national unification and in the meantime relying on the police to keep the nationalities in hand."[6]

In all these ways, the various offsprings of the "two-tiered" model have explained and provided insights into the nature and character of the Soviet nationality question generally and, in particular, with reference to Transcaucasia. Yet, as an approach or a way of conceptualization, the model has obvious limitations. First, the identification of "elites" is in itself a rather problematical undertaking. Deciding who is and who is not a part of them is not easy because there is no necessary unanimity on policy among such a large group and, even when the ruling elite did enjoy a significant degree of unanimity, its policies did not always prevail (for example, the preservation of the garden plots allotted to the collectivized peasants' individual households despite the desire for complete collectivization; or the ban on the subordination of women in Moslem areas that has been only sporadically and on the whole unsuccessfully enforced).[7] Therefore, a construct that conjures up a picture of the "nationality question" in which a united elite draws up and implements a policy that is then reacted to by the local nationality may not provide the best answers and may, in fact, sometimes be quite wrong. Our growing awareness of ethnicity in America teaches us that nationality has many other sides than the political one, and that these sides sometimes may be even more fundamental for our understanding of what the nationality problem really represents.

The Stalinist political system in relation to Transcaucasia could, for example, be described not only as totalitarian but, even better, as one of "clientelism," a "feudal" or in some ways "traditional" conglomeration of group loyalties based on patron-client ties. Political authority in this region of the Soviet Union inherited certain features of the traditional political and social culture of prerevolutionary Transcaucasia, which is to say that "political authority (came) to resemble (there) more closely the kind of authority that is found in the family."[8] Moreover, in Transcaucasia, where various local languages strengthened group affinities, protecting the "family" from outside dangers and promoting that family's specific interests, ethnic identity and national consciousness, have been strengthened rather than diminished, in Stalin's time.[9] "Clientelism," rooted in peasant tradition and earlier czarist practice, was strongly reinforced by the continuous disorganization of society during the Revolution, Civil War, invasion, and terror (especially the randomness of the Great Terror). It has, in fact, effectively replaced formal institutional protection from arbitrariness perpetrated by the powers that be. The "enormous demands" and "crushing penalties for failure to perform" forced the officials themselves to take part in, or even to create, cohesive networks of mutual relationships as otherwise they would be left without defense in the face of the sweeping purges.[10]

"Clientelism" serves well the purpose of "putting human beings back into the Soviet system," but it does not explain which social factors, and how, gave rise to particular patron-client ties. The patronage system apparently grew up rather naturally within the new Soviet elite created in Transcaucasia during the "Stalin revolution" of the 1930s. The older upper classes, along with the more radical and undisciplined elements promoted in the 1920s, were then eliminated with a ferocity seldom encountered in history. New professional "red experts," who most often were offsprings of the lower social classes, rose rapidly through the ranks after having received some technical training. Through these new "cadres" in Party, army, bureaucracy, and other leading strata Soviet society in Transcaucasia was quite drastically recast. As Matzak Papian, one-time chairman of the Central Executive Committee of Armenia, said at a Kremlin reception for an Armenian workers' delegation in 1935:

> I am the son of a poor peasant, whom the kulaks in our village counted as a nobody. In 1921 I entered the Red Army. I spent three years in it and learned a great deal . . . If formerly in the eyes of the village kulaks I was the last man, now I lead the village.[11]

The rise of such men and women to power and prominence was spectacular indeed. A person who was a housekeeper in 1917 could easily become in the 1930s a secretary of a Party committee and a Party organizer of the Party's Central Committee in an Armenian factory. The greatest winners in the Stalin revolution were those who had been promoted from the humble backgrounds of poor peasants and manual workers to administrative positions of some prominence by 1935, along with their children who got preferential access to higher education. In Armenia, for example, the children of such parents constituted only 7 percent of the total number of people in the same age groups but they accounted for about one-half of all students in higher educational institutes of that republic. Also the proportion of manual workers and their children in the industrial technicums (35.9 percent) exceeded their proportion in the total population of Armenia.[12] "As engineers and agronomists they could enter the growing ranks of the 'Soviet intelligentsia.' But only on one condition could they 'get ahead': they must imbibe deeply of the new Soviet culture, a compound of Russian culture, Marxist-Leninist theory, and Soviet experience."[13]

The biography of Aram Pirouzian, the one-time chairman of the Armenian Council of Ministers, is typical for a person whose success in life was shaped by the 1930s. Pirouzian started out as a laborer in the copper rolling mill in Alaverdi. During two stays in Moscow (1927 and 1932), he was trained as an engineer and accepted into the Party. He returned to the Caucasus to become director of the copper sulphate factory in Alaverdi, and in 1937 became director of the Department of Industry of the Central Committee of the Armenian Communist party. Later the same year he took over as head of the Armenian government.[14] For many, as for Pirouzian, promotion into the elite was abrupt. As a result of the Great Purge the thus formed new elite rapidly moved into Party and government posts, and although Russians came to hold some important positions in Armenia, "on the whole Armenians were appointed to fill the vacancies created by the Great Purge."[15]

The new elite in Transcaucasia had, as a rule, strong local roots. Many who were promoted to it had never been to Moscow. They held positions in the provinces, which may have left them somewhat less sophisticated than their Moscow and Leningrad counterparts, but which ensured that the influence of the new Soviet Transcaucasian elite reached down to the very bottom of provincial society. As patrons, the new leaders—the watchers-over, or Those Admitted to the Table, in the colloquial Abkhazian phrase—represented in the law courts, in the bureaucracy, in meeting the demands from Moscow, etc., the interests of many local people with whom they were related or associated. The former, entrenched already on all levels of Soviet hierarchy, tried to secure protection or achieve a redress of grievances for the latter, and often with some success.

The new bosses with strong local roots appear in literary works as prominent dignitaries presiding over special occasions—such as births, weddings, funerals of their workers—or even celebrating their own arrival in a town or village. At harvest time on the new collective farms they feasted with the humble folk as masters of the banquet table, seeking to be as expert in fulfilling the traditional role of *tamada*, the toastmaster who sets the model in holding liquor and making speeches, as they were expert in the work of office or factory. These *Soviet* Armenians, *Soviet* Georgians, *Soviet* Azeris, as well as their many clients, could indeed see the value and use in considering themselves Soviet. As the young Soviet Armenian poet Hovhannes Shiraz wrote in 1935:

> The old world is unknown to me,
> I knew it not in youth.
> What would recall it to me
> Out of the obscurity of dust and murk?
> But when I look into

My gray-haired mother's eyes,
It rises menacing with death,
And the filth and misery replete.
The old world is unknown to me,
I knew it not in youth,
But in the dimming pupils of her eyes
Its mists do hover still.[16]

Thus, the vertical links of Transcaucasian society were not always and invariably oppressive. In the uncertainty and fluidity of the newly forming Soviet elite, loyalty and close personal attention to specific individuals could span the vast distances of the USSR. A Beria, Mikoyan or Ordzhonikidze became the focus of intense loyalties of many a local resident who acquired through them an influence on Soviet policies they had never enjoyed before. Patronage gave them the opportunity to provide not only for themselves but also for their region. Stalin could be the greatest father of the motherland, but they, not Stalin, directly promoted the local welfare. Thus, while Transcaucasians were told to regard the Russians as big brothers, some of them could be themselves the big brothers (and big sisters) in their localities. It is noteworthy that during the purges in Armenia a Party secretary, Bouniatian, was accused of "surrounding herself with flatterers," while another official, Haroutiunian, was criticized for moving regally amidst "crawlers" and "flatterers."[17] The Transcaucasian patrons appearing in public came to include a dense and admiring crowd.

What effect did these patron-client loyalties, generated in the social and economic revolution of the 1930s, have on national consciousness? While it may be impossible to answer this question definitively, it is instructive to note that in 1952, when attacking the disintegrative tendencies that could result from patron-client relationships, the then first secretary of the Georgian Communist party explained that "divisive" patronage working against "progress" should be eliminated because if it were tolerated, "Georgia would have been broken up into a number of "province principalities," which would have had the "real" power, and nothing would have remained of the Communist party of Georgia and the government of the Georgian SSR."[18]

In retrospect, the success of Soviet integration of Transcaucasia rested on more than simply terror, coercion, and repression, or even on a prophylactic policy of siphoning off potential national resistance into safe channels of personal self-seeking. Of course, the rich opportunities for upward mobility gave the Transcaucasians who made good use of them vast opportunities for profiteering which was not the least reason for their acceptance of, and identification with, the Soviet regime. But Soviet policies were sometimes enthusiastically received on entirely selfless grounds, especially when these policies were compatible with traditional values such as, for example, expansion of education, support of the family, and enhancement of national customs. The use of the national language as medium of instruction in the schools was very popular in the region, too. The new Soviet elite that replaced the old one in the 1930s consisted of men and women who, on the one hand, were of genuinely local stock and, on the other, were distinguished by a "common education and their recognized achievements in the Soviet milieu."[19] Thus, it was through Soviet institutions that a number of upwardly mobile Transcaucasians acquired a sense of meaningful membership in the society at large and thus "an enhanced feeling of personal significance."[20]

II

Three main features stand out in Transcaucasia's development since Stalin's death in 1953: continued social and economic opportunity; demographic trends intensifying ethnic identity, attachment for one's native language, and the sense of lost traditional moorings in a more urbanized world; and cultural trends, emphasizing a more complex and positive approach to religion, positing basic moral and historical questions, giving a fuller and more truthful account of life, especially in villages and of the "little people" who suffered most and benefited least from the Soviet regime. These features of Transcaucasian developments clearly show, in my view, that the synthesis of the national and the Soviet worked out in Stalin's time has not proved to be either objectively satisfactory or able to take root in the national psyche as a sustaining pattern or design for life.

On the whole, economic development in Transcaucasia has retained approximately the same level of opportunity as that provided for the indigenous people of that region during the previous decades. Yet, between 1950 and 1960, the rate of industrial growth in Armenia, earlier the fastest in the USSR, had fallen behind that of eight other republics. Although in the 1960s the Armenian economy grew more quickly than the USSR's average, five other republics began to outpace its industrial growth.[21] For Transcaucasia as a whole, Soviet official indices show that gross industrial output rose during 1950–1978 at an annual rate of 8.2 percent in Georgia, 9.9 percent in Armenia, and 7.4 percent in Azerbaijan.[22] On a per capita basis, however, industrial growth in Transcaucasia lagged behind the USSR's average, which meant that, even though per capita output had increased, the gains achieved through it had a less favorable impact than they otherwise might have had. In still other terms—the ones perhaps most meaningful for Transcaucasians themselves—the total income of each republic has gone up, but not in a uniform way. The growth of national income (total and per capita) in Georgia and Armenia exceeded the USSR's average for the 1960–1978 period, while Azerbaijan stayed behind it. In per capita terms, the average annual rate of growth was 3 percent in Azerbaijan compared with 5.5 percent in Georgia and Armenia, or 6.3 percent for the entire USSR. Thus, a general economic picture shows Transcaucasia improving its economic life and raising its standard of living, yet "the relative position of Transcaucasia evidently has deteriorated in relation to all-union economic performance."[23]

While during the 1960s and up to the mid–1970s Transcaucasia did not grow as fast as some other parts of the Soviet Union, it clearly changed from being largely a producer of consumer goods to being a producer of an industrial mix that included machinery, electrical equipment, motors, and machine tools. Moreover, the private sector in agriculture progressed in Transcaucasia during that period at such a pace that by the early 1980s that sector provided two-fifths of all agricultural employment and 46 percent of total output in Georgia and 28 percent in Azerbaijan. In these and other respects, private agriculture contributes to the region considerably above the average of the USSR. Real per capita income, too, doubled by 1970 what it had been in 1950 in Georgia and Armenia and nearly doubled in Azerbaijan, although such improvement fell short of the all-union average. Transcaucasians also saved more than in earlier years.[24]

Since the supplies of high-quality goods produced in the USSR or imported into the country are extremely limited, as much in Transcaucasia as in the rest of the country, those in privileged positions busily engage in acquiring the "*defitsit*," extracting for this purpose money from those below them ("wiping themselves with money," in local parlance). The members of Transcaucasian privileged stratum also do their utmost to ensure privileged status for their children by getting them into the best schools and training, regardless of their academic qualifications. Slower economic growth, combined with the advantages accruing to the Transcaucasian elite, have led to strong working-class resentment which prompted the instigation of official "anti-corruption" campaigns in all three republics. Geidar Ali Reza Ogly Aliev, the then first secretary of Azerbaijan's Communist party, remarked in a 1969 speech: "We have no right to gloss over the immoral behavior and dissoluteness of some officials. Trouble-makers, slanderers, provocateurs and careerists who bring harm to our cause must be unmasked."[25] Such criticism is readily echoed by the members of the working classes who sometimes cynically say: "With money you still can do anything—get a vacation travel pass, or enroll your son in an institute."[26]

None the less, the evidence suggests that even with rapid population growth and immigration, the economic and social situation of Transcaucasia continues to provide some real opportunity for upward mobility of the indigenous people. This is indicated by the success the educational system has had in providing highly skilled indigenous manpower. (Georgia and Armenia ranked first and second among the union republics in the per capita number of specialists with higher education.) The out-migration of Russians from Transcaucasia also provides increased opportunities. Even in Armenia, where a large segment of indigenous specialists with higher education had in the 1960s sought employment outside Armenia, the trend now seems in line with that in Georgia and Azerbaijan: rapid urbanization in Armenia in the past twenty years has drawn many Armenians back from outside their national republic.[27]

Transcaucasians, like others, do not live, however, by bread alone, especially if the bread is gained by increasing the unwanted dependence of local Transcaucasian economies on the larger Soviet economy whose needs have pushed the economic development of the region faster than this would have been the case if the three republics had existed as independent countries. Gevork Emin, the very popular Armenian poet, has succinctly put this point in his ironical poem, "We Never Discuss Trapping Monkeys":

> You know how it's done of course
> with bottles and sugar. The monkey thrusts
> in a paw and can't extricate
> his fist without giving up his bait
> and won't. He's captured thus.
> But why should monkeys concern us?[28]
>   (1973)

To economic and social issues are added the linguistic and demographic ones. Over recent decades higher fertility, emigration by Russians from the region, and migration of local nationals to their own republics from outside their borders seem to be pushing the Transcaucasian peoples into more compact and more nationally flavored units. In a positive sense they, according to Gevork Emin, are like small particles of salt that give spice to the larger Soviet dish, or like diamonds compressed by the force of the world, small grains of "marvellous uranium which cannot be broken down, put out, or consumed."[29] But heightened ethnic awareness and greater national concentration have also nourished historic tensions. Here, too, economic progress has played a role, particularly for the Armenians of Georgia and Azerbaijan, who have been able to take advantage of Armenia's rapidly growing urban industrial life. Their immigration to Armenia helped to create a rate of urbanization there which not only surpassed that of Georgia and Azerbaijan, but exceeded that of the USSR as a whole.

Such demographic changes undermine efforts directed at protecting minority rights, especially the use of the minorities' languages in schools. Armenians accuse Azeris of forcing the Armenians of mountainous Karabagh to study only Azeri Turkish; the Azeris make the same claim against Armenian treatment of Azeris in Nakhichevan. These demographic changes also diminish the role of Russian as a primary language of the elite, to say nothing of the ordinary people. Russians respond to this by leaving the region in large numbers, which leads to an ever more overwhelming numerical domination of Transcaucasians over the Russians in the region. This is true even in Baku, where Russians made up the majority until the 1960s. Thus, anti-Russian feelings among the Transcaucasians do not arise from their fear of being inundated by them as is the case in some other Soviet republics. Personal encounters by foreign visitors bear out the demographic statistics. One American scholar visiting Armenia in 1957 found that an Armenian family of scientists habitually spoke Russian at home. In 1971 a Soviet Armenian scholar agreed that in 1957 this was not unusual, but he stressed that currently such phenomena are rapidly disappearing.[30]

These demographic changes, according to a specialist on the demography of Transcaucasia, "often have a certain dynamic of their own, more or less independent of conscious, planned policy intervention."[31] This is to say that the nationality question in Transcaucasia cannot be explained merely in terms of Russian imperialism and its alleged policy of ruling the non-Russian peoples in the name of Soviet ideology and with the sole purpose of serving Russian imperial goals. The current situation with migration, fertility, and the usage of languages reflect sentiments and perceptions that arise from the local public's consciousness.[32] These sentiments and perceptions are also willy-nilly taken into account by Soviet central policymakers. For example, the strong desire to use one's own native language, while at best employing Russian as a second language useful in the workplace, seems to have affected Soviet language policy directly, as it tries to ensure a widespread and stable bilingualism, with Russian taking at least the role of the second language. Indeed, Armenians, Azeris, and Georgians primarily learn Russian in school, where it is studied as a *foreign* language rather than as a "second mother tongue."[33] In the spring of 1978, when new constitutions of these republics were being prepared, an attempt was made to eliminate the provisions in the constitutions of the Transcaucasian republics according to which the Armenian, Georgian, and Azeri languages were designated as the official languages for the respective republics. Five thousand people in Tiblisi took to the streets in protest, producing an immediate government capitulation. This experience was repeated in Erevan. These events clearly demonstrated how unacceptable and unenforceable coerced "Russification" would be in the Transcaucasian republics and, thus, that the nationality question cannot be reduced simply to the preferences of those "above" in control of those "below" them.

Another important demographic trend already briefly mentioned above is the steadily increasing urbanization that has occurred in the Soviet period. In 1926, Armenia was the least urbanized of the Transcaucasian republics (19 percent of the total population; Georgia and Azerbaijan were 28 percent and 22 percent urbanized respectively). By 1979 Armenia had taken the lead with 66 percent of Armenians living in cities and towns. Georgia claimed 53 percent and Azerbaijan 52 percent. By American standards, the degree of urbanization is still modest, but in terms of the region's historical past the move from village to town and city has meant important changes in attitudes, first expressed in the attempts of some newcomers to city life to embrace the new Soviet culture of the 1930s; and then, since 1950, in the almost universal alienation from that culture and attempts to revive instead pre-Soviet cultural values and traditions vital for the preservation of national identity under the threat posed to it by Soviet urban life.

Such response to urbanization seems universal, and it is not surprising to find it expressed also in Transcaucasia, where people speak and write of lost values and a lost sense of place in the universal scheme of things that could have earlier be found in the village. The old people have passed away and their children have moved to the city, selling the family home and thereby somehow cutting themselves off from their roots. "And when a man is aware of his roots and has some sense of continuity in his life, he can direct it more wisely and generously. And it is harder to rob or deprive him, because not all of his wealth is carried on his person."[34] So speaks a character in *The Goatibex Constellation* by the gifted Abkhazian writer Fazil Iskander. Perhaps for this reason, too, Armenians have reacted so strongly to Azeri migration into Armenian lands, abandoned by Armenians for better opportunities in the cities.[35] Again, these developments arise from rather large trends, not just in response to particular policies emanating from the center, or from "above."

The Stalinist synthesis of the national and the Soviet in Transcaucasia left many sides of traditional life repressed and still others distorted. The Stalin generation of the Soviet Transcaucasian elite was not just philistine and raw, it was also the one which prospered under Soviet rule that heavily penalized high moral standards and put a premium on unethical but subservient behavior. Their Soviet patriotism was real, but the way of life they created in the 1930s and 1940s proved to be too sterile to deal effectively with national sensibilities in a way appealing to both a younger generation of Transcaucasia and of the Soviet Union generally.[36] Significantly, Mikoyan took the lead in the first post-Stalin years in encouraging a larger view of the past:

> Of course there are nationalist shadings in some of the works of Patkanian and Raffi, but on the basis of this can we renounce a cultural inheritance which reflects several pages of the heroic struggle of the Armenian people against the Turkish and Persian enslavers, which glorifies with love and high feeling the life and work of the people?[37]

He suggested that national writers must interpret their region for the larger audience of the USSR as a whole,[38] and some of the most successful writers have indeed done so, either in collaboration with Russian writers or by writing directly in Russian. Such collaboration goes back to the 1930s, most notably to the close association between Boris Pasternak and the Georgian poets Paolo Yashvili and Tician Tabidze.[39] More recently, Yvgeny Yvtushenko has praised and supported the writings of Armenia's most popular and prolific poet Gevork Emin, dedicating to him a quite provocative poem entitled "Oh, No" which contains the following lines:

> The day will come, I know,
> when boundaries
> are erased from this world
> and only the rainbow divides
> earth and sky,
> when I can clasp Ararat
> to my breast freely . . .
> or else
> (if rage were strength)
> lift the mountains to my shoulders
> and though crushed down
> by its sacred weight
> move it by myself here to you.[40]

Thus, the precepts laid down by Mikoyan after Stalin's death seem in some way to be at work in the cultural fermentation of recent decades. It is worth noting that Fazil Iskander, probably the most popular Transcaucasian author among readers throughout the USSR, writes in Russian.

The issue of religion also bears on the historical understanding of Transcaucasians, specifically on the problem of how being an "Armenian" or "Georgian" or "Azeri" is related to being "Soviet." For each of these peoples, their historical institutions and values were grounded in religion: monophysite Christianity for the Armenians, Eastern Orthodoxy for the Georgians, and Sh'ia Islam for the Azeris. The Bolshevik Revolution brought a new value system based on an internationalist ideology of Marxism-Leninism whose self-proclaimed intellectual roots (English political economy, German classical philosophy, and French utopian socialism) were completely Western and secular. The historical institutions that gave content to the lives of Transcaucasians were thus either violently swept away or drastically marginalized, putting the newly introduced Soviet outlook into deep conflict with historic tradition. Nearly seven decades of Soviet atheist preaching and administrative repression have not succeeded, however, in transforming Transcaucasians into Marxist-Leninist atheists. The result of them has been either a lazy indifference to religion of some or a fervent embrace of religious belief, tied to a strong public identification with the symbols of the national and religious heritage, by many others, among them, in the first place, members of the younger, Soviet-born generation.

One Armenian example will have to stand for many that might be cited for the other Transcaucasian nationalities as well. Historically the Armenians have used Christianity to draw the boundaries separating them from their neighbors, while deriving a sense of oneness in the face of outside dangers. In defending their doctrinal differences, "Armenians preferred slavery or death to any compromise on dogma, and kept getting their preferences."[41] In this way religion importantly defined Armenian ethnic identity and shaped the determination of the Armenians to assure their national survival. National-religious symbols such as Echmiadzin (the current residence of the Catholicos and, according to traditional beliefs, the site where Christ, the "only begotten," descended to St. Gregory in a vision and exhorted him to establish a church); Mount Ararat; the mystery of liturgical ritual; communion; the prayers of St. Nerses; *miuron* or consecration of holy oil, one of the Armenian church's most sacred and reverential ceremonies; and certain historical figures and events that, too, had acquired such a symbolic meaning (e.g., St. Vardan and the battle of Awarair in 451, where victory in defeat forever merged religion and ethnic survival) provide Armenians with a firm integrating pattern that is stressed by the new generations of Soviet Armenians with renewed fervor and with proud insistence on Armenia's primacy among Christians.[42]

Suppressed since the Stalin years, this integral part of Armenian national heritage resurfaced so powerfully that even the authorities were forced into granting it a degree of official recognition. In 1975, for example, a statue of St. Vardan by Yervant Kochar, Armenia's most decorated sculptor, was erected in Erevan. The unveiling took place in the presence of the first secretary and members of the Armenian Communist party's Central Committee, the mayor of Erevan, academicians, writers, artists, and a huge crowd. The Armenian clergy has gradually come to occupy a place in Armenian life in ways consistent with its historical role, too. Often, in their long history the Armenian people have relied on their clergy to play the role of intermediary between the national community and its many enemies, a role that was essential for the survival of the Armenians as a consistent religious and national entity. The continued importance of the clergy's intermediary role in recent Soviet times was demonstrated during the quasi-legal demonstration of Armenian students in Moscow on 24 April 1965, the fiftieth anniversary of the attempted Turkish genocide of the Armenians. The students marched on the Turkish embassy and compelled its staff to lower the Turkish flag. They justified their daring action quoting the encyclical issued by the Catholicos for the occasion. Meanwhile, at the Opera House of Armenia's capital, Erevan, where an officially approved public commemoration of the tragic events in 1915 was going on, a mass outburst was brought to a peaceful end only when the Catholicos' Vazgen I rose and calmly addressed the demonstrators. Wildly cheering his words, the crowd heeded his advice to leave quietly and wait patiently.[43] In this way, the Armenian clergy, and in the first place its head, the Catholicos at Echmiadzin, proved both useful to the authorities in controlling the masses and to the Armenian nation in obtaining leverage for expanding the boundaries of its religious-national life. A few years later, a new impressive monument dedicated to the memory of those who died in the 1915 holocaust was erected in Erevan.

What recent trends in Transcaucasia since Stalin's death suggest is that the nationality question cannot be adequately analyzed by relying only on the various "two-tiered" models most often employed. Just as the relative popularity in Transcaucasia of prospects for rapid upward mobility during the Stalin era expressed some genuine national aspirations and helped to mediate and diffuse Soviet values quite widely in the region, so the more recent trends affect in complex ways the relationship between Transcaucasia's Soviet elite and the broader population. One should qualify, for example, explanations insisting that in "the last three decades . . . the national elites of the union republics have fostered a base of support within the population by making concessions to the ethnic majority. . . . But once it takes the form of public protest or political organization, it becomes dissident or unorthodox nationalism."[44]

The assumption here seems to be that "unorthodox" ideas do not emerge from the elite itself, yet it is apparent that many such ideas can in fact be traced to that source. For example, the native Armenian leadership shares and promotes the popular desires of Armenians to return mountainous Karabagh from Azerbaijan to Armenia to such an extent that Armenian communist leaders put themselves at odds with Communist leaders in Karabagh and in Azerbaijan. In 1975, Iasha Bablian, an Armenian Komsomol

secretary in Karabagh, publicly read a poem expressing Armenian nationalist sentiments offensive to Karabagh's Party secretary and as a result was
fired from his job. Sergo Khazandian, a prominent Soviet writer and high
Communist official, when sent from Armenia to Karabagh to investigate
a national incident, ended his mission by writing a letter to Leonid Brezhnev
contesting as false and baseless Azeri justifications for retaining Karabagh
in Azerbaijan. It seems that common national sentiments unite the Communist elite and the masses of a certain nation over the many divisions
that separate them and make suspicious of each other. For this reason, the
1976 statement of the then first secretary of the Georgian Communist party,
E.A. Shevarnadze, should not be read simply as a declaration of elite
unhappiness with the new trends in Transcaucasian life described above.
His following words are equally an admission that the new attitudes are
widespread and can be found in the ranks of the elite as much as in other
strata:

> Over the last fifteen or twenty years, the inner world of the individual has
> suffered even more from voluntarism and subjectivism than from the economy.
> For it is an open secret that there has occurred among the young a certain
> reappraisal of our convictions and our values; the soul and the consciousness
> of our youth have been seriously undermined.[45]

Underlying broad trends in Transcaucasia's demography, economics,
religious, and cultural consciousness emphasize now, perhaps more than
ever before, the crucial significance of the "nationality question" in this
region. The search for a meaningful past within a Soviet present provides
the Transcaucasians with a fuller awareness of what is to be demanded for
ensuring their deeper and more satisfying expression of national identity
in the future. To quote Fazil Iskander, "We may not recognize it, but in
idealizing a vanishing way of life we are presenting a bill to the future. We
are saying, 'Here is what we are losing; what are you going to give us in
exchange?' "[46] Will the Soviet regime be able to find a satisfactory answer
to this basic question in which all the fundamental problems of nationality
in Transcaucasia are expressed? Only the future will tell. But if the regime
does not find such an answer, the prospects for solving the nationality
problem in Transcaucasia within the Soviet context will be rather dim. It
is the ability to answer this question fully and satisfactorily, which is most
likely to determine the nature of "transition" in this region of the Soviet
"empire" as well as the fate of that "empire" as a whole.

Notes

1. Many of the standard statistics compiled to present this picture can be found in Jeremy R. Azrael, "Emergent Nationality Problems in the USSR", in Jeremy R. Azrael, ed., *Soviet Nationality Policies and Practices* (New York: Praeger, 1978), 363–90.
2. Ronald Grigor Suny, *Armenia in the Twentieth Century* (Chico, California: Scholars Press, 1983), 62–63.
3. David Marshall Lang, *A Modern History of Soviet Georgia* (New York: Grove Press, 1962), 273.
4. Richard Pipes, "Reflections on the Nationality Problems in the Soviet Union", in Nathan Glazer and Daniel P. Moynihan, eds., *Ethnicity. Theory and Experience* (Cambridge, Mass.: Harvard University Press, 1975), 457.
5. ———, 464.
6. ———, 465.
7. Jerry F. Hough, *The Soviet Union and Social Science Theory* (Cambridge, Mass.: Harvard University Press, 1977), 208–09. Also, of course, the "ruling elite" cannot be defined in terms of Russians against the national minorities, when one sees many non-Russians in important posts even outside their titular republics.
8. Charles H. Fairbanks, Jr., "Beria, His Enemies, and Their Georgian Clienteles, 1949–1953," *Occasional Paper 119* (Washington, D.C.: Kennan Institute for Advanced Russian Studies, 1980), 25. The essay is revised as "Clientelism and Higher Politics in Georgia, 1949–1953", reprinted in Ronald Grigor Suny, ed., *Transcaucasia. Nationalism and Social Change* (Ann Arbor, Michigan: Michigan Slavic Publications, 1983), 339–68.
9. Fairbank, *"Beria,"* 21–22.
10. ———, 15–17.
11. Mary Kilbourne Matossian, *The Impact of Soviet Policies in Armenia* (Westport, Conn.: Hyperion Press, 1962), 137.
12. ———, 146.
13. ———, 132.
14. Similar careers can be found in the biographies of Matsak Papian, V.V. Khvortinian, Souren Tovmasian, Magarian, Pisounov, and Aroushianian among Armenian leaders and in the careers of P. Mzhvanadze, P.V. Kovanov (a Russian), G.D. Jakakhishvili, and M.P. Georgadze among the Georgians.
15. Matossian, *Impact*, 161–162. There were certainly many vacancies to fill. The 1938 Erevan Committee reported that in recent city elections 41.4% of those elected were elected for the first time and that on the City Committee itself there was not a single carryover from the 56 members of the previous year.
16. ———, 151, quoted from R.P. Casey, *Religion in Russia* (New York, 1946), 164.
17. ———, 156 and 200.
18. Quoted in Fairbanks, "Beria," 25.
19. Matossian, *Impact*, 215.

20. ———.
21. Zev Katz, ed., *Handbook of Major Soviet Nationalities* (New York: The Free Press, 1975), 144.
22. Gertrude E. Schroeder, "Transcaucasia since Stalin: The Economic Dimension," in Suny, ed., *Transcaucasia*, 398.
23. ———.
24. ———, 409.
25. Quoted in Steven E. Hegaard, "Nationalism in Azerbaijan in the Era of Brezhnev", in George W. Simmons, ed., *Nationalism in the USSR and Eastern Europe in the Era of Brezhnev and Kosygin* (Detroit, Michigan: The University of Detroit Press, 1977), 195.
26. ———, 197.
27. Brian D. Silver, "Population Redistribution and the Ethnic Balance in Transcaucasia", in Suny, ed., *Transcaucasia*, 385–86.
28. Diana Der Hovanessian and Marzed Margossian, eds. and trans., *Anthology of Armenian Poetry* (New York: Columbia University Press, 1978), 288.
29. Gevork Emin, "Small," in Hovanessian & Margossian, *Anthology*, 283.
30. Katz, *Handbook*, 151.
31. Silver, "Population Redistribution," 395.
32. ———.
33. ———, 390.
34. Fazil Iskander, *The Goatibex Constellation*, Helen Burlingame, trans., (Ann Arbor, Michigan: Ardis Publishers, 1975), 40.
35. Katz, *Handbook*, 159.
36. Matossian, *Impact*, 168.
37. Quoted in Matossian, *Impact*, 201.
38. Matossian, *Impact*.
39. Boris Pasternak, *Letters to Georgian Friends*, David Magarsnak, trans. and intro., (New York: Harcourt, Brace and World, 1967).
40. Translated by Diana Der Hovanessian in *The Christian Science Monitor*, 17 January 1985; 38.
41. Herbert J. Muller, *The Loom of History* (New York, 1958), 380, as quoted by Vakhan N. Dadrian, "Nationalism in Soviet Armenia: A Case Study of Ethnocentrism", in Simmons, ed., *Nationalism*, 218.
42. These paragraphs on Armenian Christianity rely on Dadrian, "Nationalism"; see also Mesrob K. Krikorian, "The Armenian Church in the Soviet Union, 1917–1967," in Richard H. Marshall, Jr., ed., *Aspects of Religion in the Soviet Union, 1917–1967* (Chicago: The University of Chicago Press, 1971), 239–56. For Georgian Christianity see Elie Melia, "The Georgian Orthodox Church," 228–38 in the same anthology.
43. Dadrian *Nationalism*, 226–35.
44. Suny *Armenia*, 78.
45. See: Basile Kerblay, *Modern Soviet Society*, Rupert Sawyer, trans., (New York: Pantheon Books, 1983), 289, quoting *Zaria Vostoka*, 23 January 1976.
46. Fazil Iskander, *Sandro of Chegem*, Susan Brownsberger, trans., (New York: Random House, 1983), 8.

7

Soviet Muslims and Self-Determination:

Trends and Prospects

ALEXANDER BENNIGSEN

For more than half a century, Soviet propaganda has been claiming that in the USSR, for the first time in world history, Marxist-Leninist ideology has solved for all times the eternal problems of relations between national groups within the Soviet multinational state. If we are to believe Soviet *agitpropshchiki*, there no longer is any national or religious antagonism in the USSR, and a new species of human life, the "New Soviet Man," is being developed. This new life form will be divorced totally from survivals of the past (*perezhitki*), and he will appear to be much the same in all parts of the Soviet Union, regardless of differences in ethnic or cultural background.

Soviet propaganda remains convinced of the eventual success of this evolution, even if it remains somewhat vague on the specifics of the process. Yet it is clear that indoctrination alone will not bring about the advent of the "New Soviet Man." This was aptly demonstrated in World War II, when almost all Muslim nationalities in the Caucasus whose territories were reached by the Germans (Crimean Tatars, Balkars, Karachais) and even those the Germans did not reach (Chechen, Ingush, Meskhetian Turks) were collectively accused of treason and deported to Siberia and the deserts of Central Asia. No one was spared; Communist cadre from these peoples were liquidated along with Muslim mullahs.

After the war, the sovietization of all nationalities was—and still is—

considered to be the right solution to the nationality problem. Sovietization was to be achieved through a complex two-stage process of *sliyanie* (ethnic "Merging"). In the first stage, all non-Russian nationalities were to be subjected to strong Russian cultural currents, which were intended to lead toward psychological assimilation. These processes would result in the following benefits to the Soviet system:

> In stage one, Russian would become the second mother tongue of all Soviet citizens; local literatures would be raised to the level of proletarian art by imitating Russian models. The cities of Central Asia would be modernized and would lose their oriental flavor, becoming similar to a Russian town. The "Muslim way of life" would eventually disappear, and Central Asians would acquire "the psychology of a Petrograd worker," as Kalinin over-optimistically predicted sixty years ago. As a corrolary, ethnic hostility would be replaced by brotherly love. Finally, migration in both directions would take place and mixed marriages between Soviet "Europeans" and the "Natives" would become commonplace, facilitating the biological symbiosis of the species.
>
> In the second stage, an "international community" will emerge with a common "Soviet" culture representing the quintessence of all the best elements of different national cultures (but obviously heavily dominated by Russian culture, although Soviet theoreticians remain somewhat vague on this point), with a unique historical tradition (also Russian), and one "Soviet" (read "Russian") patriotism. Soviet theoreticians usually conclude that the result of this happy evolution will be the immutability of the Soviet empire—"We are forever one family" (*Naveki v Sem'e Edinoi*).

After seventy years of Soviet rule, it is clear that not one of these goals has been reached. Ethnic amalgamation as a result of migration in both directions has never taken place. The massive influx of Russian immigrants to Central Asia in the 1950s had, by the 1970s, slowed dramatically, and in some areas, especially in the Caucasus where xenophobia from both sides is a real factor, Russian colonies were reduced in absolute numbers, suggesting natural increase of the native Muslim populations, the proportion of Muslims to Slavs in all Muslim territories has been growing steadily. The opposite phenomenon—the migration of Muslims to Slavic lands—is most conspicuously absent.

Nor has biological symbiosis taken place. Today in all Muslim republics the two communities coexist but do not mix. Mixed marriages remain as rare as they were forty years ago.[1]

Linguistic assimilation, however, has been more successful, Russian having become the second mother tongue of most Muslim intellectuals, but at the same time there is no evidence that Muslims are abandoning their native languages. Native language use commonly runs between 95–99 percent among Muslims in the Central Asian republics. A prominent Soviet ethnographer has recently noted that the departure of Russians from the southern republics will undoubtedly hamper the further spread of Russian language use among non-Russians.[2]

The Basis for Self-Determination

To understand the problem of self-determination among Soviet Muslims and their future relations with the Russians, three ideas are important. First, the USSR is not a Russian national state but a multinational empire, in fact, the last of its kind in the world. Russians represent 50 percent of the total Soviet population, and their demographic advantage is being rapidly eroded. It should be remembered that until WW II, the growth of the Muslim population of the USSR was slower than that of the Slavs and below the average of the USSR as a whole. One important result of the wartime conflict was that the losses suffered by Russians and other Slavs eventually had to be felt in demographic statistics. At the same time, the fertility rate of the relatively safer Muslims soared.

In 1985, Muslim nationalities number about 50 million. Estimates of their future size vary widely, but a moderate estimate places them somewhere between 68 and 78 million by the turn of the century, which will correspond to approximately one-fourth of the total Soviet population. The picture for the year 2000 thus, is a Slavic majority (Russians, Ukrainians, and Belorussians) of over 200 million and a strong Muslim minority population about twice the size of present-day Iran. Moreover, if trends continue, this Muslim population will be highly concentrated in its traditional regions, not dispersed like the Slavs. In their own regions, Muslims will, with several possible exceptions, dominate not only the countryside but also the main cities.[3] Mixed marriages probably will become even more rare that at present, and efforts at linguistic assimilation will collapse. Muslim cadre will gain greater authority in the management of their own internal affairs. Those trends are already present.

Second, it is important to remember that the Islamic peoples of the Soviet Union belong to an old and brilliant culture. Central Asia, the Caucasus and the Middle Volga region have, since the early Middle Ages, been distinguished centers of world culture and the seats of world empires. Toward Russians, Soviet Muslims have no inferiority complex, despite Russian posturing as "the elder brother," I see little chance for the Russian cultural offensive to succeed.

Third, Soviet Muslims have three levels of identity—subnational, supranational, and national. The first two are rooted in history and culture. The last, national identity, is a Soviet creation forced upon the Soviet Muslim population in the 1920s with the aim of undermining any pan-Islamic or pan-Turkic sentiment that might exist, thereby ensuring Russian control. All three levels of identity coexist today despite Soviet efforts to eradicate the first two.

Supranational identity has survived half a century of Soviet-style indoctrination. Yet, both intellectuals and masses still refer to themselves as "Muslims," but this self-appellation has stronger nationalist rather than religious overtones. Central Asians and Caucasians believe—and this is frequently reported in the works of Soviet specialists—that a non-Muslim cannot be an Uzbec or an Azeri, for example. Moreover, since Stalin's death, Muslim elites have undertaken to rediscover their historical roots and in particular their common Islamic and Turko-Iranian heritage. This search for historical solidarity, which Soviet critics call *mirasism*, is strengthened by the disappearance of traditional rivalries between nomads and sedentaries in Central Asia, between Sunni Muslims and Shiite Muslims in the Caucasus, and by the introduction of a uniform political and economic vocabulary, which has reduced dialectal differences.[4]

Finally, the purely contemporary awareness of belonging to a modern Soviet nation has become reality among most Soviet Muslims. This awareness has not yet, however, evolved to the point where Soviet Muslims feel any real national competition among themselves. As long as the Russian presence and domination continues, inter-Muslim competition is unlikely to assume great importance: nationalism, in this sense, is unlikely to impede cooperation and integration among Muslims.

The Year 2000

As noted above, by the turn of the century the Soviet Muslim population will number around 70 million or more. If the Soviets manage to crush the Afghan resistance and incorporate that country into the Soviet Empire, the number will grow another 15 million or so. One can even imagine the number of Muslims within the empire expanding further still, if the Soviets were to become rash enough to invade Iran successfully. By region, the Muslim populations will be highly concentrated: in Central Asia, Muslims will constitute approximately 50 million of the total population of about 60–65 million; in the Caucasus they will be approximately 16 million of a population of 23–25 million.

Such a situation is tolerable for Soviet leaders as long as the Muslims remain submissive and quiet. But will they? We can get a feeling for Soviet anxieties in this regard by examining the attitudes of Muslim elites toward themselves, toward their place in the Soviet Empire, and toward the Russians.

The first question—how do Soviet Muslim elites see themselves?—deals with the complex question of identity. To date, subnational feelings have survived quite well within the Communist structure, and it is logical to think that they will continue to thrive under these conditions. Entire areas of Party and government in the Muslim regions are dominated by certain tribes and clans; as long as natives are forced to compete for these positions with imported Russians this trend will continue.

Various supernational identities—pan-Turkic, pan-Islamic or Turkestani—are likely to find more adherents as Muslims rediscover their cultural patrimony and as Soviet cultural forms became even more boring and oppressive.

The strength of modern nationalism, which is a purely Muslim affair, will almost certainly grow, and it is possible that by the year 2000 one national group, the Uzbeks, who will then number about 25 million, will emerge as the dominant national force. This evolution could include the merging of Turkestani consciousness with Uzbek consciousness, a truly important merger, for it would establish the Uzbeks as *primus inter parus* among Soviet Muslims. History tells us that if Turkestan is to be united again as it has been many times in the past, in the time of the Samanide kings, the Shwarezm shahs, the Chagatay khans, the Timurid Empire, and the Shayanid khans, it will be once more around the cities of Bukhara, Tashkent, Samarkand, and under Uzbek leadership.

What might be the attitude of Muslim elites toward the Soviet state at the turn of the century? To my knowledge, for the time being at least, there is no organized Muslim nationalist dissent movement. The first expressions of religious-political dissent, symbolized by religious *samizdat* (written and cassettes), has appeared only recently,[5] but it is already possible to see the first trends in the evolution of native nationalism and to speculate on the different ways in which it could mold itself. Three options would appear to be viable for Soviet Muslim elites.[6]

The first may be described as follows. For the more cautious Soviet Muslim intellectuals, the Soviet regime, despite its negative political aspects, its economic shortcomings, and its unwillingness to provide real independence to the Muslims of the Soviet Empire, is globally a positive phenomenon in that it has achieved—the essential goals of the Muslim modernist (*jadid*) reformers of the last century: a modern secular society. These intellectuals believe that for the forseeable future the cultural and economic prosperity of the Muslim nations of the USSR is better linked with the prosperity and might of the Soviet Union as a whole. They conclude that the USSR must not maintain its present form. In exchange, Muslims have to be treated as partners and to be allowed greater access to decision-level positions in the regions and in Moscow itself. The republics must receive a great share of total capital investment. Protected by Russian power, Muslims will have time to develop their native cultures.

Those who advocate or are likely followers of this line of argument are members of the native *nomenklatura*, who will undoubtedly remain loyal to Moscow through self-interest rather than ideology. It may be assumed that their numbers and the strength of their dedication depend on the strength of Soviet international prestige and economic and political power. If the Soviet army finds it impossible to crush the Afghan *mudjaheddin* and, thus, the Afghan war goes into the next generation—as it well might— and if the technological and economic prospects of the Soviet Empire decline vis-à-vis the U.S.A. and other power centers, it is obvious that the number of partisans from the Soviet Muslim peoples who favor this "don't rock the boat" attitude will decline rapidly.

A second option might be as follows. A large portion of the native Communist cadres believe today that they are as good as, or even better Communists than the blundering Russians, that they are better qualified to run not only their own republics but to assume a larger share of the management of the USSR, as a whole. This urge will be sharpened by demographic trends which favor Soviet Muslims. At the very least, these Muslims want parity with the Russians; more likely, they want superiority in many areas of common endeavor. They may or may not express a coherent ideology, but we should not be surprised to learn of pan-Turkic or pan-Islamic leanings among them. This group could well resemble the Muslim national Communists of the 1920s.

The third option, which probably contains an important minority of the Soviet Muslims who are actively thinking about these problems, is as follows. These intellectuals—including many from the younger generations— believe that the Soviet Union will someday crumble and that the Muslim republics will be free to make other political and economic alliances. Russians and other "European" settlers will be expelled and natives will assume total responsibility for their own affairs. Events along the Soviet Central Asian borders—in Afghanistan, Iran, and increasingly, China—will encourage this line of thinking, as will the growth of the younger Muslim population.

How Do Muslims View Russians?

The present day attitude of Soviet Muslims toward their Russian masters is characterized by several contradictory aspects. In the first place, Soviet Muslims have generalized but well-camouflaged hostility toward the Russians. This feeling is due to many factors: competition for jobs, frustration at being excluded from important positions in administration, the Party, and the military, as well as a traditional sense of xenophobia. A more readily apparent reason for this hostility is the thinly disguised racism which is directed at Soviet Muslims by the Russians in their midst and in the institutions, such as the military, in which all must serve.

In the second place, Muslims have a built-in fear of the Russians as a result of the never-to-be-forgotten repression of the Muslim cadre and ordinary citizens following the 1916 revolt and proceeding throughout the 1920s and 1930s. These are vivid memories, caused by the physical extermination of thousands of Soviet Muslims at the hands of the Russian authorities and attempts at the extermination of entire nationalities, such as Crimean Tatars and North Caucasians deported during WW II. Soviet Muslims know full well that the Russians are capable of the most brutal and repressive tactics—including genocide of the kind now being practiced in Afghanistan—to bring Muslims to heel.

In apparent contradiction to these two aspects of the Muslim's attitude toward Russians, we find that most Soviet Muslims are optimistic about the future, based largely on their biological superiority. Time is on their side; they eventually will outgrow the Russian presence. Moreover, Turks have always had a feeling of cultural superiority over Russian culture, and this inclination probably is gaining more currency as the Afghan *mudja-heddin* successfully resist what is claimed to be the strongest army in the world.

If Soviet Muslims view the Russians and other Slavs in Central Asia and the Caucasus in any one way, it is, with some interesting exceptions,[7] as bearers of communism and as atheists. For the natives, Russian and atheist have finally become synonymous terms, and to fully appreciate this conjunction we must remember that even today in Turkestan "atheists" (*bidin* in Tajik, *dinsiz* in all Turkic languages) still means "scoundrel" or "idiot."

With the exception of the special Crimean Tatar case, we have no evidence of contact between potential Muslim dissidents and the dissenting Russian movements. Such contacts are highly unlikely with the "Russists" or any other right-wing or neo-Stalinist dissenters. In principle, contacts could be easier with Christians, for the Muslim still considers the Christians to be "men of the book," who have not lowered themselves to the status of animals. Thanks to the excellent research of Rasma Karklin[8] we know, for example, that Kazakhs treated deported Volga Germans quite differently because they were believers and fellow oppressed victims; Russian immigrants were, and are, treated as enemies by most Kazakhs.

The current relationship between Muslims and Russians is at least ambiguous. It needn't be emphasized that Russian power is far too strong to be challenged at this stage. But can we say that this will be the situation in the future? Certainly, if Marxism-Leninism remains the guiding ideology of the USSR, and if all kinds of more dynamic ideological and cultural trends continue to spread into the Soviet Muslim regions from abroad as is now the case, then future challenges to Russian supremacy cannot be ruled out. Marxism-Leninism has nothing to offer Soviet Muslims, at least nothing sufficiently attractive to make them reject their Islamic tradition, which is a prerequisite. We must remember that for several centuries, from the conquest of Kazan in 1552 to Nicolas Il'minski in the late nineteenth century, Russian rulers tried to convert their Muslim subjects to Orthodoxy but without attempting to russify them. There were a few successes,[9] but for the most part this program can be labeled as a spectacular failure. Most Russian Muslims remained attached to Islam despite the obvious attractions of the spiritual and cultural wealth of Orthodoxy. Can anyone honestly believe today that Soviet Muslims would be willing to discard their ancient culture, their way of life, and their religion in favor of a primitive and coarse Russian-dominated ideology like Marxism-Leninism?

Would Muslim-Russian relations be better if the Soviet Union were replaced by another form of state? I sincerely doubt it, unless the state was one in which authentic "internationalism" is finally achieved. This is an unlikely possibility, however, inasmuch as the most logical kind of successor state to the USSR is one dominated by Russian nationalism: hardly the kind of ethnic distance most Soviet Muslims desire.

Add to this the increasing attraction to most Soviet Muslims of the Muslim world abroad. It certainly has not escaped them that while 8 million Yeminis or a few hundred thousand Kuwaitis have full independence, Soviet Muslims who number more than 50 million do not.

Do the Russians Leave Any Cards to Play?

The answer is really quite simple. The Russians have one card which will work for the future—raw power. As the empire follows the historical path of all empires before it and enters into a gradual or abrupt period and becomes more repressive. Beyond this, it is quite difficult to know how the process will go.

What the Russians no longer possess—if, in fact, they ever did have any other real alternatives—is a political or sociological solution to the Muslim problem. The "new Soviet man" has not appeared in Central Asia and there is no evidence that he will. In fact, there is increasing evidence that Islam—either as an active religion or as a body of culture—has successfully thwarted Russian attempts at social engineering.

The vaunted dream of the original Bolsheviks—an *international of Proletarians*—has given way to the *Intranational of Bureaucrats*. This may be good cement for the empire at this particular stage in history, but I doubt that it will prove very strong over the long run. As noted earlier, many other factors will temper the Muslims' acceptance of subordinate status, even with greater participation.

The best Soviet ethnologists now admit that the Soviet "melting pot" doesn't work. Take the well-known Yuri Bromlei, for instance, who recently wrote:

> Despite the growing similarities in the family life of all (Soviet) nations, the greatest differences in family structure among the various nations are to be found among the intellectuals and highly qualified workers. This can be seen in the strict standards of respect for parents and elders among the nations of Central Asia and the Caucasus. These standards are respected equally among different age groups. Despite the fact that the nations of Central Asia have substantially changed their attitude on the role of women in society and the family, the division of domestic responsibilities between man and woman, and a traditional way of life are still noticeably preserved even among intellectuals.[10]

Soviet leaders are faced now, but more in the future, with the specter of an empire declining. The dynamics of the Muslim population of the empire will contribute greatly to its decline; this dynamism is unlikely to be harnessed to help preserve the empire intact. Will the empire decline gracefully, avoiding bloodshed, or will it dissolve with a maximum of violence? We cannot know, and the leaders of future Russia will have to show exceptional wisdom to avoid a major catastrophe.

Notes

1. See, for instance, B. Kalyshev, "Mezhnatsional'nye braki v sel'skikh raionakh Kazakhstana-po materialam Pavlodarskoi oblasti", *Sovetskaia Etnografia*, 1984, No. 2, 71–72. Among the Kazakhs mixed marriages decreased between 1906–1976.
2. Iu. Bromlei, "O nekotorykh aktual'nykh zadachakh etnograficheskogo izucheniia sovremennosti," *Sovetskaia Etnografia*, 1983, No. 6, 21.
3. Iu. Bromlei, O nekotorykh, 11 and 14, observed that "Urbanization does not mean that traditional peculiarities, national culture and customs disappear completely," and that "there has been very little migration from rural areas to the cities in Central Asia. Rural population in Central Asia has increased by 70 percent in the past 20 years, while in the same period the rural population of the European republics decreased by 22 percent.
4. It is significant that the most "Pan-islamic" of all Chingiz Aytmatov's novels, *The Day Longer than a Century*, was written directly in Russian, its clear

message could thus reach all the Turkestani nations and not only his fellow Kirghiz.

5. *Soviet Ozbekistoi* 26 September 1982, Tashkent, on Uzbek written *Samizdat*, analyzed by Hasan Paksoy in *Central Asian Survey*, Oxford, "The Deceivers," 3-1, 1984, 123–31, and *Turkmenskaia Iskra* of Ashhabad, 14 October 1984, on the recorded *Samizdat* produced illegally by several Turkmen studios (analyzed in *Arabia*, London).

6. I exclude from this analysis the few "russified," dedicated, authentic native Communists of the hard-line Marxist-Leninist type, because they represent an insignificant minority and play no role in the life of Central Asia, having cut all the ties with the native milieu. They are no longer considered by their countrymen as "us" but as "Russians."

7. Such as the old, prerevolutionary settlers, Orenburg, Siberian Ural Cossacks, Old Believers in Central Asia, the Molokans and the Dukhobors in the Caucasus, who often speak local languages and have remained believers.

8. Rasma Karklins, "Islam: How strong is it in the Soviet Union?" in *Cahiers du Monde russe et sovietique*, Paris 21-1, (January–March 1980), 65–81.

9. The creation of two Tatar Christian communities, the "Old Baptized" (*Staro Kryashen*) of the sixteenth century and the "New Baptised" (*Novo kryashen*) of the eighteenth–nineteenth centuries, numbering all together between 100,000 and 200,000 souls and still existing in the Middle Volga.

10. Iu. Bromlei, "O nekotorykh, 16.

The Finno-Ugrians in the Soviet Union:

Their Situation and Perspectives for the Future*

VALEV UIBOPUU

Introduction

Parallel to the term Finno-Ugric languages, the term Uralic languages is frequently found in current usage. What constitutes the unity or rather the difference between the two terms? The Samoyed languages are most closely related to the Finno-Ugric languages. Before these two linguistic groups split (prior to 4000 B.C.) they formed a unified Finno-Ugric-Samoyed proto-language which, due to geographic considerations, has been termed the Uralic protolanguage. The speakers of this protolanguage were located in the region of the Ural Mountains, the larger part to the west and the smaller part to the east.

The diverging of the Uralic protolanguage into two groups took place, according to linguistic evidence, when around 4,000 B.C. the speakers of

---

*The terminology used in this article with regard to the names of the double-named Eastern Finno-Ugric peoples is not the author's but the editors'. In the author's original text these peoples have been designated as Cheremis (Mari), Zyryan (Komi), Votyak (Udmurt), Vogul (Mansi), and Ostyak (Khanty). The author wishes to state that the editorial changes with regard to the names of these peoples were introduced without a preliminary consultation with him and have resulted in a discrepancy between the terminology of the present text of his article and that of the original sources (and consequently the footnote system) used in it, for which the author bears no responsibility.

this protolanguage started to expand, with the Finno-Ugric languages evolving among those speakers of Uralic who moved to the west, and the Samoyed languages—among those of them who moved to the east. Hence, when we speak of the Finno-Ugric languages and peoples in the strictest definition of the term, we are referring today only to the descendants of those speakers of the Uralic protolanguage who moved to the west, leaving out the Samoyeds, while when we speak about the Uralic languages we are including the Samoyeds, too. Since the Samoyed group is very small in comparison with the Finno-Ugric group (only approximately 35,000 speakers of Samoyed languages as opposed to the 22 million Finno-Ugrians) the term Finno-Ugric has become predominant and usually includes the Samoyed group. In this overview the emphasis is on the Finno-Ugrians; however, a brief overview of the Samoyeds and their situation will also be given at the end of the chapter.

The original historic territory of the Finno-Ugric peoples was the part of eastern Europe stretching from the Ural Mountains to the Baltic Sea in the west, and from the Arctic Ocean to the Caspian and Black Seas in the south. Within this immense territory, their primeval homeland was situated on the banks of the Middle Volga and its tributaries. The widespread distribution of the Finno-Ugrians can be explained by the nomadic life-style of the aboriginal tribes and as a result of historic climactic changes. There were no other peoples apart from the Finno-Ugrians living north of the tree line, with the exception of some paleoarctic tribes in the Arctic region. The Slavic peoples did not arrive from the south into the Baltic area until as late as the sixth century A.D. In the south, toward the Caspian and Black Seas, the Finno-Ugrians came into contact with ancient Indo-European tribes at a very early stage. Scores of Indo-Iranian and Indo-European loanwords attest to this fact.

From an archeological point of view the common feature unifying the territory of the Finno-Ugrians is the combed-ware style of pottery which has been discovered in all the areas inhabited by the Finno-Ugrians. After the splitting of first the Uralic tribes and then the Finno-Ugric tribes, new local centers of culture, along with newly emerging local protolanguages, emerged in the many different regions to which the Finno-Ugrians had migrated. Very shortly after the disintegration of the Uralic unity we find evidence of Finno-Ugric settlements on the shores of the Baltic Sea. This should not be surprising given that the distance from the Ural Mountains to the Baltic is not significantly greater than, for instance, the distance from southern Finland to the Arctic coast.

Among the speakers of the Finno-Ugric languages we find peoples of various racial characteristics. Modern anthropology does not allow for racial affiliation to be determined by language or vice versa. The majority of modern Finno-Ugrians exhibit predominantly Europoid racial features. Only the two easternmost small groups of Finno-Ugrians, the Mansi (Voguls) and Khanty (Ostyaks), exhibit Mongoloid traits and these they probably acquired only after having migrated into an area populated predominantly by Mongoloid groups. The Uralic protopeople were already very early characterized by a racial mix and belonged to what is generally known as the Uralic race.[1]

The following historic centers of Finno-Ugric local protolanguages have been established in the territory of the modern Soviet Union: Balto-Finnic, Volga-Finnic, Permian-Finnic, and Ob-Ugric. Understandably, the geographic distribution and ensuing historical development have affected the fates of the peoples who emerged in these centers. It is therefore fitting that we should examine these peoples according to the groups as they developed around the centers of the protolanguages and local protohomelands for here the linguistic and historic similarities are greatest.

The Balto-Finnic Peoples and Languages

In the area of the Baltic Sea in very close proximity to each other live Finno-Ugric peoples whose linguistic relationship is noticeably close. Their languages have all evolved from a common protolanguage. These peoples are: the Finns, Estonians, Izhors (together with the Ingrian Finns), Carelians, Vepsians, Votes, and Livonians. All of these peoples are Europoid as regards their anthropological type and descend ethnically from a unified Balto-Finnic prototribe which settled in this area at least 5,000 years ago. These peoples are referred to as the Balto-Finns. (Within the Soviet Union there are also approximately 70,000 Finns proper, scattered all over the country. However they are mostly "Russian Finns" as the inhabitants of the areas of Finland annexed by the Soviet Union during the last war were almost 100 percent evacuated to Finland.)

Related to them, though not anthropologically, are small groups of Lapps inhabiting the northern parts of the same area (the coastal area between the White and Arctic seas) and belonging to a separate Lapponoid group. The majority of the Lapps live in Norway, Sweden, and Finland, and only a small part live in the Kola Peninsula of the Soviet Union.

The Estonians

The Estonians are the only Finno-Ugric people in the Soviet Union who have enjoyed national independence (from 1918 to 1940). Their native territory lies to the south of the Gulf of Finland between Lake Peipus and

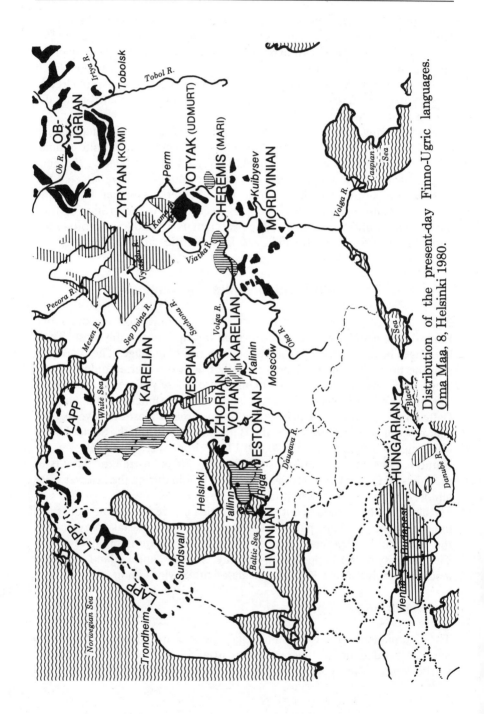

Distribution of the present-day Finno-Ugric languages.
Oma Maa, 8, Helsinki 1980.

the Baltic Sea and formerly covered 47,000 km². The Estonians are linguistically and racially the closest relatives of the Finns. Racially they are in part of Western and in part of Eastern Baltic racial type, which is fairly typical of the majority of peoples living in the Baltic area. The Estonians have practiced agriculture since very early times, and definitely prior to the beginning of the period of Christianization (thirteenth century). The land was administered through a tribal confederation consisting of eight counties at the head of which was an elected elder.

The history of the Estonians can be divided into the following periods: (1) the ancient tribal confederation until 1208; (2) the period of the Baltic crusades (the ancient war of independence), 1208–1227; (3) the period of rule by the Teutonic Order, 1227–1561; (4) the period of Swedish rule, 1561–1721; (5) the period of Russian rule, 1721–1917; (6) the period of independence, 1918–1940; (7) the period of Soviet occupation, 1940 to the present.

The Estonian War of Independence (1918–1920) against Soviet Russia culminated in the establishment of the Estonian Republic as the northernmost of the three Baltic republics of which the other two are Latvia and Lithuania. The period of independence is of far-reaching importance, the effects of which are still strongly felt today under an occupation which has lasted for almost half a century. The most important result of the period of independence was the establishment of a democratic system of government and the intensive development of national culture. The most noteworthy achievement was the land reform which abolished the holding of large areas of land in the form of estates by the Baltic nobility. Of special importance was the legislation enacted in 1925 concerning the cultural autonomy of minorities, which guaranteed to all minorities schools in their own native languages. Notable, too, was the law concerning the allocation of generous grants for the arts enacted at the same time.

Although by the Treaty of Tartu, concluded in 1920, Soviet Russia accorded to Estonia the right of self-determination and pledged to respect the integrity of her borders "forever," it tried in 1924 to bring about a *coup d'état* in Tallinn with forces brought in from outside. However, this attempt to "sovietize" Estonia, being sectarian in nature and not backed up by a full-scale Soviet intervention, failed abysmally. The liquidation of the Estonian Republic's sovereignty by a full-scale Soviet intervention took place later, in 1940. It was carried out in accordance with the Molotov-Ribbentrop Pact concluded between the Soviet Union and Nazi Germany on 23 August 1939. By a Secret Protocol accompanying this pact, the two signatories divided the territories of the European states lying between their countries between themselves, ostensibly as spheres of influence but in fact as territories destined for annexation. Soviet occupation of Estonia and her incorporation into the USSR resulted in a large loss of life through mass arrests and deportations. The war between the Soviet Union and Germany of 1941–1945 resulted likewise in large losses of life in Estonia. However, during the final phases of the war many thousands of Estonians managed to escape to the West. Following the Soviet reoccupation of Estonia new mass arrests and deportations took place. The deportation that took place in conjunction with the forced collectivization of agriculture in 1949–1950 was especially devastating—during its course about 90,000 rural inhabitants or nearly one-tenth of the total population of Estonia was deported to Siberia. During both Soviet occupations the country lost by executions, deportation, and exile approximately 200,000 people or one-fifth of its total population. Although the Soviet rulers do not allow the examination of the history of these two occupations objectively, the scars left by them are felt very strongly by every Estonian even today, determining to a large degree the political consciousness of the Estonian people and its aspirations for the future.

Estonia or, as it is known today under the ongoing Soviet occupation, the Estonian Soviet Socialist Republic (ESSR), is actually the only member republic of the Soviet Union whose indigenous population is Finno-Ugric. The territory of the present-day Estonian SSR encompasses 45,215 km^2, which is approximately 2,000 km^2 smaller than the territory of the republic during its period of independence. This is the result of the incorporation, in 1945, of the areas to the east of Narva and Pechory into the territory of the Russian Soviet Federated Socialist Republic (RSFSR) proper. In 1979 the population density was 32.9/km^2 (in 1934 it was 23.1). The increase in density has arisen through the immigration of foreign people into the area. The capital, Tallinn, has a population of 442,400 (1981); in 1940 this figure was 176,000. Here, too, the increase is the direct result of an influx of foreign people, most of whom are Russians.

The population figures for the Estonians have fluctuated greatly over the centuries. Until the counting of souls of 1782 the figures were only approximate and conjectural. According to the existing evidence, the population figures for the Estonians are as follows: in the year 1200—150,000; 1550—240,000; 1625—100,000; 1695—325,000; 1710—100,000; 1782 (the year of the counting of souls)—490,000; 1897 (census)—986,000; 1922 (census)—1,107,059; 1934 (census)—1,126,413; 1939 (estimated)—1,133,940. In addition to the census figures, it was estimated that in the 1930s there were Estonians living outside the borders of Estonia in the following numbers: in the Soviet Union—155,000; in North America—55,000; and in Latvia—approximately 8,000. The sharp decline in the population between the years 1550 and 1625 coincides with the Russian-Livonian War and the ensuing famine and plague. The decline in the

Table 8–1
Population Fluctuations After World War II

	1934	%	1959	%	1970	%	1979	%
Estonians	993	(88.2)	892	(74.6)	925	(68.2)	948	(64.7)
Russians	92	(8.2)	266	(22.3)	381	(28.2)	468	(32.0)
Germans	16	(1.5)	—		—		—	
Swedes	7.6	(0.7)	—		—		—	
Others	16	(1.5)	37	(3.1)	49	(3.6)	49	(3.3)
Total	1,126		1,196		1,356		1,464	

The figures represent thousands

population at the beginning of the eighteenth century coincides, accordingly, with the Northern War and its disastrous effects.

The Second World War also brought about large changes in the population and this has continued right into the post-war period[2] as can be seen from Table 8-1.

During the twenty-year period 1959–1979 the percentage of Estonians to the total population dropped by 10 percent, that is to say, from 74.6 percent to 64.7 percent. If this is compared to the prewar situation then the decrease is 23.5 percent. Comparably, the percentage of foreigners rose. The largest group of non-Estonians comprises the Russians along with Ukrainians and Belorussians. (In absolute figures there were 409,000 Russians, 36,000 Ukrainians, and 23,000 Byelorussians in Estonia in 1979; altogether 467,883 individuals of Slavic origin.) The overall percentage of non-Estonians at the time of the 1979 census in Estonia stood at 35.3 percent. Compared to the prewar situation the number of Russians has more than quadrupled. It should also be borne in mind that the largest part of the Russian minority during the period of independence lived in those areas which were annexed directly into the RSFSR. In 1979, 98.4 percent of the Estonians considered Estonian as their native language, which reflects very clearly the position with regard to national self-awareness. However, only 1.56 percent of the Russians living in Estonia in 1979 considered Estonian as their native language, which also indicates a practically negligible tendency of the Russians to assimilate. If to this figure the numbers of those who speak Estonian as their second language were added, then only 12.9 percent of the native speakers of Russian living in Estonia speak the language of the country of their residence.

Among the 72,039 Soviet Estonians living outside of the territory of Estonia (1979), 33,954 spoke Estonian as their native language. Among the immigrants to Estonia were also 17,000 Finns (1979), in all likelihood Ingrians who were prevented from returning to their former homes after the war and who later migrated from various parts of the Soviet Union into Estonia. (This process continues.) The Finns (Ingrians) are the only group of newcomers who exhibit a tendency to assimilate into the Estonian population.

As regards the increase in the numbers of non-Estonians, in addition to the census figures, the military personnel, along with members of their immediate families, must also be taken into consideration. No one knows the exact figures for these individuals, but they tend to dominate the scene in the streets and public life of the larger cities. As a result of these changes over 80 percent of the populations of Narva and many other eastern towns in Estonia are Russian. In Tallinn, the capital, this figure may be 50 percent or even more.

This change in the demographic composition of Estonia, which is the most radical one in its history to date, has produced a tendency to favor the Russian-speaking population and discriminate against the speakers of Estonian. In a secret decision of the Central Committee of the Estonian Communist party in 1978, a move to fix the dominant role of the Russian language was endorsed. As a result, Russian-language teaching is begun now in Estonian-language kindergartens. In Estonian-language elementary schools Russian is introduced as early as the first fall semester while at the same time the teaching of Estonian in Russian-language schools does not start until the fifth grade. Moreover, many students of Russian-language schools can be individually released from having to learn Estonian. The increase in Russian-language instruction in Estonian-language schools is usually provided at the expense of time allocated to the teaching of Estonian and Western languages.

V.U.

As of 1975 all theses and dissertations written at Tartu University (one of the oldest universities in the whole of the Soviet Union, established by the Swedish king Gustavus Adolphus II in 1632) must be written in Russian (even if they deal with the Estonian language or Estonian literature). At the university there are three departments dealing with Russian subjects: the department of Russian language, the department of Russian literature, and a department specially dealing with the methodology of teaching the Russian language. In the academic year 1984–85, the faculty of these three departments together numbered fifty-six. At the same time the faculty of the Estonian-language department and of the department of Estonian literature and folklore numbered only forty-six. Tartu University also has a special department of military studies whose faculty numbers twenty individuals only one of whom has an Estonian name. Russian is the sole language of instruction in this department. According to the statistics, in 1980 only 17 percent of television and radio broadcasts were in Estonian. The largest Finno-Ugric ethnographic museum in the Soviet Union is affiliated with the Tartu University. Still today, 40 years after the war, the museum is housed in temporary dwellings. There are only 100 m² of space available for exhibits. Most of the material is stored in attics and basements. This situation reflects the general attitude of the Soviet authorities to disciplines dealing with the Finno-Ugric national and cultural legacy.

Russification, which has been the chief threat to the Finno-Ugric peoples throughout the ages, can occur in Estonia in one of three ways: passive Russification, i.e., a voluntary adoption of Russian on the part of the people; active Russification, i.e., the imposition of Russian onto the people by means of force or coercion; and finally, the deliberate replacement of the population of the territory in question brought about by either deportation (e.g., extermination) of the native population or by a massive influx of Russian-speaking immigrants, or a combination of both.

The first two of these above-mentioned methods have never produced any tangible results, neither during the czarist régime, under which they were the dominant ones, nor today. As a nation which has achieved a high level of indigenous culture, the Estonians are not about to Russify either voluntarily (apart from perhaps a few cases of careerists) or under pressure. Much more dangerous, however, is the third alternative, i.e., the replacement of the people of this area, which during the czarist period was not practiced extensively at all. Today, however, this seems to be the primary method in use. Deportations (and extermination) stopped after the death of Stalin, but the immigration of foreign stock, under the pretext of satisfying the ever-increasing need for labor, continues unabated. It is feared that with the Soviet continuation of such a national policy the Estonian people will become a minority in their own territory by the end of the millennium, all the more so since the average age of the immigrants is significantly lower than that of the Estonians.

The unconditional restoration of national sovereignty and secession from the USSR is the inarguable aspiration of the Estonians, a nation which has experienced independence in its living memory and has a long-standing democratic tradition. This would also solve Estonia's demographic problems by preventing the replacement of her indigenous population now pursued against the nation's will.

The Carelians

Of the Balto-Finnic peoples in the Soviet Union the Carelians are the second largest group next to the Estonians. Moreover, the Carelians are the closest relatives of the Finns and Estonians as far as both their language and ethnic origin are concerned.

A. Population and Geography

The modern-day Carelians are scattered in three national-administrative units. These are: (1) The Republic of Finland; (2) The Carelian Autonomous Soviet Socialist Republic (Carelian ASSR); and (3) the Russian Soviet Federated Socialist Republic (RSFSR). In Finland the Carelians are a group whose language is one of the eastern Finnish dialects; Carelian is not considered a separate language in Finland. With the redrawing of the borders after the Finno-Soviet Continuation War in 1944 only two or three Carelian villages were left in Finland proper. The Finnish Carelians living in the isthmus between Lake Ladoga and the Gulf of Finland were all evacuated to various parts of Finland.

The Carelian ASSR lies to the east of the border of Finland between the White Sea and Lakes Ladoga and Onega. Its southern border within the RSFSR (of which it is legally a constituent part) is formed by the Süvari (Svir) River between Lakes Ladoga and Onega. This territory encompasses the settlements of the Vepsians as well. Together with the territories the USSR annexed from Finland during the last war, the ASSR is a relatively large area, 172,400 km^2, of which over 10 percent is water in the form of larger and smaller lakes numbering approximately 40,000. The administrative center is Petrozavodsk (Petroskoi/Äänislinna) with a population of 234,000 (1980).

In the RSFSR proper, Carelians live mainly in the former government of Tver (now Kalinin Oblast) (Province) and in the regions of Tichvin and Valdai. A few Carelian settlements are situated also in Siberia where the Carelians are referred to as Koryaks. There are only hundreds of Carelian villages in Kalinin Oblast today whereas in earlier times their number must have reached into the thousands. It is thought that in Carelian settlements, scattered among Russian settlements in the Boksitogorsk Rayon (District) around Tichvin, there are approximately 2,000 Carelians, and in those around Valdai only a few hundreds of them.

According to the 1970 census there were altogether 146,000 Carelians in the USSR: 84,200 lived in the Carelian ASSR and 61,800 in the Kalinin Oblast. According to the 1979 census this figure had gone down to 138,400. In the Carelian ASSR, in 1979, from a total population of 740,000, the majority were Russians, namely 517,000 (or 71.3 percent). The number of Carelians was 82,140 (or 11.1 percent). The rest were Finns (19,980 or 2.7 percent), Vepsians (5,920 or 0.8 percent), Belorussians (59,940 or 8.1 percent), Ukrainians (24,420 or 3.3 percent), and other nationalities (19,980 or 2.7 percent). The population density was 4.3/km². The percentage decrease of Carelians in their autonomous republic can be clearly seen in the following statistics: in 1897 the percentage of Carelians among the local inhabitants was 42.3; in 1926—38.2; 1939—23.2; 1959—13.1; 1970—11.8; 1979—11.1. This same decrease can be seen in the actual numbers of Carelians (Northern Carelians and Tver Carelians together). In 1897 the Carelians numbered 208,100; in 1926 this figure was 248,000; and in 1939—253,000. After this date these figures fell sharply. In 1959 there were only 167,300, and, as mentioned above, 146,100 and 138,400 in 1970 and 1979, respectively. The percentage of Carelians who speak Carelian as their native language has also decreased. In 1959 Carelian was the native language to 71.3 percent of the Carelians. In 1970 this figure was 63.0 percent, and in 1979—55.6 percent. Carelians are mentioned today in Soviet ethnographic studies as a typical example of a people in the process of being assimilated.[3]

Racially the Carelians belong to the eastern group of Balto-Finns. According to the measurements carried out by the Estonian anthropologist, Karin Mark, they belong to the Baltic racial type, predominantly Europoid with some weak Mongoloid traits.[4]

In the Carelian SSR Carelians form 7.7 percent of the urban population and 20.9 percent of the rural population (1970). The chief means of livelihood among the Carelians of the Kalinin *Oblast* is collective farming. Of the Carelians in this area 75 percent live in rural areas.

B. History

The Slavs appeared in the neighborhood of the Carelians in the second half of the first millennium. There exist data about the Bjarmian (Perm) state along the shores of the Viena River, which Other (Ottar) the Norseman described in his report to Alfred the Great, king of England. In the ninth–twelfth centuries, the southern parts of Carelia belonged to the Kievan Russian state. In the twelfth century, however, the whole of Carelia was added to Novgorod. Carelia remained a vassal state under Novgorod until 1478, when it became part of the Principality of Moscow. During the Novgorod period Carelia underwent intensive Christianization into the Orthodox faith in the process of which the Monastery of Solovetsk, built on an island in the White Sea, played an important role.

In conjunction with the revolution of 1917 the Northern Carelians on a number of occasions desperately tried to gain independence. At a mass meeting in Uhtua on 12–14 July 1917, the declaration of an autonomous Carelia was passed which was very shortly thereafter accepted in many other Carelian centers. At the end of the Finnish War of Independence there was a general desire to join Finland; in July 1918 a meeting of the representatives of the Northern Carelian (Viena) parishes was held with that particular aim. The parish of Repola and subsequently other parishes declared themselves seceded from the former Russian Empire and integrated into Finland. However, in the fall of 1918 the Red forces got the upper hand, and the Finnish and Carelian regiments were forced to retreat back into Finland. In the early spring of 1919 the movement to free the Onega region started again with the help of volunteers from Finland. In a short time the southern and central areas of the Onega region were almost completely freed. But already by the summer of 1919 the Finnish forces had to retreat again.

In the meantime, the English and French troops participating in the Russian Civil War having taken Arkhangel gave Northern Carelia to the Russian Whites. When their grip on power in that territory proved to be weak, a Carelian-Finnish action to secede from Russia was once again undertaken in Uhtua and an interim Carelian government was established there. In the spring of 1920 the White Russian forces were totally defeated and the Carelians fled massively from the advancing Red troops into Finland. The Reds gradually took all of Eastern Carelia which, on 8 June 1920, was proclaimed the Carelian Labor Commune with the status of an autonomous *oblast* (province).

In the peace negotiations with the Soviets, Finland tried to get their agreement for establishing an autonomous Carelia which, in fact, was granted by a special article included into the Peace Treaty of Tartu. When the implementation of this agreement proved to be unsatisfactory, the Carelians attempted to rise one last time in the fall of 1921 and the early spring of 1922. At first their uprising was successful but in the end the superior forces of Soviet Russia managed to suppress it. At the instigation of Finland the Carelian question was raised in the League of Nations which passed a resolution in support of Carelian independence, but could do nothing to translate it into political reality. Between 1917 and 1922, and after 1923, when the Soviets finally conquered Carelia, approximately 30,000 Carelian refugees escaped to Finland.

On 25 June 1923, Carelia was declared an autonomous soviet socialist republic. After the conclusion of the Finnish Winter War, on 31 March 1940, its status was changed to that of the Carelian-Finnish Soviet Socialist Republic with the obvious implication of a possible incorporation into it of the rest of Finland. Carelia's status as a union republic lasted until 16

June 1956 when, for the sake of consolidation of good relations with Finland, the Soviet government demoted Carelia to the status of an autonomous SSR once again.

During the Finno-Soviet Continuation War (1941–1944) a large part of Eastern Carelia was occupied by Finnish forces and the region was administered by the Finnish military government established in Äänislinna (Petrozavodsk). This government abolished collectivization and effected a changeover to a system of private farms. The schools and the legal system were modeled after the Finnish ones. In order to make the necessary changes in the administration, the Finnish military government created an advisory committee composed of representatives of the local population. During Finnish rule over Carelia from 1941 to 1944, only about 90,000 inhabitants were left on Carelian territory. The remaining part of the population had either been evacuated or had fled.

C. Language and Culture

The oldest linguistic document in Carelia is a piece of birchbark from the thirteenth century discovered in 1957 in Novgorod. It consists of a few short lines containing a litany to thunder. Later, in 1960, another piece of birch-bark was discovered, again in Novgorod; it is dated to the fourteenth century and contains a text written partly in Russian and partly in Carelian. The Russian text is a promissory note while the Carelian text is a commentary on the Russian text.

Despite such early beginnings (at least in comparison with the other Balto-Finnic languages) the Carelian written language has remained underdeveloped. The number of books printed in this language is very small and very few readers use them.

At the beginning of the Soviet period Finnish and Russian were adopted as the written languages in the Carelian ASSR. A written language in the Latin alphabet based on the Tolmatshu dialect was created for the Carelians living in the Tver (Kalinin) *Oblast*. During the period 1931–1937 over 50 books (mainly schoolbooks) and a newspaper, *Karjala Tozi* (Carelian Truth), appeared in this language. This written language was abolished in the course of the linguistic reforms of 1937, when a unified written language in the Cyrillic alphabet for the Carelians of both the Tver (Kalinin) *Oblast* and the Carelian ASSR was created. The linguist D.V. Bubrich (1890–1949) worked out a plan for this language, which was put together of elements taken from a number of dialects.[5] Between the years 1938–39 quite an extensive list of textbooks on, and other literature in, that language were published. Unfortunately, these books did not circulate widely as the experiment was terminated by 1940. Simultaneously with the formation of the Carelian-Finnish SSR in March 1940 it was decided to reintroduce Finnish as the official language of the republic. With this decision the Carelian written language virtually disappeared. The use of this language had already been eliminated among the Tver Carelians in 1939 when the sole medium of instruction in local schools became Russian. There is some literary production in Finnish appearing in the Carelian ASSR, a newspaper, *Neuvosto-Karjala* (Soviet Carelia) and journals, including the organ of the Carelian ASSR Writers' Union, *Punalippu* (Red Flag).

There is no doubt that the erratic experimentation with the Carelian language has resulted in the significant decrease in its use even as a spoken language. What is surprising, however, is that in the Kalinin *Oblast*, where the Carelians are surrounded by a massive majority of Russian speakers, the Carelian language has managed to survive as it has for over 300 years. The assimilation in the Carelian ASSR seems to be moving in two directions—first a changeover to the Russian language and secondly a somewhat lesser changeover to Finnish, especially as regards the use of a written language.

Even though the Carelians lack any published literature of any significance, their oral folk tradition is all the richer. The indigenous folk songs have survived in Carelia longer and more completely than anywhere else among the Finno-Ugric peoples. Not without reason is Carelia called the song-land of the Kalevala. Elias Lönnrot has compiled the Kalevala on the basis of materials largely collected in Carelia.[6] From the folksinger Arhippa Perttunen in Latvajärvi village alone he recorded over 4,000 verses which formed almost one quarter of the proto-Kalevala. Moreover, the Carelian songs form the largest part of the great Finnish collection of folk songs, *Suomen Kansan Vanhat Runot.*

The indigenous Carelian culture and literature live on to a certain extent in the medium of Finnish. However, certain Carelian writers have published some poetry in their native dialects, too.

*   *   *

In recent history the Carelians have affirmed their desire and aspirations for independence. The large territory inhabited by them is rich in natural resources, such as forest reserves that are among Europe's largest, abundant sources of hydroelectric power, and large fishing grounds, which should be able to ensure an independent economy sustainable by today's small population without the need to import a foreign work force. As a comparison, Iceland, which gained its independence following World War Two, or the Micronesian and Marshall islands of the Pacific Ocean, which have recently won self-determination, can be cited. A negative factor is, of course, the assimilation that has taken place over the last few decades and the threat of replacement of the population of this large territory. For the Carelians the present time is in this respect much more critical than even for the Estonians. The Carelians do not have much time to wait for a change in their situation and fortunes. Now they are still a sufficiently large ethnic entity with enough self-confidence to preserve their separate identity. However, it is doubtful that the Carelians would be able to preserve this position for much longer without separating from Russia. Today there are no signs indicating the possibility for such a separation taking place. However, under more propitious conditions, the Carelians would certainly look for support to the cause of their independence across their western border, and, first of all, to their closest relatives, the Finns.

The Vepsians

A. Population and Geography
The Vepsians, nearest neighbors of the Carelians, are located between Lakes Ladoga and Onega and the White Sea, where they live in three groups separated one from the other. The first of these, known as the northern group, lives in the territory of the Carelian ASSR on the shores of Lake Onega, south of Petrozavodsk and, according to earlier sources, consisted of twenty-four villages. The second and largest group are the so-called Middle Vepsians located in the Russian SFSR in the Leningrad *Oblast*. They are far removed to the southwest from the previously mentioned group, living in the region of the Ojatti River which flows into Lake Ladoga. The third, the Southern Vepsian group, is located territorially also in the RSFSR, on the north-western edge of the former Novgorod government and the present-day Vologda *Oblast*. It consists of only some dozen or so villages. The Southern and Middle Vepsians have direct contacts, but the Northern Vepsians live far away and are removed from the more southernly Vepsians by the Süvari (Svir) River and numerous Russian settlements.

The Vepsians who in the past had been considered as a vital and significant group of Balto-Finns, have now retreated to the point of being a people on the verge of extinction. All the existing data from censuses speak of the continuous decrease in their numbers, which has been especially noticeable between the years 1959–1970: 1926—32,785; 1959—16,400; 1970—8,000. According to the detailed analysis of the 1959 census only 41.6 percent of the Vepsians spoke Vepsian as their native language. In the 1970 census speakers of Vepsian were not even listed separately. The figure of 8,000 was gleaned by looking at the combined statistics of the Carelian ASSR and the RSFSR. In the Carelian ASSR there were 5,800 Vepsians at the time of the 1979 census. The Finnish demographer Seppo Lallukka has given the figure of 8,100 as the total number of Vepsians living in the Soviet Union, of whom only 38.4 percent speak Vepsian as their native language.[7]

The decline of the Vepsians has been rapid. When the Finnish linguist Lauri Kettunen visited the Vepsian settlements in the Soviet Union in 1934, the number of Vepsians was estimated to be close to 50,000.[8] Only in the settlement of Pyatina, which was removed from other Vepsian settlements, was there any Russification to be noticed. Otherwise Vepsian was spoken in the homes, and in the Middle Vepsian areas there were even Vepsian schools. Families tended to have many children.

Racially the Vepsians belong to the White Sea group of Balto-Finns of the eastern Baltic type. As regards primary racial traits they resemble the eastern Finns, who are considered to be predominantly Europoid with weak Mongoloid traits. The primary means of livelihood of the Vepsians is agriculture in collective farms, forestry and, among the Onega Vepsians, fishing as well.

B. History

The Vepsians were mentioned among other independently established peoples in the Chronicles of Jordanes in the sixth century. They were also mentioned in the Chronicles of Nestor where they are listed among those people who, in the ninth century, had invited the Swedish Varangians to rule over them. References to Vepsians are made in passing in the travelogue of the Arab, Ahmed ibn Fadlani, who traveled in Europe in 921–922, as well as in the four-volume Hamburg History of the Church which was written by Adam of Bremen in 1075–1080. A discussion of the Vepsians in the "Gesta Danorum" of Saxo Grammaticus in the thirteenth century was followed by a long period of silence until A.J. Sjögren, who visited and described Vepsian settlements in 1824, reintroduced them to the world.[9]

After the Slavs began to encroach into their territory, the Vepsians increasingly became dependent on first the Novgorodian Slovenes and then the Russians. There were, however, no Russian settlements in the territory of the Northern Vepsians before the fourteenth–fifteenth centuries.

At the time of the Finn-Soviet Continuation War during World War II (1941–1944) the territory of the Northern Vepsians was separated from that of the Middle and Southern Vepsians by the front which, for a long time, ran along the Süvari (Svir) River. The Finns took control over the Northern Vepsians' territory, organizing a local administration and introducing the Finnish school system. Finnish textbooks were procured and among other things excursions to Finnish cities were organized for the children. Soviet prisoners of war from local Carelian and Vepsian areas formed a volunteer corps in the Finnish army, called the Brother Battalion. The retreat of the Finns brought much suffering and many human tragedies to the Northern Vepsians. Cruel punishment was meted out by the Soviet authorities to those of them who had lived under Finnish rule and a great many of them were accused of cooperating with the enemy. After the signing of the peace treaty with Finland, the remains of the Brother Battalion were surrendered to the Soviets. A few individual Vepsians, however, did manage to escape and reach Sweden through Finland as refugees.

The Vepsians are today a people without a written language even though a short-lived attempt was made to create one (1932–1937). The creation of a written language for Vepsian was carried out by the Department of Minority Peoples under the jurisdiction of the executive committee of the Leningrad *Oblast*. The department worked out an orthography in Latin alphabet that resembled the one created for the Carelians of the Kalinin *Oblast*. The central dialect of Vepsian, with some concessions to its southern dialect, was taken as the basis of the Vepsian language. The first book was *Ezmäne vepside azbuk i lugendknig* (First Vepsian ABC and Reader [Leningrad, 1932]). Altogether, close to thirty elementary school texts were written in the Vepsian language. These were compiled or translated by native Vepsian pedagogues such as M.M. Hämäläinen, F.A.Andreev and others. The aforementioned also compiled a small Vepsian-Russian dictionary which appeared in 1936.[10] The trial period for the written Vepsian language was suddenly terminated in the late 1930s, and it thus shared the fate of other small Finno-Ugric languages.

From the last All-Union census (1979) one may gain the impression that Vepsian is a language on the verge of extinction. However, local data from the Carelian ASSR and the relevant regions of the RSFSR show that the number of Vepsian-speaking Vepsians is nonetheless many times larger than, for example, the number of Lapps of the Kola Peninsula. Therefore, Vepsians may justifiably claim for themselves national autonomy and schools. Their autonomous status could be modeled on that of the Swedish minority in independent Estonia or on the present-day situation of the small community of Swedes in Finland. If the present situation of the Vepsians in the USSR is not changed soon enough, the Vepsians as an ethnic entity may become extinct.

The Izhors and the Ingrian Finns

The name Ingrian (Est. ingerlane, Finn. inkeriläinen, Swed. ingermanländer) generally refers to the people of Balto-Finnic origin who live in Ingria regardless of what Finno-Ugric language they speak. In addition to the Izhors, Ingria is populated by the Äyrämöis, who are former immigrants into the area from the parish of Äyräpää in Finland, and the Savakkos, who are immigrants from Savo County, also in Finland. These are the groups which are generally known as the Ingrians.

Finnish linguists consider all the languages spoken in Ingria to be merely dialects of Finnish. (To be sure, there is some controversy among them concerning the Izhor language or, as they call it, the Ingeroinen dialect.) Estonian linguists, on the other hand, consider Izhor (Ingeroinen) to be an independent language. The Izhors, however, call themselves Carelians and their language, Carelian.

The name Ingria derives from the name of a southern tributary of the Neva River which in Finnish and the Ingrian dialects is called Inkere and in Russian—Izhora. Accordingly, the dialect is called either Inkeroinen/Ingeroinen (from the Finnish variant) or Izhor (from the Russian variant). The valley of the Inkere River is considered to be the original area of habitation of the Izhors (the speakers of the Inkeroinen/Ingeroinen/Izhor dialect).

A. Population and Geography

Ingria (Ingermanland), the historic territory of the Ingrians is now a part of the Leningrad *Oblast* in the RSFSR. It encompasses the stretch of land on the southern coast of the Gulf of Finland from Narva to Leningrad. It is a relatively low-lying area, with a coastline of about 150 km, with many forests, bays, and river valleys. Historically, the borders of Ingria stretched from the Narva River to Lake Ladoga, including the area on both sides of the Neva. Leningrad, formerly St. Petersburg (and Petrograd), is a relative newcomer in the area having been founded among Finno-Ugric villages in the year 1703. In earlier times the area was home to the Balto-Finns until, in the sixth and seventh centuries, the Slavs reached the same latitudes and became the immediate neighbors of the indigenous Finno-Ugric population.

The Izhors are on the verge of extinction. In the All-Union census of 1959 their number was given as approximately 1,100. In the next (1970) census they were not even mentioned. The number of Izhors is given as 1,000 in the Estonian Soviet Encyclopedia. According to Arvo Laanest, their number was 800 in 1970.[11] And in Lallukka's summary of the latest (1979) census, the number of Izhors is given as 700.[12] From the same sources it also is apparent that the percentage of Izhors considering Izhor (Ingeroinen) as their native language is the lowest among Soviet Finno-Ugrians (32.6 percent).

Linguistic statistics of minority peoples is something that the Soviet central authorities very rarely disclose in sufficient detail. Nonetheless, quite detailed information concerning the Balto-Finnic population of Ingria exists from the time of czarist Russia. According to the census that was carried out in 1848, there were at that time in Ingria 17,800 Izhors, 29,344 Äyrämöis, 42,979 Savokkos, and 5,148 Votes, altogether approximately 100,000 individuals from various Balto-Finnic groups. According to the Finnish scholar, Professor Honko, there were 200,000 Balto-Finns in Ingria just before the Revolution in 1917.[13] According to *Iso Tietosanakirja* (the Great Finnish Encyclopedia), in the 1930s approximately 20,000 speakers of the Ingeroinen dialect lived in 130 Ingrian villages (which, in comparison with the 1848 data, is an increase of over 2,000). The periodical *Inkeriläisten Viesti* (The Ingrians' News),[14] which is published in Finland, estimated that the number of Balto-Finns in Ingria during the period of German occupation (1941–1944) was approximately 100,000. The decline as compared to the figures before the Revolution can be explained by Russification, deportation, and imprisonment during the interwar years and just prior to the last war. Only during the period of 1929–1931 (the initial stage of collectivization), 4,000 Ingrian families or altogether 18,000 Ingrians were deported. At the time news of this created a sensation in Finland. In April 1935 another 7,000 individuals were deported and in May to July 1936 all of the parishes of Northern Ingria were emptied of people, affecting altogether 50,000 individuals. The preponderance of these people were shipped to the areas between the Yenisei and Lena rivers, some to Sakhalin and some to the mining areas of the Kola Peninsula. News of these deportations again caused unrest and protests in Finland.

The First World War inflicted huge losses in human lives on the Balto-Finnic groups of Ingria, and the Second World War was an absolute catastrophe for them. Thousands died of starvation and diseases or were killed, as Ingria represented the immediate scene of the siege of Leningrad by the Germans. According to Lauri Honko and another authoritative work on Ingria 65,000 Ingrians managed to escape to Finland during the last war.[15]

The last boatload of Ingrians had scarcely arrived when Finland was forced to sue for peace, which meant, among other things, the repatriation of the Ingrian evacuees. Under the terms of the peace treaty, 55,000 Ingrians were repatriated from Finland after the war. However, before the repatriation, 5,000 of them escaped to Sweden, where they now live scattered throughout the country. The Ingrians constituted the majority of the soldiers of the Brother Battalion, whom Finland was forced to surrender to the Soviet Union. Just before their repatriation some of them managed to escape to Sweden.[16] A few years after the war, Finland was forced to repatriate even those orphans of Ingrian descent who had been adopted into Finnish families during the war.

The Ingrians repatriated from Finland, contrary to their expectations, were not sent back to their former homes. According to Lauri Honko, a part of those repatriated ended up in the region of the southern Volga and its tributaries, while another part was sent to prison camps in Siberia.[17] Later data indicate that as of 1956 many former Ingrians returned from various parts of the Soviet Union to Estonia where they are now registered as Finns. According to the latest (1979) census, the number of Finns in Estonia is 17,753. In all likelihood the large majority of these Finns are former Ingrians. According to the same census, in the whole of the Soviet Union there are 77,000 Finns. This figure includes the Finns living in Carelia and elsewhere in the Soviet Union, the people who speak Äyrämöinen and Savakko dialects, and probably also some Izhors.

By forbidding the Ingrians to return to their former homes the Soviet authorities had, in fact, liquidated them as an ethnic and linguistic entity.

History

As has been mentioned already, the Izhors call themselves Carelians, which shows that they share with the latter their ethnic origins and Old Carelian as the language from which both Carelian and Izhor derived. The same, no doubt, applies also to the ancient history of the Izhors which coincides with that of the Carelians.

After the 1917 Revolution the Izhors attempted to secede from Russia and achieve autonomy. During the Estonian War of Independence two Ingrian battalions were formed, one in Finland and another in Estonia. They were both subordinated to the Estonian commander in chief. The fate of the Ingrians was sealed, however, by the Soviet-Estonian Peace Treaty concluded in Tartu in 1920, according to which only the smaller portion of Western Ingria fell into Estonia. This consisted of the areas around the rivers Rosona and Luga, where a thousand or so Ingrians lived in thirteen villages. The rest of Ingria became an integral part of Soviet Russia. In 1933–1938 the Soviet authorities made an effort to create a written language for the local inhabitants of Ingria. They introduced it into schools and tried to bring it into general usage in that area. This written language was based on Izhor (the Ingeroinen dialect). According to the bibliography compiled by I.A. Selitskaya in Leningrad in 1965,[18] 25 textbooks in the Ingeroinen patois were published in this period for use in Ingrian elementary schools. In 1938 this experiment was abruptly terminated and was followed up by a wave of deportations and arrests which took their toll on the authors of the above textbooks, too. Since the same had happened with the new written languages of the Samis (Lapps), Carelians, and Vepsians it must be assumed that this was a centrally directed action.

Although the Izhorian written language has never been allowed to develop properly, the Ingrians have none the less made in their dialects a very significant contribution to the history of Finno-Ugric culture. The most extensive collection of Finnish folk songs, *Suomen Kansan Vanhat Runot*, devotes a total of nine volumes with 6,500 pages and 45,000 verses to Ingria. Thus Ingria can be considered as a true homeland of Finno-Ugric song. One should also note that many noteworthy authors, scholars, and public figures have risen from among the Ingrian refugees scattered in Finland and Sweden.

Despite their relatively large numbers and territorial compactness, neither the Izhors nor the Ingrian Finns have ever been able to achieve any sort of autonomy to say nothing of more far-reaching self-determination. Their rather unfortunate geographic location has been the cause of the huge tribulations and losses by which this group of Finno-Ugric peoples has been so irreparably damaged. It is doubtful that they will be able to recover from the wounds inflicted upon them and become a viable ethnic entity again. However, if in the future, Finland and Estonia were in the position to provide the Ingrians with adequate help, their remaining communities may be saved and preserved. After all, Finland and Estonia have been traditionally the nations upon whom the Ingrians throughout their history looked as their haven and on whose support in favorable circumstances they could count.

The Votes

The Votes are the nearest relatives of the Estonians. Their original territory lies to the east of Estonia, on the other side of Lake Peipus.

A. Population

The present-day territory of the Votes consists of only a few places in Western Ingria that are incorporated into the Kingisseppa *Rayon* of the Leningrad *Oblast* of the RSFSR. They comprise the former parishes of Kattila, Kaprio, Soikola, and Narvusi. We are dealing here with an extremely small number of people that is inexorably moving toward total extinction in the near future. According to Soviet Estonian scholars, the number of Vote speakers is only a few dozen; Paul Ariste, for example, writes that there were only thirty-five good speakers of Vote left in 1959.[19]

The territorial spread of the Votes was considerably larger in the past, stretching at one time from Eastern and Northeastern Estonia to Lake

Ladoga in the east and reaching all the way to Novgorod in the south. For the greater part, the territory inhabited by the Votes coincided with Ingria. The earliest scientific record of the numbers of Votes comes from the overview by Peter van Köppen in 1848, in which he enumerates thirty-seven villages in Ingria where a total of 5,148 Votes lived. The number of Votes was, however, given in the census of 1917 as 500 and in the census of 1926 as 705 individuals. The Votes were no longer mentioned in the census of 1959.

The decrease in the numbers of Votes in recent times has been caused, on the one hand, by Russification and, on the other, by assimilation with the Estonians, the Finns, and the Ingrians. The deportations of 1929–1931 which affected the Votes as much as the other Finno-Ugric peoples of the area must also be mentioned as an external cause of their decline. The same has to be said of World War II since the home territory of the Votes was the scene of many battles.

B. History

The territory of the Votes, according to the ancient chronicles, formed the northernmost part of eleventh-century Novgorod. In the fourteenth century, when this territory was incorporated into the principality of Moscow, it was called the *"Vodskaya Pyatina"* (the Votic fifth). It formed a large triangle with its head angle pointing to Novgorod from the north, its eastern border running along the Volkhov River to Ladoga, and its western border stretching along the Luga to the Bay of Narva. In the north it encompassed a part of the Carelian Isthmus and of Border Carelia (*Raja Karjala*). In Novgorod itself there was a street called Chud ("Chud" is the Russian generic term for Balto-Finnic people), which went northward.

After the crusaders had conquered Estonia, they often made incursions into Ingria and established there, in 1240, a frontier garrison at Kaprio which was later captured by the Russians. Between 1444–1447 the German Knights of the Teutonic Order were very active in Ingria. During one battle they deported a group of Vote prisoners of war to Courland and settled them near the town of Bauske. The local Latvians called the deported Votes Krevins, a term derived from a pejorative Latvian nickname for the Russians, "krievs." Since these prisoners were brought from Russia the local population assumed them to be a kind of Russians. The last of the Krevins were documented in 1846 when the Finnish linguist Sjögren undertook an expedition to the Bauske area and found there a few individuals who could still speak the language. The Estonian linguist Wiedemann, when launching an expedition in the same area in 1870, was already unable to find any more speakers of the language—by that time the whole Krevin community had been completely Latvianized.[20]

When at the end of the fifteenth century Novgorod was forced to submit to the rule of Moscow, the Votes suffered more deportations. This happened in 1484 and 1488, when masses of Votes were taken into the interior of Russia and settlers were brought from other parts of Russia to replace them. The cause of the deportations may have been Moscow's mistrust of these foreign people. When Moscow in 1617, according to the Peace of Stolbovo concluded that same year, conceded Ingria to Sweden, Votes in large numbers fled to Russia in order to avoid forced conversion to the Lutheran faith by the Swedes. Finns from Lutheran parishes near the border were brought to fill the Vote villages that had been left empty.

The Votes have never had schools in their native language and therefore were easily assimilating with the neighboring peoples—Russians, Finns, Izhors, Estonians, and Latvians. Famines, deportations, and wars have completed the destruction of the Votes as a people. Their territory shrank to a very small piece of land in the northwest corner of Ingria, between the Bay of Narva and the Fortress of Kaprio. Only in two separate villages could speakers of Vote still be found at the time of World War II.

C. Language and Culture

The Votes have never had a written language of their own, but they possess nonetheless a rich folklore and folk art. When in the 1930s the Soviet authorities artificially established written languages for the Carelians, Vepsians, Samis of the Kola Peninsula and the Votes' closest neighbors, the Izhors, the Votes were the only group in this area to be excluded from that experimental linguistic reform.

Although the Votes must be looked upon as a Finno-Ugric people who by now have disappeared forever, they have nonetheless left a clear and concise warning to posterity—a warning about what can happen to small peoples who are surrounded by larger ones. Vote history vividly portrays the chief factors causing the destruction of small ethnic communities. These are: deportations organized by larger neighbors, the replacement of the indigenous population by immigration, and exclusion from receiving an education in the native language. We must conclude from this that in order to protect ethnic minorities one must in the first place safeguard the ethnic integrity of their respective territories.

The Livonians

At the time of the Christianization of the Baltic area (from the beginning of the thirteenth century), the Livonians were among the most significant of the local peoples. The whole territory from the Gulf of Riga right up to the Gulf of Finland in the north bore its name (Livland, Livonia). Only later did this area divide into Latvia and Estonia.

The territory inhabited by the Livonians encompassed the whole coastal region of the Gulf of Riga—the northern march of the eastern coast reached as far as the present Estonian border on the Salatsi River, in the east it stretched to the upper part of the Daugava River, and in the west it went as far as to encompass the present-day Latvian city of Ventspils. The Daugava River and the Gulf of Riga divided the Livonians into two groups—the Livonians of Courland (Couronia) and the Livonians of Livonia proper. In Courland, especially in its northern end, the Livonians were isolated from the Latvians by a protective zone of forests, and consequently they preserved their identity longer. In contrast, the Latvianization of the Livonians of Livonia was accomplished much more rapidly. It is thought that the last Livonians of Livonia died out in the middle of the nineteenth century.

As regards the numbers of Livonians, it is estimated that at the beginning of the period of Christianization (approximately 1186) the Livonian tribe was significantly larger than the Latvian tribes. However, not even an approximate figure can be given. On the other hand, it is quite possible that the number of Livonians was the same or even slightly less than the numbers of the Southern Estonians, the Ugalans, or their nearest neighbours directly across the sea, the people of Saaremaa, who likewise were seafarers and fishermen. The earliest verifiable information about the Livonians comes from Peter von Koeppen, according to whom the total number of Livonians in 1835 was 2,074.[21] Next, T. dePauley mentions the total number of Livonians in Courland in 1862 as being around 2,000.[22] According to Setälä, in 1888 there were in Courland 2,939 Livonians.[23] According to the Latvian census in 1925 there were 1,238 Livonians in Latvia. Lauri Kettunen has estimated the number of Livonians in the 1930s as being around 800–1,000.[24] Most of them lived in the twelve Livonian villages situated along the eastern and western coasts of the Domesnäs Peninsula in Northern Courland. The number of Livonians appear as 200 in the Soviet census of 1959. In the 1970 census the Livonians are no longer mentioned. Nonetheless, Estonian scholars have maintained contact with Livonians up to the present. According to Arvo Laanest, their number was 150 in 1975.[25] It seems that the majority of them live in Riga. The Livonians are the most Europoid of all of the Finno-Ugric peoples.

The period following the First World War is considered to be the period of national awakening for the Livonian people. In independent Estonia and Latvia approximately fifty publications appeared in the Livonian language—calendars, religious literature, and readers. Among them is *Livô lôlôd* by the poet K. Stalte, which was published in Tallinn in 1924 and which is the only collection of poetry in Livonian. Between the years 1931–1939 a hectographed newspaper, *Livli*, was published.

The Livonians, who throughout their history have been subjugated by their bigger neighbors, did not have the opportunity of developing an adequate national self-consciousness and of promoting an educational system in their own language. Their national awakening, accompanied by attempts at creating a separate cultural identity in their own language, came about too late, just before the final catastrophe of the Second World War.

The Sami (Lapps)

In the Soviet Union, to the north of the Balto-Finns, live small groups of Samis (Lapps). They are linguistically related to the Balto-Finns although racially they are not related to them at all.

The Samis inhabit the northern part of the Finno-Scandinavian Peninsula in a territory which stretches in the form of a crescent from Dalarna (Sweden) northward along the Arctic coast through Norway and Finland and out to the eastern end of the Kola Peninsula in the Soviet Union. This territory is about 2,000 km long and its width is estimated to be 150–200 km. The total territory in question covers close to 400,000 km². The Samis occupy pockets of land in the following regions: in Norway—in Tromsa and Finnmark; in Sweden—in Härjedalen, Väster—and Norr-botten; in Finland—in Lapinlääni; and in the Soviet Union—in the Kola Peninsula.

Conflicting data concerning the numbers of the Samis have been presented depending on the criteria used to determine their ethnic affiliation, one of which has often been reindeer-herding as the chief means of livelihood. According to the most recent source, the following figures are considered to be more or less exact: in Finland—4,000; in Sweden—17,000; in Norway—25,000; and in the Soviet Union—2,000; in total—48,000.[26] It must be taken into consideration that of this number only about two-thirds, approximately 32,000, speak Sami as their native language. According to the 1979 Soviet census, only 55 percent of the Kola Samis spoke Sami as their native language.

Racially the Samis belong to the Lapponoid branch of the Uralic race, but there is a marked difference in the racial characteristics of the Western and Eastern Samis. As regards primary anthropological traits the Finnish

Samis have approximately 27 percent Mongoloid traits while the Kola Samis have 39 percent. Thus, while both groups have predominantly Europoid traits, they do not have enough to belong to the Europoid races, which maximally allow about only 20 percent of racial mix.[27]

Divided into splintered groups between four nations, the Samis have never been able to maintain close contacts with one another nor have they been able to establish any sort of administrative organization for themselves. In recent years, however, there have been attempts made in this direction and at least in the three Western countries where they live, there are now Sami central organizations functioning. Their umbrella organization is the *Nordiska Sameradet* (The Northern Sami Council) (est. 1953) which tries to protect the interests of the Swedish, Norwegian, and Finnish Samis. In the last few decades the ethnic identity and self-awareness of these Western Samis has risen quite noticeably.

Among the Kola Samis there are two main dialect groups: these are the Kildin and Tarja dialects. The latter derives its name from the easternmost Sami place named Tarje. In all of the Russian Sami dialects there are copious Slavic loanwords whereas in the western dialects there are relatively few. Russian loans are thought to have started entering the Sami language in the fifteenth century, when the first Orthodox monastery was established in Petsamo and its monks began to proselytize among the Samis. One part of the Russian loanwords has entered the language through Carelian. Literature began to appear in the Kola Sami dialects in 1878 when the Gospel of Matthew appeared in the Kildin dialect. This and later religious literature were all written in the Cyrillic alphabet. In 1933–1937 an attempt was made in the Soviet Union to establish a written language for the Russian Samis, using the Latin alphabet, but the experiment was terminated in 1938, at the same time when similar experiments were terminated with regard to the Izhors, Carelians, and Vepsians.

The small group of Kola Samis are the most assimilated of all the Sami groups. The future of this group is thinkable only in terms of its close association with the Samis of Finland, Sweden, and Norway who freely cooperate with each other across national boundaries and are well advanced on the path of attaining their cultural autonomy.

* * *

Of the six Balto-Finnic ethnic groups in the Soviet Union (the Estonians, Carelians, Vepsians, Izhors, Votes, and Livonians), the four smallest ones have either become totally extinct or are on the verge of extinction precipitated not so much by physical destruction, which has been quite considerable, too, as by linguistic-cultural assimilation with their larger neighbors. Their small numbers also have prevented them from establishing in the course of their long history any sort of national autonomy at even the lowest level, which could have provided them with at least the opportunity of obtaining an education in their native languages.

The above study allows one to conclude that the ability of an ethnic group to survive and to consolidate into a nation directly depends on the number of people of which this ethnic group consists. As the example of the Carelians demonstrates, the critical number allowing for an ethnic group's survival and consolidation even in the adverse conditions of it being ruled by foreigners and surrounded from all sides by more numerous and powerful neighbors, is about 100,000 people.

The Volga-Finnic Peoples and Languages

From the common Volga-Finnic language and tribe that once may have existed, two completely different languages and two peoples, the Mordvins and the Maris (Cheremis), have developed.

The Mordvins

The name Mordvin is actually the common name for two quite distinct groups, the Erza and the Moksha, both of whom have their own written languages.

A. Population and Geography

The Mordvins are the most fragmented of the Finno-Ugric peoples. The territory of the Mordvins consists of larger or smaller pockets of settlements scattered from Central Russia to Siberia and reaching as far as Central Asia. An autonomous province (*oblast*) for the Mordvins was established in 1930 in the territory between the rivers Oka and Volga. In 1934 this autonomous province was reorganized into an autonomous republic (Mordvin ASSR) within the RSFSR, but only 28 percent of the Mordvins live there (approximately 385,000). The territory of the Mordvin autonomous republic covers 26,200 km². The capital is Saransk, with a population of 263,000 (1980). But even in their "own" republic the Mordvins are a minority. In 1979 the total population of the republic was 991,000 of which Mordvins constituted 34.2 percent and Russians 59.8 percent; the remaining 6 percent consisted of Chuvashes, Tatars and other nationalities. The Mordvins living outside the Mordvin ASSR are present in rather large numbers in the Kuibyshev (approx. 115,300), Penza (approx. 109,400), Orenburg (approx. 95,000), Ulyanovsk (approx. 73,000), and Gorki (approx. 63,000) oblasts. According to the 1979 census, there were altogether

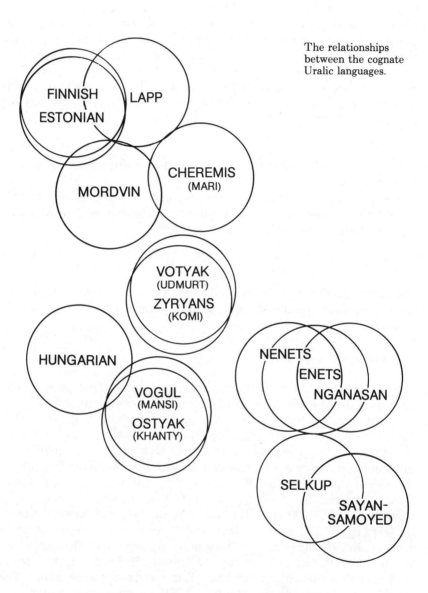

The relationships
between the cognate
Uralic languages.

By Pétér Hajdú from "Ancient Cultures of the Uralian
Peoples", Budapest 1976.

1,191,800 Mordvins of whom 72.6 percent spoke one or the other of the Mordvin languages (Erza or Moksha) as their native language. In 1959 one of these two languages was the native language of 78.1 percent of the Mordvins. Thus, over a period of twenty years there had been a 5.5 percent decrease in native speakers of the Mordvin languages.

In terms of total population figures, the Mordvins, after the Hungarians and Finns, are the third largest Finno-Ugric people in the world. However, as far as the numbers of native speakers are concerned, the Estonians are more numerous than the Mordvins and firmly occupy the third place (in absolute terms there are 855,216 native speakers of Mordvin and 972,199 native speakers of Estonian). Looking at the national statistics, it seems that the number of Mordvins has been steadily decreasing over a long period of time. The Mordvins achieved the maximal level of their population in 1939 when 1,481,000 Mordvins were enumerated. In 1959 this figure was 1,285,000; in 1970, 1,263,000, and most recently 1,191,000. Thus, the decrease over 40 years has been 265,000, or approximately 18 percent. At the same time there has been a decrease in the numbers of native speakers of the language, too.

This decrease is not especially surprising given the scattered distribution of the Mordvins and the events which shaped their history. Rather, one should be surprised at the tenacity with which assimilation has been avoided despite ample conditions favoring it. The fact that the Mordvins are split into two groups, the Erza and the Moksha, is in its own right detrimental to their ethnic well-being and ability to withstand assimilation. The difference between the two languages is as great as the difference between Estonian and Finnish. The Erzas make up approximately two-thirds of the Mordvins, while the Mokshas make up the other one-third. In the Mordvin ASSR Mokshas live predominantly in the western and southern parts of the territory while Erzas inhabit the eastern and northern parts. The infamous Mordvin prison camps of which Potma is best known are located in the territory of the Mokshas (that is, in the western part). Both groups of Mordvins live predominantly in villages where their chief occupation is agriculture as it is practiced in collective farms. The urban population consists mainly of Russians. The percentage of Mordvins in the Mordvin ASSR's urban areas was 16.8 percent in 1970. Mordvin cultural institutions, such as language institutes for both languages, are located in the Mordvin ASSR's capital, Saransk.

In the Gorki (formerly Nizhny-Novgorod) *Oblast* between the Volga and the Oka rivers there are twenty-five villages of Russified Mordvins (altogether 12,000 individuals) called Teryuhans. While they speak Russian, the findings of the Finnish scholar H. Paasonen reveal that here we have a group of former Mordvins whose language still retains many Mordvin elements. Along the Volga River in the Tatar ASSR a separate group called the Karatai live in three villages not far from Kazan. They speak Tatar but linguistic investigation has revealed that these are actually Tatarized Moksha Mordvins.[28]

Not only do the Erza and Moksha Mordvins differ as regards dialect, but they differ anthropologically and to a certain extent culturally as well. The Erza Mordvins are considered to be the nearest relations to the Balto-Finns. The racial traits of the two groups coincide for the greater part. However, according to the findings of Karin Mark, the Erzas belong to the blond Europoid race whereas the Mokshas are more heavily pigmented.[29]

B. History

According to the Hungarian scholar, Gyula Décsy, the following periods can be distinguished in Mordvin history:

1) 700–1236: period of Bolgaro-Turkic influence
2) 1236–1552: period of Tatar domination
3) 1552 to the present: period of Russian domination (Gyula Décsy sees no significant difference in the situation of the Mordvins between the czarist and Soviet periods of Russia's history.)[30]

The Bolgaro-Turkic influence on the Mordvins was limited by the loose contacts the Mordvins maintained with the Volga Bolgar state. Even in this period a bigger threat to the Mordvins came from the Russians who relentlessly tried to achieve dominance over the area. In Nestor's Chronicles it is mentioned that in 1103 Prince Yaroslav of Murom attempted to conquer the Mordvins but was defeated. The Mordvins defended themselves against the continuing onslaughts of the Russians within their walled fortifications. There is documentation that in 1172 the Russians conquered a Mordvin fortress called "Abramov Gorod" which in all likelihood was a center of some local Mordvin tribe. Around the year 1220 the Russians established the town of Nizhny-Novgorod at the mouth of the Oka River which was inhabited by the pagan Mordvins. The Mordvin struggle against the Russians was made difficult by their lack of any strong central administration and the rivalry among the Mordvin tribal leaders. In the northern area the tribal leader was Purgas (an Erza) and in the southern—Puresh (probably a Moksha). Puresh allied himself with the Russians and with their help managed to defeat Purgas. The Russian advance was, however, stopped in 1236 when Russia was conquered by Mongol and Tatar forces. Following this, the lands of the Mordvins fell to the so-called Golden Horde (a Mongol-Tatar Khanate of the thirteenth–fifteenth centuries) and later partly also to the Kazan Khanate.

The Tatars left the economic and social structure of the Mordvins relatively untouched which partly explains the rather peaceful coexistence between the two peoples. In fact Mordvin soldiers participated in the Tatar attacks into Eastern and Central Europe. However, by the fourteenth–fifteenth centuries, the Tatars were no longer able effectively to prevent the Russian encroachment into Mordvin territory. A part of the Mordvins allied themselves with the Russians and fought against the Tatars. When in 1552 Ivan IV (the Terrible) conquered Kazan, the power of the Tatar Khanates over Mordvin territory was finally broken and the area fell under the sway of the Russians. Tatar influence had been greatest in the territory of the Mokshas.

The victory of the Russians in Mordvinia created a solid foundation for further Russian expansion. In order to secure the eastern borders of Russia a series of fortresses were built such as Saransk, Insari, Penza, and others. These developed into Russian administrative centers. At the same time intensive proselytizing was carried out with the use of coercion as well as sheer force. In 1585 the monastery of Pomyshevaya Polyana was established as the center for missionary activities in Mordvinia. Mordvin leaders upon adopting Christianity were admitted into the Russian nobility and were given appropriate economic prerogatives. This of course hastened Russification. Soon the Mordvins began to be heavily taxed and their lands were confiscated by the nobility and clergy. After a time the Mordvin peasants became serfs. Due to these insufferable conditions, the Mordvins began to leave their homes, moving eastward across the Volga. Thus new Mordvin settlements were established in the regions of Ulyanovsk (formerly Simbirsk), Samara (present-day Kuibyshev), Utka, and along the Ingris River right into Siberia. Russian colonists, stimulated by special governmental incentives, replaced the Mordvins on their land. The government's attitude is exemplified by the fact that, for example, in 1737, the tax per head for Mordvins (taxes were paid in wheat) was twice as large as the tax per head for Russians. It is therefore not surprising that the Mordvins often rose in rebellion against Russian rule and also allied themselves with Russian peasant uprisings. They played a prominent part in the Sten'ka Razin (1667–1671) and Pugachev (1773–1775) rebellions as well as in a number of lesser ones. One of the last Mordvin uprisings occurred in the government of Nizhny-Novgorod in 1804. In conjunction with the 1905 Revolution there was very great unrest among the Mordvins too—for instance one-fifth of all of the landed estates in Mordvinian territory were destroyed by the rebellious Mordvins.

The opposition to the Russian colonists limited the influence of Christianity to such an extent that the general mass of Mordvins was converted to that faith only in the eighteenth century. The Mordvins were in actual fact the very last pagans of Europe.

At the end of the czarist period the territory of the Mordvins was so heavily infiltrated by the Russians that many Mordvins lost all hope of maintaining their identity and started to see in complete Russification the only viable solution to the problems of their existence in the Russian Empire.

C. Language and Culture

In the Soviet period separate written languages were created for both Mordvin dialects. According to many scholars (e.g., the Estonian linguist Julius Mägiste), this official and artificial creation of two written languages for the Mordvins represents a typical example of the old policy of *divide et impera* (divide and rule).[31] It cannot be doubted after all that the existence of two written languages for one nation can only foster separation and lead to a further split of an already critically small nation. This appears to be clear to many Soviet scholars as well. The Soviet Estonian linguist E. Päll feels that it largely depends on one's choice whether to refer to languages like Mordvin and Mari (Cheremis) as two written languages or as two forms of one literary language. In his opinion one would refer to the latter if one had sufficient hope that in a given linguistic area there is hope of creating a unified written language, and to the former if there were no such hope any more.[32] The Soviet policy of developing in Mordvinia two separate written languages seems to indicate that the Party was not interested in creating a unified Mordvin nation with a common written language. According to Päll, this is due to the fact that a suitable dialectal base for a unified written language has not been found. However, he refers to the historic unification into one written language of Northern and Southern Estonian, languages which were quite far apart, too, but, given the political will to unite the nation, were successfully driven into becoming mere dialects of one single Estonian language.

Both Mordvin written languages were officially created at a roundtable conference of Mordvin schoolteachers in Moscow in 1925, where it was decided that the basis of the Erza language should be the dialect of Koslovska village in the Atyasheva *Rayon*, and the basis of the Moksha language the dialect of the Krasnoslobodski-Temnikovo *Rayon*. In 1932 the Mordvin Research Institute was established. The chief function of this institute was to develop the Mordvin language. The question of a unified written language was addressed to more than once but in spite of it the Institute worked in full force to establish two separate written languages for the Mordvins. The first conference to discuss the grammar of the two written languages took place in Saransk in 1933. At the second conference, in 1934, terminology and syntax were discussed. At the third, in 1935, the same was continued. A fourth conference was held in 1938 where orthography, morphology and terminology were reviewed. The government of the Mordvin ASSR formally ratified the decisions of this conference on 28 April 1938. Thus both Mordvin written languages are in their entirety the result of conferences. It should also be noted that the Cyrillic alphabet was adopted for the Mordvin languages. This is contemporaneous with the time of termination of the short-lived experiment of introducing the Latin alphabet for the written languages of the Balto-Finnic peoples.

The two Mordvin languages are different as regards the strata of their loanwords. Russian loanwords started to enter the Moksha language before they entered the Erza language. As a result, there were differences in the older Russian loans as they were adapted to the local Mordvin sound systems. Older Russian loanwords are estimated at around 120. Today the newer Russian loans have become the dominant layer of loans in both languages. These are thought to number around 500. Loanwords that refer to concepts of the Soviet period have entered the Mordvin languages without any significant phonological changes. The result is a larger degree of Russification in the modern usage of the Mordvin languages.

The original and copious folklore of the Mordvins has captivated scholars, especially the Finnish ones. Beside the original Finno-Ugric elements there are in it many Russian elements expressed at their best in the syllable structure. The most comprehensive publication of Mordvin folk songs was collected and published in eight volumes by Heikki A. Paasonen and Paavo Ravila during the years 1938–1981.[33]

The beginning of modern literature in Mordvin is associated with the period between 1921–1926, when it began to germinate in the pages of, and around, the Erza language newspaper, *Jakstere Sokistja* (The Red Field Worker). It has proliferated since. Julius Mägiste, who has followed Mordvin literature enthusiastically and avidly, states, however, that "Mordvin literature is typically soviet," which means that it is permeated by Party propaganda.[34] Mägiste, whose review of Mordvin literature extends to 1956, feels that in Erza literary works there are more elements in keeping with the Mordvin spirit than in Moksha works. He has found in both written languages a great deal of Russian words as well as new loanwords which have not in any likelihood been readily adopted in the spoken language. According to the journal *Druzhba Narodov* (The Friendship of Peoples) (November 1957), 257 literary titles appeared in the Mordvin languages between the years 1918 and 1956. According to newer sources, twenty-two newspapers are published in the Mordvin ASSR of which only two are in the Mordvin languages. There are likewise in these languages only two journals dealing with cultural matters—*Syatko* (Spark) in Erza, and *Moksha* in Moksha. Both have a very heavy political content. Over the last decades, however, Mordvin belletristics has become more lively both in the poetry and prose areas.

*   *   *

The Mordvins are a large enough people with a unique culture of their own which, given the opportunity, would be able and willing to form a nation-state either fully independent from, or at least genuinely autonomous in regard to, the colonial powers. This would in all likelihood not only stop the present tendencies toward assimilation but reverse them into a tendency of re-Mordvinization of both the Mordvins who are currently being Russified and of Mordvinia as a territorial entity.

The Maris (Cheremis)*

A people called Imiscaris-Sremniscars mentioned in Jordanes Chronicle in 551 is thought to refer to the Maris as well as to some other Finno-Ugric people living in their neighborhood.

The original territory of the Maris has been the area around the Middle Volga between the Vyatka and Vetluga rivers, to the northeast of the territory of the Mordvins. This territory is now within the RSFSR and since 1936 has enjoyed the status of an autonomous republic—the Mari ASSR. Scarcely one half of the total number of Maris live within their ASSR (23,200 km^2). According to the 1979 census, the population of the Mari autonomous republic was 703,000, with a population density of 30/km^2. Of this population 43.5 percent were Maris, 47.5 percent were Russians, and 9 percent Tatars, Chuvashes, and other minorities. The Maris are settled mainly in villages, while the Russians live in the cities. The Maris live also in the Bashkir ASSR as well as in the Tatar and Udmurt ASSRs;

---

*Cheremis is a name which the Maris themselves do not use (nor have they ever done so). This name has entered other languages through the old Russian form *Cheremisy* which appeared for the first time in Nestor's Chronicle. The name Cheremis was officially dropped in Russian usage in 1936 when the Mari ASSR was established. (Prior to this, as of 1920, the area had been the Cheremis Autonomous *Oblast.*) In Western Finno-Ugric studies, however, the name Cheremis is the one which has predominantly remained in use with a few authors (e.g., the present writer) adding in parentheses alongside it the name Mari. Bearing in mind that this book is addressed not specifically to the students of Finno-Ugric but to a mainly lay audience of people interested in the Soviet Union as a whole, the editors decided to avoid confusion, between the official name of the national territorial unit and its people, by consistently using the name Mari for both.

they are scattered in various other areas, too. The Mari settlements (as well as their dialects) are divided into three main groups: the Hill Maris in the west, on the highlands south of the Volga; the Meadow Maris on the lowlands, north of the Volga; and the Eastern Maris who are separated from the other two groups since they live in Bashkiria, where they settled in the seventeenth and eighteenth centuries. In 1959 there were almost 100,000 Maris in that area.

According to the statistics provided by the 1979 census, there were in the USSR altogether 622,000 Maris of whom 86.8 percent spoke Mari as their native language. Among Soviet Finno-Ugric peoples they rank second to the Estonians in maintaining their own language. A strong sense of national identity and the relatively compact territory of their habitation has resulted in the Maris being one of the few Finno-Ugric peoples in the Soviet Union to show real growth and to preserve well their native language (although there is in this respect a slight decrease; if, according to the 1959 census, 91.2 percent of Maris spoke Mari as their native language, in 1979 only 86.8 percent of them did so). The statistics provided by the census conducted in the czarist period, in 1899, indicated that there were in Russia 366,033 Maris; the 1939 census gave that figure as 481,300; the 1959 census—504,000; and the 1970 census—598,600.

The Maris' chief occupation is agriculture with the largest part of their activity within the collective-farm system being devoted to animal husbandry and agriculture. The largest properly agricultural areas are located in the northeastern part of their territory where wheat, rye, barley, buckwheat, linen, hemp, potatoes, and hops are cultivated. The Maris are the largest hop growers in the Soviet Union.

The capital of the Mari Autonomous SSR is Yoshkar-Ola (formerly Tsarevokokshaysk), with a population of 201,000 (1979), the majority of whom are Russians. The Mari Research Institute for the Sciences, established in 1930, is located there. At the institute language, literature, ethnography, and history are studied. The folk art of the Maris is especially prized for the embroidery with which the women embellish their clothes. The wood carvings and old wooden architecture of the Mari menfolk is also outstanding.

Anthropologically the Maris are comparable to the Moksha Mordvins with perhaps slightly stronger Mongoloid tendencies and a shorter stature. According to Karin Mark's measurements, the index of Mongoloid traits for the Maris is 41–42, which is equal to about a 20–25 percent Mongoloid mixture.[35]

According to Décsy,[36] Mari history can be periodized in the same way as Mordvin history:

1) 700–1236: Bolgar-Turkic period of domination
2) 1236–1552: Mongol-Tatar period of domination
3) 1552–present: Russian period of domination

It is also in substance very similar to Mordvin history. The Mari areas which had formerly belonged to the Khanate of Kazan were annexed into the Russian czarist state. As was the case with the Mordvins, so here too the indigenous nobility upon its conversion to Christianity was accepted into the Russian nobility. The result was a hastening of Russification. In order to safeguard the new southeastern borders of the empire a number of Russian garrison towns were established in the Mari territory, such as Urzhum, Yaransk, Kukarka, Tsarevokokshaysk (the precursor to the present-day capital, Yoshkar-Ola), and others. On the Mari land many Russian peasants were newly settled, and a lot of it was given to monasteries established for proselytizing Orthodox Christianity among the Maris. Special "Cheremis regiments" were formed in the czar's army following the Tatar example. In the Livonian-Russian War of 1558–1561 and in Russia's wars against Poland the Cheremis cavalry was an especially feared component of the Russian army.

The Mari peasants, whom the new Russian masters submitted to the yoke of serfdom, took part, as the Mordvins had done, in very many uprisings. Under Catherine II waves of Mari emigration to the east took place, especially to the area around Ufa. Thus the Eastern Mari settlements in Bashkiria were established, far removed from the Maris' original territory but closer to the Permian and the more distant Uralic proto-homeland. Forced Christianization, which was strongly resisted, was also one of the factors motivating Mari emigration.

After the October Revolution, the Cheremis Autonomous *Oblast* was established on 4 November 1920; on 5 December 1936, it was reorganized into the Mari ASSR.

C. Language and Culture

Linguistically the Maris belong to the Volga-Finnic group. Their nearest neighbors are the Mordvins, who live in the same general area, and the Permian-Finns, who are situated to the east and northeast of the Maris. Three very distinct dialects exist: Meadow, Hill and Eastern Mari. As is the case with Mordvin, the Mari language has a basic underlying stratum of ancient Finno-Ugric vocabulary. There are a number of old Indo-European loanwords as well. Of the other strata of loans, the oldest are the Chuvash (Volga-Bolgar) loans followed by Tatar loans. It is estimated that there are up to 1,200 Russian loanwords which first, from 1446, appeared in Hill Mari (i.e., when the Hill Maris allied themselves with the Russians against the Khanate of Kazan). The older loanwords have been adapted into the Mari sound system and earlier stress system. The later loans have been taken unchanged into the language. Budenz in 1865 estimated the number of Russian loans to be 370.[37] Thus the largest influx of Russian loans has occurred in the last 120 years. Eastern Maris have the least number of Russian loans.

The beginnings of the Mari written language are relatively late. The first Mari (Cheremis, as in the book's title) grammar (by an unknown author) appeared in Russian in St. Petersburg as early as 1775, but while it did have a certain significance from the linguistic point of view, it did very little to alleviate illiteracy among the Maris. Today research in the Mari language is chiefly carried out at the Mari Research Institute established in Yoshkar-Ola.

Right from the beginning the Mari written language has used the Cyrillic alphabet. In the nineteenth century some symbols were added which represented sounds that Russian did not have (ö, ü, ä, ng). It is, however, little known that the Mari, too, have two distinctly different written languages which became established after years of debate and discussion at the language conference in 1937. There it was concluded that it was not possible to find a common base for the two main Mari dialects—Meadow and Hill Mari—and that two written languages had already been developing. The decision to create two different languages for the Maris produced catalyzing conditions for splitting the Maris into two parts, which, of course, put the survival of such a small people at great risk.

The folklore of the Maris is rich and interesting. There are songs, fairy tales, riddles, and proverbs. In the more eastern areas a certain Tatar influence is felt. Mari pre-Soviet literature has been very modest, consisting for the most part of translated religious works (the first translations of the New Testament in the Hill dialect appeared in 1821 and 1827), school books, books on medicine, and almanacs. The only original Mari writer of that period is S. Chavain (1882–1942). The Soviet sources say that "his literary output was disrupted by the 'personality cult.' "

Today twenty-nine newspapers are published in the Mari ASSR, of which fifteen are in Mari, e.g., the main Party official newspaper, *Mari Kommuna* (The Mari Commune). The Mari Writers' Union publishes a literary journal in Mari, *Onchyko* (Forward). After 1917, the publishing of original literature intensified—an estimated three hundred titles were published up to 1965.

*   *   *

In addition to the Mordvins and Maris two other groups of Finno-Ugric peoples, the Muromas and the Merjas, belonged to the Volga-Finnic branch. They lived to the northwest of the others, i.e., in the territory between those of the Volga- and Balto-Finns. Information about them is to be found in the Russian chronicles as late as 1000 A.D. Their extinction was brought about by a linguistic assimilation with the surrounding Russians.

The Mordvins and Maris together form the largest group of ethnic Finno-Ugrians in the Soviet Union. Both are modern, nationally self-aware peoples with a well-developed culture. Nonetheless, there are a few differences between the two. The Maris have demonstrated by their firm language retention that their national self-awareness is higher than that of the Mordvins. A similar difference exists with regard to their respective demographic situations. It seems that the demographic and linguistic-cultural aspects of an ethnic group are mutually interdependent. The more compact and numerous the ethnic society the less vulnerable to linguistic-cultural assimilation it is. The geographic scattering of the Mordvins is their "Achilles' heel" while at the same time the compact nature of the Maris' settlements works to their advantage. An even more negative factor consists in the Mordvins being a minority (28 percent) in their own territory (the Mordvin ASSR), whereas the number of Maris in their territory (the Mari ASSR) is more or less equal to the number of Russians (43.5 percent Maris to 47.5 percent Russians).

Both the Mordvins and Maris are, however, sufficiently large and self-aware peoples for being able and willing to claim their independence or at least total and realistic autonomy from Russia. This is for them a vitally important claim for only under independent or truly autonomous conditions of existence can they hope to preserve in the long run their ethnic identity and integrity. Furthermore, the establishment of such conditions should create a powerful incentive for the Mordvins and the Maris to migrate back from the areas of their present diaspora to their respective national homelands (in just the same way in which large numbers of Estonians scattered around Russia returned to Estonia after she, during 1918–1920, gained independence). On the other hand, the conditions of true independence or autonomy, under which the prerogative of decision making would be concentrated in the hands of the representatives of the indigenous population, might cause a large Russian emigration from these areas (especially those Russians who were established there in administrative positions would be likely to leave), which would also contribute to the ethnic consolidation of both the Mordvins and the Maris. The independent or autonomous national administrations could then take the necessary steps for unifying the many artificially created written languages into one unified written language for every nation (as, again, happened in Estonia where the two written languages that had existed for hundreds of years were united in the eighteenth century into one written language which immensely strengthened the Estonians' ethnic identity and integrity and allowed them to develop into a full-fledged modern nation). Considering the specific traits of the phonetic system of the Finno-Ugric languages, which makes them so vastly different from the Slavic languages, it would be expedient for the Mordvins and Maris to abandon the Cyrillic and introduce the Latin alphabet. This would create an additional barrier against Russification and bring these peoples into closer contact with the better-established Finno-Ugric peoples.

The Permian-Finnic Peoples and Languages

Two peoples are the descendants of this once unified language. They are the Komis (Zyryans) and Udmurts (Votyaks). Geographically they occupy a territory which to a great extent coincides with the territory of the proto-homeland of the Finno-Ugric peoples.

The Komis (Zyryans)*

The Komis (Zyryans) actually consist of two ethnic groups, the Komis proper, and the Komi-Permyaks, or just Permyaks. On the basis of geographic distribution they could also be called the Northern and Southern Komis respectively.

A. Population and Geography

The territory of the Komis is situated in the northeastern corner of Europe, along the western foothills of the Ural Mountains and the Arctic coast. In the west the Komis scatter on to the Kola Peninsula and the regions around Arkhangel, and in the east on to the other side of the Urals where they

---

*The name Zyryan derives from the language of their neighbours, the Mansis (Voguls), who call them Saran. Through the intermediary of Russian this name has been taken into other languages. The old name Permyak has been retained by the Komi-Permyaks and it is derived from the place name Perm (the province and the city). The present-day self-designation, Komi, means "human being." In Western Finno-Ugric studies, however, the name Zyryan continues to be used for designating Komi in the same way as Cheremis is used to designate Mari. As in that latter case, it was also here the editors' decision to break with this established Western scholarly tradition and, in the interests of the lay readers, to use the name Komi consistently for both the national-territorial unit and its people.

live among their Ugric relatives, the Mansis (Voguls) and Khantys (Ostyaks). Their central and original territory is the basin of the Vychegda,
Pechora and Izhma rivers, all of which flow into the Arctic Ocean. The
southern group of the Komis, the Permyaks, have inhabited the valley
between the Kama and the Vyatka rivers since prehistorical times.

The Komis are among the most successful of the Finno-Ugric peoples
in the Soviet Union; their number has been increasing at a steady rate. In
1835, 123,169 Komis were enumerated. In 1897 this figure had increased
to 258,336. According to the 1926 Soviet census, there were 375,700 of
them (with both groups being counted together). The figure in the 1939
census was 422,300, and in the 1970 census—475,500, of which 153,500
were Permyaks. According to the 1970 census, 84.2 percent of the Komis
considered Komi to be their native language. The latest, 1979 census,
indicates that there were 477,500 Komis living in the USSR of which
150,800 were Permyaks. Thus, the latter group has shown a slight decrease
while the former has shown a comparable increase. In this latest census,
77.1 percent of the Komis considered Komi to be their native language,
while the percentage for the Komis proper was 76.2 percent. Thus, the
position of the Komi language as native to the Komis has weakened by 7–
8 percent over the last decade.

The whole large territory of the Komis lies within the RSFSR and is
divided into two administrative units. The first is the present-day Komi
ASSR (established in 1936) where the majority of the Komis proper live,
and the other—the Komi-Permyak Autonomous *Okrug* (Region) where
the majority of the Permyaks live. The Komi ASSR is, in relation to its
population, an immense territory encompassing 415,900 km^2 and is thus
only a little bit smaller than Sweden (438,000 km^2). The northern part of
this territory is covered by perpetually frozen tundra, the central part by
taiga, and the southern part by massive mixed forests. The climate is
continental.

According to the 1970 census, the population of the Komi ASSR was
965,000 with a density of 2.3/km^2. In that same year Komis formed 28.6
percent of that population, Russians—53.1 percent, Ukrainians—8.6 percent, and Belorussians—2.6 percent. The demographic picture for the same
region was altogether different in 1939. Then, of the total population (approximately 318,900), 70 percent (223,000) were Komis. During and after
the Second World War the population of the territory literally exploded
(there has been an increase of 300 percent) and, at the same time, the
demographic pattern has changed radically with the Russians, formerly a
minority, having become the completely dominant majority.

This sharp and profound change was the result not only of political but
also of economic developments. The Komi ASSR is a part of the chain of

prison camps which Solzhenitsyn introduced to the world by the name of the "Gulag Archipelago." During the Second World War and in the years following it, prison and forced-labor camps were set up in this area in numbers the likes of which had never been seen before. Here were to be found the notorious camps of Kotlas, Inta, Ukhta, Vorkuta, and others, some of which are today well-established cities. Using the cheap labor force of the prisoners, the central authorities began to exploit the territory's natural resources such as coal, oil, natural gas, and the enormous wealth of forest and timber. The same work force was used in 1941–1945 to build the railroad from Kotlas to Pechora, and, during 1945–1960, another one to Vorkuta and on to Labytnangi. These projects, as evidenced by Solzhenitsyn, cost millions of human lives and also changed the local demographic structure. First of all the network of prison and forced-labor camps required an administrative structure as well as managers and specialists to man the industries that were to be built. These were mainly imported to Komi ASSR from the outside regions of Russia and were predominantly Russians.

The capital of the Komi ASSR is Syktyvkar (formerly Ust'-Syssol'sk), a town which was established at the end of the sixteenth century. In 1979 the city's population was 171,000. The river harbor of Syssola as well as a logging central and factories manufacturing forest products are all located within the city. The local university is relatively young: it was established in 1972. The population of the capital has grown as rapidly as the infrastructure of the whole region and here, too, Russians form the majority. Other larger cities in the Komi ASSR are Vorkuta (population 100,000 in 1979), Inta (51,000 in 1969), Ukhta (76,000 in 1975), and Pechora (38,000 in 1970). Of these the infamous Vorkuta lies on the northern edge of the Komi ASSR, 160 km to the north of the Arctic Circle. A settlement was established here in 1931 and was given city status in 1943. This is a center for coal mining and forestry, and in the camps in the surrounding areas, hundreds of thousands of political prisoners still could be found as late as in 1955. The same goes for Inta. Ukhta is a center for the production of oil and natural gas, while Pechora is a center for the forestry industry and the location of a river port on the Pechora River.

Of the population of the Komi ASSR 62 percent live in cities but only 15.3 percent of them are Komis (1970). The main occupation of the Komis is agriculture which produces chiefly oat, barley and potatoes—crops with a short growing period. Animals—oxen, pigs, goats and sheep—are also raised. Additional occupations are trapping and fishing. In recent times the Komis proper were introduced to reindeer herding which they learned from their northern neighbors, the Samoyeds.

A major part of the Komi-Permyaks, the southern group of the Komis, lives in the Komi-Permyak Autonomous *Okrug*. It is 32,900 km² large and located in the upper regions of the Kama River. Komi-Permyaks formed 58 percent of the population of the Autonomous *Okrug* (1959), the capital of which is Kudymkar (26,000 inhabitants in 1970). Kudymkar is located on the banks of the Inva River, one of the tributaries of the Kama. This is one of the few areas where the Russian population has decreased over the past few years. According to the 1979 census, Russians formed only 34.7 percent of the population of the Komi-Permyak Autonomous *Okrug*, whereas according to the previous census (1970) they formed 36 percent. The percentage of other nationalities in 1979 was 3.9 percent whereas in 1970 it was 5.7 percent. Thus the number of Komi-Permyaks has increased to 61.4 percent in the area, but at the same time the use by them of their native language has decreased to 77.1 percent (according to the 1959 census it was 87.1 percent). In addition to the two groups already mentioned (the Komis proper and the Komi-Permyaks), there is a third distinct group of Komis living in the region around the Yazva River and therefore called Yazva Komis. They number 4,000.

According to K. Mark, the Komis are anthropologically more Europoid than, for instance, the Maris. They display a weaker mixture of Mongoloid features with a Mongoloid index of 26–43.[38]

The earliest evidence of settlements comes from the Paleolithic age. The region has been home to the speakers of the Permian branch of Finno-Ugric languages presumably since 3,000–2,000 B.C. The first written documents attesting to the Permians, ancestors of the Komis, come from the Russian chronicles of the eleventh and twelfth centuries. The Komis began to move northward from their original area of settlement around the seventh century. According to the Russian chronicles, the Komis had already reached the area of the Vychegda River by the eleventh century, and by the fourteenth century they were settling in the region around present-day Kotlas. The forefathers of the Komis were successful merchants who, along the northwestern trade route, established contacts with the forefathers of the Vepsians and Carelians. Concrete proof of these contacts are Vepsian loan-words in the idiom of the North-Western Komis. Very soon, however, the Komis were separated from the Vepsians and Carelians by a wedge of Russians who came from the southwest and colonized the area stretching between them. In Novgorod and Rostov the Komis were constantly trading with the Russians already in the twelfth and thirteenth centuries. They were paying tribute to Novgorod between the twelfth and fourteenth centuries. Later the influence of the Principality of Moscow strengthened and in 1478 the land of the Komis was annexed by it.

Christianization of the Komis was one of the major tasks undertaken by their Muscovite rulers. In this Bishop St. Stepan (called Stepan of Perm in Soviet sources) played a significant role. In 1383 Moscow named this successful missionary the bishop of Old Permia, i.e., the region around the Vychegda River and its tributaries. His seat was in Ustvym. The success of his activities was based in part on his phenomenal knowledge of the Komi language for which he created the first alphabet (the so-called Abur alphabet). After Bishop St. Stepan's death, Moscow continued to name his successors even though the territory belonged to Novgorod until 1471.

With the advent of Christianity a large part of the land was given to the Orthodox church and to the Russian nobility. Simultaneously Moscow took away the freedoms of the Komis. In 1558 Moscow presented huge areas of land on both sides of the Kama River to a salt manufacturer, Stroganov, who established the town of Sol'vychegodsk there. As a result of this a large part of the Southern Komis became serfs.

During the Russian Civil War there was intense opposition to the Bolsheviks in the Komi territory. In August 1918 Soviet power was toppled by local people in Mezin and in Pechora, and by November 1919 the Russian Whites had taken control over large parts of the present-day Komi ASSR. The Reds were able to win back the territory only in March 1920. An autonomous *Oblast* was formed for the Komis on 22 August 1921, which in 1936 was reorganized into the Komi ASSR.

C. Language and Culture

Komi, together with its closest relative, Udmurt, belongs to the Permian branch of the Finno-Ugric language family. Both of these diverged from the Permian protolanguage in about 3,000–2,000 B.C. The Komi branch has two main dialect subbranches, the Northern and Southern, or, in Soviet terminology, Komi-Zyryan and Komi-Permyak. Both these branches of Komi have many subdialects. As in the cases of Mordvin and Mari, the Soviet authorities found it expedient to create two separate written languages for the Komis. Both use the Cyrillic alphabet which has been supplemented by some symbols for sounds that are lacking in the Slavic languages. In the 1930s, for a short period, the Latin alphabet was introduced, but soon afterward, as everywhere else, it was replaced again by the Cyrillic alphabet.

Komi, after Hungarian, is the second Finno-Ugric language to have written documents dating from the fourteenth century. They are in the alphabet created by St. Stepan of Perm, which was used by the Komis between the fourteenth and seventeenth centuries but later fell into disuse.

It is estimated that there are approximately 1,000 words of Finno-Ugric origin in Komi. Other loans are: the oldest and rarest ones from Iranian and Volga-Bolgar (Chuvash), and the largest and newest ones—from Russian, adapted to fit the Komi sound system. According to some Estonian linguists, the Komi newspapers are so full of Russian words that a Russian with very little knowledge of Komi can still understand them.

Today the center for studying the Komi language is at the Komi Research Institute established in Syktyvkar in 1930. Here, in addition to linguistics, Komi history, literature, folklore and archeology are studied, too.

The folk poetry of the Komis is predominantly lyrical. Epic songs are much fewer. The classic author of Komi literature is I. Kuratov (1838–1875). Because of the pressures from Russian censors, the publication of his works during his lifetime was selective. In addition to writing his original works, he translated many classical texts of world literature into Komi. A solid foundation for Komi professional prose and poetry was already laid before the First World War.

With the establishment of the Soviet regime the possibilities for literary activity opened up quite widely, and better outlets for publishing were provided. But in exchange for this a political forfeit had to be paid, which in its broad outline was the same as in the cases of Mordvin and Mari literatures.

In the Komi ASSR, twenty newspapers are published of which only four are in the Komi language (1970).

* * *

Both groups of the Komis have demonstrated a remarkable vitality and ability to resist assimilation despite the influx of large numbers of foreigners into their huge territory. As is the case with the Mordvins and Maris, in the long run the possibility for the Komis to survive as a separate people depends on their achieving independence or at least authentic autonomy. Theirs is a sufficiently large and strongly self-aware ethnic entity for putting, in favorable conditions, a claim to this effect with due force.

The Udmurts (Votyaks)*

The Udmurts (Votyaks) are the Permian-Finnic people living in the northeast corner of the European part of the Soviet Union. Udmurt means "people of the meadows."

*Votyaks is the name which was given to the Udmurts by the Russians and which has thus spread into other languages. As in the cases of Mari (Cheremis) and Komi (Zyryan), the name Votyak is the one the Western Finno-Ugric scholars continue to use to designate Udmurt. Here too, the editors have reversed the traditional Western scholarly ways and, for the same reasons and in the same way as they did with regard to the Mari and Komi, are naming the people, the present writer deals with in this section, Udmurt.

A. Population and Geography

The main territory of the Udmurts is the hilly plateau stretching westward of the foothills of the Ural Mountains and encompassing the areas situated between the Vyatka and Kama rivers in the basin of the Volga. About 47 percent of the whole region is covered by forests. Many scholars consider this territory to be the heartland of the protohomeland of the Finno-Ugric peoples. The Udmurts thus appear to be the only Finno-Ugric people that refused to wander away and who stayed on right to the present time in the territory of their protohomeland.

For the most part the actual territory of the Udmurts coincides with the territory of the Udmurt ASSR which is 42,100 km^2 large. The average density of the population is 34.1 persons per km^2. Outside their ASSR there are Udmurts scattered in the Perm and Kirov (former Vyatka) *Oblasts* and in the Bashkir and Tatar ASSRs. According to the 1979 census, there were 713,000 Udmurts of whom 76.4 percent considered Udmurt to be their native language. In the previous census (1970) 704,300 Udmurts were enumerated of whom 82.6 percent considered Udmurt to be their native language. In the 1959 census the percentage of Udmurts who considered Udmurt to be their native language had been yet a bit higher—89.1 percent. As in the case of the Komis, the Udmurts have experienced growth in population but a decrease in retention of the native language.

According to the 1979 census, the population of the Udmurt ASSR was 1,494,000. Of these 32.3 percent were Udmurts, 58.3 percent Russians and the rest other nationalities (Tatars, Chuvashes, Maris, etc.). In 1939 the indigenous people there formed 52 percent of the population, 43 percent were Russians, and 5 percent were other nationalities. As in the Mari ASSR, here too the majority people have become a minority with the immigrant Russians becoming the majority. Approximately 24 percent of all the Udmurts live outside the territory of the Udmurt ASSR. In 1970 there were 30,600 of them in the Perm *Oblast*, 27,900 in the Bashkir ASSR, 24,500 in the Tatar ASSR and 29,400 in the Kirov *Oblast*.

A distinct group in the northern part of the Udmurt ASSR, around Glazov, are the Bessermans of whom it is estimated there are 10,000. Some scholars consider them to be Udmurt-assimilated Tatars but others think that they are Volga-Bolgars (Chuvashes) who have changed their national identity to that of Udmurt.

The main occupation of the Udmurts is agriculture now practiced in the form of collective farms. Today the main crops consist of rye, barley, and, more recently, of wheat, but a very prominent part traditionally belongs to apiculture. The natural resources of the territory are iron, oil, coal, and lignite.

The capital of the territory is Izhevsk (recently renamed Ustinov) with a population of 549,000 (1979). This city, which is located on the shores of the Izha River (a tributary of the Kama), grew around an iron foundry established in 1760. The next largest centers are Glazov, Votkinsk, Sarapul, Kambarka, and Mozhga. Only 16.9 percent of the Udmurts live in cities (1970) where Russians form 71.4 percent of the population. The proportion of Russians and Udmurts is reversed in the rural areas.

Anthropologically the majority of Udmurts are more Europoid than, for instance, the Maris. According to K. Mark, their Mongoloid index wavers between 34–39 corresponding to a 25 percent Mongoloid mix[39] (the index of the Maris is 41–52). Close to 80 percent of the Udmurts are blond but at the same time they are short in stature: the average height of a man is 162cm. Among the Udmurts living in the southeastern parts of the territory there are stronger Mongoloid traits. The Mongoloid index of the Bessermans in the north is 32–33 which indicates that they are more Europoid than the other Udmurts. This speaks against them being originally a Tatar group and confirms the theory according to which they are the descendants of Volga-Bolgars.

B. History

The historic fate of the Udmurts is in many ways similar to that of the Volga-Finns (the Mordvins and the Maris) and therefore the periodization of their history could be equally applied to the Udmurts. From the eighth–ninth century to 1236 they belonged to the Volga-Bolgar tribal confederation. Numerous Volga-Bolgar (Chuvash) loanwords attest to the strong influence that the Bolgar contacts had on agriculture, architecture, and the social fabric. The profound Bolgar-Turkic influence on their culture is one of the most important features which distinguishes the Udmurts from the Komis, who, having retreated to the north, were in the periphery of that influence.

The Russians started to infiltrate into the territory of the Udmurts from the 11th century onward. Their aim was to establish a separate Vyatkan state there. Formally the territory was declared a part of the Principality of Moscow but in reality Moscow was able to take it over only after Ivan IV had conquered the Khanate of Kazan in 1552.

The period of Russian rule saw the Russification of the Udmurt nobility and intense Christianization which went along with the establishment on Udmurt territory of Orthodox Christian monasteries. In all lands possessed by Russian or Russified nobles and the monasteries, the Udmurt peasants were turned into serfs. Russian colonists were brought into the territory to settle on the land confiscated from the Udmurts. The spreading of

Christianity from 1636, when the Bishopric of Vyatka was established, although frequently conducted by force, was not especially fruitful. The old pagan beliefs survived for very long. As late as in 1897, it was estimated that there were 31,488 unbaptized Udmurt souls (the total Udmurt population at that time being 420,976). But even among the baptized the majority still practiced their pagan cults.

In response to Russian colonization and oppression the Udmurts repeatedly rose in rebellion, frequently allying themselves with other national rebellions, such as the Bashkir uprising of 1705–1711, which attracted almost all of the peoples living around the Volga. Many Udmurts participated also in the peasant insurrection led by E. Pugachev (1773–1775). The eighteenth-century administrative reforms divided the Udmurts among five different governments: Vyatka, Kazan, Ufa, Perm, and Samara.

When in August 1919 the Red Army expelled the White Russian armies from Izhevsk and established Soviet control in Udmurt territory, the government of Soviet Russia created there, by a decree issued on 4 November 1920, the Votyak Autonomous *Oblast*, with the administrative center in Glazov. It was later transferred to Izhevsk. In 1932 the Votyak Autonomous *Oblast* was renamed the Udmurt Autonomous *Oblast*. From this time on the name Udmurt has been in official usage in the Soviet Union. In December 1934 the Udmurt Autonomous *Oblast* was reorganized into the Udmurt ASSR.

C. Language and Culture

Udmurt belongs to the Finno-Permian group of languages and its nearest relative is Komi. Udmurt derives directly from the Finno-Permian proto-language having developed into an independent language when the dialects of the ancestors of the Volga-Finns diverged, with the Komis migrating to the north and the ancestors of the Udmurts remaining in the original homeland. This is thought to have occurred between 800–900 A.D. at which point the independent development of the two languages began. The difference between Komi and Udmurt is at present at the same stage as the difference between Estonian and Finnish.

The Udmurt language includes loanwords from Iranian, then from Chuvash, Tatar, and Bashkir and, finally, from Russian. The number of Russian loans is especially high. Chronologically they can be divided into three layers: 1) the old loans (fourteenth–seventeenth centuries), 2) the newer loans (eighteenth–nineteenth centuries), and 3) the modern loans. While the older loans have usually been adapted into the phonological and morphological system of Udmurt, the modern ones, consisting mostly of Soviet terminology, are less so adapted.

The first attempt to describe the Udmurt language in a scholarly fashion was a Russian-language manual of the Udmurt language written by an unknown author and published by the St. Petersburg Academy in 1775. In this book the declension system, the use of the possessive suffixes and the verbal conjugations are described. There is also a glossary of about 1,000 words in the book.

The center for the study of Udmurt is today at the Udmurt Research Institute established in 1930 in Izhevsk. A unified Udmurt written language based on the Cyrillic alphabet, with a few extra symbols added, was introduced in 1927.

Udmurt folklore is rich and interesting. A path-breaker in its collection and publication was the Russian ethnographer/linguist G. Vereshchagin (1854–1930). Folk poetry is predominantly lyrical. The epic form is unknown.

The first original works of Udmurt literature appeared in the beginning of the twentieth century. Its predominant genre was prose which has been translated to some extent into other languages. The Udmurt Writers' Union was established in 1926. According to the Hungarian literary scholar Peter Domokos,[40] it became suspect in the eyes of the authorities and was banned in 1941, with the majority of writers arrested. The Udmurt Writers' Union was reopened in 1954, and the repressed writers were rehabilitated. In 1974 the union had a membership of 24 authors.

In 1975 there were 45 newspapers published in the Udmurt ASSR, of which 18 were in Udmurt. The Udmurt Writers' Union publishes a literary magazine, *Molot* (The Hammer).

*   *   *

The Udmurts as a modern and ethnically self-aware eastern Finno-Ugric people have all the prerequisites for an independent or genuinely autonomous future. The conclusions reached above in this respect with regard to the Komis apply even more to the Udmurts.

The Ugric Peoples and Languages

The Hungarians

The Hungarians are the largest Finno-Ugric people (approximately 14.5 million). They live along the middle part of the Danube River in the People's Republic of Hungary, and in Transylvania, which is under Romanian control. What is not generally known, however, is that there is a relatively large group of Hungarians living in a compact area in the Soviet

Union. According to the figures of the 1979 census, the number of Hungarians living in the USSR was 170,000.

The USSR's Hungarian minority resides in the so-called Carpathian Ukraine (the Ciscarpathian *Oblast* of the Ukrainian SSR). Before the First World War this area of Hungarian settlements was part of the Austro-Hungarian Empire. After the First World War it became a part of Czechoslovakia and in 1939 was annexed by Hungary. During the Second World War this area was occupied by, and incorporated into, the Soviet Union. The national identity of the Soviet Hungarians, although they do not have their own autonomous area, is very strong: 95.4 percent of them use Hungarian as their native language (1979).

Two ethnic groups linguistically closely related to the Hungarians belong to the Ob-Ugric group—they are the Mansis (Voguls) and the Khantys (Ostyaks).

The Mansis (Voguls)*

A. Population and Geography

The Mansis (Voguls) live in the western region of the territory situated between the lower part of the Ob River and the Ural Mountains. The southernmost villages lie along the banks of the Tavda River with its tributaries, at approximately 57 degrees latitude, while the northernmost lie in the Lyapin Valley of a tributary of the Sosva River, at approximately 67 degrees latitude. Mansi villages lie predominantly in the Sosva, Sygva, Lozva, Vagilski, Pelymka, Konda, and Tavda valleys. In this territory, nearly 1,000 km long and 300 km wide, human settlements are extremely sparse. The territory is a part of the Khanty-Mansi Autonomous *Okrug* of the Tyumen *Oblast*, which in turn is an administrative area within the RSFSR. All of the present-day Mansis live east of the Ural Mountains. In addition to the Tyumen *Oblast*, there are Mansis living in the Sverdlovsk *Oblast*, too.

The chief occupation of the Mansis even today is hunting, fishing, and, to a certain extent, reindeer herding (mainly in the regions around the Sosva and Upper Lozva rivers). Agriculture is practiced only in the southernmost villages situated along the Tavda River, where rye, barley, oats, potatoes, rape, and, more rarely, linen are grown. Horses are quite common, but cows and sheep are very few.

*The name Vogul has also spread into other languages by the way of Russian and is continued to be used in Western Finno-Ugric scholarship for the designation of Mansi. Here, too, the editors have reversed this traditional usage by naming one of the peoples living in the Khanty-Mansi Autonomous *Okrug* in preference to naming them Vogul.

According to the censuses there were 7,600 Mansis in 1897, 5,700 in 1926, 6,400 in 1959, 7,700 in 1970, and 7,600 in 1979. These figures show that over the last 80 years the Mansi population has been relatively stable. However, as regards native-language retention, there seems to be a marked tendency toward assimilation, especially strongly manifested during the last few years. In 1959 59.2 percent of the Mansis considered Mansi as their native language. By 1979 this figure had been reduced to 49.5 percent. Russification has been especially noticeable in the southern areas.

In 1938 only 6.2 percent of the total population of the area were Mansis; in 1959—4.6 percent, in 1970—2.5 percent, and in 1979—1.1 percent. The percentage of Russians, according to the last three censuses, was respectively, 72.5 percent, 76.9 percent, and 74.2 percent, and of other nationalities—13.7 percent, 16.1 percent and 22.7 percent, respectively. The Mansis are a rural people. Only 0.8 percent (1970) live in urban areas. Their rapid decline in comparison with the total population of the autonomous Okrug is the result of its explosive repopulation that came along with the discovery there of natural resources (mainly oil and gas) during the last decades—in 1938 only 98,300 people lived there, whereas in 1979 the population was already 596,000.

Anthropologically the Mansis, as well as their closest relatives, the Khantys, are furthest removed from the general Finno-Ugric type. The Mongoloid index of Karin Mark for the Ob-Ugrians indicates a Mongoloid mixture of over 50 percent.[41] More Europoid traits are found among the Southern Mansis living in the region of Konda. The Northern Mansis living in the region of the Sosva River are mixed with the Mongoloid peoples living in that region and therefore their Mongoloid component is much higher.

B. History

The Mansis emerged as a separate people when the common ancestors of the Hungarians and the Ob-Ugrians separated, with the Hungarians moving westward from the area of their common origin. According to one theory this separation took place around 1000 B.C.,[42] whereas another theory places this event at 600 B.C.[43] Even more interesting is the question about when the common Ob-Ugrian ancestors of the Mansis and Khantys separated from each other, beginning to coalesce into two separate peoples. The first historical mention of the Ob-Ugrians is in the Chronicle of Nestor describing the events of the eleventh century A.D. However, no distinction was made there between the Mansis and the Khantys. Such a distinction begins to emerge only by the fourteenth century. It is known that in 1265 the Jugrans (i.e., the Ob-Ugrians, including both the Mansis and Khantys) were paying tribute to Novgorod. It is also known that in the fourteenth century both the Mansis and the Khantys, led by their respective princes, resisted the Russian colonists penetrating from the west and the Tatar conquerors pressing from the south. In 1364 Novgorod forces penetrated into the area around the Ob River, but later the Mansis managed to launch a counteroffensive against them, which, under their Prince Asyka, achieved considerable success. In 1455 Asyka led an attack against an outpost of Moscow on the Vychegda, west of the Urals, where his forces killed the bishop of Perm, Gerasim. Gerasim was the first missionary who attempted to Christianize the Eastern Ugrians. In 1499 the Muscovites conquered the regions around the Ob River and their ruler, Ivan III, received in honor of that conquest the additional title of the "Jugrian." However, Ivan III's victory over the "Jugrians" was not final. The Mansis successfully resisted the Muscovites for at least another hundred years or so until the Russian "conqueror of Siberia," Yermak Timofeyevich, in the end of the sixteenth century firmly put them under Moscow's rule, which has lasted until the present time. In all these struggles the Mansis were the chief source of opposition to the Russians whereas the Khantys had already retreated to the eastern regions of Siberia, beyond the Ob River.

There was no significant conversion of the Mansis to Christianity until 1712–1715, when Monk Feodor who later received the name of Bishop Filofey became the "Voguls' apostle." By all the means in his power, inclusive of coercion and force, he baptized the majority of the Ob-Ugrians. Conversion was, however, only nominal and the old religious practices lived on tenaciously.

With the spread of Christianity, Russian officials and merchants began to arrive in the Ob region in ever-increasing numbers. Very soon the Mansis, who were not used to trading practices, fell into debt, becoming economically totally dependent on the Russian colonists.

The Revolution of 1917 introduced into the life of the Mansis only certain formal changes. The establishment in 1930 of their autonomous national area (till 1940 Ostyako-Vogul National Okrug and at present Khanty-Mansi Autonomous Okrug) achieved for these people much less than one might have expected. The influx of foreigners grew even more with the percentage of the indigenous people continually falling. The small-scale agriculture was collectivized and the fishers were banded into cooperatives. The Mansis supply a significant percentage of the work force in the industries of the nationalized timber trade, fishing concerns as well as in the collective farms and fishers' cooperatives of the area.

C. Language and Culture

Mansi is a Finno-Ugric language belonging to the Ugric branch. Together with its nearest relative, Khanty, it belongs to the Ob-Ugric subbranch of the Ugric languages.

Due to the Mansi people's wide geographic spread the Mansi language is splintered into four main dialects: the northern, western, eastern, and southern dialects. The difference between the northern and southern dialects is so great that mutual understanding is very difficult (this difference is considered to be equal to the difference existing between Estonian and Finnish).

There are approximately 800 roots in Mansi which have cognates in other Finno-Ugric languages. As a result of linguistic contacts, loans from Komi occupy a dominant place in the language, especially in its northern dialect (over 100 loans). Since the same loans are present in Khanty, it is thought that they were introduced in the period predating the separation of the Mansis from the Khantys. There are significantly less Samoyed loans in Mansi than in Khanty, which shows that the Khantys were more susceptible to influence by their immediate neighbors than the Mansis. There are, however, numerous Tatar loans in Mansi, altogether 500, which is about the same as in Khanty. In the common Mansi language there are approximately 600 Russian loans. The oldest are from the period of Christianization, the later ones are cultural words loaned into the recently created written language. Today Russian is the chief assimilator of Mansi.

It was only in the 1930s that a written language was worked out for the Mansis. It was based on the northern dialect as this was the most widespread one. The creator of this written language was the Russian linguist V.N. Chernetsov who introduced the Latin alphabet for it. A number of textbooks were published in this language. In 1938, as everywhere else in the Soviet Union, the Latin alphabet was abolished and replaced by the Cyrillic alphabet.

Today the literature that is published in Mansi consists for the most part of schoolbooks and literature translated from Russian. Indigenous folklore has been published, too. Finnish and Hungarian scholars consider it to be rich and interesting. The most important genres are birth songs, songs of heroes, bear songs, dramatizations of the bear wake, offering of prayers, songs of fate, fairy tales, and riddles.

Authors writing in Mansi have appeared in the past few years. The best known of them is Yuvan Shestalov (born 1937), who has published lyrical poetry and prose. Recently he switched over to writing in Russian and is now primarily a Russian writer.

The Khantys (Ostyaks)*

A. Population and Geography

The Khantys (Ostyaks) live to the east of the Mansis in the basin of the Ob and Irtysh rivers in northwestern Siberia. Their settlements are in the Khanty-Mansi and Yamalo-Nenets Autonomous *Okrugs* of the Tyumen Oblast, but they are also settled in parts of the Tomsk Oblast of the RSFSR. Their territory stretches approximately 1,500 km in length from the source of the Vashyuga River, a tributary of the Ob, to the mouth of the Ob River. The northernmost villages are in the Nadymi River valley, along the south shore of the Ob Delta as it reaches into the Arctic Ocean. The Khanty-Mansi Autonomous *Okrug* covers a vast and very sparsely populated territory of 523,100 km², with a density of 1.07/km². The capital of the autonomous *okrug*, Khanty-Mansiisk (Ostyako-Vogulsk until 1940), is a port on the Irtysh River approximately 25 km from its mouth. The settlement was given city status in 1930. In 1968 the population was 25,000.

The number of Khantys has remained relatively stable. In 1897, 19,700 Khantys were enumerated. In 1939 this figure was 18,500, and in 1950—19,400. In the census of 1970 the number of Khantys was given as 21,100 and in 1979—20,900. At the same time over the last twenty years native language retention among the Khantys has declined significantly. In 1959 77 percent of the Khantys considered Khanty to be their native language, and in 1979 this figure was 67.8 percent—a 10 percent decrease over twenty years. This tendency is paralleled by the increase of the number of Russians in the territory of the Khanty-Mansi Autonomous *Okrug*. In 1959 the total population of the autonomous *okrug* was 124,000, but by 1979 this figure had risen to 569,000. In 1959 the Khantys formed 9.2 percent of the total population, but in 1979 the comparable figure was only 2.0 percent. The predominance of the Russians is especially noticeable in the towns, where they form over 80 percent of the population. The increase in the total population, as well as the increase in the number of Russians, is the result

---

*The name Ostyak comes from Russian, where it was encountered for the first time in written form in the chronicles of 1572. From Russian the name spread into other languages and is still predominantly used in the West today. This Russian name in turn comes from the Khantys' neighbors who commonly called them "as-yah," i.e., the people of the Ob River. The Russians made the form Ostyak from this, which means the same thing. In Tatar, on the other hand, "ushtyak" means a foreigner or stranger.

The self-designation of the Western Ostyaks is "Hanty," while that of the Eastern Ostyaks is "Kantyk"—hence, Khanty as the common name for both.

Here again the editors have chosen the name Khanty for one of the peoples living in the Khanty—Mansi Autonomous *Okrug*, in preference to that of Ostyak.

of the discovery of oil in Ust-Balyk, Megion, Shaim, and later Surgut; and of natural gas in Beryozov. To give an example, the population of Surgut in 1967 was 19,000, whereas, according to the 1979 census, it was 107,000. The number of Khantys among the urban population is very small—in 1959 it was 2.4 percent and in 1979 only 1.1 percent. The Khantys still live by fishing and hunting, and to a certain extent by reindeer herding which they learned from their neighbors, the Samoyeds. A certain number of Khantys earn their living as lumberjacks in the nationalized forestry industry. Agriculture in the form of collective farms is practiced only in the southernmost villages.

Anthropologically the Khantys are in every way similar to their nearest neighbors, the Mansis. According to the findings of Karin Mark, the Mongoloid index of the Ob-Ugrians ranges between 71–92 indicating a racial mix of over 50 percent.[44] Racially they are so removed from the other Finno-Ugrians that the Ob-Ugrians can in no way be considered to be anthropologically related to them. The society of the ancient Khantys was divided into a clan system where each clan was led by an elder. Many clans had a common prince. Members of one clan were not allowed to marry into their own clan. In the north the Khantys and the Mansis were divided into two big clans which were called "Por" and "Mosh." According to one theory, this allows us to presuppose that the Ob-Ugrians derive from two different ethnic groups: one was the common prototribe of the Khantys, Mansis and Hungarians, while the other was a Mongoloid people of Siberia. The Khantys' prohibition of marrying into their own clan resulted in their prolific mixing with the neighboring Mongoloid tribes.

B. History

The territory of the Khantys, despite of its peripheral location, became the object of expansion of two foreign powers. The Tatars tried to conquer the area from the south. The high point of the hegemony of the Tatar Khanate over the Khantys was in the fourteenth–sixteenth centuries; while the Tatars taxed the Khantys, they nonetheless left their indigenous tribal and social structure intact. The Tatar Khan Kutshum, who named himself the emperor of Siberia in 1563, ruled over most of the Khanty territory. The Russians, on the other hand, came as conquerors from the west. Russian forces launched their first offensive against the Khantys in 1364, but a more serious offensive was launched in 1483, when a large number of tribal chiefs were taken hostage. Ivan III agreed to free the hostages only if all the Jugrian chiefs recognized the sovereignty of Moscow over them and paid taxes to its treasury. Apparently Ivan III was not satisfied with this result, for in 1499 he launched another attack into Jugria, conquering territory in the lower reaches of the Ob as well as above the mouth of the Irtysh. For some time Jugria was simultaneously under the jurisdiction of Moscow and of the Tatars, but in 1582 the Russians conquered the capital of the Tatar Khanate, Sibir, on the right bank of the Irtysh, and from that time on Russian power over Jugria remained without competition. Administrative centers started to grow in the area: in 1585 Tyumen was established; in 1587—Tobolsk. Later, in 1593 and 1595, Beryozov, Surgut and Obdorsk were founded.

Christianization of the Khantys began relatively late, in the eighteenth century, during the reign of Peter the Great. During 1712–1726 Bishop Filofey, formerly the monk Feodor, known as the "Vogul Apostle," had organized massive Christening expeditions in Khanty areas, which resulted in formal baptism of the people, but did not achieve much else as the majority of the Khantys retained their pre-Christian faith up to the beginning of the twentieth century.

Russification, which coincided with Christianization, prevented the Khantys from developing into a consistent ethnic entity. The nationalities' policy of the Soviet regime was implemented in Khanty territory by establishing there in 1930 a common autonomous *okrug* for the Khantys and the Mansis. But by that time the Russian colonists had achieved such a large majority and the role of the local peoples had become so insignificantly small that this "autonomy" could have meaning only on paper.

C. Language and Culture

Khanty belongs to the Ugric branch of the Finno-Ugric language family and its nearest relative is Mansi. The similarity between the two is approximately the same as the similarity between Estonian and Finnish. Khanty and Mansi began to diverge from the common Ob-Ugric protolanguage in about the twelfth century A.D. There are, however, differing opinions as to when the split actually occurred. Numerous dialects and sub-dialects have formed due to the sparse population spread over an immense territory. The dialects of Khanty are divided into three main groups: 1) the northern dialects (in the regions of Obdorsk, Beryozov, Kazymi, and Serkala); 2) the southern dialects (in the regions of Nizyam, Irtysh, Demyakin, and Konda); 3) the eastern dialects (in the regions of Salym, Surgut, and Vahin-Vashyuga). There are approximately 7,000 speakers of the northern dialect, 4,000 of the southern, and 8,000 of the eastern.

The oldest loanwords in Khanty are Iranian, which entered the language even earlier than the Iranian loans entered the languages of the Finnic branch. In historic times Khanty has received loanwords from Komi, Tatar, and Russian. Komi loans are estimated at around 350, and Tatar loans at around 200. The Russian loans can be divided into the older and the recent ones. The older ones, which were introduced before the nineteenth century, have been modified to fit the sound pattern of Khanty. The recent loans have, however, been taken over with the Russian pronunciation. In their entirety the Russian loans form the largest stratum of loanwords in the Khanty language.

As of 1920 a special institute in Leningrad worked on creating written languages for the backward nationalities of the Soviet Union. A written language for Khanty, based on the Kazym dialect, was created there in 1930. The Latin alphabet was used until 1937. In this alphabet approximately 30 volumes of various kinds were published. P. Hatanzeyev compiled the first ABC book in this language (1930–1931). However, in 1937 the Latin alphabet was abolished and, as everywhere else, replaced by the Cyrillic alphabet. In 1940 a new written language was added to the already existing one. It was based on the dialect of the Middle Ob (Sherkal). In 1950 written languages were created on the basis of the Vah, Surgut, and Shuryshkar dialects as well. Thus, for 19,000 Khantys there are now five (!) different languages. The literature published in these languages consists above all of textbooks, translations of literature from Russian, and later also of original poetry.

The folklore of the Khantys, which is considered to be very rich, overlaps to a great extent with Khanty mythology. Since the Khantys retained their pre-Christian religion until the beginning of the twentieth century, their folk poetry still contains very strong shamanistic and totemistic elements. Their songs are about heroes and sages (shamans); they recite stories, fairy tales and real events. A special genre are the bear songs. The most important songs are about the ancient heroes, who have become demigods. These songs relate their voyages, battles, and other glorious deeds. Originally, they were performed to the accompaniment of reed instruments. They are rhythmically recitative and do not have a fixed syllable structure or meter. Repetition is an especially important element in these songs. The central theme in Khanty mythology is familial ancestor worship. The animistic element figures in it very prominently for the ancestors are depicted there as having been transformed into animals or other people.

In more recent times young authors writing in Khanty have appeared on the Khanty cultural stage. They are first and foremost poets. The first lyric poet to write in Khanty was D. Lazarev who also was the editor of the only Khanty-language newspaper published in Khanty-Mansiisk. The younger Khanty authors are almost as old as their young written language.

*   *   *

The huge size of the Khanty-Mansi territory, over which these two small peoples are scattered, together with that territory's large-scale colonization and the strong tendency shown by both the Khantys and Mansis to assimilate with the colonizers, indicate that the chances for preservation of the ethnic future of these peoples are rather bleak. However, if the Mansis and Khantys were to acquire cultural autonomy on the scale of the small Swedish minority in independent Estonia, with schools operating in their own languages and some institutions of their self-government being established, these peoples may not only survive but even become stable and progressively develop ethnic entities.

The Samoyed Peoples and Their Languages

A. Population and Geography
Geographically as well as linguistically the Samoyed peoples and languages are divided into the northern and southern groups (the latter is also called the Sayan Samoyed group). To the northern group belong: the Yurak Samoyeds (Nenets), the Yenisei Samoyeds (Enets), and the Tavgi Samoyeds (Nganassans). The southern group consists of the Ostyak Samoyeds (Selkups) and, earlier, the now extinct "Kamassians" belonged to it. The Motor, Koibal, Karagassian, Taigi, and Sojod Samoyed languages became extinct even earlier than the Kamassian.

The tribes speaking the various Samoyed languages live in scattered groups over an immense territory that stretches along the Arctic coast from the White Sea by the Kola Peninsula to the Sea of Laptevit in the east. Thus there are Samoyeds living in Europe and Samoyeds living in Asia. The heart of their territory is northeastern Europe and western Siberia. There are also Samoyeds living on the island of Novaya Zemlya and on the islands of Kolguyev and Vaigach. In the south their territory (where the Selkups live) stretches to the Ket, a tributary of the Ob. Administratively all the territories of the Samoyeds belong to the RSFSR. Samoyeds are to be found predominantly in the Nenets and Yamalo-Nenets Autonomous *Okrugs* (the Yurak Samoyeds) and in the Taimyr (or the Dolgano-Nenets) Autonomous *Okrug* (the Yenisei and Tavgi Samoyeds). There are Samoyeds also living in the Khanty-Mansi Autonomous *Okrug* (the Selkups). Altogether, there are approximately 35,000 Samoyeds in the Soviet Union, more or less as many as there are Lapps.

The Yurak Samoyeds (Nenets) live in the territory stretching from the Kanin Peninsula on the eastern coast of the White Sea to the mouth of the Yenisei. Additionally they can be found in the islands of Kolguyev,

Novaya Zemlya, Vaigach, and Belyi as well as in the territory between the lower part of the Ob and the Yenisei rivers. There are also small Nenets family groups living on the Kola Peninsula. The White Sea part of their territory belongs to the Arkhangel *Oblast* and the Yenisei part to the Tyumen *Oblast*. The administrative center of the Nenets Autonomous *Okrug* of the Arkhangel *Oblast* is Naryan-Mar, a port city on the right bank of the Pechora River. It was established in 1933. The population in 1972 was 17,000. The administrative center of the Yamalo-Nenets Autonomous *Okrug* of the Tyumen *Oblast* is Salekhar (formerly Obdorsk), a port city on the mouth of the Poluy River and the right bank of the Ob. The original settlement was established in 1595, in conjunction with the Russian conquest of Siberia. It was granted the rights of a city in 1938, and in 1974 its population was 26,000.

The number of Yurak Samoyeds in both autonomous *okrugs*, according to the 1970 census, was 29,000 and, according to the 1979 census—30,000. In 1970, 83.4 percent of this group considered Samoyed to be their native language whereas in 1979 this figure was reduced to 80.4 percent. Numerically the Yurak Samoyeds are the largest group of Samoyeds.

From time immemorial the Yurak Samoyeds have derived their livelihood from reindeer herding and to a lesser extent from hunting and fishing. Although today they are members of collective farms, they still roam, as they have always done, along the tundra with their huge reindeer herds.

The Yenisei Samoyeds (Enets) live in the Taimyr (or Dolgano-Nenets) Autonomous *Okrug* of the Krasnoyarsk *Kray* (Territory) on the eastern bank of the Yenisei Delta. They subsist on hunting and fishing. They chiefly hunt the wild reindeer. Domesticated reindeer are used mainly as draught animals. Due to the harsh climate (from −30 degrees C. in the winter to only +2–13 degrees C. in the summer), any other means of livelihood is hardly thinkable, let alone possible.

According to the 1959 census, there were 400 Yenisei Samoyeds. They were no longer mentioned in the 1970 and 1979 censuses. Presumably their numbers have dropped to below 400 which seems to be the critical borderline figure in Soviet censuses as regards the small peoples of the east.

The Tavgi Samoyeds (Nganassans) are the northernmost people of the USSR. They live in the northern part of the Taimyr Peninsula, between 84 and 100 degrees latitude. In addition to the Yenisei Samoyeds the nearest neighbors of the Tavgi Samoyeds are the Yakuts. The Tavgi Samoyeds are considered to be indigenous inhabitants of the Taimyr Peninsula who later mixed with the local Paleo-Asiatic population. Their source of livelihood is fishing and hunting, as is the case with the Yenisei Samoyeds. Likewise, they chiefly hunt the wild reindeer. Domesticated reindeer are very seldom kept.

In the 1970 census 1,000 Tavgi Samoyeds were enumerated of whom 75.4 percent considered Samoyed their native language. In the 1979 census there were 900 Tavgis of whom 90.2 percent considered Samoyed to be their native language. This small people is one of the few whose rate of assimilation has decreased and, by that, on quite a substantial scale.

* * *

The Ostyak Samoyeds (Selkups) live in a broad territory along the Taz River between the middle flow of the great rivers, the Ob and the Yenisei. Administratively they are located in the Tomsk *Oblast* and the Krasnoyarsk *Kray* with their groups being present also in the Yamalo-Nenets Autonomous *Okrug*.

According to the 1970 census, there were 4,300 Ostyak Samoyeds of whom 51.1 percent considered Samoyed to be their native language. In the 1979 census the figure was 3,600 of whom 56.6 percent considered Samoyed to be their native language. Thus we can see that this people, despite of its numerical decrease, has slightly strengthened its native-language retention.

The Ostyak Samoyeds are much more sedentary in their life-style than their northern relatives, the Yurak, Yenisei, and Tavgi Samoyeds. They subsist likewise on hunting and fishing. They hunt squirrels, arctic foxes, sable, wolverines, and wild birds. Domesticated reindeer are kept mainly for draught purposes but the Ostyak Samoyeds use them as mounts too. In the winter they live in log huts built into the ground and in the summer in four-cornered teepees.

The Kamassians are the group of southern Samoyeds which has most recently become extinct. As late as in 1970 a representative of the Kamassians, Klavdiya Plotnikova, attended the Third International Congress of Finno-Ugricists held in Tallinn. She came from the village of Ablakovo on the Sayan hills. She was the last Kamass as well as the last speaker of Kamassian.

Genetically, all of the Samoyeds have very strong Mongoloid traits. They cannot be considered as genetic relatives of the Western Finno-Ugric peoples. But the Samoyeds differ racially among each other as well. The Northern Samoyeds have broader faces and are squatter than the others. The average height of a Yurak Samoyed man is 158cm. and they have short craniums (index 84.4). The majority have dark hair and dark brown or black eyes. Generally, they have more Mongoloid traits than the Ostyak Samoyeds (Selkups), who resemble more the Ob-Ugrians. The average height of the Ostyak Samoyed is 158.1cm. and their cranium index is 82.6. They do not exhibit the epicanthic fold.

B. History

The oldest source that mentions the Samoyeds is the Chronicle of Nestor in the eleventh century. Plano Carpini (1246), emissary of Pope Innocent IV, who in 1245–47 visited the "land of the Mongols" and wrote a report about it, speaks for the first time of the Eastern Samoyeds. Northern Samoyeds lived under the rule of the Tatars, until in 1582 the Russians conquered the Tatar Khanate. Then they came under Russian rule. In order to rule Siberia, the Russians built a series of forts which were at the same time centers of administration for the Samoyeds. Such forts were Beryozov (1593), Surgut and Obdorsk (1595), Narym (1596), and Ket (1597). After the Russian conquest, the Samoyeds actively joined in the uprisings against Russian rule. It was from the Russians that the Samoyeds learned how to use firearms. With the establishment of Krasnoyarsk (1628), the Southern Samoyeds fell into the orbit of the Russians, too. In Europe the last full-scale armed confrontation between the Russians and the Samoyeds occurred in 1746. The Samoyeds, who had laid siege to Pustozersk, were beaten, and about 100 Samoyeds who had been captured ended their lives at the gallows.

The Russians started Christianizing the Samoyeds as late as the Ob-Ugrians. As a result the Samoyeds' pre-Christian concept of the world (shamanism and the cult of the dead) is still very much alive.

The Soviet regime imposed a collective-farm system upon the Samoyeds and, with it, centralization and a more sedentary way of life. No longer do family units wander with their reindeer herds. Only the herders do so, the others live in the villages of the collectives. Here schools have been established. The first Samoyed school was opened in 1925. Later Samoyed schools spread quite widely, especially so in the areas inhabited by the Yurak Samoyeds. The national (now autonomous) *okrugs* established for the Samoyeds in the 1930s are, however, not of much significance in terms of Samoyed self-government, since in all of them the Samoyeds are a small minority beside the Russian and other colonists.

C. Language and Culture

The Samoyed languages belong to the Uralic language family in which different languages are interrelated much more closely than is the case with the various groups of Finno-Ugric languages. It is thought that the original features of the Uralic languages are better preserved in the Samoyed languages than in the Finno-Ugric languages. For this reason many Finno-Ugricists have become interested in Samoyed. A common feature shared by the Samoyed and Finno-Ugric languages are their inflectional and derivational systems, but there are many phonological similarities as well. In 1932 a written language was created for the Yurak Samoyed using the Latin alphabet. Its development was halted in 1937 when the Cyrillic alphabet replaced the Latin one. Primarily school textbooks have been published in the Yurak Samoye language along with translations from Russian, but there have been some original literary works, too. Altogether approximately fifty works have appeared in this language. Ostyak Samoyed (Selkup) was the second Samoyed language to receive a written language. An ABC book and a few school textbooks have been published in this language. These are used in the preparatory and elementary schools. There are no written languages for the Yenisei and Tavgi Samoyeds; instead Yurak Samoyed is developing into the common written language that should encompass these two as well.

Due to intensive contacts with foreigners many loanwords from other languages were introduced into the Samoyed languages. There are especially many loans from Russian which, in fact, is so dominant that the well-known Samoyed scholar, Professor Ago Künnap, is of the opinion that all Samoyed languages are in great danger of assimilation with Russian.[45]

Samoyed folklore is considered to be rich and original, especially in the territory of the Northern Samoyeds. Folklore art is mainly performed in the form of *joigs*. The joigs' poetry does not differ much from prose since it lacks alliteration, rhyme, and repetition. The songs when presented in joig form are difficult to understand owing to the use of extra syllables as filler material. The joigs are often sung by two people where one of the two usually repeats certain words or phrases. There are many different genres of joigs: 1) legends about heroes and sages; 2) narrative joigs (songs accompanied by rhythmic movements or dancing) of a general nature; 3) shaman joigs accompanied by the drum; 4) narrative laments, in which the difficulties and sufferings of life are related; 5) drinking joigs which are comparable to the songs of fate of the Ob-Ugrians. Legends, fairy tales and riddles exist separately from and alongside with the joigs. They are not necessarily performed.

The beginnings of original literature can be found in the Yurak Samoyed language. A newspaper is published in the Yurak Samoyed language in the Yamalo-Nenets Autonomous *Okrug*, which is the only Samoyed-language newspaper in the world.

* * *

In order to protect the Samoyed languages and tribes from extinction a comprehensive system of autonomy is required, which should be organized by representatives of the Samoyeds themselves and not their colonial and foreign "guardians."

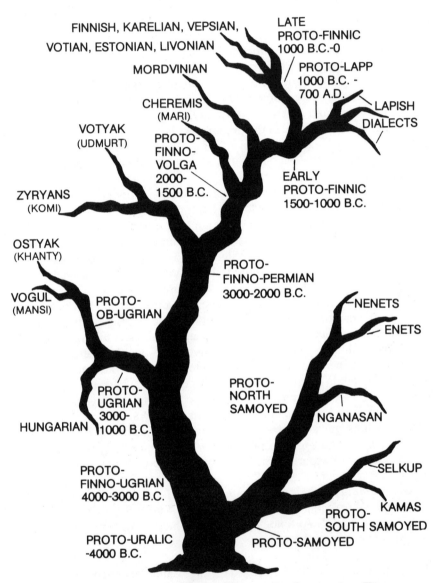

The most recent family tree of the Uralic peoples. From
Johdatus lapin kielen historiaan (Introduction to the History
of the Lappish Language), Korhonen, Mikko. Helsinki, 1981.

Conclusion

The Finno-Ugrians in the Soviet Union number 4.45 million people (1979) who are scattered over a very large geographical area. Different geographic locations create different conditions for development. This is why the various Finno-Ugric peoples have such divergent histories and dissimilar social, political, and economic backgrounds. This heterogeneity determines different perspectives for the future of these peoples regardless of whether the future unfolds in unchanged or changing circumstances. It is simply impossible to come out here with any single prognosis equally applicable to all peoples considered. In any case the present situation and the historical past that underlies it are providing the sole frame of reference within which the future can be reliably discussed.

When looking at the past, one sees that a certain number of Finno-Ugric peoples and languages have either become extinct in the distant or not so distant past, or are on the verge of extinction. Of the Balto-Finnic group this includes the Votes, Livonians, and Izhors. So, too, the Vepsians have stopped to be accounted for in Soviet censuses, even though smaller groups than the Vepsians still continue to figure in them. In the Volga-Finnic area the Merjans and Muroms, and in the Samoyed group, the Karagassians, Koibals, Motors, Soyods, Taigins and most recently the Kamassians, have disappeared. Altogether eleven or twelve Uralic peoples are missing from the original lot, which amply demonstrates the existential danger the peoples of this language family face.

Overall, however, the present state of the Finno-Ugric peoples in the USSR need not be assessed too pessimistically. The numerical size of some of these peoples is equal to or even bigger than that of some independent peoples of the world. When one takes into consideration the number of languages and the number of human beings in the world, a people of one million appears to be not small but rather average sized. Of the 62 languages of Europe, Hungarian is in the 12th position, Finnish—in the 20th, Mordvin—in the 30th, Estonian—in the 36th, Udmurt—in the 39th, Mari—in the 42nd, and Komi—in the 43rd (Décsy). As a comparison, let it be mentioned that Icelandic, with its 210,000 speakers (1972), holds the 48th place among the languages of Europe. Today, however, who would even consider denying the rights of the Icelanders to their independence on account of their size, let alone predicting their disappearance?

Of the nineteen peoples speaking Uralic languages only the Hungarians, Finns, and Estonians enjoy the status of nations with a well-developed culture in the Western sense. Some of the other Finno-Ugric peoples should have been in a similar position but historical, geopolitical, and geographical factors have created impassable obstacles to their development. Of the three nations with a well-developed culture mentioned above, the Finns are the only ones who are independent and have a democratic system of government. This makes them a part of the Western world with all the advantages that follow from it. Of the Finno-Ugric peoples living in the Soviet Union, the Estonians are the only ones to have the status of the so-called union republic with all the relative advantages this status gives to a Soviet-ruled nation. The other Soviet Finno-Ugrians do not enjoy this status and find themselves in much more adverse conditions than the Estonians. These "advantages," however, do not really eliminate the actual danger the Estonians face through the subordination of their culture to Soviet ideological demands and the unfavorable demographic development which dilutes the Estonian ethnic society through an uncontrollable influx of foreigners. In a nation enjoying the rights of self-determination, such a situation threatening the nation's existence would have been unthinkable. While the Finnish people need not experience the danger of demographic change, just as it is not necessary for the Hungarians to be afraid of it, it is the biggest fear of the Estonians. Cultural subordination to Soviet ideological demands, again, is minimal in Finland, and much lighter in Hungary than in Estonia. But it is the continual decrease of the Estonians as the majority population in their own republic that makes the situation of the Estonians begin to resemble that of the lesser Finno-Ugric peoples of the Soviet Union. Indeed, compared to the situation before the Second World War, the relative number of Estonians in their own territory has decreased by 23.5 percent. It goes without saying that the Estonians cannot reconcile, and have not reconciled, themselves with this situation. They realize full well that in order to ensure the unhindered existence of their nation it is necessary for them fully to restore their right to self-determination which they then could use to disengage their country from the USSR and establish it as a fully sovereign nation-state. Only thus would they be able to free their national development from the foreign-imposed ideological fetters and provide for effective restrictions on the nationally devastating foreign immigration. In the same way it is vitally important for the Estonians to assume sovereignty over their natural resources, which are now thoughtlessly squandered by the foreign-imposed exploitative and ineffective economic system. Radical political change is required for achieving all these goals and, if the Estonians are to survive as a viable nation, this change has to take place in the not too distant future.

The position of Soviet Finno-Ugric peoples who have in the USSR the status of an ASSR (autonomous republic) is relatively similar for all. Differences are mainly in the size of the particular group, its location, and areal compactness or scatteredness. The vitality and the potential level of cultural self-expression of the respective peoples is dependent on these

Table 8–2
Relative Size of the Five Finno-Ugric
Autonomous Republics (ASSRs)

Name of ASSR	Total population in millions	Indigenous peoples % of total population	
		1959	1979
1. Udmurt	1.494	35.6	32.2
2. Komi	1.119	30.4	25.3
3. Mordvin	0.991	35.8	34.2
4. Mari	0.736	43.1	43.5
5. Carelian	0.703	13.1	11.1

Table 8–3
Relative Size of the Five ASSRs in Urban Areas

Name of ASSR	Indigenous peoples % of urban population (1970)
1. Udmurt	16.8
2. Komi	15.3
3. Mordvin	16.8
4. Mari	15.6
5. Carelian	7.7

factors. There are altogether five such Finno-Ugric autonomous republics in the Soviet Union. Characteristic to all of them is the minority position of the indigenous population, while the position of the Russian and other immigrant peoples increasingly gains in importance and strength. This is demonstrated in Table 8–2.

It follows from it that the Mari autonomous republic is the only one in which over the given 20-year period the indigenous population has managed to maintain its position and, in fact, somewhat improve it (by 0.4 percent).

An even greater imbalance between the indigenous and immigrant peoples exists in the urban population, which is demonstrated in Table 8–3.

Since the cultural and educational life as well as the government agencies that administer these areas are centered in the cities, this so-called "autonomy" does not give to such a small minority much opportunity for full self-expression, to say nothing of self-determination. The autonomy thus

Table 8–4
Decline in Native Language Retention among the Finno-Ugric Peoples

People	Native language retention %		Decrease %
	1959	1979	
1. Udmurt	89.1	76.4	− 12.7
2. Komi	89.3	76.2	− 13.1
3. Mordvin	78.1	72.6	− 5.5
4. Mari	95.1	86.8	− 8.3
5. Carelian	71.3	55.6	− 15.7

becomes illusory or merely formal, even if discounting the fact that the Soviet system of government is incompatible with any genuine autonomy for anyone or anything. This is exacerbated by the linguistic situation of the indigenous population. We are dealing here with young, artificially created written languages, all of which originated in the 1930s. In the beginning the written languages made use of the Latin alphabet, but by the end of the 1930s all were switched to the Cyrillic alphabet. Oddly enough not one but a number of different written languages were created for most of these people. The Mordvins, Maris, and Komis all have two written languages while the Khantys were given a total of five written languages. In place of their native language the Carelians use Russian or Finnish as their written language, and the written language that had previously been created for them was abolished altogether. The existence of a number of written languages based on different dialects prevents the effective development and consolidation of homogenous national societies characterized by at least a common written language, which is conducive to the evolution, in due course, also of a common oral language. The status of the native languages of the Finno-Ugric peoples of the autonomous republics is low anyway, and this splintering makes it even lower and also practically less usable. The result is the continually ongoing switch of the respective Finno-Ugric peoples to Russian, which is the largest cause of their assimilation. The decreasing rate of retention of the native languages is clearly established by the results of the last two Soviet censuses, which are demonstrated in Table 8–4.

In the case of the smaller administrative autonomous units (autonomous *okrugs*) the situation in broad outline is the same. The scantiness and inexactness of the statistical material is all the more noticeable the smaller the respective unit.[46]

Table 8–5
Native-Language Loss Among the Non-Autonomous Finno-Ugric Peoples

Peoples	Numbers in thousands	Native language retention%		Decrease
		1959	1979	
1. Finns	77.1	59.4	40.9	− 18.5
2. Vepsians	8.1	46.1	38.4	− 7.7
3. Lapps	1.9	69.9	53.0	− 16.9
4. Izhors	0.7	34.7	32.6	− 2.1

There are two so-called autonomous okrugs for the Finno-Ugric peoples of the Soviet Union: the Komi-Permyak and the Khanty-Mansi, for the Mansis and Khantys together. In the Komi-Permyak Autonomous *Okrug* native language retention during 1959–1979 decreased by 10.5 percent. For Mansis the figure is 9.7 percent and for the Khantys 9.2 percent. It appears that in the Soviet Union the hard and fast rule is as follows: the smaller the people the faster the rate of assimilation. This comes, no doubt, from the lower status and possibilities of practical usage of the languages in question.

Native language loss is generally even higher among those Finno-Ugric peoples who have no national administrative unit of their own (Table 8–5).

More than half of the Izhors, Vepsians, and Finns have abandoned their native languages and thus remain within the Finno-Ugric group only nominally. They are in fact former Finno-Ugrians who, speaking Russian as their native language, have become Russians by all relevant standards. The decrease in the number of Vepsians resembles a sudden collapse over a short period of time. Between 1959–1970 the numbers of Vepsians dropped by nearly one half (from 16,400 to 8,300). The Second World War took the bottom out from under the Izhors (who numbered 16,100 people in 1926). The situation of the Samis as a whole is different in that the major parts of their population live as minorities on the territory of Finland, Sweden, and Norway, where the developments over the past few years have dramatically improved their ethnic situation. The future perspectives for the Soviet Samis could become more favorable if they were allowed freely to cooperate with their compatriots across the border. A system of cultural autonomy, such as was prevalent in independent Estonia for the Germans and Jews who did not possess any territorial units, would be a possible solution to the problem of survival for those

Finno-Ugrians who lack their own territorial units (the Finns, Vepsians, Izhors).

Even though the system of national autonomy for the minorities in the Soviet Union is, at least in principle, a big step forward compared to czarist Russia, this system has not borne out the results that one might have expected it to produce. The political and ideological atmosphere in the USSR has never been, and is not, favorable to the formation of strong national communities. In fact the Soviets condemn the slightest attempts at strengthening such communities as chauvinistic or "bourgeois-nationalistic" manifestations.

The Marxist-Leninist ideology which sees in the disappearance of ethnic distinctions (*sliyanie*) a necessary phase in the development toward communism, is one of the most negative factors here. The policy-wise induced changeover to the use by all peoples of one common language, for which Russian apparently has been the chosen one, is taking place in the USSR in strict accordance with this ideology.

The survival of the Soviet Finno-Ugric peoples can be therefore ensured only by their acquiring a fully independent or, at least, authentic autonomous status. These peoples, facing the situation of "to be or not to be" and naturally seeking to solve it in favor of "to be," surely realize this fact better than anyone else, and thus must be fully committed to ascertaining themselves as entities entirely independent from, or, at least truly autonomous within, Russia. One international example of such an authentic autonomy within another nation's state should be well known to the Soviet Finno-Ugrians as it is established in Finland to which they are used to look for positive examples and leads. The case in point is the autonomy granted by Finland to Aland. According to the established rules governing Aland's autonomy, immigration of Finnish-speaking population onto Aland is severely restricted with the view of permanently ensuring that Aland remains Swedish speaking. These rules were sanctioned in 1922 by the League of Nations, which placed the Swedish-speaking population of Aland under international protection. Finland replaced these rules in 1951 with similar internal laws on autonomy which also guarantee that the 25,000-strong population of Aland remains Swedish speaking and that, in addition, some specific privileges and rights of self-determination are accorded to it. The above-mentioned solution would be one way of ensuring the ethnic survival and prosperity of those Finno-Ugric peoples for whom it is not possible to become fully independent or, at least, to dissociate themselves from Russia by joining a related Finno-Ugric nation outside Russia.

The legal protection afforded to the Swedish minority in Finland proper, especially as regards the educational system, could in many ways serve as an example of how the Finno-Ugric minorities, who live in Russia but do not have within it a territorial unit of their own, should be treated by the Russian state and its dominant nation-state.

The Soviet Finno-Ugric peoples' demands for independence, or, in some cases, for genuine territorial autonomy, or, yet in other cases, for adequate protection by law of their ethnic minority rights within the Russian state would be, no doubt, eagerly supported also by the many Russian friends of the Finno-Ugric and other oppressed peoples. The merciless assimilatory policies the Soviet regime pursues with regard to these peoples cannot find genuine support among these Russians, not least for the reason that the Russians themselves are the victims of Soviet assimilatory policies aiming to transform them into a new "historical community of Soviet people."

Notes

1. Karin Mark, *Zur Herkunft der finnisch-ugrische Völker vom Standpunkt der Anthropologie*, (Tallinn: "Eesti Raamat," 1970), 72, 79–105.
2. Seppo Lallukka, *Suomalais-ugrilaiset kansat Neuvostoliiton uusimpien väestönlaskentojen valossa*, (Finno-Ugric Peoples in the Post-War Soviet Censuses), (Helsinki: Neuvostoliitto-instituutti (The Soviet Institute), 1982), 20, 22, 29–33.
3. For relevant examples see, Lallukka, *Suomalais* 20, 22, 25–28; for substantiating figures see Tsentral'noe statisticheskoye upravlenie RSFSR. *Karel's-kaya ASSR: 60 let. Statistichesky sbornik*, (The Central Statistical Directorate of the Russian SFSR. The Carelian ASSR: 60 years. A statistical collection), (Petrozavodsk: Kareliya, 1980.)
4. Mark, *Zur Herkunft* 48–49.
5. D.V. Bubrich & A.P. Barantsev, *Karel'skaya piśmennost'*, (Written Carelian), (Leningrad: Pribaltiysko-finskoe yazykoznaniye, 1967), 89–104.
6. Elias Lönnrot, *Kalevala*, (Helsinki: Suomalaisen Kirjallisuuden Seura, (Finnish Literature Society), 1835–36).
7. Lallukka, *Suomalais* 28–29.
8. Lauri Kettunen, *Suomen lähisukukielten luonteenomaiset piirteet*, (Characteristics of the languages near-related to Finnish [Balto-Finnic]), (Helsinki: Suomalaisen Kirjallisuuden Seura, 1960).
9. A.J. Sjögren, *Tutkijan tieni*, (My Way as Scientist), edited and translated from Swedish into Finnish by A.J. Joki, (Helsinki: Suomalaisen Kirjallisuuden Seura, 1955).
10. F.A. Andreev, *Vepskijan grammatikan openuzkirj*, (The Vepsian Grammar Textbook), (Leningrad: 1934); M.M. Hämäläinen & F.A. Andreev, *Vepsä-Venähine vajehnik*, (Vepsian-Russian Dictionary), (Moscow-Leningrad: 1936).
11. Arvo Laanest, *Sissejuhatus läänemeresoome keeltesse*, (Introduction to the

Balto-Finnic Languages), (Tallinn: The Academy of Sciences of the Estonian SSR, 1975), 11.

12. Lallukka, *Suomalais*, 20, 29.

13. Lauri Honko, *Geisterglaube in Ingermanland*, (Helsinki: Academia Scientiarum Fennica, 1962), 42.

14. *Inkeriläisten Viesti*, (The Ingrians' News), No. 2, Helsinki 1983, 12–14.

15. See, Honko, *Geisterglaube*, and *Inkerin suomalaisten historia*, (The History of the Finns of Ingria), (Jyväskylä: Inkeriläisten Sivistyssäätiö Helsingissä, [The Ingrians' Educational Foundation in Helsinki], 1969).

16. For documentation on this shocking incident see, Eino Hanski, *Brödrabataljonen*, (The Brother Battalion), (Stockholm: Askild & Kärnekull, 1979).

17. Honko, *Geisterglaube*.

18. I.A. Selitskaya, "Bibliography of Literature in the Izhorïan Language," in *Sovetskoe Finno-ugrovedenie* (Soviet Finno-Ugristics), Vol I, No 4, 1956, 302–305.

19. Paul Ariste, "Vajalaisten nykyisyydestä" (The Votes at the Present Time), Viritäjä (Initiator), Vol. 61, No 1, Helsinki, 1951, 119–23.

20. J.A. Sjögren, "Bericht über eine im Auftrage der Russischen Geographischen Gesellschaft während der Sommermonate des Jahres 1846 nach dem Gouvernement Livland und Kurland unternommene Reise zur genauen Untersuchung der Reste Liven und Krewingen," *Denkschriften der Russischen Geographischen Gesellschaft zu St. Petersburg*, I, (Weimar, 1849), 453–605; F. J. Wiedemann, "Uber die Nationalität und die Sprache der jetzt ausgestorbenen Krewinen in Kurland," *Mémoires de l'Académie Impériale des Sciences de St. Pétersbourg*, 7th series, 8, No. 2, (St. Pétersbourg: L'Académie Impériale des Sciences, 1871), 1–119.

21. Peter von Koeppen, "Die Bewohner Kur- und Livlands im Allgemeinen und die Liven insbesondere," *Bulletin de la classe des sciences, historiques, philologiques et politiques de l'Académie Impériale des Sciences de St. Pétersbourg*, 3, (St. Pétersbourg: L'Académie Impériale des Sciences, 1847), 259–260.

22. T. de Pauley, *Description ethnographique des peuples de la Russie*, (St. Pétersbourg: L'Académie Impériale des Sciences, 1847), 10.

23. E.N. Setälä, "A liv nép és nyelve" (Livonia. People and Language), *Nyelvtudomínyi Közlemények*, (The Linguistics Bulletin), 21, (Budapest, 1890), 241–64.

24. Lauri Kettunen, *Livisches Wörterbuch*, (Helsinki: Suomalais-Ugrilainen Seura, (Finno-Ugric Society), 1938), VIII-IX.

25. Laanest, *Sissejvhatus*, 12.

26. Mikko Korhonen, *Johdatus lapin kielen historiaan*, (Introduction to the History of Lappish), (Helsinki: Suomalaisen Kirjallisuuden Seura, 1981), 15.

27. Mark, *Zur Herkunft* 49, 73.

28. Heikki Paasonen, "Die sogenannten Karataj-mordwinen oder Karatajen," *Journal de la Société Finno-ougrienne*, 21, Helsinki, (1903), 3–51.

29. Mark, *Zur Herkunft*, 73.
30. Gyula Décsy, *Einführung in die finnisch-ugrische Sprach-wissenschaft*, (Wiesbaden: Otto Harrassowitz, 1965), 96.
31. Julius Mägiste, *Idasoome-ugri rahvaist, keelist ja kirjandusist*. Seminariet för finsk-ugriska sprak vid Lunds universitet. (On the Eastern Finno-Ugric Peoples, their Languages and Literatures. Seminar of Finno-Ugric Languages, University of Lund), (Lund: University of Lund, 1958), 4.
32. Eduard Päll, "Jooni nõukogude fennougristika arenemisest," (Some outlines of the development of the Soviet Finno-Ugristics), *Looming*, (The Creation), 10, Tallinn, 1972, 1704–5.
33. Heikki Paasonen & Paavo Ravila, *Mordvinische Volksdichtung*, (Helsinki: Suomalais-Ugrilainen Seura, 1938–1981), 1–8.
34. Mägiste, *Idasoome-ugri*, 11.
35. Mark, *Zur Herkunft*, 46.
36. Décsy, *Einführung*, 107.
37. Jószef Budenz, "Orosz eredetü szók a cseremisz nyelvben" (Words of Russian origin in the Cheremis language), *Nyelvtudomány Közlemények* (Linguistics Bulletin), 4, Pesten 1865, pp. 429–39.
38. Mark, *Zur Herkunft*.
39. ———.
40. Péter Domokos, *Itäisten suomalaisugrilaisten kansojen kirjallisuudesta*, (On the Eastern Finno-Ugrians Literature), (Helsinki: Suomalaisen Kirjallisuuden Seura, 1983), 195–207.
41. Mark, *Zur Herkunft*.
42. See E.N. Setälä, "Suomensukuisten kansojen esihistoria," (The Pre-History of the Finnish-Kindred People), *Suomen Suku*, 1, (The Finnish-Kindred People), Vol. I, (Helsinki: Suomalaisen Kirjallisuuden Seura, 1926), 172.
43. See Péter Hajdú, "Sukulaisuuden kielellistä taustaa," (The Linguistic background of affinity), *Suomalaisugrilaiset* (The Finno-Ugrians), (Helsinki: Suomalaisen Kirjallisuuden Seura, 1975), 43.
44. Mark, *Zur Herkunft*.
45. Ago Künnap, "Kamassid," (The Kamassians), *Saaremaast Sajaanideni*, (From Csel to Sajan Mountains), (Tallinn: Valgus, 1970), 205–206.
46. See Lallukka, *Suomalais*, 9.

9

Russia and the Jews

MIKHAIL AGURSKY

This topic is too complicated, too wide and too controversial to be adequately covered in a single chapter.[1] However, one may at least try to put forward here a few impressionistic views in an attempt at drawing up a balance sheet for Russian-Jewish relations.

I

Before the Revolution, Russian Jews were the victims of the cruel discriminatory policies of the czars as well as of popular anti-Semitism. They were therefore vitally interested in the liberalization of the Russian state which would naturally include the abolition of discrimination against Jews. Since demands to this effect had been consistently rejected by the authorities, while a wave of pogroms began in 1881, Jewish youth was quickly revolutionized. But it would doubtlessly be a grave distortion of reality to regard revolutionary Jews as anti-Russian. Indeed, whoever among them was disappointed with Russia and ceased identifying with it had a very simple solution: to emigrate; and in fact before the Revolution hundreds of thousands of Jews left Russia, scattering in all directions. Those who remained, and especially those who risked their freedom and their lives by participating in the revolutionary movement, regarded their destiny as inseparable from that of Russia and the Russian people. One must add that in the Russian Empire there were also some Jews who identified with Poland and a few other non-Russian nations, but the majority clearly

608

identified with Russia. These Jews, together with their like-minded Russian compatriots, could strongly oppose some Russian traditional institutions and values (as well as also some Jewish ones), but they regarded Russia as their mother-country and wished her well.

Radical Jews, such as Rosa Luxemburg, could have had vested interests in the abolition of national boundaries, but they actively opposed the very idea of dismembering the Russian multinational state. The same, though for entirely different reasons, applied to the non-radical Jewish bourgeoisie, first of all because its economic prosperity to a great extent depended on the territorial integrity of the Russian Empire. For example, the economic activity of Polish and Baltic Jews was entirely oriented to the captive Russian market. Many Jewish businessmen served as brokers between Russia and the West, relying on the Jewish international economic network. The separation of Poland from Russia was a mortal threat for Jewish business in Poland (this was aptly noticed by the dissident Bolshevik, Grigory Alexinsky, before the Revolution[2]). The desperate economic situation of the Jews in independent Poland after World War I was, in fact, caused by Poland's separation from Russia—an economic blow from which the Polish Jewry has never been able to recover.

Apart from the economic interests, the dissolution of the Russian Empire into separate nation-states undermined Jewish communal unity and cultural integrity generally. The five million Jews inhabiting the Russian Eempire were closely interrelated regardless of where they lived there; indeed their family links transcended all provincial boundaries and made the Jewish community across the whole empire one single national entity cemented by common cultural and religious centers such as those in Warsaw, Vilna, Odessa, Berdichev, etc.. The Lithuanian Mitsnagdic *yeshivot* even supplied religious leadership for the whole of the East European Jewry. In the same way, Hassidic ramifications were extraterritorial, too. The survival of this entire Jewish infrastructure could have been secured only by the continuous territorial-political unity of the Russian Empire and, conversely, that infrastructure was unable to survive the collapse of that empire.

It is important to stress these points as they effectively destroy the various primitive Russian anti-Semitic myths which ascribe to the Jews a sinister wish to destroy Russia as a great power.[3]

Many Jews, in spite of living among the non-Russian nations of the empire, chose to identify themselves with the great imperial Russian culture in preference to that of the particular local nation, which they usually regarded as being "parochial," and, within the framework of an imperial Russian state, of not much practical use anyway. Because of that, local anti-Russian nationalism was in many cases directed also against the Jews as conductors of the "alien Russian cultural influence," which amplified locally bred anti-Semitism quite substantially. It is therefore not surprising that many Jews, regarding the imperial Russian state as their protector against the wrath of the local nations, abhorred the prospect of Russia's disintegration. That these fears of the Jews were not entirely unjustified was aptly demonstrated by the 1919–1921 anti-Jewish pogroms in the Ukraine. It was thus only natural for a significant number of Jews who lived in the non-Russian areas (mainly in the Ukraine and Belorussia) to join the Bolsheviks in their determined struggle against local nationalisms. This significantly complicated the situation of the Soviet Jews in many respects, especially when the Soviet state started to use anti-Semitism as one of its national policy instruments.

We will come to the discussion of these matters below. Here it suffices to say that as difficult and complicated as the situation of the Jews under the Soviet regime has been, that of the Jews who remained outside the boundaries of the new Soviet state, especially in Poland, was not all that easy either. During World War II, the impoverished Polish Jewry was almost totally exterminated by the Nazis, mainly because a relatively small Poland, being unable to defend itself against Hitler, could not manage to protect from him her Jews either, while a considerable part of the Soviet Jewry managed to survive by escaping from the advancing Nazi troops into the Russian hinterlands. This was yet another example of the danger for the Jews of living in a small state.

II

A comprehensive solution to the Jewish problem in Russia was suggested by the most powerful socialist organization of the Russian Jews, the Bund. The Bund always wanted the Jews to remain an organic part of Russia, without them losing, however, their national identity. For this the Bund relied on the concept of cultural-national autonomy, seeing in it the most appropriate foundation for a new Russian multinational state. This concept, which the Bund borrowed from the Austrian social democrats,[4] stipulated for every citizen of a multinational state, wherever he lived, equal cultural-national rights combined with those of equal political participation and representation. According to this concept, any diaspora nationality should have a representative political body elected by all its members regardless of their geographical location, and also possess its own national schools and other cultural institutions wherever sufficient groups of members of this nationality existed. The Bolsheviks declared this concept to be bourgeois nationalist,[5] and therefore it was never implemented.

III

The attraction of Russian culture for many Russian Jews was overpowering indeed. It could be described in terms of an unrequited love. This unhappy but fruitful love story is not over yet. The reasons why so many Jews in the Russian Empire suddenly fell in love with the Russians and their culture are not entirely clear, although there are several sophisticated theories which try to explain them, for example, by the affinity of the Jewish and Russian psyches, etc..

Of the over five millions Jews who lived in the Russian Empire, only 67,000 spoke Russian in 1897.[6] We can assume that the vast majority of Yiddish-speaking Russian Jews were indifferent to Russian culture. But since the Russian-speaking Jews belonged to the Jewish intellectual elite, their importance greatly exceeded their numerical strength.

The first Jewish declarations of sincere love for Russia and her culture could be traced back to the beginning of the nineteenth century. The powerful Russian Empire, which captured Poland with her Jews, seemed to some of these Jews to be the force which would free them from oppression by the arrogant Polish nobility. Itzhak Baer Levinson, the father of the *Haskala* movement in Russia, appealed to the Russian Jews to study Russian as a vital part of their education.[7] Almost at the same time a Volynian Jew, Barukh Tsatskes, translated for the first time a piece of Russian literature into Hebrew. His choice was the now almost forgotten Russian poet of the eighteenth century, Mikhail Kheraskov.[8] Thus the Jewish interest in Russian literature has a tradition going back more than 150 years. Levinson, who did not break with Orthodox Judaism, tried to find theological legitimacy for the rapprochement between the Jews and the Russians: As Christians, the Russians were sons of Noah; if they were to fulfill Noah's seven commandments, they would have a share in the world to come.[9]

In spite of all the vicissitudes of Russian-Jewish relations during the nineteenth and twentieth centuries, the Russian-Jewish intelligentsia arrived at a consensus whereby it somehow managed to separate the artistic genius of great Russian writers, and the substance of the Russian culture generally, from any of the anti-Semitic traits that this culture contained. It is almost impossible to find any repudiation by a Jew of a Russian writer or artist of genius because of his anti-Semitism. Russian Jews listened only to that writer's universal message; like genuine lovers they paid no attention to the dark sides of the object of their love. When stressing the universalism and ignoring the narrowness of a Dostoyevsky or a Gogol, the Russian Jews perhaps reflected their own universalist attitudes more than those of the subjects of their love and praise.

Many Russian Jews were deeply involved with Russian culture, but a central place among them probably belongs to Mikhail Gershenzon. A Bessarabian Jew, he became not only one of the best historians of Russian culture, but took a special interest in the most nationalistic aspect of it, Slavophilism. His work exerted a great influence on the whole Russian intellectual history. Some Jews accused Gershenzon of an excessive involvement in Russian affairs,[10] but he rejected this accusation and was very proud about his biography being included in the *Jewish Encyclopedia*. Indeed, along with the work exploring the problems of Russian culture proper, Gershenzon did quite a lot to popularize the new Hebrew poetry in Russia.[11] However, latterly he started preaching total assimilation of the Jews, seeing in it the best contribution they could make to the world's culture and history, which naturally elicited a negative Zionist reaction.[12] The Israeli historian Itzhak Maor, however, defended Gershenzon; according to him, Gershenzon's philosophy was common to many other European Jews and he was not the only Jew who fell in love with the Russians, and even with the Slavophiles.[13]

Even such a committed Zionist as Vladimir Zhabotinsky was deeply involved with Russian culture. Although he pointed out in his work the anti-Semitic trends inherent in that culture, he never stopped admiring Russian poetry and was an excellent Russian essayist and poet in his own right. Even his translations of Bialik and other Hebrew poets into Russian demonstrate that the Russian language was his natural milieu.

Some Orthodox Jews, including certain members of the rabbinate, were not immune from Russian cultural influence either. An Orthodox Habad rabbi, Abraham Hen, who escaped from Russia after the Revolution and later became the rabbi of the Yeshurun Synagogue in Jerusalem, referred, for example, to Dostoyevsky in an essay against capital punishment. In this essay, Rabbi Hen approvingly cites Dostoyevsky's views, according to which the value of human life is absolute and consequently its taking by the deliberate action of another man cannot be justified.[14] One should add that Rabbi Hen wrote this essay in Hebrew for a solely Jewish, even Orthodox Jewish, readership. Thus he cannot be accused of flirting with the Russian reader by quoting a Russian author. Furthermore, it was not necessary for him to refer to Dostoyevsky's authority to persuade his Jewish readers of the absolute value of human life. It is therefore quite obvious that Rabbi Hen chose to base his arguments on this writer's works and ideas out of sheer admiration for them—an admiration which he felt in spite of his knowing perfectly well what Dostoyevsky's attitude to the Jews was. Apparently Rabbi Hen did not consider the admiration for the anti-Semite Dostoyevsky to be sacrilegious at all. (Dostoyevsky was not Rabbi Hen's only Russian favorite. He also used to cite Tolstoy and even the

Russian anarchist Peter Kropotkin, calling him "a saint of the new world."[15])

Among Orthodox Jews, Rabbi Hen as an admirer of Russian culture was not alone. The well-known Jewish religious leader Yehuda Leib Don-Yahia did not hesitate to refer positively to Tolstoy in his sermons in a Soviet Russian synagogue in the 1920s, in spite of the fact that this great writer was a Christian *par excellence*. Moreover, Rabbi Don-Yahia referred to Tolstoy's most Christian essay, "Confession."[16] Certainly, the rabbi did not share Tolstoy's beliefs, but, following Yehuda Halevi, he considered Christianity as partly stemming from the Torah and therefore tried to find a common denominator among all believers in God.[17] Don-Yahia also held in high esteem the radical Russian literary critic, Dmitry Pisarev, in spite of the fact that Pisarev was a committed atheist.[18]

Rabbi Shmuel Aleksandrov (killed by the Germans in Bobruisk in 1941) provided a general cabbalistic theory for the acceptance by the Jews of non-Jewish culture and knowledge. According to him, the Jews are exclusive owners of the fruits of the tree of life (i.e., the Torah), and the Gentiles—of the fruits of the tree of knowledge. The world's historical process consists in the mythical exchange of the fruits of the two trees, and therefore, by accepting the fruits from the Gentiles (i.e., their philosophical ideas, literary and artistic achievements technology, scientific accomplishments), the Jews give them a new spiritual meaning, thus sanctifying the Gentiles themselves.[19] Hence, according to Aleksandrov, to absorb all new trends proceeding from the Gentiles is an important Jewish objective. Among Aleksandrov's favorite authors were the Russian religious philosopher Vladimir Solovyev and Tolstoy.[20]

Taking a look at current Orthodox Jewish thought we see Rabbi Abraham Bik (Shauli) among the great admirers of Russian culture. Rabbi Bik composed a bibliography of Yiddish writings on Tolstoy.[21]

One should stress once more that Rabbis Hen, Don-Yahia, Aleksandrov, and Bik wrote only in Hebrew (or sometimes in Yiddish), that is with no intention of courting the Gentile reader, but out of deep internal persuasion. However, these Orthodox admirers of Russian culture and thought did not represent the mainstream of Jewish interest in that culture. That mainstream was, of course, represented by the secularly minded Jews.

There were also such Jews who expressed negative attitudes to Russia and Russian culture. They belonged, however, to marginal groups. Some Jewish extremists announced, for example, that any Jewish interest in Russian or any other Gentile culture represents a threat to Jewish national identity and therefore should be outrightly condemned. There were also selective Jewish criticisms of Russian culture whereby only some of its trends were rejected: for example, the Slavophiles. Nonetheless, the overall balance of the Jewish attitudes to Russian culture is overwhelmingly positive.

IV

With regard to the Russian attitude toward the Jews, it would also be unfair to claim that Jews experienced only Russian hostility. Many Russians of different background and education and of various political persuasions—liberals, radicals, and conservatives alike—accepted Jews on equal terms and defended their civil rights and human dignity. Such people as Gorky, Stasov, Korolenko, Vladimir Solovyev, Pirogov, Mordovtsev, Kuskova, Ivan Tolstoy and many, many others were champions of Jewish rights.[22] Naturally, the majority of Russian radicals and revolutionaries also struggled for Jewish equality. All this, however, did not save Russian-Jewish relations from considerable asymmetry. While the Jews were deeply involved in Russian culture and its spiritual content, only a handful of Russians were consciously interested in the Jewish national tradition and spiritual culture. The Jewish world did not exist even for many sincere Russian friends of Jews. Although the Russians knew the Holy Writ, they did not perceive it as being specifically Jewish. One should also bear in mind that the majority of Russian supporters of the Jews were secular in orientation and therefore the Jewish religious heritage was for them largely irrelevant. For these people, the Jews were survivors of a distant past and also victims of unjust and cruel persecutions, no more.

Some Russians were, however, obsessed by the Jewish idea in various ways. The negative role ascribed to the Jews by Christianity, combined with the massive Jewish presence in Russia, impressed a great many Russians. Eventually some of them developed a very ambivalent attitude towards Jews, hesitating between hating and loving them and vice versa.[23] Even such self-avowed anti-Semites as Gogol and Dostoyevsky were not entirely free from this ambivalence. Once Dostoyevsky had even appealed for friendship between Russians and Jews, but his ambivalence with regard to the Jews showed itself not so much in this episodic appeal[24] as in his constant obsession with the idea of the exclusive Divine election of the Russians. For Dostoyevsky the Russians had replaced the Jews as the Chosen People. Although, according to Christian theology, after Christ the Jews lost their "chosenness," no other nation had been proclaimed by the New Testament as their successor. There were different attempts to claim such succession, for example in seventeenth–eighteenth-century England, but Dostoyevsky was the first to claim this right exclusively for the Russians. In his view the Russians had a unique faculty in their relations with other nations—they could better feel and absorb the best ideas of others and that was why they were genuine universalists. Their vocation, he said, was All-Humanity (*vsechelovechnost'*) and they were therefore the only real Europeans.[25]

An almost identical claim was made for the Jews by the above-mentioned Shmuel Aleksandrov on the basis of the Cabbala.[26] (Incidentally, the most elaborate theological justification of Jewish All-Humanity belongs to the Italian Sephardic Rabbi Eliahu Benamozegh who, in 1884, emphasized that it was a Jewish obligation to achieve a religious synthesis from all the best that was produced in the Gentile world, including the religious achievements of ancient Egypt, Greece, Persia, and so on. It was not by chance, said Benamozegh, that Jethro and Avimelech stay so near the cradle of Judaism, symbolizing the transfer of ancient wisdom to the Jews, which they later integrated in the world religion.[27]) Dostoyevsky knew nothing about contemporary Jewish thought, but as a genius he felt acutely the Jewish religious "chosenness," and for that reason he built his theology of Russian election to be the Chosen People in competition with the analogous Jewish claim.

Another extremely ambivalent attitude to the Jews was expressed by Rozanov, also without doubt a man of genius. Sometimes he stressed the superiority of Judaism over Christianity because of the former's more realistic attitude to family life. He accused Christianity of bringing to earth nonrealistic forms of life. Suddenly he switched to wild anti-Semitism, accusing the Jews of the blood ritual during the Beilis trial. Then several years later he became an extreme Judeophile again, even inviting the Jews to rule Russia . . . but with delicacy . . .[28]

V

Russian-Jewish relations have transcended Russia's geographical frontiers. Russian culture has always had a very great impact on both the Israeli and the Jewish diaspora cultures. Aharon Gordon, inspired by Tolstoy and by the ideas of Russian peasant socialism, managed to transplant these ideas to Israel: the Israeli kibbutz movement is a grandiose monument to the Russian cultural legacy.[29]

Russian literature has been a permanent focus of Israeli cultural interests. Many first-rate and even some second-rate Russian writers and poets have been translated into Hebrew. The poetic translations of Pushkin made by Abraham Shlonsky are considered this poet's best translations. A Hebrew reader who does not know Russian has an excellent chance to discover Russian literature.

The late Leah Goldberg, who chaired the Russian Department in the Hebrew University, composed a bibliography of Russian and Soviet writers translated into Hebrew.[30] Here one finds the best selection of Russian literature: Tolstoy, Dostoyevsky, Gogol, Turgenev, Goncharov, Hertzen, Chekhov, Leonid Andreev, Bunin, Merezhkovsky, Prishvin, Gorky, Aleksey Tolstoy, and many others. We can now add such writers as Solzhenitsyn, Bulgakov, Maximov, Voynovich, and others.

All this has certainly influenced Israeli culture. It is not difficult to single out Amos Oz, the Nobel Prize winner for literature, as probably the most Russian-influenced contemporary Israeli writer: Oz himself acknowledges this. One of his most excellent essays is devoted to a Russian theme.[31]

In analyzing the content of some of the great Jewish writers and thinkers of the diaspora, one would certainly also become aware of their permanent interest in Russian culture. Probably one of the most remarkable expressions of this is to be found in Saul Bellow's *Herzog*. The Russian dimension is implicit in the life of this American-Jewish intellectual. Russian books separate Bellow's *Herzog* from his wife in their bed and, when in a state of emotional distress, *Herzog* writes to various Russian dead writers and thinkers, among them Rozanov.

Another example of a diaspora Jew greatly influenced by Russian culture is Sir Isaiah Berlin, who is full of admiration for Hertzen, Tolstoy, Turgenev, Belinsky and others.[32] Berlin is very sensitive to the slightest reverberation of Russian thought.

It is also necessary to put some Western Jewish Communists, including Israeli Communists, in a somewhat different perspective. Sometimes one might ask whether Jewish communism today is not a kind of sublimated Russophilism.

The recent controversy in Israel over Richard Wagner cannot help but excite feelings concerning the relations between Jews and Russians as well. Indeed, Wagner's case must be seen in a broader perspective than that of Jewish-German relations alone. It is very difficult to make any quantitative comparisons among anti-Semites; there is no such thing as a scale for anti-Semitism. But there is no doubt that Dostoyevsky will be awarded an honorable place among the most distinguished anti-Semites, and Gogol can successfully compete with him in this worldwide contest.

Nevertheless, both Dostoyevsky and Gogol are favorite writers of the Israeli readership. Their works have been widely translated into Hebrew and proliferate on the stages of Israeli theaters. A Hebrew version of a Dostoyevsky play was broadcast on Israel's television. Nobody has dared to proclaim these Russian writers *personae non gratae* in Israel, and, one could add, if this were done, it would cut Israeli culture off from the most powerful and most productive source of influence, thus putting the whole history of Israeli culture into question.

VI

After the Revolution of 1917 the situation of Jews in Russia changed drastically. The Provisional Government (not the Bolsheviks and their Soviet government, as many still tend to believe) abolished the Pale of Settlement and all other discriminatory regulations concerning the Jews which were enforced and maintained in Russia by the czarist régime. When, after the February 1917 Revolution, the democratic and revolutionary political parties gained a preponderant role in Russia's public life, the Jews, who played an active and in many cases a leading role in these parties, suddenly surged to the top of Russia's political establishment, too.

This situation did not change much after October 1917, when the Bolsheviks seized power in Russia, for among the leading stratum of the Bolshevik party the Jews were numerically and functionally as prominent as they were in all other Russian anti-autocratic revolutionary and democratic parties. The nonpolitical Jewish intelligentsia, being predominantly anti-czarist, was prepared to accept the rule in Russia of any revolutionary party and therefore acquiesced to Bolshevik rule much more easily than its purely Russian counterparts. The pro-Bolshevik attitudes among the Jews were substantially reinforced by the experience of the Civil War during which the "Whites" in many instances indulged into anti-Semitic practices or condoned them, whereas the "Reds" actively suppressed anti-Semitic outbursts and otherwise demonstrated their intolerance of anti-Semitism.

This was one of the reasons why the great exodus of Russian intelligentsia during and after the Civil War did not affect its Jewish part as drastically as it affected its Gentile majority. As a result, the Jewish element among the remnants of Russia's educated classes within the USSR became, if not predominant, then at least unprecedentedly significant even in terms of sheer size.

It was perhaps not too surprising that in the early period of Russia's Soviet development the politically engaged Jews, those who constituted the Bolshevik Old Guard or joined the Bolsheviks during the Revolution and Civil War, occupied a prominent place in the Soviet political and military elite and played a leading role in the cultural revolution aimed at changing the traditional Russian identity into a Marxist-Leninist one. Much more surprising was the fact that many thousands of Jews suddenly appeared in the top echelons of the Russian culture-makers (writers, musicians, artists, actors, etc.) and of experts on traditional Russian culture (historians, archeologists, literary and art critics, linguists, etc.).

In this respect it suffices to mention the names of the poets and writers Boris Pasternak, Osip Mandel'shtam, Yury Tynyanov, Ilya Ehrenburg, Venyamin Kaverin, Semyon Marshak, Nikolay Erdman; of literary critics Boris Eikenbaum and Viktor Shklovsky; of the theater director Vsevolod Meyerkhol'd; of the composers Isaak Dunaevsky, brothers Pokrass, Matvey Blanter of the cinema directors Sergey Eisenstein, Dziga Vertov, Mark Donskoy, Leonid Trauberg, Mikhail Romm, Abram Room, Yuly Rayzman; of the artists Natan Al'tman, Aleksandr Tyshler, Robert Fal'k, Eli Lysitsky; of the actors Serafima Birman, Lev Sverdlin, Arkady Raykin, Faina Ranevskaya, Mark Prudkin, Mark Bernes, Sergey Yursky; of the musicians David and Igor Oistrakh, Samuil Feinberg, Emil Gilels, Yakov Flier. These and hosts of other Jews belong to the flower of what grew on Russian soil during the Soviet years. It goes without saying that all these people did not participate in Russian cultural life as Jews—indeed, the great majority of them were almost entirely Russified.[33]

In the initial period of Bolshevik rule there was nothing in the policies of the Soviets that could be qualified as specifically anti-Semitic. One could rather say that Bolshevik policies were antinational with regard to all nations equally. The Bolsheviks' main target was to provide a universal Marxist-Leninist melting pot in which all national-cultural and religious traditions would be annihilated and from which all nations would emerge as a single sociopolitical entity held together by a monolithic and uniform "proletarian culture." With this goal in mind the Bolsheviks launched a violent attack against the traditional Russian culture in which, together with the Russian Communists, the Jewish ones assumed a very prominent role. The same Jewish Communist zealots, along with their Russian and other counterparts, did their utmost in order to annihilate also, for the same reasons, the traditional Jewish culture. As a result, many Russians blamed the Jews for the Soviet regime's attempts at destroying Russian culture and for the damage that was thus inflicted on Russia, whereas many Jews blamed the Russians for the Soviet regime's attempted destruction of their identity.

Hence, the massive and almost total Jewish involvement into all aspects of Russian life which has taken place under the Soviet regime, instead of providing for a genuine Russian-Jewish rapprochement, has, on the contrary, greatly intensified Russian-Jewish animosity, bringing it to an unprecedentedly high and tense level.

The Marxist-Leninist melting-pot installed by the Soviet regime has not only failed to produce on the intended scale the assimilatory results with regard to the Russians or any of the other territorial nations of the USSR, but provoked in these nations the exactly opposite effect, that of stimulating the nationalist attitudes and, moreover, of enhancing their most extreme forms. The Soviet melting pot has achieved better results with regard to nonterritorial national minorities, most prominently the Jews, or, to be more precise, with those significant elements among them, which were traditionally striving for assimilation with the dominant territorial nation, that is chiefly with the Russians. Stalin was quick to realize the persistence and even growth of Russian nationalism despite all efforts to liquidate it and, in order to gain some more popularity for his regime, from the mid–1930s relented the Bolshevik anti-Russian drive and gradually started to flirt with some Russian nationalist sensitivities. The necessity for Stalin to appeal to Russian nationalism was greatly amplified by the war, and after the war Stalin sought new ways in which the, by now irrepressible, Russian national sentiments, could be so channeled that, instead of representing a threat to Bolshevik totalitarianism, they could be used for its further enhancement. Anti-Semitism was chosen by Stalin as one of the means to that end, and it has remained part and parcel of Soviet policy ever since. Naturally enough, official anti-Semitism amalgamated with multiplying expressions of popular anti-Semitism caused a powerful resurrection of Jewish national consciousness. Russian-Jewish relations in the USSR have thus come to the brink on both sides.

However, the regime's efforts to establish its genuinely Russian (not Jewish as many Russians believe) national credentials by means of embracing anti-Semitism did not succeed sufficiently well either. Some Russian nationalists were not convinced and they continue to see in the Jews the force which still dominates the Soviet Union and which, with the regime's connivance, has infiltrated all pores of Russia's culture and life with the determined view of thus eventually destroying what has been left of true Russia altogether.[34]

The anti-Semitic attitudes of these Russian nationalists, now vigilantly controlled and, with regard to putting them into practice, effectively suppressed by the regime, would inevitably come out into the open in the event of the Soviet regime's demise. This is to say that there is no real future for the Jews in Russia, and perhaps in a non-Soviet Russia even less so than in the present USSR. It seems therefore that the only realistic way out of this Russian-Jewish impasse would be a mass and final exodus of the Jews from Russia. That many Soviet Jews have realized the hopelessness of their situation in Russia and accepted the prospect of exodus is evidenced by the fact that the resurrection of Jewish national consciousness in the USSR has taken the form of a movement for Jewish emigration. There is little doubt that the nationalistically oriented new Russia will be happy to see the back of the Jews, too, and, in contrast with the present

Soviet regime, which bars the freedom of Jews to emigrate, will do its utmost to encourage the Jews to leave Russia.

Also, there would hardly be a different future for the Jews in most of the non-Russian nation-states that would succeed the USSR. Exodus would, no doubt, be the best fate awaiting the Jews living in the Moslem republics because of these republics' natural solidarity with the Moslem-Arab cause. Anti-Semitic trends in the Ukraine are even stronger than in Russia and all the arguments about Russian-Jewish relations would even, to a larger extent, apply to the Ukrainian-Jewish relations. The Belorussians, whatever their own attitude to the Jews may be, will most probably follow the Russians in this respect. Among the non-Russian nation-states which would be likely to succeed the USSR perhaps only Georgia and the Baltic States would accept the continuing presence of Jews without too much controversy.

VII

The tragic history of Jews in Russia is thus nearing its end. This history was very beneficial for the Jews, as beneficial perhaps, as the not less tragic history of the Jews in Spain. In spite of the fact that the Jews were eventually expelled from Spain, the several-centuries-long period during which they lived in that country was extremely fruitful for them in terms of both the acquisition of universal culture and the consolidation of the specific Jewish national-cultural identity. But what about Russia? What would the consequences of the final Jewish exodus be for her? Would "Jewishless" Russia not share the destiny of Spain which, after the expulsion of its Jews, found itself in the situation of a constant relative decline? It seems that with that question asked, the brief and somewhat scattered attempt at drawing in this chapter the balance sheet of Russian-Jewish relations may be properly concluded.

Notes

1. I dealt with this topic in more detail in other works. Cf., M. Agursky, *The Third Rome*, Boulder, CO: Westview Press, 1987; M. Agursky, "The Prospects of National Bolshevism", in Conquest R. ed., *The Last Empire: Nationality and the Soviet Future*, Stanford, CA; Hoover Institution Press, 1986.
2. Alexinsky G., *La Russie et la guerre*, (Paris: A. Colin, 1915), 177–178.
3. For an account of a few such myths, see my *The Third Rome* which also

contains an abundant bibliography. See also M. Agursky, "The Intensification of Neo-Nazi Dangers in the Soviet Union," in Meerson-Aksenov and Shragin eds., *The Political, Social and Religious Thought of Russian "Samizdat"—An Anthology*, (Belmont, Mass.: Nordland Publishing Co., 1977).

4. The leading exponents of this concept were Rudolf Springer (Karl Renner) and Otto Bauer.
5. Cf., J. Stalin, "Marxism and the National Question," in J. Stalin, *Works*: 2, (Moscow, Foreign Language Publishing House, 1953).
6. See: Y. Slutsky, *Ha-itonut ha-yehudit b'mea ha-tsha-esrei* (The Jewish-Russian Journalism in the 19th Century), (Jerusalem: Mosad Bialik, 1970), 35.
7. M. Agursky, "Universalist Trends in Jewish Religious Thought," in *Immanuel*, No. 18, (Fall 1984), 44–47.
8. See J. Raisin, *The Haskala Movement in Russia*, (Philadelphia: The Jewish Publication Society, 1913), 124.
9. Agursky, *Universalist Trends*, 46.
10. M. Lazerson, *Pravo na banal'nost'*, (The Right to Banality), (Riga: Kul'tura, 1925), 26–27.
11. See his introduction to V. Khodasevich ed., *Evreyskaya antologiya*, (The Jewish Anthology), (Moscow: Safrut, 1918).
12. M. Gershenzon, *Sud'by evreyskogo naroda*, (The Fate of the Jewish People), (Petrograd-Berlin: Epokha, 1922).
13. I. Maor, "Gershenzon v'ashkafotav al'ha-yahdut," (Gershenzon and his Views on Judaism), in *He-avar*, 15, 1969.
14. See in Agursky, *Universalist Trends*, 51.
15. ———, 52.
16. ———.
17. See, for example, H. Schoeps, *The Jewish-Christian Argument*, (London: Faber and Faber, 1963), 68.
18. Cf., A. Bik, "Sifrut toranit v'hagut datit ivrit b'Brit-Ha-Moazot," (Torah Literature and Hebrew Religious Thought in the Soviet Union), in *Shvut*, 1, 1973.
19. For more details, see: Agursky, *Universal Trends*, 49–51.
20. ———.
21. A. Bik, "Tolstois werk in Yiddish," in *Yiddishe Kultur*, 15, No. 9, 30–31.
22. Cf., M. Agursky and M. Shklovskaya, *Gor'ky. Iz literaturnogo naslediya*, (Gor'ky. From the Literary Legacy), (Jerusalem: The Hebrew University of Jerusalem, 1986).
23. A most remarkable example of such an ambivalent anti-Semitism can be found in writings of Vasily Shul'gin. Cf., Shul'gin V., *Chto nam v nikh ne nravitsia*, (What We Do Not Like in Them), (Paris: Russie minor, 1929).
24. F. Dostoyevsky, *The Diary of a Writer*, (London: Cassel and Co., 1949), 2, 651–53.
25. ———, 784–85.
26. Agursky, *Universalist Trends*, 50.
27. E. Benamozegh, *Israel et l'humanité*, (Paris: Albin Michel, 1961), 109–12.

28. Rozanov always had Jewish admirers. One of his recent admirers was the late Pavel Goldshtein who published the Russian-language Jewish Orthodox magazine *Menora*. Cf., V. Rozanov, "Dva pis'ma," (Two Letters), in *Menora*, No. 8, 1975, V. Rozanov, "Tuflia" (Shoe), in *Menora* No. 15, 1978; P. Goldshtein, "Bozhestvennyi dar tvorcheskoy svobody," (God's Gift of Creative Freedom), in *Menora* No. 2, 1973.

29. Cf., H. Rose, *The Life and Thought of A.D. Gordon*, (New York: Bloch Publ. Co., 1964).

30. L. Goldberg, *Sifrut yafa clamit b'tirgumim b'ivrit*, (World Literature in Hebrew Translations), (Tel-Aviv: Ha-merkaz l'tarbut, 1953).

31. A. Oz, "Ivan Illitch's Sillogism," in *Harpers Magazine*, (September 1979).

32. I. Berlin, *Russian Thinkers*, (London: The Hogarth Press, 1978).

33. Cf., J. Miller ed., *Jews in Soviet Culture*, (New Brunswick-London: Transaction Books, 1984).

34. There were a lot of accusations like this, both implicit and explicit, in Soviet publications. One can mention such authors as V. Kozhinov, I. Belza, V. Petelin, Y. Seleznev, L. Zhukov, Y. Loshchits, and others who made this point.

Cf., M. Agursky, *Contemporary Russian Nationalism—History Revised*, Research Paper No. 45. (Jerusalem: The Soviet and East European Research Center, the Hebrew University of Jerusalem Press, 1982)

B

THE SOVIET BLOC

10

A Possible Impact of a Change in the USSR upon East European Systems

RADOSLAV SELUCKY

The principal economic limit of the Soviet system lies in its present declining rate of growth which oscilated, during the past five years, around some 2–3 percent per annum. Such a slow economic growth cannot, at the same time, sustain Russia's huge military spending and at least maintain the present living standards. If this slow pace were achieved through innovations and a steady increase in productivity of labor and capital or, to use the Russian term, through an intensive economic growth, it would allow for the restructuring of the entire national economy and for a future revival of the lost dynamics. The intensive growth, however, cannot be achieved in the condition of the command economic system. This conclusion has been established some twenty years ago by economic theory[1] and since then has been accepted by some ruling Communist parties.[2] What is more, the command economy combined with the totalitarian political system became the main obstacle for an overall modernization. Modernization needs computer technology on a mass scale. A system in which information is strictly rationed, distorted by propaganda and/or kept secret, cannot master that technological change. A system which cannot afford a free flow of information, a free access to copying machines and computers with data banks, automated electronic telecommunication system and an overall mobility required by the recent technological changes, has to become more and more backward in comparison with the advanced Western systems.

Some scholars would disagree with that statement. They would point out that the Soviet Union was capable of modernization under the old system (i.e., totalitarianism and command economy). They would argue that the Soviet Union has become, under the old system, a superpower. Though I do not deny that the Soviet Union is a military superpower, I would like to look at the achievement from a different angle.

Command economic system is a *sui generis* war economy.[3] A war economy is always an emergency system in which all the resources are mobilized irrespective of costs, for an achievement of one objective only. That is why a command economic system has to rely on the method of the "main link," on one priority at a time. On top of it, while in all the other branches of a command economy there is the monopoly of the producer, the military industry enjoys a special status: in this particular sector, it is the consumer who has an absolute monopoly. The consumer, in this case, is the country's ruling elite. That is why the Soviet Union could have become a military superpower under its command economic system. Moreover, as a country with a medium level of economic development, it became a military superpower at the expense of low-living standards of the people and of an underdeveloped infrastructure. The Soviet technological base is too low to turn the country into an economic superpower. Therefore, the superpower status of the Soviet Union is shaky and distorted: the USSR is only a one-dimensional superpower.

The country—rather semi-developed though overindustrialized—has become a military superpower by spending some 33 percent of its annual national income for investments and some 17 percent of its annual national income on military expenses. If compared with the golden rule of Western market economies (some 12 percent of the GNP for investments, some 3–8 percent for military spending), it becomes transparently clear that such a high proportion of the national income taken from the people's consumption can be explained only by the country's totalitarian dictatorship. Under no other system would the population comply with such deprivation.

To know the cause of the problem is one matter and to resolve it is another matter. One may remember the famous dictum coined first by Mr. Amalrik: In order to survive, the system has to change; in order to survive, the system must not change.[4] The dilemma lies in that any systemic change conducive to an overall modernization requires a market economic system free from an ideological and political straitjacket provided by the Party apparat, by the partocracy; and in the political sphere, a systemic change would have to turn the totalitarian dictatorship at least to a sort of authoritarian system. At the first look, that is a subtle change; in reality, it would be a profound revolutionary systemic change, a *sine qua non* of any attempt to take the task of modernization seriously.

At the moment, there is little indication that the Gorbachev's leadership is attempting to initiate any structural reform.[5] On the contrary, the leadership seems to believe that the system might be improved by a better managerial and labor discipline. One might admit that an improved discipline could contribute to a higher rate of economic growth for a limited period of time. But even in the best circumstances, the growth would have to rely again on the traditional extensive sources which are almost exhausted. If the new leadership is unable to achieve, let us say before the end of this decade, a clearly visible economic revival, the Soviet regime might become destabilized to such an extent that it could no longer fully control its East European satellites.

There could be yet another change, however. If the Soviet regime failed to deal with its systemic problems within the framework of Marxist-Leninist ideology, it might lose its Communist identity and acquire a more traditional Russian nationalistic identity instead. That would mean that the Party yielded its power and control to another group capable of ruling the country. The group in question could be the military in a combination with a technocratic and scientific elite allied with young professionals in the state security apparat. Though such a change would have an open-ended scenario, it would no longer require that East European satellites maintain the rigid patterns of the Soviet system. If—in such an event—the present "proletarian internationalism" dogma were abandoned, East and Central European satellites would acquire more freedom to shape their domestic systems according to their indigenous needs and traditions providing that they remained friendly to Russia along the lines of a sort of Finlandization within the Soviet bloc. In his fascinating paper[6] Alexander Shtromas put forward the hypothesis that the Soviet system may be approaching a point of systemic change. Because the traditional system led by the partocracy is unable to renew Russia's dynamic development and properly (i.e., in an intensive way) utilize the country's material and intellectual resources, the partocrats are to be replaced by the technocrats. To make a clear distinction between the two strata, I wish to use an analogy from Karl Marx's writings. In the third volume of *Das Kapital*,[7] Marx drew a clear dividing line between "capital as function" and "capital as ownership." From the point of view of a functional capitalist, capital is management, innovation, enterpreneurship. From the point of view of an institutional capitalist, capital is private property with the right to appropriate surplus. Power of the functional capitalist is derived from his function while power of the institutional capitalist is derived from his ownership of the property. Functionally speaking, the former is essential for the system while the latter may become, under certain circumstances, dysfunctional and redundant. The circumstances under which the institutional capitalist becomes redundant may vary but one thing is important: if the institutional capitalist becomes an obstacle to the functioning of the system, he ought to be removed from the position of power.

Analogically, the same distinction applies to a socialist system, too. The partocracy does play the part of institutional capitalists: they control property relations, have the right to decide how the socialized property is to be used, who would manage it and how he would manage it. The technocracy is subordinated, in the Soviet system, to the partocracy. To be a technocrat in the system that is based on social (socialized) capital, however, means to perform as entrepreneur, manager, and innovator. While the partocrats are guardians of the system's entrance gate, the technocrats are doers. The guardians do sit on the system's ideology which legitimizes their power. Because they do have the right to interpret the ideology, they do so in such a way which would enhance their positions and their power, which would make the system's legitimacy dependent upon the part performed by the partocracy. The technocrats play the second fiddle: they serve the system without having direct access to the top decision-making power.

While the partocracy relies on ideology, the technocracy relies on performance. The technocrats do not care too much about ideology; they do care about results. Caring about results, particularly in the sphere of the national economy, requires pragmatism rather than an ideological straitjacket. If the system led by the partocracy lost its dynamism and became incapable of modernization, a systemic change would be necessary. The only alternative ruling class in the Soviet system is that of technocrats. For my purpose, I include in the term all the experts and innovators working in various spheres of society. In the particular Soviet case, technocrats may be found everywhere—even in the Party apparat. Though their functions are indispensable, they do not rule: that position is kept by the partocracy.

According to Leninism, the leading role of the vanguard party is the principal dogma of the system. The entire power of the partocracy is derived from the dogma. The dogma gives legitimacy to the partocracy's rule. While all the technocrats working in different social sectors do the real job, they are supervised, selected, appointed, and rewarded at the pleasure of the partocrats. In a sense, they compete with each other for favors distributed by the partocrats. Those of them who joined the ranks of the partocracy have to give up their technocratic functions in the sense that they must give preference to the dogma rather than to common sense, performance, and results. If they did not, they would be expelled from the ranks of the partocracy.

The dogma of the leading role of the Party is based on the assumption that the working class is unable to reach, on its own, a level of class political consciousness. In this respect, Lenin has radically revised Karl Marx's belief that the workers can free themselves, that they are able to make the revolution on their own, that they are able to organize themselves as the ruling class in a postrevolution society. According to Lenin, the working class cannot do it without a vanguard party, without professional revolutionaries, without the partocracy.[8]

The second reason for Lenin's revision of Marx was caused by the fact that the prerevolutionary Russia was an agricultural country with a tiny working class. If—as Lenin argued—the vanguard party can substitute for the working class, then even a country which, according to Marx's criteria, is not ripe for socialism because of its lack of capitalist industrial development, may implement a revolutionary change.

Lenin's concept of the leading role of the Party, and of a specific nature of the vanguard party, is *the* core of Leninism. Lenin even went so far that he claimed that while democracy and decentralization is the principle of opportunism, bureaucracy and centralization is the principle of revolutionary Marxism.[9] This Lenin's legacy is the main source of the partocracy's legitimacy. While partocracy and bureaucracy goes hand in hand, technocracy is a foreign element in the system. Though it is needed for doing the necessary managerial functions, it must not do them on its own: the partocracy has to prevail.

Another part of the Leninist legitimacy refers to economics. Socialism is, by definition, a higher socioeconomic stage of development than capitalism. To definitely win over capitalism, said Lenin, socialism has to achieve higher productivity than any capitalist country. Moreover, socialism is supposed to achieve, on the basis of the higher productivity, higher living standards than capitalism. And finally, because a higher productivity requires a higher and more comprehensive innovation and modernization, socialism has to be ahead not only in terms of economic performance, but also in terms of its thoroughly dynamic socioeconomic development.

From this point of view, the Soviet system is not legitimate enough in terms of the Leninist orthodoxy. On top of it, its ideology lost its ability to mobilize the masses. Its totalitarian political system led by the partocracy lost its appeal to the toiling masses of the world. In a word: the Soviet system is already facing an economic, political, and ideological crisis.

In view of the systemic dilemma—either to comply with the leading position of the partocracy or to meet Lenin's economic criteria of the system's legitimacy—the Soviet system would have to make a choice under the Amalrik's sort of catch-22 situation. That is why Alexander Shtromas titled his paper "How the end of the Soviet system may come about?"[10] In Shtromas's view, there is just one viable alternative ruling class in the Soviet system: the technocracy. The term does not include all the people who occupy the functions which are usually held by technocrats. Many of the so-called technocrats are just bureaucrats appointed because of their loyalty to the principle of the leading role of the partocracy while some Party officials represent, by and large, technocratic values. If there is to be a systemic change in the Soviet Union in a foreseeable future, it would be a shift to the rule of technocracy, accompanied by a sort of market economy and an authoritarian (rather than the present totalitarian) political system. Shtromas suggested several possible scenarios for the change. In this chapter, I would consider just two of them: a technocratic regime combined with an adjustment of the Leninist ideology to the badly needed modernization, or a technocratic regime relying on a more traditional Russian nationalistic ideology. The power shift may be either smooth or have the form of a military takeover, and modernization could take place either under the condition of a sort of reconciliation with the West, or without it. I wish to look at the ramifications which the change, under the alternative scenarios, will have for Eastern Europe. But before I open my argument, I wish to make few a comments on the viability of an adjustment of Leninist ideology, of a return to a traditional Russia's nationalistic ideology, and of a military takeover.

Adjustment of Leninism

Whoever tried to adjust Leninism to a market economic reform, he would have to turn to Lenin's New Economic Policy (NEP). Of course, Lenin's argument for NEP—Russia's underdevelopment and backwardness of the early 1920s—would have to be changed. That could be easy—incidentally, Hungarians have already legitimized their market reform by reinterpreting the economic theory of Leninism.[11] There is however another problem: a new interpretation of Lenin's concept of the leading role of the Party. Natural representatives of such revision would be the technocrats within the Party *apparat* disguised as partocrats. It would be their task to render Leninism compatible with their technocratic rule. The reinterpretation of the leading role of the Party would have to meet one condition only: to allow for (at least) an authoritarian political system which would yield an autonomy to the national economy and sciences from the political and ideological control of the partocracy. If the economic source of the Leninist legitimacy were used for the purpose, the problem would scarcely become insurmountable.

Return to a Traditional Nationalist Identity

Although Marxism is formally an ideology of internationalism, its Soviet practice has always been nationalistic. Proletarian internationalism has been identified with each Communist's first loyalty to the Soviet Union rather than to his own nation. The entire history of the Comintern testifies to the fact that whenever a national interest of the USSR conflicted with interests of the international Communist movement, the Soviet national interest got the precedence.[12] If I say "Soviet" national interest I do mean "Russian" national interest because the Soviet Union is first of all the Russian national state ruled by the Russians rather than by other nationalities of the union. If Russia turned openly to its traditional nationalism instead of practicing it in the disguise of the proletarian internationalism, nothing would actually change. During World War II the Soviet Union openly relied on Russian nationalism, on Russian national values. Russia was the only country in which World War II was named the "Great Patriotic War." Even today, Russian Marxism-Leninism is practiced in a nationalistic manner in the USSR. If the switch to an open nationalism were completed, it would have one advantage for the member countries of the Soviet bloc. An open shift to Russian nationalism cannot be extended beyond the Soviet borders. If a technocratic regime in Russia were using an official ideology of Russian nationalism, it would not be interested in imposing it upon East European nations. The hitherto "universal" Soviet model of socialism would be reduced to a national model not obligatory for other nations in the Soviet bloc. As a result, Communist countries within the Soviet bloc would be given more room for their own structural reforms.

Military Takeover

Leninism does not allow for Bonapartism. The army is supposed to be kept under the strict control of the Party. Before the Polish crisis of 1980–81, it was impossible for an army general, i.e., for a professional military man, to become anything more than minister of defense and, at best, member of a ruling Politburo. When General Jaruzelski was appointed prime minister of Poland, all the accepted rules were broken. And when he also became first secretary of the Polish Party, the rigid rules were broken completely.

In no Warsaw Treaty Organization (WTO) member country, could preparation for a military rule which, in itself, contradicts all the widely recognized rules and norms of the Soviet-type system, happen without the knowledge and supervision of the Supreme Command of WTO troops, i.e., without the knowledge of top Soviet military leaders. In turn, their approval of such an action is unthinkable without prior approval by the ruling Soviet Politburo. How is it then, that the Soviet Politburo has allowed a military takeover in a satellite country to be executed in a manner which indicates that the Party is unfit to rule?

There is a distinction between an open foreign military intervention by Soviet army and a military takeover by a national army in a satellite country. If the Soviet army gets commands to intervene, the commands are given by the Soviet Politburo. No one, in such circumstances, must overlook that the Soviet army would act on behalf of its political masters. If we study the *form* of the Polish military takeover of December 1981 however, we clearly see a different pattern. Though Mr. Jaruzelski had been, at that time, not only a general, minister of defense and prime minister but first secretary of Polish Communist party also, he had conspicuously acted in his military capacity only. The military council that had assumed the full executive power in Poland was made up of military personnel only. There was no public announcement that the Politburo, let alone the Central Committee of the Polish Communist party, remained in control of the military, that they had approved beforehand the military takeover. General Jaruzelski was referred to not as First Secretary of the Party but as a general. He wore his military uniform all the time. Why was the action of the military not formally authorized and legitimized by a top Party body within a few hours after the *fait accompli?*

The manner in which the army took over was to indicate that the army did not act in the Party interest but in the Polish national interest. Though one may question whether the *appearance* of the military takeover had been identical with its *essence*, the message to the nation was clear: the general public was led to believe that, in the final analysis, Polish national interests were better represented by the military, that the Polish military (rather than the Party in Moscow) were the ultimate saviors of Polish national *and* socialist values.

I suspect that the *form* of the military takeover deviated from the *assumed* scenario, which had been approved by the Soviet Politburo. I would go even further and contend that at least some of the Soviet military leaders had a prior knowledge about, and approved of, the deviation. Though the manner of the action did not change its final outcome, the manner *did* matter: we have got a precedent in which the army, subordinated to the Party, had legitimately acted on its own in the condition of a deep national crisis, in the condition of an ultimate national emergency.

Legitimation given to the Polish military takeover by virtue of a joint Soviet bloc approval of it rendered this precedent applicable also to other satellite regimes and, because of the specific manner in which the Polish military took over, to the Soviet Union itself. After the Polish December 1981, no one can easily dismiss Shtromas's hypothesis about the viability of a military takeover in the Soviet Union providing that the country were hit by a crisis, by a power-vacuum, and instability caused by the partocracy's impotence to make the Soviet economy move again. That is not to suggest that such a military takeover is likely. It is merely to suggest that such a military takeover is *possible* and, after the Polish event, it could and would be deemed legitimate under the above circumstances.

A Flexible Scenario

Because Russia's world position depends much more on its system's performance than on its obsolete ideology, a technocratic alternative to the present system seems the only viable systemic change within the realm of the possible. The technocratic alternative, however, may take different forms. It may be achieved by a sort of military takeover if the necessary reforms are again postponed, if the present stagnation and decay continues, if the partocratic regime is unable to make the Soviet Union move again. If the technocrats managed to transfer power from the partocracy without any open political crisis, the transition could be smooth. If a technocratic regime *adjusted* Leninism to the requirements of an overall modernization, the revised Leninism would have to rely on a sort of Russian nationalism. If nationalism were to *replace* Leninism, it would have to formally retain at least some of the latter's tenets. And finally, the systemic change may or may not be accompanied by a sort of reconciliation with the West. Though both alternatives are viable, the reconciliatory one seems more likely. Any serious process of a thorough modernization would have to render Russia a much more inward-looking country. Domestic modernization and external confrontational policies do not mix too well. On top of it, to expedite domestic modernization, Russia would need genuine economic cooperation with the West.

If Russia changed its system along the lines mentioned above, it could be scarcely interested in preserving partocratic systems in its bloc. It would be even less interested in subsidizing their economic inefficiency. An intensive economic growth in East European countries would improve both quality and technological parameters of Russia's imports from the region and, at the same time reduce the quantity of raw and energy materials that the region imports from the Soviet Union. As a result, East European countries would be free to follow Russia's suit. Though the East European Communist countries would be free to implement their structural reforms, one limit of systemic changes in the region will remain in force: a friendly, cooperative coexistence of the bloc countries with the Soviet Union. Though this limit might seem cumbersome, it would offer enough room for the change.

Though I do assume that, if a technocratic systemic change takes place in the USSR, a sort of reconciliation with the West will be likely, there is a possibility that external political circumstances will not change from the present state of affairs. In such conditions, the USSR's control of the region will remain—at least in military matters—rather strict. Under such conditions, systemic changes in Eastern European countries will have to be compatible with their membership in the WTO. For the sake of argument, let me explore both scenarios, the flexible one and the limited one. The former refers to changes that would take place in the satellite countries if their freedom of choice were less restricted; the latter refers to changes which the satellite countries would be allowed to pursue under Russia's strict supervision.

Czechoslovakia

As a Russificated ideology, Marxism-Leninism does not have any appeal to some four-fifths of the Czechoslovak society. Unlike in Russia, the ideology has not been shaped by domestic (Czech and Slovak) traditions, by domestic political culture. Though Czechoslovakia is the only satellite country where the Communist system has been initially introduced by domestic political forces rather than by the Soviet army, the popular perception of socialism had been based on democratic principles rather than on the crude Soviet-type totalitarian dictatorship executed by the partocracy. Even a majority of the Communist party of Czechoslovakia did not want the Soviet-type economic and political system of socialism after the World War II. In fact, they believed—as did some Communist leaders too—in a specific Czechoslovak way to socialism. Though the concept of the Czechoslovak way had been, in 1947, rather vague, it was specified in the 1968 reform program and, yet later on, by some concepts of Eurocommunism in the 1970s. As far as the non-communist part of the Czechoslovak society was concerned, it would have rather accepted, in 1948, the democratic socialism of a West-European fashion.

When the Soviet-type system was imposed upon Czechoslovakia in the early 1950s, it did not work. The country with a strong tradition of liberal and social democracy, with a high level of industrial development, highly skilled labor, and a well-educated population was turned, by the inadequate Soviet model, to the stage of primitive industrialization, forced collectivization, one-party totalitarian dictatorship, and rigid Byzantine version of Communist ideology. As an industrialized country, Czechoslovakia needed an economic system conducive to an intensive type of growth with a well-developed infrastructure. All the limits of the Soviet-type command economic system had become clearly visible in Czechoslovakia by the late 1950s and early 1960s. As to the totalitarian political dictatorship, its inadequacy in Czechoslovakia had been visible since the very beginning of the Communist rule.

Yet some twenty years ago, Czechoslovak society was willing to accept a revised concept of Marxian socialism combined with democratic freedoms and civil rights, with a sort of economic self-management and popular political participation, a socialism economically efficient and welfare oriented. The 1968 slogan, "Socialism with a human face," did reflect the then popular political sentiments.

In 1986, I am afraid, the very idea of a Marxian socialism, with or without the humane face, lost its former popular appeal. I do not even speak about Leninism, which is seen as an asiatic ideological import by the Czechoslovak people. Formerly a prosperous liberal democracy, one of the ten most industrialized countries in the world, Czechoslovakia declined to the position of a Russian colony which is backward in comparison with the previously poorer and less democratic neighboring Austria. What is more: Czechoslovakia is gradually slipping, from its previous prominent position in Central Europe, to the level of semideveloped Balkan countries.

Because Czechoslovakia does not have as yet any alternative (spare) ideology to the failed Marxism-Leninism, some people turned to humanistic values of civil rights and freedoms, others to religion, and still others, to an ideology of survival. The latter group is by far more representative of the Czechoslovak society than the two former.

Very soon after the reimposition of the Soviet-type system, the Party leadership concluded, quite informally and tacitly, a *sui generis* social contract with the society. As long as you do not interfere with our government business, implied the leaders, we will not interfere with your private life. Moreover, we are willing to trade your passive acceptance of the system for relatively high living standards, for a sort of consumer society. Though we will not restore either private businesses or market-type material incentives, we will tolerate, albeit within limits, an unofficial "second" economy with its black market of goods, services and labor, with kickbacks and universal tippings, with an exchange of mutual favors and privileges.

This social contract perfectly fits the pattern of the ideology of survival. As a result, active dissidents are few and far between. Though the Czechoslovak society scarcely believes in official politics and policies, a majority pretends that they either do believe, or at least that they do not mind. For the first time ever, the regime let those who prefer to do so, live at the margin of the official system or even without the official system. That is a remarkable authoritarian feature in the otherwise totalitarian system. It is not yet the exact replica of Kadar's slogan, "He who is not against us is with us," but it is close to the pattern.

This pattern brought about a general decline in ethical standards of Czechoslovak society. Widespread corruption has been tacitly accepted as *the* way of life. People refer to this phenomenon previously alien to Czechoslovak culture as to a sort of sovietization, or *asianization* of Czechoslovakia. The phenomenon is threatening Czechoslovakia's future as a (central) European country more than the direct Soviet domination. As a result, private and public life have become strictly separate from each other, and a utilitarian consumerism has become the most visible feature characteristic of Czechoslovak society. An existential alienation of the nation has been widely recognized as a logical by-product of the so-called normalization (i.e., of the forced reimposition of the partocratic system) under the condition of the Soviet military occupation.

That is why any ideology derived from Marxism, or any reform model derived from the so-called Marxist-Leninist scientific socialism, is under deep suspicion in Czechoslovak society. This is a far cry from the universal euphoria of the "Prague Spring," when the Czechoslovak people were sympathetic to socialism though terribly disappointed with one (the Soviet one) of its possible forms. Because all the shortcomings of the Soviet-type socialism are perceived as a result of its politics and ideology, freedom and democracy appear a much more important issue than yet another experiment with an unproven model of a humanized Marxian socialism.

If the flexible scenario of systemic change were available, there is every reason to expect that the popular consensus would approach the Austrian pattern: a neutral, decent, central European political democracy with a mixed, yet relatively efficient economy, combined with a well entrenched comprehensive welfare system. In the Austrian-type system, nothing is exceedingly good, but almost everything is reasonable. What is more, the Austrian political culture shares some common features with the Czechoslovak one, including the famous *Schlamperei*.

Hungary

At present, Hungary is the only Soviet bloc country experimenting with a quasi-market economic reform while its political regime is closer to authoritarianism than totalitarianism. It seems that Hungary has already started the change, which all the other Soviet bloc countries are supposed to follow; that is, to marketize their economic systems and adjust their political systems to a new economic mechanism.

While Hungarian leaders are cautiously trying to adjust the country's system to the social fabric of Hungarian society, one cannot say that the change has been an overwhelming success. The main reason for its rather moderate results lies in the fact that the Hungarian national economy consists of two parts: one is tied to the CMEA countries with their command planning, while the other is consistently more open to the new system. The two principles (command plan vs. market) are mutually exclusive. It seems as if the system, which is in need of an accelerated market reform, has already reluctantly accepted the present transitory stage as a substitute for the initially more radical concept. Even the country's move from totalitarianism to authoritarianism is slow and inconsistent. One may explain the government's halfheartedness not only by the pressure from the Hungarian partocracy, but also by the fact that while the New Economic Mechanism (NEM) has been tolerated both by the Soviet Union and other CMEA countries, it has not yet been fully legitimized in the documents of the Soviet bloc ideological conferences.

Despite the halfhearted implementation of the reform, the very fact that Hungary was able to continue with its NEM after the Soviet invasion of Czechoslovakia has been recognized as one of the greatest achievements of the Kadar regime. Of course, if compared with the objectives of the 1956 revolt, it is a compromise. Under the circumstances, however, it does not seem worse than was the compromise achieved by Mr. Kadar's predecessors in 1867 through the *Ausgleich*. In both cases, a favorable compromise followed a defeated revolt. Mr. Kadar masterfully exploited all the avenues—within the realm of the possible—which remained at his disposal. At the same time, his success required a price. For a cautiously drafted mini-reform, Hungary had to give up its more ambitious objectives which had been, and are, unacceptable to the Soviet partocracy. Instead of using the term "marketization," Hungarians would use the term "monetary-commodity relations," instead of talking about the "market mechanism," they would talk about the "new mechanism." In November 1967, when discussing some aspects of market reforms with Hungarian economists and officials, I had been warned many times that Czechoslovakia was going "too far, too fast," that it was better to compromise, that it was always better to gain a little than to lose too much. The result is that, at present, Hungary is having a minireform, while Czechoslovakia is having a restored command system of the 1950s.

If Soviet technocrats take over and start a market-type economic reform, one can predict an immense acceleration of the Hungarian reform. Moreover, the Austrian pattern appeals to the Hungarians no less than it appeals to the Czechs. That is why one cannot rule out that the two countries might coordinate their reforms under the flexible scenario.

Poland

If Marxism-Leninism were a scientific theory, all the Marxists-Leninists would hurry to examine, in an impartial way, a few empirical tests undertaken in Poland in the early 1980s. While Karl Marx believed that the working class can become a "class for itself," i.e., reach the level of class *political* consciousness, Lenin was more skeptical: according to his theory, the proletariat on its own can reach, at best, just a *trade union* level of class consciousness. Marx has stated that if the proletariat failed to free itself, no one else would free it; Lenin maintained that the proletariat needed a vanguard party to reach its class political consciousness to win, under its guidance, socialist revolution.

In 1980, a protest workers' strike in the city of Gdansk evolved, in a few weeks, into a 10 million member strong trade-union organization, independent from any vanguard Communist party. What was more, the trade union acted as a political party. It offered the government its cooperation in introducing economic reforms, in participating in economic management and decision making. To obtain the latter, the trade union was willing to accept its share of responsibility for the Polish national economy. Solidarity was established against the will of the ruling party in the political vacuum which had to be filled by a decisive political force. Leaders of Solidarity realized all the constraints: if they went too far, there would be Soviet military intervention.

Solidarity was thus much more than a trade union. In a system where there was no chance to establish an open political party, an independent trade union (even if forced by court to recognize, albeit formally, the leading role of the Polish Communist party in society) went as far as the political limits of the system allowed. The Polish case has therefore confirmed the view of Karl Marx rather than that of Vladimir Lenin.

Compared with other revisionistic (or dissident) movements in central Eastern Europe, the emergence of Solidarity was a revolutionary deed. It was possible to argue that reforms in Czechoslovakia or in Hungary had been initiated by intellectuals, or by ambitious revisionist Communists. In Poland, no one could have denied either the spontaneity of the event or the nonprofessionalism of Solidarity's leaders. If the Soviet Union intervened directly, the entire world would have seen that the Soviet army was sent to crush the 10 million member strong workers' organization. In addition, the USSR had been afraid that, if a direct military intervention had taken place, all the political gains the USSR had achieved in the battle against the deployment of American intermediate range missiles in Europe, would have been lost in Western Europe, in a matter of hours. Thus, yet another scenario of a military takeover was prepared. Despite its appearance, the takeover eventually saved the power of the Polish partocracy.

Since 1956, Poland has been distinct from other Soviet-type regimes in the Soviet bloc because of two deviations. First, the Polish Catholic church was able to retain its spiritual autonomy from the Party and the state and become a truly national institution that speaks on behalf of the Polish society. Second, a mostly decollectivized agriculture became a reality with which the Party had to find a *modus vivendi*.

As far as the Church is concerned, the Polish uniqueness can be attributed to the position taken by the country's Catholic church, during the three partitions of Poland whose main benefits went to Orthodox Russia and Protestant Prussia, a position which had coincided with the Polish national interest. (This can't happen in either Czechoslovakia or Hungary. In Bohemia the Church stood with the Hapsburgs against the Protestant Czechs while in Hungary the Church sold out Hungarian national interests to the more powerful interests of Austria.)

The two-centuries-old coincidence has produced, when the Catholic church was confronted, under the Communist rule, with the official and would-be monopolistic Marxist-Leninist ideology, a logical result. Marxism-Leninism as a strictly atheistic and militantly antireligious ideology is identified primarily with the USSR, i.e., with a mainly Russian national state. Everybody in Poland knew that Marxism-Leninism was first the ideology of the "center of the center" (i.e., the CPSU) and only secondary also the ideology of the "center of the periphery" (i.e., of the Polish Communist party).

While in other East European countries of the Soviet bloc the only major alternative to the official ideology is either revisionism or nationalism, the Poles have enjoyed the advantage of having a third major ideology in Catholicism. Because the Polish Catholic church represents the country's national interests and, at the same time, also European cultural and spiritual values, Poles realized that to be a Pole *and* a European means to be a Roman Catholic.

When mentioning this unique position of the Catholic church in Poland, I do not intend to hide the fact that the Church is a rather conservative institution. As a matter of fact, there are two rather conservative institutions within the Polish context: the Party and the Church. Unlike the Party however, the Church represents Polish national interests and values, stands for the traditional civil society and is a staunch defender of human rights. This extraordinary part played by the Church depends on an absence of another major autonomous social (or political) institution which would offer an ideological and/or political platform. During the period of the legally functioning Solidarity, there had been a certain decline in the Church's social influence, while after Solidarity had been banned, the role of the Church was substantially increased and its authority strengthened.

During the Polish crisis of 1956, Party leaders had been faced with a dilemma: To which major social group should they yield a concession? The workers had demanded workers' councils, a sort of self-management. Intellectuals demanded freedom of press, freedom of expression and an autonomy of educational, cultural, artistic and scientific institutions from the Party and the state. Peasants demanded privatization of the Polish agriculture.

The Party leaders could have not fought all the major social groups at the same time. From the point of view of the partocracy, the least dangerous was the concession yielded to the countryside. Unlike workers, peasants are dispersed in small villages and hamlets. They do not have a social organization (e.g., trade unions) on their own. They do not have an easy access to centers of power which are concentrated in the nation's capital and regional cities. Peasants do not have an easy access to the mass media to make public their feelings, opinions and demands. Even when working on private farms in an individual manner, they may be easily controlled by procurement prices, supplies of agricultural machinery and fertilizers. What is more, farmers are not only isolated from decision-making bodies of the centralized society. They are even unable to leave their farms and miss their daily chores to organize collective actions outside their villages. By and large, even if the peasants are allowed to disband collective farms and work on their own, their potential challenge to the ruling partocracy will be less than that one of the two remaining groups. Workers self-management might undermine the control of the economy exercised by the Party. Intellectuals do have a persuasive power and may easily influence the society at large from their workplaces. From a purely power-political point of view, the peasantry—in a densely populated central European country—has limited room for an independent and nationwide coordinated action. On balance, a concession yielded to the peasantry is less dangerous for the preservation of the system than a concession given to the proletariat or the intelligentsia.

Ever since 1956, every Polish leadership has faced a painful decision: If there is private agriculture, we must not support it to the extent it becomes prosperous. If the private agriculture demonstrated its superiority over the collectivized one, it would be tantamount to an ideological defeat of the Party. The best thing, therefore, would be to keep the peasantry on a short leash and try to recollectivize it at the nearest convenient point of time.

The convenient point of time, however, failed to come. Because the Party was doing its best to prevent private agriculture from becoming prosperous, it has gradually undermined the agricultural base of the country's industrial system. It suffices to remember the crises of 1970, 1976 and

1980 caused by food shortages and intended food price increases to understand the vicious circle felt by every consecutive Polish government after 1956.

On the other hand, Polish partocracy was unable to pacify Polish workers, students and intellectuals either. Since the mid 1960s, the regime has been irresistibly heading to a major confrontation with the Polish society. In 1968, there was a confrontation with students and intellectuals. The crisis of 1970 caused by workers revolt in Baltic cities removed Gomulka and installed Gierek. In 1976, another workers' riot caused a minicrisis. During the entire decade of 1970–80, Gierek's regime tried to substitute Western credits and transfer of technology for a domestic structural economic reform. The attempt ended in the country's economic collapse because the command nonmarket economy has been unable to organically absorb foreign-made innovations. As the result, Poland faced another political and economic crisis, in which the working class established itself as an autonomous social and political movement within the civil society. Instead of an attempt at national reconciliation, and a speedy implementation of radical systemic economic and political reforms, the partocracy both in Warsaw and Moscow has chosen confrontation with Polish society by a proxy—i.e., by the action of Polish army and security forces. Though the *status quo ante* has been formally restored as the result, no single systemic problem has been solved.

Thus, Poland offered *the* evidence that the working class may become an independent political force under the rule of partocracy. Second, that any system which does not care about its agriculture—irrespective of its socioeconomic structure—cannot avoid deep economic and political troubles. Third, that even under the rule of partocracy, the Church may function independently; at the same time, agriculture may remain decollectivized. And fourth, that each major social group in society—peasants, workers, intellectuals, students, and the church—may escape, at least temporarily, from the totalitarian political structure and turn it into a pluralistic yet authoritarian entity.

All these lessons ought to be carefully studied by official Marxism-Leninism. After forty years of Communist rule, Poland's social, economic, political, and ideological crisis reached the state of terminal disease. Unlike Czechoslovakia and Hungary where economic reforms of the 1960s had been initiated from above, Polish demands for economic, social, and political reforms came from a spontaneous action of the working class supported by the entire society. Moreover, the Polish working class expressed directly, without any outside mediator, its strong demand for an active participation in the administration of public affairs. In this respect, Polish workers have shown a much higher degree of political consciousness than their brethren elsewhere in the Soviet bloc. What is more, the Polish working class has reached the point of its own political emancipation. Workers' demands for self-management in their working place and for a share in the macropolitical decision-making process have come from their ranks rather than having been imposed upon them from without as was the case of Czechoslovakia in 1968.

Therefore, under the flexible scenario, a wide variety of pluralistic alternatives is open to Poland. One of them is a mixed economic system combined with employees' participation in management, with a strong private sector in agriculture, crafts, services, and professions. As far as political aspects of the change are concerned, a guided (regulated) democracy based, in the beginning, on a sociopolitical contract between Solidarity, rural Solidarity, the Church and the technocratic wing of the Party could lead to a two-(three) party system, to a mixed national economy with public but not necessarily state-owned large enterprises combined with a comprehensive welfare system.

Romania

In the West, Romania is seen as a maverick of the Soviet bloc. The reason for Romania's special treatment by the Western powers is a certain degree of the country's nationalistic deviation from the bloc's economic and foreign policy patterns. I am talking about the deviation from traditional policies rather than about the deviation from the system. Ceausescu's Romania is just a more transparent replica of a neo-Stalinist model of totalitarianism whose regime pursues Romania's rather than Russia's national objectives.

In the early 1960s, Mr. Khrushchev suggested a kind of specialization in the Soviet bloc economic organization—CMEA—which would halt Romania's and Bulgaria's ambition to start a full-scale industrialization. In fact, the suggestion would have rendered the two countries agricultural and raw-material suppliers for CMEA. While Bulgaria accepted the pattern, Romania did not. When Mr. Ceausescu succeeded Mr. Georghiu-Dej, he decided to legitimize Communist rule in Romania by an overall domestic industrialization. Unlike the early 1950s when the USSR sided, within CMEA at least, with the least developed bloc countries, Mr. Khrushchev reversed his country's previous position and shifted his support to the most developed bloc countries, i.e., the GDR and Czechoslovakia. Despite the general policy of CMEA, Mr. Ceausescu decided to industrialize Romania with the assistance from developed Western countries.

The shift in policy led to an adjustment of Marxist-Leninist doctrine for both domestic and international consumption. Romania has subscribed to the concept of national sovereignty, which identifies the transition to so-

cialism with a full-scale industrialization of each particular national economy, and mightily objected to any attempt to be pushed into any close
economic and political integration within the Soviet bloc. Because of Romania's visible deviation from the common policy in the Soviet bloc, mainly
in the sphere of domestic economic development and the country's foreign
policy, the West readily offered its generous assistance to Mr. Ceausescu's
ambitious program.

Because Mr. Ceausescu maintained that each Communist country had
both the right and the duty to follow its own national interests, the Romanian regime has become a natural ally of Yugoslavia, China, and in
1968 of Czechoslovakia without having any sympathy for Yugoslavia's market reforms combined with workers' self-management, for Mao's great
leap forward and cultural revolution, for Czechoslovakia's attempt to build
"socialism with a human face" or for Deng-Xiao Ping's reversal of Mao's
policies after 1979. In political terms, Romania had to support, or at least
tolerate, any deviation from the rigidity of the Soviet model even if it did
not agree with the nature of the deviation. If it failed to do so, its own
deviation would have lost any legitimitcy.

At present, Romania is at the edge of bankruptcy—economic, political,
and ideological. In economic terms, Romania's totalitarian political regime
prevented any genuine modernization despite the tremendous transfer of
Western technology. The only result of the latter is a foreign debt which
the regime tries to service and repay by drastically cutting down the already
low, and elsewhere in Eastern Europe unacceptable, living standards. Politically, the Ceausescu's regime is resented by the nation. Ideologically,
Ceausescu's attempts to gain his people's support by draping the country's
neo-Stalinist system in national colors failed. During the recent period,
even some members of the ruling elite have been unhappy with Mr. Ceausescu's stubborn policies.

It seems likely that the present regime cannot survive if Ceausescu, for
whatever reason, departs from the political scene. Because Ceausescu's
economic system is in direct opposition to market-type reforms, as well as
the fact that his political system is in the direct opposition to any relaxation
leading to authoritarian rule, probably no radical domestic change in Romania will take place under Mr. Ceausescu's leadership. The only way
now to open a reconciliatory, less dogmatic and more efficient economic
development would be Ceausescu's removal. One may perceive his removal
if, for instance, there are major riots against food and energy shortages,
price increases or another series of drastic cuts in living standards. Any
major economic disruption might turn into an open political protest against
the inflexible dictatorship of Ceausescu's family.

Because democratic traditions are almost nonexistent in Romania, any substitute for Ceausescu's regime will likely be authoritarian rather than liberal. A sort of military-technocratic regime, which would relax the disparity between accumulation and consumption and visibly improve both living standards and the human rights record, would fit well into the flexible scenario.

Bulgaria

Rightly or wrongly, Bulgaria is considered the closest ally of the Soviet Union in Eastern Europe with good feelings about Russia shared by the general public. Unlike other Balkan countries, Bulgaria has always been relying on its reputation as a diligent country with hard working peasants and practically nonexistent remnants of feudalism in its agriculture. In some central European countries, they would still use—instead of saying "he works like a beaver" yet another metaphor for hard work: "He toils like a Bulgarian." However, despite this rather positive tradition, neither the country's national economy nor the country's political reputation at home and abroad reflects this positive heritage.

By the end of 1970, Bulgaria began flirting with the idea of a market-oriented economic reform which would give more autonomy to agricultural units, to cooperative brigades of peasants and, finally, to the families of collective farmers. Similar changes were supposed to be extended to the industrial sector as well. While technocrats and economists widely support a major extension of the scope of "the new mechanism," the partocracy is reluctant to go too far with the changes that might undermine its power. That is why the halfhearted reform failed to improve the country's economic performance. Even the Soviet Union recently criticized the low quality of Bulgarian goods exported to the USSR, failures in investment priorities, and difficulties in Bulgarian agriculture which forced the country to import food stuffs from Yugoslavia and the West. Shortages in energy and food supplies led, in 1985, to another food price increase and cuts in the consumption of electricity.

As everywhere else in the Soviet bloc, there is a visible tension between the partocracy and the technocracy in their approach to badly needed systemic changes. While the partocracy is interested in preserving the old system just with some cosmetic changes, the technocracy is willing to risk a systemic change to improve the country's overall economic performance.

Instead of paying close attention to economic problems, the partocracy decided to "Bulgarianize" the entire population. Previous assimilation policies aimed at the Macedonian minority have been extended to the Turkish minority which makes up some 10 percent of the population. Bulgarian Turks have been forceably displaced, their mosques closed, their names

"Bulgarianized," their language, and cultural rights curtailed. This action recalls Ceausescu's treatment of Romania's Hungarian minority and testifies to the fact that the official Marxism-Leninism in Bulgaria has been reinforced by a shift to nationalism. If one adds to the picture a series of terrorists acts (e.g., a blowup of a train, blowups of cars, etc.), it will become clear that the Party leaders failed to preserve a stable social balance in the Bulgarian society.

Bulgaria's image abroad is even worse than that of their neighbor; Romania. A series of "umbrella assassinations" of Bulgarian émigrés living in the West, an alleged Bulgarian connection to the attempt to assassinate the pope, the country's complicity with international terrorism, and alleged drug and arms smuggling had been continuing during the recent period. Though the country's domestic crisis is not as profound as those in Poland and Romania, trends in economic, political, and human rights point to a continuing deterioration.

Because there is no evidence about a democratic change under the flexible scenario, the only statement that can be made with a fair degree of certainty is as follows: If there is a profound change in Moscow, Bulgaria will follow suit along the lines of technocratic authoritarianism.

East Germany

There is always an exception to a rule. For instance, Japan's economic performance even during the last worldwide depression has been an exception to the rules determining the functioning of mixed market systems. Analogically one may say that the GDR's economic performance is an exception to the rules that determine the functioning of command economies in the Soviet bloc. Though I did analyze elsewhere[12] the reasons why the GDR's national economy has been performing better than any other command economy in the Soviet bloc, there is no comprehensive explanation why the otherwise dysfunctional system works in the GDR. With my tongue in cheek, I do accept the explanation offered by an eminent Western scholar: "I have yet to see a system in which Germans would not perform relatively well."[13]

In addition to many beneficial circumstances in which the command economy functions in the GDR, East Germany is *de facto* both a CMEA and an EEC member through the so-called inter-German trade. Though such a position may explain a great deal of the country's relatively good economic performance, it cannot explain the latter in full. It seems that, in addition to the country's particular tradition and political culture, the fact that the East German command economic system is the most technocratized command planning ever known may explain the puzzle. Indeed, if there were an ideal, rationally constructed model of the command economy, then undoubtedly the East German command economy would represent its closest approximation.

When stating the obvious, I by no means ignore another important aspect to the case: if there were no Berlin wall, and if East German borders with West Germany were free and wide open, the East German population would have shrunk by a few million because of massive emigration. However well the East German economy may perform if compared, let us say, with the neighboring Czechoslovakia, its performance is unable to offset other negative features of the country's regime, especially in the sphere of politics, ideology, and civil and human rights.

If there were a technocratic change in Moscow combined with an authoritarian rather than the present totalitarian political regime, East Germany would have no problem to follow suit. As a matter of fact, that would be the trend introduced first in East Germany some twenty years ago, albeit in a cautious rather than a radical manner. One thing would change the East German pattern however: the future technocratization would be combined with a degree of marketization. I do say with a degree of marketization because the very trend in the direction of marketization would be rather risky in political terms: if East Germany started a market economic reform, it would move closer to the West German economic system without its corollary, i.e., without political democracy. If this were the case, the existence of two German states would appear even more artificial than it does at present, and the question if and how to reunify Germany might become topical on both sides of the artificial border. I personally think, however, that a possible reunification of Germany might be perceived under yet another scenario which is well beyond the limit of this chapter.

*   *   *

If the USSR replaced its Marxist-Leninist totalitarian political system with its traditional partocratic command economy by an authoritarian/technocratic system, Eastern Europe's response to the change would be positive on the side of the people though not necessarily so on the side of the partocratic rulers. Depending on domestic political cultures, traditions, and readiness for domestic change, East European reforms would oscillate about technocratic/authoritarian to pluralistic/democratic/participatory patterns. The best candidates for a more open and far reaching reform are Poland, Hungary, and Czechoslovakia.

Because one cannot be sure about the East European partocracy's response to the change in the USSR, one has at least to mention briefly yet another part of the flexible scenario consisting of a quasi-Albanian solution. Theoretically at least, one should consider a case in which a domestic partocracy decided to maintain the pre-reform system in defiance of the USSR and other regional powers. Though academically conceivable, such an alternative does not seem feasible. The Albanian case had been unique for several reasons. First, Albania had a Stalinist regime which the leaders were able to defend against the rest of the bloc because they could have relied on then-Maoist and anti-Soviet China. They did not have contiguous borders with the USSR and the country had never been too much open to the outside world—neither in terms of trade nor in terms of political and cultural relations. In addition, Khrushchev's USSR was allied with Yugoslavia at the time when Albanian leaders tried to add their anti-Yugoslav policies to their legitimacy. In addition, the country did not need, due to the lack of its specialized economic development, any sizable foreign trade nor any other forms of external economic cooperation.

There are no reasons why any present East European country might follow Albania's pattern. True, one may suggest that Ceasescu's Rumania is both Stalinist and nationalistic. But Romania depends on its good image in the eyes of the rest of the world—of the Western as well as Third World countries. If it were to play the role of another Albania, its rulers would act against their vested interests. Another potential candidate might be seen in a sometimes very orthodox East Germany. But East Germany does not have any ambition to isolate itself from the rest of the world, neither in the Soviet bloc nor in the West. On top of it, its national interest, as well as the interest of the ruling partocracy/technocracy, depends on good relations with both West Germany and the USSR; the latter power is instrumental for protecting the very nationhood of the German Democratic Republic.

In addition to one feature of Albania's system—an almost thorough isolation from the world—there is yet another consideration for anyone who wanted to play the part of another lonely remnant of Stalinism: no national economy of a small country that has already reached a certain level of industrialization could survive without economic reforms pointing to a kind of marketization. Save Albania, no other country in the world pursues today the policy of *strict* command planning. This is another reason why one may safely rule out any East European attempt to follow the Albanian pattern under the flexible scenario.

I might be asked yet another question however: What if a country, let us say Romania or Bulgaria, faced a popular uprising against the existing regime with a lot of anti-Communist and privatization demands, especially by the peasantry? As there is no indication that, in either country, there is a movement capable of organizing and winning such an upheaval, my former suggestion for the countries—a kind of autocratic dictatorship capable of a more efficient economic policies—would hold. The ruling East

European partocrats may be dull, selfish, and power oriented, but they are by no means fools who would disregard, in the case of major reforms in the Soviet Union, the new political reality in the region and the general mood of their population. One thing is to expect that the partocrats would slow down reform trends, another thing is to expect that they would act not only against the national interests of their respective countries, but also against the interests of the USSR, and—last but not least—against the interests of their own political and physical survival. Since any attempt at an "Albanian" solution seems doomed from the very beginning, one may wonder where would the defeated leader try to seek refuge? One does not see too many countries available for the purpose.

A Limited Scenario

Given the fact that Leninism is the only source of legitimacy in the USSR; that the non-Russian population of the USSR approximates one-half of the whole; that the USSR cannot attract, with a more traditional and openly Russian national ideology, either the non-Russian part of its inner empire or the very unbalanced and diversified East European outer empire; that any Russian government would scarcely resign from its part as superpower or as spokesman for a group of countries, a more limited scenario seems more likely than the flexible one.

The limited scenario would have to rely on an adjustment of Leninism to both economic and political modernization of the USSR *and* Eastern Europe. Revival of centrifugal forces through marketization/decentralization on the one hand, and loosening of the political control through the transformation to an authoritarian system (the two minimum conditions for modernization) on the other hand would have to be balanced by an internationally viable political ideology, which would have to help keep the Soviet bloc together. That is why the satellite countries will have little elbow room for their systemic changes, approximately just along the hypothetical lines of the change "in the center of the center."

In the recent stage of development of the Soviet bloc, even totalitarianism with its rigid and orthodox ideology was unable to prevent various deviations from the Soviet pattern in individual East European countries. It is even less likely that an adjusted system, a sort of market pluralism with a mere authoritarian rule, could prevent a further diversification of the Soviet bloc. Systemic changes, once initiated, cannot be stopped. They could, however, be kept under control by the Soviet rulers. Though the limited scenario would allow for less radical changes only, some East European countries would try to go faster and further than the others. They would explore new avenues, albeit cautiously. Because we do know that authoritarian political systems are more open to liberalization and democratization, and that democratic systems are by far more conducive to modernization than the authoritarian ones, the trend seems to point, though more slowly and reluctantly, to the same objectives as would be the case under the flexible scenario.

There is still one thing that has to be given serious consideration. In all the Soviet-type national command economies, the second economy functions almost openly not only in the narrow sphere of private consumption and services, but also along the lines of centrally planned macro-economics. The results of the second economy are scarcely recorded by official statistics. It seems that some raw materials, parts, and semifinished products are not just wasted but utilized in the second economy. The fact that command system works at all lies in that it had absorbed, in early 1931, a sort of market through *khozraschyot* (economic accountability); at present, it has absorbed, through the second economy, certain market and entrepreneurial practices which, though officially not recognized, are beneficial to the societies concerned. If official reforms would be combined, under the limited scenario, with unrecognized but tolerated pragmatic practices, even the limited scenario might make room for far-reaching systemic changes. The first deadly sin—an adjusted and/or revised Leninism—would have to lead to more and more sinful practices. The better each individual country masters such practices, the better its chance to proceed with its process of overall modernization.

No doubt, the limited scenario would at the outset bring about fewer and less radical changes than the flexible one. Moreover, the changes will be less transparent. But in view of the above considerations, the limited scenario seems more likely than its flexible alternative to pave the way to an overall systemic change.

Notes

1. See among others O. Sik, *Plan and Market under Socialism* (New York: IASP, 1967), R. Selucky: *Marxism, Socialism, Freedom* (London: Macmillan 1979); R. Selucky, *Economic Reforms in Eastern Europe*, (New York: Prager, 1972); F.A. von Hayek: *Collectivist Economic Planning* (London: Routledge, 1935); B.E. Lippincott (ed.): *On the Economic Theory of Socialism* (New York: McGraw-Hill, 1964), etc.

2. Hungary, Czechoslovakia in 1965–1968 and China after 1979 accepted the view that a market oriented economic reform is the only solution to problems created by command economic planning.
3. Oscar Lange, *The Political Economy of Socialism* (Warsaw, 1957), 16.
4. A. Amalrik: *Will the Soviet Union Survive Until 1984?* (New York: Harper & Row, 1970), 22.
5. According to a text obtained by Seweryn Bialer and Joan Afferica, Gorbachev delivered a closed door speech to an audience of economic officials from Eastern Europe in August 1985 in which he said: "Many of you see the solution to your problems in resorting to market mechanism in place of direct planning. Some of you look at the market as a lifesaver for your economies. But comrades, you should not think about lifesavers but about the ship, and the ship is socialism." *Newsweek,* 3 March 1986, 45. Similarly, in the same text, Yegor Ligachev, the number two man on the Gorbachev's Politburo said: "There will be no shift toward a market economy or private enterprise."
6. Alexander Shtromas: *How the End of The Soviet System May Come About: Historical Precedents and Possible Scenarios*, in Vol. I of the present series.
7. Karl Marx, *Capital III*, (New York: International Publishers 1973), 436 ff.
8. See V.I. Lenin: *One Step Forward, Two Steps Back* (Moscow: Progress Publishers, 1969).
9. ———, 192–93.
10. See Alexander Shtromas, *How the End.*
11. See e.g., Laszlo Szamuely, *First Models of the Socialist Economic Systems* (Budapest: Akademiai Kiado, 1974).
12. See R. Selucky, *Economic Reforms in Eastern Europe*, (New York: Praeger Publishers, 1972).
13. Professor Alec Nove used this explanation to students at Carleton University in Ottawa during his guest lecture in the 1970s.

11

How Developments in Eastern Europe Affect the Stability of the Soviet Regime

AUREL BRAUN

It may seem odd and perhaps even ironic that one would speak of the East European developments having an impact on the stability of the Soviet regime, given the fact that the Soviet Union imposed the current political systems on the East European states and continues to define the parameters for political and economic behavior in the region. Nevertheless in any relationship in the international system, no matter how unequal the partners, there is bound to be mutual input. In this case what is of importance, of course, is whether the input from Eastern Europe is significant enough that it would have a substantive impact on Soviet régime stability. Furthermore, this essay deals with evolutionary or "normal" rather than revolutionary or traumatic developments in Eastern Europe in order to determine their past, current, and potential effects on the Kremlin.

It is often assumed that the developments in Eastern Europe that are likely to have the greatest effect on the stability of the Soviet régime are those which involve major political and economic upheavals such as those in Hungary in 1956 or Czechoslovakia in 1968. But it is entirely possible that long-term evolutionary developments including economic reforms, such as the New Economic Mechanism (NEM) in Hungary, may have as great, or perhaps even greater, impact on the Soviet Union, posing a more subtle but ultimately far more potent challenge to the stability of the Soviet regime. In part this chapter will attempt to test the latter hypothesis. In

651

order to assess the effect on the USSR of development in Eastern Europe though, it is important to examine the Soviet mechanisms for maintaining stability, and Soviet vulnerabilities to inputs from Eastern Europe. This in turn leads us to an examination of the entire relationship between the Soviet Union and Eastern Europe and particularly Soviet perceptions of that relationship. Lastly, it may be useful to look at specific developments and try to gauge the impact of these on the stability of the Soviet regime.

The Soviet Union and its East European allies are all too often beset by contradictory impulses. Moscow has sought to achieve both cohesion and viability throughout its domain in Eastern Europe. The Soviet elite has also been interested in the stability and maintenance of its domestic system and, as Dimitri Simes has pointed out, the two are not necessarily compatible.[1] Structural similarities would tend to minimize differences in the Soviet bloc, and the Kremlin has always been on guard to ensure that the East European environment was not contaminated either by ideas or structures which were inimical to the Soviet system and to Soviet interests. Still differences persist and these may prove to have significant implications ultimately to Soviet regime stability.

The Transmission of Innovations from Eastern Europe

It is not easy for smaller states to transmit their innovations to a larger partner, especially when the latter is a superpower viewing itself as innately superior to them, a state which has pioneered, and is leading, the "world's socialist system," to which they all belong. Moscow has always felt more comfortable in the role of a hegemon or teacher and, consequently, not only the type of innovation emanating from Eastern Europe, but also the way in which it is presented, is bound to have a seminal impact on the success of that innovation's transmission to the Soviet Union. For example, since the Soviet Union is constantly concerned about the possibility of undesirable "spillovers" from technological or economic developments into political and social areas, a purely technological innovation, clearly defined as such, would be far more easily transferrable.

Although the Soviet system functions in a substantively different fashion from other political entities acting on the international scene, it shares with them, in broad terms, some of the criteria for the successful transmission of innovations. Among these are the requirements that innovations should demonstrate relative advantage, compatibility, and divisibility.[2] The first one, which involves innovations that have developed an advantage over an extant idea or institution, is very difficult to transmit to the Soviet Union for, as the self-proclaimed guardians of the purity of Marxism-Leninism and leaders of the first and most developed socialist state, the Soviets are bound to maintain that the Soviet Union already has developed and possesses the best possible systems of ideas and institutions. The second criterion of compatibility has to take into account existing values as well as the past experience of the potential adopter, and in the case of the Soviet Union compatibility with the Marxist-Leninist ideology and the leading role of the Party is *conditio sine qua non*. The third criterion, divisibility, is particularly important to the Soviet Union for it must be assured that innovation may be tried on a limited basis. Despite the frequent use in the Soviet Union of the term "comprehensive," changes there usually have been introduced in a piecemeal fashion. The Soviet system is extremely conservative and therefore the divisibility of innovations by diminishing the danger of "spillovers" make them more palatable to the Soviet leaders.

Others have suggested that in general a political unit is more likely to adopt innovations from another unit if that innovation has been adopted successfully by the first and is viewed by key decision makers in the second as a point of legitimate comparison.[3] Therefore, the respect that an East European state enjoys in the eyes of the Soviet Union becomes an important element in the diffusion of innovation. Even if the Soviet Union allows a particular policy innovation in an East European state and it is successfully applied there, it is much more likely that Moscow would be willing to adopt this innovation if it perceived key developmental similarities between itself and the East European state in question. Therefore, states such as the German Democratic Republic (GDR) and Hungary would have a significant advantage over a state which is regarded with such utter contempt by Moscow as Romania. This brings us to another factor determining the successful diffusion of innovation, namely the perception of the communicator. If the leader of an East European state enjoys the confidence and the respect of the Soviet regime, as, for example, Janos Kadar of Hungary did, Moscow might be far more willing to view innovations introduced by him in a favorable light.

Furthermore, the personality of the Soviet leader or of those forming a collective leadership is an important element as well. Some have a far greater penchant for innovation such as Khrushchev, Andropov or, apparently, Gorbachev. One can contrast the approach and the attitudes of these individuals with the rigidity of others, such as Chernenko. And an ebullient, adventurous leader, one who might be willing to take some risks in the Soviet Union, may exhibit not only more flexibility but also may be more easily persuaded that the innovations are not imposed by any outside forces but rather occur in a somewhat symbiotic fashion. This would allow Moscow to present adoption as another "creative" development of traditional values and forms.[4] Moreover, such a leader as Gorbachev may also be more confident in predicting the consequences of adopting an innovation. If the consequences are nonthreatening and the "spillover" effect can be minimized, such measures would become more acceptable. Furthermore, and very importantly, as James Q. Wilson has pointed out in his study of organizations, these innovations would be adopted far more readily if there is a crisis.[5] In a large system though, ongoing difficulties may act more as a positive catalyst than the threat of collapse. Although it would be greatly overstating the case to suggest that the Soviet political and economic system is on the verge of collapse, Moscow is experiencing major difficulties. Some have suggested that, in fact, the Soviet economy is in a state of "permanent crisis."[6] This is well exemplified in the atomic energy sector where new generating sets are delayed for up to four years while the atomic engineering factories work all-out trying to meet an insatiable demand for their product.[7] Against this background the Chernobyl disaster looks more like a logical manifestation of this permanent crisis than a mere accident. Therefore, there may be extra pressures on Gorbachev for reform and the innovations proliferating in Eastern Europe may become more attractive as models for implementation in the USSR.

Moscow, however, still has the ability to take active steps against the diffusion of innovation from Eastern Europe. Any society can draw on certain sources in order to resist changes in the social system, and totalitarian ones have particularly well-developed mechanisms for the task. Some scholars have listed several sources of resistance to change: 1) conformity to norms or habits; 2) systemic and cultural coherence; 3) vested interests; 4) the "sacrosanct" ("the greatest resistance concerns matters which are connected with what is held to be sacred"); 5) rejection of "outsiders."[8] Others, such as Karl Deutsch, have found that a nation-state can reduce or stall the inflow of external inputs by counting on the disappearance of the external source of input, reducing linkage groups or institutions, cutting off contact with the input source, making the domestic system more stable and hence more impervious to external inputs, or trying to effect a change in the environment itself.[9]

The Soviet Union has at its disposal all of the resources to resist change and at one point or another it has employed all the tactical methods suggested by Deutsch. The Soviet system with its innate conservatism and insistence that its interpretation of the Marxist-Leninist doctrine is sacrosanct is adept at dealing with external challenges to change. Ultimately, when other methods failed, it has used force to change the challenging environment itself as in the case of Hungary in 1956 and Czechoslovakia in 1968.

Furthermore, the Soviet regime has been particularly concerned with the possibility of the spread of dissent through the linkage of dissident groups in Eastern Europe and the Soviet Union. Nor should one in any discussion of Soviet resistance mechanisms overlook the factor of size. A very large state, particularly one which has instituted a totalitarian system controlling the population very tightly, is extremely well equipped to withstand many an impact of external development, and the great asymmetry in size between the Soviet Union and the East European states gives Moscow additional protection.

Thus Moscow has enormous resources that it can mobilize in order to resist the spread of innovation from Eastern Europe. It has shown a ready willingness to use various mechanisms to suppress what it perceived as dangerous developments and thereby prevent contamination. On the other hand, it has also demonstrated an inclination to tolerate what it perceived as controlled experiments, the primary example of such toleration being the attitude taken by the Kremlin to the introduction of the New Economic Mechanism (NEM) in Hungary in 1968. It would seem therefore that East European innovations would have the best chance of penetrating into the Soviet Union if the Kremlin did not perceive in them potential dangers and thus did not activate the resistance mechanisms against them. Consequently, long-term evolutionary developments in Eastern Europe that are subtle in their challenge, rather than blatant in attacking the core Soviet interests, are likely to have the greatest impact on the Soviet system. But the diffusion is still dependent to an extent on the kind of "transmission belt" or "linkage process" that is available for the flow of East European innovations or other inputs to the Soviet Union. James Rosenau delineated three basic types of linkage processes:

1) Penetrative—where members of one polity actually participate in the political process of another.
2) Reactive—the actors who initiate the output do not participate in the allocated activities of those who experience the input but the behavior of the latter is nevertheless a response to behavior undertaken by the former.
3) Emulative—this corresponds to the so-called "diffusion" or "demonstration" effect whereby political activities in one country are perceived and emulated by another.[10]

Though these types as defined by Rosenau cannot be applied precisely to the Soviet Union, key aspects of these linkages have been employed as two-way transmission belts. Whereas penetrative processes represent more of a one-way flow from the Soviet Union to Eastern Europe, emulative processes represent two-way flows with considerable potential.

The two-way flow on the East-European—Soviet transmission belt becomes even more important as the standard of living increasingly determines regime legitimacy also in the Soviet Union. But the closeness of the linkages also helps to determine the type of possible input-flows from Eastern Europe to the USSR. As noted, the Soviet Union has always been concerned with East European cohesion and viability and the "Brezhnev Doctrine" merely reaffirmed the principle of Soviet ideological supremacy and Moscow's role as the ultimate arbiter of doctrinal orthodoxy in the socialist camp under its control. Yet, more than that, the Kremlin has also perceived Eastern Europe as a vital and indispensable domestic factor.[11] In that context, Moscow has sought a closer integration with the East European states through various mechanisms such as the Council for Mutual Economic Assistance (CMEA). It has, however, fallen significantly short of the goals of "socialist integration," and Soviet society itself has remained largely insulated from Eastern Europe. This shows that the East European states do not function in the same way as the Soviet union republics and that Moscow assigns a different degree of importance to its relations with particular Soviet bloc states.

The Kremlin's approach to integration, though, has varied since the late 1940s and so has the acquiescence, enthusiasm or resistance of the various East European states. Khrushchev introduced the concept of the socialist commonwealth (*sodruzhestvo*) which allowed for some difference in means as long as the Leninist goals and principles were maintained. Increasingly this has, however, given way to the use of the term socialist community (*soobshchestvo*) which connotes less equality and more control.[12] Some East European leaders, particularly Todor Zhivkov of Bulgaria, have always supported integration enthusiastically. He has asserted that "Bulgaria and the Soviet Union will act as a single body, breathing with the same lungs and nourished by the same blood stream."[13] Others have been far less enthusiastic. The Romanians have been most visible in their opposition to socialist integration,[14] but others have also expressed strong, if more subtle, stands against supranational integration, including the Hungarians.[15]

Moscow is now aware of the difficulties of promoting supranational integration or integration "from within." Its attempt at introducing in 1962 the "basic principle" for integration failed in the face of strong East European opposition. But not only opposition was the cause of this failure. The "basic principle" had to fail because it relied mainly on mutual trade and exchanges, while the integration of command economies cannot be brought about on the basis of trade alone—trade flows in such economies are only the by-product of the production plan,[16] and, hence, true socialist integration would involve the creation of a single command economy encompassing all member-states.

In the latter part of the 1960s Soviet economists began to come to grips with that problem. Their new prescriptions came close to eventually creating a single integrated economic unit with division of socialist labor, joint forecasting and joint planning.[17] They implied, however, a much more gradualist approach, and in 1971 the Soviet Union settled for a hybrid integrative plan in the CMEA called "the comprehensive program" which sought to promote integration through joint economic planning and joint production ventures in only the key areas of the economy. The success of this venture has been mixed at best. CMEA has undertaken a number of large joint projects which were designed to provide for closer links between the Soviet Union and the bloc states. The cost of ten of these large projects launched in 1975 was 9 billion transfer rubles (US $12.2 billion).[18] And the Soviet Union has continued to push strongly for further integration. At the thirty-second CMEA session in 1978, for instance, the late Soviet premier, Aleksei Kosygin, urged members to move more decisively toward the overall integration of their individual economies.[19] And in 1983 Yuri Andropov further contended that in order to ensure a strengthening of the economies of the member-states there had to be a "qualitatively new level" of integration within the CMEA and that such integration must be "increasingly deep, comprehensive and effective."[20]

Nevertheless, the level of integration in the CMEA continues to fall short of Soviet goals. There continues to be greater emphasis on bilateralism than on multilateralism. There is no effective joint transferrable currency and delays in production, lack of coordination and the cumbersome, interlocking barter trade system have all hindered progress. The quantum increase in OPEC oil prices in 1973–74 eventually had a profound and extremely detrimental impact on the East European economies and created new strains in the relations of East European states with the Soviet Union.

On the other hand, it should also be recognized that the integrative process continues. The current economic difficulties of the East European states created for the Soviet Union, along with additional economic burdens, new integrative opportunities. The June 1984 "extraordinary" thirty-eighth CMEA session, the first meeting of the highest representatives of the member countries of the organization to deal primarily with economic matters since April 1969, confirmed some of the Soviet leverage.[21] The conference participants agreed mutually to develop ways in which the major economic problems affecting them all may be collectively resolved. As in the past, the members agreed to intensify further and in an all-out way the efficiency of production and to improve its quality in all branches of the economy, but this time also with the specific view of providing the member-states with adequate supplies of fuel, power, raw materials, industrial goods and, particularly, of fostering their technological progress.[22] This would still have been pretty much standard fare had not the joint statement contained the ominous section, which indicated that the East European states agreed that in order for them to receive supplies of fuel and raw materials from the Soviet Union, they would have "gradually and consistently to develop their production and export structure and carry out the necessary measures for this in the area of capital investment and in the construction and rationalisation of their industry *so as to supply the Soviet Union* with the products it needs, notably foodstuffs and manufactured goods, some types of construction materials, machines and *high quality world class equipment*"[23] (emphasis added). In order to supply the Soviet Union with "high quality world class equipment," the East European states would have to redirect a good deal of their trade to the USSR.

Yet greater involvement on the part of the East European states in the Soviet economy could allow these states to have a larger input in Soviet developments despite obvious asymmetries. This input would be in addition to all other political, ideological, psychological inputs, and even those that result from economic failures in the bloc states. If that were to materialize, the East European states would become for the Soviet Union even more of an "internal" factor than previously. In the process of increasing control over Eastern Europe, the Soviet Union may thus also be creating greater opportunities for the East European states to influence Soviet developments and, in that sense, making itself more vulnerable to Eastern Europe. It should be worthwhile, therefore, to explore some of the specific areas in which East European developments have, or can have, significant effects on the stability of the Soviet regime. These should include at least the political/ideological, the economic, the military, the psychological, and the cultural dimensions.

The Political/Ideological Dimension

Despite the problems that the Soviet Union has encountered in Eastern Europe, the political arrangements that it managed to impose on the region have been on the whole satisfactory for the Kremlin which has gone to significant lengths to preserve these arrangements. The Kremlin had to do its utmost to ensure the viability of Marxist-Leninist regimes in the countries of the region not only for the sake of maintaining bloc cohesion but, also, as a means of preserving the legitimacy and, ultimately, stability of the Soviet regime in the USSR itself.

There have been attempts at separating Soviet political behavior and goals from the ideological objectives proclaimed by the Soviet regime. For example, Robert Daniels has argued that within the Soviet Union there is only one real source of emotional support for the regime, that of old-fashioned Great Russian nationalism, "defensive in its primary instinct but proud of the global role that the country has won by virtue of its military power."[24] Furthermore, Daniels contends that Marxism-Leninism is a spent force which is vainly used to try to justify the policies of the Soviet leaders and to legitimize their rule.

Ideology and politics cannot, however, be easily separated, and certainly not in the case of the Soviet Union. As Seweryn Bialer succinctly put it, "to distinguish analytically between the various elements of ideology and the many dimensions of Soviet nationalism is in essence to separate artificially factors that are not separate, distinct or counteropposed to one another, but inseparably intertwined. . . ."[25] It is the combination of ideology and Soviet nationalism, of ideology and *Realpolitik* that represents the Soviet leaders' view of the world. And in this view of the world the regime is committed to retaining the empire that Stalin built in Eastern Europe, to defending it at all costs, to treating it as the borderline of their own defensive preoccupation. To quote Bialer again, it is as if the slogan "socialism in one country" had expanded into "socialism in one empire."[26]

Since the USSR regards Eastern Europe as an extension of its own system, Soviet ideological relations with Eastern Europe inevitably acquire a political dimension. As noted above, the maintenance of a Marxist-Leninist system in Eastern Europe is considered by Moscow to be crucially important in legitimizing the Soviet system itself both in the eyes of the Soviet population and in the minds of outsiders.[27] Political and ideological functions are inseparable here. Socialism must either be seen as coherent and irreversible everywhere or, if it were not, if it could be reversed at least in one place, then the days of the socialist system would be numbered in all other places, too, including the Soviet Union itself. Hence, by ensuring the survival of the ideology throughout the empire, the Soviet Union helps assure the continuous survival of the Soviet system of rule at home.

Although, as noted above, the transfer of innovative ideas and reforms from Eastern Europe to the Soviet Union has been rarely explicit, the potential for such transfer is clearly there. The realization of this potential may be substantially facilitated by distinguishing between the socialist system as such and its particular implementation in a specific political regime (or a specific pattern of institutional relationships). By employing such distinctions one may help to legitimize the search for new and more effective forms of political organization in the Soviet Union itself.[28] That this is indeed the case has been already proven on a few occasions.

In the 1960s East European reforms, at least in their theoretical formulations, went beyond Soviet proposals. This was particularly evident in such areas as agriculture or balancing between consumption and investment which logically led to a more "permissive" attitude toward private enterprise.[29] In the socialist world, the East Europeans were also the innovators in working out their societies' response to the challenge of the scientific-technological revolution. A study by the Czechoslovak Academy of Sciences in 1966 came to the conclusion that the urgency of embarking and succeeding in the scientific-technological revolution was impeded by a "directive system of management" which as part of the superstructure was incapable of nourishing the free spirit of enquiry and conflicts of views essential to the optimal development of science.[30] The East Europeans, particularly the Czechs and to a lesser extent the Hungarians, also concluded from the studies they have undertaken that advanced socialist societies were in danger of experiencing a restratification and reemergence of alienation.[31]

The East Europeans took the initiative even in areas with clear political implications. They suggested, for example, electoral reform; revitalization of representative institutions; broadening of trade union rights; and easing of censorship.[32] Prior to 1968, Moscow took quite a flexible view of such East European developments, benevolently seeing in them creative contributions to the socialist experience. But following the invasion of Czechoslovakia in 1968, and particularly after 1971 (that is in the wake of the Twenty-fourth Congress of the CPSU), the Soviets claimed that there is only one scientific model of socialism common to all countries, which is represented most fully by the Soviet Union, as it was at a higher stage of socialist development than any other socialist country.[33] Though local conditions may militate for some differences, the Soviets contended, the general direction had to be the one elaborated by Moscow. It was only in the latter part of the 1970s, when acute problems multiplied both in Eastern Europe and in the Soviet Union itself, that the Soviets started to show again a greater receptivity for East European innovations and reforms. Moreover, following Andropov's ascension to power, the Soviets themselves started to propel innovative ideas, most of which could clearly be traced back to East European thinking of the 1960s.[34]

This is not to imply that Soviet wariness of East European ideological and political innovations came to an end. Moscow continues to be highly concerned about the emphasis many of the East European theorists put on the significance of introducing the rule of law and securing the independence of the judiciary powers, which challenges the Marxist-Leninist view about the law and the state being in an organic relationship in which supremacy belongs to the state. And, as far as reforms are concerned, the Soviets continue to stress their unwillingness to allow smaller CMEA coun-

tries to move significantly ahead of Moscow in solving their internal problems.[35] The Soviet Union, of course, would find it particularly dangerous
if some of the more radical East European ideas filtered through to Soviet
dissidents, forming between them and their counterparts in Eastern Europe
a transnational link. For the Soviet Union dissent in Eastern Europe presents, therefore, a major challenge.[36] Hence, the more subtle the reforms
introduced in Eastern Europe are, the less the Soviets will perceive them
as a challenge, and the better chance these reforms will have to penetrate
into the USSR.

Periods of succession usually increase the chances for penetration of
innovative experience as Gorbachev's succession has already proved to
some extent. Successions in Eastern Europe may also bring significant
changes. In three states, Bulgaria, the GDR, and Czechoslovakia, the
leaders are in their seventies. The leadership structures are rigid and major
changes may occur with each succession. It is also likely that developments
in Eastern Europe would have a far greater impact on the stability of the
Soviet regime if it had to face a coincidence of several crises. In the past
the Soviet Union had the luxury of dealing with one crisis at a time. Now
a multiple-crises scenario is becoming evident not only in terms of the
forthcoming successions but also in those of economic reality where the
Soviet Union, in addition to being challenged by the penetration of East
European innovations, would have to confront the economic burdens that
it has incurred there.

The Economic Dimension

From the very aftermath of its victory in World War II, the Soviet Union
developed close economic links with Eastern Europe. The nature of this
economic relationship has, of course, evolved, but it has been estimated
that in the first postwar decade, Moscow extracted from East European
states goods and resources worth about $14 billion, a sum in the same
order of magnitude as the aid the United States gave to the Western
Europeans under the Marshall Plan.[37] Despite that, the East Europeans
were on the whole more successful in coping with their economic problems
than the USSR. And, given the Marxist-Leninist belief in the role played
by economics in determining social mechanisms, it is not surprising that
the Soviet Union monitored economic reforms in Eastern Europe very
closely. Economics is thus an area where the transmission of innovations
from Eastern Europe to the Soviet Union may play an important role in
the development of both.

The Hungarian Model

Of all the East European states Hungary stands out as the one which has implemented, though in a limited way, economic decentralization and achieved by so doing a certain degree of economic success. With the Czechoslovakian experiment of 1968 brutally terminated and the movement for democratization in Poland in 1980–81 suppressed, Hungary in terms of reforms occupies at present the front line. By having satisfied the basic economic needs of Hungary's population, the Kadar regime achieved a considerable degree of legitimacy and stability, which set it apart from the other Soviet bloc states.

How did Hungary manage successfully to accomplish the move from *"Gulag"* to "Goulash" communism while other states, particularly Czechoslovakia, have failed? The Hungarians from the beginning were very careful to deemphasise the value-related and ideological elements of their reform, stressing instead the material benefits it could produce. Kadar sold himself to the Soviet Union as the indispensable leader. The innovations were introduced by him gradually and in a calm atmosphere which allowed the Budapest leadership to appear stable, united, reliable and trustworthy.[38]

The Hungarians also placed great emphasis on assuring the Soviet Union that the economic reforms would by no means affect the leading role of the Party. In contrast to Czechoslovakia, "radical" rhetoric was avoided while substantial measures changing many an aspect of the institutional pattern were introduced, first by endowing the existing institutions with new rights and powers and only then by creating some new institutions. Economic reform was also incrementally extended to the agricultural sector. At the same time political changes to accompany that economic reform were very limited. For example, contested elections were introduced, but even though the elected representative bodies are practically powerless, only 49 of 352 seats were, in fact, contested in the parliamentary elections of April 1971.[39]

The timid impression that the Hungarians managed to convey was vital for the success of their reforms. Budapest's message was that reforms were a preventive measure rather than an emergency response to an impending crisis. They were measures "taken rather deliberately, as something which ought to be done sooner rather than later to avoid the kind of system breakdown confronting the Czechoslovaks. This enabled the Hungarians to present their reforms more as a technical adjustment in the system than as a major overhaul and reevaluation of its basic machinery and workings."[40]

This is how the Hungarians created the necessary environment for a favorable Soviet response. Moscow has viewed their reforms as a "controlled market mechanism," and some Soviet economists, including Academician Abel Aganbegyan and his colleagues from the Institute for Economics and Organization of Industrial Production in the Novosibirsk branch of the USSR's Academy of Sciences, have proposed to introduce economic reforms in the USSR, which can be traced back to measures initiated by Hungary's NEM. Support for Hungary came not only from Soviet academics or high-ranking bureaucrats but from Brezhnev himself when, in the Report to the Twenty-sixth Congress of the Party he explicitly praised Hungarian agricultural achievements.[41] It has been argued moreover that since the general secretary's report for these occasions is the product of a collective effort, the secretary in charge of agriculture would very likely be the one who initiated that statement.[42] The Party secretary in charge of agriculture in 1981 was Mikhail Gorbachev. On several occasions, he has given indications that he is sympathetic to Hungarian reforms, particularly in the area of agriculture, although so far he has been cautious in introducing substantive changes.

Indeed, the diffusion of Hungarian innovations to the Soviet Union encounters a variety of problems. First of all, Hungarian economic reforms are incomplete and by Western standards the Hungarian system is not performing efficiently. Moreover, Budapest seems to have reached the limits of Kadarism. Further reforms may already endanger the leading role of the Party and threaten to provoke Soviet action. Even though, on the whole, Moscow views the Hungarian experiment benignly, it was willing in the past to use pressure to limit that experiment when it deemed it was going too far. In 1974, for example, the Kremlin apparently succeeded in having the Hungarian economist and "father" of NEM, Reszo Nyers, removed from his post.[43] Furthermore, during the last few years, living standards in Hungary have been stagnating, growth rates have declined sharply, and Hungary has incurred the highest per capita hard currency debts in the bloc.[44]

Nevertheless, Hungarian innovations continue to present a set of wide-ranging challenges to Moscow. In the case of the CMEA, Hungarian proposals to institute a truly convertible currency, restructure trade by allowing enterprise-to-enterprise exchanges, and revise the banking system, imply the restructuring in the long run of other CMEA economies along Hungarian lines. But for the Soviet Union a wholesale adoption of the Hungarian-style reforms would be extremely dangerous for, if these reforms were to undermine the Party's power monopoly, there is no external intervention force that could come to the rescue of the Soviet Communist party. A spillover of economic reform into the political arena in the Soviet Union could spell a disaster for the Soviet regime.

The Hungarians have become, in some ways, a little less cautious in certain policy areas as they have become increasingly more frustrated. Matyas Szuros, the Central Committee secretary responsible for international policy, subtly rejected supranationality and Soviet control following the June 1984 Economic Summit.[45] Nyers wrote that for integration in the socialist bloc to proceed successfully there would have to be reform both of the CMEA and of the economic mechanisms of its member-states bringing them closer to the Hungarian NEM. But he came to pessimistic conclusions finding that systemic, size-related and developmental barriers stood in the way of CMEA's further integration.[46] Lastly, the Hungarians have been also somewhat less than cautious in their public statements on the problems of the spillover. For example, following the 8 June 1985 elections to Parliament where rival candidates already contested 352 of the 387 seats (though each of them had to endorse the Communist party's basic program), the Deputy Prime Minister Josef Marjai stated that "more economic freedom requires more political freedom to debate choices."[47] But this is precisely what the Soviet regime fears. A major reshuffle of the Hungarian leadership in June 1987, though, indicates that the Soviet Union need not be concerned yet. A well-known hard-liner, Karoly Grosz, was appointed prime minister and Janos Berecz, more moderate, but not a reformer, was brought into the Politburo. Although since assuming office Grosz has taken a surprisingly pragmatic approach, he has supported only economic but not political reform. True reformers, such as Imre Pozsgay, are still in the background as Hungary pursues a rather cautious road. In terms of political reform, Poland has already moved further ahead than Hungary. Thus, for the time being, Hungarian reforms operate within parameters that are acceptable to Moscow.

Hungary is not the only model that the Soviet Union may draw on. By East European standards the GDR has also enjoyed considerable success. And yet East Berlin did not move toward market socialism. In the reforms of 1964, and again of 1971–81, it introduced some decentralization between the ministry and the *kombinats* or trusts.[48] The *kombinats* were first made operational in 1972 as institutions combining vertical and horizontal integration of enterprises, and thus moving economic management beyond vertical ministerial control and shortening the planning ladder. To a certain extent these "intermediary institutions" have also broken up the state monopoly of foreign trade. But these are very limited reforms, and the GDR's achievements in building a relatively successful economy is the result of a multiplicity of factors. Not least among these is the GDR's peculiar relationship with the Federal Republic of Germany, which grants it special credit and trade concessions. Neither this fact nor the specific German cultural and historic traditions, as well as the skills of the German population, can be replicated elsewhere. Therefore, for a reform to be successfully introduced in the USSR, the GDR model would simply not be adequate.

Economic Burdens

Moscow, though, has to cope not only with successes in Eastern Europe but also with failures, and by this we mean more than the general systemic problems affecting the whole Soviet bloc. Economic disasters and policy-making mistakes also place a burden on the Soviet Union, which may have a potential destabilizing effect on the Soviet regime.

In the 1970s various East European states in order to promote economic growth and to raise their standard of living borrowed massively from the Western nations. They ran up enormous hard currency debts and by the end of the decade some, like Poland and Romania, faced such massive economic failures that they were unable to service these debts. Some Western observers concluded that the East European states had therefore become major financial burdens to Moscow. But this in some ways overstates and in other ways understates the case.

Although the Soviet Union in the first postwar decade mercilessly exploited the East European states, it gradually moved to a position where in effect it was providing them with economic subsidies. The surplus of Soviet exports and the higher than world market and intra-CMEA prices paid by Moscow for East European manufactured goods have become part of what has been called the USSR's "implicit subsidies" to Eastern Europe. There is controversy as to the actual amount. Michael Marrese and Jan Vanous contend that "the Soviet Union transferred resources equivalent to $87.2 billion to Eastern Europe during 1960–1980; the bulk of these resources—$75.5 billion—was transferred during 1971–80."[49] But Paul Marer argues that the subsidy came to only $14 billion for the six East European CMEA states between the period 1971–78.[50] I find the Marer assessment more persuasive but what is clear overall is that the Soviet Union had been providing subsidies on a large scale. Just as importantly, there is also a consensus among economists that since 1981 these subsidies have been declining.[51]

Therefore, what we see is that, despite the worsening economic performances of East European states, the Soviet Union managed to decrease its economic burden. And if we use the Marer figures then, even at its height, this burden represented only about 10 percent of the cumulative total exports to the six East European states.[52] The examination of Soviet subsidies shows as well that Moscow used quite a sophisticated approach to the providing of subsidies, which rewarded the more loyal members of the bloc. In the 1971–78 period, for example, loyalist Bulgaria received by far the highest per capita subsidy whereas dissident Romania received no such benefit and, as a result, incurred a small net loss.[53]

It is true that the Soviet Union, faced with instability in Poland following that country's economic collapse, had no choice but to provide economic aid. In 1982, for instance, Moscow agreed to a rescheduling of Polish debt payments and granted Warsaw credits of 2.7 billion rubles, an amount representing 73.8 percent of the value of Poland's exports to the Soviet Union for the year.[54] But this was in certain ways less of a burden than the adjustments that Western creditors had to make in order to try to preserve their enormous hard currency loans to Poland. The Soviet leadership must have watched with considerable amusement the development by Western states of a very strong interest in maintaining the stability of the Polish regime in order to protect their loans. In the case of the other economic cripple, Romania, the Soviet Union did little, and the Bucharest regime itself undertook a series of draconian measures aimed at reducing its foreign debts.

Therefore, the Soviet Union, at least so far, has managed to carry its economic burden in Eastern Europe quite successfully, and has taken rather effective steps to diminish it. It may be argued that this could also weaken Soviet leverage over Eastern Europe, but I would suggest that, given the essential nature of the commodities that the Soviet Union supplies on a barter basis to most East European states (oil, natural gas), Moscow is likely to be able to continue to exercise its influence in Eastern Europe independently of providing substantial subsidies. As far as mounting rescue operations, the situation in Poland did not place too heavy a burden on the Soviet Union although the Soviets were clearly unhappy about that situation. What is correct though is that the Soviet Union's ability to supply even that kind of aid may diminish in the future as its own economic difficulties increase. If there are multiple failures that it has to tend to, this could create a crisis. Nevertheless, as things stand, and given developments over the past ten years, it is unlikely that economic burdens in Eastern Europe will in the near future become a major factor affecting the stability of the Soviet Union.

The Military, Psychological and Cultural Factors

As John C. Campbell has suggested, among the fundamental interests that the Soviet Union continues to have in Eastern Europe is its ability fully to exercise on East European territories physical power, including the stationing of military forces in most East European countries and backing them up with the might of the entire Soviet military machine.[55] The WTO created by the Soviet Union in 1955 has helped to draw the East European states closer to the Soviet Union militarily. After 1960 the Soviet Union placed greater emphasis on the military utility of the East European forces even as it integrated them further with its own military force. In terms of foreign policy coordination, by 1971 Brezhnev did declare that the WTO was "the main center for coordinating the fraternal countries' foreign policies."[56] But the late WTO Chief of Staff, Sergei Shtemenko, had also contended that a key function of the alliance was the "suppression of counter-revolution" in Eastern Europe.[57]

Although consultation within the Warsaw Pact may provide something of a political safety valve—and there has been considerable evidence of disagreement, particularly on the part of Romania—the WTO remains very much a Soviet creature. With the exception of Romania which has formulated an independent military doctrine of "people's war," which is in some ways similar to the territorial defense doctrine of Yugoslavia,[58] the other East European armies have become little more than mere components of the larger Soviet-led unit. There is thus no WTO doctrine but only a Soviet doctrine. If anything, Soviet military control over Eastern Europe has been increasing. As far as Bucharest is concerned, the Soviet Union appears willing to tolerate its military deviation in part because Romania is in the strategically less significant southern tier of the WTO region and in part because of an attitude of superiority vis-à-vis the Romanians which includes confidence that in case of need the Soviet Union can easily acquire control over Romanian territory.

The latter stance is also an indication of the Soviet psychological attitude towards Eastern Europe. Superpower status, as equal with that of the United States, combines well with Great Russian feelings of national superiority. The superpower psychology can also function as a cohesive force within the Soviet Union, as all the groups in it share that status despite domestic inequalities. This would help the regime to resist the destabilizing impact of certain East European developments. On the other hand, a diminished status vis-à-vis the United States as Soviet economic performance declines relative to that of the West (and if United States has the will and the skill to deny it equal status) would deprive the Soviet regime of the cohesive benefits the superpower status entails. In that case problems of nationalism in the Soviet Union would multiply. For the Soviet Union a dramatic rise in national awareness among the minority groups, particularly as demographic trends turn against the Great Russian majority, is dangerous to say the least. The history of empires is in this respect not encouraging either. In Eastern Europe there has been already an increase in nationalism. Ceausescu has found it to be a very useful rallying force, although it has become subject to its own laws of diminishing returns. But even in Hungary, as economic growth has stagnated, the regime has developed far greater interest in the welfare of Hungarian-speaking minorities in Romania and Czechoslovakia. There is, therefore, the potential that, under certain circumstances, East European nationalism could encourage nationalism in the various non-Russian Soviet republics. But, along with all the factors discussed in this chapter, the diffusion of nationalism would also be dependent on cultural and people-to-people links.

Although the Soviet Union has done much to isolate its population from the rest of the world, it maintains relatively close cultural and even tourist links with the East European states. Over 100,000 students from Eastern Europe study in the Soviet Union, and many thousands of cultural exchanges, together with strong cooperation and competition in sports, take place on a regular basis.[59] That "inter-linking" may have been designed to enhance Soviet control over Eastern Europe, but practically the flow of influence inevitably became a two-way one. And lastly, Soviet tourism has been almost exclusively directed toward Eastern Europe with millions of Soviet citizens visiting these states. The Soviet Union has thus made itself a little more permeable.

Conclusion

First of all, it should be noted that, though Eastern Europe may be regarded as a source of potential instability for the Soviet system, its impact on the USSR, given the size of the Soviet Union, its many resistance mechanisms and the general difficulties of transmitting innovations to it, will tend to be limited. Nevertheless, the potential for serious destabilization remains. The East European states are suffering from what may be called permanent legitimation and economic crises. The stability of these regimes in large part rests on a fragile legitimacy which, in turn, is based on economic progress that is more and more difficult to obtain. Although the Soviet regime can base its legitimacy, and thus also its stability, on a broader set of factors, its problems become increasingly similar to those of Eastern Europe.

Development over the past several years would tend to indicate that the Soviet Union is likely to face increased domestic and foreign dilemmas (particularly in Eastern Europe) which will further complicate the Soviet policy-making process. In many ways the Soviet Union has shown itself to be far more adept in dealing with such challenges in which the dangers and the outcomes can be identified with some certainty. It has been less well able to cope with subtle and prolonged challenges that are not easily amenable to quick and decisive solutions. Yet the Soviet Union on the one hand, in order to avoid destabilization, needs to introduce fundamental reforms but, on the other, is afraid of doing so, as such reforms are likely to carry the risk of undermining the totality of power of the regime to the degree of forcing its demise. Moscow is thus likely to embark on the course of structural reforms only if it becomes convinced that it is in desperate need of doing so; that is, to use Edmund Burke's words, if it would feel the need to make a choice between the disagreeable and the intolerable—and if the regime is sufficiently confident that it can control the momentum of such reforms and protect itself from its side effects.

This is where the role of the East European states may become important. Crises of stability in the region would put additional pressure on Moscow but, far more importantly, under specific circumstances, certain innovations may become attractive to Moscow as crisis-deterring or crisis-management means. The Hungarian experiment becomes in this respect especially salient. It is not that Moscow is not aware of many of its shortcomings and risks. But it appears to be a palatable experiment, and the Soviet Union, at a certain stage, may risk to transfer it, or at least its key components. Gorbachev, who is apparently very much aware of the enormous difficulties facing the Soviet Union and who appears to be supremely confident in his ability to manage situations, may become the Soviet leader who might after all, when he sufficiently consolidates his power, dare ride the tiger of reform. But if in Hungary the reform is well controlled—the possibility of the Soviet Union's intervention working there as both a controlling and an enabling factor—in the Soviet Union, which is devoid of external checks, the equivalent of the Hungarian NEM would have to be open-ended. This is to say that there it could more easily precipitate the process of the regime's radical and irreversible transformation.

Notes

1. Dimitri K. Simes and Associates, *Soviet Succession: Leadership in Transition*, The Washington Papers, 6, No. 59 (Beverly Hills and London: Sage Publications, 1978), 20–21.
2. Everett M. Rogers, *Diffusion of Innovations* (New York: Free Press, 1962), 124–31.
3. Jack L. Walker, "The Diffusion of Innovations Among the American States", in *American Political Science Review*, 63, No. 3 (September 1969), 897.

4. With regard to Khrushchev this thesis was advanced by Zvi Y. Gitelman, *The Diffusion of Political Innovation: From Eastern Europe to the Soviet Union*, (Beverly Hills, CA: Sage Publications, 1972), 16.

5. James Q. Wilson, "Innovation and Organization: Notes Toward a Theory," in James D. Thompson, ed., *Approaches to Organizational Design* (Pittsburgh: University of Pittsburgh Press, 1966), 208.

6. David Wilson, *The Demand for Energy in the Soviet Union* (London: Croom Helm, 1983), 15.

7. ———.

8. Goodwin Watson, "Resistance to Change," W.G. Bennis, K.D. Benne and R. Chin, eds., *The Planning of Change* (New York: Holt, Rinehart & Winston, 1969), 142.

9. Karl Deutsch, "External Influences on the Internal Behavior of States," in R. Barry Farrell, ed., *Approaches to Comparative and International Politics* (Evanston, Ill.: Northwestern University Press, 1969), 11.

10. James N. Rosenau, ed., *Linkage Politics: Essays on the Convergence of National and International Systems* (New York: Free Press, 1969), 45.

11. Andrzej Korbonski, "Eastern Europe," R.F. Byrnes, ed., *After Brezhnev: Sources of Soviet Conduct in the 1980s* (Bloomington, Ind.: Indiana University Press, 1983), 293.

12. Peter A. Toma, ed., *The Changing Face of Communism in Eastern Europe* (Tucson: University of Arizona Press, 1970), 8.

13. *Rabotnichesko Delo* (Sofia), 20 September 1973

14. See: Aurel Braun, *Romanian Foreign Policy Since 1965: The Political and Military Limits of Autonomy* (New York: Praeger, 1978).

15. See: *Nepszabadsag* (Budapest), 3 September 1969. The Hungarians suggested that integration should involve the creation of a free trade area in the CMEA.

16. Peter J.D. Wiles, *Communist International Economics* (Oxford: Oxford University Press, 1968), 1–2, 376.

17. See, for example, P.M. Alampiev, O.T. Bogomolov, and Y.S. Shiryaev, *A New Approach to Economic Integration* (Moscow: Progress, 1974), 82–83. In 1987 these ideas were strongly reemphasized by Gorbachev who in his speech to the heads of CMEA governments assembled in Moscow said that "in the activities of CMEA a more organic combination of coordinated cooperative planning with direct productive links between enterprises and research institutions should be secured." He also congratulated the decision of CMEA's session to elaborate "a collective conception of the socialist division of labour," stressing that the "definition of long-term orientation for collaboration, specialization and cooperation will allow . . . to accelerate social-economic development and to help solving the common tasks of the socialist community" (*Pravda*, 15 October 1987, 1).

18. *The Times* (London), 3 January 1976.

19. *Scinteia* (Bucharest), 28 June 1978.

20. *Politika* (Belgrade), 21 June 1983; *Foreign Broadcast Information Service*, 23 June 1983.

21. See for more details a report published in *World Marxist Review*, 28, No. 8 (August 1984), 6–11.
22. *Izvestiya*, 21 June 1984.
23. Report in *World Marxist Review*, 8–10.
24. Robert V. Daniels, *Russia: The Roots of Confrontation* (Cambridge, Mass.: Harvard University Press, 1985), 360.
25. Seweryn Bialer, "The Political System," in Byrnes, ed., *After Brezhnev*, 10.
26. ———, 9.
27. Korbonski, "Eastern Europe," in Byrnes, ed., *After Brezhnev*, 322.
28. For a detailed substantiation of such an approach, see: Fyodor Burlatsky, *Lenin, Gosudarstvo, Politika*, (Lenin, the State, Politics) (Moscow: Nauka, 1970), 136–39, and his "Lenin and the Art of Management," in *New Times*, No. 51 (1968), 6–9.
29. See: Sarah M. Terry, "Theories of Socialist Development in Soviet-East European Relations," in Sarah M. Terry, ed., *Soviet Policy in Eastern Europe* (New Haven: Yale University Press, 1984), 227–28, 239.
30. Paul M. Cocks, "Retooling the Directed Society: Administrative Modernization and Developed Socialism," J.F. Triska and Paul M. Cocks, eds., *Political Development in Eastern Europe* (New York: Praeger, 1977), 54–55.
31. Zdenek Mlynar, "Problems of Political Leadership and the New Economic System," in *World Marxist Review*, No. 8 (December 1965), 75–77.
32. Terry, Theory of, 237–38.
33. D.A. Kerimov, ed., *Sovetskaya demokratiya v period sotsializma*, (Soviet Democracy in the Period of Socialism) (Moscow: Mysl, 1976), 89–92, 139.
34. See, for instance, Fyodor Burlatsky, "Karl Marx and Our Times," in *New Times*, No. 23 (1983), 18–20 or A. Aganbegyan, "Stimulirovanie i rezervy: Vnedrenie resheniy Noyabr'skogo Plenuma Tsentral'nogo Komiteta KPSS," *Trud*, 12 December 1982.
35. "Soviet Signals on Economic Management Picked up in Hungary," *Radio Free Europe*, RAD Background Reports/68 (31 March 1983).
36. Vratislav Pechota, "East European Dissent, the U.S. and the Soviet Union," in J.L. Curry, ed., *Dissent in Eastern Europe* (New York: Praeger, 1983), 205–12.
37. Paul Marer, "Soviet Economic Policy in Eastern Europe," in John P. Hardt, ed., *Reorientation and Commercial Relations of the Economies of Eastern Europe*, compendium of papers submitted to the Joint Economic Committee, Congress of the U.S. (Washington, D.C.: U.S. Government Printing Office, 1974).
38. Gitelman, *Diffusion*, 42.
39. "L'Unita Interviews Reszo Ryers", *Radio Free Europe* Report of 22 July 1969.
40. Gitelman, *Diffusion*, 44.
41. Leonid I. Brezhnev, *Otchetny doklad Tsentral'nogo Komiteta KPSS XXVI s'ezdu Kommunisticheskoy partii Sovetskogo Soyuza*, (Report of the Central

Committee of the CPSU to the 26th Congress of the CPSU) (Moscow: Gospolitizdat, 1981), 9.

42. Archie Brown, "Leadership Succession and Policy Innovation," A. Brown and M. Kaser, eds., *Soviet Policy for the 1980s* (London: Macmillan, 1982), 244–45 and 269.
43. Terry, Theory of, 245–46.
44. Charles Gati, "Soviet Empire: Alive But Not Well," in *Problems of Communism*, March-April 1985, 77; and *The Globe and Mail* (Toronto), 20 November 1987.
45. *The Guardian* (London), 22 July 1984.
46. Reszo Nyers, "Hagyomany es ujitas a KGST-egyuttmukodesben," (Tradition and Innovation in CMEA Cooperation), in *Koszgazdasagi Szemle*, (Journal of Economics) (Budapest), No. 4 (1982), 385–403.
47. *New York Times*, 23 June 1985.
48. For details, see: T. Weiskopf, "GDR," in *East Europe*, 20, No. 10 (1981).
49. Michael Marrese and Jan Vanous, *Implicit Subsidies and Non-market Benefits in Soviet Trade with Eastern Europe* (Berkeley: University of California Press, 1982), 3; also cited by *Wall Street Journal*, 15 January 1982.
50. Paul Marer, "The Political Economy of Soviet Relations with Eastern Europe," in Terry ed., *Theory of*, 175–179.
51. Charles Wolf, Jr. et al., *The Cost of the Soviet Empire*, R. 3073-1-NA (Santa Monica, CA: The Rand Corporation, 1983).
52. Marer, *The Political Economy*, in Terry (ed.), Soviety Policy, 179.
53. ———, *Soviet Policy*.
54. *Zolnierz Wolnosci* (Warsaw), 23 March 1982; *Foreign Broadcast Information Service*, 1 and 2 April 1982.
55. John C. Campbell, "Soviet Policy in Eastern Europe: An Overview," in Terry (ed.), *Theory of*, 21.
56. Quoted from Aurel Braun, "The Warsaw Treaty Organization," in *Yearbook on International Affairs, 1984* (Stanford, CA: Hoover Institution Press, 1984), 418 and 423–25.
57. *Za rubezhom*, (Abroad) (Moscow), 7 May 1976.
58. Aurel Braun, "The Yugoslav/Romanian Concept of People's War," in *Canadian Defence Quarterly*, 7, No. 1 (Summer 1977), 39–43.
59. Robert L. Hutchings, *Soviet-East European Relations* (Madison, Wis.: University of Wisconsin Press, 1983), 224–25.

12

Eastern Europe:

An Examination of Political
and Socioeconomic Alternatives

ZDISLAW M. RURARZ

Under the term "Eastern Europe" are included all the six Soviet-dominated countries of the area (Bulgaria, Czechoslovakia, Eastern Germany, Hungary, Poland and Romania), as well as the three Baltic States incorporated into the USSR (Estonia, Latvia and Lithuania).

The examination of political and socioeconomic alternatives of the area in a post-Soviet Eastern Europe is based in this chapter on a most advantageous assumption, namely the possibility of a peaceful and prompt phasing out of Soviet domination in the countries under consideration. This comprises also the absence of civil war or any other violence. On the contrary, the chapter assumes that such a phasing out would be accompanied by a process of national consensus, supplemented by friendly relations among the nations of the area, as well as the successor of the present Soviet state. Quite naturally, this would mean that no changes in the present frontiers among the nations of the area would take place.

Such a scenario may look highly unlikely, yet not impossible either.

It is further assumed that all the world democracies would help Eastern Europe to enter the path of freedom and democracy and would extend their helping hand to it.

Finally, the chapter treating on three distinct issues, though undoubtedly interrelated, runs a risk of certain simplifications or even contradictions. Political ambitions, social heritage and expectations, as well as hard economic realities may conflict with one another and complicate the choice of proper alternatives.

Moreover, a post-Soviet Eastern Europe will certainly be confronted with issues bridging the past, present, and future in conditions having no parallel in history. Still it is necessary to have a certain vision of that process, however controversial it may be.

Political Alternatives

It is assumed that the political underlying conditions for the alternatives enumerated below are the same for all countries of the area, although it is quite evident that this cannot be the case in practice. Still, such an assumption is better than making distinctions between various countries of the area, something inviting unnecessary polemics by various nationals belonging to it.

The present state of political affairs in Eastern Europe cannot provide any indication for future developments in the area, with the possible exception of East Germany, which might style its political institutions on those existing in the Federal Republic of Germany (though even here sheer adoption of such institutions without certain adaptations seems unlikely).

Taking all this into account, one has to suggest, nevertheless, a few most likely, from today's point of view, political alternatives in a post-Soviet Eastern Europe.

Contrary to possible alternatives in social and economic domains, those in the political domain seem to be more numerous and less clearly definable.

Having all the above-mentioned reservations in mind, the following political alternatives seem to be possible:

1. Continuation of the present political system.
2. A slight shift in the present system, perhaps more in rhetoric than in reality.
3. An important change of the present political system which, nevertheless, remains basically "socialistic" in nature, with some tendencies for dictatorship preserved.
4. A shift toward the social-democratic system, with an unabridged multiparty pattern in sight and free elections postponed for not too long; this accompanied also by some reprivatization of the economy.
5. A clear discontinuation of "socialistic orientation" and adoption of a liberal course, with both the Left and the Right in minority.

6. The emergence of a clearly Christian-democratic, moderately conservative, and nationalistic political system.
7. A chauvinist-nationalist, religiously orthodox, and extremely conservative political system.
8. A military dictatorship, with Fascist tendencies, in some countries even a return to monarchy.
9. A kind of Fascist system, with some odd ideology in the background.
10. Complete anarchy, interrupted by periodic swings from one extreme to another.

Without excluding *per se* any of the above alternatives, and many intermediate ones not specifically mentioned, it seems that the first alternative has the least chances, as the Soviet-imposed political institutions in Eastern Europe would most likely fall victim to agitated people of the area with no regard to how useful these institutions sometimes might have been and still could be.

Moreover, in the present Soviet-dominated Eastern Europe, communism has nowhere come to power in an orderly manner, but was either brought on the Soviet bayonets, or through a Soviet-directed *coup d'état* as was the case in Czechoslovakia in February 1948.

Hence the political institutions existing at present in Eastern Europe are rightly considered by the people as an instrument of Soviet domination and as such would be most likely spontaneously dismantled.

In other words, the disappearance of the Soviet presence in Eastern Europe could lead almost instantly to the disappearance of Soviet-type communism and its institutions, at least in name for sure.

Even alternative No. 2 seems to have no chance, or at any rate could not prevail for too long (the latter may perhaps be the case in Bulgaria, Romania, and Latvia. In Latvia because of the fact that the nonnative population is close to a half of the total population and could resist drastic change).

Alternatives Nos. 7, 8, and 9 also have little chance, especially since, after the disappearance of communism, democracy would surely strengthen its position all over the world.

As to alternative No. 10, perhaps the most disastrous in the short run, though highly improbable in the long run, it may have some chance of materializing in some of the countries of the area at the starting point of their transition to democracy.

Alternatives Nos. 3, 4, 5, and 6 are the ones to be seriously reckoned with should Soviet domination in Eastern Europe cease. Some extreme solutions apart, it seems quite probable that in many countries of the area, if not in all, the passage from one political system to another would develop in the form of a gradual process, despite radical action that might be taken to dismantle the existing political institutions. Such a process could run at a changing tempo and in zigzags.

This assumption stems from certain political realities. The formal and practical absence of oppositional political parties in the presently Soviet-dominated Eastern Europe (such an opposition party, of liberal-democratic orientation—the PKN—was established in Poland on 11 November 1984, but little is known about its activities), is such a reality.

The absence of opposition political parties in Eastern Europe could very likely be turned into a spontaneous mushrooming of non-Communist parties, once Eastern Europe would go free. Yet it is by no means certain that their political maturity would be similarly instantaneous (in Poland, after the birth of Solidarity and before martial law, there was no tendency for any mushrooming of political parties, but this can be explained by the fact that nobody believed even then that Poland had ceased to be Soviet-dominated).

For this simple reason, any uniformity when it comes to the adoption of the before-mentioned most likely political alternatives, seems rather improbable and one has to be prepared both for the lack of clarity, as well as the volatility of certain political alternatives crudely defined above.

The most difficult development to foresee in this connection is the very "political mood" of the people. They may be quite eager to be engaged in the destruction of the presently existing political order, at least its facade. But it is not certain that they would be equally interested in remaining active in the process of creation of the alternative political order. One must remember that the people of Eastern Europe, if not outrightly contemptuous of, are fed up with, politics, a reaction to artificially overdosed pseudo-political activism under communism.

But it may equally be true that once the people discover that they are truly politically free, their energies for genuine political activism may be released on a scale unimaginable today.

This great unknown seriously complicates any educated guess about the political future in Eastern Europe when freed from Soviet domination.

There is another set of factors to be reckoned with seriously when it comes to the shaping of the area's political alternatives. These are social and economic factors which would certainly play a decisive role. If the socioeconomic situation remains strained, or even deteriorates, then political extremism and perhaps anarchy, too, may gain sufficient prominence for making a strong impact on the emerging alternative political system. If, however, the world democracies helped post-Soviet Eastern Europe to cope with its political reconvalescence, then a more orderly process toward democratization would most certainly be assured.

One must also assume that once the process of democratization is put in motion it can not only gain in experience, but most likely become more imaginative than are the political parties in mature democratic societies, lacking, as a rule, in vigor and originality.

In the end one additional positive factor should be stressed. This is the fact that Eastern Europe is actually an integral part of Western civilization, something communism and Soviet domination have not erased. On the contrary, paradoxical as it may sound, that link has even been strengthened. This is so because the oppressed peoples of Eastern Europe, in their inner opposition to Communist rule, have attached themselves more strongly to the West, even to the extent of idealizing it. This in turn may lead to almost noncritical copying of certain democratic institutions practiced in the West and at a pace much faster than presently thought.

Social Alternatives

Although the title of the chapter does not separate social alternatives from economic ones, the presentation does. This is because of the fact that social demands often clash with economic realities and both tend to clash with political realities, while at the same time greatly influencing their shaping.

If political alternatives in a post-Soviet Eastern Europe to a large extent remain a matter for speculation, social alternatives seem to be more predetermined by the presently existing situation which is going to be inherited *in toto* by any new politico-economic system. This inheritance may even prove to be the most resistant to change, especially if in the short run people considered its change as an encroachment on their privileges, no matter how illusory these privileges may be.

The social reality in Soviet-dominated Eastern Europe is regarded by the people as basically just but malfunctioning. Eastern European communism especially is very much identified with the concept of a "welfare state." In fact it is a "pauperized welfare state." Yet the people believe that the state should take care of them and if they complain about this it is only because the state either cannot keep its promises or the people's expectations outpace such promises.

At any rate, certain "social achievements," like full employment, free education and medical care (once very low housing rents as well) have taken deep root in people's minds and any future politico-economic system will have to take serious account of such a left-over from earlier times. The people may simply consider certain social privileges, whatever their quantity and quality, as something untouchable.

It follows from the above that the continuation of the "social contract" evolved under the Communist regime may favor those politico-economic alternatives that allow for strong state intervention in social affairs. Moreover, paradoxical as it may sound, it is also very probable that with communism and Soviet domination gone, the constituency in any free elections may demand in fact that the past Communist social promises, right in their gist, be fully implemented by a true democracy.

But the above social reality is not the only one to be seriously reckoned with once Eastern Europe goes free and democratic.

Another one is man's peculiar ethics, work ethics in particular, which has been devastated under Soviet-imposed communism. Many people in Soviet-dominated Eastern Europe, as in Communist countries elsewhere, consider their workplace not so much as a place where they should work but as an institution that should take care of them, or even serve them as a place for their amusement (alcoholism, dating or cardplaying is common, to say nothing about leaving the workplace for shopping). Although the workplace is not truly a "nationalized property," as the official propaganda maintains, still many people believe that the workplace is, in a sense, theirs and they may behave there as they please. Even absenteeism, a real plague, is considered as socially justified. Many people are truly absent from work for health reasons but many are forced to do so because of being unable to cope with many of their daily affairs otherwise. Since for the above reasons absenteeism is on the whole tolerated, many try to capitalize on this attitude, inventing various reasons not to come to work whenever possible.

Any change in that kind of work ethic can represent a real problem under the conditions of full employment, but unemployment could hardly be tolerated either.

There are a few other social problems as well. One is widespread theft of "national property." In the situation of chronic shortages of practically everything, and taking into acount the meager wages paid, it is quite natural that the above phenomena flourish and are even socially accepted as moral (theft of "national property" is not even outrightly condemned by some churches).

Insolence is another problem, especially in the service sector. The cause of it is mainly economic but over the decades it has become a way of life.

Both phenomena are widespread and as such represent a grave social problem that will have to be dealt with seriously in the future (as all the efforts to deal with it at present inevitably end in failure).

Yet another social problem is the impression that upward mobility is natural and promotion easily attainable. Such an impression, originating in early periods of the Communist rule, coupled with rapid urbanization, is solidly anchored in people's minds. Especially because so many mediocrities, and *lumpen*-proletarians in general, have indeed been promoted upwardly without much difficulty. In the past also the young generation enjoyed ample opportunities for quick promotion.

Moreover, Soviet-imposed communism has created in Eastern Europe (as elsewhere where Communist regimes were established) many odd jobs for "white-collar" employment. (Members of the repressive organs, though they officially belong to the "working class," are, no doubt, also "white-collar" employees.) Many such jobs give their holders an air of "social importance," they look like some sort of "mini-*nomenklatura*," to say nothing about the *nomenklatura* proper. According to various estimates, almost one-fourth of all employees believe that they are "important," as they have subordinates or feel that way for some other reason.

This is, in fact, a kind of compensation for the absence of private property—a specific social status is created for many that enables them to regard themselves as belonging to a privileged stratum. Those who are not part of this stratum know only too well what they have to accomplish to join it. Hard work, integrity, and intelligence are not necessary here. But for many it is precisely this which makes "people's power" socially attractive.

Finally, there is the problem of the solidly entrenched sense of egalitarianism. Although in reality all Communist societies are strictly stratified, it is nevertheless true that very rich people there are not only very rare, but also that they are commonly despised. Even anti-Communists in Eastern Europe do not wish to see any capitalists or landowners return and are, in general, highly suspicious of foreign private capital. Communist propaganda, over the decades, has succeeded in convincing most of the people that the rich are villains, thus raising egalitarianism to the level of faith.

This author believes that in contrast with the whole panoply of political alternatives, in the social domain, at least in the initial stage of transition, only one alternative can be seriously proposed: namely, that of establishing self-governing bodies at all possible levels.

Any passage from a Communist-ruled society to a democratic society has not yet been historically recorded. But a certain historical evidence to this effect was provided by Poland between August 1980 and December 1981. At that time, when Solidarity was legal, self-government was practically the only preached alternative to a Communist-ruled society. The self-governing bodies, though, for obvious reasons, drastically limited in their executive power, were popular not only in the workplace, but also locally and regionally. They practically entered, or at least attempted to enter, all walks of life and went far beyond trade-unionism only. They were releasing the dormant energies of the people who earlier had been socially and politically inactive.

Moreover, many social ills, like the lack of work and behavioral ethics mentioned above, were frontally attacked and the initial success was stunning (alcohol consumption dropped by one-third during the 16 months of Solidarity's legal existence).

Although at present it is rather premature to speculate on the precise form that the said self-government may take, a few suggestions of a general nature can nevertheless be spelled out.

In the West, or rather in Western Europe, it was already tried, some time ago, to put to practical use, the concepts of *"Mitbestimmung"* and *"la participation."* This failed because it was a departure from capitalism, pointing in the direction of some ill-defined socialism.

In a post-Soviet Eastern Europe the above still-born concepts could perhaps be successfully applied because they would serve an opposite purpose, namely the departure from "socialism." Whether the destination would be classical or present-day capitalism is difficult to guess (although initially something like *"Volkskapitalismus"* should not be totally dismissed as utopian).

Self-government, as practically the only social alternative that is most likely to be wholeheartedly accepted by the people, should be actively encouraged by all those who really wish Eastern Europe to become de-communized and de-Sovietized, despite all the flaws of that idea.

One must remember that people in Eastern Europe, though neither starving nor destitute, are relatively poor and feel socially insecure. Any change depriving them of the minimum they already have in their possession, even temporarily, will inevitably be met by them with hostility. At the initial stage they would trust no individuals or groups, only themselves. And this is what self-government provides for.

Self-government poses, of course, many dangers, especially when its role is preponderant as it is most likely to be the case in a post-Soviet Eastern Europe. With political parties hardly existing, or immature, and with the economy not immediately reprivatized, the influence of the self-governing bodies would be truly immense. Any misconception and misuse of power by the self-governing bodies could be highly detrimental to the process of democratization but one has to take such a risk. There is simply "no alternative to this alternative."

Politically speaking, self-governing bodies, as a "mass training in the school of democracy," could be even very helpful in settling many thorny problems, especially the social ones.

Economically speaking, however, the issue would be much more complicated.

Economic Alternatives

Whatever political and social solutions a decommunized and de-Sovietized Eastern Europe is to adopt they will, in the end, be determined by economic factors. Although politico-social solutions may be conducive or detrimental to the economic situation, it is the economic situation which will in the end be decisive for the success of the process leading to democratization.

Central planning, no matter how nuanced from country to country in Soviet-dominated Eastern Europe, is a visible failure. The area, whose per capita GNP is less than half of the West's, has problems related not only to further economic growth, but to keeping the achieved level of development. In Poland the GNP, calculated on a per capita basis, is now roughly 20 percent below the 1978 level, and there are no responsible forecasts as to when that level can be really achieved. Moreover, Eastern Europe, especially Poland and Romania, do not offer any hope with regard to their being able to repay their debts, or even substantially to reduce the level of debt.

It is also more than certain that the past pattern of economic relations with the USSR, based primarily on Soviet fuel and raw material supplies in return for manufactured goods, has gone forever. Hence, Eastern Europe is facing several dire economic dilemmas which with time will become even more ominous and more difficult to settle. This is because of the fact that wrong industries have been built in the wrong places, that agriculture has been greatly neglected and the infrastructure, including the protection of the natural environment, heavily underinvested. On top of all this, housing has become a problem of utmost acuteness, not to mention the hopelessly inadequate resources for meeting all other needs of individual consumers.

In such circumstances, and mainly due to the lack of competitiveness, Eastern Europe's involvement in international trade has become seriously handicapped. Whenever such involvement takes place, it is either in traditional primary products or in heavily subsidized manufactured goods.

The very fact that Soviet-dominated Eastern Europe has been forced to adopt the central-planning system and has been for various reasons deprived of full participation in the international flow of goods, services, and capital, has led to the situation in which, despite some openings to the West (rather a failure), the prospects for participation of that area in the Third Industrial Revolution have become dubious.

Yet any dramatic overhaul of the economy in a post-Soviet Eastern Europe seems to be limited by several constraints.

The first one is the social situation mentioned above which may not favor either the reprivatization of the economy or the discontinuation of guaranteed full employment as well as many other social allowances and fringe benefits.

The second one could be a very uncertain outlook with regard to the economic relations between Eastern Europe and its former metropoly, namely the present USSR. Whatever the shortcomings of the present pattern of those relations are, certain realities existing in this domain are hard to change. For example, Poland imports all her natural gas as well as roughly 80 percent of her oil and iron ore from the USSR. Any drastic change in this import pattern is impossible because of the lack of alternative transport facilities. Similar conditions exist elsewhere in Eastern Europe.

The same applies to Eastern Europe's exports of manufactured goods to any future post-USSR. Should such exports cease suddenly, the alternative markets would not be promptly found.

The third constraint is an unknown as to how a post-Soviet Eastern Europe would be accommodated in international trade and finance by the West and the developing countries.

More specifically, the central issue in this respect is whether the West and the international financial institutions could come to the rescue of the area and bail it out from serious economic troubles, already present and bound to be compounded in the future.

This particular issue requires some elaboration.

Eastern Europe is rather poorly endowed with natural resources; it has very little fertile lands, a not too-well developed infrastructure and a seriously inadequate system for the protection of the natural environment. Moreover, its industries are high-energy and material-intensive and turn out internationally uncompetitive items. All this is accompanied by seriously insufficient supplies of goods and services for consumers.

Any change in that situation, especially a rapid one, is absolutely impossible without the infusion of foreign capital and know-how. That infusion would have to be accompanied by the rescheduling, or perhaps even cancellation, of the area's external debt.

In other words, two measures seem indispensable:

—a sort of Marshall Plan for Eastern Europe;

—the opening up of Eastern Europe to foreign investment.

Insofar as the first issue is concerned, the West would not in fact be taking upon itself an economic burden. The disappearance of tension in Europe, and elsewhere in the world, would release substantial funds for some other purposes. In fact, the Western aid program for Eastern Europe could even cushion certain adverse effects caused by the falling demand for defense items.

Moreover, a rapid emancipation of Eastern Europe could even stimulate the flow of goods, services, and finance internationally and thus contribute to the well-being of all nations. In the case of a reunited Germany the benefits from aiding former Eastern Germany would be more than obvious.

Besides, Eastern Europe, despite all the shortcomings plaguing its economy at present, is the area where the multiplier effect of well-thought-out economic assistance could be really higher than elsewhere in the world. After all, many factors guaranteeing this are already in place.

If this is so, the new Marshall Plan, of substantial magnitude, should be seen as a worthwhile investment.

Eastern Europe as of today has, on a per capita basis, the GNP level similar to that Western Europe enjoyed in the late forties. Not all Western Europe was helped and not all the help was from the Marshall Plan. As today's economic potential of the West by far exceeds that of the U.S.A. in the late forties, one should repeat the experience and come out with a sum similar to the one apportioned in the past. This would mean that, at today's prices, the sum should roughly be 50 billion dollars over a four-to-five-year period. This would amount to, on a yearly basis, slightly more than 0.1 percent of the West's combined GNP, a proverbial peanut compared to the burden the Marshall Plan imposed at the time on the GNP of the U.S.A.

Such an assistance program would not only neutralize certain political and social pressures in a post-Soviet Eastern Europe, something already mentioned, but it would create favorable conditions for the inflow of private capital from abroad, especially for direct investments.

Having accomplished the two preconditions mentioned, a post-Soviet Eastern Europe could embark on the path of thorough reforms of its economy.

In this connection, it is quite obvious that Eastern Europe would be looking for avenues facilitating its joining the European Economic Community and, in general, all available schemes liberalizing international exchange and cooperation.

Still, several purely domestic economic problems would remain acute and various alternative solutions of these problems should be discussed.

Those alternatives are, in fact, confined to the basic question, namely to what extent the post-Soviet economies would become market economies, and under this term the reprivatization of the economy is meant, not any toying with "socialist market economy," as is the case today in Hungary and even partly in Poland.

Despite the obvious advantage of adopting the system of market economy, the accomplishment of this task may prove to be not too easy in a post-Soviet Eastern Europe. Also, all the politico-social aspects apart, the area is hardly prepared for such a shift on purely technical grounds. Most of the people, including managerial and technical staff, have no idea about money and commodity markets or any other phenomena common in the market economies (even economically enlightened people do not understand most of these phenomena or even the terminology related to them).

There is also the virtual absence of a properly trained entrepreneurial class and of a middle class in general. The ordinary people are also hardly familiar with capital markets; they even distrust anything that is not cash (preferably "greenbacks").

Moreover, many people, even ardent anti-Communists, honestly believe that certain industries and utilities, as well as the banking system, should be state-owned.

In such a situation, any basic overhaul of post-Soviet Eastern European economies into market economies, would be a highly complicated task.

Still, such a task must be undertaken and accomplished rather promptly.

When it comes to purely domestic measures the following alternatives should be examined:

1. Decollectivization of agriculture and lifting of all the restrictions (this refers to Poland) on the acreage of privately owned land. State-owned farms should be sold (on credit) to private peasants or genuinely organized peasant cooperatives.
2. All services other (at least initially) than railway transportation and urban transit, as well as communications and certain utilities (mostly water supplies) should be eligible for reprivatization. Foreign capital should be invited here in the first place.
3. All industries employing no more than fifty people should be immediately made available for reprivatization; the rest gradually.
4. Banking and finance should be reprivatized wherever possible and money and commodity exchanges established (the latter if commercially feasible).
5. State monopoly for trade should be immediately abolished and foreign-exchange control gradually phased out (quite obviously the money reform would be indispensable).

Yet even the above would not suffice, especially when it comes to "big business" and the role of foreign capital in it.

It goes without saying that the reprivatization of "big business," even by changing it into publicly owned stockholding companies and not truly privately owned ones, would be a long process during which many unknown circumstances would undoubtedly arise.

The only exception to this solution could be the admission of foreign private capital in the said "big business."

There are three subalternatives to the above:

—minority interests;
—majority interests;
—wholly-owned foreign subsidiaries.

The first subalternative would certainly be the most acceptable domestically, but internationally it would be the least attractive. Even the majority interests could be not sufficiently attractive to foreign private capital, although, domestically, it would not be easily accepted.

The best economically and the most controversial politically and socially could be, of course, the third subalternative.

The discussion of the pros and cons in this connection seems to be aimless at present, but one has to point out a problem.

The successful solution of this particular problem is, nevertheless, very instrumental for the success of all other alternatives mentioned above.

Under the best of circumstances, wholly owned foreign subsidiaries could revolutionize the functioning of the area's economies by infusing capital, know-how, and managerial skills into them, to say nothing about the marketing facilities abroad that would be thus opened.

But under all circumstances, best or worst, any serious effort in post-Soviet Eastern Europe to change properly and rapidly the extant economic systems into market economies, seems to be dependent on how foreign private capital will be treated. The availability of a new Marshall Plan may be made conditional on solving this particular problem.

East Germany apart, all other countries of the area may find some difficulties in settling this very problem (if only because they lack the expertise in negotiating the conditions on which foreign private capital would be admitted to them).

Many of the dilemmas to this effect could be solved by people reemigrating from the West to their native countries. Many have expertise in the said domain and a few even have capital.

In this connection another observation should be made. Namely, that the West and other democratic nations should treat a post-Soviet Eastern Europe as an ill person, going through a period of reconvalescence and asking for real and disinterested help, rather than as a full-fledged business partner who could be cheated whenever a propitious opportunity for that arose.

Returning to domestic preconditions for various economic alternatives, where the reprivatization issue is pivotal, one has to take into consideration the purely psychological factor. Namely, should the affluence of the people be rising, wastefulness of the economy disappearing and overall politico-social situation improving, many social ills inherited from the past and lying in the way of reprivatization would fade away, perhaps even rapidly.

To sum it all up: the alternative choices in the economic domain are basically between remaining a central-planning system or adopting a market economy. All the rest is only the problem of the scope and tempo of change, the alternative to which is no change at all. The latter option seems to be excluded and the former simply must be tried.

Some Other Alternatives

Eastern Europe is far from being a homogenous unit. In fact the USSR has never been interested in encouraging closer contacts and cooperative links between particular Eastern European countries and has discouraged anything like that between the Baltic States and the remainder of Eastern Europe.

For this simple reason, to say nothing about some other realities, a post-Soviet Eastern Europe will perhaps not try, or even be capable of trying, to form anything like a federation, confederation or even a common market or a free trade zone.

Apart from East Germany, which would most certainly be reunited with West Germany, all other countries may therefore look to Western Europe for associating themselves with it.

Communism and Soviet domination have transformed the nations of Eastern Europe immensely and anything to do with their hopeless nationalism, let alone chauvinism, is to a large extent gone. Those nations want to live decently and are ready to surrender a lot of their sovereignty, if not all of it, should they be sure that they would be living in a community of nations where broadly understood human rights, which include also a decent standard of living, were respected and solidly anchored.

Moreover, should the USSR end its domination over Eastern Europe peacefully, there is good reason to believe that the relations between Eastern Europe and the USSR's successor, no matter how unhealthy and artificial they were in the past, could continue and perhaps even flourish. It could well be that a new Eastern Europe could serve as a bridge between Western Europe and a successor of the USSR. Such a solution could be among the most cheerful scenarios.

But whatever the future shape of relations between a post-Soviet Eastern Europe and the remainder of the world, especially Western Europe, would be, the issue should not be left to its spontaneous solution.

The West, particularly Western Europe, should be interested in involving the present Eastern Europeans in its endeavors wherever possible in order to keep them familiar with the issues which one day in the future may prove highly helpful in solving various issues standing between the East and the West.

One thing seems clear—Eastern Europe has no alternative but to go the Western way, that is to be free and democratic. And it must be helped to achieve this end.

Concluding Remarks

The disintegration of the Soviet Empire, which might not be too far away, will most certainly free Eastern Europe from Communist bondage. It is even quite likely that it will be precisely Eastern Europe, which will contribute the most to that disintegration.

But even under the best of circumstances, certain important facets of the past Soviet domination will remain in Eastern Europe and may pose many serious problems before being completely erased.

Soviet-dominated Eastern Europe is a badly ill area in many respects. This is true and should be remembered when the time for change comes.

But, at the same time, the peoples of Eastern Europe may both have a healthy instinct for change, more sharpened than elsewhere, and once their dormant energies are released they could surprise the world by how quickly they may catch up with certain lost opportunities.

It was not this author's intention to paint any rosy picture of the future and beautify certain realities. By emphasizing certain difficulties and ills, the present writer was eager to focus attention on certain issues that it is easier for an Eastern European to raise than for anybody else, as the latter might be unwilling to create the impression of offending the former.

Yet even the frank mentioning of some dilemmas does not give any reason for pessimism. In fact, there is a solid ground for optimism once Eastern Europe goes free and democratic. If anything can be truly disputable, it is only the pace at which an optimistic vision will come into being. There can be no question about this vision not coming into being at all.

13

The Potential of East European Political Institutions in Exile to Assure Eastern Europe's Smooth Transition from Dependency to Sovereignty— A Commentary on Chapter 12

TADEUSZ A. MUSIOL

In his analysis of possible scenarios for change in a post-Soviet Eastern Europe, Dr. Zdislaw Rurarz omits one variable which needs to be taken into consideration. This is the existence of East European national governments and other political structures in exile, that will inevitably be an important factor under any conditions of change.

Apart from Russia, which would seem to be the sole exception, all the nations of Eastern Europe under Soviet domain, whether incorporated in the Soviet Union or not, have their political structures surviving in exile. These structures constitute the only genuine bodies of political representation of the nations considered and could provide the necessary framework for the transition from the Soviet-type political systems to the newly forming national ones.

If Poland is taken as an example, then the position of the government-in-exile is quite unequivocal. When a regime subservient to Moscow was formed in Warsaw, the president of the Republic of Poland, the late Wladyslaw Raczkiewicz, declared in a proclamation to the Polish nation issued in London on 29 June 1945:

> . . . The law of the Republic laid upon me the obligation of handing over the office of President of the Republic, after the conclusion of peace, to a successor appointed by the nation in free democratic elections, devoid of all force and threat. I shall do so directly circumstances permit the nation to make such a choice.[1]

This declaration was issued in accordance with Article 24 of the 1935 Constitution of the Republic of Poland which states:

> (1) In time of war the term of the President's office shall be prolonged to three months after the conclusion of peace; the President of the Republic shall then by special act, promulgated in the Official *Journal of Laws*, appoint his successor, in case the office falls vacant before the conclusion of peace.
> (2) Should the President's successor assume office, the term of his office shall last up to the lapse of three months after the conclusion of peace.[2]

Therefore, within three months after cessation of Soviet control (that may be equated by analogy to the conclusion of peace), the president of the Republic of Poland would be obliged to hand over the office to his successor "appointed by the nation in free democratic elections."[3] Such an arrangement provides a coherent framework for filling the political vacuum during the period of transition.

Just as the continuity of legitimate political authority is provided by the president of the Republic of Poland in exile, the continuity of party political structure and corresponding ideas is provided by the existence of various political parties such as the Polish Socialist party (PPS) and the Polish Peasants' movement (PSL), who continue their activities in exile on behalf of their respective constituencies in the country and who endeavor to maintain as close links as possible with the nation at home.

As Rurarz suggests, the actual character and political persuasion of any future free government can at this stage be only the subject of speculation, albeit informed. Nevertheless, by transposing the national political institutions in exile—whether both governmental and party-political, as in the cases of Poland and the Baltic States, or only party-political, as in most other cases—to their respective countries for the interim period, one could assure the transition to a proper democratic order based on fair electoral proceedings, thereby immediately excluding the following options considered by Rurarz:

1. Continuation of the present political system.
2. A slight shift in the present system, perhaps more in rhetoric than in reality.
3. An important change of the present political system which, nevertheless, remains basically "socialistic" in nature, with some tendencies for dictatorship preserved.
8. A military dictatorship, with Fascist tendencies, in some countries even a return to monarchy.
9. A kind of Fascist system, with some odd ideology in the background.
10. Complete anarchy, interrupted by periodic swings from one extreme to another.[4]

Consequently, one of the four remaining options suggested by Rurarz would then be able to materialize and achieve full legitimacy.

Contrary to Rurarz's expectations, the transition from the present imposed political order to its successor would be, under the above conditions, effected much more speedily while also obviating the necessity of proceeding "at a changing tempo and in zig-zags"[5] between different political alternatives before arriving at a point of political consensus.

In analyzing the political maturity of the nations in question, Rurarz also seems unduly pessimistic. As he quite rightly discerned, the absence of evidence for any sort of tendency "for any mushrooming of political parties"[6] in Poland during the Solidarity period can be explained "by the fact that nobody believed even then that Poland had ceased to be Soviet-dominated."[7] By its own terms of reference (i.e., a self-limiting revolution), Solidarity precluded the formation of such parties which, by their very nature, would have been in direct open political opposition to the ruling Polish United Workers' party (PZPR). Nevertheless, the intense political debate which erupted into the open during the Solidarity period, gave evidence (not for the first time) of the existence in Polish society of a wide spectrum of political opinion displaying in most instances a remarkable level of political maturity and clarity of vision. It is worth noting also that, despite different opinions, the essentials of a common national purpose served as a viable force providing for Poland's overall social and political unity.

Even in the pre-Solidarity period there were many instances of acute political awareness being translated into positive action despite the threat of repression. The "Manifesto of the 59 Intellectuals" in December, 1975, concerning the proposed changes to the Constitution of the Polish People's Republic, which stipulated the leading role of the PZPR and the adherence of Poland to the Soviet Union, and which were eventually implemented on 10 February 1977, is one such example. This manifesto, in fact, heralded a spate of other similar open letters from a wide cross-section of the population, openly expressing opposition to the proposed changes and, if only by implication, to the enforced political order. After demanding that the basic civil rights, including the freedoms of conscience and religious practice; of work; of speech and exchange of information; and of education, should be guaranteed and observed by the state, the signatories of the "Manifesto of the 59 Intellectuals," further stated that the assurance of such basic freedoms was irreconcilable with a system of state authority which gave a leading role to one party. Furthermore, they maintained that a "constitutional assertion of this type would give to the political party the role of an instrument of State authority, not responsible to nor controlled by the public. Under such conditions Parliament cannot be regarded as the highest instrument of authority, the Government is not the highest executive body, and the courts are not independent. All citizens must be assured that they will achieve their right to nominate and vote for their representatives according to the accepted democratic principles of free elections. The courts must be assured of their independence from the executive power, and the highest legislative power must effectively be given to Parliament."[8]

Also in the early months of 1976, almost as a natural sequel and enlargement upon the postulates expressed in the "Manifesto of the 59 Intellectuals" there appeared a samizdat document in Poland entitled "The Programme of the Polish League for Independence." The league is known to have linked people of various backgrounds and their document, which was widely circulated not only in Poland but also in neighboring countries, was regarded by many to be the most important of its kind to be issued since the subjugation of Poland by the Soviet Union after the fraudulent referendum in 1946 and the falsified elections of 1947.

The following excerpts from their twenty-six point program are self-explanatory:

1. . . . We consider all post-war agreements . . . limiting the sovereignty of the Republic, to have been made under duress without consulting the will of the people and therefore to be invalid. The right to assume obligations which would be legally and morally binding on all Poles, can only be exercised by a freely elected Polish Parliament whose activities are not subject to foreign pressure.

17. . . . The free collaboration between Polish organizations and communities at home and abroad is prevented. The Polish emigration is a priceless national fund of opportunities and experience . . . and their familiarity with the functioning of contemporary democratic states might help us to eliminate the consequences of many years of totalitarian government in Poland.[9]

The spontaneously emerging bodies of political opinion at home combined with the national political structure transposed from abroad can thus provide an adequate political form which would take care of all the needs of political transition from the imposed Soviet-type to a genuine national democratic polity. Once this is taken into account, assessments suggesting the unlikelihood of a viable political structure emerging in the immediate aftermath of freedom and independence being regained, seem hard to sustain.

I should like to conclude by noting that I am also much more optimistic than Rurarz on the following points concerning the socioeconomic alternatives in a post-Soviet Eastern Europe.

The attitude of the people may indeed be such that they would seek a continuation of social-welfare provision which, as Rurarz feels, may then "favor those politico-economic alternatives that allow for strong State intervention in social affairs."[10] It is, nevertheless, difficult to ascertain how psychologically dependent the respective populations will feel toward some form of social-welfare provision by the State, or indeed toward the actual level of such provision. However, it is worth considering the fact that all the nations under consideration, including Russia, have displayed a strong and deep-rooted entrepreneurial instinct whenever the opportunity has permitted, and have always tended to rely on themselves in preference to reliance on the State.

Social and economic delinquency is also, as Rurarz observes, a feature which is endemic in the present system of a Soviet-dominated Eastern Europe. However, the Solidarity period in Poland was notable, among other things, for introducing a moral regeneration, affecting personal behavior throughout the whole spectrum of social activities, not least of all, in the workplace. It was this socially mature attitude which underpinned the efforts of Solidarity and which, as Rurarz points out, made self-government a popular and "practically the only preached alternative to a Communist-ruled society."[11]

Finally, the transposal of specialists within the émigré communities to their respective countries, as well as the mobilization of help from the émigrés in general, in order to regenerate the economy of their nations should not present a problem. As has already happened many times in the past, this will inevitably take place and should produce the initiatives capable of ensuring the economic viability of the countries in question, at the same time easing their integration within the Western world's economic system.

Notes

1. See Tadeusz Pelczynski, et al. eds., *Armia Krajowa w Dokumentach, 1939–1945*, (The Home Army in Documents, 1939–1945). Vol. 5, *1944–1945*. London: Studium Polski Podziemnej, 1981. Document no. 1580, 466–67. This gives the English text of the presidential proclamation. Also on 467–78 is the Polish text as published in the *Dziennik Polski i Dziennik Zolnierza*, (*The Polish Daily & Soldier's Daily*), London: 2, No. 153, 30 June 1945. The original text of the proclamation is held in the archives of the Foreign Affairs Ministry of the Polish Government-in-Exile, London. Document no. 336 (MSZ).
2. Quoted from *Ustawa Konstytucyjna z dnia 23 kwietnia 1935r*, (*Constitution of the Republic of Poland*). Bilingual publication. (London: The Polish Government in-Exile, 1967). 16.
3. Excerpt from Wladyslaw Raczkiewicz's presidential proclamation, as quoted in T. Pelczynski, et al. eds., *Armia* (no. 1), p. 467.
4. Rurarz, p.
5. Ibid., p.
6. Ibid., p.
7. Ibid., p.
8. A. Ostoja-Ostaszewski, T. Musiol, K. Stepan, R. Zakrzewski Eds. *Dissent in Poland*, 1976–77. (Second revised impression). (London: Association of Polish Students and Graduates in Exile, 1979) 14. (For some elaboration of the issue see also T. Musiol, et al. *The Changing of the Constitution of the Polish People's Republic*. London: The Association of Polish Students and Graduates in Exile, 1976.)
9. ———, pp. 166, 169.
10. Rurarz, p.
11. Ibid., p.

14

Problems of Legitimacy in Poland: Party-State, Civil Society and Church, and the Lessons of Solidarity

CHRISTOPHER G.A. BRYANT

There is in contemporary Poland a legitimation problem of exceptional proportions. Crisis would be a more apt term were it not for its association with acute conditions when the problem is a chronic one. According to Weber, legitimate domination rests on rational grounds when there is "a belief in the legality of enacted rules and the right of those elevated to authority under such rules to issue commands."[1] Many in Poland question that legality and that right. More generally, as Habermas puts it, "Legitimacy means that there are good arguments for a political order's claim to be recognized as right and just; a legitimate order deserves recognition. *Legitimacy means a political order's worthiness to be recognized.*"[2] It is, as he says, a "contestable validity claim," and there are plenty in Poland ready to contest it. Legitimacy refers, then, to a social relation; regimes may claim legitimacy but the claim is hollow unless the people agree to it. Legitimation is also a process, not a state; claims have to be made, and conceded, on a continuing basis. Indeed, regimes can forfeit their legitimacy if they fail to meet certain basic expectations the people have of them. Finally, legitimation is a process which can operate at different levels; legitimacy may be claimed and granted at one level while it is denied at another. The economic success of a regime, for example, may compensate for more fundamental objections to it; conversely popular dismay at economic failure may be kept within bounds if a regime is, in some more fundamental sense, still regarded as legitimate. Legitimation becomes a serious problem when it fails to operate at any level; it becomes exceptionally serious when no remedies for these failures appear practical. This is the bleak prospect in Poland today.

Some Poles have always contested the legitimacy of the Communist party-state. Many workers and peasants, however, found good reasons for supporting it so long as it offered them extensive opportunities for collective and individual advancement.[3] For three decades after the war, the transformation of an agrarian into an industrial economy, the growth of cities and the expansion of education afforded such opportunities on a large scale. The standard of living steadily improved. In the 1970s, however, changes in the occupational structure slowed down, affording less scope for upward social mobility. In addition, following imprudent borrowing from the West to finance major capital projects, the economy went into decline and income levels fell. Bereft of economic success, the regime faced a situation in which no other claim to legitimacy found favor with any major group of the people.[4]

It is the common misfortune of all the state-socialist regimes of Eastern Europe that their vanguard ideology obliges them to refuse workers their right to autonomous organizations even as they propagate an ideology which constantly reminds workers of their power. Solidarity is the most dramatic demonstration yet that the workers know that Poland is not a workers' state. It is the peculiar misfortune of the Polish regime to have so to refuse workers fortified by the religious faith which sustained their forebears through the tribulations of centuries.[5] The Church presents itself as the true guardian of the Polish nation; the party-state, by contrast, is a usurper beholden to a foreign power.

European sociologists have generally agreed that industrialization and urbanization are accompanied by secularization, that rationalization entails the disenchantment of the world. Where this appears not to have been the case—America, the Herberg thesis notwithstanding, is the best known example—they have inclined to suppose that secularization is merely delayed for some local reason and is still to be expected in the longer term.[6] Leaders of the Communist regime in Poland used similarly to console themselves; however strong the Roman Catholic church is now, the argument went, it is destined eventually to wither away.[7] The passing of the years since the election of a Polish pope in 1978, and the prescription of Solidarity in 1982, has made this appear less likely than ever. On the contrary, no amount of party-state directed industrialization and urbanization will lead to the extensive secularization the party-state desires because it is the comportment of the party-state itself which continually reinforces the strength of the Church. Indeed, the Church is the one institution in Poland to have emerged stronger from the rise and suppression of Solidarity. It is reported, for example, that a record eight million people made the pilgrimage to Czestochowa in 1985.[8] This is ominous for the party-state because the Church does more than care for the souls of the faithful; it is also the main contributant to a civil religion which undermines the party-state.

In sum, the regime's claims to legitimacy foundered on two main obstacles, the political maturation of the working class and the alternative view of history favored by the Roman Catholic church. It is the thesis of this chapter that, in the given circumstances, no resolution of the legitimation problem in Poland is possible because, *inter alia*, the civil religion of Poland denies support to the party-state. In order to substantiate this thesis, I shall first consider Solidarity and relations between civil society and the party-state. Then I shall examine the identity of Church and nation, the character of the Church and relations between the Church and civil religion. Finally, I will argue that there is no prospect of the civil religion affording the party-state support. The rights of rulers, it transpires, are of limited value to rulers without rites.

Solidarity and Civil Society

Was Solidarity in 1980–81 a trade union, a political party, a social movement, a movement for national liberation, or what? It is best regarded as an independent self-governing trade union whose objectives could only have been secured within an economic reform which required not only self-management at the level of the enterprise but also social and political guarantees inseparable from a general democratization of society.[9] In particular, the parameters for self-management would have had to have been determined by a national economic policy which enjoyed popular support. And for informed consent to be possible, there would have had to have been freedom of information and proper procedures for the articulation and representation of popular opinion. Thus it was that Solidarity took on more and more of the character of a social movement. In its challenge to the prerogatives of the party-state, Solidarity presented a very different conception of politics, but it always denied that it was itself a political party because its aim was to roll back the state and to liberalize, to depoliticize, civil society. The Party, Solidarity contended, had no place in the factory, no right to form all unions in its own image, no right to maintain the *nomenklatura* system, no right to control school syllabuses, no right to rewrite Polish history, no right to control the media, no place in voluntary associations and no right to obstruct religious belief and practice. Solidarity represented the determination of a working, not a bourgeois, class to limit the prerogatives of the state, to open up and expand civil society and to assert the cause of civil liberties and human rights. It sought to free Poles from the controls of a party-state which was additionally resented because, notwithstanding a tradition of national communism which had given rise to (the idea of) a Polish road to socialism, it was ultimately Moscow's creature, not theirs. If ever there has been a working class which truly became a universal class, it was in Poland in 1980–81.

Solidarity's identification with society, and its opposition of society to the state, though foreshadowed in many unofficial publications in the late 1970s, presented a notable challenge to long-held theoretical assumptions in political science and sociology. Society refers here to civil society not in the Scottish Enlightenment sense of civilized society in contrast to barbarian or uncivilized society, or Rousseau's idea of the civil state in contrast to the state of nature, but to the Hegelian conception of a social space between household and state in which to prosecute particular interests—economic, religious, cultural, etc.—subject only to legal regulation by the state in the universal interest. The opening up of civil society in the seventeenth and eighteenth centuries was an achievement of a propertied bourgeoisie committed to capitalism. No wonder the spectacle of propertyless workers who were presumably committed to socialism attempting it in the late twentieth century was hard to credit.

It was also hard to grasp at first just how total was Solidarity's opposition to the state. Lech Walesa may not have been the most cogent of speakers but, as Garton Ash has pointed out, his continued references to the suffering of "society" at the hands of the "authorities" had great resonance.[10] Just as KOR, the Committee for the Defense of Workers, which was established in 1976 to protect workers arrested in the disturbances of that year from reprisals by the party-state, transformed itself into KSS, the Committee for Social Self-Defense, in 1979, so Solidarity broadened from a union for the defense of workers interests against the party-state to a social movement for the defense of society's interests against the state. The state was regarded quite simply as an instrument for the service of Party interests. Solidarity—indeed Polish public opinion—still favored social ownership of most means of production but interpreted this to mean ownership by society, not the state. The aim was to develop forms of public ownership other than state ownership which allowed self-management by the workers and ensured responsiveness to real social needs. At the same time Solidarity recognized that it had to be a self-limiting movement dedicated to a self-limited revolution; that is, in deference to Soviet sensibilities, it had to allow the Party to keep control of defense and foreign relations and those internal functions which properly remain the preserve of the state. The term self-limiting revolution was originated by Jadwiga Staniszkis, the sociologist adviser to the Gdansk strikers, and amplified by Jacek Kuron, the best-known member of KOR, but the idea could be said to go back to an article of Kolakowski's, published in exile in 1971.[11] Even so, Party diehards feared the emergence of "dual power." The term is Trotsky's and refers to the development of soviets alongside the apparatus of the state between the February and October Revolutions of 1917.[12] Their fears had more genuine point after the adoption of a "Program" in September 1981 committing Solidarity to pursuit of a self-governing republic.

The declaration of martial law in December 1981 and the subsequent suppression of Solidarity disappointed the immediate hopes of workers for autonomous organizations of their own. Equally, it crushed the hope of all Poles for the democratization of Polish society. However, it has not, and cannot, remove the idea of a society which the experience of Solidarity made vivid for so many millions. In effect, Solidarity showed that outside the private space of the household there are two public spaces—civil society and the state—and not just one—a society so penetrated by the party-state as to have become little more than an extension of it. Some independent social organizations, and the unofficial press, continue to operate—albeit at a lower level of activity than in 1980–81—in a society whose repossession by the party-state is effectively incomplete, thanks to the noncooperation of a sullen and defiant people.

Suppression of Solidarity has also left the Church stronger than before. This is not just because the Church brings comfort to those in despair at ever seeing a free Poland, or because Poles have returned to the only opposition they have traditionally known, but rather because the social significance of the Church is now plain for all to see. The party-state has always tried to confine the Church to matters of theology and individual faith and morals—in effect to the private matters of the home. It has always resented and resisted the Church's pronouncements on the public matters of politics, economy, and social structure which it jealously regards as its preserve. But if Poles come to think in terms of two public spaces, only one of which—the state—is the preserve of the Party, then the Church is free to exert influence on the other.

Church and Nation

There is in Poland an identity of nation and Church in the consciousness of the people, which is not as perfectly founded historically as is commonly believed but which nonetheless has ample justification. It is symbolized in the title Queen of Poland conferred on the Virgin Mary. This identity is to the experience of the partitions of Poland between 1772 and 1918. In this period Poles suffered political, cultural and linguistic repression and economic exploitation, and of the three partitioning powers the most repressive were Protestant Prussia and Orthodox Russia. The Church, at least at the parish level, stayed close to the people in all their sufferings and became a focus for national identity. The Vatican, by contrast, stood aloof from Polish national aspirations and refused to support successive uprisings; it started to have second thoughts on this policy only when it saw that the promotion of nationalism by Polish socialists, all of whom were professedly materialists, and some of whom were anticlerical, was aiding their cause.

During the Second Republic, between 1918 and 1939, the Church generally aligned itself with the Right, and from 1926 with the Sanacja, although it was not directly involved in politics. The Sanacja, an authoritarian regime founded by Marshal Pilsudski, fixed elections but never went so far as to eliminate the opposition. It engaged in a good deal of repression of workers, adopted a policy of "pacifying" ethnic minorities (31 percent of the population by language according to the 1931 census) and tolerating, when it did not actually instigate, anti-Semitism.[13] "Sanacja" refers to a return to the (political) health of the nation, health which was sullied by non-Polish elements—Jews, Belorussians, Ukrainians and Germans, who, except for the Uniates, were non-Catholics—and by socialists who challenged its conception of nationalism and who were also, by virtue of their ideology of materialism, suspect to the Church.[14] If the history of the Church between the wars gives some offense, however, its conduct during the Second World War was often heroic. There are objections that it did not do all it could to protect the Jews but many of those who did survive owed their lives to Catholic help. Certainly the Church stood side by side with all other ethnic Poles in their darkest hour. One in three of the clergy perished—compared with one in five for the population as a whole.[15]

The transfers of population after the Second World War left Poland ethnically and religiously homogenous for the first time in its history. The builders of People's Poland thus had to contend with a Church that enjoyed the allegiance of more than 90 percent of the people and an association with a spectacularly intense nationalism. In an effort to weaken the Church, between 1948 and 1956, they resorted to a succession of anticlerical measures of which the arrest of Cardinal Wyszynski, and his confinement within a convent between 1953 and 1956, was only the most obvious. After 1956, Gomulka emphasized that a Polish road to socialism would have to include a *modus vivendi* with the Roman Catholic church. Ever since Church and party-state have been jockeying for relative advantage. The two main items of contention have been provisions for religious education and permits for the building of churches in new centers of population. For all its complaints, however, the Church has not done badly. As Davies has drily noted, "An establishment which in 1972 counted 2 cardinals, 45 seminaries, 73 bishops, 13,392 churches, 18,267 priests, 35,341 monks and nuns and over 20 million weekly communicants, could not claim to be living out a persecuted existence among the catacombs."[16]

In some respects, the Church would like to endorse the idea of rendering to Caesar the things which are Caesar's, if only the party-state would reciprocate by allowing the people to render to God the things which are God's. The trouble is that neither side can agree where the division between God and Caesar should lie; in particular, each makes its claims on society. With its own official and unofficial publications, its own associations, its own university (the only one in the socialist bloc), its token representation in the Sejm, and, above all, its authority in the eyes of the people, the Church continues to have a pervasive presence in Polish life.

To many Poles, including some unbelievers, the Church alone represents constancy and moral integrity. By contrast, four factors have combined to make the party-state intolerable. First, there is the official insistence upon Poland's indissoluble friendship with the Soviet Union, which from 1976 till 1988 was even enshrined in the Constitution itself. Most Poles regard the Russians as the authors of at least half of their historic misfortunes and all their contemporary ones. The fourth partition of Poland in 1939–41, Katyn and the other unknown Katyns, the failure to assist the Warsaw Uprising of 1944, the detention of 200,000 Polish soldiers and others in Siberia until 1956, the forced imposition of communism after 1945, the economic exploitation of Poland between 1945 and 1956 and the hostility to Poland's attempts to reform itself after 1956 and in the Solidarity years, are just part of a litany of complaints. Second, there is the rewriting of history which accompanies the first but goes far beyond it. It includes the understatement of Poland's Western and Catholic heritage, the misrepresentation of the plight and the achievements, however limited, of the Second Republic (where it is mentioned at all), and the devaluation of the role of the Home Army in the Second World War. Third, there was the official contradiction of the daily experience of ordinary Poles which culminated in the extravagant rhetoric of economic success in the later Gierek years as the economy accelerated toward ruin and massive foreign indebtedness and the people stood on line for food and searched for other basic goods. How false the rhetoric of new socialist man compared with the impossible reality of corruption, connections, moonlighting, multiple price systems, foreign currency shops, and the privileged access to scarce goods and services enjoyed by the functionaries of Party and state and those who protect them, such as the hated ZOMO. Fourth, there is the transparent ideological bankruptcy of the Party. When Gierek's bid for economic growth failed, the party-state had nothing left except fear of Soviet intervention, or, as it turned out, martial law. Between February 1980 and February 1983, the Party lost 800,000 members—around a third of the total.[17] Significantly, the new, post-Solidarity Party-controlled unions have attracted little support. Most damaging of all, Poles remember how the party-state ceased to function in the summer and autumn of 1981—a veritable withering away of the state, though clearly not the one Engels had in mind. It was as if all the pretenses were set aside. The Party was ideologically bankrupt, remains ideologically bankrupt, everyone knows it and no one any longer bothers to pretend otherwise.

The ideological bankruptcy of the Party and the paralysis of the state in the summer and autumn of 1981 provide a fascinating example of Parsonian "power deflation." Parsons argued that power is as much a circulating medium in the goal attainment subsystem (polity) as money is in the adaptation subsystem (economy). Power is the "generalized capacity to serve the performance of binding obligations by units in a system of collective organization when the obligations are legitimized with reference to their bearing on collective goals."[18] It is a means of getting things done and can grow just as wealth can. Leaders who forfeit the trust placed in them, by failing to honor the binding obligations the community imposes upon them, can find themselves impotent. Confidence in power can collapse just as surely as confidence in money; when this happens leaders find themselves impotent because no one heeds them. Parsons assumes communities choose their leaders and their collective goals. Neither assumption holds in Poland. Nevertheless he is right that recourse to violence, or the threat of violence, on the part of leaders, is a sign of weakness in a modern society. Although it can enable leaders to retain office, it cannot secure the willing compliance without which leaders cannot get things done to maximum, or sometimes even moderate, effect. Martial law in 1981–82 confirmed this.

While the party-state has lied, and lied, and lied again, the Church, it seems, upholds eternal verities. Its very doctrinal backwardness appears to be an asset. The more the party-state attacks the Church, the more attractive the Church becomes. The party-state demeans human values and dignity; the Church upholds them. The party-state persecutes those who protest; the Church offers them protection.

Finally, I doubt whether the Party is right to take comfort from the evidence for Adamski's practical secularization thesis which states that while many workers continue to attend mass they reject the Church's teachings on contraception, abortion, and divorce.[19] On the contrary, by providing facilities for contraception, abortion, and divorce the party-state has helped to ensure that those at practical odds with the Church's family teaching can obtain what they need from state services and remain unembittered within the Catholic fold. Indeed, they are more likely to blame the party-state for their transgressions than to criticize the Church for maintaining its ideals. It is the party-state, for example, which is held responsible for the chronic housing shortage and the cramped conditions in which so many millions live.

What Sort of Church?

I have argued that the only institution to emerge stronger from the Solidarity years is the Church—but what sort of Church is it? The question has been framed most pointedly by Adam Michnik on behalf of the left opposition to the regime.[20] The Left opposition was long suspicious of the Church. It remembered the Church's questionable associations in the Second Republic, its mixed record in opposing anti-Semitism in the Second Republic and in the early years of People's Poland and in defending the Jews during the Holocaust, its historic hostility toward Polish socialists (many of whom were neither atheist nor anticlerical) and its general cultural backwardness and anti-modernism—what might be called its Syllabus of Errors mentality.

Outside and inside Poland opposition intellectuals, such as Kolakowski and Michnik, have in the 1970s come to reappraise their attitude to the Church in recognition of its consistent support for human rights and the care and succor it has offered the individual victims of the regime and their families, whether Church members or not.[21] They have concluded that today's bishops, and today's priests, better educated than those between the wars, and, in any case, the inhabitants of a different world, should be regarded for what they are and not for what their predecessors were. Even so, doubts remain.

Michnik, in a famous essay on the Church and the Left, drew upon Cywinski's distinction between a Constantine and a Julian church:

> The idea of Constantinism derives . . . from the name of the emperor Constantine, under whose rule the theory of the dual powers, the spiritual and the temporal, found expression for the first time. Julianism (from the

name of the emperor Julian the Apostate, who rejected Christianity and sought to destroy the church') offers a model of a political situation which is diametrically opposed to the Constantine model. Instead of the collaboration of the dual powers, there exists a conflict. The church finds itself in the opposition. It is deprived of political power, but it retains its moral authority and it derives its strength from this fact. . . . Moral authority is the foundation of the Julian church, in the same way power is the foundation of the Constantine church. The Julian church is morally pure, since persecution purges it of opportunists and surrounds it with a special halo: the tradition of Julianism is both indestructable and beautiful . . .

. . . Constantinism is a participation in power; Julianism is characterized by regret and indignation over the loss of this power, and never by a free renunciation of power. That is why, for all its spiritual power, the Julian church is never in complete solidarity with society, or fully identified with it. . . . Having been deprived of political power, it fights to retain spiritual leadership over the nation. Thus it does not recognize the existence of other means of achieving the spiritual or ideological integration of the nation, nor does it admit the existence of other forms of opposition against the secular power in addition to those controlled and instigated by itself. If the presence of such outside opposition becomes evident and creates some other ideological alternative for society, allowing the dissidents to organize apart from the church hierarchy, then the Julian church condemns this opposition, or refuses to treat it seriously and disparages it publicly. The Julian church is never eager to collaborate with independent centers of dissident thought. In its conflict with the secular government, the church wants to act alone, without partners, for whom it can feel no solidarity.[22]

Is the Roman Catholic church in Poland today Julian or does it renounce power freely, recognize the existence of alternative means of achieving the integration of the nation than its own and show solidarity with the proponents of these alternatives? Michnik, writing in 1977, felt confident that the Church had rejected Julianism as much as Constantinism. Since then it has shown solidarity with Solidarity which it certainly did not organize, nor even exclusively advise, and it has found words of praise for other opponents of the regime in the name of human rights. Indeed, as the 1980s progress the Church is providing more protection than ever to opposition elements of all kinds, and more facilities for groups to meet and disseminate ideas. Even so, for many clergy respect for the humanist and the secular expert cannot come easily. I doubt whether renunciation of Julianism is complete.

Civil and Political Religion

The idea of a civil religion is prefigured in classical writings, in Augustine and doubtless in other places too. The term "civil religion," however, originated with Rousseau. It rests upon a distinction between the "religion of man," which is a private matter between the individual and God, and the "religion of the citizen," which is a public matter of the individual's relation to society and government. There is, according to Rousseau, ". . . a purely civil profession of faith of which the Sovereign should fix the articles, not exactly as religious dogmas, but as social sentiments without which a man cannot be a good citizen or a faithful subject."[23] Civil religion should bind all members to society, tell them their duties, even move them to fight for their society where necessary. Rousseau's ideas clearly influenced Durkheim, but the term "civil religion" found contemporary currency only with Bellah's work on the United States.[24] In his original essay, Bellah neglected to define civil religion. This omission was remedied by J.A. Coleman as follows: civil religion is "a set of beliefs, rites and symbols which relates a man's role as citizen and his society's place in space, time and history to the conditions of ultimate existence and meaning."[25] To this I would add that civil religions must set out the proper relationship between (civil) society and the state in the securing of a society's place in space, time, and history.

The term "political religion" was coined by Apter, but it is Christel Lane's use of the term in her work on the Soviet Union which is more relevant here.[26] She distinguishes between "civil religion" and "political religion" on two counts.[27] First, civil religion connects the political order to a transcendent power, such as God, derived from the religion(s) of the society concerned, whereas political religion simply makes holy the existing political order. Second, civil religion confines itself to the political order and even then uses terms so general as to avoid conflict both with conventional religious and with political values and norms, whereas political religion claims authority over all social life and specifies values and norms accordingly. I doubt whether the twin distinction holds when applied to cases like the United States. There the sacralization of the American way of life connects the political order to a transcendent God; it also extends far beyond the political order to the celebration of free enterprise and the social order generally.

Rousseau contrasted his civil state to the state of nature. Later theorists divided the civil state into civil society and the state. This distinction is currently, and for good reasons, reentering the political vocabulary in both parts of Europe. It can, I suggest, provide us with a better way of distinguishing civil and political religion than Lane's. Society is the prime mover of civil religion; the state the prime mover of political religion. The collective representations in a civil religion are genuinely representative of society as a whole, or at least of many sections of it; of course, politicians who control the apparatus of the state exploit them, but they also ignore them at their peril. By contrast the collective representations of a political religion are superimposed on society by those who control the state. The one is historically rooted; the other is politically contrived. Alternatively, with civil religions it is ultimately the state which heeds society; with political religions it is ultimately society which heeds the state. Both have a critical potential, but in one the roles of critic and criticized are the reversal of the other. In sum, where Lane concludes that "Civil religion is celebrated in societies where the individual is dominant, and political religion evolves where society is primary," I would argue that civil religion is celebrated where civil society is predominant, and political religion is developed where the state is primary.[28]

Although I reject reference/non-reference to a transcendent power as a criterion for distinguishing between civil and political religion, I agree with Lane that those political religions which make no such reference are still political *religions*. The conception of religion which she and I both use is the Durkheimian one. Where many sociological definitions of religion depend upon a distinction between the supernatural and the natural, Durkheim's hinges on a distinction between the sacred and the profane.[29] Things, persons, representations sacred are set apart from things, persons, representations mundane. They are treated with awe, reverence, special respect. Though often supposedly of divine origin, they are, in reality, social constructions; thus in acknowledging the authority the sacred has over them, men and women acknowledge their individual dependence on society. For Durkheim, the unbelieving son of a rabbi, no avowedly secular system of values and norms could easily secure the respect due to a system believed to contain the word of God. Nevertheless, those who would establish secular ideologies could still be expected to try to vest elements of their systems with sacredness, thereby placing them, insofar as they succeeded, beyond criticism. Within this perspective, there need be no surprise, for example, that Stalin's 1936 Constitution for the Soviet Union makes several references to the sacred.

Integral to Durkheim's theory of religion is a theory of ritual which emphasizes that ritual regulates our contact with the sacred and prevents us from profaning it. Rites, ceremonies, also celebrate values and help fix them in the minds of each new generation of celebrants. Even the stylized words, acts, music, dance or whatever of the ritual remind those who participate, and those who witness, that the occasion is extraordinary—set apart from ordinary life. On return to the routines of mundane life, recall of the experience is also recall of the values celebrated. Civil and political religions include political rituals, or what Lane, following Goodin, calls "the rites of rulers."[30] Civil religions, because they represent the whole of society or at least most sections of it, afford political legitimacy. Political religions only do so where the whole of society, or at least most sections of it, willingly accedes to them.

I do not want to argue here whether a civil or political religion is a necessary feature of any social and political order; I merely wish to consider the Polish experience as compared with the American and the Soviet. Bellah's famous account of "Civil Religion in America" centers on America's self-understanding of her obligation to carry out God's will on earth. It refers to a covenant between God and nation, to America as the new Israel and Americans as a chosen people, and to an understanding of American history in which the Revolution represents exodus, the Civil War death, sacrifice, and rebirth—and the cold war a Manichean conflict between righteousness and evil. In the course of his essay, Bellah alludes to statements from the founding fathers, the Declaration of Independence, presidential inaugural addresses from Washington's to Kennedy's, the Gettysburg Address and other pronouncements; symbols and monuments (I would say sacred places) such as the motto of the United States "In God We Trust," the Lincoln Memorial and the Arlington National Cemetery; and celebrations and rituals such as Thanksgiving Day, Memorial Day, Veterans Day, saluting the flag, and ceremonies in schools.

Bellah acknowledged that there had always been a danger that the high moral content of American civil religion would degenerate into national self-idolatry, and in subsequent writings he referred ever more astringently to the "broken covenant."[31]

The Soviet Union presents the relevant example of a political religion. Notwithstanding my criticism of her method of distinguishing political from civil religion, I accept Lane's argument about the structure and functioning of political religion in the Soviet Union and the place of ritual in the legitimization, even sanctification, of the existing political order. She quotes Moore's comment that ritual "communicates the non-negotiability (the unquestionability), the sacredness of certain interpretations of social life,"[32] and concludes from her study of Soviet ritual that

> The official ideology of Soviet Marxism-Leninism which emerges . . . is clearly no longer a revolutionary ideology mobilizing people for fundamental social change. It has become a very conservative set of rationalizations which support and legitimate the existing order. The association of this ideology with a revolutionary past is utilized to mask the conservative policies of the present.[33]

Lane discusses the sacralization of the October Revolution, the Great Patriotic War and the heroic achievements of labor, and the accompanying symbols and rites, such as October parades, visits (pilgrimages?) to the Lenin mausoleum, the placing of Lenin photographs (icons?) in every public office, war memorials and remembrances, and Labor Days. She also carefully examines references to the motherland and to Soviet endeavor in familial life-cycle rituals, rituals of initiation into social or political collectives, labor ritual, holidays of the calendric cycle and their ritual, ritual of the military-patriotic tradition, and the mass political holidays of the revolutionary tradition.

There are those who claim that the Soviet Union is a country without Communists, that convinced Marxists-Leninists no longer exist—not even in the CPSU. They would say that Soviet political religion is hollow, that it has no resonance with the people. Be that as it may, Soviet political religion is sensible in national, as well as Communist ideological, terms. There may be a few who take Party ideology to their hearts, but equally there can be few who are unmoved by the magnitude of a distinctively Soviet industrialization and modernization of the motherland and who can find nothing to celebrate in it. I realize that other nationalisms are a complicating factor in the Baltic, Trans-Caucasian and Central Asian republics, and may be also in parts of the Ukraine, but elsewhere at least, Soviet political religion does celebrate truly Russian achievements.

But what of Poland? What rites have her rulers? To grasp their predicament, one has to remember the forging of Polish national consciousness during the partitions. During this period, there developed a civil religion which celebrates freedom and democracy and laments the suffering of the nation. "In exile," Garton Ash reminds us, "Romantic poets like Adam Mickiewicz developed a Messianic allegory in which Poland, the 'Christ among nations,' suffered, was crucified, but would rise again for Europe's redemption. The Church, the insurrectionary tradition, the cultural work of the intelligentsia and romantic Messianism forged what can best be described as the Polish national consciousness."[34] Poles expect Poland to suffer but not to abandon hope. Something of these sentiments is found in the national anthem, in origin a marching song of Dabrowski, the Polish legionary who commanded forces for Napoleon in Italy and Haiti. It says:[35]

Poland has not perished yet
So long as we still live.
That which alien force has seized
We at swordpoint shall retrieve . . .

It is notable that Solidarity, in its efforts to roll back the party-state and to open up civil society, also took on elements of a movement of national liberation. It adopted, for example, the song "So that Poland shall be Poland," i.e., itself and not Russian.

Establishment by the party-state of a political religion of its own has never been a practical possibility, while invocation of the civil religion is impossible without damage to itself because the civil religion denies legitimacy to any government which sets itself against the Church. The Church, it is true, still presumes to speak on the responsibilities of the individual citizen and on Poland's place in history. Moreover, it does so in a way which usually allows the necessary accommodations with the party-state, and in so doing it may thereby indirectly afford the party-state some service, but it disallows unqualified loyalty to a state committed to atheism. When it comes to ritual support for the political system, Poland's rulers have to get by with those few rites which command national respect (for example, certain war remembrances) and the respect of the diminishing Party faithful for the party-state's own rites such as May Day parades. When it comes to mobilizing the people for difficult reforms this is not enough. Lane could speak of the rites of rulers in the Soviet Union. What strikes me as extraordinary about Poland is how few rites her leaders have.

The problem is not new. Poland dates its nationhood from 966 when Prince Mieszko I accepted Christianity on behalf of his people in return for help from the Christian Czechs in resisting the eastward migration of German tribes. In 1966 the Church duly organized celebrations of the Polish millennium, a millennium in which the union of nation and Catholic faith remained unbroken. The highlight of the celebrations was to have been the celebration of Mass at the shrine of the Black Madonna in Czestochowa by Pope Paul VI, but the regime refused entry to the pope and organized commemorations of its own. The Church went ahead without the pope but with massive popular participation. By contrast, the party-state's events generated little interest. In 1979 and 1983 Pope John-Paul II visited Poland and drew the biggest gatherings Poland has ever seen. The Party did not choose to hold rival rallies of its own; it had long since given up trying to compete in demonstrations of popular enthusiasm.

I will give another example of the difficulty. On 16 December 1980, at a time when talk of a Soviet invasion was intense, society, Church and party-state came together to commemorate those workers killed by the militia in 1970 at the new memorial in Gdansk. Erection of the memorial was one of the demands of the Gdansk strikers. It consists of three metal crosses, 140 feet high, representing the revolts of 1956, 1970, and 1980. At the top of each cross is an anchor, symbol in Poland of hope, and also the emblem of the Home Army. At the base of the monument are bas-reliefs of workers' lives, including workers striking under the banner of Solidarity. There are also inscriptions. One is of lines from Czeslaw Milosz, the exiled poet who won a Nobel Prize. They say:

You, who have wronged a simple man,
Bursting into laughter at his suffering . . .
Do not feel safe. The poet remembers,
You may kill him—a new one will be born.
Deeds and talks will be recorded.[36]

Another presents words of Pope John-Paul II. Andrzej Wajda, Poland's greatest film director, staged the ceremony and Krzystof Penderecki, her greatest living composer, wrote a lacrimosa for it. The head of state, Henryk Jablonski, the local Party secretary, and the provincial governor then stood with Lech Walesa and 150,000 others as the archbishop of Cracow celebrated Mass. The rite, televised live, brought the nation together—but the terms in which national unity could be expressed were not the party-state's.

Polish messianism is more evident still at the Church of St. Stanislaw Kostka in Warsaw. It was here that Father Popieluszko celebrated his masses for the nation, and here that, following his murder by the secret police, he was buried. The masses continue with packed congregations raising crucifixes and Solidarity victory signs in roughly equal numbers. The tomb is a place of pilgrimage and Solidarity banners adorn the church and the inside of the railings which enclose the graveyard.

Not far away at Victory Square you might expect the party-state to draw strength from ceremonies at the tomb of Poland's unknown warrior—given the scale of Poland's suffering in the last war and the respect in which the army was generally held at least until martial law. But appearances are deceptive. For a start, the unknown warrior may be unknown but the enemy he died fighting is not—it was the Russians during the Russo-Polish War of 1920–21 which the Poles Marshal Pilsudski won, under following the miracle on the Vistula. Then the tomb itself is backed by a ruined colonnade—all that is left of Marshal Pilsudski's military headquarters. And now, completing the picture, General Jaruzelski has restored to the soldiers guarding the tomb the prewar uniforms of Pilsudski's army including the famous four-cornered caps.

From these and other examples, it is possible to draw the extraordinary conclusion that the civil religion of Poland lends no support to the regime, that her rulers are rulers without rites and that this is an important element in the chronic legitimation problem.

Conclusion

For more than a decade prior to 1980, a specter haunted the leaders of the Polish United Workers party, the specter of a working class whose maturation removes the justification for the vanguard role of the Party. The specter was not simply one of a working class increasingly composed of skilled, second-or-more generation workers educated in a socialist system; it was also one of workers resistant to Party control insofar as they had participated in autonomous workers organizations in 1966, 1970–71 and 1976 and were likely to want to do so again. In 1980–81 the specter was made flesh by Solidarity, which at its height organized ten million workers, 80 percent of the labor force. It haunts it still. One of the devices which made Solidarity so formidable was the interfactory strike committee—the very embodiment of solidarity—and of all the banners displayed by participating factories the most shocking was the one that proclaimed "Proletarians of all factories - unite!"[37] But now another specter looms even larger, all society—workers, peasants, intellectuals, white-collar employees and the Church—ranged once again against the party-state.

Unable to deliver economic growth, unwilling to resort to systematic terror, and unsuccessful in ideological manipulation, the Polish regime has had to fall back on fear of Soviet intervention, martial law and now the exhaustion of the people—plus a little help from the Church—to retain its rule. The regime and its functionaries want to keep the Soviet Union at bay partly in response to a tradition of national communism which has been much mocked by hardliners but never extinguished, but also because Soviet intervention would displace many of them from positions from which they profit.

Keeping the Soviet Union at bay also remains a prime objective of the Church, not only because it believes a defective Polish state to be better than none at all, but also because it believes it has only to compare the lot of Polish Catholics with their coreligionists in Lithuania to assure itself that things could always be worse. It also believes time is on its side. The real threat to the Roman Catholic church in Poland would come from honest and popular government, economic liberalization (consumer sovereignty knows no bounds) and the cultural expansiveness that accompanies economic success. In these circumstances Poles would have less call for the protections of a defensive Church. Given the weight of Polish history, lapsing might well even then be slow but it would be sure, or at least surer than it is now in the face of a hostile party-state. The church need have no fear for the moment that this scenario is about to unfold; changes in the Soviet Union must come first. Instead the Church can rely on the party-state to protect it from the ravages of secularism and the party-state can rely on the Church to restrain the antagonisms of the people.

Postscript

This chapter was written for humble staff and postgraduate seminars in the sociology departments of the Universities of Salford and Exeter in January and May 1986. The original title was "Rulers without Rites: the Legitimation Problem in Poland." When Alex Shtromas kindly said he would like to include it in this volume he did not ask for significant changes, except for the addition of a postscript on possible future developments. I have few credentials to provide one but have done my best by suggesting, as briefly as possible, some of the conditions which would, I think, have to be met for different outcomes to be possible.

Could another self-limiting revolution succeed? Solidarity's 1980–81 self-limiting Revolution came to grief for want of a constructive response from the party-state. When the latter failed to honor agreements there were bound to be those who argued that self-limitation should be abandoned. Staniszkis contends that this is what happened from mid–1981 onward.[38] It might be thought that Solidarity made a mistake in not involving itself with those who were trying to reform the Polish United Workers' party—particularly Iwanow in Torun who challenged the Leninist principle of Party organization by establishing a consultative commission of Party secretaries from factories in the region on the model of Solidarity's interfactory strike committees. This horizontalism was anathema to the Party. Iwanow's expulsion from the Party in November 1980 did not stop other reformers. Garton Ash has written of the "pentecostal excitement of that autumn."

> Horizontal structures would be permitted. All party officials would be elected on a free, secret ballot with a real choice of candidates. They would be directly accountable and there would be strict limits to the time they could hold office, and the number of offices they could combine. In short, the party would control the apparatus.[39]

The reformers, however, were defeated bit by bit, martial law finally halting their cause even more effectively than it did Solidarity's. Solidarity's disinclination to link up with them therefore made no difference in the end. From this we may conclude that continued support for the self-limiting character of a Revolution depends on a constructive response from the Party; without it the self-limiters cannot show such a policy to be effective.

To get that response there must be an element in the Party in favor—not just at the local level, but at the top—and that element must secure the approval, however grudging, of the Soviet Union. In 1981 Kuron and some other KSS/KOR members counseled caution; so did the Church. In any future attempt at a self-limiting revolution, the Party could not be expected to trust some analogue of KSS/KOR as a guarantor; on the other hand, it might trust the Church. The Church has a legitimacy which the Party lacks, it is as much respected by the workers as by other sections of Polish society and it has its own interest in maintaining some sort of symbiotic relation with the party-state. The chances of the conditions necessary for a self-limiting Revolution to succeed being met are currently remote. And if they were to be met, other options might also be possible.

Could an unlimited Revolution succeed? For this to happen the Party would have to crumble still further and the Church would have to give its unequivocal support. Revolution involves calling the Soviet bluff—if it is a bluff. The economic and political cost of suppressing an uprising in Poland would make the cost of the Soviet invasion of Afghanistan pale into insignificance, but the partocrats at the top of the Soviet Party might still be willing to pay that price even if the technocrats were not. If the technocrats were seen to be in control, also currently a remote prospect, then who knows . . .

Could economic reform succeed? At the moment this looks doubtful, but who in 1956, or even five years later, would have credited what Kadar was to achieve in Hungary by the 1980s? It took Kadar twelve years to rebuild the Hungarian Party to a point at which it felt secure enough to allow some decentralization of economic decision making and greater use of the market.[40] The Polish economy in the 1980s faces even greater difficulties than the Hungarian in the 1960s but I would not rule out economic reforms in the longer term, particularly if there is some support from Western creditors and some from the Soviet Union. Exactly what such reforms might yield is too ramifying a question for a quick postscript but if the Hungarian example is any guide it would certainly be complex. The Hungarian sociologist, Hankiss, has written of the emergence of a second society. This is much more than just a complement to the second economy. It represents protopluralism within the one-party system, and is informal and diffused (whereas the first society is formal and centralized). The upshot is a society in which Hungarians live according to a variety of social paradigms:

> A citizen may work in a state-controlled factory as a wage-laborer. He then goes home and may work in some family enterprise for the market under a different set of norms. He then may have to approach the town hall for

permission to construct some building and he approaches there as a 19th century scared subject of an almighty bureaucracy as if in an absolutist state. Perhaps also he wants to send his son to university so he goes to find a client as in a neo-feudalistic society.[41]

There would seem, then, to be not just two public spaces—society and state—but many, with each one operating according to different norms.

Finally, might there not be an indefinite continuation of the present stalemate? The stalemate might well continue for some time yet—never underestimate apathy and inertia bred of disillusionment—but I do not think it will endure indefinitely. The maturation of the working class is irreversible; the memories of 1956, 1968, 1970–71, 1976, and 1980 are unforgettable; and the total repossession of society by the party-state probably impossible. This last might prove especially important. Polish sociologists have taken up the idea of new social movements associated with Offe and others in Germany.[42] Such movements are located in Hankiss's second society; they are relatively informal, diffused, variously visible and invisible, and at the edge of legality. (Some of them might even undermine the traditional authority of a very conservative Church.) Regardless of what happens in the Soviet Union, or in international economic relations, I think they will prove sufficiently irrepressible to make some changes inevitable in the longer run. These might well prove more piecemeal than dramatic, but insofar as they contain elements of a socialist civil society—socialism without the state, or at least with a much reduced state—they would have lessons for the West, too.

Acknowledgements

Drafts of this chapter were presented to staff and postgraduate sociology seminars in the Universities of Salford and Exeter and I am grateful for comments made on those occasions. I must also thank Stephen Edgell and Alex Shtromas for their careful scrutiny of earlier versions. Finally, I am indebted to Polish colleagues who commented on some of my arguments when I presented them in another context; they will know who they are. Needless to say, responsibility for the end product is mine alone.

Notes

1. M. Weber, *Economy and Society* (German, ph. 1922), Berkeley (University of California Press), corr. edn. 1978, 1, 215.
2. J. Habermas, "Legitimation Problems in the Modern State" (German, 1976), in his *Communication and the Evolution of Society*, (London: Heinemann, 1979), 178.
3. On social mobility, and advancement, see W. Wesolowski and K.M. Slomczynski, *Investigations on Class Structure and Social Stratification in Poland 1945–1975*, (Warsaw: Polish Academy of Sciences, 1977); R. Andorka & K. Zagorski, *Socio-Occupational Mobility in Hungary and Poland; Comparative Analysis of Surveys 1972–1973*, (Warsaw: Polish Academicy of Sciences, 1980); C.G.A. Bryant, "Worker Advancement and Political Order in a State Socialist Society: a Case Study of Poland," *Sociological Review*, 28 (1980), 105–28. On the workers, see G. Kolankiewicz, "The Working Class," in D. Lane & G. Kolankiewicz (eds.), *Social Groups in Polish Society*, (London: Macmillan, 1973), chap. 3; G. Kolankiewicz, 'Poland, 1980: the Working Class Under 'Anomic Socialism,' " in J.F. Triska & C. Gati, *Blue-Collar Workers in Eastern Europe*, (London: Allen & Unwin, 1981); A. Pravda, "The Workers," in A. Brumberg, (ed., *Poland: Genesis of a Revolution*: New York Vantage Books, 1983).
4. On the economic crisis at the end of the Gierek era, see I. Shapiro, "Fiscal Crisis of the Polish State: Genesis of the 1980 Strikes," *Theory and Society*, 10 (1981), 469–502; J. Figa, "Societal Sources of Polish Renewal," *Economic and Industrial Democracy*, 3 (1982), 117–39; B. Minc, "The Reasons for the Polish Crisis of 1980–81," *Economic and Industrial Democracy*, 3, (1982), 141–57; P.G. Lewis, "Obstacles to the Establishment of Political Legitimacy in Communist Poland," *British Journal of Political Science*, 12, (1982), 125–47.
5. This is the conclusion to Bryant (1980).
6. W. Herberg, *Protestant-Catholic-Jew*, (Garden City, NY: Doubleday, 1955).
7. For an extensive account of the Marxist and Catholic sociologies of religion in Poland and their competing findings, see M. Pomian-Srzednicki, *Religious Change in Contemporary Poland: Secularization and Politics*, (London: RKP, 1982). I have given my own response to this flawed but fascinating book in a review in *American Journal of Sociology*, 90 (1984), 685–87.
8. "The Hammer and the Cross: Poland," BBC TV, 16 February 1986.
9. On Solidarity, see N. Ascherson, *The Polish August: What Has Happened In Poland*, (Harmondsworth: Penguin, 1st edn. 1981, 2nd edn. 1982); T. Garton Ash, *The Polish Revolution: Solidarity 1980–2*, (London: Cape, 1983); A. Brumberg ed. (1983); A. Touraine with F. Dubel, M. Weiviorka & J. Stzelecki, *Solidarity: Poland 1980–1* (French, 1982), (Cambridge: CUP, 1983).
10. Garton Ash (1983), chap. 2.
11. J. Staniszkis, "The Evolution of Forms of Working-Class Protest in Poland: Sociological Reflections on the Gdansk-Szczecin Case, August 1980"; *Soviet*

Studies 33, (1981), 204–31; Touraine cum al. (1983), 64, give priority in the use of the term to Kuron; also see L. Kolakowski, "Hope and Hopelessness," *Survey* 18 (1971), 37–52.

12. L. Trotsky, *The History of the Russian Revolution* (Russian, 1932–33), (London: Gollancz, 1965), chap. 11; also see Garton Ash (1983), 99.

13. N. Davies, *God's Playground: a History of Poland*, (Oxford: OUP, 1981), 2, 406.

14. On the Sanacja, in addition to Davies (1981), see A. Polonsky, *Politics in Independent Poland 1921–1939*, (Oxford: Clarendon Press, 1972).

15. C. Cviic, 'The Church', in Brumberg, ed. (1983), chap 7; see p. 93. On the church, also see Davies (1981), 2, chap. 7.

16. Davies, *God's Playground*, (1981), 2, 613.

17. R. Taras, *Ideology in a Socialist State: Poland 1956–1983*, (Cambridge: CUP, 1985), 217.

18. T. Parsons, "On the Concept of Political Power," *Proceedings of the American Philosophical Society*, 107 (1963), 232–62; see p. 237.

19. The thesis is discussed in Pomian-Srzednicki (1982), 146–47.

20. A. Michnik, "The Church and the Left" (French, 1977), in F. Silnitsky, L. Silnitsky and K. Reyman, eds, *Communism and Eastern Europe: a Collection of Essays*, (Brighton: Harvester, 1979), 51–95.

21. L. Kolakowski, "La revanche du sacre," *Centrepoint*, no. 13, (1977), 48–60.

22. Quoted in Michnik, *The Church*, (1979), pp 83–84.

23. J.J. Rousseau, *The Social Contract* (French, 1762), (London: Dent, 1963 reprint), 114.

24. R.N. Bellah, "Civil Religion in America," *Daedalus*, 96 (1967), 1–21.

25. J.A. Coleman, "Civil Religion," *Sociological Quarterly*, 31 (1974), 67–77, see p. 70.

26. D.E. Apter, "Political Religion in the New Nations," in C. Geertz, ed, *Old Societies and New States* (New York: Free Press, 1963); C. Lane, *The Rites of Rulers: Ritual in Industrial Society—the Soviet Case*, (Cambridge: CUP, 1981).

27. Lane *The Rights*, (1981), p. 42.

28. ——, 44.

29. E. Durkheim, *The Elementary Forms of the Religious Life* (French, 1912), (London: Allen & Unwin, 1915).

30. R.E. Goodin, "Rites of Rulers," *British Journal of Sociology*, 19 (1978), 281–99.

31. R.N. Bellah, *The Broken Covenant*, (New York: Seabury, 1975) and "Religion and Legitimation in the American Republic," in T. Robbins and D. Anthony, eds., *In Gods We Trust*, (New Brunswick, NJ: Transaction Books, 1981), chap. 2.

32. Unpublished paper by S.F. Moore quoted in Lane (1981), 32.

33. Lane *The Rights*, (1981), 24.

34. Garton Ash (1983), 3. Also see Davies (1981), 2, chap. 1; and G. Schopflin "Hungary: an Uneasy Stability," in A. Brown & J. Gray, eds., *Political*

Culture and Political Change in Communist States, (London: Macmillan, 1977), chap. 5, for an interesting comparison with Hungary.

35. This translation is from Davies (1981), 2, p. 16.
36. This is the translation given in R. Laba, "The Political Symbolism of the 'Solidarity Movement,' " paper given to seminar on Folklore and the State: Contemporary Eastern Europe, sponsored by ACLS and Rockefeller Foundation, Bellagio, 27 August–1 September 1984. Also see Garton Ash (1983), 101–3; and J. Kubik, "The Role of Symbols in the Legitimization of Power and Social Order: a Polish Case," paper given to Bellagio seminar.
37. Garton Ash, *The Polish Revolution*, p 63.
38. J. Staniszkis, "Institutional Revolution," published as "Poland on the Road to the Coup," *Labour Focus on Eastern Europe*, vol. 5, nos. 1–2 (1982), 19–25.
39. Garton Ash *The Polish Revolution*, pp 171–72.
40. On the Hungarian New Economic Mechanism and subsequent reforms, see W.F. Robinson, *The Pattern of Reform in Hungary: a Political, Economic and Cultural Analysis*, (New York: Praeger, 1973); B. Belassa, "The Firm and the New Economic Mechanism in Hungary," in M. Bernstein, ed., *Plan and Market*, (New Haven: Yale University Press, 1973); D. Stark, "A Comparative Model of Internal Labor Markets: New Insights in Light of Recent Hungarian Experiences," paper given to 5th International Conference of Europeanists, Washington D.C., October 1985.
41. Quoted in B. Dent, "Knowledge on the Black Market: How Barriers to the Study of Change in East Europe are being Broken by Sociologist Elemer Hankiss," *Times Higher Educational Supplement*, 7 March 1986, 11.
42. B. Misztal ed., *Poland After Solidarity: Social Movements Versus The State*, (New Brunswick, NJ: Transaction Books, 1985); C. Offe, *Contradictions of the Welfare State* (German, 1977–83), (London: Hutchinson, 1984).

15

The Prospects for Poland in the Event of a Cessation of Soviet Control

STANISLAV ANDRESKI

Despite the wastefulness of the economic system, the vast natural resources of the USSR might permit some improvement in the standard of living, given the worldwide technical progress, particularly as the birthrate is falling. But even if the condition of the people became much worse, the empire can continue to exist as long as the machinery of coercion remains efficient. Nor is there much chance of its destruction from outside. At the stage of mutually assured destruction nobody would dare to attack possessors of a large quantity of nuclear missiles. Only an invention of a gadget capable of preventing a use of nuclear weapons could create a possibility of a total defeat of a superpower. It is impossible to foretell whether such an invention will be made or by whom, and what would happen then.

The Soviet Empire could also disappear through voluntary liquidation. However, we could expect this to happen only if the USSR itself became a liberal polity because it would be strange if the Russian rulers were willing to relinquish their control over the satellites while withholding civic rights from their own nation. And if the USSR became a liberal and prosperous real federation, the nations of Eastern Europe might not wish to dissociate themselves from it. Their present discontent is not due to a dislike of the Russian people but to the repellent nature of the system. If an evolution in the said direction did occur, the satellite regimes would also undergo a gradual liberalization more or less in step with the changes in the USSR.

The empire would cease to exist through a process of transforming itself into something completely different. Unfortunately, there are no signs that a change of this magnitude is likely in the foreseeable future, even on the reasonable assumption that the progress of civilization, which has occurred since the death of Stalin and involved an abandonment of the most barbarous forms of coercion, will continue.

A sudden collapse of the empire seems possible to me only if there is a violent split at the top which, by spreading downward, rips asunder the entire machine of coercion, and makes a rebellion of the masses possible. The increasing smoothness of succession at the top indicates a solidification of the ruling class, and reduces the likelihood of such an event.

Even if for some unforeseeable reason the Soviet control over Eastern Europe vanished, the satellite regimes would not necessarily disappear all at once. Franco survived the fall of his protectors, and the Communists still rule Yugoslavia and Albania without outside support. Even in the only country where there is some open resistance, the rise of *Solidarnosc* might be difficult to repeat because the machine of coercion has been greatly strengthened. Only paralyzing mutinies could impair its ability to hold the nation down. These, however, are unlikely because the mercenaries have strong incentives to stick together: not only the desire to keep their jobs and perks but also the fear of punishment. One of the conditions which made the rise of *Solidarnosc* possible, was the attenuation of hostility between the rulers and the ruled that occurred during Gierek's reign, in consequence of his policy of buying popularity with money borrowed from abroad. Now the popular dislike of the Party, the police and the officers seems much stronger, although some people give Jaruzelski some credit for holding the most ferocious guard dogs on the leash. An economic improvement, brought about by thorough reforms, would permit a mollification of the coercion and a partial reconciliation with the masses, thus increasing the chances of a peaceful liberalization in the event of a cessation of Soviet domination. In contrast, if the necessary reforms remain blocked by the vested interests of the bureaucratic mass, the ineptitude of the rulers or a veto from the Kremlin, the Party will have to step up coercion to contain growing discontent. This would deepen the hatred surrounding them and strengthen their incentive to hang together and on to power even without Soviet control and support.

In such an eventuality the repression would become much more brutal—rising, perhaps, to a Stalinist level—because without a Soviet presence the Polish police alone would have to inspire enough fear to restrain the masses. At present, the regime can survive a degree of repression, which is very mild by the Communist standards, because the majority of people realize that overthrowing the Polish Communists would be futile, as this would bring the Soviet troops into action. As the Soviets know that most people apart from the very young know it, they feel less need to be so quick on the draw as they would have to be to be able to maintain themselves in power without an external protection.

They would have to be much more on the alert than now also because the hatred surrounding them would be greatly strengthened by the disappearance of the only justification of their function. Nobody takes seriously the invocations of Marxism which even the party stalwarts make only as an obeisance to Moscow. The only argument, which convinces anyone in Poland is: "you better let us govern you or your fate will be much worse under a direct Soviet rule." Although the message is wrapped up in various euphemisms, people understand perfectly that the generals try to justify their action in December 1981 and their present function by saying that without them there would have been a Soviet invasion. The majority of older people accept this at least partially and, although it does not make them like the government, it dampens their dislike or hate. If the Party succeeded in maintaining itself in power by force without this excuse, it would have a good reason to fear mass lynchings in the event of a revolution.

In Spain the dismantling of the dictatorship could be done peacefully because power was first given to the king who could not be blamed for what went on before. The Spanish Church could not have played the role of a conciliator because it had been one of the main pillars of Franco's regime. The Polish Church might be able to play such a role because it is regarded by the enemies of the regime as their only shelter.

Now let us imagine that the miracle has happened: the Soviet domination has come to an end and the Party relinquished power. What would be likely to happen next? I am pretty confident about predicting the first stage: some kind of a provisional government would emerge from among the surviving former leaders of *Solidarnosc* and it would hold elections. Nobody would think of inviting the funny old men from the so-called government in London. No former Party member would have a chance of being elected. The contest would be between the various components of *Solidarnosc*. There could well be arguments about how to treat the Party members: whether to punish them all or to forgive most, whom to imprison and for how long or have a general amnesty. Another controversial issue might be the position of the Church. Now there are people who criticise Cardinal Glemp for being too conciliatory but nobody can be against the Church, which is the only bulwark against totalitarianism, without appearing to side with the Party. However, a disappearance of the totalitarian menace might revive anticlericalism among people inclined toward liberalism and free thought.

I doubt whether any grave problems would arise about the relations with the neighbors. The ethnic boundaries were made to correspond with the political frontiers of Poland by mass expulsions. To change frontiers without recourse to Hitler's and Stalin's methods would recreate frictions with minorities which bedeviled the politics of independent Poland between the two World Wars. I also doubt whether there would be any enthusiasm among the Germans for a reconquest of the eastern provinces of the Reich, particularly as even a reconquest would be of little use without reviving the practice of mass expulsions and replacing the present Constitution of West Germany by totalitarianism. Probably the only issue of foreign policy which would generate mass enthusiasm in Poland would be an application to join the EEC, which could well be seen as the only escape from the frightful economic predicament brought about by decades of misgovernment.

Notwithstanding the disagreements which began to emerge toward the end of the brief open existence of *Solidarnosc*, there was absolute unanimity (even among those who were too prudent to join) on the crucial issue: people did not want to be governed by the Communists. However, apart from a few economists and sociologists, people had very hazy, naive, and self-contradictory notions about what to put in the place of the hated system. Despite the unpopularity of the word "socialism" (let alone "communism") because of its association with oppression, exploitation and deceit, most supporters of *Solidarnosc* were naive socialists at heart, in the sense of wanting a government which would look after them. Their view of the causes of their distress was simplistic: they attributed it more or less wholly to the low moral and intellectual quality of the leaders and managers, while giving little thought to the inherent disadvantages of a statist economy. The general opinion was (and is) that the Party is a gang of moronic, thievish, and mendacious traitors who make people poor by taking either for themselves or their Russian masters everything that they have not wasted through their stupidity. This view is expressed in countless jokes and limericks like for example one about the replacement of Edward Gierek by Jaruzelski which ends with a rhyme: "come back Eddy to the pork barrel, better a thief than a bandit." Another illustration is the joke about why there is no big time gansterism in Poland. The answer is "because all the gangsters are at the top." The remedy for the economic ills envisaged by the rank and file of *Solidarnosc* was equally simple: it would be enough to replace the ruling gangsters by honest Christian patriots. It is a common view that there would be enough for everybody if only the workers were allowed to keep the products of their labor instead of having to surrender most of it to their Polish and Russian exploiters. In a way the Polish workers have accepted the basic idea of Marx's theory of value (that the value of everything is determined by the amount of simple labor put into making it) and applied it to the Communist system, casting their bosses into the role which Marx and his followers reserve for the capitalists.

Oversimplifications are popular everywhere but in Poland (and no doubt in other Communist states) the economic notions of the masses are even more primitive than in the West because they are uninfluenced by expert opinion, as any expert, who is allowed to make public pronouncements, is regarded with suspicion. So people commonly overestimate the consequences of exploitation (grave enough in reality) and underestimate the effects of inefficiency and their own shoddy work. They have an exaggerated view of the affluence of the West but little understanding of how it was achieved and is sustained.

The dominant strand of this hazy thinking can be described as Christian socialism, although nobody would use the latter word because of its repugnant associations. The name "Solidarity" reveals an attitude remote from the spirit of capitalism. Despite its abysmal failure in most respects, the official propaganda had been successful in preaching the ideal of equality but this has alienated people further from the regime, stimulating the hatred for the privileged bosses and the police, as the natural human envy came to be reinforced by the contempt for liars and hypocrites. It was no coincidence that, among the various proclamations of *Solidarnosc*, one which was most persistently made was the call for truthfulness. Outraged at being cheated, people seem to resent more bitterly the mediocre privileges of the Party elite than they did the much grander style of living of the prewar rich who did not spout about equality.

The common belief, that everything would be alright if only honest Christian patriots were in charge, albeit naively one-sided, is not without foundation because one of the most important causes of the economic collapse was the practice of putting incompetent Party stooges into top positions. Because the Party is generally despised, and because it imposes on its members the obligation to pay lip service to the doctrine in which nobody believes, it attracts only morally turpid opportunists. This has very far-reaching effects because it would be strange if we found general honesty and conscientious work among people willing to tell obvious lies knowingly for the sake of personal advantage.

For a time the generals' government appeared to be trying to break with the habit of telling obvious lies. They were ready, for instance, to admit the country was no workers' paradise but very poor. However, as the old hacks creep back into power, the old bad habits also reappear: an example is the newly erected monument to the Katyn "victims of the German fascists." Somebody who tells obvious lies, will not be believed even when he tells the absolute truth.

The distrust of and disrespect for the authority is amply justified by the long and bitter experience. But it has become so ingrained that it would be likely to persist even if the Communists were replaced by elected leaders. Even the best statesmen would not be able to avoid disappointing the expectations aroused by newly won freedom, and would soon have to face suspicions and accusations as well as the awesome task of maintaining order in a nation whose ethos is oriented toward resisting the authority and circumventing its commands.

Equally grave is another inheritance from the system which offers few rewards for honest work: the almost complete absence of conscientiousness and pride in work. The sense of duty operates only within the family and the circle of relatives and friends (where it appears to be stronger than is the case in the West) or within a clandestine group. The Church and the nation are objects of intense loyalties, but the state is regarded as something completely distinct from the nation and unworthy of loyalty. As the state is the only employer, people's attitude to it molds their attitude to work. Shoddy work and playing hooky are a perfectly excusable reaction to exploitation and mismanagement, but can we expect people, who throughout their lives have been devoting their ingenuity to shirking work and cheating the employer, to change the habits of a lifetime as soon as they have an elected government?

Although robbery, burglary and picking pockets appear to be less common than before the war (probably because there is no mass unemployment), stealing from the workplace is almost universal. People seem to have accepted the Communist slogan "property is theft" and are applying it to their relationship with the rulers, who are often called "the owners of People's Poland." Pilfering from the workplace is often described as "taking back from them what they have stolen from us." If the proceeds are distributed among friends, it is regarded as a patriotic deed. Again, this is an understandable reaction to the circumstances, but the habit has become so ingrained that it would be a miracle if it disappeared quickly under an elected government.

While totally alienated from the present system, people are ill-prepared for a market economy despite the fact that (in contrast to the prewar contempt for commerce instilled into the entire nation by the gentry) now almost everybody trades and barters. Paradoxically, the Communist rule has turned the Poles (including the Party functionaries) into a nation of small-scale businessmen. Nevertheless, it has placed a big obstacle to a development of market economy by spreading hostility to profit . . . that is, the other fellow's profit. Envy is a natural human propensity and the official propaganda succeeded on the purely negative point of stimulating it and directing it against people who make a gain by buying and selling.

The popular resentment of enterprise and profit is reinforced by the unsavory ways in which private enterprise often operates. A combination of a bureaucratically controlled economy with interstitial enclaves of private enterprise opens the field to many kinds of abuses. As the state monopolizes most raw materials and gives preference to state-owned industry, the small private artisans and traders can seldom obtain them without bribing the officials in charge of selling them. Often only stolen materials can be bought, because large state-owned factories also bribe their suppliers. Furthermore, hedged by all kinds of persnickety restrictions, plagued by endless red tape, harassed by overbearing officials and policemen, and subject to arbitrary tax assessments, the interstitial businessmen (even those who are licensed) can survive only by bribery and fiddling. They are open to blackmail by bribe-extorting functionaries because most of them could, in fact, be charged with illegal dealing. It is said that only relatives or friends of policemen can remain in business officially. Even if this is an exaggeration, there is probably something in it.

Vastly more numerous are casual producers and traders who operate entirely outside the law, albeit many of them buy surreptitious tolerance with bribes. They have little workshops or stores at home and sell what they have bought on the black market or stolen from their workplace, or made with materials of such an origin. Some even use the official premises for this purpose. I have heard, for example, of a dentist in a military clinic who lets in private patients through the back door.

One kind of business that provokes ire among those disappointed people waiting on line, is the practice of shop assistants who hide the goods, which they are supposed to sell at the official prices, sell them outside at a higher price and put the equivalent of the official price into the cash register. This could not be done in a market economy, but the resentment that this practice generates plays into the hands of the official antimarket propaganda.

Given the widespread desire for equality and the hostility to profit, it would be very difficult—I guess, impossible—for an elected government to organize a planned and gradual transition to a market economy. Nor could such a government gradually dismantle the command economy because it would collapse as soon as its only prop—the massive coercion—disappeared. A democratic socialism—which is what most people desire under a different name—could not function owing to the attitudes to authority and work described above. No doubt, large-scale industry, agriculture and distribution would be taken over by the workers. Unable to control them, an elected government would have no choice but to make the factories and shops the property of the personnel. They would probably split into the smallest workable and localized units and would have to begin to barter and trade. This would probably be the only way of preventing their dismantling through massive grabbing. Having a stake in their workplace, the workers would watch one another and put an end to pilfering and shirking, as well as to carelessness when they discovered that they cannot sell shoddy goods. Such cooperatives would have a better chance of surviving than the cooperatives in the West because they would face no competition from more efficient capitalist big business. Nevertheless, it would be a long time before such cooperatives could learn how to conduct their business. So, for a long time their productivity would be so low that many worker-shareholders would leave to try to make a living independently as hawkers, gardeners or agricultural laborers. Many establishments would have to close because they could produce nothing that could be sold. Others would founder because of demagoguery and squabbles. However, there would be no dearth of talent because many capable people have been kept out of important positions for political reasons.

There would be a tremendous proliferation of small business fed by a vast exodus from bureaucratic employment. It would be impossible for an elected government to squeeze out enough taxes to pay for more than a fraction of the present number of functionaries. It is unlikely that any welfare services (apart from the most rudimentary, like soup kitchens) could be maintained. Fortunately, the upheaval would be smallest in agriculture which is mostly in the hands of peasant owners. So, a mass starvation could probably be avoided. In other respects, however, the standard of living would fall far below its present dismal level. A sudden dismantling of the prison can leave a lot of people with no shelter whatsoever. Nevertheless, this would be better than the present hopelessness and impotent grumbling. The example of Germany shows that a nation can lift itself from a ruin quickly if it is not burdened by a parasitic ruling class and people are free to try to help themselves.

16

The Situation in Afghanistan

How Much of a Threat to the Soviet State?

ANTHONY ARNOLD

Soviet efforts to transform Afghanistan into a docile satellite have gone through several broadly definable stages. As each Soviet approach in turn was faced with probable failure, it impelled Moscow to invest more heavily and commit itself more inextricably. Thus, the original effort to "buy" Afghanistan with a massive aid program in the 1950s (an economic investment) was followed in the 1960s by support for a fledgling Communist party, the People's Democratic party of Afghanistan (PDPA), founded on 1 January 1965. When this political investment failed to result in a legal takeover or in successful manipulation of a non-Communist dictator (President Daoud), the Party seized power in a bloody coup d'état (1978), later dignified as "the Great Saur Revolution." At this point, like it or not, the Soviet investment had become ideological. It would not be a profitable commitment.

As Soviet ideologues themselves later conceded, Afghanistan was not ready for socialism. The PDPA was founded more than forty years after the next youngest Communist party in a country bordering the USSR (Norway's, in 1923). Like most revolutionaries, the Afghan intellectual theoreticians who built the PDPA were far more concerned with the techniques of seizing power than with understanding the workers and peasants in whose name they plotted.

Moreover, the Party suffered from a very Afghan political malady, factionalism, which was manifest from the outset. Although in-house disputes are scarcely unique to Afghanistan, political hostilities in this land of traditional feuding swiftly become irreconcilable, often mortal conflicts. The two major groups, *Parcham* (Banner) and *Khalq* (Masses) were virtually identical ideologically, both pledged to unswerving Marxism-Leninism as interpreted by Moscow. Tactically, the main difference was only that *Khalq* made little effort to conceal its Marxist/Leninist orientation, whereas *Parcham* pretended to be more "modernist-reformist," an effort that continues down to the present day.

Parcham coalesced around Babrak Karmal, the Kabul-born son of an Afghan general, and it attracted urban intellectuals from relatively affluent families. *Khalq*'s leader was Nur Mohammed Taraki, son of a small-town herder and trader, whose following consisted mainly of the less wealthy rural intelligentsia. Both parties were most successful in recruiting among students who were either estranged from traditional Afghan values because of their more sophisticated upbringing (*Parchamis*) or were physically removed from their normal cultural milieu in the countryside to attend boarding school in Kabul (*Khalqis*). The conflict between rural and urban values, the "country mouse/city mouse" phenomenon, is common to most cultures, but in Afghanistan it is overlaid with traditions of violence and feuding that give it especially sharp and enduring characteristics.

By mid–1967 there were organizationally separate *Khalq* and *Parcham* PDPAs, each with its own Central Committee, recruitment program, and other organizational trappings. In the best (or worst) Afghan tradition, the bitter personal animosity between the two leaders was enthusiastically adopted by their respective followings who were more than satisfied to sacrifice the benefits of unity in the interests of feuding. Only the intercession of the CPSU in 1976 and 1977 finally forced a marriage of convenience on *Parcham* and *Khalq*, enabling the reunited PDPA to stage the coup that unseated President Daoud in April 1978.

The weaknesses of the new regime were instantly apparent as it fractured anew into its constituent *Parcham* and *Khalq* factions. Largely thanks to the machinations of its second-in-command, Hafizullah Amin, within weeks *Khalq* emerged triumphant from this struggle, banishing the most prominent *Parchamis* into diplomatic exile and hounding those who remained in Afghanistan. They also undertook ill-conceived reforms that aroused popular ire by threatening the basic political, economic, and especially religious underpinnings of Afghan society. By September 1979, popular rejection of the Communist government had become so widespread that only radical measures seemed capable of preserving the new Democratic Republic of Afghanistan (DRA). These measures took a peculiarly Soviet conspiratorial turn.

Amin, driven by personal ambition and committed to the socialist transformation of his country, had already usurped a great deal of the practical political power the PDPA originally bestowed on the fuzzily intellectual Taraki. Amin thus became the ideal intended scapegoat in an involved plot that would have combined renewed reconciliation between Karmal and Taraki with the liquidation of Amin as the alleged architect of all DRA failures since 1978. Both Afghan and Soviet participants in the conspiracy bungled their assignments, however, and instead of Amin it was Taraki who was killed. Moscow was left in the embarrassing position of dealing with an ideologically loyal Amin who remained as bitterly anti-*Parchami* as ever and who was patently unable to halt the political disintegration of his discredited regime.[1]

During the final three months of 1979, as the security situation deteriorated still further, the Soviets prepared a quantum jump in the stakes: a military invasion and occupation that were supposed to salvage all the economic resources, political prestige, and ideological allegiance that they had invested in Afghanistan in the previous decades. Over the Christmas holidays, there was a massive, quiet, and unopposed infusion of Soviet troops across the border from Central Asia, by ground and air. Believing that their government had authorized these movements, the DRA army offered no resistance. On 27 December 1979, the Soviet forces launched their armed attack with an assault on Radio Kabul and a simultaneous strike by a special commando unit against Amin's headquarters in Darulaman Palace.

First Impact of the Invasion

Soviet military doctrine believes in overkill, particularly when international considerations demand swift and total victory. The tank armies that crushed the Hungarian Revolution in 1956 and the Prague Spring in 1968 were much larger than needed for certain victory, but they were committed in the interests of speed, to deny the resistance any chance to mobilize its own resources or, especially, to call on outside help. In Soviet thinking, where challenges to authority must be met with force, that force must be swift, demonstrative, decisive, and overwhelming—not only for the benefit of the outside world but perhaps first of all for the Soviet public itself.

Thus, it is logical to assume that the Soviet General Staff in late 1979 considered the 70,000 troops committed to the Afghan invasion entirely adequate for their mission. As insurance, there were available another 30,000 in reserve just across the border in the USSR. The well-equipped and well-supported invaders and reserves slightly outnumbered the entire disorganized DRA army which, for all its weaknesses, still controlled about two-thirds of the country's provinces. The plan probably envisioned a swift military victory followed by withdrawal of most combat troops as soon as a government to Moscow's liking was firmly seated. After a suitable period of political consolidation, Afghanistan could then become an equivalent of Mongolia, all but annexed to the USSR. Its role would be both that of a controlled buffer against possible infusions of Islamic nationalism into Soviet Central Asia from the south and an offensive strategic base threatening both South Asia and the Middle East energy reserves.[2]

Whatever the ultimate Soviet intentions, the immediate military goals were to save Afghanistan for Moscow by (1) liquidating Hafizullah Amin and his closest *Khalqi* advisors, (2) installing the *Parchami* leader Babrak Karmal as chief of a newly forged *Parcham-Khalq* coalition to run the DRA, and (3) annihilating or intimidating the ragtag collection of *mujahideen* (holy warriors) who had been such gadflies to the DRA and its Soviet friends.[3] The invaders accomplished the first two tasks on schedule: Amin and his bodyguard died within hours in a dramatic firefight with Soviet forces, and Karmal, after a somewhat embarrassing slip in Soviet timing, took over in triumph.[4]

The third task—disposing of the armed resistance—has now been under way for over five years, longer than the USSR fought in World War II. It has become an almost purely Soviet fight, with the Afghan troops, not the invaders (as originally intended and attempted), playing the support role. At risk are not only all of Moscow's previous investments in Afghanistan but a measure of internal Soviet stability as well.

The extent of the Kremlin's miscalculation can only be guessed. Soviet optimists probably expected that Karmal and his relatively lenient *Parchamis* would be welcomed by the Afghan people if not with enthusiasm then at least with relief; Amin's use of torture and execution in the name of social progress had not been popular. Pessimists, recalling Stalin's wartime popularity in spite of his 1930s blood purges, would have been more skeptical; the domestic tyrant, they might have noted, whatever his record is usually more acceptable than the foreign invader.[5]

The initial Soviet politico-military tactics seemed to reflect these concerns. To guarantee quick disposal of Amin, Soviet forces had to be used, but this could never be admitted. (To this day Soviet and DRA media make a point of denying any Soviet role in his removal.) News coverage in Afghanistan about the Soviet troops was kept to a minimum. In combat, Soviet airpower, armor, and artillery—their operators anonymous and relatively secure—supported the DRA, but the frontline infantry used for actually seizing ground was always Afghan. Soviet armor was also used for intimidation: convoys of tanks and armored personnel carriers would roar into a village, park, and remain for some hours before abruptly leaving again. But although this behavior did serve to avoid direct Soviet/Afghan firefights (and also to minimize Soviet casualties), it was interpreted by the Afghans not as restraint but as cowardice.

In spite of these precautions, the pessimists were right. From the outset, Afghan resentment against the aliens was wholehearted and universal. The *mujahideen* instantly grew in stature, both domestically and abroad, for their willingness to defy a superpower. Civilian attitudes toward them, previously discreet if not even occasionally hostile, became entirely supportive, and were soon manifest in Kabul itself.

On 21 February 1980, the merchants of Kabul declared a strike to protest the invasion. They were soon joined by the rest of the population, including the DRA's own civil servants, and the city's economic life came to a standstill. Martial law was declared, but no one heeded orders to return to work. The Islamic cry *"Allah Akhbar"* (Allah is great) rose eerily after curfew from Kabul rooftops and continued all night long during the strike, in spite of flares dropped from helicopters and automatic weapons fire intended to stop it. During daytime protest marches, the same watch cry was sounded, seriously embarrassing the authorities: on the one hand Karmal had proclaimed that the DRA was an Islamic republic and on the other, no one could mistake the anti-regime and anti-Soviet nature of the chant. After ten days that saw hundreds killed in clashes between civilian demonstrators and security forces, Soviet and DRA troops were able to break the strike, but the unrest continued through the spring. In April and May high school girls led student marches that resulted in tragedy when troops again opened fire. Scores of protesters were reported killed.[6]

Meanwhile the Soviet high command had its own peculiar disciplinary problems. Whatever hopes it might have entertained that its Central Asian reservists, called up on short notice in November 1979 to take part in the invasion, would bring socialist enlightenment to their backward Afghan kin were soon dashed. On the contrary, a brisk black market in Korans and hashish soon sprang up in the bazaar, and the fraternizing that developed worked if anything to the detriment of Soviet interests. When the Central Asians were sent home on completion of their 90-day service, their replacements generally came from non-Islamic parts of the USSR.[7]

The Changing War—1980–1985

The failure of the USSR and DRA to establish quick and effective control over Afghanistan's alpine Islamic society was no surprise to those familiar with the area and its peoples. The country is made up of some 25,000 quasi-independent, self-sufficient village-states, largely isolated from each other and from the capital by giant ridges and plunging valleys. Securing their allegiance requires a skillful blend of diplomacy and brute force.[8] Afghan kings and presidents have never found the job easy; foreigners—and the puppets of foreigners—have always found it all but impossible. The Afghan villager's loyalties are strictly local, and when challenged by outsiders his traditional response is armed resistance. Add to the problem the religious dimension of the USSR's official atheism and its reputation among Afghans for cruel suppression of Islam in neighboring Central Asia, and, as one observer noted,

> The ideological element is more profound and conducive to desperation than perhaps has ever before been expressed in Afghan warfare. . . . The obligation to resist has become implacable, suggesting that while the intensity of the fighting may rise and fall . . . , hostility will not cease as long as the intruder is present.[9]

Growing Soviet comprehension of the seriousness of its problem is reflected in the military and political changes that have occurred since the invasion.

Quantitatively, the 70,000-strong original troop contingent has grown steadily during this period to number between 115,000 and 140,000.[10]

Tactics and deployment of forces have also changed. By 1984, the DRA soldiers who in earlier years were used for direct combat had proven so untrustworthy that Soviet troops were replacing them. During the April 1984 Panjshir offensive, 20,000 Soviet ground troops were accompanied by only about 2,000 DRA soldiers, of whom about 400 reportedly defected on their way to the front.[11]

The makeup of Soviet troops has also changed. In 1983–1984 there was an ever greater use of airborne troops. Though they often suffered heavy casualties, they at least earned the *mujahideen* respect as fighting men. Soviet casualties have risen (some 500 were killed in the April 1984 Panjshir offensive alone) largely as a result of their more aggressive tactics and because of extensive *mujahideen* use of antivehicle and antipersonnel-mines. The latter tactic has led to greater Soviet deployment of casualty prone sappers where none was needed before.

Similarly, improved *mujahideen* antiaircraft capabilities against low-flying targets has led to higher operational altitudes for helicopter gunships and fixed wing ground attack planes, and to the employment of high-altitude strategic bombers for carpet bombing of certain areas. Meanwhile, however, the Soviet air force has been field testing its arms and munitions, from the SU-25 ground support plane to concussion bombs and a "liquid fire" incendiary substance that remains inert until stepped on or driven over, whereupon it bursts into flames.[12]

Soviet mistrust of their DRA allies is shown in many ways. When large-scale offensives are launched, the DRA command is not informed until the last possible minute. Where the range of the aircraft permits, air strikes originate in Central Asia, presumably to ensure the ground security of the planes and to guarantee that the targets are surprised.[13]

Guerrilla operations have become more aggressive. Whereas in earlier times Kabul and some other major centers were relatively safe for the occupiers, urban attacks have now reached such levels that there are no safe havens for Soviet troops in the country. Even the well-guarded air base at Bagram was attacked during a snowstorm in January 1985, a season that in previous years would have seen a hiatus in guerrilla activity.[14]

The Soviet answer to the stepped-up resistance has been an unacknowledged scorched-earth policy designed to destroy the *mujahideen*'s civilian-support base. The previous policy of executing hostages (especially village elders) in areas where the resistance had been active slowly grew into wholesale terror against all adults of a given village. During 1982 this became exemplary annihilation of selected villages and all their living inhabitants, human as well as animal. In late 1983 the policy broadened again into total devastation of whole areas from the air, in order to destroy the agricultural infrastructure, make the countryside uninhabitable, and force the resistance to support itself. Civilian survivors were impelled to migrate either abroad as refugees or into the cities, where they could be more easily controlled. It is still too early to judge how effective this policy will be, but history shows that the selfsame Russian strategy, attempted during the nineteenth century in the Caucasus Mountains against a foe extraordinarily like the Afghans, did not result in the anticipated quick victory.[15]

If the military circumstances in Afghanistan are still unresolved, the political situation since the invasion has been chaotic. On the *mujahideens* side, independent groups have set themselves up in Pakistan, competing with each other for whatever foreign military aid is offered. Their fighting contingents inside Afghanistan have tended to be concentrated in certain areas, and those making their way to or from their home territories have often had to pass through hostile groups' provinces. Armed clashes between *mujahideen* associations have been common. Furthermore, in the early stages of the conflict the leaders in the field had little interest in anything but warfare, be it against the Soviets, the DRA, or guerrilla competitors. Most of the country had no effective civil government.

Over time, however, certain more responsible figures have begun to emerge. One such is the Panjshir Valley's Ahmad Shah Massoud, a dynamic young Islamic republican who has proven capable of leading in both military and civilian affairs. Under his guidance, by mid–1985 the strategic Panjshir had survived nine major offensives by Soviet and DRA troops. Massoud also organized the valley into districts, each of which was self-governing in most matters but responsible to Massoud for levies of fighting men and support of *mujahideen* operations. Schools and mosques were opened, and an Islamic judicial system was set up. Military service was either full-time or dovetailed with farming obligations. Moreover, Massoud was able to mobilize neighboring independent *mujahideen* groups to co-operate in joint military operations against the common enemy. In April 1984, on the eve of the Soviets' seventh Panjshir offensive, such combined operations closed down the vital Kabul Kunduz road link, delaying the assault and requiring an airlift of fuel before it could be launched. Similar preemptive strikes by the resistance occurred in late March 1985.[16]

Other *mujahideen* leaders have also been successful in setting up civil administrations. As each has become established, he has extended the area under his control. So far there have been no known clashes in the few cases where these territories have abutted on each other. The potential for conflict is there, but the new leaders seem to have a better understanding of the need for cooperation than most of the purely military field commanders or the exiles in Pakistan. A slow coalescing of the resistance seems to be occurring, even though the prerequisite for an alternative government to the DRA—a political program and organization that is acceptable to a convincing majority of the resistance groups—has yet to be devised.

In contrast to the factionalism in the resistance, which in most cases seems to be relatively recent, tactical, and still somewhat open to compromise, the previously noted cleavage in the PDPA and DRA—the fight between *Parcham* and *Khalq*—has acquired the solidity of a traditional Afghan family feud. The fundamental personal hostility between Nur Mohammed Taraki and Babrak Karmal has been adopted as a matter of course by their respective followers, whose upbringing demands that they continue to visit vengeance on one another without regard to time or space. Personal animosities are the natural offspring of politics anywhere, but in the Afghan context they descend to the level of physical violence and not infrequently to murder. The *Parcham/Khalq* controversy already has outlived one of the original protagonists (Taraki) and doubtless will outlive Karmal as well.[17]

The relative strength of *Parcham* and *Khalq* has varied over the years, but at the time of the Soviet invasion *Khalq* held the overwhelming edge in numbers. In 1980, however, *Parcham* had the crucial Soviet backing that allowed it to take over the most critical leadership positions. As in previous uneasy unions between the two, there was an effort to alternate *Parchamis* and *Khalqis* in the most important leadership posts, in order to produce an apparent balance. Unlike the *Parchamis*, however, the *Khalqis* in such positions were those who had taken little part in the internecine struggle in earlier years and whose loyalty lay more to the USSR than to any given faction. Nevertheless, an Afghan feud takes on a life of its own, and Minister of Interior Sayed Mohammed Gulabzoy, for example, the unacknowledged head of *Khalq* since the death of Amin, appears to retain his grudge toward the *Parchamis*, which is returned with interest.[18] The rivalry is even fiercer at lower levels.

Since the invasion, the *Parchamis* have steadily gained in relative strength, from around twenty-five percent of the PDPA in 1980 to about forty percent in 1984.[19] They have a dominant position in KhAD, the intelligence service, an advantage offset by *Khalqi* control of Gulabzoy's security police service, Sarandoy. What remains of the army after casualties and desertions is probably mostly *Khalq*, but *Parcham* doubtless has increased its representation in recent years because of the power of its patronage.

Even were the PDPA united, it would not be viable in Afghanistan. According to its own claim, it had 134,000 members as of mid–1985, less than 1 percent of the population, and that figure is unquestionably exaggerated by a factor of two to five.[20] The Party survives only through the support of the Soviet occupation forces. Estimates of the territory controlled by the government hover around 10–20 percent, but in neither provincial seats nor the national capital can security be guaranteed at all times, even with Soviet help. Political anniversary dates are as important nowadays to the DRA as they have always been to the USSR, yet in 1984 celebration of Saur Revolution Day (26 April) was canceled in Herat and Kandahar, the second two most important regional centers after Kabul. In two other cities where parades were held, Ghazni and Charikar, they were the occasion for *mujahideen* attacks that inflicted heavy casualties. Even more embarrassing to the regime, in Kabul itself the gala celebration of the PDPA's twentieth anniversary—the topic of lyrical DRA media coverage since mid-1984 and an occasion to which distinguished guests from all over the Communist world were invited—was postponed without explanation from 1 January to 10 January 1985. Continuous *mujahideen* rocket attacks on the capital at the end of December, by day as well as by night, undoubtedly caused the delay.[21]

Despite Soviet protection, in 1984 the PDPA claimed to have Party committees in only 61 of Afghanistan's 89 cities and "large administrative districts," a decrease of 9 since a similar tabulation in 1983. Moreover, of 285 medium and small districts, only 114 had Party committees in 1983, though this number allegedly jumped to 207 in 1984.[22] If one accepts these official figures (and they almost certainly are inflated, at least in reference to the smaller, rural districts), they show that there is nominal PDPA representation in only about 70 percent of the country.

In the latter half of 1985, there were signs that Soviet strategies at last were beginning to enjoy some marginal success. Certain Afghan villages were declaring "neutrality," wishing to be associated neither with the government nor with the *mujahideen*. Mikhail Gorbachev's dynamic approach to politics and his belligerence toward Pakistan, expressed not only verbally but in transborder air and artillery attacks on Afghan refugee settlements inside that country, raised worries of possible new Soviet aggression. There were some indications of intelligence successes: individual homes where transient *mujahideen* had enjoyed hospitality were being destroyed, showing that an informant network was finally beginning to function in some villages. There was a steady drain of Afghan intelligentsia both from their homeland and from Pakistan, seeking a new life further afield.

Counteracting these factors, however, were others at least as important. The *mujahideen* were starting to get better weapons. Their manpower was better trained and more effective. In the summer 1985 offensive in Paktia, where the USSR was attempting to close off the weapons supply lines from Pakistan, the resistance actually forced Soviet forces to retreat in some salients. Aircraft losses were mounting steadily. Pakistan, which had stonewalled Soviet threats, received a shipment of Stinger antiaircraft missiles to ward off the Soviet transborder raids. Overall, the security situation for the Soviet forces appeared to be deteriorating, in spite of their more aggressive tactics.

Meanwhile, casualties have already risen because of these maneuvers, and they will doubtless rise again as the resistance gets the greater foreign aid that has been promised. Probably more important in the long run than any momentary field success on either side is the mounting army of Soviet eyewitnesses, military and civilian, to the falsity of their own propaganda and the inability of their arms to crush the resistance. By 1986, nearly a half million Soviet persons will have gained firsthand knowledge of the real situation in Afghanistan. In spite of the oaths of silence extracted from all who served there, the knowledge of what is going on inevitably will spread.

Domestic Soviet Perceptions of the War

In a country where public opinion is only the sum of its guarded private opinions, there is no easy way to determine what that opinion is. The problem is not just one for external observers but for the Soviet leaders themselves. To paraphrase the late Andrey Amalrik, the KGB spends

Table 10–1
Reported Losses in Afghanistan from Three Ukrainian Districts[34]

District	Population	Killed	Badly Wounded	Lightly Wounded	Total
Irshava Rayon	94,200	111	45	91	247
Sualyava Rayon	52,300	52	—	—	52
Muchachevo Rayon	103,000	122	145	—	267
TOTAL	249,500	285	190	91	566

millions to stifle all dissent, then spends millions more to find out what people are really thinking.

On the subject of Afghanistan, however, there are five general sources of information, each of them skewed in its own way, that cast some light on both official and unofficial Soviet views of their Afghan adventure: official Soviet media; Soviet dissidence as reflected in *samizdat* publications; interviews with prisoners and deserters from the Soviet forces in Afghanistan, as well as with other Soviet defectors; encounters that Western journalists and others have had with Soviet citizens still in the USSR; and surveys of Soviet citizens traveling abroad. Though each of these sources is liable to exaggerate or suppress information—or even deliberately misinform its audience—the aggregate of their various, often sharply differing views is instructive. By far the most prolific of the sources is, of course, Soviet propaganda, and this section of our study will focus on its description and interpretation.

Before embarking on a study of individual themes, it is important to look at the overall volume of reporting and to hazard some interpretations as to the significance of changes in it.

For the first three days after Soviet troops commenced hostilities, the Soviet media remained silent about the invasion; the first acknowledgments came only on 30 December. During January, however, the coverage was extensive. A count of Soviet items on Afghanistan translated by the Foreign Broadcast Information Service (FBIS) (Table 10–1) shows the pattern of coverage that followed over the next months and years.[23]

At the outset, about two-thirds of the coverage was in non-Soviet languages, reflecting a perceived need to meet the storm of international outrage on its own ground. As long as the Soviet leaders still believed that their arms would soon prevail, they probably thought there was less reason to address the domestic than the foreign audience. When victory did not materialize, however, and when the Afghans continued to make international headlines by fighting back, the proportion of propaganda for use at home and abroad was reversed.

During 1980, there was a general downward trend in the volume of reporting, both for foreign and domestic audiences. Ignoring the most prominent peaks and valleys, the overall level seemed to stabilize during 1981 and 1982 (Brezhnev's last years) before dipping again in 1983 (Andropov's administration). There was a rise under Chernenko, peaking just before the dismissal of Marshal Ogarkov in October 1984, and trending down again thereafter. So far in Gorbachev's administration the level has remained low.

It is probably significant that in 1981 more attention was given to the Soviet than the foreign audience, and with only a few exceptions that predominance has prevailed ever since. This seems to indicate that since that time the leaders have perceived a greater need to redress unfavorable opinion about the war at home than abroad, a change from an offensive to a defensive propaganda posture.

The brief increase in coverage following Brezhnev's death in November 1982 appeared to be part of Yury Andropov's program to open up certain controversial areas to more public scrutiny. Projection of the official view for both domestic and foreign audiences was increased, and for the former there was somewhat more realism in the reporting. After only a brief surge, however, the coverage declined again, reaching a nadir in September, before starting a general upward trend that peaked during the second half of 1984, reaching levels unseen since 1980.

The volume and targeting of Soviet propaganda held at roughly constant levels through January 1985, but in February and March, when Konstantin Chernenko entered his final decline, there was a sharp drop. It appeared as if Mikhail Gorbachev might be examining his Afghan options closely before committing himself to his predecessors' policies. Thereafter, the volume resumed its former level, its content reflecting on the one hand a dogged perseverance to achieve total conquest, yet on the other some intriguing hints of preparation for an eventual retreat.

In examining these data, it is important to understand that the *absolute* volume of reporting, even during its most intense periods, has been relatively insignificant. During the peak month of September 1984, FBIS showed Moscow television and *Pravda* carrying only nine pieces each on Afghanistan, and only six of the eighteen had an immediate human interest dimension, that is a personalized account of life in Afghanistan as opposed to reiterations of dry political positions or propaganda clichés. (Of the other thirty-two Afghan-related items FBIS noted in domestic media that month, only five had a human interest angle.) Even though Soviet papers are much briefer and television time is more limited than in the United

States, it is startling that peak reporting in the USSR's most important news outlets would each give only twice-weekly, largely impersonal coverage to an active war zone where Soviet troops were engaged in daily, mortal combat.

(Subsequently, Moscow television has shown occasional cautious coverage of what purports to be combat action in Afghanistan, though without any bloodshed depicted on the screen. When this article was written, it was still too early to reach any conclusion whether such coverage represents an important trend.)

Regarding reporting from other sources, it has been much more limited. The most incisive *samizdat* criticism of the invasion has come from several documents most of which, interestingly, appeared in the Baltic States and western Ukraine. This may be a reflection of a disproportionate allocation of troops from these areas to serve in Afghanistan, as well as of greater restiveness by the local populations there. In terms of time distribution, *samizdat* coverage spans the whole period since the invasion.

Prisoners and deserters from the Soviet occupation forces provide another limited pool of information. In addition to those who have appeared in Western Europe and the United States, some 200–300 are thought to be in *mudjaheddin* hands, but unfortunately there has been no known effort to interview them systematically. Because the resistance took no prisoners in the early days of the occupation, those who survive today mostly date from 1982 or later. Although their willingness to be interviewed at all presupposes a degree of anti-Soviet bias, there is enough consistency in their accounts to lend confidence in their overall reliability.[24]

Interviews with Soviet citizens by American visitors to the USSR and by journalists posted there present a picture of Soviet public opinion that is at best inconsistent and at worst contradictory. The extent to which this reflects the biases of the various reporters, the true opinions of their Soviet contacts, or the latter's chameleon-like adaptation to the most politically secure coloration when talking to a foreigner can only be guessed. Certainly it is fair to ascribe more weight of honesty to the Soviet person who dares criticize his regime openly than to one who parrots the Party line verbatim. It is probably significant that reports of wholehearted condemnation of the Afghan invasion by Soviet individuals to Western contacts seemed to swell immediately after Andropov's "open door" policy of more comprehensive and accurate reporting.

Two public opinion surveys carried out among Soviet travelers to the West provide more clearcut attitudes. The first, conducted during 1984, showed approximately 50 percent of the sampling (over a thousand persons) had no fixed opinion about the war. Another 25 percent supported the Soviet position unreservedly. The last 25 percent were resolutely opposed to their government's involvement. The "opposed" category is higher than might have been expected among a Soviet group that by its very presence abroad implied that it enjoyed the trust of the highest authorities. Communist party members in the above sampling were more loyal: 55 percent supported their government, 8 percent opposed the war, and 37 percent had no opinion. Nevertheless, given the duty of every Communist to support the official line, the "no opinion" in this case must be taken as an indirect expression of dissent. A less formal, ongoing poll by an émigré organization in 1984 reflected very much the same distribution of opinion, but through 1985 showed an every greater polarization. Virtually no Soviet citizens remained without an opinion, and there was a radical swing toward rejection of the war, with over 90 percent of those contacted voicing opposition to their government's policies.[25]

The Official Line

Some basic features of the line taken in Soviet media have remained constant and continue to be repeated regularly: the Soviet force consists of a "limited contingent" invited "repeatedly" during 1978–79 by the "legal government" of the DRA under the terms of the 1978 Soviet/Afghan Treaty of Friendship and Cooperation and/or under Article 51 of the UN Charter; the troops will be there "temporarily" (later modified to "as long as outside interference in Afghan internal affairs continues from abroad," an interesting catch-22 formulation); Soviet troops doing their "internationalist duty" are needed merely to bolster the DRA while it continues to be victorious in the "undeclared war" that has been waged against it since 1978 by the United States, China, and their various allies; the immediate enemy are small groups of "bandits," "mercenaries," and/or "counterrevolutionaries," led by disgruntled representatives of the former ruling class; they are trained in Pakistan by U.S. instructors to murder, torture, rape, and pillage, with special attention to attacks on women, children, and the elderly; armed by these same instructors with modern weapons made in the United States and Egypt, including "neuroparalytic" and other chemical warfare weapons as well as toy-shaped boobytrap mines, they concentrate on destroying schools, hospitals, and mosques; although they have deceived or bullied a small part of the civilian population into collaboration, they have lost all popularity with the Afghan public; to an ever greater degree Afghans are pledging allegiance to the DRA government and showing their gratitude to the Soviet troops.

Almost all of the above is instantly recognizable as lies to the Soviet soldier on the scene. True, he is unlikely to concern himself with the larger political justifications for his presence in Afghanistan; even if he could unravel the propagandists' misinformation in this respect, his immediate misfortunes eclipse the philosophical base for it all, be that base right or wrong.[26] Most of the rest of the official line, however, he knows from personal experience to be false, especially the Afghans' alleged fondness for their Soviet "protectors."

Having been forced to commit exactly the kind of attack on civilians and villages that Soviet propaganda ascribes to their foes, the soldiers are not inclined to take seriously other "mirror-image" atrocity stories. This is particularly true when the accusation involves such sophisticated weapons as nerve gas or small, toy-like antipersonnel mines, whose use by Soviet forces roused international condemnation before Soviet propaganda tried to turn the tables. Even soldiers with no personal knowledge of their own forces' use of such weapons are aware that their employment by the barefoot guerrillas would be little more than an unnecessarily complicated way of committing suicide.

The reverse-image compulsion of Soviet propagandists also permits some deductions concerning little-known realities. For example, at a time before there were many prisoners available for firsthand accounts, suspiciously frequent pictures of smiling, happy soldiers shown in *Krasnava Zvezda* already had caused some cynical analysts to conclude that there were serious morale difficulties among the troops. These were soon confirmed by deserters who had found their occupation duties unbearable.[27]

Another indirect sign of trouble is what seems like a careful effort to portray racially integrated units working smoothly as a team. In almost all *Krasnava Zvezda* descriptions of military squads there is a racial mix of Soviet nationalities, all of whom enjoy an easy camaraderie with each other. Those who have served in Afghanistan confirm that this picture is less than accurate. Central Asians stick to themselves and display contempt for their ethnically alien comrades, even when the latter themselves represent an oppressed minority. Some Western visitors to Central Asia have also noted a quiet contempt for Russians that is expressed indirectly. For example, even among Tajiks who consider themselves intellectually beyond the attraction of Islam and culturally superior to the Afghans, there is outright scorn for the Soviet propaganda line that the *mujahideen* are Chinese or American mercenaries.[28]

What is not said in propaganda is as important to Soviet perceptions as what is said. For example, the deliberately vague phrase "limited contingent" seems to evoke an image of even more troops than are there. Among Soviet citizens willing to hazard a guess, the estimates seem to run 50 to 100 percent higher than those ascribed to Western intelligence sources.[29]

The media say very little about another problem consistently described by defectors, the widespread use of drugs by young soldiers never before exposed to them.[30] So far this does not seem to have caused noticeable problems in the USSR, but it could well prove to be a social time bomb.

Yet another silent issue is the question of casualties. Until 1982, the Soviet media ignored this matter almost completely. In fact, casualties were implicitly denied in repeated statements that "not a single Soviet unit has taken part in suppressing counterrevolutionary bands."[31] In 1981, in an obvious effort to conceal losses, the practice of shipping home war dead in zinc-lined coffins was abruptly suspended. When the first news of deaths finally was released, it was in provincial papers that usually avoided mentioning Afghanistan; the soldiers simply had died "doing their internationalist duty." With one (probably accidental) exception it was not until 1983, over three years after the invasion, that the central organs unambiguously listed a few specific combat fatalities in Afghanistan. Only in 1988 the overall official figures on the number killed were released. Till then the occasional human interest story or the presentation of a posthumous medal acknowledged the casualties that Western estimates already in 1984 put at roughly 10,000 killed and 40,000 wounded.[32]

To the Soviet citizen this prolonged reticence meant only that the dimensions of the losses were huge. Estimates of up to 50,000 killed were not uncommon. Even when aware of the lower Western estimates, some former Soviet soldiers derided them as baseless guesses made in offices far from the battlefield.[33] For some regions of the USSR whose conscripts seem to have been singled out for Afghanistan duty—and where losses have been disproportionately high—the price of the war has been heavy indeed. In three rural Ukrainian districts, for example, incomplete data on casualties published in mid 1984 in the *samizdat* journal *Chronicle of the Catholic Church in the Ukraine* indicates losses of slightly more than one killed per thousand population (Table 10–1).

These figures, if extrapolated for the whole Soviet population, would imply losses of over a half million killed and wounded, a toll that not even the optimistic *mujahideen* would claim. Whether by accident or design, the USSR seems to have concentrated on using its national minorities in the western part of the country to fight its Central Asian War. This impression is confirmed, in part, by reports that those conscripts chosen for duty in the 40th Army—the unit responsible for Afghanistan—almost invariably come from rural districts in northern and western USSR, probably on the theory that geographic removal and rural isolation will help disperse and lower the impact of losses.[35]

One peculiarly Soviet quirk in the reporting of casualties is that they all appear to have occurred during *defensive* operations, an insistent note that seems to fulfill a basic need for self-justification. To this day, Soviet media have never admitted directly that their forces have engaged in offensive strikes. Since 1983, the only descriptions of hazardous operations have been actions such as mine clearing, helicopter rescue missions, or convoy escort duty. At no point has any mention been made of air strikes, of offensive armor probes, or of infantry attacks, all of them standard missions for the occupation forces. In order to describe them the press has resorted to an extraordinary euphemism: The "attackers" and "defenders" (both carefully hemmed by quotation marks) have been supposedly part of training exercises that happen to be occurring in Afghanistan. The fact that some of the "attackers" have been decorated for combat heroism and even for calling down fire on their own positions leaves little doubt that the activities being described transcended maneuvers.[36]

No such inhibitions are in evidence when it comes to describing DRA military activities. In fact, in operations such as the Panjshir offensive in April 1984, all credit was given to the 2,000-man Afghan contingent and none to the 20,000 Soviet troops who bore the brunt of the conflict. Inasmuch as the DRA forces lost almost as many men (400) to desertion on their way to the front as the Soviets lost killed in action after the battle commenced (500), the allocation of credit cannot have appealed to any Soviet soldier who survived and read the official accounts.[37]

There were signs in 1984 that the government was cautiously trying to sample public opinion about the war. A letter in *Komsomolskava Pravda*, allegedly from a Soviet sergeant on duty in Afghanistan, complained that not enough was being published about what life was really like for the troops there. He also complained about the army's low prestige, as illustrated by a girl in the USSR who had written to a colleague saying she found it embarrassing to be seen on the street with a man in uniform. He hastened to add that he himself had no hesitation about fulfilling his internationalist duties, but he also made a point of noting that some of his fellow citizens used high-level connections to avoid service. The editors solicited readers' opinions on his letter, but they waited for nearly five months before publishing a brief summary of a few readers' comments.[38] The weak results and the delay in publishing them may indicate that relatively few of the responses were favorable to the government's position.

Another February 1984 *Komsomolskava Pravda* letter, however, touched a much more responsive nerve. It dealt with the tribulations of a paraplegic veteran returning to a cold reception by the local Komsomol and Party bureaucrats. This produced an overwhelming reaction among readers (5,000 letters to the paper plus hundreds of phone calls, letters, and packages to the veteran himself), which were written up in considerable detail, spread over many columns of subsequent issues. Moreover, the follow-up articles also appeared much sooner than in the case of the sergeant.[39] From the public reactions to these two letters, it appears that there is widespread sympathy for the war's victims without any corresponding support for the war itself.

The frequency distribution of Soviet human interest stories on the Afghan war during 1984 may also possibly reflect a somewhat hesitant probing of public opinion. Two or three such stories would appear within a few days of each other in such outlets as *Krasnava Zvezda*, to be followed by ten days to two weeks of reporting limited to the impersonal, political aspects of the fray. Gradually increasing throughout the first eight months of the year, the human interest stories peaked during the last ten days of September, then fell off in October and November. From the latter part of December until at least mid-summer 1985, they all but vanished. The possible reasons for this pattern can only be conjectured, but they could include a determination that too much emotionally charged news about the war was bad for the Soviet people. Far from firing them with enthusiasm for the drama of combat, such coverage may only have stiffened their opposition to it. If so, the dismissal in October of Chief of Staff Marshal Ogarkov, the most public-relations oriented Soviet military figure in recent history, may be taken less as a cause for the decline of such stories than as an effect of their counterproductivity.[40]

Tying in with the "defensive" note has been the consistent effort to present Afghanistan as some kind of a logical sequence to the Civil War and Great Patriotic War, with the ghosts of preceding generations of soldiers looking down approvingly on their descendants. There is little indication that this appeal to bygone patriotic fervors has had much effect; conjuring up a *mujahideen* menace to the fabric of the Soviet state that would match that of the White Guards or the German *Wehrmacht* is asking a bit too much of the most persuasive propagandist. It does, however, seem to reflect a somewhat desperate effort to sound some note that would increase popular enthusiasm for the Afghanistan venture.

Most of our unofficial Soviet sources have regarded service in Afghanistan in somewhat less patriotic lights:

—An opportunity for excitement, foreign travel, and the glamor of heroism on return. This motivation has not been admitted by anyone, but two of the prisoners/defectors interviewed in Pakistan said they thought this might have played a role for some of their comrades.[41]

—An opportunity to make money or get consumer goods not otherwise available in the USSR.[42]

—A duty to be accepted "if the Fatherland asks" (from a teenager in uniform, apparently just out of basic training).[43]

—A duty which does not concern me (because I have a deferment) but is accepted with aplomb or even relish "by all my friends."[44]
—A duty to be avoided by all possible means.[45]

The last authoritative full statement of the Soviet position on Afghanistan before Chernenko's death appeared in a *Pravda* editorial article in mid-February. It summarized all of the various well-known rationalizations and justifications for the invasion and continued occupation, but it did break new ground in one respect: in explaining Afghanistan's importance to the USSR it put in first place the need to deny to the United States the use of Afghan territory to spy against the sensitive areas of Uzbekistan, Tajikistan, Turkmenistan, and Kazakhstan. Only in second place did it list the "rendering of international assistance" to the DRA "national democratic regime."[46] This is the first time since 1981 that state interests have been advanced as a rationale for Soviet actions in Afghanistan, and the priority they seem to enjoy in this article over ideological considerations may possibly be a harbinger of how the Gorbachev team will approach the issue. Not only was the problem put on a state basis, but the purported imperialist intentions—establishment of an espionage base—is both more negotiable and less emotionally charged than earlier, totally unreasonable allegations that Afghanistan would be turned into a base for armed aggression against the USSR.

Balancing Soviet propaganda against the evidence of unofficial Soviet sources permits the following conclusions:

1. The gradually more realistic—if still not objective—appraisal of the war in the Soviet press may reflect a better understanding by the leaders of its potential difficulties.
2. Vacillations in the volume of propaganda at various times may indicate leadership hesitations over the cost of the Afghan operation and concerns about public reaction. Such a conclusion would belie the commonly held belief that the USSR since 1980 has proceeded with great confidence in Afghanistan.
3. Morale at home and in the field has been a problem, most especially for the soldiers who have been conscripted for occupation duty. There appears to have been a sharp increase in domestic revulsion against the war during 1985. Even those Soviet veterans who otherwise support the Soviet position must be furious that the DRA forces get most of the combat credit. The diminution since late 1984 of the "glory" angle to Soviet reporting may reflect a concern that too much blood and thunder might become counterproductive in justifying the war to the Soviet people.

4. The prominence of the "state" rationale for the occupation (defense of the USSR's southern flank) over its ideological dimension ("internationalist duty") could herald a significant change in Moscow's official view of the war. If the ideological element is allowed to fade away, the chances for a negotiated settlement will improve markedly.

5. Racial tensions, especially between Soviet non-orientals on the one hand and Central Asians on the other, have grown sharper and will not subside as long as the war drags on.

The View from the Top

As defectors have noted, subordinates in the Soviet system are loath to report bad news to their superiors, especially if that bad news reflects in any way on their own or the superiors' judgment. There is a built-in incentive to forward only information that supports the wisdom of the decision maker, at least within one's own chain of command. This is a human condition that perhaps deserves a term of its own (Westmoreland's Contortion?), and it is present to some degree in all societies. In a rigid command structure like the USSR's, with decision-making responsibility concentrated to an inordinate degree at the top of the power pyramid, it is more noticeable than in most other societies. As Ronald R. Pope has argued persuasively, it is highly probable that the Soviet leaders were misinformed before they marched into Afghanistan, and that they very likely continue to be misinformed today.[47]

Despite this built-in insulator, there are now some signs that the dimensions of their Afghan dilemma are being forced on the Soviet leaders' consciousness. One indication is the DRA's seeming decline in official favor. Year by year Soviet visitors to Kabul on important Party occasions have been steadily less prestigious. For the 1980 Saur Revolution anniversary, Central Committee member Zimyanin and Deputy Chairman of the USSR Council of Ministers Arkhipov attended. In 1981 there seems to have been no Soviet representation, possibly due to urban unrest in Kabul, but in 1982 the second secretary of the Moscow *Obkom* and another, lesser known deputy chairman of the USSR Council of Ministers, Borisenkov, appeared. By 1983, a fifth anniversary and thus presumably worthy of special attention, the rank was down to a first secretary of the Uzbek Communist party (I. Usmankhodzhayev) and a deputy chairman of the RSFSR's—not USSR's—Council of Ministers. The 1984 Saur anniversary had no known Soviet representation. Finally, the 1985 gala celebration of the PDPA's 20th anniversary, the subject of a huge propaganda buildup, again found Usmankhodzhayev, now under something of a cloud in the wake of the disclosure of widespread corruption in the Uzbek Party and state *apparats*, as the ranking Soviet guest.[48]

As noted above, the security situation in Kabul would not permit holding the PDPA's 20th birthday on schedule. Whatever other displeasing information about Afghanistan might have been concealed from Soviet leaders by their subordinates, this was one demonstration of *mujahideen* strength that could not be ignored. Afghan Communists consider anniversary dates as sacred as do their Soviet mentors, and the postponement must have given the lie to soothing assurances from the field as nothing else could have.

Opinion into Action?

Conventional wisdom says that the Soviet people not only accept their country's foreign policy but—in contrast to their view of domestic affairs—they accept or even applaud it.[49] Having endured multiple foreign invasions over the centuries, czarist Russia bequeathed to the USSR an uncharitable view of the outside world that the events of the first quarter century of Soviet rule did little to dispel. The common Soviet predisposition to believe the worst of foreigners is, unfortunately, based on firsthand experience by at least the older members of the society, and it seems to be accepted to a large degree by the younger generation as well.

Support for Soviet foreign policy is not, however, total and unquestioning. According to Alexander Shtromas's analysis, popular acceptance of Soviet international behavior is qualified by a concern that too abrasive an approach to the outside world might trigger exactly the sort of nuclear conflict that the people know must be avoided at all costs. The logic by which the Kremlin translates the need for domestic defense against foreign aggression into an expansionist policy of commitment to national liberation movements and to support for remote regimes does not sit easily with most Soviet citizens. Not only are such policies threatening to peace but they are perceived as an expensive luxury, especially when modest improvements in domestic Soviet living standards are no longer the order of the day.[50]

The crucial question is whether in any area of commitment there is a clear foreign threat to the Soviet homeland. If the Kremlin can make the people believe that such a threat exists, then there will be a willingness for sacrifice on behalf of the state. This is certainly a more believable line when speaking of an adjacent territory like Afghanistan than of an Ethiopia or Nicaragua. It also explains the peculiarly warped nature of the Afghan War as portrayed in official propaganda, with its insistence on the "defensive" nature of Soviet actions and its identification of the current conflict with earlier, more popular wars.

As we have noted, however, it is asking too much of a Soviet soldier to equate his *mujahideen* opponent with a Nazi storm trooper. It is clear to all who serve in Afghanistan that it is they who are the aggressors. More to the point, they are *unsuccessful* aggressors. They have been put not only morally but physically on the defensive, and their task of pacification stretches into an indefinite and uncertain future.

Unlike the Soviet forces who in the 1920s and 1930s eliminated resistance in Central Asia and Mongolia, today's troops are driven neither by revolutionary enthusiasm nor by Stalinist terror. Their primary motivation is simply individual survival. Moreover, they do not have the luxury of conducting their operations in private, screened from the eyes of the rest of the world. Although the USSR has done all in its power to monopolize information about Afghanistan, including a program of disinformation in the Western world[51] and frank death threats to journalists who accompany resistance groups,[52] news of Afghan developments cannot be contained or shaped to Soviet liking. Not only in the free world, but in the USSR itself, the truth of what is happening is spreading inexorably. Given the roughly half million eye witnesses who have returned from service in the country, there are perhaps five million other Soviet citizens who have heard their firsthand accounts. That audience will grow, as will the rumor market for secondhand versions.

The question, however, is not so much what the Soviet public knows as how it acts. Here again, conventional wisdom says that the average Soviet citizen has only an apathetic reaction to official policies that are against his interests. The hopelessness of voicing opposition leads to grudging silent acceptance, an attitude that carries its own long-term social costs. According to Pope, these include absenteeism, alcoholism, poor work habits, and moral degradation, to name but a few.

Although in the early 1980s some Western journalists wrote of the Soviet public's ignorance of and apathy about the Afghan war,[53] with the passage of time it was seen more and more quite literally as a life and death matter for draft-age citizens. Reports of draft dodging, of attempted bribery of assignment officers and even of extortion by those same officers were becoming more frequent. As early as late 1982, handmade fliers in Russian protesting the war were posted almost simultaneously in European Russian centers as well as in Central Asia, the Ukraine, and the Baltic States. Dissident associations like the Helsinki Watch Group, the independent trade union organization SMOT, and a feminist group registered their protests. Reports of demonstrations at isolated mobilization points were becoming more common in 1985.[54]

In 1984, five persons were reportedly arrested in Dushanbe, capital of Soviet Tajikistan, for distributing protest leaflets about the war. Said to have links with the Afghan *mujahideen*, the five were supposed to have been taken to Moscow for interrogation.[55] Although there has been no subsequent confirmation of this incident, the fact that Soviet citizens believed and reported it is significant; the *perception* of dissent in the USSR is at least as important as its objective existence.

Reference has already been made to the desertion of Soviet soldiers. Most are still in Afghan hands as prisoners, some have found their way to the West, and a few have then decided to return home. Until early 1985, the USSR did not publicly acknowledge that anyone had deserted to the enemy. In January, however, after the return to Moscow of Nikolai Ryzhkov, TASS released a horror tale of what supposedly had happened to him after he defected, including allegations that the U.S. had ransomed him from the resistance, that it had drugged and nearly starved him, and that it had promised him a variety of sexual favors and a "new life" in return for anti-Soviet propaganda. The Western accounts of TASS's tirade, however, failed to note that it came out only in English, for foreign audiences. Not a word about Ryzhkov or his experiences appeared in the Soviet press.[56] Presumably there was some high-level concern that troops in the field might, on balance, find the treatment allegedly given him more attractive than odious.

Even more significant than simple deserters are those who have defected with the clear purpose of collaborating with the *mujahideen* against their former comrades. How many have made this decision is unknown; by taking such a step the men risk not only their own lives but they jeopardize the security of their families as well, and most have an understandable desire to remain anonymous. In 1983, some soldiers deserted because they thought they could join a free Russian regiment of which they had heard. By 1984, there was serious talk among the resistance of forming such a unit.[57] For Soviet officials old enough to recall the World War II Vlasov movement, such discussions must have raised unnerving specters.

A measure of the regime's concern about support for the war is evident in its exceptionally harsh treatment of Soviet citizens who have started or joined various pacifist movements in recent years. Forceful suppression of dissidence in the USSR is scarcely a new phenomenon, but the oppressive measures taken against an independent peace movement that started in 1982 were unusual even by Soviet standards. For example, a pregnant woman who helped found it was abducted and beaten by KGB personnel who refused to display their documents—and then was accused of attacking a policeman. In August 1985 penalties for draft dodging and for abetting draft dodgers were sharply increased.[58]

A Look to the Future

At this writing making predictions about Soviet policies is even riskier than normal. Mikhail Gorbachev is a new quantity, and there is doubt both whether and how he can reshape the USSR. The most that can be said is that he seems intent on doing so, and he has probably the best opportunity of any leader since Khrushchev. Concerning Afghanistan, he should take into account the following Afghan phenomena and their relation to other considerations of his leadership:

—The problem of Afghanistan will not go away for the USSR. On the contrary, it will almost surely intensify as outside support for the resistance increases and more sophisticated weapons find their way into *mujahideen* hands. The deteriorating military situation will call for a greater infusion of troops and equipment, raising the price of the war in blood and material. Indeed, in mid-1985 Gorbachev threatened to put in up to a half million troops to achieve a decisive victory, but so far has not followed up on his threat, which probably would only increase Soviet casualties without achieving the goal. The failure of the Soviet summer offensive in 1985, however, with its limited task of shutting down resistance supply lines, shows that the troops he has in the field are not adequate for their mission.

—Foreign assistance to the *mujahideen*, though quietly increasing, so far has been far from massive. Any increase in Soviet commitment will see a corresponding rise in arms deliveries, a relatively inexpensive strategic investment on the part of the West compared to the price the USSR would have to pay.[59]

—The conflict's economic cost to the USSR, though still relatively low, is both growing and assuming more relative importance because of other economic shortfalls. Meanwhile, the voice of the military in higher Kremlin councils, though still very loud indeed, has been muted to some degree in the past year by the dismissal of Marshal Ogarkov and the death of Defense Minister Ustinov. Gorbachev has a freer hand to reassert the supremacy of Party control over the military than any predecessor in recent decades.[60]

—If the level of conflict in Afghanistan rises, so too will its newsworthiness, both in the outside world where Soviet prestige continues to erode because of it, and, domestically, among increasing numbers of citizens with friends or relatives among the veterans. It is impossible to contain or completely to control information on such a charged subject. This is part of a much larger problem, the information explosion and how deal with it in a totalitarian state, but the Afghan issue presents an especially sharp challenge.

—A limited backlash against the war is already evident; a broader movement is increasingly likely. Unlike most previous dissident issues in the USSR, which have related to relatively narrow intellectual, ethnic, or religious interests, the Afghanistan War poses a potential threat to very broad segments of the population. Even such universal issues as violation of human rights, though affecting every citizen to some degree, are not as politically explosive; most Soviet citizens can avoid trouble with the authorities simply by keeping quiet and doing as they are told. Service in Afghanistan, on the other hand, threatens the silently obedient at least as much as the noisily dissenting. An issue that united the intelligentsia and broad masses of the people in opposition would be an unprecedented threat to the Party and state.

How Gorbachev will confront these dilemmas is anyone's guess. It seems likely that for the immediate future it will be too politico-ideologically expensive for him to organize a retreat. The status quo, however, appears to be increasingly untenable, and escalation—e.g., an aggressive push against Pakistan—would be fraught with extremely serious international risks without really solving the Afghan problem.[61]

As the pressures inside the USSR against further involvement in Afghanistan build, so too will repressive measures against any who try to voice them. At what point the resulting tensions become destabilizing, and what form that destabilization might take, can be predicted only in the most general terms. As long as state control is perceived by most citizens as increasingly efficient and invincible, the chances for a Novocherkassk type of scenario—a spontaneous explosion of popular outrage leading to a breakdown of state control—seem unlikely. The key word here, however, is increasingly. Unless the state increases its repression to keep pace with dissent, it will be perceived as losing control, yet that repression bears its own heavy costs. Inevitably there will come a time when further official duress will seem counterproductive, especially if there is no open opposition. Historically, it is just such times that produce flashpoints, e.g., the Hungarian Revolution in the wake of Khrushchev's secret speech at the 20th CPSU Congress.

Even before such a flashpoint is reached, however, there will be an impetus for conspiracy within the *nomenklatura* itself. Under the most stable conditions, intrigue is a dominant feature of Soviet politics; times of change, like the present, encourage would-be leaders to scheme for the future, and an acute unresolved dilemma, domestic or foreign, is an essential nucleus around which to build a dissenting faction. Afghanistan, with its relentless toll of blood, wealth, and national prestige certainly qualifies as one of the most obvious embarrassments inherited by the Gorbachev team. It unquestionably will prove an important catalyst in whatever political chemistries are bubbling behind the USSR's facade of placid conformism.

In the end, the critical factor will probably prove to be time. Many analysts have concluded that time is on the side of the USSR. Soviet military superiority and what is seen as infinite Russian patience are assumed to be adequate to crush the resistance in the long run. Indeed that line has even appeared in the Soviet press.[62] The USSR's own long-range intention to prevail is reflected in its wholesale destruction of rural Afghanistan and such programs as taking eight- and nine-year-old Afghan children to the USSR for ten years of schooling.[63] It is very much an open question, however, whether these measures can succeed before the divisive effects of the war inside the USSR itself force a change in policy. The Afghans are incredibly durable, and their culture is one that takes little account of time.

An old saying sums it up: "The Afghan waited a hundred years to take his vengeance—and cursed himself for his impatience."

Postscript

In the three years that have passed since this chapter was originally completed, there have been some fundamental changes in both the USSR and Afghanistan.

Mikhail Gorbachev's twin campaigns of *glasnost* (controlled candor in admitting shortcomings) and *perestroika* (restructuring) have survived their birth pains but have not yet produced a better standard of living for the Soviet people. One of the many reasons for this is that the workplace enthusiasm and discipline Gorbachev needed to bolster the economy were unattainable as long as the country was waging an unpopular foreign war.

In 1986, the erosion of official Soviet support for the war was signaled by Gorbachev's referral to it in February as a "bleeding wound" at the 27th Party Congress, by his appointment in May of ex-Khad chief Najib to replace Babrak Karmal as his Afghan viceroy, and by his symbolic (if largely false) withdrawal of six Soviet regiments in October. His disenchantment with the Afghan adventure was heightened in autumn by the appearance on the battlefield of sophisticated Stinger antiaircraft missiles. Soviet aircraft losses soared, as did ground troop casualties. DRA troop morale plummeted, and cooperation among the various *mujahideen* groups tightened markedly.

Nevertheless, in December 1986, Gorbachev turned out virtually the entire CPSU CC's Politburo and Secretariat to greet Najibullah and his matching entourage of PDPA officials. The reason for this surprising endorsement became apparent the following month, when Najibullah proclaimed a unilateral ceasefire, called for a "government of national reconciliation," and welcomed (in principle, at least) some sort of limited coalition with the less radical resistance movements. Such betrayal of revolutionary ideals might well have provoked the surviving *Khalqis*, still a majority in the army and regular police, into attempting a coup, if the Soviets had not demonstratively endorsed the new program.

It was a huge gamble by Gorbachev, and it did not pay off. The resistance ignored the ceasefire (as indeed did the DRA and Soviet forces), and as 1987 wore on, the level of fighting rose sharply. Regime calls for the refugees in Pakistan and Iran to return home went almost totally unheeded. An amnesty for regime opponents, including unnamed ranking *Khalqis* of the Amin regime, was announced in May, as was a sweeping modification of land reform that would permit many big landowners to reclaim their property. None is known to have accepted the offer. Concessions to businessmen, traders, and other bourgeois elements were proclaimed but without marked effect on the regime's security. Efforts to enlist popular support by building and repairing mosques and by asserting that the government was truly Islamic fell on deaf ears. Step by step, the regime was retreating, appearing to base its few remaining hopes for survival on appeasing all its foes.

In November, a political parties law and a new Constitution were proclaimed. Both had some trappings of democracy but—like everything else associated with the regime—were fatally tarred by their association with the Soviet occupiers. That same month the UN vote demanding a Soviet withdrawal rose to a new record high.

Early 1988 saw an amnesty for the leading *mujahideen* field commanders, until then under sentence of death. Finally, in February Gorbachev announced his intention to remove Soviet troops from Afghanistan within nine months of the signing of an agreement at the UN-sponsored "proximity talks" between Pakistan and the DRA in Geneva. The withdrawal started on 15 May, and half the troops were supposed to be out by 15 August. Although the retreat was somewhat behind schedule by the first days of August, the reason is believed to be more a combination of Soviet logistical ineptitude and mujahideen harassment than deliberate delaying tactics.

In short, Gorbachev's resolution of his Afghan dilemma is unquestionably one of retreat from the ill-advised military investment made by his predecessors, including not only the officially despised Brezhnev but Gorbachev's own personal mentors, Suslov and Andropov.[64]

The full price of this retreat has yet to be established. In the narrow focus of Afghanistan, military defeat has also meant ideological capitulation; Soviet commentators have bluntly acknowledged that, contrary to earlier beliefs, Afghanistan is not ready for socialism. At this writing, there seems to be a faint and dimming hope that the regime can somehow survive a Soviet withdrawal, but in effect Moscow is also abandoning its political investment as well. There remains only the economic connection, and the USSR has been feverishly trying to bolster old aid and trade links and establish new ones while it still can wield decisive influence. To the extent that the Afghan economy is tied to that of the USSR—and the major links were forged well before the 1979 invasion—the chances for survival of a viable economic connection appear relatively good.

At an immense price in blood and misery, Afghanistan has bought another era of independence. How long it will last cannot be predicted, but if the USSR itself survives, the economic links of today will inevitably grow into political pressures tomorrow. Whether these will ultimately result in a new military thrust is up to Kremlin leaders perhaps yet unborn.

Meantime, the implications of the retreat for the USSR are immense. Already the fires of nationalism are burning brightly in the Baltic States, Armenia, and Azerbaijan and there are more than a few embers glowing in Central Asia. Poland is smoldering ominously, and the rest of Eastern Europe has yet to realize the full implications of the announced termination of the Brezhnev Doctrine.

For average Soviet Russians, however, the uncertainties of *perestroika* may well be more important than the opportunities it offers. As many have noted, the authoritarian mechanism remains in place in the USSR, and until it is dismantled there can be no assurance that today's liberalization is permanent. Nevertheless, every day of its continued survival makes a return to absolutism less likely. It is a time of both hope and instability.

For Gorbachev personally, the period of retreat from Afghanistan may be, paradoxically, a time of relative security; as long as the withdrawal is incomplete, any usurper of power in the Kremlin must take responsibility for its final stages, and hence for at least a part of the defeat. Once it is over, however, Gorbachev's enemies can lay all the blame for "losing" Afghanistan on him. It is unlikely that they will overlook the opportunity. There is no reason to retract the judgment that political intrigue is bubbling just under the surface in the Kremlin, or that the potential for an intra-Party coup remains high.

Over the past decade Afghanistan has been usually viewed as the more or less passive target of initiatives taken by Moscow. The reverse, however, is also arguable: that events in that land are perhaps more important as causes than as effects. For example, if the Afghans' heroic resistance had not confounded Soviet expectations of a quick victory in 1980, today's Kremlin leader would more likely be the sabre-rattling Grigory Romanov or sinister Viktor Chebrikov than Gorbachev. Poland, which was only a whisker away from a Soviet invasion in 1981, would almost surely have suffered that fate. International tensions, which have eased in the last few years, would be at an all-time high, and the threat of a U.S.A.-USSR nuclear exchange, intentional or unintentional, would be much more immediate.

To the extent that these judgments are valid, the people of the world, perhaps first and foremost the citizens of the USSR, owe an immense debt of gratitude to the Afghans for their refusal to accept defeat. That debt must not be overlooked. The danger is that the world will lose interest in Afghanistan once it has ceased to be an East-West issue, and the Afghans will have to shoulder the immense task of rebuilding their war-shattered economy on their own.

Notes

1. Anthony Arnold, *Afghanistan's Two-Party Communism: Parcham and Khalq*, (Hoover Institution Press, 1983); and *Afghanistan: The Soviet Invasion in Perspective*, (Hoover Institution Press, 1985, second ed.). In retrospect, I believe that the *Parcham/Khalq* split may even have preceded the formal founding of the Party. The equality between *Parcham* and *Khalq* representation in the first Central Committee, like that which followed the Saur coup, seems too neat to be natural, and may well represent a compromise effort to achieve unity at an early stage. Regarding any doctrinal differences within *Khalq*, I have found none. Later Soviet efforts to ascribe different political outlooks to Taraki and Amin are unsubstantiated, although it seems likely that Amin viewed his nominal superior with benevolent contempt and intended making him merely a figurehead leader. It is quite probable that Karmal and the Kremlin had exactly the same views and intentions about Taraki when constructing their conspiracy.

2. Predictable controversy over the "offensive" versus "defensive" nature of the Soviet invasion broke out almost immediately in the West. George F. Kennan saw the Soviet involvement in Afghanistan as "primarily defensive," because they had gotten "sucked into (the invasion) involuntarily" after having "meddle(d) in Afghan politics" (*U.S. News and World Report*, 10 March 1980, 33). This rather curious definition of "defensive" is echoed by a few other analysts who see Soviet fear of Islamic nationalism spilling over into Soviet Central Asia as the dominating reason for the invasion. Indeed there is little question that the Soviet official position toward Islam changed after Khomeini came to power in Iran. As trenchantly analyzed by Professors Alexandre Bennigsen and Hélène Carrère d'Encausse, from the late 1960s to the late 1970s the

Kremlin regarded Islam as something to be manipulated in the interests of Soviet foreign policy, but thereafter it was treated ever more seriously as a rival ideology. Nevertheless, there was little danger of Islamic nationalist contagion from Afghanistan so long as a traditional government remained in power in Kabul; most Afghans are Sunnis, and there is no Afghan tradition of trying to proselytize in neighboring states. It was only the escalating—and only partially successful—Soviet economic, political, and ideological offensives that ultimately resulted in the birth of the *mudjaheddin* movement, thus actually helping to *create* such a danger for the USSR where none had existed before the Soviet-inspired Saur Revolution. If resistance successes since then have served to undercut Moscow's domination of Central Asia, that development is the result of the USSR's own ill-advised expansionist policies, not of Islamic ideological aggression.

3. A fourth, political goal—paradoxically—was to save Afghanistan for socialism by having Karmal retreat from some of the more upsetting *Khalqi* "socialist" reforms, including economically disruptive land reform, anticlerical activities, adoption of a blood-red national flag, and the very claim of socialism itself. These measures were either repealed or quietly allowed to stagnate, but the retreat did not materially improve the regime's popularity.

4. The Soviet plan had been to storm Radio Kabul and silence its transmitter (by destruction if necessary) so as to prevent any call to arms by Amin supporters. At the same time, a recording by Karmal announcing his takeover would be broadcast on Radio Kabul's frequency by a transmitter in Tashkent. Because Radio Kabul employees resisted stoutly (they thought they were being attacked by *mujahideen*), the Soviet takeover was delayed, and the two stations continued to broadcast simultaneously for some time, to the confusion of all listeners.

5. As exemplified in the privately expressed saying purportedly voiced by Soviet citizens in territories occupied by Hitler's Nazis during the war, "Stalin, *konechno—svoloch, no vse-taki* nash!" (Of course Stalin's a bastard—but *our* bastard!)

6. *New York Times*, 24 February 1980, 1; *Washington Post*, 14 August 1980.

7. Henry S. Bradsher, *Afghanistan and the Soviet Union* (Durham, N.C.: Duke University Press, 1983), 212. In general, the percentage of Central Asian conscripts and reservists in construction battalions or other support services in Afghanistan seems higher than in combat units. Even without entrusting most of their Muslim troops there with arms, however, the Soviet high command had good reason to be concerned about the psychological impact of fraternization with the militantly Islamic Afghans.

8. See Leon B. Poullada, *Reform and Rebellion in Afghanistan, 1919–1929: King Amanullah's Failure to Modernize a Tribal Society* (Ithaca, N.Y.: Cornell University Press, 1973), and Anthony Arnold, "The Stony Path to Afghan Socialism: Problems of Sovietization in an Alpine Muslim Society," *Orbis* 29, No. 1 (Spring 1985): 40–57.

9. Nake M. Kamrany and Leon B. Poullada, eds., *The Potential of Afghanistan's*

Society and Institutions to Resist Soviet Penetration and Domination (Santa Monica, CA.: Fundamental Books, 1985), 43.

10. The lower figure is that of the U.S. Department of State (*Afghan Resistance and Soviet Occupation: A Five Year Summary*, Special Report No. 118, December 1984, 2), and refers only to troops in Afghanistan. At least one foreign service officer recently stationed there felt that that estimate was too low, especially in view of the thousands who must be committed to servicing Soviet aircraft staged against the *mujahideen* from Central Asia (personal conversation with the writer in October 1984).

11. *1985 Yearbook on International Communist Affairs* (Stanford: Hoover Institution Press, 1985), 147.

12. *Literaturnava Gazeta*, 22 February 1984, 10; *Janes Defense Weekly*, 26 May 1984, 819; *New York Times*, 27 May 1984, 6.

13. *Janes Defense Weekly*, 19 May 1984, 768.

14. *Sueddeutsche Zeitung*, 23 January 1985.

15. In 1819, following failure of a terror campaign that also involved execution of hostages and destruction of entire villages, the Russian generals Yermolov and Vilyaminov began destroying their foe's agricultural base—orchards, irrigation systems, and flocks as well as standing crops—as a means of crushing Chechen and Daghestani resistance "in five years." In fact, the war dragged on for over 30 years in spite of continuing Russian depredations.

16. *London Times*, 2 June 1984, 2; *Afghanistan Forum* 12 no. 3 (June 1984): 4. *San Francisco Chronicle*, 29 March 1985, 17.

17. United States Department of State, *Afghanistan: Five Years of Occupation*, Special Report No. 120, December 1984, p. 2. In August 1983 a firefight between *Parcham* and *Khalq* representatives in the army and police near Kandahar is supposed to have caused 100 casualties (*New York Times*, 7 September 1983, I–4), and in April 1984 Karmal had to warn a police audience that "the equipment and military means given to you are not to be used in the party," (*Kabul New Times*, 14 April 1984). His more poetic brother-in-law, Mahmud Baryalai (the PDPA's ideological expert) was moved to scold what he heard as "the tingling noise of struggle in the party," *Kabul New Times*, 5 May 1984). In 1985 there has been less open recognition of the problem, but there is no reason to believe it has gone away.

18. Arnold, *Afghanistan's Two-Party Communism*, 125–26, 229n.

19. ———, 100; United States Department of State, *Afghanistan: Five Years of Occupation*, Special Report No. 120, December 1984, 5.

20. Radio Kabul, 6 July (FBIS, 8 July), 1985; *Yearbook*, 143.

21. United Kingdom Foreign and Commonwealth Office, *Background Brief*, "Afghanistan Chronology: November 1983–April 1984," July, 1984, 6; *Kabul New Times*, 29 December 1984 through 20 January 1985; *New York Times*, 31 December 1984, 3.

22. *Kabul New Times*, 24 April 1983 and 5 May 1984, and Radio Kabul, 12 February (FBIS, 17 February), 1984.

23. It is acknowledged that relying only on FBIS coverage for statistical analysis

involves certain obvious pitfalls: the FBIS priorities for translation may change at certain times of crisis, temporarily pushing the Afghan issue aside; some items, such as a TASS release in English that I have listed as a foreign-audience-oriented piece, may also appear in *Pravda* or *Izvestiia* in Russian as well; other TASS items may show up in several different Soviet organs yet be carried only once by FBIS. To some extent these various aberrations cancel each other out, and for the purpose of the rough generalizations given here, FBIS provides an adequate yardstick. Spot checks of available Soviet publications and a review of other translation services (*Current Digest of the Soviet Press* and extensive articles from the Joint Publications Research Service) also confirmed impressions gained from the study of FBIS alone.

24. *Los Angeles Times*, 8 August 1984, 1; *New York Times*, 18 February 1983, 3. The latter source notes that the resistance, which was holding most of the prisoners at various secret locations inside Afghanistan, did not expose Western reporters to those who continued to support the Soviet position.

25. *Christian Science Monitor*, 10 September 1985, 18. The two polls were by Radio Liberty (AR-4-85, "The Soviet Public and the War in Afghanistan: Perceptions, Prognoses, Information Sources," June 1985) and by the Russian émigré organization NTS, officials of whom informed the author in August 1985 of the new wave of antiwar sentiment among Soviet travelers to the West.

26. Not all Soviet citizens have been as uninterested. Immediately after the invasion, an open group letter signed by seventeen Lithuanians, three Estonians and a Latvian addressed to the chairman of the Supreme Soviet, the secretary-general of the UN, and the "Afghan nation" drew telling parallels with the Soviet takeover of the Baltic States in 1939–40 and demanded an immediate Soviet withdrawal from Afghanistan. ("Baltic Activists Condemn Invasion of Afghanistan," Radio Liberty Research Bulletin RL-97/80. 6 March 1980.)

27. "Morale Boosters for Soviet Troops in Afghanistan," Radio Liberty Research Bulletin RL-192/82, 10 May 1982.

28. *Materialy Samizdata*, "Tragediya v Afganistane. Intervyu s estontsem, byvshim v Afganistane," Radio Liberty, Arkhiv *samizdata* document AS-5395, Issue 6/85, 4 February 1985. This transcript of a 1983 tape-recorded interview in Estonia is one of the most moving documents to emerge from the Afghan War. See also "Moscow's Muslim Challenge," BBC Current Affairs Research and Information Section Caris Report No. 29/82, 24 August 1982, and *Der Spiegel*, 16 June 1980, 112–14. Particularly the last provides a sense of the calm superiority that many Central Asians seem to feel toward the Russians.

29. "Tragediya." The interviewee, a simple private who had recently completed his obligatory military service as part of the Soviet occupation, had no idea how many troops were in the country, but when pressed guessed the number to be about 150,000. The accepted figure in the West at that time was 100,000. Other former soldiers have guessed 200,000 or even more.

30. *Los Angeles Times*, 8 Aug 1984, 1.

31. Moscow TASS, 6 March (FBIS 7 March), 1980; *Christian Science Monitor*, 15 August 1980, 10. See also *Posev* No. 4, 1983 that quotes a specific denial of a Soviet combat role from V. Kassis and L. Kolosov, *Iz taynikov sekretnykh sluzhb*, Moscow, 1981.

32. *New York Times*, 3 December 1984, 3. *Krasnaya Zvezda* of 30 September, 1981 described the death of a Soviet Lieutenant Losev in action, but it was almost certainly a contravention of propaganda orders to have published the account; nothing like it had appeared before, nor would there be anything similar in this official defense ministry publication for nearly 18 months after. Aside from this aberrant slip, one of the first casualties to be lionized post-humously was a Ukrainian, Lt. Oleksandr Stovba, who was identified in February 1983 in *Komsomolskaya Pravda* as having been killed in Afghanistan. A year earlier his obituary had appeared in *Molod' Ukrainy* but without details as to where or when he met his fate. From his birthdate in one obituary and his age at death in another, it is clear that he must have been killed before July 1980, in the first months of the war.

33. Ronald R. Pope, "Afghanistan and the Influence of Public Opinion on Soviet Foreign Policy," *Asian Affairs*, July–August 1981, 347; "A Soviet Soldier Opts Out in Afghanistan," Radio Liberty Research Bulletin RL-121/84, 19 March 1984. In late 1981 or early 1982 students in a Soviet army sergeants' school had calculated that there had already been 20–25,000 killed in action (*Posev* 39, No. 6 (June 1983): 15). See also 40, No. 4 (April 1984): 16.

34. "Ukrainian *Samizdat* Journal Gives Details of Casualties in Afghanistan," Radio Liberty Research Bulletin RL-9/85, 10 January 1985.

35. Conversations with NTS officials, August 1985.

36. *Krasnaya Zvezda*, 18 January 1983.

37. *New York Times*, 2 May 1984, 3; 27 May 1984, 6. The DRA soldier's reputation among Soviet troops for desertion, cowardice, and treachery is well known. Most are unwilling conscripts, physically or mentally incapable of avoiding press gangs. As one Soviet source put it, they are the "seniles and the halfwits" ("Tragediya," 6).

38. *Komsomolskaya Pravda*, 10 February and 30 May 1984. The 30 May article contained abstracts from only 12 of the 3,000 responses the paper said it received.

39. *Komsomolskaya Pravda*, 26 February and 28 April, 1984. The bureaucrats were dismissed from their posts and expelled from the Party.

40. Obviously, many other factors contributed to Ogarkov's downfall, but this could well have been one of them. Since his dismissal, there have been continued efforts to glorify the military, but only rarely in terms of contemporary battles in Afghanistan.

41. "Interviews with Soviet Defectors in Peshawar," Radio Liberty Research Bulletin RL-205/84, 24 May 1984. This is a motivation that the Soviets probably try to cultivate subtly.

42. RL-205/84. After their arrival in Afghanistan, at least some Soviet troops are also motivated by the chance for plunder. See "Tragediya," 13, and "A Soviet

Soldier Opts Out in Afghanistan," *Radio Liberty Research Bulletin* RL-121/84, 13 March 1984.

43. *Christian Science Monitor*, 6 August 1981, 12.

44. *Christian Science Monitor; New York Times*, 11 April 1980, A1, and 3 December 1984, 3.

45. "Interviews with Two Soviet Defectors—Igor Rykov and Oleg Khlan," *Radio Liberty Research Bulletin* RL-220/84, 1 June 1984.

46. *Pravda*, 14 February 1985.

47. Ronald R. Pope, "Moscow's Potential for Miscalculation in Asia," *Asia Pacific Community*, Fall 1981, 93–102. 107–24. My own passing acquaintance with the Soviet ambassador to Afghanistan during the years before the invasion leads me to conclude that if the Kremlin was relying on him for accurate, unbiased, thoughtful appraisals, it had seriously misjudged its man.

48. *Kabul New Times*, 14 January 1985. One has the suspicion that the selection of Usmankhodzhayev as Soviet delegate was as much a sign of Moscow's cooling toward him as toward the DRA. With Soviet troops unable to guarantee the security of Kabul, he was probably considered the most expendable of the available ranking representatives. In any case, although the decline in prestige of representatives to Kabul seems significant, it should not be taken as definitive until Mikhail Gorbachev signals more clearly what his Afghan policy will be.

49. I am indebted to Ronald R. Pope and Alexander Shtromas for their early recognition of how Soviet public opinion might be affected by Afghanistan. See Ronald R. Pope, "Afghanistan and the Influence of Public Opinion on Soviet Foreign Policy," *Asian Affairs, An American Review*, (July-August 1981), 346–54; and "The Soviet Public and Moscow's Foreign Policy," *Asian Pacific Community* No. 22, (Fall 1983), 96–103. See also Alexander Shtromas, "The Soviet Union and the Politics of Peace," in Peter van den Dungen (ed.), *West European Pacifism and the Strategy for Peace*, (London and Basingstoke: MacMillan, 1985.)

50. Shtromas, *The Soviet Union*, 132–41.

51. Arnold, *Afghanistan*, 121–25. Direct and indirect evidence of Soviet attempts to warp reporting in the West about Afghanistan would make a fascinating study.

52. After the capture and subsequent release of the French journalist Jacques Abouchar in September–October 1984, events whose clumsy handling by the Soviets managed to lose them even the support of the normally loyal French Party (PCF), Soviet ambassador to Pakistan Smirnov warned that in the future Soviet forces would not distinguish between journalists and "bandits," and would "eliminate" both (*Christian Science Monitor*, 27 December 1984, 28).

53. One journalist who usually gives the USSR the benefit of the doubt, Fred Halliday, went so far as to assert that the Soviet policy decision in 1981 to cease sending their war dead home was "a result of popular indifference" (*New York Times*, 14 September 1981, A-25), surely as defamatory a comment about the Soviet people as has ever been made.

54. "Interviews with Two Soviet Defectors," *Turkmenskaya Pravda*, 8 July 1983, as quoted in *Posev* No. 9, September 1983, 12; *London Times*, 27 January 1983, 12; conversations with NTS officials, August 1985.

55. *London Times*, 30 April 1984, 13.

56. *New York Times*, 17 January 1985, 5; *London Times*, 17 January 1985, 6. This silence contrasts sharply with an *Izvestiia* article that appeared only a month before, describing two other soldiers who had fallen into mujahideen hands. Unlike Ryzhkov, these two had not deserted but had been captured. Although they willingly gave interviews to émigré papers and to Radio Liberty before being flown to England for resettlement, they apparently could not cope with adjustment to a free society, especially because they had drug addiction problems. After several weeks they voluntarily turned themselves in to the Soviet embassy in London for repatriation. *Izvestiia* all but made heroes out of them, possibly with an eye to luring others back home or dissuading potential deserters. The subsequent failure to mention Ryzhkov except in an English language release may indicate that the authorities had more negative than positive results from this effort.

57. *Christian Science Monitor*, 10 August 1984, 9.

58. "Unofficial Peace Movement in USSR Under Attack" and "Appeal by Olga Medvedkova," Radio Liberty Research Bulletins RL-256/82 (24 June 1982) and RL-90/84 (24 February 1984), respectively; *International Herald Tribune*, 15 August 1985, 3.

59. *Christian Science Monitor*, 1 October 1985, 16. Joseph C. Harsch, who wrote this piece, sees a motivation by both sides to avoid escalation. The more active Soviet offensive actions in recent times, and the subsequent authorization by the U.S. Congress of $200 million in secret arms aid to the resistance, however, seem to indicate that both sides are willing to raise the ante somewhat.

60. Alexander Shtromas notes that the Soviet military is neither monolithic nor necessarily pleased to be engaged in Afghanistan. He points out that the Portuguese army in Angola and the Greek army on Cyprus counseled escape from conflicts they knew they could not win. These are worthy arguments, but my own belief is that the Soviet high command, though embarrassed at its inability to win the war quickly, would be far more embarrassed to withdraw from it. Moreover, at least some ranking officers must welcome the unsurpassed opportunity to blood the troops and test new equipment in battle conditions.

61. Up to mid-1985 it appeared that Moscow hoped to intimidate Pakistan into curtailing its support to the resistance. The effort appears to have been ineffective, however. There are limits to how much pressure the USSR can bring to bear; certainly there seems little likelihood of an extension of the Soviet military thrust into Pakistan, which would only confront the USSR with the problem of subjugating yet more millions of untameable Muslims.

62. "And still, time has always been, is, and remains the best medicine. Even

against political ailments . . ." *Krasnaya Zvezda*, 17 December 1983, as quoted in "Soviet Propaganda on Afghanistan," Radio Liberty Research Bulletin RL-142/84, 5 April 1984.

63. *Kabul New Times*, 18, 19, and 20 November 1984.
64. *New York Times*, 30 March, 1988.

Notes on Contributors

Mikhail Agursky is Associate Research Professor in Soviet Studies, the Hebrew University of Jerusalem, Israel

Stanislaw Andreski is Emeritus Professor of Sociology, University of Reading, Reading, England

Anthony Arnold is Associate of the Hoover Institution, Stanford University, Stanford, California

Alexander Bennigsen was Professor and Director of Studies, University of Paris (Sorbonne), Paris, France

Aurel Braun is Associate Professor of Political Science, University of Toronto, Toronto, Canada

Christopher G.A. Bryant is Professor of Sociology and Chairman of the Department of Sociological and Anthropological Studies, University of Salford, Salford, England

Christie Davies is Professor of Sociology and Chairman of the Department of Sociology, University of Reading, Reading, England

Dennis Deletant is Senior Lecturer, School of Slavonic and East European Studies, University of London, London, England

William C. Fletcher is Professor in Soviet Studies, University of Kansas, Lawrence, Kansas

Maurice Friedberg is Professor of Russian Literature and Chairman of the Department of Slavic Languages and Literatures, University of Illinois at Urbana-Champaign, Urbana, Illinois

Vladimir Frumkin is a Researcher and Instructor in Russian at Oberlin College, Oberlin, Ohio

Alexander Gershkovich is a Fellow of the Russian Research Center, Harvard University, Cambridge, Massachusetts

Darrell P. Hammer is Professor of Political Science, University of Indiana, Bloomington, Indiana

Nicholas P. Hayes is Associate Professor, The Associate Colleges of Twin Cities, Minneapolis, Minnesota

Peter Kelly is a free-lance author and researcher, Seaford, East Sussex, England

Michael B. Kreps is Associate Professor of Russian Literature, Boston College, Chestnut Hill, Massachusetts

W. Bruce Lincoln is Research Professor in Russian History, Northern Illinois University, De Kalb, Illinois

Sergei Maksudov is a Fellow of the Russian Institute, Boston University Boston, Massachusetts

Mihajlo Mihajlov is Professor of Russian Literature and Philosophy and a journalist with Radio Free Europe-Radio Liberty, Washington, D.C.

Tadeusz A. Musiol is Assistant Lecturer in Politics, University of Salford, Salford, England

Robert L. Nichols is Professor of History, St. Olaf's College, Northfield, Minnesota

Nikolai Poltoratzky is Professor of Russian History and Philosophy, University of Pittsburgh, Pittsburgh, Pennsylvania

Zdislaw M. Rurarz is former Polish Ambassador to Japan, who refused to return to Poland in 1981 (after the crushing of "Solidarity"); now he is a free-lance author, researcher and consultant in Washington D.C.

Radoslav Selucky is Professor of Political Science, Carleton University, Ottawa, Canada

Alexander Shtromas is Professor of Political Science, Hillsdale College, Hillsdale, Michigan in 1989–90.

Victor Swoboda is Senior Lecturer at the School of Slavonic and East European Studies, University of London, London, England

Valev Uibopuu is Associate Professor in Finno-Ugric Studies, University of Lund, Lund, Sweden

V. Stanley Vardys is Professor and Chair of the Department of Political Science, University of Oklahoma, Norman, Oklahoma

Andrzej Walicki is Professor of Russian History and Philosophy, University of Notre-Dame, Notre-Dame, Indiana

Index